Microsoft

Jim Buyens
Popular author, Internet expert, and
Microsoft FrontPage Most Valuable Professional

Microsoft® Office FrontPage® 2003

PUBLISHED BY
Microsoft Press
A Division of Microsoft Corporation
One Microsoft Way
Redmond, Washington 98052-6399

Library of Congress Cataloging-in-Publication Data
Buyens, Jim.
Microsoft Office FrontPage 2003 Inside Out / Jim Buyens.
p. cm.
Includes index.
ISBN 0-7356-1510-1
1. Microsoft FrontPage. 2. Web sites--Design. 3. Web publishing. I. Title.

TK5105.8885.M53B875 2003
005.7'2--dc21 2003052669

Printed and bound in the United States of America.

1 2 3 4 5 6 7 8 9 QWT 8 7 6 5 4 3

Distributed in Canada by H.B. Fenn and Company Ltd.

A CIP catalogue record for this book is available from the British Library.

Microsoft Press books are available through booksellers and distributors worldwide. For further information about international editions, contact your local Microsoft Corporation office or contact Microsoft Press International directly at fax (425) 936-7329. Visit our Web site at www.microsoft.com/mspress. Send comments to *mspinput@microsoft.com.*

Acquisitions Editor: Alex Blanton
Project Editor: Kristen Weatherby
Series Editor: Sandra Haynes

Body Part No. X09-69498

This book is dedicated to the homeless mentally-ill persons of America. Why do we lavish health care dollars on victims of other, less debilitating illnesses while condemning these unfortunates to the streets and gutters?

Contents At A Glance

Table of Contents

Part 3
Editing Basic Page Content

Chapter 7
Creating, Opening, Saving, and Deleting Web Pages 187

Chapter 8
Adding and Formatting Text 199

Part 4
Creating Web Sites Automatically

Chapter 13
Creating Web Sites with Navigation View 331

Chapter 14
Creating Web Sites with Templates and Wizards 363

Chapter 19
Using HTML Tables for Page Layout 515

Chapter 20
Using FrontPage Themes 561

Chapter 21
Managing Appearance with Cascading Style Sheets 579

Chapter 22
Positioning Content with Cascading Style Sheets 621

Part 7
Creating and Editing Web Pictures

Chapter 23
Editing Pictures in FrontPage 635

Chapter 24
Using FrontPage Photo Galleries 655

Part 8
Incorporating Advanced Content

Chapter 29
Organizing Reusable Web Site Content 749

Chapter 30
Using Automatic Web Content Components 767

Chapter 31
Monitoring and Reporting Site Activity 777

Chapter 32
Using ActiveX Controls and Java Applets 785

Chapter 35
Processing Data Submitted from Forms 859

Chapter 36
Accessing and Updating Databases with FrontPage 877

Part 10
Collaborating with Teams and Workgroups

Part 12
Customizing Your Copy of FrontPage

Part 13
Appendixes

Appendix D
Interpreting FrontPage Reports A45

Appendix E
Design Tips for Choosing Colors A71

Appendix N
Looking at the Web—Inside Out A169

Appendix O
Installing and Configuring a Web Server A193

Appendix P
Understanding the FrontPage Server Extensions A217

Part 14
Insider Extras

Insider Extra 1
ASP Self-Diagnosis Web Page IE3

Insider Extra 2
ASP. NET Self-Diagnosis Web Page IE9

Insider Extra 3
Picture Sizer IE17

Insider Extra 4
Converting Text to GIF Format IE23

Insider Extra 5
ASP.NET Picture Library IE29

Insider Extra 6
Scripting Dynamic Tables of Contents IE35

Insider Extra 7
Scripting Web Searches IE41

Acknowledgments

Many thanks to my wife, Connie, who kept the family together while I devoted countless hours to this long, long project. When things got tough she revived me, and when I feared possession she restored my sanity. She's truly my friend, my helpmate, and my life's love.

Thanks as well to my children, Lorrill, Justin, and Lynessa, for their support and for bearing all the antics and absences involved in writing such a book. Thanks as well to my parents, my brothers, and their families: Harold, Marcella, Ruth, Dave, Connie, Michael, Steven, Rick, Jenny, Matt, and Claire. We should visit more often.

At Microsoft Press, thanks to Alex Blanton, who set up the business details, to Sandra Haynes, the series editor, and to Kristen Weatherby and Laura Sackerman, the project editors, for their ceaseless confidence, encouragement, and assistance.

Thanks to the entire team at Studioserv Book Publishing Resources, especially Steve Sagman, whose experience and professionalism shined brightly at every moment. Thanks as well to Jennifer Harris, the copy editor, and to Jack Beaudry and Chris Russo, the technical editors, all of whom contributed heavily to the overall quality of the book. Working with such a gifted group of people was a true delight.

Most of all, thanks to you, the readers, who make an effort such as this both possible and worthwhile. I hope the book meets your expectations and that we meet again.

We'd Like to Hear from You!

Our goal at Microsoft Press is to create books that help you find the information you need to get the most out of your software.

The INSIDE OUT series was created with you in mind. As part of our ongoing effort to ensure that we're creating the books that meet your learning needs, we'd like to hear from you. Let us know what you think. Tell us what you like about this book and what we can do to make it better. When you write, please include the title and author of this book in your e-mail, as well as your name and contact information. We look forward to hearing from you!

How to Reach Us

E-mail: nsideout@microsoft.com
Mail: Inside Out Series Editor
Microsoft Press
One Microsoft Way
Redmond, WA 98052

Note: Unfortunately, we can't provide support for any software problems you might experience. Please go to http://support.microsoft.com *for help with any software issues.*

About the CD

The companion CD that ships with this book contains many tools and resources to help you get the most out of your Inside Out book.

What's On the CD

Your INSIDE OUT CD includes the following:

- **Complete eBook** In this section you'll find the electronic version of *Microsoft Office FrontPage 2003 Inside Out*. The eBook is in PDF format.
- **Insider Extras** This section includes sample files referenced in the book, including the sample Web pages used in the book's examples. Install these files to your hard disk, and use them to follow along with the book's examples or as a starting point for your own work.
- **Microsoft Tools and Information** In this section you'll find resources, demos, and tools for the following applications: FrontPage, InfoPath, OneNote, and Publisher.
- **Extending FrontPage** In this section you'll find great information about third-party utilities and tools you can use to further enhance your experience with FrontPage.
- **Microsoft Computer Dictionary, Fifth Edition, eBook** Here you'll find the full electronic version of the *Microsoft Computer Dictionary, Fifth Edition*.

The companion CD provides detailed information about the files on this CD, and links to Microsoft and third-party sites on the Internet.

> **Note** Please note that the links to third-party sites are not under the control of Microsoft Corporation and Microsoft is therefore not responsible for their content, nor should their inclusion on this CD be construed as an endorsement of the product or the site.

Using the CD

To use this companion CD, insert it into your CD-ROM drive. If AutoRun is not enabled on your computer, run StartCD.exe in the root of the CD.

System Requirements

Following are the minimum system requirements necessary to run the CD:

- Microsoft Windows XP or later or Windows 2000 Professional with Service Pack 3 or later.
- 266-MHz or higher Pentium-compatible CPU

- 64 megabytes (MB) RAM
- 8X CD-ROM drive or faster
- Microsoft Windows–compatible sound card and speakers
- Microsoft Internet Explorer 5.01 or higher
- Microsoft Mouse or compatible pointing device

Note An Internet connection is necessary to access the some of the hyperlinks. Connect time charges may apply.

Support Information

Every effort has been made to ensure the accuracy of the book and the contents of this companion CD. For feedback on the book content or this companion CD, please contact us by using any of the addresses listed in the "We'd Like to Hear From You" section.

Microsoft Press provides corrections for books through the World Wide Web at *http://www.microsoft.com/mspress/support/*. To connect directly to the Microsoft Press Knowledge Base and enter a query regarding a question or issue that you may have, go to http://www.microsoft.com/mspress/support/search.htm.

For support information regarding Windows XP, you can connect to Microsoft Technical Support on the Web at *http://support.microsoft.com/*.

Conventions and Features Used in This Book

This book uses special text and design conventions to make it easier for you to find the information you need.

Text Conventions

Convention	Meaning
Abbreviated menu commands	For your convenience, this book uses abbreviated menu commands. For example, "Choose Tools, Track Changes, Highlight Changes" means that you should click the Tools menu, point to Track Changes, and select the Highlight Changes command.
Boldface type	Boldface type is used to indicate text that you enter or type.
Initial Capital Letters	The first letters of the names of menus, dialog boxes, dialog box elements, and commands are capitalized. Example: the Save As dialog box.
Italicized type	Italicized type is used to indicate new terms.
Plus sign (+) in text	Keyboard shortcuts are indicated by a plus sign (+) separating two key names. For example, Ctrl+Alt+Delete means that you press the Ctrl, Alt, and Delete keys at the same time.

Design Conventions

This text identifies a new or significantly updated feature in this version of the software.

InsideOut tips

These are the book's signature tips. In these tips, you'll find get the straight scoop on what's going on with the software—inside information on why a feature works the way it does. You'll also find handy workarounds to deal with some of these software problems.

Tip

Tips provide helpful hints, timesaving tricks, or alternative procedures related to the task being discussed.

Troubleshooting sidebars

Look for these sidebars to find solutions to common problems you might encounter. Troubleshooting sidebars appear next to related information in the chapters. You can also use the Troubleshooting Topics index at the back of the book to look up problems by topic.

Cross-References Cross-references point you to other locations in the book that offer additional information on the topic being discussed.

On the CD
This icon indicates sample files or text found on the companion CD.

Caution
Cautions identify potential problems that you should look out for when you're completing a task or problems that you must address before you can complete a task.

Note Notes offer additional information related to the task being discussed.

Sidebars

The sidebars sprinkled throughout these chapters provide ancillary information on the topic being discussed. Go to sidebars to learn more about the technology or a feature.

Part 1

Introducing Microsoft FrontPage 2003

Chapter 1

Presenting Microsoft FrontPage 2003

As the Web approaches its tenth birthday, its rate of change at least persists and arguably accelerates. New kinds of content and even new kinds of applications arise daily. Sites containing over 100,000 pages are commonplace, as are sites delivering millions of Web pages per day. Conducting business on the Web is the mainstay of today's most exciting new businesses and has become a requirement for all the rest. Meanwhile, artistic standards, page layout complexity, and demands for uniformity constantly evolve. The Web has become not only mass media, but an art form and a technological tour de force as well.

All of this is more than anyone—or any assemblage of people—could accomplish using only text editors or the page-at-a-time tools of a few years ago. And this, in turn, explains why Microsoft Office FrontPage 2003 undergoes more change with each release than any other Microsoft Office System program.

The people who design Web pages and entire Web sites are as diverse as the Web itself. Some have never used a computer before, whereas others are longtime computer experts. Some lean toward the artistic side of Web design, and some tend toward details of implementation. Some have no idea of what constitutes a computer network, and some are experienced Intrnet specialists.

In the past, FrontPage sought primarily to accommodate beginning Web designers seeking to leverage their skills from other Office applications. All those features are still available in FrontPage 2003, but the emphasis this time is on meeting the needs of professional Web designers. This, however, is good news for everyone. After all, sooner or later, everyone hopes to be an expert, and FrontPage makes the transition as smooth as possible.

Using This Book

You can, of course, be a proficient computer user and still be new to Microsoft FrontPage. The first few chapters of this book, therefore, present a whirlwind tour of basic FrontPage features that will get you started with the proper mind-set. After that, you'll probably read the book randomly on a sort of "need to know" basis. The index and table of contents will guide you to the specific information you need.

Wherever possible, multiple ways of doing the same thing appear consecutively in the text. This should make it easier to contrast, compare, and pick the right tool for the job at hand.

If you're not an intermediate or advanced computer user, or if you just prefer a bit of hand holding, a book such as *Microsoft Office FrontPage 2003 Step by Step* (Microsoft Press, 2003) might better suit your needs. Then, when you need help with those pesky details, *Microsoft Office FrontPage 2003 Inside Out* will be waiting for you. The porch light is always on.

FrontPage Overview

At its core, FrontPage is a visual editor that Web designers use to design Web pages. When the designer saves the page, FrontPage converts the design to Hypertext Markup Language (HTML)—the stuff of which Web pages are actually made.

The Web's basic operating approach is quite simple. It involves the exchange of information between a computer that requests information, often called a *client*, and one that delivers the information, usually called a *server*. The client's software, called a *browser*, requests Web pages from a server located somewhere on a network, whether it's a corporate intranet or the global World Wide Web.

At the most fundamental level, browsers expect Web pages to be coded in HTML. HTML consists of plain text "marked up" with tags such as <p> for new paragraph, <ul> for unnumbered list, and <li> for list item. This is a format anyone can produce using a simple text editor, such as the Microsoft Notepad accessory that comes with Microsoft Windows.

Many new Web designers have neither interest nor aptitude for coding HTML. Instead, they want to create Web pages with high-level tools as sophisticated and easy to use as their favorite word-processing, spreadsheet, or desktop-publishing applications. FrontPage provides this facility.

Expert Web designers, in contrast, are extremely proficient with HTML and with other kinds of code as well. This includes cascading style sheet (CSS) code that controls typography, various kinds of program code that runs either on the browser or on the Web server, and Extensible Markup Language (XML) code that contains data, formatting instructions, or configuration settings. FrontPage therefore provides ways of working with any kind of Web-related code you can imagine. Furthermore, it can switch rapidly between visual edit mode and code editing mode and even display both modes at once.

Because HTML, CSS, XML, and program code are often quite cryptic, the experts who create it are usually fastidious about formatting code to fit their personal definition of easy reading. Not only does FrontPage preserve this formatting; it tries to match its own code to that around it.

Unlike most Office documents, Web pages usually consist of multiple files. In addition to the "main" file (the one you specify in the browser's Address bar), each picture on the page is a separate file, as is each animation or sound. CSS typography instructions might reside in yet another file, as might additional scraps of HTML or program code. Managing the relationships among all these files is a complex and tedious task, but wait—it gets worse. Not only do Web pages refer to their constituent parts; they refer to other Web pages by means of *hyperlinks*. In its simplest form, a hyperlink is a string of underlined text that you click to display a different Web page. The set of all Web pages that refer to a single topic is called a *Web site*.

The relationships among text, pictures, and other kinds of files in a typical Web site is highly detailed and complex. Errors result if a single file is misnamed or misplaced. Initially creating such a structure is difficult, but maintaining it over time can be daunting. FrontPage helps you deal with this complexity by organizing sets of related Web pages into *FrontPage-based Web sites*. Each such site is a folder tree on your disk or Web server that FrontPage manages as a unit. Based on the code within each Web page, FrontPage figures out the relationships among all the files in a site. Then, whenever you update, move, or delete one of those files, FrontPage automatically changes other Web pages in the same site so that they still work properly.

All in all, from design to coding and on to Web site management, FrontPage provides the tools that beginners and experts alike need to efficiently create and maintain spectacular Web sites.

Editing Web Pages

At some fundamental level, word-processed documents, spreadsheets, slide-show presentations, and database reports are all documents. Nevertheless, each of these types represents a different mind-set and requires a different program to handle its unique requirements. So it is with Web pages.

The basic unit of Web content is the *Web page*. Physically, Web pages consist of plain ASCII text interspersed with *markup tags* that control structure and format. Most Web pages use no more than 20 or 30 HTML tags. Because these tags are fairly easy to memorize, many Web designers create pages using nothing more than a text editor. If this works for you, great—FrontPage will support you every step of the way. In fact, FrontPage supports direct hand-coding in ways that far exceed the capabilities of any text editor.

If, however, you'd rather bypass the mechanics of HTML and just create pages visually on your screen, FrontPage provides a great WYSIWYG editor. The next three figures illustrate these points visually. Figure 1-1 shows FrontPage editing a Web page in WYSIWYG view, Figure 1-2 shows FrontPage editing the same page in HTML view, and Figure 1-3 shows Microsoft Internet Explorer displaying the same page.

Figure 1-1. FrontPage closely matches Internet Explorer's display of a Web page (see Figure 1-3) and also provides a great assortment of editing commands and tools. Notice that the Design view tab is selected at the bottom of the screen.

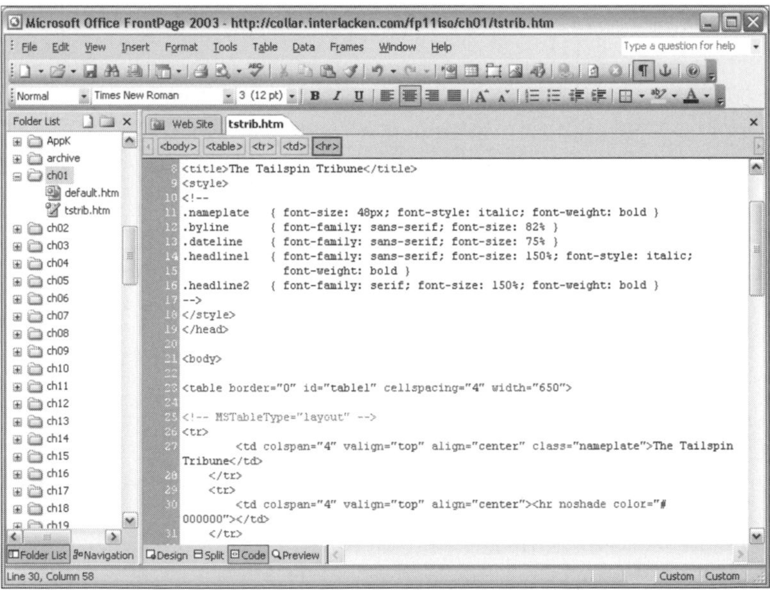

Figure 1-2. Select the Code tab at the bottom of the Editor window to view the HTML behind the current page. You can edit the code directly and then return to Design view to see the results.

Presenting Microsoft FrontPage 2003

Figure 1-3. Internet Explorer displays the Web page edited in Figure 1-1.

> **Note** FrontPage will either format HTML the way you like it or preserve the HTML formatting of any page you open. The choice is yours.

For more information about editing HTML code directly, refer to Chapter 40, "Working with HTML Code."

Figure 1-2 shows FrontPage displaying the HTML code that actually creates the Web page shown in Figure 1-1. As you can see, for the vast majority of Web page creators, editing with FrontPage offers tremendous advantages over editing raw HTML code with an ordinary text editor.

If you compare Figure 1-1 and Figure 1-3, it's apparent that FrontPage also displays certain structural elements that the browser doesn't. FrontPage, by design, displays invisible table borders, invisible line breaks, and in some cases even invisible colors, all as aids to editing. Even though the Web visitor won't see these elements, *you* need to, in order to edit them.

The FrontPage 2003 user interface follows all the style and organizational conventions of other Microsoft Office 2003 applications. If you're familiar with other Office applications, you'll find most of the commands and toolbar icons in FrontPage 2003 are just as you expect them to be. In addition to similarities such as overall appearance, menu organization, icon assignment, dialog box similarity, keyboard shortcuts, and drag-and-drop operations, FrontPage also supports the following:

- **File format conversion to and from Microsoft Office formats and HTML** These capabilities include inserting entire Microsoft Office files into Web pages as well as copying content from an Office application and pasting it into FrontPage. For example, if you copy a Microsoft Word table, a range of Microsoft Excel cells, or a block of Microsoft Access table records, FrontPage pastes any of them as an HTML table.

- **Uniform layout commands** Wherever possible, FrontPage uses familiar Office commands and dialog boxes for aligning objects, setting fonts, and controlling bullets and other paragraph properties.

HTML supports a variety of user interface objects such as text boxes, drop-down lists, option buttons, and push buttons. A related group of such elements constitutes an *HTML form*. FrontPage provides a WYSIWYG, drag-and-drop environment for designing HTML forms, form wizards, and menu-driven configuration of all form elements.

For more information about editing Web pages with FrontPage, refer to Chapter 2, "Editing Web Pages."

FrontPage provides extensive support for dragging objects from one location on a page to another, from one Web page to another, and from Windows Explorer onto Web pages.

All in all, producing Web pages is a task with unique requirements and challenges. As you'll discover from this book, FrontPage 2003 provides the most powerful and most compelling set of features in the industry for creating not only Web pages but also entire sites.

Managing Web Sites

Each Web page contains a relatively small amount of content. Hyperlinks provide easy navigation from one page to another and unify groups of pages into a cohesive whole. Nevertheless, the information that most applications would keep in a single file—such as a Word document, an Excel spreadsheet, or a PowerPoint presentation—generally resides in dozens or hundreds of Web pages. Keeping all these pages properly arranged can be a real challenge. Keeping all the hyperlinks up-to-date can be even worse.

Note Short Web pages minimize transmission time and maximize the amount of information the Web visitor can see without scrolling up and down the browser window.

Just to complicate the situation, most Web pages have several constituent parts, and each of these parts is a separate file. To load a Web page, the browser first requests the file name that appears in the Uniform Resource Locator (URL), then any files (such as frames and pictures) specified within that file, then any files specified within those files, and so forth. As a result, representing a single technical manual, presentation, or sales catalog on the Web might require dozens, hundreds, or thousands of files.

Note A URL identifies each page on the World Wide Web. In the URL *http://www.interlacken.com/fp11iso/default.htm*, *http* identifies the retrieval method (Hypertext Transfer Protocol), *www.interlacken.com* identifies the Web server, *fp11iso* identifies a folder path on that server, and *default.htm* identifies a file in that folder.

Dealing with all the files that make up a Web site presents three kinds of challenges:

- The first challenge relates to changing linked objects. Changes you make to one file might require changes to other files that refer to it. If you change a file's name or location, for example, you must correspondingly change every hyperlink that refers to it. If you have half a dozen files that link to the file /common/contacts.htm, and you then rename contacts.htm to email.htm, you must locate all six files and change the hyperlinks. The same is true for the names of pictures. In addition, changing the size of a picture often requires changing the height and width attributes in every file that uses that picture.
- The second challenge relates to uniformity. In virtually every case, all Web pages in the same body of content should share a common appearance. They should use the same general page layout, the same fonts, the same colors, the same hyperlink conventions, and so forth. Even the most fastidious Web designers find maintaining this level of consistency extremely difficult, especially if the work spans a long period of time.
- The third challenge relates to changes that should apply to more than one page. All sites change their appearance from time to time, and when this happens, updating dozens, hundreds, or thousands of pages all at once can be a daunting task.

Fortunately, all these challenges involve repetitive work on computer files and are therefore amenable to software solutions. However, such a solution is possible only if all the files to be processed are somehow grouped into a common area. In the case of FrontPage, this common area is called a FrontPage-based Web site. Physically, a FrontPage-based Web site is a designated folder tree in your computer's file system or on a Web server.

A FrontPage-based Web site that resides on your local disk or at a network location you access by file sharing is said to be *disk-based.* To open such a Web in FrontPage, you'd specify a file location such as C:\My Documents\My Web Sites\testweb\. Disk-based Web sites are very easy to use and are sufficient for many kinds of Web development. However, you can't use a disk-based Web site to test—and in some cases develop—Web pages containing features that require active participation of a Web server.

If your Web server has Microsoft Windows SharePoint Services or the FrontPage Server Extensions installed, and if you have the required security permissions, you can create and manage FrontPage-based Web sites without using any kind of ordinary file access. Instead, FrontPage reads data from the server in the same way that browsers do and writes data in the same way that HTML forms do. To open such a Web in FrontPage, you specify a network location such as *http://myserver.mydomain.com/testweb/*. FrontPage-based Web sites accessed this way are said to be *server-based*. Because server-based Web sites, by definition, involve the active presence of a Web server, they support development and testing of Web pages that use all FrontPage features.

FrontPage-based Web sites can be *nested*. This means that one Web site can physically reside within the folder tree of another. When this occurs, a *parent-child relationship* exists. Suppose, for example, that the /groceries site contains a site named /groceries/produce:

- The /groceries site is the parent of the /groceries/produce site.
- The /groceries/produce site is a child of the /groceries site.

A Web site that has no parent is a *root Web site*. The first Web site you create in a given file area or Web server must, by definition, be a root Web site. Any Web sites you create within a given root Web site are, by definition, *child Web sites* or *subwebs*.

No Web page or, for that matter, any other file can belong to two sites. This means that any operations you perform on a parent site have no effect on any child sites it contains. To apply changes to a parent site and all its children, you must open and change each site individually.

If all of this seems a bit abstract or vague to you, rest assured that you have plenty of company. Most new FrontPage users think immediately about creating or editing individual Web pages and not about creating Web sites to organize groups of Web pages. That's OK—if you want to start out editing individual pages, FrontPage can do that very well. Sooner or later, however, you'll want to start working on groups of Web pages as a unit, and that's when you'll start to appreciate FrontPage-based Web sites.

Supporting FrontPage on Your Web Server

Any general-purpose Web server can deliver Web pages you create in FrontPage. This includes Windows-based Web site servers as well as UNIX servers running Netscape or Apache Web server software. The universal nature of HTML and other file formats guarantees this will work. Nevertheless, in terms of capabilities related to FrontPage, Web servers fall into three categories:

- **Non-extended Web servers** These have no special FrontPage software installed. FrontPage can upload files to such a server using the Internet File Transfer Protocol (FTP), Distributed Authoring and Versioning (WebDAV), or Windows file sharing, and the server can deliver your Web pages, multimedia files, and other kinds of content to any and all Web visitors. Because non-extended Web servers lack FrontPage software, FrontPage features such as counting and displaying page hits, collecting data from HTML forms, sending e-mail, and processing databases won't work.

> **Tip** **Use Non-FrontPage Components on Non-FrontPage Web Servers.**
> Nothing in FrontPage prevents you from using whatever hit counters, form handlers, and other components might be available on a given Web server, extended or not. However, FrontPage won't automatically create the code that invokes non-FrontPage components.

- **FrontPage-extended Web servers** These have a collection of software called the FrontPage Server Extensions installed. These extensions support hit counters, data collection, e-mailing, database processing, and other FrontPage features that non-extended servers don't. They also support advanced file upload software and the ability to open and save Web files using Internet protocols only.

  Unlike earlier versions of Microsoft FrontPage, FrontPage 2003 doesn't come with a new version of the FrontPage Server Extensions. Versions of the FrontPage 2002 Server Extensions for Windows 2000, Windows XP Professional, Windows .NET Server, and many UNIX operating systems are still available from Microsoft's Web site.

- **Windows SharePoint Services 2.0 servers** These provide most of the features of FrontPage-extended Web servers but support database access in a much different way. Whereas FrontPage-extended Web servers use Active Server Pages (ASP) or Microsoft ASP.NET technology for database access, Windows SharePointServices uses XML data sources and formats them using Extensible Style Sheet Transformation (XSLT).

  Windows SharePoint Services 2.0 also supports the use of *Web Parts*, which are fragments of Web content that site designers, administrators, and even suitably authorized visitors can add, configure, or remove from pages. Finally, Windows SharePoint Services includes a portal application named SharePoint Team Sites.

  Windows SharePoint Services 2.0 is a feature of Windows .NET Server 2003. Therefore, you won't find any SharePoint installation files on your Microsoft FrontPage or Microsoft Office CD. Instead, you must obtain and install Windows .NET Server 2003.

NEW FEATURE!

Windows SharePoint Services—A Break from the Old

When Microsoft created Windows SharePoint Services 2.0, it decided that achieving maximum benefit required a clean break from the past. Here are some of the new approaches in this release of SharePoint:

- Most Web pages in a Windows SharePoint Services 2.0 site are so-called Web Part Pages that present no content of their own. Instead, they define an overall page layout and display one or more components called Web Parts.
- A Web Part is a program that creates HTML to display the current version of some data. Suppose, for example, that Web Parts were available to display your company stock price, a list of near-term critical dates for your project, the weather report for your city, and sports scores for your favorite team. You could add all these Web Parts to a single Web Part Page and view your life with a glance.
- Although the Windows SharePoint Services 2.0 environment is fully .NET-compliant, it won't run ASP or ASP.NET pages. Instead, you would write your own Web Parts and then add them to Web Part Pages.
- SharePoint doesn't store Web pages, pictures, document files, or anything else in the Windows file system. Instead, it stores each file as a SQL Server or Microsoft Data Engine (MSDE) database record.

- SharePoint applications can't deal with Access databases located within a Web site. This is because Access databases must reside in the Windows file system, not inside a SQL Server database.
- SharePoint's XSLT formatting engine creates HTML, which, although fully standards-compliant, doesn't always work well with older browsers.
- Some SharePoint administration pages use browser features that only Internet Explorer supports.

If these restrictions present a problem, you should probably locate your application on a server running the FrontPage 2002 Server Extensions, or in a disk-based Web site located within a Web server's content tree.

When you install the FrontPage desktop software, you don't need to know what category of Web server you'll be using. You'll need this information when you start creating pages so that you can take full advantage of the features your Web server provides and avoid those that it doesn't. And of course, the features you need should guide the requirements you place on your company's IT department or Internet service provider (ISP).

Frequently Asked Question

What's a Portal Anyway?

Contrary to folklore, a portal isn't one of those little round windows you find scattered along the hulls of ships. In fact, a portal is more like a self-customizing home page.

The home page of a portal usually displays one or more Web Parts, depending on the configuration and preferences of each visitor. Each of these Web Parts acts like a miniature, freestanding Web page. The Web Part developer doesn't typically know exactly which portal pages or which visitors will display the finished component. The portal server (Windows SharePoint Services, in this case) receives the output of each Web Part and assembles the consolidated page. (Microsoft calls a Web page that displays Web Parts a *Web Part Page*.)

By displaying only the information and links each visitor needs or wants, portals function as a single point of entry to far more options that would ever be practical on a conventional Web page. In addition, they frequently provide access to shared document libraries and other services that facilitate interaction and workflow.

Introducing SharePoint Team Sites

Each copy of Windows SharePoint Services 2.0 includes a very useful application called SharePoint Team Sites. This application provides a portal-style home page that can display Web Parts. The default configuration for this home page has links to the following built-in features:

- **Lists** These include announcements, event listings, member lists, to-do lists, contact lists, and so forth. Windows SharePoint Services includes an initial collection of lists that you can use without changing or that you can modify to your heart's content. You can also create entire lists that contain whatever data you want.
- **Discussion lists** Team members can post new comments and respond to existing ones.
- **Surveys** These collect information from anyone you authorize.
- **Document libraries** Team members can deposit, categorize, and retrieve files of any kind.
- **Pictures libraries** These are similar to document libraries except that they contain pictures. Knowing that the files are pictures, Windows SharePoint Services can display thumbnail selection lists and slides shows.
- **Annotation features** These allow collaboration, as follows:
  - The member can post a document for review.
  - Other members can view the document using only a Web browser and post annotations at the document or paragraph levels.
  - The document creator can open the annotated document and view all comments made to date.
- **Subscription features** Authorized users can ask Windows SharePoint Services to send them e-mail whenever someone updates given lists or document libraries.

Choosing an Operating System for FrontPage

FrontPage 2003 runs on any Windows 2000, Windows XP, or later operating system. Specifically, it won't run on Windows NT, Windows Me, Windows 98, or Windows 95. Microsoft suspended support of these older operating systems before it released Microsoft Office 2003.

If you need to run a personal Web server, you should also avoid Windows XP Home Edition. No personal Web server is available for this operating system. If you plan to customize Web database pages, develop pages, or develop other server-side processes on your own PC, you should use Windows 2000 Professional, Windows XP Professional, or their successors.

Windows SharePoint Services 2.0 runs only on Windows .NET Server. If you plan on using its features, you'll need a machine running this operating system in your environment.

In general, the decision to install Windows SharePoint Services on a given Web server won't be yours. Instead, a system administrator, a Webmaster, or someone else in your IT department or your service provider will probably have this prerogative. If you fulfill one of these roles, you can make your own decision. Otherwise, if the Windows SharePoint Services feature set appears valuable, you can certainly ask those people to install Windows SharePoint Services for you or find someone else who will.

Installing FrontPage

In its most complete form, FrontPage follows a client/server software model. The FrontPage editing and Web site management software that runs on your desktop is the client. The FrontPage Server Extensions or Windows SharePoint Services provide the server functions.

Deciding When to Install Your Own Web Server

Many beginning Web developers test their Web pages by loading them into their browser directly from disk. This process is fine for many kinds of Web pages, but it doesn't work for pages that expect special programs to run on the Web server every time a Web visitor requests them. If you want to see these features in action before you publish the pages on your production Web server, you'll need a separate Web server for testing.

For a listing of FrontPage components that require FrontPage software on the Web server, refer to Appendix B.

If you decide, based on these criteria, that you need a FrontPage-enabled Web server for development, the first place to look is your ISP or your IT department. It's quite possible they have Web servers ready and waiting for this kind of work.

If neither your ISP nor your IT department can provide a suitable test server—or if your bandwidth to that server is insufficient—you'll need to configure your computer as a Web server. To do this on Windows 2000 or Windows XP Professional:

1. Go to Control Panel.
2. Double-click Add/Remove Programs
3. Click Add/Remove Windows Components.
4. Select Install Internet Information Server.

Because Windows 2000 and Windows XP Professional predate FrontPage 2002, their Web servers don't come with the FrontPage 2002 Server Extensions. Therefore, don't install the server extensions that come with the Web server. First get the Web server up and running without extensions, and then install the FrontPage 2002 Server Extensions from Microsoft's Web site. Browse *www.microsoft.com/frontpage/downloads* and follow the links.

To install the FrontPage desktop software, first make sure you're running Windows 2000 or Windows XP. None of the Office 2003 applications run on Windows 95, Windows 98, Wndows Me, or Windows NT, so if you haven't upgraded your operating system in the past five or six years, now is probably the time.

Setup will start automatically when you insert the FrontPage 2003 installation CD. Enter your product key and name, accept the license agreement, choose Install Now, click Next, and wait. When Setup is complete, FrontPage 2003 is installed on your system.

If you want more control over the setup process, choose Custom instead of Install Now. Click Next, make sure FrontPage is selected, click Next again, and review the options shown in Figure 1-4. To expand and contract the headings, click the plus and minus icons. To change installation options, click the down arrow next to any disk icon, and choose the option you want from the drop-down menu.

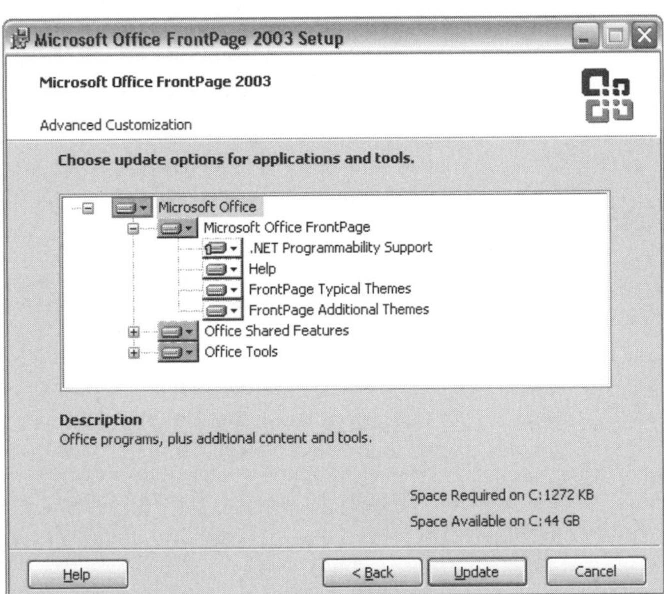

Figure 1-4. Be sure to include FrontPage when you install Microsoft Office.

Table 1-1 explains all the possibilities. The actual options available will vary depending on the circumstances. The following choices are significant:

- **Microsoft FrontPage For Windows** You should almost certainly choose Run From My Computer for this installation option. If you choose Not Available, FrontPage won't be installed.
- **Help** Again, you should almost certainly choose Run From My Computer, or no online help will be installed.
- **.NET Programmability Support** Choose Run From My Computer if you plan to work with ASP.NET Web pages or with Windows SharePoint Services. Otherwise, choose Installed On First Use.

- **FrontPage Additional Themes** Choose Run From My Computer if you'd like to expand the normal selection of *FrontPage themes*. A FrontPage theme is a prefabricated set of color and graphic designs you can apply to Web pages.

Table 1-1. Custom Installation States

State	Description
Run From My Computer	Setup installs the feature on your hard disk.
Run All From My Computer	Setup installs the feature and all components on your hard disk.
Run From Network	Setup configures the selected feature to use program files located on a network file server. If the file server isn't available when you use the feature, the feature won't work.
Run All From Network	Setup configures all components of the selected feature to use program files located on a network file server. If the file server isn't available when you use the feature, the feature won't work.
Run From CD	Setup configures the selected feature to use program files located on the product's CD. If the CD isn't available when you use the feature, the feature won't work.
Run All From CD	Setup configures all components of the selected feature to use program files located on the product's CD. If the CD isn't available when you use the feature, the feature won't work.
Installed On First Use	Setup doesn't install the feature, but instead installs a placeholder. The first time you use the feature, the application installs it from the original setup location (CD or file server).
Not Available	Setup doesn't install the feature. You can run Setup again to install it later.

For more options that affect your use of FrontPage, scroll down to the Office Shared Features item. Figure 1-5 shows these options.

Expand this heading by clicking its plus icon, and then review the following options:

- **Alternative User Input** This option controls the availability of speech recognition and handwriting as alternatives to keyboard input. Install these options as you want.
- **Clip Organizer** This is the new name for clip art. Most Web designers want all the clip art they can get and thus choose Run All From My Computer.
- **Converters And Filters** This option specifies which file format converters Setup installs on your system. FrontPage uses these converters for importing and exporting files used by other programs. If any file formats you're likely to use are marked Not Available, change them to Run From My Computer or Install On First Use.

- **Digital Signature For VBA Projects** This option installs software that digitally signs Microsoft Visual Basic for Applications (VBA) modules so that other users can detect possible tampering. This option is irrelevant to FrontPage because FrontPage makes no use of VBA Projects.

> **Note** VBA is the language most often used to write macros for Office applications. VBA Projects are modules users can distribute among themselves to add features to most Office applications. Although FrontPage supports VBA, it doesn't support distribution by means of VBA Projects.

- **Microsoft Handwriting Component** This option installs Windows Ink Services for Pen (WISP). If you're using a device like a TabletPC that supports ink input, this component adds handwriting features to FrontPage.
- **International Support** If you need to have fonts installed for languages other than your primary Office language, expand this option and mark those languages Run From My Computer.
- **Office Assistant** This option refers to the animated Clippit that appears when you start Office Help. If you specify Not Available, the animation won't pop up at all.
- **New and Open Office Document Shortcuts** This option adds shortcuts to the Windows Start menu for creating and opening Microsoft Office documents.
- **Office 2003 Web Components** This feature installs subsets of the Excel Spreadsheet, Chart, and PivotTable features that you can use as components in Web pages. They work only if the Web visitor is running Microsoft Internet Explorer 5 or later on a Windows computer, and they have reduced functionality if the Web visitor doesn't have Excel 2003 installed.
- **Proofing Tools** Use this option to choose the dictionaries you want to use for translation and spelling.
- **Microsoft Office Download Control** This feature downloads Office clip art and templates from Microsoft's Web site and opens them automatically in the associated program.
- **Themes** This option controls how many themes are installed for use by the Office suite in general.
- **Visual Basic For Applications** This option installs the files necessary to run Office 2003 macros. Select Not Available if you're sure you'll never want to create or run any FrontPage macros and you want to minimize the risk of viruses.
- **Office SOAP toolkit** This option provides a way to work with XML Web services from within Microsoft Office.

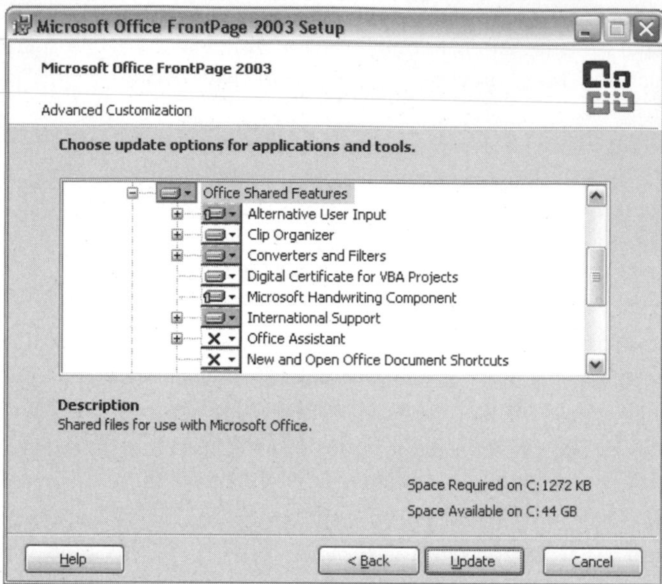

Figure 1-5. Many Office Shared Features affect the capabilities available in FrontPage.

Using VBA and Avoiding Viruses

In today's world of global connectivity, transmission of malicious computer programs (viruses) is a constant concern. Any facility that runs code can run malicious code, and VBA is no exception. Several high-profile e-mail viruses have, in fact, been VBA-based.

Having VBA on your system can be safe if the following conditions are true:

- You never execute VBA code automatically, even if it arrives as an e-mail attachment or as part of an ordinary Office document.
- When asked whether to run a VBA macro, you reply No if the macro arrived from an untrusted or unknown source.
- You keep up-to-date on the names of any VBA-based macros that are currently circulating.

Not having VBA on your system means you won't execute any VBA viruses. It also means you won't execute any Office 2003 application macros. The choice is yours.

If you're working at home or in a small office environment, or if your support staff can't provide a development Windows SharePoint Services or FrontPage Web server, you might need to install the Web server software and the FrontPage Server Extensions on your own computer or find an ISP that supports them.

Installing and configuring a FrontPage-extended Web server on your own computer is a two-step process:

1. Obtain and install Web server software. This can run on any computer that's accessible to your PC and that runs an operating system for which FrontPage Server Extensions are available.

For more information about installing Web server software, refer to Chapter 49, "Installing and Configuring a Web Server."

2. Obtain and install the FrontPage Server Extensions on the Web server you installed in step 1. In general, you should run the most recent version of the server extensions. For example, the FrontPage 2002 Server Extensions are newer than the server extensions versions that come with Windows 2000. Microsoft's Web site (*msdn.microsoft.com/library/en-us/dnservext/html/fpovrw.asp*) provides the latest version of the server extensions for FrontPage.

For more information about installing FrontPage Server Extensions, refer to Chapter 50, "Understanding the FrontPage Server Extensions."

Discovering What's New in FrontPage 2003

This section will be most interesting to designers who've used FrontPage 2002—or even older versions of FrontPage—in the past. If you're new to FrontPage, every feature in FrontPage 2003 will be new and you don't need to worry about differences between versions. If this is your situation, you might prefer skipping to the next section or just skimming this one.

FrontPage 2003 introduces professional authoring tools and makes it quick and easy to build data-driven Web sites. FrontPage 2003 provides the freedom and controls customers have been asking for.

- **User interface** FrontPage 2003 has a new overall appearance plus numerous features that make it even easier to use than previous versions.
- **Page design** These new features make it easier to build richly designed Web pages based on HTML tables, work with pictures, and add more interactivity than ever to your site.
- **Coding tools** These tools help you apply your knowledge of HTML to the authoring process. Even if you don't know HTML, these features make it easier than ever to learn.

  FrontPage 2003 also gives you more control than ever over the appearance of code that the WYSIWYG editor creates. This ensures that the HTML code is just what you want.
- **Data-driven Web sites** By providing first-rate support for XML, FrontPage 2003 makes it simple to create great-looking data-driven Web sites. Specifically, FrontPage 2003 provides visual tools that create formatting instructions for data from XML files, XML Web services, and many other XML data sources. FrontPage saves these instructions in an XML-based format called Extensible Style Sheet Transformations (XSLT) but you never need to look at the XML-based code (unless you want to).

This feature makes it easy for a FrontPage Web site to present external data inline with other content. You can use it to create your own site from scratch, to customize default SharePoint sites, or to customize SharePoint sites that other Microsoft Office services create. It does, however, require Windows SharePoint Services 2.0, which is available only as part of Windows .NET Server 2003.

Note Extensible Style Sheet Transformations (XSLT) is a language that describes how to transform one kind of XML document into another. With care, the resulting documents can also serve as HTML.

- **Publishing** FrontPage 2003 simplifies uploading your Web site via FTP or Web Distributed Authoring and Versioning (WebDAV). Of course, it still supports publishing to servers running the FrontPage Server Extensions and collaborative functions on servers running Windows SharePoint Services.

Operating the User Interface

The biggest change you'll notice when you start FrontPage 2003 is the lack of a Views bar. In FrontPage 2000 and 2002, this was the vertical bar that offered six views of a Web site: Page, Folders, Reports, Navigation, Hyperlinks, and Tasks. To conserve screen space, Microsoft replaced this bar with a much smaller set of tabs that appear below the main editing window when you click the new Web Site tab. (The Web Site tab, by the way, appears above the main editing window, in the same row as the tabs for each open Web page.) A new Remote Web Site view on the Web Site tab displays the status of the remote site to which you last published the current Web site.

In FrontPage 2003, Microsoft has added three new toolbars and removed two that were present in FrontPage 2002. Table 1-2 itemizes these changes.

Table 1-2. Toolbar Changes in FrontPage 2003

Status	Toolbar	Description
New	Code View	Commands for entering, analyzing, and scrolling through code
New	Dynamic Web Template	Commands for managing which regions of a dynamic Web template are editable in pages that use that template
New	XML View	Commands for formatting and validating XML code that you open in FrontPage
Removed	Navigation	
Removed	Reporting	

FrontPage 2003 has retained the four task panes that were present in FrontPage 2002, subject to certain modifications. In addition, FrontPage 2003 has 13 totally new task panes. Table 1-3 lists the complete set.

Tip To change the task pane currently on display, open the drop-down list at the top of the task pane area. If no task pane is on display, press Ctrl+F1.

Table 1-3. Task Panes in FrontPage 2003

Status	Task Pane	Description
Retained	New	Provides basic options to initialize a new Web page or a new Web site.
Retained	Basic File Search	Searches local file locations for specified file names or text. (To display this task pane, choose File Search from the File menu.)
Retained	Clip Art	Searches local file locations or a Microsoft Web site for clip art and then optionally adds it to the current Web page.
Retained	Clipboard	Displays up to 24 selections cut or copied to the Microsoft Office Clipboard.
New	Getting Started	Provides basic options browse or search the Microsoft Office Web site for information. This task pane appears by default whenever you start FrontPage.
New	Search Results	Displays results from searching the Microsoft Office Web site for information.
New	Help	Searches for answers in local Help files or on Microsoft's Web site.
New	Layout Tables And Cells	Manages precise settings for HTML tables and table cells that control page layout.
New	Cell Formatting	Controls special formatting effects—such as rounded corners—for HTML table cells.
New	Theme	Applies or removes Theme formatting from a FrontPage-based Web site or an individual Web page.
New	Layers	Creates and manages HTML *layers*. These are rectangular zones that float in front of or behind normal Web content, and that script code can show, hide, or reposition while the Web page is on display.
New	Behaviors	Attaches or removes interactivity from elements on a Web page. For example, you can specify actions that should occur whenever a visitor clicks on a given element or when the mouse passes over it.
New	Data Source Catalog	Displays a list of data sources compatible with commands on the Data main menu. Each data source can contain one or more database tables or XML files that you can query and display.

Table 1-3. Task Panes in FrontPage 2003

Status	Task Pane	Description
New	Find A Data Source	Searches for XML Web services and other data sources at network locations.
New	Data Source Details	Displays detailed information about a given data source.
New	Conditional Formatting	Changes the formatting of a reported data source element, depending on values in that data source.
New	Web Parts	Displays a list of Web Parts available within a Windows SharePoint Services site. Web Parts are essentially components that you can add to Web pages.

In addition to eliminating the Views bar and adding lots of new task panes, the FrontPage 2003 adds the following features to its user interface. In total, these changes provide a major improvement to the FrontPage authoring experience.

Web Site tab

This new screen element, which appears in the main editing window, replaces the Views bar that formerly occupied the left side of the FrontPage window. This increases the size of the design surface and generally provides more room to work.

For more information about the Web Site tab, see "Opening a FrontPage-Based Web Site," page 85.

Split pane

A new Split pane divides the main editing window to show Design view and Code view displays at the same time.

When you're editing in the Design view window, FrontPage immediately updates the Code view window. This makes it easy to monitor the code you're creating or to learn about HTML.

When you're editing directly in the Code view window, FrontPage doesn't immediately update the Design view window because the results would change dramatically as you type. However, the FrontPage does update the Design view display when you click it or press F5.

For more information about the Split pane, see "Understanding the Main FrontPage Window," page 41.

Editor configuration

You can configure multiple editors for each type of content you use in FrontPage 2003. This makes it easy to choose the correct editor for any job.

You can, for example, associate several picture editors with a single filename extension such as *.gif*. Then, when you right-click a *.gif* file and point to Open With, the next menu will display a selection list of the editors you specified.

For more information about editor configuration, see "Configuring External Editors," page 1118.

Configurable editing mode

When you configure FrontPage as the editor for a given filename extension, you can specify whether FrontPage should open the file as HTML, CSS, text, or XML.

For more information about configuring the FrontPage editing mode, see "Configuring External Editors," page 1148.

Text file editing

FrontPage 2003 can now open text files (such as JavaScript or XML files) directly in the FrontPage editor. Of course, all the great new code editing features are fully available.

For more information about text file editing, refer to "Configuring External Editors," page 1118.

Designing Web Pages

FrontPage 2003 has a number of completely new features that give you pixel-precise control over the layout elements on a page. It also provides new tools for adding rounded corners, shadows, borders, and other visual elements to the cells of a page layout.

Dynamic Web Templates

FrontPage 2003 supports a new kind of Web site template much richer than those of the past. When you create such a template, you specify which regions are editable. Then, in pages that use the template, designers can only add content to and modify the editable regions. FrontPage stops the designer from changing any other regions on the same page. If you subsequently change a template, FrontPage will propagate new versions of the non-editable region to all pages that use that template.

FrontPage 2003 Web Templates are syntax-compatible with templates from Macromedia Dreamweaver 4. Therefore, you can easily move your Dreamweaver Web site to FrontPage 2003 or collaborate with Dreamweaver designers working on the same site.

For more information about Dynamic Web Templates, see "Using Dynamic Web Templates," page 322.

Table Layout Tools

FrontPage 2003 provides a special set of tools for creating and manipulating tables that control page layout. Tables you create using these tools work equally well in different types of browsers and different browser versions.

- An Autostretch feature prevents distortion of columns and rows under diverse viewing conditions, such as different browser resolutions and window sizes. For example, you could create a Web page with a fixed-width column on the left and an Autostretch column on the right. Then, when the visitor resized the browser window, only the column on the right would automatically resize itself and wrap text to fit the new window size.
- Other tools insert *spacer.gif* files to set and maintain the size of fixed-width columns and fixed-height rows, set specified columns to the same width, and otherwise format table columns and rows.

Layout tools appear exactly when you need them, without requiring an additional mode to display them. Clicking a table border displays the tools, and moving the cursor within a cell or outside a table turns them off again.

For more information about using layout tables, see "Using Layout Tables," page 58.

Layout Tables And Cells Task Pane

This tool adds a layout table to your page. You can select from a variety of predesigned styles, or you can use the table pencil to create custom layout tables.

For more information about using layout cells see "Creating Layout Cells," page 550.

Layout Detection

FrontPage 2003 inspects the tables in each page it opens and automatically engages the layout tools for tables that obviously contain a layout. Because tables that contain repeating patterns of cells and normal, tabular data don't need the layout tools, FrontPage doesn't display the layout tools in that case.

FrontPage provides complete control over the Layout Detection feature. You can turn the layout tools on or off for a given table or for every table you edit. (In the latter case, you would always control the layout tools manually.)

For more information about Layout Detection, see "Inserting a Table Using Menus," on page 528, and "Configuring General Options," on page 1125.

Cell Formatting Task Pane

This feature controls a range of visual elements in the area surrounding a table cell. This eliminates the time spent hand-coding the many table cells otherwise needed to achieve these effects. For example, FrontPage 2003 can easily create rounded cell corners. You don't have to create your own corner elements in a graphics editor, and you don't have to create extra table rows and columns to position them.

If you move or resize a formatted cell, FrontPage 2003 resizes and rearranges the layout table, including corners, shadows, and other decorations.

For more information about the Cell Formatting Task Pane, see "Modifying Layout Tables," page 553.

Integrated Browser Size Settings

FrontPage 2003 Design view has an integrated browser sizing feature that makes it simple to target a particular browser or resolution or to see how your page will look in different sized windows. Select the target browser size from a menu on the status bar, and FrontPage 2003 resizes the Design view window to approximate the target.

If the target width is narrower than the editing window, FrontPage displays gray borders on each side. In addition, FrontPage draws a dotted horizontal line showing how much of the page will be visible when it first appears.

For more information about the Integrated Browser Size Settings, see "Simulating Browser Size in Design View," page 58.

Tracing Pictures

If you have a scanned picture or sketch that shows how your Web page should appear, FrontPage 2003 can display it as a background in the editing window. This is useful if, for example, you're working from an artist's rendition of a site: you can use the scanned picture as a guide!

You can vary the transparency of the tracing picture to differentiate it from your real content. However, the tracing picture is visible only in Design view. Even if you don't remove it when you finish editing, your Web visitors won't see it.

For more information about Tracing Pictures, see "Displaying a Tracing Image," page 59.

Rulers and Layout Grid

FrontPage 2003 now supports rulers and a visible layout grid in Design view. You can position the rulers, the grid, or both anywhere you want—for example, you can line them up with existing page content or a tracing picture. You can set the ruler scale, view or hide the grid, snap objects to the grid, and change the grid's granularity.

For more information about displaying rulers and layout grids, see "Displaying Rulers and Layout Grids," page 58.

Layer support

FrontPage 2003 now supports design-time layers. This makes it easy to work with overlapping content that occupies the same space and becomes visible or invisible as the Web visitor views the page. You have complete control over layer creation, placement, and visibility. The new Behaviors tools in FrontPage 2003 can create code that changes the visibility of layers. It also creates sophisticated visual effects such as expanding menus.

For more information about using layers in FrontPage 2003, see "Using Layers," page 630.

Improved themes

FrontPage 2003 always uses CSS instead of HTML to apply themes. This makes FrontPage 2003 themes much less intrusive on the HTML code. (In other words, the HTML for themed pages is smaller and simpler to understand than before.)

Inside Out

Farewell to HTML-Based Themes

FrontPage 2003 can no longer apply HTML-based themes. These themes were designed before CSS was invented and are simply too cumbersome to use in a post-CSS world. Pages with existing HTML themes, however, will still work fine.

A Theme task pane now appears in place of the dialog box that earlier versions of FrontPage used. This means that you can try different themes and see the effect of each without closing and reopening a dialog box. In addition, you'll find a number of new contemporary themes that will give your site an up-to-date look. Finally, Microsoft has improved many of the themes it retained from earlier versions.

For more information about using themes, see "Using FrontPage Themes," page 561.

Improved graphics support

FrontPage 2003 has a number of new tools for working with graphics from other applications. The new interfaces and default behaviors make it clearer what will happen when you add a picture to your Web site. You have more control over the way FrontPage saves pictures in your Web site and the actions that occur when you edit a picture. Resizing a picture displays a smart tag with choices that resample and compress the picture or leave it alone.

For more information about using FrontPage 2003's improved graphics support, see "Editing Pictures in FrontPage," page 635.

Movies in Flash format

A new menu option and drag-and-drop support make it simple to create Web pages that display movies in Flash format. In addition, a new Movie in Flash Format dialog box helps you set properties for such movies, and the new Behaviors feature (described later in this chapter) supports scripting them.

For more information about using Flash content, see "Incorporating Movies in Flash," page 706.

Interactive buttons

With this release, FrontPage 2003 finally supports rollover buttons, one of the most common visual effects on the Web. These are basically hyperlinked pictures with a DHTML script that displays a different picture when the mouse passes over them. FrontPage 2003 provides a large selection of button backgrounds and tools for specifying, formatting, and placing the button text. Because the buttons are actually pictures, you can use any tools you want to fine-tune their appearance.

Inside Out

Farewell to Hover Buttons

FrontPage 2003 can no longer create Hover Buttons, a type of interactive button that used a Java applet to perform the animation. If you have pages that use these relics, FrontPage 2003 will continue to display them properly and even reconfigure their properties. Nevertheless, the new Interactive Button component should be your choice for all new work.

For more information about using interactive buttons, see "Using Interactive Buttons," page 685.

Accessibility checking

FrontPage 2003 provides built-in accessibility checking, so you can ensure that your Web sites are accessible to all users. You can check specific pages or all pages in your Web site, and you can select which accessibility guidelines you want to follow (including U.S. Government section 508 guidelines). Each of the accessibility suggestions is shown in a list, and you can jump back and forth between that list and your site to address the issues.

For more information about checking Web site accessibility, see "Checking Web Site Accessibility," page 478.

Picture Library Integration and Office Imaging Services

Windows SharePoint Services 2.0 supports a new type of document library designed for pictures. FrontPage 2003 makes it simple to work with these picture libraries. You create a new picture library in the same way you create a document library. In addition, if you have Office 2003, you can use the new Microsoft Picture Library program to optimize and upload pictures into the library.

For more information about integrating SharePoint and Office picture libraries, see "Using Windows SharePoint Services Picture Libraries," page 665.

Preview In Multiple Browsers

FrontPage 2003 has enhanced support for previewing pages in the browser by making it simple to configure multiple browsers in multiple sizes for previewing Web pages. You can set up as many browser and size combinations as you want. To view any of these combinations, click the Preview In Browser button or on the File menu, point to Preview In Browser and choose one of the browser configurations. You can easily preview the same page in multiple browsers simultaneously.

For more information about configuring and invoking previews in multiple browsers, see "Previewing in External Browsers," page 55.

Editing Code

FrontPage 2003 leverages your knowledge of Web technologies not only in Design view, but in Code view as well. Consequently, FrontPage now makes working at the code level as easy and powerful as possible, including HTML, CSS, JavaScript, ASP.NET, and so on. Here are the new capabilities:

Quick Tag Selector

This toolbar displays a text icon for the HTML element that contains the insertion point, plus another icon for each element that surrounds it, ending at the <body> tag. If, for example, the insertion point is in an HTML table cell, the Quick Tag Toolbar would display these icons: <body> <table> <tr> <td>.

Clicking an icon on the Quick Tag toolbar selects the corresponding element in Design view. This makes it very easy to select just the table or cells you want, even if you're working on a page that contains nested tables or other elements that are usually difficult to select. Drop-down options on each icon can also select the tag's contents, edit or remove a tag, insert additional HTML, wrap a new tag around the existing one, or display a dialog box for editing the tag's properties.

For more information about using the Quick Tag Selector, see "Understanding the Main FrontPage Window," page 41.

Quick Tag Editor

This feature can insert or edit tags in your document directly in the editing window. You can select the text and edit the tags that surround it, wrap the text in a new tag, insert new HTML, or remove a tag.

For more information about using the Quick Tag Editor, see "Working with HTML While in Design Mode," page 67.

Code IntelliSense

FrontPage Code view now provides Microsoft IntelliSense technology for HTML, CSS, XSL, JavaScript, and VBScript code. IntelliSense displays pop-up selection lists that show and explain whatever parameters are valid at the current point in the code. This makes writing code much easier and less prone to errors.

For more information about using IntelliSense with different kinds of code, see the sidebar, "IntelliSense Language Support in FrontPage," page 65.

Typing aids

In addition to IntelliSense, FrontPage 2003 provides a number of other new or improved typing aids in Code view. These tools are available on the new Code View toolbar, and most are also available through hot keys. The tools include:

- **Line Numbers** Code view now supports line numbers.
- **Word Wrap** You can now set lines to wrap in Code view so that they don't extend off the screen to the right.
- **Autoindent** You can specify whether new lines in Code view are aligned with the line above or begin at the left margin.
- **Code Indentation** Selecting a block of text and pressing Tab or Shift+Tab changes the indentation of the block.
- **Balancing Braces** There's now a command for expanding the selection to the extent of the surrounding braces. Subsequent calls will expand the selection out to the next set of braces, and so on.
- **Matching Tags** This command finds the tag that matches the current tag. For example, you can jump from a start tag like <b> to its corresponding end tag </b>.
- **Improved Paste** Pasting code into Code view now works the way a code developer would expect. For example, you get <b> rather than *<b>*.
- **Typing Shortcuts** There are hot keys for inserting start tags, end tags, and comments and for placing the insertion point in the correct portion of the tag.
- **Temporary Bookmarks** You can create bookmarks in your code and jump back and forth between portions of the Code view window. For example, you could move between the script block at the top of the page and the script invocation at the bottom.

- **Tab Setting** There's an improved interface for setting the number of spaces that Code view inserts when you press Tab.

For more information about the new Code view typing aids, see "Configuring the Code View Display," page 1037.

Code snippets

FrontPage 2003 can store chunks of code in a code snippet library and then insert them into other documents. These code snippets can be anything that you can insert in Code view (HTML, CSS, and so forth).

For more information about storing and inserting code snippets, see "Storing and Inserting Code Snippets," page 1049.

Support for ASP.NET controls and script authoring

FrontPage 2003 correctly detects and previews ASP.NET controls, which makes it both safe and easy to use FrontPage 2003 and Microsoft Visual Studio .NET for working on the same Web site. This takes perfect advantage of FrontPage's more powerful and flexible design features as well as Visual Studio's more powerful programming environment.

FrontPage Design view previews, repositions, and resizes ASP.NET controls. FrontPage Code view provides IntelliSense scripting that can easily create, modify, or delete ASP.NET intrinsic controls.

For more information about using FrontPage 2003 and Visual Studio .NET together, see Chapter 43, "Using FrontPage 2003 and Visual Studio .NET Together."

Smart Find And Replace

FrontPage 2003 provides basic find and replace functionality as well as a rules engine for performing HTML searches. You can quickly and accurately search and replace based on attributes or tags across your entire site or on specific pages. For example, you could specify a rule to "Find all pages in the site that lack a keyword meta tag and add a keyword tag before the </head> tag." You can save search and replace settings as queries so that you and coworkers can run them again in the future.

For more information about using the new Smart Find And Replace, see "Finding and Replacing Text," page 229.

Behaviors

If you want to provide more interactivity on your Web site, you can use new Behaviors functionality to create JavaScript without writing a line of code. Such scripts can, for example, show and hide pictures or jump to another page depending on the visitor's browser type. Just select the functionality you want from a task pane, and FrontPage 2003 writes the script for you.

This feature is extensible. If you or your team writes a certain script often, you can extend FrontPage to offer that script.

For more information about using Behaviors, see "Scripting DHTML Behaviors," page 694.

Minimal HTML reformatting

When you modify a page in Design view, FrontPage makes as few changes as possible to your HTML code. Furthermore, when integrating new code, FrontPage 2003 strives to use the same formatting as the rest of the same Web page. Microsoft's goal is to make the generated HTML identical to what you would code by hand.

For more information about configuring HTML formatting rules, see "Personalizing HTML Format," page 1040.

Simple HTML creation

When you modify a page in Design view, FrontPage also strives to create the simplest possible HTML. When you create a new HTML table, for example, FrontPage 2003 by default creates the simplest "vanilla" HTML table.

This is quite a contrast to FrontPage 2002, which tried to make default tables looked like Word tables. Every new table contained the following properties:

```
style="border-collapse: collapse" bordercolor="#111111"
```

and there was no padding between a table cell's contents and its borders. Most designers found these settings a nuisance, and Microsoft has therefore removed them. Of course, it's easy to switch back to Word-style tables if that's what you want.

For more information about HTML tables, see "Using HTML Tables for Page Layout," page 515.

HTML cleanup

If your existing HTML is a mess, FrontPage 2003 can clean it up. FrontPage 2003 does this by merging adjacent tags, by removing various elements such as empty tags and unused styles, and by removing comments and white space. Furthermore, FrontPage can do this either a page at a time in Design view or a site at a time when you publish your site to another location. Table 1-4 lists the optimizations available in each scenario.

For more information about cleaning up HTML code, see "Optimizing Published HTML Code," page 454, and "Optimizing HTML Code at Design Time," page 475.

Table 1-4. HTML Optimization Types

Element	In Design view	When publishing
All HTML comments		
Author-time Web component comments	❍	●
Theme and Shared Border comments	❍	●
Browse-time Web Component commands	❍	●
Dynamic Web Template comments	●	●
Layout Tables and Cell Formatting comments	●	●
Script comments	●	●
All other HTML comments	●	●
White space		
HTML leading white space	●	●
HTML all white space	●	●
Unused content		
Merge adjacent tags	●	❍
Empty tags	●	❍
Unused styles	●	❍
Generated HTML		
FrontPage Tracing Image attributes and Interactive Button attributes	●	●
Generator and ProgID tags	●	●
Delete VML content	●	❍
Word HTML	●	❍

When Less Is More—Optimizing HTML

The last two items in Table 1-4 warrant special mention. First, VML graphics content comes from various Microsoft Office programs that create line drawings. When you save such documents as HTML, Office saves the line drawing information in an XML format called VML. If you don't want to send this drawing information to Web visitors, FrontPage 2003 can remove it.

Second, Word HTML comes from saving a Microsoft Word document in HTML format. If you've ever looked at the resulting HTML code, you know it's fairly ugly. This occurs because the Microsoft Word development team never intended the HTML for human reading, and also because the HTML contains extra information so that if anyone ever opens the HTML file in Word, all the word-processing features of the original document are still available. Of course, if you want to work on the document as an HTML page, all this extra information gets in the way. That's why FrontPage 2003 has an option to remove it.

Fine-grained feature control

FrontPage 2003 has several features that create code that follows all the rules for well-formed HTML but is difficult to read or manipulate manually. If you don't want to use these features (or don't want coworkers using them), FrontPage 2003 can turn the features off, either through the application or through policy. Here are some of the features you can control this way:

- **Office Drawing Toolbar** The Office Drawing toolbar creates graphics in VML format. FrontPage can turn this feature off.
- **Themes** The original Themes mechanism in FrontPage used numerous comments and HTML tags to apply theme properties. FrontPage 2003 avoids this problem by using much truer and cleaner CSS code. However, you can still turn off themes completely if you want.
- **FrontPage Components** FrontPage saves the parameters for most FrontPage components as HTML comments, and saves these plus the corresponding HTML when you save the page or recalculate hyperlinks in the Web site. FrontPage 2003 can optionally strip out such comments when you save the page or when you publish the Web site. It can also completely disable features that insert FrontPage Component comments.

For more information about configuring FrontPage component availability, see "Matching FrontPage Capabilities to Browser Capabilities," page 471, and "Administering User Rights," in Appendix O.

Developing Data-Driven Web Sites

When you use FrontPage 2003 along with Windows SharePoint Services 2.0, you can easily create Web sites that accept, organize, and distribute documents and data that Web visitors upload using only a browser. In this context, the term *data source* refers to any document library or database that Windows SharePoint Services provides. FrontPage can access, query, and display any such data source; it calls the result a data view.

Windows SharePoint Services sends the contents of a data source to FrontPage 2003 in XML format. Front Page 2003 then uses XSLT technology to transform the raw XML into HTML code that the browser can display.

This approach avoids any kind of proprietary code or markup. In fact, if you understand XSLT code, you can even modify what FrontPage produces (with, of course, the support of IntelliSense code completion). Normally, however, you'll create the XSLT code by working with live data directly in Design view. This assures you'll always get an up-to-date WYSIWYG view of the results.

Here are the individual components that FrontPage provinces for creating data-driven Web sites.

Data Source Catalog

This component makes it easy to select data views and add them to a page. Supported data sources include:

- Windows SharePoint Services lists and document libraries
- XML files in your Web site
- URLs that return XML
- XML Web services
- Microsoft SQL Server databases
- Microsoft Access, Oracle, and most other databases accessible via OLE DB.

For more information about accessing the Data Source Catalog, see "Accessing the Data Source Catalog," page 986.

Details view

FrontPage 2003 provides a Details view for each available data source. This view displays the structure of the data in the data source and even the content of individual records. This makes it easy to verify the data you'll be accessing before you add a view to a page.

For more information about accessing data source details, see "Accessing Data Source Details," page 998.

Data View Web Part

When you add a data view to a Web page, you're actually inserting something called a *Data View Web Part*. You do this working with live data directly in the FrontPage 2003 editing window.

Data View Web Parts are transparent in both Design and Code view; they look just like regular FrontPage 2003 content. You can format the data by selecting columns or other end points and then using standard FrontPage tools like the Formatting toolbar. FrontPage responds by creating XSLT code that applies the given format to the display. This code appears directly in the HTML file. If you want to edit it directly, you can do so in FrontPage 2003 Code view.

For more information about creating and using Data View Web Parts, see "Creating and Configuring Data View Web Parts," page 999.

Data view styles

In addition to manually formatting your data, you can also apply prebuilt data view styles. This makes it easy to quickly and easily change the overall look of your data. Applying a style preserves any applicable manual formatting you've already specified. In addition, you can still apply manual formatting after you apply the style.

For more information about controlling data view styles, see "Controlling Data View Styles," page 1002.

Conditional formatting

This feature can show, hide, or reformat data items based on a field's value or its position in the Data View Web Part. Conditional formatting in one field can depend on another, even if that field doesn't appear in the display.

For more information about applying conditional formatting to a data view, see "Applying Conditional Formatting to a Data View," page 1008.

Sort, filter, and group

You can select which data is presented and how it's presented by applying these features:

- **Sorting** You can sort your data in either ascending or descending order by a field in the data, even if that field doesn't appear in the display.
- **Filtering** You can include or exclude records based on data values.
- **Grouping** You can group your data based on data values, even for fields that don't appear in the display.

The processing for these features occurs on the Windows SharePoint Services or database server. This is very efficient because, for example, if you filter your data, FrontPage 2003 or the browser receives only the filtered records.

For more information about sorting and grouping data views, see "Sorting and Grouping Data Views," page 1005.

Connecting Web Parts

You can connect multiple Web Parts and then change the data or formatting in one Web Part when the contents or selection of the other Web Part changes. This creates sophisticated master/detail views of your data. For example, when a Web visitor selects categories in one Web Part, another Web Part might display items in that category.

For more information about connecting Web Parts, see "Connecting Web Parts," page 981.

Web Part Gallery and Web Part Zone Creation

FrontPage can work with almost any kind of Web part that exists on your server. This includes the Data View Web Part, of course, but also Microsoft Office 2003 Web Parts and Windows SharePoint Services Web Parts. You can add these Web Parts directly to your page or put them in Web Part Zones that you define. If you use Web Part Zones, Web visitors can add Web Parts without even starting FrontPage 2003.

For more information about creating Web Part Zones, see "Creating Web Part Zones," page 976.
For more information about using the Web Part Gallery, see "Adding Web Parts to Zones," page 978.

Save form results as XML

You can save results from your HTML forms in an XML file in your Web site. Just specify XML as the save results format and pick a file name. The Data View Web Part can then treat the file as a data source.

For more information about saving form results as XML, see "Configuring File Results Options," page 863.

Publishing Your Site

FrontPage 2003 can publish your Web site more easily, more efficiently, and to more kinds of destinations than ever before. In addition to publishing files to a customary (remote) destination, you can reverse-publish files to the local site or synchronize both sites to the most recent version of each file. Here, in detail, are the new features that make this possible.

Support for FTP and WebDAV

The last several versions of FrontPage have supported publishing Web sites to another server by FTP. However, this capability has been hard to find and limited in flexibility. FrontPage 2003 has a rich, new, integrated set of publishing tools that work with any type of destination server: SharePoint, FrontPage, FTP, or WebDAV.

Note WebDAV is a set of extensions to HTTP that make it easy for groups of Web designers to collaboratively edit and manage files on remote Web servers. These extensions provide ways of locking, downloading, and uploading Web content.

When you publish to a Web server via SharePoint, the FrontPage Server Extensions, or WebDAV, FrontPage 2003 uses the file-locking features built into those tools.

When you publish to an FTP server, FrontPage supports file locking through the use of *.lck* files. These files are fully compatible with the ones Macromedia Dreamweaver uses. Therefore, FrontPage designers and Dreamweaver designers can use the same FTP server without accidentally overwriting each other's changes.

For more information about publishing to various kinds of Web servers, see "Publishing Your FrontPage-Based Web site," page 443.

Remote Site view

FrontPage 2003 includes a new, fully integrated Remote Site view that shows the status of a partner Web site. After FrontPage opens your development Web site, for example, Remote Site view would typically show your production Web site. In fact, however, Remote Site view can display any site you specify.

When you publish a Web site, Remote Site view provides the default destination. However, Remote Site view can also copy files from the remote site to the currently open site. Remote Site view can synchronize both sites; when this operation is complete, both sites will have identical content based on the most recent version of each file.

Remote Site view also provides filters that show which files are out of date on each server, whether any files are marked to not be published, which files are in conflict, and so forth.

For more information about using Remote Site view, see "Using Remote Site View," page 435.

Web import

An improved Web Import dialog box makes capturing content from remote sites easier than ever. It now includes options to specify the type of connection, how to deal with SSL (Secure Sockets Layer), whether to use passive FTP (PASV), and other connection settings.

Note PASV is a variant of FTP that works better through firewalls than the normal FTP connection mode.

For more information about importing Web sites, see "Importing Web Files and Folders," page 175.

Web Packages

FrontPage 2003 can export and import collections of Web pages, Windows SharePoint Services lists, and Windows SharePoint Services list content as single files called *packages*. This makes it easy to copy your work from one Web site to another. Whenever you import or export, FrontPage 2003 automatically includes dependent files so that the deployed package will work seamlessly on the new Web site.

For more information about exporting and importing Web packages, see "Exporting And Importing Web Packages," page 461.

In Summary…

FrontPage 2003 provides not only a powerful, visual Web page editor, but also a myriad of features for managing the hundreds or thousands of cross-related files that comprise a typical Web site. The latest release includes a multitude of new features that make creating Web pages easier and more productive than ever, regardless of whether you work visually in Design mode or directly with the underlying code.

The next chapter provides a rapid introduction to the process of creating Web pages with FrontPage.

Chapter 2

Editing Web Pages

This chapter and the next introduce the major components of Microsoft Office FrontPage 2003, explain their purpose, and provide an overview of how they work. This chapter is primarily about creating individual Web pages, and Chapter 3 addresses the management of multipage sites.

Be forewarned, however: these chapters present only a broad introduction to the process of using FrontPage to create Web sites. Once you understand the general mind-set of working with FrontPage, you'll be ready for the details—presented in later chapters—that will give you mastery over Web development.

HTML and Text Editors

The inventors of HTML intended it for publishing scholarly and technical papers—and simple ones at that. There was no way to know what size screen or which fonts each Web visitor would have, so the inventors left these details to the discretion of each visitor's browser and system configuration rather than to the Web page designer. Text would flow within whatever document window the visitor chose. Control over fonts was generic. The designer could, for example, assign style codes such as <h1> through <h6> for progressively smaller headings, but each computer could theoretically display these styles in a different font, size, and color. HTML offered no provision for publishing equations, charts, or tables. Today, of course, style and appearance have become at least as important as content—no one wants to look at ugly pages—and the idea that certain kinds of content can't be displayed seems ridiculous.

The HTML specification from those early days still provides the basis for the most complicated Web pages we see today. In fact, plain text editors remain among the most common tools for creating Web pages, no matter how complex the page or how cryptic the HTML codes might be.

Objectively, HTML is one of the worst page description languages around. Its greatest strength and its greatest weakness are one and the same: simplicity. Its simplicity lets anyone with a plain text editor (such as Notepad) create Web pages and anyone with a browser on any computer system read those pages. But at the same time, it constrains page designers so harshly that designers can spend huge amounts of time trying to overcome its limitations. Page designers should be designers, stylists, and artists, not technicians who create intricate program code.

Designing effective Web pages today requires a two-pronged approach: first, use tools that simplify the coding of complex Web pages; and second, accept the fact that every Web visitor's browser is going to display your work a little differently.

WYSIWYG Editing in FrontPage

Web designers working with a text editor typically keep a browser running in the background to display the page they're working on. To preview the appearance of a page, the designer saves it from the editor to disk and then clicks the browser's Refresh button to reload the file into the browser. "But this is crazy," you say. "Why doesn't someone invent a Web page editor that displays what the visitor will see—in true WYSIWYG fashion—and not a bunch of HTML gibberish?" FrontPage 2003 has done just that.

With FrontPage 2003, you can quickly create Web pages with all the familiarity and ease of use found in other Microsoft Office applications, such as Microsoft Office Word and Microsoft Office PowerPoint. To the maximum extent possible, FrontPage's menu structure, toolbar icons, dialog boxes, and working conventions strongly resemble those in other applications. With the visual tools built into FrontPage, you can concentrate fully on your message and let FrontPage handle the mechanics. As a result, you can also create great-looking Web pages without seeing a scrap of HTML.

The end result of all this visual editing is, of course, code, and many kinds of it. Developing a modern Web site requires using more different kinds of code than almost any other endeavor: HTML code for page layout, CSS code for typography and positioning, JavaScript code for interaction at the browser, and various programming languages for processing submissions and customizing output at the Web server. Sooner or later—and regardless of whether you're an expert, an old-timer, a beginner, a show-off, or a wannabe—you're going to encounter some requirement that's easier to do in raw code than in visual design mode.

As the section "Working with Code," later in this chapter, will illustrate, FrontPage 2003 provides great tools for working directly with all the kinds of code that appear on Web pages. The remainder of this section, however, will concentrate on visual tools.

Understanding the Main FrontPage Window

The first time you start FrontPage, it displays an application window much like the one shown in Figure 2-1.

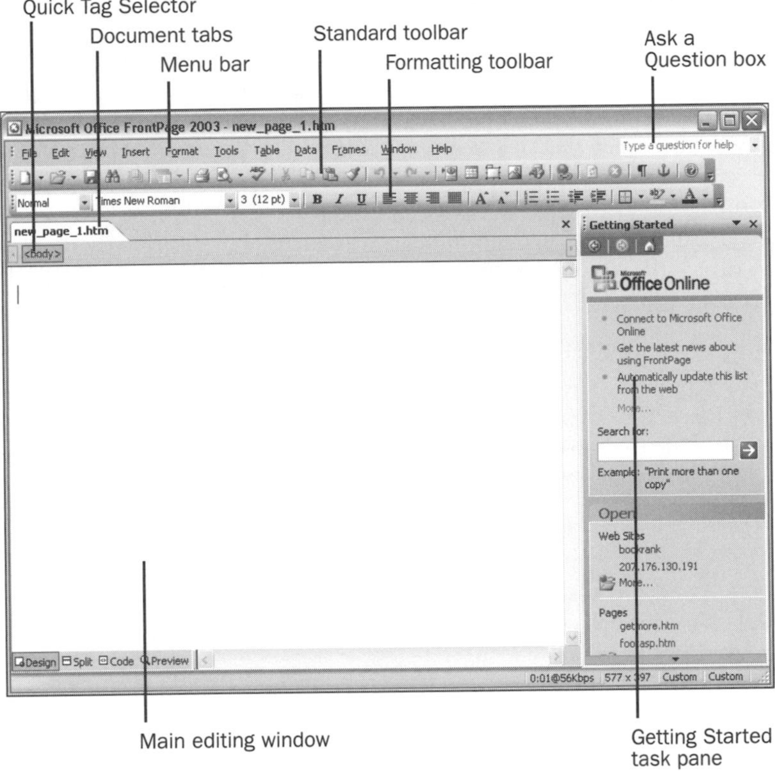

Figure 2-1. By default, the main FrontPage window contains these elements on startup.

Here are the functions of each element:

- **Menu bar.** The FrontPage menu bar is typical of those found in all Microsoft Windows programs since the advent of the Windows, Icons, Mouse, and Pointers (WIMP) interface. File, Edit, and View are on the left; Help is on the right. You can customize the menu bar by choosing Customize from the Tools menu.

  By default, FrontPage 2003 displays personalized menus. This means that the commands you use most appear when you first display a menu, and the rest appear after you leave the menu open for a few seconds or click the double arrow at the bottom of the menu. If you find personalized menus more distracting than useful:

  1. Choose Customize from the Tools menu.
  2. Click the Options tab.

3. To see full menus all the time, select the Always Show Full Menus check box.
4. To see full menus only when you click the double arrows, clear the Show Full Menus After A Short Delay check box.

> **For more information about customizing FrontPage menus and toolbars, refer to "Customizing Menus and Toolbars," Appendix M.**

- **Standard toolbar** The most fundamental and most often used FrontPage commands—New, Open, Save, Cut, Copy, Paste, and so forth—appear on this toolbar.

> **For more information about the Standard toolbar, refer to "The Standard Toolbar" in Appendix A.**

FrontPage, like many other Windows applications, features dockable toolbars. This means that you can rearrange toolbars, lengthen them, shorten them, dock them at any side of the window, or let them float anywhere on the screen. To display or hide a particular toolbar:

- Choose Toolbars from the View menu, and select or deselect the appropriate toolbar.
- Right-click a toolbar, and choose the toolbar you want from the shortcut menu.

> **For more information about positioning and modifying toolbars, refer to "Customizing Menus and Toolbars," Appendix M.**

Be alert to down arrows in any toolbar. A down arrow beneath a pair of greater than symbols (>>) means that part of the toolbar is hidden. Clicking the down arrow displays the hidden portion, as shown here:

- **Formatting toolbar** This toolbar contains buttons for the most often used formatting commands: Style, Font, Font Size, Bold, Italic, and so forth. This toolbar is one of the easiest to use because it provides the same buttons and functions as most other Microsoft Office System applications.

> **For more information about the Formatting toolbar, refer to "The Formatting Toolbar" in Appendix A.**

- **Ask A Question box** At any time, you can type a plain-English question about using FrontPage in this box, and FrontPage will try to answer it.

- **Getting Started task pane** This element provides the options listed in Table 2-1. Unless you take the following actions, the Getting Started task pane appears whenever you start FrontPage:
  1. Choose Options from the Tools menu.
  2. When the Options dialog box appears, click the General tab.
  3. Clear the Startup Task Pane check box.
  4. Click OK.

  Table 2-1. Options on the Getting Started Task Pane

Section	Description
Microsoft Office Online	Provides some useful links to the public Microsoft Office Web site, and a form that searching that site for keywords you specify.
Web Sites	Provides hyperlinks for opening the two Web sites you opened most recently. If you need to work on some other site, click the More link. This will display an Open Site dialog box where you can specify any Web site you want.
Pages	Provides hyperlinks for opening the two Web pages you opened most recently. To work on any other page, click the More link, and specify the page you want in the resulting Open File dialog box.
Create A New Page Or Site	Display a New task pane that contains options for creating new Web pages and Web sites.

  You can display the Getting Started task pane at any time by clicking the Home icon on any task pane, or by clicking the drop-down arrow in the title bar of any task pane and then choosing Getting Started. If no task pane is currently visible, choose Task Pane from the View menu or press Ctrl+F1.

- **Editing window** This is where the most important work occurs—the work of actually creating Web pages. By default, the window displays an editable preview of what your Web visitors will see. Most of the FrontPage menu commands are dedicated to creating, configuring, and formatting elements in this window.

  The tabs at the top of the editing window identify each currently open page by name. To edit a particular open page, click the tab for its file name.

  The tabs at the bottom of the editing window control how the current Web page appears:

  - **Design** displays the Web page in editable WYSIWYG view.
  -  **Split** displays an editable view of the code in the top half of the main window, and an editable WYSIWYG view of the current page in the bottom half.
  - **Code** displays an editable view of the HTML code for the current Web page.

- **Preview** saves the current page to a temporary disk area, and then starts Microsoft Internet Explorer and tells it to display the saved page in the FrontPage editing window.

- **Quick Tag Selector bar** displays an icon for each tag that surrounds the current seection in the editing window. For a new, blank Web page, it displays only one icon: <body>. If the current selection were text inside a table cell, however, the Quick Tag Selector bar would display <body>, <table>, <tr>, and <td> icons. Clicking these icons would select the entire Web page, the current table, the current row, or the current cell, respectively. Drop-down arrows on each icon present further options.

  If the Quick Tag Selector bar doesn't appear when a Web page is open in Design view, choose Quick Tag Selector from the View menu.

Initializing a New Web Page

The next few sections step through the process of creating a simple Web page. The purpose of this exercise is to introduce the FrontPage editor, not to describe it exhaustively, and not to produce a stunning, award-winning, real-world page. Here's how to begin:

1. Start FrontPage. If FrontPage automatically opens a Web, close it by choosing Close Site from the File menu.

> **Tip** To determine whether a FrontPage-based Web site is currently open, click the File menu, and inspect the Close Site command. If it's enabled, a Web is currently open. If it's dimmed, no FrontPage-based Web site is open.

2. If no task pane is visible, press Ctrl+F1 to display one.
3. If the current task pane isn't the New task pane, click the drop-down arrow near its top right corner, and select New from the resulting list.
4. If a new Web page isn't already open and ready for editing, go to the New task pane, locate the section titled New Page, and click the Blank Page link.

> **Tip** In Figure 2-1, a new, blank Web page named new_page_1.htm is ready for editing. This file name appears in the tab along the top left edge of the editing window.

5. If the New task pane is still open, close it by clicking the Close button in its top right corner.

Editing Web Pages

Entering and Formatting Text

FrontPage should display a blinking insertion point in the top left corner of the Design view window. Because Web pages "grow" from the top left corner, this is your starting point for adding content. In this respect, creating Web pages is more like entering text in a word processor, such as Word, than like arranging objects in a graphics program such as PowerPoint or Microsoft Visio. Here are the familiar steps for entering text:

1. To create some heading text, type **My Accessories.**
2. Press Enter to start a new paragraph of body text, and type **Here are some of my favorite gadgets.**
3. To format the heading, set the insertion point anywhere within the My Accessories heading, and then choose Heading 1 from the Style box on the Formatting toolbar.

Normal

Style box

The Web page should now resemble Figure 2-2.

Figure 2-2. In Design view, adding text to a Web page is as simple as typing in a word processor.

Drawing Tables

The next area of the Web page will contain three pictures arranged vertically, with a caption to the right of each one. Arranging these items neatly requires a grid with three horizontal rows (one for each picture) and two vertical columns (one to align the pictures and another to align the captions).

Creating any sort of grid on a Web page—even an invisible one—generally involves creating an HTML table. FrontPage offers two distinct toolsets for working with HTML tables and gives the impression that the resulting tables are fundamentally different objects. In fact, however, the HTML standard defines only one kind of table and this is the kind that both toolsets create.

- **The Conventional Table toolset** creates the sort of results that Web designers have been using for years. By default, the table itself, its rows, its columns, and its cells have no predetermined size; they size themselves automatically in response to their current contents, to the size of each Web visitor's browser window, and to the size of each Web visitor's fonts.
- **The Layout Table toolset** mimics the practice of arranging page elements on a ruled typesetter's grid or desktop publishing program. Little, if any, of the composition is self-sizing; instead, the measurements are fixed and absolute. For page designers accustomed to print media, this is a much easier paradigm to follow.

The section "Using Layout Tables," later in this chapter, will explain how to arrange the three pictures and their captions using the Layout Table toolset. In the meantime, to format the page using the conventional table toolset, follow these steps:

Insert Table

1. Move the insertion point to the end of the Web page. (Press Ctrl+End, or click anywhere below the last existing content.)
2. Click the Insert Table button on the Standard toolbar. A drop-down grid appears. Move the mouse over the grid until it darkens an area two cells wide and three cells high and then click the last darkened cell.

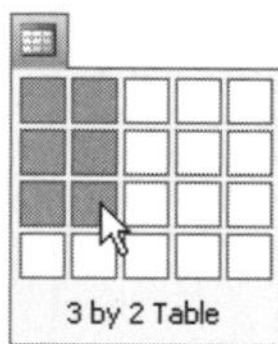

> **Tip** **Choose from two ways of using the Insert Table toolbar button**
>
> There are two ways to use the Insert Table button. The first method is to click the button, move the pointer to the last desired cell in the drop-down grid, and then click again. The second method is to click the button, point to the first cell, hold down the mouse button, drag the pointer to the last desired cell, and then release the mouse button. The difference is that the first method can't expand the drop-down grid, and the second can.

3. By default, FrontPage creates a table with 2 pixels between cells, 1 pixel between the edges of each cell and its contents, and no visible border. To override these settings, right-click anywhere in the table, and choose Table Properties from the shortcut menu. The Table Properties dialog box shown in Figure 2-3 appears.
4. When the Table Properties dialog box appears, under Layout tools, make sure the Disable Layout Tools option is selected.

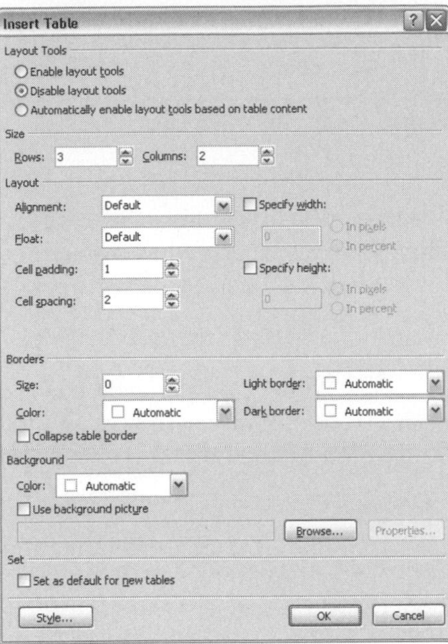

Figure 2-3. This intuitive dialog box controls table properties in both Design view and Code view. There's no need to memorize and manually enter cryptic HTML codes.

5 Under Layout, make sure these settings are in effect:

Property	Setting
Alignment	Default
Float	Default
Cell Padding	1
Cell Spacing	2
Specify Width	Cleared
Specify Height	Cleared

6 Under Borders, verify these settings:

Property	Setting
Size	0
Color	Automatic
Light Border	Automatic
Dark Border	Automatic
Collapse Table Border	Cleared

7 Under Background and Set, make sure all the controls are set to Automatic or cleared, and click OK.

For more information about working with HTML tables, refer to "Creating and Editing Tables" on page 515.

At this point, the table exists but contains no next or pictures. The three pictures will all come from the Microsoft Office clip art library. Here's the procedure for adding the first picture and its caption:

1. Click in the top left cell—column 1 of row 1—of the HTML table.
2. Choose Picture from the Insert menu, and then choose Clip Art.
3. In the Clip Art task pane, type **mouse** in the Search For box, and then click Go. The Clip Art task pane should now resemble Figure 2-4.

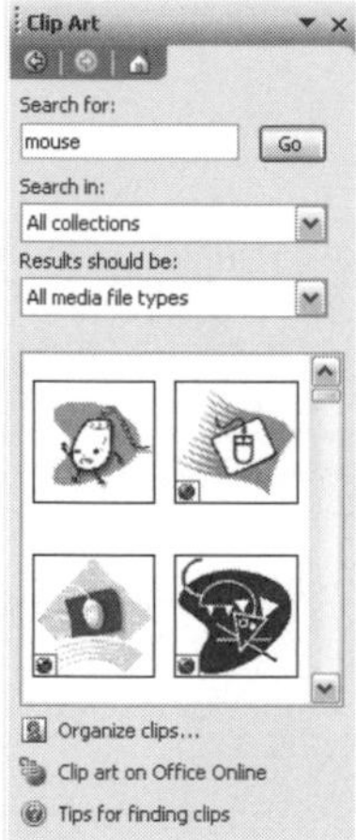

Figure 2-4. The Clip Art task pane makes finding and inserting clip art a breeze.

4. Select the mouse picture you like best, and then take one of these actions:
   - Right-click the picture.
   - Hover the mouse over the picture, and click the down arrow that appears to the right of the picture.

   In either case, continue by choosing Insert from the shortcut menu. The picture you selected should appear in the cell you selected in step 1.
5. To adjust the size of the newly pasted mouse picture, right-click it and choose Picture Properties from the shortcut menu. This displays the Picture Properties dialog box, shown in Figure 2-5.

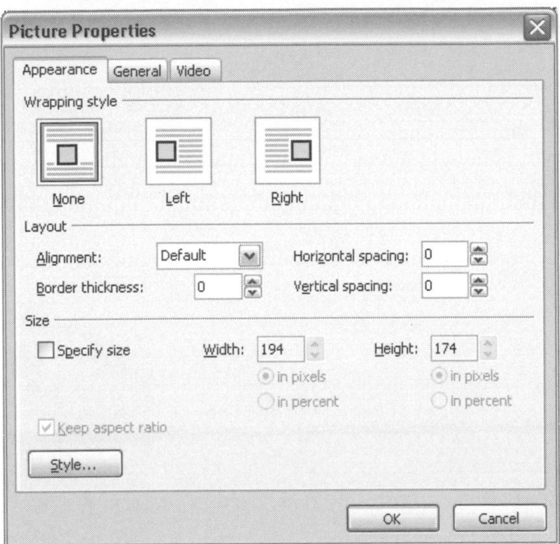

Figure 2-5. With this dialog box, you can easily modify the characteristics of a picture.

6. Under the Size heading, select the Specify Size check box, and then change the Height value to 75 In Pixels.
7. Click the General tab, and then click the Picture File Type button. When the Picture File Type dialog box appears, choose GIF.
8. Click OK twice to close the Picture File Type and Picture Properties dialog boxes.
9. With the picture still selected, look for the Pictures toolbar. If it isn't visible:
   - Choose Toolbars from the View menu, and then choose Pictures, or
   - Right-click the picture, and choose Show Pictures Toolbar from the shortcut menu.
10. Now, with the mouse picture still selected, click the Resample button on the Pictures toolbar. This will create a true bitmap 75 pixels high (the height you specified in step 6).

Resample

For more information about working with pictures, refer to Chapter 10, "Adding and Formatting Pictures."

Repeat these steps to locate, insert, and resize a keyboard picture and a monitor picture. Add the keyboard picture to table column 1, row 2, and the monitor picture to column 1, row 3.

To add captions for the graphics, follow this procedure:

1. Click column 2 of row 1 of the table, and type **Maureen the Mouse**.
2. Add the captions **Kenny the Keyboard** and **Monty the Monitor** in the same manner for the remaining pictures. Your page should now resemble Figure 2-6, on the next page.

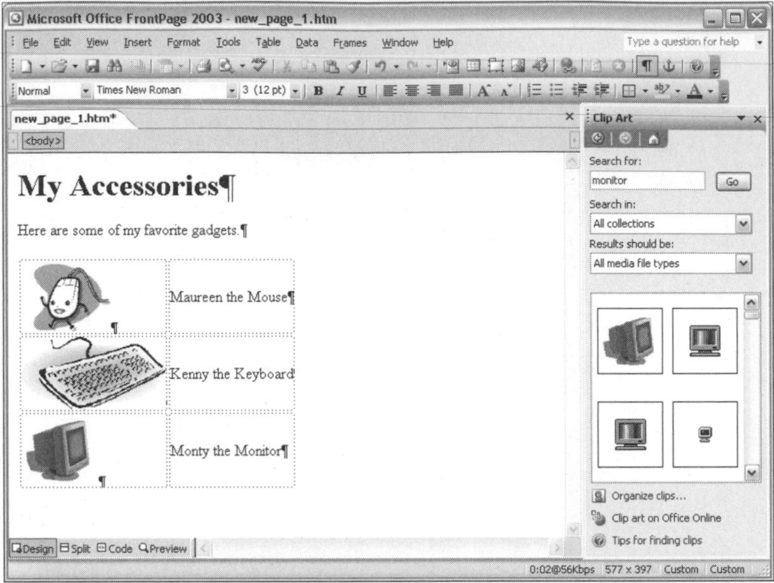

Figure 2-6. HTML tables are a great way to align elements spatially on a page. Using a text editor to create even simple compositions like this can be difficult. Using Design view makes it a snap.

Adding a Hyperlink

FrontPage makes it easy to add hyperlinks. To see how this process works, follow this procedure:

1. Click anywhere below the HTML table, and then type **Microsoft Office Tools on the Web.**
2. Select all the text you just typed. You can do this either by dragging the mouse across the text or by clicking the margin area to its left.
3. Right-click the selected area, and choose Hyperlink from the shortcut menu. (Clicking the Insert Hyperlink button on the Standard toolbar has the same effect.)

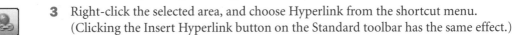

Insert Hyperlink

4. When the Insert Hyperlink dialog box shown in Figure 2-7 appears, type **http://office.microsoft.com** in the Address box, and then click OK.

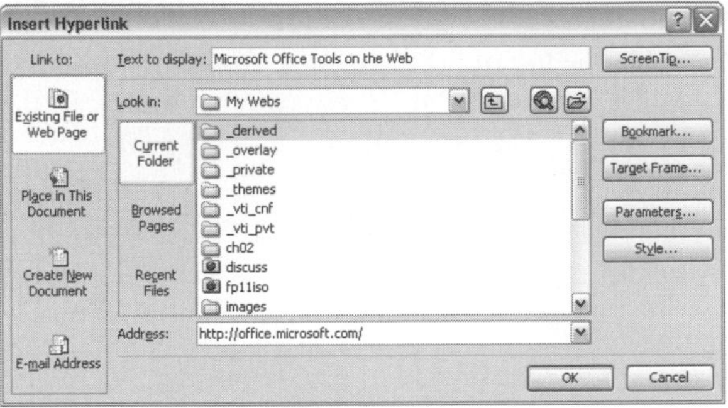

Figure 2-7. This FrontPage dialog box provides a rich array of tools for locating Web locations with point-and-click methods. If you prefer, you can also fill in the Address box by hand.

For more information about working with hyperlinks, refer to Chapter 11, "Building Hyperlinks."

Saving the Web Page

Saving this page on disk requires more steps than you might suspect, because there are actually four files to save: the Web page itself and three picture files. Here's the procedure:

Save

1. Click the Save button on the Standard toolbar.
2. When the Save As dialog box shown in Figure 2-8 appears, click the My Documents icon on the My Places bar. This will display the contents of your My Documents folder.

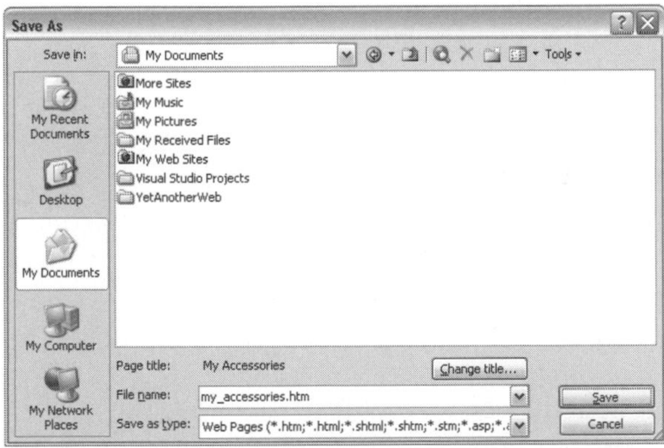

Figure 2-8. The My Places bar on the left in the Save As dialog box sets the Save In location to one of several common starting points.

3. If your My Documents folder already contains a My Web Sites subfolder, double-click it. Otherwise, click the Create New Folder button, and create a subfolder named My Web Sites. Either way, the Save As dialog box should now display the contents of your My Web Sites folder.

Create New Folder

4 Click the Create New Folder button, and create a subfolder named ch02.

5 The Save In location at the top of the dialog box should now specify the new ch02 folder. If the name **my_accessories.htm** doesn't already appear in the File Name box, type it in. In any event, click the Save button.

6 The Save Embedded Files dialog box shown in Figure 2-9 appears next. This box initially suggests that you save the three converted clip art files in the same folder as the my_accessories.htm page with the names in the Name column of the dialog box.

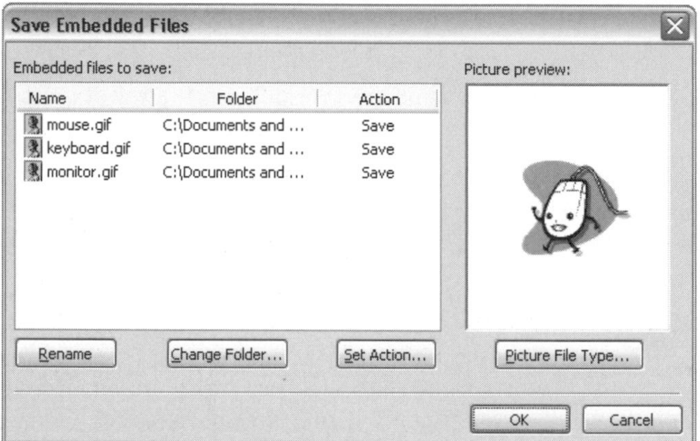

Figure 2-9. Saving a Web page can require saving not only the main HTML file, but several constituent files as well. FrontPage displays this dialog box when you save a Web page that contains unsaved constituent files.

7 The file names that appear in the Save Embedded Files dialog box will probably be quite obscure. To correct this:

- Select one of the cryptic file names. A thumbnail of the corresponding picture will appear in the Picture Preview box.
- Click the Rename button. The selected file name will become editable.
- Rename the files as follows:

Mouse picture:	mouse.gif
Keyboard picture:	keyboard.gif
Monitor picture:	monitor.gif

- Repeat this procedure for each of the remaining pictures.

8 Click OK to close the Save Embedded Files dialog box. This completes the entire Save operation.

Using the My Places Bar

The area Microsoft calls the My Places bar occupies the left side of most Office 2003 file-oriented dialog boxes. By default, the My Places bar offers these icons as quick starting points for locating folders.

- **My Recent Documents** Clicking this icon displays a list of documents, folders, and Web sites you recently accessed with FrontPage.
- **Desktop** Clicking this icon displays the file locations that normally appear on your desktop: My Computer, My Documents, My Network Places, and so forth.
- **My Documents** Clicking this icon displays the contents of your My Documents folder.
- **My Computer** Clicking this icon displays the same drive letter selections as the My Computer icon on your desktop.
- **My Network Places** Clicking this icon displays a list of Web servers that have Windows SharePointServices or the FrontPage Server Extensions installed. Servers appear in this list for two reasons: because you opened a FrontPage-based Web site on that server or because you used the Add Web Folder or Add Network Place Wizard to add the server manually.

To include more locations on the My Places bar, follow this procedure:

1. Select the location in the main file list window in any file-oriented dialog box.
2. Click the Tools button on the dialog box toolbar.
3. Click Add To "My Places" in the drop-down menu.

Tools

Tools

To remove, move, or rename an icon in the My Places bar, right-click the icon, and then choose Remove, Move Up, Move Down, or Rename from the shortcut menu.

More Save Embedded Files Options

The Save Embedded Files dialog box has additional options:

- To save a file in a different folder, select the file, and click the Change Folder button.
- To change a file's action from Save to Don't Save (or back again), click the Set Action button.
- To change a picture's format from GIF to JPEG or to change other format properties, click the Picture File Type button.

Click OK when all these options are set the way you want them.

When the Save operation is complete, you might notice that a new Web Site tab appears above the Design view window and that a Folder List pane appears at the left side of the main

FrontPage window. This is because the my_accessories.htm page and the three picture files now belong to the same FrontPage-based Web site. Chapter 3, "Managing Web Sites," will introduce the concept of FrontPage-based Web sites more fully.

> **Note** A FrontPage-based Web site is a folder tree full of Web pages and related files that FrontPage manages as a unit. The terms *FrontPage-based Web site* and *Web site* aren't really synonymous, but they're close enough that people tend to use them interchangeably.

Checking Your Work

FrontPage Design view provides a reasonable preview of what a visitor with browser settings similar to yours would see. Nevertheless, there are limits to the extent that any HTML editor can provide a WYSIWYG view. Your Web visitor's system still controls the screen resolution, color depth, page width, font, font size, and other visual aspects, according to its operating system, browser software, installed fonts, and so forth. No HTML editor can predict what these settings will be at display time, so no HTML editor can preview them 100 percent accurately.

To preview the Web page as Microsoft Internet Explorer would display it, click the Preview tab at the bottom of the editing window. This saves the current Web page as a temporary file on disk, loads Internet Explorer into the editing window, and tells Internet Explorer to display the temporary file. Figure 2-10 shows a preview of the current page. To resume editing, click the Design tab at the bottom of the editing window.

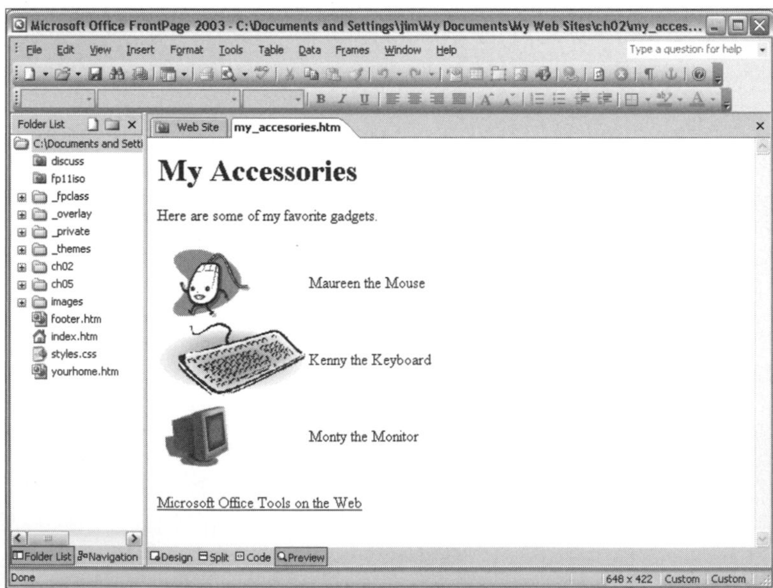

Figure 2-10. Clicking the Preview button at the bottom of the editing window displays a temporary copy of the current page as Internet Explorer would present it.

Previewing in External Browsers

To view your Web page in a browser outside of FrontPage, choose Preview In Browser from the File menu, or click the drop-down arrow to the right of the Preview In Browser button on the Standard toolbar. Either action displays the submenu shown in Figure 2-11. Choose the combination of browsers and window sizes you want to view. If none of the available selections satisfy you, choose Edit Browser List to customize the choices.

> **Note** All experienced Web designers test their pages in multiple versions of multiple browsers. You might notice some startling differences when you do this, but that's the point. Make sure that your pages are at least legible for everyone and that they look their best in the browsers most of your Web site's visitors use.

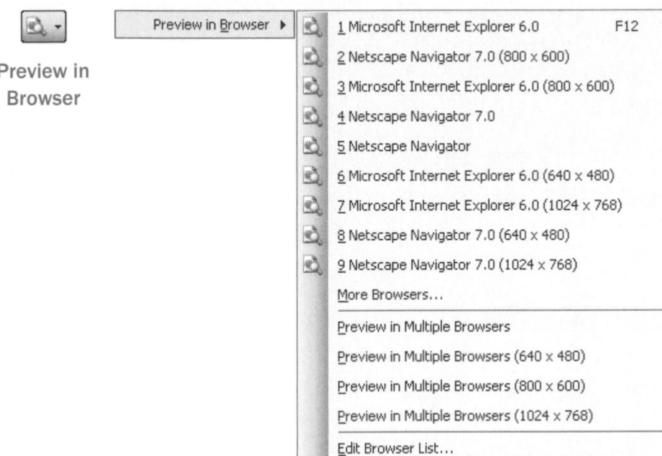

Figure 2-11. If you have several browsers installed on your computer, FrontPage can display the current Web page in any one of them, or in several at once.

FrontPage checks to see whether you've made any changes since you last saved the page, prompts you to save the page if necessary, starts the selected browser if it isn't already running, and then tells the browser to display the page. Figure 2-12 shows the sample page developed in this chapter displayed in Netscape Navigator.

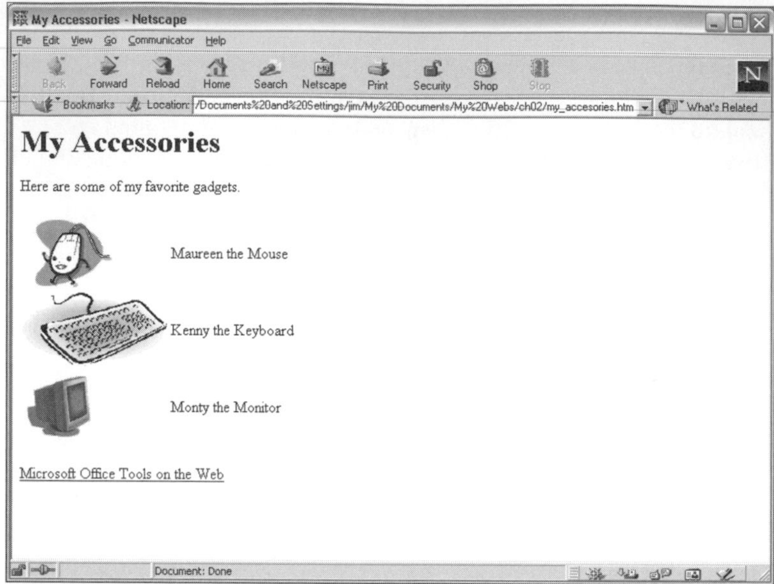

Figure 2-12. FrontPage is quite capable of creating Web pages that are compatible with Netscape Navigator.

The fastest way to end an editing session is simply to close its editing window by clicking the Close button in the window's top right corner or by choosing Close from the File menu.

Opening an Existing Web Page

If you need to work on a Web page that already exists, and if you worked on that file in FrontPage recently, you can open it using either of these methods:

- Choose Recent Files on the File menu, and then select the file you want.
- Display the Getting Started task pane, and then, under Pages, click the file you want.

The most flexible way to open pages, however, is by using the Open File dialog box, shown in Figure 2-13.

There are several ways to display this dialog box:

- Press Ctrl+O.
- Click the Open button on the Standard toolbar.
- Choose Open from the File menu.
- Display the Getting Started task pane, and then, under Pages, click More.
- Display the New Site task pane, and then, under New Page, click From Existing Page.

Open

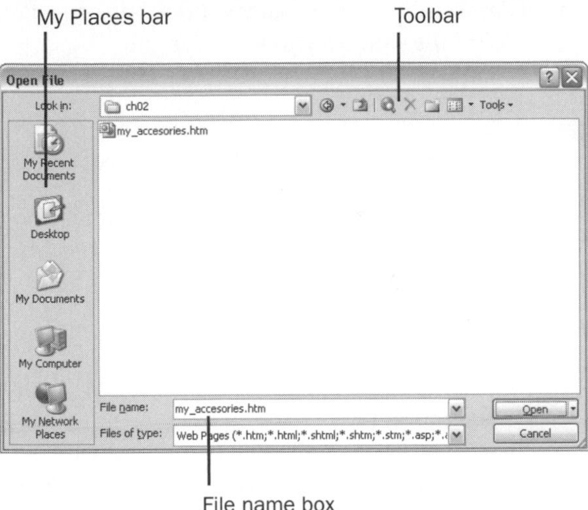

Figure 2-13. The FrontPage Open File dialog box provides a My Places bar and enhanced toolbar controls, just like those in the Save As dialog box.

For more information about opening Web pages, see "Opening an Existing Web Page" on page 56.

The Open File dialog box can open any type of Web page located on your computer, on a file server, or on the World Wide Web. If you type a file name in the File Name box, FrontPage opens that file via the Windows file system. If you type a Web address, such as *http://www.interlacken.com/fp11iso/default.htm*, FrontPage retrieves all the files from that location just as a browser would and then loads them into the editing window.

Note Just because you can load a page from the Web into the FrontPage editing window doesn't mean you can save changes back to the same location. For you to do that, the Web server needs software capable of receiving file updates, and the server's administrator must grant you permission to use it.

The remaining controls in the Open File dialog box save you from having to type file names in the File Name box—in other words, you can use these controls to specify file names by pointing and clicking. For the most part, these controls work like those in any other Windows application.

For more information about the Open File toolbar, refer to "The File Dialog Box Toolbar" in Appendix A.

When you open several pages at the same time, they all normally appear within the same FrontPage window. To edit a particular page, click its tab at the top of the editing window, choose its name from the Window menu, or press Ctrl+Tab until the page you want appears.

If you want two editing sessions to be visible at the same time, first open an additional FrontPage window by choosing New Window from the Window menu, and then open one page in each window. Repeat this process to open as many windows as you want. To switch between windows, press Alt+Tab until the window you want appears.

Using Layout Tables

To experience the mind-set of using Layout Tables, first make sure that the my_accessories.htm page you saved in the "Saving the Web Page" section is still open. If not, choose Recent Files from the File menu, and then click the my_ accessories.htm option.

Displaying Rulers and Layout Grids

The next step is to activate all the FrontPage user interface elements that go along with Layout Tables. You can create and manipulate layout tables without turning on these options, but having them around is handy. They're less handy when you're working with conventional HTML tables and other types of content, but you can leave them in place if you want. Proceed as follows.

1 Choose Ruler and Grid from the View menu, and then choose Show Ruler. This displays horizontal and vertical rulers, graduated in pixels, across and along the Web page.
2 Choose Ruler and Grid from the View menu, and then choose Show Grid. This displays vertical and horizontal guide lines every 50 pixels across the Design view window.

Simulating Browser Size in Design View

FrontPage 2003 has a new capability that simulates the area a Web visitor would see when viewing the current page. With this feature in effect, Design view always displays the page with the width you specify. If the Design view window is wider than the width you specify, gray areas will appear on either side of the WYSIWYG display. If the Design view window is narrower than the width you specify, you'll need to scroll the Design view window right or left. FrontPage also draws a horizontal dotted line across the page, indicating the bottom of the Web visitor's browser window.

To experience this feature during the upcoming example, choose Page Size from the View menu and then choose 600 x 300 (640 x 480 Maximized) from the resulting menu.

This tells FrontPage to size the Design view display exactly 600 pixels wide and to draw a dotted line across the page 300 pixels from the top. In real life, you'll probably simulate larger screen sizes, but for now, using a small size keeps the example simple.

Displaying a Tracing Image

If you have the task of re-creating an existing document or layout, you might find it helpful to use a copy of that artwork as a background picture in Design view. FrontPage calls this a *tracing image*. Here's the procedure for using one:

1. Scan or otherwise convert the sample layout to a picture file. This might be a GIF or TIFF file for line drawings or a JPEG file for photographs.
2. In FrontPage, open the Web page you want to design.
3. Choose Tracing Image from the View menu, and then choose Configure.
4. When the Image Tracing dialog box shown in Figure 2-14 appears, click the Browse button, and locate the picture file that contains the sample layout.

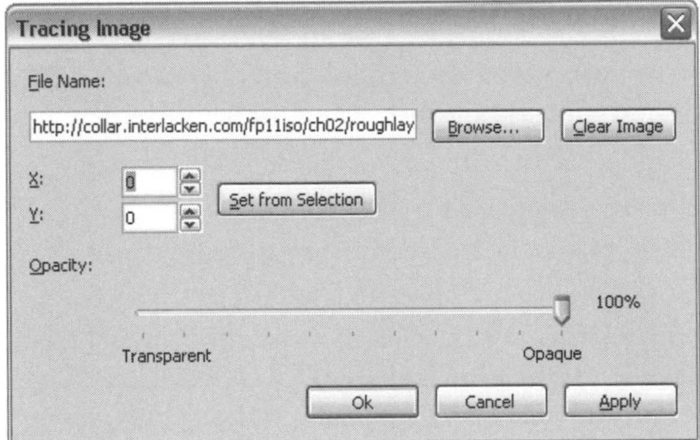

Figure 2-14. To ease the job of converting artwork or sketches to Web format, FrontPage can superimpose a tracing image over the normal page background.

In addition, you can modify these settings:

- **X** The distance from the left edge of the Design view window to the left edge of the tracing image.
- **Y** The distance from the top of the Design view window to the top of the tracing image.
- **Opacity** The extent to which the tracing image will mask out the normal page background. If you set this to 100, the default, the tracing image will completely mask out the normal page background. If you set it to 50, the tracing image and the normal background will each show at 50 percent intensity, and so forth.

5. Click OK when your choices are complete.

After you've specified a tracing image for a page, you can display or hide it by Choosing Tracing Image from the View menu and then choosing Show Image.

Drawing a Layout Table

To practice creating a layout table, first make sure the My Accessories page is still open. Then, to delete the existing accessories table, follow this procedure:

1. Click anywhere inside the table.
2. On the Quick Tag Selector bar, click the <table> icon.
3. Choose Delete Cells from the Table menu.

The next task is to create a layout table similar to the original accessories table you created with conventional HTML tools. Proceed as follows:

1. Choose Toolbars from the View menu. Then, if the Tables command on the submenu isn't checked, choose it.
2. If no task pane is currently visible, press Ctrl+F1.
3. Click the drop-down arrow at the top of the current task pane, and choose Layout Tables And Cells from the resulting list.
4. In the task pane under Work With Layout Tables And Cells, click the Draw Layout Table button (and *not* the Insert Layout Table hyperlink).

   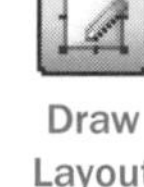

   Draw Layout Table

   When the mouse pointer is on the Design view window, it will now resemble a pencil.
5. Move the mouse pointer below the line that reads *Here Are Some Of My Favorite Gadgets*, and then, holding down the left mouse button, drag the pointer down and to the right. Release it when the table is about 300 pixels square. Don't worry if your dimensions aren't exactly 300 by 300. The screen should now resemble Figure 2-15.

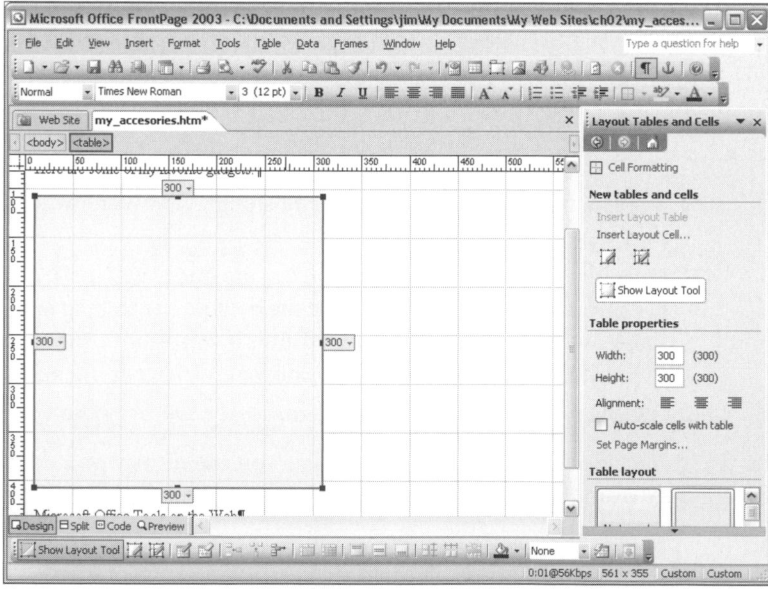

Figure 2-15. The new Layout Tables featurein FrontPage 2003 eases the job of creating tables with fixed dimensions.

6 Choose Draw Table from the Table menu, and then drag the mouse pointer from just below the top center of the new layout table to just above the bottom center. (Make sure the mouse pointer is a pencil before you start dragging.) A dotted line should now divide the table in half.

7 Similarly, drag the mouse pointer from just inside the left edge to just inside the right edge. Perform this operation twice, dividing the table into three rows. Check your work against Figure 2-16, again disregarding exact measurements.

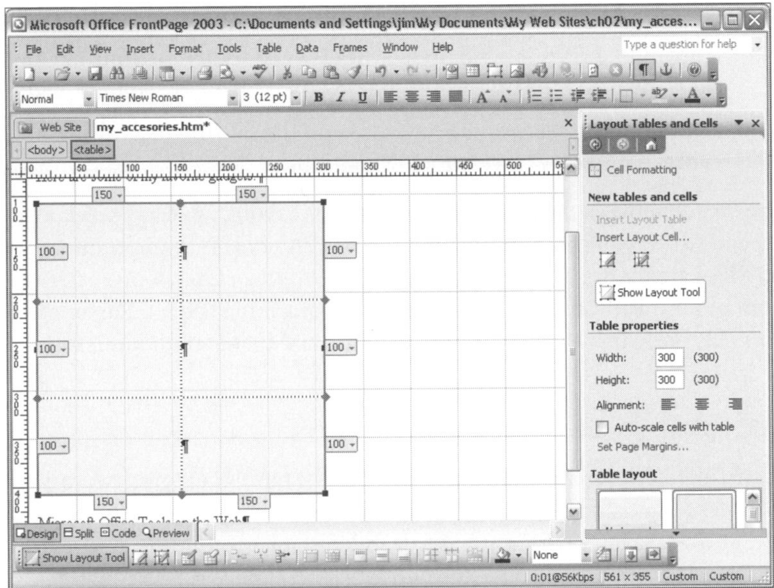

Figure 2-16. With Layout Tables, you can apply fixed cell heights and widths without leaving Design view.

8 Right-click anywhere in the table, and then choose Table Properties from the shortcut menu. When the Table Properties dialog box appears, specify the following settings, and then click OK:

Cell Padding:	1
Cell Spacing:	2
Borders Size:	0

9 If the Folder List isn't visible at the left of the FrontPage window, choose Folder List from the View menu.

10 Locate the mouse.gif file in the folder list, and drag it into the top left table cell. Similarly, drag the keyboard.gif and monitor.gif files into the middle and bottom left table cells.

11 Enter the same captions as before: Maureen the Mouse, Kenny the Keyboard, and Monty the Monitor.

12 If either of the columns look too wide or too narrow:
   1 Click anywhere inside the table.
   2 Click the <table> tag on the Quick Tag Selector bar. (If this bar isn't visible, choose Quick Tag Selector from the View menu.)
   3 Click the drop-down arrow to the right of the column measurement you want to change, and then choose Change Column Width from the shortcut menu.
   4 When the Column Properties dialog box appears, specify the Column Width measurement you want, and then click OK.

13 If any of the rows look too tall or too short, modify the Row Height using essentially the same procedure described in step 12 for changing column width.

14 To save your work, choose Save As from the File menu, and specify a different file name, such as my_accessories_layout.htm.

The choice between the Conventional Table or Layout Table toolsets is a personal one, largely depending on your background and the task at hand. Web programmers and long-time HTML veterans are likely to stick with Conventional Table tools; designers transitioning from other media are likely to prefer the Layout Table toolset. Fortunately, FrontPage supports both approaches, and you can mix and match both kinds of tables at will.

Working with Code

Recurring concepts are an interesting aspect of human progress. If you watch a given specialty long enough, the same trends fall in and out of favor, in about the same sequence, over and over again. This is just as true for computer technologies as it is for clothing fashions and the stock market. Sooner or later, everything old is new again!

So it is with the code behind Web pages. Early practitioners worked entirely with code, generally using ordinary text editors. Graphical editors then burst onto the scene, fought for acceptance, and finally achieved respect. And now, the pendulum is swinging back to code. There are two main reasons for this trend:

- Ultimately, the purpose of a graphical editor is to produce HTML code. Sometimes, working directly with code provides more flexibility than working at arm's length through a graphical editor.
- More and more of today's Web sites are actually front ends to database-driven information systems. With this arrangement, a single Web page can display information about thousands or even millions of different items. This is possible because program code on the Web server customizes the outgoing HTML to contain the correct item information. This approach then requires working with at least two kinds of code: program code and HTML code.

None of this implies that graphical editors like FrontPage are going away. It only means that in addition to a great visual editor for designing the visual aspect of Web pages, today's Web developers also need a great code editor for working with lines of code. FrontPage 2003 therefore includes three improved ways of working with code:

- A code editor that understands the syntax of your code and uses this information to help you write code correctly on the first attempt.
- Tools that create code based on specifications you supply through dialog boxes.
- Tools that operate in Design view but work directly with HTML code.

The next three sections will briefly introduce these toolsets. This book, however, isn't a primer on HTML or any other coding language. The material here tells you how to use FrontPage for coding, and not about the programming languages themselves.

Using the FrontPage Code Editor

To view and modify the HTML code for any Web page, open the page as usual, and then click the Code tab at the bottom of the main editing window. Figure 2-17 shows how the code will then appear on your screen. To change the code, just set the insertion point and start typing.

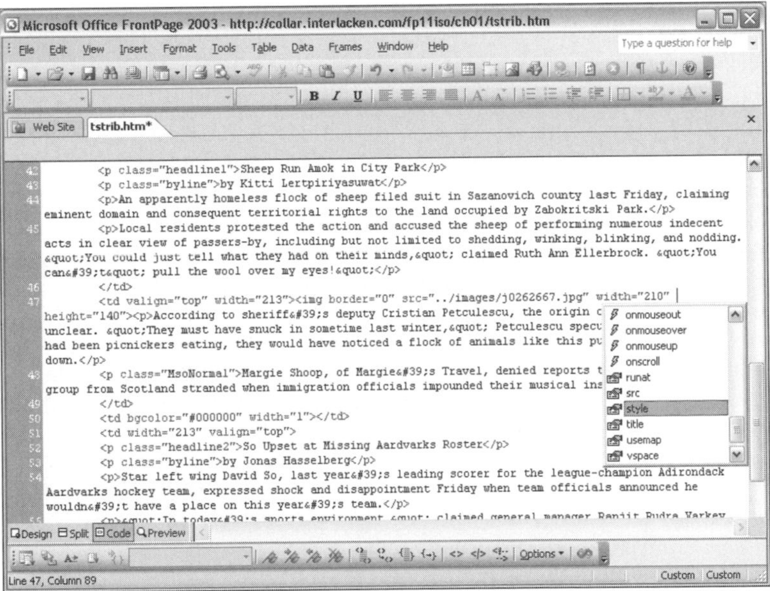

Figure 2-17. As you type code, Microsoft IntelliSense displays lists of valid options. The choice is yours whether to keep typing, double-click one of the IntelliSense options, or select an option and press Tab.

Viewing and Bookmarking Code

For your convenience, FrontPage can display line numbers at the left of the Code view window. This makes it easier to find your place as you scroll back and forth between various parts of the code listing.

Toggle Bookmark

If you find yourself scrolling frequently to a certain line of code, you might want to select it and press Ctrl+F2. This sets a *bookmark* at the given line. Once you have bookmarks set, pressing F2 will jump forward to the next bookmark, and pressing Shift+F2 will jump backward to the previous bookmark. The Code View toolbar visible at the bottom of Figure 2-17 also provides Toggle Bookmark, Previous Bookmark, and Next Bookmark buttons that work just like these keystrokes.

Next Bookmark

FrontPage also has a Word Wrap feature that displays code on several lines even if it physically occupies one long line. Figure 2-17 shows this option in effect. The on-screen lines that have no line number are actually continuations of longer lines in the HTML file.

Previous Bookmark

Although it might be difficult to see in a monochrome screen shot, FrontPage also color-codes each language element. This makes the code easier to read. HTML tag names are purple, attribute names are red, attribute values are blue, and so forth. You can customize these colors by choosing Page Options from the Tools menu, and then clicking the Color Coding tab.

Automating Code Entry with Intellisense

The pop-up list on the right in Figure 2-17 shows the IntelliSense feature in action. On line 47, the designer typed a space after `width="210"`, and FrontPage intelligently sensed (so to speak) that the next valid element would be an attribute of an <img> tag. The IntelliSense feature therefore displayed a pop-up list of valid <img> attributes. Rather than typing the full attribute name, the designer can simply just select it from the list.

When you supply an attribute name and its following equals sign, IntelliSense provides a list of acceptable values that you can select in just the same way. (Of course, this is only possible for attributes that have a discrete list of acceptable values. For attributes such as *height=* and *width=*, you must still type the numeric measurement you want.)

When the insertion point is between tags and you type an opening angle bracket, IntelliSense also provides a list of valid tag names. Altogether, this means that you can create a lot of HTML without much typing. IntelliSense will correctly type the tag names, attributes names, and most attribute values for you, and even remember for you what choices are possible and valid.

IntelliSense Language Support in FrontPage

The FrontPage Code view window supports IntelliSense processing only for HTML code, CSS code, intrinsic ASP.NET controls, and for JavaScript and VBScript code that runs on the browser.

To get IntelliSense support for JavaScript and VBScript code that runs on the Web server, including Active Server Pages (ASP) and Microsoft ActiveX Data Objects (ADO), start Microsoft Script Editor by pressing Alt+Shift+F11 with the page open in Design, Code, or Split view.

To get IntelliSense support for C#, Microsoft Visual Basic .NET, Microsoft ASP.NET, and Microsoft ADO.NET, you'll need to open the page with Microsoft Visual Studio.NET.

For more information about using FrontPage 2003 and Visual Studio .NET together, refer to Chapter 43, "Using FrontPage 2003 and Visual Studio .NET Together."

IntelliSense can also type end tags and attribute quotes for you. Typing end tags means, for example, that after you type the closing angle bracket in <table>, IntelliSense will automatically type </table> for you and set the insertion point between <table> and </table>. Typing attribute quotes means that after you type **height=**, IntelliSense will type two quotation marks and set the insertion point between them. To activate or suppress these features, choose Page Options from the Tools menu, and then click the IntelliSense tab.

Formatting and Optimizing HTML Code

People who create code by hand—whether HTML or some other language—are usually fastidious about it. Even if the browser doesn't care about capitalization, line endings, and indentation, human beings do. As a result, FrontPage is very careful not to reformat or oherwise change your code. This applies to switching in an out of Code view as well as to opening and saving files. FrontPage can, however, reformat the code for the current page if that's what you want. Just display the page in Code view, right-click anywhere in the code, and choose Reformat HTML from the shortcut menu.

Tip To change the rules FrontPage uses when reformatting HTML code, choose Page Options from the Tools menu, and click the Code Formatting tab.

If your HTML has problems that go beyond code formatting, FrontPage can fix them for you. Switch to Design view and then choose Optimize HTML from the Tools menu. This will display the Optimize HTML dialog box shown in Figure 2-18. To use this dialog box, simply select the types of cleanup you want FrontPage to perform and then click OK.

For more information, refer to "Optimizing HTML Code at Design Time," on page 475.

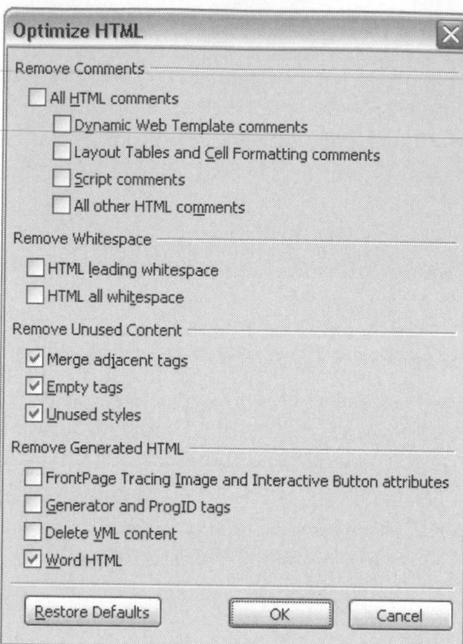

Figure 2-18. FrontPage can correct and improve your HTML code in a variety of ways.

Of course, the features presented here are nothing but the highlights. FrontPage also has features for automatically selecting the contents of a tag, for moving the insertion point between matching start and end tags, for inserting prewritten snippets of text, and many other common tasks.

For more information about customizing FrontPage menus and toolbars, refer to "Customizing Menus and Toolbars," Appendix M.

Using Split View

If you frequently switch between Design view and Code view, Split view might provide the happy medium you're seeking. This view divides the editing window in half horizontally. The top half displays the current page in Code view, and the bottom half displays it in Design view.

If you make changes in the Design view pane, FrontPage immediately updates the Code view pane accordingly. Changes you make in the Code view pane, however, don't show up in Design view so quickly. To do this, FrontPage would have to update the Design view pane after each Code view keystroke, and that would present great problems as FrontPage tried to display half-coded tags and other structural elements. Instead, FrontPage updates the Design view pane only when it receives the focus (that is, when you click the pane) or when you press F5.

Split view is also helpful while you're learning HTML. As you work in Design view, you can watch the HTML form as if by magic!

Using Code-Creation Tools

HTML is the most obvious form of code that FrontPage creates. The major reason Design view exists, after all, is to create HTML code. FrontPage can also create and modify Cascading Style Sheet (CSS) code; to use this feature, choose Style from the Format menu.

In addition, FrontPage can create bona fide program code in a number of ways. Here are some examples:

- Anytime you use FrontPage database features, FrontPage creates ASP or ASP.NET program code that implements your specifications.
- Anytime you set up validation rules for form field objects, FrontPage creates JavaScript code that checks the values of those fields every time a Web visitor submits the form.
- Adding certain FrontPage components to your Web page actually adds bits of HTML and JavaScript code. The new Interactive Button component is a case in point. This component creates the HTML to display a picture, plus JavaScript code that displays a different picture when the Web visitor moves the mouse over it or clicks it.
- The Behaviors task pane creates JavaScript code that responds to various events that might take place on your Web page. This is useful if, for example, you wanted some text to change color or font when the mouse passed over it.

Inside Out

Leave Machine-Generated Code to the Machines.

Useful as the code-generating features of FrontPage might be, don't get the idea of using them to initialize code that you would then modify. Almost without exception, FrontPage doesn't create the kind of code a human being would write (or can read without difficulty).

Working with HTML While in Design Mode

Through its last several releases, FrontPage has included features that work directly with HTML code even when you're in Design view. These include:

- **The Reveal Tags command** This feature adds HTML tag icons to the Design view display, showing where each tag occurs in the underlying HTML. Clicking a tag icon selects the tag itself, its matching tag, and any enclosed content. Figure 2-19 shows this option in effect.
- **The Paste Without Conversion command** If you have some HTML on your clipboard, this commands pastes it directly into your Web page at the current insertion point. Design view then displays the new HTML as if you'd created it in Design view, or as if you'd pasted it into Code view. This is handy if, for example, you're copying some code from another Web page and pasting it into yours.

Figure 2-19. The Reveal Tags command displays icons for most of the HTML tags in a page. These tag icons do take up space, however, and degrade the WYSIWYG nature of the display.

To use this command:

1. Set the insertion point, and choose Paste Special from the Edit menu.
2. In the Convert Text dialog box, click the Do Not Convert option button, and click OK.

- **The HTML Markup component** This feature also pastes HTML into your Web page but marks it so that the Design view editor doesn't display it or modify it in any way. This is useful if you have a chunk of HTML code that FrontPage handles incorrectly. To use this component:
  1. Choose Web Component from the Insert menu.
  2. When the Insert Web Component dialog box appears, choose Advanced Controls in the Component Type list on the left.
  3. Choose HTML in the Choose A Control list on the right, and then click Finish.
  4. When the HTML Markup dialog box appears, type or paste the HTML you want your Web page to contain. (Use Ctrl+V to paste.) Finally, click OK.

- **Quick Tag Selector** The Quick Tag Selector bar provides several new ways to work with code from Design view. This bar displays an icon for the tag that encloses the current selection, plus an icon for each additional enclosing tag up to and including the <body> tag. Selecting any of these icons selects the corresponding element in the Design view display. In addition, hovering the mouse over any Quick Tag Selector icon displays a drop-down arrow that reveals the following commands:
  - **Select Tag** selects the start tag, the end tab, and all content between them.

- **Select Tag Contents** selects any content between the start and end tags, but not the tags themselves.
- **Edit Tag** displays the Quick Tag Editor dialog box shown here. To modify the tag or its attributes, click inside the central text box and start typing. To save your changes, click the check mark button. To quit without saving, click the X button.

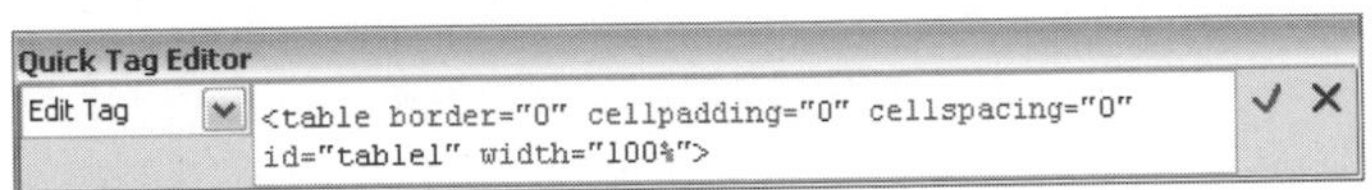

- **Remove Tag** deletes the start and end tags but not any content between them.
- **Insert HTML** adds text or HTML code just before the selected HTML start tag. Selecting this command displays the Quick Tag Editor dialog box as before.
- **Wrap Tag** surrounds the current start and end tags with a new pair of matching tags. The Quick Tag Editor dialog box prompts you for the new start tag, and FrontPage automatically supplies the end tag.
- **Tag Properties** displays the FrontPage dialog box for configuring the current tag type. For example, if you click the Quick Tag Selector icon for a <table> tag and select Tag Properties, FrontPage will display the Table Properties dialog box.

Inside Out

Avoid Revealing Tags

Although instructive, the Reveal Tags command isn't terribly useful for everyday work. Compared to working with tags hidden, it offers little additional capability. Also, the presence of the tag icons distorts the WYSIWYG view.

Using FrontPage Web Components

To help you produce sophisticated Web pages quickly, FrontPage includes a powerful collection of intelligent Web components. FrontPage inserts these components wherever you specify, prompts you for any variable information, and then generates the corresponding HTML code when it saves the page. Along with the HTML, FrontPage saves the dialog box values you specified so that it can redisplay them in future editing sessions or re-create the HTML if some other factor changes.

In almost every case, Web components provide active output (that is, their content or appearance changes automatically based on events beyond the Web page that contains the components). These changes may occur for any of the following reasons:

- The generated HTML includes a browser-side or server-side script that produces variable output.

- The generated HTML runs a program on the server, such as a database query or full text search.
- The generated HTML reflects information located elsewhere within the FrontPage-based Web site. If you change the information located elsewhere, FrontPage automatically corrects all the Web pages that reference it.

All Web components depend on FrontPage to run them whenever the designer saves a page. If you make changes to your Web site using a different editor, FrontPage won't be there to run the Web component and the component might not function correctly. Scheduled Web components take effect only if you save the affected pages on or after the specified start and stop dates.

Using Design-Time and Browser Components

The following components operate totally within either the FrontPage design environment or the Web visitor's browser and don't require that any FrontPage software be installed on the Web server.

> **Note** Unless stated otherwise, you can insert these components by choosing Web Components from the Insert menu and then selecting the appropriate component.

- **Comment** This component displays text that's visible only in FrontPage. The same text doesn't appear when visitors view the Web page in their browsers. To insert a Comment component, choose Comment from the Insert menu.

  For more information about the Comment component, refer to "Inserting FrontPage Comments," on page 212.
- **Date And Time** FrontPage replaces this component with the date and time of the last update to the page. To insert a Date And Time component, choose Date And Time from the Insert menu.

  For more information about the Date And Time component, refer to "Using the Date and Time Component," on page 721.
- **File Upload** If a page contains this component, Web visitors can upload files along with other HTML form input. To insert this component, choose Form from the Insert menu, and then choose File Upload.

  For more information about the File Upload component, refer to "Setting File Upload Options," on page 848.

- **Interactive Button** This component displays a button picture that you select from a list and also creates JavaScript code that changes the picture when the mouse passes over it or the Web visitor clicks it.

  For more information about the Interactive Button component, refer to "Using Interactive Buttons," on page 685.

- **Banner Ad Manager** This component displays a series of pictures, each for a specified number of seconds. When Web visitors load the page, their browsers load a FrontPage Java applet that continuously retrieves and displays the specified pictures.

  For more information about Java applets, see the section "Java Applets," later in this chapter.
- **Photo Gallery** This component organizes groups of pictures by creating and displaying miniature versions (thumbnails) of each one. Web visitors scan the thumbnails until one catches their interest and then click the thumbnail to display the full-sized picture.

  For more information about the Photo Gallery component, refer to "Creating a New Photo Gallery," on page 655.
- **Substitution** This component replaces itself with a page-level or Web-level configuration variable.

  For more information about the Substitution component, refer to "Using Site Parameters and the Substitution Component," on page 759.
- **Include Page** FrontPage replaces this component with the contents of another page in the same site. When the same features appear in many Web pages and you might need to change them in the future, you should consider using the Include Page component.

  For more information about the Include Page component, refer to "Using the Include Page Component," on page 750.
- **Scheduled Include Page** FrontPage replaces this component with the contents of another Web page (or page segment) every time the page is saved during a specified time period. After the time expires, FrontPage no longer displays the included page.

  For more information about the Scheduled Include Page component, refer to "Using the Scheduled Include Page Component," on page 755.
- **Scheduled Picture** This component works like the scheduled Include Page component except that the Scheduled Picture component replaces itself with a picture instead of a Web page. Figure 2-20 shows the dialog box that controls the Scheduled Picture component. In this example, the component labels an element on the Web page as *New!* for a period of six months.

  For more information about the Scheduled Picture component, refer to "Using the Scheduled Picture Component," on page 758.
- **Page Banner** This component inserts a text or graphic object containing the current page's title, as specified in various Page Properties dialog boxes. The Page Banner component is particularly useful when you're constructing page templates or standard page headings. Each time you use the template, the Page Banner component displays the title of the current page.

  For more information about the Page Banner component, refer to "Using Page Banners," on page 359.

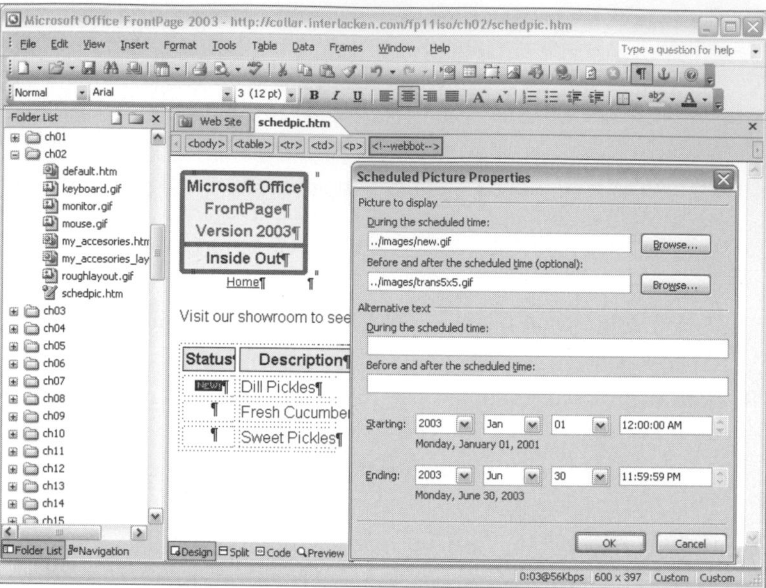

Figure 2-20. The Scheduled Picture component starts and stops displaying a picture based on a specified date.

- **Link Bar** This component builds a set of text or graphic hyperlinks and inserts them wherever you want on the current Web page. A single Web page can contain any number of Link bars, and they can be of two different types.
  - **Link Bar Based On Navigation Structure** This type of link bar gets its hyperlinks from a diagram you draw in another part of FrontPage called, logically enough, Navigation view. You can only configure links generically with this type of link bar; you specify, for example, whether to include links to the current page's Navigation view children, parents, left and right siblings, and home page. Changing the structure in FrontPage's Navigation view updates the link bars—automatically—in any relevant pages.

    For more information about Navigation view, refer to Chapter 13, "Creating Web Sites with Navigation View."
  - **Link Bar With Custom Links** You configure the hyperlinks in this type of link bar entirely by hand. This provides the look and feel of link bars without forcing you to diagram the site.

    For more information about Link bars, refer to "Using Link Bars with Navigation View," on page 348, and "Using the Link Bar Component," on page 306.
- **Table Of Contents For This Web Site** This component creates an outline with hyperlinks to each page in your Web site. It also updates the outline whenever the Web changes.

  For more information about the Table Of Contents For This Web Site component, refer to "Using the Table Of Contents For This Web Site Component," on page 722.

- **Table Of Contents Based On Page Category** Given one or more category codes, this component builds a list of hyperlinks to pages in those categories. You can categorize Web pages either as you edit them or from the Folder List in Folders view. (Right-click the file, choose Properties from the shortcut menu, and then choose Workgroup.)

  For more information about the Table Of Contents Based On Page Category component, refer to "Using the Table Of Contents Based On Page Category Component," on page 727.

- **HTML Markup** If you know how to code HTML and want to insert some special code into a Web page, this component provides the means to do so. FrontPage inserts any HTML you provide directly into the Web page without interpretation, validation, or correction.

  For more information about the HTML Markup component, refer to "Using the HTML Markup Component," on page 1050.

> **Tip** **Paste Standard HTML into Code view.**
>
> To fully integrate your HTML with the HTML generated by FrontPage, insert the new HTML lines after switching FrontPage to Code view. This technique permits subsequent WYSIWYG viewing and editing. Use the Insert HTML component only for HTML that you don't want FrontPage to process in any way.

Locating Web Server Components

Some Web components operate at least partially on the Web server, and you need to be sure your Web server has Windows SharePoint Services or the FrontPage Server Extensions installed before using these components. For list of these components, refer to Appendix B.

Understanding Programmed Components

The fact that computers deliver Web pages on demand and display them interactively means that computer programming instructions can be inserted at any step of the process: when storing pages to the server, when processing Web visitor requests, when delivering requested pages, or when displaying the pages. This flexibility is one of the significant differences between the Web and other mass media. Newspapers, magazines, books, radio, and television all provide very little interactivity or opportunities for customization.

Developers have invented a wide range of technologies for adding programmed intelligence to the Web experience. These include the following:

- Server-side scripting
- Script languages
- Java applets
- ActiveX controls
- Plug-ins

Server-Side Scripting

Common Gateway Interface (CGI), Netscape Server Application Programming Interface (NSAPI), and Internet Server Application Programming Interface (ISAPI) are three interfaces that programs running on a Web server can use to receive data from Web visitors and produce Web pages as output. A Web visitor starts such programs by submitting a special Web page request, and the Web server returns the generated page to that Web visitor. Creating such programs is beyond the objectives of FrontPage, but FrontPage does provide a useful, prewritten set of them—the FrontPage Server Extensions.

For more information about the FrontPage Server Extensions, see Chapter 50, "Understanding the FrontPage Server Extensions."

ASP is a higher-level technology for creating special Web pages containing both HTML code and script code that runs on a Web server. FrontPage supports the development of ASP in three scenarios:

- If you create a Web page that contains a database results region, FrontPage generates ASP code and saves the Web page with an .asp filename extension.

For more information about database results regions, refer to "Using the Database Results Wizard," on page 884.

- If you open the Web Site Templates dialog box and run the Database Interface Wizard, FrontPage creates a group of ASP pages collectively called a *database editor*. A database editor can display, add, change, and delete database records at will.

For more information about the Database Interface Wizard, refer to "Using the Database Interface Wizard," on page 911.

- By switching to Code view, you can add ASP code to any Web page. This code won't prevent you from returning to Design view and resuming WYSIWYG editing for any fixed portions of the page.

For more information about ASP, refer to "Working with ASP Database Result Search Forms," on page 900, and "Saving Form Results as Files or E-Mail," on page 861.

Script Languages

Scripts are short sections of program code inserted directly into Web pages and set off by special tags so that the source code doesn't appear on the displayed page. Scripts can run on either a browser or a Web server, subject to the design of the script and the capabilities of the environment.

Two common uses for scripts are inserting variable information, such as the current date or the date a page was last saved, and responding to Web visitor events, such as resizing the browser window or clicking a button. Script languages can also interact with ActiveX controls and Java applets on the same page, and with the browser or server itself.

For more information about using scripts, refer to Chapter 41, "Working with Script Code."

FrontPage supports script languages by providing a way to insert developer-written scripts into Web pages and by automatically generating script code for common functions, such as field validation. FrontPage supports both VBScript and JavaScript, the two most popular browser script languages. Figure 2-21 shows several lines of JavaScript inserted into a Web page.

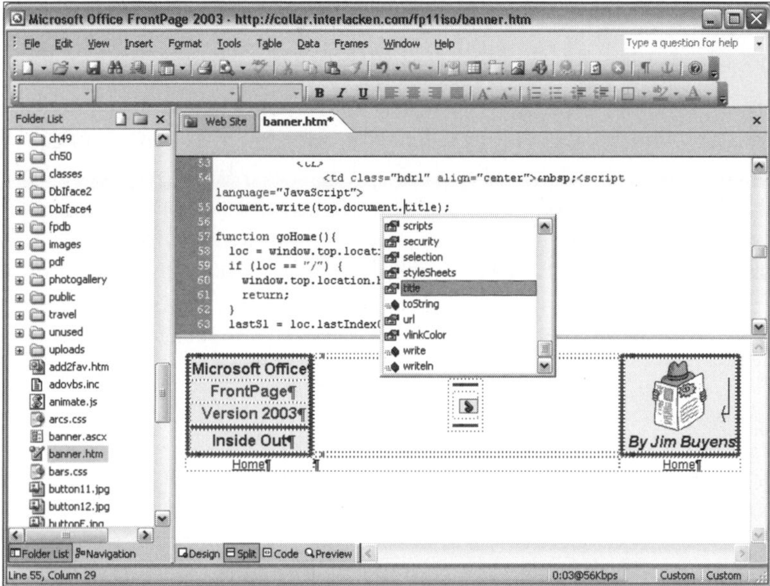

Figure 2-21. FrontPage can insert JavaScript or VBScript code anywhere on a Web page.

The DHTML Effects toolbar creates script code that changes the format of an HTML element based on an event—such as a click or move movement—that occurs on the same element or a different one. To display the DHTML Effects toolbar, choose Toolbars from the View menu, and then choose DHTML Effects.

The new Behaviors feature in FrontPage 2003 can respond to an amazing variety of events that occur for almost any element on a Web page. Like the DHTML Effects toolbar, Behaviors can modify most page element, but it can also instigate actions such as jumping to another Web page. To display the Behaviors task pane, choose Behaviors from the Format menu.

**For more information about the DHTML Effects toolbar, refer to, "Using DHTML Effects," on page 690.
For more information about Behaviors, refer to, "Scripting DHTML Behaviors," on page 694.**

Java Applets

Java applets are small programs written in the Java programming language. Programmers convert their Java programs to a format called *bytecode*. The bytecode files can run on any computer on which a piece of software called a *Java bytecode interpreter* is installed. The interpreter creates an environment called the *Java Virtual Machine*, which, at least in theory, can run any Java program. This approach frees programmers from having to write different versions of their programs for each type of computer. The interpreter must be matched to the type of computer, but the Java program need not be matched.

Java applets are designed to run as part of a Web page. An applet usually occupies a portion of the browser window, controls its contents, and responds to any Web visitor events that occur there. For security reasons, applets can't access files and other resources on the local computer, and they can initiate network connections only to the server from which the applet was downloaded. (These restrictions are frequently compared to a "sandbox," in which Java applets must play.) FrontPage isn't a development environment for Java applets, but it can add existing applets to a page and display them in their initial state.

For more information about using Java applets, refer to "Incorporating Java Applets," on page 803.

ActiveX Controls

Like Java applets, ActiveX controls are programmed objects capable of providing a given function in a variety of contexts. Unlike Java applets, however, ActiveX controls are based on the OLE approach developed for Windows. ActiveX is a very flexible specification that defines not only Web page objects but also objects that run in all sorts of Windows environments. In fact, most ActiveX objects are background components with no visible display.

Controls designed to run within a browser window occupy a portion of the Web page and accept input from HTML code, the Web visitor, or other controls. In response, the controls change their appearance and make results available for transmission back to the Web server. ActiveX controls running on a Web server don't create visual output directly, but instead perform server-side functions such as writing and retrieving data in files and databases. They typically get their input from requests originating from a browser client or from a script that invokes them. As output, they might return values to the script that invoked them or write HTML for transmission to the Web visitor.

ActiveX controls are compiled for a specific type of computer and a specific class of operating system. A separate version is therefore required for each environment. Currently, almost all ActiveX controls run on X86 processors and Microsoft Win32 operating systems.

There's no sandbox limiting what an ActiveX control can do, but each control is digitally signed so that the Web visitor can verify that it arrived both intact and from a trusted source. Although FrontPage isn't a development environment for ActiveX controls, it supports placing such controls on a page and displaying them in their initial state.

For more information about using ActiveX controls, refer to "Incorporating ActiveX Controls," on page 785.

Plug-Ins

Plug-ins are another category of software modules, first developed by Netscape Communications Corporation, that integrate into the display of a Web browser. Plug-ins typically provide interactive and multimedia capability. Here's how the process of displaying content with a plug-in works:

1. The Web page contains special HTML coding that tells the browser to retrieve a file and display it using a plug-in. However, the HTML coding doesn't tell the browser which plug-in to use.
2. The browser requests the specified file from the Web server.
3. The Web server sends the requested file and identifies it with a MIME type.

Note MIME stands for Multipurpose Internet Mail Extensions, and a MIME type is a text string such as *audio/wav*. Windows-based Web servers usually derive the MIME type from the file extension.

4. The browser looks up the MIME type in a table and determines whether any available plug-ins can display that MIME type.
5. The browser loads the first suitable plug-in and tells it to display the downloaded file.

The fact that the HTML coding doesn't tell the browser what plug-in to use is very disturbing to many Web designers. It means that designers have much less control with plug-ins than they have with Java applets and ActiveX controls. With applets and ActiveX controls, designers can specify—and the browser can download—all the software needed to display the object. With plug-ins, designers can only tell the Web visitor what plug-in the page requires and provide a manual link to the plug-in vendor's download site.

For more information about using plug-ins, refer to "Incorporating Plug-Ins," on page 711.

In Summary…

This chapter explained the essentials of creating a Web page with FrontPage. FrontPage provides a rich array of powerful tools that make it easy for both beginners and experts to create Web pages that look the way they want. For more details on these techniques and others, please refer to this book's later chapters.

Chapter 3 explains how FrontPage works not only with individual Web pages, but also with entire Web sites.

Chapter 3
Managing Web Sites

Creating Web pages one-by-one is certainly a useful task, but realistically, you can't present much content on a single page. All but the simplest projects require interrelated Web pages numbering in the dozens, hundreds, or more. Additionally, because each Web page typically uses several constituent files, the total number of files to create, interconnect, and maintain over time can be intimidating.

Site management is an area that many beginning Web designers fail to appreciate. Hard experience is frequently the best teacher in this regard, so if you want to try creating and maintaining Web pages as if they have nothing to do with one another, please go ahead. But if you'd rather follow the lead of most experts and deal with Web pages as members of a set, consider the approaches this chapter describes.

Microsoft Office FrontPage 2003 comes with a broad collection of highly useful tools that can help you create a well-organized site and keep it organized over time. The descriptions in this chapter provide only a brief overview, but that should be enough to get you started. As your expertise grows, you'll probably come to appreciate these and other features even more than the WYSIWYG editor that possibly drew you to FrontPage in the first place.

Planning Your Web Environment

For most projects, it makes perfect sense to have two FrontPage environments: a development environment where you develop and test new or updated pages, and a production environment that delivers finished pages to Web visitors. When new content is ready for world consumption, you transfer it from your development environment server to your production environment server.

Initially, your development environment could be a small collection of freestanding Web pages and associated pictures located in a folder on your hard disk. For sites consisting of more than just a few pages, however, you'll benefit greatly from using a FrontPage-based Web site. This could be a disk-based Web site not involving a Web server, a server-based Web site that someone else administers, or a Web site on a personal Web server you administer yourself.

In general, the more alike your development and production environments, the more effective your testing will be and the fewer problems you'll encounter. This situation argues strongly for two Web servers, both running the FrontPage Server Extensions or Microsoft Windows SharePoint Services. At the same time, other configurations are certainly possible, workable, and in many cases preferable, depending on your circumstances. The remainder of this section will describe some of these scenarios.

If your needs are simple, and formal control over content changes isn't critical, a single server might suffice. If your needs are complex, you might need a battery of servers. Your development environment might be disk-based or Web-server-based. Your production server might be Microsoft Windows or UNIX, and in either case, it might or might not have the FrontPage Server Extensions installed. If your production server doesn't have the server extensions, publishing your Web site won't be quite as smooth, and FrontPage services that run at browse time—such as Search, Save Results, and Database Access—won't be available. This might or might not present a crisis, depending on your requirements. All in all, these are decisions only you, your organization, or your client can make. Here are some common scenarios:

- You create Web pages in your home or small office and connect only periodically to the network where your production Web server resides. Your development Web site is disk-based.

  An ISP, a Web presence provider, or your corporate IT department operates the production server. Your service provider doesn't have the FrontPage Server Extensions installed, and so you have to publish using either an external FTP program or the FTP or DAV features built into FrontPage. Neither your development nor your production environment supports server-based Web components such as Hit Counter, Web Search, and Save Results.
- You create Web pages in an office or on a campus using a permanent network connection. Your development and production Web sites both reside on Windows servers running the FrontPage Server Extensions. To get a FrontPage-based site created on either machine, you submit paperwork to a system administrator. All FrontPage functions work on both machines.
- Your development environment consists of a personal Web server running on your home computer. The FrontPage Server Extensions are installed on your personal Web server.

  Your production environment is a UNIX server operated by your ISP, and the server doesn't have the FrontPage Server Extensions. This means that although all Web components work perfectly in your development environment, they fail in production. However, if your ISP supplies sample HTML for hit counters, forms processors, or other components supported on the UNIX Web server, you can paste it into FrontPage's Code view.

For more information about installing a personal Web server, refer to Appendix O, "Installing and Configuring a Web Server."

- You're one of several programmers working on a Web-based or an e-commerce business system. You run a Web server on your own PC, developing visual designs in FrontPage and program code in Microsoft Visual Studio .NET. When your Web pages are ready, you copy them to a shared, central Web server that contains a test version of the entire system. When a new release of the entire system is ready for production, a program librarian or administrator copies the test system to the production server.

If you've decided you need a personal Web server and you're working remotely, or if you're cursed and have to *be* the network administrator, you'll need to learn how to install a Web server yourself. Later chapters explain in detail how to choose the proper Web server for your platform and how to coordinate installation of the Web server, the FrontPage Server Extensions, and the FrontPage client.

For more information about installing the FrontPage Server Extensions, refer to Appendix P, "Understanding the FrontPage Server Extensions."

Creating a FrontPage-Based Web Site

Many of the most powerful features in FrontPage work not just on single Web pages, but also on all Web pages in a given set. This invites the question of what constitutes a set, and the answer is, a FrontPage-based Web site.

A FrontPage-based Web site consists of all the individual pages and folders that reside within a specially designated folder tree on your hard disk or Web server. The only exception is that no one file or folder can be a member of two Web sites. You can physically locate one site inside another, but operations on the "outer" site won't affect the "inner" site (as they would if the "inner" site were an ordinary folder.)

For more information about FrontPage-based Web sites, refer to Chapter 6, "Creating and Using FrontPage Web Sites."

In general, you should create a different Web site for each group of pages you want to treat as a unit. As to what constitutes such a group, the decisions is yours; it could be all pages for a given topic, all pages formatted a certain way, or all pages with the same security. Typically, FrontPage-based Web sites contain from a few dozen to a few hundred Web pages, plus pictures and other ancillary files. Here's the procedure for creating a FrontPage-based Web site:

1. Start FrontPage and press Ctrl+F1 if no task pane is visible.
2. If the current task pane isn't titled New, click the drop-down arrow on the current task pane's menu bar, and choose New.
3. Under New Web Site, click One Page Web Site. This displays the Web Site Templates dialog box shown in Figure 3-1.

Tip In lieu of steps 2 through 4, you might prefer clicking the drop-down arrow on the Create A New Normal Page icon in the Standard toolbar and then choosing Web Site.

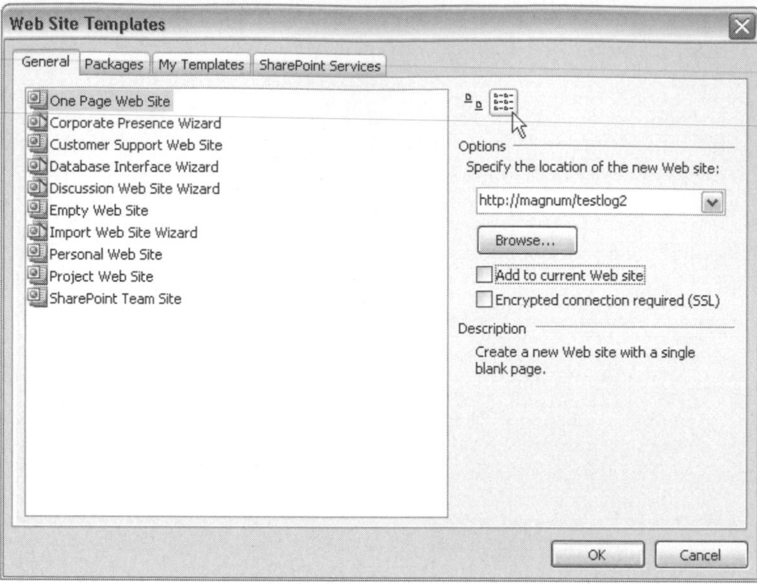

Figure 3-1. The Web Site Templates dialog box lists templates containing good starting points for your new Web.

4 The templates on the left side of the Web Sites tab provide various kinds of initial content for your new Web site. To view the full name of each template, click the List button in the right side of the dialog box. In Figure 3-1, the mouse pointer indicates this button.

5 Make sure that the selected template is the one you want. The most common choices are:

- **One Page Web Site** Creates a new Web site that contains a blank home page.
- **Empty Web Site** Creates a new Web site that contains no initial content at all.

The options on the right side of the General tab specify the location of the new Web site and other options. In the box titled Specify The Location Of The New Web Site, type the full path to the location where you want the Web site to reside:

If you enter a file location, such as C:\Documents and Settings\<*username*>\My Documents\My Webs\fp11iso or \\spike\webshare\fp11iso, FrontPage creates a disk-based Web site.

If you enter a Web address, such as *http://www.interlacken.com/fp11iso*, FrontPage creates a server-based Web site.

Note You can create server-based Web sites only on a Web server that has the FrontPage Server Extensions or Windows SharePoint Services installed. In addition, you must have the necessary security permissions to access the Web server.

By default, the first Web site that FrontPage creates is named *myweb* and is located in C:\Documents and Settings\<*username*>\My Documents\My Webs\. If you create additional Web sites, their default names will be *myweb2*, *myweb3*, and so on, and their paths will be as follows:

```
C:\Documents and Settings\<username>\My Documents\My Webs\myweb2
C:\Documents and Settings\<username>\My Documents\My Webs\myweb3
```

However, if you create a Web site somewhere else, such as *http://www.interlacken.com/fp11iso*, the default location for the next Web site you create will be *http://www.interlacken.com/fp11iso2*.

6. If you prefer to specify the Web site location by pointing and clicking rather than by typing, click the Browse button. Clicking Browse displays the New Web Site Location dialog box. (This box looks much like the Open File dialog box mentioned in Chapter 2.) Navigate to the location you want, and then click Open.
7. Select the Add To Current Web Site option if you've already opened a Web site and want to add the contents of the template to that site.
8. Select the Encrypted Connection Required (SSL) check box if you're creating a server-based Web site and that server's security policy requires the use of Secure Sockets Layer (SSL) communication. Click OK to create the new site.

Reviewing the New Task Pane

When you need to start creating a new Web page or Web site, the New task pane often provides just the command you need. Here are commands this task pane provides.

- **New Page** This group of commands creates new files that will reside within your Web site:
  - **Blank Page** Opens a new, blank Web page in Design view.
  - **Text File** Open a new, empty text file in Code view.
  - **From Existing Page** Opens a new copy of an existing Web page. Saving this copy doesn't overwrite the original file.
  - **More page templates** Displays a Page Templates dialog box that lists each template currently available to FrontPage.
- **New Web Site** These commands create new Web sites that will reside on your local disk or on a Web server.
  - **One Page Web Site** Displays the Web Site Templates dialog box with the One Page Web Site template selected.
  - **SharePoint Team Site** Displays the Web Site Templates dialog box with the SharePoint team site template selected.

- **Web Package Solutions** Displays the Web Site Templates dialog box with the Packages tab selected. (In FrontPage terminology, a package is a complete FrontPage-based Web stored and compressed into a single file.)
- **More Web Site Templates** Displays the Web Site Templates dialog box with the first available template selected.

- **Templates On Microsoft.com** These commands search for page or Web site templates on Microsoft's Web site:
  - **Search Office Online** Searches the Microsoft Office Web site for templates matching given keywords.
  - **Templates Home Page** Displays the Microsoft Office Templates home page in your browser.
- **Recently Used Templates** Displays a list of the last few templates you've used.

For more information about creating and managing FrontPage-based Web sites, refer to Chapter 6, "Creating and Using FrontPage Web Sites."

Chapter 6 presents much more information about creating and managing Web sites, but here are some quick tips to get you started:

- If the file or network path to a new FrontPage-based Web site contains an existing site, the new Web site will be a subweb. Suppose, for example, that you have a Web site at
C:\Documents and Settings\<*username*>\My Documents\My Webs\Statues
and then you create a new site at
C:\Documents and Settings\<*username*>\My Documents\My Webs\Statues\Grecian
The Grecian site becomes a subweb of the Statues site.

Note **Use subwebs to manage your content.**

A *subweb* is a FrontPage-based Web site that physically resides within another FrontPage-based Web site.

A new FrontPage Web server contains one site: the so-called *root* Web site at URL /. If you create additional sites on the same server, those sites will have URLs like /flora and /fauna, and they' be subwebs of the root site.

Breaking a server's content into subwebs provides granular control over permissions, visual appearance and other aspects of each body of content.

The terms subweb and subsite are synonymous.

Another—even easier—way to create subwebs is to follow these steps:

1 Use FrontPage to open the Web site that will contain the new subweb.
2 If necessary, display the Folder List by choosing Folder List from the View menu.

3 Create a folder where you want the subweb to reside (that is, right-click the parent folder, choose New from the shortcut menu, and name the new folder as you want).

4 Right-click the new folder in the Folder List, and choose Convert To Web from the shortcut menu. Click Yes when prompted.

The more files a Web site contains, the longer certain operations will take. This particularly affects Web site publishing. Try to keep the size of your Web sites down to a few hundred files if possible, or a few thousand files at most. When a site gets to large, break it into subwebs.

You should update FrontPage-based Web sites only by using an HTTP location in My Network Places or by using FrontPage itself. Updating a site by any other means doesn't update all the file indexes and cross-references that FrontPage needs for proper operation and doesn't maintain consistency among files the way FrontPage can.

Tip If you must update a Web site by means other than FrontPage, you need to take corrective action by opening the site in FrontPage and choosing Recalculate Hyperlinks from the Tools menu.

Security needs are another issue to consider when planning your Web sites. FrontPage user security operates at the site level. This means one part of a Web site can't be open to a different set of users—whether for authoring or for browsing—than another part of the same site. Each different security requirement necessitates its own Web site or subweb.

Opening a FrontPage-Based Web Site

The first step in working with a FrontPage-based Web site is to open it. Here's one way to do this:

1 Choose Open Site from the File menu. The Open Site dialog box shown in Figure 3-2 appears.

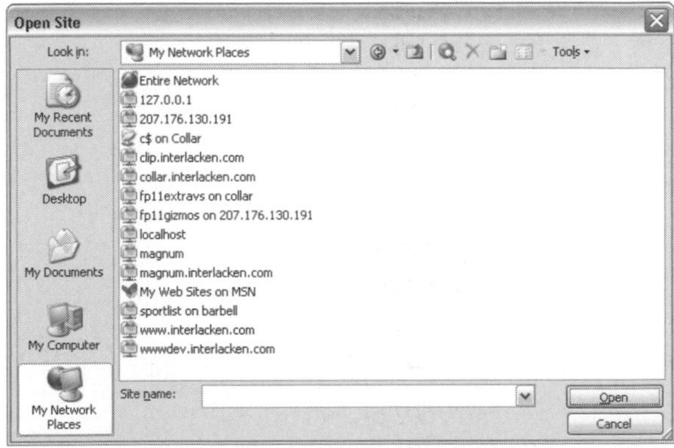

Figure 3-2. The Open Site dialog box is very similar to the Open File dialog box shown in Figure 2-13. Rather than opening a single file, however, this box opens a group view of many files.

2 Locate the site you want using either of the following techniques:

- To locate a disk-based Web site, click the My Recent Documents, Desktop, My Documents, or My Computer icon.
- To locate a server-based Web site, click the My Network Places icon.

Note The first time you try to open a server-based Web site, its server might not appear in the My Network Places list. FrontPage can't display a list of Web servers in your environment, because your environment might be the entire Internet! If the folder you want doesn't appear in the My Network Places list, just type its URL in the Site Name box, and then click Open. This both opens the site and adds it to the list for next time.

Note In folder listings, the icon for a FrontPage-based Web site looks like a folder with a globe on it. This visually distinguishes FrontPage sites from regular folders.

3 Double-click the name of the Web site, or select the name and click the Open button.

Opening a Web site is such a common task that FrontPage provides many ways to do it. Here are some additional ways to open a site:

- Open a Web page that resides in a FrontPage-based Web site. FrontPage opens both the specified file and the site that contains it.
- Choose Recent Sites from the File menu. If the Web site you want to open appears in the list, simply select it.

For information about opening individual files in FrontPage, refer to "Opening a Page from Design view," on page 193.

Note In the case of server-based Web sites that support user-level security, FrontPage might prompt you for a user name and password. If you don't know what to enter, contact the Web server's administrator.

- Locate the Web site within the Folder List of another Web site, and double-click it.

Opening a regular folder in FrontPage displays that folder's contents in the same window. Opening a FrontPage-based Web site creates a new window displaying that site.

Figure 3-3 shows a Web site open in FrontPage.

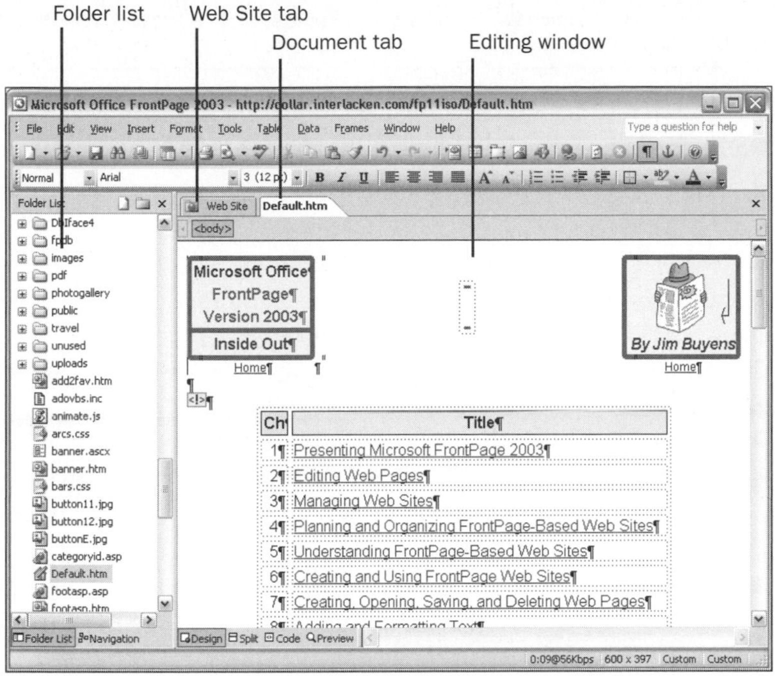

Figure 3-3. The Folder List at the left of the FrontPage window displays the files and folders in the current Web site. The tabs above the document area select documents, and those below select views.

Below the toolbars are four important areas:

- **Folder List** This frame displays the Web site contents as a folder tree. To hide or display it, choose Folder List from the View menu.
- **Editing window** This frame displays the current document, report, or work area.
- **Web Site tab** Whenever a Web site is open, this is the first tab above the editing window. Clicking this tab displays one of six views in the editing window. To change views, click the corresponding icon in the Views bar below the Editing window. Here are the choices:
  - **Folders** Displays a tabular list of files in the site, organized by folder.

  - **Remote Web Site** Displays a comparison of files in the current (local) site and next higher (remote) site in your working environment.

    An example should clarify this. Suppose that on your own PC you have a copy of a site that resides on a service provider's Web server. To make updates, you open the local copy. When the updates are complete, you copy the changed pages to the service provider's Web server.

    If, in this scenario, you opened the local site in FrontPage and displayed Remote Web Site view, the display would show the difference between your local site and the copy on the service provider's Web server.

For more information about Remote Web Site view, refer to the section "Publishing Your Web Site," later in this chapter.

- **Reports** Displays an assortment of tabular listings useful for site management.
- **Navigation** Graphically displays the logical hierarchy of pages in a Web site.
- **Hyperlinks** Graphically displays files in a Web site, organized by hyperlink reference.
- **Tasks** Displays a list of reminders about completing or correcting pages.

- **Document tabs** A tab for each open document also appears above the editing window, extending from the Web Site tab to the right. To display any open document in the editing window, click the corresponding document tab. Depending on the document type, as many as five views may be available:
  - **Design** Displays Web pages in WYSIWYG view for editing.
  - **Split** Divides the editing window in half horizontally. The top half displays the current document in Code view. The bottom half displays the same document in Design view.
  - **No Frames** This view is available only when the current document is a frameset. In that case, No Frames view shows the page as a browser that doesn't support frames would display it.
  - **Code** Displays the HTML and any embedded program code for a Web page.
  - **Preview** Starts an instance of Microsoft Internet Explorer, and uses it to display the current Web page.

Note For text files other than Web pages, the only available view will be Code view.

Working with Web Folder Lists

The Folder List normally appears whenever a FrontPage-based Web site is open. It occupies the left pane of the main FrontPage window and provides access to all files and folders in the site. In addition to providing information, the Folder List has two main uses: manipulating the files and folders in the site, and opening files with the appropriate editor.

In some cases, a Navigation pane might appear in place of the Folder List. The Navigation pane displays the same information as Navigation view but in a smaller format that FrontPage can display simultaneously with an open Web page. To display the Folder List instead of the Navigation pane, choose Folders from the View menu or click the Folder List tab located at the bottom of the Navigation pane.

For more information about Navigation view, refer to the section "Creating a Web Site in Navigation View," later in this chapter.

Manipulating Files and Folders

The left pane in Figure 3-3 shows a typical Folder List. As the following list illustrates, all the normal Microsoft Windows Explorer commands work as expected:

- To open a collapsed folder, double-click it or click the preceding plus icon.
- To collapse an open folder, double-click it or click the preceding minus icon.
- To load the Clipboard with a file to be copied, select the file, and then press Ctrl+C or Ctrl+Insert or choose Copy from the Edit menu.
- To load the Clipboard with a file to be moved, select the file, and then press Ctrl+X or Shift+Delete or choose Cut from the Edit menu.
- To complete a move or copy operation, select the desired folder, and then press Ctrl+V or Shift+Insert or choose Paste from the Edit menu.
- To move a file from one folder to another, drag the file to the destination folder's icon.
- To copy a file from one location to another, hold down the Ctrl key while dragging the file to the new location.
- To move or copy a file or folder and control the operation from a shortcut menu, drag the file or folder to the desired location using the right mouse button, release the button, and then make a selection from the shortcut menu.
- To rename a file or folder, either select it and press F2 or right-click it and choose Rename from the shortcut menu.
- To delete a file or folder, select it and press Delete, select it and choose Delete from the Edit menu, or right-click it and choose Delete from the shortcut menu.

Maintaining Hyperlink Locations

When you use FrontPage to move or rename files in an open Web site, FrontPage locates and updates all hyperlinks that use the affected files. Suppose, for example, that you have a picture file named clown.jpg that's located in a FrontPage-based Web site. If you open the site in FrontPage and rename the file joker.jpg, FrontPage displays the Rename message box shown here, offering to change any picture tags, hyperlinks, or other references to the clown.jpg file within that site so that they point to joker.jpg instead:

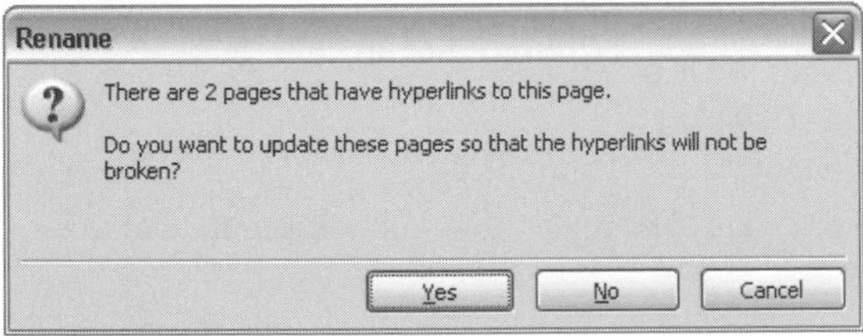

Of course, this works for any type of file, not just picture files, and it also works when you move a file from one folder to another.

You can also cut, copy, and drag files to transport them between two Web sites and between a disk location and a Web site. However, the following special precautions apply:

- You can't move files into or out of a Web site. You can only copy them.
- You can't copy or drop files or folders onto a site icon that a parent site displays in its Folder List, or in any of its views. To copy between Web sites, you must open each site in a separate FrontPage window.
- When you drag or copy a file out of a Web site and onto your Windows desktop, Windows creates an Internet shortcut to the file. Clicking this shortcut launches your default browser and displays the file.

  You can't copy a file from a FrontPage Web site to a physical location on your hard disk by dragging it out of a FrontPage Folder List or view. However, there are three other ways you can do this:

  - Select the file in the Folder List or in Folders view, and then choose Export from the File menu.
  - Open the file in the FrontPage editor, choose Save As from the File menu, and specify a location on your hard disk.
  - On your desktop, open My Network Places, select the location that contains your Web site, and then open any necessary subfolders. Finally, drag the file from the resulting window and drop it into Windows Explorer.

Tip To control the specifics of a dragging operation, drag with the right mouse button, and choose a command from the shortcut menu that appears when you release the button.

Figure 3-4 shows the shortcut menus you see after right-clicking a file, a folder, and a subweb icon in the Folder List.

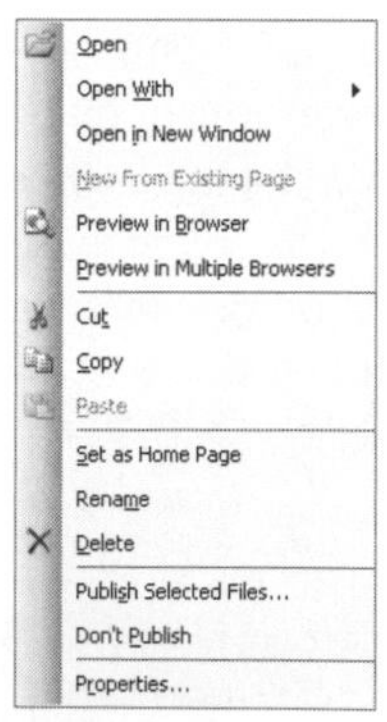

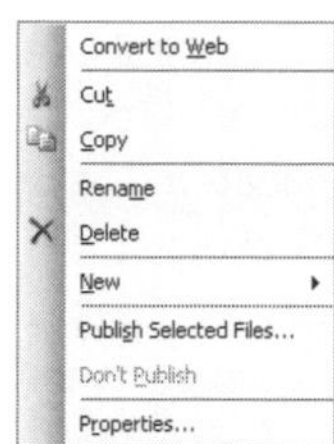

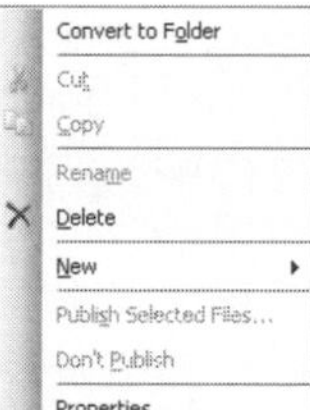

Figure 3-4. Right-clicking a Folder List file, folder, and subweb produces these shortcut menus, respectively.

Notice the Convert To Web option on the Folder shortcut menu and the Convert To Folder option on the Web menu. These are reciprocal operations, but as explained in Chapter 6, "Creating and Using FrontPage Web Sites," both operations alter or discard information about a Web site. After converting a folder to a site, converting the resulting site back to a folder might not restore all the files and FrontPage indexes back to their original condition.

For more information about conversion between folders and Web sites, refer to "Converting a Folder to a Web Site," on page 173, and "Converting a Web Site to a Folder," on page 174.

Whenever you move or rename files in FrontPage, FrontPage automatically corrects all hyperlinks, image tags, and other references in the same Web site. Suppose, for example, that 23 pages in your site use a picture named boots.gif. For some reason, you decide to rename the file from boots.gif to shoes.gif. When you rename the file from within FrontPage, FrontPage updates all 23 pages so that they reference shoes.gif rather than boots.gif. FrontPage also warns you before it deletes a file used by other files in your site.

Caution FrontPage can't correct references from outside your Web site to files within it. First, this would require searching the entire Internet. Second, even if FrontPage *could* locate such references, you probably wouldn't have the authority to update them. You can minimize this problem by organizing related Web pages into the same FrontPage-based Web site.

To add an external file to the current Web site, select the folder in which it should reside, and then choose Import from the File menu. If the site isn't on the local machine, the Import command copies the file across the network. The Import command also updates FrontPage with appropriate file information, an operation that wouldn't occur if you simply copied the file to the site's physical location using some other method.

The Add Task option, available from the Tasks submenu of the Edit menu, creates a Tasks entry for the selected page. The section "Working with Tasks View," on page 1015, discusses this feature in detail.

Choosing an Editor

Double-clicking any file in the Folder List opens that file using the appropriate editor. Unfortunately, FrontPage's idea of what constitutes an appropriate editor might be different from yours, and this can lead to confusion. Here's how FrontPage chooses an editor:

- Normally, FrontPage opens Web page files—identified by file extensions such as .htm, .html, and .asp—in FrontPage Design view.
- Recent versions of most Office applications can directly save their native documents as pages in a FrontPage-based Web site. FrontPage opens all such files in the same application that created them, even if the file extension is .htm, .asp, or something else that FrontPage would normally open in Design view. You can tell what application FrontPage will start by looking at each file's icon. Figure 3-5 shows examples of Folder List icons representing .htm files saved by Microsoft PowerPoint, Microsoft Excel, and FrontPage.

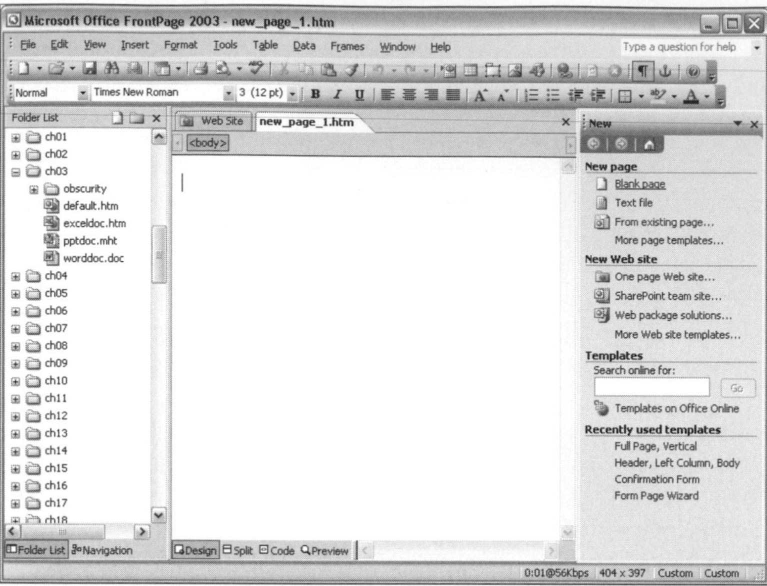

Figure 3-5. FrontPage detects which Office application created a Web file, displays a corresponding icon, and opens files in that same application.

Chapter 3

Tip **Open All Office Web Pages In Design View**

If you want FrontPage to open all Web pages in Design view, regardless of the application that created them, choose Options from the Tools menu in FrontPage, click the Configure Editors tab, and clear the Open Web Pages In The Office Application That Created Them check box.

- For other kinds of files, FrontPage first tries looking up the file extension in a list of configured editors. To revise this list, choose Options from the Tools menu, and then click the Configure Editors tab.

For more information about the Configure Editors tab, refer to "Configuring External Editors," on page 1118.

- If all else fails, FrontPage chooses an editor by using Windows file associations (that is, it uses the same program Windows would use if you double-clicked the same type of file in Windows Explorer).

There are two ways to temporarily override FrontPage's normal choice of editors (that is, to use an editor other than the one FrontPage would use if you double-clicked the file):

- If the application you want to use has a My Network Places choice in its Open File dialog box, simply start the application and open the file you want.

- Right-click the file in the Folder List or in Folders view and then choose Open With from the shortcut menu. If the application you want doesn't appear in the resulting dialog box, add it to the list on the Configure Editors tab just described.

Building a Web Site

FrontPage supports five primary ways of populating a new Web site with content. The best choice for a particular job depends, of course, on the nature of the job. Here are the five ways:

- **Manual** You create all your Web pages and the hyperlinks that connect them by hand.
- **Navigation view** You diagram your site in Navigation view and let FrontPage create the individual Web pages automatically. Components called *link bars* use the Navigation view structure to automatically create hyperlinks from one page to another.
- **Web Site templates** You tell FrontPage the type of content you want, and FrontPage supplies a typical collection of Web pages. This provides a starting point for developing your own pages.
- **SharePoint Team Sites** FrontPage creates a generic portal site complete with document libraries, picture libraries, and lists. You can customize this site by adding any libraries, lists, and Web parts you require and by removing those that you don't.
- **Web packages** FrontPage includes a number of prewritten applications as Web packages. When you create a new Web site, you can initialize its content from these packages.

Manually Building a Web Site

The time-honored, classic way of building a Web site is first to create a home page, then create pages that the home page will link to, then add the appropriate hyperlinks to the home page, and so forth, for as many levels as the site requires.

Despite the fact that it's 100 percent manual, this approach to building a Web site remains the most common. It's fast, it's flexible, and it's simple. FrontPage makes it easy to create as many pages as you want, to create hyperlinks by pointing and clicking, and to move things around without breaking links as your site changes and evolves. In return for doing all the work yourself, you have complete control over the results.

For more information about creating hyperlinks, refer to Chapter 11, "Building Hyperlinks."

Rank beginners tend to choose this method because it requires the least amount of technology to learn. Experts choose it because they want complete control. If learning curves and control don't concern you, FrontPage provides three ways to build a Web site automatically. The next few sections describe these approaches.

Creating a Web Site in Navigation View

For Web sites of moderate size, you can save yourself some work, but sacrifice some flexibility, by creating the site in Navigation view. At a high level, here's how this works:

1. Create and open a new, empty Web site.
2. Click the Web Site tab above the editing window, and then click the Navigation tab below it. The editing window will then display a Navigation view of your site. You can recognize this view by the word *Navigation* at the left of the toolbar that appears just below the Web Site tab.
3. Right-click anywhere inside the Navigation view display, point to New on the shortcut menu, and then choose Top Page from the resulting submenu. This creates an icon representing your home page. This page is named Home Page, and it has a little Home icon in its lower left corner.
4. To change the name of the home page, make sure that it's selected, press F2, type the new name, and then press Enter. This name eventually becomes the title that appears in large type at the top of the Web page.

New Page

5. To add a second page to the Web site, click the home page you just created, and then click the New Page button on the Navigation view toolbar. This will add a new page that's a child of your home page. As before, press F2, give the page a meaningful name, and press Enter.
6. To create additional pages, repeat step 5 as often as you want. Each new page will appear as a child of whatever page you select before clicking the New Page button. To move any page beneath a different parent, drag it in the Navigation view window until a line connects the page you're dragging to the parent page you want.

At this point, your screen should look similar to the one pictured in Figure 3-6. To physically create the pages so that they appear as in the Folder List, click any Web Site tab other than Navigation. This creates a new, blank page for each node you diagrammed in Navigation view. The pages will become visible in the Folder List at this time.

New, blank pages might be interesting—or not—but the real payback from creating your Web site in Navigation view comes when you add shared borders, Web components, and themes to the site, as the next sections describe.

For more information about Navigation view, refer to Chapter 13, "Creating Web Sites with Navigation View."

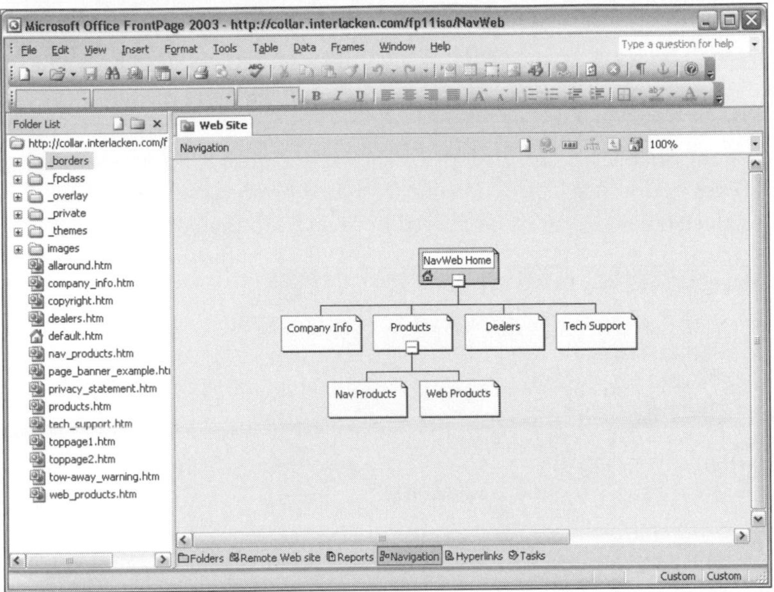

Figure 3-6. Navigation view provides an electronic storyboard for designing Web sites.

Adding Shared Borders

Shared borders are a high-powered way to replicate content throughout a Web site. A site can have up to four shared borders located at the top, left, right, or bottom edge of each page in the site. Whatever you put in, say, the top shared border appears in the top border of every page in that site. Whatever you put in the left shared border appears at the left of every page, and so forth.

Shared borders would be boring, mundane, and downright monotonous if not for some special Web components that display different content depending on the page in which they occur. These Web components include:

- **Page Banner** This component displays the title you gave a Web page in Navigation view. Putting a Page Banner component in a Web site's top shared border displays—in one fell swoop—each page's Navigation view title at the top of each page.
- **Link Bar** This component is even more exciting. It automatically displays a series of hyperlinks to pages above, below, to the left, or to the right of the current page as diagrammed in Navigation view. This saves you the work of manually building the hyperlinks that Web visitors use for traversing your site.
- **Date And Time** This component automatically displays the date—and optionally, the time—of the last update to the page that contains it.

Here's the procedure for adding shared borders to a Web site:

1 Open the site in FrontPage and choose Shared Borders from the Format menu.

Tip If the Shared Borders command is dimmed, choose Page Options from the Tools menu, and then click the Authoring tab. Then select the Shared Borders check box and click OK.

2 When the Shared Borders dialog box shown in Figure 3-7 appears, make sure that the All Pages option is selected. Otherwise, shared borders will apply only to any pages you selected before you chose Shared Borders from the Format menu.

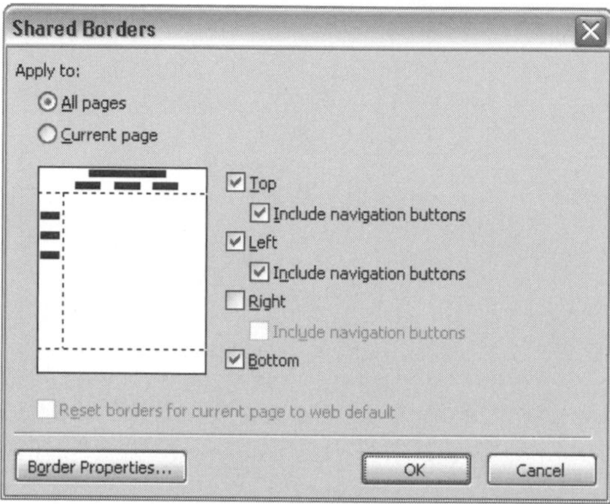

Figure 3-7. Shared borders are reserved areas of content that FrontPage replicates to all or selected pages in a Web site.

3 Select the check boxes for each shared border you want to use. For purposes of this example, select the Top, Left, and Bottom borders.

If you select the Include Navigation Buttons check box under Top, FrontPage adds a Page Banner component and a Link Bar component to the top shared border. If you select the Include Navigation Buttons check box under Left or Right, FrontPage adds a Link Bar component to the respective border.

4 Click OK to apply the shared border.

For more information about shared borders, refer to "Using Shared Borders," on page 761.

Adding Shared Border Content

To add content to the shared borders you just created, open any page in the current Web site and take the following actions. This example assumes you've opened the home page, default.htm, and that it appears as shown in Figure 3-8.

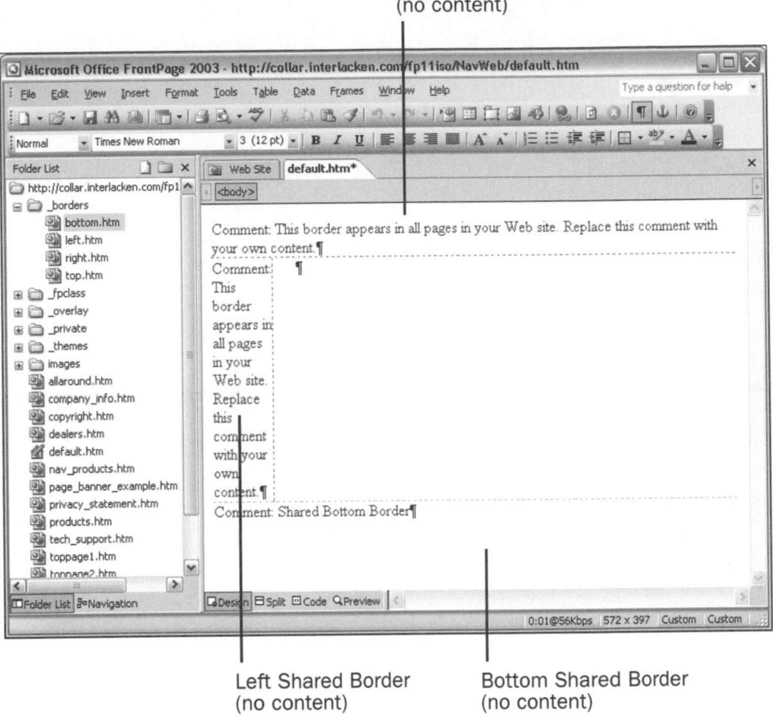

Figure 3-8. This Web page contains three shared border areas: top, left, and bottom. None as yet contain displayable content.

To add a Page Banner component to the top shared border, proceed as follows:

1. Set the insertion point inside the top shared border. If a comment appears within this border, click it, and then press Delete.
2. Choose Web Component from the Insert menu.
3. When the Insert Web Component dialog box appears, choose Included Content in the Component Type list at the left, and then choose Page Banner in the Choose A Type Of Content list at the right.
4. Click Finish. When the Page Banner Properties dialog box appears, accept the default property settings, and click OK.

Follow the next procedure to add a Link Bar component to the left shared border:

1. Set the insertion point inside the left shared border. If a comment appears within this border, click it, and then press Delete.
2. Choose Web Component from the Insert menu. This displays the Insert Web Component dialog box.

3 Click Link Bars in the Component Type list at the left, and then click Bar Based On Navigation Structure in the Choose A Bar Type list at the right.

4 Click Finish. When the Link Bar Properties dialog box shown in Figure 3-9 appears, make sure that the General tab is visible. Select the Child Level option if necessary, and then select the Home Page and Parent Page options.

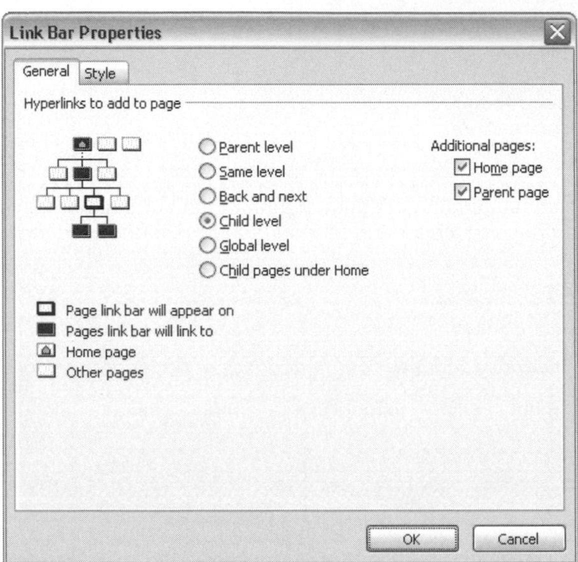

Figure 3-9. Link bars can derive their content from a structure you draw in Navigation view. If you need more than one category of hyperlinks on the same page, include two or more Link Bar components.

5 On the Style tab, make sure that Use Page's Theme is selected in the Choose A Style list. (To see this choice, you might need to scroll the list to the top.)

6 Under Orientation And Appearance, select the Vertical option. If you selected a Theme that can provide animated buttons, FrontPage will enable the Use Active Graphics check box; select that box if you want such buttons. Finally, click OK.

The next procedure adds a Date And Time component to the bottom shared border. Follow these steps:

1 Set the insertion point inside the bottom shared border. If a comment appears within this border, click it, and then press Delete.

2 Type the phrase **This page last modified on** and a space.

3 Choose Date And Time from the Insert menu.

> **Tip** Because various countries specify month, day, and year in different orders, a date like 2/3/4 can be quite ambiguous. February 03, 2004 is much more specific.

4 Under Display, select Date This Page Was Last Edited. For Date Format, select a format that displays the name of the month and a four-digit year.

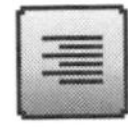

Align Right

5 Click OK. To right-align the contents of the bottom shared border, click the Align Right toolbar button.

The Web page should now appear as in Figure 3-10.

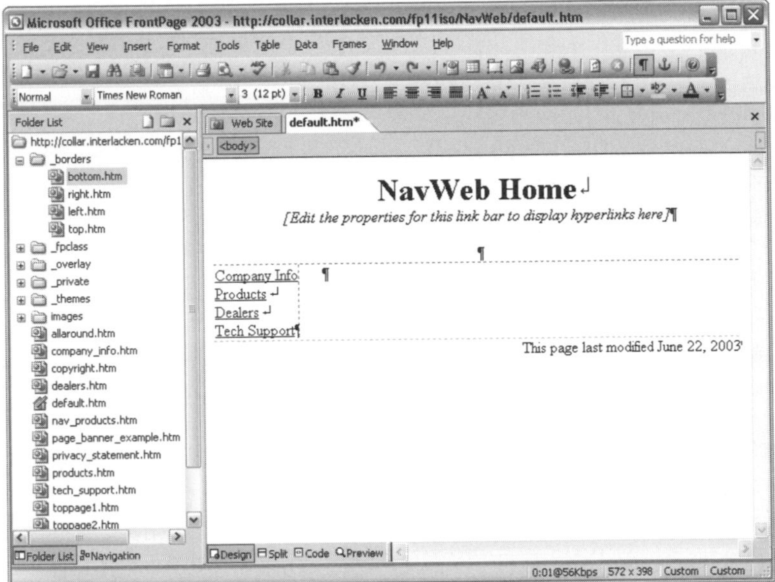

Figure 3-10. Here the Web page pictured in Figure 3-8 has some typical content added to it.

Applying a Theme

The sample Web site is now functional but hardly attractive. FrontPage themes provide an excellent way—again in one fell swoop—to improve the appearance of all the pages in a given site. Here's the procedure for applying a theme to a site:

1 Open the site in FrontPage, and choose Theme from the Format menu.

2 When the Theme task pane shown in Figure 3-11 appears, select the options you want. For example, you might select the theme Axis and then, below the list of themes, select Vivid Colors, Active Graphics, and Background Picture.

3 If a warning dialog box appears, click Yes.

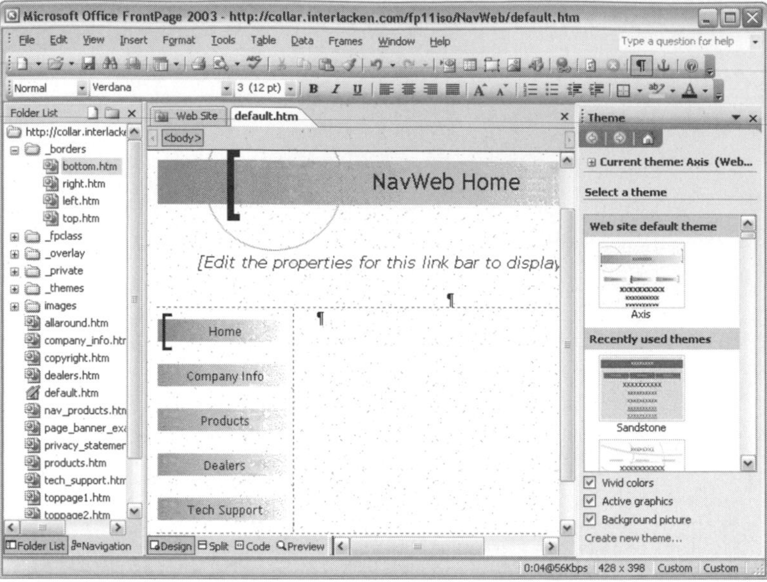

Figure 3-11. This Theme task pane lists and displays previews of all available FrontPage themes.

You can now preview the Web page in Internet Explorer to see the results shown in Figure 3-12. This is quite an improvement over the spartan Web page shown in Figure 3-10. In addition, the right bracket that appears just to the right of the Company Info hyperlink actually slides up and down as the mouse pointer hovers over each menu choice. All that remains is adding the detail content for each page.

Creating Web sites with Navigation view, shared borders, Web components, and themes has many advantages. You can add, rearrange, or delete pages at any time; FrontPage will update the link bars in all your pages automatically. All page banner and link bar choices will use consistent names for each page. All your pages will share a consistent, attractive appearance.

Of course, there are disadvantages as well. If a site contains only a few pages, it might be quicker to lay it out by hand. If the site consists of hundreds or thousands of pages, Navigation view can become unwieldy. If some pages need to be formatted quite differently from others, the forced uniformity of themes can become a real hindrance. And finally, if your home page, like so many today, contains dozens of tiny hyperlinks grouped by function, link bars might not generate the appearance you need. Despite these disadvantages, an automatic FrontPage-based Web site works quite well for many kinds of sites and is definitely an option to consider.

For more information about themes, refer to Chapter 20, "Using FrontPage Themes."

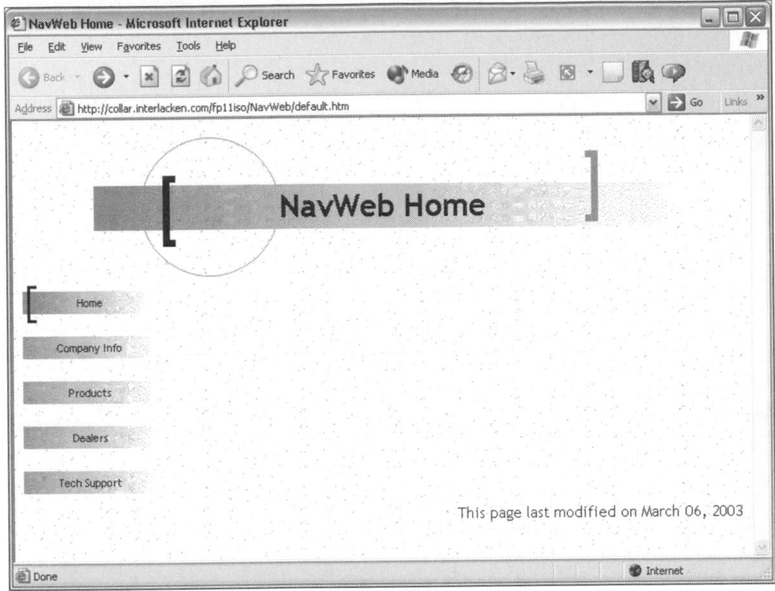

Figure 3-12. Here's how the Web page in Figure 3-10 looks with a theme applied. The improvement is striking.

Working with Web Templates

Earlier in this chapter, the section "Creating a FrontPage-Based Web Site" briefly mentioned the Empty Web Site and One Page Web Site options that appear after you display the New task pane and then click More Web Site Templates. The following list describes the remaining options in that dialog box. The wizard templates prompt you for information; the remaining templates create exactly the same results every time you create a new site with them:

- **Customer Support Web Site** Creates a Web site that provides customer support services, particularly for software companies.
- **Import Web Site Wizard** Creates a Web site filled with documents from your local computer or the Internet. Choosing this option is equivalent to creating an Empty Web Site, choosing Import from the File menu, and clicking From Site in the Import dialog box.
- **SharePoint Team Site** Creates a SharePoint Team Web site. This is a prefabricated site that centralizes information for groups of people working together. It supports upload, display, and download of a shared document library; discussion groups; and lists of contacts, tasks, announcements, events, and Web links.
- **Personal Web Site** Creates a prototype Web site that describes you. It includes pages to describe your interests, show photos, and list your favorite Web sites.
- **Project Web Site** Creates a Web site for coordinating project members and activities. It provides a list of members, a schedule, status, an archive, and discussions.

- **Database Interface Wizard** Creates a Web site that contains a database editor. This is a group of Web pages that work together to display, modify, add, and delete records in a database.
- **Discussion Web Wizard** Creates a discussion group with threads, a table of contents, and full-text searching.
- **Corporate Presence Wizard** Creates an archetypal site that represents your organization on the Internet.

For the most part, these templates aren't terribly exciting. The Corporate Presence Wizard, Customer Support Web Site, and Personal Web Site options provide basic starting points for your work but no real flashes of brilliance. You can run the Import Web Site Wizard just as easily after creating a new, blank Web site or, for that matter, on a Web site with existing content. If your Web server supports it, a SharePoint Team Site provides much better features than a Discussion Web Site or Project Web Site.

> **Tip** You can create a SharePoint Team Site only on a server running Windows SharePoint Services.

Creating a SharePoint Team Site

The SharePoint Team Site option is the real star among FrontPage Web Site templates. Figure 3-13 illustrates the home page for such a site.

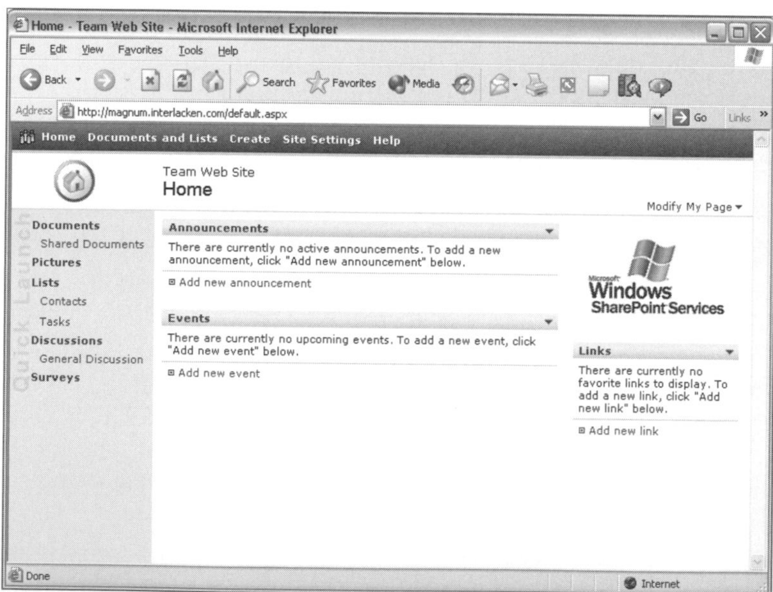

Figure 3-13. SharePoint Team Sites provide a wide assortment of features that enhance collaboration.

Here are descriptions of the major options SharePoint Team Sites have to offer:

- **Documents** This heading identifies special folders that make it easy for people to share documents. Initially, a SharePoint Team Site has one document library, named Shared Documents, but you can create as may document libraries as you want. Each library displays documents in a list that Web visitors can sort, filter, and possibly—depending on the file format—display.

  For documents saved as HTML (remember, all Office applications can save their native document types as HTML with no loss of intelligence or appearance), people using only a browser can review documents, insert comments about the document in general, and insert comments inline with document text. When the originator later opens the document, comments from all reviewers appear in a single copy of the document.
- **Pictures** This heading identifies libraries where people share and exchange picture files. Windows SharePoint Services provides special support for such libraries, such as displaying reduced-sized "thumbnail" pictures for selection. A new SharePoint site, however, has no default picture libraries.
- **Lists** A SharePoint list contains any set of repetitive items you want. You can create as many lists as you want, each containing whatever columns are appropriate. A new SharePoint Team Site contains two default lists.
  - **Contacts** This list displays the names, addresses, telephone numbers, and other information for your team members and the people they work with.
  - **Tasks** This task list keeps track of work that you or your team needs to complete. You can expand a task list by adding columns relevant to your line of work.
- **Discussions** This feature makes it easy for team members to conduct newsgroup-style discussions about any topics they like. A new SharePoint Team Site has one discussion group, named General Discussion.
- **Survey** This feature makes it easy to poll team members. Creating surveys is easy; just use the supplied Web pages to enter a list of questions and acceptable answers.
- **Announcements** This feature provides a place for team members to notify each other of news and other information by posting it to a list.
- **Events** This is a schedule of upcoming meetings, deadlines, and other events that team members need to keep in mind.
- **Links** This section contains a list of Web sites that are interesting or useful to SharePoint Team Site members.

The main menu appears on each page in the site. It contains a link to the home page, plus the following commands:

- **Documents And Lists** This command displays a tabular listing of all document libraries, picture libraries, lists, discussion boards, and surveys in the site. A link for each item jumps to the entry page for that item.

- **Create** This command displays a page with options to create new document libraries, picture libraries, built-in lists, discussion boards, surveys, Web pages, and custom lists.
- **Site Settings** This series of Web pages configures the site name and description, the list of authorized users, the characteristics of the built-in lists, and other settings related to the SharePoint Team Site.
- **Help** This command opens a new browser window that displays generic help about SharePoint Team Sites.

Team site lists are actually database tables, and team Web sites have facilities to upload and download these tables as Microsoft Excel worksheets. This makes it easy to use the data in other applications or to effect mass changes.

The information contained in a SharePoint Team Site actually resides in a Microsoft SQL Server or Microsoft Data Engine (MSDE) database. This database contains all the data you see in lists and surveys, plus many kinds of information about files that reside in document libraries.

Subscriptions are another important feature of SharePoint Team Sites. Subscribing means that you receive e-mail whenever someone changes a SharePoint Team Site list. You can receive notifications when someone adds a new item, changes an existing item, or deletes an item—or any combination of the three.

For more information about SharePoint Team Sites, refer to Chapter 37, "Using SharePoint Team Sites."

Creating a Web Site from Packages

Microsoft provides a number of prewritten Windows SharePoint Services applications as Web packages. To initialize a new Web site with one of these packages, follow the procedure for using a Web template, but when the Web Site Templates dialog box appears, click the Packages tab, and then select any of the available choices.

If you receive a package from another source, just open a new or existing Web site, choose Packages from the Tools menu, and then click Import. This starts the process of adding the package files to the current site.

The packaging facility only works with Web servers running Windows SharePoint Services. You can only export packages from—and import pages to—such Web servers.

Managing Page Appearance

Most, if not all, Web designers readily agree that all Web pages in the same body of content should share a common appearance. There is, however, much less agreement on how to achieve this lofty goal. The problem isn't a lack of tools or methods, but a glut of them.

FrontPage provides four methods for maintaining a common appearance among multiple Web pages. One method is sure to be right for whatever job you have in mind.

Manually Managing Appearance

Most beginning Web designers learn how to format text, assign colors, and otherwise modify page elements one element at a time. If they want a heading to be blue Arial font, they select the heading, choose Font from the Format menu, and specify that font name and color. This approach works well for small numbers of pages but generally falls apart when you want a large collection of pages to look alike. Maintaining uniformity becomes increasingly difficult if you create the pages over an extended period of time, or if several people do the work.

If you want to format page elements manually, FrontPage supports you with a rich set of toolbar buttons, commands, and dialog boxes that implement almost every capability of HTML. These features look and behave much like those in other Office applications and are therefore very easy to learn and use.

Unfortunately, no matter how easy a command structure might be, applying it dozens, hundreds, or thousands of times to as many Web pages is tedious and error-prone. For this reason, you'll almost certainly want to learn and adopt one of the broader formatting approaches described in the next few sections.

For more information about entering and formatting text, refer to Chapter 8, "Adding and Formatting Text."

Applying Themes

Its collection of themes is the most pervasive, all-encompassing style facility FrontPage has to offer. Themes control overall page properties such as colors, fonts, bullet styles, graphical buttons, and backgrounds. Applying a theme to a page or Web site locks in a professionally designed appearance and disables any command that could override it. If you want to guarantee that your site has consistent style and colors, nothing else has the force of FrontPage themes.

The earlier discussion of building a Web site with Navigation view explained how to apply a theme to every page in a FrontPage-based Web site. Those steps established a given theme as the default for all pages in a site. If you want some pages to be exceptions and present a different appearance, you must exclude them from the default theme. Here are the necessary steps:

1. Select the page in Design view, in the Folder List, or in Folders view.
2. Choose Theme from the Format menu. When the Theme task pane (shown previously in Figure 3-11) appears, locate the Apply Theme To setting and, if necessary, choose Selected Page(s).
3. Select the theme you want the selected page to have, or if you don't want any theme applied, select (No Theme).

The greatest disadvantage of themes is their all-or-nothing nature; a theme can be applied in its entirety or not at all to a given page. After you apply a theme, FrontPage deactivates most normal formatting options and prevents overriding options set by the theme.

You can create and modify themes directly within FrontPage. However, don't fall into the trap of creating numerous, slightly different themes to accommodate different kinds of pages. The more different themes you use, the more difficult each theme is to manage, update, and apply as intended.

For more information about themes, refer to Chapter 20, "Using FrontPage Themes."

Working with Cascading Style Sheets

To overcome the many stylistic limitations of HTML, the World Wide Web Consortium (W3C) devised a new specification that fills in most of HTML's gaps. (The W3C is the international standards body that controls the definition of HTML.) This specification, as you might have guessed from the heading of this section, is called cascading style sheets (CSS), and it consists of two levels:

- **CSS Level 1** This level is primarily concerned with typography. Compared to HTML, CSS provides powerful control over typefaces, colors, and paragraph formatting.
- **CSS Level 2** This level is primarily concerned with positioning (that is, the ability to locate elements precisely on a page).

You can apply either set of CSS features—or both—to individual Web page elements, to portions of Web pages, to whole Web pages, or to groups of Web pages. FrontPage supports all these options. In Figure 3-14, for example, FrontPage is modifying a CSS style named *.hdr1*

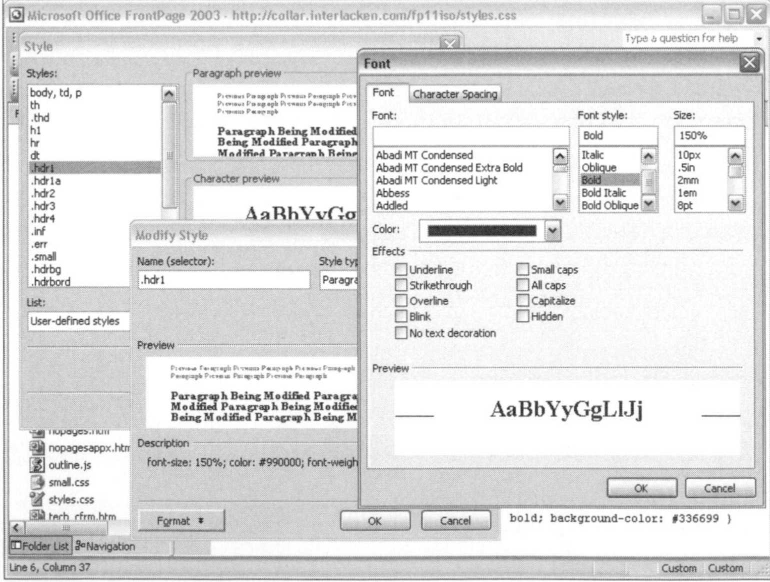

Figure 3-14. These dialog boxes are building a new style named *.hdr1*. After you create this style, it appears in the Style list on the Formatting toolbar.

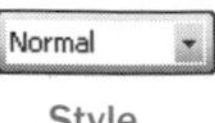

Style

After you create this style, it will appear in the Style list on the Formatting toolbar, and you can apply it to anything on the Web page.

There are two kinds of CSS styles: *inline* and *named*. An inline style pertains to one and only one HTML element, such as a paragraph or table. FrontPage uses inline styles to apply some of the settings available with Format menu commands such as Font, Paragraph, and so forth. You can specify inline styles directly by right-clicking a page element, choosing Properties from the shortcut menu, and clicking the Style button.

Using inline styles might provide more typographical control than using HTML attributes but offers no opportunity for managing overall appearance at the page or Web site level. For that, you must initialize a style sheet, define one or more named styles, and then apply those styles to the pages or page elements you want.

The official term for the name of a CSS style is a *selector*. There are three kinds of selectors:

- **Type selectors** These have the same names as (and control the appearance of) HTML tags. To modify the appearance of all page elements defined by a given HTML tag, simply assign properties to a type selector named after that tag. Here are two examples:
  - To change the appearance of all Heading 1 text in a page, set up an *h1* type selector and give it the properties you want.
  - To change the appearance of all normal paragraphs, set up a *p* type selector and assign it the desired properties.

  A type selector is a very powerful facility. Using type selectors, you can create Web pages that have no special formatting commands mixed into the HTML but that nevertheless appear with rich and consistent formatting.
- **Class selectors** These begin with a period (.), and using them involves a two-step process: First you define the class, and then you apply it to each HTML element you want.

  Class selectors are very useful for styling specialized content. You might, for example, set up a class selector named *.errmsg* and then assign this class to any part of a Web page that displays error messages. If you were publishing the script of a play, you might set up class selectors for scene headings, stage directions, character names, speech text, and so forth.
- **ID selectors** These begin with a pound sign (#), and using them involves a slightly different two-step process: First you give the desired HTML element an ID, and then you define a corresponding ID selector that specifies the CSS properties you want that element to have. In practice, this type of selector receives very little use.

For more information about controlling typography with CSS, refer to Chapter 21, "Managing Appearance with Cascading Style Sheets."

Creating Page-Level Styles

To create a style sheet for a single page, open the page in Design view, and then choose Style from the Format menu. This displays the Style dialog box shown in Figure 3-15.

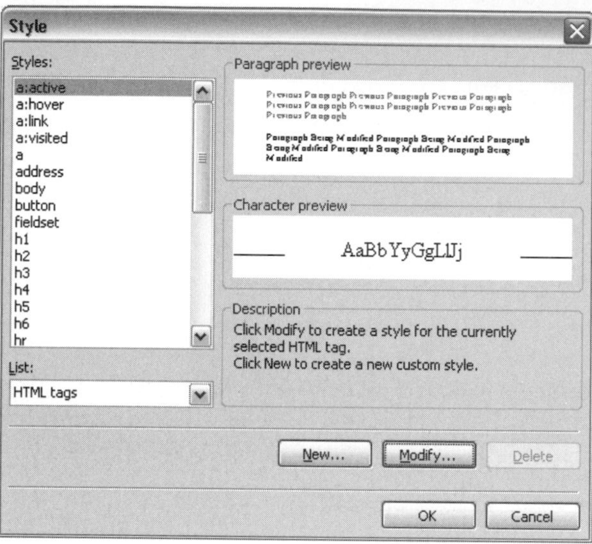

Figure 3-15. CSS can override the default appearance produced by any HTML tag.

Here's how to use the controls in this dialog box:

- To create or modify a type selector, make sure that HTML Tags appears in the List drop-down list, select the name you want from the Styles list, and then click the Modify button.
- To modify an existing class or ID selector, select User-Defined Styles in the List drop-down list, select the name you want from the Styles list, and then click the Modify button.
- To create a new class or ID selector, click the New button, and enter the class or ID name in the Name (Selector) box.

After completing any of these actions, you should see the Modify Style dialog box, shown in Figure 3-16. (The New Style dialog box, if it appears, works essentially the same way.) Click the Format button to display the list of style types, select a style type, and then use the resulting dialog box to set the properties you want.

For more information about creating page-level styles, refer to "Formatting Single Web Pages," on page 591.

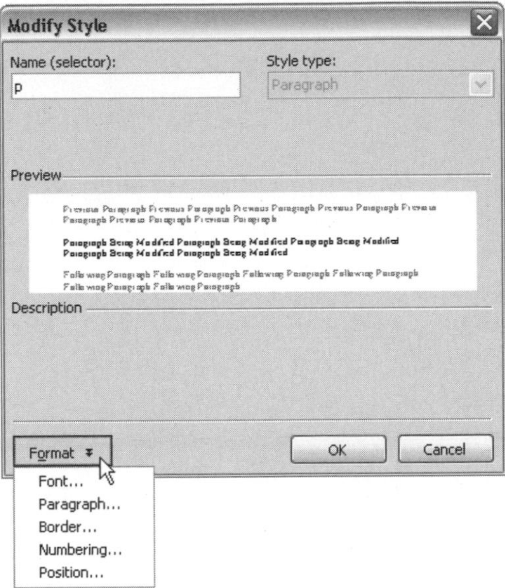

Figure 3-16. The commands that modify CSS styles aren't visible when you first display this dialog box. To see them, you must click the Format button.

Creating Shared Style Sheets

The procedure in the previous section described how to modify and create CSS styles that apply to a single Web page. The first time you create or modify a named style, FrontPage automatically adds a style sheet to the page and uses that sheet or any styles you define.

Styles that apply to multiple pages must reside in a file that's separate from any of them. Such files have a .css file extension. To create such a file in FrontPage, follow these steps:

1 Open the Web site that contains the pages the style sheet should affect, and choose New from the File menu. This displays the New task pane. Then, on that pane under New Page, click More Page Templates.

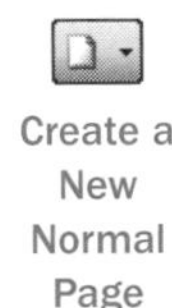

Create a New Normal Page

2 Alternatively, click the drop-down arrow for the Create A New Normal Page button on the Standard toolbar, and then choose Page from the resulting menu.

3 When the Page Templates dialog box shown in Figure 3-17 appears, select the Style Sheets tab, select Normal Style Sheet, and then click OK.

4 A new, blank style sheet page appears in the editing window. Save this page in the Web site's root folder with a name that denotes its use. If this style sheet should apply to most pages in your site, a good name is styles.css.

5 To create styles, choose Style from the Format menu, and proceed as you did when creating and modifying styles for a single Web page.

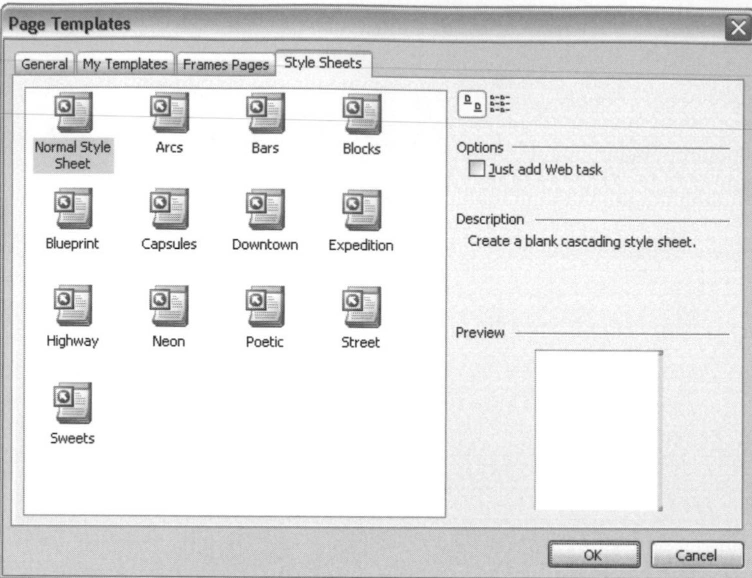

Figure 3-17. FrontPage provides this assortment of prefabricated style sheets.

Because style sheet files don't contain any content, FrontPage can't display styles in WYSIWYG view. Instead, as illustrated in Figure 3-18, FrontPage displays the file in Code view. No other views are available.

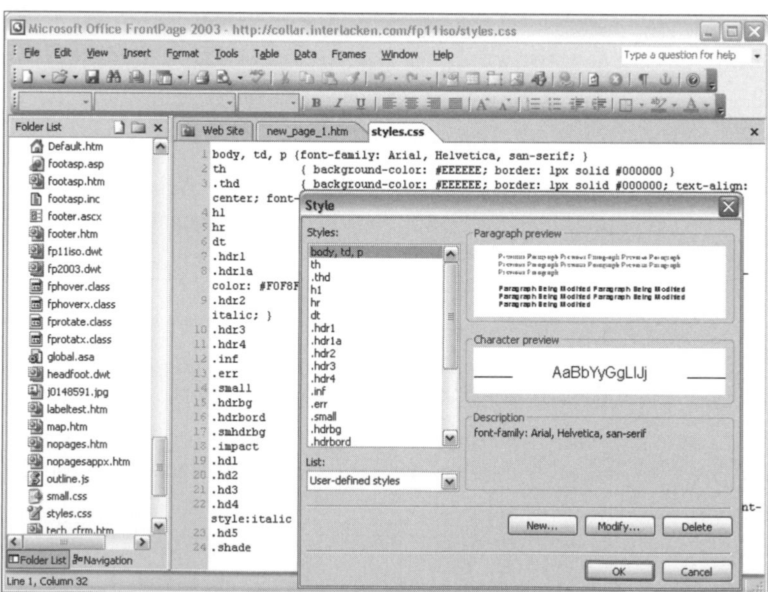

Figure 3-18. Even though FrontPage displays style sheet files as code, you can modify their styles through commands on the Format Style menu.

Tip After a while, you might become familiar enough with CSS to modify the code directly, but until then, don't make any changes you might have difficulty undoing later.

After you create a style sheet file, the next step is designating each Web page that will use it. Here's the procedure for doing this:

1. Select the page or pages that should use the style sheet. You can do this by clicking on a page that's open in Design view, on one or more pages or folders that appear in the Folder List, or on one or more pages or folders that appear in another FrontPage view.
2. Choose Style Sheet Links from the Format menu. This will display the Link Style Sheet dialog box, shown in Figure 3-19.

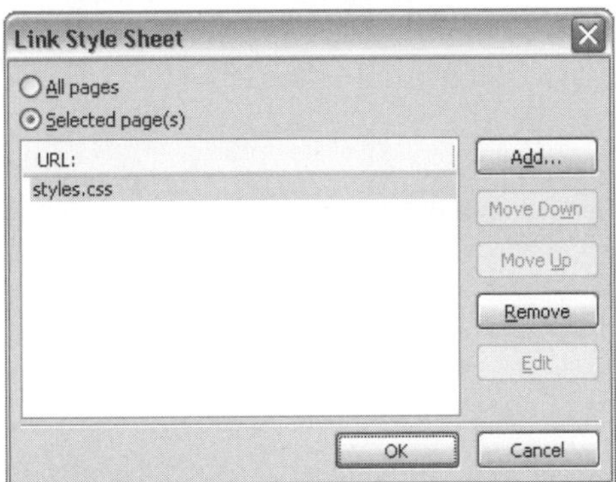

Figure 3-19. To apply a shared style sheet to a Web page, select the page, and then choose Style Sheet Links from the Format menu. Click the Add button to browse the current Web site for CSS files.

Note If the Style Sheet Links command on the Format menu is dimmed, you haven't selected any files that can use style sheets. You can't apply style sheets to picture files, for example.

3. Make sure that the Selected Page(s) option is selected.
4. Click the Add button, find the style sheet file you want in the Select Style Sheet dialog box, and then click OK.
5. To remove a style sheet, select it in the URL list, and click the Remove button.
6. If a given page uses multiple style sheets and you need to change the order or precedence, select one of the style sheets, and use the Move Down and Move Up buttons to reposition it.
7. When you're satisfied with your changes, click OK to close the Link Style Sheet dialog box.

Note When two style sheets modify the same property for the same selector, the definition that occurs last prevails.

To apply a style sheet to every page in a site, skip step 1, and then, in step 3, make sure that the All Pages option is selected.

Setting up shared style sheet files and applying them to Web pages might at first seem convoluted compared to just formatting each page the way you want it. The payback comes when you have many Web pages that you want to look alike—if they all use the same style sheet, they will.

Shared style sheets are both more flexible and less commanding than themes, yet they offer a similar degree of site-level control. This is the approach most experienced Web designers use for at least part of their work.

Browsers earlier than Internet Explorer 3 and Netscape Navigator 4 ignore CSS commands and therefore display Web pages using default fonts and colors. However, the number of Web visitors using these older browsers is constantly declining. What's more, although those Web visitors won't see your well-chosen fonts and colors, they'll at least see a legible version of the page.

For more information about creating shared style sheets, refer to "Formatting Multiple Pages," on page 597.

Using Page Templates

Another way FrontPage can provide a consistent Web site appearance is through its Templates feature. There are two kinds of page templates: *static* and *dynamic*. Both types provide content for a new page, but after that:

- A static template steps out of the way. The entire page, including the parts the template provided, becomes editable. Changing the template has no effect on pages it previously created.

- A dynamic template designates one or more areas on the page as editable; these are the only areas that pages using the template can modify. If you later change a non-editable portion of the template, FrontPage will automatically update each page in the same Web site that used that template.

Creating and using a static template is simple. Here are the steps you need to perform:

1. Use FrontPage to create a Web page with the color scheme, background, and other standard features you want in the template.
2. To save the page as a template, choose Save As from the File menu. Select FrontPage Template in the Save As Type drop-down list and then click Save.
3. When the Save As Template dialog box shown in Figure 3-20 appears, review the title, name, and description fields, and then click OK.
4. When creating a new Web page that should have the given template features, select that template in the Page Templates dialog box.

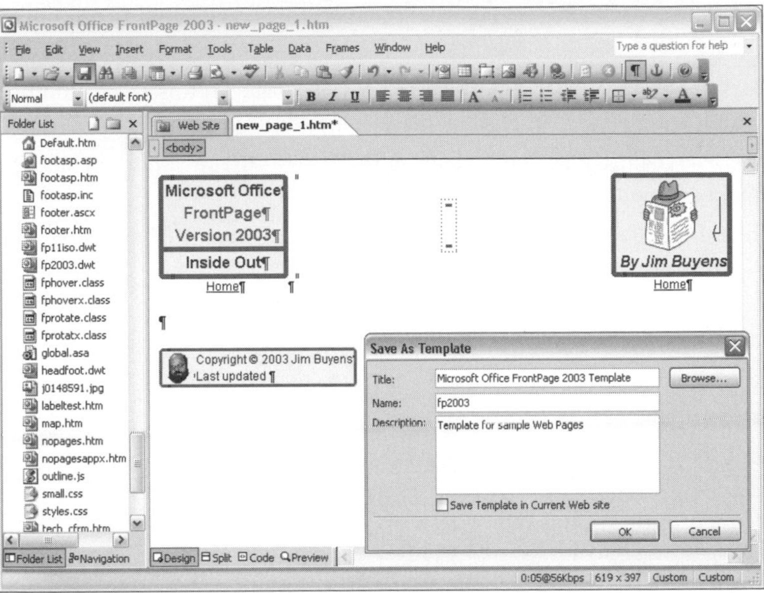

Figure 3-20. FrontPage can save pages as templates, which are models for other pages.

For more information about templates, see Chapter 14, "Creating Web Sites with Templates and Wizards."

After you save a static page template, it appears in the My Templates tab of the Page Templates dialog box. Figure 3-21 illustrates this.

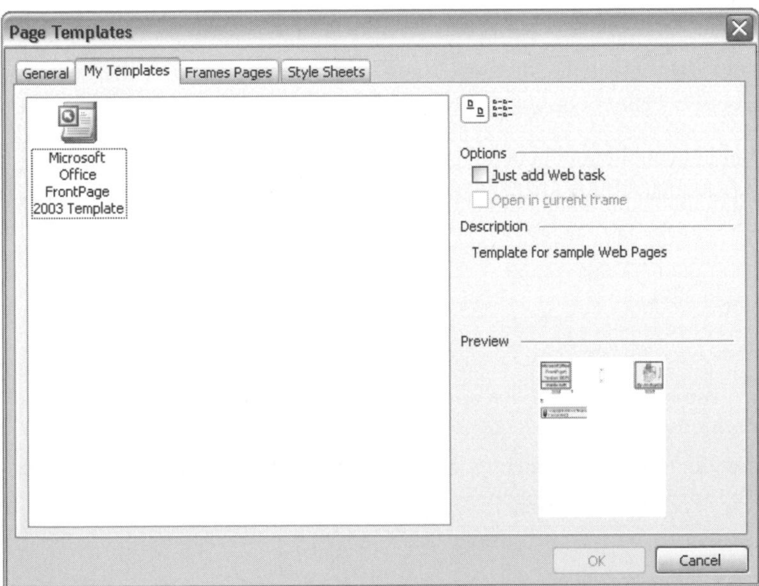

Figure 3-21. You can choose any template as the starting point for a new Web page.

To create a dynamic template, add whatever content you want, just as you did for a static template. Then, however:

1. Select the first area that will vary from page to page. (If this area contains no other content, enter and then select an empty paragraph.)
2. Choose Dynamic Web Template from the Format menu, and then click Manage Editable Regions.
3. When the Editable Regions dialog box shown in Figure 3-22 appears, type a name for the region selected in step 1 in the Region Name box.

Figure 3-22. This dialog box gives the current selection a name and flags it as an editable dynamic Web template region. The Remove button cancels an editable region, and the Goto button scrolls to one.

4. Click Add to make the region part of the template, and then click Close to close the Editable Regions dialog box. An orange border will surround the new editable region.
5. Repeat steps 1 through 4 for each additional editable region.

The number of editable regions you create is entirely up to you, but in general, there's no reason for two adjacent areas to be separate editable regions. Creating one editable region that includes both areas is simpler and therefore, in all likelihood, better.

When you've finished designing the template and designating editable regions, use this procedure to save it:

1. Choose Save As from the File menu.
2. When the Save As dialog box appears, make sure that the Save As Type box specifies Dynamic Web Template (*.dwt).
3. In the File Name box, specify a short, easy-to-remember name that contains no spaces or special characters. Click Save.

Using the saved dynamic Web template in another Web page is easy. Just follow these steps:

1. Open the page that should use the template. Most often this will be a new, blank page, but in fact it can be any page you want.
2. Choose Dynamic Web Template from the Format menu, and then choose Attach Dynamic Web Template.
3. When the Attach Dynamic Web Template dialog box appears, locate and double-click the template you want to use. (This dialog box looks and acts very much like an ordinary File Open dialog box.)
4. When the Choose Editable Regions For Content dialog box shown in Figure 3-23 appears, the table with the column headings Old and New shows which areas on the open Web page FrontPage will display in each area of the template.

   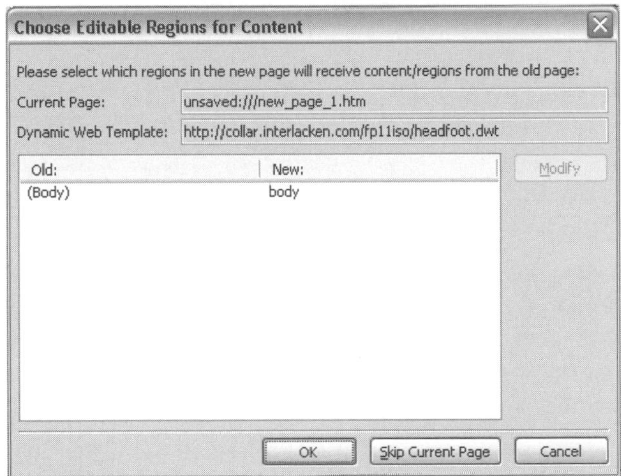

   Figure 3-23. This dialog box appears when you attach a dynamic Web template to an ordinary page. It maps regions on the ordinary Web page to editable regions in the template.

   In Figure 3-23, for example, the entire body of the existing Web page will appear in the editable region named *body*. This is the simplest situation. Life would be more complicated if the existing page already used a dynamic template that had several editable regions, and the new template had more, fewer, or differently named regions. If you're not happy with the matches FrontPage proposes, select the incorrect matchup, click the Modify button, and specify the new region where the existing content should go.
5. Click OK to apply the template and close the dialog box.
6. To save the updated Web page, choose Save from the File menu.

The Dynamic Web Template submenu (the one that appears after you choose Dynamic Web Template from the Format menu) contains these additional commands for Web pages that use a dynamic Web template:

- **Detach From Dynamic Web Template** Dissociates the current page from the template, but leaves the template's content in place (and now editable).
- **Open Attached Dynamic Web Template** Opens the template file for editing.

These additional commands propagate changes from any dynamic Web templates you select in Design view, Folders view, or the Folder List:

- **Update Selected Page** Propagates changes to any other pages that use the template, and that are currently selected.
- **Update All Pages** Propagates changes to all pages that directly or indirectly attach the selected template. To appreciate this option imagine that Page1.htm attaches Template1.dwt and Template1.dwt attaches Template 2.dwt.

  If you change Template2.dwt, then the Update All Pages command will update both Template1.dwt and Page1.htm.
- **Update Attached Pages** Propagates changes to all pages that directly attach the selected template. In the preceding example, this command would update Template1.dwt but not Page1.htm.

Regardless of editable regions, a dynamic Web template always seizes control of most options on the General, Formatting, Advanced, and Language tabs of the Page Properties dialog box. You'll also find that the Style, Style Sheet Links, Shared Borders, and Background tabs on the Format menu are dimmed. Any page that attaches a dynamic Web template inherits these settings from the template; you can't override them.

Dynamic Web templates are a very powerful new feature of FrontPage 2003—so powerful that many Web designers will likely adopt them in favor of themes, static templates, and include files for reusable layouts such as page headers and footers.

For more information about using page templates, refer to Chapter 14, "Creating Web Sites with Templates and Wizards."

Laying Out Pages

FrontPage provides a full complement of intuitive dialog boxes for applying colors, fonts, alignment, and other properties to the content of your Web pages. Virtually every feature of HTML is available for making your pages look their best; you can access these features through the familiar Office user interface.

Despite all this flexibility, members of a group should generally be united by a common appearance—rock bands notwithstanding. FrontPage offers a number of tools that impart a unified and attractive style to all your pages. And anyway, why format Web pages one at a time when you can do them all together in bunches?

Working with Tables

Most page designers—Web or print—use grids as the basis for all page layout. A *grid*, in this sense, is a series of columns and horizontal lines—visible or invisible—that serves to line up the elements in the composition. Layout grids are most obvious in newspapers and magazines, but if you look closely, most brochures, display ads, and posters use them as well.

For Web pages, an HTML table is the closest analog to a physical layout grid. Page layout tables usually fill the entire page width, and they normally have invisible borders and backgrounds. Their only purpose is to align page elements horizontally and vertically.

Envisioning the appearance of an HTML table can be a real challenge when you're working with raw HTML code. The code is one-dimensional—top to bottom—but the table, having height and width, is two-dimensional. Fortunately, the WYSIWYG editor in FrontPage makes working with tables not only two-dimensional and intuitive, but even enjoyable.

The sample Web page developed in Chapter 2 used an HTML table to organize its elements. Another more complex and realistic example appeared in Figures 1-1 through 1-3.

For more information about using HTML tables for page layout, refer to Chapter 19, "Using HTML Tables for Page Layout."

Working with Shared Borders

The Shared Borders feature applies any combination of top, bottom, left, and right borders—including the content within them—to selected pages or to an entire site. Shared borders are very handy for applying standard heading styles, standard footers, and standard margin content to an entire site. The procedure for applying a shared border to an entire site was covered earlier in this chapter, in the section "Adding Shared Borders."

Working with Frames Pages

A *frames page* is a special kind of Web page whose sole purpose is to divide the browser window into several rectangular areas called *frames*. Each frame has a *name* and a *target*; the name identifies the frame, and the target identifies the Web page the frame should display.

Hyperlinks clicked in one frame can load pages into another frame. A common application of frames pages is to define a menu as the target of one frame and corresponding content as the target of another. Clicking a hyperlink in the menu frame changes the target in the content frame. This avoids the need to keep menus up to date on each content page. Of course, many other applications are possible as well. Anytime you want to replace only portions of the browser window, a frames page is an option worth considering.

Figure 3-24 shows a frames page open in FrontPage. Frames pages and default targets appear in fully editable, WYSIWYG view. Notice the title frame at the top of the page, the menu bar at the lower left, and the large content frame at the lower right. This is a fairly typical arrangement.

For more information about frames, refer to Chapter 15, "Creating Web Sites with Frames."

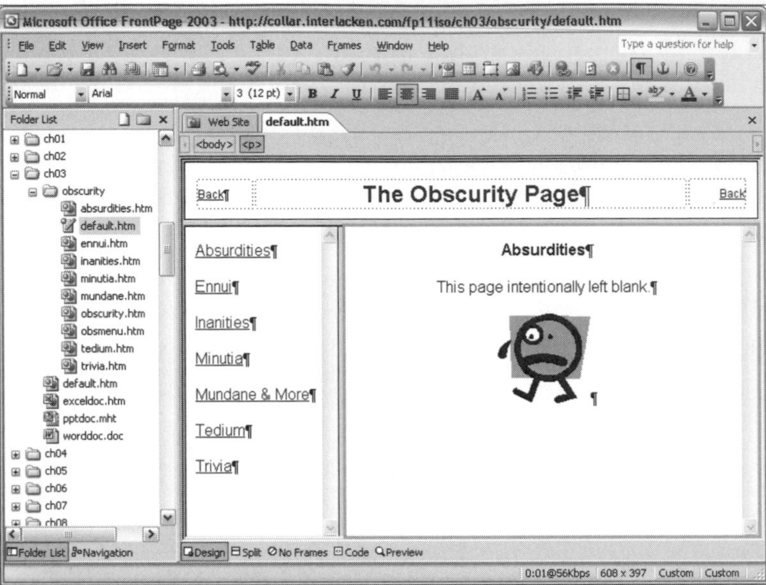

Figure 3-24. FrontPage 2003 provides full WYSIWYG editing of frames pages. Four Web pages are open in this example: a frames page that defines three frames, and a separate, ordinary Web page in each frame.

Positioning

The "Working with Cascading Style Sheets" section earlier in this chapter introduced CSS Level 2, but this topic deserves further discussion in terms of layout. CSS Level 2 (CSS2 or CSS positioning) is primarily concerned with positioning Web page elements.

In some of its documentation, Microsoft likes to call CSS2 "pixel-perfect positioning." This is because CSS2 can position Web page elements precisely on the page based on measurements in pixels or, for that matter, in inches, centimeters, percent of available space, or obscure measurements like ems and points that come from the printing industry.

CSS2 uses two positioning strategies: *absolute* and *relative*. Absolute positioning displays page content a specified distance from the upper left corner of its container. Relative positioning displays content a specified distance from its normal position (that is, from where it would appear if no positioning were in effect).

Note Within a Web page, a *container* is any page element that limits the space available to another page element. The default container is the browser window but table cells, layers, frames, and certain other elements can also be containers.

The dialog box for CSS positioning (that is, CSS2) is shown in Figure 3-25.

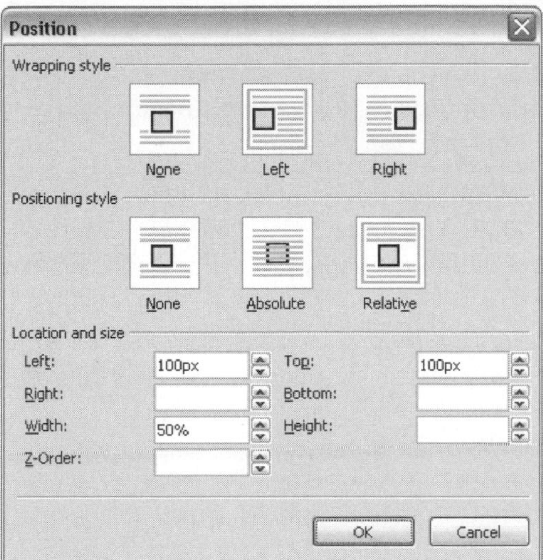

Figure 3-25. This FrontPage 2003 dialog box specifies CSS2 positioning for the currently selected content.

Absolute Positioning and the *Z-Index* Attribute

Absolute positioning is a feature of browsers that support the CSS2 specification. CSS2 provides a way to locate elements at specific locations, measured either from their normal location or from the upper left corner of their container.

A CSS property called *z-index* governs the visibility of overlapping page elements. When several page elements on the same Web page overlap, the element with the highest *z-index* appears on top (that is, unobstructed), and those with lesser *z-index*es appear in order behind it.

Normal page elements have the default *z-index*, which is 0. Elements with positive *z-index* values appear superimposed over normal page content, and those with a negative *z-index* value appear behind it.

Positioning a block of content can be as easy as this:

1. Open the Web page in Design view, and select the elements you want to position.
2. Choose Position from the Format menu.
3. When the Position dialog box appears, select the position settings you want, and click OK.

If parts of your Web page are positioned and parts aren't, the parts that aren't might not flow properly around the ones that are.

Publishing Your Web Site

Most Web designers maintain at least two copies of each site they develop: a development copy and a production copy. The development copy is for implementing and testing changes; the production copy is for Web visitors to access.

Unless you keep fastidious records of each file you change on the development site, copying all the changed files to the production server can be a real challenge. It's very likely you'll forget to copy some files that you should, and also that you'll mistakenly copy some files that you shouldn't.

> **Tip** Some of the hardest files to remember to copy are those that FrontPage creates automatically. In normal use, you might not even realize these files exist. This is one of the best reasons to let FrontPage publish your Web site for you.

In FrontPage parlance, *publishing* is the process of copying one FrontPage-based Web site to another. To begin the publishing process:

1. Open the sending Web site.
2. Click the Web Site tab above the FrontPage editing window.
3. Click the Remote Web Site tab below the FrontPage editing window.

NEW FEATURE!

If you've never published the current Web site, the editing window will be nearly blank, containing only the message *Click "Remote Web Site Properties" to set up a remote Web site.* If this happens to you:

1. Click the Remote Web Site Properties button on the toolbar at the top of the Remote Web Site window.
2. When the Remote Web Site Properties dialog box shown in Figure 3-26 appears, choose the Remote Web Server Type value, and then, in the Remote Web Site Location box, type the network location.

   Here's the correct format for the destination network location:

Remote Web Server Type	Network Location Type
FrontPage, SharePoint, or Distributed Authoring and Versioning (WebDAV)	*http://* URL
FTP	*ftp://* URL
File System	<Drive letter>/<path> or //<server>/<sharename>/<path>

3. Click OK. (This saves the new settings but doesn't publish any files.)
4. If the location you specified in step 2 isn't a FrontPage-based Web site, FrontPage will ask if you want to create a site at that location. Unless you misspelled something, click Yes.

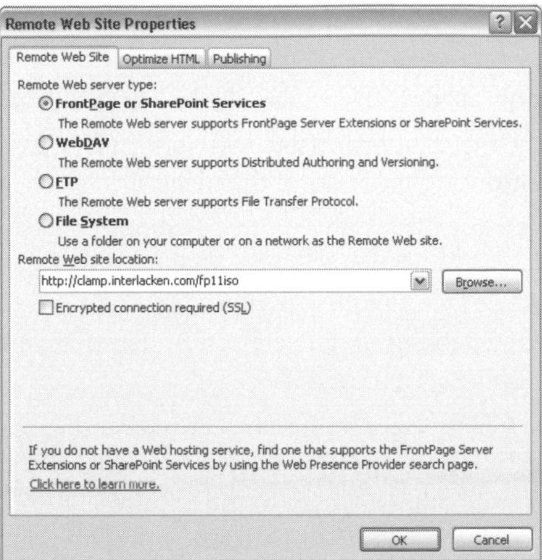

Figure 3-26. The Publish Web Site command can copy Web sites using any common network protocol.

The remote Web site display should now resemble Figure 3-27. The list box at the left displays the contents of the local Web site (the publishing source), and the list on the right displays the contents of the remote Web site (the publishing destination). In each case, the Status column shows the publishing status of each file: Unchanged, Changed, Unmatched, Conflict, Don't Publish, and so forth. To view the status of files in a listed folder, double-click that folder icon.

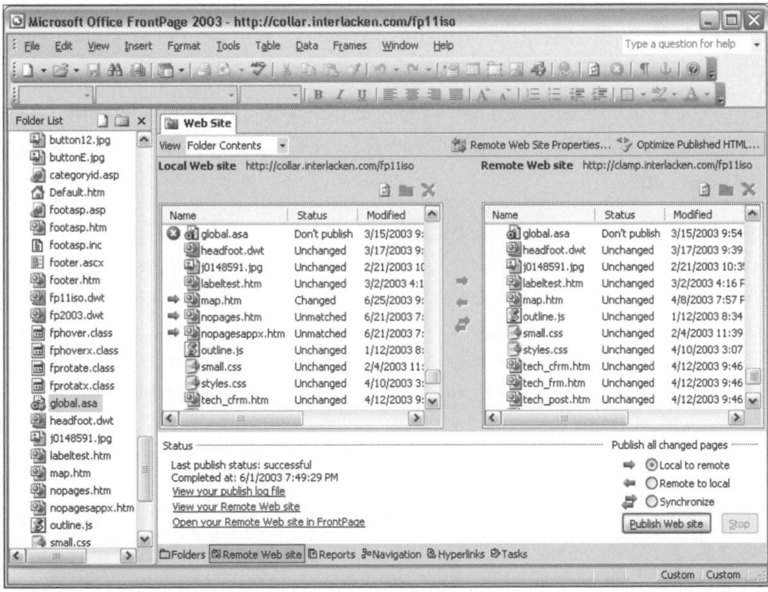

Figure 3-27. Remote Web Site view compares and contrasts the contents of the current Web site with the contents of another. Clicking the Publish Web Site button transfers the necessary files so that both sites are identical.

The View list box in the Remote Web Site toolbar can change the display to any of four formats:

- **Folder Contents** Displays the default format (the one that appears in Figure 3-27.)
- **Files To Publish** Lists the files that FrontPage will publish if you click the Publish Web Site button in the bottom right corner of the display.
- **Files Not To Publish** Lists any files you've indicated should never be published. (To indicate this, you would right-click the file in either list box, in the Folder List, or in Folders view and then choose Don't Publish from the shortcut menu.) Typically, these would be Microsoft Access databases or data collection files that you don't want to overwrite when you publish new Web pages.
- **Files In Conflict** Lists any files where both the local and remote copies have changed since a publishing operation last synchronized them. This makes it likely that publishing the local site will overwrite other changes to the remote site, such as changes by another developer. If you proceed with the publishing operation, FrontPage will ask which version to keep.

To actually publish a site, choose one of the options at the bottom right corner of the Remote Web Site window, and then click the Publish Web Site button. These options are:

- **Local To Remote** Publishes changed pages from the local site to the remote site.
- **Remote To Local** Publishes changed pages from the remote site to the local site. You might think of this as a "reverse" operation; it resets the local site to the contents of the remote site.

- **Synchronize** Compares the contents of both sites and takes the most recent copy of each file. When the operation finishes, both sites will be identical, but each might contain a mixture of file versions from each site.

If the need arises, you can also publish individual files or folders. To do this, right-click the file or folder in either list box, in the Folder List, or in Folders view, and then choose Publish from the shortcut menu.

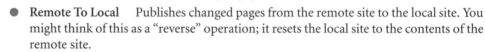

If you want, FrontPage can clean up and simplify your HTML as it publishes your site. To activate this feature, click the Optimize Published HTML button at the far right of the Remote Web Site toolbar. This displays the Optimize HTML tab of the Remote Web Site properties dialog box, shown in Figure 3-28. Just remember, anything you remove from your pages while publishing in one direction won't be present if you later retrieve the same pages in the opposite direction. Also, you might be uncomfortable modifying your tested pages en route to the production server.

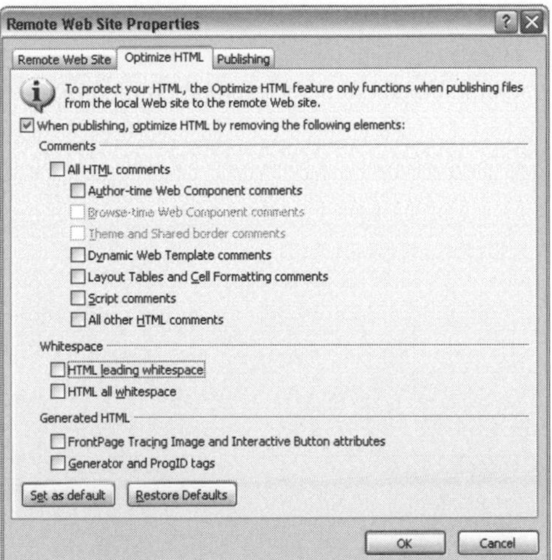

Figure 3-28. FrontPage 2003 can clean up your HTML and remove unnecessary comments as it publishes your Web site.

For more information about publishing FrontPage-based Web sites, refer to Chapter 16, "Publishing Your FrontPage-Based Web Site."

In Summary...

This chapter introduced the wide assortment of tools that FrontPage provides for managing Web sites. It explained how to create FrontPage-based Web sites, how to fill them with content, and how to avoid repetitive, manual work both when creating Web pages and when maintaining them over time.

The rest of this book delves into these topics in much greater detail and presents many additional features, tips, tricks, and advice on what to do when things go wrong.

Part 2

Planning and Organizing Your Web Site

Chapter 4

Planning and Organizing FrontPage-Based Web Sites

Whatever your site's size and purpose, proper advance planning will produce a better appearance, more organized content, faster construction, and easier ongoing maintenance. More importantly, a well-planned site will attract more visitors, better meet the site's original goals, and be cheaper to run.

This chapter addresses the core aspects of planning and producing a Web site. These aspects are closely interrelated: You can't plan without understanding the work to be done, and without a sound plan you can't properly do the work. That's why learning to organize and produce Web sites is an iterative process that considers increasing levels of detail.

Most of all, keep in mind that design of any kind—Web, print, or other—is a human process requiring human judgment to obtain human objectives. No piece of software—not even Microsoft Office FrontPage 2003—can design your site or judge it ready for public consumption. Beauty is a human concept, and not a mechanical one.

Defining Your Site's Content

All successful Web sites start out with a well-defined mission. This leads to a well-organized, well-defined body of content and ultimately to effective communication. Taking the time up front to understand your mission will certainly pay off in timely, effective results later.

Identifying Your Message

Step one in building or maintaining a Web site is to understand why the site's sponsors want it to exist. Some sites send an overt or implicit message; some provide a business function; some are hobbies in and of themselves. If you don't understand a site's true purpose, you are very unlikely to achieve it. Instead, you might end up sending a message like, "I'm just learning HTML," "I'm scatterbrained," or "I'm trying to increase ugliness and confusion in the world."

"Establishing a presence" is probably the most common reason for starting a Web site, but this is terribly vague. It usually means following a perceived trend, keeping up with competitors, or responding to requests from others. Here are more focused (and more useful) reasons for starting a Web site:

- Promoting a desired public image
- Advertising products and services
- Selling products or services directly to Web visitors
- Providing post-sale services and support
- Increasing knowledge and awareness of a person, a topic, or an organization
- Releasing information in accordance with law or an organization's charter

You'll almost certainly need to drill through several levels of detail to fully understand your site's mission. Investigating each level generally leads to questions for the next. The end result should be a mission statement, even if informal, that describes the site's purpose and objective.

Understanding the Audience

As important as knowing your site's message is knowing its audience. "Everyone on the Web" is too vague an audience to be useful; you should have some particular *kinds* of people in mind—perhaps even specific people to use as models. The following are typical audiences:

- Everyone in a certain industry
- Practitioners of a certain skill
- Purchasers of a certain type of product or service
- Users of a specific product or service

After you decide who your audience is, you should learn whatever you can about them. Are they technical, artistic, or people-oriented? What are their skills and interests? What's their level of vocabulary and education? Do they respond more to detailed text or to color, style, and visual metaphors?

You hope, of course, that your audience will find your site's message inherently interesting and attractive. Often, however, they'll need some other enticement. Perhaps you can entice visitors with a free clip art library and then, while they browse, sell them your graphics program. Perhaps you can sell art supplies as people browse a library of works or techniques. If they come for information about a product they already own, perhaps you can sell them another.

The ultimate enticement, according to recent thinking, is to make your site the meeting place for a community of some kind—presumably a community with an interest in your product or message. The goal is then to make your site such a valuable resource—such a compelling place for people in your target audience to find each other and interact—that the site becomes a "must visit." This generally requires some sort of added content that's updated frequently and not readily available elsewhere. It also requires a means for visitors to enhance the site themselves and to find other visitors without invading anyone's privacy. This sort of community is more often talked about than achieved in practice, although it remains a lofty goal. It also illustrates the importance of providing a magnet to attract targeted visitors.

Identifying Content Categories

If your site is typical, the home page will be the most time-consuming of all to construct. There are several reasons for this:

- The home page presents the site's first impression; therefore, it's usually the most elaborate page in the site. Remember the old saying: "You get only one chance to make a first impression."
- Despite being the site's most elaborate page, the home page must download quickly. Otherwise, Web visitors will give up after a minute or two and go elsewhere.
- The home page often serves as the prototype for the entire site's visual appearance. It sets the tone and image for every page that follows.
- If you're new to creating Web pages, a home page will probably be your initial learning experience.
- The options on the home page intrinsically represent the site's primary structure.

The first four issues usually work themselves out, but the last one is critical. If you can identify the top few options in your site, you probably have a good understanding of its message and audience. If you can't get your home page organized, your content plan probably isn't organized either.

FrontPage provides built-in templates and wizards that create typical pages for many kinds of sites, but at best they produce only starting points. No two sites are exactly alike; your site's content and organization are ultimately your unique creation.

Here are some terrible ways to organize a site:

- Offer an option for each member of the design committee
- Provide an option for each person who reports to the top executive
- List an option for each category someone thought of, in chronological order
- Repeat the same options you used at a previous site

All of the above share the same problem: They ignore the target visitor's likely interests and mind-set. They indicate a lack of defined message, defined audience, or both.

Defining Your Site's Style

Every site should have a consistency suited to its purpose. Pages should be unified by a common theme, a common organization, and a common style. The words, pictures, colors, and layout should lead the visitor to the messages—both overt and subtle—that justify the site's existence.

Artists and computer specialists usually embody completely different mind-sets. Nevertheless, both types of skills are needed to produce an effective Web site. To reduce the gap between art and science—at least in a small way—this section introduces a few topics regarding pleasing and effective visual design.

Elements of Design

Artistic design isn't an exact science, so many technically inclined people conclude that it's beyond them—or at least that it gives them a headache. If you lack the talent to become a professional artist, however, you can use certain principles of good design to enhance your work and communicate your message more effectively. Contrast and symmetry are two such principles, and they appear in a variety of contexts.

Contrast vs. Clash

The polar bear at the North Pole and the black cat in the coal bin figure in two old jokes involving contrast. In both cases, lack of contrast makes the key element indistinguishable from its surroundings. Graphic contrast serves two important purposes in Web pages or, for that matter, any other document:

- **Contrast enhances legibility.** For example, the black type and white background in this book make it easier to read than if one color were gray.
- **Contrast visually communicates distinctions among various page elements.** In this book, for example, contrasting typography makes it easy to distinguish headings from body type.

The contrast knob on your monitor or TV set controls the difference in brightness between the lightest and darkest parts of a picture. Contrast, however, occurs in many other dimensions as well: contrast between adjacent colors, contrast between differently sized or shaped fonts, contrast between positions on a page, and many more. The total contrast between two page elements thus involves the number of contrasting attributes as well as their individual extents.

The need for contrast is generally intuitive; document creators ordinarily realize that items like titles, headings, body text, and captions are intrinsically different and that a unique appearance should identify each such element. They run into greater problems deciding what kind of contrast to provide and how much. Too much or too little contrast can be illegible, confusing, or just irritating to the eye.

To understand the need for contrast, look at the Web page shown in Figure 4-1. Other than the contrast of black text on a white background and normal paragraph formatting, this page has no contrasting elements. There's nothing to guide the eye to various kinds of content, and certainly nothing interesting to look at.

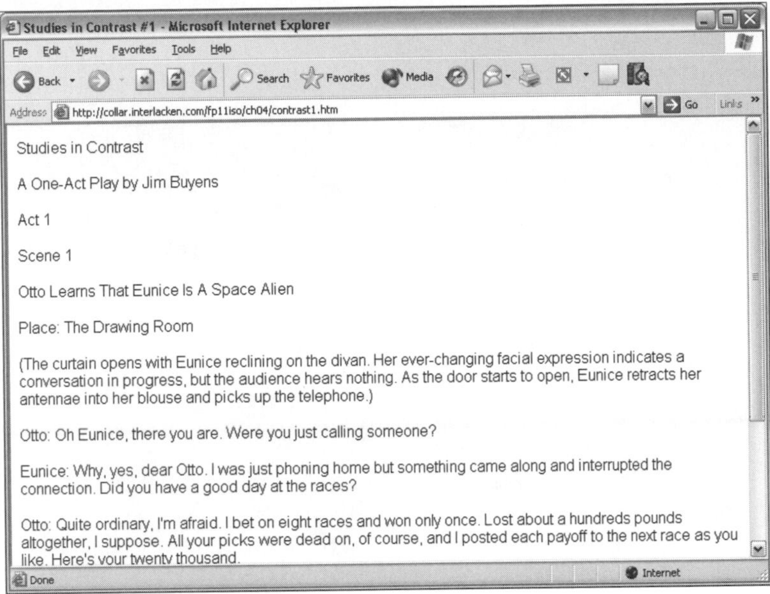

Figure 4-1. This Web page provides no contrast among the various kinds of content it contains. Not only is it boring to look at, but it also communicates poorly.

The Web page shown in Figure 4-2 has plenty of contrast—but please, please don't try this at home, or in the office, or anywhere else. The contrast in the background image overpowers the text, despite the use of a boldface font and a white-on-dark color scheme. Notice as well how white and near-white areas in the background blend into the text, making it hard to read. Use of strong backgrounds is the number one cause of ugly and illegible Web pages. (Use of blue text on black is probably number two.)

Figure 4-3 shows another Web page loaded with contrast.

The rampant use of fonts in this page produces an appearance experts call a "ransom note." Creating a page like this might be an interesting exercise for a Web designer who just discovered the Fonts dialog box, but the use of so many different fonts, without any clear rationale, is very distracting. This page shows some effort at page design—not everything is flush left—but the alignment of page elements is essentially random.

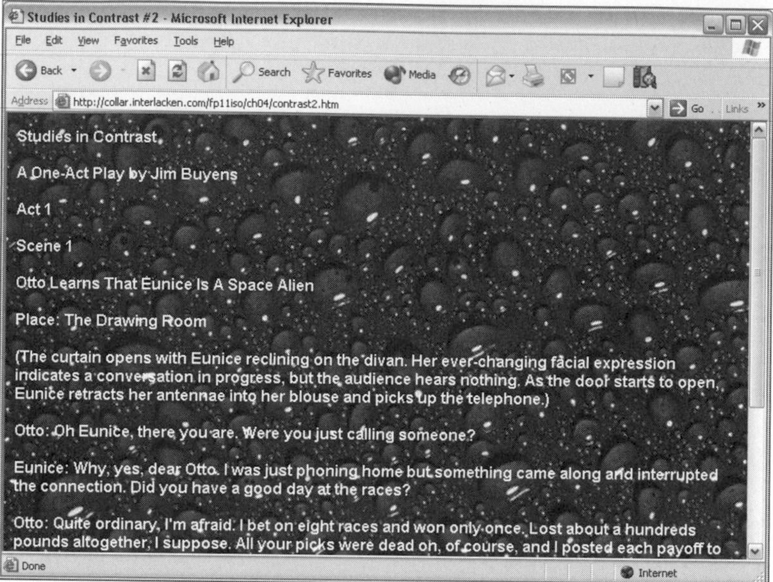

Figure 4-2. The high-contrast background in this Web page overwhelms and obscures the content. Today's expert Web designers use very soft backgrounds, if any.

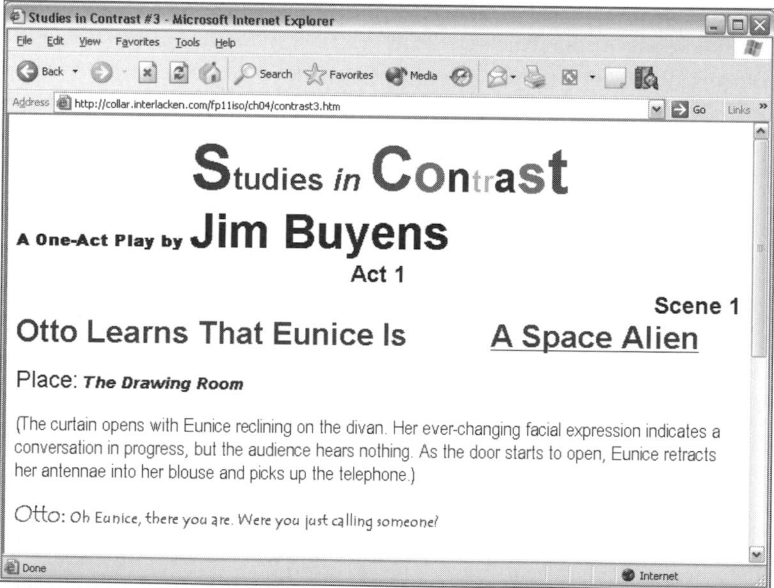

Figure 4-3. The many fonts and varied page placements in this Web page provide lots of contrast. Unfortunately, contrast this random is a distraction rather than a way to communicate.

Chapter 4

None of the previous examples used appearance to enhance content. Even worse, the appearance of the second and third examples actually detracted from content. Figure 4-4, in contrast (sorry), shows a Web page where contrast truly enhances the content and makes it easier to understand.

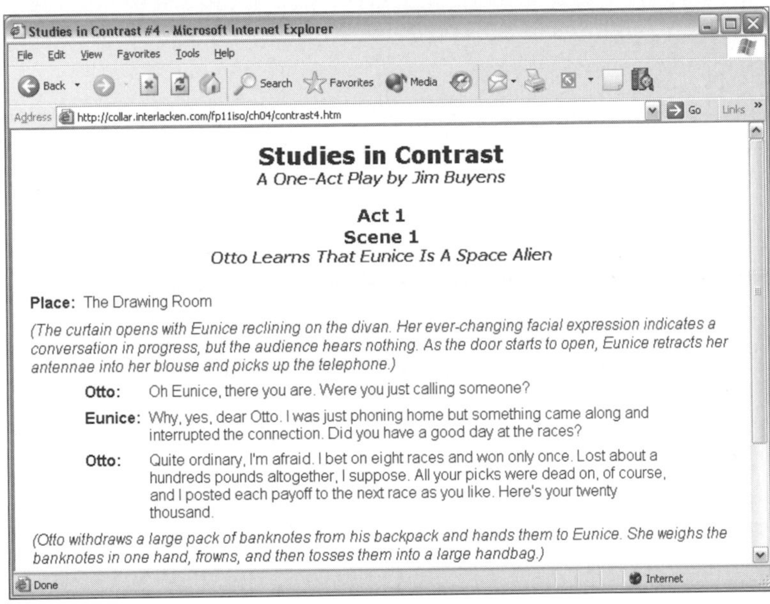

Figure 4-4. Contrasting styles in this Web page clearly distinguish various kinds of content. Consistencies in the style and alignment of similar items provide symmetry.

Note the following features:

- The fonts are interesting yet simple. Because computer monitors are low in resolution, complex fonts generally don't appear clearly.

> **Note** In print media, serif fonts are usually easier to read. The serifs, which are tiny horizontal lines at the end of each character stroke, create a horizontal "track" for the eye to follow. Because computer monitors are much less precise than a laser printer or typesetting machine, they generally do a poor job of displaying serifs. That's why most designers now believe that sans serif fonts are more legible on the Web. Just remember to provide enough line spacing whenever you use a sans serif font.

- All major titles use the same font. Smaller font sizes indicate lower-level titles and larger font sizes indicate more significant ones.
- Subtitles (some people call them "kickers") are universally indicated by italics.
- Specific formatting identifies the "place" line, stage directions, and speeches. All speeches look alike, for example, and nothing else looks like a speech.

- Notice the alignment of elements along invisible gridlines. These alignments occur at the left margin, at the left edge of the speaker names, at the left edge of the speech text, at the right edge of the speech text, and at the right margin.
- Speeches occupy less than the full page width not only to give them a distinct appearance, but also to make them easier to read. If text is too wide, the eye has trouble jumping from the end of one line to the beginning of the next. This is especially true when line spacing is tight.

Real life offers—as does Web design—a countless variety of potential contrasts. Contrasts of color, of size, of alignment, and of motion immediately come to mind. If something doesn't look right, consider increasing or reducing the number of contrasts as well as varying their intensities. And remember, the visual equivalent of screaming in someone's face isn't necessarily the best way to communicate your message. When contrast is required, don't be a wimp, don't be a screamer, and don't mix signals.

For more information about choosing colors for Web pages, refer to Appendix E, "Design Tips for Choosing Colors," and "Achieving Accurate Rendition—Safe Colors," on page 507.

Symmetry vs. Monotony

In any page layout, similar elements should have a similar appearance, and elements that differ should have a different appearance. Neither contrast nor uniformity should be random. This is the principle of symmetry.

All chapter headings in this book are set in the same font, color, size, and position on the page. When you encounter some text that visually resembles the other chapter headings, you assume that that text is a chapter heading as well. You also assume that any text with a different appearance is *not* a chapter heading.

Note that chapter headings are similar to each other, but not to body text. Because chapter headings and body text are quite different elements, there's a lot of contrast between them. There's essentially no contrast (other than distance) between one chapter heading and another, because all chapter headings are alike.

The same reasoning applies to this book's figures, tables, and side notes such as warnings and tips. Each element has a unique style that helps identify it and generally makes the book appear cohesive. It would be confusing if notes in this chapter and the next appeared differently.

The principle of symmetry (or parallelism) applies equally to Web pages. Make all your top-level headings look the same, for example, not just within each page but also within an entire Web site or major section. Use the same color scheme, the same typography, the same alignment (left aligned, centered, right aligned, or justified), the same menu appearance, the same title conventions, and so forth. Avoid monotony by adopting (and testing on your eyes and the eyes of others) an attractive set of designs up front, not by making each page look completely different.

The same is true for pictures. If your site has a logo, use exactly the same logo file in every page that requires one. This not only ensures uniformity but also minimizes download time: The browser downloads the same file (the same URL, actually) only once, no matter how many different pages use it. However, don't use the same picture to communicate different concepts, even if they're in different places. Do try to use an assortment of pictures all done in the same style, however.

An overall site design should be a guide, never a straitjacket. Certainly you'll have several different types of pages, and each page type should have unique elements that visually alert the Web visitor. The number of page types and their corresponding appearances are strictly your decision, but each page type should have the following elements:

- Symmetry that unifies it with all other pages in the same site
- Distinctive contrasts that visually identify each unique type of page or content
- Symmetry among similar types of page or content

In short, similar types of content call for fewer contrasting elements having a narrower range of contrast. Dissimilar types call for a greater variety and degree of contrast.

Choosing a Visual Concept

Visual appearance plays a critical role in the way visitors perceive your site and receive its message. No matter how interesting, well-organized, and useful your site's content might be, a drab presentation will provide a poor viewing experience for your Web visitors and indicate a lack of interest on your part. Because most Web sites devote the best visual presentation to the most important content, many Web visitors now associate drab presentation with boring, outdated information.

Visual presentation is no substitute for well-organized and useful content; both are necessary to produce an effective site. Except for a few highly specialized sites, content doesn't *consist* of presentation; instead, presentation is a means to *convey* content. HTML is such a weak page description language that the challenge of achieving visual appeal frequently overshadows that of developing content. Don't let this happen to you.

Your site's graphic design should complement its message and appeal to its audience. An abstract, garish design patterned after a CD cover might be appropriate for a rock group, but certainly not for a bank or a brokerage house. A site's overall graphic design conveys messages just as surely as its text and pictures, and you should strive to have those messages reinforce each other rather than clash.

If it happens that you're not an experienced graphic design professional, don't despair. In many cases, the site's organization will already have logos, colors, and style guidelines designed by professionals for use in other media. If so, you can adapt these for use on the Web. This might even be a requirement of the Legal department.

In the absence of other guidelines, choose a theme related to some aspect of the site's content. For a school, consider the school colors, emblem, and mascot. For an athletic league, consider the colors and textures of the playing field or equipment. For a restaurant, consider the scenes and colors related to the cuisine or locale, the style of the restaurant's menu, fixtures and objects from the restaurant's decor, or ingredients and cooking utensils.

Beyond these relatively obvious approaches, consider a theme based not on products themselves, but rather on settings where the product is used, cities or sites where it's manufactured or sold, or aspects of the organization's history or technology. Your site's theme should suggest colors, pictures, and icons you can use throughout the site or its principal sections. If a particular theme doesn't suggest a set of workable colors and pictures, move on to another. You'll probably get an "aha!" feeling when you've found it.

The default colors on most browsers are black on gray or black on white. This is every bit as interesting as black-and-white slides projected on a basement wall. Black, white, and gray aren't necessarily colors to avoid, but they *do* deserve augmentation with adjacent frames, pictures, and borders. When choosing text and background colors, choose dark text on a light background. Bright text on a dark background is harder to read, especially for small type sizes. It's usually a good idea to maintain color contrast as well as brightness contrast between text and background.

For information about choosing colors that display correctly on Web pages, refer to "Achieving Accurate Rendition—Safe Colors," on page 507.

Planning Your Pages

Given a mission, an audience, a content plan, management go-ahead, a visual concept, and knowledge of what HTML can and cannot do, you're finally ready to design pages in detail. To at least some extent, this will probably involve storyboards and sketches.

The classic storyboard consists of index cards pinned to a wall. You write up an index card for each Web page, annotate it to indicate planned content, and then arrange all the cards in some kind of hierarchy or sequence. Web visitors will traverse the site along these sequences and hierarchies. Team members and your project sponsor will review the chart, suggest revisions, and someday pronounce it worthy of prime time.

Actual storyboards of this type are rare, but the concept is sound. Your storyboard might be notes on a yellow pad, an outline in a word processor, a preliminary set of Web pages containing only headings and hyperlinks, or even a Navigation view in FrontPage. No matter: The key result is a well-organized set of pages, not the method used to achieve it.

Note FrontPage Navigation view provides an excellent means to record and modify your storyboard electronically. Navigation view has the added bonus of building and hyperlinking your pages for you.

For more information about Navigation view, refer to "Creating a Web Site in Navigation View," on page 994, or Chapter 13, "Creating Web Sites with Navigation View."

It's easy to go wild with menu structure. Visitors are unlikely to find pages more than two or three clicks away from the main page, however, so don't nest menus too deeply. Avoid long pages of hypertext links by using drop-down lists, option buttons, check boxes, and other HTML form elements. Together, a drop-down list of 10 product names and another with 4 kinds of information can efficiently support 40 menu choices.

You should also start sketching or drafting pages at this point. Identify each type of page you plan to use, and then make up a draft or template for each type. Identify changeable components that will exist on multiple pages—menu bars, signature blocks, contact names, and the like. Then plan site parameters and include blocks to support them. Accumulate pictures from stock collections, too. These are logos, icons, buttons, bars, and theme pictures that, if standardized, will help the site achieve a unified appearance.

Lengthy text, either as content or as HTML commands, is seldom the cause of excessive download times. Pictures, Java applets, and Microsoft ActiveX controls are far more often the culprits. As you plan your pages and accumulate your pictures, keep a rough total of download bytes for each type of page. There are no hard-and-fast rules on the size of Web pages, and this is less a consideration on high-bandwidth intranets than on public Internet sites that Web visitors access by dial-up. Most designers consider pages with more than 25,000 to 30,000 download bytes too large for dial-up Web visitors. This is equivalent to 15 to 20 pages of double-spaced plain text, or one uncompressed picture that's 170 pixels on a side.

A final bit of planning advice: You *can* have too much of a good thing. All Web sites are always under construction, so trying in advance to nail down every nit for every page is probably a futile exercise. If you try to plan too much detail, the site's rate of change will exceed the rate of planning. Don't let "paralysis by analysis" happen to you.

Achieving Effective Page Layout

The normal progression of topics on a Web page should be the same as that in your morning paper. For Western languages, this is top to bottom and left to right. Every Web page should have both a meaningful title and a meaningful heading. As Figure 4-5 illustrates, the title appears in the browser's title bar, and the heading appears somewhere near the top of the page. The title serves to identify the page externally to processes such as FrontPage and to search engines such as Yahoo!, Lycos, AltaVista, and MSN Search. The heading immediately informs the Web visitor what content appears on the page. A visitor who has chosen a wrong link can immediately jump back to the previous page. Otherwise, the heading confirms that the visitor has arrived at the correct page. If the page is long, bookmark links should provide pathways to each major subsection, to avoid extensive scrolling (at least on the home page).

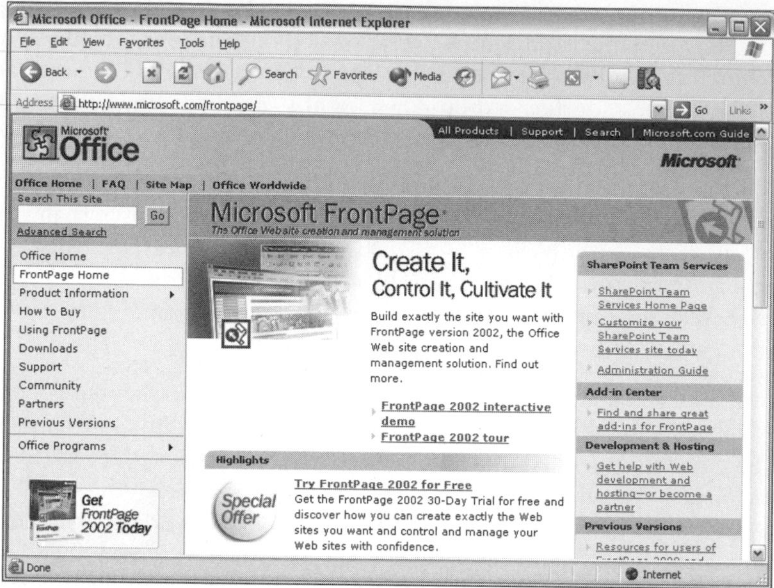

Figure 4-5. The title of this page is "Microsoft Office—FrontPage Home," and its heading is "Microsoft FrontPage."

Experienced page designers often find HTML's weak page-layout features extremely frustrating. This reflects a fundamental conflict between the HTML goal of device independence and the artistic desire for precise control. This conflict isn't likely to subside any time soon, although FrontPage does support a number of recent HTML page-layout facilities:

- **Alignment tags** The normal flow of HTML text is down the left margin, wrapping lines automatically when they reach the right margin, a hard-coded line break, or an explicit or implied paragraph ending. Pictures, Java applets, and ActiveX controls retain their relative positions within the HTML text.

  Implied paragraph endings occur in several situations:

  - Before and after tables
  - At transitions in paragraph style
  - Before and after numbered and bulleted lists

  Recent versions of HTML support attributes to left-align or right-align pictures and other objects, flowing text around them. A centering attribute centers the same kinds of objects, but no text flows to the right or left of the centered picture. Additional attributes align non-text objects vertically with the surrounding text flow. FrontPage supports all of these attributes.

- **HTML tables** Originally designed to display tabular data, HTML tables have become one of the premier means to place items spatially on a page. Any time you want to draw an imaginary grid on a page and align items within it, an HTML table should be your choice.

- **Cascading style sheet (CSS) positioning** This technology finally gives Web designers pixel-precise positioning and layering control over their work. FrontPage provides access to CSS positioning though the Position choice on its Format menu.
- **Frames** This feature provides a way to divide a Web page into tiled rectangles and to independently control the content of each rectangle. One Web page defines a *frames page*—an object that controls the number, sizes, and placement of the frames—while additional Web pages provide the content for each frame. Standard frames have visible borders between them and scroll bars for moving up, down, left, and right within each frame. Borderless frames have no visible borders and are simply page-layout areas that corral your text where you want it.

For more information about using alignment attributes to control page placement, refer to "Aligning Text," on page 216.

For more information about using FrontPage to create HTML tables, refer to "Creating and Editing Tables," on page 515.

For more information about CSS positioning, refer to "Positioning Content with Cascading Style Sheets," on page 621.

For more information about frames, refer to Chapter 15, "Creating Web Sites with Frames."

In Summary...

This chapter described the process of Web design at a very high, human-oriented level. It also introduced some useful concepts for giving your site a uniform, attractive, and effective visual appearance.

Chapter 5 examines FrontPage-based Web sites, a facility that groups Web pages together for convenience, group processing, accountability, and security.

Chapter 5

Understanding FrontPage-Based Web Sites

Although most new designers understand that creating a Web site means creating and linking many Web pages, many of them intuitively look for tools that work on one Web page at a time. Such tools can make the page creation process faster, more enjoyable, and generally more successful, but they provide no help in keeping the site organized, uniform, and functional. Only when things get out of hand do beginners look for software that can manage and organize the site as a whole.

The best use of Microsoft Office FrontPage 2003 avoids this page-at-a-time mentality. Rather than creating and managing each page independently, you first designate a file area where FrontPage can manage new or changed pages as you develop them. This provides much better results than any manual or after-the-fact analysis can hope to achieve, but it does catch new FrontPage designers by surprise. Learning to think in terms of first creating an empty Web site and then filling it with pages is probably the greatest single challenge new FrontPage designers face.

This chapter broadly describes what constitutes a FrontPage-based Web and what a FrontPage-based Web can do. The next chapter continues this discussion by explaining in some detail how to create and operate FrontPage-based Web sites. If you're reading the book sequentially and prefer to jump directly into the details of creating individual pages, skip ahead to Part 3, "Editing Basic Page Content."

Organizing Web Pages and Sites

Web sites are more than the sum of their parts. When Web pages work together effectively, their organization, their cohesion, and their ability to provide for each Web visitor's mind-set and interest is what makes hypertext such a different experience from print.

To manage and administer your Web content in FrontPage, you organize Web pages into units called *FrontPage-based Web sites.* Physically, a Web site is a folder tree located somewhere on your local hard disk, on a file server, or on a Web server. Logically, it's a file area gifted with intelligence about the files it contains and the relationships among them. FrontPage leverages this intelligence to make your job as a Web designer easier.

The next three sections compare and contrast the three ways FrontPage can store and retrieve Web pages: as individual files, in disk-based Web sites, and in server-based Web sites.

Creating Web Pages as Individual Files

Creating Web pages as individual files is the simplest approach for beginners because to create a page, you simply start FrontPage, add the text and pictures for the page, apply formatting, and save the page just like any other Microsoft Office document (that is, you save it with the Save or Save As command and open it with the Open command). Unfortunately, as the number of pages grows, memorizing the function of each page and all its relationships to other pages becomes harder and harder.

Note For purposes of this discussion, files on a network file server are equivalent to files on your local hard disk.

You can partially resolve this problem by faithfully maintaining written documentation and by using tools like the Search For Files Or Folders command that comes with Microsoft Windows. Sooner or later, however, most designers end up wanting more.

Using Disk-Based Web Sites

The simplest kind of FrontPage-based Web site is just a designated folder on your hard disk. FrontPage calls this a disk-based Web site. The folder itself can be almost anything: a new empty folder you create yourself, a new folder FrontPage creates and perhaps populates with sample pages, or an existing folder full of Web pages, pictures, and other files you've already created.

For more information about the mechanics of creating FrontPage-based Web sites, refer to Chapter 6, "Creating and Using FrontPage Web Sites."

After you've defined a disk-based Web site, FrontPage can perform global operations on it. These operations include things like checking spelling in the entire Web site, checking all the hyperlinks within the Web site, and copying the Web site to another computer.

Figure 5-1 shows Windows Explorer displaying the root folder of a disk-based Web site named *My Web Sites*. To make all the files and folders visible, the Hidden Files option is set to Show All Files.

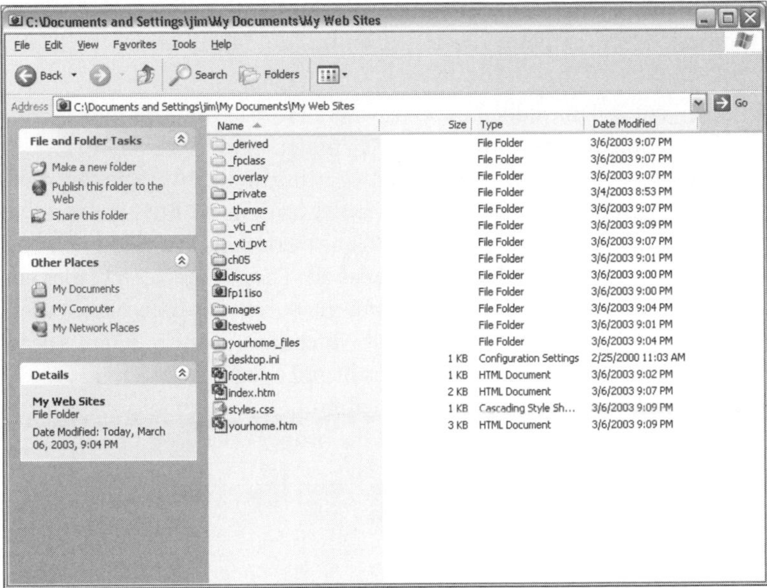

Figure 5-1. Blue globe icons identify folders that contain FrontPage-based Web sites. Each Web site contains not only the content folders that Web designers use, but also the hidden folders that FrontPage uses.

This view of a FrontPage-based Web site is instructive because it exposes some of the inner workings. Here's a guided tour:

- The folder icon at the left of the title bar contains a blue globe. This indicates that the folder contains a FrontPage-based Web site.
- The discuss, fp11iso, and testweb folder icons also contain globes. These indicate that these folders contain additional Web sites.
- The ch05 folder and the footer.htm, index.htm, and yourhome.htm files contain ordinary Web content. The yourhome_files folder contains content files that FrontPage created because yourhome.htm contains a drawing. These folders and files are fairly easy to understand, but FrontPage has added some special folders to this Web site as well:
    - **_derived** Contains pictures that certain FrontPage components create automatically. In this case, this folder contains the pictures that appear in a FrontPage Link Bar component on the Web site's home page.
    - **_fpclass** Contains any Java applets FrontPage uses as part of a component.
    - **_overlay** Contains additional pictures that FrontPage creates automatically.
    - **_private** Contains data files you don't want Web visitors to access. If, for example, you add a Hit Counter component to one of your Web pages, the file that stores the current count goes in the _private folder. This is also a good place to store data that HTML forms submit.

- **_themes** Contains one folder for each theme you use in a Web site. Each of these folders contains all the files and subfolders necessary to display the given theme.
- **_vti_cnf** This hidden folder is where FrontPage stores information about the files that make up your Web site. To understand how this works, refer again to Figure 5-1. The C:\Documents and Settings\jim\My Documents\My Web Sites folder contains four files, named footer.htm, index.htm, styles.css, and yourhome.htm. The _vti_cnf folder also contains four files with these names, but they aren't HTML or CSS files at all. They're special text files where FrontPage stores information about the corresponding content files. In Figure 5-2, for example, Microsoft Notepad shows the contents of the _vti__cnf/ index.htm file that describes index.htm. FrontPage creates and maintains all the files and file contents that reside within the _vti_cnf folder. Disturbing this information might interfere with the proper operation of FrontPage.

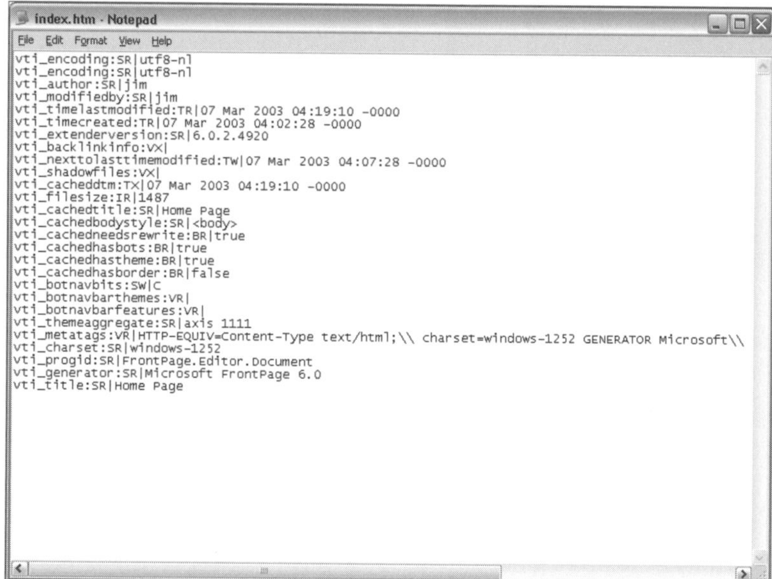

Figure 5-2. This file, located in a _vti_cnf folder, describes a Web page named index.htm.

- **_vti_pvt** Another hidden folder. This is where FrontPage stores Web settings, the Navigation view structure, the Task List, and other information about the current Web site.
- **images** Contains pictures and graphics you want to use in your Web pages.

The reason for presenting this information isn't because you need to work with these special files and folders yourself. The point is rather to show that FrontPage maintains a great deal of information about the pages in your Web site. The term for this information is *metadata*, or data about data. If you change files manually (for example, without going through

FrontPage), the metadata will be incorrect, and FrontPage will malfunction in any number of major or minor ways. This situation leads to the following advice:

- After you create a FrontPage-based Web site, always use FrontPage to change it. If you want to use an editor other than FrontPage occasionally, identify it to FrontPage in this way:
  1. Choose Options from the Tools menu.
  2. When the Options dialog box appears, click the Configure Editors tab.
  3. On that tab, associate the editor with the appropriate file type.

  Having done this, right-click the file you want to edit, choose Open With from the shortcut menu, and select the editor you want.

For more information about configuring FrontPage to invoke external editors, refer to "Configuring External Editors," on page 1118.

- If you must change a FrontPage-based Web site directly, finish your changes, open the Web site in FrontPage, and then choose Recalculate Hyperlinks from the Tools menu. This will regenerate all the metadata FrontPage depends on for proper operation.

Note FrontPage isn't the only program that can maintain the integrity of a FrontPage-based Web site while making changes. Any program that uses FrontPage client software to update a server-based Web site will preserve the correctness of that site. This includes *http://* locations that you open from the My Network Places desktop icon, *http://* locations that you specify in file-oriented dialog boxes, and *http://* locations that you specify in Microsoft Visual Studio and other programs.

Figure 5-3 shows the Web site selected in Figure 5-1 open in FrontPage. With the exception of the _private and images folders, FrontPage doesn't show any of its special folders because you, as the Web designer, should never need to modify them. FrontPage does the modification automatically, silently, and unobtrusively.

One FrontPage-based Web site can contain another. A site that contains another Web site is a *parent*, and the Web site it contains is a *child* or a *subweb*. A site that has no parent is a *root Web site.*

There are no concrete rules or technical requirements that dictate how many Web sites a server should have or what they should contain. Certain principles do, however, apply:

- Pages with many hyperlinks among themselves usually belong in the same Web site (that is, distinct bodies of content should generally reside in the same Web site).
- If different people administer groups of Web pages, those pages should generally be in different Web sites.
- The larger the Web site, the longer it will take to upload and update. For purposes of both performance and content management, FrontPage-based Web sites generally shouldn't exceed a few thousand files.

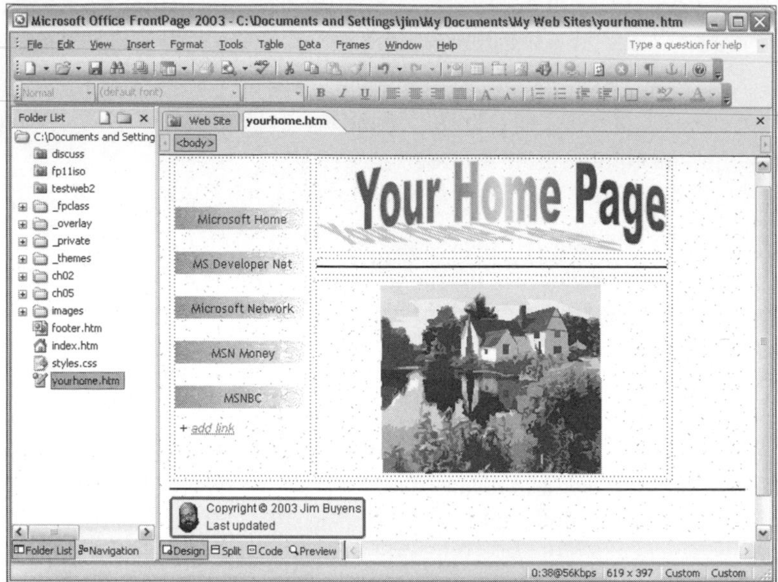

Figure 5-3. This is how FrontPage displays the Web site shown in Figure 5-1. FrontPage hides its special folders because Web designers have no need to work with them directly.

Using Server-Based Web Sites

Disk-based Web sites are very suitable for many kinds of work, but they can't emulate active processes designed to run on a Web server. These processes include displaying hit counters, using an HTML form to search for content, processing data from HTML forms, and working with databases. The programs that do these things on the World Wide Web are designed to run on a Web server and not on your disk—it's as simple as that. If you want these functions to work in your development environment, your environment must include a Web server.

A FrontPage-based Web site that resides on a Web server is called, logically enough, a *server-based Web site*. Of course, the Web server should be one you can access through your network connection. This connection could be a dial-up network connection, a local area network (LAN) at your office, or a home network that connects the computers in your house. The FrontPage desktop software reads files from the Web server instead of from your local disk and writes files to the Web server as well. Whenever a FrontPage client changes a file, software on the Web server updates the necessary FrontPage cross-references and indexes. FrontPage achieves its maximum potential when the Web server you use for development and the Web server that delivers those pages worldwide both utilize server-based Web sites.

Tip **Make sure your computer has TCP/IP networking.**
Neither Web servers nor Web browsers can operate on a computer that lacks a TCP/IP network connection. If you already connect to a TCP/IP network, either on a LAN or by dialing in to an ISP, this network software is already installed. If not, go to Control Panel, open Network, and add the TCP/IP protocol.

FrontPage 2003 can work with two very different kinds of server-based Web sites. They are:

- **FrontPage-extended Web sites** These Web sites reside on Web servers that have the FrontPage Server Extensions installed. What you see as files and folders in FrontPage are physical files and folders on the Web server.

  FrontPage-extended Web sites can contain any kind of files, including ASP pages, ASP.NET pages, and Microsoft Access databases. However, such Web sites don't support the new, XML-based data-handling features in FrontPage 2003, and they don't support Web Parts or any other portal features.

A *portal* is a special kind of home page (or Web site) that displays information and options customized to each visitor. Designers program each information display or option as a reusable component that can occupy space in any number of Web pages. For more information about portals, refer to, "Introducing Portals," on page 921.

Note Windows XP Home Edition doesn't support a Web server, and therefore it can't support a server-based Web. If you have this operating system and want to install a server-based Web site, you'll need to upgrade to Windows XP Professional.

FrontPage Server Extensions are available for a variety of popular Web servers and computing platforms, including Windows 2000, Windows XP Professional, and UNIX. There's no new version of the extensions to accompany FrontPage 2003. For now, at least, the FrontPage 2002 Server Extensions will remain the most current.

For more information about installing the FrontPage Server Extensions, refer to "Obtaining and Installing the FrontPage Server Extensions," in Appendix P.

- **Windows SharePoint Services Web sites** These Web sites reside on Web servers that have Windows SharePoint Services installed. They might or might not be SharePoint Team Sites. A SharePoint Team Site is only one of many applications—prewritten or custom—that can run under Windows SharePoint Services.

  When you open a Windows SharePoint Services Web site in FrontPage, it appears to contain files and folders. This, however, is an illusion. The files are actually SQL Server or MSDE database records that SharePoint manipulates in response to commands from FrontPage or other programs.

Note MSDE stands for Microsoft Data Engine, which is a stand-alone version of Microsoft SQL Server equipped with only the most rudimentary management tools. Microsoft bundles MSDE with other products, so you don't have to buy those products *and* SQL Server. In addition, developers can distribute MSDE with applications they create using certain Microsoft development tools.

Because the files in a Windows SharePoint Services Web site don't reside in the Web server's file system, accessing a file-oriented database like Microsoft Access is impossible. Such Web sites won't process ASP or ASP.NET pages, but they do support FrontPage 2003's new data-handling features, Web Parts, and other portal features.

Windows SharePoint Services is a feature of Windows .NET Server 2003 and only runs on that operating system (or a successor).

For more information about Windows SharePoint Services, refer to Chapter 37, "Using SharePoint Team Web Sites."

The choice between these alternatives won't be confusing if you let your requirements drive your selection:

- If you need to develop portal applications or if you want to use FrontPage 2003's new data manipulation tools, then ask your IT department to install Windows SharePoint Services or seek out a service provider who will provide it.
- If you want to use the database tools included in the last few releases of FrontPage, want to write ASP or ASP.NET pages, or need to support a server-based Web site on an operating system other than Windows Server 2003, install or seek out a Web server that has the FrontPage Server Extensions.

Both the FrontPage Server Extensions and Windows SharePoint Services provide various centralized services—such as data collection, mailing, and search capabilities—that Web visitors can use when they visit your site. One of these, for example, is the FrontPage Hit Counter. When you tell FrontPage to create the HTML for a hit counter, FrontPage generates code that tells the Web server it should run the FrontPage Hit Counter program every time a visitor requests the page. That Hit Counter program, in turn, is part of the FrontPage Server Extensions or Windows SharePoint Services .

Using either type of server-based Web site is very easy if a suitably equipped Web server is already on your network. Just ask the server's administrator to create a Web site for you, specify its HTTP location in FrontPage's Open Site dialog box, and away you go. Unfortunately, not everyone is in an office with existing Web servers and administrators. If such is your fate, you might need to be your own Webmaster and install the necessary software yourself.

On Windows Server 2003, the Web server software and the FrontPage 2002 Server Extensions are built-in options. To locate these options:

1. Open Control Panel and double-click Add Or Remove Programs.
2. In the Add Or Remove Programs dialog box, select Add/Remove Windows Components.
3. On the Windows Components page of the Windows Components Wizard, select Application Server and then click Details.
4. When the Application Server dialog box appears, select Internet Information Services (IIS) and then click Details.

In you want to install Windows SharePoint Services, don't install the FrontPage 2002 Server Extensions. Instead, complete the Web server installation without them, then obtain and install Windows SharePoint Services. Microsoft plans to distribute this software through the Windows Update process.

For more information about installing a Web server, refer to Appendix O, "Installing and Configuring a Web Server."

If you don't have Windows Server 2003 but you do have Windows 2000 or Windows XP Professional, you can still install the Web server software that came with your operating system and the FrontPage 2002 Server Extensions. Here's an overview of the procedure:

1. Open Control Panel and double-click Add Or Remove Programs .
2. In the Add Or Remove Programs dialog box, select Add/Remove Windows Components.
3. On the Windows Components page of the Windows Components Wizard, select Internet Information Services (IIS), and then click Details.
4. In the Internet Information Services (IIS) dialog box, make sure that the World Wide Web Service check box is selected and that the FrontPage 2000 Server Extensions check box is cleared. (There's no point in installing the FrontPage 2000 Server Extensions initially and then upgrading them a few minutes later.)
5. Click OK to close the Internet Information Services (IIS) dialog box, and then click Next on the subsequent pages to complete the wizard.
6. Download and install the FrontPage 2002 Server Extensions from Microsoft's Web site. To do this, browse www.microsoft.com/frontpage/downloads/ and then click the FrontPage Server Extensions link.

Regardless of whether you install the FrontPage Server Extensions or SharePoint Team Services, checking Microsoft's Web site for hot fixes and new versions is to your advantage.

You can install the FrontPage desktop software, a Web server, and the FrontPage server extensions all on one machine. Figure 5-4 illustrates this arrangement.

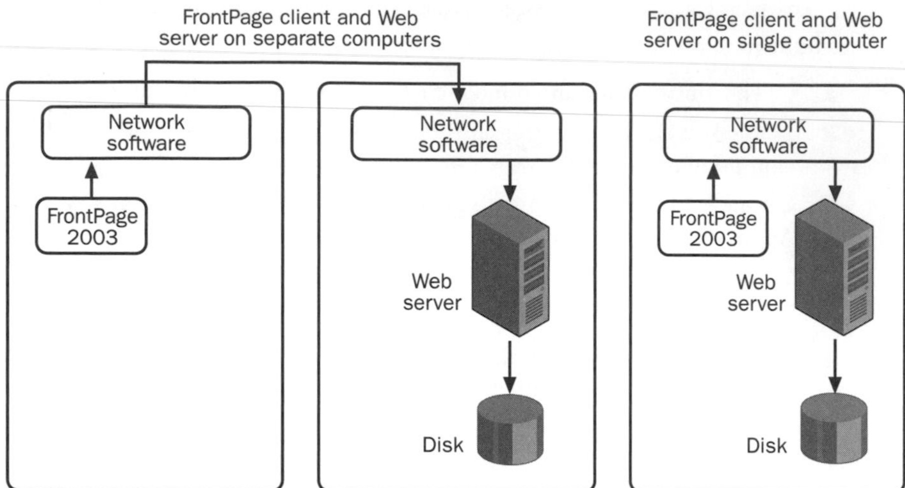

Figure 5-4. The FrontPage 2003 client and a Web server used for authoring can reside either on separate computers or on the same computer.

Because Windows 2000 Professional and Windows XP Professional support at most one Web server, installing the FrontPage Server Extensions applies the extensions to that server.

Windows 2000 Server and Windows .NET Server can run any number of Web servers, and these can support any combination of non-extended servers, FrontPage-extended Web servers, and SharePoint Team Services Web servers.

For more information about installing the FrontPage Server Extensions, refer to, "Obtaining and Installing the FrontPage Server Extensions," in Appendix P.

Extending a Web server creates a single Web site that includes the server's entire existing content. The root Web site's administrator will initially be the Web server's administrator. The root Web administrator can then create subwebs—either new, empty subwebs or subwebs covering existing content—and grant appropriate permissions for administration, authoring, and browsing.

Appreciating FrontPage Web Sites

The natural FrontPage way of doing things is to first create a Web site and then put pages in it. This is often confusing at first, and for two quite logical reasons. First, FrontPage-based Web sites are rather abstract entities. Second, the need to manage and organize Web pages might not be obvious when you don't yet *have* any Web pages!

Chapter 3, "Managing Web Sites," described a variety of features that FrontPage can provide only by treating your files and folders as a group (that is, as a FrontPage-based Web site). In all, the features FrontPage offer for a Web site fall into these general categories:

- Correcting hyperlink locations when you relocate or rename the target files
- Automatically creating site maps and other kinds of Web pages based on Web content
- Including one file within another, and adjusting hyperlinks so that links in the included content are correct even though the pages that include them reside in different folders
- Scanning for errors and omissions
- Finding and replacing text throughout a group of pages
- Reporting activity statistics
- Stopping one designer from changing a given page before another designer has finished with it
- Recording who last changed each file in a Web site
- Maintaining task lists
- Intelligently transferring files from one site to another

Altogether, these features provide a powerful incentive to deal with Web pages as members of a FrontPage-based Web site and not as individual files.

In Summary…

This chapter introduced the operating concepts of FrontPage-based Web sites and explained how they can be valuable to you, the Web designer. Hopefully, it convinced you that the first step in creating any group of Web pages is to create a FrontPage-based Web.

The next chapter explains in some detail the procedures for creating, configuring, and deleting FrontPage-based Web sites.

Chapter 6

Creating and Using FrontPage Web Sites

Describing FrontPage-based Web sites and justifying their existence might be very interesting—or not—but the essence of understanding Microsoft Office FrontPage 2003 is knowing how to create them and start using them. The use of FrontPage-based Web sites permeates almost everything described in this book. This chapter therefore explains in some detail how to create FrontPage-based Web sites.

When creating a new Web site, you should think in terms of first creating a site in FrontPage, and then filling it with all the Web pages, pictures, and other files that constitute a working unit. If you'd rather read about creating individual Web pages, jump ahead to Part 3, "Editing Basic Page Content."

Creating a Web Site for New Content

When you're ready to create a new Web site, you should first initialize it in FrontPage. FrontPage can create new Web sites on your computer's hard disk or on a Web server, with or without sample content. This section explains the necessary procedures.

This section doesn't explain how to create a new site for content that already exists. For those procedures, refer to the section "Creating a Web Site for Existing Content" later in this chapter.

Here's how to initialize a Web site populated with no content at all, with just a home page, or with sample content designed for common situations:

1. Choose New from the File menu. This will display the New task pane, shown in Figure 6-1.
2. If you want to create a new Web site that takes all defaults, click the One Page Web Site option under New Web Site. Then, when the Web Site Templates dialog box appears, click OK and skip the rest of this procedure. The new Web site has these features:
   - FrontPage supplies a home page with no initial content.

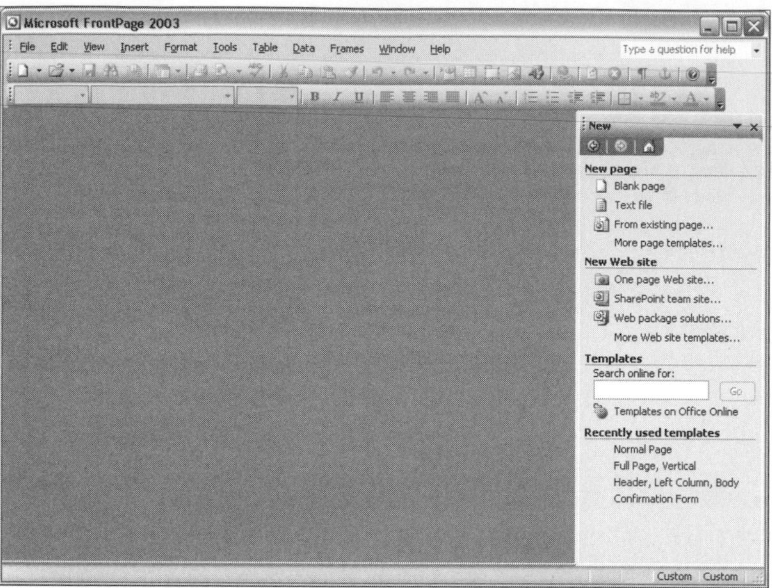

Figure 6-1. The New task pane provides quick access to features that create new pages or Web sites.

- FrontPage chooses a location for the new Web site based on the folder or server location of the last Web site you created. If you've never created a Web site before, FrontPage normally creates one at C:\Documents and Settings\<*username*>\My Documents \My Web Sites\myweb or at *http://127.0.0.1/myweb*. FrontPage uses the HTTP location, known as a *loopback address*, only if the computer is running a Web server that supports server-based Web sites.

> **Note** The loopback address, 127.0.0.1, is a special IP address that always means *this computer*. For more information about the loopback address, refer to the sidebar titled "Talking to Yourself—The Loopback Address," in Appendix N.

- When creating the second or any subsequent Web site on a given machine, FrontPage creates a new site name based on previous new site name plus 1. If the previous name didn't end in a digit, FrontPage appends the digit 1. If it did end in digits, FrontPage adds 1. After creating a site named pizza, for example, FrontPage would name the next few sites pizza1, pizz2, and so forth.

3 If you want to gain more control over the new Web site you're creating, look in the New task pane under New Web Site heading, and click the More Web Site Templates link. This displays the Web Site Templates dialog box, shown in Figure 6-2.

Tip To skip steps 1 through 3 and arrive directly at step 4, on the Standard toolbar, open the Create A New Normal Page button's drop-down menu and then choose Web Site.

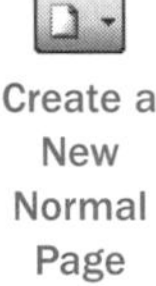

Create a New Normal Page

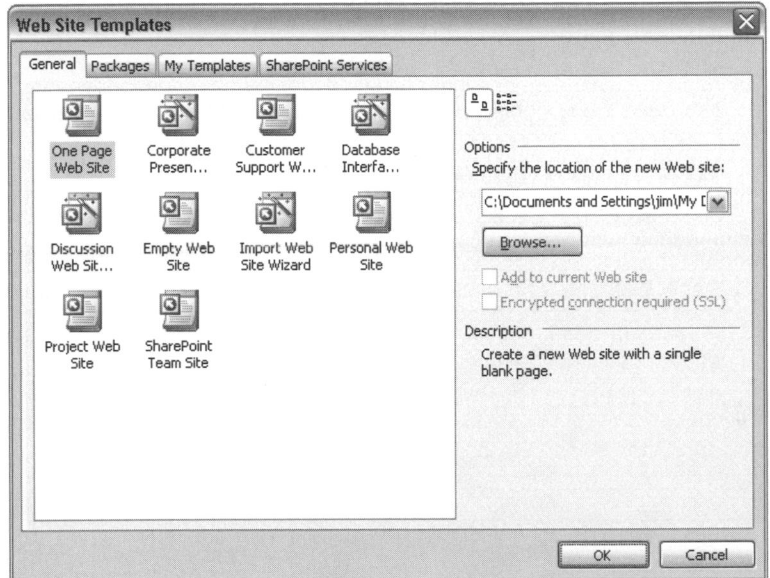

Figure 6-2. To create a new Web site, choose the initial content you want, specify an HTTP or a disk location, and then click OK.

4 Click either the General tab or the Packages tab, and then select the type of initial content you want in your Web site. The large area at the left of Figure 6-2 lists the available types. As you select each choice on the left, FrontPage provides relevant information under the Description heading on the right. Table 6-1 summarizes the choices available on the General tab. Table 6-2 summarizes those on the Packages tab.

The SharePoint Services tab will only contain entries after you specify the name of a Web server running Windows SharePoint Services in the box titled Specify The Location Of The New Web Site, and then tab to another field. The list of templates in this case comes from the SharePoint server, and not from your local installation of FrontPage. Table 6-3 lists some typical SharePoint templates.

Table 6-1. General Web Site Templates and Wizards

Template or wizard	Description	Windows SharePoint Services
Corporate Presence Wizard	A comprehensive Internet presence for your organization.	Compatible
Customer Support Web Site	A Web site for providing customer support services.	Incompatible
Database Interface Wizard	A set of Web pages that displays, adds, modifies, and deletes information in a database.	Incompatible
Discussion Web Wizard	A discussion group with threads, a table of contents, and full-text searching.	Incompatible
Empty Web Site	A Web site with nothing in it.	Compatible
Import Web site Wizard	A Web site populated with content from an existing location. FrontPage prompts for the existing location, and then either readies the content for publishing into the new Web site or—depending on the source—copies it immediately.	Compatible
One Page Web Site	A Web site containing only a blank home page.	Compatible
Personal Web Site	A personal Web site, with pages for your interests, photos, and favorite Web site sites.	Incompatible
Project Web Site	A Web site for a project team; it includes Web site pages for the project members, status reports, the project schedule, an archive area, and ongoing discussions.	Incompatible
SharePoint Team Site	A database-driven Web site that maintains lists and document libraries for project or workgroup members.	Required

Notice the Windows SharePoint Services column in Table 6-1. Here's what the entries in this column mean:

- **Compatible** The Web site will work on Web servers running either Windows SharePoint Services or the FrontPage Server Extensions.
- **Incompatible** The Web site will work only on Web servers running the FrontPage Server Extensions.
- **Required** The Web site will work only on Web servers running Windows SharePoint Services.

All the templates in tables 6-2 and 6-3 require a Web server running Windows SharePoint Services.

For more information about using SharePoint Team Sites, refer to Chapter 37, "Using SharePoint Team Sites."

Table 6-2. Packaged Web Site Templates

Template or wizard	Description
Issue Tracker	An issue tracker complete with issue organization, multiple display configuration, and graphical feedback
Review Site	A review site complete with review page, voting facility, discussion board, and cross-product comparison
Web Log	A Web log complete with hot topics, favorite links, news log, and link depot discussions

Table 6-3. Typical Windows SharePoint Services Templates

Template or wizard	Description
Team Site	A site for teams to create, organize, and share information quickly. Includes a document library and basic lists for announcements, contacts, events, and so forth.
Blank Site	A site with a blank home page. You can use FrontPage to edit this page and add other SharePoint features.
Document Workspace	A site where co-workers work together on documents. It includes a document library, a tasks list, and a links list.
Basic meeting Workspace	A site for planning, organizing, and tracking a meeting. Such a site contains tree lists: objectives, attendees, and agenda.
Blank meeting Workspace	A blank site you can customize with any features you need to plan a meeting.
Decision meeting Workspace	A site for reviewing relevant documents and recording decisions. It includes lists of objectives, attendees, agenda, document libraries, tasks, and decisions.
Special meeting Workspace	A site for planning social occasions. It includes a discussion board and pictures library as well as lists of attendees and things to bring. It also uses directions, weather, and image/logo Web parts.
Multipage Meeting Workspace	A site with multiple pages for planning, organizing, and tracking a meeting. Such sites include objectives, attendees, and agenda lists, plus two blank pages you can customize.

5. Under the Options heading, in the Specify The Location Of The New Web Site box, indicate where you want the new site to reside. Two types of locations are valid:
   - To create the site on a local disk or file server, enter a drive letter and folder name. If any of the folders you specify don't exist, FrontPage will create them. Here's an example:

     ```
     C:\My Web Sites\creating\new\web
     ```

   - To create the site on a Web server, enter an existing Web's URL, plus any intermediate folders, plus one new or existing folder. (This works only if the creating folder and the new folder already exist.) For example:

     ```
     http://www.interlacken.com/creating/new/web
     ```

6. Select the Add To Current Web Site check box if you don't want to create a whole new Web site, but instead want to add new features to the current site. This option is dimmed unless a Web site was open when you started this procedure.
7. Select the Secure Connection Required (SSL) check box if you specified a Web server location in step 5 and the server you specified requires SSL communication for authoring. This option is dimmed unless you specified an HTTP location in step 5.

FrontPage begins building your Web site. If it's a server-based Web site, FrontPage might prompt you for the parent Web site's administrator name and password, as shown in Figure 6-3.

Figure 6-3. Enter the parent Web site's administrator name and password here.

Note FrontPage doesn't prompt for parent Web site account information under three circumstances: first, if you're creating a disk-based Web site; second, if your Web server has no security in effect; and third, if your computer automatically supplies a password from a previously successful network or HTTP logon.

If you specify a Windows SharePoint Services Web server and a template that won't run on that platform, a dialog box such as the following will appear:

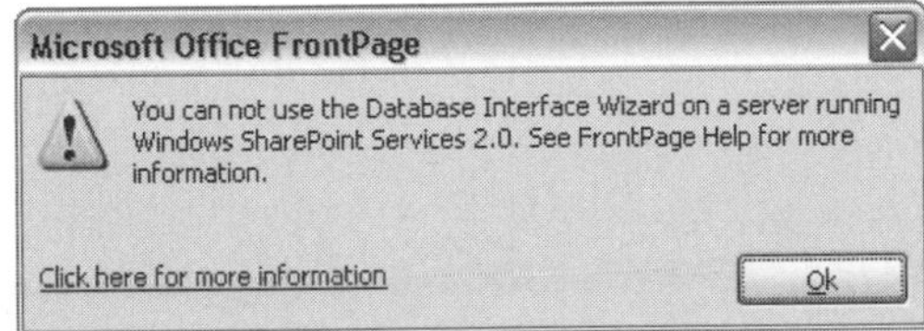

Likewise, if you specify a FrontPage-extended Web server and a template that requires Windows SharePoint Services, this dialog box will confront you:

In either case, your options are to use a different template or locate a compatible server.

If you chose a wizard in step 4, FrontPage now prompts you for additional input. Figure 6-4, for example, shows one screen from the Corporate Presence Web Wizard. Answer the questions to the best of your ability, but don't agonize—you can always delete the new Web site and start over. In fact, you *should* expect to delete the new Web site and start over several times until you get the results you want.

Note When creating a new Web site on a given server, FrontPage uses that server's default page name as the file name of the new Web site's home page.

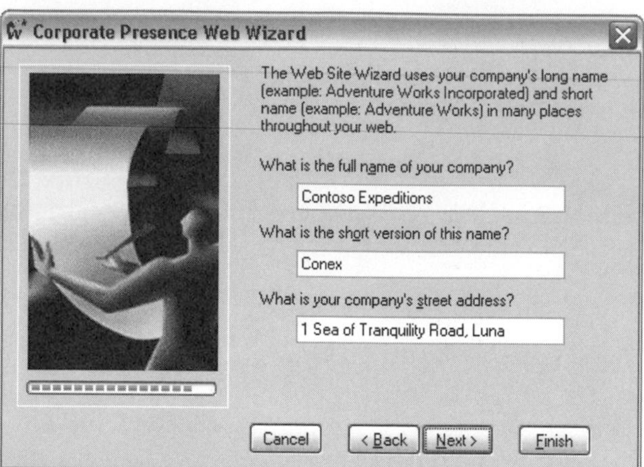

Figure 6-4. This is a prompt from the Corporate Presence Web Wizard. Your answers determine the initial content of the new Web site.

When it finishes building the new Web site, FrontPage displays it, as shown in Figure 6-5.

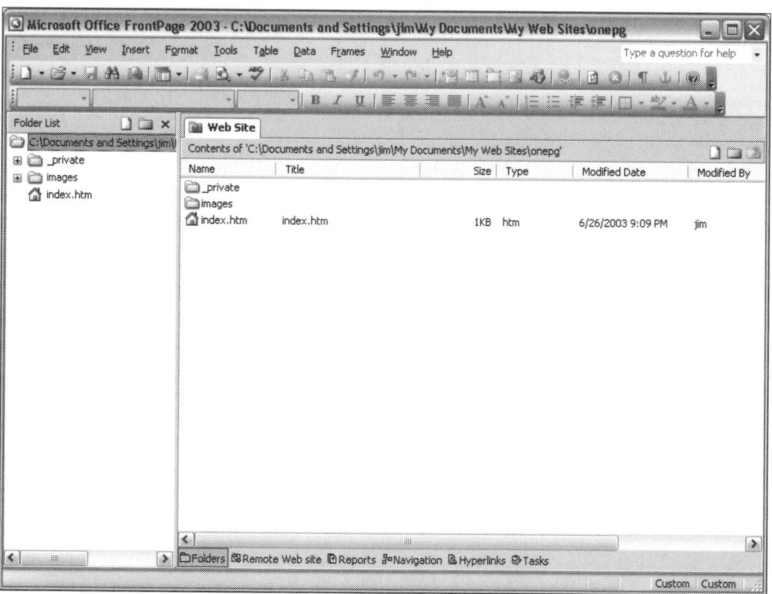

Figure 6-5. FrontPage Explorer displays a new FrontPage-based Web site like this. The drive letter and folder-path location mark this as a disk-based Web site. The One Page Web site template produced these results.

Creating a Project Web Site, for example, produces the 23 generic Web pages shown in Figure 6-6. This is a server-based Web site named *collar.interlacken.com/fp11-iso/ProjWeb.*

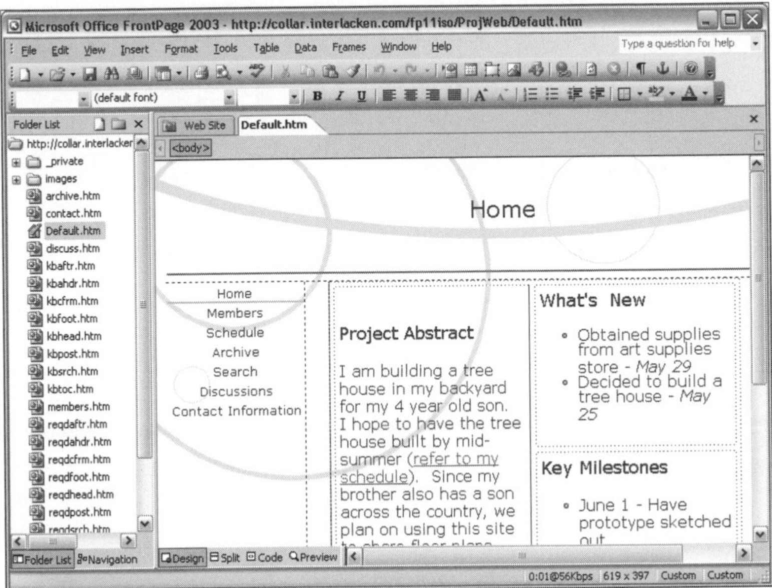

Figure 6-6. All the pages in this Web site resulted from choosing the Project Web site template.

Figure 6-7 shows an unmodified page from this Web site: the Discussions page.

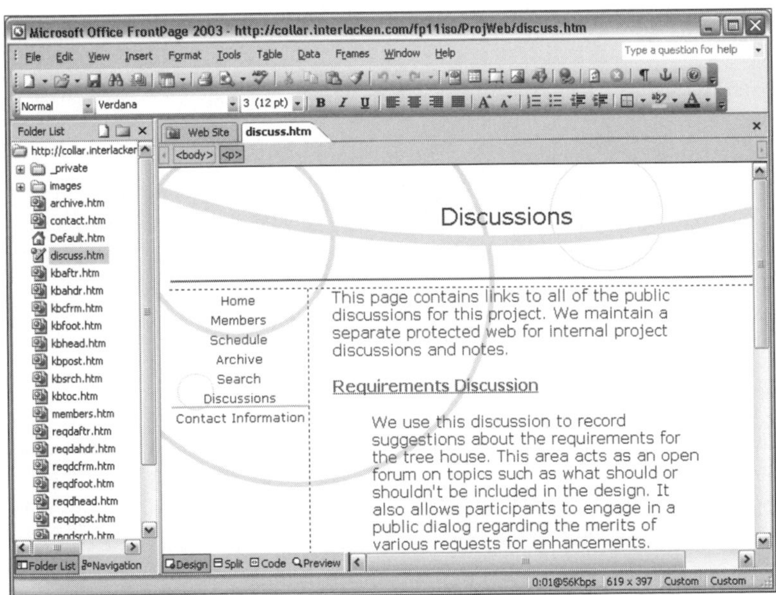

Figure 6-7. This is a typical Discussions page in a new FrontPage-based Project Web Site.

Naming FrontPage-Based Web Sites

You can name a FrontPage-based Web site anything that's valid as a folder name on your disk or Web server, but the following restrictions will minimize later problems:

- Use only lowercase letters or numbers.
- Don't use any spaces or special characters.
- Create a name that's meaningful, but no longer than 8 or 10 characters.

You should choose a Web site name, folder names, and file names for your Web site that are valid on any server that will host it. This is one reason to avoid special characters, spaces, and uppercase letters when choosing these names.

The difference between wizards and templates lies in their degree of automation. A template is relatively static and preformatted; a wizard prompts you for local information and then custom-builds your site accordingly. The Corporate Presence Web Wizard, for example, displays 15 pages of prompts for information such as company name, company address, color scheme, and background, which affect the resulting site. It also presents lists of pages you can choose to generate or not. Although detailed discussion of these wizard prompts is beyond the scope of this book, the prompts are fairly self-explanatory, and there's on-screen Help for each one.

Figure 6-8 shows that the Corporate Presence Web Wizard has created site parameters for changeable information and Tasks view items to remind you to finish the Web site's pages.

For more information about Tasks view, refer to "Working with Tasks View," on page 1015.

Figure 6-9 shows FrontPage displaying the Corporate Presence home page that the wizard generated; notice the boilerplate text suggesting information you should enter under each heading. This Web site's appearance resulted from specifying the Journal theme while running the wizard, but you can change themes at will by using the Theme task pane.

For more information about topics mentioned in this section, refer to:
Chapter 20, "Using FrontPage Themes"
"Using Link Bars with Navigation View," on page 348
"Using Site Parameters and the Substitution Component," on page 759
"Using the Include Page Component," on page 750.

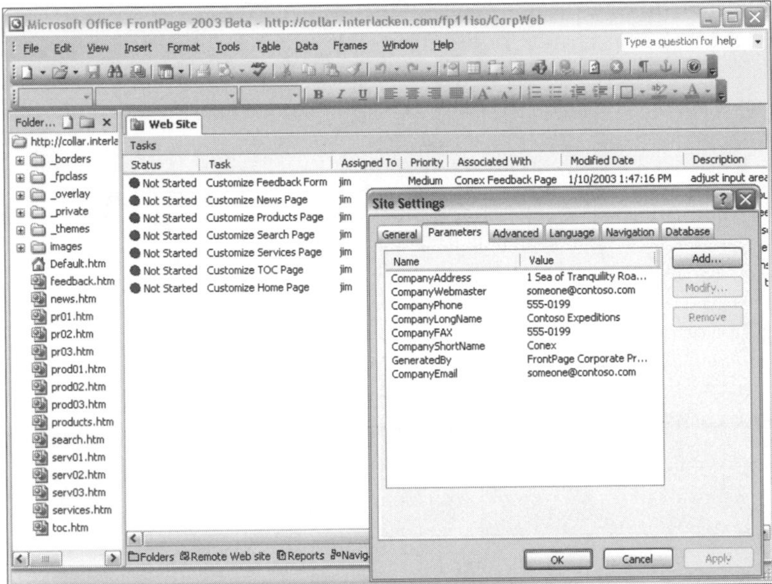

Figure 6-8. Creating a Corporate Presence Web site initializes the FrontPage Tasks list (shown in the background) with a list of themes you need to complete manually. Changing the Value column in the foreground dialog box automatically updates references throughout the Corporate Presence Web site.

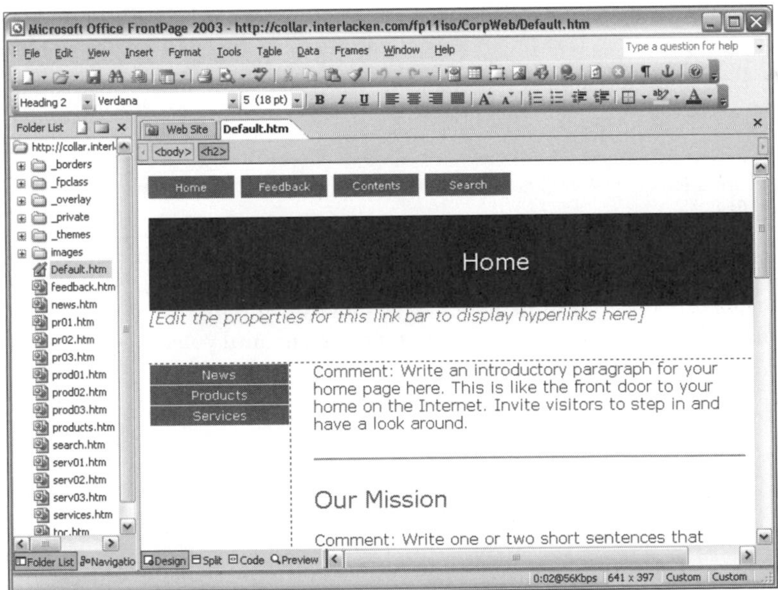

Figure 6-9. FrontPage is ready to modify the default Corporate Presence home page. Boilerplate text suggests typical content.

Figure 6-10 shows the Navigation view of the Corporate Presence Web site. The wizard prompted the Web site's creator for the number of press releases, products, and services. The Feedback, Contents, and Search pages aren't actually part of the hierarchy; they're peers at the Web site's top level and, by virtue of a Link Bar component included in a Shared Border component, are available from every page in the Web site.

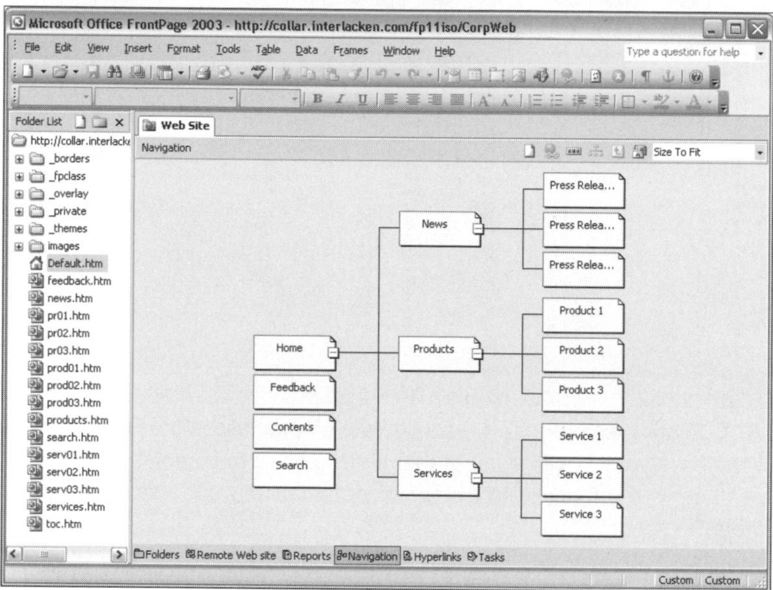

Figure 6-10. This is the Navigation view of a Corporate Presence Web site. The right-most button on the Navigation toolbar toggles the diagram between portrait and landscape orientation.

For more information about Navigation view, refer to Chapter 13, "Creating Web Sites with Navigation View."

The wizards in FrontPage for creating a new Web site can produce so many unique variations that describing them all is impossible. The best advice is simply to try them and judge the results for yourself. Create, decide, delete, and re-create until you have the starting point you want, and then begin your own modifications.

FrontPage and the File System

Within the root Web site, FrontPage maintains information not only about the site itself, but also about each subweb. In addition, each subweb maintains indexes and other information about itself. You should be extremely cautious about moving, renaming, or otherwise updating file areas under the control of FrontPage.

After you've created a Web site using FrontPage, you should use FrontPage for making changes whenever possible. If you add, change, or delete any content files without going through FrontPage, be sure to open the Web site afterward with FrontPage and verify your changes by choosing Recalculate Hyperlinks from the Tools menu.

Never use Microsoft Windows Explorer or any other program to update FrontPage system files or folders. This might create situations that are very difficult to recover from.

Creating a Web Site for Existing Content

Creating new Web sites in FrontPage is relatively straightforward, but converting an existing Web site to FrontPage is perhaps a more common task. This is especially true for designers new to FrontPage, who frequently have an existing body of work. The following sections therefore describe scenarios for initializing a new Web site with existing content, and then one related topic:

- Initializing a disk-based Web site that's already in place
- Initializing a Web site with files from a file system folder
- Importing content from an existing Web site
- Converting a folder to a Web site
- Converting a Web site to a folder

Initializing a Disk-Based Web Site in Place

If you already have a set of Web files in a folder tree on your computer, FrontPage can directly convert it to a disk-based Web site. Here's all you need to do:

1. Choose Open Site from the File menu.
2. Use the Look In drop-down list or any of the My Places bar icons to locate the folder that contains your existing files, and then click Open.
3. FrontPage displays the Add FrontPage Information To The Folder dialog box, shown in Figure 6-11. The information this dialog box refers to is the information, other than content files, that makes up a FrontPage-based Web site. In a manner of speaking, the dialog box offers to "Webify" the chosen folder.

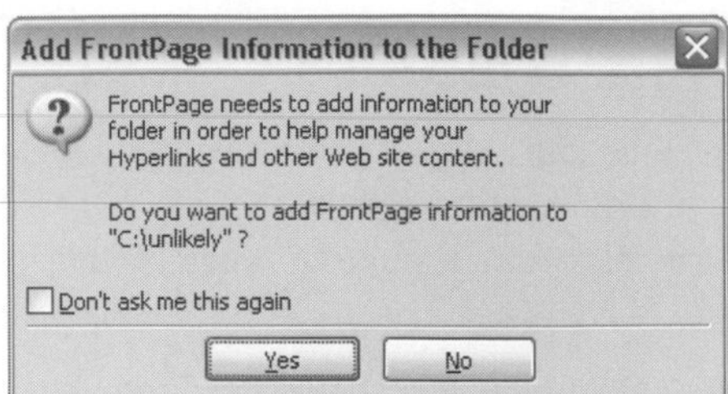

Figure 6-11. To convert an existing disk folder to a disk-based Web site, simply tell FrontPage to open it as a Web site and then reply Yes to this prompt.

4 To convert the folder to a disk-based FrontPage-based Web site, click Yes.

Converting a folder to a Web site doesn't remove or modify any existing files. It does, however, add a great many files. If you change your mind about making this folder a disk-based Web site site, removing all these files can be a nuisance. If you think you might change your mind, make sure you have a good backup of the folder in question, or do your work on a copy.

Initializing a Web Site from a File System Folder

If you need to creating a new Web site and initialize it with existing content from your hard disk or file server, you have a choice of two general procedures. Here's the first.

1 Create an empty Web site as the previous section titled "Creating a Web Site for New Content," explained.

2 Add the existing files and folders to this site, as the later section titled, "Importing Web Files And Folders," explains.

The second procedure is even easier: Use Window Explorer to create a copy of the existing Web site, and then use the procedures in the preceding section to open the copy as a Web site.

Running the Import Web Site Wizard

The Import Web Wizard unifies three procedures you could invoke separately if you want; the wizard just makes it easy to use them together. In sequence, these procedures are:

1 Creating A New Blank Web Site. The preceding section, "Creating a Web Site for New Content," explained how to do this.

2 Associating a remote site with the new local site from step 1. Chapter 16, "Publishing Your FrontPage-Based Web Site," will explain this procedure in detail.

3 Copying the remote site to the local site. Chapter 16 explains this process as well.

The Import Web Wizard can populate a new Web site with content from any of these sources.

- A FrontPage disk-based Web site on your hard disk or on a network file server.
- A FrontPage server-based Web site on that resides on any Web server.

- A Windows SharePoint Services Web site that resides on any Web server.
- Any Web site consisting of files accessible by FTP.
- Any Web site consisting of files accessible by WebDAV.
- Any Web site you can access with a browser.

Tip Create local copies of any Web sites you access by FTP or WebDAV.
If you attempt to open an WebDAV or FTP as a FrontPage based Web, FrontPage responds by starting the Import Web Wizard. Consider this a gentle reminder that to update a site, you should create a local copy, update it, and then publish your changes back to the original location.

In all cases but the last, FrontPage can populate a new Web site from an existing site with 100% accuracy. This is possible because FrontPage uses its so-called publishing features, which are the fastest and most accurate way to copy a Web site from one location to another. Fortunately, the publishing features in FrontPage 2003 are more flexible and easier to use than ever before.

The last case is a last resort for importing Web sites you can't access any other way. The sidebar titled "Importing Pages by Imitating a Browser" explains the limitations of this approach.

Importing Pages by Imitating a Browser

FrontPage can download the contents of almost any Web site by imitating a browser and saving the resulting files in a FrontPage based web site. Here's how this process works.

1. FrontPage requests the home page, just as a browser would. It also requests any pictures and other files the home page uses.
2. Next, FrontPage checks the home page for hyperlinks within the same site, then downloads those pages and their support files as well.
3. Finally, FrontPage check the pages from step 2 for hyperlinks, downloads those pages and their support files, and repeats the process until no more pages remain or until FrontPage reaches a limit you specify.

In almost every case, this process doesn't achieve the same results as retrieving files directly from the Web server's file system. For one thing, the site might contain files that don't appear in any URLs. For another, if the site contains any ASP or ASP.NET pages, any Web Part Pages, any Web Parts, or any other executable content, you'll receive the results of executing that content and not the executable code itself.

If you can access your existing site by any of these means, the following procedure will copy it into a new or existing FrontPage Web site located anywhere you want.

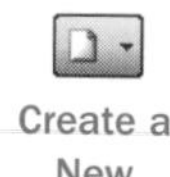
Create a New Normal Page

1. Display the Web Site Templates dialog box. For example:
   - Click the Create A New Normal Page drop-down button on the Standard toolbar, and then choose Web Site.
   - Display the New task pane and then, under New Web Site, click more Web Site Templates.
2. When the Web Site Templates dialog box shown previously in Figure 6-2 appears, make sure the General tab is selected and then select the Import Web Wizard icon.
3. Under Options, the Specify The Location Of The New Web Site box controls where the new Web site will reside. Specify a location as follows.
   - If you want the new Web site to reside on a local disk or a file server, specify a drive letter and path.
   - If you want the new Web to reside on a FrontPage or SharePoint extended Web server (even one running on the local computer) specify an http:// location.

   You should also check the status of the Add To Current Web Site check box.

   - If no Web site was open was open in FrontPage when you started this procedure, the check box will be dimmed.
   - If a Web site was open and you don't want to replace its existing contents, make sure the box is cleared.
   - If a Web site was open and you want to replace its existing contents, select the check box.

   Finally, if you specified an http:// location and that Web server requires the use of Secure Sockets Layer (SSL) check the box titled Encrypted Connection Required (SSL)
4. Click OK. If you specified a location on a FrontPage or SharePoint based Web site, FrontPage might display the Connect To dialog box shown previously in Figure 6-3. This prompts you for a username and password that has permission to create the new Web site.
5. When the Import Web Wizard – Welcome dialog box shown in Figure 6-12 appears, click one of these options under How Do You Want To Get The Files?
   - **FrontPage Server Extensions Or SharePoint Services** Click this option if the existing Web site resides on a Web server running the FrontPage Server Extensions or Windows SharePoint Services.
   - **WebDAV** Click this option if the existing Web site resides on a server accessible using WebDAV.
   - **FTP** Click this option if the existing Web site resides on a server accessible using FTP.
   - **File System** Click this option if the existing web site is a FrontPage disk-based Web site that resides on your local disk or a network file server.
   - **HTTP** HTTP Click this option if the existing Web site is available only by browsing the Internet. Note that in this case, you will import pages as browsers receive them, and not as they exist in the Web server file system.

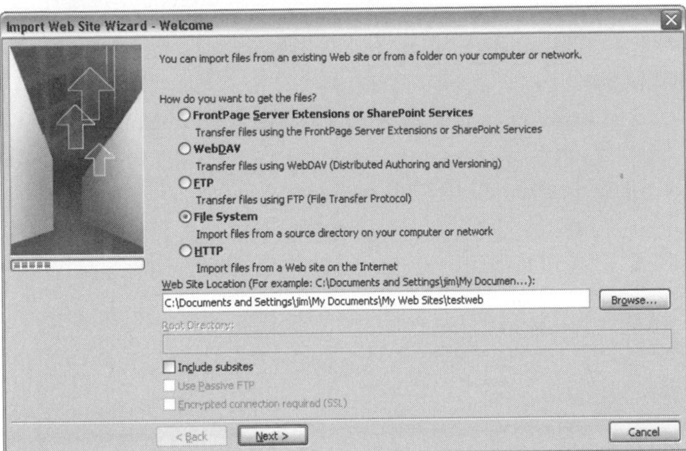

Figure 6-12. FrontPage can populate a new Web site with files from a remote Web site, from an FTP site, or from a local disk.

6 Use in the Web Site Location box to specify where the existing Web pages should come from:

- If you chose FTP in step 5, enter the FTP server's URL in the Web Site Location box. Then, in the Root Directory box, enter the FTP path to the start of your existing Web site. If accessing this location requires the use of Passive FTP (PASV), check the Use Passive FTP box.
- If you chose File System in step 5, enter the drive letter and path that identifies the start of the existing FrontPage disk-based Web site.
- In any other case, enter the HTTP URL of the folder where the existing site begins. This is normally the URL of the site's home page, minus the name of the home page itself. If accessing this Web location requires the use of SSL, click the Encrypted Connection Required (SSL) box. Remember that not all FrontPage Web sites start at the Web server's root folder.

7 Check the status of the Include Subsites check box.

- If in step 5 you chose WebDAV or FTP as the way to get files, this check box will be dimmed.
- If you chose FrontPage, SharePoint, or File System, the location you specified in step 6 might contain subwebs. To retrieve the first (outermost) Web site plus any sites nested within it, check the Include Subsites box. To retrieve only the outermost site Web, clear the box.

Note All Web servers running the FrontPage Server Extensions contain at least one FrontPage-based Web site: the *root Web site*. The root site's URL is *http://<servername>/*. Authorized designers can designated folders within the root as separate Web sites—called *subwebs*—for purposes of administration, security, or content management.

8 Click Next to display the Choose Your Destination Web Location page shown in Figure 6-13. This page gives you one last chance to change your mind about where the copied files will go:

- **Local Copy Location** Overrides the target location.
- **Add To Current Web Site** Adds the files to the Web site—if any—that was open when you began this procedure.
- **Secure Connection Required (SSL)** Specifies that the server you named in Local Copy Location requires SSL communication for authoring.

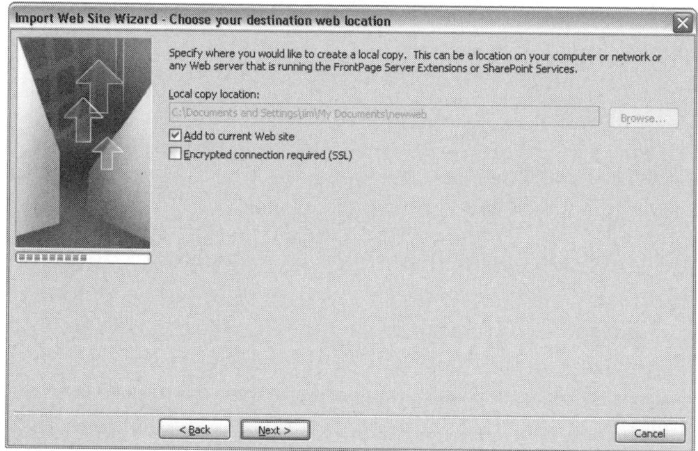

Figure 6-13. The second page of the import web site wizard confirms the receiving location.

9 Click Next. If you chose anything but HTTP in step 5, this will display the final (and congratulatory!) page of the wizard. Otherwise, it displays the Set Import Limits page shown in Figure 6-14. Configure these settings as you want and then click Next:

- **Import The Home Page Plus Linked Pages** To limit the depth of retrieval, select this check box, then specify the maximum number of levels between an imported page and the home page. Specifying 1, for example, means that FrontPage will import the home page and any files from the same site that have hyperlinks within it. Specifying 2 means that FrontPage will also import any pages that have hyperlinks within level 1 files, and so forth.
- **Import A Maximum Of** To limit the number of kilobytes FrontPage will download, select this check box, and specify the maximum number you want.
- **Import Only HTML And Image Files** Select this check box to download Web pages and picture files only, ignoring any content such as ZIP files and executables.

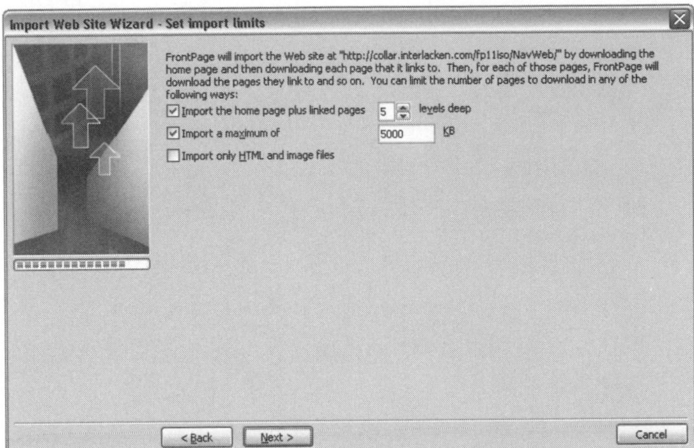

Figure 6-14. FrontPage provides three ways to avoid excessive downloading when importing an existing Web site.

10 Click Finish to complete the wizard.

Unless you chose HTTP in step 5, the main editing window will now display Remote Web Site view, which appears in Figure 6-15. This is the focal point for all FrontPage publishing commands.

- A list box at the left will display the content of the new site you specified in step 3, FrontPage considers this the *local* Web site.
- A similar list box at the right will display the contents of the existing site you specified in step 6. FrontPage considers this the *remote* Web site.

In most cases, you'll want to copy the entire remote site to the new local site. Here's the necessary procedure:

1. Look under the Publish All Changed Pages heading at the lower right.
2. Select the Remote to Local option.
3. Click the Publish Web Site button.

If you want, you can also copy selected portions of the remote site; to do this, just right-click the files or folder you want in the right-hand list box, then choose Publish Selected files form the shortcut menu.

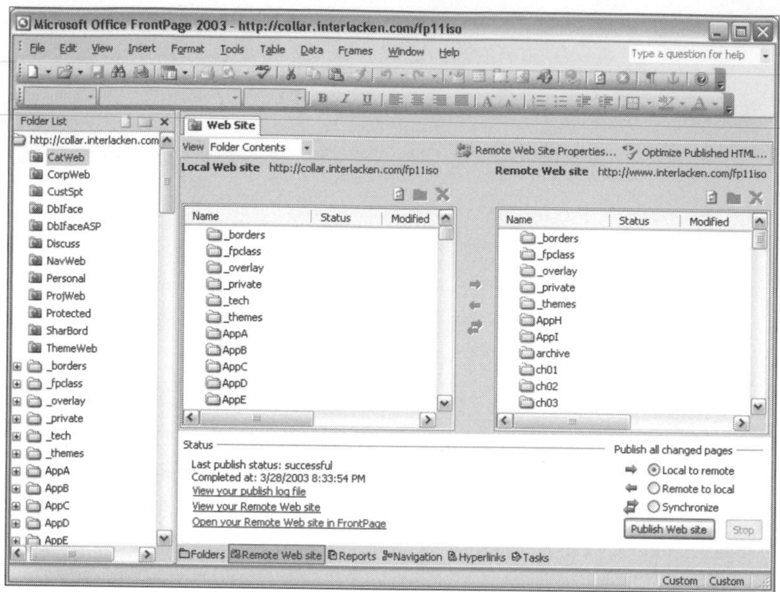

Figure 6-15. Remote Site View can transfer content between two sites in full or in part, and in either direction.

At all costs, avoid publishing an empty, local site to the existing, remote site. This erases all the files in the existing, remote site. Once you have a full local copy, however, you can leave Remote Site View, change the site any way you want, and then publish the results to any authorized location you want (including, of course, the original location).

After clicking Remote To Local, clicking Publish Web Site, and waiting for the process to complete, you'll have a new FrontPage-based Web site that contains all your former pages. You might also have a mess. Unless you've been extraordinarily meticulous in the past, the many views and organizing tools FrontPage provides will likely reveal inconsistent file names, missing page titles, files not residing in the most logical location, and other regrettable situations. It's like a new TV showing what a bad antenna or cable connection you have. Fortunately, FrontPage makes it easy to reorganize files without breaking hyperlinks among pages.

For more information about repairing a poorly organized Web site, refer to "Planning and Managing Folders," later in this chapter.

Copying FTP and WebDAV Content

Strictly speaking, copying Web content from an FTP or a WebDAV location to another FTP or WebDAV has nothing to do with creating a new FrontPage-based Web site. You can't use the Publish command for copying content from one to the other, but you do have two alternatives:

- Create and open a new disk-based Web site, switch to Remote Web Site view, point the remote Web site location to the source Web site, and publish Remote To Local. Then set the remote Web site location to the target Web site and publish Local To Remote.
- Open both locations in Windows Explorer, and drag files from one window to another.

To open an FTP location in Windows Explorer, type its location in the Address box of any Windows Explorer or Internet Explorer window. For example, type **ftp://ftp.contoso.com/whatever**, where *ftp.contoso.com* is the FTP server's network name and *whatever* is a path.

If you need to specify a username and password, either right-click the body of the window and choose Login As from the shortcut menu, or specify the URL as *ftp://<username>@ftp.contoso.com*.

To open a WebDAV location in Windows Explorer, open My Network Places, click Add A Network Place, and then complete the wizard, specifying an *http://* location as the Internet or network address.

Converting a Folder to a Web Site

As Web sites grow in size and complexity, it often becomes apparent that what started as an ordinary folder deserves to become a Web site in its own right. This breaks your content into more manageable units, both in terms of data volume and administrative responsibility, and it sets limits on FrontPage functions that process an entire Web site.

Here's how to convert a folder in an existing Web site to its own FrontPage-based Web site:

1. Open the existing Web site in FrontPage, and right-click the existing folder.
2. Choose Convert To Web from the shortcut menu.
3. When the confirmation prompt shown in Figure 6-16 appears, click Yes.

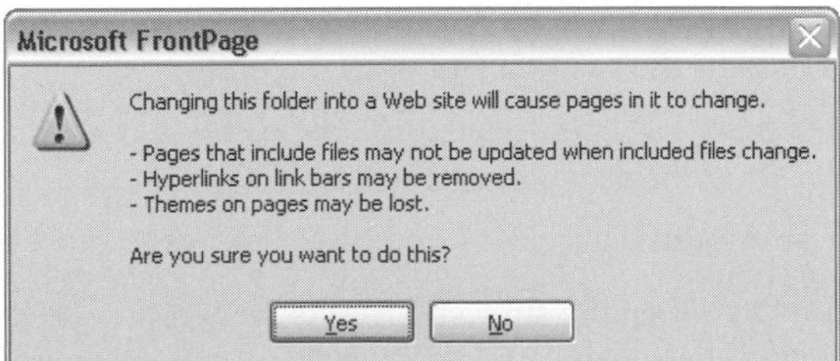

Figure 6-16. This prompt warns you that making a new Web site out of a folder in an existing Web severs ties between the converted folder and the existing Web site.

Recall that no file or folder can belong to two Web sites, even if one site physically resides within another. This explains the confirmation prompt in Figure 6-16. Suppose, for example, that the Web page default.htm has a hyperlink to the page birds/ducks.htm:

- If these pages are in the same Web site, renaming birds/ducks.htm to birds/geese.htm would update the hyperlink in default.htm.
- If you converted the birds folder to a subweb and *then* renamed ducks.htm to geese.htm, FrontPage would *not* update the hyperlink in default.htm, because the two files would then be in different Web sites.

The second part of the prompt reminds you that for each file included in the new Web site, any references from the old Web site will become *external* (that is, those references will now point to locations outside the old Web site).

Converting a folder to a Web site can be a relatively major change. Planning is the key. Here are some things to consider:

- Organize your content *before* creating the new Web site, while FrontPage can still fix hyperlinks as you move things around. Make sure your content is clearly and logically divided between the old and new areas.
- Don't forget to organize pictures and other files as well as Web pages. Create a folder named images inside the folder you plan to convert, and then move or copy any required pictures into that images folder. Again, do this while FrontPage can still fix hyperlinks for you.

If the existing Web site is server-based and uses Windows SharePoint Services or the FrontPage Server Extensions 2002, you can also convert folders to subwebs using the administration Web pages.

For more information about converting folders to subwebs by means of the administration Web pages, refer to "Creating a Subweb," in Appendix P.

Converting a Web Site to a Folder

Just as you can convert folders to Web sites, you can also convert Web sites back to ordinary folders. There is, however, one significant catch: Any Web site you convert to a folder must already reside within another Web site (that is, you can convert a subweb to a folder, but you can't convert a root Web site to something dangling in space). Here's the procedure:

1. Open the Web site that contains the subweb you want to convert.
2. Locate the subweb in the Folder List, right-click the subweb's folder icon, and then choose Convert To Folder from the shortcut menu.
3. When the confirmation prompt in Figure 6-17 appears, click Yes to proceed.

   The warning reminds you that when the subweb loses its identity, it also loses its unique security, its Navigation view data, and its Tasks list. Furthermore, if you've applied a theme to the entire parent Web site, that theme might not apply to pages in the converted Web site.

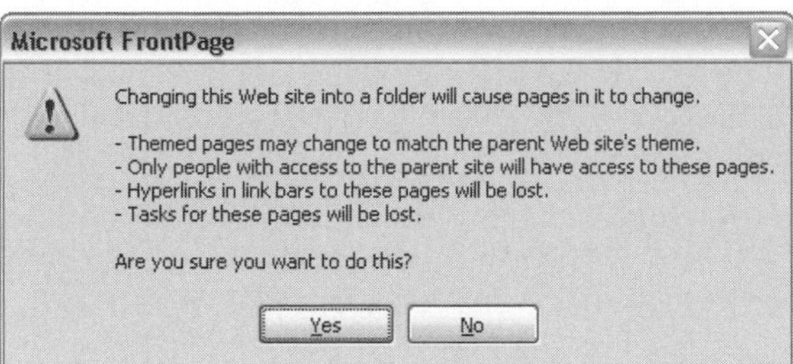

Figure 6-17. This prompt warns that converting a FrontPage-based Web site to an ordinary folder discards any information unique to that Web site.

Importing Web Files And Folders

Adding existing Web pages, pictures, and other files to a FrontPage-based Web site is a common requirement. FrontPage calls this process *importing* and can perform it at the file or folder level. There are two importing methods: the menu method and the dragging method.

Importing files using menus is a two-step process. First you must build a list of files to import, and then you must actually import them. To build the list:

1. Open the receiving Web site in FrontPage, and select the Web folder you expect to receive the most files.
2. Choose Import from the File menu to display the dialog box shown in Figure 6-18.

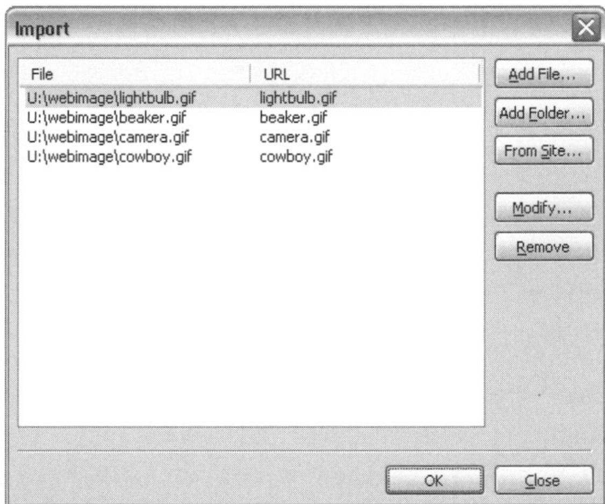

Figure 6-18. Use this dialog box to build a list of items to import.

3. Depending on what you want to import, choose any of these options:
   - To add individual files, click the Add File button. When the Add File To Import List dialog box appears, find the files you want to import, and then click Open. FrontPage will add the selected files to the import list shown in Figure 6-18.

Chapter 6

- To add all the files in a given folder (and all its subfolders), click the Add Folder button. When the File Open dialog box opens, locate the desired folder, and click Open. FrontPage will add all the files in the selected folder, including subfolders, to the import list.
- To add the files from an existing local, intranet, or World Wide Web site, click the From Site button. This transfers control to the Import Web Wizard. Refer to the section "Running the Import Web Site Wizard," earlier in this chapter, for instructions on using this wizard.

4 Normally, FrontPage imports all files to the current folder in FrontPage. To change the destination of an individual file, select the file, and click Modify. (You won't have this option if you're importing a Web site.) When the Edit URL dialog box shown in Figure 6-19 appears, change the displayed destination, and click OK.

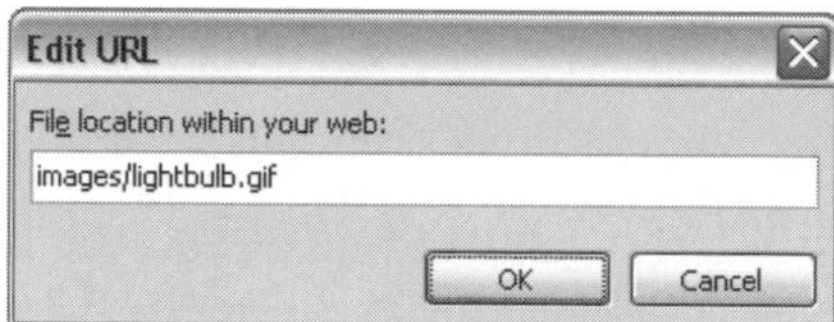

Figure 6-19. Use the Edit URL dialog box to change the planned destination of an imported Web file.

5 To remove a file you've placed in the import list, select it and click Remove.

Caution Imported pages frequently contain incorrect or nonstandard HTML, especially if they were previously maintained by hand. FrontPage might interpret these questionable elements differently than a browser would. Keep the original files until you view the imported versions in FrontPage, save them, and review the results with your browser. If they need more than a minor cleanup, you might want to correct the originals and reimport them.

When you're ready to import the files in the list, click OK. To abandon or postpone importing, click Close. FrontPage will remember the import list for the current session. To import the list later in the same session, choose Import from the File menu.

To import Web files by dragging:

1 Open the receiving Web site with FrontPage.

2 Use Windows Explorer to locate the files or folders you want to import.

3 Drag the files or folders from Windows Explorer to the desired destination in FrontPage.

To copy content between two Web sites, open both Web sites in FrontPage, and then drag the desired content between the two FrontPage windows.

Of course, you can also move content into, out of, and among FrontPage-based Web sites using the Web Folders feature that comes with Microsoft Office XP. The default drag operation is Copy, as long as the source and target locations are on different drives, on different servers, or on one drive and one server. If both locations are on the same drive or server, the default operation is Move. You can reverse these defaults by holding down the Ctrl key while dragging, but it's often less confusing to drag with the right mouse button instead.

Tip After you drag something with the right mouse button, Windows displays a shortcut menu asking whether to copy, move, create a shortcut, or cancel.

Publishing, Packaging, Copying, and Importing: What's the Difference?

The FrontPage Publish command is the best way to interactively copy a FrontPage-based Web site from one location to another. Publishing a Web site ensures that the target location contains not only 100 percent of your content files, but also a full set of well-structured cross-reference and index files as well.

Packaging is a way of transporting Web sites from one location to another when an interactive approach isn't possible. Packaging a Web site means exporting some or all of its files or folders into a single file that you can transmit offline: by FTP, by e-mail, or by compact disc, for example. Whoever receives the package can then import it on another Web server. You can only export packages from Web sites that reside on Windows SharePoint Services servers, any you can only import pages to such sites as well.

If your Web site resides on a local disk or file server, copying files into the Web site file area with Windows Explorer or the command prompt might seem quicker and easier than importing them with FrontPage. The difference is this: When FrontPage imports a Web file, it copies the file into place and also updates all the necessary FrontPage indexes and cross-reference files. Externally copying the files into place doesn't perform the FrontPage updates.

Creating a new Web site and then importing an existing one imports the home page, then all pages and files referenced on the home page, then all pages and files on those pages, and so forth. This bypasses any files that aren't explicitly mentioned in hyperlinks. For example, it doesn't usually import database files or files mentioned in JavaScript or VBScript code. It also bypasses FrontPage files that contain information such as Web site settings and the Navigation view structure. If the source Web site contains any ASP pages or other components that execute on the Web server, you will most likely import the result of running those pages rather than the source files.

By far, the best procedure for copying a FrontPage-based Web site is to open the source Web site, choose Publish Site from the File menu, specify a target location, and click the Publish Web Site button.

To restore a FrontPage-based Web site to consistency after an external process has changed it, open the Web site in FrontPage, and choose Recalculate Hyperlinks from the Tools menu.

Planning and Managing Folders

Other than the hidden folders used by FrontPage, there are no requirements and no limits on the number of folders your Web site can use. Most sites use folders to segregate and categorize their content, but the extent of such use is a matter of judgment and preference.

When a FrontPage wizard or template creates a site, it normally places all HTML files in the root folder of the current Web site and all pictures in an /images folder. There are several good reasons for having an /images folder:

- At most sites, HTML files require more structure and management than picture files. Keeping all the pictures in one folder reduces clutter and makes it easier to manage folders of Web pages.
- Many pictures are stock items used on several pages. Keeping all pictures in one folder makes it easy to locate and use stock pictures when creating new Web pages.
- Most browsers cache Web files to eliminate unnecessary downloads. If you store the same picture in two different folders, however, the browser has no way of knowing the two pictures are identical, and it downloads them both. Keeping all pictures in one folder eliminates duplicate downloads.

It's often a good idea to put all pages for a given topic in one folder, and to name the topic's home page with the server's default page name. That way, you can nest subtopics in subfolders to form a topical tree. This keeps individual folders small enough to review their contents at a glance and it also provides a navigational aid for Web visitors. When Web visitors see a URL such as www.interlacken.com/fruit/citrus/lemons.htm they expect that shortening it to www.interlacken.com/fruit/citrus/ will bring up a Citrus Fruit home page, and that shortening this further to www.interlacken.com/fruit/ will produce a Fruit home page.

This isn't to say that every page—or even every menu page—should reside in its own folder. This is poor practice. It's also poor practice, however, to locate all pages in a large site in a single folder. The organization you choose depends on the structure of your content, but there should be organization of some kind.

Folder names are again a matter of preference, but long dual-case names containing special characters usually create more problems than clarity for the following reasons:

- Users do sometimes type URLs by hand—perhaps copying them out of magazines or even computer books—and long names are simply hard to type.
- Dual-case names create confusion because some systems (particularly UNIX) are case-sensitive and others (such as Windows) are not. To UNIX, /Potions and /potions are two completely different folders—as different as /potions and /notions. To a Windows Web server, however, /Potions and /potions are the same thing. Always using lowercase avoids such confusion.
- Many special characters, even though acceptable as folder names, require special encoding when used in URLs. The coding consists of a percent sign (%) followed by the hexadecimal value of the character's ASCII code. If you create a folder name containing a space, for example, you'll have to represent the space as *%20* in all URLs—ungainly and hard to fathom.

Working with Web Site Views

Keeping all but the smallest Web page collections organized would be difficult without a graphical organizer like FrontPage. To suit various needs, FrontPage provides six distinct views of a Web site. To select a particular view, click the Web Site tab *above* the main editing window, and then click the view tab you want *below* the main editing window. The six views are:

- **Folders view** In this view, you can see a more complete list of a Web site's files and folders than Design view's simple Folder List.
- **Remote Web Site view** This view compares the contents of the current Web site to those of another and provides commands for transferring content between them.
- **Reports view** This view displays interactive reports that help you manage your site.
- **Navigation view** In this view, you can create and display the hierarchy of the pages in your site. You create the hierarchy by dragging rectangles representing Web pages into a diagram that resembles an organization chart. Adding a Link Bars component to any Web page then creates a menu corresponding to your hierarchy.
- **Hyperlinks view** This view is, in some ways, the reverse of Navigation view. With Navigation view, you create the structure, and the Link Bars component creates the hyperlinks. With Hyperlinks view, FrontPage analyzes your existing hyperlinks and graphically displays links to and from any page.
- **Tasks view** This view displays a list of tasks that have been created for the current Web site. In essence, it's an electronic, multi-user to-do list.

Regardless of which view is in effect, however, FrontPage's menu bar and toolbars provide rich options to:

- Create, globally modify, or delete Web sites.
- Import pages from existing sites not controlled by FrontPage.
- Check spelling and search text throughout a site.
- Copy sites from one server to another.
- Control security.

The next section will explain the basics of working with Folders view. The remaining views are more specialized, and for that reason, their descriptions appear later in this book (although you've already seen some examples using Remote Web Site view).

For more information about Remote Web Site view, refer to "Publishing Your Web Site," on page 120.
For more information about Navigation view and Link Bars components, refer to "Using Link Bars with Navigation View," on page 348.
For more information about Hyperlinks view, refer to "Using Hyperlinks View," on page 467.
For more information about Tasks view, refer to "Working with Tasks View," on page 1015.

Working with Folders View

Folders view provides a representation, strongly resembling Windows Explorer, that displays the files and folders in a Web site. It also displays properties such as file date and file size. Figure 6-20 shows an example of Folders view. Notice the Title column, which isn't present in Windows Explorer.

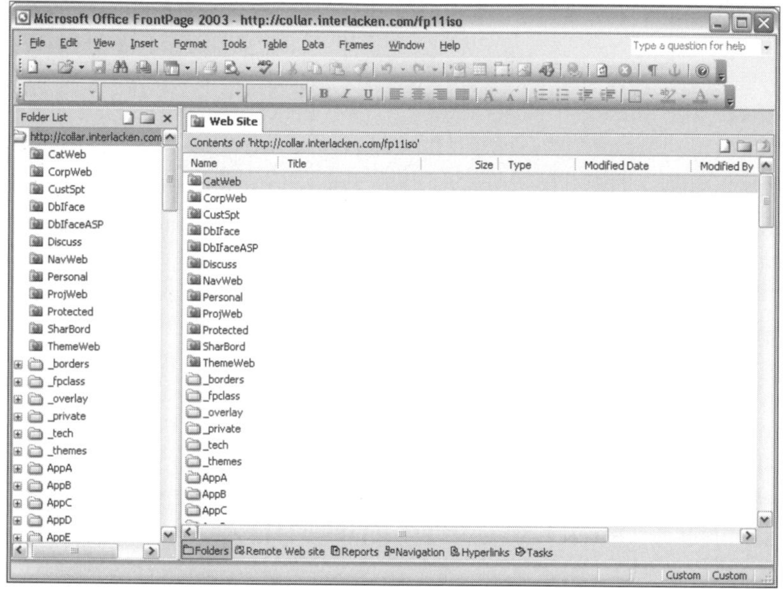

Figure 6-20. FrontPage's Folders view gives a graphical view of the files and folders that make up a FrontPage-based Web site.

This view provides a way to view or manage the physical arrangement of files and folders that make up your Web site. It supports all the cut, copy, paste, and drag features that the Folder List provides. The difference is in the display: Folders view presents a tabular view of one folder at a time. To display the contents of a specific folder, either select it in the Folder List or double-click it in the Folders view window.

Double-clicking individual Web pages opens them in Design view, and double-clicking a picture file opens your default picture editor.

> **Tip** You can maintain the list of available editors by choosing Options from the Tools menu and clicking the Configure Editors tab in the Options dialog box.

To sort the Folders view listing on any column, click its column heading. Repeatedly clicking the same column heading switches between ascending and descending sequence.

Right-clicking a file in Folders view displays a shortcut menu that contains these commands:

- **Check Out** Creates a backup copy of the current file, and then locks the file so that no other designer can change it. Later, you can change the file, revert to the backup copy, or use a Check-In command to relinquish control. This command is present only for Windows SharePoint Sites and for FrontPage-extended Web sites with the Document Check-In And Check Out feature in effect.

For more information about document check-in and checkout, refer to "Using Document Check-In and Check-Out," on page 1023.

- **Open** Opens the file in Design view, or another program appropriate to the file type.
- **Open With** Opens the file with another editor of your choice.
- **Open In New Window** Opens the file in a completely new FrontPage window.
- **New From Existing Page** Opens a new file initialized with the contents of the current file. The Save command doesn't default to the current file name.
- **Preview In Browser** Starts your browser if necessary and then tells it to display the file you right-clicked.
- **Preview In Multiple Browsers** Displays the current page in each browser installed on your computer.
- **Cut** Moves any selected files or folders to the Clipboard and adds a Paste option for storing them elsewhere. After pasting, the original file or folders disappear.
- **Copy** Like Cut, moves the selected files or folders to the Clipboard and adds a Paste option. However, the original files or folders is retained after pasting.

Tip When you move or rename a file by any means in FrontPage, FrontPage updates references from other files in the same Web site.

- **Paste** Creates a copy of a file previously moved to the Clipboard.
- **Set As Home Page** Designates the current page as the home page in Navigation view. (Because the home page must reside in your Web site's root folder, this command is unavailable for files in subfolders.)
- **Rename** Selects the file name for editing.
- **Delete** Permanently removes the file. (There's no Undelete.)
- **Publish Selected Files** Displays a dialog box showing a proposed remote web site location. If you click OK, FrontPage will publish the selected files to that location. If you click Cancel, no publishing takes place.

- **Don't Publish** Excludes the currently selected files from any future publishing operations. Use this option when you don't want files at the destination—such as data collection files—to be overlaid with files from the source.
- **Properties** Displays a dialog box showing the object's characteristics and settings.

FrontPage's Folders view supports all the dragging operations you've grown accustomed to in Windows. The difference is that if you move or rename a file in Windows, you have to manually locate each hyperlink from other pages in your site to the moved or renamed one, and you have to update each of these pages manually. When you move or rename a file in FrontPage, FrontPage automatically updates the other pages in your Web site.

Referring again to Figure 6-20, notice the Title column in the right pane. For Web pages, FrontPage obtains this title from the HTML code itself. To update the title of a Web page:

1. Double-click the file name to open the Web page in Design view.
2. Choose Properties from the File menu, and update the Title field on the General tab. Click OK, and save the file.

To update the title of any file, HTML or not, just right-click the file name in the Folder List or Folders view, and choose Properties from the shortcut menu. Update the Title field on the General tab, and click OK. Figure 6-21 illustrates this updating process.

Figure 6-21. Use the Properties command to update the title of any file in your Web site.

To change the comments for any type of file, right-click the file, choose Properties from the shortcut menu, and then select the Summary tab, shown in Figure 6-22. Finish by entering or updating the comments and clicking OK.

Figure 6-22. On the Summary tab of the Properties dialog box, you can modify the Comments field for a FrontPage-based Web site file.

Deleting a FrontPage-Based Web Site

To delete a FrontPage-based Web site:

1. Open the parent Web site (that is, the Web site that contains the Web site you want to delete).
2. In the Folder List, select the Web site you want to delete.
3. Choose Delete from the Edit menu (or right-click the Web site you've selected and choose Delete from the shortcut menu).
4. Click Yes in the resulting Confirm Delete dialog box.

Caution Deleting a FrontPage-based Web site deletes absolutely everything it contains—Web pages, pictures, text files, FrontPage system files, and all folders. If you want to save the Web pages, pictures, and other content, back them up before deleting the Web site.

In Summary…

This chapter explained how to create FrontPage-based Web sites under various circumstances. It also introduced two of the ways of viewing FrontPage-based Web sites: Design view and Folders view.

The next chapter explains how to enter a new site's structure in Navigation view so that FrontPage can create the Web pages automatically.

Part 3

Editing Basic Page Content

Chapter 7

Creating, Opening, Saving, and Deleting Web Pages

Performing basic file operations on Web pages is a mundane but necessary task. Without the ability to save and reopen work, the value of your efforts would be fleeting indeed.

File operations in Microsoft Office FrontPage 2003 parallel those in most other Microsoft Windows applications, and especially those of other Microsoft Office applications. Still, with their ability to read and open Web pages over the Internet, to create new preformatted Web pages, to save and manipulate files in FrontPage-based Web sites, and to detect and save unsaved Web page components, the basic FrontPage file features are worth a look.

This chapter doesn't address filling new Web pages with content. For that, skip ahead to the next chapter.

Creating a New Web Page

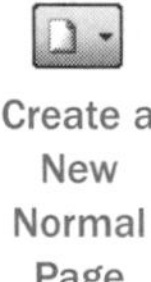

Create a New Normal Page

If you can click a button, you can create a new Web page. All you need to do is start FrontPage and click the Create A New Normal Page button on the Standard toolbar. FrontPage displays a blank Web page ready for text, pictures, or anything else you care to toss in. Figure 7-1 illustrates the default, blank Web page, ready for input.

Clicking the Create A New Normal Page toolbar button is far from the only way to create new Web pages. Here's the complete list:

- **Use the Create A New Normal Page button on the Standard toolbar.** This is the method just described. It always creates an empty Web page.
- **Use the keyboard. Press Ctrl+N.** This works exactly like clicking the Create A New Normal Page button on the Standard toolbar.
- **Use the right mouse button.** This creates a new page in any view except Tasks or Reports view. Here are the steps:
  1. Right-click a folder icon or a blank space in any folder or file list.
  2. Choose New from the shortcut menu, and then Blank Page from the resulting submenu. This method always creates a normal, empty Web page.

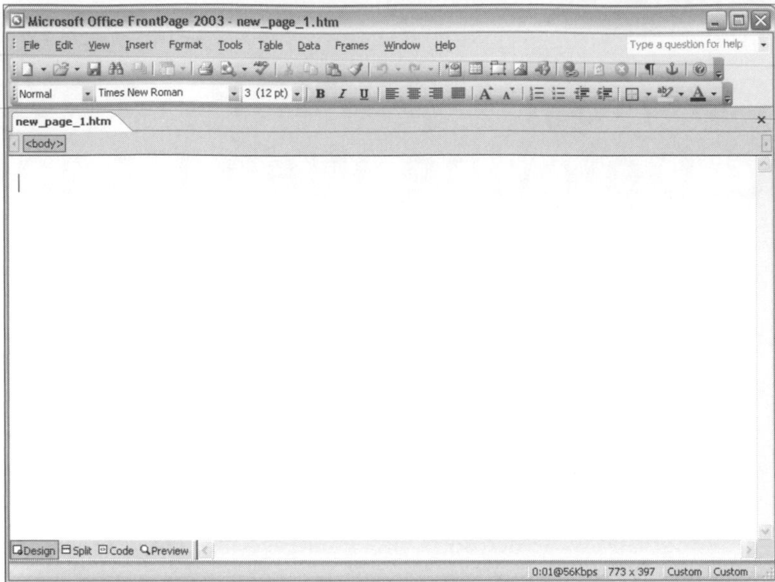

Figure 7-1. FrontPage presents a new, blank Web page, ready for content.

- **Use the New task pane.** This creates a blank page or a way to choose a page template:
  1. Choose New from the File menu. This displays the New task pane shown in Figure 7-2.

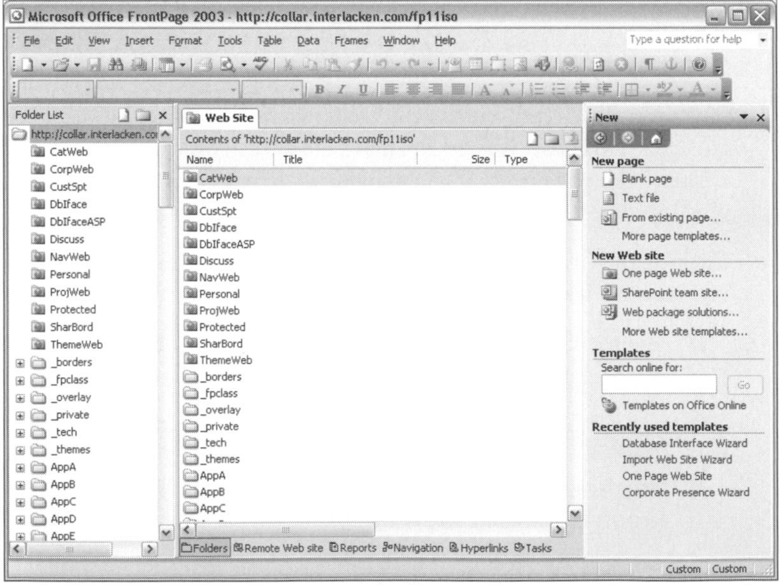

Figure 7-2. Click Blank Page to create a new, empty Web page, and click More Page Templates to display the Page Templates dialog box (shown later, in Figure 7-3).

2 Under New Page, click the Blank Page link to create a new, blank page. Click the More Page Templates link to create a page with preformatted content, a frames page, or a CSS file.

- **On the Standard toolbar, display the Create A New Normal Page button's drop-down menu, and choose Page.** This method creates pages using a variety of page templates, including standard pages with preformatted content, frames pages with various arrangements, and CSS files.

> **Tip** To display one of several pages open in Design view, click the page's tab above the Design view window, choose the page from the Window menu, or press Ctrl+Tab.

- **Click the New Page button in either the Folder List or Folders view.** This method adds a new blank page to the file list.

In all views except Design view (discussed shortly) and Tasks view (where you create new tasks rather than new Web pages), creating a new Web page means creating an HTML file in the current folder, giving the file a default name, and leaving the file name ready for renaming. FrontPage *doesn't* switch to Design view and open the new file; for that, you have to double-click or in some other way open the new file yourself.

> **Tip** Remember, if you haven't opened a Web site, Folders view, Remote Web Site view, Reports view, Navigation view, Hyperlinks view, and Tasks view won't be available.

In Design view, clicking the Create A New Normal Page toolbar button immediately creates and displays a new, blank page. If a blank page isn't what you want, click the New command on either the File menu or the Standard toolbar's Create A New Normal Page drop-down menu. FrontPage then presents the opportunity (or nuisance, depending on your mood) to select page designs from a choice of templates. The dialog box that shows all the available templates appears in Figure 7-3.

The tabs at the top of the left pane divide the templates into the following categories:

- **General** This tab provides a list of currently available page templates. Single-clicking any template selects it, displays its description in the Description area at the right of the dialog box, and displays a visual preview in the Preview area.

  If you don't know which template or wizard to choose, select Normal Page. This produces a blank page with no special features or attributes.

For information about creating your own Web page templates, refer to "Creating Your Own Static Templates," on page 319.

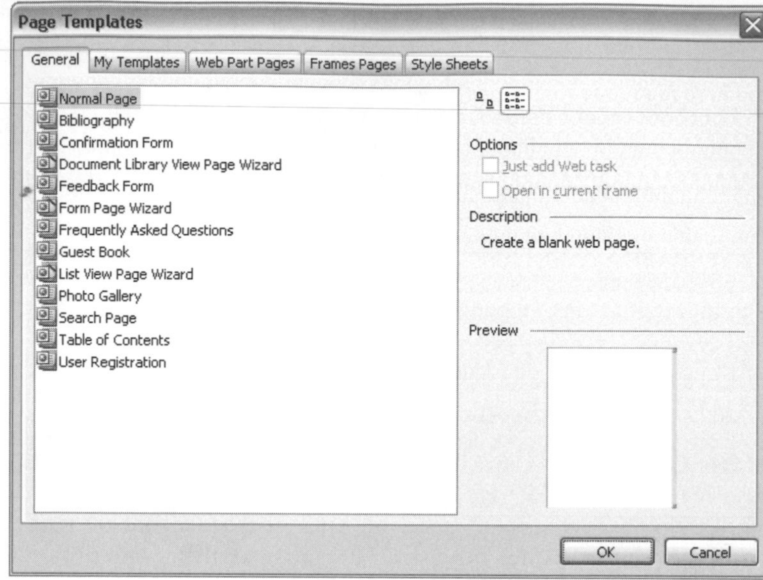

Figure 7-3. The Page Templates dialog box offers a choice of types and formats for initializing new Web pages.

- **My Templates** If you've created any custom templates and saved them in the current Web site, this tab will present them as options. If there are no such templates, this tab won't appear.
- **Web Part Pages** This tab only appears if the current Web site resides on a Web server running Windows SharePoint Services. In that case, it displays a list of page arrangements that can display Web Parts. (A Web Part is an independent unit of content that a designer or programmer creates without knowing exactly which page might display it.)

For more information about Web Parts and Web Part Pages, refer to Chapter 37, "Using SharePoint Team Sites."

- **Frames Pages** This tab works much like the General tab, except that the listed templates create frames pages.

For information about frames pages, refer to Chapter 15, "Creating Web Sites with Frames."

- **Style Sheets** This tab initializes a CSS file. Such files have a .css file extension and contain instructions for overriding the appearance of standard HTML elements such as normal paragraph, heading 1, table heading, and table cell. CSS files can also define custom styles. Any number of Web pages can reference the same CSS file and thus assume a common appearance.

For more information about style sheet files, refer to Chapter 21, "Managing Appearance with Cascading Style Sheets."

Other useful options appear on the right side of the Page Templates dialog box:

- **Large Icons and List buttons** Located above the Options area, these change the format of the main selection window. Figure 7-3 illustrates the List option.
- **Just Add Web Task option** This adds a task to the Tasks list rather than initializing a new page in Design view.
- **Open In Current Frame option** This is available only if the active document in Design view is a frames page. Ignore this for now.

It's important to note that creating a new page in Design view *doesn't* create an physical file. It creates only an unsaved file, open for editing. To create the actual file, you must save it.

> **Caution** If you create a new page in Design view and then close it without making any changes, FrontPage won't ask whether you want to save it. To save a new, empty page, choose either Save or Save As from the File menu.

Opening an Existing Web page

You can open a Web page for editing in many ways, which vary somewhat depending on the view you're using. The following sections detail your options for each view.

Opening a Page (General Procedure)

Each of the following actions opens a page in Design view. They all require that the FrontPage-based Web site that contains the page already be open, and they work in any view except Tasks view.

- Double-click the file name or icon of the page you want to open.
- Right-click the file name or icon of the page you want to open, and then choose Open from the shortcut menu.
- Select the file name or icon of the page you want to open, and then press Enter.
- Double-click a file icon in Navigation view, or select the icon and then press Enter. (If the Navigation view icon refers to a page outside the current Web site, this action displays the Edit Hyperlink dialog box.)

The following ways of opening an existing page for editing work even if no Web site is currently open in FrontPage.

- Choose Recent Files from the File menu. This displays a submenu of your most recently opened files. To open a specific file, just choose it from the Recent Files submenu.
- In the Open area of the Getting Started task pane, under Pages, click one of the recent files or click the More link.

  To display the Getting Started task pane, press Ctrl+F1. If some other task pane appears, click the task pane's drop-down arrow, and select Getting Started.

Caution You can't open a Web page by dragging it out of the Folder List or the Navigation Pane and dropping it onto an open Web page in Design view. That operation does something else: it modifies the open page by adding a hyperlink to the page you dragged.

- Use the Open File dialog box, shown in Figure 7-4. There are three ways to do this:
  - Choose Open from the File menu.
  - Press Ctrl+O.
  - Click the Open button on the Standard toolbar.

Open

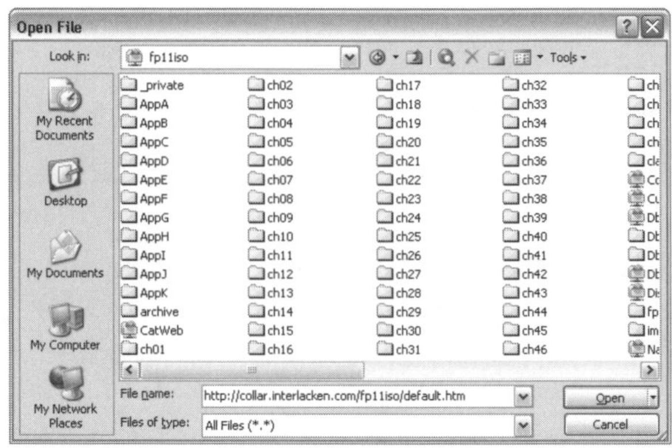

Figure 7-4. The FrontPage Open File dialog box accepts either a local file location or the URL of a page on the Web site.

The icons along the left edge of the Open File dialog box provide the usual five ways to locate a Web page. No matter which place you choose to browse, selecting a file name enters it in the File Name box at the bottom center of the dialog box. The file name can be either a file location, such as C:\Documents and Settings\<user-name>\My Documents\My Web Sites\mypage.htm, or a Web site location, such as *http://www.interlacken.com/default.htm*. FrontPage opens file locations as Windows applications have been doing for years. It opens Web site locations by reading the necessary files over the network.

Tip Don't forget the prefix *http://* when you enter a Web site location. If you omit it, FrontPage tries to open the URL as if it were a local folder location.

If convenient, you can also enter file locations and Web site locations by hand (that is, by typing or pasting them into the File Name box). In any event, when the file name is entered, the Open button becomes active, and clicking Open tells FrontPage to open the file.

The Files Of Type drop-down menu works as in most Windows Open dialog boxes: It controls which filename extensions appear in the file listing. Table A-15 in Appendix A describes the remaining icons in the Open File dialog box toolbar.

Opening a Page from Design View

If you're starting from Design view, the following additional procedures will open a Web page:

- Right-click a hyperlink in a page that's already open, and then choose Follow Hyperlink from the shortcut menu.
- Ctrl+click a hyperlink in a page that's already open.

Opening a Page in a New Window

FrontPage normally creates one main window for each Web site that you open. If you open several Web pages in the same Web site, the pages are identified by tabs that appear along the top edge of the Design view window. Figure 7-5 illustrates this arrangement.

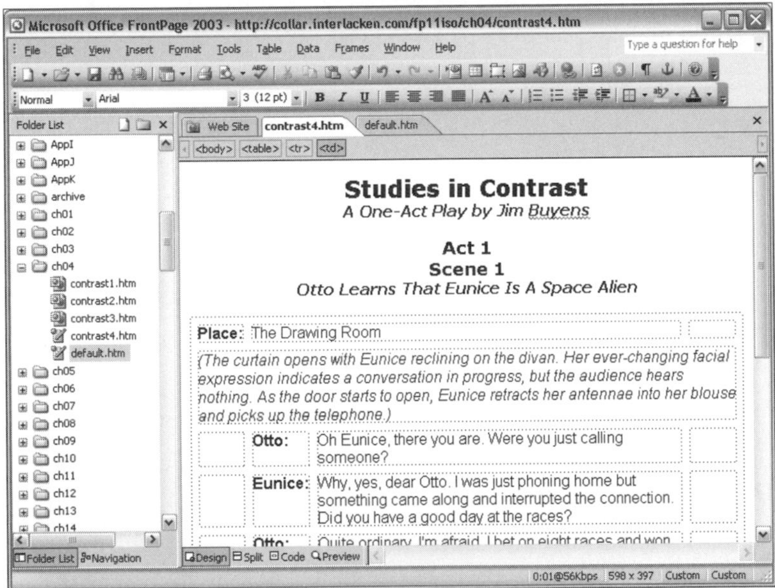

Figure 7-5. Two Web pages are open in this screen shot, but only one page is visible. To display either page, click the corresponding tab at the top of the document area.

To open multiple pages in the same Web site and display them in separate main windows, follow this procedure:

1. Open the first file normally.
2. Open the second file by right-clicking it in the Folder List or in Folders view and then choosing Open In New Window from the shortcut menu.

or this one:

1. Open the Web site that contains the two pages you want to open.

2 Create a new window by choosing New Window from the Window menu.

3 Open one page in each window.

Figure 7-6 shows the results from either procedure.

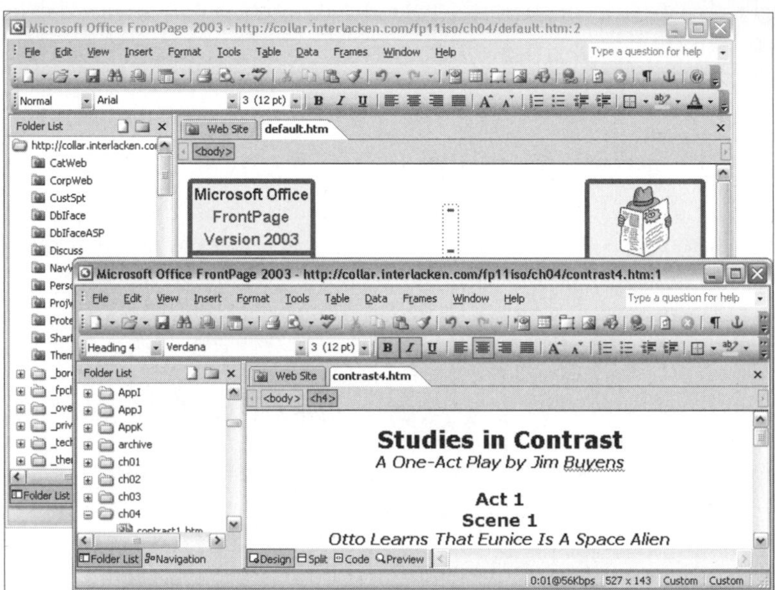

Figure 7-6. If you prefer, FrontPage can open pages from the same Web site in different windows.

Opening a Page from Tasks View

Because Tasks view displays tasks, not Web site files, the procedure for opening a file is unique. Do either of the following:

- Right-click a task that references the page, and then choose Start Task from the shortcut menu.
- Select a task that references the page, point to Tasks on the Edit menu, and then choose Start Task.

For more information about Tasks view, refer to "Working with Tasks View," on page 1015.

Opening a Copy of a Page

Consistency among pages in the same Web site is a beautiful thing. Many designers almost never create a new page from scratch. Instead, they open an existing page that has the appearance they want, modify it, and then save it under a new name. Unfortunately, this approach has a common pitfall: mistakenly using the Save command rather than Save As the first time the designer saves the page.

To avoid this situation, right-click the existing file in the Folder List, in Folders view, or in Reports view, and then choose New From Existing Page on the shortcut menu. This initializes a new page with the content of the existing page. The new page will have a default name of New_Page_1.htm—a name that FrontPage will prompt you to change the first time you save the page.

Saving Pages

Save

If you fail to regularly save your files, all your hard work could be for naught. To save a file that's open in Design view, choose Save from the File menu, click the Save button on the Standard toolbar, or press Ctrl+S.

If no one has previously saved the Web page or any of its components in the current Web site, FrontPage displays Save As dialog boxes for them.

To save a page using another name, choose Save As from the File menu. The resulting dialog box is almost the same at the one that opens Web pages, with all the same options plus two:

- **Page Title** Displays the name of the page in words. Although this is an optional field, for optimal user-friendliness, don't omit it. A page's title appears whenever a Web site visitor browses the page, and in many FrontPage contexts.
- **Change Title** Displays the page title in a Set Page Title dialog box so that you can change it. Click the Change Title button to display the dialog box. Figure 7-7 shows this facility in action.

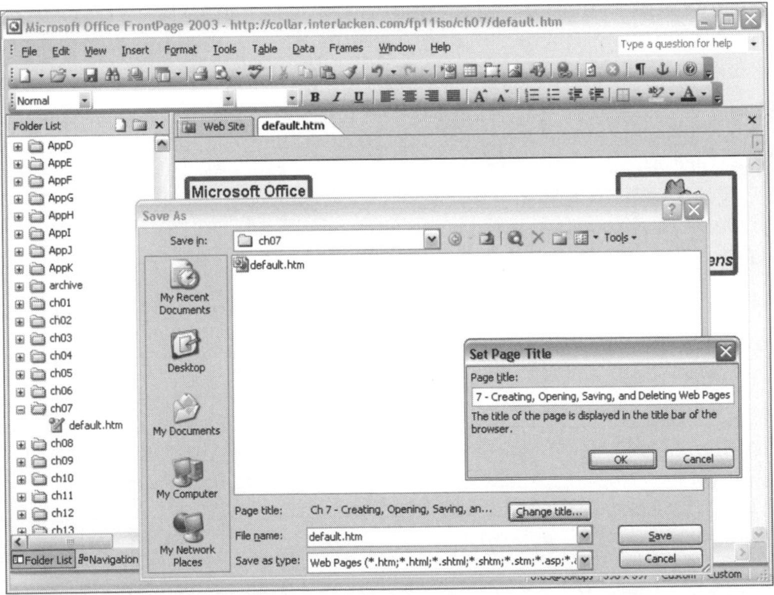

Figure 7-7. This is FrontPage's Save As dialog box, with the Set Page Title dialog box also open.

As when opening files, the File Name location can be either on a local disk or file server or within a FrontPage-based Web site. If the specified Web site isn't already open, FrontPage opens it.

Occasionally, when you save a Web page, FrontPage displays a Save Embedded Files dialog box like the one in Figure 7-8.

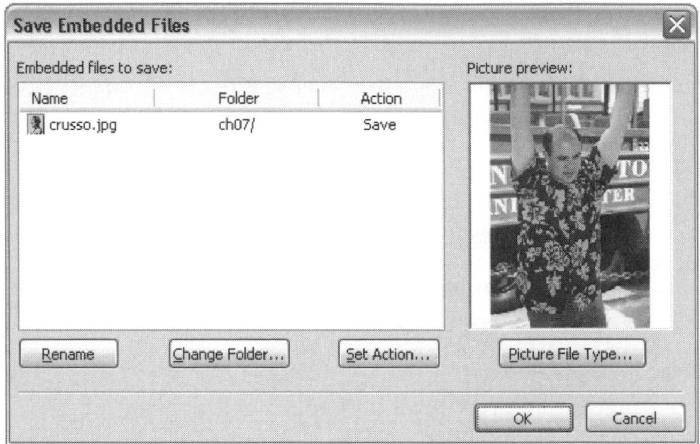

Figure 7-8. When Design view saves a Web page containing elements held only in memory, it displays this dialog box asking what to do with them.

This means that Design view has an object in memory—in this case, a picture pasted from the Clipboard—and FrontPage doesn't know where to save it. This also happens after using some of FrontPage's picture processing tools. The original picture might reside on disk but the modified version doesn't; FrontPage therefore has to ask where to put modified version.

For more information about FrontPage's picture processing tools, refer to Chapter 23, "Editing Pictures in FrontPage."

To change the proposed Save properties for any file listed, first select the file, and then do any or all of the following:

- To change the file name, click the Rename button, and edit the proposed name.
- To change the folder location of the saved file, click the Change Folder button, and select a folder from the resulting dialog box.

> **Tip** If a file's Folder column is blank, FrontPage saves the file in the same folder as the Web page itself.

- To change the action for the given file, click the Set Action button, and select either Save This File or Don't Save This File from the resulting Set Action dialog box.
- To change the picture file type—for example, from GIF to JPEG—click the Picture File Type button. This displays (what else?) a Picture File Type dialog box where you can specify the picture type and other settings you want.

Deleting an Existing Web page

Sooner or later, everybody has to carry out the garbage. Along with the successful pages you create and add to your Web site will be the inevitable failed experiments, schemes gone awry, and pages gone obsolete over time. There are three ways to delete a page; however, you must be in Folders view, Reports view, Navigation view, or Hyperlinks view to use any of them. Here are the three techniques:

- Select the file name or icon by single-clicking it, and then press Delete.
- Select the file name or icon, and then choose Delete from the Edit menu.
- Right-click the file name or icon, and then choose Delete from the shortcut menu.

In each case, FrontPage will ask you to confirm the deletion before it erases the page.

Saving and Opening Files in Microsoft SharePoint Team Sites

If, in any Microsoft Office file-oriented dialog box. you specify an http:// path that points to a SharePoint Team Site, you can open and save documents in the SharePoint Team Site's shared document areas quite easily. Simply save them or look for them in the Web site's Shared Documents folder. Figure 7-9 shows how the Open File dialog box displays a shared document library in a SharePoint Team Site. Because the publicity file (as indicated by its icon) was created in FrontPage, it opens in FrontPage. The other files open in the applications that created them.

For more information about SharePoint Team Sites, refer to Chapter 37, "Using SharePoint Team Sites."

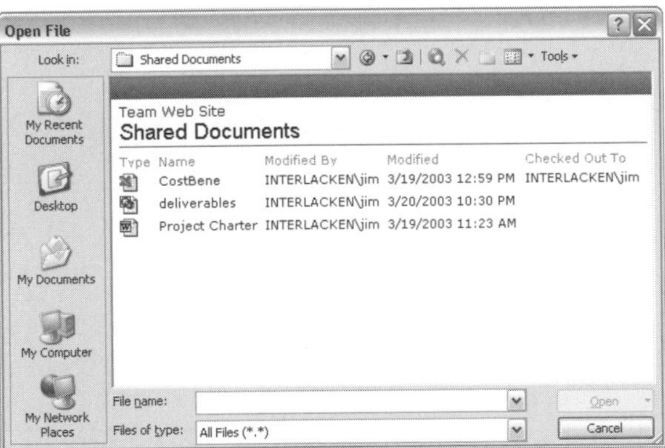

Figure 7-9. Microsoft Office file-oriented dialog boxes can directly access the shared libraries of a SharePoint Team Site.

The Save As dialog box provides a similar interface for saving files in a shared document library. With either technique, be aware that you must open the library (that is, double-click it) before you can view or update its documents.

Displaying the SharePoint Team Site View

When you use an Open File or a Save As dialog box to access a SharePoint Team Site, the dialog box might display the Team Site's normal file structure by default.

To see the SharePoint Team Site view, click the Views drop-down arrow on either the Open File or Save As dialog box toolbar, and choose WebView.

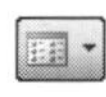
Views

Alternatively, click the Views button repeatedly until the dialog box displays the view you want.

In Summary…

This chapter explained how to create, open, save, and delete Web pages, and explained the special features available when working with SharePoint Team site libraries.

The next chapter is one of several concerned with adding content to Web pages. It devotes itself particularly to entering and formatting text.

Chapter 8

Adding and Formatting Text

This chapter explains how to add text to a Web page. At one level, this is a very simple task: Just create a new Web page and start typing. Of course, the task becomes more complex when you start pasting text from other programs, formatting text with different fonts and paragraph styles, and inserting symbols and special text elements. This chapter addresses those issues as well. Given that most Web pages consist mainly of text, this is an important chapter.

What you won't find here are instructions on page layout. For that, refer to "Defining Your Site's Style," on page 129, and Part 6, "Formatting Your Web Pages."

Word Processing Conventions Used in FrontPage

Entering text in Microsoft FrontPage is very much like typing into a word processor. Follow these steps in Design view:

1. Set the insertion point on the page by clicking the desired spot. The insertion point will jump to the nearest location where text can appear.
2. Start typing.

> **Tip** FrontPage accepts input like a word processor, and not like some picture editing and publishing programs. You can't just click in the middle of some white space and locate objects there.

To end a paragraph and start another, press Enter. To begin a new line within the same paragraph, press Shift+Enter.

Copying and Pasting Text

You cut, copy, paste, and delete work in standard fashion, as shown in Table 8-1. In addition, you can drag selected text anywhere on the page that text can normally appear. Simply dragging text moves it, and holding down the Ctrl key and dragging copies it.

Table 8-1. Copying, Moving, and Deleting Text

Operation	Preparation	Standard toolbar	Menu command	Keystroke	Drag and Drop
Cut	Select source text		Edit/Cut	Press Ctrl+X or Shift+Delete	N/A
Move	Select source text		Edit/Cut, set insertion point, Edit/ Paste	Press Ctrl+X, move insertion point, and press Ctrl+V	Drag to new location
Copy	Select source		Edit/Copy	Press Ctrl+C or Ctrl+Insert	Hold down the Ctrl key and drag to additional location
Paste	Set insertion point		Edit/Paste	Press Ctrl+V or Shift+Insert	N/A
Paste Special	Set insertion point		Edit/Paste Special	N/A	N/A
Clear	Select source text		Edit/Delete	Press Delete	N/A

Paste Options

When you paste text directly into FrontPage, FrontPage normally does its best to preserve all formatting that was present when you copied the same text. To override this behavior, look for a Paste Options button below newly pasted content and open its drop-down menu. Figure 8-1 shows the options this reveals after pasting a highly formatted Microsoft Word table into FrontPage.

The following Paste Options are available:

- **Use Destination Styles.** Formats the pasted text with styles in effect in the destination document.
- **Keep Source Formatting.** Formats the pasted text with styles that were in effect in the source document.
- **Keep Text Only.** Removes all formatting—including table cell divisions—from the pasted text.

Depending on the circumstances, other options might appear. If you're not sure which option to select, try each of them. The Paste Options button won't disappear until you start working on another part of the Web page.

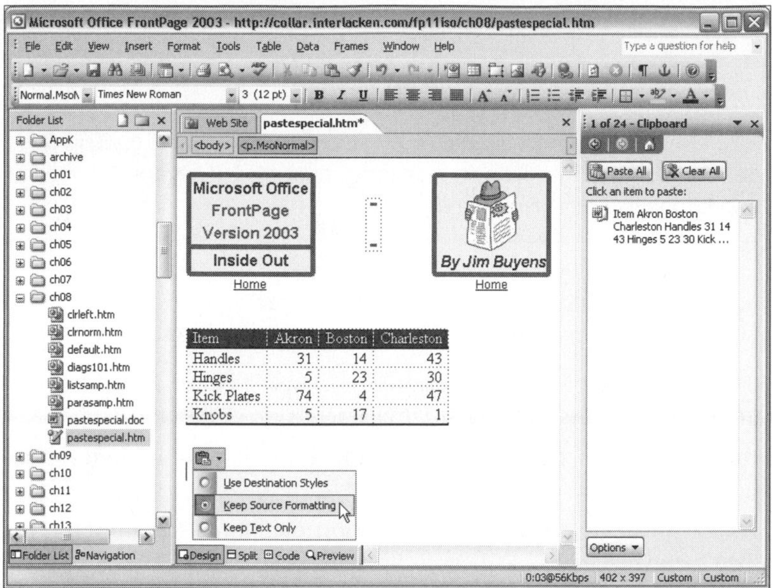

Figure 8-1. To change the format of something you've just pasted into Design view, open the drop-down menu on the Paste Options button.

The FrontPage Paste Special command can paste text in the four special formats described in Table 8-2 or as HTML.

Table 8-2. Paste Special Options

Command	Result of Pasting:			
	Paragraph endings	**Line breaks**	**Paragraph style**	**Font**
One Formatted Paragraph	Line breaks	Line breaks	Formatted <pre>	Monospaced
Formatted Paragraphs	Line breaks	Line breaks	Formatted <pre>	Monospaced
Normal Paragraphs	Space	Space	Normal <p>	Proportional
Normal Paragraphs With Line Breaks	Line breaks	Line breaks	Normal <p>	Proportional

Inside Out

Two For One!

The One Formatted Paragraph option and the Formatted Paragraphs option appear to produce identical results. This behavior has persisted through several versions of FrontPage and remains somewhat of a mystery.

When pasting text, the Paste Special options first remove all typographical formatting such as boldface, italics, underlining, font, and font size and then apply one of these paragraph styles:

- **Formatted** This style displays text in a monospaced font—usually a form of Courier—and honors all white-space characters present in the data.

  A white-space character is any character that's invisible but occupies space. This includes spaces, tabs, carriage returns, and linefeeds.
- **Normal** This style displays text in a proportional font—usually a form of Times Roman—and displays all sequences of white-space characters as if the data contained one space.

In addition, the Paste Special command can paste paragraph endings either as paragraph endings (no surprise there!) or as line breaks. The difference is that most browsers display a blank line after each paragraph ending, but not after a line break.

The Paste Special command can also paste HTML code directly into your page. This is quite useful if someone sends you a piece of HTML that does some special job. Follow this procedure to insert such HTML:

1. Open the file that contains the HTML code in Microsoft Notepad or another text editor.
2. Select and copy the HTML code.
3. In FrontPage, open the Web page that should contain the special HTML.
4. Set the insertion point where you want the HTML to appear.
5. Choose Paste Special from the Edit menu.
6. In the Convert Text dialog box, choose Do Not Convert, and click OK.

Using the Office Clipboard

The Clipboard task pane, shown in Figure 8-1, displays up to 24 items copied onto the Clipboard from various applications.

- To show the Clipboard task pane, choose Office Clipboard from the Edit menu, or choose Clipboard from the drop-down menu at the top of any other task pane.
- To paste any item in the Clipboard, either:
  - Click it.

- Move the mouse pointer over its right edge, click the shaded arrow to display a drop-down menu like the one below, and then choose Paste.

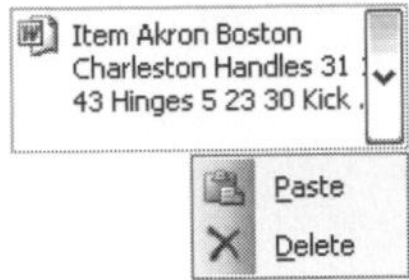

- To delete an item from the Clipboard task pane, display the drop-down menu, and choose Delete.

The Clipboard task pane also contains these buttons:

- **Paste All** Pastes all items in the Office Clipboard into the current document.
- **Clear All** Removes everything from the Office Clipboard.
- **Options** Displays a drop-down menu that controls Office clipboard settings.

The Options button provides access to the following settings. The first three of these affect global settings for all Office programs

- **Show Office Clipboard Automatically.** If this option is selected, the Office Clipboard automatically appears whenever one of the following occurs:
  - You copy or cut two different items consecutively in the same program.
  - You copy one item, paste the item, and then copy another item in the same program.
  - You copy one item twice in succession.
- **Show Office Clipboard When Ctrl+C Pressed Twice.** With this option in effect, the Office Clipboard automatically appears when you copy the same item twice in succession.
- **Collect Without Showing Office Clipboard.** If this option is selected, all cut and copy operations update the Office Clipboard even if it isn't displayed. If this option is cleared, cut and copy operations don't update the Office Clipboard unless it's visible.
- **Show Office Clipboard Icon On Taskbar.** If this option is selected, displaying the Office Clipboard in FrontPage also displays the Office Clipboard icon in the tray area on the Microsoft Windows task bar.

  The icon in the Microsoft Windows tray appears as shown below whenever at least one active Microsoft Office program is displaying the Office Clipboard task pane. If another Office application occupies the foreground and isn't displaying the Office Clipboard task pane, clicking the Windows tray icon causes it to do so.

  9 of 24 - Clipboard
  10:05 PM

- **Show Status Near Taskbar When Copying.** If this option is selected, the message *Item collected* appears under the Clipboard counter whenever a Clipboard operation is in progress.

The Office Clipboard and the normal Windows Clipboard are two separate facilities. Here's how they're related:

- When you copy multiple items to the Office Clipboard, the Windows Clipboard always contains the last item you copied.
- Any content you paste from the Office Clipboard appears not only in the document, but also on the Windows Clipboard.
- Clearing the Office Clipboard clears the Windows Clipboard as well.
- When you use the Paste command, the Paste button, or the shortcut keys (Ctrl+V), you paste the contents of the Windows Clipboard, not the Office Clipboard.

Selecting Text

Table 8-3 lists the procedures for selecting text. These are the same procedures that most other Office programs use.

Table 8-3. Text Selection Procedures

Operation	Procedures
Select range	Do one of the following: · Drag the mouse pointer across the range. · From the insertion point, hold down Shift and click at the end of the range. · Hold down Shift and use the arrow keys to highlight the desired selection.
Select word	Double-click the word.
Select paragraph	Hold down Alt and click anywhere in the paragraph.
Select entire document	Choose Select All from the Edit menu, or press Ctrl+A.

Table 8-4 lists the keyboard commands for changing the insertion point. Again, these are much the same as the procedures in any word processor. Holding down Shift while changing the insertion point extends the current selection.

Table 8-4. Keyboard Commands for Changing the Insertion Point

Operation	Key Combination
Move one character right or left	Right Arrow or Left Arrow
Move one word right or left	Ctrl+Right Arrow or Ctrl+Left Arrow
Move to start of line	Home
Move to end of line	End
Move up or down one line	Up Arrow or Down Arrow

Table 8-4. Keyboard Commands for Changing the Insertion Point

Operation	Key Combination
Move to beginning or end of current paragraph	Ctrl+Up Arrow or Ctrl+Down Arrow
Move up or down one paragraph	Ctrl+Up Arrow or Ctrl+Down Arrow from beginning or end of paragraph
Move to top of Web page	Ctrl+Home
Move to bottom of Web page	Ctrl+End

Importing Text

FrontPage is remarkably capable at accepting whole files or selected portions—in almost any format—and converting them to HTML. To add such content to a Web page, open the page in FrontPage, and take the following actions:

- To insert an entire file by dragging it, locate the file's icon in Windows Explorer and drag it to the desired location in Design view.
- To insert an entire file using commands:
  1. Set the insertion point where you want the file to appear in FrontPage.
  2. Choose File from the Insert menu, and locate the file you want to insert.
  3. Double-click the file name, or select it and click the Open button.
- To insert less than an entire file by dragging: Open the file in its normal application, select the desired content, and then drag the selection into FrontPage Design view.
- To insert part of a file using commands:
  1. Open the file in its normal application.
  2. Select the desired content, and copy the selection to the Clipboard.
  3. In FrontPage Design view, set the insertion point where you want the content to appear, then choose Paste from the Edit menu or press Ctrl+V.

Frequently Asked Question

How does FrontPage interpret pasted text and pictures?

When asked to incorporate content that isn't in HTML format, FrontPage first determines whether the data is character-based or pictorial. If the data is character-based:

- FrontPage consults the table of standard file translators installed on the local computer.
- FrontPage translates the data to Rich Text Format (RTF).
- FrontPage translates the RTF to HTML.

Tabular data, such as a spreadsheet, becomes an HTML table. Other data becomes free-flowing text. FrontPage attempts to retain formatting instructions in the original data.

If the data is pictorial:

- FrontPage converts the data to a Windows bitmap for display.
- When you save your Web page, FrontPage identifies pictures that originated outside the current Web and displays a Save Embedded Files dialog box listing each one.
- If a picture uses transparency or contains no more than 256 colors, FrontPage saves it, by default, as a GIF file. If the picture contains more than 256 colors and no transparency, it's saved in JPEG format.

For more information about HTML tables, refer to "Creating and Editing Tables," on page 515. For more information about using pictures in Web pages, refer to Chapter 10, "Adding and Formatting Pictures."

Text Conventions Unique to HTML

The preceding section might have convinced you that entering text in FrontPage is no different than using virtually any word processor. This is no accident, and in fact it's a unique strength of FrontPage. Nevertheless, the nature of HTML introduces a number of unique restrictions:

- HTML considers tab characters the same as word spaces. Outside of creating a table, there's no facility for setting "tab stops" to line up text in columns.
- HTML treats all strings of white-space characters as a single space. White-space characters are spaces, tabs, linefeeds, carriage returns, and so forth. FrontPage counteracts this behavior by detecting any repeating spaces you enter and replacing all but the last with nonbreaking spaces (that is, spaces neither FrontPage nor the browser will suppress).
- HTML provides no direct control over first-line indentation, paragraph indentation, line length, or line spacing. (You can, however, control these properties with cascading style sheets.)

Inserting Special Text Elements

The Insert menu in FrontPage can add four kinds of special text elements: line breaks, horizontal lines, symbols, and comments.

Inserting a Line Break

Choosing Break from the Insert menu displays the dialog box shown in Figure 8.2.

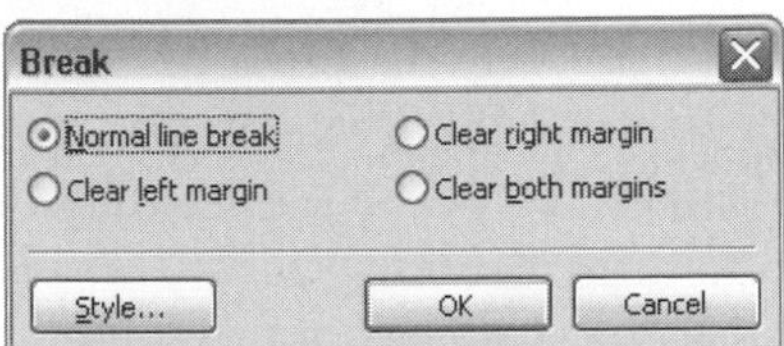

Figure 8-2. The Break dialog box inserts a line break at the current insertion point. Clearing a margin means resuming text flow just beyond any non-text objects aligned at that margin.

This dialog box inserts four kinds of line breaks:

- **Normal Line Break** This is an ordinary line break, just as you would create by pressing Shift+Enter. Text resumes flowing normally exactly one line below the line containing the break.
- **Clear Left Margin** If this break occurs in text flowing around a picture or other object aligned at the left margin, text following the break will start flowing immediately below that object.
- **Clear Right Margin** If this break occurs in text flowing around an object aligned at the right margin, text following the break will start flowing immediately below that object.
- **Clear Both Margins** If this break occurs in text flowing around objects aligned at either or both margins, text following the break will start flowing immediately below them.

For more information about using pictures in Web pages, refer to Chapter 10, "Adding and Formatting Pictures."

Clicking the Style button in the lower left corner of the dialog box displays FrontPage's Modify Style dialog box, discussed in Chapter 20. Any CSS properties you specify will apply to the current line break.

For more information about CSS, refer to Chapter 21, "Managing Appearance with Cascading Style Sheets."

Figure 8-3 shows a Normal line break.

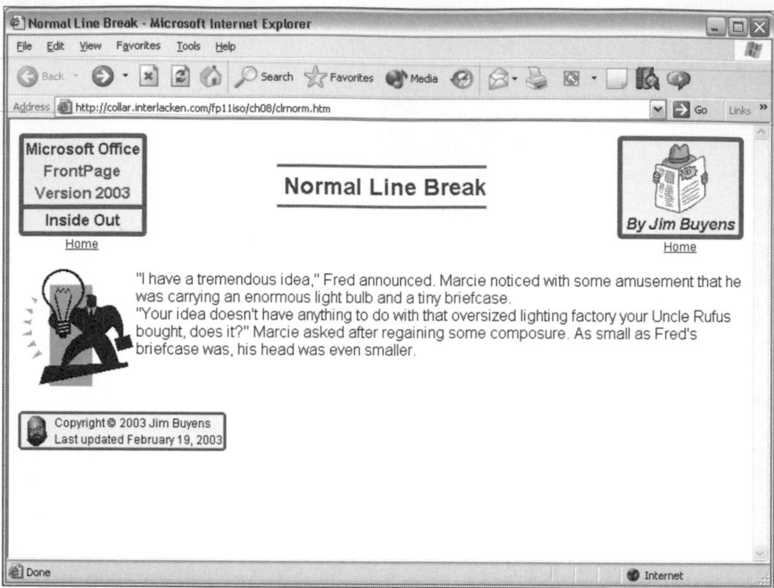

Figure 8-3. This page illustrates a Normal line break after the words *tiny briefcase*.

Figure 8-4 shows a Clear Left Margin break for clearing an object on the left margin.

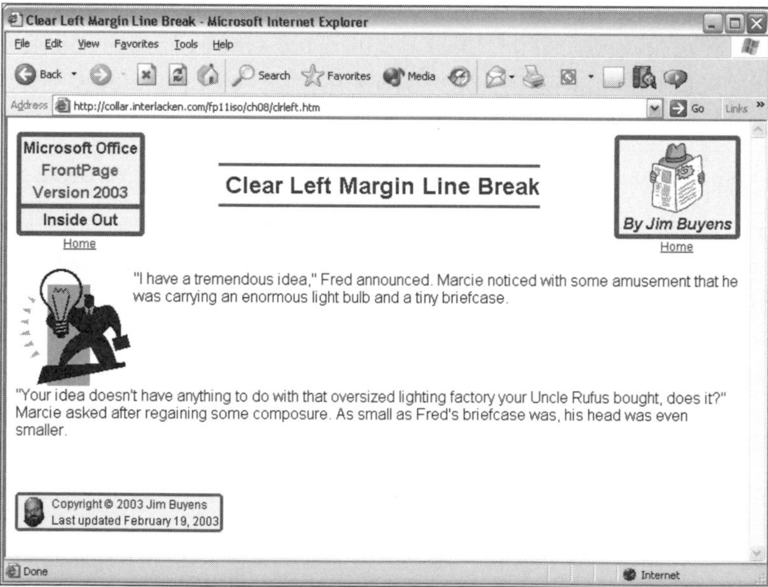

Figure 8-4. Text following a Clear Left Margin line break jumps around any object on its left and resumes flowing at the true left margin below the object.

Frequently Asked Question

Is there any way to make the browser display two or more spaces in a row?

By design, browsers compress all strings of white-space characters down to a single space before displaying them. This means there's no way, in HTML, to provide extra word spacing by adding extra spaces. If you really want to insert extra spaces—for instance, to align program code or to provide extra word spacing—you have several options:

- Use the Formatted paragraph style, which provides an exception to HTML's normal handling of white space. FrontPage uses the HTML <pre> tag to format paragraphs assigned this style. The <pre> tag displays content in an unattractive monospaced font but with all spaces and carriage returns honored, as if you were using a typewriter. You can't, however, use heading levels or other elements within a Formatted style paragraph, and you should avoid tabs because different browsers might assign different numbers of spaces to them. But if you don't mind the monospaced font, if you stick to using spaces rather than tabs, and if you want to control the alignment of each character on a line, the Formatted style might be acceptable.
- HTML provides a special, *nonbreaking space* character that browsers don't compress. A nonbreaking space appears in HTML code as the string * *. Every time a browser sees this code, it displays a space, no matter how many appear consecutively. There are three ways to enter nonbreaking spaces in FrontPage:
    - When you type multiple spaces in FrontPage, FrontPage inserts nonbreaking spaces rather than ordinary spaces for all but the last of them.
    - When you're entering text, FrontPage treats pressing Tab the same as pressing Spacebar four times.
    - When you want to insert nonbreaking spaces one at a time, press Ctrl+Shift+Spacebar.

Despite the presence of these features, spacing text or other objects by using multiple space characters still constitutes bad style. Repeating spaces will seldom produce the results you want, given HTML's use of proportional fonts, variable page width, and automatic line wrapping.

The practice of inserting two spaces between each pair of sentences is a carryover from the days of typewriters when, because of monospaced fonts, letter spacing within words tended to be wide. Nowadays, with proportional fonts, letter spacing is narrower, and one space provides plenty of separation between sentences.

Inserting Horizontal Lines

HTML provides a special horizontal line object that's often useful for breaking pages or other blocks of content into sections. The horizontal line forces line breaks before and after itself and normally occupies the entire width of its container (typically the browser window or a table cell). Figure 8-3 and Figure 8-4 each contain two horizontal lines, one just above and one just below the page titles Normal Line Break and Clear Left Margin Line Break. In each case, the horizontal lines fill the width of a table cell.

For more information about HTML tables, refer to "Creating and Editing Tables," on page 515.

To insert a horizontal line, set the insertion point where you want the horizontal line to appear, and choose Horizontal Line from the Insert menu.

To modify the properties of a horizontal line, right-click it, and choose Horizontal Line Properties from the shortcut menu. This will display the Horizontal Line Properties dialog box, shown in Figure 8-5.

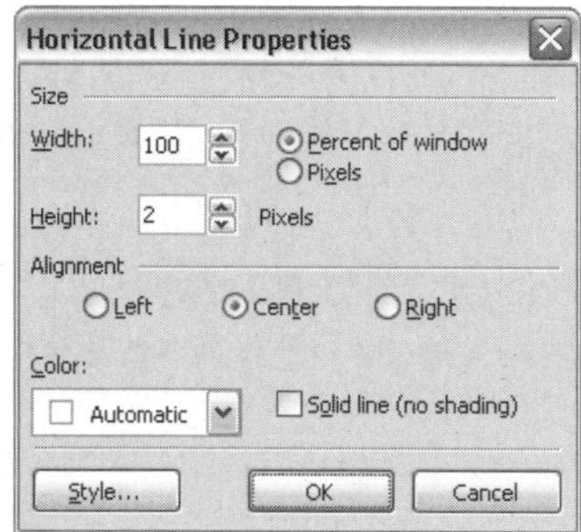

Figure 8-5. This dialog box sets the properties of a horizontal line.

The options in this dialog box work as follows:

- **Width** Specifies the width of the horizontal line in pixels or as a percentage of the available display width. The default is 100 percent.
- **Height** Specifies the height or thickness of the line in pixels. The default is 2 pixels.
- **Alignment** Sets the line's alignment to the left, to the right, or in the center.
- **Color** Selects the line's color.

For more information about using FrontPage color dialog boxes, refer to "Using FrontPage Color Dialog Boxes," on page 509.

- **Solid Line (No Shading)** Eliminates the normal three-dimensional effect along the edges of the line.
- **Style** Opens the Modify Style dialog box, where you can select any applicable CSS properties for the horizontal line.

Inserting Symbols

You can easily insert special characters—those that don't appear on your keyboard—using the Symbol dialog box, shown in Figure 8-6.

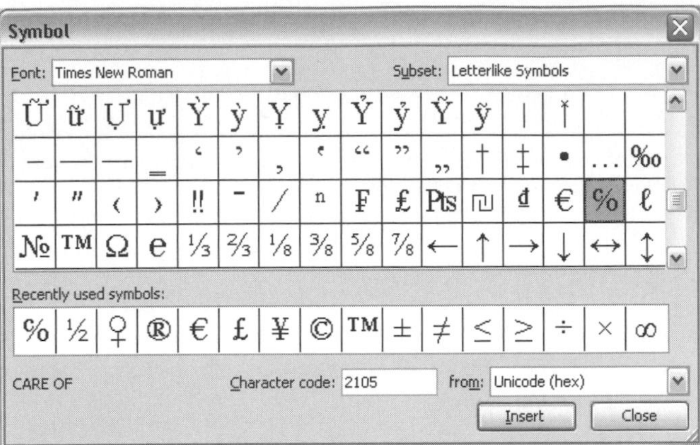

Figure 8-6. To insert characters not on the keyboard, choose Symbol from the Insert menu.

To insert a special character:

1. Set the insertion point where you want to insert the symbol.
2. Choose Symbol from the Insert menu.
3. Double-click the desired character, or select the desired character and click Insert.
4. Close the dialog box.

HTML provides three ways of coding special characters: single-byte characters, name codes, and number codes. Each of the following forms, for example, will display a U.S. cent sign: ¢, *¢ ¢*.

- For most symbols that have a number code between 32 and 255, FrontPage inserts a normal character.
- For symbols between 32 and 255 that have special significance to HTML, FrontPage inserts a name code. When you insert a less than sign, for example, FrontPage actually adds *<* to the HTML.
- For symbols that have a number code of 256 or higher, FrontPage inserts a number code. When you insert a c/o symbol, for example, FrontPage adds *℅* to your HTML. The decimal value 8453 equals the hexadecimal value 2105 that appears in the Character Code box shown in Figure 8-6.

Don't be surprised if you find that a certain browser doesn't display characters with codes of 128 or higher the way you expect. Not all browsers support all name codes, not all browsers support all number codes, and not all versions of the same font contain all the same special characters. If you encounter problems displaying a certain character, try this:

1. Select the problem symbol in Design view.
2. Switch to Code view. You should find that the problem character is still selected.
3. Change the problem symbol's notation. If the character is ¢, for example, try changing it to *¢* or *¢*.

4. Save the page and then, on the File menu, choose Preview In Browser and then Preview In Multiple Browsers.
5. Check how the problem symbol appears in each browser.

For a cross-reference listing of common HTML characters, name codes, and number codes, browse *hotwired.lycos.com/webmonkey/reference/special_characters/*.

Inserting FrontPage Comments

FrontPage comments display text in Design view but display nothing to Web visitors. As Figure 8-7 shows, comments typically contain notes (preferably the scrutable kind) about the page for yourself or others on your team.

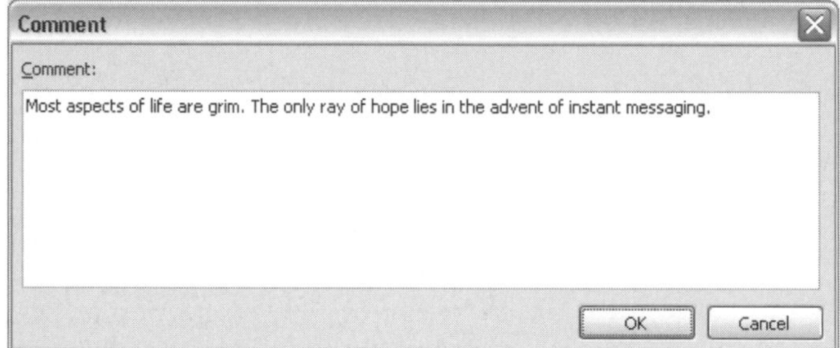

Figure 8-7. Comments you insert here won't be visible to viewers of your Web site.

To add comments to a Web page:

1. Set the insertion point where you want the comment to appear.
2. Choose Comment from the Insert menu.
3. Enter your comments in the Comment dialog box, and click OK.

In Design view, FrontPage comments appear as purple text. To modify a comment, either double-click it or right-click it and select Comment Properties from the shortcut menu. To delete a comment, click it, and then press Delete.

HTML itself and programming languages like JavaScript and Microsoft Visual Basic each have their own syntax for entering comments. None of these appear in Design view, but you can easily view them in Code view and, if you're willing to do the typing, enter them as well.

By default, when the Web server sends visitors the HTML for your Web page, it also sends visitors your FrontPage comments, your HTML comments, and any comments you put in program code that runs on the browser. These comments won't be visible in the normal browser display, but they *will* consume bandwidth and they *will* be visible if the visitor uses the browser's View Source command.

> **Warning** From a security standpoint, sending internal comments about your Web Site to visitors is a very bad idea. The more malicious visitors can learn about your site, the more problems you'll likely experience.

Fortunately, FrontPage can automatically remove comments from the published versions of your Web pages. To activate this feature:

1. Open the FrontPage Web site that contains your pages.
2. Click the Web Site tab that appears above the main editing window.
3. Click the Remote Web Site tab that appears below the main editing window.
4. If necessary, on the Remote Web Site toolbar, click the Remote Web Site Properties button to specify where your published Web site should reside.
5. Click the Optimize Published HTML button on the Remote Web Site toolbar.
6. When the Remote Web Site Properties dialog box shown in Figure 8-8 appears, make sure that the Optimize HTML tab is selected.

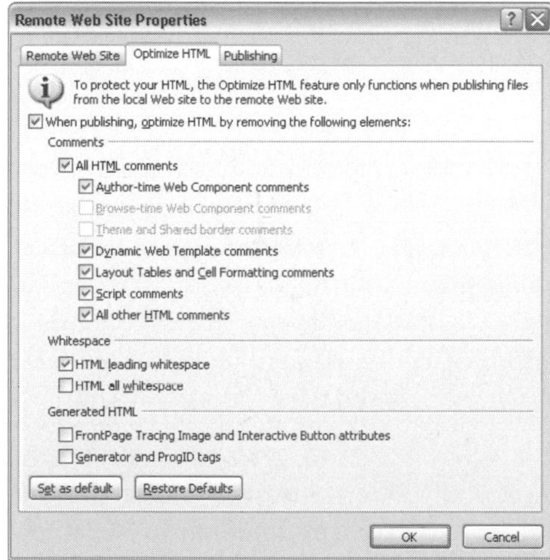

Figure 8-8. FrontPage can optimize the HTML in your Web site as you publish it to another location.

7. Select the When Publishing, Optimize HTML By Removing The Following Elements check box.
8. Under Comments, select the types of comments you don't want Web visitors to receive.
9. Click OK to close the Remote Web Site Properties dialog box, and then click Publish Web Site to publish the Web site without comments.

Inside Out

Don't Discard Comments by Mistake.

If you remove comments from a Web site during a publishing operation and then open the published copy, you might find that FrontPage has "forgotten" the configuration of various components. This is because FrontPage uses HTML comments to record these settings. Pages without comments will still work correctly, but you should avoid opening and directly modifying pages in the remote location. Instead, make your changes to the local Web site (which still contains the comments), and then republish to the remote site.

Removing comments as you publish to a remote site, and then publishing the remote site back to your local site effectively erases every comment in your site, and therefore a great many component configurations. Think twice before placing yourself in this situation.

Formatting Paragraphs

The arrangement and layout of paragraphs—or any blocks of text—are key elements of page layout and visual communication. FrontPage therefore provides a rich assortment of tools that control paragraph appearance.

Using HTML's Basic Paragraph Styles

FrontPage supports the basic HTML paragraph styles shown in Figure 8-9. These are paragraph styles and not font styles; they modify the appearance of an entire paragraph and not of any specific text. HTML was designed to specify the structure of a document's elements, not the explicit formatting of a given element; therefore, each browser will display these elements according to its own settings and the system configuration on which it's running.

Headings 1 through 6 are for successively lower-level titles. In practice, any page with six levels of titles is probably too long and an excellent candidate for separation into multiple pages. Nevertheless, the availability of six styles provides more flexibility in selecting sizes. (You might, for example, choose to use Headings 1 through 3, or 4 through 6.) Heading 1 generally uses the largest font, and Heading 6, the smallest.

The Normal style is for ordinary text. Like the heading styles and most of the other styles, it specifies no fixed line width but instead wraps within its container.

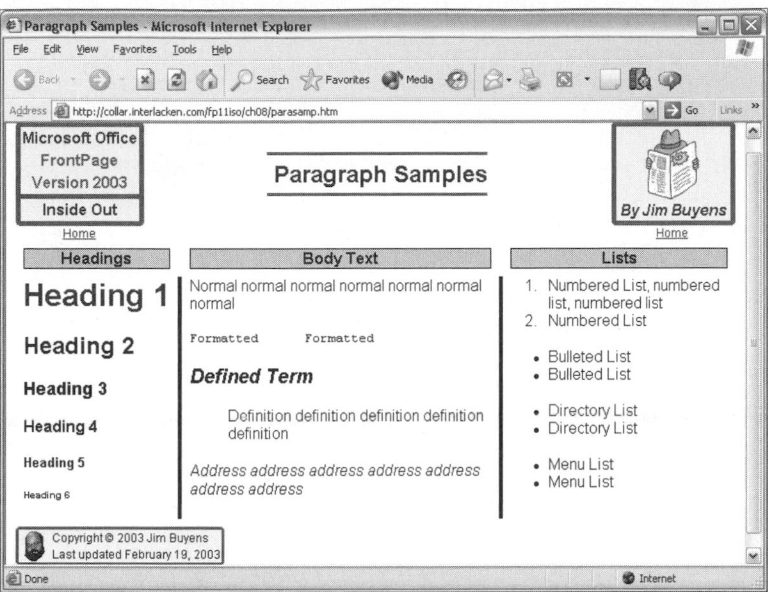

Figure 8-9. FrontPage supports these standard HTML paragraph styles.

> **Note** In HTML parlance, a *container* is any object that limits the space for displaying another object. The default and most common container is the browser window, but table cells, divisions, frames, and other objects can also be containers.

The Formatted style is unique in three respects: It uses a monospaced font; it preserves and displays multiple spaces; and it doesn't wrap within the browser window. Because of these characteristics, the Formatted style is useful for applications like tabular data and program listings, where preservation of columns and letter spaces is vital.

The Address style identifies Web addresses. Its most common use is making e-mail hyperlinks stand out from ordinary text. Web address paragraphs frequently appear in italics.

To assign any of these basic styles to a paragraph, click or select any part of the paragraph, and then select the desired style from the Style drop-down list on the Formatting toolbar.

Normal

In addition, there are two style shortcut keys:

- **Ctrl+Shift+N** Applies the Normal style.
- **Ctrl+Shift+L** Applies the Bulleted List style.

The following buttons on the Formatting toolbar also modify the appearance of text:

Button	Name	Description
	Align Left	Left-aligns text in selected paragraphs.
	Center	Centers text in selected paragraphs.
	Align Right	Right-aligns text in selected paragraphs.
	Justify	Aligns text in selected paragraphs to both right and left margins.
	Numbering	Creates a numbered list.
	Bullets	Creates a bulleted list.
	Decrease Indent	Decreases the paragraph indentation or nesting level of selected list items.
	Increase Indent	Increases the paragraph indentation or nesting level of selected list items.
	Outside Borders	Adds or removes visible borders around or between paragraphs.

Aligning Text

HTML provides only five settings for aligning paragraph text: Default, Left, Center, Right, and Justify. There are three ways to apply these settings:

- Use the Align Left, Center, Align Right, and Justify buttons on the Formatting toolbar. When an alignment is in effect, its button will remain selected. To specify default alignment, click the selected button again to clear it.
- Choose Paragraph from the Format menu and then, in the Paragraph dialog box, select the appropriate alignment from the drop-down list. (See Figure 8-10.)
- Right-click the paragraph, choose Paragraph from the shortcut menu, and in the Paragraph dialog box, select the appropriate alignment from the drop-down list.

> **Tip** The following keystrokes also align text: Ctrl+R toggles right alignment; Ctrl+L toggles left alignment; and Ctrl+E toggles centering.

Fine-Tuning Paragraph Properties

Use the Paragraph dialog box with caution. If you need to format a particular paragraph beyond HTML's defaults, you'll most likely need to format other paragraphs in your Web the same way. If you format each of these paragraphs individually, you'll probably miss a setting or two in at least some of them. Changing all the individually formatted paragraphs later will cost you even more time and leave you prone to further errors. For these reasons, you should always consider using themes or shared CSS to control specialized paragraph formatting.

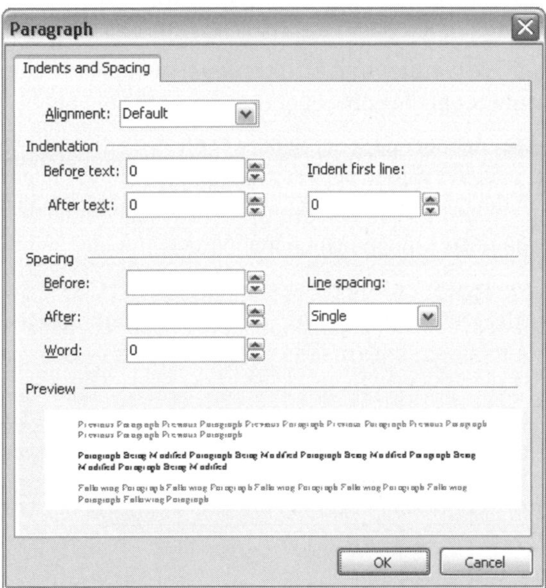

Figure 8-10. Use the Paragraph dialog box to configure paragraph styles.

> **For more information about themes, refer to Chapter 20, "Using FrontPage Themes." For more information about CSS, refer to Chapter 21, "Managing Appearance with Cascading Style Sheets."**

The Paragraph dialog box controls the following settings:

- **Alignment:**
  - **Default** Each line within a paragraph will butt against the default border.
  - **Left** Each line will butt against the left border.
  - **Right** Each line will butt against the right border.
  - **Center** The browser will center each line between the left and right borders.
  - **Justify** The browser will add enough word spacing so that each line butts against both the left and the right borders.
- **Indentation:**
  - **Before Text** Controls the amount of blank space that appears between the left edge of a paragraph and its container. This is actually the left margin setting. (CSS only.)

- **After Text** Controls the amount of blank space that appears between the right edge of a paragraph and its container—in other words, it controls the right margin. (CSS only.)
- **Indent First Line** Specifies first-line paragraph indentation. Negative numbers produce "outdents," where the first line extends to the left of second and subsequent lines. (CSS only.)

- **Spacing:**
  - **Before** Controls the amount of blank space that appears above a paragraph—that is, the paragraph's top margin. (CSS only.)
  - **After** Controls the amount of blank space that appears below a paragraph—that is, the paragraph's bottom margin. (CSS only.)
  - **Word** Adjusts the normal spacing between words. Positive values increase spacing, and negative values decrease it. (CSS only.)
  - **Line Spacing** Specifies the amount of vertical space reserved for a line. A common value is the font size times 1.2. (CSS only)

The effects flagged *CSS only* appear only in browsers that support CSS; other browsers ignore them. For all the settings flagged *CSS only*, you can enter a unit of measure as well as a numeric value. The values *1* and *1px* both mean 1 pixel, but you can also enter measurements such as *0.5in* and *3mm*.

For more information about CSS units of measure, refer to Table 21-12, "CSS Units of Measure," on page 617.

Formatting Lists

In HTML terminology, *lists* are collections of paragraphs the browser will format with leading bullets or numbers. Because lists inherently have a structure to them, creating and updating them is slightly trickier than working with normal paragraphs. Fortunately, FrontPage takes care of this complexity for you.

Creating Bulleted and Numbered Lists

As shown in Figure 8-11, Figure 8-12, and Figure 8-13, FrontPage supports three kinds of bulleted and numbered lists:

- **Picture Bullets** FrontPage uses a picture that you select as the item identifier.
- **Plain Bullets** FrontPage instructs the browser to display a standard bullet character.
- **Numbers** FrontPage instructs the browser to sequentially number the list items.

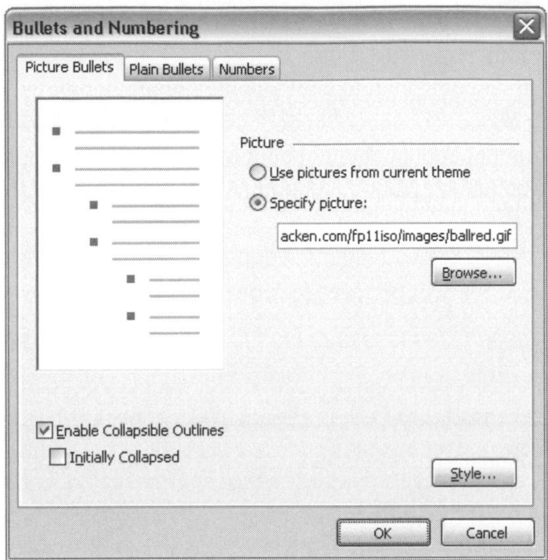

Figure 8-11. If you choose Bullets And Numbering from the Format menu, you can insert picture bullets from this dialog box.

Numbering

To convert existing paragraphs to a list:

1. Select the desired paragraphs.
2. Do one of the following:

Bullets

   - Choose Numbered List or Bulleted List from the Style drop-down menu on the Formatting toolbar.
   - Click the Numbering button or the Bullets button on the Formatting toolbar.
   - Choose Bullets And Numbering from the Format menu.

Note You can't create a picture bulleted list from the Formatting toolbar. To create a picture bulleted list, choose Bullets And Numbering from the Format menu, and then select the Picture Bullets tab, as shown in Figure 8-11. You can also select the Picture Bullets tab by right-clicking an existing plain bulleted list and then choosing List Properties from the shortcut menu.

You can create a new list in two ways. The first is to create normal paragraphs and convert them as just described. The second is this:

1. Set the insertion point where the list should begin.
2. Do one of the following:
   - Click either the Bullets button or the Numbering button on the Formatting toolbar.
   - Choose Bullets And Numbering from the Format menu, select a style, and then click OK.

3. Enter the text for each item in the list, and press Enter to continue to the next item.
4. To end the list and return to Normal paragraph style, press Enter twice. (If you don't want an extra blank line, press Backspace to delete it.)

Note Remember the convention that two consecutive paragraph endings denote the end of a list. This explains many otherwise curious behaviors that occur around the ends of lists.

From the Picture Bullets tab, you can select pictures for your bullets in two ways:

- If the current Web or page uses themes, choose the Use Pictures From Current Theme option to use the bullet pictures supplied with the theme.
- Choose the Specify Picture option if there's no theme in effect or if you don't want the standard theme bullets. Continue either by typing the picture's URL or file path or by clicking the Browse button to display a standard Select Picture dialog box. As usual, this dialog box can browse local file locations, browse locations in server-based Webs, or receive URLs you locate using Microsoft Internet Explorer.

Figure 8-12 shows the Plain Bullets tab of the Bullets And Numbering dialog box. Here you can select any one of several bullet styles that use text symbols rather than pictures. Click the style you want, and then click OK. Click the Style button to set CSS properties.

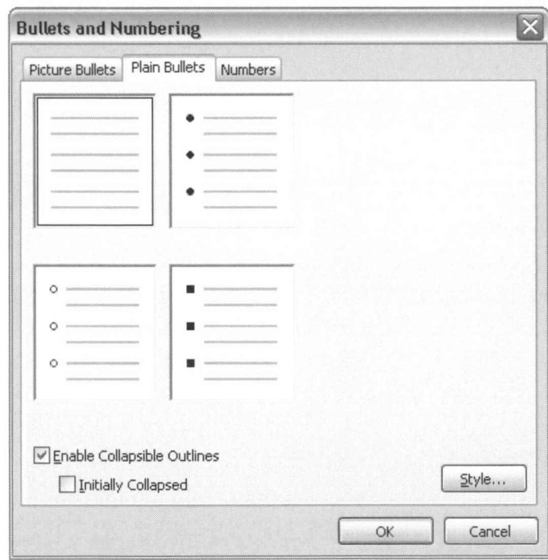

Figure 8-12. FrontPage assigns the properties of normal bulleted lists according to the settings made here.

Figure 8-13 shows the Numbers tab of the Bullets And Numbering dialog box. Click the numbering style you want, verify or change the Start At value for the first paragraph in the list, and then click OK. Click the Style button to set CSS properties.

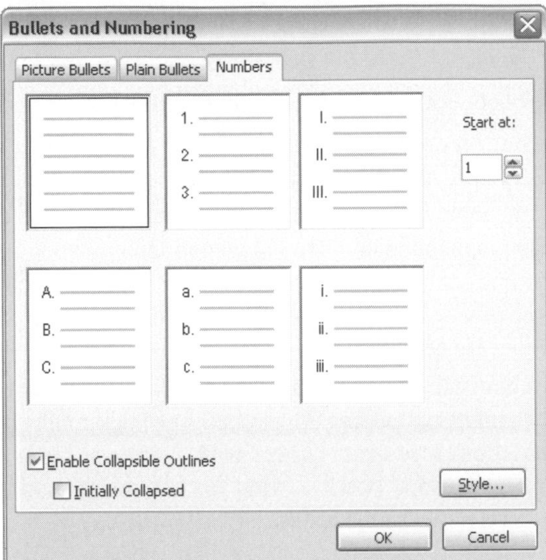

Figure 8-13. The Numbers tab of the Bullets And Numbering dialog box controls the properties of numbered lists.

Figure 8-14 shows examples of indented lists using plain bullets, numbered lists, and picture bullets. These are actually lists inside of lists; each sublist is part of the text for the item just above it.

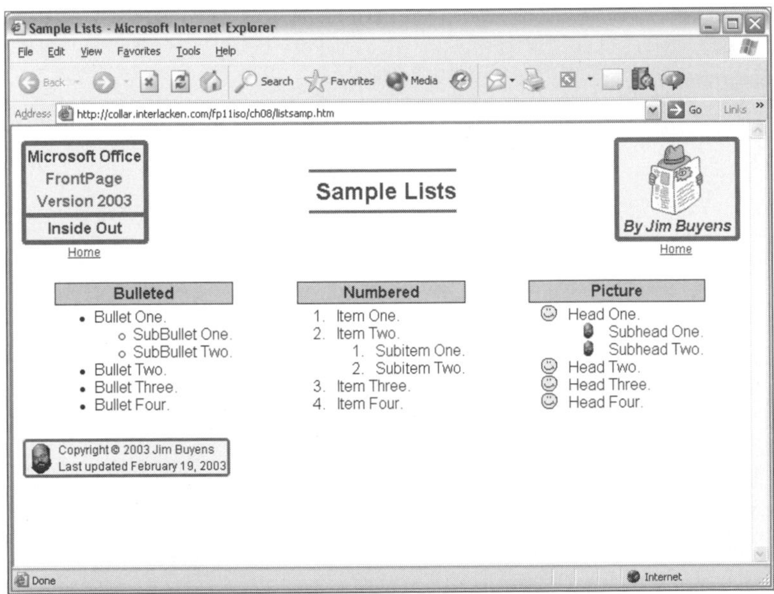

Figure 8-14. Each sublist is included within a parent list.

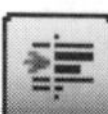
Increase Indent

To begin a sublist:

1. Set the insertion point at the end of the bullet that will precede the first indented bullet.
2. Press Enter to create a new list item.
3. Click the Increase Indent button on the Formatting toolbar twice. The first click creates a Normal style paragraph, and the second click creates a sublist bullet.

Caution You can't add multiple items to the end of a list without entering text as you go. Setting the insertion point at the end of the list and pressing Enter once will create a new item, but pressing Enter *again* will delete the newly created item and terminate the list.

Decrease Indent

To convert any item in a list to a Normal style paragraph, first select it, and then click the Decrease Indent button on the Formatting toolbar. More than one click might be necessary, depending on the original indentation. If you experiment with successive clicks of the Increase Indent and Decrease Indent buttons, you'll see that you can move from level to level, passing through a Normal style level between list levels.

To continue adding new items at the current list level, simply press Enter at the end of each preceding item.

To change an existing list's overall style, right-click anywhere in the list, and choose List Properties from the shortcut menu. Figure 8-15 shows the resulting dialog box.

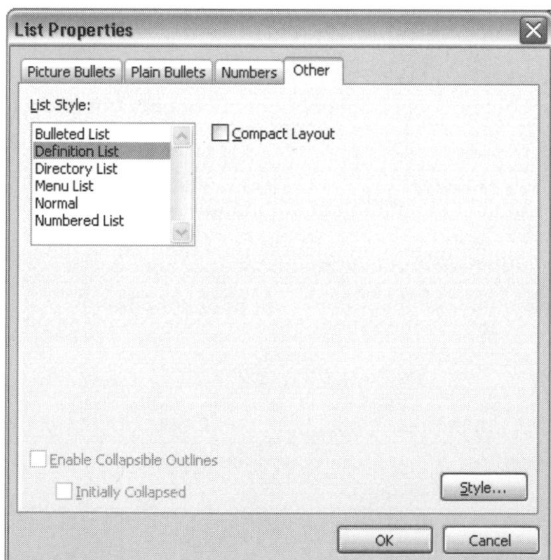

Figure 8-15. The Other tab of the List Properties dialog box contains additional list choices.

On the Other tab of the List Properties dialog box, choose from the following options:

- **List Style** Changes the list's overall style.
- **Compact Layout** Appears only for definition lists. For an explanation of Compact Layout, refer to "Using Other List Types," in the next section.

Creating Collapsible Lists

FrontPage can make multilevel lists *collapsible*. This means that sublists appear and disappear as the visitor clicks their parent list items. Figure 8-16 provides an example. FrontPage, running in the back window, displays the collapsible list in its entirety. Internet Explorer, running in the front window, displays details only for entries the visitor has clicked.

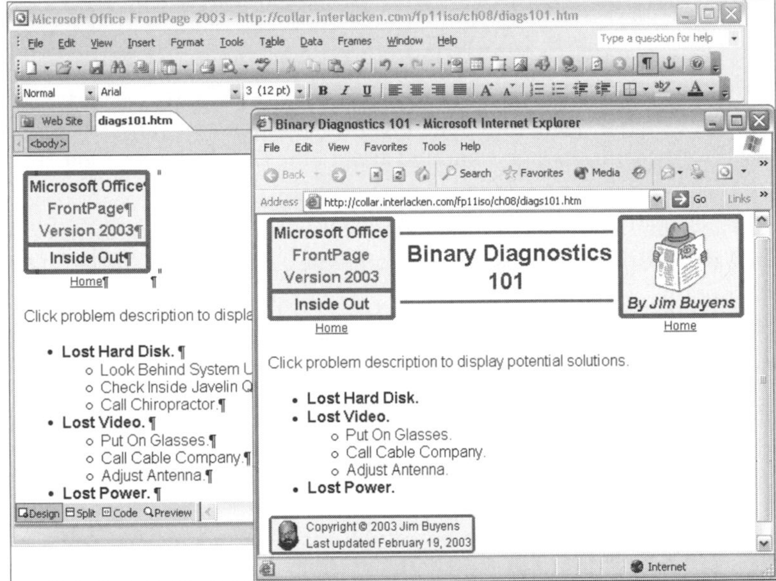

Figure 8-16. Collapsible lists expand and contract as the Web visitor clicks headings.

Two settings control the behavior of collapsible lists. For convenience, they appear on all four tabs of the List Properties dialog box last shown in Figure 8-15:

- **Enable Collapsible Outlines** If selected, means that sublists should appear and disappear as the visitor clicks their parent list items.
- **Initially Collapsed** If selected, means that the collapsible portions of a list will initially be hidden. Otherwise, they initially appear.

> **Caution** Collapsible lists don't collapse in Netscape Navigator, at least not through version 7. For Internet Explorer, they require at least version 4. This is because collapsible lists use dynamic HTML (DHTML) features first introduced in Internet Explorer 4.

Using Other List Types

The Other tab of the List Properties dialog box shown previously in Figure 8-15 presents some alternative options for formatting a list. Among these are directory lists and menu lists, which current browsers seem to display identically to bulleted lists. Nevertheless, you can use this tab to assign the directory or menu list types to be used if the need arises. Bulleted lists are by far the most common of the three and therefore the most universally supported.

The Definition List option in the List Styles list on the Other tab combines two HTML styles, Defined Term and Definition, to create a special type of list. The browser displays a Defined Term paragraph flush left, followed by an indented Definition paragraph. (Glance back at Figure 8-9 to see how the Definition style appears.) To create a defined term and its definition:

1. Type the term you plan to define.
2. Select Defined Term from the Style drop-down list on the Formatting toolbar. This formats the paragraph as a defined term.

Normal

Style

3. Set the insertion point at the end of the Defined Term paragraph, and then press Enter. FrontPage starts a new line and applies the Definition style, indenting the new line.
4. Type the definition of the term, and press Enter. FrontPage starts a new line and begins a new defined term so that you can type a list of terms and definitions without interruption.
5. When you've finished with the entire definition list, terminate the list by pressing Enter twice at the end of the final definition line.

If you want your definition list to take up less space, select the Compact Layout check box on the Other tab of the List Properties dialog box. This displays the definition on the same line as the defined term, provided the defined term is short enough not to overlap.

Formatting Text Fonts

Controlling fonts on Web pages presents unique difficulties. For one, there's no way of knowing what fonts or font technologies a given Web visitor will have available. For another, it's unlikely that all the same fonts will be available to any two Web visitors. Finally, even fonts that appear identical down to their names might have subtle differences when obtained from different vendors or even from the same vendor when used on different platforms.

The original HTML specification tried to avoid font confusion by avoiding fonts. Instead of providing a way to specify fonts by name, it provided ways to flag blocks of text by their structural use in the document. Responsibility for assigning specific fonts then fell to the Web visitor's browser.

For information about how to format small amounts of text as pictures, refer to "Adding Text to Pictures," on page 635.

Some newer versions of HTML *do* support specific font name assignments, as does FrontPage. However, just because FrontPage lets you specify font names such as Estrangella Edessa and Palatino Linotype doesn't mean those fonts are available to your Web visitors. If the Web visitor's system doesn't have a font with the name you specify, it will substitute another font—usually the default browser font, which, if not stylish, will at least be legible.

Recommendations for Using Fonts on the Web

Consider these five commonsense suggestions for using font attributes effectively in your Web pages:

- **Use fonts large enough to read.** Small print is for lawyers. If the text isn't important enough to present legibly, omit it.
- **Don't waste space with large fonts.** Large amounts of text in a large font slow down the reader and lead to excessive scrolling. In addition, they have far less impact than a pleasing and effective page design.
- **Stick to mainstream fonts.** If Web visitors don't have the artistic font you want, their browser will probably substitute an ugly one.
- **Avoid ransom notes.** Stick to a few well-chosen sizes and styles of type.
- **Aim for contrast, not clash.** Achieve a pleasing contrast between background and text.

Most browsers correctly substitute a local version of Arial, Helvetica, or Times Roman for any known variation of those names. Font substitution for less common names, however, can be problematic.

There's another reason to approach font attributes with caution. If you need to use a special font in a particular situation, you should use exactly the same font settings everywhere in the same page and everywhere in the same Web site where the same situation occurs. If you format all this text manually, you'll almost certainly miss some spots and make some errors. Furthermore, changing the specified font later will be difficult at best. Thus, for reasons of reasons of consistency and maintainability, always consider using global facilities like themes and shared CSS to control typography.

For more information about themes, refer to Chapter 20, "Using FrontPage Themes." For more information about CSS, refer to Chapter 21, "Managing Appearance with Cascading Style Sheets."

FrontPage provides seven font-related icons on the Formatting toolbar. Each icon applies an attribute to the selected text or removes an attribute previously applied.

Button	Name	Description
Times New Roman	**Font**	Applies a selected font name.
3 (12 pt)	**Font Size**	Increases or decreases font size.
B	**Bold**	Toggles boldfacing on and off.
I	**Italic**	Toggles italicizing on and off.
U	**Underline**	Toggles underlining on and off.
ab	**Highlight**	Controls a text area's background color.
A	**Font Color**	Controls the color in which the browser displays text.

You can also toggle boldfacing, italicizing, and underlining of selected words on and off by pressing Ctrl+B, Ctrl+I, and Ctrl+U, respectively. Press Ctrl+Shift+greater than sign to increase the font size of selected words, and Ctrl+Shift+less than sign to decrease it. Ctrl+Shift+plus sign formats text as a superscript, and Ctrl+equal sign formats it as a subscript.

For maximum control of font settings, select the text you want to modify, and then choose Font from the Format menu. The resulting dialog box contains a Font tab, shown in Figure 8-17, and a Character Spacing tab, shown later in Figure 8-18.

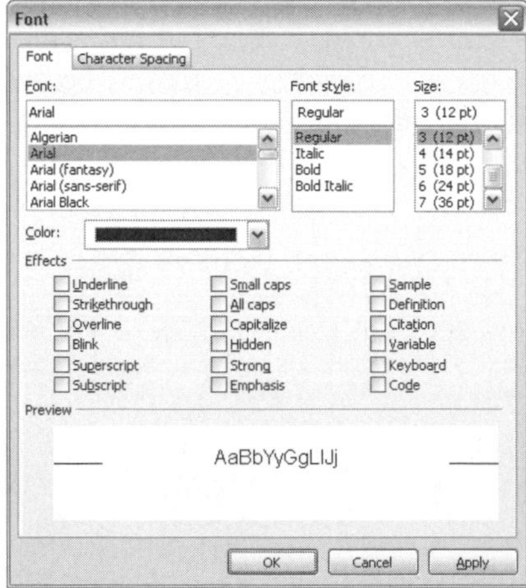

Figure 8-17. The Font tab of the Font dialog box provides controls similar to those of any word processor.

Tip You can display the same Font dialog box by right-clicking a block of text and choosing Font from the shortcut menu.

The Font tab controls the following settings:

- **Font** Selects a specific font name.
- **Font Style** Controls the following effects: regular, italic, bold, bold italic.
- **Size** Specifies a code from 1 through 7, indicating the relative size of the font. The dialog box lists typical point-size equivalents for convenience, although these can vary by browser and system configuration.
- **Color** Provides the usual FrontPage color dialog boxes, beginning with a drop-down list of 16 colors.
- **Underline** Underlines text. This setting has no effect on the underlining of hyperlinks.
- **Strikethrough** Draws a horizontal line through the selected text.
- **Overline** Draws a horizontal line above the selected text. (CSS only.)
- **Blink** Displays flashing text. Web browsers that can't display blinking text will ignore this setting.
- **Superscript** Reduces text in size and shifts its baseline upward, like the 2 in $e=mc^2$.
- **Subscript** Reduces text in size and shifts its baseline downward, like the 2 in H_2O.
- **Small Caps** Displays reduced-size capital letters in place of any lowercase letters in the actual text. (CSS only.)
- **All Caps** Displays all letters in uppercase, even if the actual text is lowercase. (CSS only.)
- **Capitalize** Displays the first letter of each word in uppercase, even if the actual text is lowercase. (CSS only.)
- **Hidden** Suppresses display of the selected text. (CSS only.)
- **Strong** Enhances text to convey a stronger meaning. Most browsers use boldface for this.
- **Emphasis** Enhances text to convey extra emphasis. Most browsers use italics for this.
- **Sample** Displays a sequence of literal characters in a monospaced font, usually some variation of Courier.
- **Definition** Indicates a definition, typically in italics.
- **Citation** Indicates a style designed to be assigned to a manual, section, or book, typically in italics.
- **Variable** Indicates a variable name, typically in italics.
- **Keyboard** Indicates typing by a visitor, as when following a procedure. This is usually similar to the monospaced (Courier) font.
- **Code** Indicates a code sample. This is usually similar to the monospaced (Courier) font.

Effects flagged *CSS only* appear only in browsers that support CSS; other browsers ignore them. You can preview the results of setting the various Font controls in the Preview area.

For more information about applying fonts to an entire page or Web site, refer to Chapter 21, "Managing Appearance with Cascading Style Sheets."
For more information about configuring FrontPage to reflect the capabilities of various browsers, refer to "Matching FrontPage Capabilities to Browser Capabilities," on page 471.

Figure 8-18 shows the Character Spacing tab.

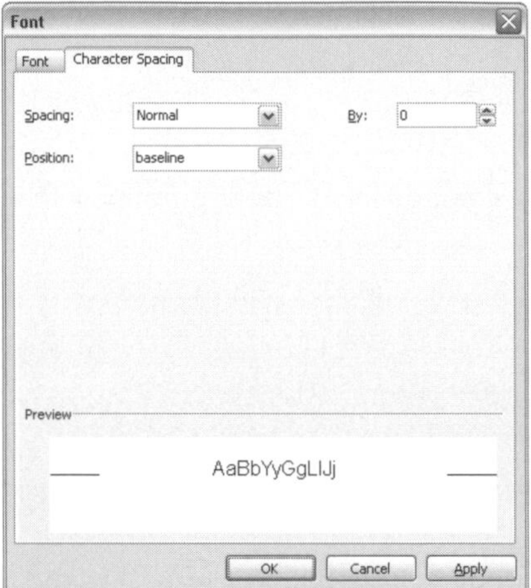

Figure 8-18. The Character Spacing tab controls space between characters, as well as character position relative to the baseline.

This tab controls the following font settings, each of which requires a numeric value:

- **Spacing** Choose Normal for the default spacing, Expanded for extra space between letters, or Condensed for less than the normal spacing. (Appears only in browsers that support CSS; other browsers ignore it.)
- **By** Enter a CSS measurement for the amount of extra or lesser spacing you want.

For more information about valid CSS measurements, refer to "Specifying Style Sheet Measurements and Colors," on page 617.

- **Position** This setting dictates the vertical position of the text. Options include Baseline, Sub, Super, Top, Text-Top, Middle, Bottom, and Text-Bottom.

To preview the results of setting Character Spacing controls, see the Preview area at the bottom of the dialog box.

In Summary…

This chapter explained the basics of entering and pasting text and of formatting paragraphs and fonts.

The next chapter explains how to find, replace, and check the spelling of text.

Chapter 9

Finding, Replacing, and Checking the Spelling of Text

Once you've developed a collection of Web pages and other text files, it's a sure bet that sooner or later you'll want to change them. Finding all the spots you need to change can, of course, be a problem. Regardless of whether your interest is in a single file, a group of files, or an entire Microsoft FrontPage–based Web site, mechanical assistance finding certain strings of text is a major source of help.

Fortunately, FrontPage can search for, replace, and check the spelling of text in a single Web page, in selected pages, or on an entire Web site. FrontPage even provides a thesaurus to help you find the exact word you mean. This chapter explains how to use these tools.

Finding and Replacing Text in an Open Page

This section examines the simplest and most common cases of finding and replacing text—those involving a single Web page. The section "Finding and Replacing Text in Multiple Pages," later in this chapter, will explain how to extend these techniques to search multiple files.

Searching for Text

The simplest type of search is for text in a page that you've opened in the FrontPage editor. Here's the procedure:

1. Set the insertion point where you want the search to begin. Pressing Ctrl+Home, for example, sets the insertion point at the start of the Web page.
2. Choose Find from the Edit menu, or press Ctrl+F. The Find And Replace dialog box shown in Figure 9-1 appears.
3. In the Find What box, type the text you hope to find.

The Regular Expressions button to the right of the Find What box displays the menu of common special expression characters shown in Figure 9-2. These work like wild card characters, but only if you select the Regular Expressions check box further down in the dialog box. To add any of these characters to your Find What search string, either type them into the Find What box or click the corresponding menu option.

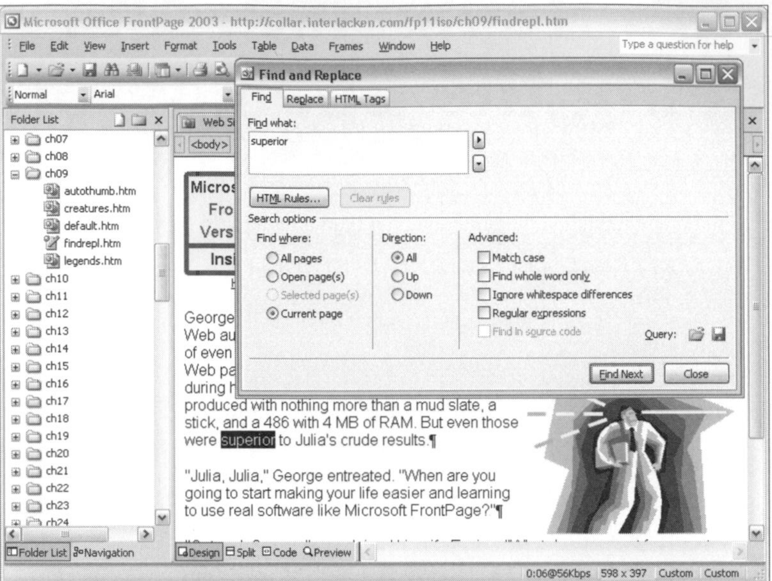

Figure 9-1. The Find And Replace dialog box searches your Web page for a specified text string.

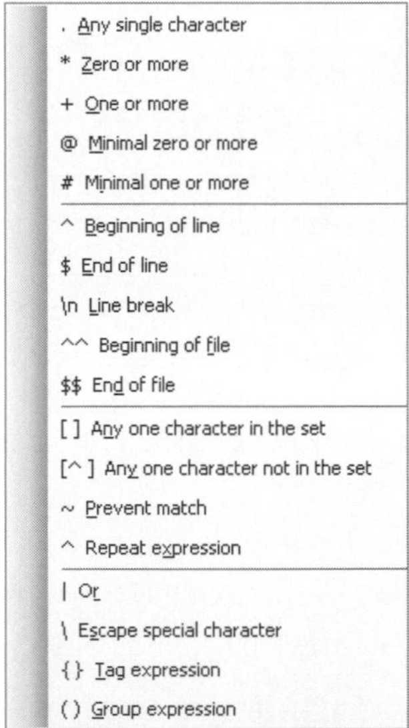

Figure 9-2. FrontPage interprets these regular expression characters as pattern indicators during a search.

The Most Recently Used button to the right of the Find What box displays a list of previous Find What strings. To reuse any of these strings, select it from the list.

4 Under Find Where, specify which pages you want to search. Table 9-1 itemizes the options.

Table 9-1. Text Search Location Options

Option	Description
All Pages	Searches the entire FrontPage Web site
Open Page(s)	Searches all pages that are currently open in the FrontPage editor
Selected Page(s)	Searches all pages that are currently selected (in the Folder List or in Folders view, for example)
Current Page	Searches the current page

5 Under Direction, specify the direction to search. Table 9-2 summarizes your options.

Table 9-2. Text Search Direction Options

Option	Description
All	Searches from the insertion point to the end of the document and then from the top of the document down to the insertion point
Up	Searches from the insertion point to the top of the document
Down	Searches from the insertion point to the end of the document

6 Under Advanced, specify any of the additional options listed in Table 9-3.

Table 9-3. Text Search Advanced Options

Option	Description
Match Case	Makes the search case sensitive. A search for *walker*, for example, wouldn't stop at *Walker*.
Find Whole Word Only	Ignores partial word matches. A search for the word *walk*, for example, wouldn't stop at the word *walking*.
 Ignore Whitespace Differences	Treats all consecutive runs of spaces, tabs, and line endings—in both the search string and the text—as if they were a single space. This has the effect of searching for a series of words rather than a specific sequence of characters.
 Regular Expressions	Treats the Find What text as a regular expression.
Find In Source Code	Searches for the Find What string not only in ordinary page text, but also within the HTML code. This option is unavailable if the Find Where location is Current Page. To search for source code in the current page, first switch to Code view.

7 Click the Find Next button.

Coding and Using Regular Expressions

In addition to searching for specific characters, FrontPage 2003 can search for text that matches a generalized pattern. You specify the pattern by coding a regular expression.

Regular expressions are a bit like wildcard characters on steroids. Most characters represent themselves, but others have special meanings. Here are a few examples:

- A period means "any character." Searching for the string *r.ng* will stop at the string *r.ng*, but also at *rang*, *ring*, *rung*, *r?ng*, and any other four-character string beginning with *r* and ending with *ng*.
- A backslash means that the character following it is literally that character. Thus, searching for *r\.ng* would match only *r.ng*.
- An asterisk means zero or more of the character that precedes it. Thus, *so*n* matches *sn*, *son*, *soon*, *soooooon*, and so forth.
- A plus sign means one or more of the character that precedes it. For example, *so+n* matches *son* and *soon* but not *sn*.
- Square brackets signify any single character that appears between them. Searching for *th[ia]s* would find *this* and *that* but not *ths*, *thias*, or *thus*.
- A hyphen inside angle brackets indicates a range. The expressions *Room [012345]* and *Room [0-5]* are equivalent.

Regular expressions are an extremely powerful facility, but they involve a unique mind-set, and beginners often have trouble with them. For more information, search FrontPage Help for the keywords *regular expression*.

To search for additional occurrences of the Find What text, keep clicking the Find Next button. To edit the page, you don't need to close the Find And Replace dialog box; just move it out of the way.

Tip After closing the Find And Replace dialog box, you can still perform a Find Next by pressing the F3 key.

Searching with HTML Rules

FrontPage 2003 can search for text in specific parts of your HTML code. For example, it can search for text only within certain HTML tags, only within certain HTML attributes, or outside any HTML tag.

To perform such a search, display the Find And Replace dialog box shown previously in Figure 9-1, and then click the HTML Rules button. This displays the HTML Rules dialog box, shown in Figure 9-3.

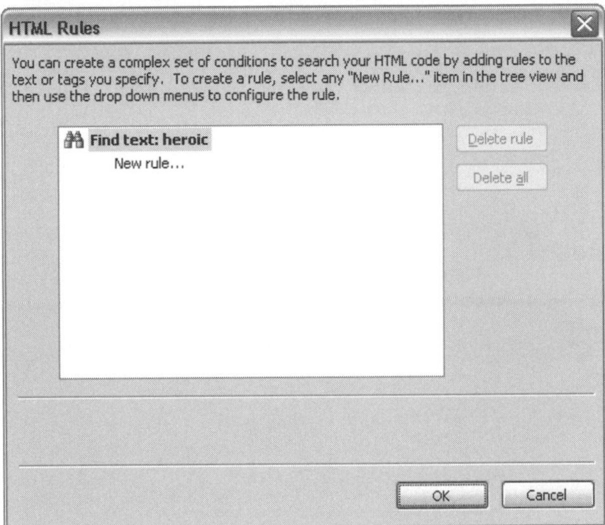

Figure 9-3. Use this dialog box to specify the exact HTML elements you want to find and replace.

The rules tree in the middle of this dialog box shows the current HTML rule. Initially, the only rule will be the search condition you specified in the Find And Replace dialog box. This is the situation that Figure 9-3 illustrates.

To add an HTML rule, click any New Rule item in the rules tree. (Figure 9-3 shows only one new rule line, so that's the one you'd click.) This displays an additional drop-down list offering these choices:

- **New Rule** Specifies that the current line in the rules tree is ready to receive a new rule. No rule for that line in currently in effect.
- **Inside Tag** Specifies that you want to search for text enclosed between any pair of matching HTML tags, or between matching HTML tags of a specific type.

  Choosing this option displays yet another drop-down list. This one has an [Any Tag] choice, plus choices for each valid HTML tag. If you select [any tag], FrontPage will search for text only between matching start and end tags of any type. If you select the name of a specific type of tag, FrontPage will search for text only between start and end tags of that type. The rule shown in Figure 9-4, for example, searches for the text *george* between <a> and </a> tags (that is, it searches for the word *george* in a hyperlink).

Tip When dealing with Web pages, searching for text enclosed by any HTML tag (or not enclosed by any HTML tag) isn't terribly useful, because <html> and </html> tags, at least, enclose almost everything in a Web page.

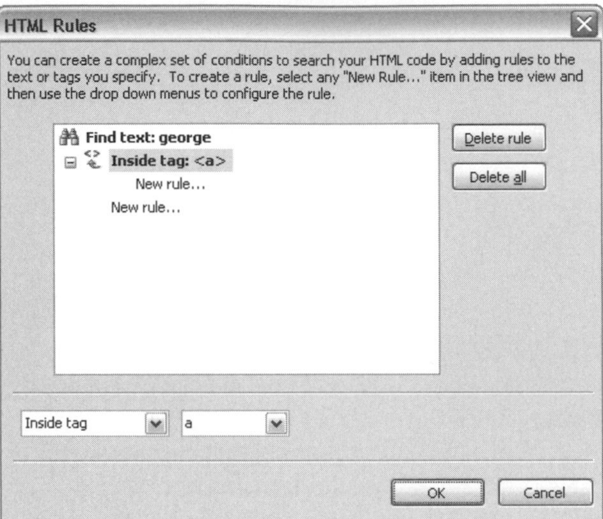

Figure 9-4. You can add additional HTML rules at any level of the decision structure.

- **Not Inside Tag** Specifies that you want to search for text not enclosed by any HTML tag, or by any specific HTML tag. For example, you could search for text outside the range of any <a> and </a> tags (that is, text that doesn't appear in a hyperlink). As before, selecting this option displays a list of tags: Select the one you want the search to ignore.

Notice that two New Rule lines appear in Figure 9-4. Indentation shows that configuring the rule on line 3 adds additional conditions to the rule on line 2. Six such conditions are possible:

- **With Attribute** The parent rule will apply only to tags that contain a certain HTML attribute. Selecting this option displays an additional box where you can specify the attribute name you want. You can also configure a comparison operator and value. This would be useful if, for example, you wanted to search for text inside <a> and </a> tags where the start <a> tag had the attribute *target="_top"*.
- **Without Attribute** The parent rule will apply only to tags that *don't* contain a certain HTML attribute. Otherwise, this option works like the With Attribute option.
- **Containing** The tags in the parent rule must enclose another string of text or tag. Suppose, for example, that the parent rule searched for the text *Edna* inside <a> and </a> tags. A containing rule could further specify that the <a> and </a> tags must enclose the text *Kansas* or must also contain an <img> tag. FrontPage will display additional boxes so that you can configure these options.

- **Not Containing** The tags in the parent rule must *not* enclose a given string of text or tag. Otherwise, this option works like Containing.
- **Inside Tag** The tags in the parent rule must reside within another pair of tags. If, for example, the parent rule searched for text between <a> and </a> tags, an Inside Tag rule could specify that those tags must appear between <td> and </td> tags. Selecting Inside Tag displays another drop-down list for specifying the tag you want.
- **Not Inside Tag** The tags in the parent rule must *not* reside within another pair of tags. Otherwise, this option works like Inside Tag.

Configuring the rule on line 4 of Figure 9-4 adds additional conditions to the rule on line 1. Use the same procedure you used on line 2, keeping in mind that a search hit requires both conditions to be true. HTML rules always combine with *And* conditions, never *Or* conditions. Adding rules always narrows the search, and never widens it.

Realistically, HTML rules are hard enough to configure that when searching a single Web page, it's usually easier to specify a simpler search and bypass the extra hits manually. This facility is much more useful when searching an entire Web site, or at least a group of pages.

Replacing Text

Choosing Replace from the Edit menu (or pressing Ctrl+H) displays the Replace tab of the Find And Replace dialog box. Figure 9-5 illustrates this tag.

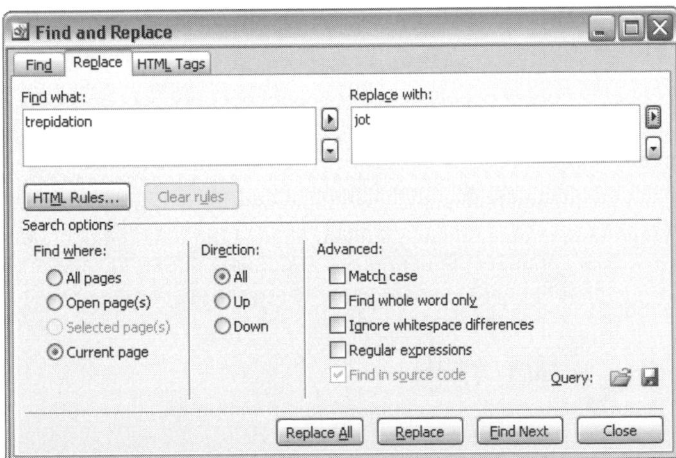

Figure 9-5. The Replace function works much like Find, except that clicking either the Replace or Replace All button modifies the original text.

With two exceptions, the Replace tab works just like the Find tab. Here are the exceptions:

- After finding a match, you can click the Replace button to replace the found text (with the contents of the Replace With box, of course). Clicking Replace All replaces all occurrences of the Find What string with no further prompts.

- Clicking the Regular exceptions button near the Replace With box displays ten choices identified \0 through \9. Here's how these work.
  - \0. FrontPage replaces this sequence with the entire currently found text. Suppose, for example, that you ran the following Find and Replace:

Find What	**Replace With**
st.ff	\0ing

    Here are some typical results:

staff	staffing
stiff	stiffing
stuff	stuffing

  - \1 through \9. FrontPage replaces \1 with the first portion of the Find What text that you surrounded with curly braces. Here's an example:

Find What	**Replace With**
{.o}ad	text \0 begins with \1

    Again, here are some typical results:

goad	goad begins with go
load	load begins with lo
road	road begins with ro
toad	toad begins with ro

    Similarly, FrontPage replaces \2 with the second portion of the Find What text that you surrounded with curly braces, \3 with the third portion, and so forth. The curly braces have no effect on the Find portion of a Find and Replace operation. They serve only to mark text for inclusion in the results.

Finding and Replacing HTML Tags

Unlike earlier releases, and in addition to HTML rules, FrontPage 2003 has special features for finding and replacing HTML tags. If this seems attractive, proceed as follows:

1. Use any method you want to display the Find And Replace dialog box. For example, press Ctrl+F.
2. Click the HTML Tags tab. Figure 9-6 shows the controls that appear on this tab.
3. In the Find Tag drop-down list, select the HTML tag you want to find.
4. In the Replace Action drop-down list, specify the type of change you want to make. Table 9-4 lists the possibilities.

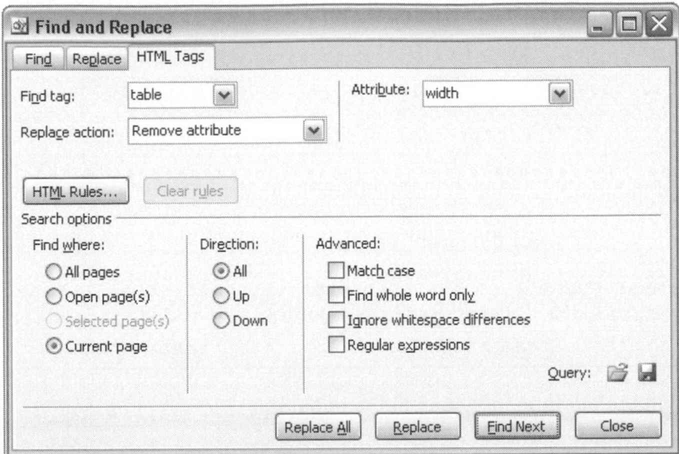

Figure 9-6. FrontPage 2003 has special features to search and replace HTML tags.

Table 9-4. HTML Tag Replacement Actions

Action	Effect	Example	
		Before	**After**
(None)	Finds instances of the tag, but makes no changes		
Replace Tag And Contents	Replaces the start tag, the end tag, and anything between with an arbitrary string	<b>big</b>	large
Replace Contents Only	Replaces any content between the start and end tag	<b>big</b>	<b>large</b>
Add After Start Tag	Adds text after the start tag	<b>big</b>	<b>very big</b>
Add After End Tag	Adds text after the end tag	<b>big</b>	<b>big</b> enough
Add Before Start Tag	Adds text before the start tag	<b>big</b>	Very <b>big</b>
Add Before End Tag	Adds text before the end tag	<b>big</b>	<b>big shot</b>
Remove Tag And Contents	Deletes the start tag, the end tag, and everything between	<b>big</b>	
Remove Tag	Deletes the start and end tags, but retains everything between them	<b>big</b>	big

Table 9-4. HTML Tag Replacement Actions

Action	Effect	Example	
		Before	**After**
Change Tag	Changes one tag name to another	<b>big</b>	<i>big</i>
Set Attribute Value	Adds or replaces an attribute of the given tag, including the attribute value	<table>	<table width="100%">
Remove Attribute	Deletes an attribute of the given tag	<table width="100%">	<table>

5 Look in the top right corner of the HTML Tags tab. Here FrontPage will display one or more drop-down lists or boxes so that you can finish specifying the replace action you want. The exact controls that appear will depend on the replace action you specify. If you're adding or replacing text, for example, FrontPage will display a With box. If you're changing one tag to another, FrontPage will display a To drop-down list of tag names.

6 Configure HTML Rules and Search Options just as you would for a normal find or replace operation.

7 To find each occurrence of the given tag, repeatedly click the Find Next button.

To perform the replace action on any found occurrence, click the Replace button.

To perform the replace action on all occurrences of the find tag, click the Replace All button.

Finding and Replacing Text in Multiple Pages

Within a single Web page, finding and replacing text are handy and useful operations, but you could probably search a Web page by eye just as quickly. Most Web pages just aren't very long. Searching and replacing text across multiple pages is a much more valuable technique, and that's what the topics in this section describe.

Searching for Text Across Multiple Pages

From time to time, you'll no doubt find it valuable to search your Web site for all instances of a certain word or phrase. You might need to locate all instances of a person's name, a product name, an address, or some other text expression and check those pages for accuracy. The Find In Site feature in FrontPage provides an excellent facility for such searches.

Don't confuse the Find In Site feature with ordinary file system utilities or with the FrontPage Web Search component. Here are the differences between Find In Site and file system search utilities:

- Find In Site offers one-click access to editing Web pages in FrontPage.

- A file system search locates word or phrase instances in FrontPage index and cross-reference files, as well as in Web pages.
- A file system search misses phrase instances that contain carriage returns, line feeds, tabs, or extra spaces.

Find In Site differs from the Web Search component in the following respects:

- The Web Search component operates at run time, using a browser, and has no direct links to authoring tools. Also, it must be activated in advance as part of your Web.
- Find In Site operates in the FrontPage environment. When you find a matching page, a single mouse click opens it in Page view. Find In Site is always available.

For more information about the Web Search component, refer to "Using the Web Search Component," on page 733.

Finding or replacing text in multiple files is a two-phase process. Phase 1 creates a list of Web pages that match the given criteria, and phase 2 opens each page in the list for editing. To run Find In Site on your site:

1. Open your Web site in FrontPage.
2. To ensure accurate results, save any pages that are open for editing.
3. If you want to search only certain files or folders, select them in the Folder List or in Folders view.
4. Choose Find from the Edit menu.
5. When the Find And Replace dialog box shown previously in Figure 9-1 appears, type the word, phrase, or pattern you hope to find in the Find What box.
6. Configure the Find Where, Direction, and Advanced sections in compliance with Table 9-1, Table 9-2, and Table 9-3. However, *don't* specify a Find Where location of Current Page.

   Note that if Find Where is All Pages or Selected Pages, a Find In Site button replaces the Find button that otherwise appears in the bottom right corner of the Find And Replace dialog box.
7. After completing the entries in the Find And Replace dialog box, click the Find or Find In Site button. The Find And Replace dialog box then assumes the form shown in Figure 9-7.

   Searching all the pages you specify might take a noticeable amount of time. During this time, Stop and Cancel buttons appear in the bottom right corner and progress messages appear in the status line. Click Stop to pause the search or Cancel to abandon it.

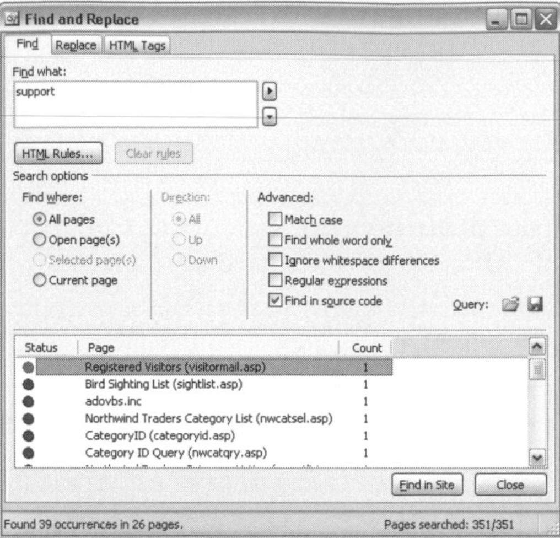

Figure 9-7. This dialog box displays Find In Site progress and results. The two buttons in the bottom right corner read Stop and Cancel while a search is in progress.

8 When the search finishes, the buttons in the lower right corner revert to their normal names. The large results list displays these column entries for each page containing the Find What text:

- **Status** Initially displays a red circle, indicating that no action has yet been taken.
- **Page** Displays the title and name of each page that contains the Find What text you specified in step 5.
- **Count** Reports the number of matches on each page.

9 To view or edit a found page, double-click its entry in the list. As shown in Figure 9-8, FrontPage opens the page and highlights the first instance of the Find What text.

The options in Figure 9-8 default to the values you assigned in the Find And Replace dialog box. Any changes you make apply to your search of the current page only. Repeatedly clicking the Find Next button searches the document from top to bottom or bottom to top, depending on the Direction setting.

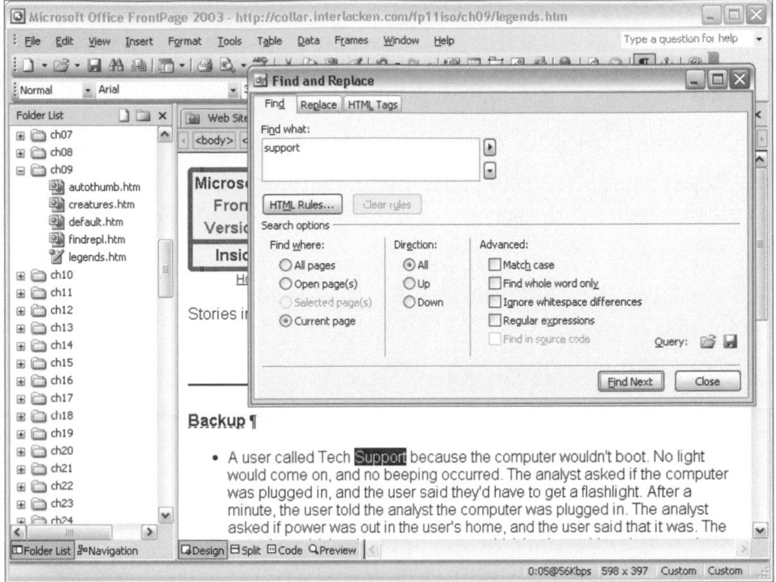

Figure 9-8. Double-clicking a page located with Find In Site opens it in Page view.

10 Clicking the Back To List button or searching to the end of the page displays the Continue With The Next Page? dialog box shown in Figure 9-9.

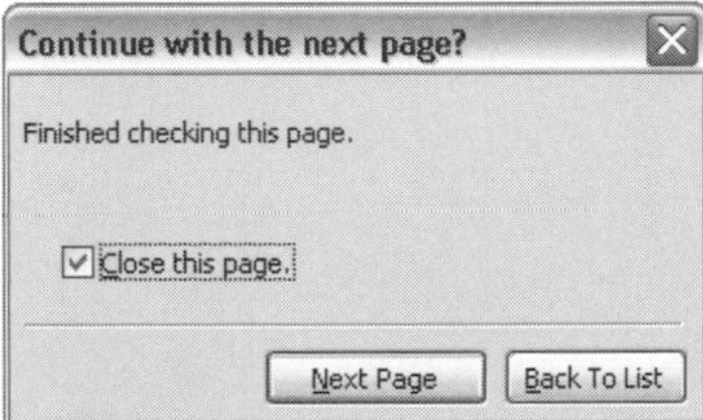

Figure 9-9. This dialog box prompts for the disposition of Web pages found and opened by Find In Site.

This dialog box has three options:

- **Close This Page** If selected, closes the editing window for the current page. If you clear this box, FrontPage keeps the page open for further editing.
- **Next Page** Opens the next document in the Find In Web list shown in Figure 9-7.
- **Back To List** Terminates the process of opening successive documents in the Find In Site list. It also leaves the current page open for further editing.

11 Opening a found page in FrontPage changes its Status icon (in Figure 9-7) from a red circle to a yellow circle followed by the word *Edited*.

Replacing Text in Multiple Pages

As you might expect, the process of replacing text in multiple files resembles that for finding text. There are, however, two major differences:

- When specifying the text to find, you must also specify the text to substitute.
- When you open a Web page from the find results list, FrontPage displays both the search text and the substitution text in the resulting Find And Replace dialog box.

A Replace In Site operation can be unattended or prompted. An unattended Replace In Site operation scans all the files you specify, unconditionally replacing all instances of one string with another.

Here's the full procedure for performing an unattended multiple-file Replace In Site:

1. Open your Web in FrontPage.
2. Save any pages that are open for editing.
3. Choose Replace from the Edit menu.
4. When the dialog box shown in Figure 9-10 appears, configure the settings as you would for a Find In Site procedure.

   There's one additional box—namely, the Replace With box—in which you specify the word or phrase that should replace the found text.

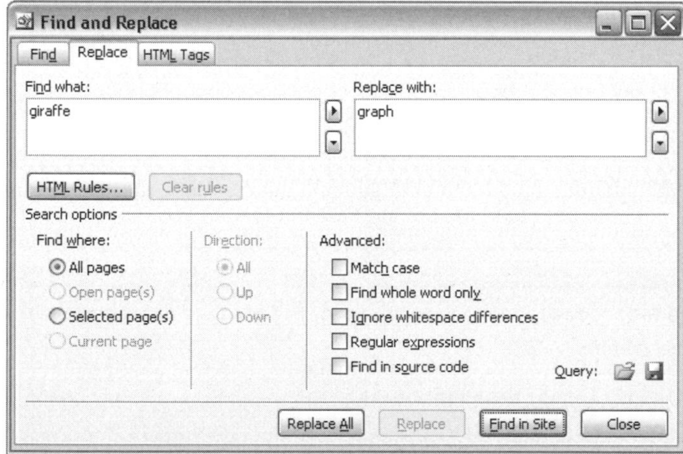

Figure 9-10. Begin a Replace In Site operation with this dialog box.

5. Click the Replace All button. FrontPage displays the following warning. If you click the Yes button, FrontPage summarily replaces all instances of the Find What string with the Replace With string.

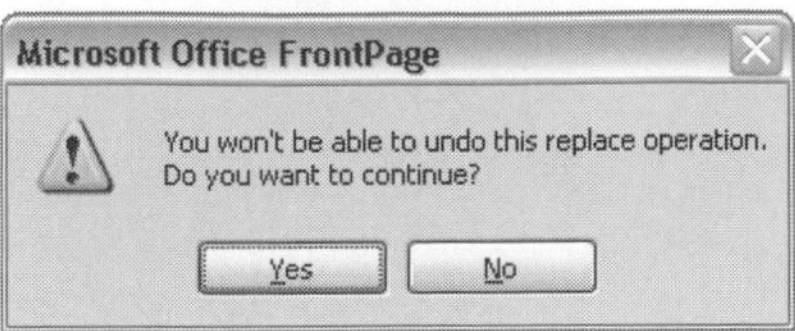

FrontPage can't undo an unattended Replace In Site, but it does display a list of the files it modified. You should at least spot-check the results before deleting this list.

A prompted Replace In Site, like a Find In Site, involves two phases. The first phase searches your entire Web for all instances of the Find What string. (In fact, this phase of a Replace In Site *is* a Find In Site. You can run it with the Find tab selected and then click the Replace tab to run phase 2.)

The second phase begins when a find results list is displayed and you click the Replace button. FrontPage sequentially opens each page in the list and displays a Find And Replace dialog box that applies only to that page. This dialog box is yours to operate. When the Find and Replace operations for the current page are finished, FrontPage asks whether to display the next matching page or suspend the entire operation.

Here's the detailed procedure for performing a prompted Replace In Site:

1. Perform steps 1 through 4 of the previous procedure.
2. Click the Find In Site button. FrontPage runs the Find In Site procedure and changes the Find And Replace dialog box to the form shown in Figure 9-7.
3. At this point, no actual replacements have been made. Click the Replace button to begin replacing text in the first listed page.

   To begin replacing text on a different page, first select that page, and then click the Replace button. Alternatively, double-click the desired page.
4. As shown in Figure 9-11, FrontPage opens each page for editing, finds the first instance of the Find What text, and offers to replace it.

   You can then do any of the following:

   - **Replace All** Click this to replace all instances in the current page without prompting.
   - **Replace** Click this to replace the current instance of the Find What text and advance to the next instance in the same page.
   - **Find Next** Click this to advance to the next instance of the Find What text in the same page.
   - **Back To List** Click this to redisplay the Replace In Site results list.

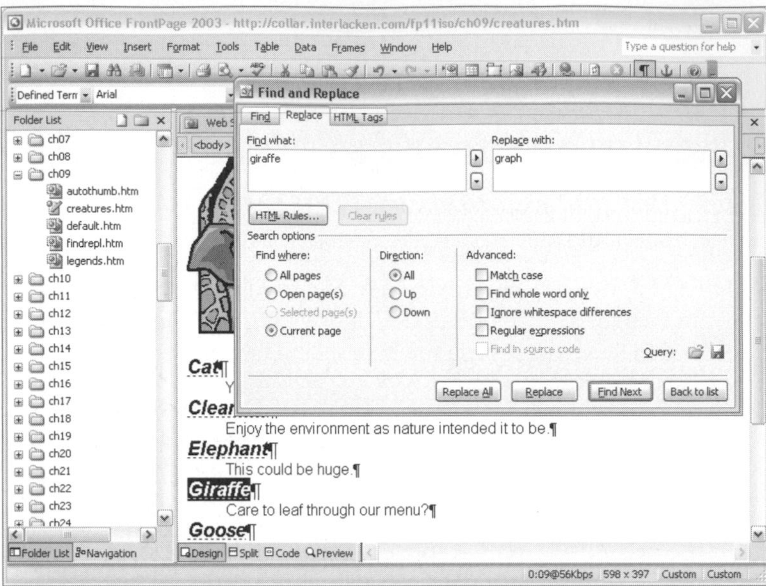

Figure 9-11. To replace text on a given page, double-click its entry in the Replace In Site results list. FrontPage displays the Find And Replace dialog box.

5 If you click Replace All or click either Find Next or Replace past the end of the page, FrontPage offers to save the current page and open the next page containing the found text, again using the dialog box shown in Figure 9-9.

Each page you examine will be marked *Edited* when you return to the list of matches, even if you don't make any changes.

When FrontPage displays the Replace In Site results list, the Replace and Replace All buttons work globally (that is, they affect the entire Web site). When a Web page is open and the results list is hidden, the buttons work only on the current page. Table 9-5 summarizes these differences and provides a reference to other related commands as well.

Table 9-5. Find And Replace Dialog Box Buttons

Button	Replace In Site results list absent	Replace In Site results list present
Find In Site	Searches the entire current Web for pages that contain the Find What string and displays a Replace In Site results list. This command is available only when Find Where is set to All Pages or Selected Page(s).	
Replace All	Replaces all instances in the current page without prompting.	Replaces all instances in all listed pages without prompting.

Table 9-5. Find And Replace Dialog Box Buttons

Button	Replace In Site results list absent	Replace In Site results list present
Replace	Replaces the current instance of the Find What text and advances to the next instance and in the same page.	Opens the current (or first) page in the results list, displays a normal Find And Replace dialog box, and finds the first instance of the Find What text.
Find Next	Advances to the next instance of the Find What text in the same page.	N/A
Back To List	Redisplays the Replace In Site results list.	N/A

Saving and Retrieving FrontPage Queries

By now, you should appreciate that the Find And Replace dialog box provides a great deal of power. This power, however, comes at a cost: Configuring a complex search involves quite a few settings.

Fortunately, FrontPage has a form of short-term memory for Find And Replace dialog box settings. Closing and reopening the dialog box doesn't erase its settings; instead, FrontPage remembers the settings until you change them or quit the program.

FrontPage 2003 can also save search settings in a file for later retrieval. Follow these steps:

1. Get the search (or search and replace) working the way you want.
2. Click the Save Query button on any tab of the Search And Replace dialog box. This button appears just above the Close or Back To List button. It's visible, for example, in Figure 9-11 above the Back To List button.
3. In the File Save dialog box, type a file name in the File Name box then click Save. FrontPage calls this a FrontPage Query file and gives it a .fpq file extension.

To restore settings you previously saved, use this procedure:

1. Open the Search And Replace dialog box. (For example, press Ctrl+F.)
2. Click the Open Query button on any tab of the dialog box. This is another button just above the Close or Back To List button.
3. In the File Open dialog box, locate the file that contains the search specifications you want and double-click it. Alternatively, select the file, and then click Open.

Unfortunately, you can't save a FrontPage Query file in a server-based Web site. This would be handy if you wanted to share the file with other designers working on the same Web site, but alas, it's impossible. By default, FrontPage saves query files at C:\Documents and Settings\<*username*>\Application Data\Microsoft\FrontPage\Queries. This makes the query available only to you, but for any Web site you open.

Checking Spelling

FrontPage 2003 supports two kinds of spelling checking: First, it can check the spelling of words as you type them, and second, it can scan an entire Web page, selected pages, or an entire Web site for errors. Theirs know eggs cues four amiss spilt whirred inn Annie sight Yukon troll.

Checking Spelling as You Type

This is the feature that displays squiggly lines under each misspelled word in your document. In Figure 9-1, for example, the word *anthropological* is misspelled and therefore underlined. To configure this feature, choose Page Options from the Tools menu. The following check boxes appear in the Spelling section on the General tab:

- **Check Spelling As You Type** Controls whether FrontPage immediately checks the spelling of each word you type. You might want to clear this option because it slows down your system or if your page content contains a lot of nonstandard words. This option is selected by default.
- **Hide Spelling Errors In All Documents** Controls whether FrontPage displays squiggly lines under the misspelled words. Why check spelling as you type and not display the squiggly lines? Well, maybe you don't like squiggly lines but you do like very rapid spelling checks later.
- **Default Spelling Language** Controls which national language spelling dictionary FrontPage should use in the absence of any other language specification.

When you right-click a misspelled word—one with a squiggly underline—FrontPage displays a shortcut menu that suggests possible spellings, an Ignore All choice that temporarily accepts the questionable word as correct, and an Add To Dictionary choice that adds the questionable word to the spelling dictionary.

Inside Out

Misspelled words interfere with context menus.

The misspelled word shortcut menu appears in place of any normal shortcut menus. For example, you can't change paragraph properties by right-clicking a misspelled word and choosing Paragraph, because all you'll get is the spelling correction menu. To access the other shortcut menus, right-click some other part of the paragraph that lacks squiggly underlining.

Checking Spelling on Demand

At your command, FrontPage can explicitly check all the spelling in an open Web page. To do this, simply Choose Spelling from the Tools menu. If FrontPage finds any misspelled words, it displays the Spelling dialog box shown in Figure 9-12.

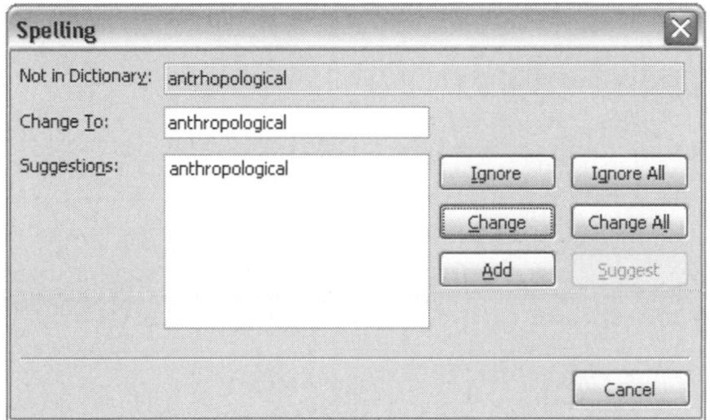

Figure 9-12. FrontPage uses the same spelling checker as the rest of the Microsoft Office System 2003 family.

The Spelling dialog box provides the following options:

- **Not In Dictionary** Displays the misspelled word.
- **Change To** Supplies a corrected word. You can accept the word FrontPage suggests, type a word on the keyboard, or pick a word from the drop-down list of suggestions.
- **Suggestions** Provides a list of possible corrections to the misspelling.

After reviewing these options, click one of the buttons on the right in the dialog box. Table 9-6 describes these buttons.

After you click any button in the table, FrontPage resumes checking with the next word in the page. To stop the spelling check, click the Cancel button.

Table 9-6. Spelling Correction Buttons

Button	Description
Ignore	Makes no change to the questionable word and continues the spelling check.
Ignore All	Works the same as Ignore, except that the spelling checker won't stop if it finds additional occurrences of the same questionable word during the current spelling check.
Change	Replaces the questionable word with the word in the Change To box. You can accept the spelling checker's initial suggestion, select another word from the Suggestions list, or type your own corrected word.
Change All	Works like Change, except that for the remainder of the spelling check, it makes the same replacement whenever it finds the same questionable word.

Table 9-6. Spelling Correction Buttons

Button	Description
Add	Adds the questionable word to the spelling checker dictionary.
Suggest	Checks the spelling of the word in the Change To box and, if it can't be verified, offers suggestions.

Checking Spelling in Multiple Pages

Front Page can also check spelling in all or part of your Web site. In a two-phase process similar to finding and replacing text in multiple files, the spelling checker first builds a list of pages containing misspelled words and then provides choices for editing pages or adding them to the Tasks view. If you choose to edit a listed page, FrontPage steps through the misspelled words. Here's the procedure to check spelling in all or part of a Web:

1 Close any pages that are open for editing.

2 If you plan to check less than the entire Web, select the pages you want to check.

3 Choose Spelling from the Tools menu, or click the Spelling button on the Standard toolbar. This displays the Spelling dialog box shown in Figure 9-13.

Spelling

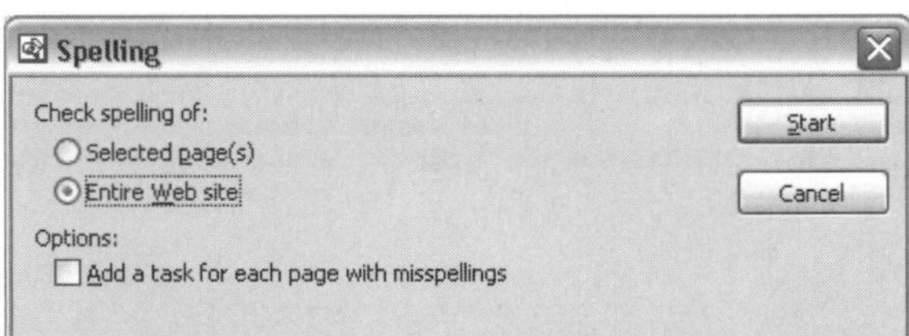

Figure 9-13. Use this dialog box to initiate Check Spelling In Site.

Configure the following settings:

- **Check Spelling Of** Specifies the range of pages to check for correct spelling: Selected Page(s) checks only the pages you specified in step 2, and Entire Web checks all pages in the current Web.
- **Add A Task For Each Page With Misspellings** Indicates that you want to bypass the list of pages containing misspelled words and instead add each page to the Tasks view.

4 Click Start. FrontPage checks the specified pages for spelling errors and then displays the result list in the Spelling dialog box as shown in Figure 9-14. This itemizes all selected pages containing misspelled words.

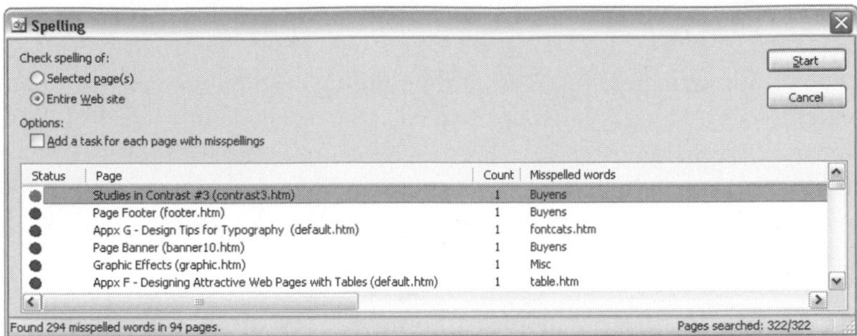

Figure 9-14. FrontPage displays this dialog box to identify pages with spelling errors.

The Status column displays the following:

- If you selected Add A Task For Each Page With Misspellings, FrontPage displays a yellow circle and a status of Added for each page that failed the spelling check.
- If you didn't select Add A Task For Each Page With Misspellings, FrontPage displays a red circle and no status for each page that failed.

5 As with the Find In Site and Replace In Site operations, scanning for errors doesn't correct them. To actually resolve spelling errors, double-click the entry for the first page you want to correct, or select it and then click Start.

6 FrontPage opens the page you selected in step 5, advances to the first spelling error, and displays the Spelling dialog box shown previously in Figure 9-12. As when checking a single page, the following options are available:

- **Not In Dictionary** Displays the misspelled word.
- **Change To** Supplies a corrected word.
- **Suggestions** Provides a list of possible correct spellings.

Set these controls, and then click one of the buttons on the right. (Table 9-6 explains the buttons.) Clicking any button except Cancel advances to the next spelling error in the same page.

7 When FrontPage reaches the end of the current page (or if you clicked the Cancel button), it displays the Continue With The Next Page? dialog box, shown previously in Figure 9-9. If you need help with these buttons, refer to the instructions near that figure.

> **Note** FrontPage uses the Microsoft custom dictionary. Because this file is on the FrontPage designer's local machine, dictionary additions made by one designer won't be available to other designers working on the same Web.

Using the Thesaurus

As you're thinking great thoughts and pounding out text, finding just the right word is frequently a problem. Or perhaps you need the opposite of a word. To resolve both dilemmas, FrontPage 2003 has a built-in thesaurus. Neither prehistoric nor reptilian, a *thesaurus* is a dictionary of words with like and opposite meanings. FrontPage uses the same thesaurus as the rest of the Microsoft Office 2003 suite. To use the thesaurus:

1. Select the word you want to replace.
2. Choose Thesaurus from the Tools menu. This displays the Thesaurus dialog box, shown in Figure 9-15.

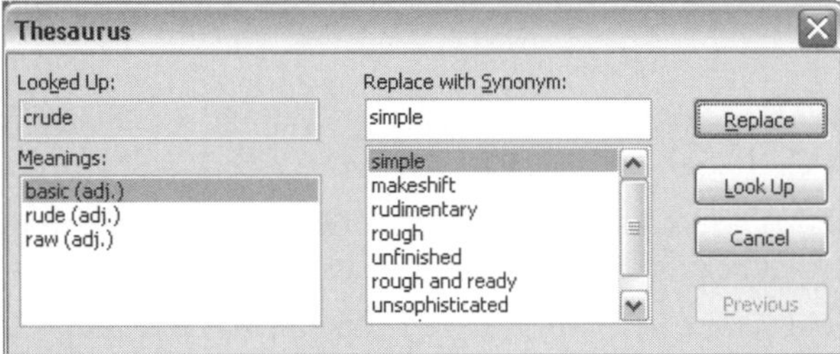

Figure 9-15. The thesaurus searches for words with like and unlike meanings.

FrontPage automatically displays the selected word's synonyms (words with like meanings). When the original word has several meanings, the Meanings box will have an entry for each. In the example, clicking the *basic* meaning at the left displays a different list of synonyms at the right than clicking the *rude* meaning.

3. If the Replace With Synonym list contains a word you want in your Web page—or even a word that seems closer to a good fit—click that word. The word you clicked will then appear in the Replace With Synonym box.
4. To check for synonyms of the word in the Replace With Synonym box, click Look Up.
5. If step 4 takes you further from your goal rather than closer to it, click the Previous button.
6. To look up synonyms for an entirely new word, enter it in the Replace With Synonym box, and then click the Look Up button.
7. When the best word appears in the Replace With Synonym box, click the Replace button. This closes the dialog box and replaces the word you selected in step 1.
8. To exit the thesaurus without replacing the original word, click Cancel.

In Summary…

This chapter explained the basics of finding, replacing, and checking the spelling of text in single Web pages, selected Web pages, or an entire FrontPage-based Web site. It also explained how to use the Microsoft Office thesaurus to finds synonyms for a word.

The next chapter explains how to add pictures to a Web page.

Chapter 10

Adding and Formatting Pictures

Pictures (also called graphics and images) are among the most important components of any Web page—so important that it's rare to see a page without them. A Web page without pictures is like a day without sunshine—a dull and dreary prospect.

Recognizing this importance, Microsoft FrontPage includes features that easily search for existing pictures, acquire new pictures from scanners or digital cameras, and in some cases, even create pictures. What's more, FrontPage can modify pictures in a variety of ways right in the Page view editing window.

This chapter provides the basic techniques for adding pictures to Web sites and to Web pages. For completeness, it also introduces a plethora of advanced techniques covered more fully by individual chapters later in this book. Feel free to jump ahead to those chapters as the mood strikes you.

Adding Pictures to a Page

FrontPage can add pictures of almost any kind to your Web pages in a variety of ways. One of these is almost sure to meet any requirements you encounter:

- **Picture files** FrontPage can insert pictures from any file location on your computer, from the Clipboard, from the Web site you're working in, or from any location on the World Wide Web. If the picture isn't in one of the usual Web file formats, FrontPage will convert it automatically.

For more information about picture file types used on the Web, refer to "Choosing Picture File Formats," on page 671.

- **Clip art** FrontPage can use the Microsoft Clip Organizer, which is the same picture gallery that the rest of the Microsoft Office System 2003 suite uses. If none of the thousands of pictures in the Clip Organizer meet your needs, you can search further on Microsoft's Web site by clicking Clip Art On Office Online in the Clip Art task pane.

- **Pictures from a scanner or camera** FrontPage can directly accept pictures from TWAIN-compliant devices such as scanners and digital cameras. This bypasses the usual steps of first capturing the picture as a disk file, then adding the file to your Web site, and finally adding it to your Web page.

> **Note** Despite reports to the contrary, TWAIN doesn't stands for Technology Without An Interesting Name. TWAIN isn't an acronym; it's simply the name of a software standard for connecting scanners and digital cameras to computers. For more information about TWAIN, browse *www.twain.org*.

- **Video files** FrontPage can add video files to a Web page as easily as it can add picture files.
- **Line art** FrontPage can add line art to a Web page. The following kinds of pictures all use Vector Markup Language (VML) to express line drawings. VML is an XML-based way to describe pictures using curves, lines, and xy-coordinates:
  - **Drawings** FrontPage can draw lines, arrows, rectangles, and other objects within a Web page.
  - **AutoShapes** FrontPage can create geometric shapes, block arrows, flowchart symbols, stars, and other shapes selected from a library.
  - **WordArt** FrontPage can provide extremely rich formatting of text. This feature has been present in earlier releases of Microsoft Word, Microsoft Excel, and Microsoft PowerPoint. The introduction of VML makes it usable in FrontPage as well.

  A line drawing expressed in VML is usually much smaller than the same drawing saved as a GIF or JPEG file. Currently, only Microsoft Internet Explorer 5 and later can display VML. Other browsers ignore the VML code and display instead a GIF version of the same picture.

After you add a picture to a Web page, FrontPage provides full access to the picture's HTML properties through easy-to-use dialog boxes. FrontPage also provides a variety of tools for modifying pictures. With these tools, you can enlarge pictures, reduce them, flip them top to bottom or right to left, and change their brightness and contrast.

No matter where the picture comes from, FrontPage prompts you for a Save As location the next time you save the Web page.

FrontPage also includes a collection of basic picture editing tools. For more information about these tools, refer to Chapter 23, "Editing Pictures in FrontPage."

Inserting Pictures by Dragging

FrontPage makes adding a picture to a Web page as easy as dragging and dropping. Figure 10-1 shows how you can drag pictures from Page view's Folder List to a page that's open in Design view. As you drag over the open Web page, the insertion point shows where the picture will appear.

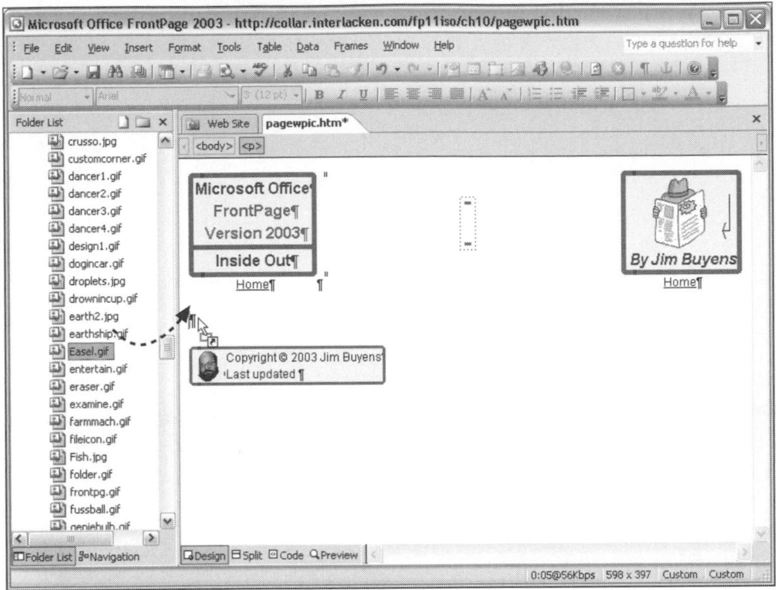

Figure 10-1. FrontPage can accept pictures dropped from the Folder List, from Windows Explorer, or from Internet Explorer.

If the picture you want to use isn't located in the current Web site, you can proceed in two ways. You can:

- Drag the file from its current location and drop it into the current Web site—for example, into the Folder List or Folders view. (If you have no reason to put the file anywhere else, the images folder is usually a good choice.) Then drag the file from its new location onto the open Web page.
- Drag the file from its current location and drop it on the open Web page. The next time you save the open page, FrontPage displays the Save Embedded Files dialog box, shown in Figure 10-2. This dialog box asks where in the current Web site you want to save the copied file.

Tip Drag and drop pictures confidently in FrontPage 2003.

In past releases, FrontPage would often mishandle pictures you dragged from a local file location and dropped onto a Web page. As a result, many Web designers formed the habit of always dragging pictures to the Folder List and then dragging the same picture from the Folder List to the open Web page. In FrontPage 2003, this problem is fixed and either procedure works fine.

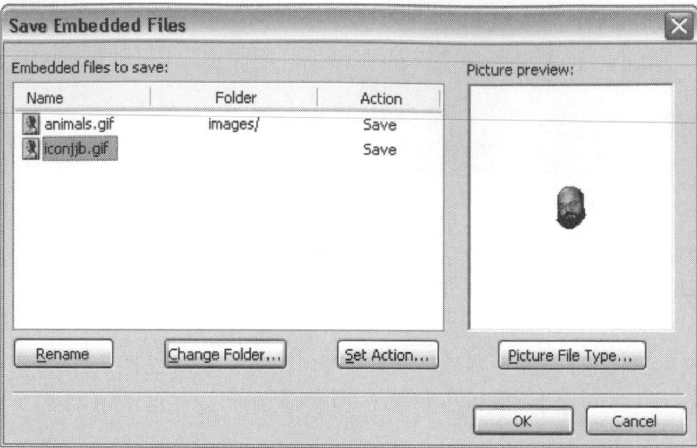

Figure 10-2. When you save a Web page that contains pictures not already saved in the current Web site, this dialog box lists and suggests a save location for each picture.

You can drag picture files—or, for that matter, any other kind of file—to and from the following locations in almost any combination:

- An open Web page
- A folder location in the same Web site
- A folder location in a different Web site
- A folder location in your local file system

Drag-and-drop operations involving the document area of an open Web page follow different rules than drag-and-drop operations among folder locations. This is because a Web page contains only a link to the picture's physical location, and not a copy of the picture itself. The rules governing drag-and-drop operations involving open Web pages are these:

- Dragging a picture from one spot on a Web page to another spot on the same page performs a *move* operation. In effect, the picture disappears from its old location and appears in the new one.
- Dragging a picture from one Web page to another in the same Web site also performs a *move* operation. The picture disappears from the page that formerly displayed it.
- Dragging a picture from an open page in one Web site to an open page in a different Web site *copies* the picture. The picture doesn't disappear from the page that originally displayed it.

Be aware that this last operation doesn't copy the picture file into the second Web site. FrontPage holds the copied picture in memory until you save the Web page and then displays the Save Embedded Files dialog box to prompt you for a Save location inside the second Web site.

Dragging a picture file from a folder location to an open Web page never copies the file physically. It creates only an instruction to display the file from its location within the same Web site. If the file doesn't reside in the same Web site as the open Web page, FrontPage again holds the copied picture in memory and displays the Save Embedded Files dialog box when you save the page.

Dragging files between folder locations in the same Web site always moves the files. Dragging files between folder locations in different Web sites always copies them, as does dragging files between FrontPage and Windows Explorer. Table 10-1 summarizes all these rules.

Table 10-1. Drag-and-Drop Results in FrontPage

Drag from	Drop on				
	Open page		Folder		
	Same Web site	Different Web site	Same Web site	Different Web site	File location
Open page	Moves link	Copies into memory	Not allowed	Not allowed	Not allowed.
Folder in Web site	Creates link	Copies into memory	Moves file	Copies file	Copies file.
Folder in file location	Copies into memory	Copies into memory	Copies file	Copies file	Copies file if drive letters are different; otherwise, moves file

If an operation would normally move a file and you actually want to copy a file, hold down the Ctrl key while you drag.

If you have trouble remembering these rules, try dragging with the right mouse button. Whenever you drop an object after dragging it in this way, Microsoft Windows displays a shortcut menu with Move Here, Copy Here, Link Here, and Cancel options.

Using the Save Embedded Files Dialog Box

The Save Embedded Files dialog box, previously shown in Figure 10-2, appears whenever you save an open Web page that contains a picture or other object that doesn't reside in the current Web site. This situation occurs when you drag or paste a picture from outside the current Web site onto an open Web page, when you insert clip art, when you use certain FrontPage picture editing tools to create a new version of a picture, and in various other situations. If there are several such files, FrontPage lists them all in one dialog box. From the Save Embedded Files dialog box, you can do the following:

- If you want to rename a file, select it, and click the Rename button.
- If you want to save one or more files in a different folder, select the files, and click the Change Folder button.
- If you want to change a file's action from Save to Don't Save (or back again), click the Set Action button. If a file with the same folder location and file name already exists in the current Web site, clicking the Set Action button displays a Set Action dialog box with these options:

- **Overwrite** FrontPage replaces the existing file with the new one and makes the current Web page refer to the new file.
- **Use Existing** FrontPage discards the picture it has in memory, retains the existing file, and makes the current Web page refer to the existing file.
- **Don't Save** FrontPage retains both the existing file and the new version in memory. The Save Embedded Files dialog box will reappear the next time you save the page.

Unless you have strong reasons not to, you should accept FrontPage's suggestion and save these files to your Web site. Rename them or change the folder where they reside, if you want, but do save them. If you don't, sooner or later they're bound to come up missing from your Web page.

- If you want to change a picture's characteristics, click the Picture File Type button. This displays the Picture File Type dialog box shown in Figure 10-3.

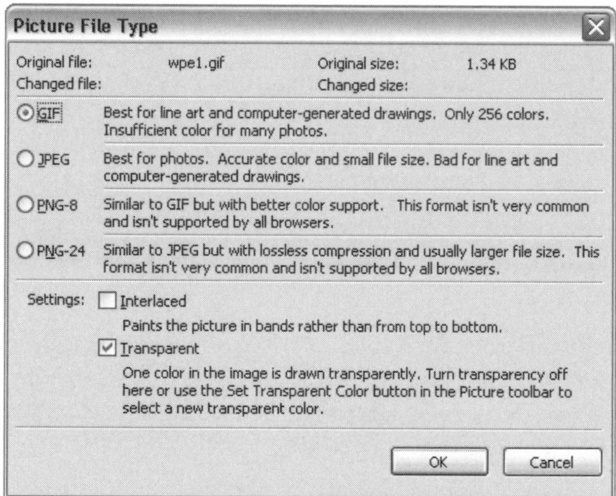

Figure 10-3. Clicking the Picture Options button in Figure 10-2 provides these options for the currently selected picture.

From this dialog box, the following options are available:

- **GIF** Select this option if you want FrontPage to save the picture as a GIF file. GIF files are preferable for pictures that contain sharp lines, flat areas of color, and at most 256 colors.
- **JPEG** Select this option if you want FrontPage to save the picture as a JPEG file. JPEG files are generally preferable for photographs and other pictures that contain many colors.
- **PNG-8** Select this option of you want FrontPage to save the picture in 8-bit Portable Network Graphics (PNG) format. This is a new format similar to GIF. Although this format does offer some advantages, not all browsers can display it.

- **PNG-24** Select this option if you want FrontPage to save the picture in 24-bit PNG format. This is a new format similar to JPEG. Again, not all browsers can display this format.

After you select one of these formats, FrontPage will display additional settings just above the OK and Cancel buttons. Table 10-2 explains these settings.

Table 10-2. Picture File Type Settings

GIF	JPEG	PNG-8	PNG-24	Setting	Description
●	❍	●	●	Interlaced	The browser will first display a coarse version of the picture and then a full-resolution version when it finishes receiving the file.
●	❍	❍	❍	Transparent	Indicates that the file might contain one color that the browser displays as transparent. Clearing this box returns the color to normal visibility. If the box is dimmed, no transparent color is in effect.
❍	●	❍	❍	Use Image As Is	Tells FrontPage to save a JPEG picture using that picture's original settings.
❍	●	❍	❍	Quality	Specifies a degree of compression. Lower numbers decrease file size but sacrifice picture quality. Typical values are 70 through 90.
❍	●	❍	❍	Progressive Passes	Specifies the number of increasingly detailed versions the browser will display before displaying the picture at full resolution. To display the picture at full resolution as it arrives, specify 0.

For more information about designating a GIF color as transparent, refer to "Setting Transparency," on page 643.

Click OK when you've set all these options the way you want them.

Inserting Pictures Using the Insert Menu

You can also insert pictures using the FrontPage Insert menu. Here's the procedure:

1. Open the page that should display the picture.
2. Set the insertion point where you want the picture to appear.

Chapter 10

3 On the Insert menu, point to Picture and then choose From File. This produces the Picture dialog box, shown in Figure 10-4.

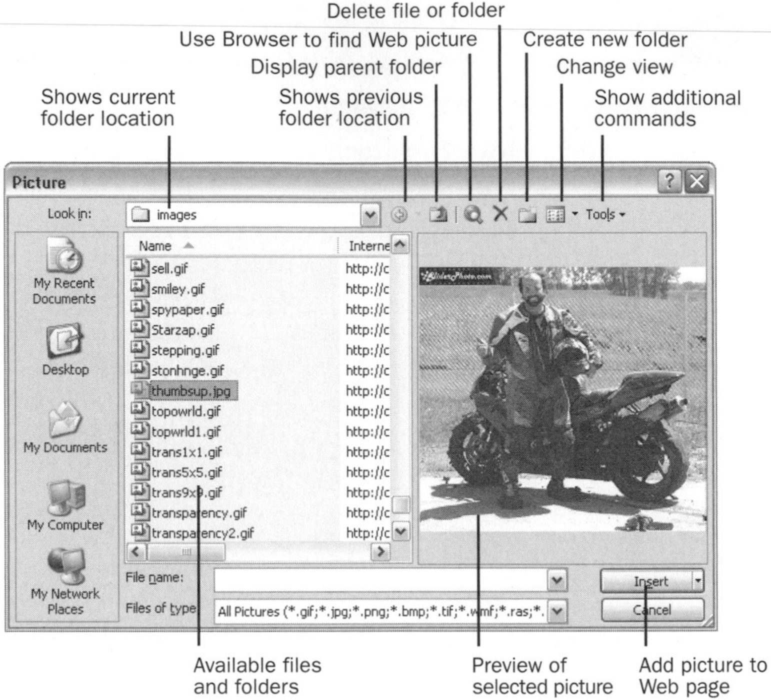

Figure 10-4. Use this dialog box to locate and insert a desired picture.

4 Select the picture file you want to display or type its name into the File Name box, then click Insert.

If the Picture dialog box shown in Figure 10-4 looks familiar, there's a reason: It's essentially a duplicate of most other file-oriented dialog boxes in FrontPage. All the toolbar buttons and other controls work as they do in other such dialog boxes.

For more information about the buttons and icons in the Picture dialog box, refer to "The File Dialog Box Toolbar" and "The My Places Bar," in Appendix A.

Views

Switching the file selection list to Preview mode is particularly useful when searching for pictures. Figure 10-4 shows the Picture dialog box in this mode previewing a picture. To select Preview mode, choose Preview from the Views drop-down menu, or repeatedly click the Views toolbar button until Preview mode is in effect.

Inserting Clip Art

If you don't have an existing picture that meets your needs, it's very likely you can find one in the extensive Clip Organizer that comes with FrontPage. The Clip Organizer is a shared resource for the entire Office 2003 suite of programs. This means any clip art you install for any Office application (such as Microsoft Publisher) is available to FrontPage as well. FrontPage can also use Office clip art that Microsoft provides on its Web site; this includes buttons, horizontal rules, backgrounds, pictures, and other figures that can enhance your Web pages.

Office 2003 provides three distinctly different ways to search for and select clip art:

- The Clip Art task pane, shown in Figure 10-5, provides a quick and easy way to search for clip art without leaving FrontPage and without obscuring the current Web page.

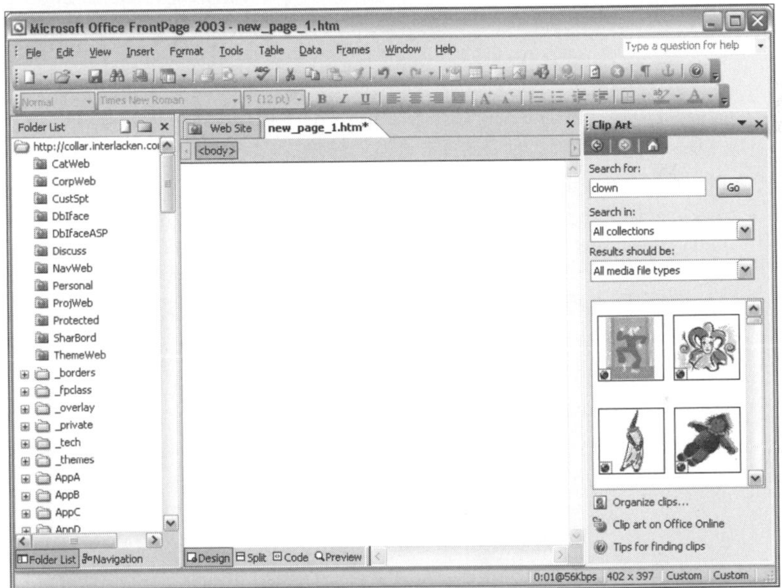

Figure 10-5. This task pane searches for clip art pictures without obscuring or disabling the main document window.

- The Clip Organizer application, shown in Figure 10-6, provides more ways to search for clip art, more screen space to display search hits, and better previewing capabilities.
- Design Gallery Live, shown in Figure 10-7, provides additional clip art from Microsoft and a community section where you can share pictures and ideas with other people. You must agree to a license agreement before accessing the Design Gallery Live clip art.

Figure 10-6. The Microsoft Clip Organizer searches for pictures and other media files. It can also add, rearrange, and delete individual files or entire collections within the gallery.

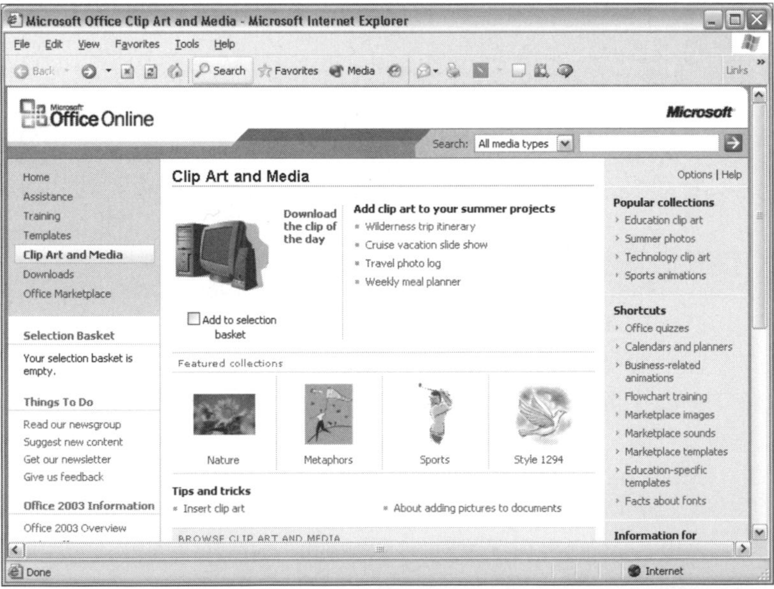

Figure 10-7. Microsoft's Design Gallery Live site offers additional Microsoft clip art and provides a way for clip art users and creators to find each other.

Here's the procedure for using the Clip Art task pane to locate and insert clip art:

1. Open the Web page on which you want to display the clip art picture.
2. Set the insertion point where you want the picture to appear.
3. Choose Picture from the Insert menu, and then choose Clip Art.
4. When the Clip Art task pane appears, as shown previously in Figure 10-5, use one or more of the following controls to describe the picture you hope to find:
   - **Search For** Enter one or more keywords that categorize the picture. Concrete terms like *man*, *woman*, *building*, and *water* usually produce better results than abstract terms like *happy* and *sad*.
   - **Search In** Display the drop-down list shown here, and modify the category selections to further refine your search. By default, All Collections is selected. To limit the search, clear the categories you don't want. To display subcategories, click the plus sign that precedes each category. The example shown here searches the entire My Collections collection and the Agriculture and Animals portions of the Office Collections collection:

     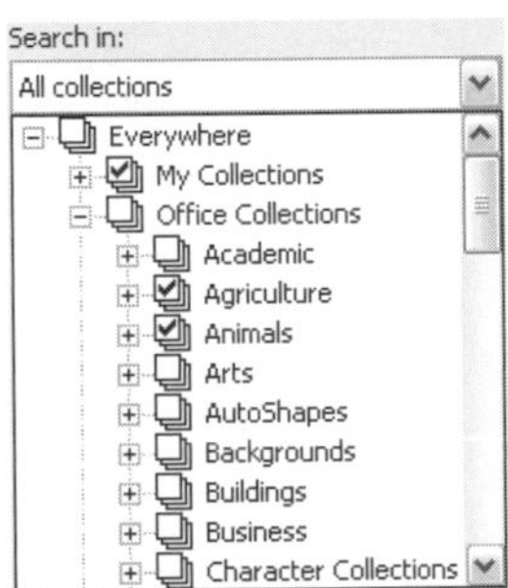

   - **Results Should Be** Display this drop-down list to specify the file formats you want: Clip Art, Photographs, Movies, or Sounds. To display subtypes, click the plus sign that precedes each file format. This list starts with all file formats selected. Clear any file formats you don't want.

     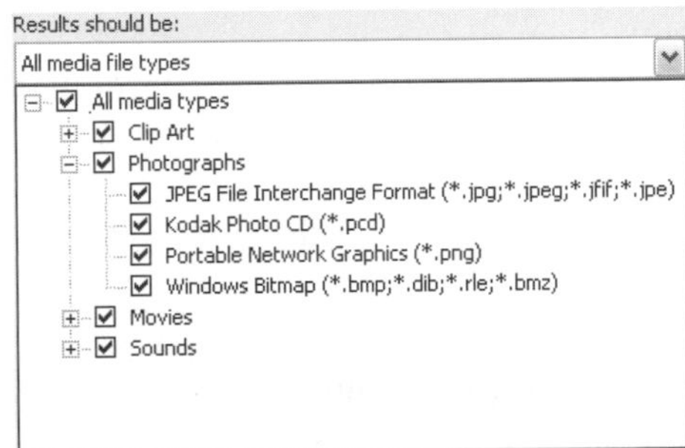

5. After you've described your criteria as completely as possible, click the Go button. The message *(Searching…)* will appear above the list in the center of the task pane, and then, after a brief wait, search results will begin to appear in that box.

> **Tip** **Resize or detach a task pane**
>
> To resize the Clip Art task pane (or, for that matter, any other task pane), drag its inner border to the right or left. To move any task pane to the outer side of the main window, drag its title bar. To detach a task pane, drag its title bar completely outside the main FrontPage window. To reattach it, drag the title bar over the left or right window border.

6 When the search is complete, the *(Searching…)* message disappears, and the results box displays a scrollable list of matching pictures. Hold the mouse pointer over any picture to display a pop-up information box and drop-down arrow, as shown in Figure 10-8. The pop-up information box lists the picture's assigned keywords, its width and height, its size, and its format.

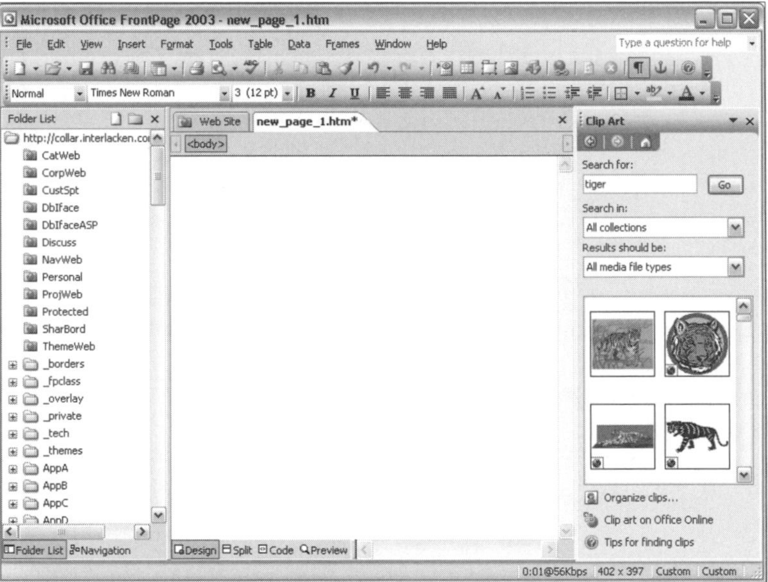

Figure 10-8. After a clip art picture appears in the Clip Art task pane, clicking it adds it to the current Web page.

7 To add any displayed clip art picture to a Web page, open the page, set the insertion point, and then click the displayed picture once. If you require more options, click the picture's drop-down arrow to expose these commands:

- **Insert** Adds the selected picture to the current Web page at the insertion point.
- **Copy** Copies the selected picture to the Clipboard. This is handy if you want to paste the clip art picture into another program, modify it, and only then paste it onto your Web page.

- **Delete From Clip Organizer** Removes the selected picture from the Clip Organizer.
- **Copy To Collection** Copies the selected picture's catalog entry to another area of the Clip Organizer. For example, you might want to create your own collection of frequently used pictures.
- **Move To Collection** Moves the selected picture's catalog entry to another area of the Clip Organizer.
- **Edit Keywords** Displays a Keywords dialog box where you can add, modify, or delete the keywords assigned to the current picture. You can use this facility to associate pictures with keywords (such as product departments or project names) that are uniquely meaningful to you.
- **Find Similar Style** Conducts a new search, this time for pictures drawn in the same style as the selected picture. Using the same clip art style throughout a Web site adds to the site's sense of unity.
- **Preview/Properties** Displays a dialog box that shows a larger version of the selected picture and a text listing of its properties (name, file format, size, creation date, keywords, and so forth).

8 Unless you're having the luckiest day of the year, the newly inserted clip art picture will almost certainly be too large, too small, too light, too dark, or too terrible to describe. Fortunately, FrontPage has built-in tools for correcting such problems. Even more fortunately, a later section in this chapter describes how to use them.

For more information about modifying pictures in Web pages, refer to "Modifying Picture Properties," later in this chapter.

9 If the search results are unsatisfactory (or if you just want to start a new search), modify any settings you want, click the Search button, and return to step 4.

Clicking the Organize Clips link at the bottom of the Clip Art task pane starts the Clip Organizer, shown previously in Figure 10-6. You can also start the Clip Organizer directly from the Programs submenu of the Windows Start menu; it's under Microsoft Office Tools.

The Clip Organizer uses three task panes that normally appear at the left side of the window. These are:

- **Collection List** Displays a list of collections in your local clip art library. This is the same information that FrontPage displays in the Search In drop-down list of its Clip Art task pane.
- **Search** Displays the same input controls as the FrontPage Clip Art task pane: a Search For box, a Search In drop-down list, a Results Should Be drop-down list, and a Go button. These controls work the same as their FrontPage counterparts.
- **Search Results** Displays options to search Microsoft's Web site for Office assistance or training, for offline help, or for clip art and media.
- **Help** Displays options to search the local Help database or Microsoft's Web site for assistance.

Chapter 10

Frequently Asked Questions About WMF Files

Many Microsoft clip art pictures arrive in a format called WMF. This gives rise to the following questions:

Is it true that WMF stands for World Mustache Federation?

No. Windows Metafile (WMF) is a file format that stores the Windows API commands required to draw something on your screen. WMF usually stores pictures as lines, curves, and shapes rather than as pixels. This makes WMF a great format for clip art because you can enlarge, reduce, or reshape such pictures with no loss of resolution. Microsoft supplies most clip art pictures in WMF format.

Is WMF a good format for display on the Web?

No. Because some browsers can't display WMF, it isn't a good format to use on Web pages. FrontPage therefore converts pasted WMF pictures to GIF or JPEG format the first time you save the receiving page.

Should I modify WMF pictures before or after FrontPage converts them to GIF or JPEG?

After FrontPage converts a WMF picture to GIF or JPEG, resizing or otherwise changing the picture will degrade the picture just as it does for any other GIF or JPEG file. Therefore, it's much better to resize, resample, or otherwise modify any new clip art pictures before you save the page that contains them. This ensures that the picture is saved with the proper size and without loss of resolution.

Is there any way to convert a WMF picture to GIF or JPEG format without saving the Web page?

Resample

Yes. After the picture is the size you want, select it, and click the Resample button on the Pictures toolbar. (If you resize the picture by dragging its handles, a Picture Actions box will appear after you release the mouse button. Open the drop-down menu on this box, then Choose Resample Picture To Match Size.)

For more information about resizing and resampling pictures, refer to "Resampling Pictures," on page 645.

Thumbnails

The Search task pane doesn't contain a results box like the one in the FrontPage Clip Art task pane. Instead, when a search yields results, the matching pictures appear in the Clip Organizer main window. This window has three viewing modes, which you can select by using either the View menu or the Clip Organizer Standard toolbar:

List

- **Thumbnails** Displays a small preview picture of each matching file.
- **List** Displays a compact list of each matching file name.
- **Details** Displays the file name, size, type, caption, keywords, duration, and date of each matching file. Duration refers to the amount of time that a sound or video file will play.

> For more information about the Clip Organizer Standard toolbar, refer to "The Microsoft Clip Organizer Standard Toolbar," In Appendix A.

To view the entire contents of a given collection:

Collection List

1. Click the Collection List button on the Clip Organizer toolbar, or choose Collection List from the View menu. This displays the Collection List task pane, shown in Figure 10-9.

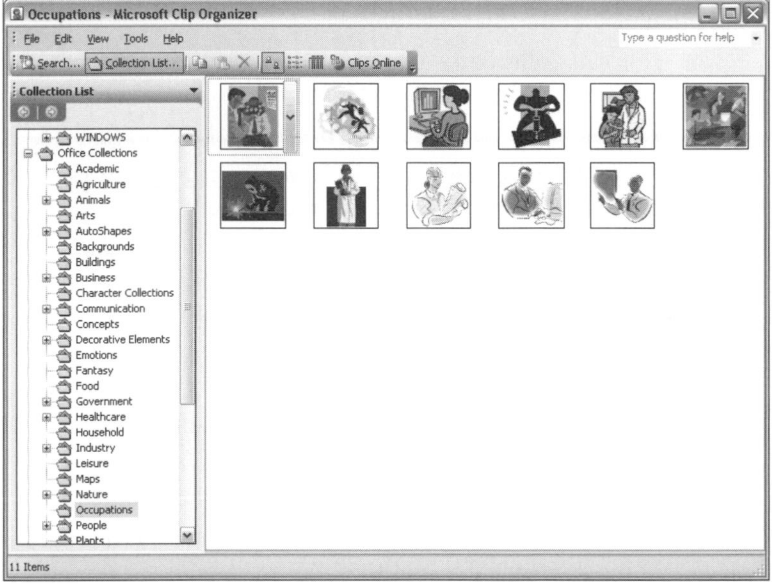

Figure 10-9. The Collection List task pane displays the names of each collection in the Clip Organizer. The main document window shows the clip art files in the current gallery.

2. Click any listed collection to display all of its files in the main document window.
3. To view files in subfolders, expand the parent folder, and click the subfolder you want to view.

Note that the main document window doesn't display files located in subfolders of a collection you select. For that, you must explicitly select the subfolder. Clicking a plus sign icon displays the subfolders of a given folder, and clicking a minus sign icon hides them.

Use the menu commands listed below to add, reorganize, or delete Clip Organizer files or collections:

- **File** The Clip Organizer File menu provides the following commands:
  - **New Collection** Creates a new collection folder and specifies its location.
  - **Add Clips To Organizer** Enlarges the gallery with new files. This command can add all media files on all or part of your hard disk, individual files, or files from a scanner or camera.

- **Send To Mail Recipient (As Attachment)** Sends an e-mail message containing the currently selected clip files to recipients you specify.
- **Collection Properties** Displays or modifies the physical location of the current collection and offers an option to update the Clip Organizer index with current information.

- **Edit** The Clip Organizer Edit menu provides these commands:
  - **Cut, Copy, and Paste** Work as they do in all other Windows programs.
  - **Move To Collection** Relocates the catalog entries of the currently selected clip files to a different collection.
  - **Copy To Collection** Duplicates the catalog entries for the currently selected clip files in a different collection.
  - **Rename Collection** Changes the name of a collection.
  - **Delete From "Collection"** Removes the catalog entries for the currently selected clip files from the current collection.
  - **Delete From Clip Organizer** Removes all catalog entries for the currently selected clip files from all collections where they occur.
  - **Select All** Selects all files in the current collection or search results.
  - **Keywords** Displays a Keywords dialog box where you can add, modify, or delete the keywords assigned to the current picture. This is the same dialog box you get by right-clicking a picture and choosing Edit Keywords from its shortcut menu.
- **View** The Clip Organizer View menu provides these commands:
  - **Thumbnails, List, Details, Collection List, and Search** Duplicate the functions of the corresponding toolbar buttons.
  - **Preview/Properties** Displays a dialog box that shows a larger version of the selected picture and a text listing of its properties. This is the same dialog box you get by right-clicking a picture and choosing Preview/Properties from its shortcut menu.
  - **Refresh** Reloads the display with current information.
- **Tools** The Clip Organizer Tools menu offers these three commands:
  - **Clips Online** Displays the Microsoft Clip Art And Media Home Page in your browser.
  - **Find Similar Style** Searches for pictures similar in style to the current selection.
  - **Compact** Reclaims wasted space in the Clip Organizer catalog.

Inserting Pictures from a Scanner or Camera

To record a picture directly from a scanner or a digital camera to a Web page, follow this procedure:

1. Open the Web page that should contain the scanned picture.
2. Set the insertion point where you want the scanned picture to appear.
3. On the Insert menu, point to Picture and then choose From Scanner Or Camera.
4. If FrontPage displays a dialog box like the one shown in Figure 10-10, select the scanner or camera you want to use, and then click Insert.

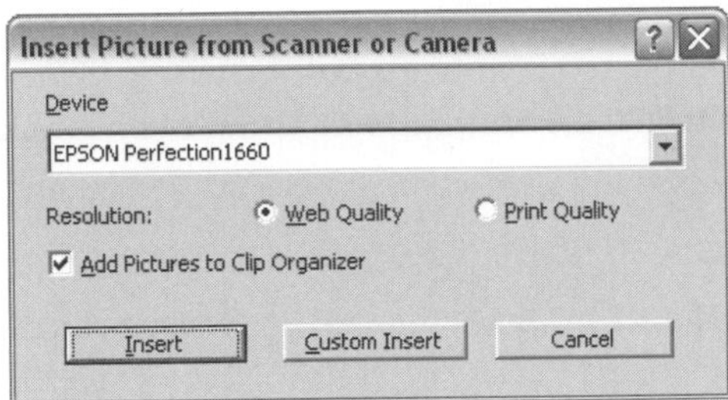

Figure 10-10. This dialog box is the starting point for capturing pictures from a digital source connected to your PC. FrontPage can add such pictures directly to a Web page.

5. The software that captures pictures from your scanner or camera might appear at this point. If so, follow the instructions that came with that software.

   Instead of the usual Save and Save As commands, most scanning software provides a command called Place Image, Insert Picture, or something similar. Choose this command to terminate the scanner or camera software and add the scanned picture to your Web page.
6. The next time you save the Web page, FrontPage will display the Save Embedded Files dialog box to confirm the file name and folder location for the captured picture.

Inserting Drawings

Figure 10-11 shows a drawing done entirely in FrontPage. The various boxes, lines, text fragments, and shading are all VML objects. Transmitting a VML drawing to the Web visitor uses far less bandwidth than transmitting a GIF or JPEG picture of the same size. This is because VML transmits instructions for drawing the objects rather than a picture of the entire diagram.

Chapter 23, "Editing Pictures in FrontPage," includes detailed instructions for creating drawings such as the one shown in Figure 10-11.

Troubleshooting

Unable to Connect to Scanner or Camera

Whenever you choose the From Scanner Or Camera command, FrontPage searches the local computer's configuration for software that complies with the TWAIN specification. If no such software is installed on the computer running FrontPage, the following message appears:

Unable to connect to scanner or camera. Check the connection and reinstall driver if necessary.

To stop getting this message, attempt the following:

- Install the Windows driver software that came with your device. (Better yet, download and install the latest driver from the manufacturer's Web site.)
- Make sure that you connected the device properly to your computer.
- Make sure that you've turned the device on.

Most scanner and camera software complies with the TWAIN specification. If yours doesn't, save the picture to disk, and then drag the disk file from Windows Explorer to your open Web page.

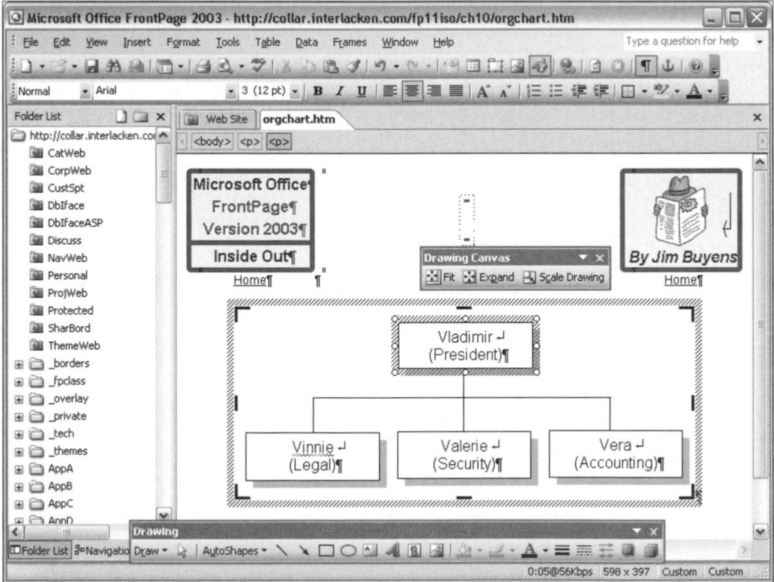

Figure 10-11. You can create line art drawing like this entirely in FrontPage. If a browser supports VML, downloading the line art will be much faster than downloading an ordinary picture file of the same size.

At a surface level, the procedure for creating this picture goes like this:

1. Set the insertion point where you want the drawing to appear.
2. From the Insert menu, choose Picture and then choose New Drawing. This creates a drawing area, which appears as the large shaded rectangle shown in Figure 10-11. A Drawing Canvas toolbar also appears; this controls the size of the drawing area (that is, the size of the canvas). If necessary, use the sizing handles to change the size of the drawing.

For more information about the Drawing Canvas toolbar, refer to "The Drawing Canvas Toolbar," in Appendix A.

3. If the Drawing toolbar isn't visible, choose Toolbars from the View menu, and then choose Drawing. The Drawing toolbar appears below the main document window in Figure 10-11.

For more information about the Drawing toolbar, refer to "The Drawing Toolbar," in Appendix A.

Text Box

4. To create each of the four text boxes shown in Figure 10-11, first click the Text Box button on the Drawing toolbar, and then drag the mouse pointer across the area where you want the text box to appear. You can alter text boxes in the following ways:
   - To resize a box, drag one of its sizing handles.
   - To reposition a box, drag it by its edge.
   - To enter text in a box, click in the center of the box and start typing.

Line

5. To draw each of the connecting lines, click the Line button on the Drawing toolbar, position the mouse pointer where you want the line to start, and then drag the pointer to where you want the line to end.

Shadow Style

6. To add the three-dimensional shading, click the Shadow Style button on the Drawing toolbar, and then select the style of shading you want.

If you plan to start working with drawings without referring to Chapter 22, you should know that drawing areas use CSS Positioning. This technology positions objects on a Web page in a variety of ways, including pixel-precise xy-coordinates. CSS Positioning is a powerful but frustrating tool because not all browsers support it equally.

For more information about CSS Positioning, refer to "Positioning Content with Cascading Style Sheets," on page 621.

Not all browsers support VML either, but this is less of a problem than you might expect. Every time you save a Web page that contains an object created using the Drawing tools, FrontPage creates a copy of the drawing as a GIF file. Then, inside the VML code, it buries an HTML tag that displays the GIF file. The result is this:

- Browsers that understand the VML code bypass the tag that displays the GIF file.
- Browsers that don't understand the VML code will ignore it and display the GIF file.

This explains how, in Figure 10-12, Netscape Navigator 4.77 is displaying the drawing created in Figure 10-11.

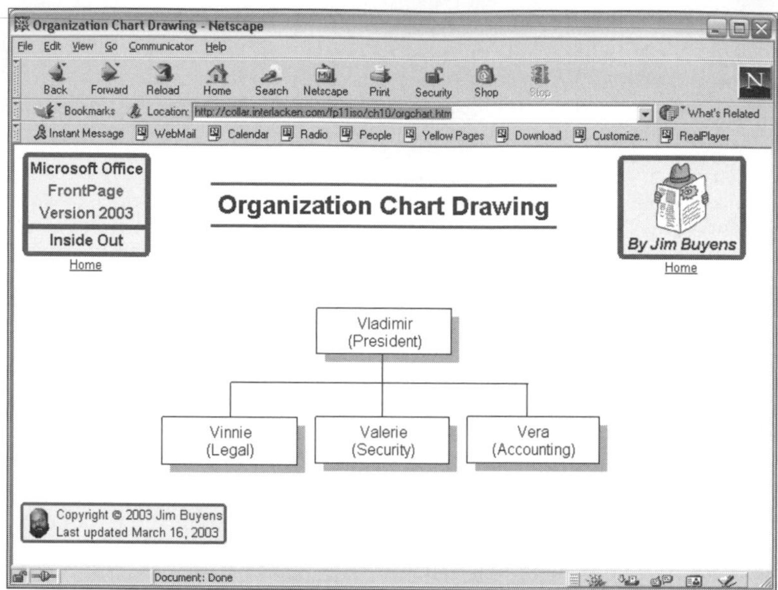

Figure 10-12. Netscape Navigator 4.77 doesn't support VML, but it does display this drawing by downloading a substitute GIF file.

For more information about creating drawings in FrontPage, refer to "Creating Drawings," on page 647.

Inserting AutoShapes

Many common objects such as arrows, banners, flowchart symbols, and charts are very tedious to draw using only basic elements such as curves, lines, and boxes. FrontPage therefore includes several collections of predrawn shapes that you can include in your Web page. Here's the procedure for inserting one of these shapes:

1. Set the insertion point where you want the shape to appear.
2. From the Insert menu, choose Picture and then choose AutoShapes.
3. When the AutoShapes toolbar appears, click any of the first six buttons to display a drop-down list of available shapes. To add any shape you want to the current Web page, click it, and then drag it in the desired direction until it's the size you want.

For more information about the AutoShapes toolbar, refer to "The AutoShapes Toolbar," in Appendix A.

4. To resize the inserted shape or change its proportions, select it, and drag the sizing handles. To move the shape around the Web page, drag it by its edge.

5 To rotate the shape, drag its rotation button (the little green handle).

6 To change any other property of an AutoShape object, right-click it, and choose Format AutoShape from the shortcut menu.

Figure 10-13 shows a Web page that contains an AutoShape object: a large gray star. Notice that the star is partially transparent and that it occupies the same space as other objects on the page. The star is actually black, but it's 95 percent transparent; the transparency is a feature of VML. The fact that it occupies the same space as, but lies behind, ordinary Web content is possible because the drawing uses features of CSS Positioning. Because Netscape Navigator, at least through version 4.7, doesn't support these features, it won't display this page properly. Netscape would, however, display a page that used AutoShapes along the lines, so to speak, of Figure 10-11.

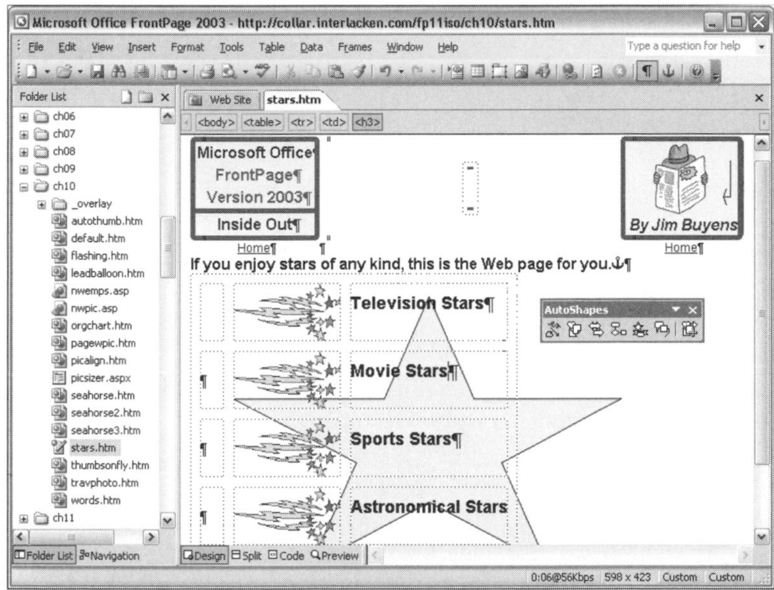

Figure 10-13. The large star in this Web page is transparent and occupies a layer behind the normal Web content.

You can avoid compatibility problems of this type by not overlapping drawings (or other objects) with other content. As long as Netscape can display a GIF file instead of the VML drawing, the page will look essentially the same on either browser.

For more information about CSS Positioning, refer to "Positioning Content with Cascading Style Sheets," on page 621.
For more information about creating AutoShape objects, refer to "Creating AutoShapes" on page 646.

Inserting WordArt

Applications like Microsoft Word, Microsoft Excel, and Microsoft PowerPoint have for some time provided a feature called WordArt that transforms text into a decorative object. FrontPage's support for drawing objects makes the WordArt feature practical on Web pages as well. A WordArt object formatted the phrase *Words for Worriers* in Figure 10-14.

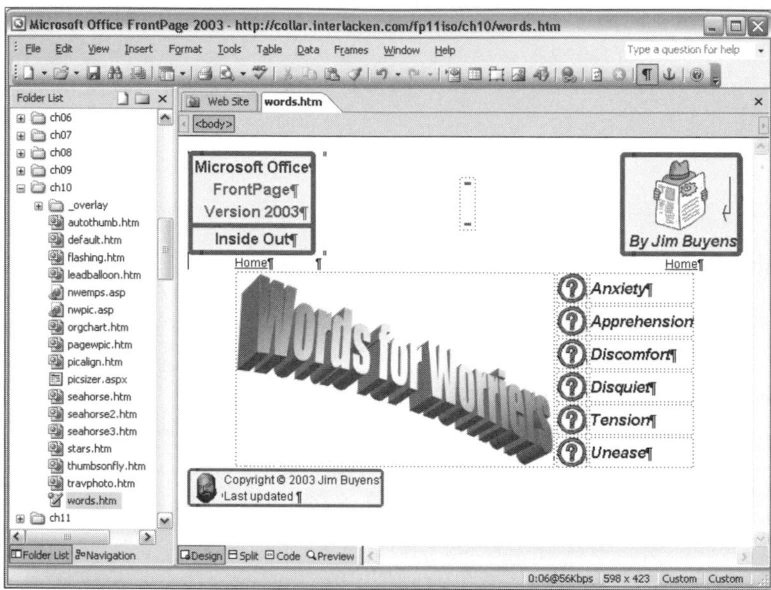

Figure 10-14. WordArt provides a stylized rendition of text.

Here's the procedure for creating such an object:

1. Set the insertion point where you want the WordArt object to appear.
2. From the Insert menu, choose Picture and then choose WordArt.
3. When the WordArt Gallery shown in Figure 10-15 appears, select one of the styles presented, and then click OK.
4. In the Edit WordArt Text dialog box, enter the text you want to display. Change the font, size, boldface, and italic properties if you want, and then click OK.
5. The WordArt object now appears on your Web page. To change its size, proportions, or rotation, use the handles that appear when you select it. To make other changes, right-click the object, and then choose Format WordArt from the shortcut menu.

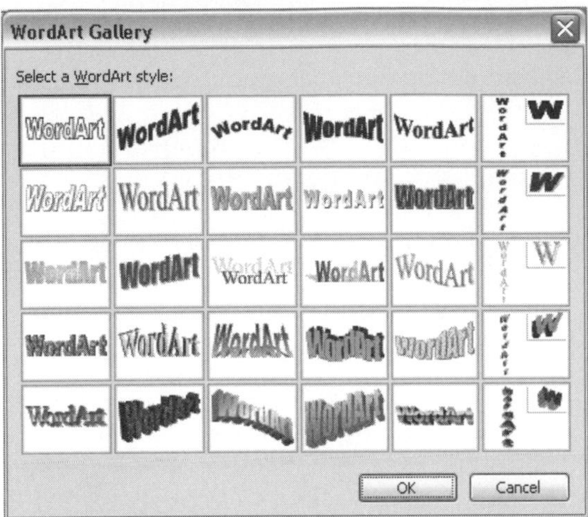

Figure 10-15. These formats are available when you create a WordArt object. You can introduce many other variations after the WordArt object exists.

As with drawing and AutoShape objects, FrontPage uses VML whenever possible to display WordArt objects. If the browser ignores the VML code, it will discover an ordinary tag that displays an equivalent (although slower to download) GIF picture.

For more information about creating WordArt objects, refer to "Creating WordArt Objects," on page 649.

Modifying Picture Properties

Very often, making a picture appear on a Web page is only half the job. The remainder involves details of placement and presentation. HTML, and therefore FrontPage, provides a variety of settings for this purpose. To open the Picture Properties dialog box, do *one* of the following while in the Design view:

- Click a picture, and choose Properties from the Format menu.
- Right-click a picture, and choose Picture Properties from the shortcut menu.
- Click a picture, and press Alt+Enter.
- Double-click a picture.

Performing any of these actions displays a Picture Properties dialog box. The next few sections will explain the tabs and controls in this dialog box.

Modifying Size and Placement Properties

The Appearance tab of the Picture Properties dialog box, shown in Figure 10-16, controls picture layout and size.

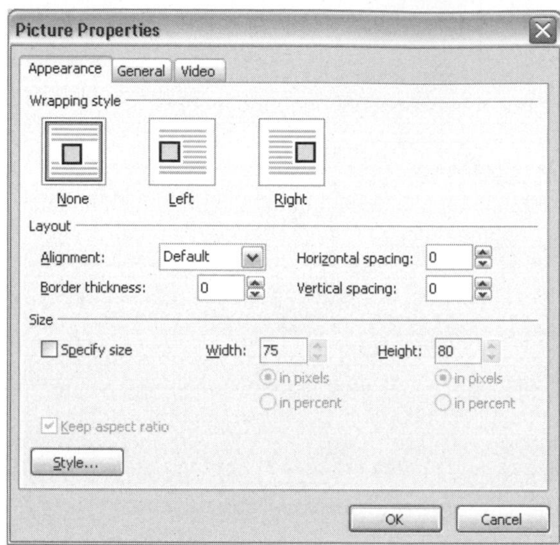

Figure 10-16. The Appearance tab in the Picture Properties dialog box controls page positioning and displayed picture size.

This tab controls the following settings:

- **Wrapping Style** This group of controls provides a quick way to set the Alignment control in the next group to the three most frequently used choices:
  - **None** Sets the Alignment control to None. The picture will default to the browser's default alignment.
  - **Left** Sets the Alignment control to Left.
  - **Right** Sets the Alignment control to Right.
- **Layout** This section positions the picture relative to any surrounding text:
  - **Alignment** Controls vertical positioning of a picture and text in the same line. Table 10-3 describes each option.
  - **Border Thickness** Specifies the width in pixels of a border that surrounds the picture. A width of zero specifies no border. Hyperlinked pictures have blue borders; others have black borders.
  - **Horizontal Spacing** Controls the separation, in pixels, between the picture and other elements on the same line.
  - **Vertical Spacing** Controls separation between the picture and any text or pictures in lines above or below.

- **Size** This frame controls the displayed size of a picture:
  - **Specify Size** If selected, indicates that you want to override the natural size of the picture.
  - **Width** Sets the amount of horizontal space the browser should reserve for the picture. Use the In Pixels or the In Percent button to denote the units of width.
  - **Height** Sets the amount of vertical space the browser should reserve for the picture. Use the In Pixels or the In Percent button to denote the units of height.
  - **Keep Aspect Ratio** Specifies that changing either the picture's height or its width changes the other dimension proportionally.
- **Style** This button accesses the Modify Style dialog box, where you can apply CSS properties to the current picture.

Table 10-3. HTML Picture Alignment Settings

Alignment	Description
Default	Sends the browser no instructions as to picture alignment. Most browsers, however, default to *baseline*.
Left	Floats the picture down and left to the next spot available at the left margin; wraps subsequent text around the right side of that picture.
Right	Aligns the picture with the right margin; wraps subsequent text around the left side of that picture.
Top	Aligns the top of the picture with the top of the tallest item in the line. See Figure 10-17 for illustrations of this and the following settings.
Texttop	Aligns the top of the picture with the top of the tallest text in the line (this is usually, but not always, the same as Top).
Middle	Aligns the middle of the picture with the baseline of the current line.
Absmiddle	Aligns the middle of the picture with the middle of the current line.
Baseline	Aligns the bottom of the picture with the baseline of the current line.
Bottom	Aligns the bottom of the picture with the baseline of the current line. This is the same as Baseline.
Absbottom	Aligns the bottom of the picture with the bottom of the current line.
Center	Aligns the vertical center of the picture with the baseline of the current line. This is the same as Middle.

For more information about assigning CSS properties, refer to "Assigning Style Sheet Properties," on page 602.

Resizing Pictures by Dragging

You can resize any picture that appears in Design view by first selecting it and then dragging its sizing handles. (These are the eight square dots that appear at the corners and sides of any picture you select.)

After you do this, FrontPage displays a Picture Actions box near the picture's lower right corner. Clicking the drop-down arrow on this box exposes two options:

- **Only Modify Size Attributes** Click this option to retain the picture file's original size, but tell the browser to display it at the size you specified by dragging. This is the default.
- **Resample Picture To Match Size** Click this option to change the picture's physical size to the dimensions you specified by dragging. The next time you save the page, FrontPage will display the Save Embedded Files dialog box prompting you for the name and location of the resulting picture file.

As Figure 10-17 illustrates, placing pictures inline with text pictures often also results in uneven, distracting line spacing. Therefore, most Web designers demand more control over picture placement than inline pictures provide.

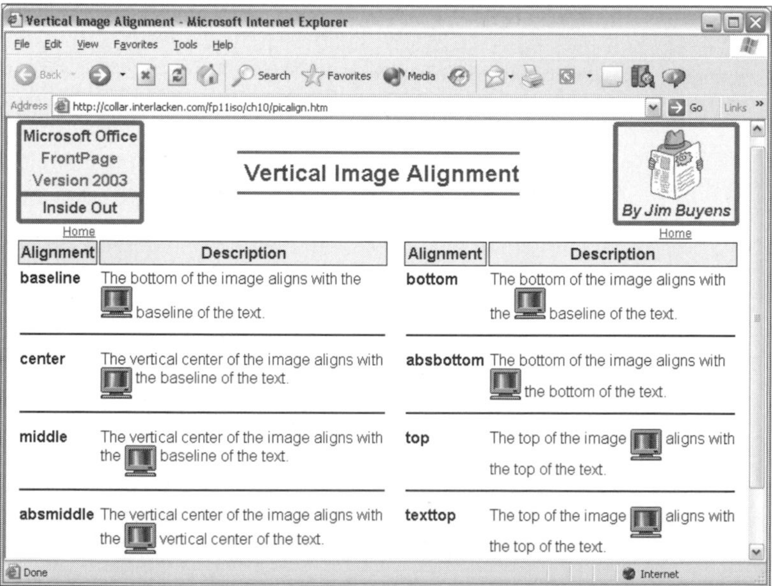

Figure 10-17. This page illustrates various HTML picture alignment settings.

This explains why, of the ten picture alignment settings, Left and Right are probably the most often used. The Left and Right settings provide at least some absolute positioning—to the margins—and they also maintain uniform line spacing.

To center a picture by itself, put it in its own paragraph. To center the paragraph, do either of the following:

Center

- Select the paragraph, and click the Center button on the Text toolbar.
- Right-click the paragraph, choose Paragraph from the shortcut menu, and set the Alignment control to Center.

By default, the browser determines the size of each picture it receives and then displays the picture at its natural size. Nevertheless, most experienced Web designers hard-code picture sizes into their HTML. Here are the reasons:

- Using the default behavior, the browser can't allocate window space to a picture until it has received enough of the file to determine the picture's dimensions. Not knowing the size of a picture might also delay placement—and therefore display—of other page elements. Specifying sizes for all pictures on a page means that many page elements are displayed sooner than otherwise might be possible.
- Occasionally, you might want to display a picture larger or smaller than its natural size. This used to be rare, because downloading a large picture and having the browser reduce it takes more time than downloading a smaller one. In contrast, downloading a small picture and having the browser expand it results in a loss of resolution. More recently, however, the practice of expanding small pictures has become surprisingly common.

  Anywhere Web designers want some blank space on a page, they display a transparent picture. Because such pictures, being invisible, can't possibly look fuzzy, designers usually specify a very small, rapidly transmitted picture and make the browser stretch it to the required size.
- Older browsers tend to have difficulty with pages containing both scripts embedded in the HTML and pictures with no preassigned height and width. These problems seem to arise from the scripts starting to run before all page element locations are determined. Therefore, always specify dimensions—in pixels—for all pictures on pages that contain scripts.

For more information about the use of transparent pictures to reserve white space, refer to "Using Transparent Pictures for Page Layout," on page 559.
For more information about scripts that run when the browser receives a page, refer to "Scripting Web Pages on the Browser," on page 1056.

Fortunately, FrontPage automatically hard-codes picture sizes in the following two cases:

- For all pictures in the current Web site, even if the Specify Size check box shown in Figure 10-16 isn't selected
- For all pictures, regardless of location, for which you select the Specify Size check box and choose a Width and Height in pixels

Modifying General Picture Properties

You can use the General tab of the Picture Properties dialog box, shown in Figure 10-18, to modify the properties of a picture. Certain options might be unavailable (dimmed), depending on the context.

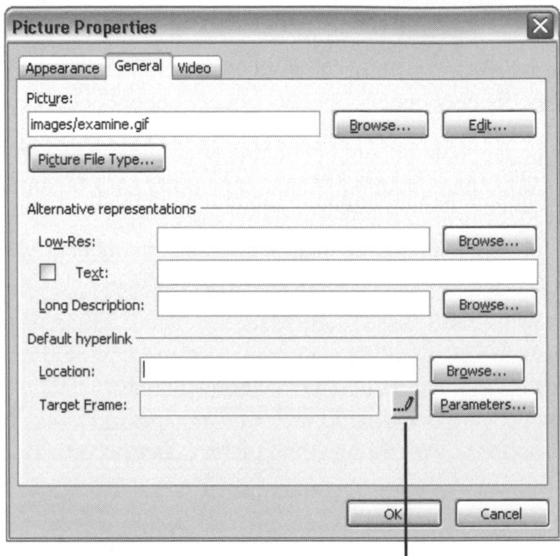

Figure 10-18. The General tab of the Picture Properties dialog box specifies the location of a picture file and other details of presentation.

The full complement of fields includes the following:

- **Picture** This box specifies the full or relative URL of the picture file being modified. It might be read-only, depending on the context.
  - **Browse** Click this button to browse the current Web site or file system to locate a picture. This option will be dimmed if the Picture box is dimmed.
  - **Edit** Click this button to modify the current picture. FrontPage chooses an editor based on the picture's file extension.

For more information about configuring FrontPage to run the picture editor you want, refer to "Configuring External Editors," on page 1118.

- **Picture File Type** This button displays the Picture File Type dialog box, shown previously in Figure 10-3. You can use this dialog box to change the file format and other properties of the current picture.

For more information about the GIF and JPEG file formats, as well as additional file formats, refer to "Choosing Picture File Formats," on page 671.

- **Alternative Representations** The fields in this section control alternative views of a picture:
  - **Low-Res** This specifies a low-resolution picture that the browser displays while downloading the larger picture file. You can use the Browse button to find such a picture file.
  - **Text** This setting specifies a line of text that browsers will display in lieu of the picture file. This might occur because the Web visitor has turned off the display of pictures, or because the picture is still downloading. Some browsers also display this text as a ToolTip when the mouse pointer is over the picture. The Text setting involves two controls: a check box and a text box. If you clear the check box, the browser will receive no alternative text. If you select the check box but don't specify any text, the browser receives an empty string. If you select the check box and specify text, the browser receives that text.
  - **Long Description** This field specifies a URL that contains more information about the current picture. This URL appears, for example, in the dialog box that opens when you right-click a picture in Netscape Navigator 7 and choose Properties from the shortcut menu. The Web visitor can click the link to get the additional information. If you want to specify a Long Description URL but don't want to type it, click the associated Browse button.
- **Default Hyperlink** This section establishes a hyperlink to another location from any part of the current picture that has no hotspot defined. This command isn't available for background pictures.

For more information about normal and hotspot hyperlinks, refer to "Creating and Managing Hyperlinks," on page 291.

  - **Location** This field contains the URL that the browser will retrieve when the Web visitor clicks the current picture. You can use the Browse button to locate it.
  - **Target Frame** This field specifies the frame in which the Location page will appear. It can also specify that the linked page should appear in a new browser window. To enter a value, either type it in the text box or click the Change Target Frame button. The value that makes a page appear in a new window is _blank.

For more information about using the Change Target Frame dialog box, refer to "Creating and Modifying Frames Pages," on page 405.

  - **Parameters** Click this button if the browser should transmit query string parameters to the Web server whenever the browser requests the specified picture. FrontPage displays the Hyperlink Parameters dialog box, shown in Figure 10-19, where you can add, modify, remove, or clear such parameters.

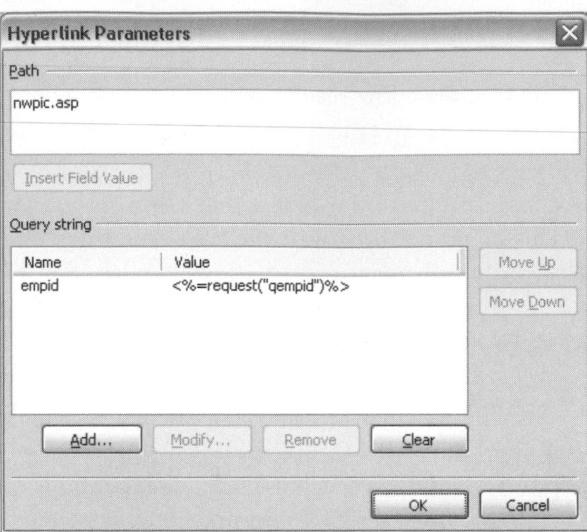

Figure 10-19. This dialog box creates, modifies, and deletes *keyword=value* expressions appended to a URL by means of a query string.

There are at least two scenarios where this might be necessary: First, if the picture source specifies not an ordinary GIF or JPEG file, but rather a program that runs on the Web server and generates a picture file on the fly. Many such programs—and hit counters in particular—use query string parameters to control their results. Second, if you're displaying pictures (such as banner ads) that certain Internet advertising sites provide, you might need to specify parameters in order to get paid.

Displaying Pictures from Programs

If you know anything about ASP, the dialog box shown in Figure 10-19 creates quite a dilemma. An ASP page is usually a special Web page that contains not only HTML, but also special script code that runs on the Web server. The script code accesses databases, files, or other resources available on the server and uses this information to customize the HTML each Web visitor receives.

The nwpic.asp file referenced in Figure 10-19 is a special ASP page that sends the browser a picture in bitmap (BMP) format rather than a Web page in HTML format. Specifically, the picture is a photo of an employee in the ubiquitous Northwind Traders database. The following HTML tag displays the photo for employee number 5:

```
<img src="nwpic.asp?empid=5">
```

Note Microsoft distributes the Northwind Traders database in Microsoft Access format. Many Microsoft products use this database in sample exercises. A copy of this database, in Access 2002 format, is in the /fp-iso/fpdb folder on the companion CD.

Interesting as this might—or might not—be, it would be even more interesting if the Web visitor could use an HTML form to select an employee and then receive not only the picture but also some associated database information. Figure 10-20 shows just such a page. The drop-down list appears as the Employee list to Web visitors, but its name in HTML is *qempid*. It lists each employee in the database. When the Web visitor clicks the Submit button, the browser transmits the list's name and a value associated with the current selection to the Web server. (In this case, the value associated with each selection is the employee ID.) The Web server then adds this name and value to a *request* object.

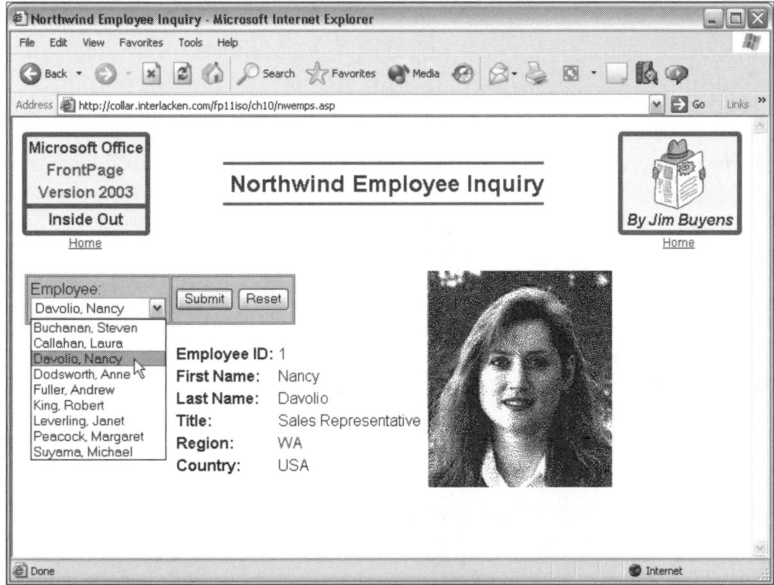

Figure 10-20. This Web page displays pictures stored as objects in an Access database. A better approach is to store only the picture name in the database.

The expression

```
<%=request("qempid")%>
```

is a small fragment of ASP code that searches for a field named *qempid* in the Web visitor's request and supplies its value.

Compare the HTML code that displays the picture for employee ID 5 with the following code, which displays the picture for the employee selected in the *qempid* drop-down list when the Web visitor submitted the form:

```
<img src="nwpic.asp?empid=<%=request("qempid")%>">
```

For more information about drop-down lists, refer to "Setting Drop-Down Box Properties," on page 840.

The Web page shown in Figure 10-20 involves quite a few advanced techniques, some of which this book touches upon only lightly. However, it does provide a somewhat realistic example of a picture location that uses query string parameters.

For more information about sending pictures stored in an Access database to Web visitors, search for article Q175261, "Retrieving Bitmap from Access and Displaying It in Web Page" on Microsoft's Web site, at *http://www.microsoft.com/search*. For information about sending pictures stored in a Microsoft SQL Server database to Web visitors, search Microsoft's Web site for article Q173308, "Displaying Images Stored in a BLOB Field."

Incidentally, the preferred method of displaying pictures associated with a database record is to store not the picture in the database, but only the picture's file name. Then when you write the ASP code that customizes the outgoing HTML, you can just insert the picture's file name into the picture tag. This way is much easier to program and much more efficient in terms of CPU usage than the method this example uses.

If you want to try running this example on your own Web server, you'll have to perform the following procedure first:

1. Log onto the Web server's console as an Administrator.
2. Locate the file named dbpic.dll that you installed from the companion CD, copy it into the \Windows\SYSTEM32 folder on the Web server's system drive.

   By default, the Sample Files setup program will put this files in a folder at [My documents]\Microsoft Press\FrontPage 2003 Inside Out\dbpic.
3. Open a command window on the Web server.
4. Change to the system drive and then to the folder \Windows\SYSTEM32.
5. Enter and run the following command:

   ```
   regsvr32 dbpic.dll
   ```

   A message box should display the message *DllRegisterServer in dbpic.dll succeeded.*
6. Close the command window, and log off the server.

If you later wish to remove the dll, change once again to the \Windows\SYSTEM32 folder on the system drive, and then run the following command.

```
regsvr32 /u dbpic.dll
```

It's then safe to delete the dbpic.dll file.

Note Be aware that the techniques used in the dbpic.dll file are unsupported. Microsoft article Q175261 states this fact quite clearly. Because of this, the dbpic.dll file itself is unsupported as well.

Organizing Pictures with Thumbnails

To minimize download time for large pictures, it's common practice to display a small preview picture (a thumbnail) on the Web page a visitor would first encounter, and display the full-size picture only if the visitor clicks the thumbnail. This gives the Web visitor the choice of whether to view a larger file, without having to wait to download it first. Thumbnails are very popular on Web pages that display a series of pictures the Web visitor can select because:

- The thumbnails download much faster than the full-sized pictures.
- The thumbnails present more options at a glance than are possible with full-sized pictures.

The next section describes the FrontPage AutoThumbnail feature, which creates thumbnail pictures one at a time. FrontPage also includes a Photo Gallery feature, which organizes an entire set of pictures into a scrollable, clickable list of thumbnails that displays one full-sized picture at a time.

For more information about using FrontPage Photo Galleries, refer to "Using FrontPage Photo Galleries," on page 655.

Using the AutoThumbnail Feature

The FrontPage AutoThumbnail feature creates one thumbnail picture at a time. Here's the procedure for using it:

1. Open the Web page on which you want to display the thumbnail.
2. Set the insertion point where you want the thumbnail to appear.
3. Using any method you want, insert the full-sized picture where you want its thumbnail to appear.
4. Select the large picture, then press Ctrl+T or select Auto Thumbnail from one of the following places:
   - The Tools menu.
   - The Pictures toolbar. (If the Pictures toolbar isn't visible, choose Toolbars from the View menu, and then choose Pictures.)
   - The shortcut menu that appears when you right-click the picture.

Auto Thumbnail

In one operation, FrontPage removes the large picture, creates the thumbnail in its place, and sets up a hyperlink from the thumbnail to the large picture.

Tip To create a linked thumbnail in one operation, use the right mouse button to drag any picture file from the Folder List to an open Web page. Then when you release the mouse button, choose Auto Thumbnail from the shortcut menu.

5. Use the thumbnail's handles to resize it if desired.
6. When you save the Web page, FrontPage displays a Save Embedded Files dialog box to prompt for the thumbnail's file name and location. By default, FrontPage names the thumbnail by appending *_small* to the original base file name.

For more information about using the Save Embedded Files dialog box, refer to "Using the Save Embedded Files Dialog Box," earlier in this chapter.

Figure 10-21 shows typical results from using the AutoThumbnail feature. Clicking the small picture in the background page displays the large picture shown in the foreground page.

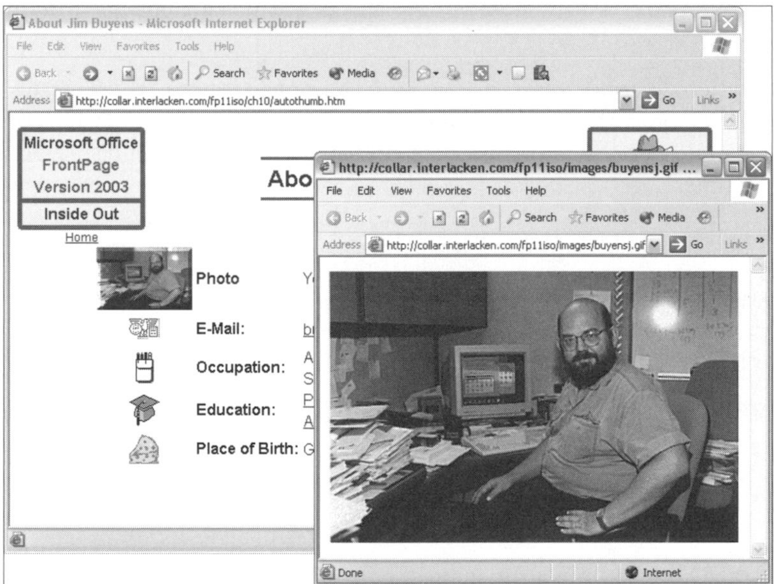

Figure 10-21. Clicking the thumbnail picture in the background Web page displays the full-sized picture in the foreground.

Double-clicking a thumbnail picture in Design view (or right-clicking it and choosing Picture Properties from the shortcut menu) displays the properties of the thumbnail and not the properties of the original picture.

For more information about configuring page options, refer to Chapter 46, "Configuring Page Creation Options."

Chapter 10

Setting AutoThumbnail Properties

As you might have noticed, the preceding discussion made no mention of the thumbnail picture's size and appearance. That's because FrontPage assumes you want all the thumbnails you create to look the same. (Surely you wouldn't want them all to look different, would you?)

To specify the default size and appearance of all thumbnails you create, choose Page Options from the Tools menu, and click the AutoThumbnail tab, as shown in Figure 10-22.

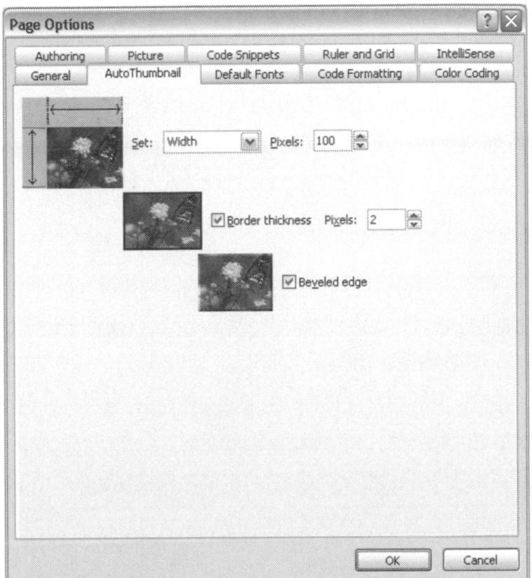

Figure 10-22. This tab in the Page Options dialog box controls how FrontPage creates thumbnail pictures.

This tab provides the following settings:

- **Set** Controls the size of the thumbnail pictures. You should specify both a sizing strategy and a measurement. The sizing options are as follows:
    - **Width** Choose this option if you want FrontPage to make all thumbnail pictures the same width.
    - **Height** Choose this option if you want FrontPage to make all thumbnail pictures the same height.
    - **Shortest Side** Choose this option if you want FrontPage to make the shortest side of each thumbnail a uniform size.
    - **Longest Side** Choose this option if you want FrontPage to make the longest side of each thumbnail a uniform size.

  No matter which strategy you choose, FrontPage sizes the remaining edge of the thumbnail in proportion to that of the full-sized picture.
- **Pixels** Specify the fixed size applied to the edge you chose.

- **Border Thickness** Select this check box if you want FrontPage to create borders around each thumbnail picture. The Pixels spin box controls the border width.
- **Beveled Edge** Select this check box if you want FrontPage to create beveled edges for each thumbnail picture.

Troubleshooting

Using the Page Properties dialog box to create a thumbnail produces no improvement in download time

You can display a large picture in a small space by opening the Picture Properties dialog box, selecting the Specify Size box on the Appearance tab, and specifying small values for height and width. This doesn't, however, create a smaller picture file. It only forces the browser to display the large picture in a small space.

If you want to create a thumbnail picture entirely by hand:

1. Add the full-sized picture where you want the thumbnail to appear.
2. Display the Picture Properties dialog box, select the Appearance tab, and specify the height and width you want the thumbnail to have.
3. Click the General tab, and then copy the URL of the full-sized picture from the Picture box and paste it into the Default Hyperlink Location box.

   (To copy the URL, select it, and press Ctrl+C. To paste it, set the insertion point, and press Ctrl+V.)
4. Click OK to close the Picture Properties dialog box.
5. With the picture still selected, click the Resample button on the Pictures toolbar.

Resample

The Resample button creates a new version of the picture with genuine, physically smaller dimensions. It also triggers the Save Embedded Files dialog box the next time you save the Web page, which in turn confirms the save location for the resampled picture. Unless you want to replace the full-sized picture, be sure to rename the thumbnail when this dialog box appears.

For more information about the Resample feature for editing pictures, refer to "Resampling Pictures," on page 645.

Creating Thumbnails on the Fly

In some cases, it might be desirable to create thumbnail pictures on the fly rather than ahead of time. This avoids issues of keeping the thumbnails in sync with the full-sized pictures, but it does require the Web server to open the full-sized picture and reduce it in memory every time a request for the thumbnail arrives.

Tip Resize any picture as much as you like.

The picsizer.aspx page can read almost any picture from the Web server's disk, resize it to almost any extent, and then send the results directly to a Web visitor's browser. For more information about the picsizer.aspx page, refer to the information about Insider Extra 3 on the companion CD.

On-the-fly thumbnails aren't a feature of FrontPage, but they're not hard to implement if you have a Windows Web server with the Microsoft .NET Framework installed. Here's the procedure:

1. Open the picsizer folder in the Inside Extra files you installed from the companion CD.
2. Copy the picsizer.aspx page out of the picsizer folder and into your Web site.
3. Open any Web page, and add the full-sized picture where you want a thumbnail to appear.
4. Right-click the full-sized picture, and choose Picture Properties from the shortcut menu.
5. In the Picture Properties dialog box, click the General tab, and then copy the location from the Picture box and paste it into the Location box. If you want the full-sized picture to appear in a new browser window, click the Change Target Frame button, select New Window, and then click OK.
6. Add the following text in front of the location that remains in the Picture box, where *<path>*/ is the relative path, if any, from the entire Web page to the picsizer.aspx file:

   ```
   <path>/picsizer.aspx?size=100&url=
   ```

   The *size*= value specifies the size in pixels of the thumbnail's height or width, whichever is larger. If you prefer, you can provide a *height*= or *width*= specification instead.
7. Figure 10-23 shows how the General tab should now appear.
   - The path, if any, in front of picsizer.aspx is the path from the current Web page to the picture aspx page.
   - The path, if any, between url= and the name of your picture file is the path from the picsizer.aspx page to your picture file.
8. Make any corrections to your page, and then click OK.

If you have a FrontPage-extended Web site on a server that has the .NET Framework installed, the thumbnail should appear in Design view within a few seconds. Otherwise, the thumbnail might look like a broken link until you publish your Web site and browse the page.

Chapter 10

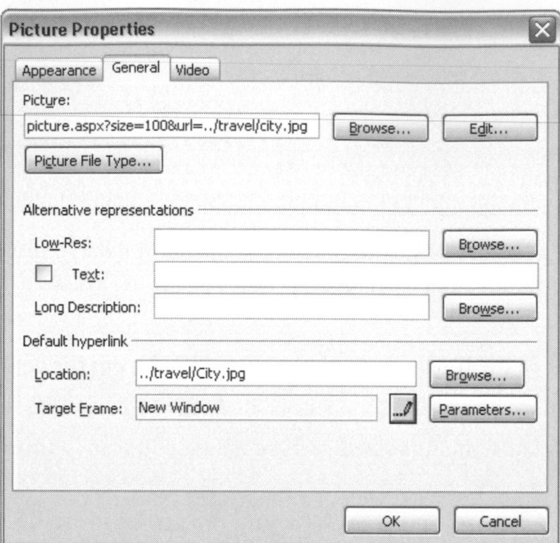

Figure 10-23. These picture properties specify that the picture comes from the picsizer.aspx page. Query parameters specify the desired size and full-sized picture location. The Default Hyperlink Location box establishes the hyperlink to the full-sized picture.

Figure 10-24 shows a completed Web page that uses this technique. An HTML table arranges the thumbnails and captions.

Figure 10-24. An ASP.NET page created these thumbnail pictures on the fly. Only the full-sized pictures reside on the server's disk.

This technique has one limitation you should know about: If you create a thumbnail for a GIF picture that specifies a transparent color, the transparent pixels will come out black. This is a limitation of the .NET classes that resize the picture.

> **A FrontPage Photo Gallery can produce results similar to those in Figure 10-24 but wouldn't automatically create new thumbnails if pictures arrived from a Web cam or other external process. For more information about FrontPage Photo Galleries, refer to Chapter 24, "Using FrontPage Photo Galleries."**

In Summary…

This chapter explained the basics of adding pictures to a Web page. It also provided an introduction to a variety of picture types and picture techniques that later chapters explain in greater detail.

The next chapter explains how to construct hyperlinks, the glue that holds the World Wide Web together.

Chapter 11
Building Hyperlinks

Hyperlinks are the essence of the Web. Without hyperlinks, there would be no point-and-click navigation among Web pages—and without point and click, the Web would be dead. Every time you click some underlined text or a picture and thereby jump to another page, you're using a hyperlink. A Web page lacking hyperlinks is truly a Web page going nowhere.

Without hyperlinks, visitors would have to manually type the URL of each page they wanted to visit. Given the length and cryptic nature of many URLs, visitors probably wouldn't visit many pages, or they'd get lost in a thicket of typos along the way.

This chapter describes the most common Web mechanisms for linking Web pages and explains how to employ these mechanisms using Microsoft FrontPage:

- **Hyperlinks** These are special areas on a Web page that hold the address of another page in waiting. When a Web visitor clicks such an area, the browser retrieves the Web page at the associated address.
- **Bookmarks** These provide a means for jumping not to the top of a Web page but to some point further within the page. Essentially, they associate a name with a spot on a Web page and provide a way of jumping to that name.
- **Hotspots** These provide a way of jumping to a different Web location depending on which part of a picture the visitor clicks. This can be useful when a set of hyperlinks lends itself to visual depiction.

Creating and Managing Hyperlinks

The most common form of hyperlink is the *anchor*. Clicking text or a picture that bears this type of link takes a Web visitor to another page. A simple anchor has the following HTML syntax:

```
<a href="/contact.html">Click here for contact information.</a>
```

The browser would display this code as follows:

Click here for contact information.

Clicking this text would take a Web visitor to the contact.html page in the current server's home folder. The *a* in *<a href=...>* stands for *anchor*, and *href* means *hypertext reference.*

Content that appears between the *<a href=…>* and *</a>* tags appears as a link, and clicking it jumps to the *href* location.

> **Tip** Hyperlinked pictures work virtually the same as hyperlinked text. Format the anchor tags just as you would for text, but put the HTML code that displays the picture between them.

Of course, a major reason FrontPage exists is to isolate you from HTML tags such as <a href=…>. The next few sections will explain how to create these tags.

For more information about the format and contents of uniform resource locators, refer to Appendix C, "Creating Uniform Resource Locators (URLs)."

Creating Hyperlinks with Drag-and-Drop

If you're working in a Web site—either disk-based or server-based—creating hyperlinks within your Web site is as easy as dragging. Here's the procedure:

1 Open the page that should contain the hyperlink.
2 Locate and select the target Web page in the Folder List.
3 Drag the target onto the open page.

FrontPage creates a hyperlink to the page you dragged, using that page's title as the hyperlink text. Table 11-1 shows the results of dragging or pasting objects of various kinds onto an open Web page.

Table 11-1. Effects of Dragging or Pasting a File Onto an Open Web Page

Drag or copy from	Type of file	Typical extensions	Results
Folder List or Folders view	Web page	.htm, .asp, .aspx	Creates hyperlink to dragged file with page title as hyperlink text.
	Picture file	.gif, .jpg, .avi	Displays dragged picture on Web page.
	Folder		Creates hyperlink to dragged folder with folder location as hyperlink text.
	Style sheet	.css	Adds the file to the list of style sheets for the page.
	Other	.doc, .pdf, .txt, .zip	Creates hyperlink to dragged file with file location as hyperlink text.

Table 11-1. Effects of Dragging or Pasting a File Onto an Open Web Page

Drag or copy from	Type of file	Typical extensions	Results
Windows Explorer	Web page	.htm, .asp	Merges HTML from dragged file into current Web page.
	Picture file	.gif, .jpg, .avi	Displays dragged picture on Web page. Displays Save Embedded Files dialog box during next page save.
	Folder		Nothing.
	Other	.doc, .txt, .zip	Translates dragged file to HTML and merges results into current Web page. Fails if the given file type has no available translator.

The following procedure is more flexible and easier to remember, and it offers more options for dragging files onto an open Web page:

1. Open the page you want to update.
2. Locate the file you want added to the open page. The file can be in the FrontPage Folder List, FrontPage Folders view, or Windows Explorer.
3. Use the right mouse button to drag the file onto the open Web page. Releasing the right mouse button displays the following shortcut menu. If current context prohibits using an option, FrontPage dims it.

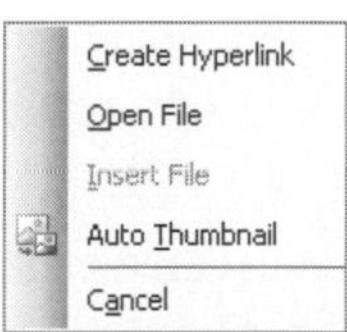

- **Create Hyperlink** Adds a hyperlink from the open Web page to the dragged file. When you drag a file from Windows Explorer, this command is dimmed. Drag the file from Windows Explorer into the Folder List, and from there onto the open Web page.
- **Open File** Loads the dragged file into the default editor for the file type. This performs the same action as double-clicking the dragged file and doesn't modify the open Web page.
- **Insert File** Performs two different actions, depending on the type of file. For pictures, it displays the picture on the open Web page as if you'd used the Insert Picture command. For other types of files, it converts the file to HTML and merges the result on the open Web page.
- **Auto Thumbnail** Creates a thumbnail version of a dragged picture, adds it to the open Web page, and hyperlinks the thumbnail to the full-sized version.
- **Cancel** Cancels the dragging operation without taking any action.

Creating Hyperlinks with Menus

You can also create hyperlinks in FrontPage using menus and dialog boxes. This is the best way to create hyperlinks that have special options or hyperlinks that point outside the current Web. The basic procedure is as follows:

1. Select the text or picture you want the Web visitor to click.
2. Choose Hyperlink from the Insert menu, or click the Insert Hyperlink button on the Standard toolbar, or right-click the selection and choose Hyperlink from the shortcut menu. The Insert Hyperlink dialog box shown in Figure 11-1 appears.

Insert Hyperlink

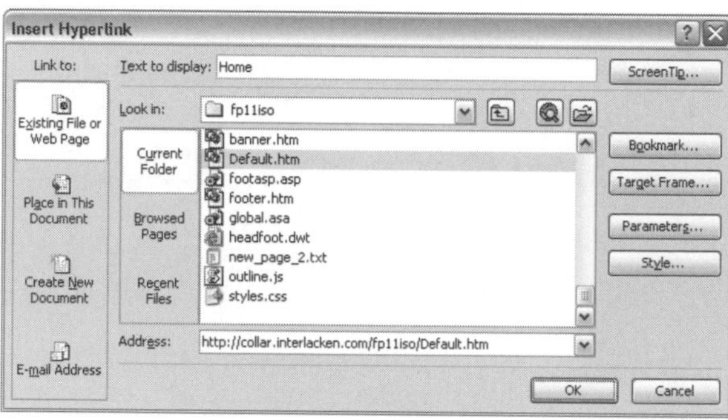

Figure 11-1. FrontPage uses this dialog box to hyperlink a selected text string or picture to another Web page.

3. Specify the hyperlink's target address in the Address box, and click OK.

All other options in the Insert Hyperlink dialog box are variations on performing step 3. There are four such variations, which correspond to the four buttons in the Link To bar at the left of Figure 11-1:

- **Existing File Or Web Page** Selects an address that points anywhere in the current Web site, an intranet, or the World Wide Web.
- **Place In This Document** Selects an address that points to a bookmark in the current Web page.
- **Create New Document** Creates an address that points to a page that doesn't exist yet. You can tell FrontPage to open a new, empty Web page at this address for editing or to defer creating the page completely.
- **E-Mail Address** Creates an address that opens the Web visitor's e-mail program and addresses a new message to a given recipient.

Clicking any of these Link To options changes the rest of the Insert Hyperlink dialog box. However, the following controls apply to all four options:

- **Text To Display** Displays and optionally modifies the clickable text the Web visitor sees. This box is dimmed if the clickable area contains a picture.

- **ScreenTip** Opens the Set Hyperlink ScreenTip dialog box shown below. Any text you enter in this box will appear as a ScreenTip (that is, as text in a small yellow box) whenever the Web visitor's mouse rests over the clickable area.

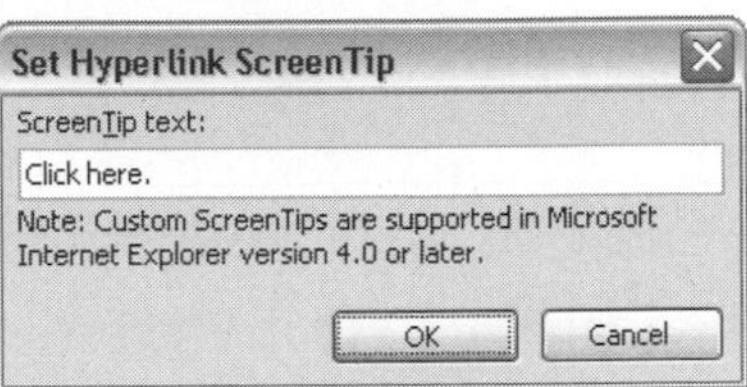

This facility is subject to two restrictions:

- If the clickable area includes a picture configured with alternative representation text, that text will supersede the hyperlink's ScreenTip text when you move the mouse pointer over the picture.
- Only Microsoft Internet Explorer 4 and later can display ScreenTip text.

For more information about alternative representation text, refer to "Modifying General Picture Properties," on page 278.

- **Target Frame** Applies to two situations:
  - If the current page will occupy one frame of a frameset, this option specifies which frame will display the hyperlink's target page.
  - This option can also specify that the target page should appear in a new window. To make this happen, click the Target Frame button, choose New Window in the Target Frame dialog box, shown in Figure 11-2, and then click OK.

For more information about framesets, refer to Chapter 15, "Creating Web Sites with Frames."

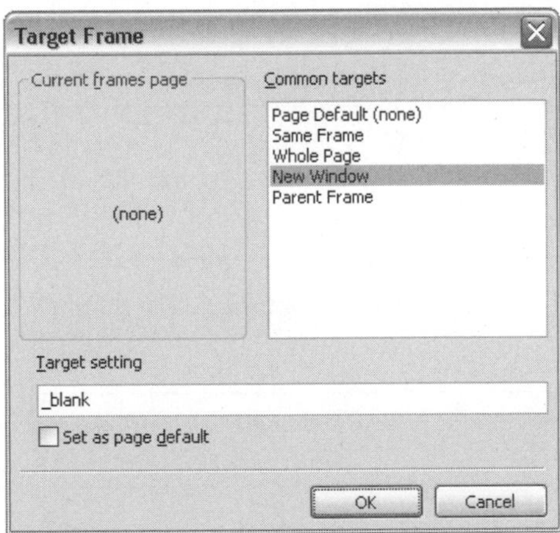

Figure 11-2. For hyperlinks on pages edited within a frameset, this dialog box specifies which frame will display the target page. Even for pages that don't appear in a frameset, it can make the target page appear in a new browser window.

- **Parameters** Displays a dialog box that creates, modifies, and deletes parameters in a URL's path information or query string.
- **Style** Applies CSS properties to the hyperlink.

For more information about CSS, refer to Chapter 21, "Managing Appearance with Cascading Style Sheets."

Linking to an Existing File or Web Page

The following controls appear only if the Existing File Or Web Page button is selected in the Link To bar shown previously in Figure 11-1. What's more, they appear no matter which of the Look In bar's buttons you click (Current Folder, Browsed Pages, or Recent Files):

- **Address** Specifies the location of the page that clicking the hyperlink will display. If you know this location and you're willing to type or paste it into this box, do so and ignore all the other controls.

Tip To paste a URL into the Address box, press Ctrl+V or Shift+Insert.

Browse the Web

- **Browse The Web** Locates the target page with your browser. To use this feature:
  1. Click the Browse The Web button.
  2. When your browser window appears, display the page you want the hyperlink to target.
  3. Copy the address in the browser's Address bar to the Clipboard. For example, select the entire address, and then press Ctrl+C.
  4. Switch back to FrontPage, select the existing address (if any) in the Edit Hyperlink dialog box, and then press Ctrl+V to paste the address you copied in step 3.

Browse for File

- **Browse For File** Displays the Link To File dialog box. Locate the target page you want, and then click OK.

Tip Linking directly to a file on your computer is usually a bad idea, because Web visitors don't have access to the files on your computer. It's better to first add the file to the current Web site and then create a hyperlink to that location.

- **Bookmark** Specifies not only a particular page, but a particular location within that page.

For more information about bookmarks, refer to "Setting and Using Bookmarks," later in this chapter.

The Current Folder button in the Look In bar displays files and folders in the current folder. Because this feature can also change the current folder to any available Web or file location, it's much more powerful than its name might suggest. The following controls appear only after you select the Current Folder button:

- **Look In box** Displays and controls the folder that appears in the large selection list in the center of the dialog box. Open the drop-down list to display and select folder locations above and below the current folder.
- **Selection list** Itemizes the contents of the current Web site:
    - Click a file or folder once to copy its location to the Address box.
    - Double-click a file to copy its location to the Address box, close the dialog box, and update the hyperlink.
    - Double-click a folder to display its contents.

Up One Folder

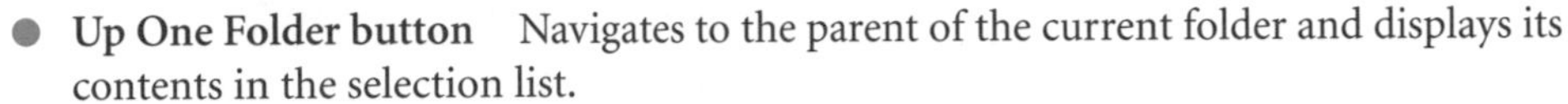

- **Up One Folder button** Navigates to the parent of the current folder and displays its contents in the selection list.

The Browsed Pages button displays a list of pages you recently browsed using Internet Explorer. Figure 11-3 shows an example of this list. To use any of the listed pages as the target of your hyperlink, either select a page and click OK or double-click the page.

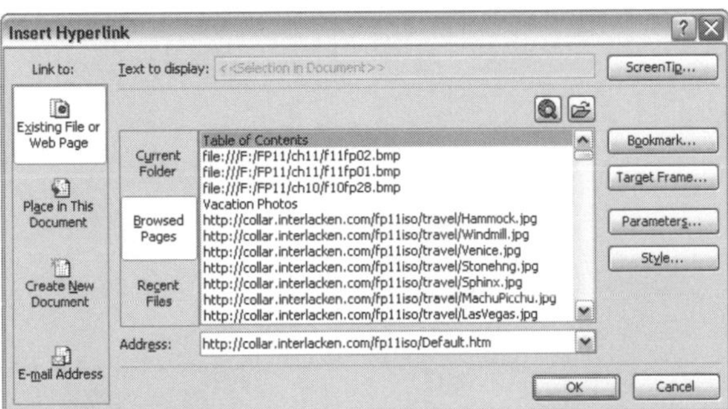

Figure 11-3. The Browsed Pages button displays a list of Web pages you recently displayed in Internet Explorer.

The Recent Files button displays a list of files you recently opened with FrontPage. Figure 11-4 provides an example. Selecting any file and clicking OK makes that file the target of your hyperlink. Double-clicking any file does the same thing.

Clicking the Parameters button—when it's available—displays the Hyperlink Parameters dialog box shown in Figure 11-5. This dialog box modifies any values that need to appear in the path information portion or the query string portion of a URL that invokes a program on the Web server.

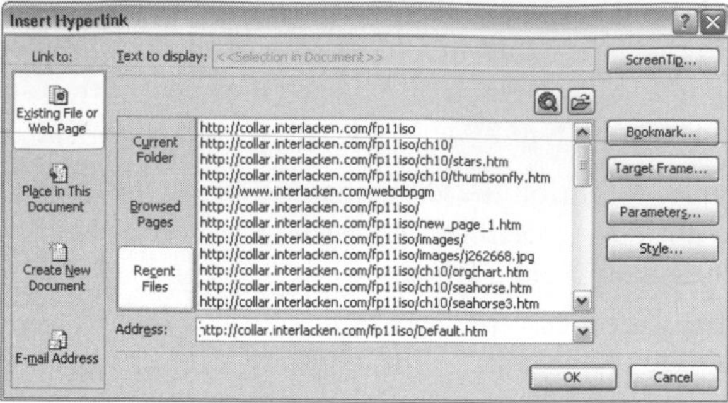

Figure 11-4. The Recent Files button displays a list of Web pages you recently opened in FrontPage.

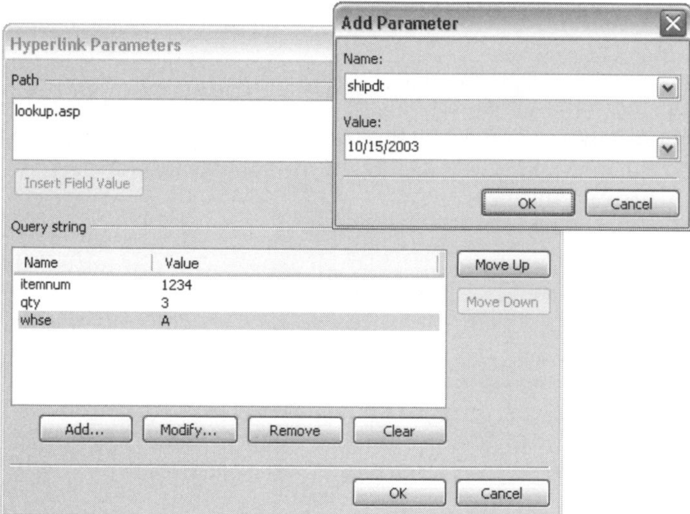

Figure 11-5. Clicking the Parameters button in the Insert Hyperlink dialog box displays the Hyperlink Parameters dialog box, which specifies parameter names and values passed to server-side programs as a query string.

For more information about paths and query strings, refer to "Coding URL Fields for Executable Programs," in Appendix C.

The options in this dialog box are as follows:

- **Path** Use this box to enter any data you want to appear between the name of the program that will execute on the Web server and the query string.
- **Insert Field Value** FrontPage dims this button unless the hyperlink appears within a Database Results region. In that case, click this button to add an expression containing the value of a database field to the *path* string.

For more information about Database Results regions, refer to "Using the Database Results Wizard," on page 884.

- **Add** Click this button to display the Add Parameter dialog box, which appends a new *keyword=value* pair to the query string. Figure 11-5 shows the Add Parameter dialog box in the foreground.
- **Modify** Click this button to change the value of the parameter currently selected in the Query String list.
- **Remove** Click this button to remove the parameter currently selected in the Query String list.
- **Clear** Click this button to remove all parameters currently present in the Query String list.
- **Move Up** Click this button to move any parameters currently selected in the Query String list one position higher.
- **Move Down** Click this button to move any currently selected parameters one position lower.

Linking to a Place in the Current Document

Clicking the Place In This Document button in the Link To bar hides all the controls described in the previous section and, in their place, displays the selection list (essentially a list of bookmarks), as shown in Figure 11-6.

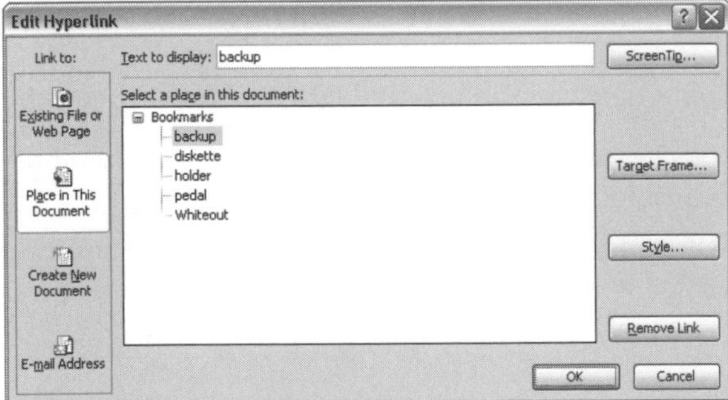

Figure 11-6. Clicking the Place In This Document button displays a list of bookmarks in the current page.

For more information about bookmarks, refer to "Setting and Using Bookmarks," later in this chapter.

Linking to a New Document

Clicking the Create New Document button in the Link To bar switches the Insert Hyperlink dialog box into the mode shown in Figure 11-7. The Create New Document mode creates a hyperlink to a Web page that doesn't yet exist.

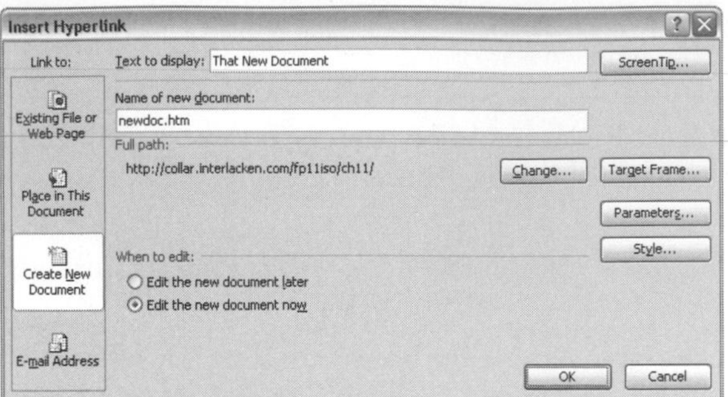

Figure 11-7. After clicking the Create New Document button, create a new page and link to it in one operation.

The following controls appear only after you click the Create New Document button. Here are the functions they provide:

- **Name Of New Document** Specify the name of the Web page you want to create. If you enter this value by hand, enter a location relative to the Full Path value.
- **Full Path** Verify that this setting correctly specifies the location where you want the new page to reside. If the path is incorrect, click the Change button.
- **Change** Click this button to change the path where the new page will reside. Then, when the Create New Document dialog box appears:
    1. Click your way to the folder location that should contain the new Web page.
    2. Enter the name of the file you want to create.
    3. Click OK.
- **When To Edit** Specify when you plan to edit the new, blank Web page.
    - **Edit The New Document Later** Click this option to create a new, blank Web page at the specified location without opening it for editing.
    - **Edit The New Document Now** Click this option to create a new, blank Web page at the specified location and open it for editing in FrontPage.

Linking to an E-Mail Address

Clicking the E-Mail Address button in the Link To bar displays the fields shown in Figure 11-8. This button creates a *mailto* URL that launches the Web visitor's e-mail program and initializes a new message addressed to the specified recipient.

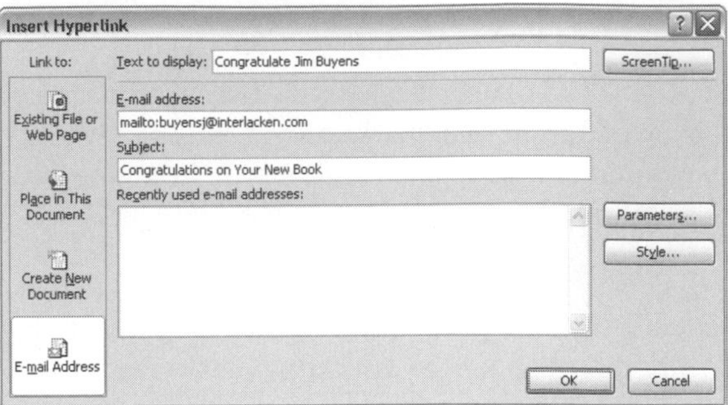

Figure 11-8. The E-Mail Address button displays the controls necessary to create a link that starts the Web visitor's e-mail program.

The input boxes listed here control this process:

- **E-Mail Address** Specifies the e-mail address that will receive the message.
- **Subject** Provides a subject line for the new message. Some mail programs ignore this field.
- **Recently Used E-Mail Addresses** Displays a list of e-mail addresses you've recently set up as *mailto* links in FrontPage. Clicking any of these addresses enters the name and subject line in, respectively, the E-Mail Address and Subject boxes.

For more information about the structure of URLs, refer to Appendix C, "Creating Uniform Resource Locators (URLs)."

Modifying Hyperlinks

Assuming that the page is already open in Design view, use any of the following procedures to modify the properties of an existing hyperlink:

- Right-click the hyperlink, and choose Hyperlink Properties from the shortcut menu.
- Select the hyperlink, and then do one of the following:
  - Click the Insert Hyperlink button on the Standard toolbar.
  - Choose Hyperlink from the Insert menu.
  - Press Ctrl+K.

Any of these actions displays an Edit Hyperlink dialog box that's essentially identical to the Insert Hyperlink dialog box shown in its many variations earlier in this chapter. All the controls and options work the same as they do when you're creating a new hyperlink.

To delete a hyperlink, click the Remove Link button that appears in the lower right corner just above the Cancel button in the Edit Hyperlink dialog box.

Tip To follow a hyperlink in Page view, Ctrl+click it. This opens the target page in Design view.

Setting and Using Bookmarks

Sometimes, especially when a Web page is long, it's desirable for hyperlinks to point somewhere other than to the top of a page. Bookmarks provide this handy function. They can jump from one location to another in the same page, or even from one page to any bookmark in another page. To define a bookmark:

1. Open the target page in FrontPage.
2. Select the spot you want displayed in the browser's top left corner. (This is where you'll insert the bookmark.) You can either set the insertion point at this location or select some text or other content there.
3. Choose Bookmark from the Insert menu to display the Bookmark dialog box, shown in Figure 11-9.

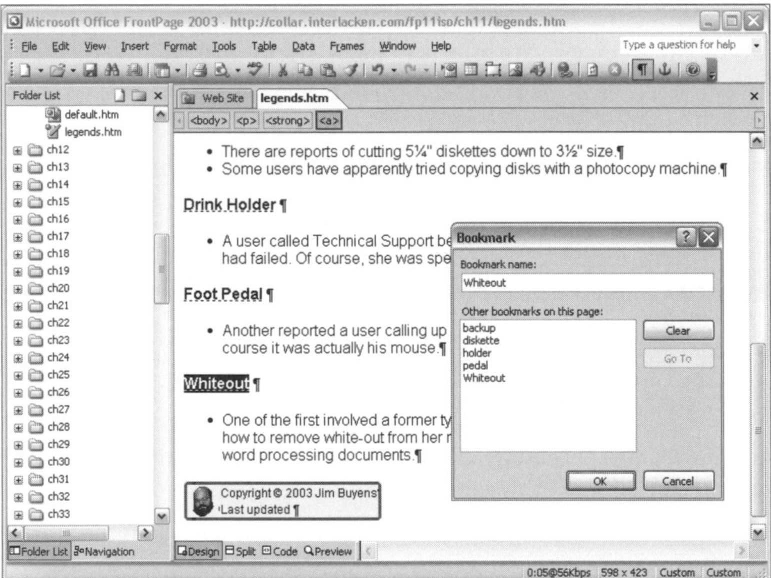

Figure 11-9. Bookmarks mark specific locations within a Web page.

4. Type the name of the bookmark in the Bookmark Name box. Use a unique name for each bookmark on a page.
5. Click OK. If you selected any content in step 2, dotted underlining, as appears in the Drink Holder, Foot Pedal, and Whiteout examples in Figure 11-9, denote the bookmark's location. Otherwise, a flag icon will indicate the bookmark.

Flag Icon

> **Note** When the browser jumps to a bookmark, it won't position the bottom of a Web page higher than the bottom of the browser window. Therefore, jumping to a bookmark near the end of the page might not position the bookmarked text at the top of the window.

Two additional buttons in the Bookmark dialog box perform useful functions:

- **Clear** To delete a bookmark, double-click it in the Other Bookmarks On This Page list. After the bookmark appears in the Bookmark Name box, click the Clear button.
- **Goto** To move the insertion point to an existing bookmark, select its name in the Other Bookmarks On This Page list, and then click the Goto button.

To set up a hyperlink that jumps to the bookmark:

1. Open the page that will contain the hyperlink.
2. To add a bookmark to an existing hyperlink, select the hyperlink. To create a new hyperlink that jumps to a bookmark, select the text, picture, or other content that will become the clickable area.
3. Choose Hyperlink from the Insert menu, or click the Insert Hyperlink button on the Standard toolbar. If you're linking to an existing hyperlink, the Edit Hyperlink dialog box appears; if you're creating a new link, the Insert Hyperlink dialog box appears.

Insert Hyperlink

To link to a bookmark on the current page, continue as follows:

1. Click the Place In This Document button in the Link To bar.
2. In the Select A Place In This Document list, select the bookmark to which the hyperlink should jump, and click OK.

To link to a bookmark on a different page, follow this procedure:

1. Click the Existing File Or Web Page button in the Link To bar.
2. Specify the Web page you want as the target of the hyperlink.
3. Click the Bookmark button.
4. When the Select Place In Document dialog box shown in Figure 11-10 appears, select the bookmark you want, and then click OK.

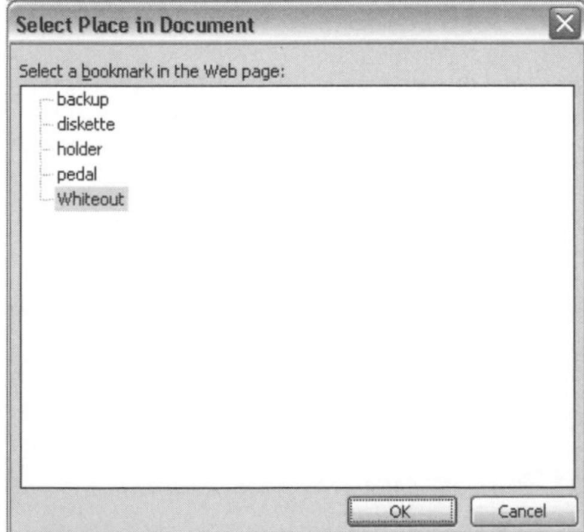

Figure 11-10. Clicking the Bookmark button displays a list of bookmarks in the current Web page.

5 Click OK a second time to apply your changes.

If the page you specify in step 2 isn't currently available, clicking the Bookmark button will produce an error message instead of the Select Place In Document dialog box. Your options at this point are:

- Establish connectivity to the target Web page, and then try again.
- Enter the bookmark manually by typing a pound sign and the bookmark name at the end of the Address box. Here's an example:

  http://www.interlacken.com/fp-iso/ch11/legends.htm#pedal

Creating and Using Hotspots

Rectangular Hotspot

Hotspots provide another form of hyperlinking—one that assigns different URLs to different parts of a picture. Another name for hotspots is *image map areas*. The most common uses for hotspots are in menu bars and maps; however, you can use hotspots for any application that requires jumping to different locations depending on which part of a picture the Web visitor clicks. Here's how to add hotspots to a picture in FrontPage:

1 Open the Web page that contains the picture, and click the picture once to select it.

2 Click the Rectangular Hotspot, Circular Hotspot, or Polygonal Hotspot button on the Pictures toolbar.

For more information about the Pictures toolbar, refer to "The Pictures Toolbar," in Appendix A.

Circular Hotspot

3 When using the Rectangular Hotspot or Circular Hotspot tool, drag the mouse pointer over the portion of the picture that should define the hotspot. When using the Polygonal Hotspot tool, draw a polygon by clicking the mouse pointer at each corner of the shape you want. To close the polygon, double-click the next-to-last point; FrontPage draws the final line to the starting point.

Polygonal Hotspot

4 When dragging is complete, FrontPage opens the Insert Hyperlink dialog box, the same dialog box you would use for setting up ordinary hyperlinks. Define the hyperlink as explained in the earlier section "Linking to an Existing File or Web Page."

5 Repeat steps 2, 3, and 4 to define additional hotspots for the same picture.

6 To define a hotspot for the picture as a whole, click any portion that's not already a hotspot, and specify its URL in the usual way.

When you select a picture that has hotspots, FrontPage displays the clickable areas, as shown in Figure 11-11. This figure shows a single picture with eight hotspots.

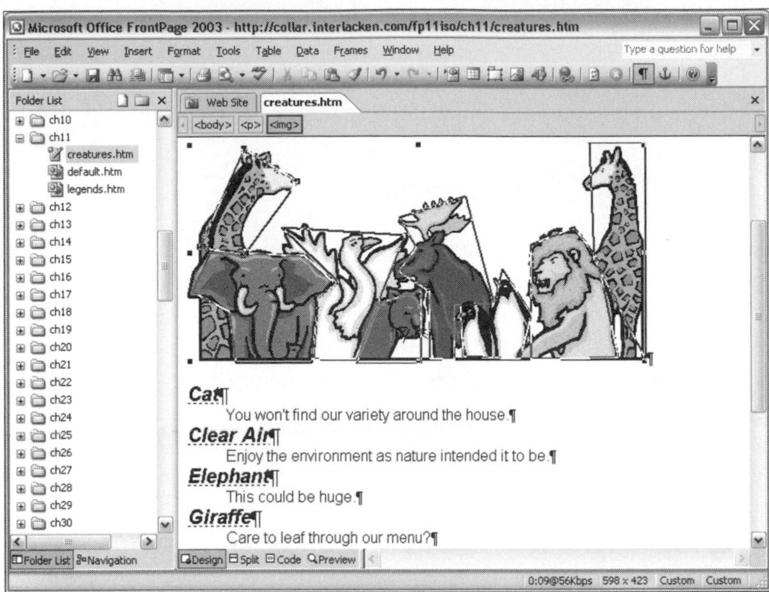

Figure 11-11. The irregular lines around each animal enclose hotspot areas. Each hotspot area jumps to a different URL.

Here's how to perform some common operations on existing hotspots:

- If the picture's hotspots are difficult to see, click the Highlight Hotspots button on the Picture toolbar. This toggles the picture to a solid white background.
- To modify a hotspot area, select it once, and then drag the edges or corner handles.
- To modify a hotspot hyperlink, double-click the hotspot area, or right-click it and choose Picture Hotspot Properties from the shortcut menu.

Tip **Provide visual clues for hotspots.**

A frequent criticism of hotspots—and of picture hyperlinks in general—is the lack of visual clues they provide. Visitors are reduced to moving the mouse pointer over a picture and watching for the pointer to indicate a hyperlink, or to clicking pictures at random to discover what they do. If the picture you're hyperlinking lacks obvious visual clues, be sure to provide instructions in the surrounding text.

Early implementations of hotspots transmitted the xy-coordinates that the Web visitor clicked to a program on the Web server. That program read an *image map file*, determined which area the Web visitor clicked, identified the corresponding jump location, and sent that information back to the browser. The browser would then request the resulting page. Newer browsers can translate hotspot clicks to hyperlink locations using image maps coded into the HTML. This is a much cleaner and more efficient approach than server-side image maps and is now the only approach that FrontPage supports.

Lack of server-side image map processing means that hotspots created in FrontPage won't work in certain very early browsers. Visitors with visual disabilities will have no use for hotspots, and fully sighted visitors frequently overlook them. These are all good reasons not to rely exclusively on hotspots for navigation through your Web site.

Using the Link Bar Component

Several FrontPage components create hyperlinks automatically. The most common of these is the Link Bars component, which creates an array of hyperlinks based either on a structure you diagram in Navigation view or on freestanding "mini-structures" called *custom link bars*. If you like to create Web sites by diagramming them in Navigation view or if you just like the highly formatted appearance of link bars, this component will probably grab your attention.

For more information about Link bars, refer to "Using Link Bars with Navigation View," on page 348.

Hyperlinking to Adobe Acrobat and Other Special File Types

Nothing about the Web stops it from delivering any kind of electronic content known to humankind. In addition to Web pages and pictures, it can deliver Microsoft Office documents in their native formats, Adobe Acrobat (PDF) files, ZIP archives, and essentially any kind of file you can think of. In most cases, the procedure for delivering such files is amazingly simple:

1. Open your FrontPage Web site.
2. Drag the file from its location in Windows Explorer, and drop it into the Folder List or Folders view.
3. Open the Web page your visitors will view before retrieving the special file.
4. Using the right mouse button, drag the file from the Folder List and drop it onto the open Web page.
5. When the shortcut menu appears, choose Create Hyperlink.
6. If you want, edit the hyperlink text.

This will create a hyperlink that delivers the file to your Web visitor. It doesn't, however, guarantee that the Web visitor's computer will handle the file the way you want. This depends on two factors:

- The Web visitor's computer must have the proper software installed. If the Web visitor's computer doesn't have a copy of Adobe Acrobat reader installed, for example, it can't possible display any Acrobat files you send.

  To avoid this problem, any Web page that provides special kinds of content should inform visitors what software they need to view it. If possible, the page should also provide a link to obtain that software.

- The Web server must correctly tell the browser what kind of file is arriving. In some cases, the file extension might provide all the information the browser needs, but in others, the Web server must also send the browser a *MIME type*.

For more information about MIME types, refer to, "MIME Types and Other Curiosities," in Appendix N.

In Summary...

This chapter explained how to create and modify hyperlinks, the mechanism that sends Web visitors from one page to another when they click on designated areas of a Web page. It also completes Part 3 of this book, which explained the fundamental processes of creating new pages, adding text, incorporating pictures, and linking pages together.

The next chapter explains how to create Web pages with a predetermined appearance, predetermined content, or both. Depending on your situation, this can be much easier than creating each page from scratch.

Chapter 12

Using Page Templates

The easiest way to finish any task is to reuse work someone else has already done. This is the simple concept behind templates. Templates eliminate duplicate work and improve consistency by supplying initial content for new Web pages.

There are two times to think about page templates: once when you're just starting a page, and again when you finish one. When you start a new page and a template can give you a head start, you might as well take advantage of it. When you finish a page and it seems likely you'll be creating more pages like it, that's an excellent time to consider saving the page as a template as well. Just save the page normally, and then remove all the content that's unique to the current instance, and then save the results as a template. As this chapter explains, creating templates is almost as easy as using them.

In past releases, Microsoft FrontPage templates helped you create pages but provided no special assistance maintaining them. Now, however, the new Dynamic Web Templates feature in Microsoft Office FrontPage 2003 changes all that. When you create pages from a Dynamic Web Template and then change the template, FrontPage can update those pages to reflect the new template styles and content. This is a fabulous capability because, sooner or later, every Web site needs a new look. If you created the site using Dynamic Web Templates, you simply update the template, congratulate yourself, and get back to that important hobby.

Creating Pages with Static Templates

Chapter 7, "Creating, Opening, Saving, and Deleting Web Pages," described several ways to create a new Web page ready for editing. Two of those procedures can create not just a blank page, but also a page initialized with content, formatting, or both from a previously stored template. Here's the first of these procedures:

1 Choose New from the File menu.
2 When the New task pane shown in Figure 12-1 appears, under New Page, click More Page Templates.

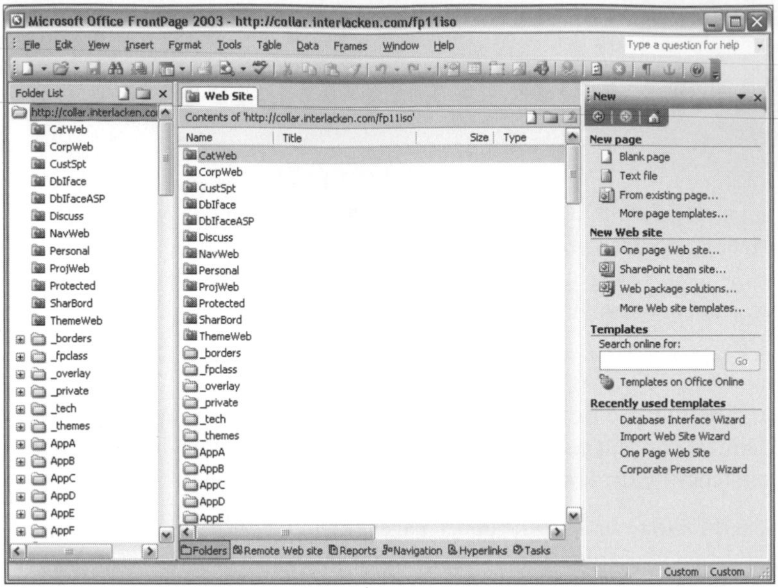

Figure 12-1. Click the More Web Site Templates option on this task pane to display a selection of available templates.

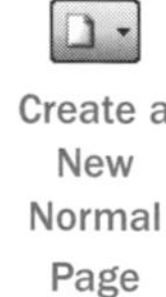

Create a New Normal Page

The second procedure is even simpler: On the Standard toolbar, click the Create a New Normal Page drop-down arrow, and then choose Page.

Regardless of which procedure you choose, FrontPage displays the Page Templates dialog box, shown in Figure 12-2.

To continue creating a Web page that uses any available template, take these steps:

1. Click the General, My Templates, Web Part Pages, Frames Pages, or Style Sheets tab to select the general category of page you want to create. Later sections in this chapter describe each of these categories. Two of the five tabs are optional:
   - The My Templates tab will be present only if you previously saved any static FrontPage templates and if one or more of those templates are available.
   - The Web Part Pages tab will be present only if the Web site resides on a Web server running Microsoft Windows SharePoint Services.
2. Review the list of templates, and select the one you want.
3. Check the Preview area. If a preview of the selected template is available, it will appear here.
4. Click OK. FrontPage loads the template into the Design view editing window as a new Web page. Make any changes you want, and then choose either the Save or Save As command from the File menu to save the page for the first time.

Large icons
List

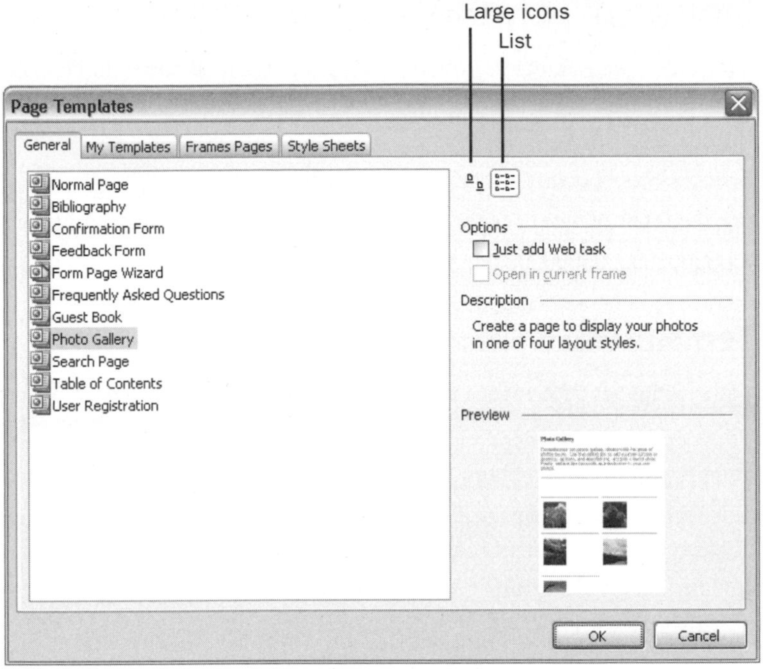

Figure 12-2. This dialog box offers a choice of types and formats for initializing new Web pages.

The following controls provide additional flexibility to the Page Templates dialog box:

- **Large Icons** This button, located above the Options area, displays a full-sized icon for each available template. The name of each template appears beneath its icon.
- **List** This button displays columns of available template names. A small icon precedes each name. This is the view shown in Figure 12-2.
- **Just Add Web Task** This option adds a task to the Tasks list rather than creating a new page in Design view.

For more information about the Tasks list, refer to "Working with Tasks View," on page 1015.

- **Open In Current Frame** This option is available only if the active Design view document is a frames page. If this option is both available and selected, the new page will appear in the last frame you clicked before you displayed the Page Templates dialog box. In any other case, the new page will be a freestanding Web page.

For more information about the using frames pages, refer to Chapter 15, "Creating Web Sites with Frames."

Selecting General Templates

This category of templates creates ordinary Web pages (that is, pages that consist of a single HTML file containing text, pictures, components, scripts, and anything else you care to add). Within this grouping are three subtypes:

- Static templates that contain nothing but ordinary content
- Component templates that use Web components supplied with FrontPage
- Form templates that create pages containing an HTML form

Using Static Templates

Each template in this group creates a perfectly ordinary, self-contained Web page. The templates are:

- **Normal Page** Creates a blank Web page ready to receive whatever content you want.
- **Bibliography** Creates a page illustrating the correct format for citing references to the printed or electronic works of others.
- **Frequently Asked Questions** Creates a page that answers common questions about some topic.

Figure 12-3 shows a page that the Bibliography template created. It incorporates no high-tech wizardry, but it does remember the standard format of a bibliography entry.

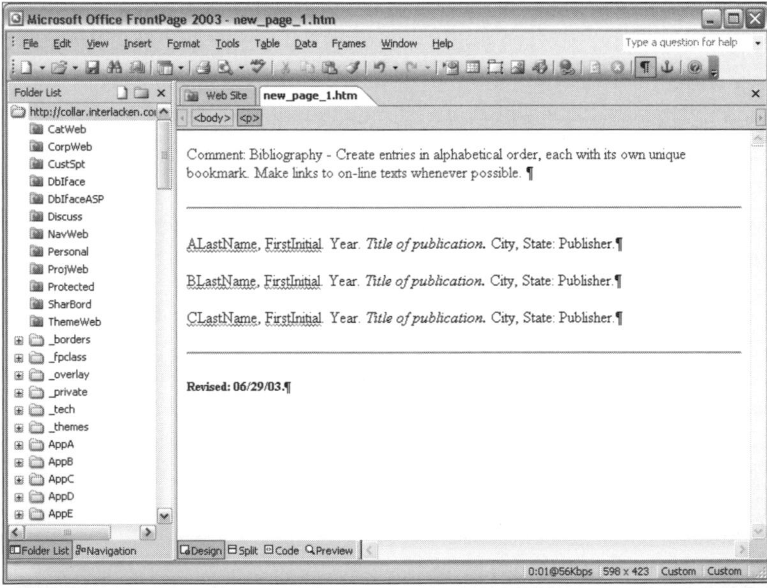

Figure 12-3. If you have trouble remembering the format of a bibliography entry, the Bibliography template is for you.

Using Component Templates

These templates each create a Web page that contains a specific FrontPage component. You can achieve essentially the same result by adding the given component to any page. There are two such templates:

- **Photo Gallery** Creates a page containing a Photo Gallery component. This component displays collections of photographs in any of four layout styles.

For more information about the Photo Gallery component, refer to Chapter 24, "Using FrontPage Photo Galleries."

- **Table Of Contents** Creates a page that contains a Table Of Contents For This Web Site component. This component displays an outline with links to every page in your Web site.

For more information about the Table Of Contents For This Web Site component, refer to "Using the Table Of Contents For This Web Site Component" on page 722.

Using Form Templates

The templates in the next group create HTML forms (that is, groups of text boxes, list boxes, check boxes, options, and buttons that submit data to a Web server). If these forms suit (or even approximate) your needs, choosing a template might be easier than designing your own form from scratch.

For more information about creating and modifying HTML forms, refer to Chapter 34, "Creating and Using Forms."

Of course, creating an HTML form is only half the battle. You must also arrange for a program on the Web server to receive and process any form data that the form submits. Here are some possible sources of such programs:

- **The FrontPage Server Extensions** Provide the following form-processing components on the Web server.
  - The FrontPage Save Results form handler
  - The FrontPage Discussion form handler
  - The FrontPage Registration form handler (non–Microsoft Windows servers only)
  - The FrontPage Wide Area Information Service (WAIS) Search Engine
- **Windows SharePoint Services** Provides most of the same form-processing features of the FrontPage Server Extensions, plus additional services for accessing XML data sources; managing lists, document libraries, and picture libraries; and assembling Web Part Pages from Web Parts.
- **Microsoft Indexing Service** A full-text search engine that comes with all recent Microsoft operating systems.

- **Custom ISAPI, NSAPI, CGI, and ASP scripts** Various ways of writing programs that run on Web servers when visitors submit suitably formatted requests. Here's what the acronyms mean:
  - ISAPI: Internet Server Application Program Interface
  - NSAPI: Netscape Server Application Program Interface
  - CGI: Common Gateway Interface
  - ASP: Active Server Pages

  Custom server-side scripts provide tremendous flexibility, but creating them requires writing program code. If you can't do this yourself, you'll need to find someone who can or purchase a third-party solution.

For more information about processing submitted HTML forms, refer to Chapter 35, "Processing Data Submitted from Forms."

Here are the specific FrontPage templates that create HTML forms:

- **Form Page Wizard** Prompts you for the type of information you want a form to collect, creates a form with typical form elements for that information, and incorporates that form into a new Web page.

  Both Windows SharePoint Services and the FrontPage Server Extensions can save data from this type of form into a file or send it as an e-mail message. If you want to save the data in a database, you'll need a Windows Web server that can run ASP. A custom script can also process input from this type of form.

For more information about the Form Page Wizard, refer to "Using the Form Page Wizard," on page 854.

- **Feedback Form** Creates a form that collects comments about your Web site, products, or organization. Feedback forms require the same kind of program on the Web server as forms that the Form Page Wizard creates. By default, feedback forms record their information in a file in your Web site named _private/feedback.txt.
- **Guest Book** Creates a form that Web site visitors can use for appending comments to a public list. Like feedback forms, guest book forms require the same kind of programming as forms from the Form Page Wizard. By default, guest book entries appear in a Web page named guestlog.htm and located in the same folder as the guest book page.
- **Search Page** Creates a page that contains a Web Search component. This provides a way for visitors to search your Web site for given words or phrases. To view or change the Web Search component's configuration, double-click anywhere within the dotted lines. A search page requires one of the following environments
  - Microsoft Indexing Service installed on the Web server and configured to monitor the area where the Web site resides.
  - The FrontPage Server Extensions installed on the Web server. (In the absence of the Indexing Service, the FrontPage WAIS Search Engine provides the full-text search capability.)

Figure 12-4 shows a page that this template created.

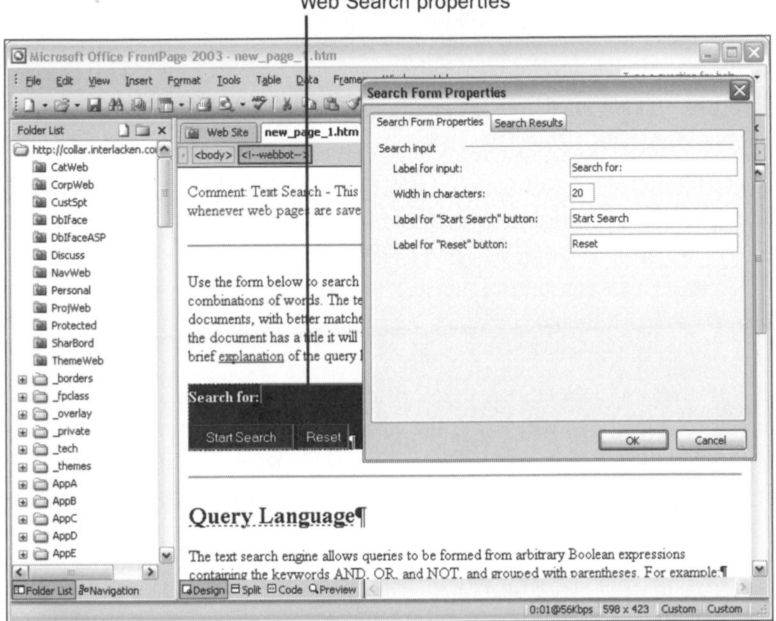

Figure 12-4. To configure the properties of a Web Search component in the Search Form Properties dialog box, double-click its area on the Web page.

For more information about the Web Search component, refer to Chapter 28, "Providing a Text Search Capability."

- **User Registration** Creates a form where visitors can create their own security accounts for accessing protected Web sites (that is, sites that require entry of a user name and password for access). Use of such forms is subject to these restrictions:
  - They must be located in the root Web site of a FrontPage-extended Web server that contains the protected Web site. Locating them within the protected site is useless because—by definition—unregistered visitors have no access there. Protecting sites and setting up self-registration forms are usually jobs for an administrator of the server's root Web site.
  - The Web server must be running an operating system other than Windows. Windows-based Web servers use the same user account database for authenticating both Web access and system logons. It would be a major security loophole if unknown Web site visitors could use self-registration to create accounts that permit system logons.

For more information about self-registration, refer to "Enabling User Self-Registration," on page 820.

- **Confirmation Form** This template, despite its name, doesn't create a form. Instead, it creates a Web page that's formatted as a thank-you letter and contains six confirmation components: Username, MessageType, Subject, UserEmail, UserTel, and UserFAX. This might be useful if all of the following are true:
  - You've developed another page that contains an HTML form.
  - The form uses the FrontPage Save Results component to save data on the Web server.
  - The form contains six form fields named Username, MessageType, Subject, UserEmail, UserTel, and UserFAX. The more your form fields differ from these, the more editing you'll have to do.
  - You want to acknowledge receipt of the data by showing a Web page that looks like a thank-you letter. Again, the more the desired format differs, the more editing you'll have to do.

  If there's a lot of editing to do, you'll probably have more success creating a blank page, formatting it as you want, and inserting a confirmation component for each field on the HTML form.

  Confirmation forms work only on servers with Windows SharePoint Services or the FrontPage Server Extensions installed.

Refer to the sidebar "Using Confirmation Components" for more information about confirmation components.

Using Confirmation Components

Whenever the FrontPage Save Results, Discussion, and Registration components process data from an HTML form, they send a *confirmation page* to the Web site visitor. If any errors occurred, the confirmation page reports them. If no errors occurred, the confirmation page shows the Web site visitor what data was saved.

For more information about the Discussion component, refer to "Creating and Managing Discussion Web Sites," on page 807.

Normally, the form handlers of the Save Results, Discussion, and Registration components create their own confirmation pages on the fly. This approach is easy on the Web designer but not on the eyes; the pages are rather plain in appearance and usually bear no resemblance to other pages in the same Web site.

To avoid these problems, Web designers can create confirmation pages. These are ordinary Web pages—formatted as the designer wants—that contain one or more confirmation components. Each confirmation component is coded with the name of one field on an HTML form. When a Save Results, Discussion, or Registration form handler processes the form, it also processes the confirmation page, replacing each confirmation component with the form field value having the same name.

Using Page Templates

Selecting Custom Templates

Each time you display the Page Templates dialog box, FrontPage determines whether any custom FrontPage static templates are available in the current FrontPage-based Web site or on your disk. These are templates that you or another designer saved as described later in this chapter, in the section "Creating Your Own Static Templates." If there are any such templates, FrontPage adds a My Templates tab to the Page Templates dialog box and lists the custom templates on that tab.

To use a custom template, select its name on the My Templates tab of the Page Templates dialog box, and then click OK. FrontPage will initialize a new page with whatever styles and content the template contains.

Selecting Web Part Pages Templates

Whenever you're working with a Web site that runs on Windows SharePoint Services, the Page Templates dialog box will contain a special Web Part Pages tab. Figure 12-5 shows an example of this tab.

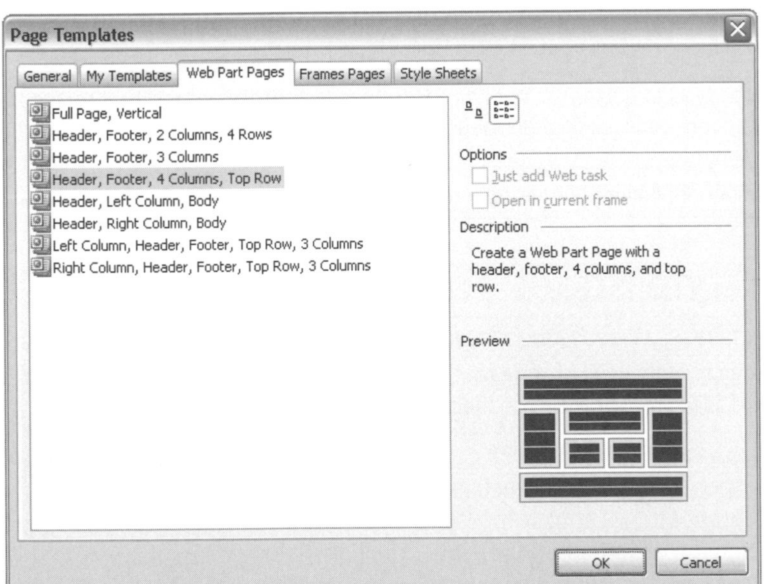

Figure 12-5. The Web Part Pages tab of this dialog box appears only for Windows SharePoint Services Web sites.

A Web Part Page is basically an empty page layout that can display one or more Web Parts. Programmers and Web designers create each Web Part independently, often without knowing which Web Part Pages—or even how many Web Part Pages—will display it. System administrators—and in some cases, even Web visitors—actually decide which combination of Web Parts will appear on a given page.

Using the Web Part Pages tab on the Page Templates dialog box is easy enough; just find the page layout that's closest to what you need, select it, and click OK. Chapters 37 and 38 will explain how to add Web Parts, save the page, and integrate it with the rest of your Windows SharePoint Services Web site.

For more information about adding Web Part Pages to Windows SharePoint Services Web Sites, refer to "Using SharePoint Team Sites," on page 921.

Selecting Frames Page Templates

These templates create frames pages. A frames page—or, by its official name, a *frameset*—is a special kind of Web page that divides the browser window into two or more rectangular areas called, naturally enough, *frames*. Each frame typically displays a different Web page.

Because they consist of multiple files, frames pages are somewhat more difficult to create and manage than ordinary Web pages. They do, however, make it easy to update one part of the browser window (one frame) in response to clicks in another part of the window (another frame).

FrontPage contains a wealth of features that make working with frames pages easy, beginning with a useful assortment of starting points. That's the purpose of the templates on this tab.

To select the best template for your needs, select each offering by clicking it or by using the arrow keys, and watching the Preview area. When the correct layout appears, click OK.

For information about frames pages, refer to Chapter 15, "Creating Web Sites with Frames."

Selecting Style Sheet Templates

Templates in this category create CSS files. These files have no visual appearance of their own; instead, they contain lines of code that change the typographical properties (that is, the style) of standard HTML objects or of objects that depend on a custom style.

If you're fairly new to creating Web pages, you might want to ignore CSS for a little while. As you gain experience, however, you'll probably recognize the futility of trying to maintain uniform appearance throughout your Web site when you apply typographical formatting to a word, a sentence, or a paragraph at a time. You'll wish there were some way to specify formats centrally and have any number of pages refer to them. When this happens, it'll be time to take another look at CSS.

For now, take it on faith that FrontPage provides an assortment of sample CSS files—templates—already coded and ready for use.

> **For more information about style sheet files, refer to Chapter 21, "Managing Appearance with Cascading Style Sheets."**

Creating Your Own Static Templates

Creating and using FrontPage templates is both easy and productive. Templates relieve designers of repetitive tasks when they create new pages. To create a template:

1. Use any convenient method to create a Web page with the desired components and features. When in doubt, it's usually better to include optional page features than to omit them. Deleting features you don't need is easier than adding those you do.
2. With the page open in Design view, choose Properties from the File menu, make sure the General tab is visible, and enter the template title in the Title box. This is the name you (or other Web authors) will later use to select the template. Click OK after you've entered the title.
3. Choose Save As from the File menu to display the Save As dialog box, shown in Figure 12-6.

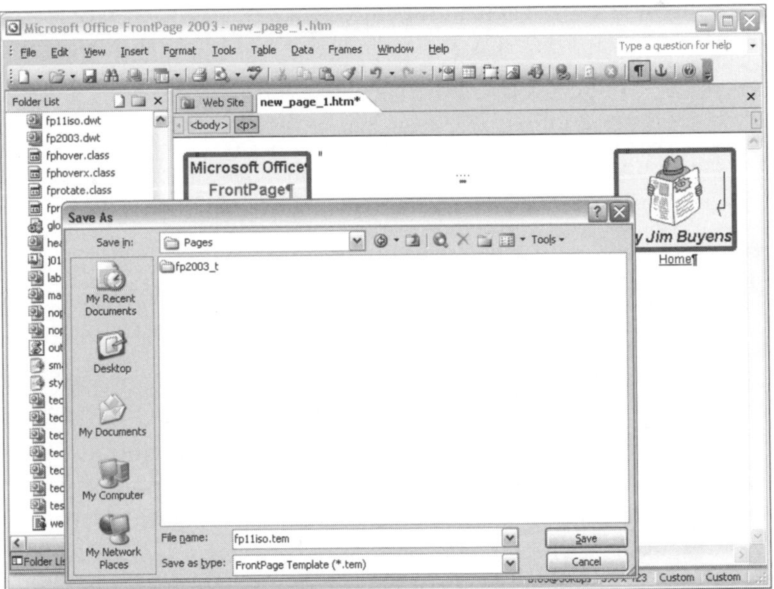

Figure 12-6. To save any Web page as a template, set Save As Type to FrontPage Template.

4. In the Save As dialog box, set Save As Type to FrontPage Template, verify that the file name is acceptable, and click Save.

5 When the Save As Template dialog box shown in Figure 12-7 appears, enter or verify the following information:

- **Title** The name by which you or other FrontPage designers will select the template. This text will appear on the My Templates tab of the Page Templates dialog box, shown previously in Figure 12-2.
- **Name** The base file name used for saving the template's files and folders.
- **Description** Any verbal explanation or notes.
- **Save Template In Current Web.** If selected, saves the template in the current Web site. This instantly makes the template available to all designers of that Web site, but only when creating pages in that site.

If this check box isn't selected, FrontPage stores the template on your hard disk. This makes it available only to you, but it's available no matter what Web site you open.

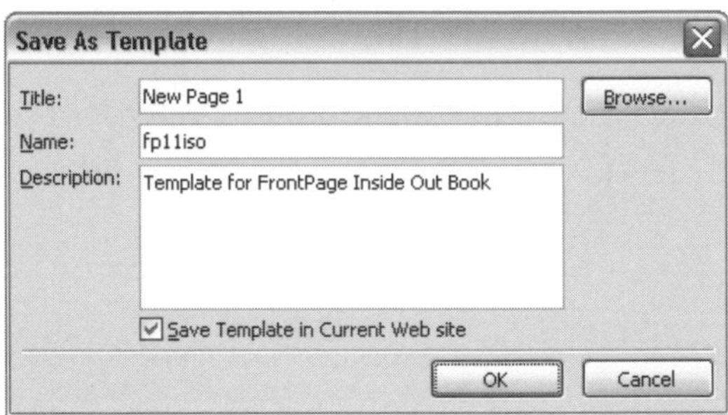

Figure 12-7. Specify the template's name, description, and location in this dialog box.

6 Click OK to save the template.

7 If the Save Embedded Files dialog box shown in the background of Figure 12-8 appears, the new template makes reference to other files in the current Web site.

For each such file, click the Set Action button, and then, in the Set Action dialog box shown in the foreground of Figure 12-8, choose one of the following options:

- **Save** Retains a copy of the file along with the template. When you or someone else uses the template and saves the resulting page for the first time, FrontPage optionally adds a copy of the embedded file to the new page's Web site.
- **Don't Save** Doesn't retain a copy of the file. Anyone who uses this template will be responsible for providing the given file.

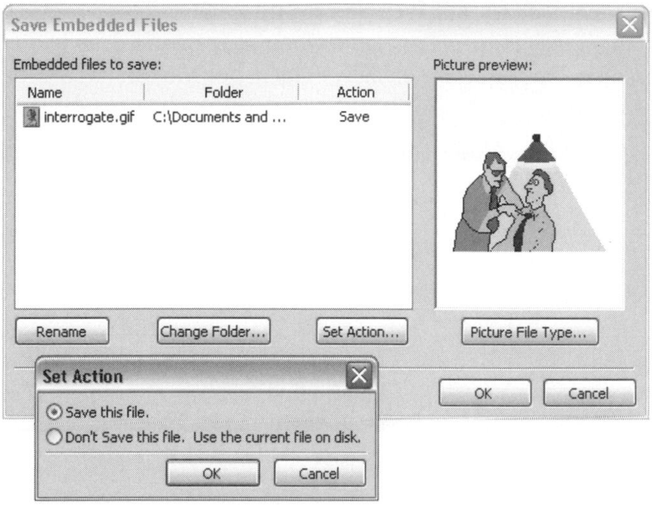

Figure 12-8. This dialog box controls which component files FrontPage saves as part of a template. Click the Set Action button to display the Set Action dialog box in the foreground.

The procedure for modifying a template is somewhat less intuitive. Here it is:

1. Use the template to create a new page.
2. Make whatever changes you believe are necessary.
3. Repeat the procedure described for creating a new template. When FrontPage prompts for permission to replace the existing template, click Yes.

When you save a template to your hard disk, FrontPage saves it in a folder that's usually located at C:\Documents and Settings\<*username*>\Application Data\Microsoft\FrontPage\<*type*>\<*template*>.tem, where:

- <*username*> is your Windows logon account.
- <*type*> is CSS, Frames, or Pages, depending on the type of template.
- <*template*> is the name you specified when saving the template. The <*template*>.tem folder normally contains a file named <*template*>.inf, and possibly a second file named <*template*>.dib.

> **Tip** **Reveal the hidden Application Data folder.**
> The Application Data folder is usually a hidden folder. Make sure you configure Windows Explorer to display hidden files and folders before you look for this folder. To do this, in Windows Explorer, first choose Folder Options from the Tools menu. Then, when the Folder Options dialog box appears, click the View tab, select the Show Hidden Files And Folders option, and click OK.

When you save a template to your Web site, FrontPage saves it in a folder located at /_sharedtemplates/<*type*>/<*template*>.tem, where <*type*> and <*template*> have the same meanings as on disk. This folder is normally hidden, but you can use the following procedure to make it visible:

1. Choose Site Settings from the Tools menu, and click the Advanced tab.
2. Make sure the Show Hidden Files And Folders check box is selected.

There are two reasons for knowing where FrontPage keeps templates:

- To delete a template, you must delete its .tem folder from the location just described.

> **Tip** Show Hidden Folders is an option on the View tab of the Folder Options dialog box in Windows Explorer. Choose Folder Options from the Tools menu to display this dialog box.

- To distribute a template stored on disk:
  1. Copy the <*type*>\<*template*>.tem folder to an intermediate location.
  2. Have the other designers copy it to their C:\Documents and Settings\<*username*> \Application Data\Microsoft\FrontPage\<*type*>\<*template*>.tem folder). In an organizational setting, this is something you could automate through a logon script or a Systems Management Server (SMS) package.

Changing a static FrontPage template doesn't change any pages it previously created. Of course, any variables, Include Page components, or shared style sheets specified by the template remain as such on created pages, and you *can* maintain these components globally. But if you want changes in a template to directly affect pages that template previously created, proceed to the next section.

Using Dynamic Web Templates

Like static templates, FrontPage Dynamic Web Templates impart new pages with a predesigned visual design and prepositioned page elements. Unlike static templates, however, Dynamic Web Templates remain attached to the pages they create. When you save changes to a Dynamic Web Template, FrontPage propagates them to each page in the same Web site that has that template attached.

The body of a Dynamic Web Template can contain any number of editable and non-editable regions. These designations, however, pertain only to pages that *use* a Dynamic Web Template. When you edit the template itself, you can edit either type of region. Table 12-1 illustrates this concept.

Table 12-1. Effect of Dynamic Web Template Editable Regions

Type region	Editable in template	Editable in created page	Propagates template changes
Editable	Yes	Yes	No
Non-editable	Yes	No	Yes

Table 12-1 also illustrates that only non-editable areas receive new content when you update the template. In effect, all copies of a non-editable region remain in sync with the template. If any copies of editable regions remain in sync, however, it's simply a happy accident.

Irrespective of any editable regions you create, attaching a Dynamic Web Template dims most options on the General, Formatting, Advanced, and Language tabs of the Page Properties dialog box. It also dims the Style, Style Sheet Links, Shared Borders, and Background tabs on the Format menu. If you want to change these settings, modify the template, and let FrontPage update the attached pages. If this would affect more pages than you want, you probably need two Dynamic Web Templates—one for each set of appearance settings—instead of one.

Note One Dynamic Web Template can attach another. In this arrangement, changing the first template updates the one that attaches it, and this in turn updates any pages that use the second template.

Creating Dynamic Web Templates

Before using a Dynamic Web Template you must, of course, create it. Here's the procedure:

1. Open a new or an existing page in Design view.
2. Add or modify any content you want.

Tip In a new Dynamic Web Template, the entire page is non-editable.

3. Select the first area in the page you want to designate as editable. (If the area you want contains no other content, add an empty paragraph so that you can select it.)
4. Choose Dynamic Web Template from the Format menu, and then Click Manage Editable Regions.
5. When the Editable Regions dialog box shown in Figure 12-9 appears, choose a name for the new editable region and type it into the Region Name box.
6. Click Add to make the region part of the template, and then click Close to close the Editable Regions dialog box. An orange border will surround the new editable region.
7. Repeat steps 3 through 6 for each additional editable region.

You can create as many or as few editable regions as you want. Presumably you'll want at least one so that each page using the template can present its own unique content. At the same time, there's usually no advantage in creating lots of small editable regions that touch each other. A single, larger editable area would work just as well.

Figure 12-9. Attaching a Dynamic Web Template is as simple as opening a file.

Here's the procedure for saving a Dynamic Web Template:

1. Choose Save As from the File menu.
2. When the Save As dialog box appears, select Dynamic Web Template (*.dwt) in the Save As Type box.
3. In the File Name box, specify a short, easy-to-remember name—that same sort of name you'd give any other Web page.
4. Click Save to save the template and close the dialog box.

Attaching Dynamic Web Templates

The procedure for using a Dynamic Web Template isn't difficult, but it does require a different approach than using static templates. Proceed as follows:

1. Open the page you want the template to control. This could be a new, blank page or an existing page. If you want, create a new page based on a static template.
2. From the Format menu, choose Dynamic Web Template and then choose Attach Dynamic Web Template.
3. When the Attach Dynamic Web Template dialog box shown in Figure 12-10 appears, locate and double-click the template you want to use.
4. If your Web page has any existing content, FrontPage will display the large Choose Editable Regions For Content dialog box shown in the background in Figure 12-11. By default, this will associate the existing page content—designated *(Body)*—with the first editable region in the template.

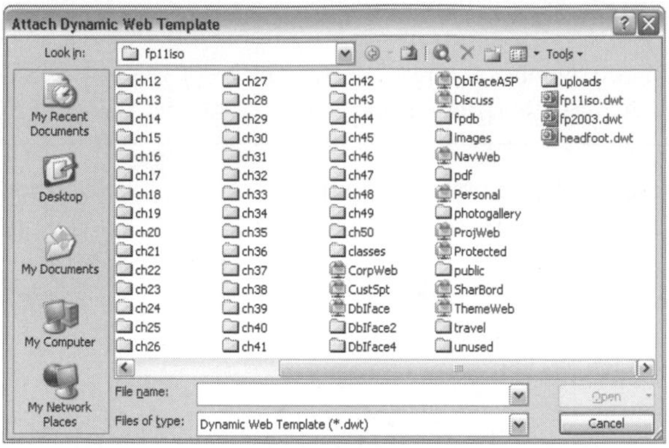

Figure 12-10. Use this dialog box to associate existing editable regions with those on a different Dynamic Web Template.

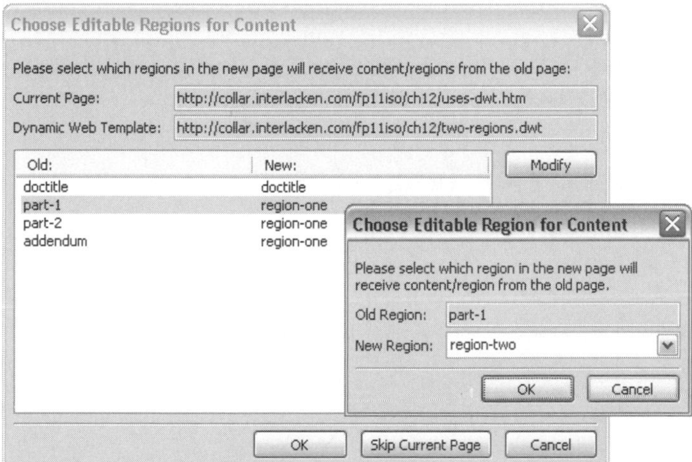

Figure 12-11. When a page uses a Dynamic Web Template and then you attach a different one, you must map content in the old editable regions to the editable regions in the new template.

If, as in Figure 12-11, the page already uses a Dynamic Web Template and you attach a different one, FrontPage will try to match up editable regions in the old and new templates based on name. If an existing editable region name in the old template doesn't exist in the new template, FrontPage matches it up with the first the editable region in the new template.

If FrontPage doesn't propose the editable region matchups you want, select any line that's incorrect, and click the Modify button. This displays the small Choose Editable Region For Content dialog box that appears in the foreground of Figure 12-11. Select the new region you want from the drop-down list, and then click OK.

Note The *doctitle* editable region appears in the Choose Editable Region For Content dialog box by default. It designates the title of the Web page as editable. (This is the title you enter in Design view after choosing Properties from the File menu.)

5 Click OK to close the dialog box and apply the template. FrontPage will display the following dialog box to confirm the operation:

6 To save the updated Web page, choose Save from the File menu.

Designating a Dynamic Web Template region as non-editable is no cure-all. In pages that attach the template, designers can modify non-editable regions in Code view, or by opening the page in any editor other than Design view. However, FrontPage will discard such changes the next time it propagates changes from the template.

Maintaining Dynamic Web Templates

When you edit and save a Dynamic Web Template, FrontPage displays a confirmation prompt similar to this:

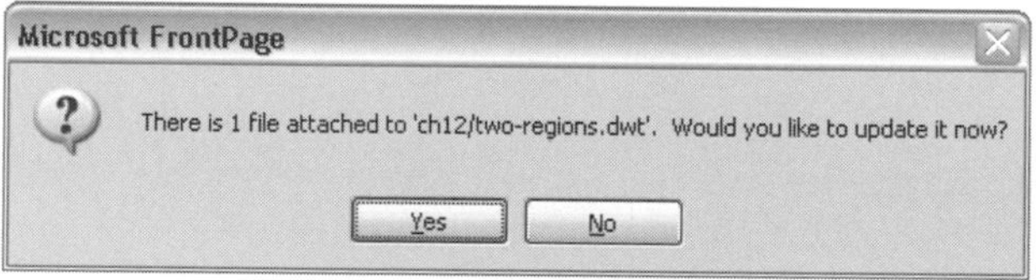

If you click Yes, FrontPage will propagate your template changes to each attached page. If you click No, FrontPage will bypass the updates. Clicking No might be useful if you're saving the template to guard against loss of work, and not because the changes are complete.

The following commands apply to any Dynamic Web Templates that you open in Design view. To access them, point to Dynamic Web Template on the Format menu.

- **Update Selected Page** Propagates template changes to the selected pages.
- **Update All Pages** Propagates template changes to all pages.
- **Update Attached Pages** Propagates template changes to all pages attached to the current template.

On the flip side, FrontPage provides the following commands whenever a page attached to a Dynamic Web Template is open in Design view. To access these commands, choose Dynamic Web Template from the Format menu.

- **Detach From Dynamic Web Template** Disconnects the current page from the template, but leaves the template's content in place (and now editable).
- **Open Attached Dynamic Web Template** Opens the template file for editing.
- **Update Selected Page** Propagates template changes to the current page.

Dynamic Web Templates are a very powerful new feature of FrontPage 2003—so powerful that many Web designers will likely adopt them in favor of Themes, static templates, and include files for reusable layouts such as page headers and footers.

In Summary...

This chapter explained how to create new Web pages based on templates, which are images of Web pages saved for future use. It also explained how to avoid repetitive work by creating templates of your own.

The next chapter begins Part 4, which explains how FrontPage can automate the creation or organization of entire Web sites. Discussion begins with the use of Navigation view, a diagramming facility that records the structure of your site and builds hyperlinks among them automatically, then continues with templates, wizards, and frames pages.

Part 4

Creating Web Sites Automatically

Chapter 13

Creating Web Sites with Navigation View

After you've created an empty Web site, the next step is, naturally, to fill it with pages. Just as naturally, you should organize and link these pages together in a way that presents your message effectively and that Web site visitors can readily understand.

Microsoft Office FrontPage 2003 has a feature called *Navigation view* that records the content you have in mind and then, together with certain Web components, creates a set of Web pages complete with titles and hyperlinks. What's more, as you revamp and reorganize your content over time, FrontPage updates all the page titles and hyperlinks automatically.

Appealing as Navigation view might be, it's not the best choice for every Web site. As so often occurs, the price of Navigation view's automation is a certain loss of design flexibility and control. Nevertheless, using Navigation view is an excellent approach for creating many kinds of Web sites and one you should consider for sites of medium size and complexity.

Working with Navigation View

Most Web designers organize their content hierarchically (that is, much like an organization chart). As Figure 13-1 illustrates, Navigation view provides a way to organize and record this structure.

Using Navigation view has several advantages over other methods of diagramming a Web site's logical structure:

- Navigation view, being electronic, is easier to revise than paper drawings.
- FrontPage automatically creates a Web page for each node you enter in the Navigation view diagram.
- If you add a Link Bar Based On Navigation Structure component to each page contained in Navigation view, FrontPage creates hyperlinks among your pages that perfectly reflect the Navigation view structure. Furthermore, if you later rearrange all or part of your Navigation view diagram, FrontPage will adjust all the link bar hyperlinks accordingly.

For more information about Link Bar components, refer to "Using Link Bars with Navigation View," later in this chapter.

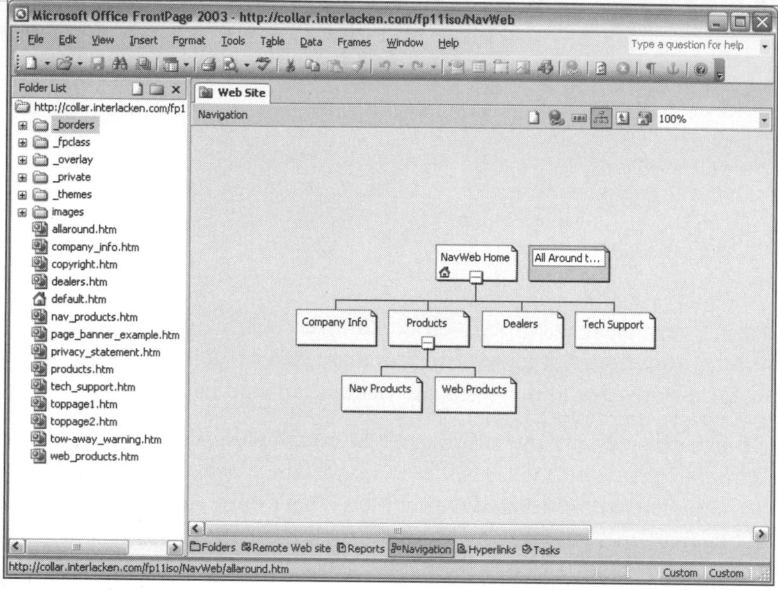

Figure 13-1. Navigation view provides a way to record and view the logical structure of a Web site.

- If you add a Page Banner component to each page you diagram in Navigation view, the text in every page heading and the text in every link bar selection will agree perfectly. This is because both components incorporate the page names you assign in Navigation view.

For more information about Page Banner components, refer to "Using Page Banners," later in this chapter.

- Constructing hyperlinks based on a diagram ensures that your Web site's design concept, its Navigation view, and the actual hyperlinks are always in sync, and that all page titles and link titles are consistent throughout your Web site.

Navigation view and the Link Bar Based On Navigation Structure component work very much hand-in-hand. After you diagram your page in Navigation view, adding a Link Bar Based On Navigation Structure component to any page creates hyperlinks that correspond to the structure you drew.

All link bars are single FrontPage components that contain multiple links. If you choose not to configure these links yourself and instead tie them to the Navigation view structure, FrontPage will automatically generate and maintain a set of hyperlinks Web visitors can use to traverse your site. In Figure 13-2, a Link Bar component in the Products page displays hyperlinks to the Web site's home page and the two child pages that appear in the diagram in Figure 13-1.

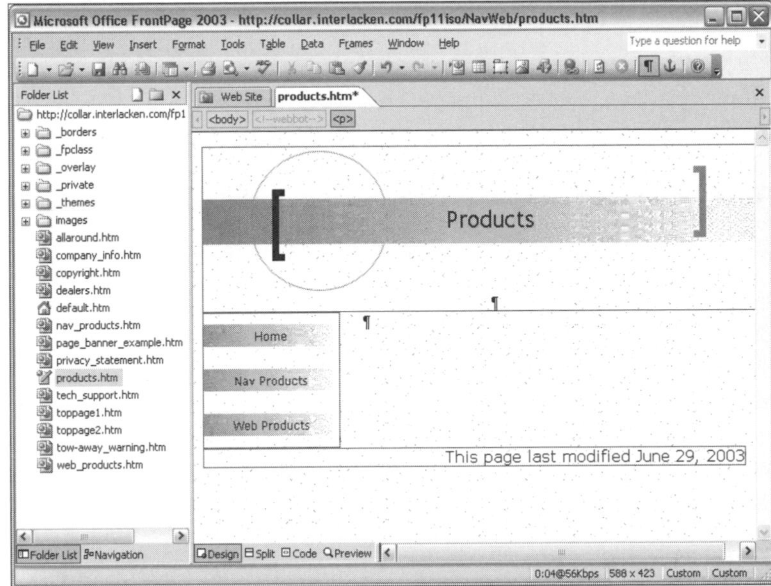

Figure 13-2. FrontPage can generate attractive link bars like these based on the site structure you diagram in Navigation view.

Documenting the structure of your Web site might at first seem like redundant work; you might expect that FrontPage should infer your site's structure by analyzing hyperlinks or folder structures. On reflection, however, you'll find that neither of these methods produces the same results as good human judgment. Here are the reasons:

- Hyperlink analysis fails because most Web pages contain hyperlinks that are convenient for the visitor but extraneous to the Web site's primary content structure.
- Folder analysis fails because most sites become disorganized over time and because utility pages often exist separately from the Web site's main structure.
- If several pages have hyperlinks to the same target page, there's no way to determine which is the target page's true parent in terms of overall structure.

For these reasons, FrontPage takes an opposite approach to eliminating double work: Rather than inducing the Web site's structure from hyperlinks among its pages, FrontPage generates HTML from information you provide about your Web site's structure—information you enter in Navigation view.

Deciding Whether to Use Navigation View

Many successful Web designers never use Navigation view, link bars, page banners, or any other FrontPage features that organize, create, and maintain a Web site automatically. Here are some guidelines to aid your decision:

- Rank beginners creating very small sites usually prefer the direct approach (that is, creating and linking a few pages by hand). Working indirectly through Navigation view might be more than they can initially absorb.
- Expert designers usually take the manual approach as well, because it gives them more flexibility over the Web site's design.
- Navigation view can neither organize nor create a site that uses frames.

For more information about frames, refer to Chapter 15, "Creating Web Sites with Frames."

- Navigation view is probably overkill for a Web site with five or fewer pages.
- Navigation view is likely to be unwieldy for a Web site with more than 100 to 200 Web pages. To use Navigation view for a larger site, break the site into multiple subwebs, each having its own Navigation view diagram.
- Link bar buttons are typically rather large, especially if you format them with a graphical theme. This makes it difficult to design pages that have more than six or eight hyperlinks to child pages. If this many links seems sufficient for any page you can think of, count the number of links on the home page of any large e-commerce or Internet portal site.

Displaying Navigation View

Because Navigation view deals with groups of Web pages, it's applicable only to FrontPage-based Web sites. A Web site defines the boundaries of the Navigation view diagram and provides the file areas that store the Navigation view structure. Here's the procedure for displaying the Navigation view structure of a Web site:

1. Open your Web site.
2. Click the Web Site tab that appears above the main editing window.
3. Click the Navigation tab that appears below the main editing window.

FrontPage can also display a condensed version of Navigation view, called the *Navigation pane*, instead of the Folder List while you're editing a Web page. Here's the procedure to display the Navigation pane:

1. Open any file in the FrontPage Editor.
2. Make sure that the editing window isn't displaying any view from the Web Site tab.
3. Choose Navigation Pane from the View menu, or click the Navigation button at the bottom of the Folder List. Figure 13-3 shows the Navigation pane displaying the same Navigation structure as Figure 13-1.

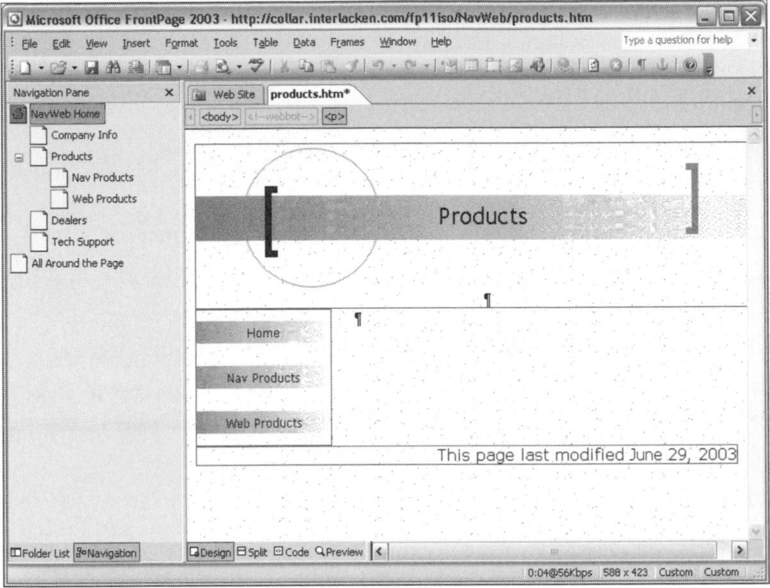

Figure 13-3. The Navigation pane displays a miniature version of Navigation view that you can refer to and update while editing a page in Design view.

Defining a Navigation View Home Page

A home page is the jumping off point for all the content and features your Web site has to offer. The home page is the initial, default, and generally most important page in a Web site. This holds equally true for your Web site's logical structure and its physical implementation.

You, your Web server, and Navigation view should all agree on the identity of the home page. As to its location, the home page always resides in a Web site's root folder. In a disk-based Web site, the home page has the name index.htm. In a server-based Web site, its name depends on the Web server's default document name. On Microsoft Web servers, the default document name is usually default.htm. On others, it's usually index.htm or index.html.

If your Web site contains a page with this name, FrontPage normally makes it the home page in Navigation view. To verify this, display Navigation view, and look for a page that appears at the top level of the hierarchy and contains a house icon like this:

If no one has drawn a Navigation view structure for the current Web site, the home page will be the only page that appears. If Navigation view can't identify a home page, it displays this message: *To create a Home Page, click New Page on the toolbar.*

View Subtree Only

If your Web site doesn't yet contain a home page, the solution is simple: Click the New Page button on the Standard toolbar. FrontPage creates a blank home page and places it at the top of your Navigation view hierarchy. Its file name is index.htm in a disk-based Web site or the Web server's default page name on a server-based Web site.

If the Web site *does* contain a home page, try the following methods, in order, of making Navigation view recognize it:

1 First try using the command FrontPage provides for this purpose:
    1 Locate your home page in Folder view or in any Folder List, and right-click the file name.
    2 When the shortcut menu appears, choose Set As Home Page.
    3 Display Navigation view, and look for the home page. If you're already in Navigation view, press F5, the Refresh key. This method will rename your home page to the name Navigation view is looking for.

4 If your home paçge still doesn't appear in Navigation view, choose Recalculate Hyperlinks from the Tools menu, and then display Navigation view, and look for the home page. If you're already in Navigation view, press F5

5 If a home page still doesn't appear, follow these steps:
    1 Rename the existing home page file and, in Navigation view, click the New Page button to create a new home page.
    2 Open both pages for editing.
    3 Copy the entire contents of the old home page file, and paste the contents into the new home page file.
    4 Save the new home page file, and close both files.
    5 Display Navigation view, and look for the home page. If you're already in Navigation view, press F5, the Refresh key.
    6 Delete the old, renamed file.

After you've designated the correct home page in Navigation view, you should probably never delete it. If you try to delete it in Navigation view, FrontPage displays the Delete Pages dialog box, shown in Figure 13-4. This dialog box presents only two options: delete the home page and all pages beneath it from Navigation view, and delete the home page and all pages beneath it. These are both extreme actions with no possibility of undoing them.

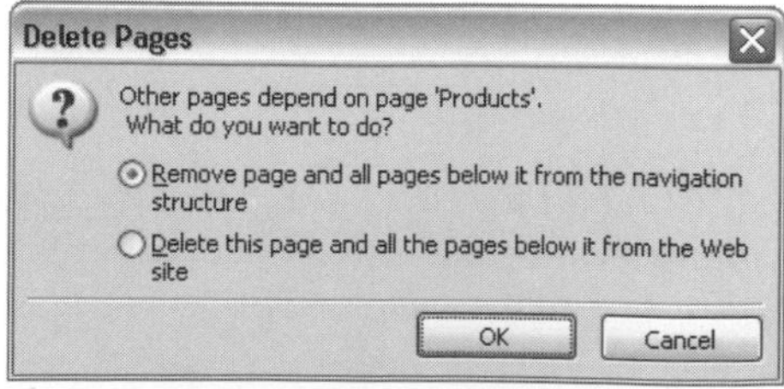

Figure 13-4. Deleting a page from Navigation view also deletes its children from Navigation view, and might delete all affected pages from your Web site.

Troubleshooting

Default page names differ on development and production Web servers

Confusion can result if your authoring environment and production Web server have different default page names. Here are two such scenarios:

- You create Web sites using a Microsoft Web server whose default page name is default.htm, but publish them on a UNIX Web server whose default page name is index.html.
- You create disk-based Web sites with home pages named index.htm and publish them to a Microsoft Windows 2000 server whose default page name is default.htm.

The cleanest and most desirable solution is to change your authoring environment, your production Web server, or both so that they use the same default document name. Unfortunately, this isn't always possible. In the case of a disk-based Web site, FrontPage has no facility to change the file name that identifies the home page. In the case of a server-based Web site, you might not have access to the Web server's configuration, the server's administrator might not be willing to make the change, or making a change might adversely affect other applications.

FrontPage renames the home page when it copies a Web site from one location to another and all the following are true:

- You use the FrontPage Publish command to copy the Web site.
- Both the source and the target locations are FrontPage-based Web sites.
- The default document name in the two Web sites is different.

Of course, just as it always does when renaming files, FrontPage adjusts all hyperlinks so that they keep working as you intend.

If you can't eliminate the discrepancy in default document names and you must publish by FTP, file sharing, or some other mechanism that doesn't rename the home page, proceed as follows:

1. Use the development server's default file name (in other words, default.htm) as the Navigation view home page.
2. Create a redirection file having the production server's default file name (in other words, index.htm). This page should redirect visitors to the default file name from step 1 (default.htm).

   For information about creating redirection pages, refer to "Configuring HTML Header Properties," on page 505.

Keep in mind that whenever you delete entries from Navigation view, you're deleting hyperlinks from link bars as well. This explains why, after deleting the home page and its children from Navigation view, any Link Bars components you've added might be blank or significantly diminished.

Adding Child Pages to Navigation View

After Navigation view correctly displays a home page, adding child pages is easy. Choose your favorite method from this list:

- To create a new page and immediately define it as the child of another:
  1. Right-click the parent page in Navigation view.
  2. Choose New from the shortcut menu, and then choose Page.

  This procedure is very handy when you're designing the initial structure of a Web site.

  New pages you create this way are just Navigation view entries, not physical files. As such, they don't appear immediately in the Folder List. However, when you update the screen, FrontPage creates all the pages using file names and titles similar to their Navigation view names. You can update the screen by using any of these four methods:

  - Right-click the Navigation view background, and choose Apply Changes from the shortcut menu.
  - Switch to another view.
  - Edit a page in FrontPage.
  - Close the Web site.

  After FrontPage creates any new files, you can change their file names by using the normal Folder List commands.

- To designate an existing page in your Web site as the child of a page in Navigation view:
  1. Drag the page from the Folder List.
  2. Drop the page under the appropriate parent in the Navigation view display.

  As you drag files near prospective parents, FrontPage draws shaded lines suggesting a relationship. When the shaded line connects to the correct parent, release the mouse button. FrontPage retains the left-to-right positioning of any nearby pages. Figure 13-5 shows this operation in progress.

- To first create a physical file and then add it to Navigation view:
  1. Select anything in the Folder List.
  2. Click the New Page button.
  3. Switch to Navigation view, if necessary.
  4. Save and rename the new page, and then drag it into position.

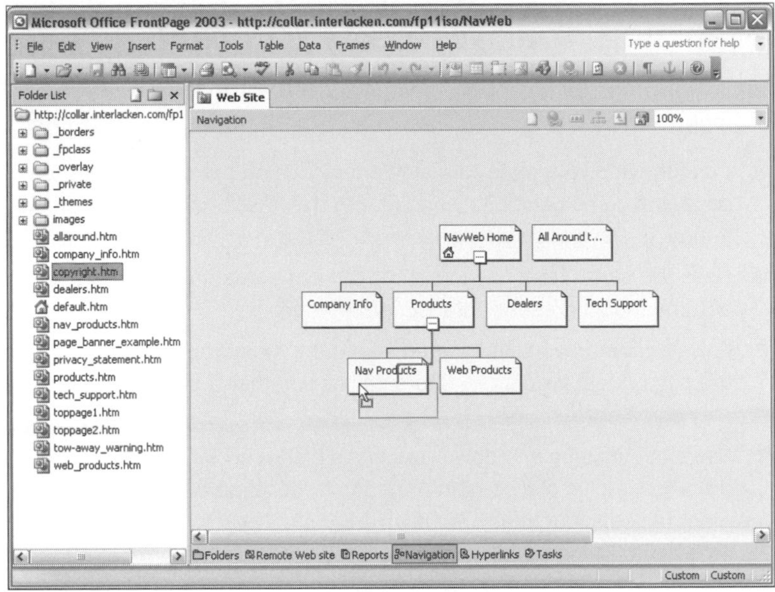

Figure 13-5. When you drag a page around in Navigation view, FrontPage draws a shaded line to the closest available parent. Drop the page when the shaded line connects it to the parent page you want.

- To add a page outside the current Web site to your hierarchy:
  1. In Navigation view, right-click the page that will be the external page's parent.
  2. Choose Add Existing Page from the shortcut menu. This displays the Insert Hyperlink dialog box shown in Figure 13-6.

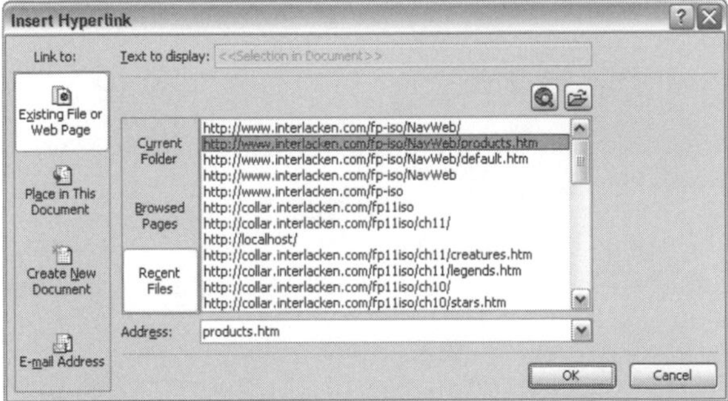

Figure 13-6. Choosing Add Existing Page in Navigation view displays this dialog box for entering locations inside or outside the current Web site.

  3. Locate or type the desired link, and then click OK.

Organizing Your Web Site Content

Here are some tips for organizing Web pages in a way that presents your message clearly and simply:

- Confine each Web page to a single topic. If you put two or more topics on the same page, the combined page won't fit into the Navigation view hierarchy. Each page can appear in Navigation view only once.
- Have the pages near the top of the structure deal in broad categories. Pages at the bottom should present detailed information.
- Put the most important hyperlinks and the most important information at the top of the page. Most Web site visitors decide whether a page is interesting long before they scroll down.
- Use clear links up and down your site's hierarchy. Most Web site visitors want to drill down to specific pieces of information rather than traversing, accepting, or rejecting many pages sequentially. For example, no one wants to locate a product or any other listing by clicking a Next button several hundred times.

Troubleshooting

FrontPage won't add a page to Navigation view

If FrontPage won't draw shaded lines to a page you drag from the Folder List, that file already appears beneath the home page or a top page. (For more information about top pages, refer to "Adding Top Pages to Navigation View," later in this chapter.) If you try to add the same page by clicking its parent and choosing Add Existing Page from the shortcut menu, you get the following message:

The page you are trying to add is already in the navigation structure. Rename this page or select a different page and then try again.

This behavior occurs because FrontPage requires each page in Navigation view to have at most one parent. Therefore, each page in a Web site can appear in the main navigation structure only once.

To avoid this restriction, add the destination page to a Custom Link Bar and then add a Link Bar With Custom Links component to the pages where you want the links to appear. The section "Creating a Link Bar With Custom Links Component," later in this chapter, explains how to create this component.

The only nodes that can have children in Navigation view are Web pages in the current Web site. However, you *can* add external links, pictures, multimedia files, CGI programs, or anything you want as the *child* of a page in the current Web site. Because FrontPage can't manipulate link bars and other components in such files, they can't be Navigation view parents.

Tip As the diagram becomes larger and more complex, you might want to zoom in, zoom out, and collapse branches and then expand them. For instructions on doing this, refer to "Controlling the Navigation View Display," later in this chapter.

Here's how FrontPage names the pages you add to Navigation view:

- When you create a new page in Navigation view, Front Page gives it a Navigation view name of New Page *x*, where *x* is a sequential number.
- When you add an existing page to Navigation view, FrontPage uses the page's title as the Navigation view name. (This is the title you assign on the General tab of an open page's Page Properties dialog box, and not the page's file name.) If the existing page resides outside the current Web site, you'll also see a small globe icon on the external page.

Even though a page's HTML title provides a reasonable first guess, in most cases you'll want to shorten the Navigation view name. HTML page titles are the strings that search engines and browsers use to identify the page. You'll probably want your HTML titles to be fully descriptive of each page and possibly to contain your company or site name as well. The Navigation view name, on the other hand, frequently becomes the menu text that appears in link bars, and you'll likely want to keep this short.

In either case—new page or existing—accepting a page's default Navigation view name is usually a bad idea. Fortunately, changing the Navigation view name of a Web page is quite simple. Just do this:

1. Highlight the page's icon by clicking it in the main Navigation view window or in the Navigation pane.
2. Right-click the page, and choose Rename, press the F2 key, or click the name.
3. Type or revise the page's Navigation view name.
4. Press Enter, or click anywhere outside the Navigation view name.

Rearranging Pages in Navigation View

Rearranging pages is even simpler than adding them. If you're working in Navigation view, click the page you want to move, hold down the mouse button while you drag, and then release the button when the shaded line connects the dragged page to the desired parent.

The procedures are somewhat different if you're working in the Navigation pane. Proceed as follows:

- To move a page under a different parent, drag the child page and drop it onto the parent page.

- To rearrange the children of a particular parent, drag one of the pages you want to move and drop it above, below, or between its siblings. A black horizontal line indicates the new page position, should you drop the page with no further movement. Figure 13-7 shows this operation in progress.

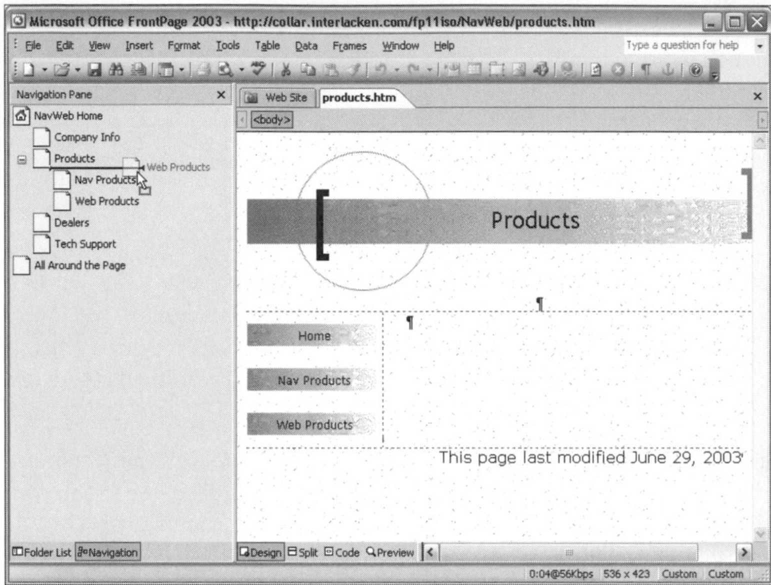

Figure 13-7. If you drop a page where a vertical bar appears, FrontPage makes the page a peer of the page above the line.

Adding Top Pages to Navigation View

Orphan pages are perfectly valid in Navigation view. These are pages that don't fall within the hierarchy beneath the home page—pages such as Search, Send Mail, and Contact Webmaster. Because these pages aren't the home page and yet have no parent, FrontPage calls them *top pages*. They appear at the top of the Navigation view diagram, adjacent but not connected to the home page. To designate an existing page as a top page:

1. Drag it from elsewhere in the Navigation view diagram or from the Folder List.
2. Drop it—just as you probably suspected—adjacent to but not beneath the home page.

You can create as many top pages as you want. Follow this next procedure to create a new top page:

1. Right-click anywhere in the Navigation view diagram.
2. Choose New from the shortcut menu, and then choose Top Page.
3. FrontPage gives new top pages names like Top Page 1, Top Page 2, and so forth. Rename the page as you would any other page in the diagram.

Top pages can have children just as the home page does. To add children, drag them beneath the top page just as you would under any other page.

The Link Bar component treats pages you draw beneath a top page much as it does pages you draw beneath the home page (that is, it honors relationships such as parent pages, child pages, and left and right pages). Link bars can also display links to all top pages in a Web site. However, you can't add special top page links to all forms of link bars as you can home page links.

> **Tip** To view the file name of a page that appears in Navigation view, right-click its icon, and then choose Properties from the shortcut menu.

Adding Custom Link Bars to Navigation View

A Custom Link Bar is a named group of hyperlinks that's not associated with any specific page. Custom Link Bars have these properties:

- Unlike most nodes in the Navigation view diagram, Custom Link Bars don't represent a specific page. They're simply a named list of links that you can use in as few or as many pages as you want.
- Custom Link Bars have at most a two-level structure: the Custom Link Bar itself, and any number of direct children. However, the children can't have children.
- The links on a Custom Link Bar can point inside or outside the current Web site.
- One page can belong to any number of Custom Link Bars. In contrast, one page can belong to the main Navigation view structure only once.
- Custom Link Bars normally reside in the Navigation view structure as peers of the home page.
- You can drag a Custom Link Bar beneath a regular page in the Navigation view diagram, but because the Custom Link Bar isn't a page, its parent can't link to it. Instead, any link bars in the parent page will link to the Custom Link Bar's first child.

To create a Custom Link Bar that's a peer of the home page:

1. Right-click anywhere in the Navigation view or Navigation pane background.
2. Choose New from the shortcut menu.
3. Choose Custom Link Bar.

This creates a new Custom Link Bar named New Link Bar that you can modify as described in the section "Creating a Link Bar With Custom Links Component," later in this chapter.

To create a Custom Link Bar that's the child of another page, right-click that page, choose New from the shortcut menu, and then (you guessed it) choose Custom Link Bar.

You can drag a page out of the main Navigation view structure and drop it beneath a Custom Link Bar, but this removes the page from the main structure. The following procedures offer better alternatives:

- In Navigation view:
  1. Drag the page you want to include out of the Folder List.
  2. Drop it beneath the desired Custom Link Bar.

  or:

  1. Select the Custom Link Bar.
  2. Click the Add Existing Page button on the Navigation toolbar.
  3. When the Insert Hyperlink dialog box appears, specify the page you want, and click OK.

Add Existing Page

- In either Navigation view or the Navigation pane:
  1. Right-click the page you want the Custom Link Bar to include.
  2. Choose Copy from the shortcut menu.
  3. Right-click the Custom Link Bar, and choose Paste.

  or:

  1. Right-click the Custom Link Bar.
  2. Choose Add Existing Page from the shortcut menu.
  3. When the Insert Hyperlink dialog box appears, specify the page you want, and click OK.
- In Design view:
  1. Open any page that uses or should use the Custom Link Bar.
  2. If the page doesn't already contain a Custom Link Bar component, add one.
  3. In the Link Bar Properties dialog box, use the Choose Existing drop-down list to choose the Custom Link Bar you want. This list contains one choice for each Custom Link Bar that appears in Navigation view.
  4. While still in the Properties dialog box, configure the links you want, and click OK.

For more information about the Link Bar With Custom Links component, refer to "Creating a Link Bar with Custom Links Component," later in this chapter.

Figure 13-8 shows a Navigation view structure that contains one Custom Link Bar. The link bar's name is Miscellaneous Links, and it contains three children.

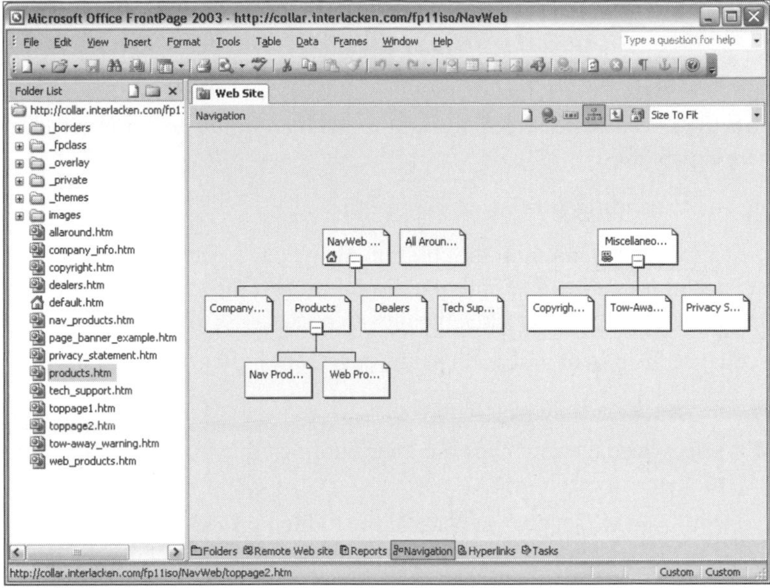

Figure 13-8. The structure on the left is a Custom Link Bar. Any Link Bar With Custom Links component that references this Custom Link Bar will display the given links.

The appearance of the following page icon differentiates Custom Link Bars from ordinary pages:

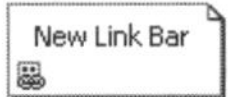

Deleting a Page from Navigation View

To delete a page from Navigation view or the Navigation pane, do *one* of the following:

- Select the page, and choose Delete from the Edit menu.
- Select the page, and press Delete.
- Right-click the page, and choose Delete from the shortcut menu.

Following any of these actions, FrontPage displays the Delete Pages dialog box shown previously in Figure 13-4. This dialog box asks whether you want to remove the page and its children just from Navigation view or completely from your Web site. Make your choice, and click OK. To also delete children of a page you're deleting, click Yes when prompted.

> **Caution** Deleting a file from the Folder List always removes it completely from the Web site. You can't undo this action.

Controlling the Navigation View Display

As the size of your structure grows, you might find it convenient to hide the parts you aren't working on or to view the diagram on a greater or lesser scale. You might even decide that the diagram fits the screen better in left-to-right mode than in top-to-bottom mode. FrontPage has all these capabilities.

Collapsing and expanding the view works like this:

- To collapse (that is, to hide) the children of any page, click the minus sign icon on that page's lower edge. The children disappear, and the icon changes to a plus sign. To display the children again, click the plus sign icon.
- To collapse the parent and peers of any page, take either of these actions.
  - Right-click a child page, and choose View Subtree Only from the shortcut menu.
  - Select the page, and click the View Subtree Only button on the Navigation toolbar.

  View Subtree Only

  A View All icon will appear in place of the hidden pages. The same two commands toggle the display back to its former appearance, as does clicking the View All icon.

For more information about the Navigation toolbar, refer to "The Navigation Toolbar," in Appendix A.

Right-clicking the background area in Navigation view displays the shortcut menu shown on the left in Figure 13-9.

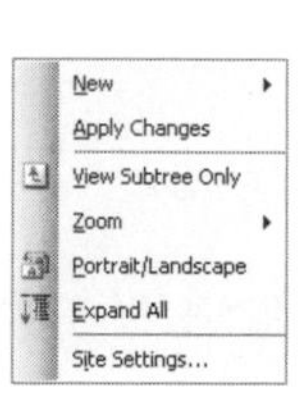

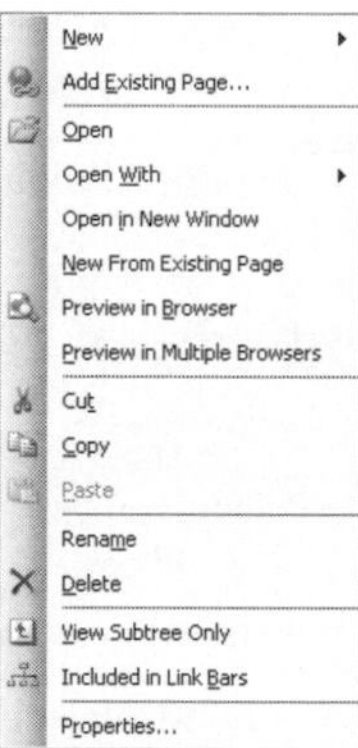

Figure 13-9. Right-clicking the Navigation view background produces the shortcut menu on the left. Right-clicking a Navigation view node produces the shortcut menu on the right.

Here's a brief explanation of what the shortcut menu commands do:

- **New** Adds a new top page or Custom Link Bar to the diagram.
- **Apply Changes** Saves the current Navigation view structure to disk. In so doing, it also creates empty Web pages for any nodes (other than external hyperlinks) that don't have them.
- **View Subtree Only** Collapses or expands all nodes above, to the left of, or to the right of the current selection.

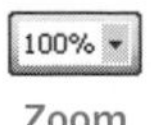

Zoom

- **Zoom** Controls the degree of magnification, as a percentage of normal size. The Size To Fit subcommand scales all visible pages into the main Navigation view window.

  The Zoom drop-down list on the Navigation toolbar provides essentially the same options.

Portrait/ Landscape

- **Portrait/Landscape** Toggles Navigation view between top-to-bottom and left-to-right display mode.

  The Portrait/Landscape button on the Navigation toolbar provides the same display options.
- **Expand All** Enlarges the view so that all pages in the structure appear. This has the same effect as clicking all the plus sign icons to show all the child pages.
- **Site Settings** Displays the same dialog box as choosing Site Settings from the Tools menu.

For information about the Site Settings dialog box, refer to "Reviewing Site Settings," on page 1137.

Right-clicking a Navigation view icon produces the shortcut menu shown on the right in Figure 13-9.

These commands work as follows:

- **New** Creates either a new page with the selected page as its parent or a Custom Link Bar.

Add Existing Paget

- **Add Existing Page** Displays a dialog box for locating a new child page for the currently selected parent. The page you select needn't be part of the current Web site.

  The Navigation toolbar includes an Add Existing Page button that also displays this dialog box.
- **Open** Opens the node using the standard editor for its file type.
- **Open With** Opens the node with an editor you select from a menu.
- **Open In New Window** Opens the node in a new FrontPage window.
- **New From Existing Page** Opens a new copy of the node. Saving the copy doesn't, by default, overwrite the original file.
- **Preview In Browser** Displays the current page in your browser. FrontPage starts the browser if necessary.
- **Preview In Multiple Browsers** Displays the current page in each browser installed on your computer.
- **Cut** Copies the current selection and all its children to the Clipboard, and then removes the selection from the Navigation view.
- **Copy** Copies the current selection and all its children to the Clipboard.
- **Paste** Adds the current Clipboard contents to Navigation view as the child of the currently selected node.
- **Rename** Changes the Navigation view name of the currently selected node. To rename the physical file, rename it in the Folder List.

Note Despite the fact that one defaults to the other, a Web page's title and its Navigation view name are two separate fields. After both exist, changing one doesn't change the other.

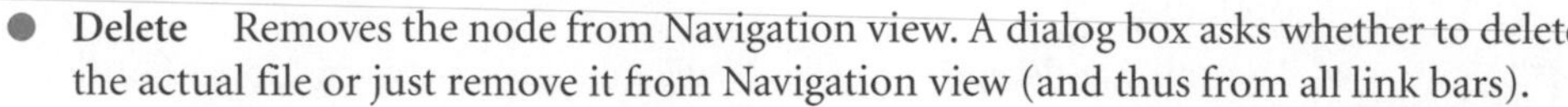

- **Delete** Removes the node from Navigation view. A dialog box asks whether to delete the actual file or just remove it from Navigation view (and thus from all link bars).

View Subtree Only

- **View Subtree Only** Collapses or expands all nodes above, to the left of, or to the right of the current selection.

  The View Subtree Only button on the Navigation toolbar provides the same function.

Included in Link Bar

- **Included In Link Bars** Toggles whether the current node appears in link bars. The color of a node indicates its state: yellow if included in link bars, gray if not.

  The Included In Link Bars button on the Navigation toolbar also controls this option.
- **Properties** Displays the Properties dialog box for the selected node's Web page. This dialog box appeared previously in Figure 6-21 and Figure 6-22.

For more information about the Properties dialog box, refer to "Working with Folders View," on page 180.

To print a copy of the Navigation view structure, make sure that the Navigation view structure is visible, and then choose Print from the File menu. To preview the printed appearance, choose Print Preview. You can also print the Navigation view structure when it appears in Print Preview mode by clicking the Print button.

Using Link Bars with Navigation View

Navigation view, the Link Bar component, and the Page Banner component all work together in the following way:

- In Navigation view, you arrange your pages and give them names.
- Link bars use the relationships and names from Navigation view to build menus that jump among your pages.
- The Page Banner component displays a page's Navigation view name as the heading of the page that contains it.

For more information about the Page Banner component, refer to "Using Page Banners," later in this chapter.

The Link Bars component automatically creates and maintains menu bars (which some people call *jump bars*) that connect the pages in your Web site. There are three kinds of link bars:

- **Link Bar With Custom Links** Displays hyperlinks based on a Navigation view Custom Link Bar.
- **Link Bar With Back And Next Links** Displays hyperlinks to the two pages immediately to the left and right of the current page, and at the same level.

- **Link Bar Based On Navigation Structure** Displays hyperlinks based on the Navigation view diagram. This means it can display links to all children of the current page, to all pages at the same level as the current page's parent, and so forth.

Creating a Link Bar With Custom Links Component

Designers using early versions of FrontPage often admired the convenience (and especially the appearance) of link bars but disdained the task of diagramming their site in Navigation view. What they really wanted, they said, was a link bar they could add to a page and then configure manually.

The Link Bar With Custom Links component not only meets this need but adds a bonus. The bonus is that when you create a Link Bar With Custom Links component, FrontPage saves its list of hyperlinks as a named object in Navigation view. That way, if you have other pages that need the same collection of links, their Link Bar With Custom Links components can get them from the same named object.

Unfortunately, the following object names are both long and confusing:

- **Link Bar With Custom Links** This is a Web component that occupies space in a Web page and displays a list of links.
- **Custom Link Bar** This is a Navigation view object that stores a list of links for use in one or more pages. It is *not* a link bar, and therein lies the confusion. A better name for this object would have been Custom Link List or Custom Link Set, for example.

  It's worth noting that you can create Navigation view Custom Link Bars first, and use them later in Link Bar With Custom Links components. The section "Adding Custom Link Bars to Navigation View," earlier in this chapter, described how to create Custom Link Bars while in Navigation view.

Here's the procedure for adding a Link Bar With Custom Links component to a Web page:

1. In Design view, open the page that should display the Link Bar With Custom Links component.
2. Set the insertion point where you want the Link Bar With Custom Links component to appear.
3. Choose Navigation from the Insert menu. This displays the Insert Web Component dialog box, shown in Figure 13-10.
4. Make sure that Link Bars is selected in the Component Type list on the left.
5. Make sure Bar With Custom Links is selected in the Choose A Bar Type list on the right.
6. Click Next to display the next page, shown in Figure 13-11.

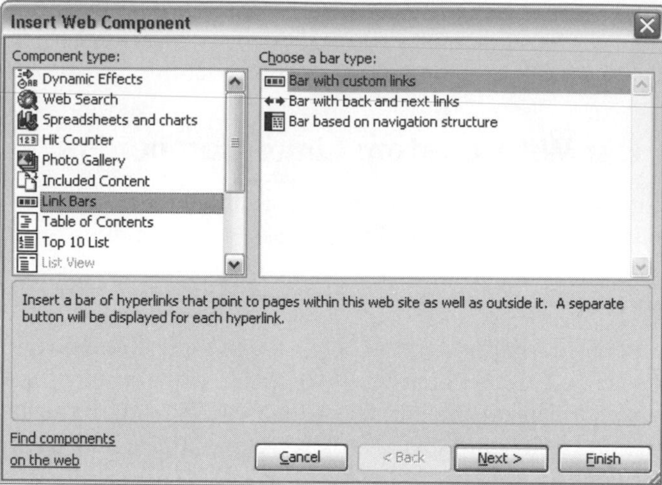

Figure 13-10. The Insert Web Component dialog box appears with the Link Bars and Bar With Custom Links options already selected for you.

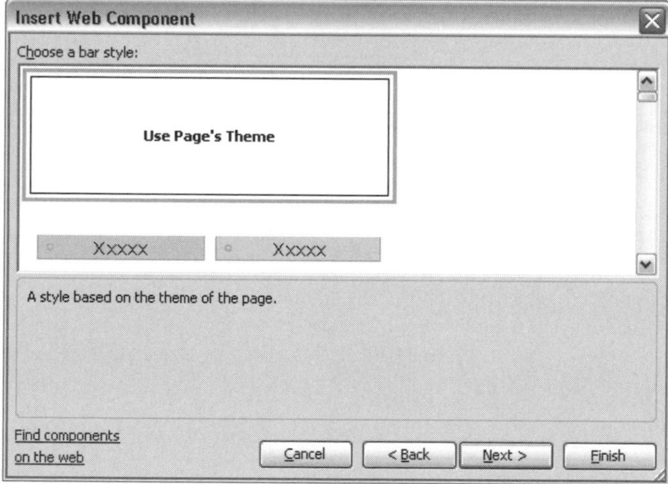

Figure 13-11. When FrontPage displays this dialog box, you can choose to use the same theme as the rest of the current page, any other theme, or various text formats.

7 Choose any of the bar styles listed in the Choose A Bar Style list. The first entry in the list uses the same theme as the Web page that will contain the Link Bar With Custom Links component. Following this are options for using any other theme available in FrontPage. Scrolling to the end of the list reveals various text-based options.

8 Click Next to display the page shown in Figure 13-12. Choose an orientation—horizontal or vertical—and then click Finish.

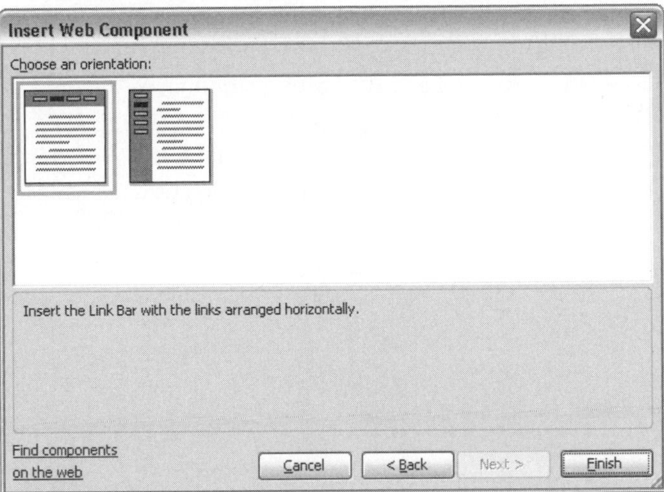

Figure 13-12. Link bars can arrange hyperlinks horizontally or vertically.

9 After you click Finish, FrontPage displays the Link Bar Properties dialog box, shown in Figure 13-13.

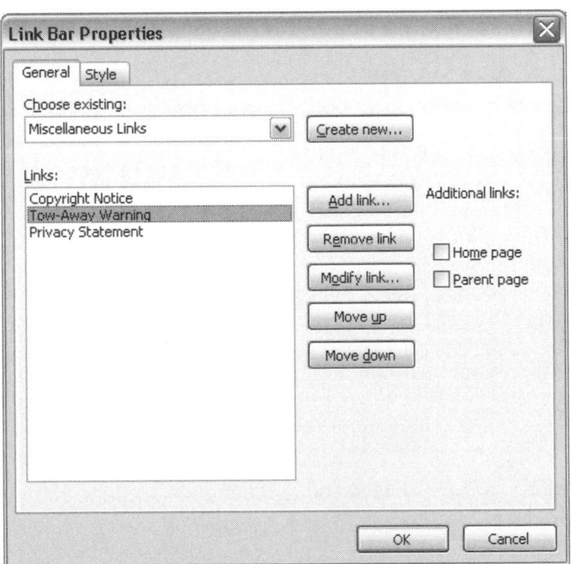

Figure 13-13. Options in this dialog box configure a Link Bar With Custom Links component. Navigation view automatically reflects any Custom Link Bars you create or modify with this dialog box.

The General tab of this dialog box contains the following options to configure the hyperlinks that the Link Bar With Custom Links component will display:

- To use the links from an existing Navigation view Custom Link Bar, select its name in the Choose Existing list.
- To create a new Navigation view Custom Link Bar, click the Create New button. This displays the Create New Link Bar dialog box, shown here. Give the new Custom Link Bar a name, and click OK.

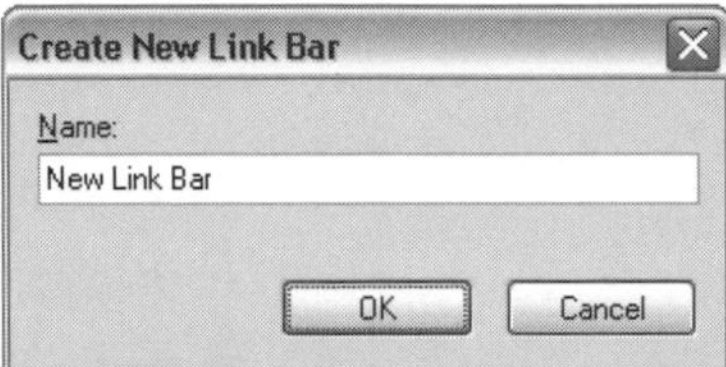

FrontPage displays this dialog box automatically if the current Web contains no Navigation view Custom Link Bars.

10 Use the following buttons to modify the links associated with the Custom Link Bar you specified in step 9. These changes will affect all Link Bar With Custom Links components—regardless of page—that use the same Custom Link Bar:

- **Add Link** Displays the Add To Link Bar dialog box, shown in Figure 13-14. In the Text To Display box near the top, type the text you want the hyperlink to display. In the Address box near the bottom, type the hyperlink location. Click OK.

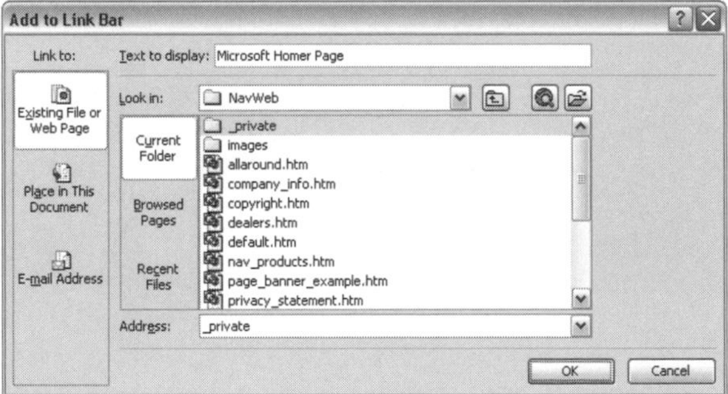

Figure 13-14. A Custom Link Bar can include locations within the current page, within the current Web, or anywhere in the world.

- **Remove Link** Deletes the selection in the Links list.
- **Modify Link** Displays a Modify Link dialog box that strongly resembles the Add To Link Bar dialog box shown in Figure 13-14. Update the Text To Display and Address boxes as required, and then click OK.
- **Move Up** Moves the selection in the Links list one position higher in the list.
- **Move Down** Moves the selection in the Links list one position lower.

11 Use the following check boxes to add links to the current Link Bar With Custom Links component. These settings will affect only the current instance of the component:

- **Home Page** Adds a link to the current Web site's home page.
- **Parent Page** Adds a link to the parent of the page that contains the Link Bar With Custom Links component.

12 Click OK.

Creating a Link Bar Based On Navigation Structure Component

This section describes how to create a Link Bar With Back And Next Links and a Link Bar Based On Navigation Structure. The section groups these topics together because the Link Bar With Back And Next variety is actually a type of Link Bar Based On Navigation Structure.

Using a Link Bar Based On Navigation Structure requires first entering structure information in Navigation view and then inserting and configuring one or more link bars in each Web page.

A Link Bar Based On Navigation Structure component that you insert in Design view reflects the current structure in Navigation view. You can insert link bars, change their appearance, and configure their options in Design view, but you can't change their hyperlinks. Instead, you diagram your site in Navigation view and then let FrontPage create the appropriate links.

Troubleshooting

Updates to the Navigation pane don't appear in Design view

After renaming or relocating pages in the Navigation pane, pages open for editing in Design view might not immediately reflect the changes. This is because the Navigation pane changes are still in a pending state.

To finalize your Navigation pane changes and update any open pages, right-click the Navigation pane background, and choose Apply Changes from the shortcut menu. Closing the Navigation pane by displaying the Folder List or another FrontPage view has the same effect.

Assuming you've already diagrammed your Web site in Navigation view, add a Link Bar Based On Navigation Structure by doing the following:

1 Open a page, and set the insertion point where you want the Link Bar Based On Navigation Structure to appear.

2 Choose Navigation from the Insert menu.

3 Verify that Link Bars is selected in the Component Type list.

4 Choose Bar Based On Navigation Structure from the Choose A Bar Type list.

If you want to create a Link Bar With Back And Next Links, choose either Bar With Back And Next Links or Bar Based On Navigation Structure. If you choose Bar Based

On Navigation Structure, be sure to select Back And Next later in the Link Bar Properties dialog box.

5 Click Next to display the next wizard page, shown previously in Figure 13-11. Choose a theme as explained in the previous section, and then click Next.

6 Choose an orientation—horizontal or vertical—and then click Finish.

7 Make your choices in the Link Bar Properties dialog box, shown in Figure 13-15. (The next section describes the options available in this dialog box.) Click OK.

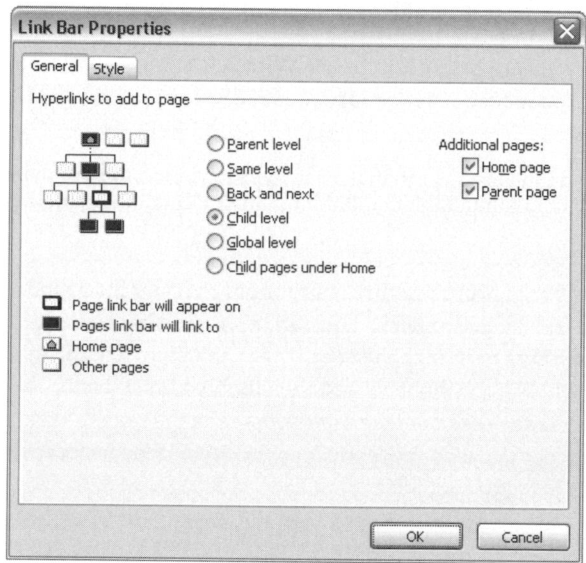

Figure 13-15. This dialog box adds a Link Bar Based On Navigation Structure to the current Web page.

Setting Link Bar Based On Navigation Structure Properties

FrontPage provides the dialog box shown in Figure 13-15 for controlling the content and appearance of a Link Bar Based On Navigation Structure component. The same dialog box applies for both creating new Link Bars Based On Navigation Structure and modifying existing ones. The following sections and controls appear on the General tab:

- **Hyperlinks To Add To Page** You can apply only one of the following six options to a single Link Bar Based On Navigation Structure. However, nothing prevents you from placing several Link Bar Based On Navigation Structure components on the same page, each configured with different options:
  - **Parent Level** Specifies that the Link Bar Based On Navigation Structure should contain hyperlinks to all pages one level higher than the current page, as positioned in Navigation view.
  - **Same Level** Specifies that the Link Bar Based On Navigation Structure should list all pages at the same level as itself.

- **Back And Next** Includes the two pages immediately to the left and right of the current page, and at the same level.
- **Child Level** Includes all pages that have the current page as their parent.
- **Global Level** Includes the home page and any other pages drawn at the same level.
- **Child Pages Under Home** Includes all the pages one level below the home page.

- **Additional Pages** You can include either or both of the following pages regardless of the choice you made in the Hyperlinks To Add To Page section:
  - **Home Page** Adds the home page to the Link Bar Based On Navigation Structure.
  - **Parent Page** Adds the parent of the current page.

To control the appearance of the Link Bar, click the Style tab of the Link Bar Properties dialog box. Figure 13-16 illustrates this tab.

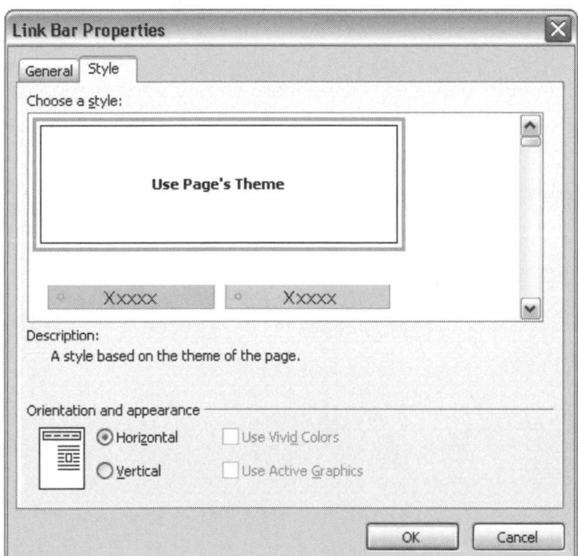

Figure 13-16. This tab configures the appearance of a Link Bar component.

Use these settings to control the link bar's appearance.

- **Choose A Style** The first option in this list tells FrontPage to format the link bar in conformance with the same theme that controls the rest of the current page. The last few options format the link bar as plain text. The options that are in between use any other available themes to format the link bar.

> **Tip** Plain-text link bars needn't be plain. You can format text link bars with all the colors, fonts, and typographical properties available for other text on your Web page.

- **Orientation And Appearance** The following options control the appearance of the Link Bar Based On Navigation Structure:
  - **Horizontal** Arranges the Link Bar Based On Navigation Structure options as a single line of text.
  - **Vertical** Arranges the Link Bar Based On Navigation Structure options vertically, with each option on its own line.

    You can choose either Horizontal or Vertical, but not both.
  - **Use Vivid Colors** If the theme you select in the Choose A Style list includes soft and vivid colors, selecting this check box selects the vivid ones.
  - **Use Active Graphics** If the theme you select in the Choose A Style list includes optional buttons that change appearance when the mouse pointer passes over them, checking this box selects those buttons.

FrontPage labels each option in the Link Bar Based On Navigation Structure component with the title of the target page as it appears in Navigation view. This provides an incentive to keep the Navigation view names short but descriptive. To change the label appearing in a Link Bar Based On Navigation Structure component, change the title of the target page in Navigation view.

The Navigation tab of the Site Settings dialog box, shown in Figure 13-17, contains options for setting the Home, Parent, Previous Page, and Next Page labels. The default labels are, respectively, Home, Up, Previous, and Next. To globally apply your own labels, choose Site Settings from the Tools menu, select the Navigation tab, and then type the text you want Web visitors to see.

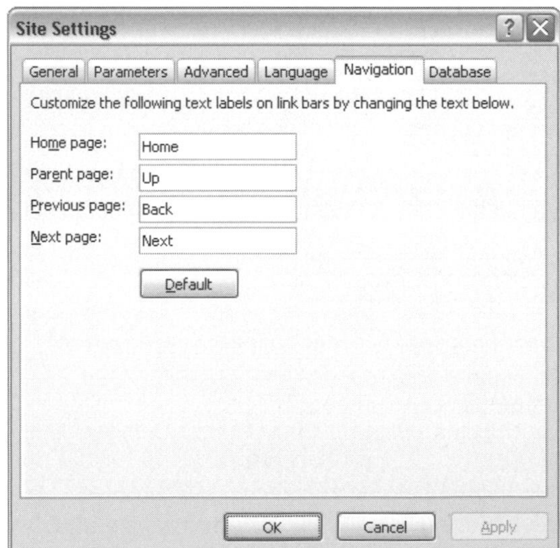

Figure 13-17. The default navigator bar names of Home, Parent, Previous, and Next can be globally customized here.

Chapter 13

Figure 13-18 illustrates a horizontal text link bar in Navigation view. The bar appears between the two horizontal lines.

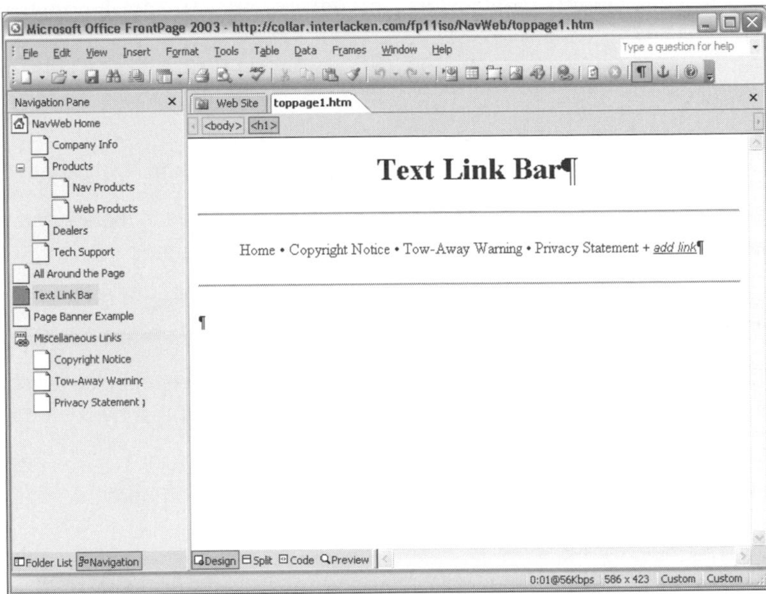

Figure 13-18. This page includes a horizontal text link bar between two horizontal lines.

Figure 13-19 shows a vertical link bar built using picture buttons. FrontPage gets the button picture from the Web page's theme. (Graphical link bar buttons are a popular feature.)

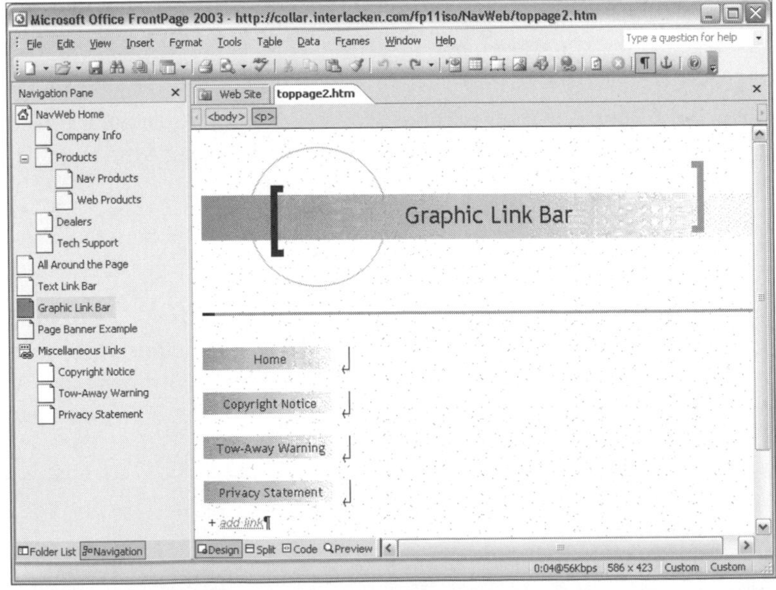

Figure 13-19. To get attractive buttons, format your link bars with themes.

Frequently Asked Questions About Link Bars

Is there any way to generate graphical link bar buttons without applying themes to a Web page?

Yes. You can select any style you want from the Style tab of the Link Bar Properties dialog box.

Is there any way to set up link bars without diagramming a site in Navigation view?

Yes. Create a Link Bar With Custom Links component as described in the section "Creating a Link Bar with the Custom Links Component," earlier in this chapter.

After diagramming a site, is there any way to add a Link Bars Based On Navigation Structure component to all its pages automatically?

Yes. The Shared Border feature can do exactly that. However, lest happiness overcome you, you'll still need to manually edit each page and take out your old, hand-coded navigation menus.

For more information about shared borders, refer to "Using Shared Borders," on page 761.

Why would a Link Bar component appear blank or missing?

If you configure a Link Bar Based On Navigation Structure with options that don't apply to the current page, the link bar will appear blank or missing when you open the page in a Web Browser. Here are some situations in which this might occur:

- The home page contains a Link Bar Based On Navigation Structure configured to display links to all parent pages. By definition, of course, the home page has no parent.
- A page contains a Link Bar Based On Navigation Structure configured to display links to all pages at the same level, but the current page is the only page at its particular level.
- A page at the bottom of the navigation structure contains a Link Bar Based On Navigation Structure configured to display all child pages. Because the current page is at the bottom of the navigation structure, it has no children.

This behavior occurs most often when you propagate identical link bars to many pages through such means as shared borders and templates. If the link bar isn't in a shared border, either reconfigure the link bar or delete it and create a new one.

Deleting or reconfiguring a link bar in a shared border will affect other pages that use the same border, and on which the link bar is working properly. In such a case, add a new link bar outside the shared border and configure it to display pages at the correct level.

Using Page Banners

The Page Banner component performs a single function requiring very little configuration: It displays a page's Navigation view title.

Using the Page Banner component has two advantages compared to just typing a heading into your Web page. First, it ensures that a page's visual heading contains exactly the same text as all link bar references to that page. This occurs because FrontPage bases both page banner text and link bar text on the same source: the page's Navigation view title. Second, if your page uses themes, FrontPage can superimpose the page banner text over the theme's designated banner picture.

Adding a page banner is a snap when you follow these steps:

1. Open the Web page in Design view.
2. Set the insertion point where you want the banner to appear, which is most frequently at the top of the page.
3. Choose Web Component from the Insert menu. This displays the Insert Web Component dialog box shown previously in Figure 13-10.
4. In the Component Type list, choose Included Content.
5. In the Choose A Type Of Content list, choose Page Banner.
6. Click Finish to display the Page Banner Properties dialog box, shown in Figure 13-20.

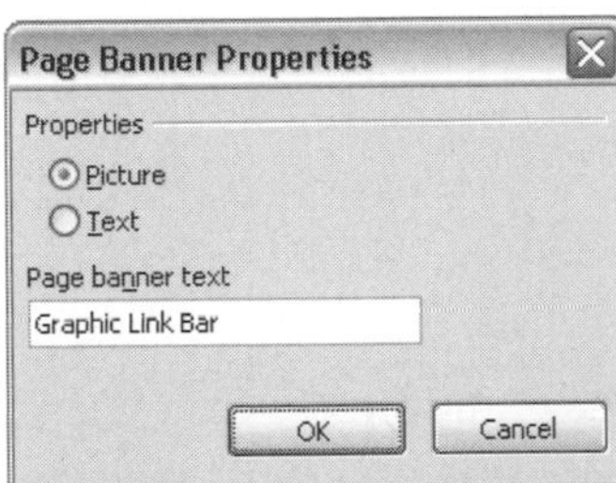

Figure 13-20. This dialog box controls the appearance of a Page Banner component. The Picture option has meaning only on pages controlled by a theme, and you can specify page banner text only for pages already entered in Navigation view.

7. Select Picture if a FrontPage theme controls the current page and you want the page banner text to appear over the theme's banner picture. Select Text if you want a plain-text banner. (This banner overrides the default banner of any themes that you might have previously applied.)

For more information about themes, refer to Chapter 20, "Using FrontPage Themes."

8. Review the suggested page banner text, and correct it if necessary.

   Initially, the Page Banner contains the current page's Navigation view title. Updating this text also updates Navigation view, and therefore all Link Bars Based

On Navigation Structure components pointing to this page. If the current page doesn't appear in Navigation view, FrontPage ignores this field and the page banner is blank.

9 Click OK.

The Page Banner component works only for pages you've diagrammed in Navigation view. You can insert Page Banner components even in Web pages not diagrammed in Navigation view, but instead of a page banner, FrontPage displays this message: [Add this page in the Navigation view to display a page banner here.]

If your Web page uses themes, the difference between a picture banner and a text banner is quite apparent. In Figure 13-21, the upper banner is a picture, whereas the lower one is text. Both banners display the text *Page Banner Example.*

> **Tip** Just because a page banner appears as text doesn't mean it has to be plain. You can apply any and all FrontPage text formatting commands to textual Page Banner components, as is done in the bordered-text example in Figure 13-21.

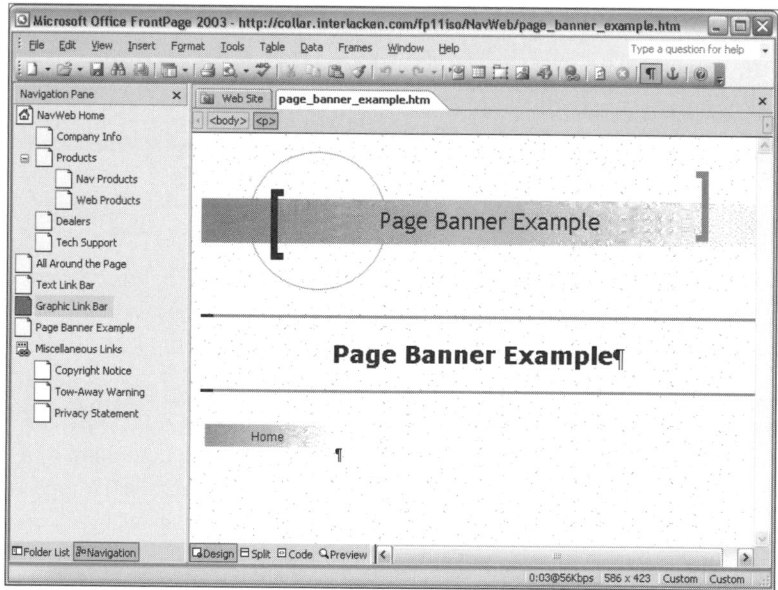

Figure 13-21. The banner *Page Banner Example* appears first as a picture and then as text with borders above and below it.

If you like using themes but don't like diagramming your site in Navigation view, you might wonder whether there's any other way to specify page banner text. There isn't. The only text a Page Banner component can display is the current page's Navigation view name. If you haven't added the page to Navigation view, that name will be blank.

To learn about superimposing text on graphics, refer to "Adding Text to Pictures," on page 635.

To insert a page banner for every page in a Web site, use either of these methods:

- Activate shared borders and place a Page Banner component in the desired border (most likely the top border).
- Add the Page Banner component to a Dynamic Web Template, select as many files or folders as you like in the Folder List, and then choose Dynamic Web Template and Attach Dynamic Web Template from the Format menu.

Of course, neither of these procedures removes any existing page headings, and both produce the message previously noted for any page not diagrammed in Navigation view.

For more information about shared borders, refer to "Using Shared Borders," on page 761. For more information on using Dynamic Web Templates, refer to, "Using Dynamic Web Templates," on page 322.

The true power of the Page Banner component lies not in formatting page headings one by one, but rather in centralizing control of link bars and page headings through Navigation view. Although initially it might seem awkward to leave Design view and configure the page banner text in Navigation view, you'll quickly come to like it. There's great power in changing a page's title once in Navigation view and having FrontPage automatically update its page banner and all link bars appearances.

In Summary...

This chapter explained how to enter a new site's structure in Navigation view and how FrontPage—using certain Web components—automatically creates Web pages that reflect that structure.

The next chapter explains another way to create Web sites automatically using Web site templates and wizards.

Chapter 14

Creating Web Sites with Templates and Wizards

During your travels around the Web, you've undoubtedly noticed that certain kinds of Web sites occur over and over again. Some are personal Web sites where people describe themselves or their families. Others provide information about businesses, government agencies, and other large organizations, or about a particular project or task force.

Microsoft Office FrontPage 2003 can't create sites like these completely on its own, and even if it could, you probably wouldn't like the results. After all, your content is unique, and you probably want your site's organization and appearance to be unique as well. No one wants a site that's just one more rubber-stamp copy of thousands of others, with just the names and a few other components changed.

At the same time—regardless of the task at hand—starting from nothing can be a daunting proposition. FrontPage therefore provides a limited collection of templates and wizards that can populate a new Web site with several kinds of typical pages. Even if you never create an actual site this way, the resulting sites provide interesting examples of a variety of FrontPage techniques.

None of the techniques in this chapter apply to sites organized with framesets. If that's your interest, skip ahead to Chapter 15, "Creating Web Sites with Frames."

Understanding Templates and Wizards

A *template* is a static unit of content saved for repetitive use. Every time you use a template, the new Web site will be exactly like all the other new sites you created with the same version of the same template. FrontPage provides the following templates for creating a new Web site:

- **Empty Web Site** Creates a Web site with nothing in it.
- **One Page Web Site** Creates a Web site with a blank home page.
- **Customer Support Web Site** Creates a Web site for a company offering customer support on the Internet. This template is designed particularly for computer software companies.

- **Personal Web Site** Creates a Web site that represents an individual, with pages for interests, favorite sites, and photos.
- **Project Web Site** Creates a Web site that members of a project team might use. It includes Web pages for a list of project members, status reports, the project schedule, an archive area, and ongoing discussion.
- **SharePoint Team Site** Creates a specialized Web site that coordinates the activities of a project or workgroup. Your Web server must be running Microsoft Windows SharePoint Services for this feature to work.

  The SharePoint Team Site option is in a class by itself. Choosing this option sets aside a dedicated part of your Web site that supports database-driven lists, document libraries, surveys, document annotation, document subscription, and all the other features of a SharePoint Team Site.

After using any of these templates to create a Web site, the next step is normally to open each page and start replacing the generic content and placeholders with your own content.

For more information about creating and modifying page content, refer to Part 3, "Editing Basic Page Content."

Wizards operate in a structured way and perform more complex operations. Each wizard first prompts you for information and preferences with a series of pages like the one shown in Figure 14-1. It then customizes its results accordingly, completing its work uninterrupted. This avoids prompts for unnecessary options and minimizes the chance of a partially completed update. Unless you give all the same answers, you'll never get the same results twice.

Figure 14-1. A wizard uses pages like this one to collect your preferences and then customize its results.

FrontPage provides the following wizards for creating new Web sites:

- **Corporate Presence Wizard** Creates a typical set of Web pages for representing a company on the Internet. This wizard contains generic pages that you can use as a starting point and leaves notes in purple text indicating what you should update and what kinds of information to include.

- **Database Interface Wizard** Creates a Web site that includes pages to add, view, and optionally update a new or an existing database.
- **Discussion Web Site Wizard** Creates a special Web site designed for interactive discussions. Visitors can submit topics by entering text in a form, review existing articles listed in a table of contents, or locate articles by searching for specific words.
- **Import Web Site Wizard** Adds an existing set of pages to a new or an existing Web site.

After you run a wizard and view its results, you might regret your answers to one or more prompts. The solution is simple: Just delete the Web site, and run the wizard again. Keep doing this until you're satisfied that the wizard has done its best. Then, as with templates, start customizing pages with your own content and preferences.

For more information about deleting Web sites, refer to "Deleting a FrontPage-Based Web Site," on page 183.

To create a new Web site based on any of the templates or wizards, follow this procedure:

1. Choose New from the File menu.
2. When the New task pane appears, click the More Web Site Templates link under New Web Site. This will display the Web Site Templates dialog box shown in Figure 14-2.

> **Tip** If steps 1 and 2 seem needlessly tedious, click the Create A New Normal Page down arrow on the Standard toolbar, and then choose Web Site.

3. Choose the type of Web site you want from one of these tabs:
   - **General** This tab lists templates and wizards that FrontPage has supported over several releases. For information on the Web server environment each of these templates requires, refer to table 14-1.
   - **Packages** Each template on this tab is a Windows SharePoint Services application bundled with FrontPage 2003. These applications only run on Web server running Windows SharePoint Services.
   - **My Templates** This tab lists any other site templates available on your computer.
   - **SharePoint Services** Each template on this tab physically resides on a Web server running Windows SharePoint Services. You can only use these templates on the SharePoint server where they reside.

For more information about creating Web sites from packages, refer to Creating Web Sites From Packages," later in this chapter. For more information about creating a new SharePoint team site, refer to, "Creating a New SharePoint Team Site," on page 927.

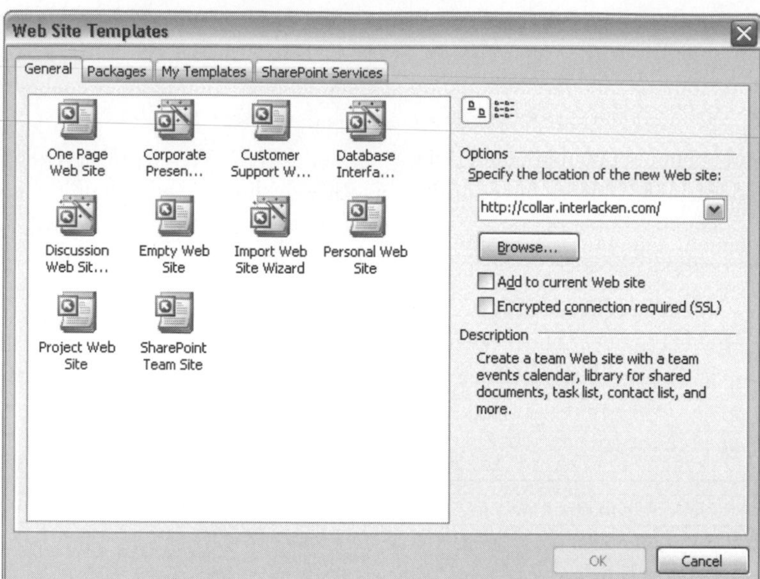

Figure 14-2. FrontPage provides this collection of templates and wizards for creating new Webs.

Table 14-1. Web Site Template Server Compatibility

Web Site Template	Non-Extended Server or Disk-Based Web Site	FrontPage Server Extensions	Windows SharePoint Services
Empty Web Site	Compatible	Compatible	Compatible
One Page Web Site	Compatible	Compatible	Compatible
Import Web Site Wizard	Compatible	Compatible	Compatible
Corporate Presence Wizard	Compatible	Compatible	Compatible
Customer Support Web Site	Compatible	Compatible	Incompatible
Personal Web Site	Compatible	Compatible	Incompatible
Project Web Site	Compatible	Compatible	Incompatible
Discussion Web Site Wizard	Compatible	Compatible	Incompatible
Database Interface Wizard	Design Only	Required	Incompatible
SharePoint Team Site	Incompatible	Incompatible	Required

In the Specify The Location Of The New Web Site box, enter the drive letter and path, the UNC path, or the Web site address where you want the new Web site to reside.

> **Note** A Universal Naming Convention (UNC) path is a Microsoft Windows file sharing location in the form \\<*servername*>\<*sharename*>\<*path*>.

If you specify a Web address (one beginning with *http://*), the Web server must have either Windows SharePoint Services or the FrontPage Server Extensions installed. Unless the Web server is operating with no security in effect, you'll also need an administrator password for the new Web site's parent site.

If you're creating a SharePoint Team Site, only a Web address is acceptable in this box. Furthermore, the Web server you specify must be running Windows SharePoint Services.

4 Click OK. FrontPage creates and opens the new Web site.

For more detailed instructions on creating a new Web site, refer to "Creating a Web Site for New Content," on page 153.

The same templates and wizards that add pages to new Web sites can add pages to existing sites as well. To do this:

1 Open the existing Web site.
2 Display the New task pane.
3 Choose Web Site Templates, and select a template or wizard for the pages you want to add.
4 Select the Add To Current Web option, and click OK.

If the template or wizard attempts to create a Web page with the same name as an existing page, FrontPage displays the Confirm Save dialog box, shown in Figure 14-3. Click Yes to overwrite the existing file with the template or wizard file. Click No to discard the new file and keep the existing one.

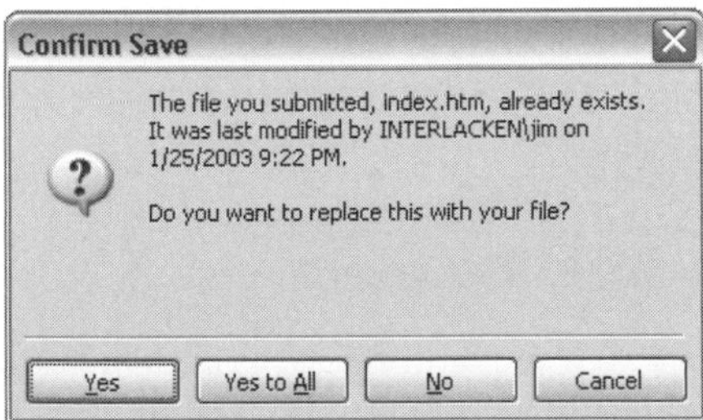

Figure 14-3. When you use a template or wizard to add pages to an existing Web site, FrontPage displays this prompt before overwriting an existing page.

Using Web Site Templates

This section explains the purpose of each Web site template that FrontPage provides. It also describes any special FrontPage features that the resulting site uses and how to modify each type of site.

Using the Empty Web Site Template

Creating a new Web site with this template provides the absolute maximum in flexibility, because FrontPage provides the absolute minimum initial content: zero. There's nothing to get in your way. The world is your oyster.

The Empty Web Site template excels at one other task—namely, converting an existing disk folder to a disk-based site. To do this, display the Web Site Templates dialog box as the previous section described, specify the existing disk folder as the location for the new site, and specify the Empty Web Site template. This creates a new site that incorporates any existing content files in the specified folder. Because the Empty Web Site template doesn't create any new content files, it won't overwrite any existing content files.

For more information about converting a folder to a Web, refer to "Converting a Folder to a Web Site," on page 173.

Using the One Page Web Site Template

This template provides all the functionality of the Empty Web Site template with the added benefit of creating a blank home page. This saves you from switching to Navigation view and clicking the Create A New Normal Page button on the Standard toolbar.

Don't laugh—the Empty Web Site and One Page Web Site templates probably account for at least 99 percent of all new sites FrontPage creates.

Using the Customer Support Web Site Template

Every time you use this template to create a Web site, FrontPage supplies the files and supporting elements that appear in the Folder List in Figure 14-4. Navigation view includes the home page (titled Customer Support Web), two top pages (Contact Us and Search), and seven children of the home page.

By default, top, left, and bottom shared borders are in effect for every page in this Web site. As shown in Figure 14-5, the top border contains a Page Banner component, and the left border contains a Link Bar Based On Navigation Structure component. The bottom border isn't visible in the figure, but it contains a second Link Bar Based On Navigation Structure component (this time formatted as text), a copyright statement, and a Date And Time component showing when someone last updated the page.

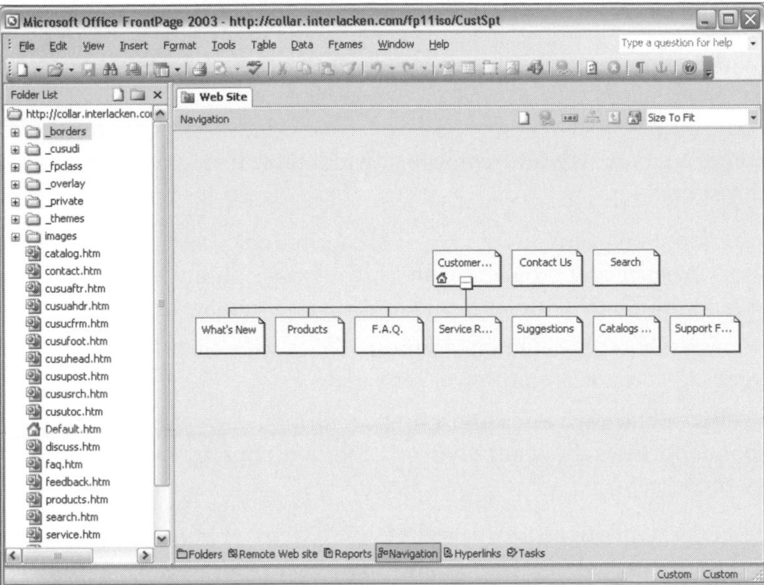

Figure 14-4. The Customer Support Web Site template creates this arrangement of pages.

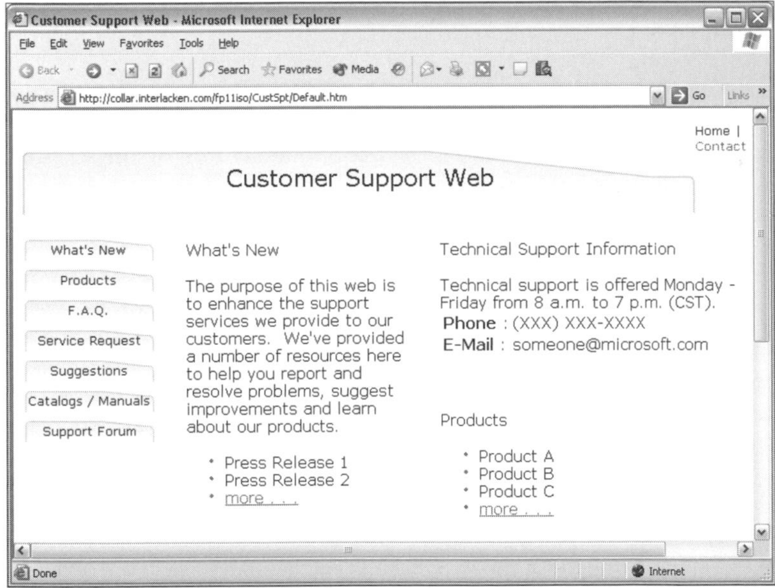

Figure 14-5. The Customer Support Web site uses shared borders, page banners, link bars, and a theme to produce an attractive and functional Web site.

Most of the 10 pages that don't appear in the Navigation view structure override the default shared border settings to omit shared borders. On the others that don't appear in Navigation view, the link bars and therefore the shared border areas are blank.

Note If a page doesn't appear in the Navigation view diagram, any Page Banner or Link Bar components that page contains will be blank. This is because the Page Banner and Link Bar components get their content from Navigation view.

The Customer Support Web Site template provides these three ways to collect information from Web visitors:

- The service.htm page contains an HTML form that collects service requests. Web visitors experiencing problems with the company's products or services can request assistance by filling in the form and clicking a Submit Service Request button.
- The suggest.htm page contains a similar HTML form that Web visitors can use to suggest new products, features, or services.
- The discuss.htm page leads into a support forum, where Web visitors can post and respond to articles about any problems, solutions, tips, tricks, pitfalls, and other tidbits they encounter.

The service request and suggestion pages both use a Web component called Save Results. This component uses the FrontPage Save Results component to receive input from an HTML form and appends it to a text file, a Web page, or a database.

For more information about the Save Results component, refer to Chapter 35, "Processing Data Submitted from Forms."

To visualize how this process works, refer to Figure 14-6. This figure shows Microsoft Internet Explorer displaying the portion of the service.htm page that contains the HTML form. When the visitor clicks the Submit Service Request button on the service.htm page, the following occurs:

1. The browser transmits the data to the Web server.
2. The Save Results program, which lives on the server and comes as part of the FrontPage Server Extensions, saves the data in whatever location the Web designer specified.
3. The Save Results program then sends the Web visitor a confirmation page so that the visitor knows that the Web server successfully received and processed the data.
4. If the designer configured the Save Results component to save the data in a Web page, visitors can view that Web page and see the effect of their submissions. For example, Figure 14-7 shows the results of appending the input from Figure 14-6 to a Web page.

   If the designer configured the Save Results component to save the data to a text file or database, visitors can view the data only if the designer also provided a Web page that queries and displays the text file or database.

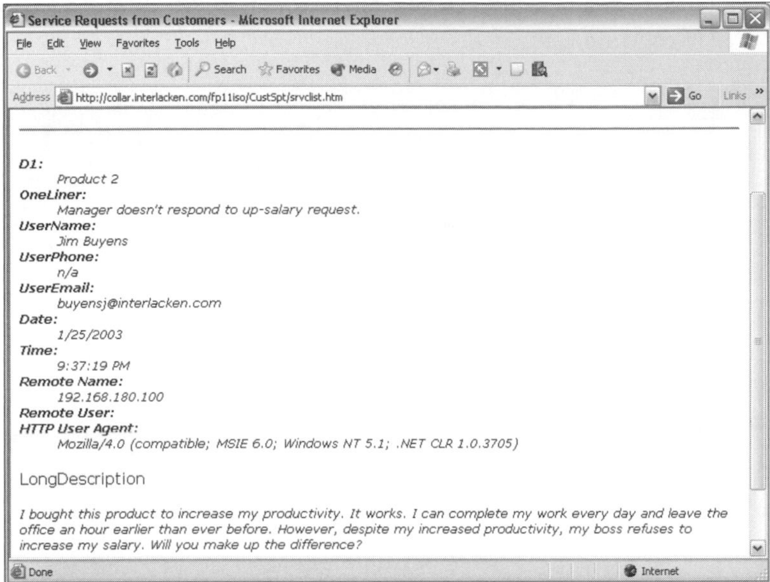

Figure 14-6. The Web server has saved the data submitted in Figure 14-6 as HTML. It also saved the data as a text file that other programs can use.

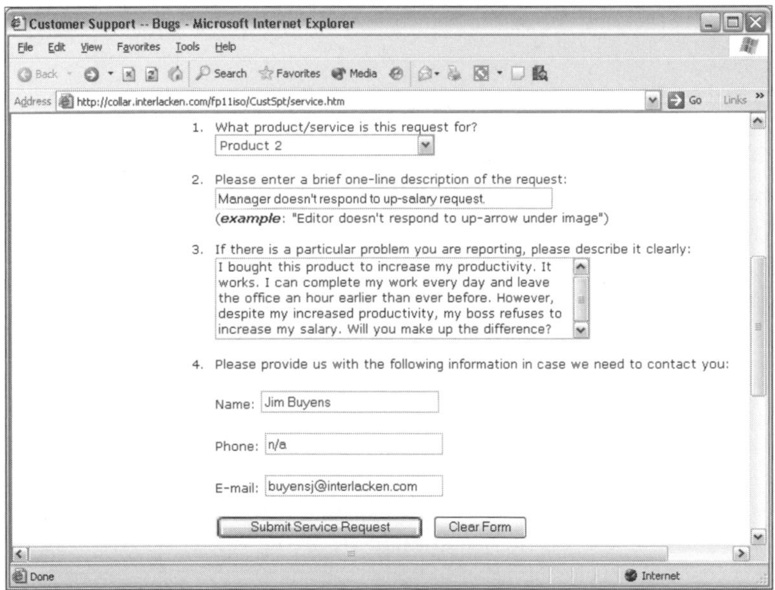

Figure 14-7. This section of the service.htm page collects data from Web visitors. Clicking the Submit Service Request button transmits the data to the Web server for storage.

The support forum uses the FrontPage Discussion Web Site feature. Figure 14-8 shows this discussion containing, so far, three postings.

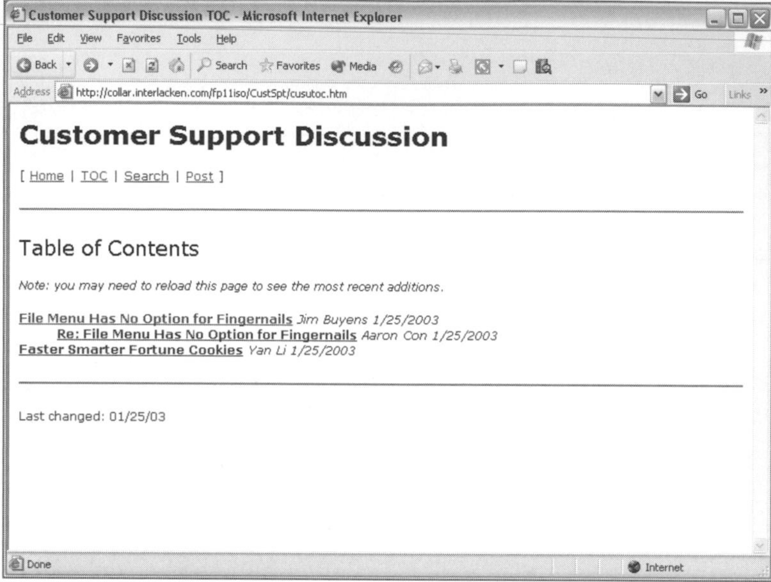

Figure 14-8. So far this discussion has three postings. Two begin new threads, and one is a response.

Here are some common actions in a FrontPage Discussion Web site:

- To start a new thread, a Web visitor would click the Post hyperlink.
- To read an existing posting, the visitor would click that posting.
- To respond to a posting, the visitor would open a posting and then click a Reply hyperlink.

For more information about FrontPage discussion sites, refer to Chapter 33, "Discussion Web Sites and Self-Registration."

Note A SharePoint Team Site provides discussion lists that are both richer in function and easier to manage than lists using the FrontPage Discussion feature. If you have access to a Web server running Windows SharePoint Services, be sure to investigate those facilities before deciding to use the FrontPage Discussion feature.

A Customer Support Web site also includes two Web search facilities:

- The search.htm page searches the entire FrontPage-based Web site and displays a clickable list of pages that contain a given string.
- The cususrch.htm page searches only the _cusudi folder for a given string and again displays a clickable list of matching pages.

The _cusudi folder contains the table of contents and all posted articles for the Support Forum. Because it's entirely controlled by FrontPage, the _cusudi folder is normally hidden. If you want to inspect it, choose Web Settings from the Tools menu, click the Advanced tab, and make sure the Show Hidden Files And Folders option is selected.

For more information about the Web Search component, refer to Chapter 28, "Providing a Text Search Capability."

Using the Personal Web Site Template

This template always creates the same six pages: those shown in the Navigation pane of Figure 14-9. FrontPage arranges these pages in Navigation view and formats them with a theme. Each page contains a Page Banner component, two Link Bar Based On Navigation Structure components (one on the left side and one at the bottom of the page), and a Date And Time component. However, the pages don't use shared borders.

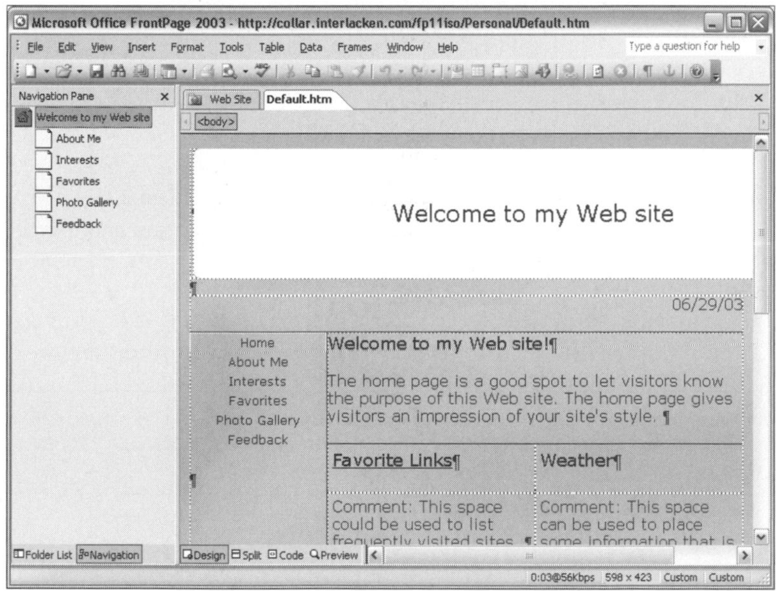

Figure 14-9. The Personal Web Site template always creates this initial set of pages.

With the exception of two pages, this template creates pages that consist entirely of ordinary HTML. The first exception occurs in the Photo Gallery page, which contains, as you might suspect, a Photo Gallery component.

For more information about the Photo Gallery component, refer to Chapter 24, "Using FrontPage Photo Galleries."

The page that might require special attention is the Feedback page, the top portion of which appears in Figure 14-10. This is an HTML form that saves its data, by default, to a file named feedback.txt, which is located in the _private folder of your Web site. The form works by using the Save Results component.

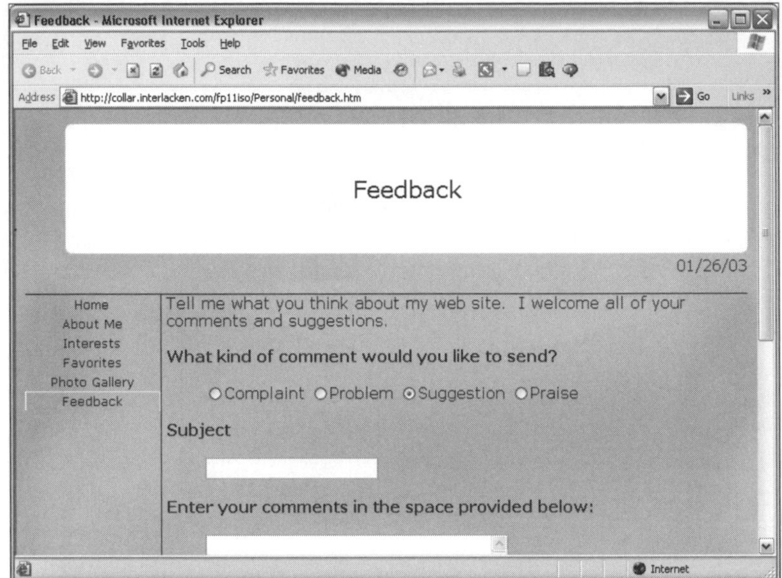

Figure 14-10. This HTML form collects comments from Web visitors and transmits them to the Web server for later viewing.

To view the comments, you'll need to download this file or display it as plain text in your browser. To clear out the file and start over, simply delete it from your Web site.

For more information about saving HTML form data as a disk file or sending it as e-mail, refer to Chapter 35, "Processing Data Submitted from Forms." For more information about saving HTML form data in a database, refer to "Saving Form Results to a Database" on page 879.

Using the Project Web Site Template

Creating a Web site with this template creates the Web pages and supporting files visible in the Folder List shown in Figure 14-11. If you click the Navigation tab at the bottom of the Folder List, you'll see seven of these pages diagrammed in Navigation view. The home page and the six pages listed in the Link Bar component at the left of the default.htm Web page use shared borders, page banners, and Link Bar Based On Navigation Structure components. A theme governs the site's appearance.

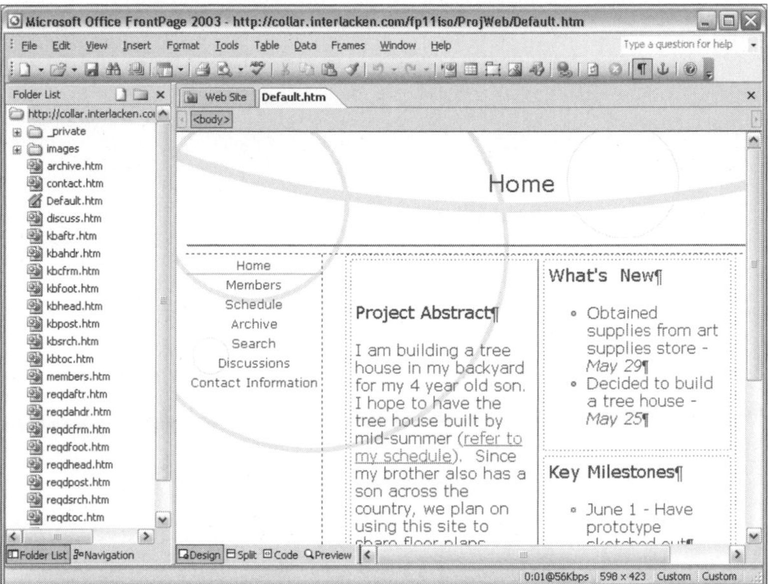

Figure 14-11. The Project Web Site template creates the pages shown in this Folder List.

The Home, Members, Schedule, Status, and Archive pages consist of ordinary HTML. The template creates some, but not all, of the pages that these pages reference. Because this Web site consists of sample pages only, you'd probably delete the missing pages anyway.

The Search and Discussions pages both use Web components that work only on Web servers that have the FrontPage Server Extensions installed. This is because both pages call programs that run on the Web server—not within the Web visitor's browser, and not within the FrontPage desktop software. The first of these is the Search page, shown in Figure 14-12.

To obtain this display, the Web visitor entered the search term form and then clicked the Start Search button. The Web Search component responded with clickable hyperlinks to three Web pages that contain this word. This is the same Web Search facility described in the section "Using the Customer Support Web Site Template," earlier in this chapter.

For more information about the Web Search component, refer to Chapter 28, "Providing a Text Search Capability."

The Discussions page has links to two threaded discussions managed by the FrontPage Discussion feature. This is the same component described in the section "Using the Customer Support Web Site Template," earlier in this chapter. The Project Web Site template creates two discussions controlled respectively by the reqdpost.htm and kbpost.htm pages.

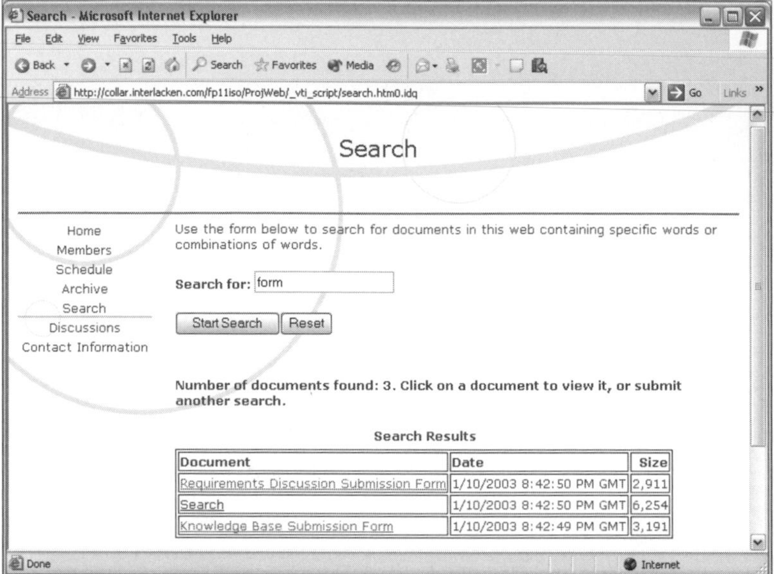

Figure 14-12. A Web visitor used this HTML form to search a Project Web Site for the word *form* The Web Search component located the matching pages listed at the bottom of the window.

SharePoint Team Sites outclass Project Web Sites in almost every respect. This is because a SharePoint Team Site stores any data it collects as database records, and not, like a Project Web Site, as lines of HTML code. Information stored in a database is much easier to leverage for other purposes than data stored in HTML format.

For more information about SharePoint Team Sites, refer to Chapter 37, "Using SharePoint Team Sites."

Using Web Site Wizards

The difference between wizards and templates is that wizards prompt you for information and then customize their output. Some of these wizards display quite a few prompts and thus produce quite a variety of results.

Reprinting these prompts and explaining the effect of each choice would produce a rather boring series of chapters with little practical use. Most of the prompts are intuitive and the on-screen text and Help explains them very well. Also, you can always delete the resulting Web and try running the wizard again until you get the Web site you want. Finally, it's fairly rare to use a Web site exactly as a wizard creates it. As a result, there's no incentive to obsess about the exact results a wizard produces.

Using the Corporate Presence Wizard

Nowadays, the rush by corporations to establish a presence on the Web is largely over. Most corporations already have a Web site—probably one with thousands or tens of thousands of pages. Even for new companies the procedure seems to be:

1. Find a domain name you can register.
2. Pick the name of the company.
3. Build a Web site.
4. Get your venture capital.

This makes the Corporate Presence Wizard less useful than it once might have been. However, this wizard produces a Web site with more FrontPage features than any other wizard or template.

Chapter 6, "Creating and Using FrontPage Web Sites," provides a brief introduction to this site. Figure 6-4 shows a page from the Corporate Presence Wizard, and Figure 6-8, Figure 6-9, and Figure 6-10 show pages from the resulting site.

For more information about the Corporate Presence Wizard, refer to "Creating a FrontPage Web Site for New Content," on page 153.

The Corporate Presence Wizard produces a variable number of pages based on how you answer its prompts. If you select all the features, a Corporate Presence Web site includes these FrontPage features:

- Navigation view includes all pages in this site.
- A theme controls the appearance of all pages in this site.
- Shared borders add uniform content to all pages in this site, including:
  - Page Banner components.
  - Link Bar Based On Navigation Structure components.
  - A page footer that includes Substitution components and a Date and Time component.
- A Feedback page that accumulates comments from Web visitors in a text file. This page uses the same techniques as the feedback form that the Personal Web Site Template creates.
- A Table Of Contents page for the current site.
- A Search page that searches the Corporate Presence Web Site. This uses the same technique as the search form that the Project Web Site template creates.
- A variable number of static Web pages for press releases, products, and services.

Substitution components are useful for displaying changeable names, addresses, titles, or other text that appears on multiple pages. Using a Substitution component is a two-step process:

1 Define a Site Parameter that contains the changeable text. Assign each different piece of text a different Web Parameter name.
2 Add a Substitution component to each page that will display the changeable text, taking care to specify the correct Web Parameter name.

For more information about site parameters and the Substitution component, refer to "Using Site Parameters and the Substitution Component," on page 759.

The Table Of Contents page from a typical Corporate Presence Web site appears in Figure 14-13. A Table Of Contents For This Web Site component derives the page names, their organization, and the hyperlink location from analysis of hyperlinks, not, as you might expect, from the Web Site's navigation structure.

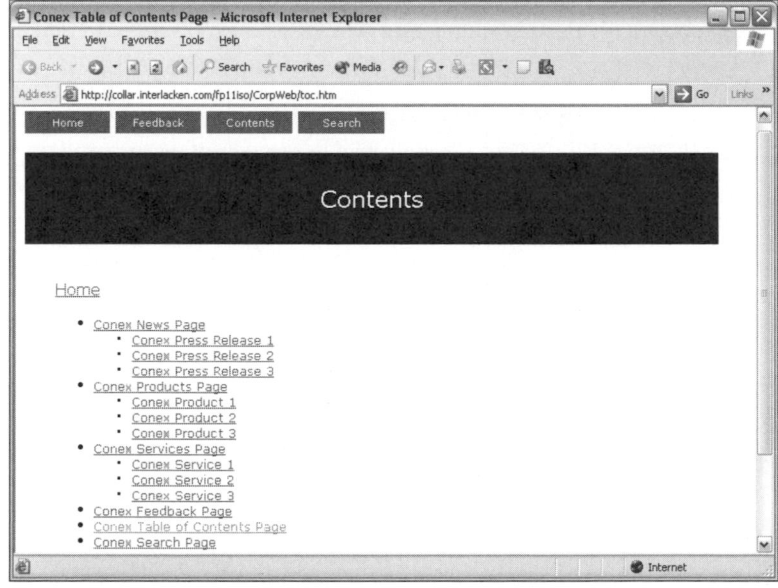

Figure 14-13. A Table Of Contents component automatically built the list of links in the center of this Web page.

For more information about Table Of Contents components, refer to Chapter 27, "Displaying Derived Content."

The Corporate Presence Wizard creates a separate Web page for each product or service. This approach offers initial simplicity, but it seldom scales very well. If your business has hundreds, thousands, or tens of thousands of salable items, you should almost certainly use a database to put your catalog on line. That way, all the pages will be uniform, and you can keep them up to date by synchronizing the catalog database with your internal business systems.

Be all that as it may, the Corporate Presence Wizard can still be useful when you're starting a new corporate site. It also provides several good examples of ways to use Web components.

Using the Database Interface Wizard

Unlike most Web templates and wizards, this one doesn't create a new sample Web site. Instead, it creates any combination you want of the Web pages that Table 14-2 describes.

Table 14-2. Application Pages in a FrontPage Database Interface

Page name	Description
submission_form.aspx submission_form.asp	Displays an HTML form that collects values from the Web visitor and uses them to add one record to a database.
results_page.aspx results_page.asp	Displays the contents of a database as a tabular listing.
database_editor.aspx database_editor.asp	Displays a selection list of records in a database. It can also add, display, modify, and delete individual records.

Unlike most FrontPage components and special features, Database Interface pages don't use programs that come with Windows SharePoint Services or the FrontPage Server Extensions. Instead, FrontPage writes custom ASP or Microsoft ASP.NET program code that meets your specifications. The choice between these technologies is yours; if you're not sure, consult the sidebar "Choosing Between ASP and ASP.NET." In addition, you should be aware of the following points:

- If you choose ASP, you get essentially the same features that were available in Microsoft FrontPage 2002.
- If you choose ASP.NET, you gain any enhancements Microsoft has added in FrontPage 2003. This conforms with Microsoft's intention to enhance the ASP.NET environment only.

Important Neither ASP nor ASP.NET pages will run on a Windows SharePoint Services Web Site. If you want to access databases using this type of Web site, refer to Chapter 37, "Using SharePoint Team Sites."

Choosing Between ASP and ASP.NET

Beginning in 2002, Microsoft has supported two ways of adding high-level, server-side programming to Web pages:

- **Active Server Pages (ASP)** Server-side programming technology that Microsoft first released in 1996 as part of Internet Information Services (IIS) 3.0. An ASP page has a file extension of .asp. It contains ordinary HTML interspersed with program code that runs (and generates additional HTML) on the Web server. The most common programming language is VBScript, but JavaScript, Perl, and other languages are suitable as well. To access system resources beyond the scope of these programming languages, programmers load Microsoft ActiveX controls. ActiveX Data Objects (ADO) provide access to database resources.
- **ASP.NET** Represents six years of progress beyond ASP pages. ASP.NET pages also consist of ordinary HTML interspersed with program code, but ASP.NET enjoys a much superior object model and much more powerful programming languages such as Microsoft Visual Basic .NET and Microsoft Visual C# .NET. ASP.NET pages can use ActiveX controls, but more often they gain access to resources by using classes in the Microsoft .NET Framework. Microsoft ADO.NET is a set of .NET classes that provide access to databases. An ASP.NET Web page has a file extension of .aspx.

As a practical matter, ASP pages are likely to work on any Microsoft Web server you encounter. If you find a Web server whose server administrator hasn't performed software maintenance since 1996—or has disabled ASP—you really ought to look for a new provider.

ASP.NET, being newer than ASP, isn't quite so ubiquitous. Microsoft has built it into the Web server that comes with Windows Server 2003, and administrators can install it on any Microsoft Windows NT 4.0 SP6, Windows 2000, or Windows XP Professional Web server. Server administrators, however, are usually very cautious people who avoid new software of any kind. As a result, don't be terribly surprised if you encounter a Web server that can't run ASP.NET pages.

If your Web server can run ASP.NET pages, you should probably make sure of this facility. Microsoft has promised to keep ASP pages working for a long time, but not forever. In addition, Microsoft has warned developers not to expect any enhancements.

If your Web server can't run ASP.NET pages, and if you're unwilling to change providers or force an upgrade, ASP pages are your only choice. ASP pages might also be a good choice if you're integrating the pages in question with an existing system based on ASP technology.

Understanding Static, Dynamic, and Data-Driven Web Pages

A *static* Web page is one that doesn't change unless you change its HTML code, one of its pictures, or some other aspect of its content. These were the earliest kind of pages used on the Web. The designer coded them, the visitors looked at them, and that was that. The WYSIWYG editor in Design view is an excellent tool for creating static pages.

A *dynamic* Web page is one that modifies itself. A dynamic Web page might, for example, change its own appearance based on the date, on the capabilities of the Web visitor's browser, or on actions taken by the visitor. Creating such pages generally requires writing scripts that modify the page while it's loading or after it's already on display. (*Scripts* are short blocks of program code written in languages such as JavaScript and Microsoft Visual Basic.)

For more information about scripts, refer to Chapter 41, "Working with Script Code."

FrontPage includes Web components that create many dynamic effects without requiring any programming on your part. By providing full access to the HTML code, FrontPage also supports development of custom dynamic effects.

For more information about creating dynamic Web pages, refer to Chapter 26, "Enhancing Web Pages with Animation."

A *data-driven* Web page is essentially a template for displaying information from another source. That source could be a simple text file, an XML file, or almost anything else, but the most common source is a database. Based on form values from the Web visitor, lookup values coded in hyperlinks, the date, the time, or some other factor, a program retrieves the correct data values, merges them into the data-driven Web page, and sends the resulting HTML to the visitor's browser for display and further action.

FrontPage can build Web pages that add, modify, delete, and display database information in a variety of ways. Of course, the more you want the Web page to change depending on data, the more likely it is that you'll need to work with both the HTML code and the program code yourself.

For more information about building Web pages that interact with databases, refer to Part 9, "Using Forms and Databases."

Figure 14-14 shows a new ASP.NET Web site that the Database Interface Wizard created. The submission_form.aspx and results_page.aspx pages are in a folder named guestdb_interface/results. The database_editor.aspx page and a number of support pages are buried even deeper, in a folder named guestdb_interface/results/editor. This structure minimizes the chance that adding a database interface to an existing Web will overwrite or interfere with any existing pages. The prefix *guestdb* represents the name of the database connection, which is something you designate when running the wizard. (This convention makes it easy to accommodate multiple database interfaces in the same Web.)

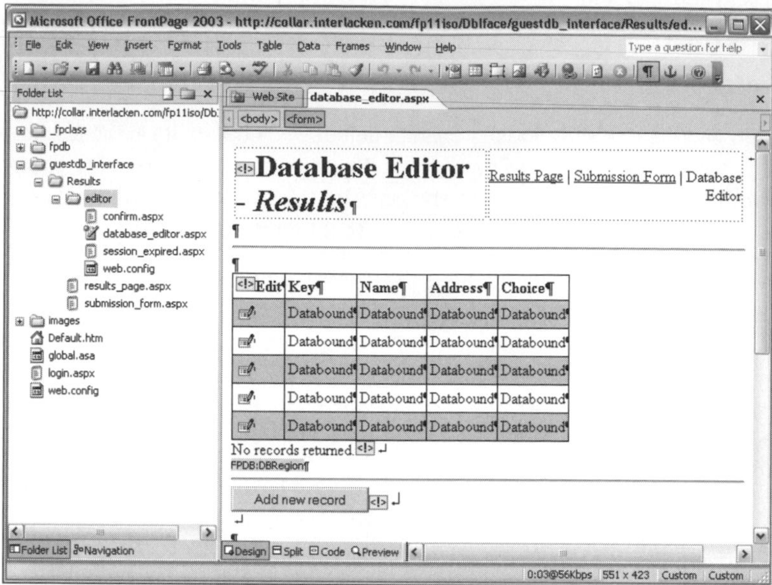

Figure 14-14. The Database Interface Wizard creates a Web page like this one for adding records to the database.

Figure 14-15 shows the corresponding ASP page. Without looking at the program code, you can tell that the ASP.NET version is more attractive and uses more advanced components.

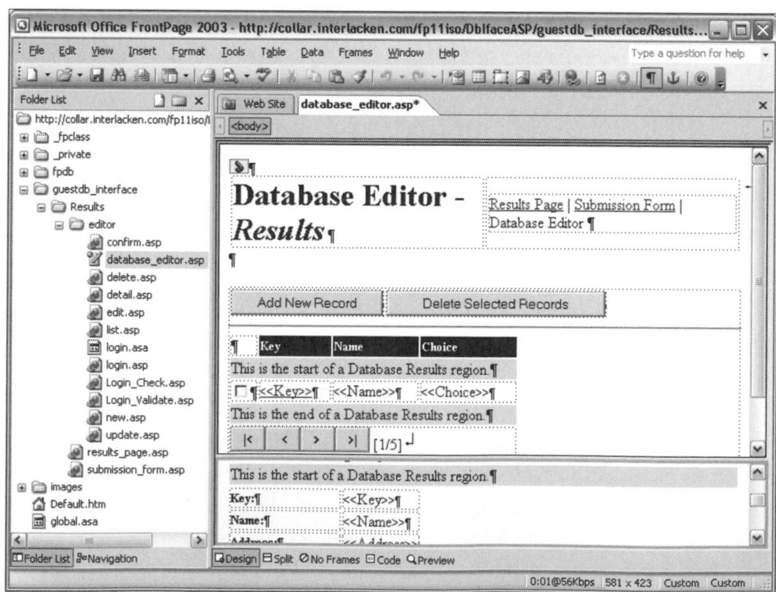

Figure 14-15. This is the ASP version of the ASP.NET page shown in Figure 14-14.

In the case of the ASP.NET page, FrontPage created not only the Web pages in the guestdb_interface folder, but the database as well. The new database, named guestdb.mdb, is a Microsoft Access database, and it resides in a folder named fpdb. The Database Interface Wizard can also connect to existing Access databases, to Microsoft SQL Server, to Oracle, and to other database systems that support Open Database Connectivity (ODBC).

Figure 14-16 shows Internet Explorer displaying the submission_form.aspx page. The page looks much different in the browser than in FrontPage because program code and ASP.NET controls create or suppress HTML each time a visitor requests the page. If FrontPage can't predict what kind of HTML an ASP.NET control will create, it displays that control as a simple gray box.

To add a record to the database, the Web visitor fills in the text boxes, selects an option, and clicks OK. While running the wizard, the designer could have selected more or fewer fields, different fields, different storage formats, and different form field types. The submission_form.aspx page uses the FrontPage Save Results To Database component. Therefore, as soon as the page exists, you can add or remove form fields, replace controls with different types, change the values assigned to radio buttons and drop-down lists, and change the page's overall appearance very easily.

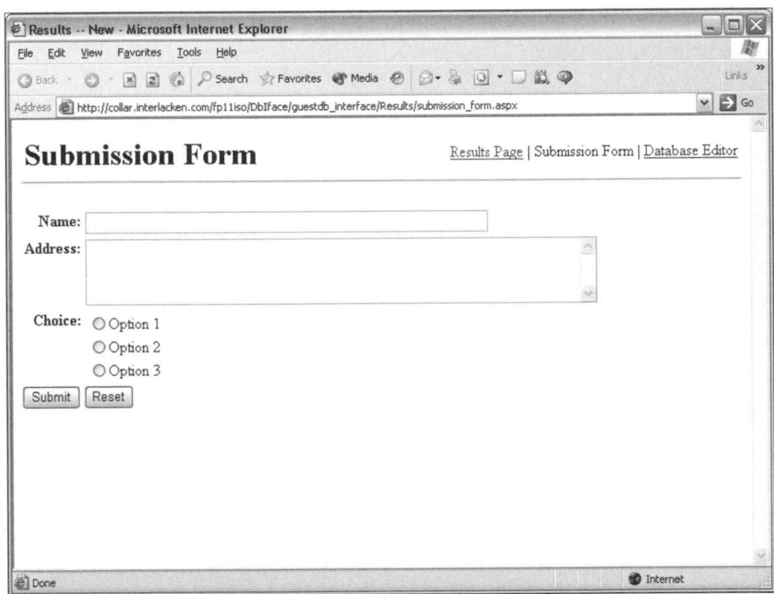

Figure 14-16. Here's how the Submission form of an ASP.NET Database Interface looks to a Web visitor.

Figure 14-17 shows the corresponding submission_form.asp page. As you can see, these pages are quite similar in both appearance and function.

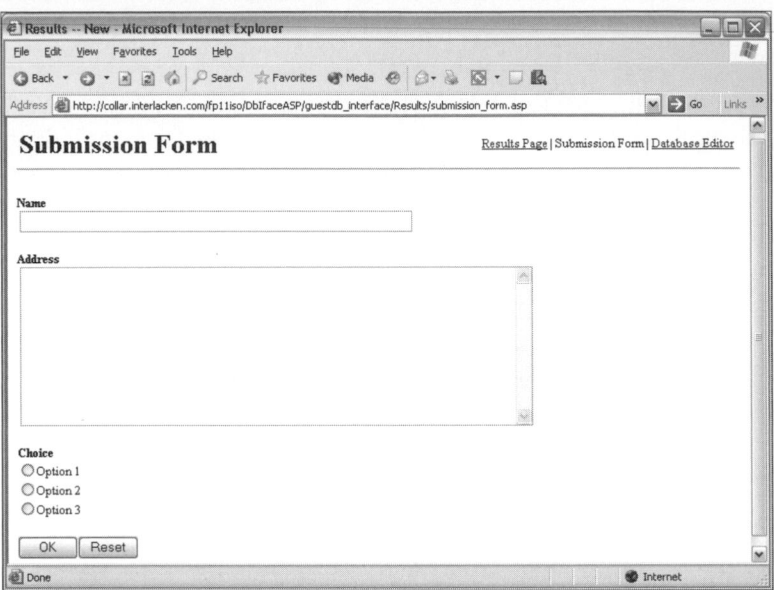

Figure 14-17. This is the ASP version of the ASP.NET page shown in Figure 14-16.

For more information about the Save Results To Database component, refer to "Saving Form Results to a Database," on page 879.

Figure 14-18 shows typical results from the results_page.aspx page. This page basically lists the contents of the database. The results_page.aspx page is a standard implementation of the Database Results component supplied with FrontPage. Therefore, you can modify the page to show a different number of records on each screen, to display the records in a different order, or whatever suits your fancy.

Figure 14-19 shows the ASP version of the same page. The default formatting is definitely on the crude side, but as with the ASP.NET version, you can edit the page and choose the appearance you want.

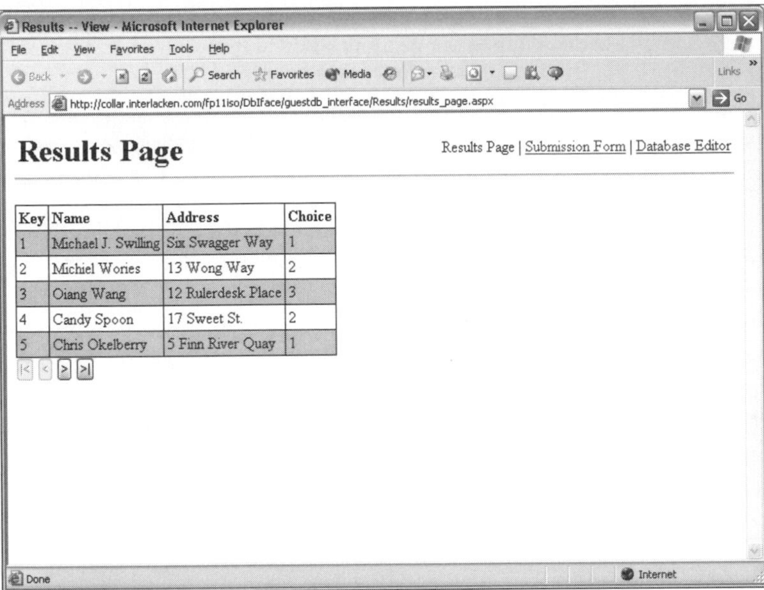

Figure 14-18. The Database Interface Wizard creates this Web page for viewing the contents of a database.

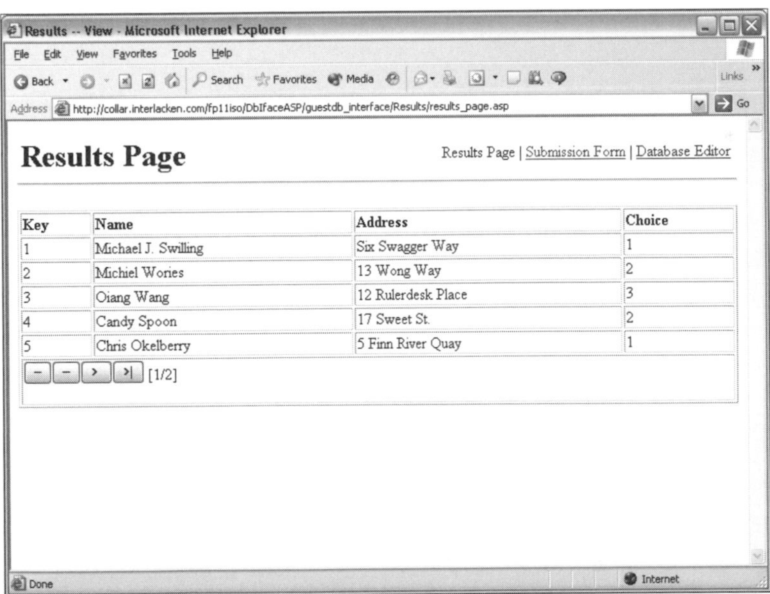

Figure 14-19. This is the ASP version of the ASP.NET page shown in Figure 14-18.

Chapter 14

The Database Results component has a powerful wizard of its own that can add and remove fields, change the sort order, change the number of lines listed on each page, reformat the page, and so forth.

For more information about saving form results to a database, refer to "Saving Form Results to a Database," on page 879.

The ASP.NET version of the Database Editor is a single Web page that contains all the program logic for viewing, adding, changing, and deleting database records. A list of existing records appears in the top half of the page. The bottom half of the page normally displays a form for adding new records. However, if you click an existing record in the top half of the page, the bottom half switches to a form for changing or deleting that record. Program code inside the Web page generates the proper display. In Figure 14-20, for example, the Web visitor clicked the hyperlink for record 4 in the top half of the page and received the change or delete form in the bottom half. The Add New Record button is dimmed. Edit and Delete buttons appear below the visible portion of the browser window.

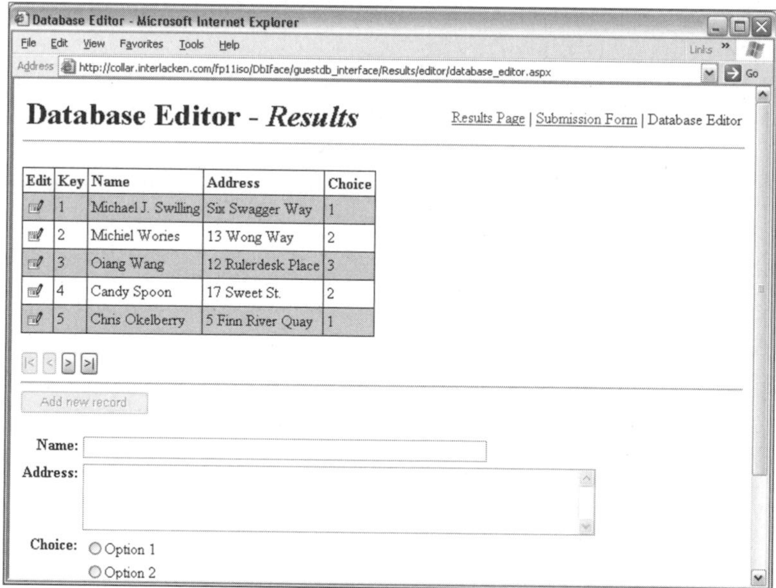

Figure 14-20. The Database Editor page can locate, display, add, modify, and delete records from a database.

The ASP version of the Database Editor page, shown in Figure 14-21, is a frames page with two frames. The upper frame provides record selection, and the lower frame provides record processing. In this version, you can also delete records by selecting the check boxes in front of each record you want to delete and then clicking the Delete Selected Records button

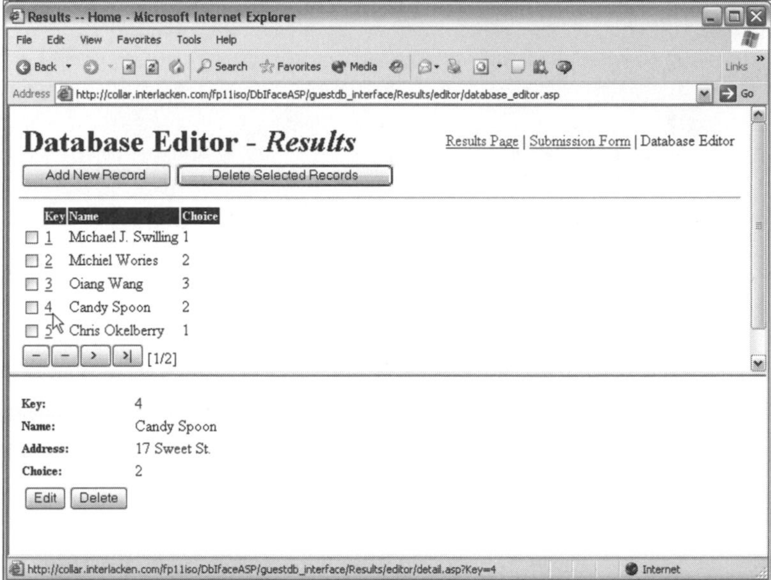

Figure 14-21. This is the ASP version of the ASP.NET page in Figure 14-20.

Here's the procedure for running the Database Interface Wizard and adding these capabilities to a new or existing Web site:

1. If you want to add a set of Database Interface pages to an existing Web site, open that site. Otherwise, just start FrontPage.
2. Choose New from the File menu.
3. When the New task pane appears, under New Web site, click More Web Site Templates. This displays the Web Site Templates dialog box shown earlier in Figure 14-2.
4. On the General tab, choose Database Interface Wizard.
5. If you're adding Database Interface components to the site you opened in step 1, select the Add To Current Web Site check box, and click OK.

   If you're creating a new Web, enter its drive letter and path, UNC path, or Web address in the Specify The Location Of The New Web box, and then click OK. FrontPage creates the new Web and opens it.
6. FrontPage starts the Database Interface Wizard, shown in Figure 14-22.

   Here are all the options on this wizard page:

   - **FrontPage Has Detected That Your Page Will Display Best Using** Click either ASP or ASP.NET, depending on which technology you want the database interface to use.
   - **Create A New Access Database Within Your Web Site** Creates a new Access database. This database contains fields you specify in subsequent wizard pages.

Chapter 14

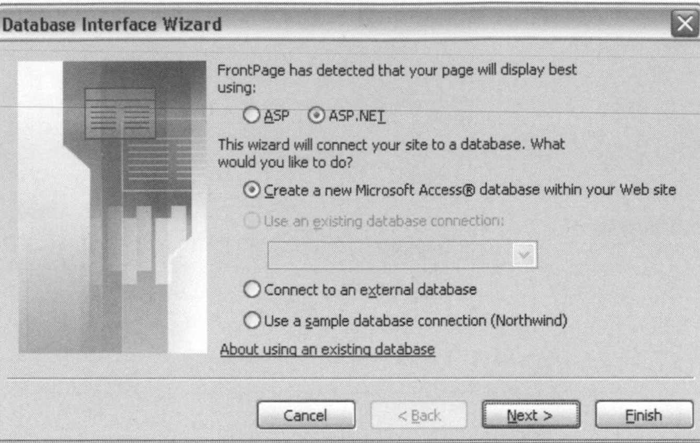

Figure 14-22. The Database Interface Wizard asks what database to use.

- **Use An Existing Database Connection (Oracle Or SQL)** Tells the wizard to create Database Interface pages using a database connection within the current Web site. Select the connection from the accompanying list. If the current site has no database connections (as a new site never will), this option is dimmed.
- **Use A Sample Database Connection (Northwind)** Adds the Northwind Traders database to the current site and creates a connection to it. This is a sample Access database that is widely used for instructional purposes.

To recreate the sample site, choose Create A New Access Database Within Your Web Site, and then click Next

7 The next page of the wizard, shown in Figure 14-23, prompts for a name for the database connection.This will be part of a directory name in URLs, so a short, lowercase name is best. To recreate the sample site, type the name **guestdb**, and then click Next.

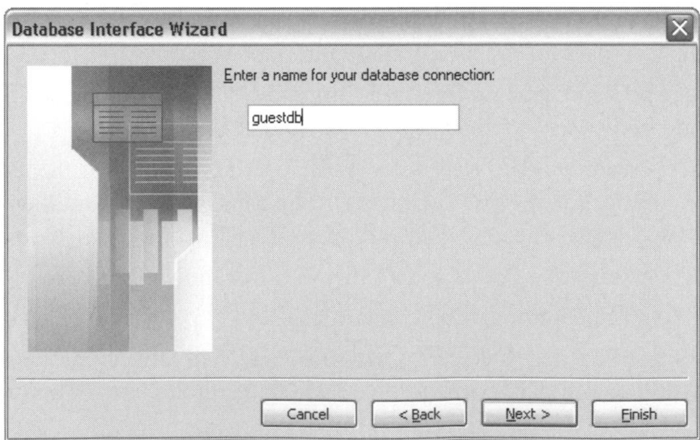

Figure 14-23. A database connection is a named, saved pathway to a database. This prompt assigns a name to the database connection that the pages in a Database Interface will use.

8 The next wizard page, shown in Figure 14-24, controls what columns the new database will contain, the format of each column in the database, and the type of form element to use on input forms.

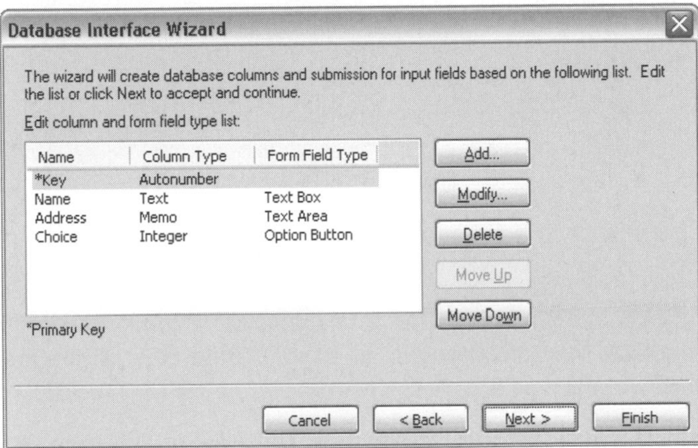

Figure 14-24. This wizard page creates or selects the fields (columns) that the Database Interface pages will use.

Note What most people call *fields*, database experts call *columns*. Humor them.

In this wizard page, you can do the following:

- To add a column, click the Add button, and specify a column name, column type, and form field type.
- To change the definition of a column, select the column you want to change, click the Modify button, and then change the column name, column type, and form field type as required.
- To remove a column, select it, and then click the Delete button.

To recreate the sample site, just take the defaults, and click Next.

9 When the wizard alerts you that it's created the database and established the connection, click Next again.

10 When the wizard page shown in Figure 14-25 appears, complete these two options:

- **Select The Table Or View You Would Like To Use For This Database Connection** This drop-down list will display a list of tables and views (named queries) that the database contains. Select the one you want.
- **Specify A Location For The New Files** This box specifies the file path where the new database interface will reside. The default is <connection-name>_interface/<table-or-view-name>. You can override this by typing a new path or using the Browse button to select one.

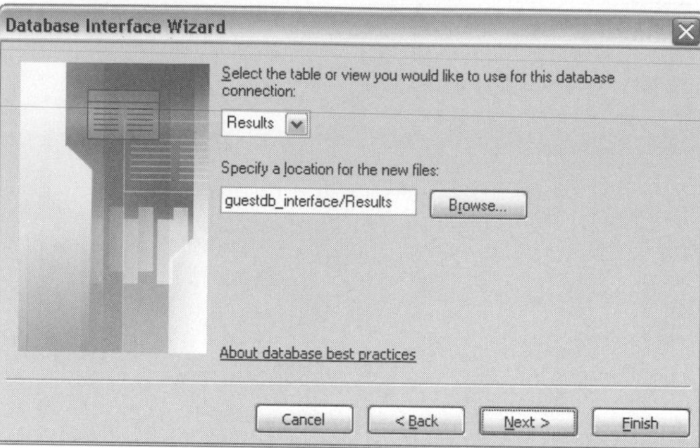

Figure 14-25. Use this wizard page to specify the table or view the database interface will maintain and the file path where the files will reside.

11 Click Next to display the page shown in Figure 14-26. This page asks which Database Interface pages you want. Select the check box for each page you want, and then click Next. The sample site includes all three pages.

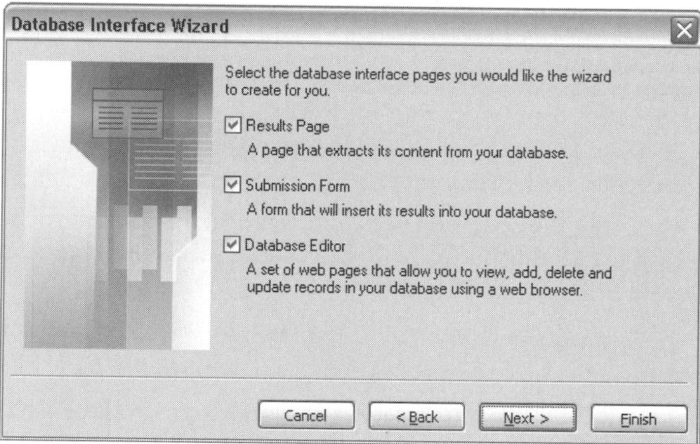

Figure 14-26. The Database Interface Wizard can create any combination of its three basic pages.

12 If you told the wizard to create a Database Editor page in step 11, the wizard displays the page shown in Figure 14-27. If you want to password-protect the Database Editor page, enter the user name and password that the Web visitor (presumably you) will need to know. You'll need to enter the password twice and spell it the same both times.

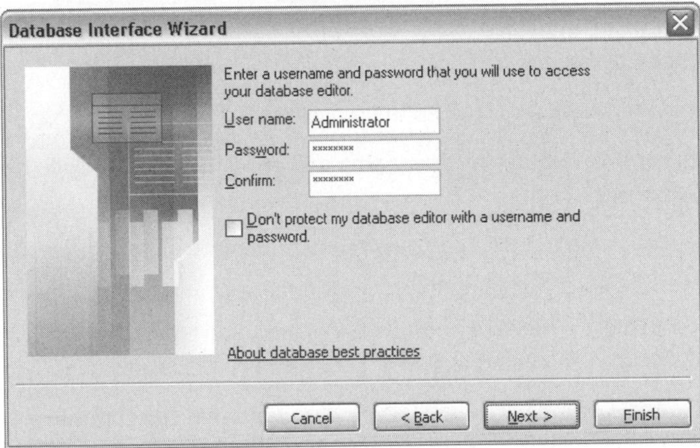

Figure 14-27. Because the Database Editor provides full access to every field in a database, the Database Interface Wizard can protect it with a password.

If you don't want to password-protect the Database Editor page, select the Don't Protect My Database Editor With A Username And Password check box.

13 Click Next to display a final confirmation page, and then click Finish.

For more information about the Database Interface Wizard, refer to "Using the Database Interface Wizard," on page 379.

Frequently Asked Questions About the Database Interface Wizard

What operating environment do Database Interface pages require?

If you choose to create ASP pages, the submission_form.asp, results_page.asp, and database_editor.asp pages will work only on Microsoft Web servers that support ASP. Generally, this means Internet Information Server 4.0 or Internet Information Services 5.0 or later (all known as IIS). The server also needs to have Microsoft Data Access Component (MDAC) drivers compatible with the database types and version you want to access.

If you choose to create ASP.NET pages, your operating system must be Microsoft Windows Server 2003, Windows XP Professional, or Windows 2000. In the latter two cases, the Microsoft .NET Framework must also be installed.

In all cases, the Web server must deliver the database interface pages to the browser. This is because the program code in an ASP or ASP.NET page executes only when a Web server delivers the page.

Why won't Database Interface pages work in FrontPage preview mode or when loaded from a disk-based Web site?

Neither of these environments meets the requirements stated above.

Where does FrontPage store the user name and password that provide access to the Database Editor page?

If you use ASP.NET pages, FrontPage puts the user name and encrypted password in the web.config file in your Web's root folder.

If you use ASP pages, FrontPage puts the user name and clear-text password in a text file named login.asa that is located in the database interface's editor folder.

Extraneous link bars and page banners are showing up in the Database Editor. Why?

You probably have shared borders turned on for the current Web site. The ASP Database Editor uses a frames page and, unfortunately, shared borders and frames pages don't live well together. This is because the shared borders show up in every page that's loaded into any frame. The only solution is to open each offending target page and override its default shared border settings.

Using the Discussion Web Site Wizard

This wizard adds a FrontPage discussion to a new or an existing Web site. The Support Forum described earlier in this chapter in connection with the Customer Support Web site is also typical of discussions that the Discussion Web Site Wizard creates.

Like the Database Interface Wizard, the Discussion Web Site Wizard slips fairly easily into an existing Web site. It won't overwrite your home page or replace your navigation structure, for example.

Discussions this wizard creates use a component called the Discussion Form Handler. This component handles new posts by updating a series of static Web pages. Facilities to sort, filter, and download postings are limited. There are no system-level facilities to delete old or objectionable postings, or to otherwise manage discussions. To perform such functions, you need to manually edit or delete the Web pages that the Discussion Form Handler updates.

Discussion lists in a SharePoint Team Site are more powerful, more flexible, and more manageable by far than FrontPage discussions. If your Web server runs (or could run) Windows SharePoint Services, this is a strong option to consider.

For more information about discussion sites, refer to Chapter 33, "Discussion Web Sites and Self-Registration."

Using the Import Web Site Wizard

This wizard creates a new Web site and then imports pages from an existing site. Chapter 6 has already described both of these operations, and there's not much more to say here. If you need to run these two functions in sequence, the Import Web Site Wizard will save you a step.

For more information about creating a new Web, refer to "Creating a Web Site for New Content," on page 153. For more information about the Import Web Site Wizard, refer to "Importing Web Files and Folders," on page 175.

Creating a SharePoint Team Site

If your Web server has Windows SharePoint Services installed, you can use FrontPage to create—and to some extent modify—SharePoint team sites. Chapter 1, "Presenting Microsoft FrontPage 2002," briefly introduced these features. Chapter 37 "Using SharePoint Team Sites," provides additional guidance on using and administering Windows SharePoint Services and SharePoint Team Sites.

Inside Out

Neither ASP nor ordinary ASP.NET pages run on Windows SharePoint Services.

By default, a Web server running Windows SharePoint Services won't run ASP, ASP.NET, or other common server-side programs. Microsoft presumes that if you want to run Windows SharePoint Services, you want to develop Web Parts and deploy them in Web Part Pages. To develop and deploy a Web Part, you must use a special Visual Studio .NET template, digitally sign your code, and then register the signed module on the SharePoint sever.

If, in fact, you want to run ordinary ASP or ASP.NET pages, you should use an ordinary (non-SharePoint) Web site with the FrontPage 2002 Server Extensions installed.

Installing Windows SharePoint Services on a Web server installs the basic Windows SharePoint Services software and one SharePoint Team Site that resides in the server's root Web site. However, it's unlikely that one SharePoint Team Site will serve the needs of all the projects, departments, teams, and task forces in your organization. More likely, each of these entities will want a site of its own. Fortunately, the process of creating a SharePoint Team Site is very simple:

1. Choose New from the File menu, and then choose Page Or Web Site?.
2. When the New task pane appears, click Web Site Templates.
3. When the Web Site Templates dialog box appears, choose SharePoint-Based Team Web Site from the list of possible Web site types.

4 In the Specify The Location Of The New Web Site box, enter the Web site address that the new SharePoint Team Site will occupy. This must be a folder on a Web server running Windows SharePoint Services. If it isn't, you'll get the error message shown in Figure 14-28.

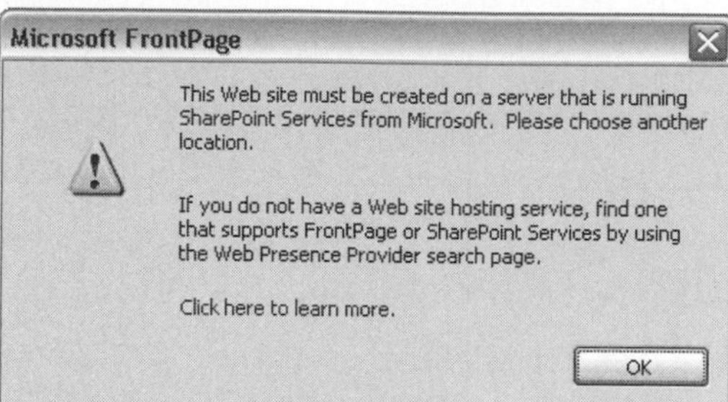

Figure 14-28. You can create a SharePoint Team Site only on a server running Windows SharePoint Services. Otherwise, this error message appears.

Figure 14-29 shows the structure of a new SharePoint Team Site. The Lists folder contains subfolders for each list, survey, and discussion. The Shared Documents folder contains the forms that process document libraries.

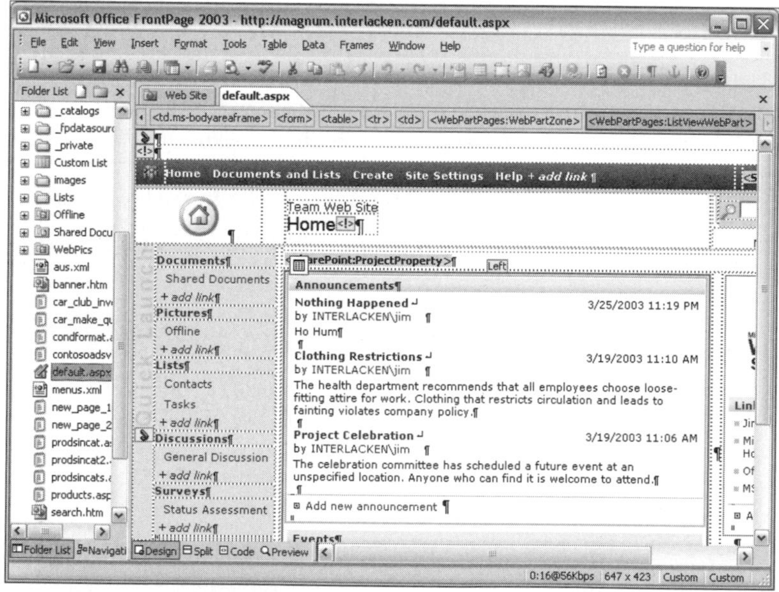

Figure 14-29. The SharePoint Based Team Web Site Wizard produces this collection of rather complex pages. For the most part, you should use these pages as is.

The Web pages that control a SharePoint Team Site are complex and contain many special elements that Windows SharePoint Services uses. You should therefore exercise extreme care when making changes to these pages. Change the appearance of the pages if you want, but not their underlying structure.

You can modify and enhance many aspects of a SharePoint Team Site using only a browser. Clicking the Create link on the home page, for example, displays the Web page shown in Figure 14-30. This page has options to create a new document library, picture library, discussion board, survey, Web page, Web Part Page, subweb, or custom list. It can also create these standard kinds of lists: links, announcements, contacts, events, and tasks. Finally, it can upload and import an existing list from Microsoft Excel.

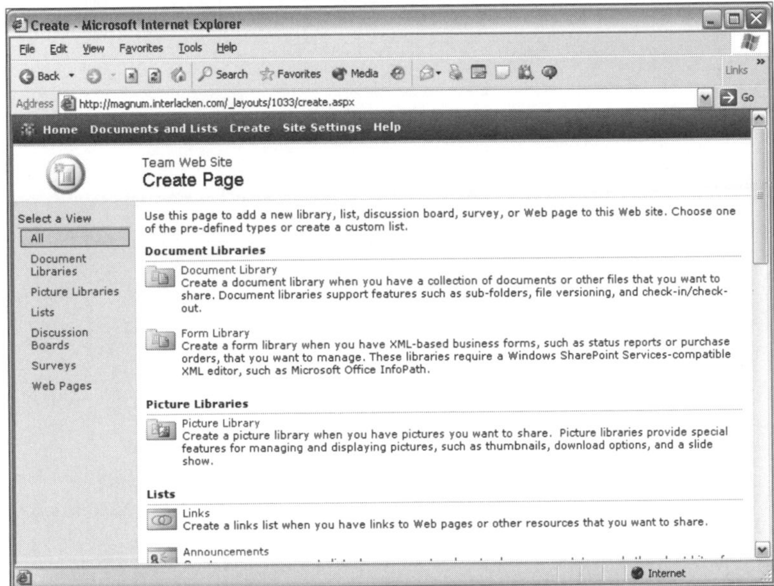

Figure 14-30. A SharePoint Team Site provides its own Web-based features for adding and maintaining lists and document libraries.

Clicking the Site Settings link on the home page displays the Site Settings Web page, shown in Figure 14-31.

This page provides the following groups of options:

- **Administration** Offers links to create, delete, or link to a subweb and to perform other administration functions. These functions include:
  - Managing users and permissions
  - Managing the catalogs of Web Parts, list templates, sites, and site templates
- **Customization** Offers links to change the site title and description; apply a new visual theme; change the design of a list, document library, discussion board, or survey; or change the appearance of the home page.
- **Manage My Information** Provides links to view and change your own user information and manage your alerts.

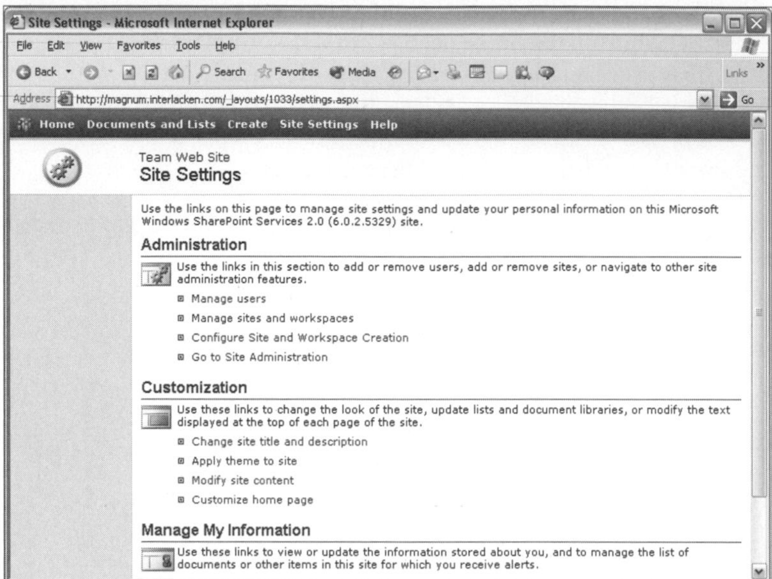

Figure 14-31. This page controls most settings that configure the daily operation of a SharePoint Team site.

For more information about Windows SharePoint Services and SharePoint Team Sites, refer to Chapter 35, "Using SharePoint Team Sites."

Creating Web Sites from Packages

A SharePoint Team Site is by no means the only application Windows SharePoint Services 2.0 can support. In fact, Windows SharePoint Services is a general-purpose portal solution that can run almost any imaginable type of application. The difference is that instead of creating ASP, ASP.NET, or other kinds of programs, you first develop Web Parts and then configure Web Part Pages to display them.

To illustrate this fact (and provide some useful applications as well), Microsoft provides the applications listed in Figure 14-32. Each of these is a SharePoint application that you can deploy either as part of a SharePoint Team Site or as a feature of any other subweb on a Web server running Windows SharePoint Services.

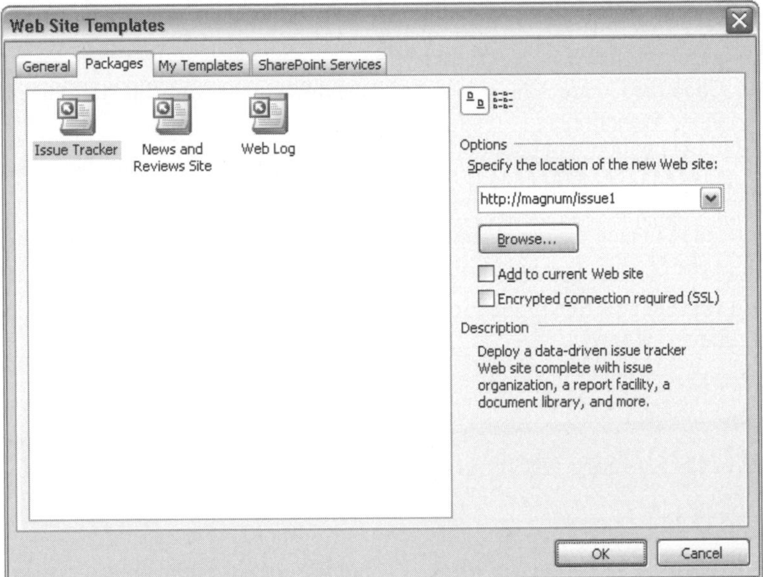

Figure 14-32. Packages contain a complete Windows SharePoint Services site or application, complete with web pages, ancillary files, and databases.

Here are the Windows SharePoint Services applications that come with FrontPage:

- **Issue Tracker** Deploys an issue tracking site complete with issue organization, a report facility, and a document library.
- **News and Reviews Site** Deploys a news site complete with previews and reviews, discussions, and voting.
- **Web Log** Deploys a blog site complete with log search, hot topics, discussions, and favorite links.

> **Note** There are as many kinds of blog sites as people in the world, but the basic concept is that of a personal Web site that includes an online diary of musings, adventures, investigations, and results. The terms *blog*, *Web log*, and *weblog* are synonymous except that *blog* is trendier and the term *Web log* can also mean a server's log files.

The procedure for installing these applications greatly resembles that for using any other template or wizard. Proceed as follows:

1. Verify that you have access to a Web server running Windows SharePoint Services.
2. If you want to add the application to an existing Web site on the SharePoint server, open that site in FrontPage.

3 Display the Web Site Templates dialog box using one of these familiar techniques:
   - Click the Web Site Templates link in the New task pane.
   - Click the Create A New Normal Page down arrow on the Standard toolbar, and select Web Site.
4 In the Web Site Templates dialog box, click the Packages tab, and then select the application you want to install.
5 If you want to create a new Web site containing the application, enter the site's full URL in the Specify The Location Of The New Web Site box.

   If you want to add the application to the current Web site, select the Add To Current Web Site check box.
6 Click OK.

NEW FEATURE! Creating Windows SharePoint Services Web Sites

Templates that create Web sites on Windows SharePoint Services can also reside on the server itself. The SharePoint Services tab of the Web Site Templates dialog box shown in Figure 14-33 lists the templates available on the server that appears in the Options area of the same dialog box.

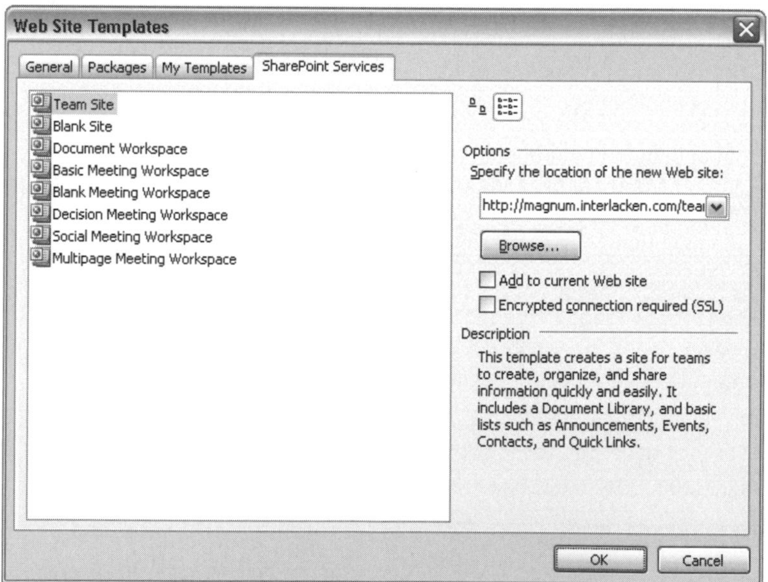

Figure 14-33. SharePoint Services templates reside, run, and create Web sites on a remote server running Windows SharePoint Services.

The procedure for using these templates is very much the same as that for using any other template. The main differences are that:

- FrontPage itself doesn't do the work of building the Web site; instead, FrontPage issues a command that tells the server to do the work.
- The list of templates can vary from one server to another. Whoever administers the server can add, change, or remove templates at will.

Tip For more information about creating Windows SharePoint Services Web sites, refer to, "Creating a New SharePoint Team Site," on page 927.

In Summary…

This chapter explained how to create FrontPage-based Web sites using the templates and wizards that FrontPage supplies. Reviewing the resulting sites also demonstrated how many FrontPage features fit together.

The next chapter explains how to create and organize Web sites that use HTML frames to divide the browser window into segments.

Chapter 15

Creating Web Sites with Frames

When you want to modify one part of the browser window without affecting the rest, an HTML technology called *frames* is worth considering. Frames divide the browser window into as many rectangular areas as you want and provide the means to update those areas individually.

In a strange way, frames address the issue of flicker. If a Web visitor clicks one link on a menu and then the whole browser window flickers, the visitor knows that a whole Web page has arrived. If both pages belong to a set, the visitor must mentally scan the new page to figure out which parts are different. For example, the menu on the second page might be exactly the same as that on the first, but the visitor must expend mental energy (and, more importantly, shift attention) to determine this. On a frames-based site, only the updated parts of the window flicker; this draws the visitor's attention to the new content. Lack of flicker assures the visitor that the rest of the window is unchanged.

The down side of frames is that a page with three frames has four URLs: one for the page that divides the window into frames, and three for the contents of the frames. This makes it difficult for visitors to bookmark content that involves a specific combination of pages displayed in each frame. Frames-based sites involve drawbacks for the designer as well—principally, they don't always scale well. A site with 8 or 10 links in one frame and corresponding content in an adjoining frame works very well, but one with hundreds of links is hard to use and even harder to manage.

Because of the drawbacks for both visitor and designer, the popularity of frames is definitely in decline. That doesn't, however, make frames obsolete. If you have occasion to work on a new or an existing frames-based site, Microsoft Office FrontPage 2003 will support you all the way.

This chapter explains how FrontPage creates and manages frames-based Web sites. It also explains how to create hyperlinks that update the frame you want or that replace the entire frames display with another page. Finally, the chapter explains some very simple scripting techniques that enhance the use of frames for both for the designer and the visitor.

Creating and Editing Frames

A major shortcoming of most Web sites is that a visitor who clicks a hyperlink receives a whole new page. Figuring out which parts have changed is a major distraction.

A *frames page* gets around this shortcoming by dividing the browser window into zones called *frames*. The frames page defines the overall frame layout but provides no actual content. Instead, each frame displays a self-sufficient Web page. The frames page tells the browser what pages to load initially; later, hyperlinks reload individual frames in response to visitor selections.

Understanding Frame Fundamentals

Figure 15-1 displays a Web page that uses frames.

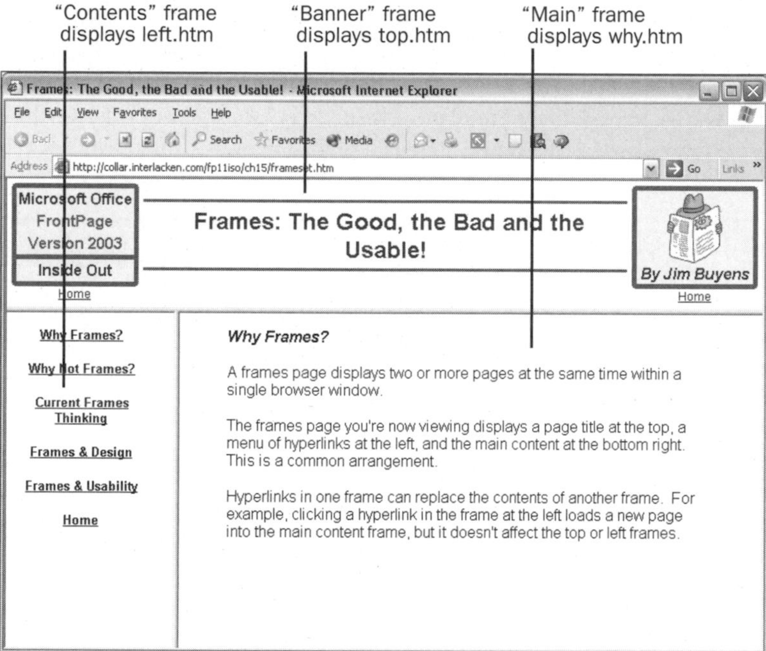

Figure 15-1. This page uses four HTML files: one to define the three frame areas, and one per frame to provide content.

Creating this display requires four HTML files:

- One HTML file defines the frame areas, giving each frame a position, name, and frame source. This file is called the frames page, and it contains no visible content of its own.
- One HTML file occupies each defined frame. In Figure 15-1, three HTML files occupy three frames. Each frame has a property, called its *frame source*, that specifies the URL of the Web page that provides the frame's content. The frames page specifies an initial frame source for each frame.

The labels in Figure 15-1 show the frame names and sources for each of the three frames that make up the frames page. The fact that Figure 15-1 displays four HTML files *at once* is a key concept. The browser's Address box shows only one URL, but three more are hidden. To see the other URLs, right-click the content area of any frame, and choose Properties from the shortcut menu. If you have the file open in FrontPage, right-click a frame, and choose Page Properties from the shortcut menu. The Page Properties dialog box appears as shown in Figure 15-2.

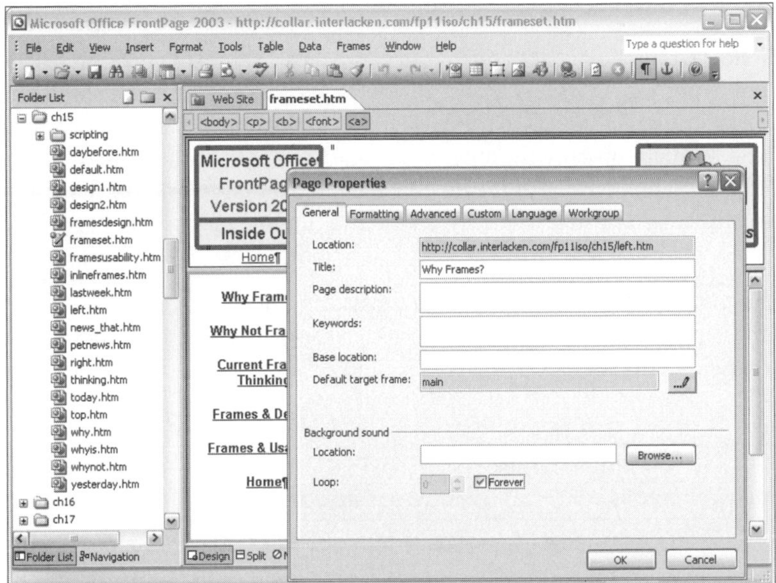

Figure 15-2. The Page Properties dialog box for the main title frame shows a URL different from that of the frames page.

A frames page can also be the source of another frame (that is, you can have frames pages within frames). This can become extremely confusing, but it works.

When a frames page and its frame sources are displayed, hyperlinks in any frame can display new content in the same frame, a different frame, the entire window (replacing the entire frameset), or a different window. A link attribute called the *target frame* specifies—by name—which frame should receive the content of a given hyperlink. The browser looks for the target frame specification in three locations. In order, these are:

- **A target on the hyperlink** Dialog boxes such as the Insert Hyperlink dialog box can specify the target frame for an individual hyperlink. Simply click the Target Frame button, and specify the name of the frame where the new page should appear.

For more information about the Insert Hyperlink dialog box, refer to Chapter 11, "Building Hyperlinks."

- **A base target in a content page** If a Web page contains a <base> tag, that tag specifies a default target frame for all hyperlinks in that page. This applies to all hyperlinks in that page that don't specify a target frame. In FrontPage, this setting appears as Base Location on the General tab of the Page Properties dialog box.

- **The current frame** If neither the hyperlink nor a <base> tag in the page that contains it specifies a target frame, the frame that contains the hyperlink receives the new content.

If you specify a target frame that doesn't exist, the browser will usually display the named HTML file in a new window. Always double-check frame name spellings, especially if a frames page isn't working properly.

Figure 15-1 illustrates the most frequent use of the target frame in current Web pages. Notice the menu of hyperlinks in the left frame. When the Web visitor clicks one of these hyperlinks, the corresponding page appears in the main frame to the right. If the content appeared in the menu frame, it might obscure the other menu choices, making them unavailable. By setting each hyperlink's target frame (or the menu page's default target frame) to main, you ensure that the menu remains visible in the left frame and that the new content appears in the right frame.

In addition to the frame names you create as part of a frames page, the four built-in target frame names listed in Table 15-1 might be useful. FrontPage sometimes identifies these by the common target names listed in the table's second column.

Table 15-1. Built-In Frame Names (No User Definition Required)

HTML code	Common target name	Browser action
_blank	New Window	Loads the hyperlink target into a new window.
_self	Same Frame	Loads the hyperlink target into the frame that contains the hyperlink. This is useful for overriding a page's default target frame on selected hyperlinks.
_parent	Parent	Loads the hyperlink target into the parent of the frame that contains the hyperlink (that is, the hyperlink target will replace the entire frames page that defines the frame containing the hyperlink).
_top	Whole Page	Loads the hyperlink target into the full window of the Web browser, replacing all prior frames pages. Designers often use this as the exit door from a frames page to a single HTML, full-page display.

An arrangement like the one shown in Figure 15-1 constantly displays your site's banner in the top frame and a menu of common hyperlinks in the left frame, no matter which page visitors browse in the main frame. However, this structure has disadvantages as well:

- Correctly specifying a target frame for each hyperlink in a Web site is a manual process. By nature, this is tedious and error-prone.

- Adding hyperlinks to specific frames page combinations can be difficult. When another hyperlink loads the entire frames page, the default frame sources will always load.
- The more hyperlinks a frameset contains (and the more page combinations it displays), the less intuitive the site becomes.
- To load the frames page with a different combination of target pages, you have to create (and perpetually maintain) a second version of the frames page or do some fancy scripting.

For more information about the use of scripting in framesets, refer to "Scripting Frames and Frames Pages," later in this chapter.

Creating and Modifying Frames Pages

Creating a new frames page in FrontPage is fairly simple. As with tables, you'll spend far more time modifying the frames than creating them. Here's the procedure:

1 Display the Page Templates dialog box using one of the following techniques:
   - Choose New from the File menu. When the New task pane appears, click Page Templates in the Other Templates section.
   - On the Standard toolbar, click the Create A New Normal Page down arrow, and then choose Page.

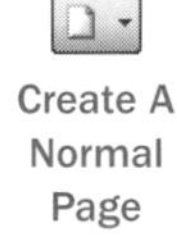
Create A Normal Page

2 When the Page Templates dialog box appears, select the Frames Pages tab, shown in Figure 15-3.

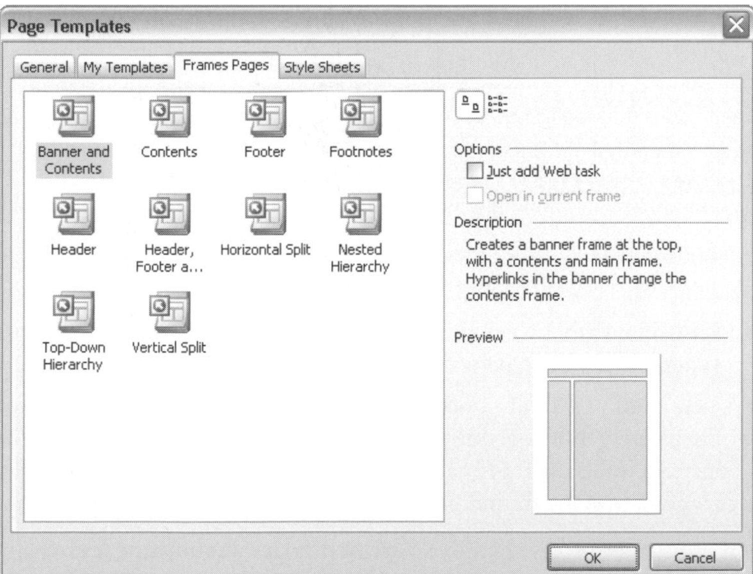

Figure 15-3. FrontPage offers a variety of prebuilt frames pages that are useful as starting points for your own work.

3 Click the available frames templates until you find the one closest to your needs. The Description area displays information about each template you select, and the Preview area depicts each selection's overall frames layout.

4 When you find a frames page that meets your needs, click OK. FrontPage displays the new frames page, as shown in Figure 15-4.

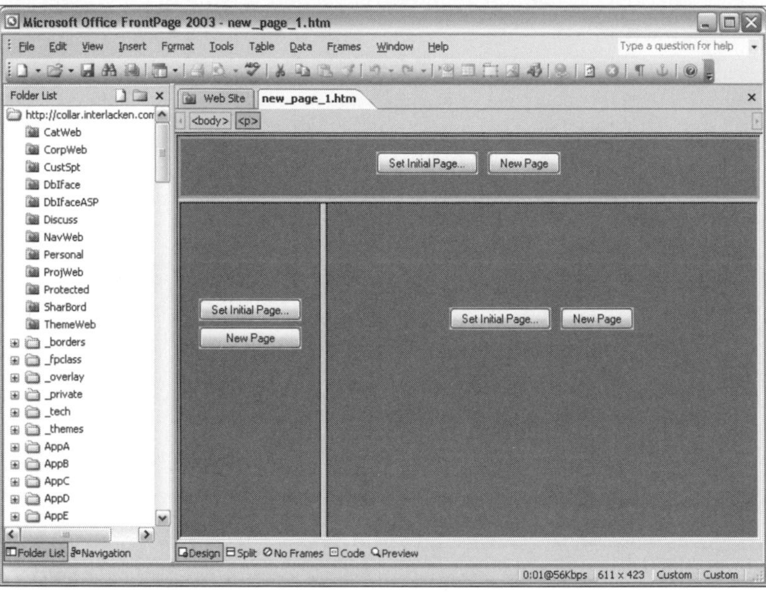

Figure 15-4. Creating a new frames page doesn't automatically create target pages for each frame.

Note The Database Interface Wizard and the Discussion Web Site Wizard are the only Web site templates that create frames pages. There are no Web templates that create general-purpose Webs organized with frames.

A new frames page contains no content. It is much like a picture frame with no picture. In place of content, FrontPage displays two buttons in each new frame:

- **Set Initial Page** Click this button to initialize the frame with an existing Web page. When the Insert Hyperlink dialog box appears, find the page, and then click OK.
- **New Page** Click this button to create a new Web page whose content will initially fill the frame. FrontPage doesn't offer templates for new pages used as frame targets; instead, it fills the frame with a blank page and prompts you for a name and title when you first save the frames page.

When FrontPage displays a frames page, it displays not only the frame windows but also their default target pages in fully editable, WYSIWYG mode. Clicking each of the New Page buttons in the frames page shown in Figure 15-4 and supplying preliminary content produces the results shown in Figure 15-5.

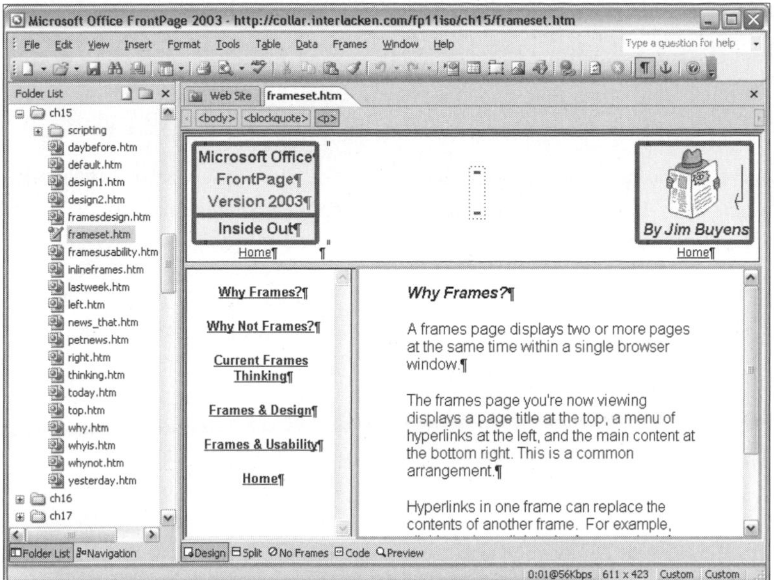

Figure 15-5. Now new target pages and some initial content populate the frames page from Figure 15-4. Saving this view saves four files: the frames page itself, and each of three target Web pages. The dark line around the top frame indicates the active frame.

When you first save the frames page, FrontPage prompts you not only for the frames page file name, but also, in turn, for the file name of each new target. When you subsequently save the frames pages, FrontPage also saves any open target pages you've modified.

Specifying Frames Page Properties

You can specify the dimensions of a frame in three ways: by percentage, by relative sizing, or by pixels. Here's the distinction:

- Percentage states what fraction of the frames page's available height or width a given frame will occupy. This has the advantage of changing the frame size proportionately, depending on the size of the visitor's browser window.
- Relative sizing assigns a sizing factor to each frame, and then divides the available space proportionately. For example, if the frames page consists of three horizontal frames with relative heights of 10, 20, and 30, the three frames receive 10/60, 20/60, and 30/60 of the browser window, respectively. (To calculate the denominator, just add the values—in this case, 10 + 20 + 30 = 60.)
- Specifying frame sizes in pixels seems at first to offer more absolute control, but only if you know in advance the size of all objects in the frame. Remember, for example, that in most cases you won't know the actual font sizes the visitor has chosen for various kinds of text.

There are two ways to resize a frame. The first of these methods resizes a frame visually:

1. Move the mouse pointer over the frame border until it changes to a double-headed arrow.
2. Hold down the mouse button and drag the border to the desired position.

The second method uses menus, and therefore controls frame sizes numerically. You can specify frame sizes relative to each other, as a percentage of available space, or as a specific number of pixels. Here's the procedure to display the Frame Properties dialog box:

1. Select the frame you want to modify.
2. Display the Frame Properties dialog box, shown in Figure 15-6, using one of these techniques:
   - Choose Frame Properties from the Frames menu.
   - Right-click the frame, and then choose Frame Properties from the shortcut menu.

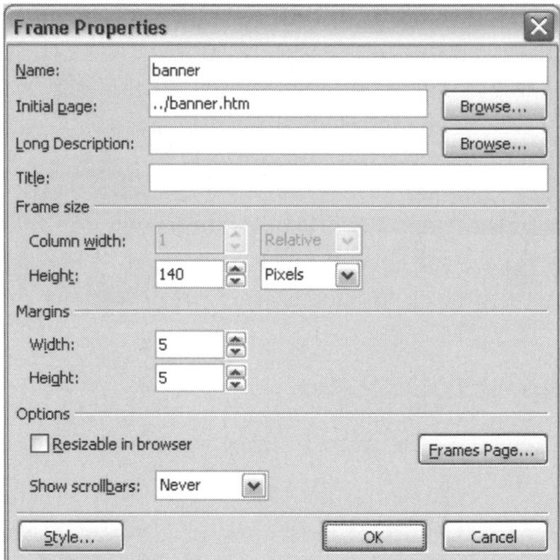

Figure 15-6. The Frame Properties dialog box controls the name, size, and other settings pertinent to a frame.

In the Frame Properties dialog box, use the following settings to control the size and other attributes of current frame:

- **Name** Enter the name that hyperlinks will specify to load their contents into the selected frame.
- **Initial Page** Specify the URL of the Web page that will initially appear in the frame (that is, when the browser first loads the frames page). Use the Browse button to locate the page.
- **Long Description** Specify a URL that contains more information about the current frame.

- **Title** Enter some text that describes the frame.
- **Frame Size** Use this group of options to control the frame's display size. As you might expect, frames have two dimensions:
  - **Width/Column Width** Use this setting to control the width of a frame or column. If the frame in a column with other frames of uniform width, the name of this box is Column Width (as it is in Figure 15-6), and the setting controls all frames in the column. Otherwise, the box's name is Width, and the setting controls one frame. In either case, specify both a width and the corresponding unit of measure.
  - **Height/Row Height** Use this setting to control the height of a frame or row. If the frame resides in a row with other frames of uniform height, the name of this box is Row Height, and the setting controls all frames in the row. Otherwise, the box's name is Height, and the setting controls one frame. In either case, specify both a height and the corresponding unit of measure.

  The preceding measurements have three possible units of measure:
  - **Relative** These units specify frame sizes relative to each other. If the frames page is divided horizontally into two frames with relative sizes of 1 and 4, the frames will occupy 1/5 and 4/5 of the available window space, respectively. Relative sizes of 2 and 8 would produce identical results, as would 5 and 20.
  - **Percent** These units allocate portions of the frames page. A frame sized at 33 percent would occupy 1/3 of the horizontal or vertical space available to the frames page.
  - **Pixels** These dimensions are straightforward. The frame will occupy the specified number of pixels or dots on the visitor's monitor.
- **Margins** Use this group of options to control the size of margins within the selected frame:
  - **Width** Use this setting to specify the number of pixels you want between the frame contents and the left and right borders. The number applies to both the left border and the right border.
  - **Height** Use this setting to specify the number of pixels you want between the frame contents and the top and bottom borders. This number applies to both the top and bottom borders.
- **Options** Use these two settings to control resizing and scroll bars:
  - **Resizable In Browser** Select this check box to let visitors resize the frame based on the size of their window. Otherwise, clear it.
  - **Show Scrollbars** Use the choices in this list to control when the browser will display scroll bars for the frame. Choose If Needed if the browser should display scroll bars whenever the frame's contents are larger than the window. Choose Never if the browser should never display scroll bars for the frame. Choose Always the browser should always display scroll bars for the frame, even if the entire contents of the page fit within the frame.

- **Frames Page** Click this button to display the Page Properties dialog box for the frames page that contains the current frame.

The Page Properties dialog box for a frames page is quite similar to that of a normal page. It consists of the five tabs that Chapter 18, "Controlling Overall Page Appearance," describes, plus the Frames tab, shown in Figure 15-7.

For descriptions of the other five tabs in the Page Properties dialog box, refer to "Specifying Page-Level Attributes," on page 493.

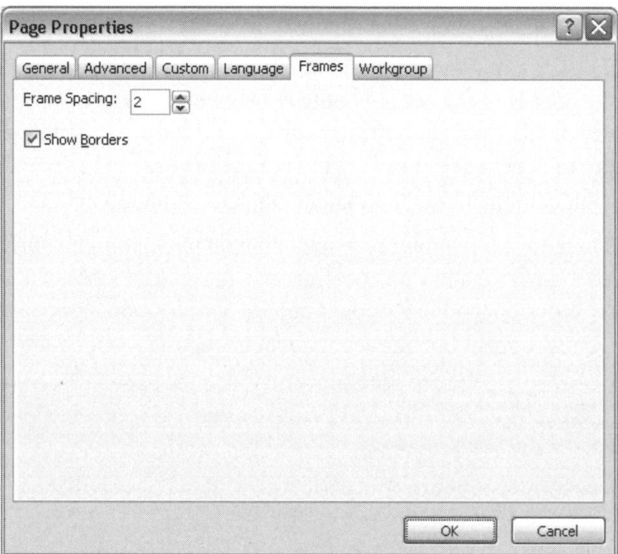

Figure 15-7. The Frames Page button in the Frame Properties dialog box opens this version of the Page Properties dialog box, which contains a Frames tab.

The Frames tab contains two settings. Both pertain to the frames page and not to individual frames or their targets:

- **Frame Spacing** Specifies the number of pixels the browser should insert between frames. If Show Borders is also selected, the space will appear as a border; otherwise, the frame contents will be separated by this amount of neutral space.
- **Show Borders** If this check box is selected, the browser will display visible borders between frames of the thickness specified in Frame Spacing.

Tip FrontPage displays borders even if Show Borders is cleared. To view the page without frame borders, click the Preview button at the bottom of the FrontPage window, or preview the page in your browser.

Creating a No Frames Page

Today, most browsers support frames, but this wasn't true when frames were new. The frames specification, therefore, provides a way to embed an ordinary Web page in a frames page. A frames-capable browser will ignore the ordinary Web page and display the frames. A frames-deficient browser will ignore the frames page information and display the ordinary Web page.

> **Note** A major tenet of HTML is that browsers should silently ignore anything they don't understand. This smoothes adoption of new HTML features by allowing older browsers to run as they always have. Unfortunately, for designers, the lack of error messages can make debugging maddeningly difficult.

To display the page that a frames-deficient browser will display, open the frames page, and then click the No Frames button at the bottom of the window (visible in Figure 15-5). FrontPage initializes the No Frames page with the message *This page uses frames, but your browser doesn't support them.*

You can replace this message with a complete Web page if you want.

Creating and Linking Additional Target Pages

When you create a new frames page, it's quite normal to create or identify its initial target pages at the same time. Then, when you save the frames page, FrontPage will save the initial target pages as well.

In almost every case, you'll need to create far more target pages than you have frames. To understand the need for these additional pages, imagine that you configure a menu frame to initially display a page with 10 or 20 links. You want each of those links to display a different page within some other frame: a frame named, most likely, main. This means you need 10 or 20 target pages for the main frame to display. Here's one way to create these pages:

1. Open the frames page in Design view.
2. Click anywhere in the main frame, press Ctrl+A to select its entire contents, and then press Delete to erase those contents. (Don't save the page after you do this!)
3. Add the new content to the blank page.
4. Choose Save Page As from the Frames menu, give the new page a new name, and click OK.
5. If you have any more pages to create, return to step 2.

In fact, few designers follow this procedure. Instead, they create and save each additional target page in an ordinary Design view window, *imagining* how it will look in the finished frameset.

Regardless of how you create the additional target pages, follow this procedure to configure the hyperlinks that display them:

1 Open the page that will contain the hyperlink.
2 Add the hyperlink text or picture to the page.
3 Select the hyperlink text or picture, right-click the selection, and choose Hyperlink from the shortcut menu.
4 When the Insert Hyperlink dialog box shown in Figure 15-8 appears, enter the target page URL in the Address box. The easiest way of doing this is usually to find and click the page in the Current Folder, Browsed Pages, or Recent Files list.

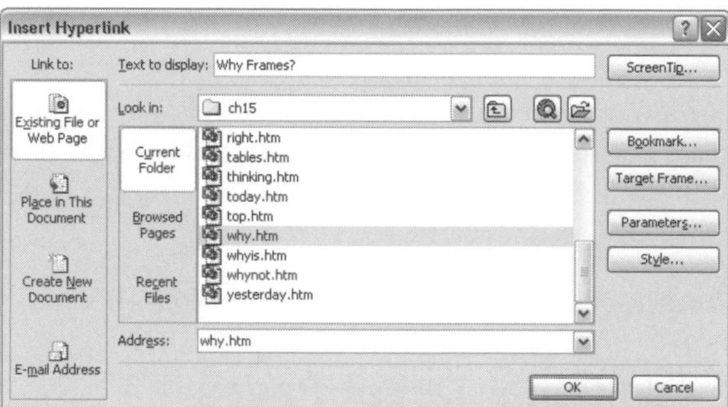

Figure 15-8. To start building a hyperlink that loads a page into a frame, specify the target page's location just as you would for any other hyperlink.

5 Click the Target Frame button. When the Target Frame dialog box shown in Figure 15-9 appears, specify the name of the frame in which you want the target page to appear.

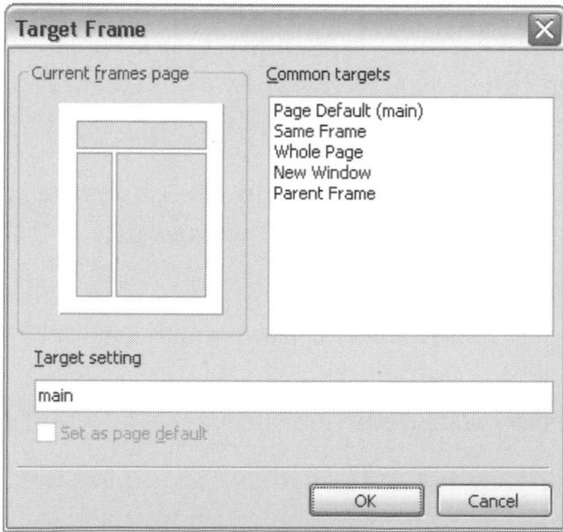

Figure 15-9. To specify which frame should display a target page, click the Target Frame button in the Insert Hyperlink dialog box, and enter the frame name in the Target Setting box.

In most cases, you can do this by clicking an entry in the Common Targets list. If that list doesn't include the frame name you want, type the name in the Target Setting box.

6 Click OK to close the Target Frame dialog box, and then click OK again to close the Insert Hyperlink dialog box.

Using Frames Pages Effectively

Here are some additional procedures you might find useful when working with frames pages:

- Save a specific target page without saving the frames page or any other target pages:
  1. Select the frame of the target page.
  2. Choose Save Page from the Frames menu.
- Save a target page under another name:
  1. Select the frame of the target page.
  2. Choose Save Page As from the Frames menu.
  3. Specify the file name, and click Save.
- Change the default target for a frame:
  1. Select the frame of the target page.
  2. Choose Frame Properties from the Frames menu.
  3. In the Frame Properties dialog box, choose a new initial page, and then click OK.

Occasionally, you might need to add a frame to an existing frames page. To do this, you must split an existing frame into two. Here's the procedure:

1. Select the frame you want to split by clicking inside it once.
2. Choose Split Frame from the Frames menu. The Split Frame dialog box appears.

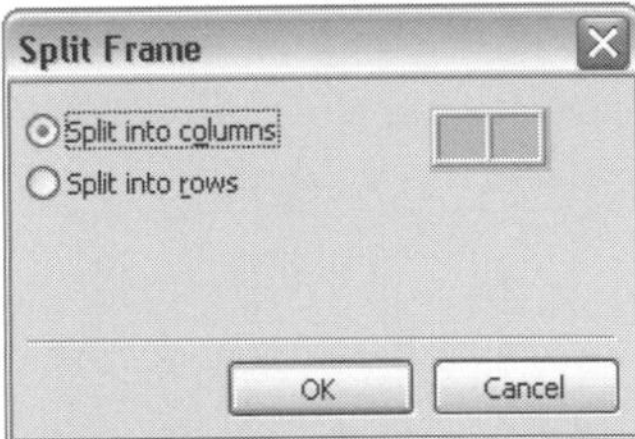

Figure 15-10. This dialog box splits a frame wither vertically or horizontally.

3. Select Split Into Columns to divide the frame vertically, or select Split Into Rows to divide the frame horizontally, and click OK.

> **Note** You can also create a new, empty frame by positioning the mouse pointer on the border of an existing frame, holding down the Ctrl key, and using the mouse to drag the border to a new location.

Chapter 15

4 FrontPage displays a new frame containing the same two buttons it displays in new frames pages. Click one of these two buttons:

- **Set Initial Page** Specifies an existing page.
- **New Page** Creates a new, blank page.

If you have a frameset open in Design view and want to edit one of its target pages in a full-sized Design view window, do either of the following:

- Click anywhere in the page, and then choose Open Page In New Window from the Frames menu.
- Right-click the page, and then choose Open Page In New Window from the shortcut menu.

Any changes you make in the full-sized window will also appear in the frameset, and vice versa.

Tip To switch among several pages open in Design view, you have three options: click the tabs at the top of the editing window, select the page you want from the Window menu, or press Ctrl+Tab.

When you click the Split or Code tab at the bottom of the Design view window, FrontPage displays the code for the frames page rather than the code for each content page. To display the code for a target page, first display the target page in its own Design view window, and then click the Split or Code tab in that window.

To delete a frame, first select it, and then choose Delete Frame from the Frames menu. This deletes the page from the frames page but *doesn't* delete the Web page itself.

Frames pages appear in Navigation view as ordinary Web pages. A frames page's default target pages aren't automatically made children in Navigation view, nor are Navigation view children automatically designated default target pages.

For more information about Navigation view, refer to Chapter 13, "Creating Web Sites with Navigation View."

Take great care when using themes and frames in the same Web ssite. Backgrounds, color schemes, and graphical elements that look good on single Web pages are often distracting when displayed multiple times, once in each frame.

For more information about themes, refer to Chapter 20, "Using FrontPage Themes."

Combining shared borders and frames is almost never a good idea, because the shared border content will appear redundantly in every frame of a frames page.

For more information about shared borders, refer to "Using Shared Borders," on page 761.

Troubleshooting

Hyperlinks load pages into incorrect frames

After displaying a Web page in a frameset in Design view, you might find that some or all of its links no longer load pages into the frame you intended.

This occurs when a <frame> tag in a frames page contains a *target=* attribute. This isn't correct HTML, and browsers will ignore it. FrontPage, however, silently copies this attribute into a <base> tag for any page you display in that frame in Design view. (*Silently* means that FrontPage adds a <base> tag to the Web page without telling you or asking whether to save.)

FrontPage templates are one source of HTML that includes *target=* attributes in <frame> tags. The templates include this attribute so that the Design view editor adds a proper <base> tag in whatever page the designer specifies should appear initially in that frame. Misguided HTML coders are another source of such attributes.

You can stop FrontPage from adding <base> tags by editing the frameset in Code view and deleting any *target=* attributes that appear within <frame> tags. This, however, doesn't remove or correct unwanted <base> tags from any target pages. To remove or correct unwanted <base> tags, you must locate and edit each page that contains them.

To learn how FrontPage can search a Web site for all occurrences of a given tag (or even a given tag and attribute combination), refer to "Finding and Replacing HTML Tags," on page 236.

Troubleshooting

Loading and saving a target page doesn't update a frame's initial page setting

The Save Page As command on the Frames menu saves the contents of the current frame using a new file name. However, it *doesn't* automatically update the frame's initial page setting. This means that FrontPage temporarily displays the *wrong* Web page in the saved frame. FrontPage recovers by reloading the last-saved version of the frame's initial page setting when you switch to another frame or, if you immediately close the frames page, the next time you open it.

Suppose, for example, that a frame's initial page is apples.htm. You modify the frame's content and then save the results as oranges.htm. FrontPage temporarily displays the contents of oranges.htm even though the frame's initial page remains apples.htm. FrontPage loads the last-saved version of apples.htm the next time you open the frameset.

This behavior is perfect if you want to open the frames page, save a modified version of one source page, and leave the original frames page and source page unchanged. Obviously, your assessment of perfection will differ if you intend something else.

To save a frame's content as a new Web page *and* point the frame's initial page setting to it, first use the Frames menu's Save Page As command. Then, with the same frame displayed, use the Frame Properties dialog box to update the initial page property.

To change a frame's content and save it under *both* the existing name *and* a new one, you have to save the target twice—first using the Frames menu's Save Page command, and then using its Save Page As command.

Scripting Frames and Frames Pages

This section explains how to work around four common stumbling blocks that designers encounter when using frames. All of these explanations involve writing simple script code, and none of them has direct FrontPage support. If you're unfamiliar with the use of scripting for the World Wide Web, you should either skip this section or read Chapter 37 before proceeding.

For more information about working with script code, refer to Chapter 41, "Working with Script Code."

Here are the stumbling blocks that the following sections address:

- Reloading two frames with one mouse click
- Loading a frames page with non-default targets
- Reloading a stand-alone page with a frames page
- Helping visitors set up shortcuts

Reloading Two Frames with One Mouse Click

Web sites that use frames often run into trouble as the number of main menu options grows. A main menu with four, eight, or twelve options might be workable, but when the number runs into the dozens, visitors run for the hills.

A common solution to the problem of too many options—and not just with frames—is to adopt a multilevel menu structure. This, however, presents another problem, because when a visitor clicks a main menu option that loads a submenu, the visitor expects *both* the menu frame *and* the main content frame to change. Think about it: After the menu frame displays the new menu, why should the main content frame display a page that pertains to the previous menu? Figure 15-11 shows a frames page experiencing this dilemma. If a visitor clicks Mineral, he or she expects to see a new content page that introduces mineral pets *and* a new menu of mineral pet choices. Normally, however, clicking a hyperlink can replace the content of only one frame.

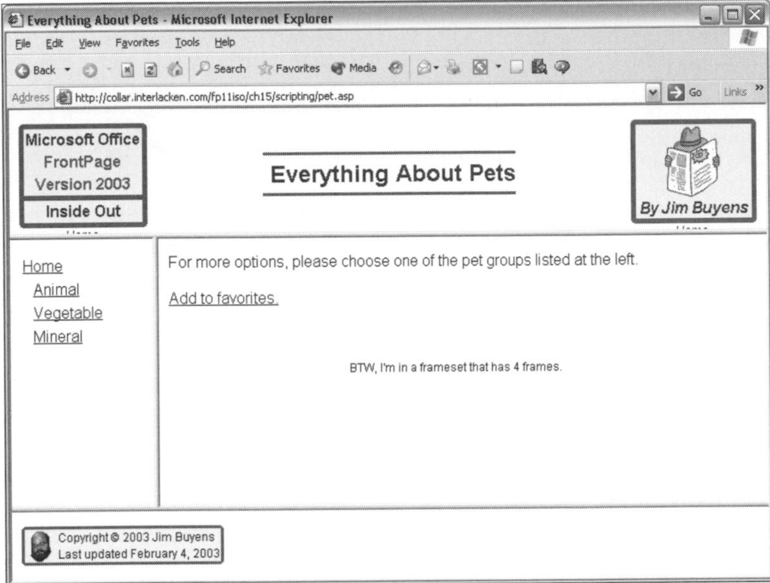

Figure 15-11. Clicking the Animal, Vegetable, or Mineral link in this layout should not only display a new menu in the menu frame, but also a new content page in the main frame.

Avoiding both prolonged meditation and self-denial, the solution to this problem is based on three facts:

- A single JavaScript statement can reload a page as easily as a hyperlink can.
- Scripts can contain as many JavaScript statements as you want.
- Clicking a hyperlink can run a script instead of requesting a new page.

The following JavaScript statements reload a given frame in a frames page:

```
parent.frames.main.location="introanimal.htm";
parent.frames.menu.location="menuanimal.htm";
```

The first statement loads the introanimal.htm page into the frame named main. The second statement loads the menuanimal.htm page into the frame named menu. The expression to the left of each equal sign says:

- Start at the parent of the current frame (that is, with the frames page).
- Go to the collection of all frames that belong to that parent.
- Go to the specified frame (main or menu, in this case).
- Go to the specified location (that is, the URL).

Loading a new URL by executing either of these statements reloads the given frame, which accounts for mentioning the first fact. As for the second fact, you can put as many JavaScript statements in a row as you want, as long as you separate them with semicolons. As for the third fact, here is the syntax for coding a hyperlink that runs JavaScript code:

```
javascript:<any javascript statements>
```

You can use the following expression as a hyperlink address, just as if it were an HTTP URL. In fact, entering this expression as the target location of the Animals hyperlink in Figure 15-10 solves the problem of content frames not displaying updated content when a visitor clicks a new menu option. Don't include a line break; the entire expression is supposed to be one line:

```
javascript:parent.frames.main.location='introanimal.htm';
parent.frames.menu.location='menuanimal.htm'
```

Figure 15-12 shows the expression entered in the Address box of the Edit Hyperlink dialog box.

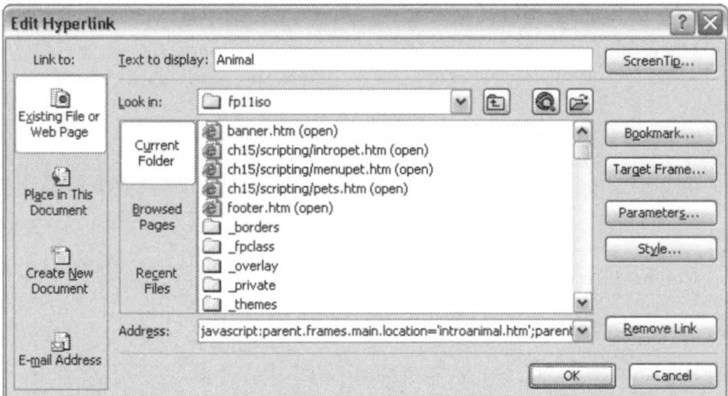

Figure 15-12. By entering JavaScript in place of a link address, you can make hyperlinks run script code.

For more information about the Edit Hyperlink dialog box, refer to "Creating Hyperlinks with Menus," on page 294.

There's just one trick to this code: FrontPage always uses quotation marks ("") to enclose URLs that appear in hyperlinks. This means that you can't put quotation marks in JavaScript statements that appear in hyperlinks; instead, you have to use apostrophes ('). Diabolical.

You can test this technique yourself by browsing the /ch15/scripting/pets.htm page in the sample Web you installed from the Companion CD. Clicking the Animal, Vegetable, or Mineral link displays a new menu and a new main content page.

While you're at it, check out the Home hyperlink on the main menu and the Main hyperlink on the submenus. These are just ordinary hyperlinks, but they provide a much better way to move back through a Web site than by using the browser's Back button. If a visitor browses 20 or 30 frame combinations and then clicks the browser's Back button, the display backs up only *one* frame combination. To get out of the frames page, the visitor has to click the browser's Back button 20 or 30 times. A Home option that returns the visitor to the page that originally loaded the frames page is a welcome feature. Coding this hyperlink with a target frame of *_top* replaces the entire frames page.

Loading a Frames Page with Non-Default Targets

A common problem with frames-based sites has been the lack of capability to jump into the site at any point. Even within the same site, there's been no way of jumping to both a frames page *and* the exact combination of target pages you want. Until now.

In its simplest form, the HTML that creates a frame specifies nothing but the frame name and a default target page. It looks like this:

```
<frame name="main" src="intropet.htm">
```

This is the code that tells the browser to name the frame main and initially load it with the intropet.htm page. If there was some way to modify the *src* location on the fly, before the browser received this code, you could make the browser load whatever page you want.

Because ASP code modifies HTML code before the browser receives it, an ASP page is perfect for the task at hand. Here's how to make an ASP frames page load any combination of target pages you want:

1. Get an ordinary frames page working as you want (except, of course, that it always loads the default target pages).
2. Rename or copy the existing frames page so it has an .asp file extension.
3. Open the frames page in Design view, and click the Code button at the bottom of the window.
4. Find the line of code that defines the frame you want to control. This will be a <frame> tag with a *name=* attribute that identifies the desired frame and an *src=* attribute that specifies the page it should initially display.
5. Replace the URL in the *src=* attribute with an expression like this:

   ```
   <%=pgMain%>
   ```

   Leave any other attributes in the <frame> tag unchanged. This will result in code that looks like the following (where the ellipsis (...) indicates any other attributes):

   ```
   <frame name="main" src="<%=pgMain%>" ...>
   ```

   The <%...%> tags mark a block of server-side scripting code. The equal sign is a shortcut notation that means, "Write the following expression into the HTML sent to the browser." The expression *pgMain* is automatically an ASP variable because it isn't anything else (such as a reserved word, function name, or built-in constant).

6 Add the following code to the <head> section of the frames page. To avoid disturbing any other tags in the <head> section, put the code either just after the <head> tag or just before the </head> tag:

```
<%
If request("main") = "" Then
  pgMain = "intropet.htm"
Else
  pgMain = request("main")
End If
%>
```

The expression *request("main")* retrieves the value of any form fields or query string values named *main* that arrived with the Web visitor's request:

- The form field, for example, could be a drop-down list named *main* that contains a list of permissible locations.
- The query string value is a *name=value* pair that you append to the URL as shown in the following code. This example specifies two query string values, *main* and *menu*. Notice that a question mark marks the beginning of the first *name=value* pair but that an ampersand marks the beginning of all others:

```
pet.asp?main=introanimal.htm&menu=menuanimal.htm
```

For the menu specification to work, you must make the same sort of changes to the menu frame that the preceding text described for the main page.

The original five lines of code in this step should now be easy to understand. If the visitor's request contains a *main* value, that value specifies the initial page the main frame should load. If it doesn't, the code identifies the initial page as intropet.htm.

7 Save the page, and then test it. To test the code in step 6, for example, you should verify that the URL

http://<yourserver>/<yourpath>/pet.asp

displays the intropet.htm page in the main frame and that the URL

http://<yourserver>/<yourpath>/pet.asp?main=introveggie.htm

displays the introveggie.htm page in the main frame.

The ch15/scripting/pet.asp page in the sample Web modifies two target frames this way: the menu frame and the main frame. In each case, a *<%=variable%>* expression replaces the normal target frame URL, and five lines of script code like those in step 5 copy a visitor-specified or default URL into that value.

One disadvantage of using such ASP code is that the Design view editing window no longer displays target pages for the modified frames, as shown in Figure 15-13. This situation occurs because Design view doesn't execute ASP code, and therefore lacks a proper target URL. This is an inconvenience, although not a serious one if you develop the frames page and default page first and subsequently incorporate the ASP modifications.

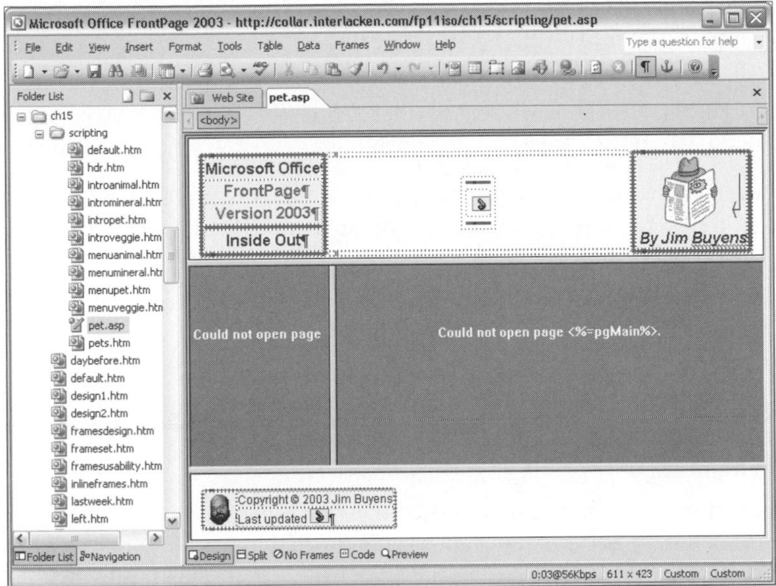

Figure 15-13. Replacing actual frame targets with ASP code prevents FrontPage from displaying a default target in WYSIWYG mode.

Because the technique that this section describes uses ASP, it requires that you use a Microsoft Web server, that the folder or folder tree that contains the ASP page be marked as executable, and that you load the page into the browser using an HTTP URL and *not* a disk location. Loading an ASP page directly from disk into a browser doesn't execute any server-side code, because a Web server isn't performing the delivery.

For more information about processing form data with ASP and ASP.NET pages, refer to Appendix J, "Processing Form Data with ASP and ASP.NET Pages."

Reloading a Stand-Alone Page with a Frames Page

Some Web visitors, desperate to create shortcuts that point somewhere inside a frames-based site, right-click an interesting frame, choose Properties from the shortcut menu to display the Properties dialog box, copy the URL, and paste it into a shortcut on their Favorites menu or desktop. Of course, when they later use the shortcut, they see only the content page and not the entire frame layout. This often leaves visitors with no access to the rest of the Web. A similar situation occurs when an Internet search engine sends visitors to one of your content frames.

To resolve this problem, a page would have to somehow determine that it had been caught in public without its frames page and immediately tell the browser to load the proper frames page. (Of course, the frames page should appear with the current page, rather than the default page, displayed in the appropriate frame.)

> **For more information about viewing a frames page with the desired target page, refer to "Loading a Frames Page with Non-Default Targets," earlier in this chapter.**

As it turns out, there are at least two ways that a script running in a Web page can determine whether that page appears solely in the browser window or as part of a frame layout:

- The script can compare *document.location* (which contains the URL of the current Web page) to *window.top.location* (which contains the URL of the top-level page displayed in the browser window).

  If these values are equal, the current page is the top-level page and therefore occupies the entire browser window. No frames page is active. (This assumes, of course, that the script is running in a content page and not in the frames page itself.)

  If the values are different, the current page is on display, but some other page controls the browser window as a whole. In other words, the current page is appearing as part of a frames layout.
- The script can evaluate the expression *window.parent.frames.length*, which returns the number of frames currently on display in the main browser window. If this value is zero, the window isn't displaying a frames page. If the value is nonzero, the value indicates the number of frames in the current layout.

The message in the center of the main frame in Figure 15-10 reflects both of these techniques. A script in the intropet.htm page, which in the figure occupies the main frame, compares *document.location* to *window.top.location*:

- If these values are equal, the script writes *I'm the top dog. There are.*
- If these values are not equal, the script writes *BTW, I'm in a frameset that has.*

The script then displays the value of *window.parent.frames.length* and the word *frames*. Displaying the intropet.htm page in and out of a frameset thus produces two different results, proving that the page can determine its environment.

To summarize, each content page needs to contain a small script that determines whether the page currently appears within a frame. If it does appear within a frame, great—end of story. If it doesn't, it needs to reload the main window with the proper frameset using the technique described in the previous section to make the current page appear in the proper window. Here's the script (five lines of code, including three that don't count):

```
<script>
if (document.location == window.top.location) {
  window.location = "pet.asp?menu=menupet.htm&main=intropet.htm";
}
</script>
```

If *document.location* equals *window.top.location*, the current page isn't in a frames layout. The script therefore changes the main window location to the URL of the pet.asp page, specifying the proper targets for the menu and main frames.

As explained thus far, the approach described in this section requires that you modify the script to specify proper target locations for each page that uses it. If you're good at scripting and willing to adopt some naming conventions, however, you could write code that inspects the *document.location* value (that is, the URL of the current page) and thereby determines the proper targets for the menu and main frames. This means that you could insert exactly the same script in every page that appears within a given frames page. And, to ease both deployment and maintenance, you could replicate that script to every required page by means of an Include Page or Shared Borders component.

For more information about the Include Page and Shared Borders components, refer to Chapter 29, "Organizing Reusable Web Content."

Helping Visitors Set Up Shortcuts

Another problem that occurs when using frames is that when Web visitors set up Internet shortcuts on their Favorites menu (that is, when they *bookmark* a page), the bookmark always points to the frames page and not to the combination of target pages on display. Although the most capable and determined visitors can dig out the URL of an interesting frame and bookmark it manually, this is no technique for the masses.

Microsoft Internet Explorer, in versions 5 and later, has a script function that can help. Here's the syntax:

```
window.external.addFavorite(<URL>,<description>)
```

Executing this statement displays the Add Favorite dialog box shown in the foreground of Figure 15-14. The Web page shown in the background contains an Add To Favorites link that runs the *addFavorite* function and thereby displays the dialog box. Web visitors can use this dialog box to add the URL and description you specified to their Favorites list.

Note You can't add shortcuts to your site without obtaining interactive approval from the Web visitor.

When the visitor later selects the shortcut, the target page will notice that it's not surrounded by the proper frames page. It'll therefore use the technique described in the previous section to load the frames page, taking care to display the original target page in the proper frame.

The only drawback is that Netscape Navigator, at least through version 7, doesn't support the *window.external.addFavorite* statement. Depending on the exact version, Netscape either displays an error message or does nothing when a script tries to use this feature. Therefore, the hyperlink that invokes it should appear only for visitors using Internet Explorer.

Figure 15-14. Clicking the Add To Favorites hyperlink displays the Add Favorite dialog box.

Fortunately, both Internet Explorer and Netscape Navigator identify themselves by a string contained in the property *navigator.appName*. Internet Explorer provides the following value:

```
Microsoft Internet Explorer
```

and Netscape provides the following value:

```
Netscape
```

The following code therefore writes a paragraph containing the phrase *Add to favorites* only if the browser is Internet Explorer. (The method *substring(0,9)* returns the first nine characters of a string.)

```
if (navigator.appName.substring(0,9) == "Microsoft"){
  document.write("<p>Add to favorites.</p>")
}
```

Surrounding the *Add to favorites* text with a hyperlink that runs the *window.external.addFavorite* method results in the following code:

```
if (navigator.appName.substring(0,9) == "Microsoft"){
  document.write("<p><a href='" +
      "javascript:window.external.addFavorite" +
      "(document.location,document.title)'>" +
      "Add to favorites.</a></p>")
}
```

Notice that this code passes the *window.external.addFavorite* method a URL of *document.location* and a shortcut description of *document.title*. The *document.location* property always contains the URL of the current Web page, and the *document.title* property always contains the text you assign that page in the Title box of the Page Properties dialog box. Using these properties rather than hard-coded values means that you can insert the script in any page you want without modifying it. Just make sure you assign each page a meaningful title; otherwise, your visitors will end up with shortcuts to pages like New Page 2.

You can use Code view to insert this code, surrounded by <script> and </script> tags, anywhere on a Web page you want an Add To Favorites hyperlink to appear. After returning to Normal view, you can drag its JavaScript icon to different locations on the page, and you can even copy the code and then paste it into other pages. To view the code and make corrections, either double-click the JavaScript icon or return to Code view.

Assessing Frames

The scripting techniques described in this section provide elegant and relatively simple solutions to real-world problems. At the same time, they clearly illustrate some of the disadvantages of using frames. If frames themselves were a simple and elegant solution, none of this scripting would be necessary.

Before you launch into designing a frames-based site, consider using shared borders, link bars, Include Page components, or dynamic templates to replicate headings, menus, and other elements throughout the site. This often produces results that are just as easy to use and clearly easier to maintain than a frames-based site.

Using Inline Frames

When you create a frames page, the entire browser window must consist of frames. This can be overkill if you just want to scroll one unit of content in an ordinary Web page. In such a case, an inline frame might serve admirably. An inline frame works like one frame in a frames page, but it's an element you can place in an ordinary Web page.

Creating an Inline Frame

Adding an inline frame to a Web page is a simple process when you're using FrontPage. The procedure is much like that for inserting any other element, such as a picture. Here it is:

1. Open the page that you want to contain the inline frame.
2. Set the insertion point where you want the inline frame to appear.
3. Select Inline Frame from the Insert menu. This creates a new inline frame, as shown in Figure 15-15.

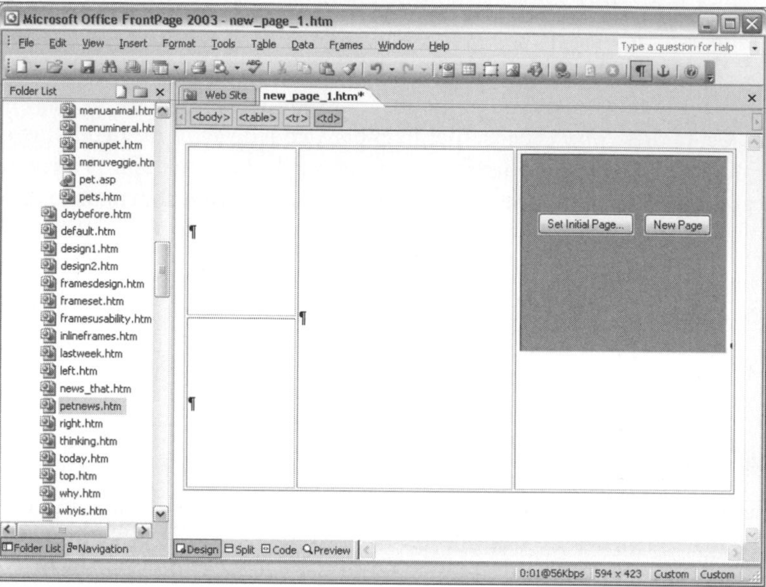

Figure 15-15. FrontPage inserts an inline frame just as it would any other frame. This page shows a new inline frame inserted into an existing table.

Note Not all browsers support the use of inline frames. Releases of Netscape Navigator prior to version 6 are a case in point. If the browser can't display an inline frame, it ignores the frame, and the information in the frame simply doesn't appear. Certain browsers might also display an error message. If a visitor clicks a hyperlink intended to reload an inline frame, a noncompliant browser will open the target page in a full browser window.

The procedure for adding content to an inline frame is the same as for a frame in an ordinary frames page. Click the appropriate button to either set an initial page or create a new one.

Modifying the Properties of an Inline Frame

As with many of the elements you add to a page, inserting an inline frame consumes much less time than modifying it, both initially and over time.

To modify an inline frame's settings, use the Inline Frame Properties dialog box:

1. Select the inline frame by moving the mouse pointer to the top of the frame border and then clicking when the pointer changes to an arrow.

2 With the frame selected, either choose Properties from the Format menu, double-click the frame or frame border, or right-click the frame border and choose Inline Frame Properties from the shortcut menu. The Inline Frame Properties dialog box appears, as shown in Figure 15-16.

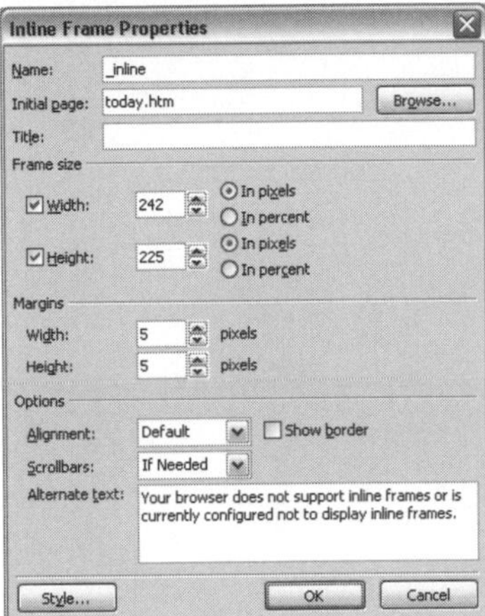

Figure 15-16. The Inline Frame Properties dialog box controls the name, size, and other settings pertinent to an inline frame.

3 Specify the Name, Initial Page, Frame Size, and Margins settings the same as you would for a regular frame. The section "Specifying Frames Page Properties," earlier in this chapter, provides information about these features.

4 In the Options section, you can set the alignment of the frame relative to its position on the page. Because a visitor's browser might not support inline frames, make sure that the Alternate Text setting contains a useful message.

The procedure for resizing an inline frame is quite simple:

1 Click one of the frame's handles.

2 Drag the frame to the appropriate size.

Figure 15-17 shows a Web page containing an inline frame as it appears in a browser.

The inline frame in Figure 15-17 appears within a table cell. This provides more control over its position on the page and over its background coloring.

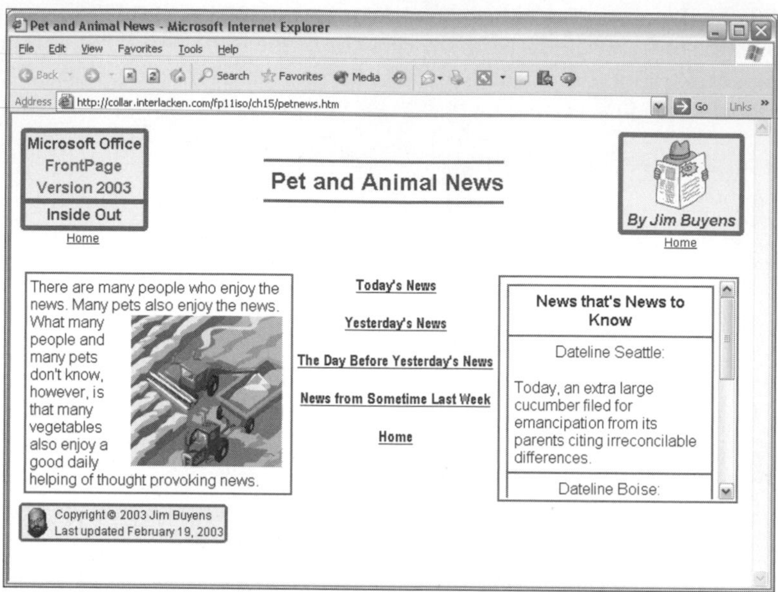

Figure 15-17. The inline frame is located at the right side of the screen, with the heading *News That's News To Know*.

Design Tips: Using Frames

Frames-based sites enjoyed a wave of popularity when the technology was new. Designers were intrigued with the idea of displaying several pages at a time to visitors. Showing all the navigational links for a site in one scrollable, unblinking list seemed like a great idea. More recently the use of frames has declined. Below is a list of some problems associated with the use of frames. Keep these issues in mind when deciding how and when to use frames:

- **Reduced viewable screen area** Keeping the contents of certain pages displayed at all times, such as menu pages in a navigation frame, reduces the main content area. This gives the visitor less screen space to see the page information. For most visitors, going to a Web site is about getting information, and not about staring at navigation buttons.
- **Misleading expectations** When visitors click a navigation button within a frame, for example, new content is generally displayed within a new frame, and the navigation frame remains. When a visitor clicks a hyperlink located within a content frame, typically the content area changes. These two different results are potentially confusing to visitors, as their expectations of "What happens when I click a link?" varies from frame to frame.
- **Inability to bookmark a page** When a visitor displays a frames page, two or more Web pages appear in the browser at the same time, but only one URL appears in the Address bar of the visitor's browser. If visitors travel through a frames site and come across a page that they'd like to bookmark, they can mark only the frames page URL, and not the specific page of content they're interested in.

- **Difficulty printing a frames page** If a frames site includes a navigation frame, chances are excellent that visitors will click only that frame. Any frame the visitor clicks becomes the active frame and by default, this is the only page that the browser's Print command prints. As a result, most visitors end up printing just the navigation buttons.

  The Print dialog box in most recent browser has an option whereby visitors case specify which frame to print, but this only works if visitors notice the option and make the proper selections. Unfortunately, no such option is available when visitors select the Print button on the browser's menu bar.
- **Slower download speed** When creating a frames site, a designer must obviously create frames pages that tell browsers how to display the target pages. This means that the browser must display one more than the total number of visible pages. This, in turn, means that displaying the pages correctly requires one more trip back to the Web server. Of course, each additional trip to the Web server takes time, potentially slowing down the display of the pages.
- **Limited search engine indexing** Most designers would like the sites they create to be found and indexed by Web search engines. Unfortunately, many search engines have trouble finding the pages of frames-based sites.

  Most search engines go to the index.htm, or home page, of a Web site and read its contents. When the search engine comes across a hyperlink, it follows that link and begins to read that Web page, looking for the page's hyperlinks. If a site uses frames, the search engine will go to the frames page looking for the links to the rest of the site, but those links are on a different page, not within the frames page. This type of setup can cause some search engines to look no further than the frames page, thus missing the full extent of the site.
- **Web visitor preference** Many usability studies show that visitors simply don't like having to interact with frames. When it comes to successful Web site design, meeting the visitor's needs and expectations should always be a designer's highest priority.

Enough Web visitors dislike frames that many Web designers provide a parallel set of non-frames pages or at least adequate hyperlinks on a single set of pages so that non-frame visitors can also navigate the site.

In Summary...

This chapter explained how to create Web pages divided into frames. Frames divide the browser window into rectangular sections, each displaying a different Web page that hyperlinks can individually replace.

The next part of this book, Part 5, "Publishing and Maintaining Web Sites," explains how to copy your Web site to another server and how to keep the site up-to-date.

Part 5

Publishing and Maintaining Web Sites

Chapter 16

Publishing Your FrontPage-Based Web Site

At some point after you've developed a Microsoft FrontPage -based Web site, you'll almost-certainly want to copy it. The most common reason is that you need to copy the Web from your development environment to a public Web server for access by the intended audience. However, there are lots of other reasons for copying Webs from place to place, including delivery to a client, a change of working environment, and precautionary backups. Some people even copy Webs to compact discs for distribution with computer books!

You might think that FrontPage-based Web sites are nothing more than sets of files, and that copying files is hardly cutting-edge technology. You can copy files with Microsoft Windows Explorer, a tape-backup program, an FTP program, or the MS-DOS prompt, just to name a few methods. None of those approaches copies every aspect of a FrontPage-based Web site, however, and none of them adjusts all the FrontPage indexes and pointers so that the Web will work properly in its new location. To do this, use the FrontPage Publish Web Site command.

This chapter explains everything you need to know about publishing FrontPage-based Web sites, even if the destination is a Web server that's not running the Microsoft FrontPage Server Extensions or not a Web server at all. What's more, one command does it all. What could be easier than that?

Web Publishing Fundamentals

While developing your Web pages, you have a choice of four ways to store them:

- As individual files on your local disk or file server.
- As a FrontPage-based Web site on your local disk or file server.
- As a FrontPage-based Web site on a Web server that runs on your computer. (Remember, this requires the FrontPage Server Extensions as well as the Web server itself.)

- As a FrontPage-based Web site or Microsoft SharePoint Team Site that runs on some other computer—a computer running a Web server plus the FrontPage Server Extensions or Windows SharePoint Services.

In the last three cases, it's certainly possible that the Web server is accessible to all your intended Web visitors; if so, your pages are ready and waiting for access the moment you finish them. It's more likely, however, that you'll need to copy your finished work to some other location for public consumption. FrontPage calls this function *publishing*.

For more information about the role multiple servers can play in a FrontPage environment, refer to "Planning Your Web Environment," on page 79.

Publishing is the only supported means of copying a FrontPage-based Web site from one location to another. Publishing copies not only your content files—Web pages, pictures, programs, applets, and the like—but also unique FrontPage information such as Navigation view and database connections. And finally, publishing won't copy certain data—such as security settings and hit counts—that ought to be different in the two locations.

If the target of your publishing operation is another FrontPage-based Web site, FrontPage 2003 can intelligently upload your finished pages a page at a time, a FrontPage-based Web site at a time, or an entire tree of FrontPage-based Web sites at a time.

Note WebDAV is an extension to the HTTP protocol that provides secure file transfer, storage of Web page information, overwrite prevention, and version management. For more information about WebDAV, browse *www.webdav.org/*.

If the target of your publishing operation is a Web server that doesn't have Windows SharePoint Services or the FrontPage Server Extensions installed, FrontPage 2003 can still upload your pages via the Internet's FTP or via Distributed Authoring and Versioning (WebDAV). However, because they are less intelligent, such transfers might take a little longer, and any FrontPage features (such as Hit Counter) that actually run on the Web server won't work.

Tip When it comes to publishing, the designations *local* and *remote* are somewhat arbitrary. The local Web site is the one you open in FrontPage, and might be a thousand miles away. The remote Web site is whatever source or destination you choose for a publish operation, and could very well be your computer. Neither the Internet nor FrontPage cares a whit about distance.

Normally, the first step in publishing is to open the Web you want to copy. Publishing considers this the *local* Web site. The *remote* Web site is the one you want to exchange content with. The remote Web site can be a server-based Web, a disk-based Web, or any WebDAV or FTP location your network can reach. Table 16-1 summarizes these possibilities.

Don't think Remote means far away.

Note Because you can't open a WebDAV or an FTP location as a FrontPage-based Web site, FTP and WebDAV locations can't be the local site in a publish operation. It can, however, be the remote site, and FrontPage 2003 can publish from remote to local.

Table 16-1. Acceptable Local and Remote Web Site Publishing Locations

Type of Web	As local site	As remote site
FrontPage or Windows SharePoint Services	OK	OK
WebDAV	Not supported	OK, but result isn't a FrontPage-based Web site
FTP	Not supported	OK, but result isn't a FrontPage-based Web site
File System (disk-based Web)	OK	OK

You should think of publishing as a *push* operation, and not necessarily as an *upload* operation. Although the most common use of the Publish command is uploading Webs from a development area to a production Web server, publishing can also *download* Webs from the production server to your local machine.

Normally, a publish operation compares the entire content of two Web sites and then makes one look just like the other. However, FrontPage can also publish individual files or folders you select. To learn the specifics about publishing single files and folders, refer to "Publishing Single Files and Folders," later in this chapter.

Note Like all earlier versions of FrontPage, FrontPage 2003 normally publishes the local Web site to the remote Web site. New in this version, however, FrontPage can also publish the remote site to the local site. This means that the local Web site isn't necessarily the source Web site, and the remote Web site isn't necessarily the destination.

Using Remote Site View

The Remote Web Site view shown in Figure 16-1 compares and contrasts the content of the current (local) Web and a target (remote) Web.

To display this view, first open the local Web in FrontPage, and then take one of these actions:

- Click the Web Site tab that appears just above the main editing window, and then click the Remote Web Site tab at the bottom of the editing window.
- Choose Publish Site from the File menu.

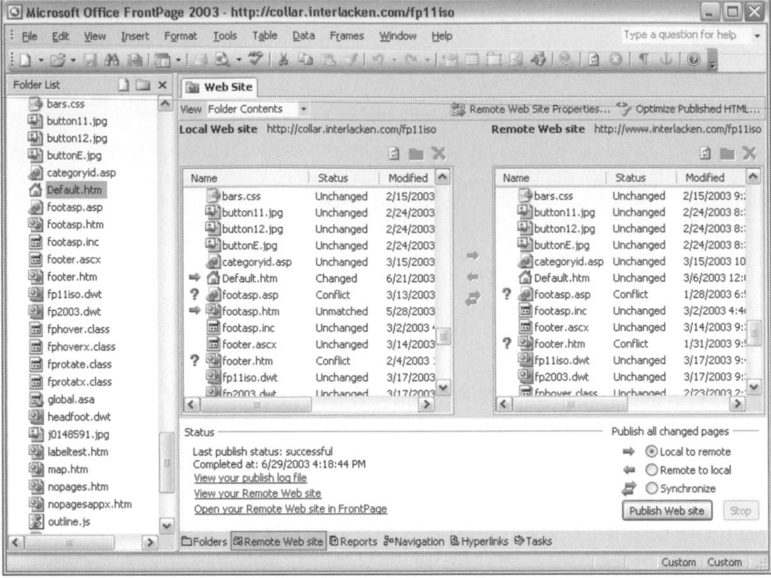

Figure 16-1. Remote Web Site view displays the content of the source and remote Web sites involved in a publish operation.

Publish Site

You can also click the Publish Site button on the Standard toolbar or click Alt+P to display Remote Web Site view, but you should probably avoid these actions for now. In addition to displaying Remote Web Site view, they immediately trigger a publish operation with all current settings.

Specifying the Remote Web Site Location

If you display Remote Web Site view for a site that no one has ever published, the main window will be blank except for the message *Click "Remote Web Site Properties..." to set up a remote site.*

It's also possible that the Remote Web Site destination (which appears above the Remote Web Site list on the right in Remote Web Site view) doesn't point to the location you want. In either case, click the Remote Web Site Properties button on the toolbar at the top of the window. This displays the Remote Web Site Properties dialog box and, more specifically, the Remote Web Site tab, as shown in Figure 16-2.

Publishing Your FrontPage-Based Web Site

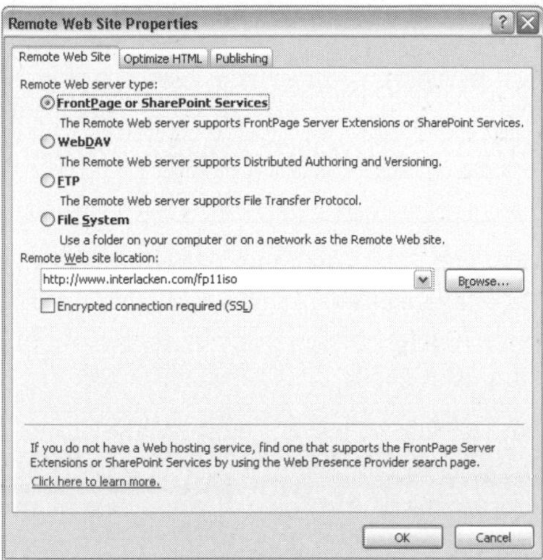

Figure 16-2. This tab specifies the communication protocol and location of a remote Web site.

The Remote Web Server Type setting controls what form of communication FrontPage will use for copying your Web site. The correct choice depends on the form of communication that the remote Web site supports. Here are the options:

- **FrontPage Or SharePoint Services** Choose this option if the remote Web site is running the FrontPage Server Extensions or Windows SharePoint Services. This option provides the most features and benefits for FrontPage designers.
- **WebDAV** Choose this option if the remote Web server supports WebDAV.
- **FTP** Choose this option if the remote Web server supports FTP.

  If your remote Web server supports only WebDAV or FTP, any sites you publish to that server won't be FrontPage-based Web sites. This leads to certain restrictions:

  You can't open a WebDAV or an FTP site by choosing Open Web from the File menu. You can, however, specify a WebDAV or an FTP site as the remote site in Remote Web Site view and then publish in either direction (Local To Remote or Remote To Local).

  Some FrontPage components won't work. Components in this category use features of the FrontPage Server Extensions or Windows SharePoint Services each time a visitor requests a page that contains them. The most common of these components involve database processing, HTML forms processing, Web search, and hit counters. However, if your Web server provides similar components from other sources, you can certainly use FrontPage to include the code for those components in your Web page.

Tip **Turn off FrontPage features your Web server doesn't provide.**

If you're worried about accidentally using components that require the FrontPage Server Extensions or Windows SharePoint Services on the Web server, you can configure FrontPage to dim those menu options. For more information, refer to, "Configuring Authoring Options," on page 1131.

- **File System** Choose this option if you access the remote Web server by means of a drive and path on your computer, or by means of Windows file sharing. This is also the correct option if you're preparing to transport a Web site by means of removable media, such as a ZIP drive or compact disc.

  You should avoid this option if the remote Web site is running the FrontPage Server Extensions or Windows SharePoint Services, even if you can access the server's file space directly. This is because a server-based Web (which you access by means of an HTTP URL) has more features than a disk-based Web (which you access though the Windows file system).

Next, enter the remote Web site's location in the Remote Web Site Location box:

- For FrontPage, SharePoint, or WebDAV sites, the location should be an *http://* or *https://* URL.
- For an FTP site, the location should be an *ftp://* URL. You should also verify correct settings in the following controls, which appear for FTP sites just below the Remote Web Site Location box:
  - **FTP Directory** Specify the directory where your Web site starts on the FTP server.
  - **Use Passive FTP** Select this check box if your FTP server or Internet firewall requires the use of passive FTP (PASV).
- For a File System site, the location should be a drive letter and path combination like C:\MyWeb or a file-sharing location like \\MyServer\MyWebShare\MyWebPath.

If you prefer to specify the remote Web site location by pointing and clicking rather than by typing, click the Browse button to the right of the Remote Web Site Location box. This displays the New Publish Location dialog box, shown in Figure 16-3. Navigate to the server and Web location you want, and then click the Open button.

Specifying FTP Locations and Passwords

Providers who offer Web servers lacking the FrontPage Server Extensions almost always provide designers with FTP access to their home directories. Accessing this location requires four pieces of information:

- The name of the FTP server.
- A user name for logging on.
- A password for logging on.
- A directory path that accesses your HTTP home directory.

To upload files, designers run command-line or graphical FTP programs. The following section is the start of a typical command-line session, with the four items just listed appearing in boldface. The put command uploads the file default.htm.

```
ftp spike.interlacken.com
Connected to spike.interlacken.com.
220 spike Microsoft FTP Service (Version 4.0).
User (spike.interlacken.com:(none)): jim
331 Password required for jim.
Password: xxxxxx
230 User jim logged in.
ftp> cd public_html
250 CWD command successful.
ftp> put default.htm default.htm
```

Fortunately, FrontPage can publish your entire Web site (or any part of it) without exposing you to any of this gibberish. To do this:

1. Open the Remote Web Site Properties dialog box.
2. Under Remote Web Server Type, choose FTP.
3. Under Remote Web Site location, type **ftp://** followed by the name of the server. To comply with the preceding code example, you would enter **ftp://spike.interlacken.com**
4. Under FTP Directory, enter the directory path that accesses your HTTP home directory. For this example, you would enter **public_html**.
5. Click OK. If FrontPage displays the Connect To dialog box shown in Figure 16-4, enter the same user name and password you would use for logging on to FTP any other way. For this example, you would enter **jim** and **xxxxxx**.

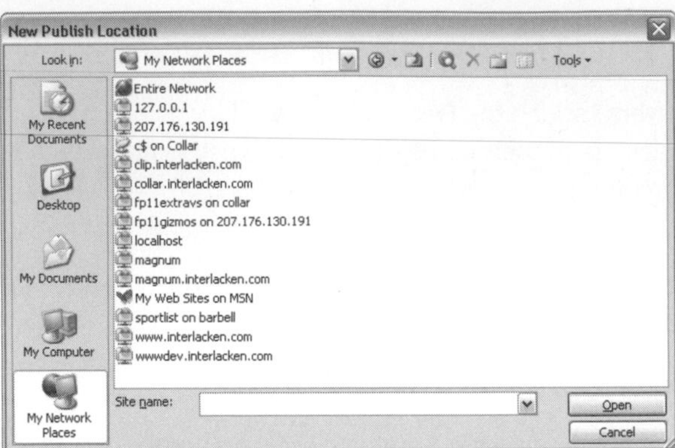

Figure 16-3. Clicking the Browse button in the Remote Web Site Properties dialog box displays this dialog box for locating a remote Web site.

If the remote FrontPage, SharePoint, or WebDAV Web site server requires SSL communication, select the Secure Connection Required (SSL) check box. The URL in the Remote Web Site Location box should then specify *https* instead of *http*.

For more information about setting up Web servers to require SSL, refer to "Creating a Virtual Server," in Appendix O.

Clicking the Click Here To Learn More link starts your browser and displays a page on Microsoft's Web site that lists Web Presence Providers (WPP) who sell Web space with the FrontPage Server Extensions installed.

To locate a WPP that offers full support for FrontPage-extended or SharePoint Team Web sites, visit either *http://www.microsoftwpp.com/wppsearch* or *http://www.actionjackson.com.*

When you click OK, FrontPage will try to connect to the remote Web site you specified. If that Web site has security controls in effect, FrontPage might display the dialog box prompt that appears in Figure 16-4, prompting you for an authorized user name and password. For updating an existing server-based Web, this must be a user name with authoring privileges. For creating a new server-based Web, the user name must be an administrator of the new Web's parent.

Figure 16-4. This dialog box asks for a user name and password combination that has access to a Web server.

Troubleshooting

Unable to open remote Web site

When you first connect to a remote Web site, the message box shown in Figure 16-5 might appear. This indicates that FrontPage couldn't establish communication with the remote Web site server.

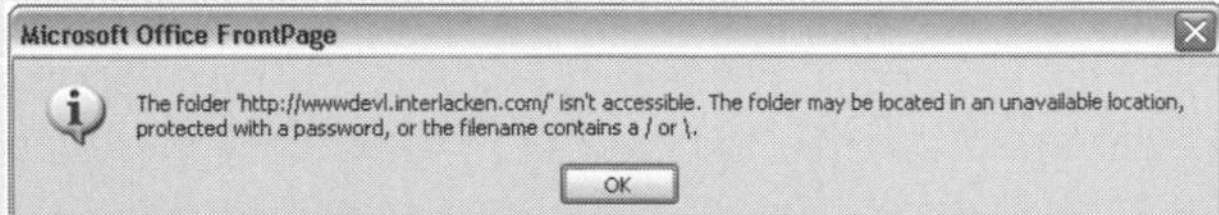

Figure 16-5. This message box indicates a failure to connect with the FrontPage Server Extensions at the remote Web site.

Here are the four most likely causes of this problem and the most likely solutions:

- **The Web server might not have the FrontPage Server Extensions installed.** If you believe that the FrontPage Server Extensions are installed on the remote Web site server, contact the server administrator and ask to have the Server Health jobs run against the remote Web site. If that fails, ask to have the extensions reinstalled.

  For more information about the checking server health, refer to "Checking Server Health," on page 481.

  If you believe that the FrontPage Server Extensions aren't installed, you can:

  - Contact the server administrator and ask to have the extensions installed.

  - Contact your Web provider or IT department and ask for space on a Web server that runs the server extensions.
  - Find a new Web provider that supports the FrontPage Server Extensions.
  - Publish your Web by WebDAV or FTP.
- **The Web server might be temporarily out of service.** If so:
  - Wait to see whether the connectivity problem goes away.
  - If you have an intermittent Internet connection (such as a dial-up line), make sure it's active.
  - Check connectivity to the remote server by pointing your browser to one of its pages. If you can't access the remote server and also can't access any other sites on the same network, contact your network provider. If you can access sites almost anywhere but the remote server, contact whoever administers the remote server.
- **If your connection is through a proxy server, the proxy server settings might be incorrect.** FrontPage uses the same Internet settings as Internet Explorer. This means that you can resolve FrontPage proxy server problems by resolving Internet Explorer proxy server problems. The location of these settings tends to change with each version of Internet Explorer, but to see the settings in Internet Explorer 6, choose Internet Options from the Tools menu, click the Connections tab, and click LAN Settings. Contact whoever administers the proxy server for the correct settings. If Internet Explorer can browse the remote server, any inability to publish in FrontPage isn't a proxy server problem. A *proxy server* is a special network device that isolates a private network from the Internet. It lets computers on the private network browse Internet sites, but blocks computers on the Internet from connecting to those on the internal network.
- **An error might have occurred in the Web server.** This is an explanation of last resort. If all else fails, contact the folks who operate the remote Web site server and ask them to check it for proper operation. Some actions they might take include checking the Event Log for unusual errors, running Check And Fix on the remote Web site, reinstalling the FrontPage Server Extensions, stopping and restarting the Web server, and rebooting the entire server.

Creating a New Remote Web Site Location

To create a new Web site on a remote FrontPage-extended or Windows SharePoint Services Web server, simply specify the path you want it to have. However, all folders but the last must already exist. For example, to create a Web at *http://yourserver/veggies/green/broccoli/* the path *http://yourserver/veggies/green/* must already exist.

If the remote Web site location you specify doesn't already contain a server-based Web, the prompt shown in Figure 16-6 appears.

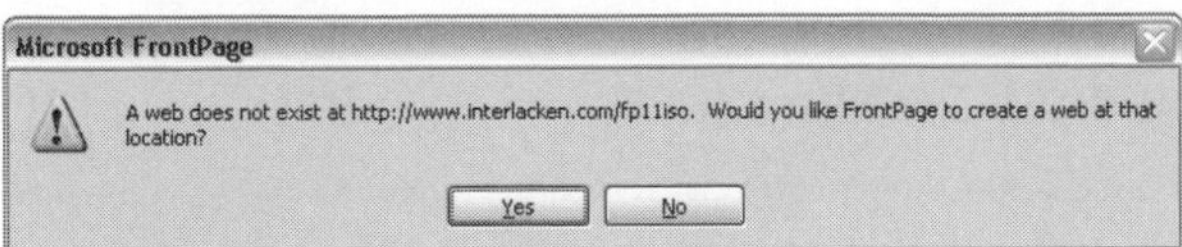

Figure 16-6. If you specify a remote Web site that doesn't exist, FrontPage displays this message box to ask whether FrontPage should create one.

Here you have the following options:

- Click Yes if you want to create a new server-based Web site at the destination location. If your current user name and password don't have authority to create a Web at the given location, FrontPage prompts you for a user name and password that does. Given the required credentials, FrontPage creates a new, blank Web site at the given location.
- Click No to quit and start over.

Neither WebDAV nor FTP servers support FrontPage-based Web sites. As a result, you can't create a new FrontPage-based Web site simply by specifying a non-existent location. In fact, you can't even create new starting folders this way. The best you can do is to fill a new, empty folder with content.

Publishing to a disk-based Web is quite handy for creating backup copies of a Web, for moving a Web to a drive with more space, and for putting Webs on a removable drive (a ZIP or JAZ drive, for example) for portability. To create a new disk-based Web:

1. Open the Remote Web Site Properties dialog box.
2. Under Remote Web Site, specify File System.
3. In the Remote Web Site Location box, enter the local or network path you want. As long as the drive letter in a local path or the server and share name in a network path exist, FrontPage will create any missing folders.
4. Click OK to create the Web site, or click Cancel to quit with no action.
5. If you clicked OK and the disk location you specify in the Remote Web Site Location box isn't already a FrontPage-based Web site, FrontPage displays a message box similar to that shown in Figure 16-6. Click Yes to create the Web site, or click No to quit.

Setting Publishing Options

Two additional tabs in the Remote Web Site Properties dialog box specify options that will apply during the publish operation. The first of these tabs, Optimize HTML, filters any elements you deem undesirable out of your Web pages. The section "Optimizing Published HTML Code," later in this chapter, will explain the options on this tab.

The Publishing tab in the Remote Web Site Properties dialog box controls the way FrontPage decides which files to publish. This tab appears in Figure 16-7.

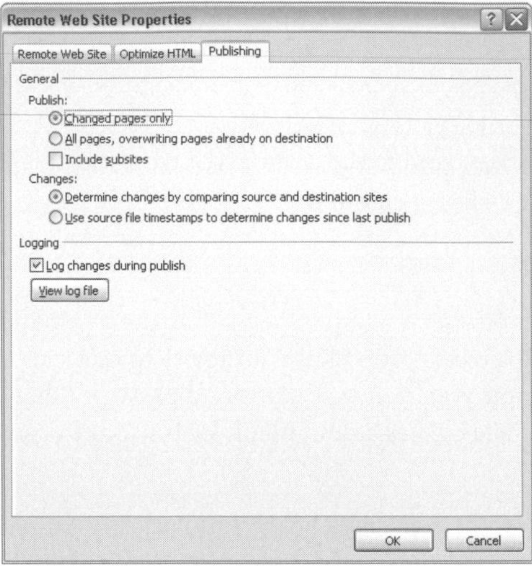

Figure 16-7. This tab configures and saves various settings related to publishing a Web site.

Specifically, the Publishing tab controls these options:

- **Publish** Determines the overall strategy for publishing content from one site to the other.
  - **Changed Pages Only** Bypasses copying any file from the source Web site to the destination Web site if the files in each site appear to be identical.
  - **All Pages, Overwriting Pages Already On Destination** Copies every file to the destination Web site that exists in the source Web site.
  - **Include Subsites** Tells FrontPage whether to publish all Web sites contained within the source Web site. To publish these sites, select this check box. To take no action regarding them, clear this check box.
- **Changes** Specifies how FrontPage should compare files in the two Web sites.
  - **Determine Changes By Comparing Source And Destination Sites** Determines which files to copy between Web sites by downloading a directory listing of the remote Web site and comparing it to current directory information for the local Web site. This method provides the most accurate results but requires time to download the remote Web site's directory listing. If the remote Web site is large and the communications link is slow, this time can amount to several minutes.
  - **Use Source File Timestamps To Determine Changes Since Last Publish.** Determines which files in the source Web site have changes by comparing each file's date and time of last update to the date and time of the last publish operation. This method is less accurate than comparing the source and remote Web sites, because in some cases it overwrites changes other people have made to the remote Web site. Of course, if you're the only person who publishes to the given

remote Web site, this isn't an issue. The primary advantage of this method lies in not having to download a directory listing from the remote Web site.

- **Logging** Tells FrontPage whether to keep a log of changes that occur during publishing.
  - **Log Changes During Publish** If selected, tells FrontPage to keep a log of each change that publishing makes to either Web site. If this check box isn't selected, FrontPage doesn't create a log.
  - **View Log File** Displays the log for the most recent publish operation.

Controlling the Publish Operation

Once you've established the location of the remote Web site, FrontPage updates Remote Web Site view to show the contents of the local Web site in the list on the left and the contents of the remote Web site in the list on the right. Each list contains more column headings than you'll probably be able to see; fortunately, both lists have horizontal scroll bars. Here's the complete list of column headings:

- **Name** The name of the file or folder. This is the only column that contains information about folders; the remaining columns pertain only to files.
- **Status** The result of comparing each page in the in current Web site to its counterpart in the other Web site. Table 16-2 lists the possibilities.

Table 16-2. Publishing Item Status Codes

Icon	Status	Description
(none)	Unchanged	The given file exists on both Web sites and the versions are equal. During a normal publish operation, which publishes changed pages only, FrontPage won't copy any such files to the other Web site.
➡	Publish	Either the given file doesn't exist in the other Web site, or it exists with an expected, older version. FrontPage always copies files with this status to the other Web site.
⊗	Don't Publish	FrontPage won't publish the given file because you or someone else told it not to.
?	Conflict	The given file exists in both Web sites, but both copies have changed since the last publishing operation. Publishing the file in either direction will overwrite someone's changes.

- **Modified** The date and time anyone last updated the file.
- **Author** The identity of the last person who updated the file.
- **Type** The file extension.
- **Size** The size of the file. The suffix *B* indicates bytes, *KB* indicates kilobytes, and so forth.

Tip **Exclude certain files from publishing**

To prevent FrontPage from publishing a given file, right-click it, and choose Don't Publish from the shortcut menu.

To cancel a Don't Publish instruction already in effect, right-click the file, and once again choose Don't Publish. This toggles off the Don't Publish setting.

You can also toggle the Don't Publish setting in the Folder List or in Folders view.

Dealing with Conflict

To understand how file conflicts occur, consider the following scenario:

1. On Monday, you publish your working copy of a Web site to its public Web server. This synchronizes the versions of all the files on the public Web server with the versions in your working copy.
2. On Tuesday, someone else in your group creates a second working copy by publishing the public Web site to another location.
3. On Wednesday, that person publishes some changed pages back to the public Web site.
4. On Thursday, you make changes to one of the files that your coworker changed and try publishing them to the public Web site. FrontPage notices that the version on the public server isn't the same version you last synchronized with your working copy of the same Web. In short, FrontPage notices that you're about to overwrite your coworker's changes.

When this occurs, Remote Web Site View displays a status of Conflict in both the Local Web Site and Remote Web Site list boxes. In addition, during a publishing operation, FrontPage displays the dialog box shown later in Figure 16-13, asking whether to overwrite the target file or leave the conflict unresolved.

Here's how to navigate through the file and folder listings for either Web site:

- To view the contents of a folder, double-click its entry in the list box.

Up One Level

- To display the folder that contains the current selection in the list, click the Up One Level icon that appears above the list.

Delete

- To delete a file or folder, select it, and then click the Delete icon above the list.
- To refresh the contents of either list, click the Refresh icon above that list. This is useful if you think that the site's content might have changed.

Refresh

Right-clicking any file or folder in either Web site displays the shortcut menu show in Figure 16-8.

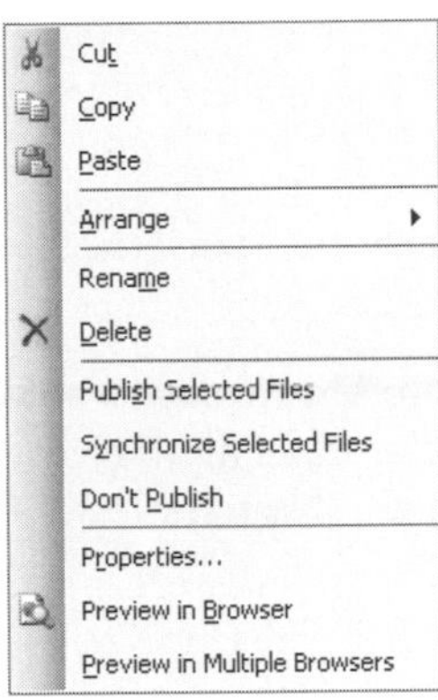

Figure 16-8. This shortcut menu appears after you right-click any file or folder in Remote Web Site view.

Here are explanations of this menu's commands:

- **Cut** Puts the selected file or folder name on the Clipboard and adds a Paste option for storing it elsewhere. After you paste it, the original file or folder is deleted.
- **Copy** Like Cut, puts the selected file or folder on the Clipboard and adds a Paste option. However, the original file or folder is retained after you paste it.
- **Paste** Copies a file or folder marked on the Clipboard to the current destination. If a Cut command put the source file or folder on the Clipboard, a Paste command deletes it.
- **Arrange** Sorts the contents of the list by any column heading. A submenu lists the available choices.
- **Rename** Makes the name of a file or folder available for editing.
- **Delete** Erases a file or folder from its current location.
- **Publish Selected Files** Immediately copies any selected files or folders to the other Web site. The site you right-clicked is always the sender.

- **Synchronize Selected Files** Immediately copies any selected files or folders so that both sites contain the newest versions of those files or folders.
- **Don't Publish** Toggles the Don't Publish state of any selected files between Publish and Don't Publish.
- **Properties** Displays the normal FrontPage Properties dialog box for the current file or folder.

Chapter 16

For more information about the FrontPage property sheet for files, refer to "Working with Folders View," on page 180, and "Using the Table of Contents Based on Page Category Component," on page 727.

For more information about the FrontPage property sheet for folders, refer to "Reviewing Folder Settings," on page 1144.

- **Preview In Browser** Displays the current Web page in the browser you most recently specified.
- **Preview In Multiple Browsers** Displays the current Web page in each browser installed on your computer.

Three buttons appear between the Local Web Site and Remote Web Site lists. Here's what they do:

- --> **(Publish Selected Files From The Local Web Site To The Remote Web Site).** This button is available only if the current selection is one or more files or folders in the Local Web Site list. In that case, clicking the button publishes the selected files to the remote Web site.
- <-- **(Publish Selected Files From The Remote Web Site To The Local Web Site).** This button is available only after you've selected one or more files or folders in the Remote Web Site list. Clicking the button publishes those files or folders to the local Web site.
- <--> **(Synchronize Selected Files).** This button is available when the current selection is one or more files or folders in either Web site list. Clicking it synchronizes those files or folders in both Web sites (that is, it publishes files in either direction so that both sites contain the most current version of each file).

The Remote Web Site toolbar provides these three controls. The first and third are available only after you've identified a remote Web site.

- **View** Select a display option from this drop-down list. Here are the possibilities:
  - **Folder Contents** Select this option to display a hierarchical list of folders and files.
  - **Files To Publish** Select this option to display a list of files FrontPage will publish if you click the Publish Web Site button.
  - **Files Not To Publish** Select this option to display a list of files you or other designers have flagged Do Not Publish.
  - **Files In Conflict** Select this option to display a list of files for which publishing one site will overwrite changes on the other.
- **Remote Web Site Properties** Displays the Remote Web Site Properties dialog box and selects the Remote Web Site tab.
- **Optimize Published HTML** Displays the Remote Web Site Properties dialog box and selects the Optimize HTML tab.

Initiating the Publish Operation

Before you start any publish operation, you should check these settings in the Publish All Changed Pages section in the lower right corner in Remote Web Site view. For an illustration, refer back to Figure 16-1.

- **Local To Remote** Select this option if you want to copy changed pages from the local Web site to the remote Web site.
- **Remote To Local** Select this option if you want to copy changed pages from the remote Web site to the local Web site.
- **Synchronize** Select this option if, when the publish operation completes, you want both Web sites to contain the newest versions of all files.

When you're satisfied that these and all other settings are correct, click the Publish Web Site button.

When you publish a FrontPage-based Web site to a WebDAV or an FTP location, FrontPage doesn't copy the site's internal files to the target location. Because the WebDAV or FTP site has no use for this information, transmitting it would be a waste of time, network bandwidth, and server disk space. This is important, however, because publishing from a FrontPage-based Web site to a WebDAV or an FTP location and then publishing from the WebDAV or FTP location to another FrontPage-based Web site will lose information. This affects any kind of information that isn't part of a Web page, database, or other normal content file—information like the Navigation view diagram and Web settings, for example.

Monitoring the Publish Operation

Regardless of the types of the local and remote Web sites, Web publishing basically occurs in four phases:

1. FrontPage determines which files need to be added, replaced, or deleted on the destinFation Web site.

   If the Publishing tab of the Remote Web Site Properties dialog box specifies Determine Changes By Comparing Source And Destination Sites, FrontPage makes this determination by comparing file and folder timestamps in the source and destination Web sites. To do this, it must first retrieve directory listings of all the files and folders in the remote site.

   If the same tab specifies Use Source File Timestamps To Determine Changes Since Last Publish, FrontPage determines which files to publish by comparing timestamps in the source Web site to the date of the last publish operation. This is less accurate but avoids retrieving file and folder information from the destination site.

   Figure 16-7 previously illustrated the Remote Web Site Properties dialog box.

2. FrontPage copies all the files that need to be added or replaced, plus instructions to delete those that are no longer needed, plus any changes to Navigation view, database connections, or any other Web settings. (If both Web sites are running either the

FrontPage Server Extensions or Windows SharePoint Services, FrontPage transmits this information in compressed form.)

3. This step occurs only if both sites are running the FrontPage Server Extensions or Windows SharePoint Services. In that case, FrontPage or SharePoint software on the destination server decompresses and processes all the updates on the remote Web site server. This includes both normal file updates, Web settings, and recalculation of hyperlinks.
4. FrontPage reports completion of the publishing process.

Figure 16-9 shows the status display for each of these steps.

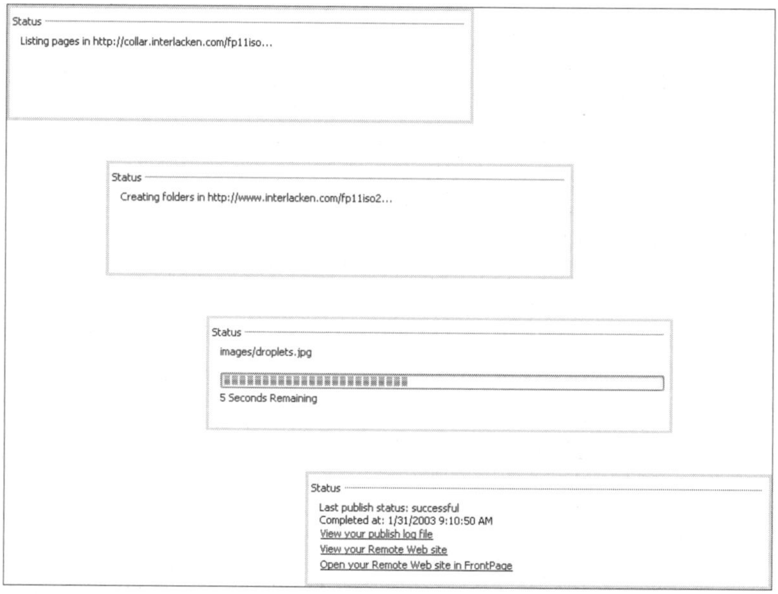

Status
Listing pages in http://collar.interlacken.com/fp11iso...

Status
Creating folders in http://www.interlacken.com/fp11iso2...

Status
images/droplets.jpg
5 Seconds Remaining

Status
Last publish status: successful
Completed at: 1/31/2003 9:10:50 AM
View your publish log file
View your Remote Web site
Open your Remote Web site in FrontPage

Figure 16-9. These are the four status messages you receive during a successful FrontPage Publish operation.

If a message like one shown in Figure 16-10 appears, it means that the Web you're publishing uses features that the remote Web site can't support. This can occur if, for example, the FrontPage Server Extensions on the destination server are outdated or absent. However, despite the error messages, FrontPage still copies the listed pages to the given destination.

> **Caution** Be very careful about publishing a Web site to a location that can't support all its features and then publishing from that location to a more capable one. In some cases, the less-capable location will discard information the features need to work. Disk-based Webs exhibit the fewest problems in this regard, but the best approach is to always publish directly to a capable site.

Figure 16-10. This dialog box warns you of any pages that won't work properly after being published to a disk-based Web.

The dialog box shown in Figure 16-11 is quite similar in appearance and function. In this case, a hidden folder is the unsupported feature. Although a Web server can automatically hide folders with names that begin with an underscore (_), the destination in this case is a disk-based Web that can't.

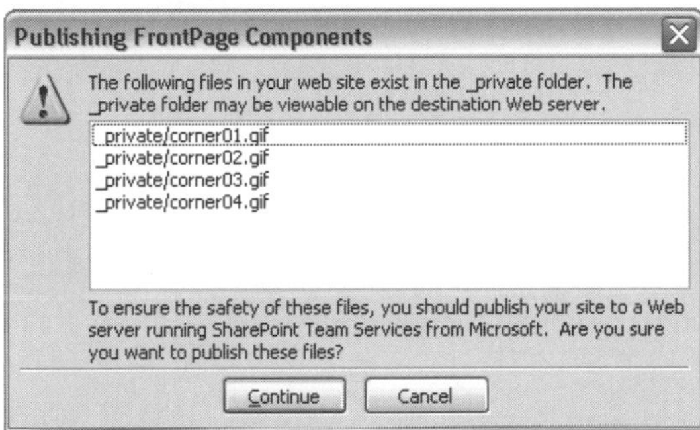

Figure 16-11. When you publish a Web site, FrontPage warns you if the source Web site uses features that the destination Web site can't support.

Frequently Asked Question

Can I publish my FrontPage 2003 Web to a server running earlier FrontPage Server Extensions?

FrontPage 2003 can publish to any Web server running any version of the FrontPage Server Extensions. To this extent, FrontPage 2003 is fully compatible with all earlier versions of the extensions. In fact, no new extensions are available for FrontPage 2003.

Of course, Web Part Pages, any other page that uses a Web Part, and any pages that use features on the FrontPage 2003 Data menu require Windows SharePoint Services 2.0. These features won't work at all on any other type of Web server.

Any features that were new to FrontPage 2002 and involve server-side processing, however, do require the FrontPage Server Extensions 2002. These features won't work properly (or at all) on earlier versions of the extensions.

For a list of features that require the later FrontPage Server Extensions, please see "Components That Require FrontPage 2002 Extensions," article 281532, in the Microsoft Knowledge Base.

If at any time you want to stop the publishing process, click the Stop button in the bottom right corner of Remote Web Site view. Otherwise, when the last set of messages shown previously in Figure 16-9 appears, FrontPage provides three convenient hyperlinks:

- **View Your Publish Log File.** Displays the log file from the publish operation that just ended. Figure 16-12 illustrates a typical log. However, this log won't be available if the Log Changes During Publish check box on the Publishing tab of the Remote Web Site Properties dialog box is cleared.

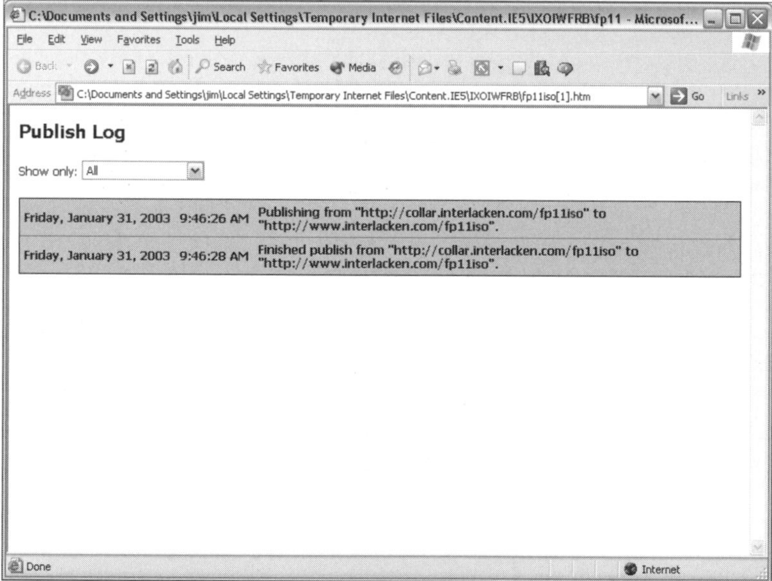

Figure 16-12. FrontPage can create a log file like this to show you the results of a Publish operation.

- **View Your Remote Web Site.** Displays the remote Web site's home page in your browser.
- **Open Your Remote Web Site In FrontPage.** Opens the remote Web site in FrontPage.

The Conflicts dialog box, shown in Figure 16-13, appears when a publish operation detects that updates to the same file occurred on both the Local site and the Remote site (that is, when the file's status in Remote Site View is Conflict).

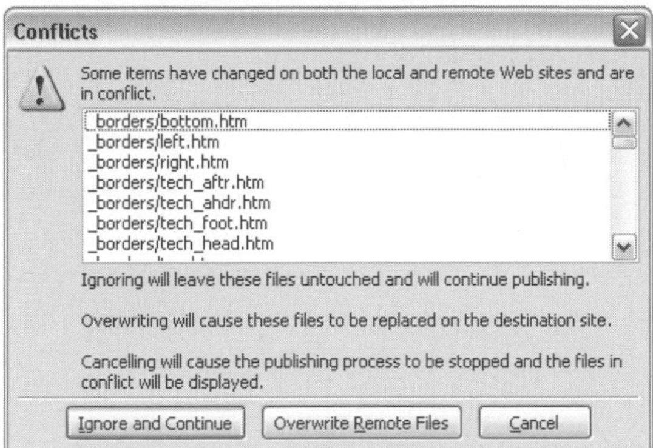

Figure 16-13. This message box appears when corresponding files on the source and remote Web sites both get updated with no intervening synchronization.

When this dialog box appears, you have three options.

- **Ignore and Continue** Click this button if you want to ignore the conflicting files on the Remote Site.
- **Overwrite Destination Files** Click this button if you want to ignore the conflicts and force your updates onto the Remote site.
- **Cancel** Click this button to abandon the publishing operation.

If you proceed with the publishing operation, FrointPage will display the following dialog box for each file in conflict.

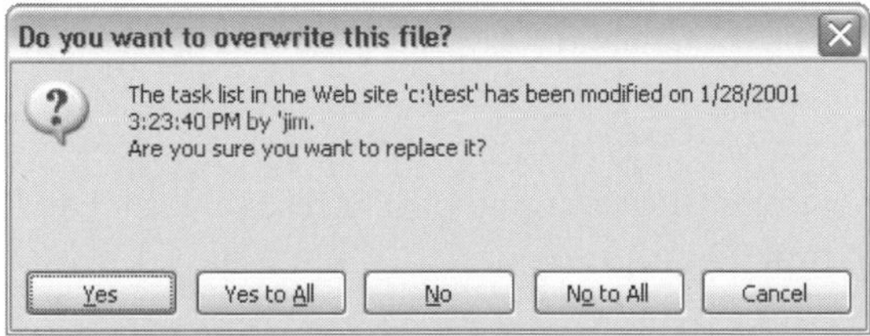

The buttons in this dialog box provide these options:

- **Yes** Replaces the existing file on the destination Web site with the corresponding file in the source Web site.
- **Yes To All** Works the same as Yes. Additionally, it applies the Yes answer to all future prompts of this type, for the duration of the current publish operation.
- **No** Bypasses the update of the questionable file, but continues the publish operation.
- **No To All** Works the same as No. Additionally, it applies the No answer to all future prompts of this type, for the duration of the current publish operation.
- **Cancel** Bypasses the update of the questionable file and terminates the publish operation.

Note that this scenario can occur even if you're the only person who updates the remote Web site. If you make spot corrections to the destination Web site or publish to the same Web from two different working copies, the roguish coworker might be you!

Figure 16-14 shows the message that appears if the remote Web site contains files not present in the local Web site. FrontPage offers you the choice of keeping or deleting such files.

Do you want to remove this file?
The file 'new_page_1.htm' exists on the destination server but does not exist in the current Web. Would you like FrontPage to remove it from 'http://www.interlacken.com/fp11iso/NavWeb'?
Yes
Yes to All
No
No to All
Cancel

Figure 16-14. When you tell the FrontPage Publish command to make two Web sites the same, it warns you before deleting any files in the destination site that don't exists in the source site.

Optimizing Published HTML Code

Many designers put things in Web pages they don't really want visitors to see. This might be intentional, as with comments and white space that make the pages easier to maintain but have no value to Web visitors. It might also be unintentional, such as component settings FrontPage saves as HTML comments or fake HTML attributes.

> **Tip** It's never a good idea to let Web visitors see HTML, JavaScript, or any other sort of comments that describe a Web page or site. Especially with malicious visitors, the less you tell them, the better.

Fortunately, FrontPage 2003 can examine every scrap of HTML it publishes and filter out various kinds of content. To activate this feature:

1. Open the Web site in FrontPage.
2. Click the Web Site tab above the main editing window, and then click the Remote Web Site tab below the editing window.
3. Click the Remote Web Site Properties button on the Remote Web Site View toolbar.
4. When the Remote Web Site Properties dialog box appears, click the Optimize HTML tab. The dialog box should then resemble Figure 16-15.

The When Publishing, Optimize HTML By Removing The Following Elements check box is a master switch. If you clear it, FrontPage will remember your settings on the Optimize HTML tab, but it won't act on them. If you select this check box, all the other settings will take effect.

The Comments section contains another, slightly less powerful master switch titled All HTML Comments. If you select this check box, the next eight settings will take effect. If you clear it, FrontPage will remember the settings but ignore them during publishing. Here are the eight settings:

- **Author-Time Web Component Comments** Select this check box if you want FrontPage to remove HTML comments that denote the beginning, end, and settings of FrontPage components that run when a designer saves a Web page or recalculates a Web site.

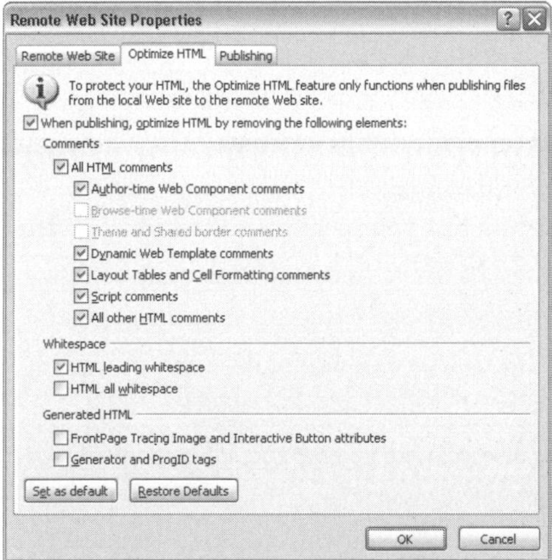

Figure 16-15. As FrontPage publishes your Web pages, it can remove elements you consider extraneous or harmful.

- **Browse-Time Web Component Comments** Select this check box if you want FrontPage to remove HTML comments that denote the beginning, end, and settings of FrontPage components that run each time a visitor requests the page.
- **Theme And Shared Border Comments** Select this check box to remove the HTML comments that record information about FrontPage themes and shared borders.
- **Dynamic Web Template Comments** Select this check box to remove the HTML comments that record information about Dynamic Web Templates.
- **Layout Tables And Cell Formatting Comments** Select this check box to remove the HTML comments that record information about layout tables and cell formatting.
- **Script Comments** Select this check box to remove comments in JavaScript or Microsoft Visual Basic code that executes in the browser.
- **All Other HTML Comments** Select this check box to remove all other HTML comments. In general, this means every pair of <!-- and --> tags, plus everything between them, provided none of the preceding options apply.

The options in the Whitespace section pertain to spaces, tabs, carriage returns, and linefeeds. Recall that HTML treats any mix-and-match series of these as if it were one space. These options affects only HTML code—not CSS rules, not script code, not anything else.

- **HTML Leading Whitespace** Select this check box if you want to remove all white-space characters between the start of a line and the first non-white-space character.
- **HTML All Whitespace** Select this check box if you want to replace all white-space sequences with a single space. This has the effect of making all of the HTML into one, long, humanly unreadable line.

The options under Generated HTML affect HTML code that FrontPage creates strictly for its own purposes. They are:

- **FrontPage Tracing Image And Interactive Button Attributes** Select this check box to remove these fake HTML attributes:
    - A *tracingsrc* attribute in the <body> tag. When you tell FrontPage to display a special Design view background for the current page, FrontPage remembers the name of that background file in this attribute.
    - Any *fp-style=* and *fp-title=* attributes in an <img> tag. These attributes remember the style and button text you specify for Interactive Button components.
- **Generator And ProgId Tags** Select this box to remove the following tags, which FrontPage adds to every Web page it saves:

```
<meta name="GENERATOR" content="Microsoft FrontPage 6.0">
<meta name="ProgId" content="FrontPage.Editor.Document">
```

  The Optimize HTML tab also provides these special buttons. Both pertain to the default settings for this tab.
- **Set As Default** Click this button to save the current settings as personal defaults.
- **Restore Defaults** Click this button to restore the settings that were in effect when you last clicked the Set As Default button.

These buttons have no special relevance to the settings for the current Web; you save those when you click the OK button. They're much more useful for remembering a certain combination of settings and applying them to other Web sites you open in the future.

There are several important things to remember about the settings on the Optimize HTML tab:

- They have no immediate effect. FrontPage removes the elements you specify when it publishes the pages between Web sites, and not before.
- They have no effect on the source Web site. FrontPage removes the elements as it reads each source page and sends it to the destination Web site.
- If you remove elements from a source Web site as you publish and then later publish the destination site back to the source, all the elements you remove will be well and truly gone. FrontPage might revert to default settings for parts of your Web page and might not recognize some components at all.
- When you optimize HTML as you publish, the HTML that arrives at the remote Web site will be different from the HTML you tested on the local Web site. The chance for a malfunction is small but non-zero, especially if you're working with an old site that contains HTML errors from antiquity.

- Even if the Web visitor is using a 9600 bps modem with no compression, the time required to transmit 1000 characters of HTML is about 1 second. If the visitor has a 56 kbps modem with compression, the time to transmit 1000 white-space characters is a tenth of a second or less. Think about this before agonizing over the size of your HTML file. In all probability, you'll achieve greater benefit from optimizing picture files.

Publishing Single Files and Folders

Sometimes it's very handy to publish just a single file or folder. For example, you might know exactly which files you changed recently and want to avoid the time required to determine changes by comparing the source and destination Web sites over a slow link. Another scenario occurs when your working copy of a Web contains both finished and unfinished changes, and you want to publish only the finished ones. FrontPage provides three ways of doing this:

- Open both Webs in FrontPage, and drag the files or folders you want to publish from one Folder List or Folders view to the other.
- If you want to publish individual files or folders to the remote Web site that Remote Web Site view is configured to use, take these steps:
    1. Right-click the file or folder in the Folder List or in Folders view.
    2. Choose Publish Selected Files from the shortcut menu.
    3. FrontPage displays the progress message shown in Figure 16-16. When this message disappears, the operation is complete.

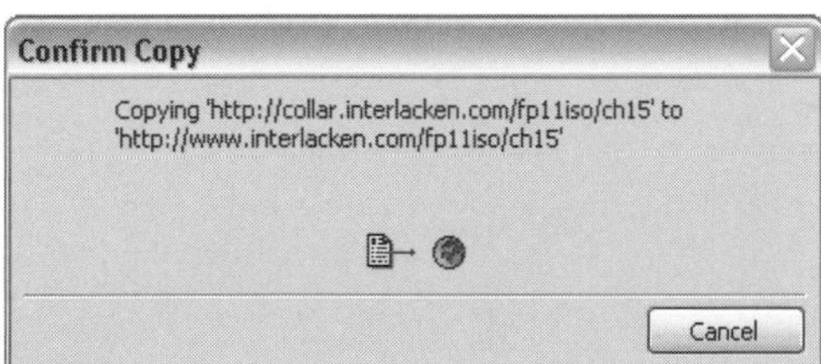

Figure 16-16. FrontPage displays this progress message while publishing individual Web pages you select.

- To publish individual files in either direction from Remote Web Site view, proceed as follows:
    1. Switch to Remote Web Site view.
    2. In the list for the source Web, select the file or folder you want to publish, and then do one of the following:
        - Right-click the selection, and then choose Publish Selected Files from the shortcut menu.
        - Click the --> or <-- button between the two Web site lists. (Only one of these buttons will be enabled, depending on which Web site list contains the file or folder you selected.

Publishing Web Content Through Web Folders

Like all Microsoft Office 2003 applications, FrontPage also supports Web publishing through a facility called Web Folders. Web Folders are HTTP locations that show up in My Network Places. Web Folders also appear when you click the My Network Places desktop icon or the My Network Places icon on the My Places bar of Office applications. Here's the procedure for using Web Folders from the desktop:

1 Double-click the My Network Places icon on your desktop.

If the Web location you want is already listed, double-click it. If not, add it by double-clicking the Add Network Place icon.

Caution Any locations you add to Web Folders must be Web servers running Windows SharePoint Services, the FrontPage Server Extensions, WebDAV, or FTP. Otherwise, the Web Folders software can't communicate with the locations.

2 Add the Web site as a Network Place per the resulting wizard's instructions.

3 The Web Folders window now resembles Figure 16-17. Instead of folder locations on your local disk or file server, this window shows Internet addresses.

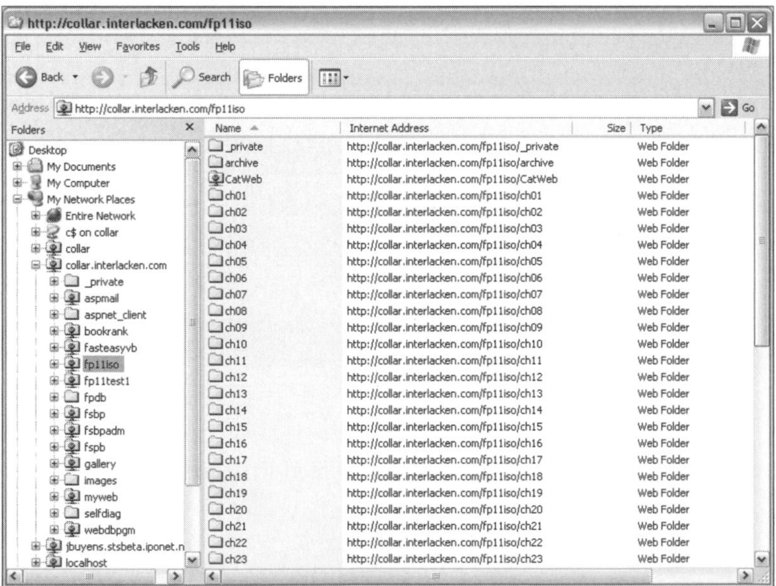

Figure 16-17. Office XP's Web Folders feature handles files on remote FrontPage Web servers as easily as those on a local disk.

4 To transfer files and folders to and from the remote Web server, drag them in and out just as you would in Windows Explorer.

Frequently Asked Questions

Why doesn't Microsoft Windows include a graphical FTP interface?

Beginning with Internet Explorer 5.5, it does. Follow this procedure to set up graphical connectivity to any FTP server:

1. Open My Network Places, and double-click Add A Network Place.
2. The Add Network Place Wizard will start. If it displays an opening page with no options appears, click Next to proceed.
3. If a page titled Where Do You Want To Create The Network Place? appears, select Choose Another Network Location; Specify The Address Of A Web Site, Network Location, Or FTP Site and then click Next.
4. Type an *ftp://* URL in the Internet or Network address box, and then click Next.
5. To log on to the FTP server anonymously, select the Log On Anonymously check box.

   To log on with a user account, clear the check box, and enter the name of the account in the User Name box.
6. Click Next to display the final page of the wizard. The value in the Enter A Name For This Network Place box will become the name of a shortcut that connects to the FTP server. The default (and an excellent choice) is the computer name in the URL you entered in step 3. Override this name if you want.
7. Click Finish to create a shortcut and connect to the FTP server. If the FTP server requires a password, Windows displays a dialog box in which you can enter the password.
8. Click OK. FrontPage connects to the FTP server and then, with the dialog box shown previously in Figure 16-4, prompts you for a user name and password acceptable to the FTP server.

To connect to the same FTP connection any time in the future, simply double-click its shortcut in My Network Places. This shortcut will also appear in the My Network Places section of most file-oriented dialog boxes in recent versions of Microsoft Office. And yes, this means that you can read Office documents from and write them to FTP servers as easily as your local disk.

That's still too complicated. Is there something easier?

OK. Click the Start menu, choose Run, type an FTP address such as **ftp://ftp.microsoft.com**, and press Enter.

I can't cope with that either. Is there an even easier way?

Type an FTP address such as **ftp://ftp.microsoft.com** in the Address bar of any Windows Explorer or Internet Explorer window.

My Internet Explorer window doesn't have an Address bar. Now what?

Choose Toolbars from the View menu, and then choose Address Bar.

Connecting through the Run menu or an Internet Explorer window always results in an anonymous logon. Is there a way to log on with an account?

Right-click the main part of the window, and choose Login As from the shortcut menu.

What if I don't have Windows 2000 or Windows XP?

The Start, Run, and Address bar method works on any system that has Internet Explorer 5.5 or later installed.

Can I use these graphical FTP windows to watch my grandmother's Web cam in Zanzibar?

No.

Transporting a Web Site on Removable Media

To transport a Web on ZIP, DirectCD, or other read-write removable media, first open the local Web site and publish it as a disk-based Web on the removable media. When the removable media arrives at its destination, open the disk-based Web site in FrontPage and then publish it to its permanent location. A similar procedure applies if you prefer to use packages. Open the local Web site, export the package to the read-write removable media, and then open the remote Web site and import the package. (The next section will explain packages.)

Transporting a FrontPage-based Web site on CD-R or DVD-R media presents additional challenges because the Publish Web Site and Export Package commands update certain files multiple times. Therefore, you must do the following:

1. Publish the Web or export the package to a temporary disk location.
2. Use your CD or DVD creation software to create a compact disc.

If you created a package, at the destination, you should:

1. Use FrontPage to open the permanent location you want.
2. Import the package.

If you created a disk-based Web, at the destination, you should:

1. Copy the disk-based Web or package from the CD or DVD to a temporary hard disk folder.
2. In Windows Explorer, right-click the temporary hard disk folder, and then choose Properties from the shortcut menu.
3. When the folder's Properties dialog box appears, on the General tab, clear the Read-Only check box, and then click OK.
4. When the Confirm Attribute Changes dialog box appears, make sure Apply Changes To This Folder, Subfolders, And Files is checked, and then click OK.
5. If you transported a disk-based Web, open it, and then publish it to the permanent location you want.

Exporting and Importing Web Packages

FrontPage 2003 provides a special way of using external media to transport content between SharePoint Team Services sites—namely *packages*. Packages can export and import not only Web pages and their associated files, but also SharePoint lists, list content, and other objects as well. In addition, packages can automatically identify and include dependent files such as pictures and style sheets. This ensures that the package will work seamlessly on the destination Web site.

Physically, a package is a single file that contains any number of logical files in compressed format. In this respect, a package is somewhat like a ZIP or Windows CAB file. Here's an overview of how packages work:

- To create a package, you open the source Web site in FrontPage and then:
  1. Choose Packages from the Tools menu, and then Export from the submenu.
  2. Specify the content you want to send and then click OK to create the package file.
- To transport the package, you send it as an e-mail attachment, upload it by FTP, carry it on a compact disc, or use any other method that's handy.
- To install the package, you open the destination Web site in FrontPage and then:
  1. Choose Packages from the Tools menu, and then Import from the submenu.
  2. Use a standard File Open dialog box to locate the package file.
  3. Choose an install location and which files from the package you want to install.
  4. Click OK to adds the package content to the destination Web site.

Here's the detailed procedure for creating a package file:

1. Open the source Web site in FrontPage.
2. Choose Packages from the Tools menu, and then choose Export from the submenu.
3. When the Export Web Package dialog box shown in Figure 16-18 appears, use the Files In Web Site list to select the content you want to send. After each selection, click the Add >> button. Any files you selected will then appear in the Files In Package list to the right. In all probability, some additional files will appear in the Files In Package list as well.

   These extra files appear because whenever you add a Web page to a package, FrontPage automatically adds any pictures, style sheets, or other files that the Web page uses. This is very cool, and a major advantage of using packages.

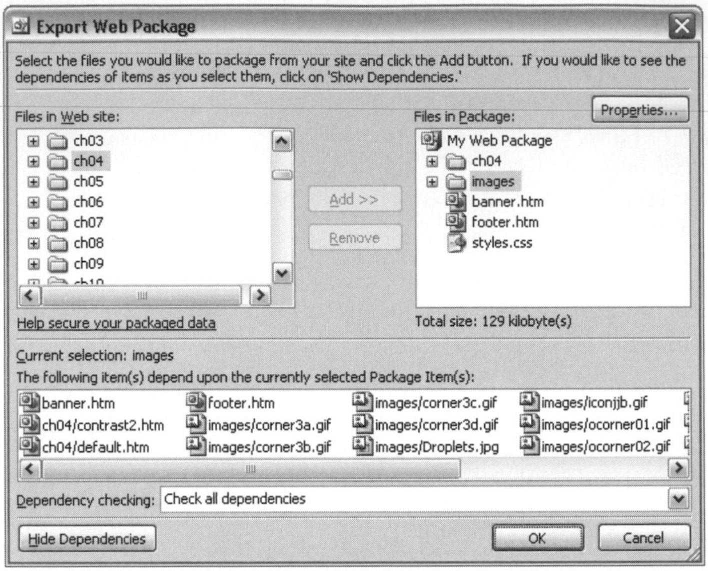

Figure 16-18. Use this dialog box to include files from the current Web in a package.

4 If FrontPage is adding more or fewer dependent files than you want, proceed as follows:

1 Look for a Show Dependencies button in the bottom left corner of the dialog box. If you find it, click it. The Show Dependencies button will change to Hide Dependencies. If the Hide Dependencies button already appears, just go to the next step.

2 Locate the Dependency Checking drop-down list. (It's just above the Hide Dependencies button.) Use this list to specify the type of dependency checking you want. The options are:

Option	Description
Check All Dependencies	Whenever you add a file to the Files In Package list, FrontPage will add every other file that your file uses. This includes pictures, style sheets, hyperlinks, and so forth (but only files in the same Web site).
Check All Dependencies, Except Hyperlinks	This works almost exactly like the previous settings, except that FrontPage won't add files that your file mentions only in hyperlinks.
Do Not Check Dependencies	FrontPage won't add any files to the package automatically. You're completely in control.

5 To preview the effect of the new Dependency Checking selection, click one or more files or folders in either the Files In Web Site or the Files In Package list. The Following Item(s) Depend Upon The Currently Selected Package Item(s) list will list the files FrontPage would add to the package along with the files you selected.

6 Changing the Dependency Checking option doesn't remove any files from the package. To remove files, you must select them in the Files In Package list and then click the Remove button.

7 Click the Properties button to add identifying information to the package. This button displays a Web Package Properties dialog box with text boxes for entering title, description, author, and company information. Click OK to close this dialog box.

8 When the package contains all the files you want, click the OK button in the Export Web Package dialog box.

9 FrontPage will display a standard Save As dialog box. Choose a file name and folder, and then click OK to create the package file. The customary file extension is .fwp.

As you might expect, the process of importing a package is similar. Here are the exact steps you need to perform:

1 Open the destination Web site in FrontPage.

2 Choose Packages from the Tools menu, and then choose Import from the submenu.

3 In the File Open dialog box shown in Figure 16-19, select the package file, and click OK.

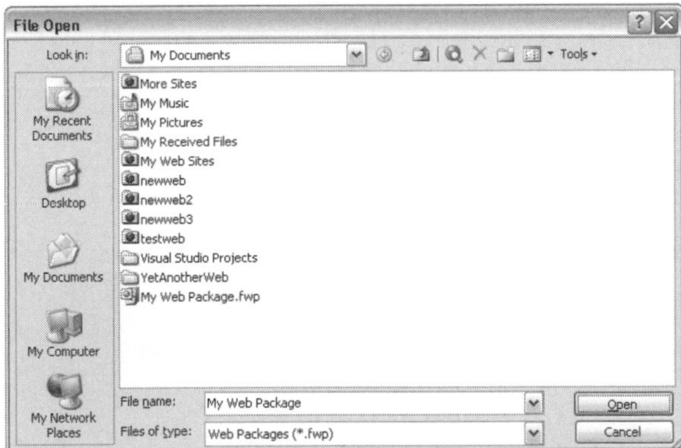

Figure 16-19. FrontPage displays a standard File Open dialog box to find files that contain a Web package.

4 When the Import Web Package dialog box shown in Figure 16-20 appears, review the list of files the package will install.

- To skip installing any file or folder, clear its check box.
- To reverse this action, select the check box.
- To select all files in the package, click the Select All button.
- To unselect all files in the package, click the Unselect All button.

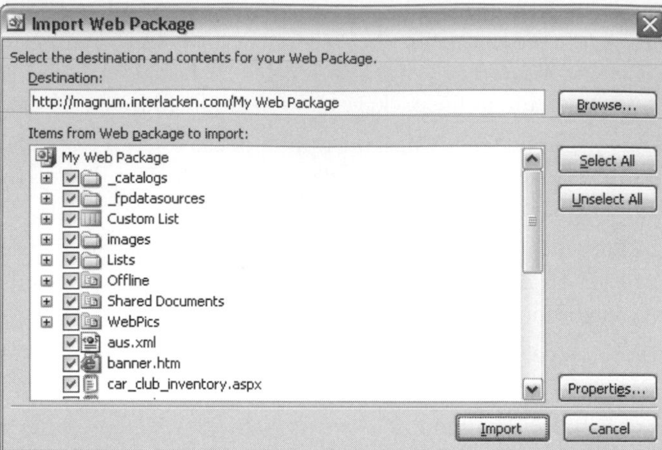

Figure 16-20. Use this dialog box to select the package files you want to install.

5 To view the package title, description, author, and company, click the Properties button. The resulting Web Package Properties dialog box will also display a listing of *external dependencies* (that is, a listing of files that the packages uses but doesn't include). Click OK to close the Web Package Properties dialog box.

6 In the Select A Destination box, enter the name of the folder where FrontPage should install the package files. To locate a folder by point and shoot, click the Browse button.

7 Click the Import button to add the package files to the current Web site. FrontPage will display this confirmation message:

In Summary…

This chapter explained how to publish a FrontPage-based Web site from one location to another. This is the only supported way of copying a Web from place to place without losing any information.

The next chapter explains how to summarize, analyze, and validate the content of a Web.

Chapter 17

Keeping Your Web Site Up-to-Date

As time passes, your Web site will likely grow in size and complexity. Pages will evolve, gaining and losing text, pictures, and hyperlinks along the way. As this process continues, the difficulty of maintaining technical and visual continuity will grow as well. Microsoft FrontPage provides a number of features to assist in ongoing maintenance. These include:

- A way to update hyperlinks automatically when you move or rename a page.
- A command for updating all cross-references and indexes for your Web site.

This chapter also explains how to use Reports view and Hyperlinks view. Reports view displays information and statistics about your Web site, locates apparent problems, and displays usage statistics. Hyperlinks view displays a graphical diagram of the hyperlinks among your pages. All these facilities help you analyze, check, and correct your Web site.

Moving, Renaming, and Reorganizing Pages

As the number of files in your Web site grows, organizing them into folders and establishing naming conventions will become increasingly important. The need to reorganize or rename pages isn't necessarily a sign of poor planning; more often, it's simply a sign that your Web site has grown. A topic that began as a single Web page might, over time, become a dozen pages and warrant its own folder. And a small collection of picture files will likely become difficult to search after growing to a hundred or so pictures.

If you have local or file-sharing access to your Web site's file area, you can move, copy, rename, or delete files with Microsoft Windows Explorer, the command prompt, or any number of utility programs. Even if you don't have such access, you can make changes with an FTP program. Unfortunately, these approaches do nothing to adjust hyperlinks from other pages to the moved or renamed files. Unless you locate and correct these links manually, your Web site won't function properly.

For more information about the mechanics of moving, copying, and deleting files in FrontPage, refer to "Manipulating Files and Folders," on page 89.

Changing file names and locations from within FrontPage avoids the problem of broken hyperlinks because FrontPage corrects links automatically. Suppose, for example, that you have a picture file named clown.jpg that's located in a FrontPage-based Web site. If you open the site in FrontPage and rename the file joker.jpg, FrontPage changes any picture tags, hyperlinks, or other references to the clown.jpg file within that site so that they point to joker.jpg instead. Of course, this works for any type of file, not just picture files, and it also works when you move a file from one folder to another.

Figure 17-1 shows this feature in action. The Web site designer has opened a Web site, switched to Folders view, and renamed the first file listed from cottage.gif to cottage2.gif. After consulting its indexes, FrontPage determines that two pages in the current Web site have links to this file and offers to correct them.

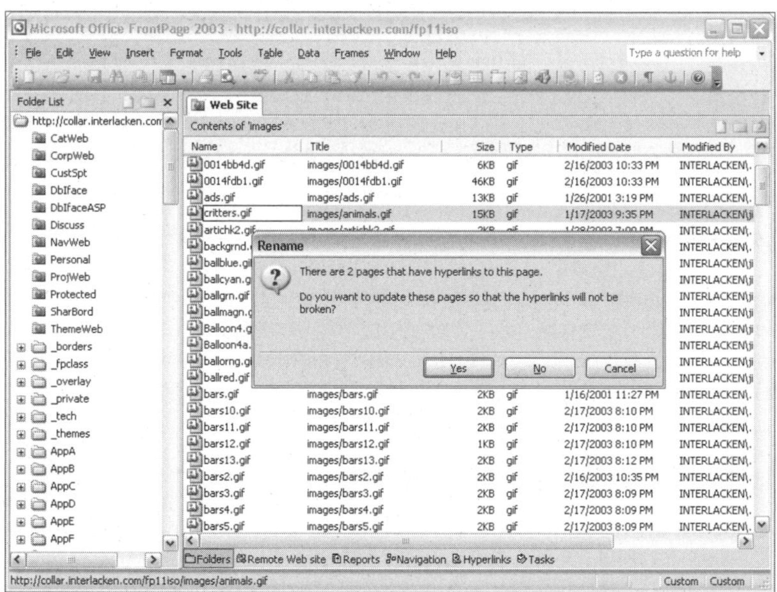

Figure 17-1. When you use FrontPage to rename or relocate a Web file, FrontPage offers to update all links in all pages that refer to that file.

For more information about using other programs to update FrontPage-based Web sites, refer to the Frequently Asked Question sidebar "How Can Programs Other Than FrontPage Safely Update a FrontPage-based Web Site?" later in this chapter.

Keeping Your Web Site Up-to-Date

FrontPage maintains indexes of all links within a Web site and uses these to find and update the necessary Web pages. To keep these indexes accurate, it's best to always use FrontPage for organizing Web pages. Here are several cautions:

- FrontPage corrects hyperlink and picture references only within the current Web site. When you reorganize pages or pictures, whoever maintains the other Web sites will need to manually correct their links to your site.
- If you suspect that FrontPage's indexes are out-of-date, run the Recalculate Hyperlinks command before reorganizing the files. The procedure is described later in this chapter. FrontPage can't update your Web site correctly if its indexes are incorrect.
- Changing a Web site by any means other than FrontPage is the number one cause of incorrect indexes.
- FrontPage can't reliably identify picture tags and hyperlinks coded as values within script code. Thus, FrontPage doesn't always update hyperlinks and picture references located within scripts.
- Close any Web pages open in FrontPage before reorganizing files. FrontPage doesn't update hyperlinks located within open pages.

FrontPage can check spelling on every page in a given Web site. To use this feature, close any pages that are open in the Design view window, choose Spelling from the Tools menu, select the Entire Web Site option, and then click Start.

For more information about site-wide spelling checking, refer to "Checking Spelling in Multiple Pages," on page 248.

Checking Links in Your Web Site

A widely accepted principle of physics is that, left to itself, order inevitably reverts to chaos. Hyperlinks provide a perfect example of such entropy at work. Although FrontPage can greatly reduce instances of broken hyperlinks within your Web site, typing errors and changes at remote sites inevitably break even the most carefully created hyperlinks. FrontPage provides the Hyperlinks report to detect and correct such errors.

All Web site designers should check hyperlinks occasionally, because there's no reliable means to catch changes as they occur throughout the entire World Wide Web. The frequency of checking will vary, depending on the number of links, their volatility, and the level of service you want to provide.

Using Hyperlinks View

Hyperlinks view provides a graphical diagram of a Web site's hyperlink relationships. This is the sort of analysis you might have expected when you first encountered Navigation view. Hyperlinks view provides a display, centered on any page in the current Web site, that illustrates graphically which other pages are related by hyperlink. This can be extremely useful when you're working with complex or unfamiliar Web sites. Figure 17-2 illustrates this view.

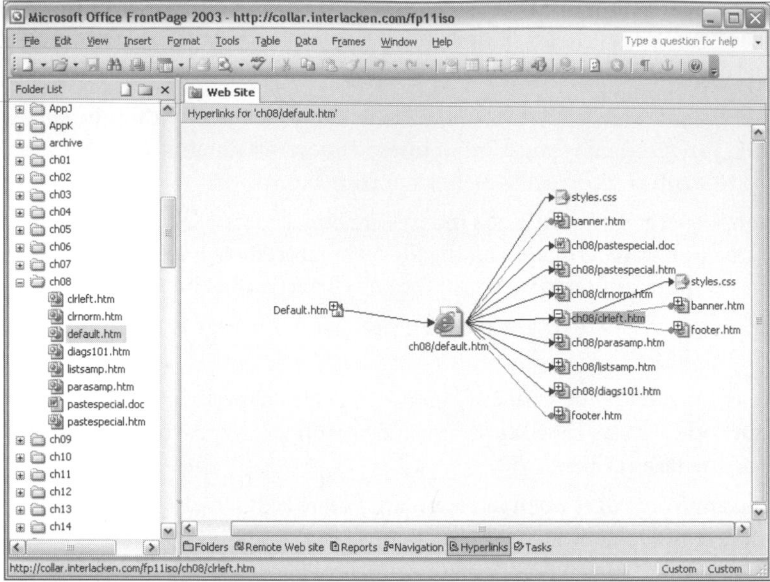

Figure 17-2. FrontPage's Hyperlinks view provides a graphical diagram of the hyperlink relationships within a Web site.

To display Hyperlinks view, first click the Web Site tab above the main editing window and then click the Hyperlinks tab below it. Alternatively, choose Hyperlinks from the View menu. Once the view is displayed, a document pane replaces the main editing window. This pane displays a chart of hyperlinks to and from a *center page.*

You can specify the center page either of two ways: by selecting it in the Folder List, or by right-clicking a page in the document pane and choosing Move To Center from the shortcut menu. Whenever FrontPage displays a new center page, it also displays:

- All pages in the current Web site with hyperlinks to the center page. These appear to the left of the center page, connected with arrows showing the direction of the link.
- All hyperlinks from the center page to any other page. These appear to the right of the center page, again connected by arrows.

Any page flagged with a plus sign icon has additional hyperlinks not displayed. To display those pages, click the plus sign icon. FrontPage will display the additional links and change the icon to a minus sign. To collapse the link display, click its minus sign icon (which will then become a plus sign).

To open any page in Design view for viewing or editing, double-click the body of its Web page icon.

Hyperlinks view identifies items by either title or file name. To toggle between these choices, right-click the Hyperlinks view window, and choose Show Page Titles from the shortcut menu. This menu also appears on the left in Figure 17-3.

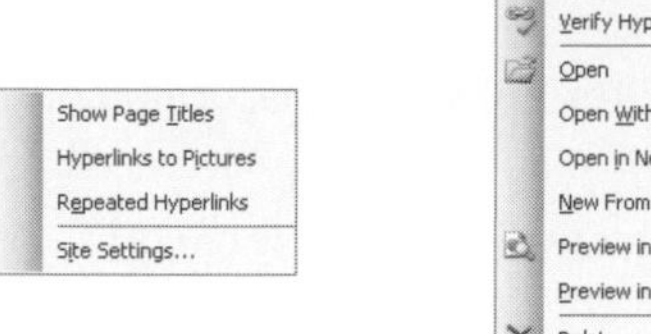

Figure 17-3. Clicking the Hyperlinks view background displays the shortcut menu on the left. Clicking a page icon in Hyperlinks view displays the shortcut menu on the right.

> **Tip** When Hyperlinks view is showing page titles, resting the mouse pointer over any page title displays the page's file name and the type of link.

To view the complete path and file name of any item in the Folder List in Hyperlinks view, right-click the item, and choose Properties from the shortcut menu. To see the file name of any item in Hyperlinks view, rest the mouse pointer over it. FrontPage briefly describes the type of item and displays its name: *Internal Hyperlink: indelinc.htm*

By default, Hyperlinks view displays only hyperlinks from one Web page to another, disregarding duplicates. To toggle display of additional items, again right-click the Hyperlinks view background, and then choose one the following commands from the shortcut menu:

- **Show Page Titles** Toggles the text that identifies Web pages between page titles and URLs.
- **Hyperlinks To Pictures** Activating this option adds picture files to the Hyperlinks view display. Designating a picture as the center of Hyperlinks view displays all pages using that picture.
- **Repeated Hyperlinks** Normally, if a page contains several links to the same target, Hyperlinks view displays only one of them. Activating this option shows all links, even duplicate ones.
- **Site Settings** Displays the Site Settings dialog box so you can view or update specifications that apply to the entire Web site.

To perform additional operations on files in either the Folder List or Hyperlinks view, right-click the page to display the shortcut menu shown on the right in Figure 17-3. Some of these options might be dimmed or omitted, depending on the context:

- **Move To Center** Designates the selected file as the center page in the right pane. This option doesn't appear for pages in the left pane or when the selected page already occupies the center position.
- **Verify Hyperlink** Validates a file or hyperlink outside the current Web site by attempting to retrieve it. This option is dimmed for locations inside the current Web site because, in that case, FrontPage has other means of verification.

- **Open** Starts the appropriate program to edit the selected page or file. Double-clicking the item accomplishes the same thing, as does choosing Open from the Edit menu. This option and the next are dimmed for links to pages located outside the current Web site.
- **Open With** Presents a choice of command editors you can use to edit the selected file. The Open With command on the Edit menu is equivalent.
- **Open In New Window** Opens the file using the default editor, but in a new FrontPage window.
- **New From Existing Page** Uses the default editor to opens a new copy of the file. If you save the new copy, FrontPage will prompt you for a new file name.
- **Preview In Browser** Launches your Web browser and tells it to request the given file.
- **Preview In Multiple Browsers** Launches all Web browsers installed on your system and tells each one to display the given file.
- **Delete** Removes a page or file from the current Web site. The Delete command on the Edit menu is equivalent.
- **Properties** Displays information about the selected file, such as its title and file name. You can also enter summary information about the page that might help you plan or maintain your Web site.

New designers are frequently enamored of Hyperlinks view, especially if they have existing Web sites. They can use this view to analyze the Web pages they've been tediously building and maintaining by hand, producing attractive diagrams as a result. This can be heady stuff, but most designers find Folders view and Navigation view more valuable for day-to-day work.

Managing Browser Compatibility

Differences in the way browsers interpret HTML are one of the greatest problems Web developers face. HTML that works perfectly well in one browser does nothing, does something different, or displays error messages in another. What's more, this problem isn't confined to browsers from different manufacturers; it also occurs between different versions from the same manufacturer.

To make matters worse, browser incompatibility isn't a black-and-white issue. Just because fonts appear larger in one browser than another doesn't make one browser better or worse, right or wrong. If one browser can display fancy hyperlink rollover effects and another can't, does that mean you should never use them?

In fact, very few Web designers aim for "least common denominator" HTML that looks the same and works the same in all browsers. Instead, they strive for HTML that takes best advantage of whatever browser a visitor might be using. This can be very tricky to achieve, and it might require HTML that's not exactly perfect for any one browser.

Of course, all this requires expertise. Most Web designers gain this expertise from years of working with various browsers, displaying their pages in each one and observing the results. Each designer develops habits and techniques that do what the designer wants and simultaneously avoid problems. Of course, each designer wants something different; as a result, the habits and techniques that work for one designer are often woefully inadequate for another.

Matching FrontPage Capabilities to Browser Capabilities

New Web designers often expect FrontPage to somehow isolate them from all the differences among browsers. In fact, because the acceptable degree of compatibility is subjective, no piece of software can do that. FrontPage can, however, remember the newest browser you want to support and then dim menu options that create HTML beyond the capabilities of that browser. To use this feature, choose Page Options from the Tools menu, and then click the Authoring tab. Figure 17-4 shows the dialog box this displays.

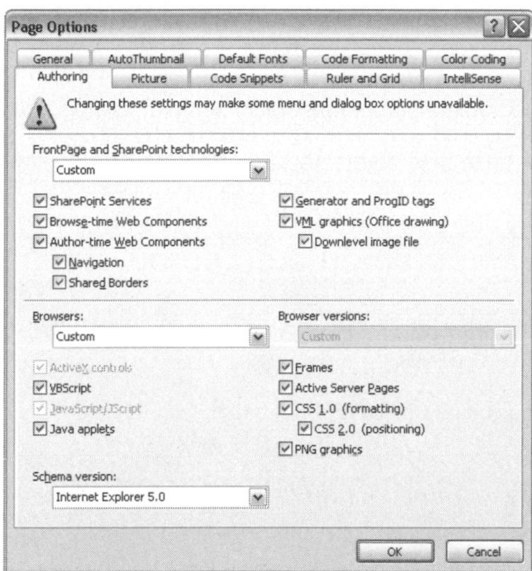

Figure 17-4. On this tab, you can specify the technologies you want your site to support. FrontPage then dims all options that would be incompatible.

Use the following settings to tell FrontPage the newest browser and browser features you want to support. FrontPage might dim some of these options, depending on other options you select.

- **FrontPage And SharePoint Technologies** This drop-down list specifies which Microsoft components you expect to be installed on the Web server. Here are the possibilities:
  - **Default** Choose this setting to select a standard combination of technologies.
  - **None** Choose this setting if you expect neither the FrontPage Server Extensions nor SharePoint Team Services to be on your Web server.

- **Complete** Choose this setting if you expect all FrontPage Server Extensions and SharePoint Team Services features to be available on your Web server. This is also the best choice if you want all FrontPage features to be available when you edit.
- **Custom** Choose this setting to specify the exact combination of FrontPage Server Extensions and SharePoint Team Services features that will be available.

In fact, each of these choices initializes a different combination of settings from the following list. You can override these settings individually at any time.

- **SharePoint Services** Select this check box if you expect SharePoint Team Services to be available on your Web server.
- **Browse-Time Web Components** Clear this check box if you don't want to use FrontPage components that run on the Web server each time a visitor requests a page. This would appropriate if neither the FrontPage Server Extensions nor SharePoint Team Services will be available.
- **Author-Time Web Components** Clear this check box if you don't want to use FrontPage components, even if those components require no special software on the Web server. (These components create fixed HTML before you publish your Web site.)
  - **Navigation** Clear this check box if you don't want Navigation view to be available.
  - **Shared Borders** Clear this check box if you don't want the Shared Borders feature to be available.
- **Generator And ProgID Tags** Clear this check box if you don't want FrontPage to add tags like this to the <head> section of your Web pages:

```
<meta name="GENERATOR" content="Microsoft FrontPage 6.0">
<meta name="ProgId" content="FrontPage.Editor.Document">
```

- **VML Graphics (Office Drawing)** Clear this check box to disable the FrontPage line drawing and WordArt features.

  Vector Markup Language (VML) is an XML-based notation that describes line drawings. VML transmits pictures such as organization charts, graphs, and diagrams much faster than a comparable GIF picture, but it only works with recent versions of Microsoft Internet Explorer.

  - **Downlevel Image File** Select this check box if you selected the VML Graphics check box and if you want FrontPage to supply a GIF version of the line art to browsers that can't display VML pictures. If you select both this option and the previous one, you get the power of line drawing plus compatibility with all browsers.

The remaining options on the Authoring tab deal strictly with features you expect your visitors' browsers to have:

- **Browsers** Choose the newest browser you want your site to support. The choices are Microsoft Internet Explorer Only, Netscape Navigator Only, Both Internet Explorer And Navigator, and Custom.

- **Browser Versions** Choose the newest version of the chosen browser you want your site to support.

  This option and the preceding one don't stop your Web site from working with newer browsers, but they do stop you from using features only newer browsers support.
- **ActiveX Controls** Clear this check box to suppress features that require displaying Microsoft ActiveX controls in the browser window. Internet Explorer is the only browser that displays ActiveX controls; all other browsers ignore them.
- **VBScript** Clear this box to suppress features that send VBScript statements to the browser for execution. VBScript is available only on Internet Explorer.
- **JavaScript/JScript** Clear this check box to suppress features that send JavaScript statements to the browser for execution. This programming language is available on all browsers.

> **Note** In practice, the terms *JavaScript*, *ECMAScript*, and *JScript* are synonymous. JavaScript was the first name for this language, ECMAScript is the official name, and JScript is the name of Microsoft's implementation.

- **Java Applets** Clear this check box to suppress FrontPage features that require Java applets to operate.
- **Frames** Clear this check box to dim all the menu options that pertain to HTML frames.
- **Active Server Pages** Clear this check box to dim all menu options that create ASP pages. This primarily affects saving form results to a database and the Database Results component. ASP pages use a type of server-side programming available only on Microsoft Web servers.
- **CSS 1.0 (Formatting)** Clear this check box to dim all options that use CSS features for typography. All but the oldest browsers support this use of CSS.
- **CSS 2.0 (Positioning)** Clear this check box to dim all options that use CSS features for positioning content on the page. This primarily affects Layers, Positioning, and DHTML effects. Support for this technology varies widely among older browsers.
- **PNG Graphics** Clear this check box to suppress the use of PNG picture files. This file format combines the features of GIP and JPEG files, but the resulting files are slightly larger. Displaying these files requires Internet Explorer 4 or later, or Netscape Navigator 4.04 or later.
- **Schema Version** Choose the version of HTML you want FrontPage to create. The choices are:
  - Internet Explorer 3.02/Navigator 3.0
  - Internet Explorer 4.0/Navigator 4.0
  - Internet Explorer 5.0

  This option might seem redundant with the earlier Browsers option, but it has a different use. The Browsers option controls which FrontPage features will be available in Design view; the Schema Version setting determines the exact syntax FrontPage will use when creating HTML.

Significantly, none of these options affect existing Web pages, pages you import from other sources, or pages you edit in Code view. If you have a frames page in your Web site, for exaple, clearing the Frames option on the Authoring tab will neither delete it nor magically convert it to a series of ordinary Web pages. To resolve this dilemma, FrontPage 2003 provides a command that searches all or part of your Web site for the use of features you've disallowed. The next section describes this command.

Searching for Compatibility Problems

FrontPage 2003 can scan your entire Web site for HTML that might not work as you expect with a given browser. To run this command:

1 Choose Browser Compatibility from the Tools menu. This displays the Browser Compatibility dialog box, shown in Figure 17-5.

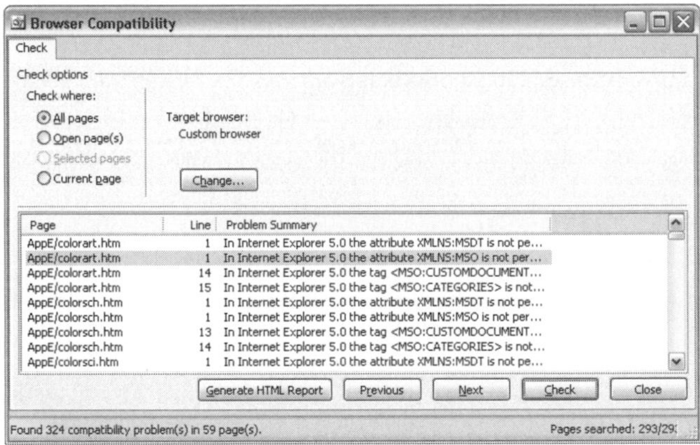

Figure 17-5. The FrontPage Browser Compatibility checker creates a list of potential problems.

2 Under the Check Where heading, specify which pages you want to check for browser compatibility. The options are:

- **All Pages** Click this option to check all pages in the current Web site.
- **Open Page(s)** Click this option to check all pages currently open in the FrontPage Editor.
- **Selected Pages** Click this option to check all currently selected files and folders (selected in the Folder List or in Folders view, for example).
- **Current Page** Click this option to check the current page in the FrontPage editor.

3 To verify the browser compatibility options currently in effect, click the Change button. This displays the Authoring tab of the Page Options dialog box.

4 Click the Check button start testing the pages you selected for compatibility. The result will be a list of Web page file names, line numbers, and problem summaries like the one shown in Figure 17-5.

5. To open, inspect, and possibly even repair the Web page that contains any error, double-click its line in the list of problem summaries.
6. Use the next three buttons at your discretion. These buttons appear only after clicking the Check button has produced results:
   - **Generate HTML Report** Click this button to save the list of compatibility problems as a Web page. FrontPage opens this page in Design view but doesn't save it to disk.
   - **Previous** Click this button to move the problem list selection up one line and then open the corresponding page in the FrontPage editor.
   - **Next** Click this button to move the problem list selection down one line and then open the corresponding page in the FrontPage editor.

When using this feature, you should be aware that FrontPage stores Authoring tab settings on a designer-by-designer, computer-by-computer basis. Suppressing features for one designer on one computer has no effect on other designers or computers. Furthermore, the same Authoring tab settings will be in effect for every Web site you edit (unless, of course, you remember to change those settings).

You should also be aware that the HTML FrontPage sees isn't necessarily the HTML the browser sees. This is because FrontPage components, ASP, ASP.NET, and Windows SharePoint Services code can modify Web pages after reading them from the server's disk and before sending then to the Web visitor. This process might "fix" apparent problems FrontPage detects or introduce problems FrontPage can't detect.

> **Tip** You can enable or suppress some FrontPage features when you configure SharePoint Team Services or the FrontPage Server Extensions. For more information, refer to "Administering User Rights," in Appendix P.

You should also be aware that after running a browser compatibility check, resolving every single problem is a lot of work and no panacea. There's no substitute for testing pages in every browser you care about and fine-tuning the results. Beauty is a thing of eye and mind, not a software report.

Optimizing HTML Code at Design Time

This feature checks the HTML in the page currently open in the FrontPage editor and removes superfluous code. This can make HTML code easier to edit in Code view and faster to download for Web visitors.

Because in some cases this feature is fairly aggressive about the code it removes, it operates only on single pages open in the FrontPage editor. That way, if you don't like the results, you can undo the change or close the editor without saving.

To optimize the HTML code in an open Web page, choose Optimize HTML from the Tools menu. This displays the Optimize HTML dialog box, shown in Figure 17-6.

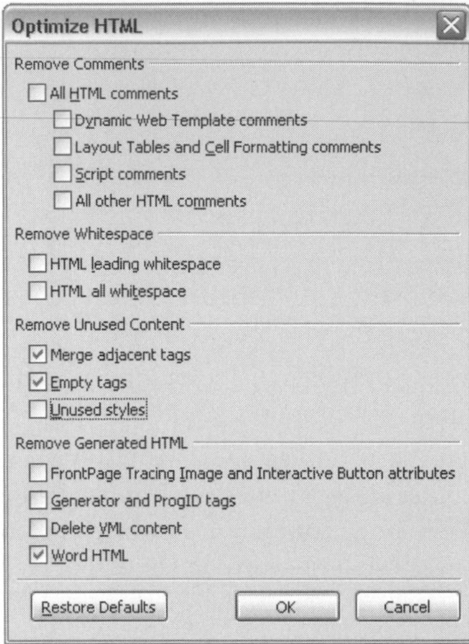

Figure 17-6. FrontPage can remove the items in this dialog box from any open Web page.

Select or clear the following check boxes:

- **All HTML Comments** If you select this check box, the next five settings will take effect. If you clear it, FrontPage will remember the settings but ignore them. Here are the settings:
  - **Dynamic Web Templates Comments** Select this check box to remove the HTML comments that record information about Dynamic Web Templates. This has the same effect as choosing Dynamic Web Template from the Format menu and then choosing Detach From Dynamic Web Template—the template content remains in the page, becomes editable, and no longer changes when you update the template.
  - **Layout Table and Cell Formatting Comments** Select this check box to remove the HTML comments that record information about layout tables and cell formatting.
  - **Script Comments** Select this check box if you to remove comments in JavaScript or Microsoft Visual Basic code that executes in the browser.
  - **All Other HTML Comments** Select this check box if you want to remove all other HTML comments. In general, this means every pair of <!-- and --> tags, plus everything between them, provided none of the preceding options apply.
- **Remove Whitespace** These options pertain to spaces, tabs, carriage returns, and line-feeds. Recall that HTML treats any mix-and-match series of these elements as if it were one space. These options affect only HTML code—not CSS rules, not script code, not anything else.

- **HTML Leading Whitespace** Select this check box if you want to remove all white-space characters between the start of a line and the first non-white-space character.
- **HTML All Whitespace** Select this check box if you want to replace all white-space sequences with a single space. This has the effect of making all the HTML into one, long, humanly unreadable line.

● **Remove Unused Content** These options remove useless HTML content.

- **Merge Adjacent Tags** Select this check box to combine multiple tags into one. For example, FrontPage would combine

```
<font face="Arial"><font size="4">Your Text</font></font>
```

into

```
<font face="Arial" size="4">Your Text</font>
```

- **Empty Tags** Select this check box to remove tags that that have no content. For example, this option would remove the following code completely:

```
<font face="Arial"></font>
```

- **Unused Styles** Select this check box to remove CSS rules that reside in the page, but that the page doesn't use.

For more information about CSS, refer to Chapter 21, "Managing Appearance with Cascading Style Sheets."

● **Remove Generated HTML** These options affect HTML code that FrontPage creates strictly for its own purposes. They are:

- **FrontPage Tracing Image And Interactive Button Attributes** Select this check box to remove the *tracingsrc* attribute, if one exists, in the <body> tag and any *fp-style=* and *fp-title=* attributes in <img> tags. FrontPage uses a *tracingsrc* attribute in the <body> tag to remember the file name of any tracing picture you specify for a page. The *fp-style=* and *fp-title=* attributes in <img> tags remember the style and button text you specify for Interactive Button components.

For more information about tracing images, refer to "Displaying a Tracing Image," on page 523. For more information about Interactive Button components, refer to "Using Interactive Buttons," on page 685.

- **Generator And ProgID Tags** Select this check box to remove the following tags, which FrontPage adds to every Web page it saves:

```
<meta name="GENERATOR" content="Microsoft FrontPage 6.0">
<meta name="ProgId" content="FrontPage.Editor.Document">
```

- **Delete VML Content** Select this check box to remove any VML pictures from the Web page.

- **Word HTML** Select this check box to remove extra HTML elements that Microsoft Word adds when it saves documents as HTML. These elements contain data that Microsoft Word would need to open the HTML document in full fidelity (that is, with losing any Microsoft Word features).

- **Restore Defaults** Click this button to restore all the preceding options to their default settings.

After selecting or clearing the options you want, click the OK button. If all goes well, the Web page will look the same as ever in Design view but much better in Code view. To clean up the overall HTML formatting in Code view, right-click anywhere in the code, and choose reformat HTML from the shortcut menu.

FrontPage can also optimize the HTML in each page you publish to another Web site. For information about this feature, refer to "Optimizing Published HTML Code," on page 454.

Checking Web Site Accessibility

FrontPage can check all the pages in a Web site to make sure they're easy to use for people with disabilities. Specifically, FrontPage checks for compliance with these standards:

- **WCAG Priority 1** *WCAG* stands for Web Content Accessibility Guidelines, a set of recommendations from the W3C. If a Web page fails to satisfy any Priority 1 guidelines, some people with disabilities will be unable to use the page.
- **WCAG Priority 2** If a Web page fails to satisfy any of these guidelines, some people with disabilities will encounter significant barriers using the Web page.
- **Access Board Section 508** These regulations refer to Section 508 of the Rehabilitation Act, a law that requires access to any electronic and information technology that U.S. federal agencies procure. The Access Board developed accessibility standards for the various technologies that the law covers, including Web pages. These standards are important if you plan to sell Web pages or Web services to the U.S. government..

For more information about WCAG and Access Board Section 508 guidelines, browse *www.w3.org/TR/WAI-WEBCONTENT/* and *www.access-board.gov/508.htm*.

Follow this procedure to check one or more Web pages for accessibility by disabled persons:

1. Open the Web site that contains the pages you want to check.
2. Choose Accessibility from the Tools menu, or press F8. This displays the Accessibility dialog box, shown in Figure 17-7.
3. In the Check Where section, specify which pages you want to check for accessibility. The options are:
   - **All Pages** All pages in the current Web site.
   - **Open Page(s)** All pages currently open in the FrontPage editor.
   - **Selected Pages** All currently selected files and folders.
   - **Current Page** The page that the FrontPage editor currently displays.

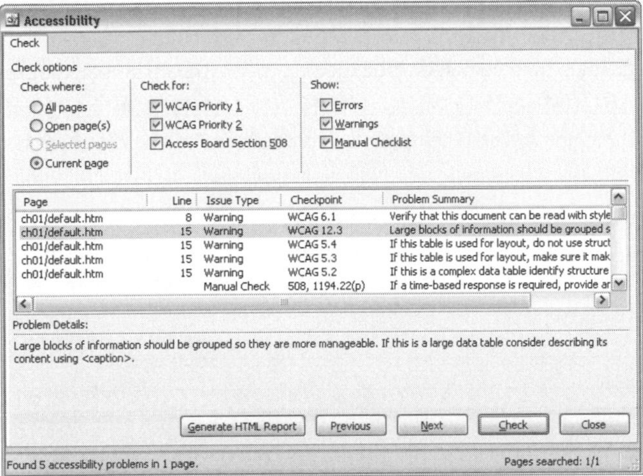

Figure 17-7. The Accessibility checker looks for elements that make Web pages difficult or impossible for people with disabilities.

4 In the Check For section, select the disability guidelines you want to satisfy. The options are WCAG Priority 1, WCAG Priority 2, and Access Board Section 508.

5 In the Show section, specify the types of problem messages you want to receive. The options are:

- **Errors** These messages report conditions that certainly conflict with the guidelines you selected.
- **Warnings** These messages report conditions that might conflict with the guidelines you selected.
- **Manual Checklist** These messages concern guidelines that involve human judgment. You must review these guidelines personally.

6 Click the Check button at the bottom of the dialog box.

If you specified All Pages or Selected Pages, checking these pages for accessibility might take some time. When the process ends, you can:

- Review the problem list that appears in the middle of the Accessibility dialog box.
- Double-click any line in the problem list to open the corresponding page in the FrontPage editor.
- Click the Generate HTML Report button to save the problem list as a Web page. FrontPage opens this page in Design view but doesn't save it to disk. (This button and next two will be absent until the problem list appears.)
- Click the Previous button to move the problem list selection up one line, and then open the corresponding page in the FrontPage editor.
- Click the Next button to move the problem list selection down one line, and then open the corresponding page in the FrontPage editor.

Reindexing Your Web Site

FrontPage maintains a number of databases and index files that cross-reference hyperlinks and other elements in your Web pages. If these files and your Web pages get out of sync, FrontPage might produce incorrect search results, incorrectly size pictures, or incompletely update hyperlinks.

FrontPage updates its indexes every time it makes changes to a Web site, but other programs and utilities don't. You should reindex your Web site every time you make changes with external tools, any time you suspect indexes of being corrupted, or in general, any time your Web site seems to be acting strangely.

Caution It's best to close any open files in your Web site before recalculating hyperlinks.

To reindex a Web site, open it in FrontPage, and choose Recalculate Hyperlinks from the Tools menu. This accomplishes three things:

- It updates the display for all current views of the current Web site.
- It regenerates all dependencies. If, for example, you used an external editor to modify an included page, any pages that include the page continue to display the old version. Recalculating hyperlinks refreshes the affected Include Page components.
- It rebuilds the text index used by the Web Search component. This can become outdated if you externally add, change, or delete files in your Web.

Stop

The Recalculate Hyperlinks dialog box, shown in Figure 17-8, appears whenever you run the Recalculate Hyperlinks command. As noted, recalculating hyperlinks can take several minutes for a large Web site. When recalculation starts, the Stop button on the Standard toolbar flashes until recalculation finishes. Only when the button stops flashing can you do further work in FrontPage.

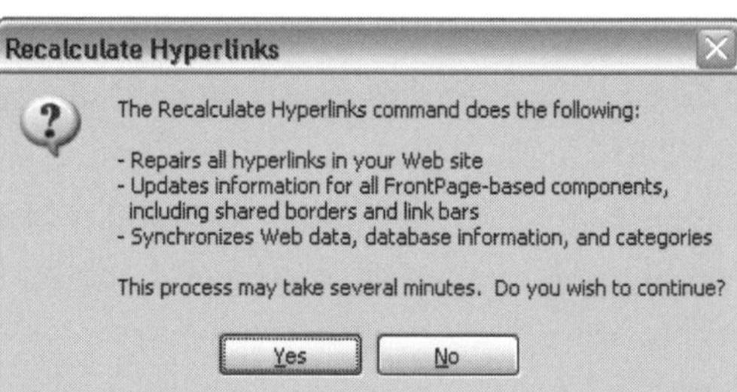

Figure 17-8. This dialog box presages a Recalculate Hyperlinks operation.

Frequently Asked Question

How can programs other than FrontPage safely update a FrontPage-based Web site?

The following methods all update FrontPage-based Web Sites or SharePoint Team Sites without invalidating the Web site's internal indexes:

- Use an HTTP location listed under My Network Places.

  You can access such HTTP locations from My Network Places, from most applications bundled with Microsoft Windows 2000, and from most Open File and Save As dialog boxes in Microsoft Office 2000 and Office XP applications.
- Have FrontPage launch the application you want to use. In this mode, FrontPage exports a temporary version of the file, runs the external program, and checks the temporary file's timestamp every time FrontPage regains the focus. If the timestamp has changed, FrontPage imports the termporary file.

  If double-clicking a file in FrontPage doesn't launch the application you want, choose Options from the Tools menu, click the Configure Editors tab, and assign the desired program to the appropriate file extension.

For more information about configuring FrontPage to launch other programs, refer to "Configuring External Editors," on page 1118.

Checking Server Health

If your Web server runs the FrontPage Server Extensions or SharePoint Team Services, commands on the server can perform a variety of consistency checks on your Web site. In many cases, these commands restore a malfunctioning Web site to proper operation. To run the full set of server health commands, you must be an administrator of the root Web site of your server. Even if you don't have authority to use this command yourself, it's worth knowing that you can ask your administrator to run the commands for you on a one-time or scheduled basis.

For more information about checking server health, refer to "Checking Server Health" in Appendix P.

Working with Reports

FrontPage provides a sizable assortment of highly useful, interactive reports for managing your Web site. To view any report, use either of these methods:

- Choose Reports from the View menu, select the report category you want, and then, from the resulting submenu, choose the specific report.
- Click the Web Site tab above the main editing window, and then click the Reports tab beneath the main editing window. This displays either the last report you requested or,

by default, the Site Summary report. To display a different report, select it from the drop-down list at the left of the Reports view toolbar.

For more information about the Site Summary report, refer to "Viewing the Site Summary Report," later in this chapter.

By their nature, reports pertain to collections of objects; one-line reports just aren't very interesting. For this reason, Reports view pertains only to FrontPage-based Web sites. If you're using FrontPage to edit just a single page and haven't opened a Web site, Reports view won't be available. If you *have* opened a Web site, the reports pertain to that site. Here are the standard FrontPage reports, grouped by category:

- **Summary report** Provides overall Web site statistics. The Site Summary accumulates and reports various high-level statistics about your Web site, such as the number of files, their total size, and so forth.
- **File reports** List Web pages and other files that meet various criteria:
  - **All Files** Lists all files in a Web site, regardless of folder.
  - **Recently Added Files** Lists all files added to a Web site within a given interval.
  - **Recently Changed Files** Lists all files changed within a given interval.
  - **Older Files** Lists files that haven't been updated within a given interval.

- **Shared Content reports** List all pages in the current Web site, with a column that shows which, if any, centralized content they utilize:
  - **Dynamic Web Templates** Lists which, if any, dynamic template each page uses.
  - **Shared Borders** Lists which, if any, shared borders each page uses.
  - **Style Sheet Links** Lists which, if any, style sheet files each page uses.
  - **Themes** Lists which, if any, FrontPage theme each page uses.
- **Problem reports** Itemize errors that exist within your Web site:
  - **Unlinked Files** Lists files your Web site might not be using.
  - **Slow Pages** Lists Web pages whose total download time, including linked components, exceeds a given amount.
  - **Hyperlinks** Reports links to files that don't exist and provides options for fixing them.
  - **Component Errors** Reports errors and inconsistencies involving FrontPage components. These can occur when, for example, you first configure the component correctly and then later delete a required file.
- **Workflow reports** Display the status of a Web site that several people are developing together:
  - **Review Status** Shows which pages are assigned for review, along with any further status the reviewer has assigned.
  - **Assigned To** Shows which pages are assigned to which designer.

- **Categories** Lists all Web pages, including a column that shows assigned Category codes.
- **Publish Status** Shows which pages are approved for publication and which are held back.
- **Checkout Status** Shows which files are checked out for updates, and by whom.

- **Usage reports** Display activity statistics collected by the Web server. These statistics are available only on Web servers running the FrontPage Server Extensions 2002 or SharePoint Team Services. In addition, an administrator must activate settings within the FrontPage Server Extensions, SharePoint, and the Web server's log files. Here are the available reports:
  - **Usage Summary** Displays overall statistics for your Web site collected since inception. The inception date is one of the reported statistics.
  - **Monthly, Weekly, or Daily Summary** Displays total visits, total page hits, total hits of all kinds, and total download bytes by applicable period since inception.
  - **Monthly, Weekly, or Daily Page Hits** Displays, by period, the number of times Web visitors requested each page in your Web site.
  - **Visiting Users** Displays the identities of Web visitors to your site. However, unless you require Web visitors to identify themselves by user name and password, this report will be blank.
  - **Operating Systems** Reports how many visits came from computers running Windows 95, Windows 98, Windows NT, Windows 2000, Macintosh, various forms of UNIX, and so forth.
  - **Browsers** Reports how many visits came from various browsers, such as Internet Explorer 5, Internet Explorer 5.5, and various versions of Netscape.
  - **Referring Domains** Reports the names of all Web sites—anywhere—that contain hyperlinks that Web visitors followed to your Web site. (No, this isn't magic. Whenever a visitor clicks a hyperlink, the browser transmits the URL of the page that contained the link.)
  - **Referring URLs** Reports the locations of all Web pages that contain hyperlinks that Web visitors followed to your Web site.
  - **Search Strings** Reports a history of keywords Web visitors entered on public Web engines just before they discovered your Web site. This report depends on information the search engine sends as part of its link to your site.

FrontPage Usage reports will contain data only if an administrator activates a process on the Web server called *usage analysis*. For information about this task, refer to "Administering Installation Defaults," in Appendix P.

Viewing the Site Summary Report

This report displays a series of statistics for the current Web site: the number and total size of all files, the number and size of all picture files, the number of files unreachable from any hyperlink in the current Web site, and so forth. Figure 17-9 shows a typical Site Summary report.

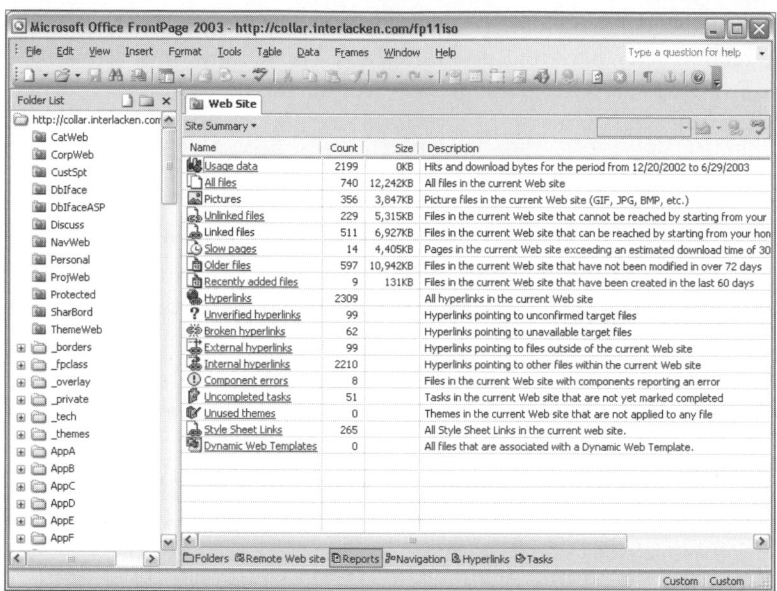

Figure 17-9. The Site Summary report displays statistics for the entire current Web site.

This report provides a wealth of information, For example, you can see at a glance how many files this Web site contains, how much disk space those files occupy, how many of the files are pictures, and how many Web pages exceed the configured maximum download time. The Description column explains the meaning of each line.

Notice the entries for recently added files, older files, and slow pages. The dialog box shown in Figure 17-10 specifies which files fall into these categories. To display this dialog box, choose Options from the Tools menu, and then click the Reports View tab.

The Site Summary report doesn't list individual files; it lists statistics tabulated from other reports. If the category name is underlined, clicking it displays the most relevant FrontPage report.

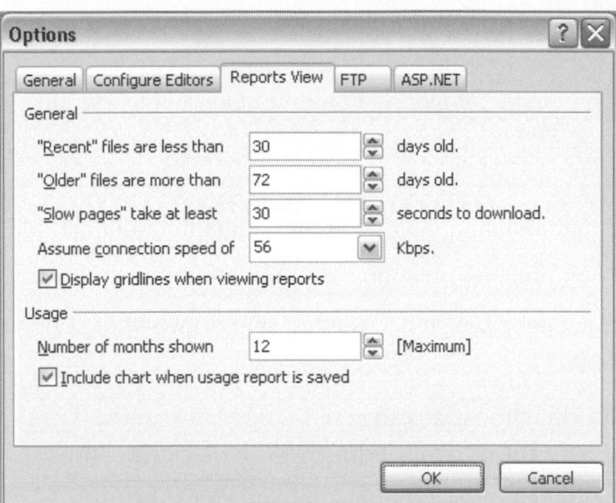

Figure 17-10. This dialog box specifies what constitutes a recent, an older, and a slow Web page for Site Summary statistics and the corresponding detail reports.

Interacting with FrontPage Reports

FrontPage reports are, in fact, highly dynamic displays. You can move files, sort and filter column displays, update displayed information, and launch other processes from FrontPage reports in a multitude of ways:

- To position any part of the report within the available window, use the scroll bars.
- To sort any report on any column, click the column heading. Clicking the same heading repeatedly alternates between ascending and descending sequence. To sort on multiple columns, click them in order from least significant to most.
- To filter a report so that it displays only certain column values, click the drop-down arrow in its heading. This displays a selection list of values like the one shown here:

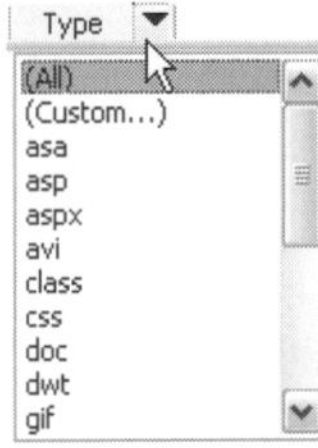

  - To filter the report on one of the listed values, select it as you would a value in any other drop-down list.
  - To remove a filter that's already in place, select (All).
  - To set up more complex filter criteria, select (Custom). This displays the Custom AutoFilter dialog box, shown in Figure 17-11.

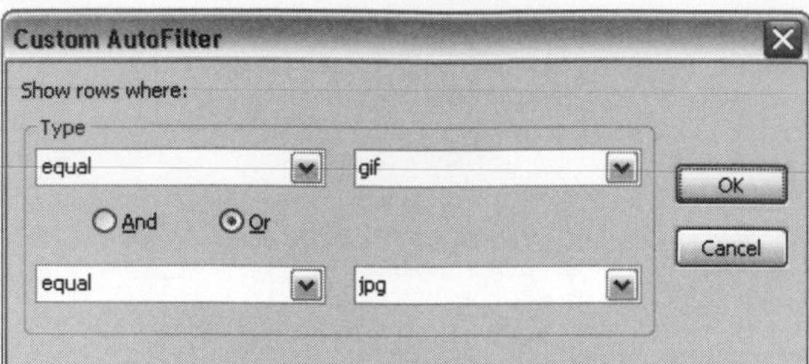

Figure 17-11. This dialog box applies either one or two filter conditions to any FrontPage report.

To enter one filter condition, choose a comparison operator in the Type section, and then select or type a value in the corresponding box to its right.

To enter a second filter condition, click either the And or Or option, select the second comparison operator, and then, as before, select or type a value in the corresponding box to its right.

Click OK to apply the filter.

In most reports, each line pertains to a file in your Web site. Right-clicking any line in such a report displays the shortcut menu shown in Figure 17-12.

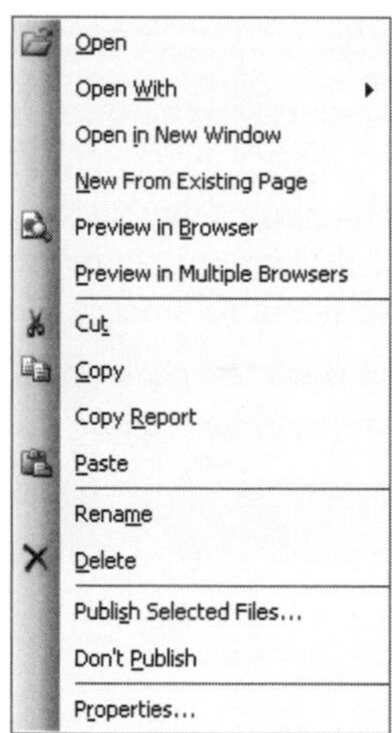

Figure 17-12. Right-clicking a line in any FrontPage report displays this shortcut menu. Depending on the context, some commands might be dimmed.

Here's an explanation of each option on this menu. Some options may be dimmed or absent, depending on the context.

- **Open** Starts the default editor for the file on the selected line. For Web pages, this is the Design view editor. For everything else, it's whatever you see configured after choosing Options on the Tools menu and clicking the Configure Editors tab.

For more information about configuring the editor associated with a given file type, refer to "Configuring External Editors," on page 1118.

Note Double-clicking any line is the same as right-clicking and choosing Open from the shortcut menu.

- **Open With** Displays a submenu with choices to open the file in various editors. If the editor you want doesn't appear, choose the Choose Program command. This displays an Open With dialog box, in which you can select the editor you want.
- **New From Existing Page** Uses the default editor to opens a new copy of the file. If you save the new copy, FrontPage will prompt you for a new file name.
- **Open In New Window** Opens the file using the default editor, but in a new FrontPage window.
- **Preview In Browser** Launches your Web browser and tells it to request the given file.
- **Preview In Multiple Browsers** Launches all Web browsers installed on your system and tells each one to display the given file.
- **Cut** Loads the Clipboard with a pointer to one or more selected files in preparation for moving them.
- **Copy** Loads the Clipboard with a pointer to one or more selected files in preparation for copying them.
- **Copy Report** Copies all the data in the current report to the Clipboard. From there, you can paste it into Microsoft Excel, Microsoft Access, or any other program for analysis.
- **Paste** Completes a pending cut or copy operation at the current location.
- **Remove Filters** Does away with any filters that were previously in effect. All possible lines will appear in the report. This option is absent when no filters are in effect.
- **Home Page** Designates the current Web page as the home page in navigation view. This option is absent if the current file isn't a web page, or if any filters are in effect.
- **Rename** Opens the file name in the Name column to editing. Pressing the F2 key is equivalent.
- **Delete** Deletes any selected files from the current Web site.
- **Publish Selected Files** Copies any currently selected files to the remote Web site specified in the last full publish operation.

For more information about publishing a Web site, refer to Chapter 16, "Publishing Your FrontPage-Based Web Site."

Don't Publish

- **Don't Publish** Toggles the Publish or Don't Publish status of any currently selected files. (A white X in a red circle visually identifies files currently flagged for non-publication).
- **Properties** Displays the Properties dialog box for the current file.

For more information about the Properties dialog box, refer to "Working with Folders View," on page 180.

Report fields other than file names might also be editable. Here's how to update an editable field:

1. Select the line that contains the field you want to modify.
2. Click the field you want to modify.
3. If the field is editable, FrontPage displays it as an editable text box, a drop-down list, or another appropriate control. The following report segment shows how FrontPage displays a drop-down list for updating a file's Publish status:

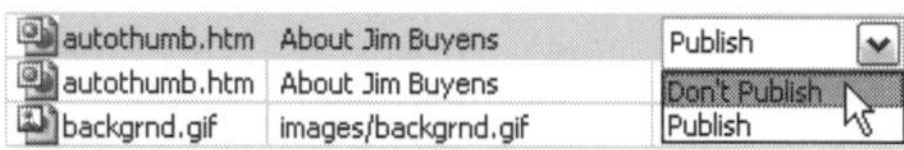

This report segment shows a text field being updated. Notice the dark border and the text insertion point.

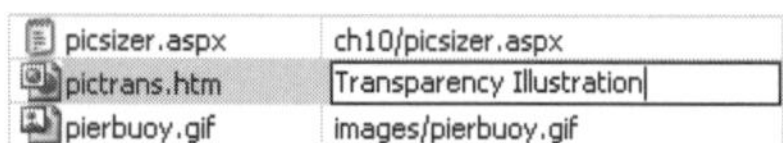

Interpreting FrontPage Reports

Figure 17-13 shows the most all-inclusive FrontPage report—namely, the All Files report. This report contains one line for each page in your Web site. Any of these methods will display this report:

- Click the All Files link in the Site Summary report.
- Choose Reports from the View menu, and then choose Files and All Files from the resulting submenus.
- Open the drop-down list at the left of the Reports view toolbar, then choose Files and All Files from the resulting submenus.

Despite minor variations, all other reports conform to this general format. Some reports also use the following controls from the Reporting toolbar:

- **Report Setting** This drop-down list box specifies the reporting interval for a Usage report. In the case of monthly reports, for example, it specifies the month to display.

Usage Chart

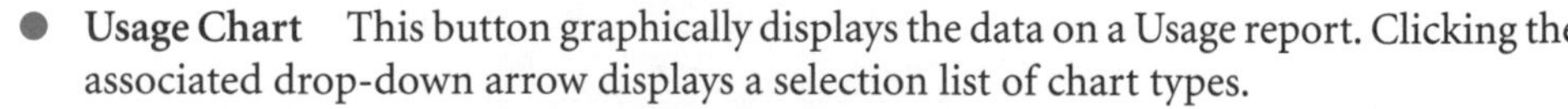

- **Usage Chart** This button graphically displays the data on a Usage report. Clicking the associated drop-down arrow displays a selection list of chart types.
- **Edit Hyperlink** When a Hyperlink report is displayed, this button displays a dialog box for changing the target of a hyperlink.

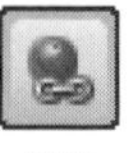

Edit Hyperlink

Keeping Your Web Site Up-to-Date

Verifies Hyperlinks In the Current Web

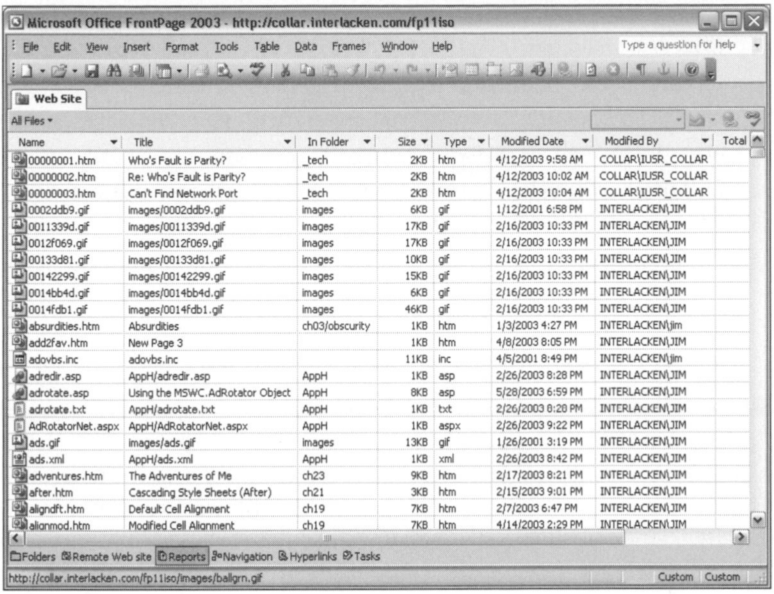

Figure 17-13. The FrontPage All Files report lists information about each file in a Web site.

- **Verifies Hyperlinks In The Current Web** This button displays the Hyperlinks report, and then starts a process that checks each hyperlink in your Web site for validity.

For more information about displaying and interpreting each report, refer to Appendix D, "Interpreting FrontPage Reports."

Testing Your Web Site

The Unlinked Files, Slow Pages, Hyperlinks, and Component Errors reports provide excellent ways to check the content of your Web, and using FrontPage produces error-free HTML. Nevertheless, there's no substitute for browsing your own Web site and testing its functions online.

Two fundamental things to check are the correct operation of all hyperlinks and reasonable page transmission times under typical conditions. However, you should also do a test drive to confirm proper appearance and operation under the following conditions:

- **Different browsers** Test your pages with at least the current production versions of Internet Explorer, Netscape Navigator, and any other browsers your visitors use, plus the previous production version and perhaps the current prerelease version of each browser.
- **Different browser settings** Remember that visitors can turn some browser features on and off, such as the ability to run scripts, run Java applets, and load ActiveX

controls. If you use these facilities, make sure your pages degrade gracefully, rather than crash and burn, if visitors turn them off.

- **Different color depths** View your pages in 256-color mode as well as 24-bit true color. Depending on your visitors' equipment, you might also want to test at 16 colors and in 64K high-color mode.
- **Different screen sizes** Make sure your pages are usable, even if unattractive, on systems with 640-by- 480-pixel displays.
- **Different servers** Don't assume that everything will work the same way on multiple servers (presuming that your environment uses more than one server, such as a Microsoft Web server for authoring and an ISP's UNIX server for production). The greater the difference between the servers, the more that can go wrong. Test and debug each server environment thoroughly.

Scripts are probably the most sensitive components in your Web site. JavaScript, in particular, began with no formal language specification or comprehensive test suite. Bugs and features seem to come and go with each browser version, so testing is an absolute necessity. Remember that Netscape browsers don't support VBScript as a browser-side programming language.

Test after each change to your Web site—each set of page changes, each publish operation, each server upgrade, each new version of FrontPage, each new browser version that appears. Even if nothing else changes, hyperlinks will; verify them periodically.

In Summary…

This chapter explained a number of ways that you can process groups of files in your Web site with one operation. This included searching, replacing, checking spelling, content analysis, usage analysis, and hyperlink analysis.

The next part of this book, Part 6, "Formatting Your Web Pages," explains how to enhance the appearance of your Web pages in a variety of ways. After all, the HTML defaults are quite dull.

Part 6

Formatting Your Web Pages

Chapter 18

Controlling Overall Page Appearance

Whenever you start working on a Web page—whether it's an existing page, a new page, or a page generated by a template or a wizard—you probably have a concept in mind that affects not only the page's content, but also its title, color scheme, and other general characteristics. Even for existing content, you might decide that this is the time to standardize pages and apply uniform page attributes. This chapter explains how to make these kinds of page-level style changes.

Of the many attributes a Web page can have, color is probably the most striking and the most obvious. This chapter therefore concludes with some tips and things to keep in mind when designing color schemes.

Specifying Page-Level Attributes

Microsoft FrontPage centralizes overall control of your page's appearance in the Page Properties dialog box. To open the Page Properties dialog box, make sure you have a page open, and then take either of these actions:

- Choose Properties from the File menu.
- Right-click anywhere in the page's window, and choose Page Properties from the shortcut menu.

The Page Properties dialog box has six tabs: General, Formatting, Advanced, Custom, Language, and Workgroup. The next series of topics explains how to use the controls on each of these tabs.

General Page Properties

The General tab of the Page Properties dialog box appears in Figure 18-1. You should always specify a meaningful title, but use of the remaining elements is optional.

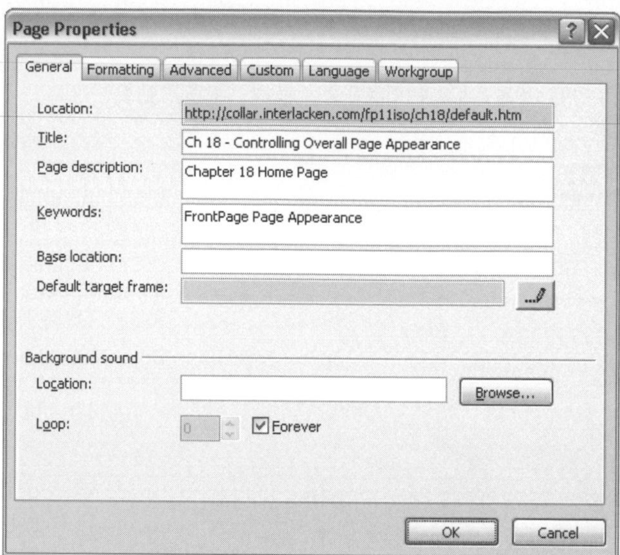

Figure 18-1. The General tab of the Page Properties dialog box controls a page's title and hyperlinking defaults.

The data options on the Page Properties General tab control the following characteristics:

- **Location** This read-only box displays the URL of the current page (that is, the URL a browser would use to retrieve it). If FrontPage opened the page from a file, a URL beginning with *file:///* appears. For new pages not yet saved, the location is *unsaved:///new_page_<#>.htm.*
- **Title** Enter the name of the page in words. This is an often-overlooked but important attribute; it appears in many FrontPage windows and dialog boxes, as a page description in search results, and in the title bars of your visitors' browsers. Be certain that every page you maintain has a meaningful title suitable for public display.
- **Page Description** Enter a brief textual description of the page. FrontPage saves this information in a <meta name="description"> tag that some search engines detect, store, and then display when your page satisfies a Web surfer's query.
- **Keywords** Enter any words that fundamentally categorize your page. FrontPage will put this information in a <meta name="keywords"> tag that search engines detect, store, and compare to search terms that Web surfers specify.

> **Tip** So many Web designers have misused the keywords meta tag that search engines have downgraded its importance. To regain some credibility, specify keywords that also appear within your page content, description, title, and alt tags.

- **Base Location** Use of this box is rare, and you should normally leave it blank. For an explanation of its use, see the sidebar "Relative Addressing and Base URLs," later in this chapter.

Change Target Frame

- **Default Target Frame** Specify the name of the frame that clicking most hyperlinks on the current page should update. (This box applies only to pages that appear within frames pages).

  Suppose, for example, that you want most hyperlinks on the current page to update a frame named main. To avoid coding a target frame on each hyperlink, you could type the frame name **main** in this box.

  To update this box, click the accompanying Change Target Frame button.

For information about using frames, refer to Chapter 15, "Creating Web Sites with Frames."

- **Background Sound** These three options select and control a sound file that the visitor's browser will play when it displays your page:
  - **Location** Enter the name of the sound file. This can be a local file or a URL. To browse the local file system or current Web, click the Browse button.
  - **Loop** Enter the number of times the specified file should play.
  - **Forever** Select this check box to have the sound file play indefinitely. This overrides the Loop setting.

Tip Avoid specifying large sound files or files in platform-specific formats. In general, MIDI files are the smallest and most widely supported.

Relative Addressing and Base URLs

Hyperlinks on Web pages needn't specify complete URLs. If a hyperlink doesn't include a host name, a browser uses the host that delivered the current page. If a hyperlink also contains no folder location, the browser uses the same folder as the current page. This is called *relative addressing*, because hyperlink locations are relative to the current page unless a full and explicit path is included. Here are two examples:

Current Page:	http://www.interlacken.com/info/default.htm
Hyperlink:	/products/toasters.htm
Jump Location:	http://www.interlacken.com/products/toasters.htm

Current Page:	http://www.interlacken.com/info/default.htm
Hyperlink:	contact.htm
Jump Location:	http://www.interlacken.com/info/contact.htm

In general, it's best to use relative addressing wherever possible. This makes it very easy to move groups of pages from one Web server or folder to another. In contrast, specifying complete URLs means updating them whenever you move pages from one computer or Web site to another.

Occasionally, you might find it convenient to base relative URLs not on the current page but on some other location. Specifying a base URL accomplishes this as follows:

Current Page:	http://www.interlacken.com/info/default.htm
Base URL:	http://www.microsoft.com/info/
Hyperlink:	contact.htm
Jump Location:	http://www.microsoft.com/info/contact.htm

To specify a base URL in FrontPage, enter it in the Base Location box on the General tab of the Page Properties dialog box.

Formatting Page Properties

Figure 18-2 shows the Formatting tab of the Page Properties dialog box. This tab controls most aspects of the page's overall color scheme

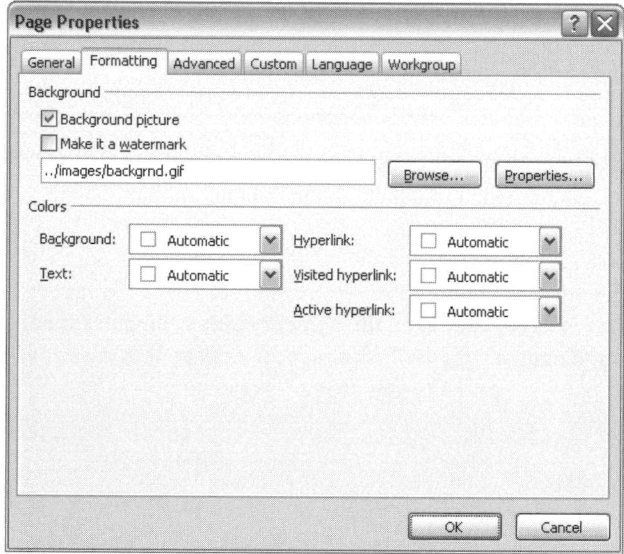

Figure 18-2. The Formatting tab of the Page Properties dialog box controls a page's overall color scheme.

The following controls appear under the Background heading. They control the background picture, should you care to use one, but not the background color.

- **Background Picture** Select this check box if you want the page to have a background picture. The associated text box specifies the location of the picture file. Rather than typing the file location, you can click the Browse button to locate it.

Note The Formatting tab doesn't appear in the Page Properties dialog box for any page controlled by a theme. The theme controls these attributes.

Tip You can also access the Formatting tab by choosing Background from the Format menu.

- **Make It A Watermark** Select this check box if, when a Web visitor operates the browser's scroll bars, you want the background picture to remain fixed and not scroll with other content on the page.

  Microsoft Internet Explorer supports this feature, as does Netscape Navigator 6 and later. Other browsers, however, might not. FrontPage itself doesn't exhibit the watermark behavior; it scrolls the background picture even though watermarking is in effect. To see watermarking in action, browse the page with Internet Explorer.
- **Properties** Click this button, when it's available, to display a Picture Properties dialog box that displays or alters the properties of the specified background picture.

For an explanation of the Picture Properties dialog box, refer to "Modifying Picture Properties," on page 273.

Using Background Pictures in Your Pages

A background picture appears behind any other pictures or text on the page. If the picture is smaller than the page, the browser repeats it left to right and top to bottom. With this "tiling" behavior, a small picture, which is fast to download, can fill the entire screen.

To keep the background picture from repeating left to right, make it wider than any typical computer screen display. A width of 1600 pixels is usually sufficient. Most picture editors have features called Add Margin or Extend Canvas that can widen pictures this way. Fill the added pixels with your background color, or make them transparent. Repeating pixels of the same color compress very well and add little to file size and download time.

Wide pictures of this kind are often used to create border designs along the left margin. The design occupies the leftmost 20 or 30 pixels, and the rest of the picture is either a solid color or transparent.

Avoid strong colors or patterns in background pictures. These can easily obscure your text.

The following controls specify the color of standard HTML elements, including the page background. They appear under the Colors heading.

- **Background** Use this setting to control the page's background color. This color appears if there's no background picture, if any part of the background picture is transparent, or if the browser is ready to start displaying the page before the background picture arrives.

For instructions on using this and other FrontPage color controls, skip ahead to the section "Using FrontPage Color Dialog Boxes," later in this chapter.

- **Text** Use this setting to control the color of ordinary text.
- **Hyperlink** Use this setting to control the color of hyperlinked text.
- **Visited Hyperlink** Use this setting to control the color of hyperlinked text whose target has recently been visited. The text reverts to Hyperlink color when its target is cleared from the browser's cache on the visitor's computer.
- **Active Hyperlink** Use this setting to control the color of hyperlinked text at the time the visitor clicks the link.

Advanced Page Properties

The Advanced tab of the Page Properties dialog box controls overall page margins, CSS styles, and settings that Microsoft Visual InterDev design-time controls (DTCs) use. This tab appears in Figure 18-3.

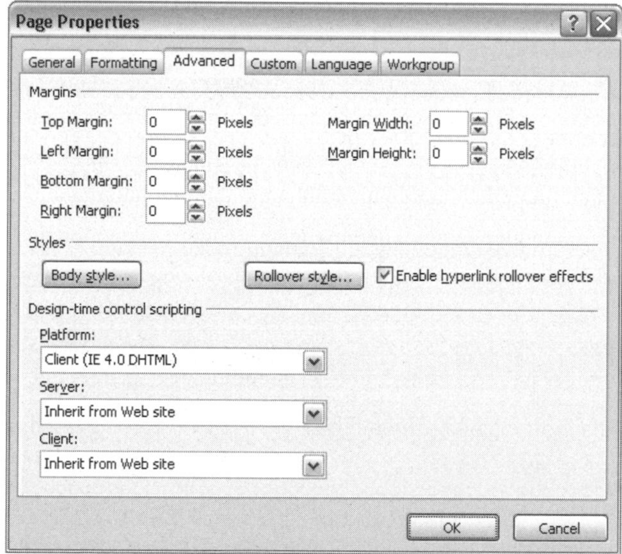

Figure 18-3. The Margins area of the Advanced tab controls the top and left margins of a Web page.

Note DTCs are a type of Microsoft ActiveX control that can enhance either FrontPage or Microsoft Visual Studio 6 with additional editing and HTML-generation features. Microsoft Visual Studio .NET no longer supports them.

The margin settings for a Web page define the number of pixels between one corner of the browser window and the closest spot where page elements could possibly appear. Most browsers have default margins of 8 or 15 pixels on all sides. If you make a picture the very first element on a page, for example, it will actually appear 8 to 15 pixels below the top of the browser window, and 8 to 15 pixels from the left edge.

Unfortunately, Internet Explorer and Netscape Navigator have never quite agreed on the proper HTML code for controlling page margins. FrontPage 2003 supports all the variations that both browsers support, but configuring the margins of a Web page is still more confusing than you might expect. The first column in Table 18-1 lists the options FrontPage provides.

Table 18-1. Page Margin Settings and Browser Support

FrontPage margin setting	Internet Explorer	Netscape Navigator 4–6	Netscape Navigator 7	Margins affected
Top Margin	Supported	Ignored	Supported	Top
Left Margin	Supported	Ignored	Supported	Left
Right Margin	Supported; defaults to Top Margin	Ignored	Supported; defaults to browser default (8 pixels)	Right
Bottom Margin	Supported; defaults to Top Margin	Ignored	Supported; defaults to browser default (8 pixels)	Bottom
Margin Width	Ignored	Supported	Supported	Left and Right
Margin Height	Ignored	Supported	Supported	Top and Bottom

Memorizing Table 18-1 could be a chore but fortunately, the arrangement of elements in the Margins section provides some assistance. Refer again to Figure 18-3 and note the following:

- Internet Explorer obeys the four settings in the left column.
- Netscape Navigator versions 4 through 6 obey the settings in the right column.
- Netscape Navigator 7 obeys both.

Thus, by always setting margin settings in both columns, you'll always get the results you want in both browsers. The settings in Figure 18-3, for example, specify zero-width margins all around for any browser. This is a popular choice for pages that use a full width, solid color page banner.

FrontPage, as you might expect, displays the top and left margins as Internet Explorer does. Figure 18-4 provides the proof.

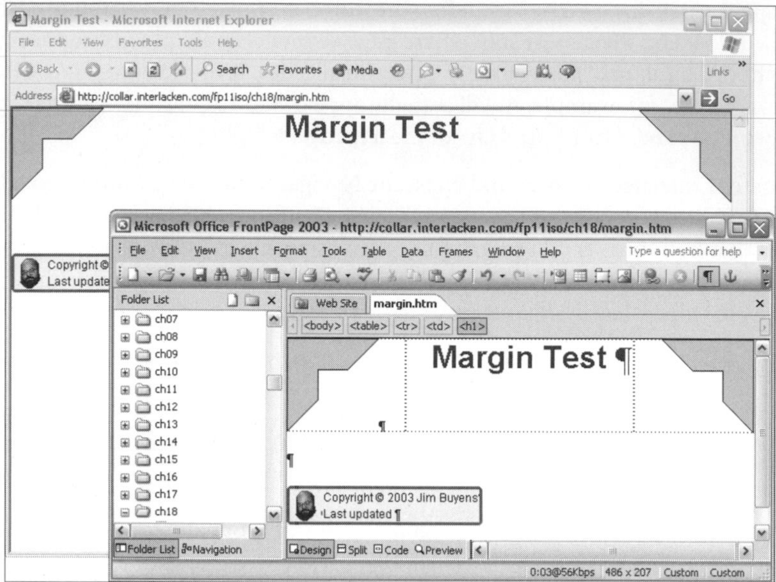

Figure 18-4. FrontPage and Internet Explorer versions 4 and later display a page with Top Margin and Left Margin settings of zero. Netscape Navigator versions 6 and earlier ignore this method of setting margins.

Figure 18-5 shows Netscape Navigator versions 4.77, 6, and 7 displaying the same page. Notice that only version 7 honors the Top Margin and Left Margin settings, and even then, the Right Margin setting doesn't default to the Left Margin value. You could make all three of these browsers display zero margins by also setting Margin Width and Margin Height to zero.

The Advanced tab also controls CSS styles that apply to the page as a whole. Here are the applicable controls:

- **Body Style** Click this button to open the Modify Style dialog box, which specifies CSS information for the body of the current page.

For information about CSS, refer to Chapter 21, "Managing Appearance with Cascading Style Sheets."

- **Enable Hyperlink Rollover Effects** Select this check box if you want text hyperlinks in this page to change appearance when the mouse passes over them. Selecting this box enables the Rollover Style button.
- **Rollover Style** Click this button to specify how text hyperlinks in this page should appear when the mouse passes over them. Clicking this button displays a Font dialog box, in which you specify how hyperlinks will look when the mouse pointer moves onto them.

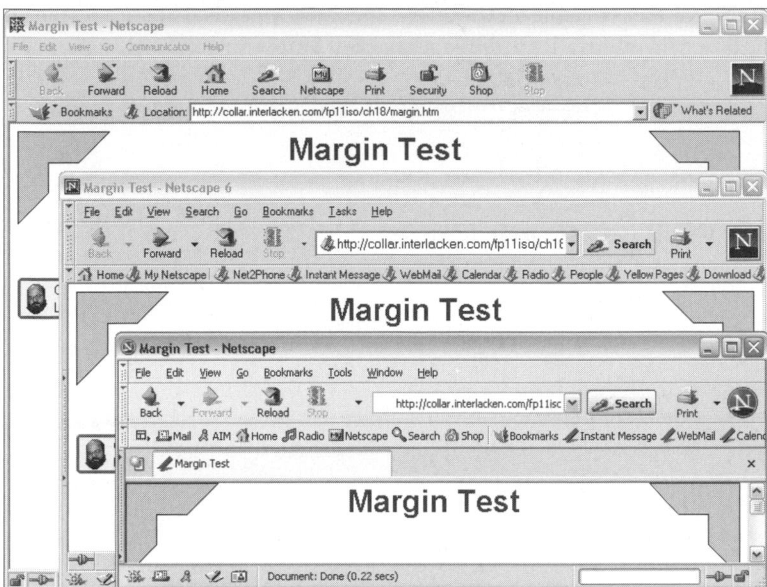

Figure 18-5. Netscape Navigator versions 4.77 and 6 ignore Top Margin and Left Margin settings (which, in this case, are zero). Navigator 7 honors the same settings, but the Right Margin setting doesn't default to the Left Margin value.

The last group of settings on the Advanced tab control the way DTCs add script code to the current page. In practice, the use of such controls in FrontPage is extremely rare.

- **Platform** Specify where scripting should occur—Client or Server.
- **Server** Specify the language that DTCs should use for server-side scripting: JavaScript, VBScript, or the Inherit From Web default setting.
- **Client** Specify the language that DTCs should use for browser-side scripting: JavaScript, VBScript, or the Inherit From Web default setting.

Custom Page Properties

Figure 18-6 shows the Custom tab of the Page Properties dialog box, which maintains two categories of variables. System variables are those defined as official HTTP headers, whereas user variables are any others you want to specify.

On this tab:

- The REFRESH system variable tells the Web visitor's browser to wait 10 seconds after displaying the current page and then jump to another page.
- The PICS-Label system variable characterizes the content of a Web page, folder, or entire site regarding violence, nudity, sex, and language.
- The GENERATOR user variable identifies the software that created this Web page. FrontPage supplies this information automatically.

- The ProgId user variable identifies the specific program that created the current page. This is another item that FrontPage supplies automatically.

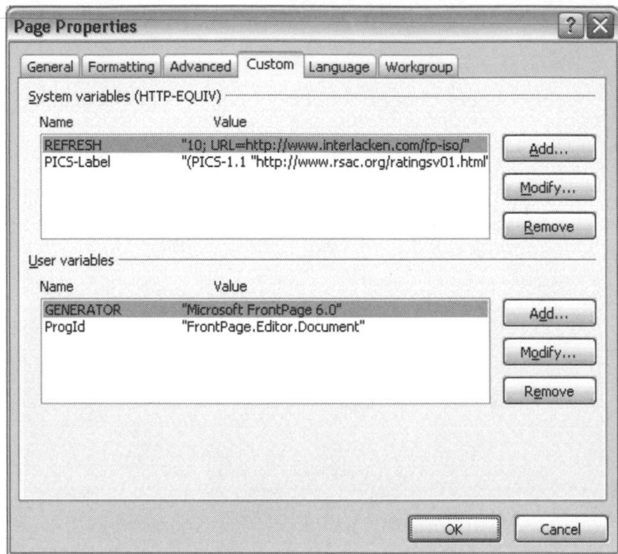

Figure 18-6. The Custom tab specifies HTTP header field equivalents and user variables. These appear in the <head> section of a page's HTML code.

To add a variable, click the appropriate Add button, and then type the variable name and its initial value in the dialog box shown in Figure 18-7.

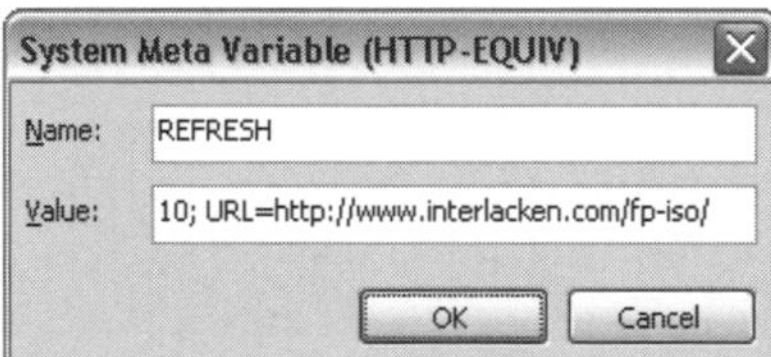

Figure 18-7. This dialog box adds a variable to the System Variables list shown in Figure 18-6.

To change the value of a variable, select the variable, click the Modify button, and replace the value. To delete a variable, select it, and then click Remove.

For information about system variables, refer to "Configuring HTML Header Properties," later in this chapter.

If you entered some text in the Page Description box of the General tab, don't be surprised if it shows up as a user variable named *description* on the Custom tab. These are simply two different ways to view of the same information. Similarly, any text you enter in the General tab's Keywords box will show up on the Custom tab as a user variable named *keywords*.

Language Page Properties

Figure 18-8 shows the Language tab, which controls the HTML character encoding for the current page (that is, the international character set).

For more information about HTML encoding, refer to "Reviewing Site Settings," on page 1137.

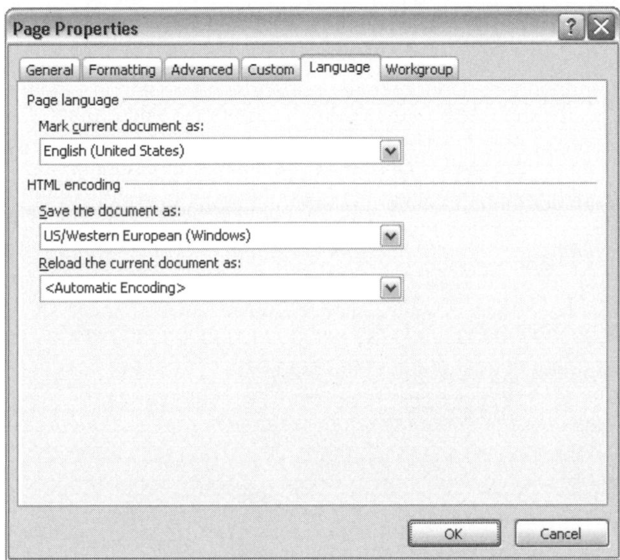

Figure 18-8. The Language tab of the Page Properties dialog box controls language usage.

The choices available depend on the languages installed with your copy of FrontPage:

- **Mark Current Document As** Specify the default language FrontPage should use when checking spelling. The default is the default language for your computer.

  To mark part of a page as being in a different language, first select it in Design view, and then choose Set Language from the Tools menu. Select the language you want from the Set Language dialog box, shown in Figure 18-9, and then click OK.

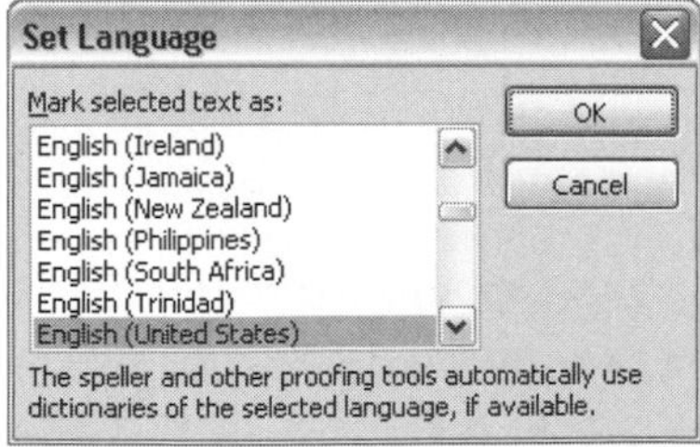

Figure 18-9. This dialog box marks the language of a selected portion of text.

- **Save The Document As** Select the character set FrontPage should use for saving the current page. The default comes from the Language tab of the Web Settings dialog box. To display the Web Settings dialog box, choose Web Settings from the Tools menu.

For more information about the Web Settings dialog box, refer to "Reviewing Site Settings," on page 1137.

- **Reload The Current Document** Select the character set a browser should use to display the current page. The default is <Automatic Encoding>, which lets the browser make this decision.

  Note that if you specify any setting other than <Automatic Encoding>, the browser must receive the page, note the character encoding, and then reload the page with that encoding.

Workgroup Page Properties

The Workgroup tab of the Page Properties dialog box appears in Figure 18-10.

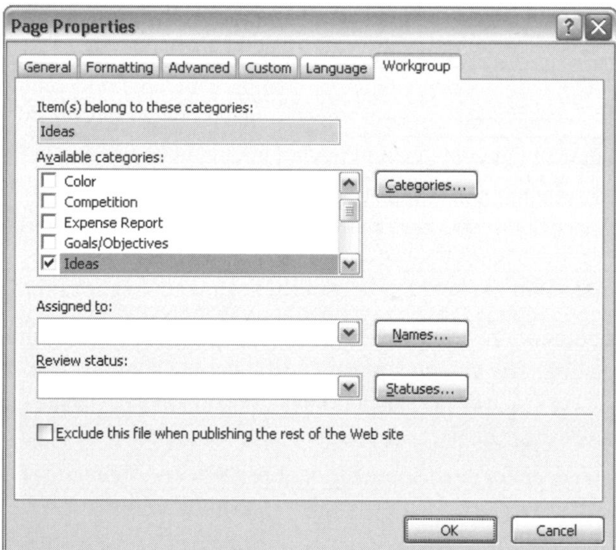

Figure 18-10. The Workgroup tab provides access to options that track a page's progress within a shared development environment.

This group of settings records and controls workgroup progress for developing the current page:

- **Item(s) Belong To These Categories** This read-only box displays a list of categories assigned to the current Web page. Use the Available Categories list to modify this information.

- **Available Categories** Check each listed category to which the current page belongs. Click the Categories button to modify the list of categories.

  This setting works in concert with any Table Of Contents Based On Page Category components on other pages in the same FrontPage-based Web site.

For more information about the Table Of Contents Based On Page Category component, refer to "Using the Table of Contents Based On Page Category Component," on page 727.

- **Assigned To** Type or select the name of the person assigned to this page. To update the selection list, click the Names button.
- **Review Status** Type or select the current review status for this page. To update the selection list, click the Statuses button.
- **Exclude This File When Publishing The Rest Of The Web** When you publish the current Web site to another location, any pages with this check box selected won't be transferred. This might be desirable for work in progress.

Configuring HTML Header Properties

This section describes a number of additional properties and features you can configure for pages in your Web site.

Note Get Rudimentary with HTTP Header Properties.

Unfortunately, FrontPage provides no convenient check boxes or drop-down lists to control the highly useful settings described in this section. One way or another, you have to configure them by hand.

Using the REFRESH System Variable

The REFRESH system variable shown previously in Figure 18-7 is a very useful one. It instructs the browser to wait a specified number of seconds—10 in that example—and then automatically jump to the specified URL. This is how some sites introduce themselves with a timed series of pages.

Another use for the REFRESH system variable occurs when you move a popular page to another location. In the page's old location, you might leave a blank or informative page containing a REFRESH system variable that automatically jumps visitors to the new location. Here are two tips for using this feature:

- An informative page should be displayed long enough for the visitor to read at least the most important parts.
- If you decide to use a blank page, set the delay for 1 or 2 seconds. Setting the delay to zero interferes with the Back button on your Web visitor's browser; the instant the visitor clicks the Back button, your REFRESH page kicks the view forward again.

Rating Your Web Site's Content

The Internet Content Rating Association (ICRA) has established a scheme whereby you can rate your Web site's content in four categories: violence, nudity, sex, and language. Web visitors can configure their browsers to display warnings or block access to sites that exceed a given level of content in the four supported categories. Here are some reasons to categorize your Web site this way:

- To be a good Internet citizen.
- To permit access by visitors who block unrated sites.
- To protect yourself from complaints by visitors offended by your content.

To use the ICRA system, you must complete a simple registration process. Here's the complete procedure for rating your site:

1. Browse the ICRA's Web site, at *www.icra.org*.
2. Follow the Label Your Site link on the home page, and complete the rating process.
3. When this process is complete, the final Web page will contain a long string of characters you should add to your Web page. (You will also receive an e-mail message containing this string.) Copy this string to the Clipboard by selecting it and then pressing Ctrl+C.
4. Use FrontPage to open the Web page you want to rate.
5. Click the Code tab at the bottom of the editing window.
6. Locate the <head> tag. This tag occupies one of the first few lines in the Web page.
7. Set the insertion point immediately after the closing angle bracket (>) in <head>.
8. Press Ctrl+V or Shift+Insert to paste the text you copied in step 3.
9. Click the Normal tab to resume editing.

Making an Icon Appear in the Favorites List

As you might have noticed, a custom icon identifies certain Web sites that you add to the Favorites list in Internet Explorer. These icons give a site additional visibility and encourage past visitors to browse your Web site again. There are two ways to make such icons appear:

- Place an icon file named favicon.ico in your Web server's root folder. For example, put the file at *www.interlacken.com/favicon.ico*.

  When the visitor adds any page from your server to his or her Favorites list, your icon will appear next to the link both on the Favorites menu and in the Favorites pane (which appears on the left in the browser window).
- If you don't have access to your Web server's root folder or want certain pages to display a different icon, add a tag such as the following to the <head> section of the Web page:

```
<link rel="shortcut icon" href="/fp-iso/iconjjb.ico">
```

This is a line of code you'll need to insert by hand. Switch to Code view, and enter it just after the <head> tag or just before the </head> tag.

This technique adds an icon that behaves just as in the first method, but only for the Web page that contains the tag.

There are two restrictions to the use of such icons. First, they work only with Internet Explorer 5 and later. All other browsers ignore them. Second, the icon must be exactly 16 by 16 pixels in size and be in Windows icon file format. Files in this format usually have a file extension of .ico.

If you don't have a graphics editor that creates .ico files 16 by 16 pixels in size, try Axialis AX-Icons. You can download and purchase this software from *www.axialis.com/order/index.html.*

Understanding RGB Color Values

The proper combination of red, green, and blue light can perfectly simulate any color humans can perceive. Computer video equipment leverages this effect to display color pictures. For each pixel (picture element) on the monitor screen, the application specifies the desired amount of red, green, and blue light. Most video equipment provides 256 intensities of red light, 256 of green, and 256 of blue. This produces 16,777,216 combinations, which is more colors than the eye can discern.

The Red, Green, Blue (RGB) system of color values describes colors just as video cards and monitors do: as three color intensities, each ranging from 0 to 255. Here are some examples:

- The RGB color 255-0-0 means pure, maximum-intensity red.
- 0-0-255 means pure, maximum-intensity blue.
- 0-0-0 means black.
- 255-255-255 means white.

Some HTML statements require RGB values coded as hexadecimal numbers. In this notation, the value *00* means none of a color and *FF* means maximum intensity. The color *#00FF00* means no red, maximum green, and no blue. The leading pound sign (#) indicates that what follows is hexadecimal.

Tip If you're not good at doing hexadecimal conversions in your head, use the Scientific mode of the Windows Calculator accessory. This mode has Hex and Dec options that toggle the calculator between these two number systems.

Achieving Accurate Rendition—Safe Colors

In the early days of the Web, display adapters capable of displaying all 16,777,216 combinations of red, green, and blue were both specialized and expensive. Most video cards of the time supported 16 fixed colors or 256 selectable colors at once. The 16-color display adapters had essentially no chance of displaying Web pages correctly, and they quickly passed out of use. The 256-color systems became the order of the day; many of these systems are still in use.

Note A video card that contains 8 bits of memory for each pixel can display 2^8, or 256, colors at once. A video card that contains 24 bits of memory for each pixel can display 2^{24}, or 16,777,216, colors at once.

Nowadays, of course, video systems that display all 16,777,216 colors are common. They typically go by the name of 24-bit color, 32-bit color, or True Color. If you know that all your visitors—or at least the overwhelming majority of them—have such video cards, you can use any colors you want and ignore the issue of safe colors. Otherwise, the safe choice is to optimize your color selections for visitors with 8-bit displays.

An 8-bit video card can display 16,777,216 different colors, but only 256 at a time. This isn't a problem when you're displaying a single Graphics Interchange Format (GIF) picture, because most programs tell the video system to display the same 256 colors that appear in the picture. However, three problems arise when you're displaying pictures on a Web page:

- On most computers with 256-color displays, not all 256 colors are programmable. On Windows-based computers, for example, 20 colors are reserved for use by Windows so that window borders, menu bars, button faces, and other elements of the user interface maintain a consistent appearance. This leaves only 236 colors that can be adjusted to match those in a picture.
- Web pages can contain any number of GIF pictures. Each GIF picture can contain only 256 colors, but two pictures on the same page—if they have no colors in common—can require a total of 512. Three pictures can require 768 colors, and so forth. This presents a problem if the display hardware can accommodate only 256 colors in total.
- A single Joint Photographic Experts Group (JPEG) picture can contain far more than 256 colors: up to 16,777,216 (but no more than one per pixel, of course). A 256-color system has no hope of rendering such a picture accurately.

Most browsers solve this dilemma by programming 256-color displays with a fixed 216-color palette. The 216 colors are all combinations of six evenly spaced intensity levels of red, the same six levels of green, and the same six levels of blue. Table 18-2 shows these six levels. These are the only colors you can be sure browsers will display as you intended, and for this reason those 216 are commonly called the *browser-safe colors*.

To display colors with RGB intensities other than 0, 51, 102, 153, 204, or 255, the browser either *dithers* or *substitutes*. When dithering, the browser displays nonstandard colors as a mixed pattern of standard-color pixels. In theory, the viewer's eye perceives the mixed pattern as a smooth area, but in practice, the perception is often grainy. Dithering usually works better on continuous-scale pictures, such as photographs. It's most objectionable on pictures with large solid areas, such as text, flood fills, and line art.

Table 18-2. Safe Palette Color Intensities for 256-Color Video Systems

Intensity	Decimal	Hex
Minimum	0	00
	51	33
	102	66
	153	99
	204	CC
Maximum	255	FF

When substituting, the browser simply replaces nonstandard colors with its idea of the closest standard color. Browsers normally apply substitution rather than dithering for background colors, because dithering a background can seriously affect the readability of text.

Why should you care about all this? Well, both dithering and substitution result in Web visitors seeing something other than what you intended. To avoid this, take one of these steps:

- Specify only the following RGB values for text, backgrounds, and solid pictures: 0, 51, 102, 153, 204, or 255.
- If you must supply RGB color values in hexadecimal, specify only values 00, 33, 66, 99, CC, or FF.

Using FrontPage Color Dialog Boxes

FrontPage provides three levels of control over most color settings. To fully exploit the use of color in your Web pages, you need to understand all three levels. They are as follows:

- A drop-down list with these choices: Automatic, the 16 original VGA colors, any other colors that already appear in the current page, and Custom.
- A second dialog box with 127 color swatches, 6 gray-scale swatches, a black swatch, a white swatch, and a button for "picking up" any color currently displayed on screen.
- The standard Windows color picker with 48 basic color swatches, 16 configurable color swatches, and controls for specifying exact colors two different ways: via the Hue, Saturation, Luminance (HSL) color model and via the Red, Green, Blue color model.

Figure 18-11 shows the first level of detail, the drop-down list that appears when you click the drop-down arrow next to any color control in a FrontPage dialog box. The Automatic choice normally means a color configured in the visitor's browser. Clicking any of the 16 color swatches arranged in two rows selects that color. To see the name of any color, let the mouse pointer rest over it.

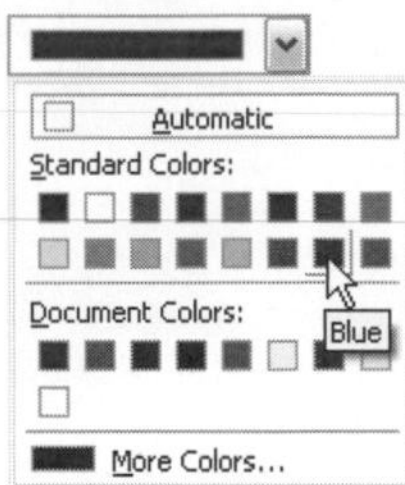

Figure 18-11. Most color choices in FrontPage begin by offering this drop-down menu.

It's usually best to choose Web colors with RGB components of 0, 51, 102, 153, 204, and 255. These are the browser-safe colors that even 256-color display systems can display accurately. Unfortunately, as illustrated in Table 18-3, only 8 of the 16 color swatches comply with this advice.

For more information on browser-safe colors, refer to "Achieving Accurate Rendition—Safe Colors," earlier in this chapter.

Table 18-3. Colors in the 16-Color VGA Palette

Safe colors					Unsafe colors				
Standard name	**FrontPage name**	**Color values**			**Standard name**	**FrontPage name**	**Color values**		
		R	**G**	**B**			**R**	**G**	**B**
Black	Black	0	0	0	Gray	Gray	128	128	128
White	White	255	255	255	Light Gray	Silver	192	192	192
Red	Red	255	0	0	Dark Red	Maroon	128	0	0
Green	Lime	0	255	0	Dark Green	Green	0	128	0
Blue	Blue	0	0	255	Dark Blue	Navy	0	0	128
Cyan	Aqua	0	255	255	Dark Cyan	Teal	0	128	128
Magenta	Fuchsia	255	0	255	Dark Magenta	Purple	128	0	128
Yellow	Yellow	255	255	0	Dark Yellow	Olive	128	128	0

Even the eight compliant colors are rather boring: black, white, the three primaries, and their complements. These are wonderful colors and, used properly, they provide plenty of contrast. However, they're hardly intriguing. You'll produce more subtle and interesting Web pages by choosing custom colors with safe RGB components. To do so, click the More Colors choice, and examine the More Colors dialog box, shown in Figure 18-12.

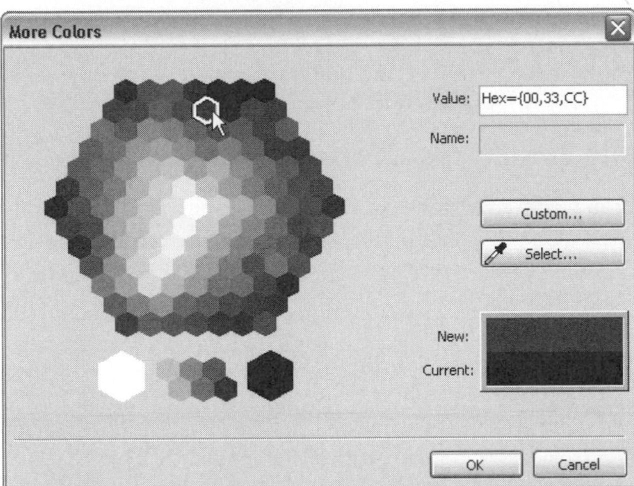

Figure 18-12. You can select any color shown in this dialog box simply by clicking the corresponding swatch. In addition, after clicking the Select button, you can use the mouse to pick up any color currently displayed on your screen.

Inside Out

Only in Windows: Artless Color

To their detriment, the FrontPage and Windows dialog boxes for picking colors both carry a lot of historical baggage. Both make it difficult, for example, to lighten, darken, or wash out colors without changing their hue. And neither has any facility for choosing combinations of colors. Oh well—maybe in the next release.

The large hexagon in Figure 18-12 is actually a color wheel with red at five o'clock, green at nine o'clock, and blue at one o'clock. Dark shades occupy the edges, light tints occupy the center, and saturated colors lie between. Below the color wheel are a white swatch, a black swatch, and between them, six gray-scale swatches.

A safe-color version of the More Colors dialog box would have black, white, 4 shades of gray, and 210 colors. Instead, this dialog box has 6 shades of gray and 127 colors, and some of each are unsafe. Rather than optimizing this feature with browser-safe colors, the FrontPage designers made it resemble the comparable one in Microsoft PowerPoint.

Fortunately, most of the 127 color swatches *are* browser-safe. To verify the browser safety of any color, hold the mouse pointer over it, and check the value displayed in the Value box. If any of the two-digit Hex values *aren't* 00, 33, 66, 99, CC, or FF, the color *isn't* browser-safe. The color selected in Figure 18-12, for example, fails the test.

HSL and the Color Dialog Box

A large part of the standard Windows dialog box for color selection displays a continuous banded rectangle of colors you can choose by clicking. Figure 18-13 shows this dialog box. This banded rectangle, plus the slider bar just to its right, utilizes the HSL color model.

Like RGB, HSL uses three numbers to denote each color. (Because the eye perceives color in three dimensions—red, green, and blue—most numerical color models use three dimensions as well.) Here's how the Color dialog box supports the HSL color scheme:

- The top edge of the banded rectangle represents a hue dimension that varies from 0 to 239. 0, at the right, means red; 80 means green; and 160 means blue. At 239, the scale wraps around to 0 (red) again.

  To select a hue, drag the crosshairs left and right within the banded rectangle, or type a number between 0 and 239 in the Hue box.
- The vertical edge of the banded rectangle represents saturation. A saturation of 240, which is the top of the scale, means that the color contains no gray. A saturation of 0, the bottom of the scale, means that the color is gray. (The bottom edge of the banded rectangle is solid gray.)

  To select a saturation value, drag the crosshairs up or down within the banded rectangle, or type a number between 0 and 240 in the Sat box.
- The slider on the right in the dialog box controls luminance. This dimension controls the brightness of gray referred to by saturation. The highest setting, 240, means white; 0 means black; and 120 produces the most vivid hue (no white or black added to the basic hue). Regardless of hue and saturation, the top of the slider is always pure white, and the bottom is pure black.

  To vary luminance, drag the slider up and down, or type a number between 0 and 240 in the Lum box.

HSL's fascination with gray stems from its origins in the television industry. Luminance is the black-and-white portion of a television signal. The inventors of color television modified the black-and-white television signal, adding hue and saturation data in such a way that monochrome sets would ignore them.

Most Web designers find the HSL system more difficult to understand than RGB. However, it does provide a way to select colors visually, and its frequent appearance in Windows color dialog boxes makes learning it worthwhile.

To pick up a color already displayed on your screen, first click the Select button, causing the mouse pointer to become an eyedropper. Move the eyedropper over the color you want, anywhere on the screen, and then click the mouse button.

Clicking the More Colors dialog box's Custom button displays the third FrontPage color picker: the Color dialog box, shown in Figure 18-13.

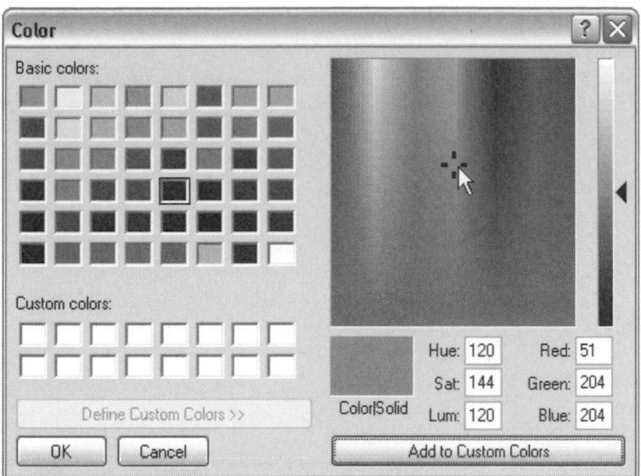

Figure 18-13. FrontPage's third color picker is the standard Windows Color dialog box.

The Color dialog box presents 48 standard color swatches (mostly unsafe), 16 configurable color swatches, and text boxes for specifying exact colors two different ways:

- Entering values of 0, 51, 102, 153, 204, and 255—and no others—in the Red, Green, and Blue boxes at last provides access to all 216 browser-safe colors.
- Dragging the crosshairs around the large banded rectangle and moving the slider on the right chooses colors by means of the HSL system. The sidebar "HSL and the Color Dialog Box" provides more information about this system.

  After choosing a color by this means, you can correct it to the nearest safe color by rounding each of the Red, Green, and Blue values to 0, 51, 102, 153, 204, or 255.

In Summary...

This chapter explained how to control the overall attributes of a Web page. It also provided advice and background material that many people find helpful when choosing color schemes.

The next chapter explains how HTML divides part of a Web page into a grid of rows and columns, and how you can use this facility for page layout.

Chapter 19

Using HTML Tables for Page Layout

Tables are one of the most useful features HTML provides. Before tables were available, HTML offered no practical means to organize content horizontally or in grids. The entire World Wide Web was left-justified.

Tables consist of horizontal *rows*, vertical *columns*, and *cells*—where rows and columns intersect. Each of these elements can have specific attributes—such as height, width, and the spacing between each cell in a table. You can also apply certain attributes to the table as a whole. For instance, you can change the table's alignment on the page or tell the browser to draw a border around it.

HTML tables can present tabular information the way a chart or spreadsheet does, but controlling page layout is their most important use. A table creates a grid on your page, and you can use the grid to position the various page elements. It's often a good idea to sketch your tables on paper before you create them in Microsoft Office FrontPage 2003. You'll save time and frustration by making most of your decisions about layout, spacing, and alignment before you create your grid.

Creating and Editing Tables

FrontPage 2003 provides two markedly different user interfaces for working with HTML tables, and in fact calls the results by two different names:

- **Conventional HTML tables** The sorts of tables FrontPage has been creating since its beginning. FrontPage provides some facilities for working with conventional HTML tables while in Design view but requires switching to dialog boxes more often than might be the case with layout tables.

- **Layout Tables** Have relative fixed dimensions and display these dimensions when you select a table in Design view. FrontPage provides rich controls for resizing layout tables; for adding and resizing rows, columns, and cells; and for other operations—all without leaving Design view

Beneath the hood, both kinds of table are the same. Whatever mess of HTML a layout table creates, the user interface for a conventional table can create as well, and vice versa. You might wonder, then which approach to use for your own work. Here are some guidelines:

Conventional HTML tables are most likely to please longtime HTML coders, longtime FrontPage designers and Web programmers. There are three reasons for this:

- They already know how to work with conventional HTML tables, and it's usually easier to stick with what you know.
- Conventional HTML tables have a more direct relationship with the HTML itself. The more you switch back and forth between Design view and Code view, the more likely you'll prefer conventional HTML tables.
- Conventional HTML tables can size themselves automatically to their contents, to the browser window, or to any other object that contains them.

  To appreciate this concern, imagine a Web page designed completely with layout tables. Because such tables have a fixed width, the browser displays them perfectly only when the visitor sizes the browser window to one perfect width. At any other width, the browser window displays extra white space to the right of the page content, or the right margin obscures some of the page content.

  A suitably configured HTML table, on the other hand, can always fill the entire browser window, no matter how wide or narrow the window might be. Variable-width content, such as running text, will likewise flow to fill the horizontal space available. Objects you configure to stay at the left window border, the right window border, or the center of the page will retain those alignments no matter the size of the browser window.

Layout tables are most likely to please design professionals coming to the Web from other media. Here are some of the reasons:

- Many such professionals feel they simply can't create anything without knowing the width of the display and the width of each design element. The design for a tall, thin poster—to cite an extreme example—would be much different from the design for a banner. Layout tables always use fixed heights and widths, and this greatly appeals to such professionals.
- Design professionals are quite accustomed to working directly on the work—as they would with pencil on paper, oil on canvas, or other traditional media—and much less accustomed to working with dialog boxes and other property sheets.

The next few sections will explain how to create simple tables of each type. Later sections will describe how to use tables for laying out more complex content. Keep in mind, however, that no matter which set of tools you use for creating a table, you can always switch to the other set later.

For additional information about using tables to design Web pages, refer to Appendix E, "Designing Attractive Web Pages with Tables."

Preparing to Create Fixed-Width Page Layouts

FrontPage 2003 has several new features that simulate the experience of arranging page layouts on a drawing table. These can be very helpful, especially when you're designing layout tables.

Setting the Design View Page Size

This feature modifies the normal Design view display to simulate a specific window size in the Web visitor's browser. This assumes, of course, that you know (or at least can surmise) what the width of the browser window will be.

Controlling the Browser Window Size

Trying to arrange page layouts without knowing the browser window size is so vexing to some designers that they look for ways to take this preference away from the Web visitor. The following script, for example, sets the width of the browser window to 800 pixels, and its height to 600 pixels:

```
<script>
<!--
function sizeWindow(){
  if (navigator.appName.substring(0,9)=="Microsoft"){
    window.resizeTo(800,600);
  }else{
    window.outerHeight=600;
    window.outerWidth=800;
  }
}
// -->
</script>
```

You can put this script almost anywhere in the page, but somewhere in the <head> section is usually best. To make it run, add an *onload* attribute like this to the <head> tag:

```
<body onload="sizeWindow();">
```

Be forewarned, however, that most Web visitors will hate you for this. They've already sized the window to suit their tastes, and by overriding their choice, you create extra work for them to drag the window back to the size they prefer.

To activate this feature, choose Page Size from the View menu. A submenu like this should appear:

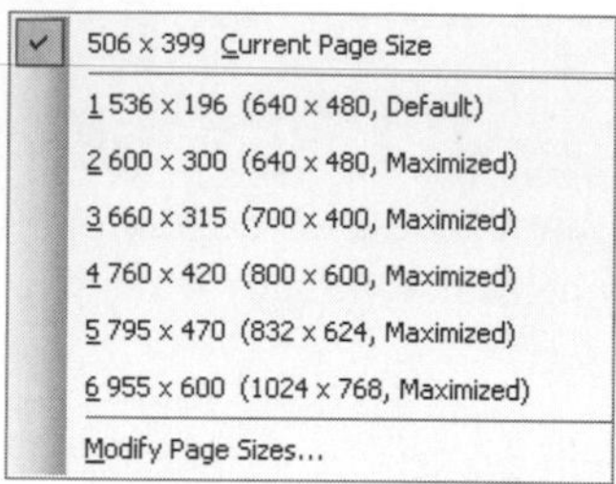

- The first choice continually resizes the Design view window to the available space, and will usually be an odd size. Choose this option to turn your back on specific height and width settings; Design view will expand or contract to fit the window size.
- Each of the next few options identifies a preset window size. If the page size you want appears here, choose it.
- Choosing the last option, Modify Page Sizes, displays the Modify Page Sizes dialog box, shown in the background in Figure 19-1.

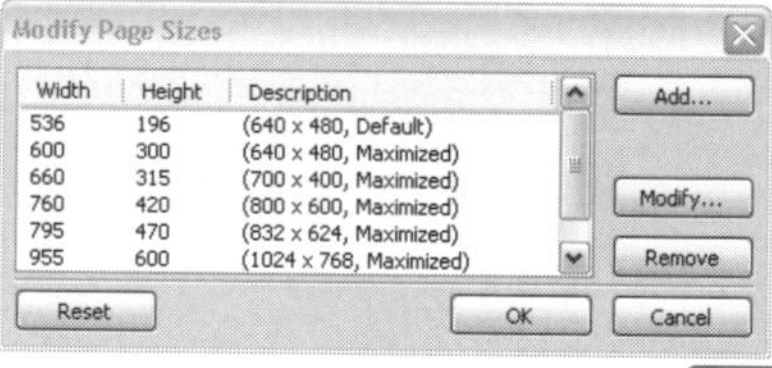

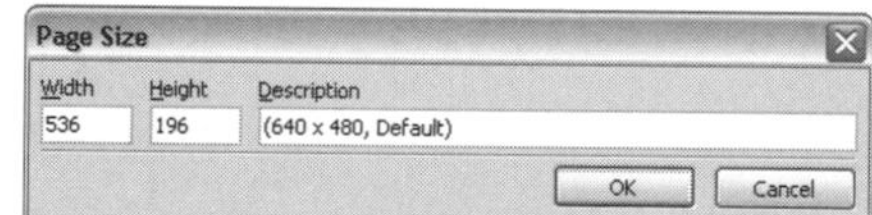

Figure 19-1. FrontPage can size the Design view window to simulate any size browser display you want.

> **Caution** Choosing a page size in Design view has no effect on the page size Web visitors use when viewing your page. Any page size you choose is simply an assumption on your part.

To add a new selection to the Page Size menu:

1. Click the Add button in the Modify Page Sizes dialog box.
2. When the Page Size dialog box shown in the foreground of Figure 19-1 appears, configure these settings:
   - **Width** The width of the document area you want to target.
   - **Height** The height of the document area you want to target.
   - **Description** A description that will identify this choice on the Page Size menu.
3. Click OK to close the Page Size dialog box.

To modify an existing Page Size menu command, select it in the Modify Page Sizes dialog box, and fill in the resulting Page Size dialog box as you would for a new command. To remove a command from the Page Size menu, select it in the Modify Page Sizes dialog box, and then click Remove.

Note that the Width and Height settings in the Modify Page Sizes dialog box specify the size of the browser's document area, not the external size of the browser window. You must exclude the browser's window borders, title bar, menu bar, toolbar, status bar, and any other such elements when you specify these settings. The windowsize.htm Web page shown in Figure 19-2 might be helpful in this regard.

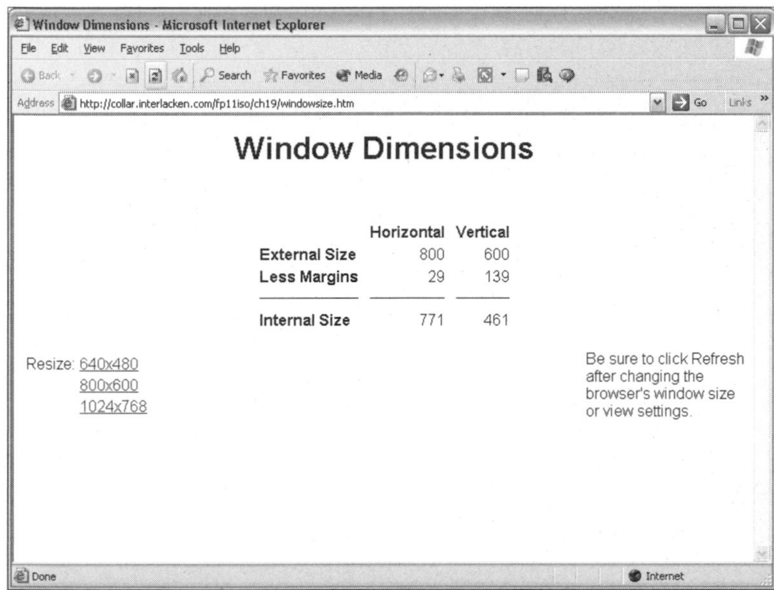

Figure 19-2. Each time you open it, this Web page displays the browser's internal and external window dimensions.

To use this page:

1. Start the browser you're concerned about.
2. Set the browser's window size and view settings as you want them.
3. Open the ch19/windowsize.htm page from the files you installed from the companion CD.
4. Use the resulting Internal Size measurements to configure a command on the Page Size menu.

Important When using the windowsize.htm page, be sure to click the browser's Refresh button after resizing the browser's window size or view settings.

With a page size setting in effect, Design view always displays pages with the width you specify. If the Design view window exceeds the width you specify, Design view displays a gray area on each side of the WYSIWYG display. If the Design view window is narrower, you'll need to scroll it left and right. To simulate the browser's document height, FrontPage draws a horizontal dotted line across the page. Figure 19-3 shows these features.

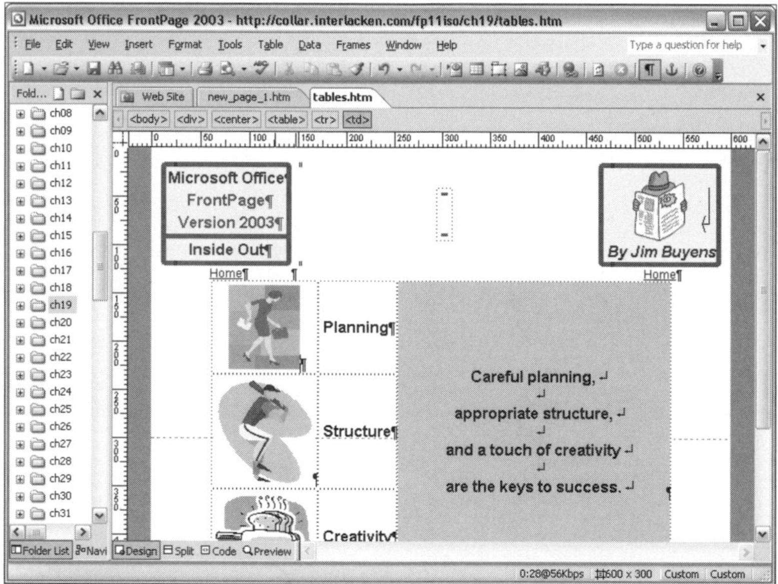

Figure 19-3. FrontPage can adjust the Design view width to simulate any size browser window. Gray areas indicate unused space at the left or right of the Design view window. The dotted horizontal line simulates the bottom of the Web visitor's window when the page first appears.

Preview mode also honors any page size settings you specify. If, however, the preview mode document area is smaller than the height and width you specify, preview mode will compress any page elements it can to make the document fit. This is also what browsers do. Figure 19-4 shows preview mode displaying the same document as in Figure 19-3, with the same page size settings in effect.

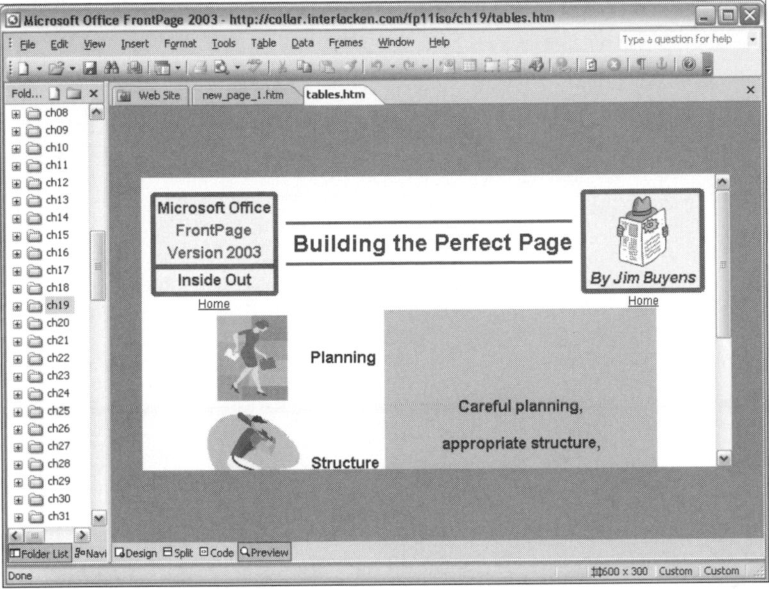

Figure 19-4. Preview mode can also simulate a given browser window size. To activate such sizing, choose Page Size from the View menu.

Displaying Rulers and Grids

If you plan to design fixed-width Web pages, you'll probably appreciate having graduated rulers along the edge of the Design view window and gridlines at convenient intervals. Here's how to get these features:

- If you want FrontPage to display horizontal and vertical rulers along the Design view window borders, choose Ruler And Grid from the View menu, and then choose Show Ruler.
- If you want FrontPage to display vertical and horizontal gridlines at regular intervals across the Design view window, choose Ruler And Grid from the View menu, and then choose Show Grid. The default is one gridline every 50 pixels.

Figure 19-5 shows the effects of choosing both options.

The View menu's Ruler And Grid submenu provides several additional options that might be helpful. These are:

- **Snap To Grid** Select this option if you want FrontPage to round all measurements to multiples of a spacing factor. The default spacing factor is 5, which means that all table and cell widths and heights will be multiples of 5. Clear this option if you want manual control of all measurements down to the single pixel.

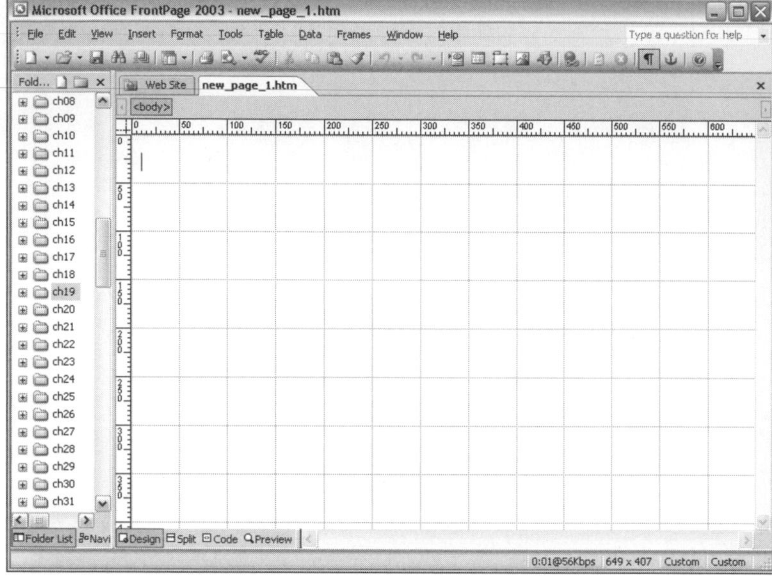

Figure 19-5. This is how Design view displays a blank Web page after you turn on rules and gridlines. These are only design guides, or course, and Web visitors never see them.

- **Set Origin From Selection** Select this option to align the horizontal and vertical rulers with the currently selected Web page element. This aligns zero on the horizontal ruler with the left edge of the selected element, and zero on the vertical ruler with the top of the selected element.
- **Reset Origin** Select this option to return the rulers to their normal state (that is, with zero aligned to the top left corner of the page).
- **Configure** Select this option to display the Ruler And Grid tab of the Page Options dialog box, shown in Figure 19-6. This is the same tab that appears if you choose Page Options from the Tools menu and then click the Ruler And Grid tab.

Here are the settings you can control by using the Ruler And Grid tab of the Page Options dialog box:

- **Ruler And Grid Units** Choose the unit of measure FrontPage should use for graduating rulers. The options are Pixels, Inches, Centimeters, and Points. (A *point* is a typographic measurement that equals 1/72 inch.)
- **Display Grid** Use these options to control the grid that appears in Design view:
  - **Spacing** Specify the number of grid units you want between gridlines. If grid units are pixels and spacing is 50, a gridline will appear every 50 pixels.
  - **Line Style** Specify the type of grid line you want: Solid, Dashes, or Dots.
  - **Line Color** Specify the color you want gridlines to be. This option uses the standard series of FrontPage color controls.

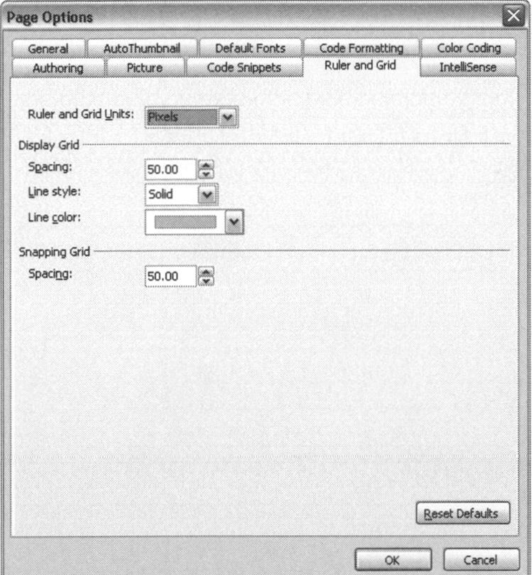

Figure 19-6. This dialog box tab controls the appearance of rules and gridlines.

- **Snapping Grid** Use this option to control the position and size of page elements when the Snap To Grid menu option is in effect:
  - **Spacing** Specify the rounding factor FrontPage should use when aligning page elements to the grid. A rounding factor of 5 (the default) means that FrontPage will force all measurements and positions to be multiples of 5.

Displaying a Tracing Image

If your starting point for a Web page is a rough sketch or other piece of artwork, you might find it helpful for FrontPage to display a copy of that art as the Design view background. This mimics the experience of working on a light table. FrontPage calls any artwork it displays this way a *tracing image*. Such images appear only when you open the page in Design view and have no direct effect on what Web visitors see.

Here's the procedure for displaying a tracing image behind the normal Design view display:

1. Convert the rough sketch or other artwork to a picture file. For example, scan it or photograph it with a digital camera. Save the picture as a GIF, JPEG, or TIFF file.
2. Convert the picture to actual size. If, for example, you want the artwork to represent 500 horizontal pixels in the browser, make the artwork 500 pixels wide.
3. In FrontPage, open the Web page you want to design.
4. Choose Tracing Image from the View menu, and then choose Configure from the resulting submenu.
5. When the Tracing Image dialog box shown in Figure 19-7 appears, click the Browse button, and locate the picture file that contains the sample layout.

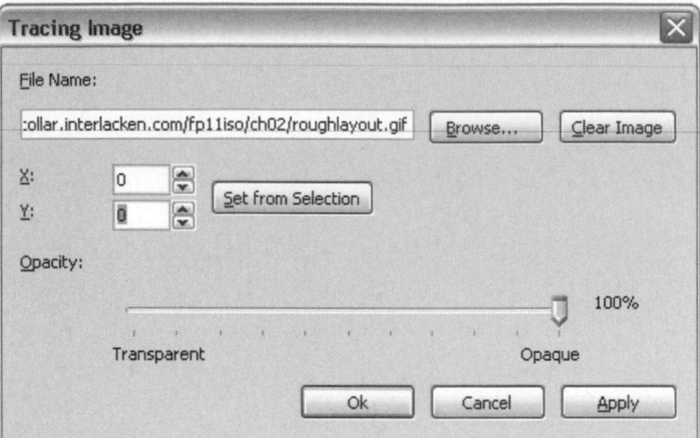

Figure 19-7. Use this dialog box to make Design view display artwork over the normal page background. Such artwork appears only in Design view.

In addition, you can modify these settings:

- **X** Specify the distance you want from the left edge of the Design view window to the left edge of the tracing image.
- **Y** Specify the distance you want from the top of the Design view window to the top of the tracing image.
- **Set From Selection** Click this button to load the X and Y settings with the coordinates of the current Design view selection.
- **Opacity** Specify the extent to which the tracing image will mask out the normal page background. A setting of 100 means that the tracing image will completely mask out the normal page background. A setting of 50 means that the tracing image will be 50 percent transparent and the normal background will show through at 50 percent intensity, and so forth.

6 Click OK when your settings are complete.

Figure 19-8 shows Design view displaying a tracing image.

Once you've specified a tracing image for a page, you can display or hide it by choosing Tracing Image from the View menu and then choosing Show Image. To remove a tracing image completely, display the Tracing Image dialog box, click the Clear Image button, and then click OK.

FrontPage remembers which tracing image to use for each page in your Web site. If you specify a tracing image that doesn't reside within your Web site, FrontPage will display it in the Save Embedded Files dialog box the next time you save the page. This prompts you to save a copy of the tracing image as part of the Web site. Normally, you should accept this offer; it ensures that the tracing image will be available to anyone who works on the page.

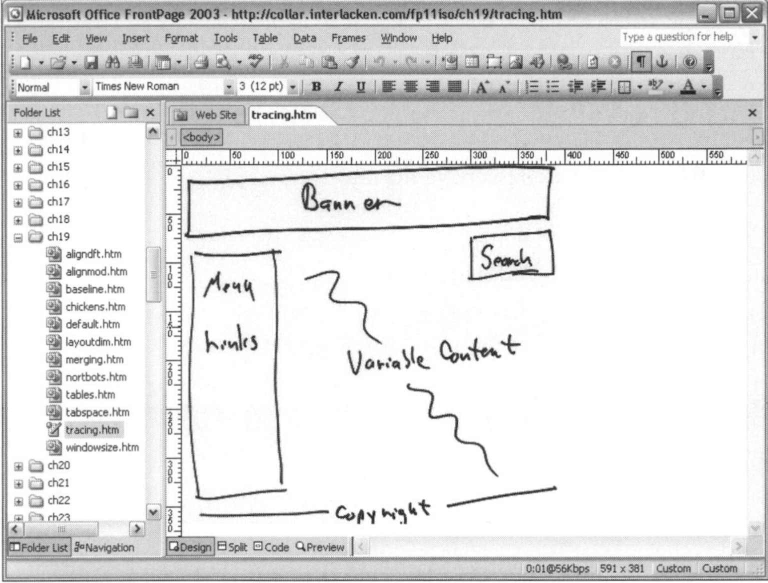

Figure 19-8. This is how Design view displays a tracing image. From here, a designer would overlay the rough sketch with actual page elements.

Creating a New Conventional Table

FrontPage provides five distinct ways to create conventional HTML tables. The method you choose depends on your preferences and the type of content you want to display. The five methods are as follows:

- Drawing with the mouse
- Using the Insert Table button
- Inserting a table using menus
- Converting text to a table
- Pasting tabular data

The remainder of this section will provide step-by-step instructions for each of these methods.

Drawing a Table with the Mouse

This method creates a one-celled table with a size and location you specify by dragging the mouse pointer across the desired area. To create more rows or columns, you subdivide an existing table, row, column, or cell by dragging the mouse pointer across it. Here's the procedure:

Draw Table

1 In Design view, choose Draw Table from the Table menu, or click the Draw Table button on the Tables toolbar. The mouse pointer will take on the shape of a pencil.

For more information about the Tables toolbar, refer to the section "The Tables Toolbar," in Appendix A.

2 Point to where you want one corner of the table to appear, hold down the mouse button, and then drag diagonally to the opposite corner of the table.

3 Release the mouse button to create the table.

Note the following:

- FrontPage sizes all such tables in pixels.
- All such tables initially consist of one cell. You can create rows and columns within the table by drawing lines with the Draw Table button.
- By default, FrontPage will position your table immediately beneath any content that precedes it. Your table will be left-aligned, centered, or right-aligned, depending on where you began to draw it.
- Drawing a line that connects two opposing sides of a table always creates a new row, column, or cell. If the line is too short or at too steep an angle, FrontPage will ignore it.
- FrontPage ignores any lines that intersect the edges of a table.
- Drawing a line that starts below an existing table and finishes inside the existing table creates a new table below the existing one.

When drawing tables, it's important to realize that the drawing pencil has two modes. And, just to make life confusing, there's no clear way to switch the pencil from one mode to the other:

- In table-drawing mode, a dotted rectangle forms as you drag the pencil diagonally across the screen. When you release the mouse button, FrontPage creates a table having approximately the same size, shape, and position as the rectangle.

  The pencil is generally in this mode when it's not near an existing table or immediately after drawing a table.
- In cell-splitting mode, a dotted line forms as you drag the pencil across the screen. When you release the mouse button, FrontPage either:
  - Slices an existing table row, column, or cell in half.
  - Discards the mouse movement if it wasn't clearly vertical or clearly horizontal, or if it didn't clearly indicate an existing table element.

  The pencil is generally in this mode when it's near an existing table.

Inside Out

Don't Lean on Drawing Tables

The table-drawing feature is a carryover from a similar feature in Microsoft Word. However, what works well for creating paper documents can be awkward for creating Web pages, and this feature is a case in point. Although it might be useful in certain instances, such as matching a tracing images, don't lock on to the table-drawing tool as your only technique for creating tables.

For information about changing a table after you've drawn it, refer to "Modifying a Conventional Table," later in this chapter.

Using the Insert Table Button

This method creates a table at the current insertion point. You specify the number of rows and columns by clicking or dragging the mouse. To use the Insert Table button in clicking mode:

1. Set the insertion point where the table should appear.
2. Click the Insert Table button on the Standard toolbar. A small grid of table cells will appear.
3. Move the mouse pointer over the grid until it shades the number of rows and columns you want.
4. Click the mouse button again to insert the table, or click Cancel to cancel table creation.

Insert Table

To use the Insert Table button in dragging mode:

1. Set the insertion point where the table should appear.
2. Click the Insert Table button on the Standard toolbar, and hold down the mouse button. A small grid of table cells will appear.
3. Drag the mouse pointer across the grid, selecting the number of rows and columns you want. The grid will grow larger if you try to drag beyond its right or bottom edge.
4. Release the mouse button to insert the table.
5. To cancel table creation, drag the mouse pointer beyond the grid's top or left edge, and then release the mouse button.

In general, the dragging method is superior because it can enlarge the supplied grid. Of course, you can always enlarge the table later with more rows and columns, should you need them. When you use either method, single line breaks will occur before and after the new table.

Inserting a Table Using Menus

Choosing a menu option and configuring a dialog box provides more control over a new table's attributes than either of the preceding methods. To take this approach:

1. Set the insertion point where the table should appear.
2. Choose Insert from the Table menu, and then choose Table from the resulting submenu. The Insert Table dialog box, shown in Figure 19-9, will appear.

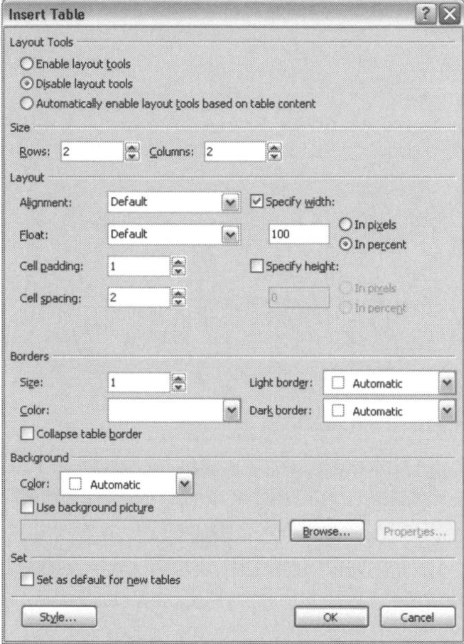

Figure 19-9. Set your table options in the Insert Table dialog box.

3. Specify the properties you want the table to have, and click OK.

Descriptions of the available properties appear in the following list. You can modify any of these properties later without re-creating the table.

Controls in the Layout Tools section show or hide layout tools for the current table.

- **Enable Layout Tools** Select this option if you always want layout tools to appear for the current table. Even with this option selected, however, FrontPage displays layout tools only after you click a table or cell border in Design view.
- **Disable Layout Tools** Select this option if you never want layout tools to appear for the current table.
- **Automatically Enable Layout Tool Based On Table Contents** Select this option if you want FrontPage to analyze the content of the table and then display layout tools at its discretion.

Frequently Asked Question

How does FrontPage mark tables as layout or conventional?

When you configure a table with the Enable Layout Tools setting, FrontPage adds the following HTML comment just before the <table> start tag:

```
<!-- MSTableType="layout" -->
```

Similarly, when you configure a table with Disable Layout Tools in effect, FrontPage adds this HTML comment just before the <table> tag:

```
<!-- MSTableType="nolayout" -->
```

If neither of these comments is present, the FrontPage editor displays layout tools or conventional tools at its discretion. This is therefore the default for tables you created in previous versions of FrontPage or in other editors that don't insert such comments.

The Size options control the dimensions of the table (that is, the number of rows and columns):

- **Rows** Enter the number of horizontal rows the table should have.
- **Columns** Enter the desired number of vertical columns.

The Layout options control page positioning and appearance:

- **Alignment** Specify the table's horizontal position on the page. The choices are Default, Left, Right, and Center. Default leaves the choice up to the Web visitor's browser—which usually results in a left-aligned table. Left and Right align a table to the corresponding margins, whereas Center positions it in the center of the page.
- **Float** This option specifies whether text will wrap around the table. The Left and Right options align the table to the left or right margin, respectively; both allow text to flow around the table. Default leaves the question of text wrapping up to the browser, which usually means it won't wrap.
- **Cell Padding** Enter the number of pixels to insert between a cell's margin and its contents.
- **Cell Spacing** Enter the number of pixels that should appear between the margins of adjacent cells.
- **Specify Width** Select this check box to control the amount of horizontal space the table will occupy. Clear it to let the browser size the table automatically, based on the contents of the table and the size of the browser window. If you select this check box, you should also specify a unit of measure and a value,
    - **In Pixels** Select this option to specify the width of the table in pixels.
    - **In Percent** Select this option to size the table as a percentage of available space in a Web visitor's browser window. A table width of 100 percent stretches the table across all available space.

Tip **Use the right container when sizing by percent.**
When you specify the dimensions of any Web page object as a percentage, that percentage is relative to the object's immediate container. Thus, depending on where it appears, an object sized at 50 percent might occupy 50 percent of the browser window, 50 percent of a frame, or 50 percent of a table cell—whichever is most specific.

- **Specify Height** Select this check box to control the amount of vertical space the table will occupy. Clear it to let the browser size the table automatically. If you select this check box, you should specify a unit of measure and a value just as you would for the width measurement.

Caution Most Web browsers treat table measurements as approximations, not as concrete specifications.

Figure 19-10 illustrates the difference between cell padding and cell spacing; they're easier to distinguish when cell borders are visible. Figure 19-10 also illustrates tables within tables.

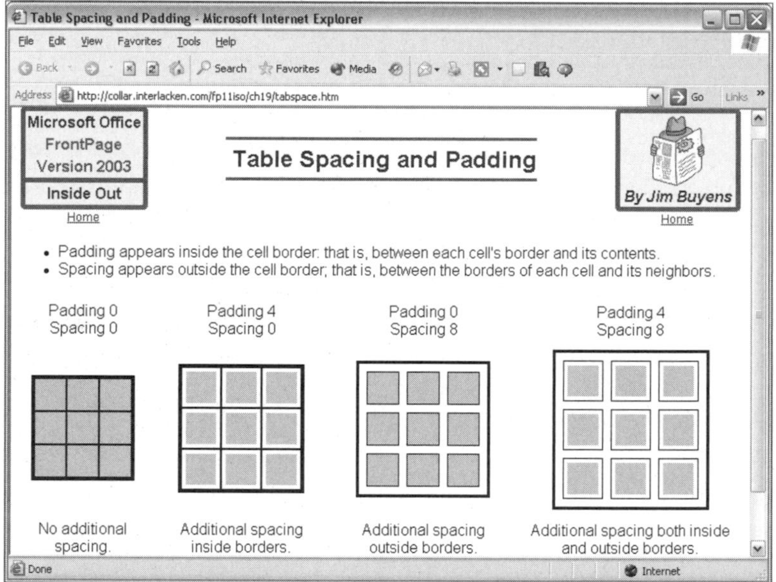

Figure 19-10. This Web page illustrates the difference between cell spacing and cell padding. Spacing occurs outside the border lines, and padding occurs within. Notice also that the four 3-by-3 tables, their headings, and their captions are located within the cells of an invisible 7-by-3 table. Columns 2, 4, and 6 contain only white space.

The Borders section of the Insert Table dialog box controls whether the table and cell edges are visible and, if so, how they appear. Here are the available settings:

- **Size** If you want a border around your table and each of its cells, enter the border's thickness in pixels. A border size of zero specifies no borders.
- **Color** Specifies a solid color for drawing the border that surrounds the table.
- **Light Border** Contributes to a three-dimensional, "raised" effect for the table by changing the color of the top and left table borders.

Tip **Provide Uniform Lighting for Three-Dimensional Objects.**

According to the Microsoft Windows user interface guidelines, the light source for three-dimensional pictures is above and to the left. Thus, to make a table, or any other object, look three-dimensional:

- Make the top and left edges light, as if catching light directly.
- Make the bottom and right edges dark, as if in shadow.

Pages take on a very confusing perspective if different objects appear lighted from different directions.

- **Dark Border** Also contributes to the 3-D effect. This setting changes the color of the right and bottom table borders.
- **Collapse Table Border** This check box controls a setting that instructs the browser how to draw borders around cells:
  - Clear the check box if you want each cell in the table to have its own four borders (top, bottom, left, and right). This is the default.
  - Select the check box if you don't want each cell to have its own border. Instead, the browser will draw a single border between any two adjacent cells.

The Background section settings control the appearance of the table background. Here are the available settings:

- **Color** Use this control to specify a background color for the table. The default setting is Automatic, which lets the page background show through. Opening the list box displays the standard set of FrontPage choices.
- **Use Background Picture** Select this option to use a picture file as the table background. Then, enter the name of a picture file in the associated text box. If the picture is smaller than the table, the picture will repeat to fill the table. If the picture is larger than the table, only the top left portion of the picture will appear.
- **Browse** Click this button to display a Select Background Picture dialog box for locating the picture file.
- **Properties** Click this button to display the Picture Properties dialog box for the current background file.

Using Collapsed Borders

Browser support for collapsed table borders is inconsistent at best. A better way of drawing single lines between table cells is to set the margin size to greater than zero, set table spacing equal to zero, and use table padding to control the amount of space between the border lines and any cell contents.

In an attempt to make HTML tables work like Microsoft Word tables, FrontPage 2002 made collapsed table borders its default. To get normal table cells, you had to display the Table Properties dialog box for the table and then select the Show Both Cells And Table Borders check box. This default proved unpopular, and as a result, FrontPage 2003 no longer collapses borders by default.

The following settings, by the way, are exact opposites. Clearing one check box is exactly the same as selecting the other.

- In FrontPage 2002: Show Both Cells And Table Borders
- In FrontPage 2003: Collapse Table Border

Despite its name, the Set section contains only one control. Without speculating how such a state of affairs ever came to pass, here's that lonely control:

- **Set As Default For New Tables** Select this check box if, when you click OK or Apply, you want FrontPage not only to apply your choices to the current table, but also to save them as defaults for creating new tables.

Tip **Set Table Defaults by Example.**
At first, it might seem inconvenient that to save defaults for creating new tables, you must create a sample table and then delete it. However, the same approach makes it very convenient to open the Table Properties dialog box for an existing table that looks just right, select Set As Default For New Tables, and click OK.

Finally, at the bottom of the dialog box and not part of any settings group, FrontPage provides the following button:

- **Style** Click this button to apply CSS properties to the table.

Figure 19-11 shows the result of inserting a table with the properties specified in Figure 19-9.

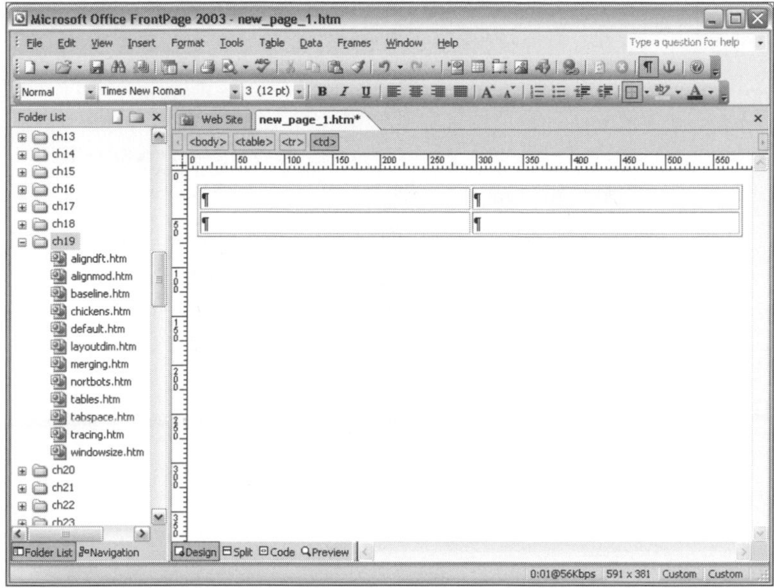

Figure 19-11. This table uses the default settings shown in Figure 19-9.

Converting Text to a Table

To create a table from existing text, follow these steps:

1. Select the text you want to convert by dragging the mouse pointer across it.
2. Choose Convert from the Table menu, and then choose Text To Table.
3. In the Convert Text To Table dialog box, shown in Figure 19-12, choose one of the following and then click OK:
   - To convert each paragraph in the text to a full row in the table, select Paragraphs.
   - To divide each row's text into columns based on the presence of tab characters or commas, select Tabs or Commas.
   - To draw a one-celled table around the selected text, select None.
   - To divide each row's text into columns based on some other character, select Other and type the character you want in the box.

> **Tip** To convert an existing table to text, first select the table, then choose Convert from the Table menu, and then choose Table To Text. Each cell in the table will become an ordnary paragraph.

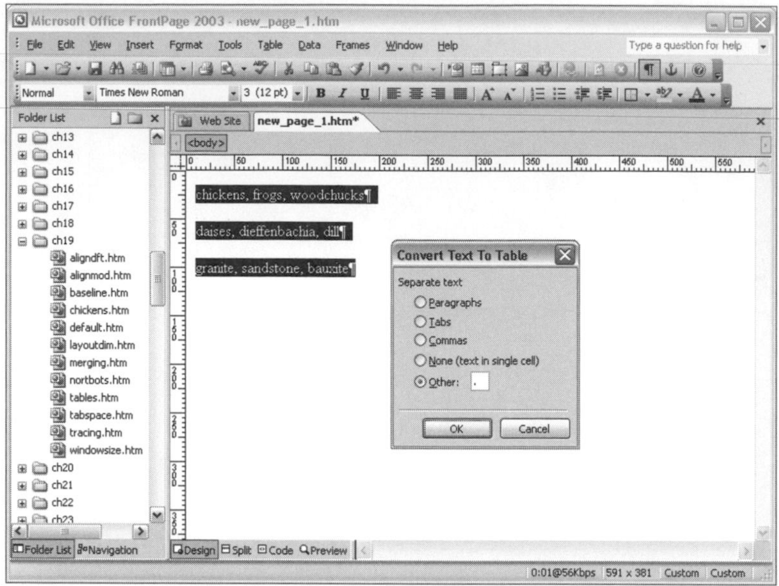

Figure 19-12. The Convert Text To Table dialog box builds a table from existing text.

Pasting Tabular Data

Another way to create a table in FrontPage is to paste tabular content from other programs, such as a table from a word processor or database, or cells from a spreadsheet. If FrontPage doesn't automatically create a table, use the Paste Special command from the Edit menu to format the text as you paste it. Then, if necessary, use the Convert Text To Table dialog box to complete the table.

Using the Table AutoFormat Feature

Within a table, you can specify different background colors, fonts, or typefaces for certain cells to create a more eye-catching presentation. FrontPage has a number of predefined table designs, and you can use the Table AutoFormat feature to add one of them to your table in much the same way you'd add a theme to a Web site. There are two ways to apply a design to your table: using the Table AutoFormat dialog box and using the Table AutoFormat drop-down list.

To use the Table AutoFormat dialog box:

1. Select the table you want to format by setting the insertion point inside it.
2. Click the Table AutoFormat button on the Tables toolbar, or choose Table AutoFormat from the Table menu. Either action will display the Table AutoFormat dialog box, shown in Figure 19-13.

Table AutoFormat

Figure 19-13. The Table AutoFormat dialog box adds predesigned formatting to an existing table.

3 Use the following options to control your table's appearance:

- **Formats** Choose a design for your table from this list.
- **Preview** When you choose a format, an example appears in this section.
- **Formats To Apply** After choosing a table format, you can customize it by selecting or clearing the check boxes listed in Table 19-1. The Preview pane will reflect your choices.

Table 19-1. Formatting Options on the Table AutoFormat Dialog Box

Format	Description
Borders	Toggles the use of borders in the table.
Shading	Specifies whether the table will contain shaded areas.
Font	Toggles the use of style-specific type for certain text in the table.
Color	Switches between gray and a background color for the shaded areas of the table.
AutoFit	Reduces the table size to fit the content of a table.

- **Apply Special Formats** These check boxes apply special formatting to rows and columns. Table 19-2 lists the choices.

Table 19-2. Special Format Options on the Table AutoFormat Dialog Box

Special Format	Description
Heading Rows	Specifies whether the top table row is shaded.
First Column	Turns shading on or off in the first table column.
Last Row	Highlights last row with shading, borders, or a combination, depending on the format you choose.
Last Column	Highlights the last column with shading, borders, or a combination, depending on the format you choose.

4 Click OK.

To use the Table AutoFormat drop-down list:

1 Select the table you want to format by setting the insertion point inside it.

Table AutoFormat

2 Choose a table formatting option from the Table AutoFormat drop-down list on the Tables toolbar.

To remove previously applied formatting from a table, select the table, and choose None from the Table AutoFormat drop-down list.

Modifying a Conventional Table

Regardless of how you create a table, you probably won't get it exactly right on the first try. Most people spend considerably more time modifying and refining existing tables than creating new ones.

The Table Properties dialog box contains settings that affect an entire table. There are two ways to open this dialog box:

- Set the insertion point anywhere in the table, choose Table Properties from the Table menu, and then choose Table.
- Right-click anywhere in the table, and choose Table Properties from the shortcut menu.

Either action displays a Table Properties dialog box that, except for its title, is identical to the Insert Table dialog box shown previously in Figure 19-9. All the settings work just as they did when creating a new table, except that they default to the setting for the current table. (Of course, they affect the current table as well.)

Adding Rows and Columns to a Table

Three methods are available for adding rows or columns to a table: using menus, using the Tables toolbar, and using the mouse.

To add rows or columns using menus:

1. Click any cell that will adjoin the new row or column.
2. Choose Insert from the Table menu, and then choose Rows Or Columns.
3. In the Insert Rows Or Columns dialog box, select either Rows or Columns.
4. Indicate the number of rows or columns to insert. The Number and Location labels change depending on whether you are inserting rows or columns.
5. For rows, specify whether to insert the new row(s) above or below the current selection. For columns, specify whether to insert the new column(s) to the right or left of the current selection. Then, click OK.

To add rows to a table using the Tables toolbar:

1. Select one or more existing rows that will appear under the new row. To learn how to select cells, see the sidebar "Selecting Table Cells."
2. Click the Insert Rows button on the Tables toolbar.

   With each click, FrontPage will insert, above your selection, the same number of rows that you selected.

Insert Rows

Tip When you insert rows using the Tables toolbar or the mouse, FrontPage inserts them above the selected rows. When you insert columns, they appear to the left of whatever columns you selected.

Likewise, to add columns to a table using the Tables toolbar:

1. Select one or more existing columns that will appear to the right of the new column.
2. Click the Insert Columns button on the Tables toolbar.

   To the left of your selection, FrontPage will insert the number of columns you selected.

Insert Columns

To insert rows or columns using the mouse:

- Right-click any part of an existing row, and then choose Insert Rows from the shortcut menu.
- Right-click any part of an existing column, and then choose Insert Columns from the shortcut menu.

Selecting Table Cells

There are four approaches to selecting cells, rows, columns, or an entire table:

- **Using menus** Click any cell in the desired range, choose Select from the Table menu, and then choose the Table, Column, Row, or Cell command.

- **Using mouse movements at the table margins** Move the mouse pointer over the top margin to select columns, or over the left margin to select rows:
  - To select a single column or row, click when the mouse pointer changes to an arrow.
  - To select multiple columns or rows, hold down the mouse button when the arrow appears, and drag along the appropriate margin.
- **Clicking cells** These procedures use mouse clicks inside a table to select cells, rows, columns, and entire tables. This provides more flexibility than any other method.
  - To select a single cell, hold down the Alt key and click the cell.
  - To select a range of cells one cell at a time, hold down Ctrl+Alt and drag the mouse pointer across each cell. As an alternative to dragging, click each cell you want to select while pressing Ctrl+Alt.
  - To select a contiguous range of cells, drag from one corner of the selection to the opposite corner. You can also click one corner cell and then click the opposite corner while holding down the Shift key.
  - To add cells to a selection, hold down the Shift key while clicking the additional cells.
  - To remove cells from a group of selected cells, click the cells while pressing Ctrl+Alt.
  - To select the entire table, click the top or left table margin while holding down the Alt key.

- **Using the Quick Tag Selector** This is the newest and coolest method of all. A covert example appeared without warning in Figure 19-11; it's the toolbar displaying a row of HTML tags above the Design view window.
  - If no Quick Tag Selector bar appears above an open Web page, choose Quick Tag Selector from the View menu.
  - To select any table, row, or cell, click its tag in the Quick Tag Selector bar.
  - If you get lost, click any element in the Design view window. This will select the corresponding tag in the Quick Tag Selector bar.

  This method is particularly useful when you're dealing with nested tables or with very small cells.

Adding and Removing Table Cells

HTML tables are quite flexible and don't require all rows to have the same number of cells. To add cells to a single row:

1. Click inside the cell just to the left of where you want the new cell to appear.
2. Choose Insert from the Table menu, and then choose Cell.

In Figure 19-14, the insertion point was in the cell numbered 5 when the Web designer inserted a cell. The new cell appeared between existing cells 4 and 5.

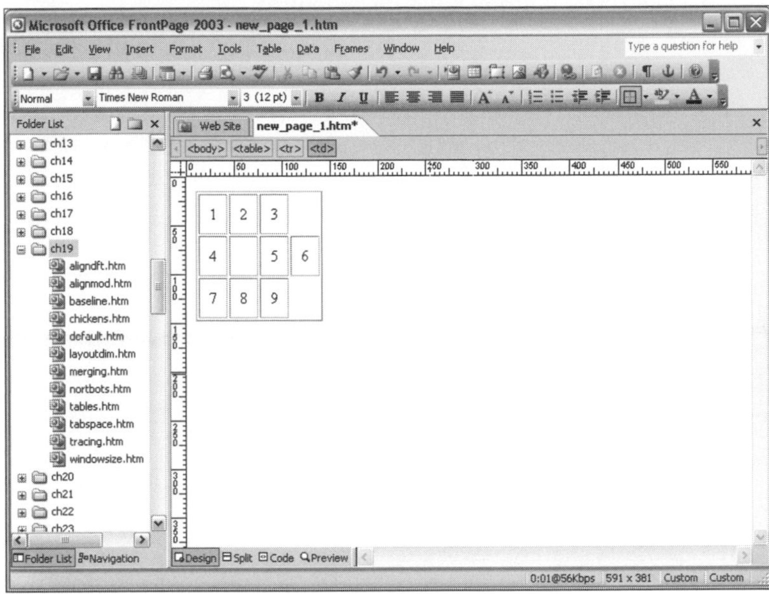

Figure 19-14. A cell was added to this table between cells 3 and 4 in the second row.

To delete cells:

1. Select the cell(s) you want to remove.
2. Choose Delete Cells from the Table menu, or click the Delete Cells button on the Tables toolbar.

Delete Cells

FrontPage can also merge adjacent cells to span several rows or columns. Figure 19-15 illustrates this concept; notice the large cells in the bottom left and top right corners that occupy the space normally occupied by two cells.

There are two basic procedures for merging cells:

- **Merging adjacent cells** This procedure combines a selected range of cells into one.
  1. Select the cells you want to merge. They must be contiguous and form a rectangular block—no L-shapes or other irregular shapes are allowed. Selecting the cells you want is the tricky part of this procedure. Refer to the earlier sidebar "Selecting Table Cells" for details.
  2. Choose Merge Cells from the Table menu, or click the Merge Cells button on the Tables toolbar.

Merge Cells

- **Erasing cell boundaries** This procedure merges two cells at a time by eliminating the barrier between them.

Eraser

1. Click the Eraser button on the Tables toolbar.
2. Drag the mouse pointer across any cell boundary. This will merge the adjoining cells.

> **Caution** Merging two cells into one produces quite a different result than deleting one of the cells. Merged cells span multiple rows or columns—whatever space the individual cells occupied before the merge. Deleting a cell forces adjacent cells to move in from below or from the right.

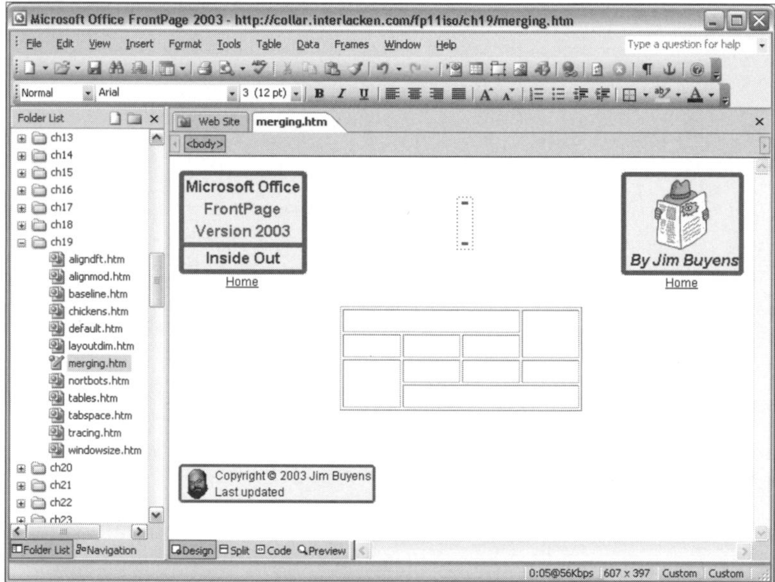

Figure 19-15. The oversized cells in the corners of this table resulted from merging cells in a 4-by-4 table.

Split Cells

To split a cell or cells into further columns or rows, select the cell(s), and then either click the Split Cells toolbar button or choose Split Cells from the Table menu. In the Split Cells dialog box, specify whether to split the selected cell(s) into columns or rows, and specify how many.

There are no restrictions on which cells you can split. If splitting a cell creates more rows or columns than its neighbors already span, FrontPage will increase the span of the neigboring cells.

Suppose, for example, that you have a column of ordinary cells, and that you split one of them into two columns. FrontPage will change each remaining cell in the same column so it spans the two cells you created from one

Adding a Table Caption

To give a table a caption, click anywhere in the table, choose Insert from the Table menu, and then choose Caption. FrontPage will create a blank caption above the table and set the insertion point there. Type the caption text you want. To move the caption below the table, follow these steps:

1. Click the caption, choose Table Properties from the Table menu, and then choose Caption. (Alternatively, right-click the caption, and choose Caption Properties from the shortcut menu.)
2. Choose the caption position you prefer—Top Of Table or Bottom Of Table—and then click OK.

Figure 19-16 shows a simple 4-by-4 table containing some data. Inserting the text was a simple matter of setting the insertion point inside each cell and then typing. The same approach works for inserting pictures and other objects—even additional tables—into a cell. You can configure the same properties for items within a cell that you can set for them elsewhere on the page.

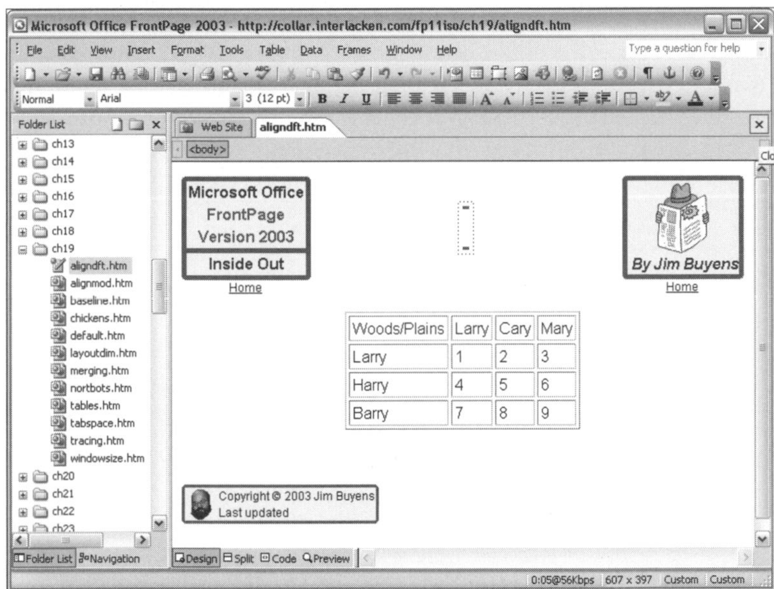

Figure 19-16. Like a browser, FrontPage adjusts default column height and row width, based on cell contents and window size.

By default, the rows and columns in a table grow in height and width to accommodate cell content. Browsers—and FrontPage as well—normally try to minimize white space by widening columns whose cells contain a lot of text. At the same time, they try to keep columns wide enough not to truncate any pictures or other fixed-width objects. If possible, the browser sizes the table horizontally to fit within the available display area.

Working with Conventional Table Cells

After you create a table, the next step is usually to format its cells and fill them with content. This section will explain how to perform such tasks.

Using the Cell Properties Dialog Box

Although the table layout in Figure 19-16 looks generally pleasing, several aspects beg improvement. The numeric entries should allow for two-digit numbers and should be right-justified, for example, and the column headings lack contrast. You can make these kinds of adjustments in the Cell Properties dialog box. To open the Cell Properties dialog box:

1. Select one or more cells using one of these methods:
   - Set the insertion point in a cell.
   - Select content in one or more cells.
   - Use any of the methods described in the sidebar "Selecting Table Cells."
2. Choose Table Properties from the Table menu, and then choose Cell. Alternatively, right-click the selection, and choose Cell Properties from the shortcut menu.

The resulting Cell Properties dialog box is shown in Figure 19-17. This dialog box controls many of the same properties as the Insert Table dialog box (shown previously in Figure 19-9), but only for the selected cells. Other properties, however, apply to cells only.

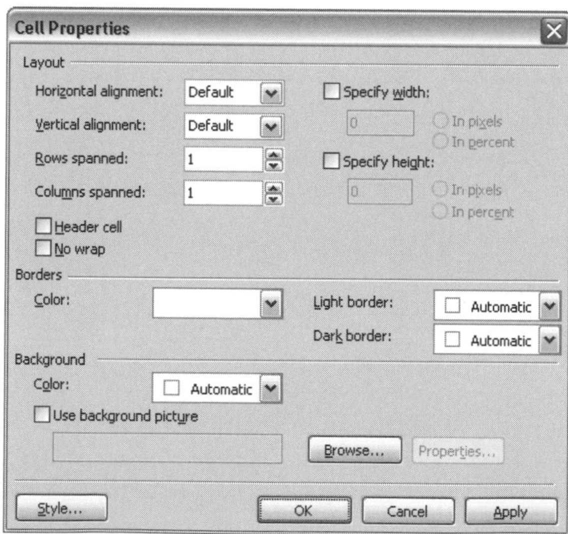

Figure 19-17. The Cell Properties dialog box exposes settings for any number of selected table cells.

The Cell Properties dialog groups options into three sections: Layout, Borders, and Background.

The Layout heading identifies the first group of settings in the Cell Properties dialog box. These settings specify where objects in the selected table cell appear. You can apply all of the following properties to a single cell or a block of cells:

- **Horizontal Alignment** Controls lateral positioning of the cell's contents. The Left and Right options align the contents to the left or right border. Center positions the contents an equal distance from the left and right borders, and Justify aligns the contents flush against both borders. Default leaves alignment to the browser, which usually aligns left.
- **Vertical Alignment** Controls vertical positioning of the cell's contents. Again, there are four possibilities:
    - **Top** Aligns the cell's contents to the top of the cell. Any white space appears at the bottom.
    - **Middle** Distributes any vertical white space half above and half below the cell's contents.
    - **Baseline** Aligns the baseline of the first line of text with the baselines in adjacent cells, as in the following example:

Baseline Baseline Baseline	Vertical Vertical Vertical	Alignment Alignment Alignment

    - **Bottom** Aligns the cell's contents to the bottom of the cell. Any white space appears at the top.
    - **Default** Leaves vertical alignment to the browser, which usually chooses Middle.

> **Note** In typography, the *baseline* is an imaginary line on which characters such as *m* and *x* rest. Characters such as *p* and *q* extend below the baseline.

- **Rows Spanned** Indicates the height of the cell in terms of normal table rows.
- **Columns Spanned** Indicates the width of a cell in terms of normal table columns.

> **Note** Merging cells and setting a span accomplish similar results, but they aren't the same. Merging combines two or more cells into one wider cell that spans multiple rows or columns; cells not involved in the merge retain their former positions. Setting a span widens one cell to cover multiple rows or columns, pushing any following cells to the right.

- **Header Cell** When selected, this option indicates that the selected cell contains headings. This normally causes any text to appear in boldface.
- **No Wrap** When selected, this option indicates that the browser mustn't wrap text in the selected cell.
- **Specify Width** This option signifies that a minimum cell width is in effect. To use this setting, you must select the check box, specify a value, and indicate a unit of measure. Click In Pixels to specify the width of the cell in pixels; click In Percent to size the cell as a percentage of the table width.

> **Caution** If you specify column widths that exceed the width of a table, the results will be unpredictable.

- **Specify Height** This option signifies that a minimum height is in effect. To use this setting, you must select the check box, specify a value, and indicate a unit of measure. Click In Pixels to specify the height of the cell in pixels; click In Percent to size the cell as a percentage of the table height.

The Borders section contains settings that control the border colors of the cell or cells you selected:

- **Color** Specifies a solid color for drawing the cell border.
- **Light Border** Specifies a color for drawing the top and left cell borders.
- **Dark Border** Specifies a color for drawing the right and bottom cell borders.

The Background section contains settings that control the background color or background picture for the cell or cells you selected:

- **Color** Specifies the color you want the cell's background to have. If you choose Automatic, the cell background will match the table background.
- **Use Background Picture** Select this check box if you want the cell to have a background picture, and then specify the background picture's file name and location in the current Web site.
- **Browse** Click this button to display a Select Background Picture dialog box. Selecting a picture in this dialog box makes it the background picture for the cell or cells you originally selected.
- **Properties** Displays a standard Picture Properties dialog box that, in this case, alters the properties of a background picture you already specified.

Finally, at the bottom of the dialog box and not part of any settings group, FrontPage provides the following button:

- **Style** Controls CSS properties for the cell(s) you selected.

Compare Figure 19-16 and Figure 19-18.

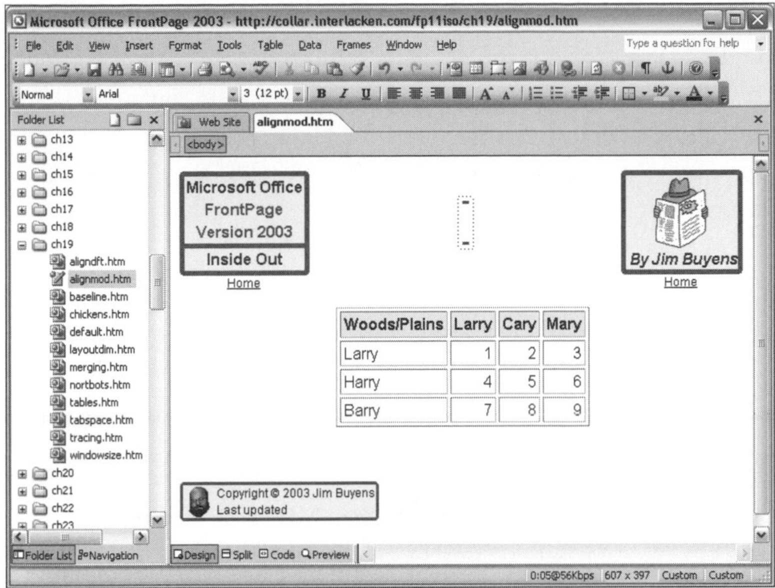

Figure 19-18. Although still simple, this table's appearance is enhanced from that in Figure 19-16.

The latter figure reflects the following edits:

- The cells in the top row have a background color of #EEEEEE.
- The text in the top row of cells is boldface.
- The cells containing numbers are right-aligned.

Adding Content to Table Cells

The procedures for adding content to a table cell are identical to those for adding content anywhere else on a Web page. You simply click inside the cell and start typing! The same procedures work for pictures and other page elements, and even additional tables. If necessary, both FrontPage and the browser will enlarge the cell to accommodate whatever content you supply.

The Table toolbar has two buttons that help propagate the same contents to several cells.

Fill Down

- **Fill Down** To use this button:
  1. Enter any repeating content in the topmost cell you want to include.
  2. Select that cell and all cells below it that should contain the same content.
  3. Click the Fill Down button on the Tables toolbar.

Fill Right

- **Fill Right** To use this button:
  1. Enter any repeating content in the leftmost cell you want to include.
  2. Select that cell and the cells to its right that should contain the same content.
  3. Click the Fill Right button on the Tables toolbar.

You can also modify the background color of an entire table or any number of cells by using the Tables toolbar. If this seems appealing:

1. Select the table, cell, or cells you want to modify.
2. Click the Fill Color button on the Tables toolbar. This displays a standard series of FrontPage color controls for choosing the background color you want.

Fill Color

Aligning Cell Content

Both FrontPage and the browser can align cell content to any border. This means that you can align content vertically to the top, bottom, or middle of a cell, or horizontally to the left edge, right edge, or center of a cell. The section "Using the Cell Properties Dialog Box," earlier in this chapter, described how to specify such alignment using the Cell Properties dialog box.

The following toolbar buttons can also align content within a cell. Be sure, however, to select the entire cell—and not just the cell content—before clicking these buttons. Otherwise, the action might apply to the content rather than to the cell.

> **Tip** When a conventional table cell is selected, Design view displays it with a solid black background. When a layout cell is selected, Design view displays a blue border with size boxes and handles.

- On the Formatting toolbar:

  - **Align Left** Click this button to align the left edge of the content with the left edge of the cell.

  - **Center** Click this button to align the horizontal center of the content with the horizontal center of the cell.

  - **Align Right** Click this button to align the right edge of the content with the right edge of the cell.
- On the Tables toolbar:

  - **Align Top** Click this button to align the top of the content with the top of the cell.

  - **Center Vertically** Click this button to align the vertical center of the content with the vertical center of the cell.

  - **Align Bottom** Click this button to align the bottom of the content with the bottom of the cell.

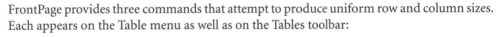

Resizing Rows and Columns

FrontPage provides a variety of techniques for specifying the height and width of individual table cells. The sad truth, however, is that the browser often overrides these. Here are some examples:

- When the browser displays a table, it forces all cells in the same row to be the same height and all cells in the same column to be the same width:
  - If either the HTML or the cell content suggests different heights for cells in the same row, the height of the tallest cell will prevail.
  - Similarly, if cells in the same column end up with different widths, the widest of these widths will prevail.
- If any cell contains a picture wider than the HTML specifies, the browser will make the cell as wide as the picture.
- If all the text and other wrapping content won't fit in the dimensions the HTML specifies, the browser will increase the height of the cell so that all the content is visible.
- If possible, the browser tries to fit the entire page within the visible document window. To do this, it uses a complex algorithm that adjusts column widths and then row heights to make the entire table visible and to minimize its height. However, the preceding rules still apply and might constrain this process.

The section "Using the Cell Properties Dialog Box, earlier in this chapter, explained how to modify cell heights and widths using the Cell Properties dialog box. Another method is to click and drag any table or cell border; when you release the mouse button, FrontPage will lock in all the cell heights and widths for the entire table.

Distribute Rows Evenly

FrontPage provides three commands that attempt to produce uniform row and column sizes. Each appears on the Table menu as well as on the Tables toolbar:

- **Distribute Rows Evenly** This command sets the height of the currently selected table to its present value in pixels, divides this value by the current number of rows, and sets the height of each cell to the resulting value.

Distribute Columns Evenly

- **Distribute Columns Evenly** This command sets the width of the currently selected table to its present value in pixels, divides this value by the current number of columns, and sets the width of each cell to the resulting value.
- **AutoFit to Contents** This command removes all sizing attributes from the current table. The browser then sizes the rows and columns to minimize the height of the table without exceeding the width of the available display area.

AutoFit to Contents

Unfortunately, the power of these commands is greatly diminished by HTML's weak control over the dimensions of table cells. Browsers consider cell dimensions specified in the HTML code as initial suggestions only. You can specify all the cell dimensions you want, but the browser, reacting to the Web visitor's current display window, will still apply its own cell-sizing logic.

Creating a New Layout Table

Using a layout table mimics the practice of arranging page elements on a ruled typesetter's grid or desktop publishing program. Few, if any, elements in the composition are self-sizing; instead, the measurements are fixed and absolute. For designers accustomed to print media, this is a much easier paradigm to follow.

From an HTML point of view, layout tables are an illusion. You can certainly tell FrontPage to create a layout table or a conventional table, and you can use different tools to do each job. In either case, however, the resulting HTML code conforms to the same HTML specification that's been in effect for years.

From another point of view, the only difference between layout tables and conventional tables lies in the toolset you use to manipulate them. In most respects, a layout table is a conventional table that you choose to modify by using the new layout table toolset.

The section "Inserting a Table Using Menus," earlier in this chapter, already described one way of creating layout tables. Briefly, that procedure is:

1. Set the insertion point where you want the table to appear.
2. Choose Insert from the Table menu, and then choose Table.
3. When the Insert Table dialog box appears, click the Enable Layout Tools option.
4. Specify any other table properties you want.
5. Click OK.

Converting any existing table to a layout table is just as easy. Take your pick of these procedures:

- Using menus:
  1. Right-click the existing table.
  2. Choose Table Properties from the shortcut menu.
  3. When the Insert Table dialog box appears, click the Enable Layout Tools option, and then click OK.
- Using the Tables toolbar:
  1. Select the existing table.
  2. Click the Show Layout Tool button on the Tables toolbar.

Show Layout Tool

Show Layout Tool

Both of these methods also work in reverse. To convert a layout table to a conventional table, click Disable Layout Tools option, or click the Hide Layout Tool button that appears in place of the Show Layout Tool button.

Regardless of the conversion method you use, the layout tools might not appear until you click a table or cell border.

Much more exciting are the specialized tools FrontPage 2003 provides for creating layout tables. These reside in a new Layout Tables And Cells task pane. To use this task pane:

1. Open the Web page that will contain the layout table.
2. Choose Layout Tables And Cells from the Table menu. (Alternatively, choose Layout Tables And Cells from the drop-down menu at the top of any other task pane.) This will display the Layout Tables And Cells task pane that appears on the right in Figure 19-19.

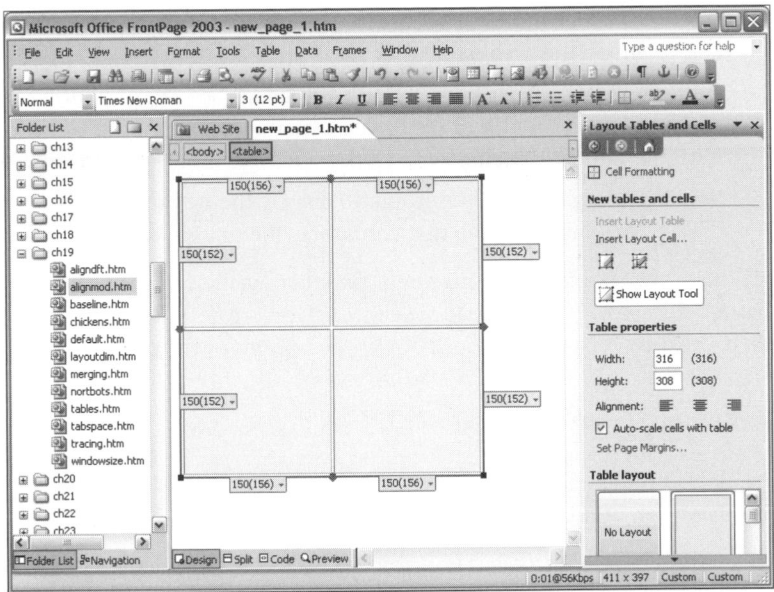

Figure 19-19. This is how a blank layout table appears in Design view. The sizing boxes and handles appear only after you select the table (for example, by clicking one of its edges).

This task pane can create layout tables three different ways. In brief, here are the three procedures:

- Click the Insert Layout Table link in the New Tables And Cells section. This creates a one-celled layout table with a default size.
- Click the Draw Layout Table button in the same section. Then:

Draw Layout Table

  - Set the mouse pointer where you want the top left corner of the new table to appear.
  - Press and hold down the mouse button.
  - Drag the mouse pointer down and to the right. When the table is as large as you want, release the mouse button.

  If you click at a spot where the rules of HTML don't allow a table to begin, FrontPage will start the table at the closest allowable spot, above and to the left of the spot you clicked.

- Click any of the templates in the Choose Layout section. This will create a new layout table with the cell arrangement you selected. The table will have a fixed width equal to that of the Design view window.

The controls in the Table Properties section modify, as you might expect, any layout table you select. Here's how to use these controls:

- **Width** Enter the width in pixels you want the layout table to have.
- **Height** Enter the height in pixels you want the table to have.
- **Alignment** Click the Left, Center, or Right button to specify the table's horizontal alignment on the Web page.
- **Auto-Scale Cells With Table** Select this check box if you want FrontPage to ensure at all times that the width of the table is equal to the sum of its cell widths, cell padding, margins, and cell spacing.
- **Set Page Margins** Click this link to display the Advanced tab of the Page Properties dialog box. This is the tab that configures the margin settings for the page.

If you use layout tables a lot, you might find it convenient for FrontPage to display the Layout Tables And Cells task pane every time you create a new page. If so, select the Show When Creating A New Page check box at the bottom of the pane. If not, clear it.

Creating Layout Cells

Like all HTML tables, layout tables consist of rows, and rows consist of cells. Within a layout table, however, FrontPage makes a distinction between ordinary cells and layout cells:

- Ordinary cells are just that: ordinary. These cells have no special properties, and if FrontPage determines that they serve no purpose, it might spontaneously delete them. No purpose, in this case, means that the cells are empty of content and contribute nothing toward positioning other content in the layout table.
- Layout cells have special properties and some very special on-screen commands. In terms of special properties, for example, you can configure layout cells to have individual borders, rounded corners, and shadows. On-screen commands can resize or reposition layout cells without affecting other layout cells in the same table.

To use layout cells effectively, think of the layout table as a drawing surface and layout cells as zones where the content appears. The ordinary cells in a layout table serve only to position the layout cells. You can create layout cells in a variety of ways, but here's the easiest:

1. Display the Layout Tables And Cells task pane.
2. If you want to draw the layout cell inside an existing layout table, select that table.
3. Click the Draw Layout Cell button in the New Tables And Cells section, or click the same button on the Tables toolbar.

Draw Layout Cell

4 Set the mouse pointer where you want the top left corner of the layout cell to appear.

5 Click and hold down the mouse button.

6 Drag the mouse pointer down and to the right. When the layout cell is as large as you want, release the mouse button.

If you drew the new layout cell inside an existing layout table, FrontPage will do its best to position the layout cell exactly where you drew it. FrontPage does this by adding new rows, columns, and cells to the existing table. Figure 19-20 provides an example.

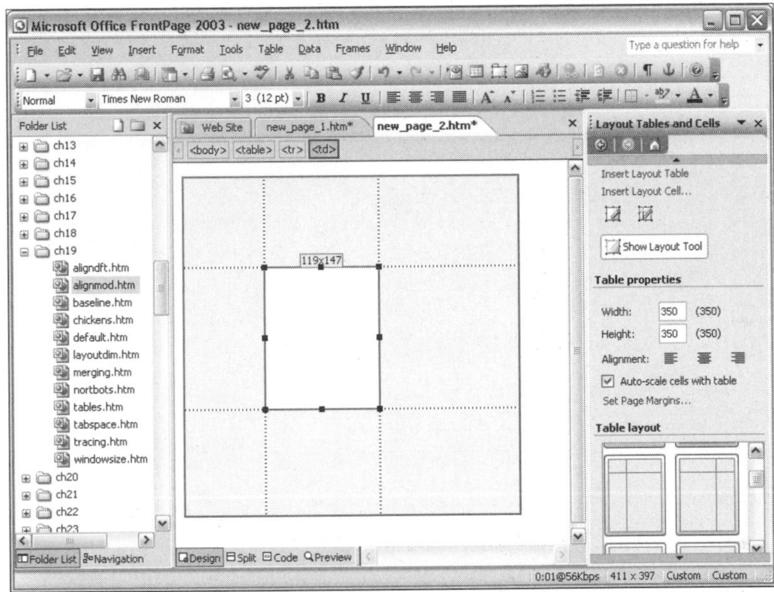

Figure 19-20. When you draw a layout cell inside a layout table, FrontPage adds and sizes enough conventional rows and columns to fix the layout cell in place.

To reproduce this example:

1 Open a new, blank Web page.

2 Display the Layout Tables And Cells task pane, click the Draw Layout Table button, and draw a table about 350 pixels on a side.

3 With the new layout table still selected, click the Draw Layout Cell button.

4 Move the mouse pointer over the new layout table and make sure the pointer looks like this:

5 Drag the mouse pointer across a rectangular area that's completely within the layout table.

Done correctly, this operation divides the table into nine cells. The center one is the layout cell you drew, and the outer eight serve only to position the layout cell where you drew it. This is rather amazing, and it gets better. Figure 19-21 shows the same Web page after drawing two more layout cells, each of which crossed existing cell boundaries. To position all three layout cells correctly, FrontPage has divided the original one-celled table into seven rows and seven columns.

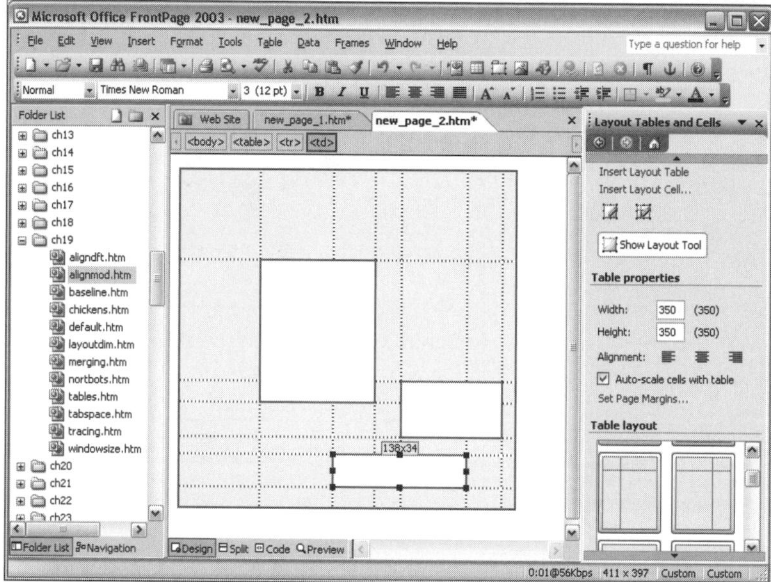

Figure 19-21. As you continue adding layout cells to a layout table, Design view keeps adding rows and columns to position them.

Inside Out

No Alignment Tools for Layout Cells

In many respects, FrontPage layout cells work like text boxes in Microsoft Publisher and Microsoft Visio. Unfortunately, FrontPage provides far fewer commands for working with layout cells than Publisher and Visio provide for working with text boxes. For example, FrontPage has no tools for:

- Cutting and pasting layout cells.
- Selecting two or more layout cells at the same time.
- Aligning the left, right, top, or bottom edges of two or more layout cells.
- Sizing several layout cells the same.
- Spacing several layout cells evenly.

Perhaps these features will appear in some future release.

Modifying Layout Tables

When you work with a layout table, FrontPage dims or hides many of the commands that add rows or columns to a conventional table. The easiest way of adding rows or columns is usually this:

1. Right-click the layout table you want to modify, and choose Table Properties from the shortcut menu.
2. When the Table Properties dialog box appears, change the number of rows and columns to the quantities you want. (Note, however, that you can't decrease the number of rows or columns in a layout table this way.)
3. Click OK to close the Table Properties dialog box.

If you're having an exceptionally lucky day, any rows or columns you create this way will be exactly the height, width, and position you want. More likely, however, you'll want to make adjustments. There are three ways of doing this: by mouse, by menu, and by task pane.

To resize or reposition a layout cell or table, you must first select it, and you must not be in drawing mode. If one of the drawing tools appears, you're in drawing mode rather than editing mode. Click the Draw Layout Cell button to change modes.

Table 19-3 shows all the mouse pointers that can appear when you're modifying layout tables and cells. If the pointer you want doesn't appear, try hovering the mouse over a different part of the table or cell edge. The corner pointer appears near the corner sizing handle, the tee pointer appears near the center sizing handle, and the move pointer appears elsewhere. Also, try selecting or deselecting the edge of the table or cell you want to modify.

Table 19-3. Mouse Pointers for Layout Tables and Cells

Pointer	Name	Action
	Draw Table	Draws a table or cells
	Draw Layout Cell	Draws a layout cell
	Move	Moves an entire cell
	Corner	Moves two adjoining sides
	Tee	Moves one side
	No entry	None available
	Double arrow	Resizes a row or column
	Heavy arrow	Selects

To resize the rows or columns of a layout table, select the layout table, and then click the tiny down arrow inside the size box that's displaying the measurement you want to change. (This refers to the blue, rectangular boxes with numbers in them, and not to the solid square sizing handles). Clicking the drop-down arrow at the left of a row will display a drop-down menu with these options:

- **Change Row Height** Choose this command to display the Row Properties dialog box, shown in Figure 19-22.

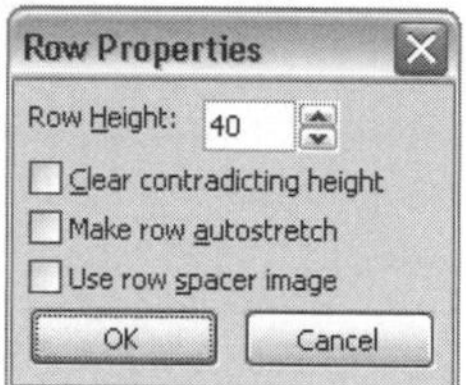

Figure 19-22. These two dialog boxes configure settings for one row or column of a layout column.

Then, modify these settings to suit:

  - **Row Height** Specify the height of the row in pixels.
  - **Clear Contradicting Height** Select this check box to correct situations where two or more cells in the same row specify different heights.
  - **Make Row Autostretch** Select this check box to let the browser determine the height of the row, depending on its contents.
  - **Use Row Spacer Image** Select this check box if you want FrontPage to control the height of the row by adding a transparent picture to the last row.

- **Make Row Auto Stretch** Choose this command to let the browser determine the height of the row, depending on its contents.
- **Use Row Spacer Image** Choose this command if you want FrontPage to control the height of the row by adding a transparent picture to the last row.

If you click the drop-down arrow at the top of a column, FrontPage will display an almost identical drop-down menu that refers to columns and widths rather than rows and heights.

Frequently Asked Question

Why does Design view display two dimensions for each row and column in a layout table?

When Design view displays two dimensions for a layout table row or column, such as 32(45):

- The first dimension is an interior size that reflects the space available for content
- The second is an external size that reports the amount of screen space the row or column will consume.

These dimensions can differ because of the space that cell spacing, border size, and cell padding occupy. Suppose, for example, that a layout table has three rows, three columns, and the following settings:

Border size	1 pixel
Cell padding	3 pixels
Cell spacing	5 pixels

Suppose also that the HTML for each cell specifies *height=32* and *width=32*. If you select such a layout table, the size boxes for each row and column won't be 32, but 45! Here's the reason, using the width of one column as an example:

	32	Cell width in HTML
+	6	Combined width of left and right cell padding
+	2	Combined width of left and right cell borders
+	5	Width of one spacing element
	45	Column width in layout table size box

Figure 19-23 illustrates this situation.

If the cells of such a table are layout cells, selecting a cell will show size box dimensions not of 32, and not of 45, but of 40. This is because when Design view calculates the height or width of a layout cell, it ignores cell spacing (which refers to space between cells, and therefore isn't part of the layout cell.)

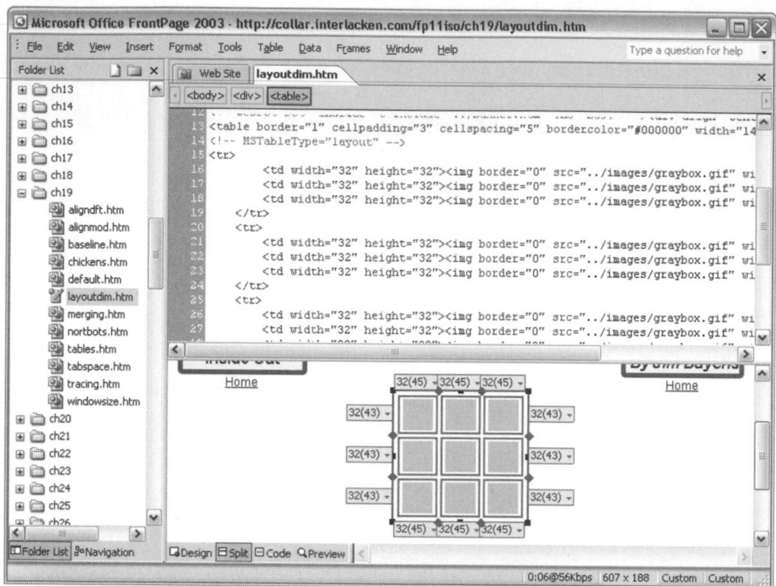

Figure 19-23. The column widths that Design view displays for a layout table take cell padding, border widths, and cell spacing into account. The corresponding HTML dimensions do not.

To resize or reformat a layout cell using the Cell Formatting task pane, first display the task pane using any of the following techniques:

- If the Layout Tables And Cells task pane is visible, click its Cell Formatting link.
- Right-click any layout cell, and then choose Cell Formatting from the shortcut menu.
- Open the drop-down menu in any task pane title bar, and then choose Cell Formatting.

The top portion of this task pane appears on the right in Figure 19-24. This is quite a long task pane—long enough that you'll almost certainly need to scroll it up and down. To do this, click the down arrow beneath the task pane or the up arrow above it. If either arrow fails to appear, the task pane is already at the top or bottom.

The top of the task pane contains these links:

- **Layout Tables And Cells** Click this link to display the Layout Tables And Cells task pane.
- **Cell Properties And Borders** Click this link to configure the size, alignment, borders, and margins or a cell.
- **Cell Header And Footer** Click this link to configure a cell's header and footer properties.
- **Cell Corners And Shadow** Click this link to configure a cell's corner and shadow properties

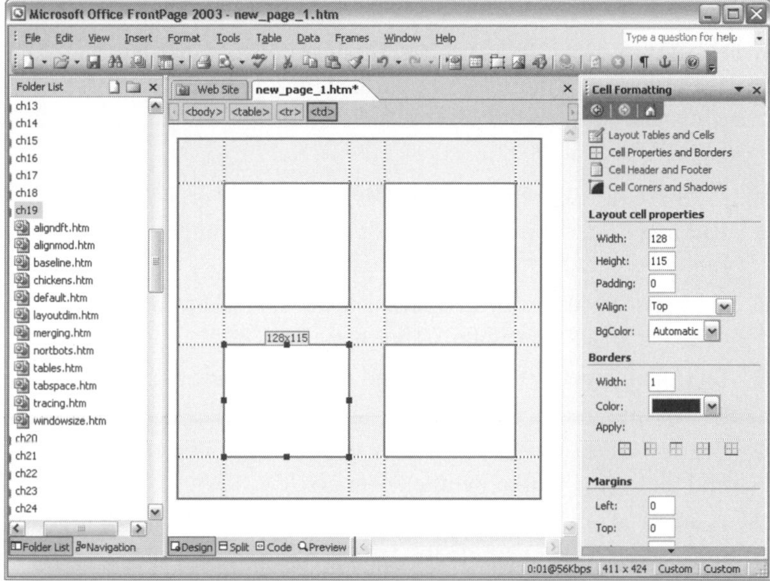

Figure 19-24. The Cell Formatting task pane controls the appearance of layout cells.

The remainder of the task pane varies depending on which of the last three links you clicked.

To modify a layout cell, first select it, and then change the settings in the Cell Formatting task pane. Click the Cell Properties and Borders link to expose the following settings:

- **Layout Cell Properties** Use these settings to change the cell's dimensions and the placement of its content:
  - **Width** Specify how wide, in pixels, you want the layout cell to be.
  - **Height** Specify how tall, in pixels, you want the layout cell to be.
  - **Padding** Specify how many pixels you want to appear between the cell border and the cell content.
  - **VAlign** Specify how you want the browser to align the cell content within the cell: top, middle, or bottom.
  - **BgColor** Specify the background color you want the cell to have. Clicking the down arrow displays a standard set of FrontPage color controls.
- **Borders** Use these settings to control lines that appear around the cell's borders:
  - **Width** Specify how thick you want the border lines to be, in pixels.
  - **Color** Specify the color you want the border lines to be. Clicking the down arrow displays a standard set of FrontPage color controls.
  - **Apply** Click a button for each side of the selected cell that you want to have borders. There are five buttons, indicating all, left, right, top, and bottom.
- **Margins** Specify the amount of background space you want to surround the cell. There are four settings, one each for the left, top, right, and bottom sides.

Click the Cell Header And Footer link to expose these settings:

- **Show Header** Select this check box if you want the layout cell to have a heading. This is an area at the top of the cell, distinguished by a different color background or other formatting, that contains title text or other distinctive content. Then, configure the following settings.
  - **Height** Specify how tall, in pixels, you want the header or footer to be.
  - **Padding** Specify how many pixels you want to appear between the header or footer border and its content.
  - **VAlign** Specify how you want the browser to align content within the header or footer area: top, middle, or bottom.
  - **Bg Color** Specify the background color you want the header or footer area to have.
  - **Border Width** Specify how thick you want the area between the cell header and the normal cell content to be, in pixels.
  - **Border Color** Specify what color the area between the cell header and the normal cell content should be.
- **Show Footer** Select this check box if you want the layout cell to have a footer. This is like a header except that it occupies the bottom of the cell. The settings for a footer are identical to those for a header.

Click the Cell Corners And Shadows link to control special visual effects. These settings are:

- **Corners** Use these settings to add rounded or custom corners to the layout cell. FrontPage implements your specification by displaying picture files in the corners of your cell.

  If you like, FrontPage will create these picture files for you. If this is what you want, click the Use Default Image option and then configure these settings:
  - **Width** Specify how wide you want the left and right borders to be.
  - **Height** Specify how thick you want the top and bottom borders to be.
  - **Color** Specify what color you want the rounded corners to be.
  - **Border Color** Specify what color you want the border surrounding the layout cell to be.
  - **Apply** Click these buttons to apply or erase corners from the layout cell. The choices are all, top left, top right, bottom left, and bottom right.

  FrontPage can also display corner files you create yourself. To proceed on this basis, look under the Image heading, click the Use Custom Image option, and then configure these settings:
  - **File Name** In this unlabeled text box, enter the Web location of the corner file you want to use.
  - **Browse** Click this button to display a standard picture box for locating the corner file by point and shoot.
  - **Width** Specify how wide you want the left and right borders to be.

- **Height** Specify how thick you want the top and bottom borders to be.
- **Apply** Click these buttons to add or remove the current corner file from one or more corners. The choices are all, top left, top right, bottom left, and bottom right.

To display a different picture in each corner of a layout cell, you must browse to the first corner file, click the corresponding Apply button, browse to the second corner file, click another Apply button, and so forth.

- **Shadows** Use these settings to add drop shadows around a layout cell.
  - **Width** Specify how thick, in pixels, you want the drop shadows to be.
  - **Softness** Specify how sharply you want the shadow to fade. The allowable range is 0 to 100, where 0 means a solid color and 100 means very light shading.
  - **Color** Specify what color you want the drop shadows to be.
  - **Apply** Click one of these four buttons to specify which sides of the layout cell should have shadows: top and left, top and right, bottom and left, or bottom and right.

> **Tip** All visual elements on the same page (or even better, in the same Web site) should have the same drop shading direction. Most often this will be bottom and right, as if light were coming from the top left corner of the Web page.

Using Transparent Pictures for Page Layout

In an effort to keep Web pages device-independent, HTML provides very little support for absolute positioning. HTML "thinks" in terms of flowing text, not in terms of objects placed on an xy-grid. This is extremely frustrating when you're presenting commercial art rather than, say, a research paper.

Tables and frames provide page designers with a rough method of xy-positioning, but for fine control, many designers have adopted the use of transparent GIF pictures. Anywhere they want some blank space on the page, they simply insert a completely transparent GIF.

> **Tip** A table cell will never be narrower than the widest picture it contains. As such, picture files exert stronger control over the size of table cells than height or width attributes you specify in the HTML.

Every pixel in a transparent GIF is the same color—transparent. Clever designers keep a 1-by-1-pixel transparent GIF, commonly called a *spacer GIF*, in their bag of tricks. This is the smallest possible file to download, and specifying an appropriate height and width for it (on the Appearance tab of the Picture Properties dialog box, shown previously in Figure 10-16) will stretch the file to any required size. Remember to clear the Keep Aspect Ratio check box so that you can independently set the width and height. You can use the same file over and over again in different locations simply by specifying an appropriate size for it each time.

Working with 1-by-1-pixel transparent GIFs presents a unique problem with WYSIWYG editors such as FrontPage: Such pictures are quite difficult to locate, select, and modify after you add them to a page. For this reason, you might find it easier to work with slightly larger files. The sample files you installed from the companion CD contain the transparent GIF files listed in Table 19-4.

Table 19-4. Spacer Files in the Sample Web.

File name	Dimensions	File size
images/trans1x1.gif	1by 1 pixels	807 bytes
images/trans5x5.gif	5 by 5 pixels	814 bytes
images/trans9x9.gif	9 by 9 pixels	821 bytes

These files will be most useful for guaranteeing the size of cells in conventional HTML tables. When you use layout table options such as Use Row Spacer Image, FrontPage creates any spacer files it needs.

In Summary…

This chapter explained the various FrontPage commands for creating and modifying HTML tables. It also provided guidance on using tables for page layout in much the same way that traditional designers use grids.

The next chapter explains how FrontPage themes can give your Web pages a uniform, professionally designed appearance.

Chapter 20

Using FrontPage Themes

Despite the fact that many beginning Web designers ignore the issue, communicating visually is something all successful Web pages must do. Human perception of information on a Web page is, after all, an artistic study, and many Web design beginners, believing that they lack artistic talent, find this issue intimidating. The task of balancing color, graphical elements such as buttons and pictures, and the text that makes up the Web's content is not only difficult, but time-consuming as well. As a result, artistic design is often an expensive task.

Microsoft FrontPage themes provide a solution for people who don't know design techniques but can recognize something they like. Themes are professionally designed style packages that include a color scheme, a font scheme, and graphical page elements that you can apply to single pages or to an entire Web site with one command.

Time and talent permitting, you can customize FrontPage themes to your heart's desire, even creating new themes if you want. To multiply the value of your efforts, any themes you create in FrontPage are available to other Microsoft Office applications as well.

This chapter first walks you through the process of applying themes to existing pages or Web sites and then covers the mechanics of customizing themes and creating new ones.

Introducing Themes

FrontPage can apply themes to a single page or to an entire Web site. Figure 20-1 shows the Theme task pane, the focal point for applying, customizing, and removing themes. To display this task pane, choose Theme from the Format menu or from the drop-down list in the title bar of any other task pane.

The Current Theme heading at the top of the task pane displays which theme, if any, is currently in effect for a page or Web site:

- If the current selection is a page open for editing or a page in the Folder List or Folders view, the Current Theme heading shows the theme in effect for that page.
- If the current selection is a folder, the Current Theme heading shows the theme in effect for the entire Web site. This is the Web site's *default theme.*

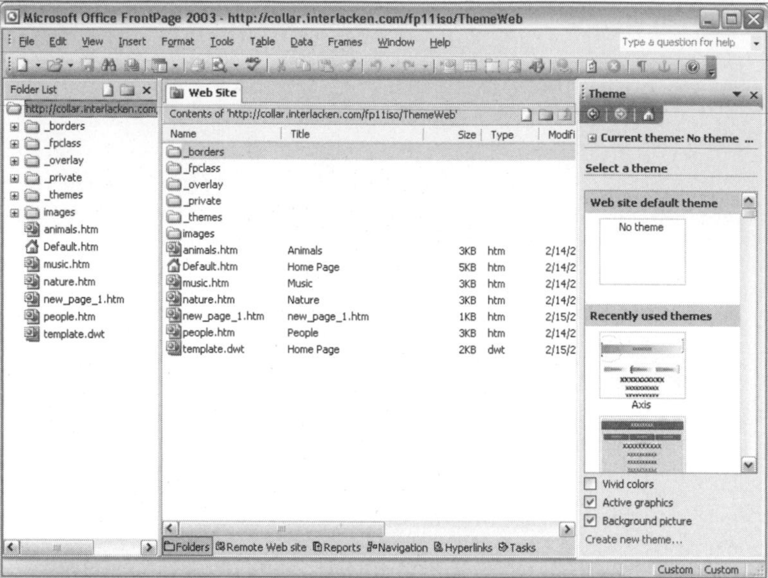

Figure 20-1. The Theme task pane imparts professional-looking designs to individual Web pages or an entire Web site.

If you click the plus sign icon to the left of the Current Theme heading, FrontPage will display specific settings in effect for that theme.

The Select A Theme section contains the controls that actually apply a theme. The scrolling list shows a thumbnail preview of each available theme, organized into three categories:

- **Web Site Default Theme** Displays a preview of the default theme for the current Web site. If no default theme is in effect, FrontPage displays a plain outline containing the words *No theme*.
- **Recently Used Themes** Displays previews of themes you recently applied.
- **All Available Themes** Displays previews of all available themes.

The three check boxes below the scrolling list control optional aspects of any theme you apply. The Create New Theme link starts a special editor for creating new themes. Later sections will explain these options.

As you'd expect, a Web site's default theme applies by default to each page in that Web site. Any theme that you apply to an individual page, however, overrides the Web site default. If you change the Web site's default theme, any themes you applied to individual Web pages will remain in effect. The next section will explain in detail how to apply themes at either level.

Tip **Apply Themes Consistently Throughout a Site**

Themes exist to give a Web site a professional and consistent look. Applying an assortment of themes to individual pages can make your Web site appear abrupt and confusing to visitors. If your Web site consists of several discrete sections and each section acts almost like a separate Web site, applying themes to the individual pages of each section might be advisable. Even then, however, you might consider creating a separate Web site for each section.

Applying a theme to an entire Web site is a somewhat irrevocable action. As indicated by the warning shown in Figure 20-2, the theme replaces all the fonts, colors, bullets, and lines in every page in a Web site, with no possibility of undoing. If you later change your mind and remove the theme, FrontPage can't restore all the colors, fonts, and other formatting your pages used to have. Instead, these properties will revert to their HTML defaults. Of course, you can always apply a different theme.

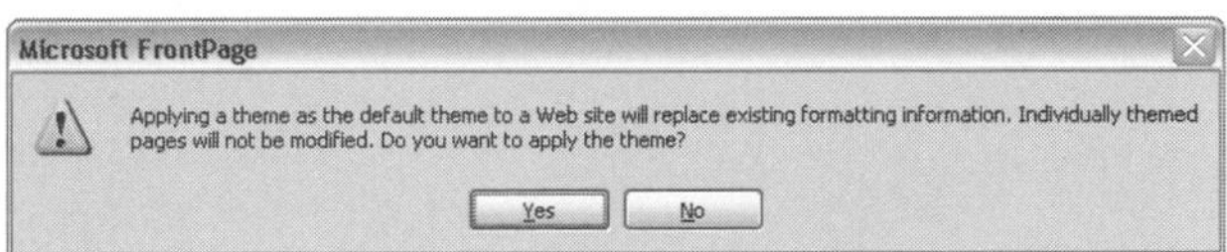

Figure 20-2. This message box warns you that applying a theme to an entire Web site overwrites formatting information that can't be restored.

Applying a theme is also a rather heavy-handed action. Themes are all-or-nothing propositions, meaning that once you apply a theme, FrontPage will dim most of the color and formatting options that would otherwise control the appearance of your page. You can't override parts of a theme. You can change the theme itself, but you can't make it control more or fewer page elements. Finally, any change you make to a theme affects *every* page that uses that theme. If these restrictions seem severe but you like the idea of centrally controlling page appearance, consider these alternatives:

- **Dynamic Web Templates** A type of "master" Web page that you can link to other pages in the same Web site. Those other pages then inherit the appearance and designated content of the template.

For more information about Dynamic Web Templates, refer to "Using Dynamic Web Templates," on page 322.

- **Linked Cascading Style Sheet files** Files that control the appearance—and optionally the position—of standard HTML elements and other items you designate. Any number of Web pages can link to the same style sheet file, thereby achieving a standard appearance. Compared to themes and Dynamic Web Templates, this alternative has the most flexibility.

For more information about CSS, refer to Chapter 21, "Managing Appearance with Cascading Style Sheets."

FrontPage 2003 themes are themselves heavy users of linked CSS files. This is the technology that FrontPage uses when it applies the color and typographical elements of any theme. Earlier versions of FrontPage could also apply themes by applying specific HTML tags, but FrontPage 2003 no longer uses such tags when applying themes. There are two reasons for this:

- The W3C has deprecated these tags.
- The HTML for pages that use CSS themes is smaller and easier to understand.

If you have existing Web sites that use non-CSS themes, those pages will still work in FrontPage 2003. Nevertheless, you should consider removing any non-CSS themes and reapplying the FrontPage 2003 equivalents before making extensive changes.

Caution Whenever you apply a new default theme—or make any other far-reaching change—to a Web site, always back up the site first, or at least test the change on an offline copy.

Applying Themes

To apply an existing theme, open a Web site in FrontPage, and choose Theme from the Format menu. This displays the Theme task pane, shown previously in Figure 20-1. The scrolling list in the center of the task pane shows a thumbnail preview of each available theme.

The procedure for applying a theme to one Web page is very simple. Here's your plan of attack:

1. Either open the page in Design view or select it in the Folder List or Folders view. Opening the page in Design view is usually the better choice—at least initially—because that way you can see what you're doing, and if you don't like the results, you can quit without saving.
2. In the Theme task pane, find the preview thumbnail for the theme you want.
3. Modify the following optional settings if you want. They appear below the list of theme previews:
   - **Vivid Colors** Select this check box to preview and apply the vivid set of colors from a theme that provides both muted and vivid colors.
   - **Active Graphics** Select this check box to activate animated pictures if a theme contains them. Tread carefully here: The novelty of flashing lights can wear off quickly.
   - **Background Picture** Select this check box if you want pages to display a background picture. A background picture is a small graphic, usually with some sort of pattern, that's tiled across the entire background of the page. Most themes substitute a solid background color if you clear this check box.

4 Apply the theme by taking one of these actions:

- Click the thumbnail preview.
- Click the down arrow that appears when you hover the mouse over the thumbnail preview, and then choose Apply To Selected Page(s) from the dropdown menu.
- Right-click the thumbnail preview, and choose Apply To Selected Page(s) from the shortcut menu.

> **Caution** After you apply a theme, there's no Undo command that restores your Web page (or Web site) to its prior appearance. Removing a theme returns pages to their default HTML state. Always back up your Web first or work from a copy.

The following shortcut menu appears when you right-click a preview thumbnail or click its down arrow. An explanation of each command follows.

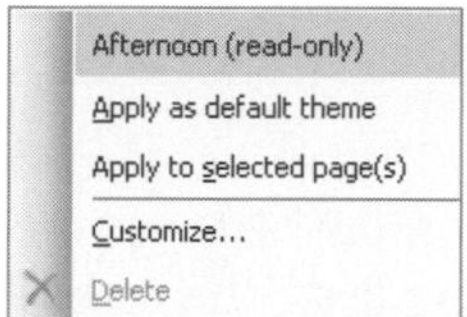

- **(Theme Name)** A title bar displays the name of the theme you're about to apply, customize, or delete. Make sure that this is the theme you want.
- **Apply As Default Theme** Choose this command if the theme you selected should become the default theme for all pages in the current Web site. This means that the theme will apply to all pages except those that have individual theme assignments.
- **Apply To Selected Pages(s)** Choose this command to apply the theme individually to one or more Web pages you've selected. This could be the current page open in Design view, or any number of pages you selected in the Folder List or Folders view. Themes you apply using this option override themes you apply with Apply As Default Theme.
- **Customize** Choose this command to modify the appearance of the theme itself. Any changes you make will affect all pages using that theme.
- **Delete** Choose this command to delete the theme from your computer. This, however, is subject to two cautions:
  - You can't use this command to delete themes that came with FrontPage or Microsoft Office.
  - This isn't the proper command to remove a theme from your Web site.

The process for removing a theme is almost identical to that for applying one. Instead of selecting a thumbnail preview, select the No Theme option at the top of the preview list.

After applying a theme, you might be surprised to find your Web pages less elaborate than the preview. This happens because the preview includes page banners, link bars, hover buttons, dividers, and other FrontPage components your pages don't necessarily contain. Alas, there's no solution but to edit each page and insert the desired elements.

For more information about link bars, refer to "Using Link Bars with Navigation View," on page 348. For more information about page banners, refer to "Using Page Banners," on page 359.

If an element on the page had a style applied to it before a theme was applied—a Heading 1 style, for example—that element takes on the Heading 1 style of any theme you apply.

For more information about applying HTML styles to text, refer to "Using HTML's Basic Paragraph Styles," on page 214.

You might also be surprised, after applying a theme, that FrontPage suppresses many of its normal formatting commands for the affected pages. You can't override colors, bullet types, and other element properties under theme control on an element-by-element, attribute-by-attribute basis. You can, of course, change the style of an element to one of the theme formats that's more to your liking.

For elements for which the theme doesn't preempt color control, FrontPage extends the color drop-down menu to include the theme colors, as shown here. This makes it easy to choose colors in line with the overall design.

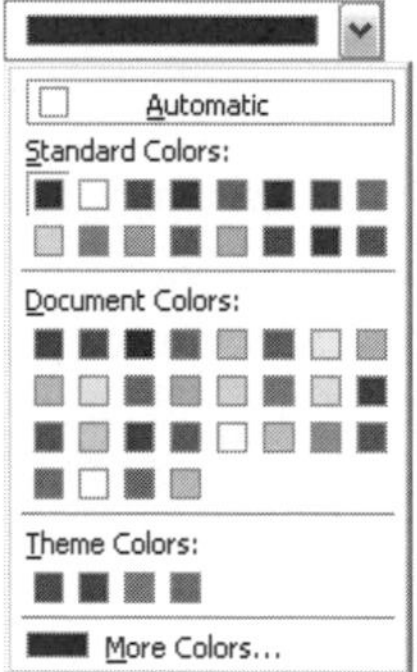

If your Web site has pages that attach Dynamic Web Templates, you'll find that FrontPage won't apply themes to those pages. This is because the Dynamic Web Template already controls the appearance of such pages. In such cases, you should apply the theme to the Dynamic Web Template and then, when you save the template, let FrontPage update the attached pages. This will propagate the theme appearance to the attached pages.

Creating and Customizing Themes

The process of creating a new theme and that of customizing an existing one differ only in one step. Here's an overview of the process:

1. Display the Theme task pane. For example, choose Theme from the Format menu.
2. To create a new theme, click the Create New Theme link at the bottom of the task pane. To customize an existing theme, right-click its thumbnail preview, and choose Customize from the shortcut menu. Either action will display the Customize Theme dialog box, shown in Figure 20-3.

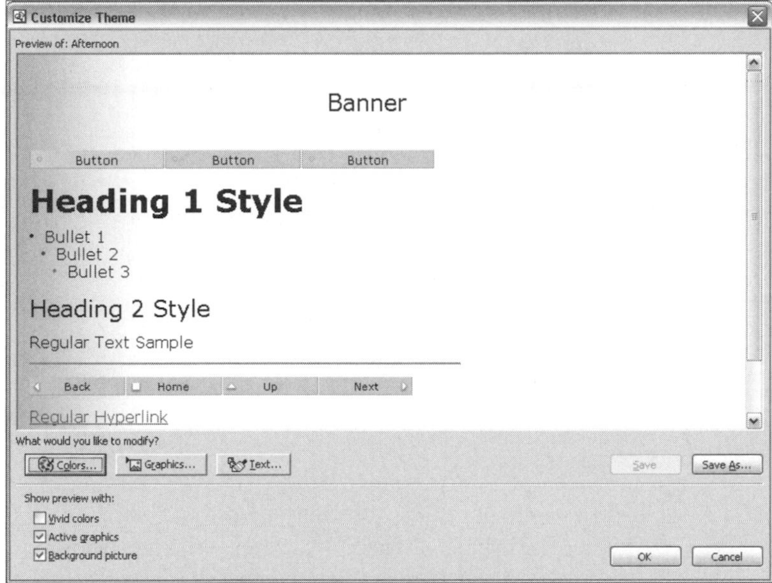

Figure 20-3. This dialog box provides the starting point for creating or customizing a theme.

3. Use the Colors, Graphics, and Text buttons to set the theme properties you want. The next three sections will provide more detail about this process.
4. Click the Save or Save As button to save your changes.

Note If you make a change to a theme and click OK without choosing Save or Save As first, FrontPage displays a warning asking whether you want to save the changes to the current theme.

Customizing Theme Colors

Clicking the Colors button shown in Figure 20-3 displays the Customize Theme dialog box shown in Figure 20-4.

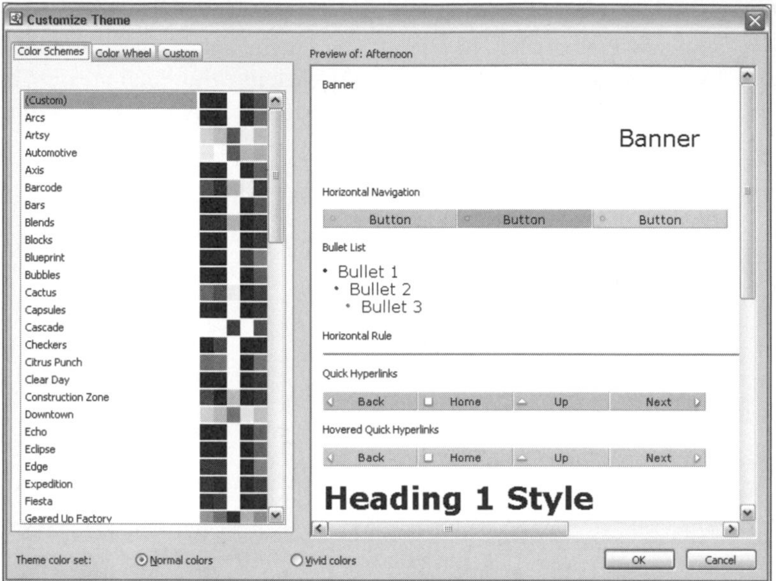

Figure 20-4. Clicking a named color scheme on the left applies a set of colors to the current theme.

The Theme Color Set option buttons at the bottom of the dialog box control which set of colors you're configuring: normal or vivid. By default, a theme's normal and vivid colors are the same. The vivid color set, should you care to define it, is usually similar to the normal set but brighter or more vibrant. A designer can switch between color sets by selecting or clearing the Vivid Colors check box in the Theme task pane.

For an explanation of color terms such as *vivid*, *bright*, and *saturated*, refer to "Design Tips for Choosing Colors," in Appendix E.

The three tabs at the upper left offer three ways to choose a color scheme. The first of these is the Color Schemes tab (shown in Figure 20-4). This tab presents preselected sets of colors grouped to look good together. To try out a given color scheme, just select its entry in the list, and view the results in the Preview Of area.

Note Although there is considerable overlap, the list of color schemes and the list of themes are different. Figure 20-4 shows Automotive and Downtown color schemes, for example, but the Theme task pane shows no corresponding themes. The color schemes that share a name with a theme show the default colors in that theme.

To use the second way of choosing a color scheme, click the Color Wheel tab, shown in Figure 20-5.

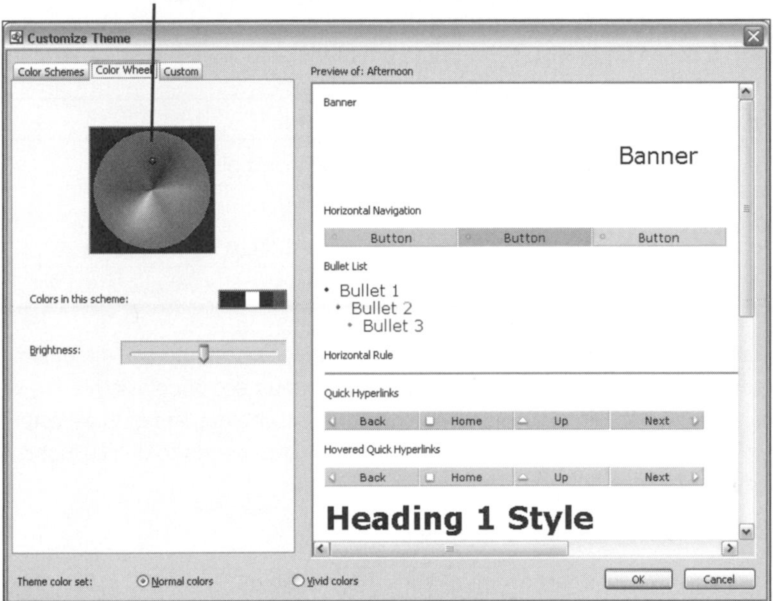

Figure 20-5. The Color Wheel tab provides an additional way to specify a color scheme.

Notice the tiny white dot superimposed on the color wheel inside the black rectangle. Dragging this dot around the circle changes the hue and saturation of a base color for the theme. The Color Wheel tab uses the Hue, Saturation, Brightness (HSB) color model. Here's how this works:

- **Hue** Refers to a true, pure color value. The color wheel represents hue as degrees of rotation around the wheel inside the black rectangle. Red, blue, and green, for example, are at 9 o'clock, 1 o'clock, and 5 o'clock, respectively.
- **Saturation** Measures the purity of a color (that is, the lack of neutral colors diluting it). To increase saturation, drag the white dot closer to the center of the circle. To decrease saturation, drag it closer to the edge
- **Brightness** Measures the intensity of a color. If brightness is zero, for example, the result is black. The Brightness slider on the Color Wheel tab controls brightness. To increase brightness, drag the slider to the right; to decrease brightness, drag the slider to the left.

Frequently Asked Question

Why can't a color wheel show all the colors?

Because the eye perceives color in three dimensions—red, green, and blue—all color measurement schemes involve at least three dimensions. Here are some examples:

Color model	Dimensions
RGB	Red, green, and blue
HSB	Hue, saturation, and brightness
HSL	Hue, saturation, and luminance
CMY	Cyan, magenta, and yellow

Because all these schemes are necessarily three dimensional, no two-dimensional arrangement can ever display a complete and continuous set of colors. A color wheel—which, being flat, is two-dimensional—can't display all combinations of three color values in any sort of continuous way. That's why the Color Wheel tab needs to display not only a color wheel, but a brightness slider as well.

Here's another way to look at this situation:

- A two-dimensional chart can graph only two variables.
- Measuring color requires three variables.
- No two-dimensional chart can ever display a continuous pattern of all possible colors.

The Colors In This Scheme bar shows the colors FrontPage uses to build the theme. These change as you drag the white dot around the color wheel. The Preview Of display changes only when you *stop* dragging (that is, when you release the mouse button).

Caution Be careful when you change the colors in a theme. Modifying colors changes only the colors of HTML elements such as text and backgrounds; it doesn't change graphics colors for elements such as buttons and banners.

You might wonder how, after you choose one color using the color wheel and slider, FrontPage loads five colors into the Colors In This Scheme bar. Here's the answer:

- The color you select is the normal text color; it appears fourth from the left in the Colors In This Scheme bar.
- The color that appears third is the background color, which can't be changed from the Color Wheel tab. To change the background color, use the Color Schemes tab or the Custom tab.

- FrontPage calculates the remaining three colors. The formulas for these calculations are buried somewhere inside the code for FrontPage, but they seem to apply the strategy of Complement And Two Similars explained in Appendix E, "Design Tips for Choosing Colors".
  - The first color applies to the Heading 2, Heading 4, and Heading 6 styles. On the color wheel, this color is 180 degrees opposite the color you select.
  - The second color applies to the Heading 1, Heading 3, Heading 5, and Active Hyperlink styles. This color is about 150 degrees counterclockwise from the color you select.
  - The fifth color applies to the Regular Hyperlink style. It's about 150 degrees clockwise from the color you select.

Choosing colors using the Colors In This Scheme bar might seem confusing at first, but it's actually quite a convenient way to create an elegant color scheme.

The Custom tab, shown in Figure 20-6, is the third and final way of choosing a color scheme.

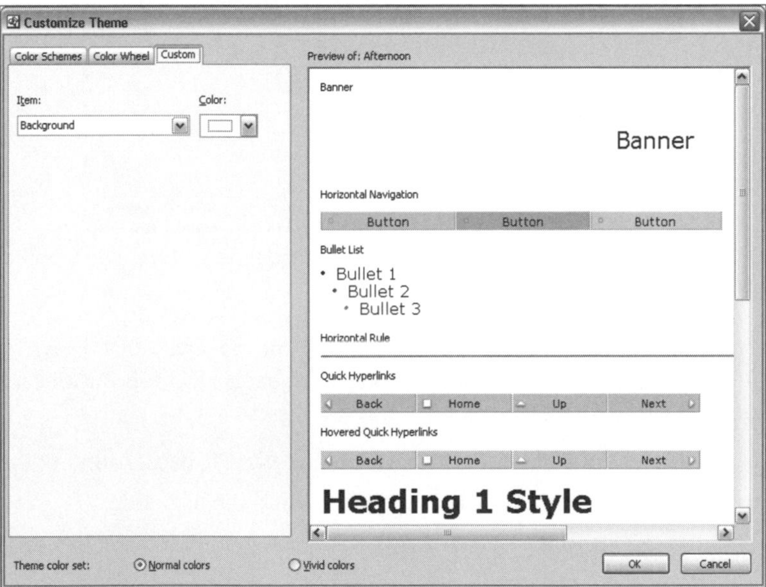

Figure 20-6. The Custom tab modifies the color of a specific element within a theme.

This tab provides direct control over 17 Web elements that a theme controls. These elements appear as items in the Item drop-down list. To change the color of any item:

1. Select it from the Item drop-down list.
2. Click the Color drop-down arrow, and choose the exact color you want.

Customizing Theme Graphics

Clicking the Graphics button in the main Customize Theme dialog box produces the Customize Theme dialog box shown in Figure 20-7. This dialog box specifies the background pictures and fonts that the theme will apply to 10 kinds of elements.

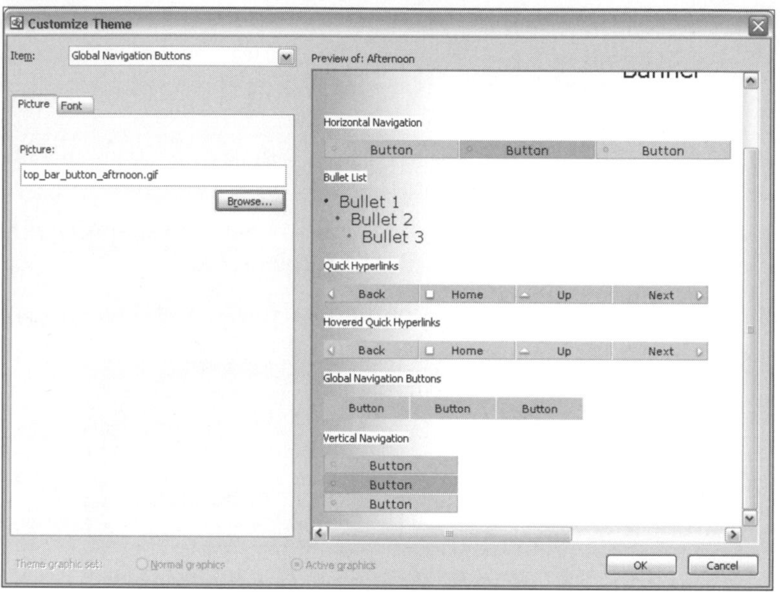

Figure 20-7. The Picture tab of this dialog box specifies the picture files FrontPage uses on pages controlled by a specific theme.

To begin customizing one of these elements, select it from the Item drop-down list at the top of the dialog box. Figure 20-7, for example, shows Global Navigation Buttons ready for modification. The three most common choices are these:

- **Background Picture** Controls the picture that fills the background of the page.
- **Banner** Controls the picture that appears behind the page title.
- **Bullet List** Controls the picture that marks each item in a bullet list.

The remaining seven picture types (Global Navigation Buttons, Horizontal Navigation, Quick Back Button, Quick Home Button, Quick Next Button, Quick Up Button, and Vertical Navigation) all apply to the Link Bars component, described in Chapter 13.

For a brief introduction to link bars and to Navigation view, which provides the data for link bars to work, refer to Chapter 13, "Creating Web Sites with Navigation View."

To specify a picture the current theme should use:

1 Select an element from the Item drop-down list.

2 In the corresponding box(es), enter or browse to the picture you want FrontPage to use:

- **Picture** Specify the graphic that will normally appear for an element.
- **Hovered Picture** Specify an alternative picture that will appear when the mouse pointer is over the element.
- **Selected Picture** Specify an alternative picture that will appear after the Web visitor has clicked the element.
- **List Bullet 1, 2, and 3** Specify the pictures you want to appear as bullets in the first three levels of a list.

3 The Preview Of area will show the effect of your choices.

Frequently Asked Questions

Themes do a great job of formatting Page Banner components. Is there any way to specify page banner text without entering it in Navigation view?

Sorry, there isn't.

For more information about the Page Banner component, refer to "Using Page Banners," on page 359.

Themes do a great job of formatting navigation bars, too. Is there any way to create a navigation bar without arranging pages in Navigation view?

Yes. FrontPage includes a feature called Link Bar With Custom Links that does exactly that.

For more information about the Link Bar With Custom Links component, refer to "Creating a Link Bar Based On Navigation Structure," on page 353.

The Font tab of the Customize Theme dialog box, shown in Figure 20-8, specifies the fonts FrontPage will use for superimposing text on the same 10 elements.

To specify the font for a given element:

1 Select an element from the Item drop-down list.

2 Specify one or more fonts in the Font box. Clicking a font name in the provided list makes it the one and only suitable font. To specify additional fonts, type their names by hand. You must separate individual font names with a comma.

> **Tip** There's no guarantee that a given font will be available on the Web visitor's computer. That's why it's best to specify multiple fonts, and to use common ones at that.

3 In the Style drop-down list, select any font variations you want, such as Bold or Italic.

4 In the Size drop-down list, select a font size.

5 In the Horizontal Alignment drop-down list, specify how to position the text laterally over the picture: left, right, or center.

6 In the Vertical Alignment drop-down list, specify how to position the text vertically within the picture: at the top, middle, or bottom.

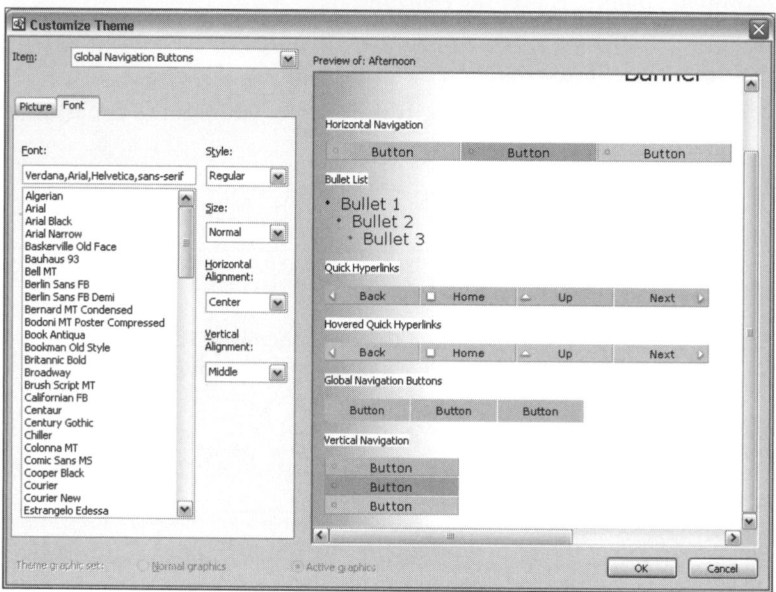

Figure 20-8. The Font tab controls the appearance of text that appears in page banners and link bars.

For more information about how FrontPage superimposes text over pictures, refer to "Adding Text to Pictures," on page 635

Customizing Theme Text

Clicking the Text button in the main Customize Theme dialog box displays the like-named dialog box, shown in Figure 20-9. This dialog box specifies the font for body and heading text that appears on pages the theme controls.

Here's the procedure for modifying these properties:

1 Select the element you want to control from the Item drop-down list.

2 Select the desired font in the Font list. The selected font name appears in the Font box.

3 To specify multiple fonts in order of preference, type the second and each subsequent font into the Font box by hand, using the list as your guide. Be sure to separate the font names with commas.

As you select new fonts from the Font list, the Preview Of area changes to reflect your selection.

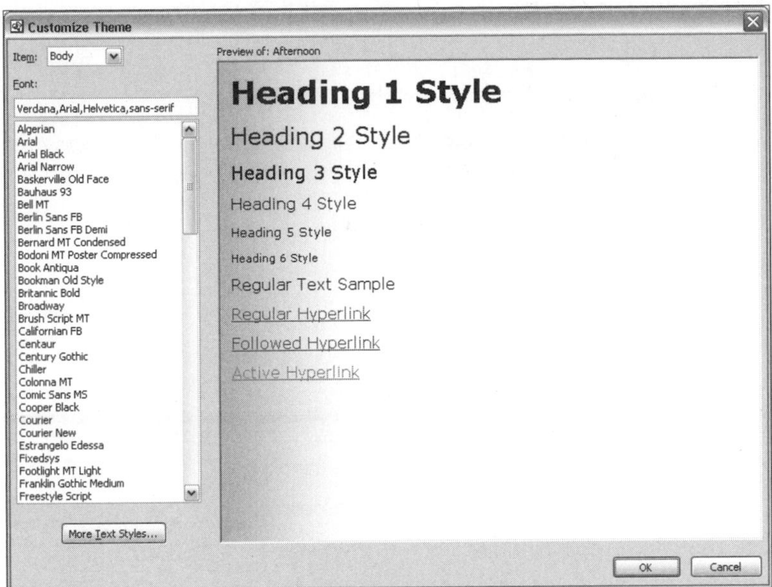

Figure 20-9. This dialog box controls the appearance of body and heading text.

The More Text Styles button provides access to more CSS properties. This button provides control not only over font family, but also over font size, weight, style, color, and all the usual CSS selectors and properties.

For more information about controlling text properties with CSS, refer to "Assigning Style Sheet Properties," on page 602.

Saving Modified Themes

When you've configured a theme to your satisfaction, click the Save button to save your theme under the same name, or click Save As to save it under a new name. If you click Save As, FrontPage displays the Save Theme dialog box shown in Figure 20-10, which prompts you for a theme name.

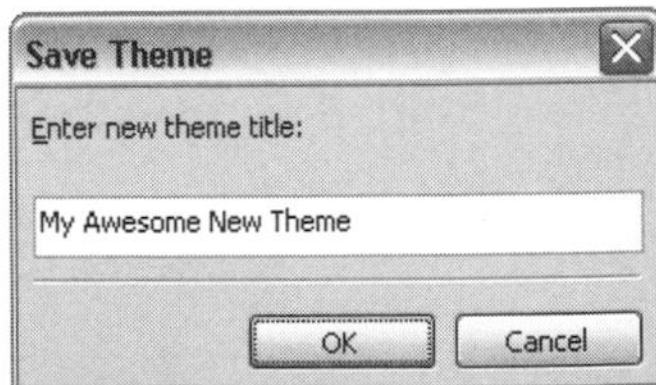

Figure 20-10. Enter a name for a newly created theme in the Save Theme dialog box.

Some themes, such as those FrontPage supplies, are flagged read-only. In these cases, the Save button will be dimmed, and you'll have to use Save As. After you've saved a theme, you can use it in any Web pages you create.

Troubleshooting

Theme task pane flashes and then disappears

When you attempt to change the themes that a Web site uses, the Theme task pane might flash into view and then disappear. This can occur for two reasons:

- The preference file, cmdui.prf, is corrupted.
- The FrontPage registry entry is corrupted.

To resolve the issue of a corrupted cmdui.prf file, first try deleting the file. Here's the necessary procedure:

1. Close all open instances of FrontPage.
2. In Microsoft Windows, choose Search from the Start menu, and then choose All Files Or Folders.
3. In the All Or Part Of The File Name box, type **cmdui.prf**.
4. In the Look In drop-down list, select the drive where FrontPage is installed, and then click Search Now.
5. When the file appears in the search results, right-click the file name in the Name column, and choose Delete from the shortcut menu. The next time FrontPage starts, it will create a new, uncorrupted version of this file.

If you find more than one .prf file, you can either delete them one at a time until the problem goes away or just delete them all. Any cmdui.prf file with a FrontPage folder in its path is a prime suspect.

If the problem persists, try deleting the entire FrontPage registry entry. This is a rather drastic action, but FrontPage will create new, uncorrupted, default registry entries the next time it starts. Here are the steps for deleting the registry entry:

1. Close all open instances of FrontPage.
2. In Windows, choose Run from the Start menu.
3. Type **regedit** in the Open box, and then click OK.
4. If necessary, click the My Computer plus sign icon to expand the registry.
5. With My Computer still selected, choose Export from the Registry menu.
6. When the Export Registry File dialog box appears, specify a safe location on your hard disk or removable drive, and then click Save.
7. When your backup is complete, expand the following folder: HKEY_CURRENT_USER\Software\Microsoft\
8. Right-click the FrontPage folder, and choose Delete from the shortcut menu.
9. Close the registry editor, and restart your computer.

Distributing Themes

Themes you save in FrontPage reside in a folder accessible to other Office applications as well. Not all Office applications use such themes, but those that do—including Microsoft Word—have access to them immediately.

There are two ways to distribute themes from one computer to another: by copying the files directly, or by transferring over the Web.

Distributing by Copying Files

Distributing a theme to computers other than your own requires copying one folder that contains four or five files. By default, this folder resides at the following path:

C:\Program Files\Common Files\Microsoft Shared\Themes\<theme name>

The folder, the theme, and three of the files generally have similar names. For example, the Afternoon theme resides in the afternoon folder, which contains files named aftrnoon.elm, aftrnoon.inf, and aftrnoon.gif.

To copy a theme from one computer to another, copy its folder to an intermediate location—such as a disk, a file server, or an FTP location—and then copy it from there into the Themes folder on the other computer. Figure 20-11 shows the Themes folder, the aftrnoon folder, and all five files in a typical Microsoft Windows XP Professional installation.

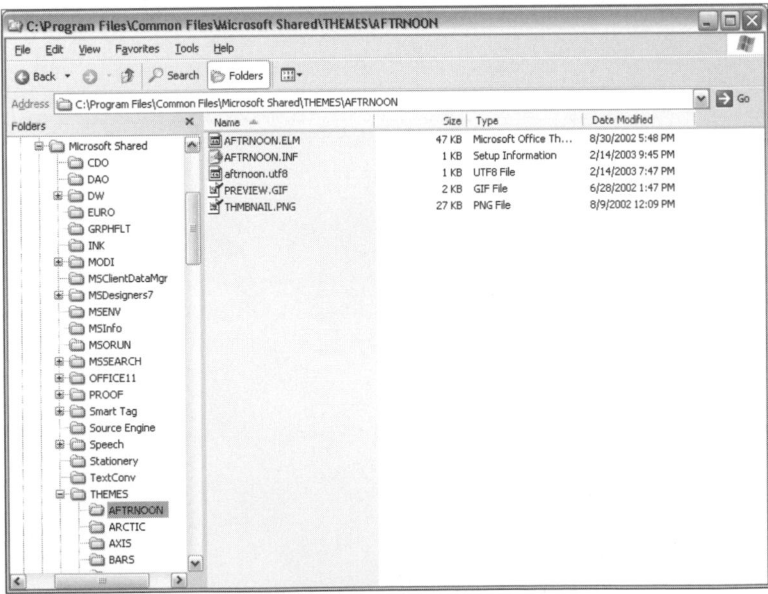

Figure 20-11. Themes reside in a common files area accessible to other Office applications. To install a theme on another computer, copy it to that computer's Themes folder.

Distributing over the Web

Applying any theme to a Web site—whether to individual pages or to the entire Web site—copies the theme into a hidden folder named, not surprisingly, _themes. This makes the theme available to anyone who opens that Web site, and overrides any like-named themes on that designer's hard disk. Distributing a theme to your entire design team is therefore as simple as applying that theme to any page in the Web site.

In fact, whenever a FrontPage designer opens a Web site, their Themes list contains two kinds of entries:

- Themes residing on their local system.
- Themes residing in the current FrontPage-based Web site.

If a designer applies a theme that resides only on the FrontPage-based Web site, FrontPage offers to download the theme and install it locally. This is an efficient way of distributing themes to those who need them.

In Summary…

This chapter explained how to apply themes to an entire Web site, how to modify themes, and how to create new themes from existing ones. Themes impart a uniform appearance to one, many, or all pages in a Web.

The next chapter explains Cascading Style Sheets, which also control the appearance of multiple Web pages from a single source.

Chapter 21

Managing Appearance with Cascading Style Sheets

The appearance of text often conveys just as much information as the words and phrases it contains. The color, shape, size, weight, pitch, and position of text visually convey document structure, levels of importance or emphasis, and special capabilities such as hyperlinking, just to name a few possibilities. This book would be much harder to read and use if all the headings, figure numbers, margin elements, sidebars, and tables looked like ordinary body text.

Although Web pages are much shorter than books, typography is just as important. Few visitors expect to read Web pages straight through, from top to bottom. Instead, they expect to scan visually, locating headings, subheadings, and further hyperlinks with great speed. To guide the visitor's eye this way requires effective layout, surely, but effective colors and fonts are just as critical.

Early versions of HTML had almost no provisions for controlling fonts, colors, indentations, line spacing, or other aspects of typography. Later versions added simple control over fonts and colors, but only for specifically marked blocks of text. Centralized control of typography for an entire page or site remained lacking.

To provide full typographical control over Web pages, the W3C denounced the early, HTML-based font tags and adopted a new technology called *cascading style sheets* (CSS, or sometimes CSS1). This technology offers two primary advantages over other methods of formatting Web pages:

- CSS can control all the same typographical properties that ordinary HTML tags control, but with greater precision. CSS can also control many typographical properties that HTML tags can't. As such, CSS offers tremendous flexibility.
- CSS can define groups of typographical properties (styles) in one place and then apply them by name to many different blocks of text located in the same Web page or in many different Web pages. In this sense, it offers tremendous control.

Of course, CSS has a few drawbacks as well. For one, not all browsers support it exactly the same way, and very old browsers don't support it at all. For another, the people who designed CSS optimized it for designers who work with lines of code. This makes CSS extremely platform-neutral but also a difficult fit for programs like Microsoft FrontPage. FrontPage does its best to shield designers from the intricacies of CSS code, but nevertheless, using some CSS features means working with code. (Fortunately, you can work with code without leaving FrontPage.)

CSS Positioning (often called CSS2) is a later development that strives to bring pixel-precise positioning to the Web. With CSS Positioning, you can specify an exact position for any page element you want, including the top-to-bottom order of any elements that overlap. Chapter 22, "Positioning Content with Cascading Style Sheets," will explain CSS Positioning.

CSS originally developed a reputation as hard to use and incompatible with many browsers. Over time, however, many more designers (and browsers) have come to know and love the facilities it provides. To see why, consider your only options for controlling typography:

- Forget typography, and make believe that Netscape Navigator 3 is the state of the art.
- Forget centralized control and the need for uniformity. Apply HTML formatting to each individual block of text.
- Make everything a picture, and force Web visitors to suffer the download time.
- Use CSS intelligently, and deal with minor browser differences.

It's hard to believe that CSS isn't the best of these solutions.

Introducing CSS Concepts

Any browser that supports CSS starts out with a default set of styles based on built-in logic and whatever preferences the visitor has in effect. Any CSS rules found in Web pages then override, on a property-by-property basis, the default styles. If several styles apply to the same element, the overrides occur in the order in which the styles appear. This is part of the *cascading* idea in CSS.

Another aspect of cascading is that some styles *inherit* properties from other styles. This is usually based on the type of HTML tag involved. When you assign a CSS property to an entire numbered or unnumbered list, for example, any subordinate list items inherit the same properties. The rules of inheritance vary somewhat among browsers, but inheritance is still a very useful aspect of cascading.

Dealing with Browser Compatibility (or Lack Thereof)

Because CSS is a relatively new technology, very old browsers don't support it. CSS support first appeared in Microsoft Internet Explorer 3 (released August 1996) and in Netscape Navigator 4 (released June 1997). Browsers older than these treat CSS instructions like they treat HTML tags they don't understand—they ignore them.

Now frankly, if you have any Web visitors still running browsers dated 1996 or 1997, they probably aren't buying very much. This makes it a safe bet that all the Web visitors in your target audience have CSS-capable browsers. Even among browsers that do support CSS, however, levels of support and details of interpretation differ.

Some designers are obsessed with the idea that their pages should look exactly the same no matter what browser the visitor uses. As a result, they use only the features that even the oldest browsers support.

Another group of designers has an opposite obsession: They exercise every feature of the very latest browsers and don't mind a bit if visitors running older versions get errors or incorrect displays. This gives the visitors an incentive to upgrade, or so goes the thinking.

The middle ground is to use features that degrade gracefully with older browser versions. That way, visitors with new browsers get the richest possible experience, and those with older browsers experience whatever they're accustomed to. The use of CSS1 fits very well into this middle-ground strategy.

The more important the page, the more important it is that you test it using a variety of browsers. This advice, of course, is universal; it applies whether or not you use CSS.

The Web page shown in Figure 21-1 uses HTML default formatting throughout. Few Web pages are actually this dull, but many come close.

Figure 21-2 shows the same content with several kinds of CSS formatting in place. Notice the borders and backgrounds in place for the three heading styles, as well as the fact that they overlap. There are no pictures at work here—just ordinary text formatted with CSS1 and locked into position with CSS2. A style sheet also specifies the paragraph indentations, picture bullets, indents, and fonts.

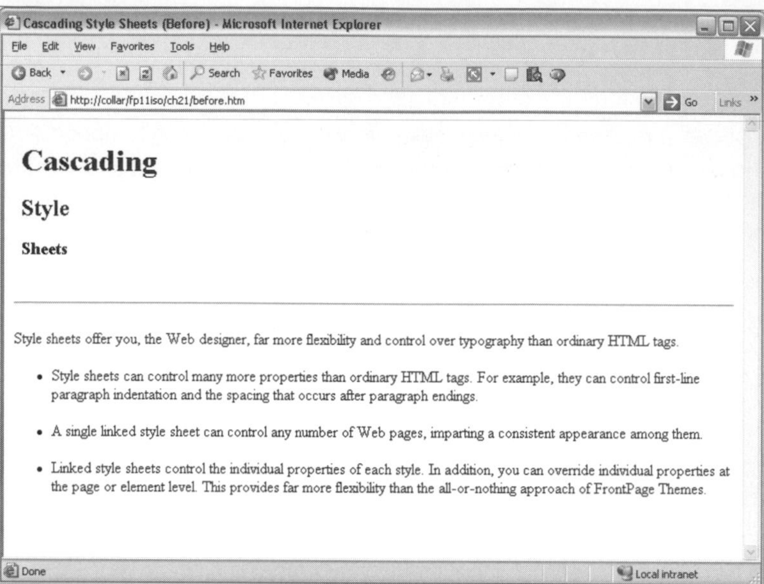

Figure 21-1. This Web page uses default HTML formatting throughout.

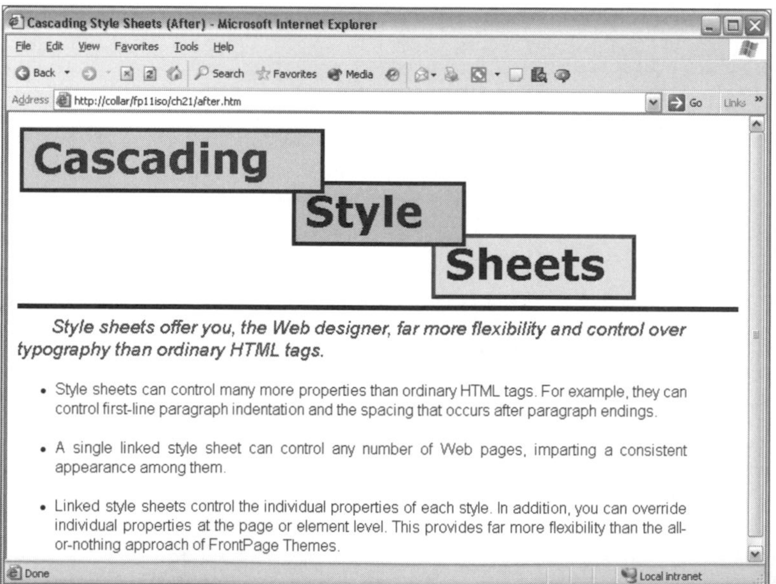

Figure 21-2. This page presents the same content as Figure 21-1, but the use of CSS styles and positioning have improved its appearance significantly.

Support for CSS in Netscape Navigator 4 lags behind that in Internet Explorer somewhat, as a glance at Figure 21-3 quickly confirms. Nevertheless, the page shown in Figure 21-3 is legible and generally follows the intended design. As all browsers increasingly conform to W3C standards, differences in page appearance should decrease.

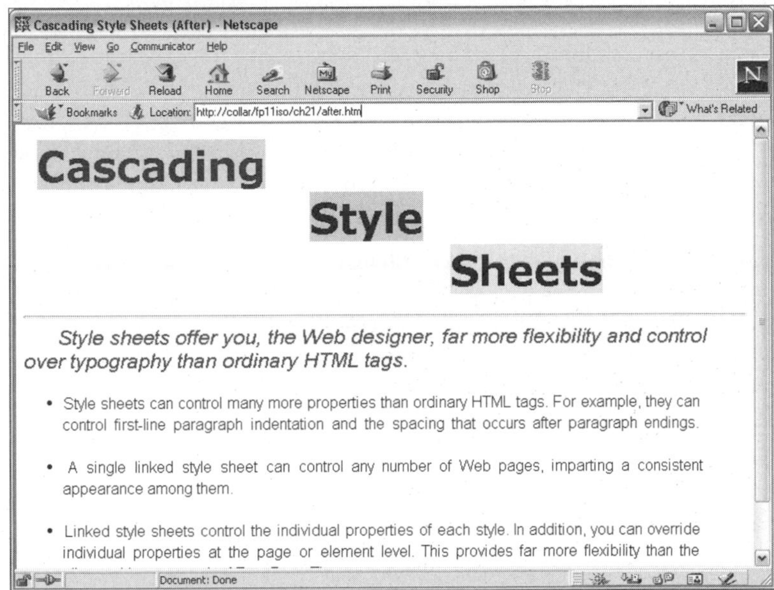

Figure 21-3. Netscape Navigator 4 supports fewer CSS features than Internet Explorer, but even so, pages formatted with CSS generally appear as designed.

Understanding Style Sheet Terminology

The CSS language consists of lines of code—code from which all the WYSIWYG editors and dialog boxes in the world can't shield you completely. Wherever possible, this book avoids showing code and displays the relevant FrontPage dialog boxes instead. But here, when considering fundamentals, code it is. Have faith, though; it'll be simple. First, some definitions:

- **CSS style** This is a collection of property names and values such as font name, font size, font weight, color, background color, border type, border width, and so forth. Here's how a CSS style looks in code:

  ```
  font-family: Arial, sans-serif; color: red;
  ```

  A colon separates each property name from its value(s). Commas separate multiple values assigned to the same property. Semicolons indicate the end of a property setting and permit the beginning of the next.
- **Selector** This is the name of a CSS rule. It specifies (that is, *selects*) the page elements to which the rule will apply.

- **CSS rule** This is a statement that assigns properties to one or more selectors.

This book focuses on three types of selectors:

- **Type selector** This selector has the same name as an HTML tag (that is, the name of an HTML element *type*). Assigning properties to a type selector modifies all text controlled by the corresponding HTML tag. The *h1* selector, for example, controls the appearance of Heading 1 text. The *b* selector controls the appearance of boldface text, and so forth. Type selectors are among the best features of CSS. With one statement, you can change the appearance of your whole Web page or of all elements that use a given HTML style. And with one command, you can make one set of type selectors control an entire Web site. Later sections in this chapter explain how to define and use type selectors.
- **Class selector** This selector has any name you choose to give it, except that the name must begin with a period and can't be the name of an HTML tag. Unlike type selectors, class selectors don't apply automatically to all similar elements of a Web page. Instead, to apply the rule, you add a class="*class-name*" attribute to the HTML tag that encloses the content you want to format. (A class selector is one you invoke with a *class=* attribute. This isn't rocket science.)

  Whenever you want text in multiple places to have a consistent format, class selectors are an excellent solution. Suppose, for example, that you want error message paragraphs to look different from normal text paragraphs. Type selectors can't do this because both kinds of paragraphs use the same tag: <p>. If, however, you defined an *errmsg* class selector, you could apply it to whatever paragraphs were appropriate. Defining the *errmsg* class selector centrally guarantees that all error message paragraphs will look the same. Later sections in this chapter explain how to define and use class selectors.
- **ID selector** This selector works somewhat like a class selector, except that the ID is the name of something in your Web page. Instead of naming a style and then invoking it from page elements, you name the page elements and then define styles for them. ID selectors can have any name you want except the name of an HTML tag. In addition, they must begin with a pound sign (#). You should never give two elements in the same page the same ID. This makes class selectors preferable for most uses. Later sections in this chapter explain how to define and use ID selectors.

Coding Style Sheet Rules

Both CSS styles and the rules that define them are rather abstract entities, not particularly amenable to WYSIWYG display. To wring every drop of function out of CSS, therefore, you'll sometimes need to click the Code tab at the bottom of the Design view window and enter the rules by hand. As seems to be the way of art, messy techniques can produce beautiful results.

For more information about using Code view, refer to Chapter 40, "Working with HTML Code."

The syntax (that is, the required format) of CSS statements is different from that of HTML. The following is a CSS rule that assigns two properties (font family and color) to the selector *h1*:

```
h1 { font-family: Arial, sans-serif; color: red; }
```

Note that in this example:

- The selector is the first item on the line.
- Curly braces enclose the entire list of properties.
- Each property consists of a property name, a colon, and then one or more values.
- Commas separate multiple values for the same property.
- A semicolon indicates the end of a property definition.

Rules and styles are many-to-many. A single rule can apply to any number of styles, and any number of rules can affect a single style. The following rule makes all Heading 1 and Heading 2 text appear in boldface:

```
h1, h2 { font-weight: bold; }
```

The comma between the two selectors implies an *or* condition, meaning that the rule applies whenever the HTML tag is *h1* or *h2*. Lack of a comma implies an *and* condition. The following rule applies only to italic text located within table cells:

```
td i { color: rgb(153,0,0); }
```

Later sections in this chapter explain how to define and use CSS rules.

For more information about the features and use of CSS, browse these locations: Microsoft: *msdn.microsoft.com/workshop/author/* and W3C: *www.w3.org/Style/*

Locating Style Sheet Styles

You can specify CSS style information in the three general locations (or, if you prefer, the three levels) listed here:

Style

- **Attached to a specific page element** You can assign CSS style properties to individual HTML elements. Styles applied this way are called inline styles.

Chapter 21

If you display the Properties dialog box for any element on a Web page, and if that dialog box contains a Style button, clicking that button displays another dialog box that applies CSS properties (font, paragraph, border, numbering, and position) to that element. In Figure 21-4, for example, the Style button in the lower left corner controls CSS properties for whatever table cells the designer selected before displaying the Cell Properties dialog box.

For more information about using styles attached to specific page elements, refer to "Formatting Individual Page Elements," later in this chapter.

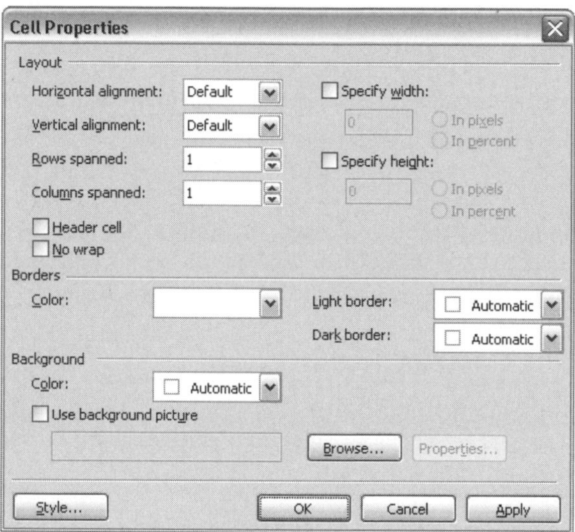

Figure 21-4. The Style button in this dialog box controls CSS properties for the selected page element.

- **In a style sheet located within a Web page** Whenever you have a Web page open in FrontPage, choosing Style from the Format menu displays the Style dialog box, shown in Figure 21-5. This dialog box can create, modify, and delete CSS rules applicable to the current page. (Clicking the Style button on the Style toolbar produces the same result.)

For more information about using style sheets located within a Web page, refer to "Formatting Single Web Pages," later in this chapter.

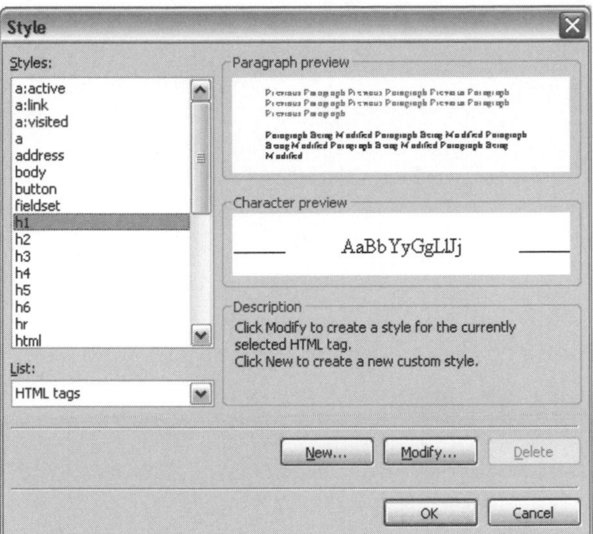

Figure 21-5. This is the launch point for creating or modifying CSS rules.

- **In a style sheet located in another file** Centrally controlling the appearance of similar elements in the same Web page is all well and good, but what if you want similar elements in an entire collection of Web pages to look alike? You could set up identical style sheets within each page, but that would be boring, mundane, error-prone, and difficult to maintain. Linked style sheet files provide a welcome alternative. Using linked style sheet files involves these overall steps:

1. Create a CSS file, most likely based on one of the CSS templates mentioned in Chapter 12.

> **For more information about creating CSS files and applying them to multiple pages, refer to "Formatting Multiple Pages," later in this chapter.**

2. Open the CSS file in FrontPage, choose Style from the Format menu, configure whatever styles you want, and save the page.

   Skip step 3 if you want to apply your style sheet to an entire Web site.
3. Select one or more Web pages that should use styles from the file you just saved. You can select an open Web page by leaving the insertion point in it, or you can select groups of files or folders in the Folder List or in Folders view.
4. In Design view, select an open Web page, and then choose Style Sheet Links from the Format menu. This displays the Link Style Sheet dialog box, shown in Figure 21-6. If the file you saved in step 2 doesn't appear in the URL list, click Add to add it.
5. To apply the style sheet to every file in the current Web, select All Pages and then click OK.

6 To apply the style sheet to pages you selected in step 3, select Selected Page(s) and then click OK.

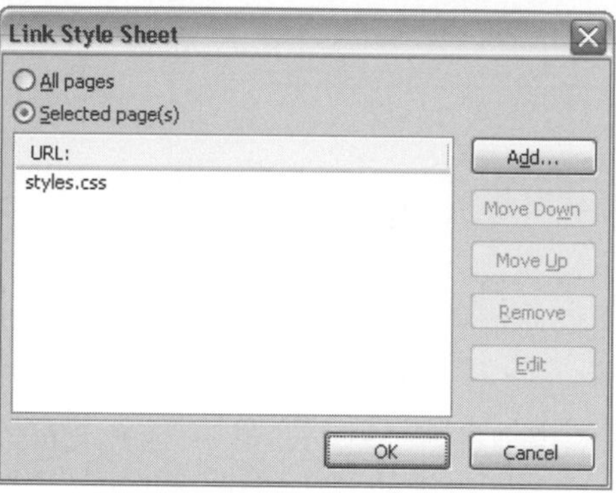

Figure 21-6. This dialog box links files containing CSS rules to selected Web pages or an entire Web site.

For more information about using one style sheet file in multiple Web pages, refer to "Linking Style Sheet Files," later in this chapter.

Formatting Individual Page Elements

The most direct way to apply CSS styles is by individual page element. CSS refers to styles used this way as *inline styles*. Here's the procedure for applying inline styles to any element in an open Web page:

1. Right-click the element you want to modify, and choose the Properties command on the shortcut menu that applies to the element you want: Picture Properties, Cell Properties, and so forth.
2. Look for a Style button in the resulting Properties dialog box. If the dialog box has multiple tabs, check each tab until you find the Style button.

   If there's no Style button, FrontPage doesn't support inline styles for the type of element you selected in step 1. Refer to the next section, "Coding Inline Styles."
3. Click the Style button to display the Modify Style dialog box, shown in Figure 21-7. The Name (Selector) and Style Type boxes are dimmed because they don't apply to inline styles.
4. If you want the element you selected in step 1 to inherit the properties of an existing CSS class, enter the class selector in the Class box or select it from the Class drop-down list. The drop-down list includes not only classes you defined in the current Web page, but classes from any linked style sheets as well.

For more information about CSS class selectors, refer to "Formatting Single Web Pages," later in this chapter.

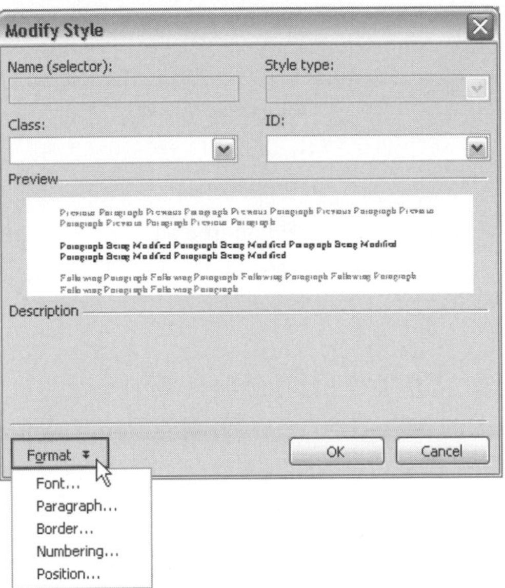

Figure 21-7. This dialog box applies a class selector, an ID selector, or inline styles to a Web page.

5 If you want to assign an ID name to the element you selected in step 1, enter that name in the ID box. Entering this name doesn't create an ID selector. It only names the current HTML element in a way that an ID selector can reference.

ID names and page elements can only be 1:1. You should never assign the same ID name to two or more elements in the same Web page, and you should never assign two different ID names to the same element.

The names in the ID drop-down list already exist on the page; therefore, don't select any of them as the name of the current element. You can refer to the drop-down list to identify previously defined ID values, but to name the current element, type a new name in the ID text box.

For more information about creating ID selectors, refer to "Formatting Single Web Pages," later in this chapter.

6 The Preview area shows a rough approximation of how text formatted with the current styles will appear. The Description area shows the CSS properties currently in effect.

7 To assign inline style properties to the element you selected in step 1, click the Format button in the lower left corner of the dialog box, and choose the category that contains the property you want to specify: Font, Paragraph, Border, Numbering, or Position.

For instructions on setting these properties, refer to "Assigning Style Sheet Properties," later in this chapter.

Here are some of the HTML element types for which FrontPage provides Style buttons:

Page	Horizontal line	Hyperlink	Bulleted list
Table	Frame	Form	Numbered list
Table cell	Inline frame	Form field	List item
Picture			

Three element types are notable exceptions to the preceding types:

- **Paragraph** The Paragraph dialog box has no Style button. FrontPage offers the following capabilities instead:
  - Setting any control in the Paragraph dialog box to a non-default setting causes FrontPage to create inline styles.
  - Similarly, FrontPage honors many of the settings in the Font dialog box by adding inline styles to the HTML. This obviates the need to set font properties at the paragraph level.
  - Scrolling to the bottom of the Style drop-down list on the Formatting toolbar displays a list of available class selectors. To format a given paragraph in accordance with any of these selectors, simply select the paragraph and choose the selector you want from the list.
- **Span** This is a special HTML element that groups arbitrary portions of a Web page. A span has no default physical appearance. It begins wherever you put a <span> start tag in the HTML code and ends wherever you put a </span> end tag. Assigning CSS properties to a span assigns those properties to all the elements contained within it.
- **Division** This element works just like a span except that it forces line breaks before and after itself. FrontPage has neither a general purpose command that directly creates a division, nor a Division Properties dialog box in which you can assign a full range of CSS properties to a division. FrontPage does, however, create divisions when you perform these actions:
  - Center an HTML table.
  - Use the Insert menu or the Layers task pane to create a Layer.
  - Use the Positioning toolbar or various dialog boxes to specify relative or absolute CSS positioning.
  - Use certain dynamic HTML features.

Inside Out

No Direct Support for <span> and <div> Tags

If you select part of a paragraph or other text element and then use the Font dialog box to change its properties, and if only CSS can control one of the properties you set, FrontPage creates a span and assigns the necessary CSS property to it. However, there's no command in FrontPage that directly creates a span, and there's no Span Properties dialog box in which you can assign CSS properties.

Lack of direct support for the <span> and <div> tags is an unfortunate FrontPage omission. Perhaps some future build or version will include this support.

Coding Inline Styles

If the Properties dialog box for a given element doesn't have a Style button (or if you're the type of person who does hexadecimal long division for fun), you can manipulate inline CSS styles directly in code. Here are the steps:

1. In Design view, select all or part of the text you want to format.
2. Click the Code tab at the bottom of the editing window.
3. Locate the HTML tag that controls the selected text. (In most cases, whatever you selected before switching to Code view will also be selected in Code view.)
4. To apply CSS properties, add a *style=* attribute to the desired HTML tag. Here's an example:

```
<p style="text-align: right">
```

For a list of available property names and acceptable values, consult the various tables in the section "Assigning Style Sheet Properties," later in this chapter.

When you return to Normal view, any inline styles you applied in Code view should be in effect. If not, you've probably misspelled something or used a property in an invalid context. (For example, specifying a font size for a horizontal line element has no effect.)

Formatting Single Web Pages

Using CSS at the page level is generally a two-step process:

1. Define rules. A rule assigns typographical properties to one or more selectors (that is, to one or more style names).
2. Apply the rules to one or more blocks of text. For type selectors, this is automatic. For class and ID selectors, you must designate the content that you want each rule to affect.

Here's the procedure for creating, modifying, and deleting CSS rules at the page level:

1 Choose Style from the Format menu or click the Style button on the Style toolbar. This displays the Style dialog box, shown in Figure 21-8.

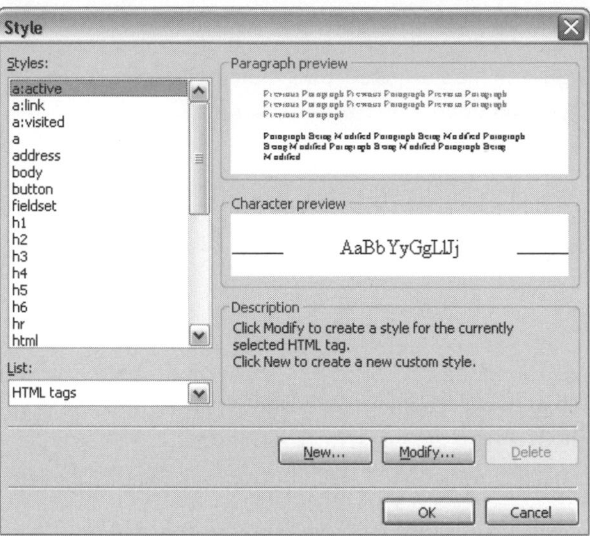

Figure 21-8. From this dialog box, you create, modify, and delete CSS style rules for the current Web page.

If the current page has no page-level styles defined, the Styles list contains the names of all valid HTML tags. Note that by definition, this is also a list of valid type selectors.

The Styles list can also display a list of existing rules for the current page. This is the default if any style rules exist. To make this happen, select User-Defined Styles in the List drop-down list below the Styles list.

To alternate between these two displays, select either HTML Tags or User-Defined Styles in the List drop-down list.

2 As you select each rule, the Paragraph Preview area shows the effect of that rule's paragraph properties, the Character Preview area shows the result of the rule's font properties, and the Description section provides a text description of the rule's properties.

The following steps explain how to create, modify, and delete rules, regardless of whether you've selected HTML Tags or User-Defined Styles in the List list:

- To create a new CSS rule of any type, click the New button. This displays the New Style dialog box, shown in Figure 21-9.

For instructions on using the New Style dialog box, refer to "Assigning Style Sheet Properties," later in this chapter.

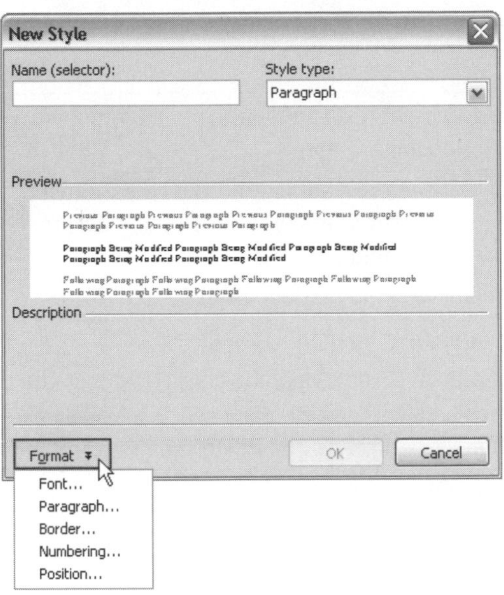

Figure 21-9. This dialog box is the entry point for setting the selector name and properties for a new CSS rule.

> **Tip** FrontPage also displays the New Style dialog box when you click the Style button in various Properties dialog boxes. However, in such cases, any properties you specify apply only to the current element.

- To modify an existing rule, highlight its selector name in the Styles list, and then click Modify. This displays the Modify Style dialog box, shown previously in Figure 21-7, which is nearly identical to the New Style dialog box shown in Figure 21-9. This dialog box displays any properties already in effect for the given style.

For instructions on using the Modify Style dialog box, refer to "Assigning Style Sheet Properties," later in this chapter.

- To delete an existing rule, select it in the Styles list, and then click Delete. You can delete any style rules you've created, including those for type and ID selectors, but you can't delete valid HTML tag names.

Choosing Style Sheet Selectors

Type selectors, because they apply to Web page elements automatically, are by far the easiest to use. Table 21-1 lists some commonly used type selectors.

Table 21-1. Common CSS Type Selectors

Selector	Description
h1–h6	Modifies the appearance of text formatted with the standard HTML styles Heading 1 through Heading 6.
body	Modifies the appearance of everything that appears in the body of the Web page. You can use this selector to control the page background color, a background picture, or a default font for the page.
p	Modifies the appearance of normal paragraphs.
td	Modifies the appearance of normal table cells.
th	Modifies the appearance of table heading cells. (To designate an ordinary table cell as a heading cell, select the cell, display its Cell Properties dialog box, and then select the Header Cell check box.)
ol	Modifies the properties of an ordered list.
ul	Modifies the properties of an unordered list.
li	Modifies the appearance of list items.
a	Modifies the appearance of hyperlinks. The *a* type selector has the following related sub type selectors: **a:active** Modifies the appearance of a hyperlink the visitor has just clicked. **a:hover** Modifies the appearance of a hyperlink when the mouse is over it **a:link** Modifies the appearance of a hyperlink the visitor hasn't yet visited. **a:visited** Modifies the appearance of a hyperlink the visitor has recently visited.

Tip To remove underlining from all hyperlinks on a page, modify the *a* selector in the Style dialog box. Click Format, and then click Font. In the Effects section, select the No Text Decoration check box.

If your page requires special formatting for certain kinds of data (such as names, titles, part numbers, warnings, or error messages), class selectors are usually the best choice. Just remember to include a leading period when you define them:

```
.warning { color: red; }
```

but not when you call them:

```
<p class="warning">
```

Most designers seldom, if ever, use ID selectors. However, if you ever need one, remember to include a leading pound sign (#) when you define the rule and not when you define the ID.

Troubleshooting

Tables and lists don't inherit body properties in Netscape Navigator 4

If you specify font properties for a *body* type selector, FrontPage, Internet Explorer, and Netscape Navigator 6 and later apply those properties, unless overridden, to all text on the page. This is because all page elements in FrontPage and Internet Explorer inherit font properties from the *body* element.

In Netscape Navigator 4, page elements such as *li* (list item), *td* (table data), and *th* (table heading) *don't* inherit text properties from the *body* element. As a result, you must control the properties of these selectors explicitly. Here are two ways of doing this:

- Use the Style dialog box to set up additional rules for *li*, *td*, *th*, and any additional selectors you require.
- Switch to Code view, and append the required selectors to the rule that already governs the *body* element. Here's an example:

```
body, li, td, th { font-family: sans-serif; }
```


Modifying Web Pages to Use CSS Classes and IDs

If you create a rule named with a type selector (that is, named with the name of an HTML tag), both the FrontPage editor and the browser will apply the rule automatically.

If you create a rule named with a class selector or an ID selector, you must specially designate any content you want the rule to affect. There are three ways to do this, the first of which involves the Properties dialog box. Proceed as follows:

1. Right-click the element you want to affect, and choose Properties from the shortcut menu.
2. Click the Style button in the Properties dialog box.
3. When the Modify Style dialog box shown previously in Figure 21-7 appears, enter the class selector name in the Class box or the ID selector name in the ID box.

   When using a class selector, remember *not* to type the leading period that's required when you define one. Similarly, when you use an ID selector, remember *not* to type the leading pound sign.

If you prefer using the Formatting toolbar, try the second method of applying a class or ID rule. Here it is:

1. Select the element you want to affect.
2. Display the Style drop-down list on the Formatting toolbar, scroll to the bottom, and choose the selector name you want. This list displays classes defined in linked style sheets as well as classes defined within the current Web page.

Here's the third way of applying a class selector or an ID selector is to do the job in Code view:

1. In the Design view editing window, select some or all of the text you want to affect.
2. Click the Code tab at the bottom of the editing window.
3. Locate the HTML tag that controls the selected text. (In most cases, whatever you select before switching to Code view is also selected in Code view.)
4. To make the tag inherit the properties of a class selector, add the following attribute inside it:

   ```
   class="class-selector"
   ```

   This paragraph tag inherits the CSS properties assigned to the class selector *onsale*:

   ```
   <p class="onsale">
   ```

5. To give the tag an ID value, add the following attribute inside it:

   ```
   id="identifier"
   ```

   The ID attribute in the following table tag assigns the identifier *scores*:

   ```
   <table id="scores">
   ```

   Remember that no two elements in the same page should ever have the same ID. To assign the same style in two or more places, use a class selector.

Troubleshooting

Random names appear as IDs of <table> tags

When you assign CSS properties to an HTML table, you might discover that the ID field is already filled in with an automatically generated name. This behavior is by design. Among their other uses, such IDs support a Microsoft Excel feature called Web Query. This feature extracts data from HTML tables anywhere on the World Wide Web and remembers which page and which table the data came from. Because Excel remembers these locations, it's easy to refresh the data at any time.

Remembering a URL is easy, but remembering a specific table is harder. Web queries can remember an ordinal position—meaning first table on the page, third table on the page, or whatever. But a better solution, if the table has an ID code, is to remember that code. To assist in this effort FrontPage, by default, assigns ID codes to every table.

There's nothing magical about the ID codes FrontPage assigns; you can change them or delete them at will. The only impact occurs if the page has been in use for some time and Web visitors have performed Web queries against it. In that case, changing the ID code might break those queries.

If you'd rather FrontPage didn't assign ID attributes to tables, choose Page Options from the Tools menu, and then, on the General tab, clear the Assign Unique IDs To New Tables check box.

Formatting Multiple Pages

CSS rules that control an entire Web page provide more consistent control over appearance than inline styles or HTML attributes applied to individual elements. Page-level CSS rules, however, provide no control over groups of Web pages, and thus no guarantee of consistency among them.

To provide such consistency, a single collection of CSS rules would have to control multiple Web pages. This is exactly what linked style sheets provide. Using linked style sheets is a four-step process:

1. Add a style sheet file to your Web site. These files contain nothing but CSS code and usually have a .css file extension.
2. Add as many CSS rules to the style sheet file as you want. Be sure to save the file after making any changes.
3. Modify any pages that should use the rules from step 2 so that they refer to the file you created in step 1.
4. If any of the rules from step 2 have class or ID selectors, modify any necessary Web page elements so that they refer to those classes or IDs.

The next four sections explain how to perform each of these steps.

Adding a Style Sheet File to Your Web Site

Using a template is the simplest and easiest way to add a style sheet file to a Web site. As usual, there are two ways to begin. Here's the first:

1. Choose New from the File menu.
2. In the New Page Or Web Site task pane, click Page Templates.

The second procedure uses the New Page drop-down menu on the Standard toolbar. Proceed as follows:

New Page Style

1. Click the New Page down arrow on the Standard toolbar.
2. Choose Page.

Following either of these procedures and then clicking the Style Sheets tab displays the Page Templates dialog box shown in Figure 21-10.

To continue creating the style sheet file:

1. Review the available templates by clicking them and reviewing the Description and Preview areas in the dialog box. Here are some guidelines for choosing a template:
   - If you're not seeking a specific predefined appearance, choose a template that controls the *kinds* of properties you want instead of one that provides correct property *values*. Values are easier to change later than the list of properties.
   - To begin with a clean slate, choose the Normal Style Sheet template. This is probably the best choice 99 percent of the time.

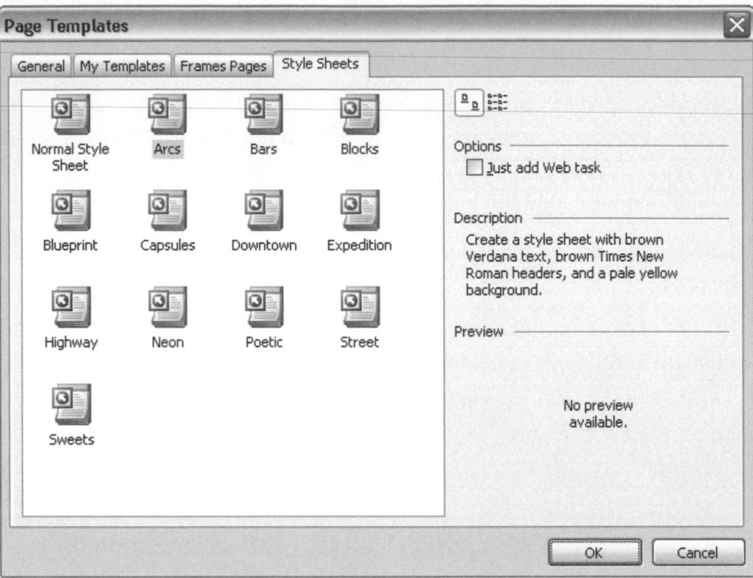

Figure 21-10. FrontPage provides a selection of page templates for creating new style sheet files.

2 When you've chosen the best available template, click OK. FrontPage loads the template into the Design view editing window, as shown in Figure 21-11. The Arcs template created the results shown in this figure.

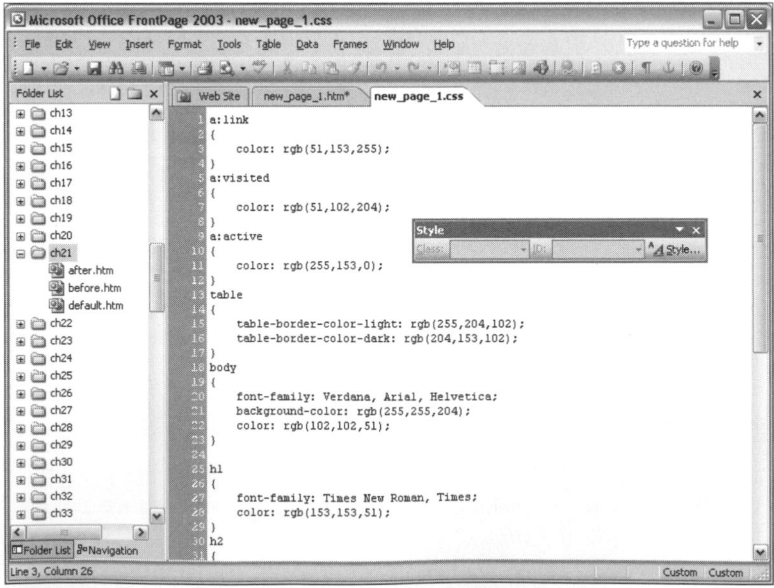

Figure 21-11. The Arcs style sheet template produces these results. Style sheets have no appearance of their own, so FrontPage displays them as code.

A quick glance at the figure reveals that CSS files don't appear in any sort of WYSIWYG view. The Design, Split, Code, and Preview tabs that normally appear at the bottom of the window are completely absent. Although style sheets definitely control the appearance of Web pages, they have no appearance of their own. FrontPage must therefore display them as code.

3 Save a style sheet file as you would any other file—for example, by choosing Save or Save As from the File menu. A common file name for a Web site's main CSS file is styles.css.

The number of CSS files you add to a Web site is totally at your discretion, but having only one such file is a good option to consider. Having only one CSS file implies that all the pages in your Web site inherit the same general appearance from the same central location. If some pages contain unique elements, set up unique class rules to accommodate them.

If you don't want to use templates for creating CSS files—not even the Normal Style Sheet template, which is blank—you can create them in Microsoft Notepad or any other text editor, save them, and then import them to your Web site.

For more information about importing files, refer to "Importing Web Files and Folders," on page 175.

Adding Rules to a Style Sheet File

The procedure for adding and modifying rules in a CSS style sheet file is the same as that for adding and modifying rules in an ordinary Web page:

1. To display the Style dialog box, shown previously in Figure 21-8, click the Style button on the Style toolbar, or choose Style from the Format menu.
2. To create a new rule, click the New button. This displays the New Style dialog box, shown previously in Figure 21-9.
3. To modify an existing rule, select it in the Styles list in the Style dialog box, and then click the Modify button. This displays the Modify Style dialog box, shown previously in Figure 21-7.
4. To delete an existing user-defined rule, select it in the Style dialog box, and then click the Delete button.

For instructions on using the New Style and Modify Style dialog boxes, refer to "Assigning Style Sheet Properties," later in this chapter.

If you understand CSS code, another option is to directly modify the CSS rules displayed in the Design view window.

Linking Style Sheet Files

The simplest and easiest way of linking a style sheet file to a Web page involves only two steps:

1. Open the page in Design view.
2. Drag the style sheet file from the Folder List to the open Web page.

If your needs are more elaborate, the longer procedure that follows might be more appropriate. This procedure always requires first selecting the Web pages you want to affect, and then assigning a style sheet to them. Here are the details:

1. Create a file containing the CSS rules you want, and then save it in your Web site with a .css file extension.
2. If you want the CSS file to control only certain files in your Web site, select them. This will probably be easiest in Folders view. To select a page that's open in Design view, click anything within it.
3. Choose Style Sheet Links from the Format menu. If, in step 2, you selected more than one Web page, the Confirm Format Style Sheet Links dialog box shown below will appear.

   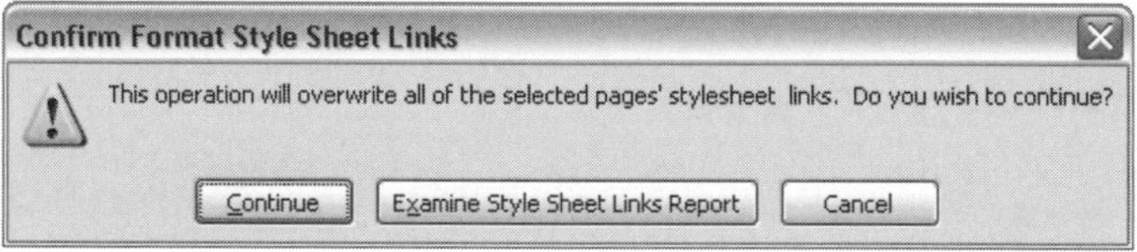

   Respond to this prompt as follows.

   - **Continue** Click this button if you intended to affect more than one Web page, and you're sure you selected the right ones.
   - **Examine Style Sheet Links Report** Click this button to display a report that shows which CSS files each Web page in your site already uses.
   - **Cancel** Click this button if you think you made a mistake and wish to go no further.

   If you click Cancel or if the prompt doesn't appear, FrontPage will display the Link Style Sheet dialog box shown in the foreground of Figure 21-12.
4. To apply a style sheet to every page in your Web, select All Pages. To apply it only to the pages you selected in step 2, select Selected Page(s).
5. If the style sheet file you want to apply isn't already listed, click the Add button to locate the file, and add it to the list. This button displays a typical file selection dialog box titled Select Style Sheet.
6. If you don't want a listed style sheet file to apply to the specified pages, select it in the URL list, and then click Remove to remove it from the list. This action doesn't physically delete the file.

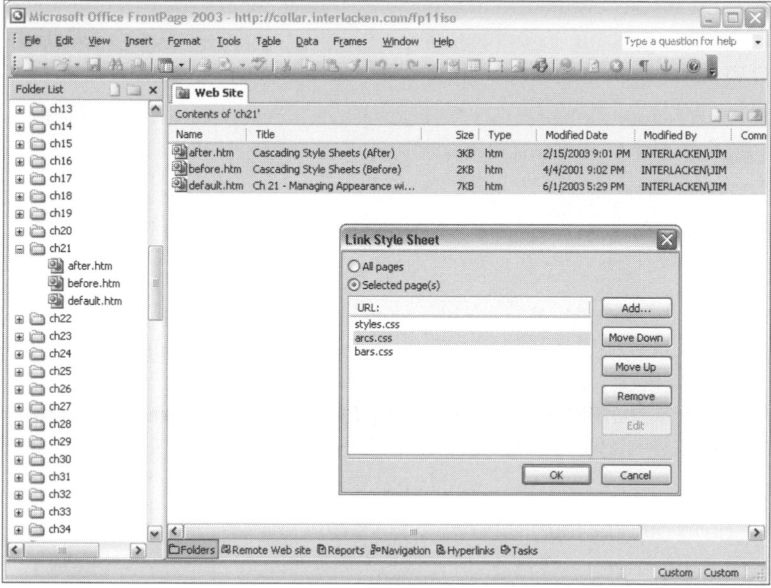

Figure 21-12. Use the options in the Link Style Sheet dialog box to apply a CSS file to one or more pages in a FrontPage-based Web site.

7. If the URL list includes more than one style sheet file, the browser will apply them in order. To change this order, select the CSS file you want to move, and then click the Move Down or Move Up button. Continue this process until all the files are in the order you want.
8. Click OK.

> **Caution** If the current Web site is server-based (that is, if the top of your Folder List shows an HTTP location), the Link Style Sheet dialog box will fail unless the Web server is running the FrontPage Server Extensions 2000 or later. Earlier versions of the server extensions can't insert style sheet links based on commands from the FrontPage desktop software.

CSS merges style sheet rules on a property-by-property basis. Consider the following series of rules. (The syntax is fairly self-explanatory and not critical to this discussion.)

```
h1 { font-family: Arial; color: red; }
h1 { font-weight: bold; }
h1 { color: blue; margin-left: 10px; }
```

The presence of these three rules produces the same result as the presence of the following single rule:

```
h1 { font-family: Arial;
     font-weight: bold;
     color: blue;
     margin-left: 10px; }
```

The same results occur whether the rules appear sequentially in one file, separated by other rules in the same file, or interspersed with others rules in various files. The last value you assign to any selector property is the value the browser applies.

Similar considerations apply when one selector inherits properties from another. Consider, for example, the following series of rules:

```
body { color: red; }
h1   { font-family: serif; color: blue; }
body { font-family: sans-serif; }
```

The first rule says that all text in the body of the Web page should be red. The second rule says that all Heading 1 text should appear in the browser's default serif font and be blue. This second rule overrides the red color specified by the first rule, but only for Heading 1 text. The third rule presents a problem by specifying that all body text should appear in the browser's default sans serif font. Does this override the more specific *font-family* setting in the second rule?

As it turns out, the third rule doesn't override properties established in the second rule because the second rule is more specific. But who needs these kinds of puzzles in life? And this is exactly what happens when you start assigning multiple CSS files to the same Web page. Save yourself the headache, and confine yourself, if not to one CSS file per Web site, to only one CSS file per page.

Assigning Style Sheet Properties

All three procedures discussed so far (that is, the procedures for inline styles, for page-level styles, and for linked style sheets) culminated in displaying the Modify Style dialog box, shown previously in Figure 21-7, or the New Style dialog box, shown previously in Figure 21-9. These dialog boxes create rules and display styles currently in effect, but actually setting CSS properties requires more pointing and clicking. Specifically, you must:

1 Click the Format button that appears in the lower left corner of either dialog box.
2 Choose Font, Paragraph, Border, Numbering, or Position from the drop-down menu.

The next four subsections describe the first four options. Chapter 22 will describe the Position option.

Fro more information about positioning content with Cascading Style Sheets, refer to Ch 22, "Positioning Content with Cascading Style Sheets,"

Assigning Style Sheet Fonts

The dialog box for assigning CSS fonts is shown in Figure 21-13. If this Font dialog box looks hauntingly familiar, you're right; it contains most of the same options that appear when you choose Font from the Format menu. The difference is that here, you're configuring an abstract style and not a specific Web page element.

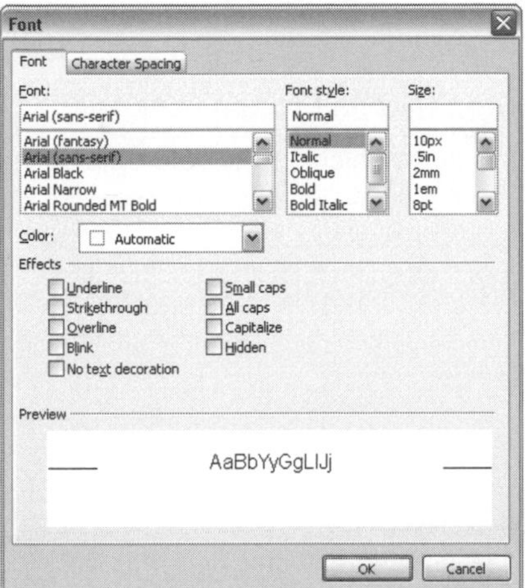

Figure 21-13. This dialog box specifies CSS fonts. Notice that you can type font names or choose from the Font list. The Size box accepts a plethora of measurement types.

Table 21-2 associates the options in this dialog box with the CSS properties they control, describes what they do, and itemizes the acceptable values. The same table also lists related CSS properties not accessible through FrontPage dialog boxes, just in case you want to engage Code view and modify your style rules directly.

Table 21-2. CSS Font Properties

Dialog box option	CSS property name	Description and values
Font	*font-family*	A list of font names available on the local system. Select any listed font, or type the name of another font. The generic fonts listed in Table 21-3 are excellent choices.
Font Style	*font-style*	Can be *normal*, *italic*, or *oblique*. Normal text is upright. Italic text is slanted, thinned, and more curved. Oblique text is slanted but otherwise resembles normal text.
	font-weight	The thickness of the strokes making up a font. Values include: ● A numeric weight from 100 to 900. ● The keywords *normal* (=400) or *bold* (=700). ● The keywords *bolder* or *lighter*, which thicken or narrow strokes compared to the object's parent.
Size	*font-size*	The height of a font, measured from the top of the tallest character to the bottom of the lowest. Any CSS unit of measurement is acceptable.

Table 21-2. CSS Font Properties

Dialog box option	CSS property name	Description and values
Color	*color*	The color in which text should appear. FrontPage controls this setting using its standard sequence of color dialog boxes.
Underline, Strikethrough, Overline, Blink, No Text Decoration	*text-decoration*	Control the following modifications to normal text: *underline*, *overline*, *strikethrough*, and *blink*. The default is *none*.
Small Caps	*font-variant*	Can be *normal* or *small-caps*. The value *small-caps* replaces lowercase letters with reduced-size capital letters.
All Caps, Capitalize	*text-transform*	Present text in a certain case, regardless of how it was entered. The options are: *capitalize* (first letter only, all others lowercase), *uppercase* (all uppercase), *lowercase* (all lowercase), and *none* (as is, the default).
Hidden	*visibility*	In most browsers, a value of *hidden* makes an element invisible, and *visible* makes it visible. Netscape Navigator 4, however, requires values of *hide* or *show*.
(none)	*font*	This is a shortcut property that accepts any of the values described above. CSS assigns each value to the correct property based on the value's syntax.

No matter what font name you assign to a CSS property, there's no assurance that the visitor has that font available. If the specified font *isn't* available, the visitor's browser does its best to pick a similar font, but this is far from an exact science. After all, if the visitor's system doesn't have a font like Gloucester MT Extra Condensed installed, how is it supposed to know enough about that font to pick something similar? There are three solutions to this problem:

- **Specify only commonly available fonts** Fonts that come with Microsoft Windows, fonts that come with Microsoft Office, and fonts installed with the visitor's browser are probably available to the vast majority of your visitors. Stick to these fonts.
- **Specify generic fonts** The generic font names listed in Table 21-3 have reasonable equivalents on every user's system. The names in the Generic Font Name are those that appear in the CSS code. The names in the Selection List Font Name column are those that appear in FrontPage dialog boxes.

  The cursive and fantasy generic fonts still leave you wondering what you're going to get, but the serif, sans serif, and monospace choices are reasonably specific and useful.

- **Specify multiple fonts** The *font-family* property can accept a list of fonts the browser should use, in order of preference. In code, it looks like this:

  ```
  h1 { font-family: Verdana, Arial, Helvetica, sans-serif; }
  ```

  This code makes the browser look first to see whether the Verdana font is available, then Arial, then Helvetica, and then any sans serif font. This virtually guarantees that what the visitor sees will conform to your original design.

  Unfortunately, FrontPage doesn't have a good facility for specifying a list of fonts. You can select the first font from the Font list in the CSS Font dialog box, but you must enter any additional fonts by hand, separating the font names with commas.

Table 21-3. Generic CSS Fonts

Generic Font Name	Selection List Font Name	Description
serif	Times New Roman (serif)	The system default serif font, such as Times New Roman or Times Roman
sans-serif	Arial (sans-serif)	The system default sans serif font, such as Arial or Helvetica
cursive	Comic Sans MS (cursive)	A font that looks like handwriting
fantasy	Arial (fantasy)	A highly decorative font
monospace	Courier New (monospace)	The system default monospaced font, such as Courier New or Courier

The Character Spacing tab of the CSS Font dialog box controls the spacing rather than the character style of text. This tab appears in Figure 21-14.

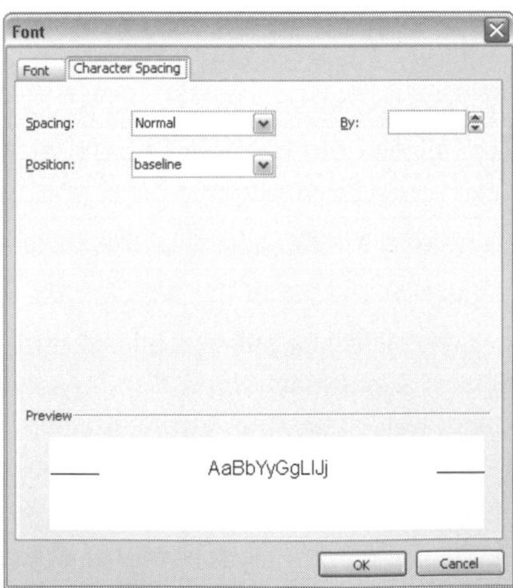

Figure 21-14. This CSS dialog box affects character spacing (kerning) and vertical alignment.

Table 21-4 details the corresponding CSS properties.

Table 21-4. CSS Letter Spacing and Positioning Properties

Dialog box option	CSS property name	Description and values
Spacing	*letter-spacing*	Expands or condenses the spacing between letters. The default measurement is in pixels. The accompanying By spinner controls the amount.
Position	*vertical-align*	A positive measurement raises the object above its normal position by the amount you choose. A negative measurement lowers the object below its normal position. See Table 21-5 for more options.

The Position property (*vertical-align*) specifies the alignment of an inline object relative to the surrounding text. Table 21-5 summarizes the permissible values. Despite its name, this property has nothing to do with CSS Positioning (CSS2).

Note The *baseline* is the imaginary straight line on which letters in a line of text rest. (The descenders of lowercase letters such as *j* and *g* extend below the baseline.)

Table 21-5. CSS Font Position Properties

Setting	Description
baseline	The baseline of the child (surrounded) object aligns with the baseline of the parent (surrounding) text.
sub	The baseline of the child object aligns with the parent's preferred baseline for subscripts.
super	The baseline of the child object aligns with the parent's preferred baseline for superscripts.
top	The top of the child object aligns with the top border of the surrounding text.
text-top	The top of the child object aligns with the top of the surrounding text.
middle	The object's vertical midpoint aligns with the parent's baseline raised by one-half the x-height (the height of a lowercase letter with no ascenders or descenders, such as *a*, *e*, *o*, and, well, *x*). In other words, the midpoint of the object would align with the midpoint of such letters as *a*, *e*, *o*, or *x* in the surrounding text.
bottom	The bottom of the child object aligns with the bottom border of the surrounding text.

Table 21-5. CSS Font Position Properties

Setting	Description
text-bottom	The bottom of the child object aligns with the bottom of the parent.
percentage	If vertical alignment is a percentage, this value raises or lowers the child's position by that fraction of the parent's line height. A setting of 50% raises the child object half a line. (Although no percentages appear in the drop-down list, you can enter a percentage by hand.)

Assigning Style Sheet Paragraph Properties

CSS provides amazing control over the layout of paragraphs. The CSS Paragraph dialog box, shown in Figure 21-15, provides access to some of the available layout properties. The Borders And Shading and Bullets And Numbering dialog boxes, discussed later in this chapter, control more such properties.

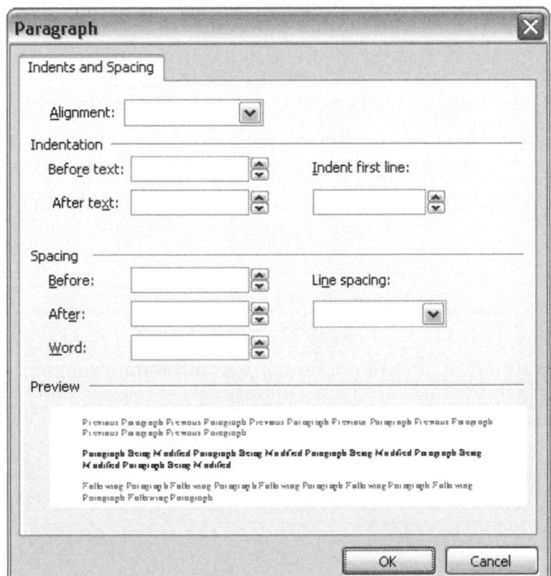

Figure 21-15. The Paragraph dialog box controls paragraph alignment, indentation, and spacing.

Table 21-6 correlates the options in the CSS Paragraph dialog box with the CSS properties they control and then describes those properties.

Table 21-6. CSS Paragraph Properties

Dialog box option	CSS property name	Description and values
Alignment	*text-align*	Controls the horizontal position of text. *left* aligns text to the left margin (left-aligned, flush-left). *right* aligns text to the right margin (right-aligned, flush-right). *center* aligns the center of each line with the center of the available area. *justify* aligns text to both the left and the right margins, spreading the required space as evenly as possible between words in the line.
Indent First Line	*text-indent*	Specifies first-line paragraph indentation. Negative numbers produce "outdents" (where the first line extends to the left of second and subsequent lines).
Indentation Before Text, Indentation After Text, Spacing Before, Spacing After	*margin-left*, *margin-right*, *margin-top*, *margin-bottom*	These four properties control the amount of blank space that surrounds a page element's border (or where the border would be, if its thickness weren't zero). If you're working in code and want all four margins to be the same, code a *margin* property like this: *margin: 10px*.
Spacing Word	*word-spacing*	Adjusts the normal spacing between words. Positive measurements increase spacing, and negative values decrease spacing.
Line Spacing	*line-height*	Specifies the amount of vertical space reserved for a line. A common value is the point size times 1.2.

The Indentation Before Text, Indentation After Text, Spacing Before, and Spacing After options control the amount of white space reserved around the borders of an element, plus a small buffer zone called *padding*. Figure 21-16 illustrates the following concepts of margins and padding:

- The *content area* is the space that a picture, text, a table, or another type of content occupies.
- *Padding* surrounds the content area, matching its background color and certain other properties.
- If there's a visible *border*, it surrounds the padding area and not just the content area.
- *Margins* surround the padding area and borders, if there are any. Unlike padding—which matches the background of its content area—margins match the background of whatever surrounds them.

Tip Starting from the outside and proceeding inward, the areas that surround a content area are margin, border, and padding: M-B-P. Remembering this acronym might be easier than remembering the CSS property names.

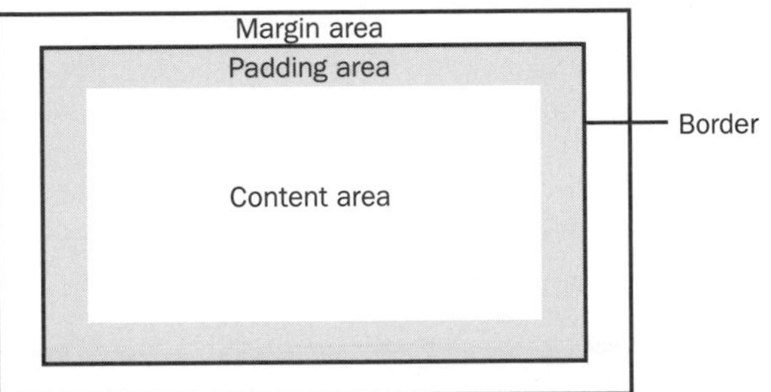

Figure 21-16. Padding surrounds a Web page object and matches its background. Margins surround the padding and match the exterior background. Borders, if specified, appear where the two meet.

You can specify margin width, border width, and padding width in terms of any CSS measurement. The most common unit of measurement, however, is pixels.

The *line-height* property controls the height of lines in a paragraph. FrontPage suggests measurements in pixels, but the CSS standard also provides for specifying a percentage or ratio of the font size (for example, either 120 percent or 1.2).

Note Typographers would call the combination of 10 point text with 12 point line spacing *10/12 spacing*. They might also speak of it as 10-point text with 2 points of leading. Leading refers to the strips of lead that early printers used to separate rows of movable type.

Assigning Style Sheet Borders

Figure 21-17 shows the Borders tab of the CSS Borders And Shading dialog box. This dialog box appears after you click Format and choose Border in the New Style or Modify Style dialog box.

To use this dialog box:

1. Choose one of the Setting options:
   - **Default** Means that the current rule will have no effect on border settings.
   - **Box** Means that you want borders on all four sides.
   - **Custom** Means that you want borders on one, two, or three sides.
2. Choose the border style you want from the Style list. The Preview area will reflect your choice.

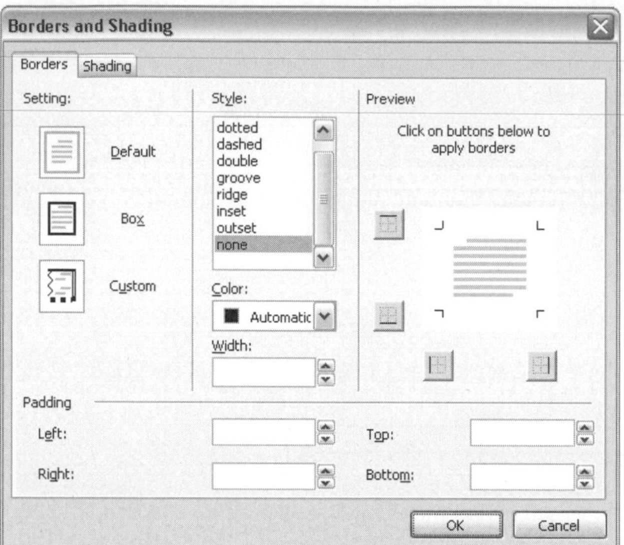

Figure 21-17. The Borders tab controls the visible border around Web page elements, as well as the amount of padding between the border and the page element's contents.

3. Use the Color drop-down list to specify what color the border should be.
4. Use the Width box to specify how thick the border should be.
5. If you chose Custom (or just changed your mind), click any of the four icons at the left of and below the preview diagram. Each icon adds or removes borders on a different side—top, bottom, left, or right.
6. Use the Padding section to control the amount of space between the border and the element's regular content. If you've forgotten what padding is, refer again to Figure 21-16.

Table 21-7 correlates each Borders tab setting with the CSS properties it controls.

Table 21-7. CSS Border Properties

Dialog box option	CSS property name	Description and values
Style	*border-style*	Specifies the type of line used to draw the border—*none, solid, dotted, double,* and so on.
Color	*border-color*	Indicates the color you want the border to be.

Table 21-7. CSS Border Properties

Dialog box option	CSS property name	Description and values
Width	*border-width*	Specifies the thickness of the border. You can specify width using generic values of *thick*, *medium*, or *thin* or specify width as a specific number of pixels. As before, the CSS specification supports additional units of measure.
Preview buttons	*border-top*, *border-right*, *border-bottom*, *border-left*	These four properties control the type of border drawn on each side of a Web page element. Accepted values are those listed in the Style list in Figure 21-17, plus *none*.
Padding Top, Padding Bottom, Padding Left, Padding Right	*padding-top*, *padding-bottom*, *padding-left*, *padding-right*	These four settings control the amount of white space reserved between a page element's border and its content.
(none)	*border-top-width*, *border-right-width*, *border-bottom-width*, *border-left-width*	These four properties specify the width of each border side independently. If all four sides should be the same width, it's much easier to use the *border-width* property.

If you're working with CSS rules by hand, it's often useful to use the *margin* and *padding* property names rather than the more detailed properties shown in Table 21-6 and Table 21-7. For example, it's perfectly OK to code:

```
.special { border: 2px solid #900; }
```

rather than:

```
.special { border-width: 2px; border-style: solid; border-color: #900; }
```

The order of any values you specify as border properties isn't important. CSS can figure out that measurements must be border widths, style names must be style values, and color values must be border colors.

If you manually code a CSS rule that uses the *border* and *padding* property names and then you modify the rule using FrontPage dialog boxes, FrontPage might rewrite the rule with detailed property names like *border-width* and *border-style*. The formatting results, however, will be the same.

In the case of border width and padding width, you can specify anywhere from one to four values. Table 21-8 shows which values control which measurements, depending on the number of values you supply.

Table 21-8. CSS Border Width and Padding Width Property Values

Number of values specified	Source of value for:			
	Top	**Right**	**Bottom**	**Left**
1	1st	1st	1st	1st
2	1st	2nd	1st	2nd
3	1st	2nd	3rd	2nd
4	1st	2nd	3rd	4th

The second tab in the Borders And Shading dialog box is—you guessed it—the Shading tab, shown in Figure 21-18.

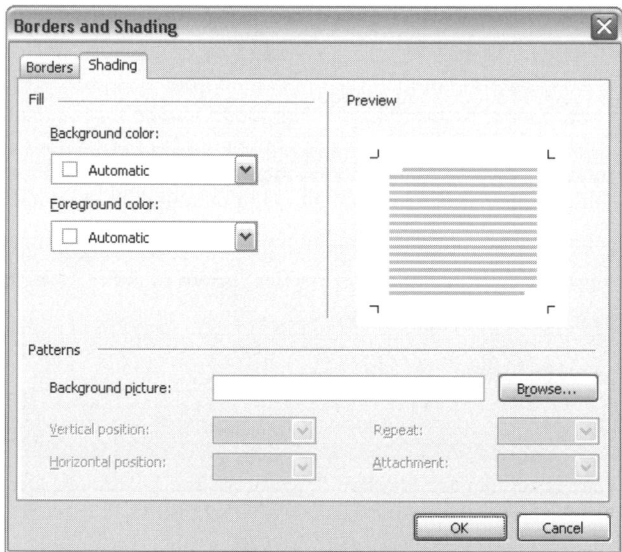

Figure 21-18. The Shading tab controls the foreground color and background appearance of styled elements on your Web page.

Table 21-9 relates the options on the Shading tab with their corresponding CSS properties and values.

Table 21-9. CSS Shading Properties

Dialog box option	CSS property name	Description and values
Background Color	*background-color*	Specifies the default color used for filling the background of an element.
Foreground Color	*color*	Specifies the color used for presenting an object's contents. For many elements, this is the color in which text will appear.
Background Picture	*background-picture*	Specifies a picture that will fill the background of an element.
Vertical Position, Horizontal Position	*background-position*	These two values control positioning of the first (or only) background picture.
Repeat	*background-repeat*	Controls the repetitive tiling of a background picture. *repeat* repeats the background picture both vertically and horizontally to fill the entire available area. *repeat-x* repeats the picture horizontally only. *repeat-y* repeats the picture vertically only. *no-repeat* displays the picture only once and doesn't repeat it.
Attachment	*background-attachment*	Scrolls the background picture or keeps it fixed. *scroll* moves the background picture along with other content. This is the default. *fixed* keeps the background picture stationary, even when other content scrolls.

The values for Vertical Position and Horizontal Position warrant some additional explanation. These values can be any of the following:

- The keywords *top*, *bottom*, *center*, *left*, and/or *right*, interpreted within the space the page element occupies.
- Percentages, again interpreted within the page element space. *0% 0%* means *top left*; *100% 100%* means *bottom right*.
- Any valid CSS measurement, interpreted from the element's top left corner.

Troubleshooting

FrontPage doesn't preserve CSS coding syntax

When you open a page that contains CSS styles, FrontPage normally saves them just as it received them. Or, as insiders would say, FrontPage accurately *round-trips* CSS code.

When you modify a rule using FrontPage dialog boxes, however, Front page often changes the rule's overall format. In most cases, these changes are relatively harmless. If you code the following rule:

```
.special { border-width: 2px; border-style: solid; border-color: 900#; }
```

and then you change it using FrontPage dialog boxes, and then you change it back, FrontPage substitutes the more compact form:

```
.special { border: 2px solid #900; }
```

This sometimes leads to curious results when CSS code contains errors. The following code, for example, tries to assign border properties to a margin:

```
.woeisme { margin: 2px solid #900; }
```

FrontPage converts this rule to the following, which is definitely not equivalent:

```
.special { margin-left:solid; margin-right:solid;
      margin-top:2px; margin-bottom:#900 }
```

The original code wouldn't have produced correct results anyway, but the modified code is valid CSS that does something other than what the designer wanted. If your CSS code doesn't seem to be working as intended, either look at the CSS code directly in Code view or review and correct all the values in CSS dialog boxes.

Assigning Style Sheet Numbering

The fourth Format option in the New Style and Modify Style dialog boxes is really a misnomer—the menu says Numbering, but the dialog box controls unnumbered bullets as well. The resulting dialog box is more accurately titled Bullets And Numbering, as you can see in Figure 21-19.

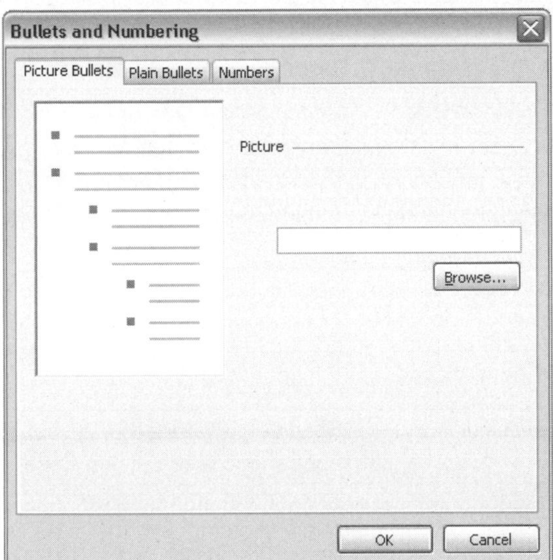

Figure 21-19. Use this dialog box to specify what kind of bullets or numbers should appear for a bulleted or numbered list.

The three tabs in this dialog box are very simple and very much alike:

- **Picture Bullets** This tab provides a text box and accompanying Browse button. Together, these controls specify a picture that the browser will use for a bulleted list. This can be any picture the browser can display, although caution suggests a small one. Browse to the picture you want to display, and then click OK.
- **Plain Bullets** This tab displays four ordinary bullet styles: none, solid round, hollow round, and solid square. Click the style you want, and then click OK.
- **Numbers** This tab displays six numbering styles: none, arabic numerals, uppercase roman numerals, uppercase letters, lowercase letters, and lowercase roman numerals. Click the style you want, and then click OK.

The Bullets And Numbering dialog box has the least direct correlation to CSS styles. Nevertheless, Table 21-10 lists the applicable CSS properties.

Table 21-10. CSS Bullets and Numbering Properties

Dialog box option	CSS property name	Description and values
Bullet Samples	*list-style-type*	Specifies the type of list bullet. Permissible values are *disc*, *circle*, *square*, *decimal*, *lower-roman*, *upper-roman*, *lower-alpha*, *upper-alpha*, and *none*.
Picture	*list-style-image*	Specifies the URL of a picture that the browser will display as a list bullet. A relative URL like *../images/ballred.gif* or *mydot.gif* is best.
(none)	*list-style-position*	Specifies whether the list bullet should appear *inside* or *outside* the text area. The default is *outside*, which produces hanging bullets like the ones in this book.
(all)	*list-style*	A shortcut property that accepts any combination of the values described above. CSS assigns the values to the correct properties based on syntax.

Assigning Additional Style Sheet Properties

Table 21-11 lists some additional CSS properties that don't pertain to any of the FrontPage dialog boxes presented so far. These might be useful if you end up being a CSS fanatic and coding rules by hand in Code view.

Table 21-11. CSS Properties Not Supported in CSS Dialog Boxes

CSS property	Description and values
width	Specifies the desired width of an element, using any valid CSS measurement.
height	Specifies the desired height of an element, using any valid CSS measurement.
float	Specifies an object's alignment: left, center, or right. Text will flow around left-aligned or right-aligned objects, but not around centered ones. If this property is blank, the object either flows inline with text or is left-aligned with text not flowing around it, depending on the type of object.
clear	Specifies that an element should be positioned far enough down the page that it clears any left-aligned elements, right-aligned elements, or both. Permissible values are *none* (the default), *left*, *right*, and *both*.

Table 21-11. **CSS Properties Not Supported in CSS Dialog Boxes**

CSS property	Description and values
display	Controls how an element is displayed. *block* means that the element starts on a new line, like a paragraph or heading. *inline* means that the element flows within a line, as occurs with boldface or italic text. *list-item* means that the element appears as an indented box with a preceding label, like a bulleted or numbered list. *none* means that the element does not appear.
white-space	Controls the treatment of spaces, tabs, linefeeds, and carriage returns. *normal* treats all strings of such characters as if they were a single-space character. *pre* leaves all such characters in place. *nowrap* compresses white-space characters like *normal*, but doesn't break lines wider than the browser window.

Specifying Style Sheet Measurements and Colors

The CSS specification provides great flexibility in the way you specify heights, widths, distances, and colors. This section explains all the available options.

Specifying Style Sheet Measurements

The values of many CSS properties involve measurements: the height of the characters, the width of a paragraph, the thickness of a border, or whatever. The format for specifying these measurements consists of a number followed by a unit of measure, with no intervening spaces. Table 21-12 lists the valid units of measure.

Table 21-12. **CSS Units of Measure**

Type	Unit	Name	Description
Absolute	mm	Millimeter	25.4 millimeters equal 1 inch.
	cm	Centimeter	1 centimeter equals 10 millimeters.
	in	Inch	1 inch equals 25.4 millimeters.
	pt	Point	72 points equals 1 inch.
	pc	Pica	1 pica equals 12 points. 6 picas equals 1 inch.
Relative	%	Percentage	Indicates a degree of magnification compared to the item's normal size. For example, 200% means twice normal size, and 50% means half normal size.
	em	Em	1 em equals the point size of the current font.

Table 21-12. CSS Units of Measure

Type	Unit	Name	Description
	ex	Ex	1 ex equals the x-height of the current font. The x-height is the height of the lowercase *x* character.
Device-dependent	px	Pixel	1 pixel equals the smallest unit of resolution on the visitor's display screen.

Here are some examples:

CSS code	Meaning
12pt	12 points
1.5in	1½ inches
7mm	7 millimeters
125%	25 percent larger than normal size

When possible, it's best to use relative measurements. That way, if the visitor's browser magnifies or shrinks the entire page, your elements retain the correct relative proportions. The same is true when you resize an element's parent and expect subordinate items to scale proportionately.

If you can't use relative measurements, the device-dependent pixel measurement should be your second choice. This at least maintains proportion to any pictures on your page, which the browser always sizes in terms of pixels. In addition, it avoids difficult-to-resolve situations involving odd pixel sizes (for example, trying to display a font that's 7.5 pixels high).

The main problem with absolute measurements, such as *1in*, lies in not knowing what the visitor's computer thinks an inch is. Most video drivers interpret 1 inch as 72 pixels, so that 1 point equals 1 pixel. This convention is far from universal, however, and is still subject to the visitor's monitor size and video setting.

The meaning of percentage measurements varies with the type of object. For most types, it's a percentage of the measurement the object would otherwise inherit. For example, a paragraph width of *80%* would make the paragraph 80 percent as wide as it otherwise would be. The following are typical exceptions to this rule:

- For colors, the range 0% to 100% corresponds to the normal RGB values 0 through 255.
- For line height, the percentage value is applied to the surrounding text's point size.

In the context of CSS, an em is a unit of distance equal to the point size of text. Thus, within 12-point text, 1 em equals 12 points, or 1/6 inch. The advantage of using ems as a unit of measure is that they change proportionately when the point size changes.

Specifying Style Sheet Colors

There are five ways to specify colors:

- **By name** You can specify colors using the names from Table 18-1, "Colors in the 16-Color VGA Palette." For example:

  ```
  { color: red; }
  ```

- **By hexadecimal 12-bit color value** To specify red, green, and blue colors on a hexadecimal scale from 0 to F, specify three hex digits preceded by a pound sign, like this:

  ```
  { color: #F00; }
  ```

- **By hexadecimal 24-bit color value** Specify six hex digits preceded by a pound sign. That's two digits each for red, green, and blue intensities, on a scale from 00 to FF. For example:

  ```
  { color: #FF0000; }
  ```

- **By decimal 24-bit color value** To specify red, green, and blue color values on a scale from 0 to 255, use this notation:

  ```
  { color: rgb(255,0,0); }
  ```

- **By percentage color value** To specify red, green, and blue color values as percentages of maximum intensity, use this notation:

  ```
  { color: rgb(100%,0%,0%); }
  ```

Tip Remember to specify browser-safe colors wherever possible. The required RGB components for the various notations are:

- 12-bit: 0, 3, 6, 9, C, and F
- 24-bit: 00, 33, 66, 99, CC, and FF
- Decimal: 0, 51, 102, 153, 204, and 255

In Summary...

This chapter explained the basics of CSS, a technology that provides far more flexibility and far more control over Web page typography than HTML tags alone can supply.

The next chapter explains how CSS can position Web page content.

Chapter 22

Positioning Content with Cascading Style Sheets

Pixel-precise positioning and layering of page elements has long been a dream of Web designers. They yearn for the relative simplicity of print design, where they can put things at specific page locations and not worry about readers changing the page dimensions after the fact. CSS Positioning (often called CSS2) provides just that capability.

Using CSS2, you can specify an exact position for any and all elements on a page, not only in terms of horizontal and vertical placement, but also in terms of overlap. (Overlap involves a *z-index* property that controls which elements appear in front of or behind others.) CSS2 is almost a dream come true for designers with experience in media other than the Web, but it suffers from three major drawbacks:

- It's seldom possible to gain complete control over every dimension that appears on a Web page. A Web visitor can change the size of fonts by using a menu command, for example, and there's nothing the Web designer can do about it. Similarly, nothing can stop Web visitors from having different-sized monitors or from resizing the browser window. And when some dimensions are fixed and others are variable, it's almost certain that something won't fit as intended.
- Browsers support CSS2 even less uniformly than they support CSS1.
- Lack of browser support for CSS2 is a more critical issue than lack of support for CSS1, as the following points illustrate:
  - When a browser that doesn't support CSS1 displays a Web page that contains CSS1 formatting, it displays the page legibly but with plain fonts.
  - When a browser that doesn't support CSS2 displays a Web page that contains CSS2 formatting, it usually displays a wild assortment of misplaced objects.

Despite the drawbacks inherent in CSS2, Microsoft Office FrontPage 2003 does a reasonable job of supporting it. This chapter explains how that support works.

Introducing Style Sheet Positioning

Level 2 of the W3C's CSS specification describes CSS positioning. This accounts for the acronym CSS2. The specification describes three kinds of positioning:

- **Static** This kind of positioning locates page elements where the browser would normally place them. In other words, CSS2 does nothing. This is the default.
- **Relative** This kind of positioning lays out the Web page normally, but then, just before displaying any positioned elements, shifts them up, down, right, or left of their normal locations. The browser still flows other content around the space where the relatively positioned element *would have been* had it not been positioned.
- **Absolute** This kind of positioning makes an element appear at specific xy-coordinates, measured from the top left corner of some container to the top left corner of the element. The browser reserves no space for the absolutely positioned element; the element just appears at the specified location. Other content doesn't flow around it.

The default container is the current Web page. You specify measurements relative to top left corner, so the CSS statement to display something 20 pixels below the top of the browser window is:

```
top: 20px;
```

The command to place something 30 pixels from the left edge of the browser window is:

```
left: 30px;
```

Combining this with the command that invokes absolute positioning produces this HTML:

```
style="position: absolute; top: 20px; left: 30px;"
```

CSS Positioning supports other properties in addition to *position*, *top*, and *left*, but these three will do for now. If you're curious about the rest, browse through Table 22-1. If you're curious about whether FrontPage makes you type code like the above, you can be sure it doesn't. Subsequent topics will get to that shortly.

Table 22-1. CSS Positioning Properties

Property	Values	Description
position	*static*	Tells the browser to position content normally. No special positioning is in effect.
	relative	Positions content relative to its normal page location.
	absolute	Positions content relative to the top left corner of its container.
top, left	*auto, <length>, <percent>*	Controls the placement of elements assigned relative or absolute positioning.

Table 22-1. CSS Positioning Properties

Property	Values	Description
width, height	*auto, <length>, <percent>*	Controls the size of positioned elements.
z-index	*auto, number*	Controls the visual precedence of positioned elements that overlap. Static elements have a *z-index* of zero.
visibility	*inherit, visible, hidden*	Controls whether an element is visible. The *inherit* value adopts the visibility of the parent container.
clip	*auto, rect* (upper-right, lower-left)	Defines what portion of an absolutely positioned element is visible.
overflow	*visible*	If an element's content exceeds its height or width, enlarges the container to display all the content.
	hidden	If an element's content exceeds its height or width, hides the additional content.
	auto	If an element's content exceeds its height or width, displays scroll bars as necessary.
	scroll	If an element's content exceeds its height or width, displays scroll bars at all times.

What can you position? Well, all browsers can apply static positioning because that's what they've been doing all along. In addition:

- Netscape Navigator 4 can apply relative or absolute positioning to spans, divisions, and block elements.
- Internet Explorer versions 4 and later and Netscape Navigator versions 6 and later can apply relative positioning to any page element, and absolute positioning to all the element types listed in Table 22-2.

Table 22-2. Valid Absolute Positioning Elements

Netscape Navigator–positionable	Internet Explorer–positionable	Internet Explorer unique elements	Form elements
Divisions	Pictures	Fieldsets	Buttons
Spans	Applets	Frames	Input elements
Block elements	Objects		Select lists
Tables			Text areas

A *block element* is anything that causes line breaks before and after itself. Normal paragraphs are the most common block elements, followed by the various heading types.

Divisions and *spans* are two HTML tags that mark sections of a Web page.

- A division starts where you put a <div> tag, ends where you put a </div> tag, and creates line breaks before and after itself. Divisions usually mark blocks of content for positioning, hiding, showing, and so forth.

Note The W3C invented the <div> tag to embrace and extend the <layer> tag that Netscape Communications originally proposed and implemented. The <layer> tag never achieved official status, but many Web designers still prefer the term *layer* over *division*. In fact, however, the tag that implements a layer is <div>.

- A span starts with <span>, ends with </span>, and flows continuously with surrounding elements. Spans usually mark ranges of content for formatting.

Both divisions and spans are normally invisible. This presents a problem for WYSIWYG editors like FrontPage, because what you see is nothing. FrontPage has a way of handling this; you'll learn about it shortly.

A *container* is any page element that establishes a coordinate system for positioned elements within it. The default container, and the only one Netscape Navigator 4 recognizes, is the body of the Web page. Internet Explorer versions 4 and later also support divisions inside one another, positioning the inner division relative to the top left corner of the outer division. In the same situation, Netscape 4 positions both divisions relative to the top left corner of the page.

To format a division, first select it, and then choose any enabled command from the Format menu. Formatting a span is trickier, because it's not visible in Design view. The trick is this: Choose Tag Properties on the span's drop-down menu in the Quick Tag Selector. This displays the Modify Style dialog box shown in the previous chapter as Figure 21-7. Use this dialog box to set any style properties you want.

Controlling Position in FrontPage

There are three ways to control positioning in FrontPage:

Show All

- Through the Position dialog box, which adds or modifies positioning properties for existing content
- Through the Positioning toolbar, which applies absolute positioning to existing content and modifies positioning properties.
- By using the mouse to drag an object's sizing handles or the object itself.

Show Layer Anchors

Tip When working with positioned content, it's best to have the Standard toolbar options Show All and Show Layer Anchors enabled.

With Show All in effect, FrontPage displays a hairline box around any positioned element.

With Show Layer Anchors in effect, Design view displays an anchor icon where the code for a positioned division (that is, a layer) actually resides.

Using the Position Dialog Box

To position elements using the Position dialog box, first select the content you want to position, and then choose Position from the Format menu. The dialog box in Figure 22-1 appears.

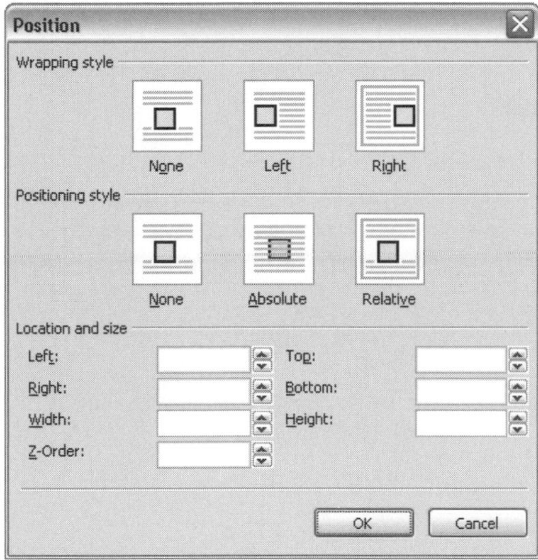

Figure 22-1. The Position dialog box controls the same properties as the Positioning toolbar, plus wrapping style and relative positioning.

The Position dialog box provides these options:

- **Wrapping Style** Controls how content outside the division or span flows around it. The choices are None (default alignment), Left (division or span aligned at the left margin, with other content flowing around it to the right), and Right (aligned at the right margin, with other content flowing around it to the left).
- **Positioning Style** Controls the type of positioning: None (the default, which CSS2 calls static), Absolute, or Relative.
- **Left** Controls the distance between the left edge of the positioned element and the left edge of its container.
- **Right** Controls the distance between the right edge of the positioned element and the right edge of its container.
- **Top** Controls the distance between the top of the positioned element and the top of its container.
- **Bottom** Controls the distance between the bottom of the positioned element and the bottom of its container.

> **Tip** If you specify a Top measurement, the browser normally ignores any Bottom measurement you specify. Similarly, if you specify both Right and Left, the browser will ignore Right.

- **Width** Controls the positioned element's vertical size.
- **Height** Controls the positioned element's horizontal size.
- **Z-Order** Controls the element's display precedence compared to that of overlapping elements (that is, it controls the element's *z-index* property).

Inside Out

Will the real z-index come to z-order?

The official name of the CSS2 attribute that controls the stack level (that is, the precedence) of overlapping elements is *z-index*. This is also the identifier that appears in CSS2 positioning code. Some portions of the FrontPage user interface nevertheless use the term *z-order* when referring to this attribute. Just remember, when FrontPage says *z-order*, it really means *z-index*.

Using the Position dialog box to modify existing properties is trickier than it might first appear. A problem occurs when:

- The positioned element is a division.
- You select an element inside that division.
- You then display the Position dialog box.

In this case, when the Position dialog box appears, it won't show the existing positioning properties. Furthermore, after you enter some properties and click OK, FrontPage creates a *new* division or span inside the existing one. This is almost certainly not what you want. If you're trying to modify existing positioning and the existing properties don't appear, try clicking Cancel and selecting the division rather than its contents. The Quick Tag Selector can be very helpful in this regard. If that doesn't work, try making your change through the Positioning toolbar.

Tip To select a division, click the margin space to its right or left.

Using the Positioning Toolbar

FrontPage provides a special Positioning toolbar for controlling position properties. Table A-10 in Appendix A describes this toolbar. All the controls on the Positioning toolbar have equivalents in the Position dialog box that the preceding section described.

The Positioning toolbar doesn't support relative positioning, but it can switch areas between static and absolute. To absolutely position one or more existing Web page elements:

1. Display the Positioning toolbar by choosing Toolbars from the View menu and then choosing Positioning.

2 Select the Web page element(s) you want to position. You can choose a single element or a contiguous set.

3 Click the Position Absolutely button on the Positioning toolbar.

Position Absolutely

Depending on the content you selected in step 2, clicking the Position Absolutely button has these effects:

- If you selected a single element (other than a block element) from the list in Table 22-2, FrontPage adds absolute positioning to that element's properties.
- In some cases, older browsers will ignore positioning commands FrontPage adds to an existing HTML tag. If you encounter this problem, choose Page Options from the Tools menu, click the General tab, and select the Use DIV tags When Positioning check box. Close the Page Options dialog box, and then remove and reapply the positioning you want.
- If you selected a block element, multiple elements, or an element not included in Table 22-2, FrontPage draws a division around the selected content and adds absolute positioning to that division's properties.

  If the selection includes only part of a block element, FrontPage extends the selection to include the entire block element:
- As usual, handles and possibly hairline borders appear around the positioned area.
- Absolutely positioning an element or area generally won't cause it to move. The absolutely positioned area, however, no longer reserves any space in the ordinary page area. This means that any elements that previously followed the now-positioned content might now flow under it, resulting in a sort of double exposure.

Width

When positioning is in effect for an element, clicking it always displays handles. There are three ways to resize an absolutely positioned element:

- By dragging the handles with the mouse.
- By typing a measurement in the Width and/or Height boxes on the Positioning toolbar.
- By selecting it, then choosing Position from the Format menu, and then changing the Width and/or Height settings in the Position dialog box.

Height

To relocate an absolutely positioned element or division, first click it to make handles appear, and then do one of the following:

- Drag the element by its edges. The move mouse pointer (shown below) appears when the mouse is in the required position.

- Click the numeric values in the Positioning toolbar's Left, Top, Right, or Bottom boxes, and type the coordinate you want.

- Choose Position from the Format menu, and then change the Left, Right, Top, or Bottom settings in the Position dialog box.

Figure 22-2 shows a Web page with absolute positioning in effect for five elements: the four mime pictures and the heading paragraph, "Great Leaping Mimes."

Figure 22-2. The four pictures and the title string are each absolutely positioned elements. Z-indexing governs the display of overlapping elements.

Getting this page to appear correctly in Netscape Navigator 4 would be a nuisance, except that FrontPage creates a division around any element you position and then applies the positioning attributes to that division. This is why Netscape Navigator 4 displays the Web page correctly in Figure 22-3.

Notice in Figure 22-2 and Figure 22-3 that three figures appear behind the title and one figure appears in front. This is an example of z-indexing. Positioned content with higher z-index values appears in front of content with lower z-index values. Both positive and negative numbers are acceptable as z-index values; ordinary page content has an implied z-index of 0. If two overlapping elements have the same z-index, the one defined first in the HTML appears behind the one defined later.

Figure 22-3. With care taken during page creation, Netscape Navigator 4 can also display positioned content.

Bring Forward

Send Backward

To assign a z-index value using the Positioning toolbar, first select the element, and then do one of the following:

- Click the Bring Forward or Send Backward button on either the Positioning toolbar or the Pictures toolbar.
- Enter a new value in the Z-Index box, and press Enter.
- Choose Position from the Format menu and then, in the Position dialog box, update the Z-Order box. (Remember, this actually refers to the z-index property.)

Using the Mouse to Position Objects

In Design view, when you click the edge of a positioned page element, FrontPage displays sizing handles around that element. After this happens, you can resize the positioned element by dragging its handles. To reposition it, move the mouse pointer over the element's outer edge and watch for it to take on this shape:

When the pointer has this shape, you can hold down the mouse button and drag the positioned content around the page.

Using Layers

FrontPage 2003 has a new Layers task pane that makes it very easy to add absolutely positioned divisions to your Web page. This task pane appears on the right in Figure 22-4.

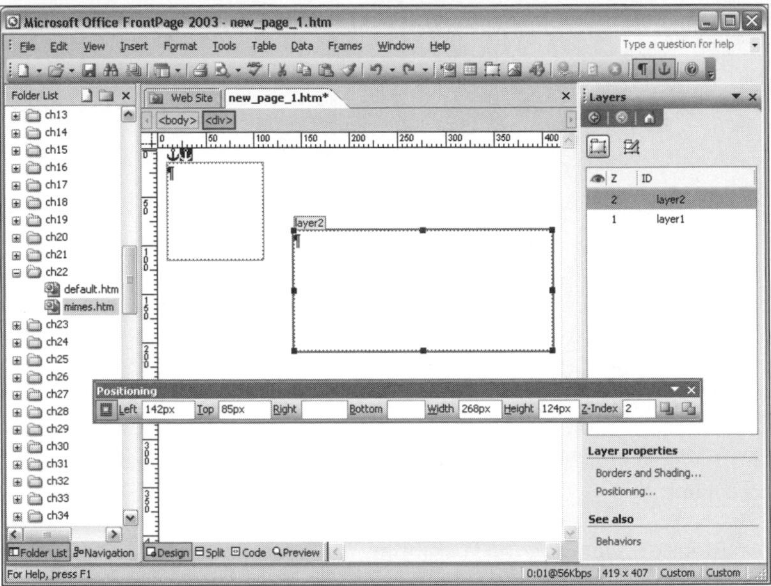

Figure 22-4. The Layers task pane creates, names, and controls z-orders or absolutely positioned divisions.

To display the Layers task pane, choose Layer from the Insert menu, or choose Layers from the drop-down menu that appears in the title bar of any other task pane.

> **Note** The term *layer* comes from a proprietary tag first introduced with Netscape Navigator 4. The W3C chose not to support this tag, opting instead to support similar features in divisions with absolute CSS2. The term *layer*, however, has persisted.

Designers usually add layers to a page so that they can make content visible or invisible. Drop-down menus are a prime example. Each menu is a layer that the designer makes visible when he or she wants the visitor to see it and makes invisible when other events occur. Such layers normally contain hyperlinks to other Web pages.

For more information about using DHTML scripts to make layers visible or invisible, refer to "Using DHTML Effects," on page 690 and "Scripting DHTML Behaviors," on page 694.

Insert Layer

You have a choice of two procedures for adding layer objects to a Web page. Here's the first:

1. Open the page that will contain the layer, and display the Layers task pane.
2. Click the Insert Layer button in the Layers task pane.

This will create a new layer of a standard size. To gain more control over a new layer you create, try this procedure:

1. Open the page that will contain the layer, and display the Layers task pane.
2. Click the Draw Layer button in the Layers task pane.
3. Drag the mouse diagonally across the Web page, from any corner to the opposite corner of the area you want the layer to occupy.

Draw Layer

No matter how you create the layer, once it exists, it works exactly like any other content you positioned absolutely using the Positioning toolbar or the Position dialog box. For example, you can resize the layer or move it around using the mouse, the Positioning toolbar, or the Position dialog box, just as earlier sections have already described.

The list box that occupies the center of the Layers task pane will display one line for each layer in your Web page. Clicking any line selects the corresponding layer. In addition:

- Clicking the eye icon to the left of any line toggles that layer's initial state between visible (eye open), hidden (eye closed), or inherit (no icon). The inherit state means that the layer will inherit its visibility from the positioned element, if any, that surrounds it.
- Clicking the Z value opens that value to editing. If two elements overlap, the one with the higher z-index will appear to be on top. Z-indexes can be positive, zero, or negative. Ordinary Web content has a z-index of zero.
- Clicking the ID value opens that value to editing. DHTML scripts and ID selectors in style sheets refer to the layer by this ID. By default, FrontPage names new layers layer1, layer2, and so forth.

The Layer Properties section of the Layers task pane identifies links to two handy dialog boxes. These links are available only after you've selected a layer:

- **Borders And Shading** Displays the Borders And Shading dialog box, shown in Figure 21-17, on page 610.
- **Positioning** Displays the Position dialog box, shown previously in Figure 22-1.

Using Positioning Wisely

When working with overlapping positioned content, selecting a particular division can be maddening. Selecting some other division that overlaps the same space is way too easy. For this reason, it's very good practice to keep divisions as short and narrow as possible, minimizing the overlap and hence the problems.

> **Tip** As with other very small or overlapping content, the Quick Tag Selector can also be very useful for selecting positioned elements.

Mixing positioned and unpositioned content is tricky as well. With part of a Web page changing with the visitor's browser environment and part being "nailed in place," it's very easy to produce a page that looks right only under the most perfect conditions. Here are a few suggestions to minimize this problem:

- Reserve white space on your page with a 1-pixel-wide transparent GIF file. Make this file as tall as your positioned content (assuming, of course, that the white space won't move and that the positioned content is fixed in height), and then locate the positioned content over the white space.
- Use a relatively positioned division as a container for your absolutely positioned content, because normal page content flows *around* a relatively positioned division. Unfortunately, Netscape Navigator 4 doesn't deal well with positioned content inside other positioned content.
- Absolutely position everything on your page. This avoids mixing free-flowing and absolutely positioned content, but it might require your visitors to adjust their browser windows.

In Summary...

This chapter explained how to use CSS2 for positioning content on Web pages. The new Layers task pane in FrontPage 2003 makes use of this technology.

The next chapter will explain how to manipulate picture files without leaving FrontPage.

Part 7

Creating and Editing Web Pictures

Chapter 23

Editing Pictures in FrontPage

Microsoft FrontPage provides a useful assortment of built-in picture editing functions. These functions certainly don't replace a full-tilt picture editor, such as Adobe Photoshop, but they conveniently provide the right tool in the right place, most of the time you need it. If a quick fix is in order, these tools might be the solution. This chapter covers the tools available within FrontPage, as well as techniques to make the best use of them.

Using Picture Editing Tools

This section describes the basic toolset that FrontPage provides for making simple changes to pictures. These tools solve many common problems quickly and easily, but they don't eliminate the need for a stand-alone picture editor.

To learn about configuring FrontPage to start your favorite picture editor whenever you double-click a picture, refer to "Configuring External Editors," on page 1118.

Inside Out

No More Dithering Over Picture Tools!

Using the picture-editing tools in earlier releases of FrontPage often made pictures look grainy. (In technical terms, the tools *dithered* most colors; they converted pure, smooth colors to a mixed pattern of similar colors.) Editing pictures in FrontPage 2003 no longer has this effect. If you've given up using these tools in the past, consider giving them a new chance.

Adding Text to Pictures

The Text On GIF component is quite a unique feature. It overlays any picture in your page with any text you want. This frees you from switching between FrontPage and a picture editor as you develop your page.

The Text-On-GIF component is useful not only for labeling pictures, but also for creating headings and titles that use special fonts or colors. To create headings and titles, you should typically choose a textured surface, solid color, or completely transparent picture as the background.

For an explanation of transparency in picture files, refer to "Setting Transparency," later in this chapter.

Here's the complete procedure for using the Text-On-GIF component:

1. Select the picture you want to overlay with text.
2. Click the Text button on the Pictures toolbar. If the picture you selected isn't in GIF format, a message box asks whether to convert it or exit.

   Text

   There's very little risk in clicking OK and proceeding with this conversion. FrontPage doesn't delete or replace the original picture file, nor does it update any other pages to use the GIF version.

   If you don't like the results, you can either undo the change or delete the Text-On-GIF component from the page and reinsert the original picture. If you keep the results and save the page, FrontPage displays the Save Embedded Files dialog box, which asks where to save the GIF version of your original file.

Note Because JPEG is a poor file format for text, the Text-On-GIF component always creates and displays GIF pictures. Unfortunately, this may degrade the colors in photographs and other artwork that has many colors.

3. Unless you exited the procedure in step 2, a bounding box and a second set of sizing handles appears within the picture area. Click inside the inner handles to set the insertion point, and then type your text. If the text doesn't fit, enlarge the text area by dragging its handles.
4. Set font, point size, alignment, color, and other attributes either by selecting the text and then choosing Font from the Format menu or by using the buttons on the Format toolbar.
5. When you've finished, click outside the picture to stop text entry and editing.

The Web page shown in Figure 23-1 includes three Text On GIF components: a FrontPage designer entered the text on all three safety nets.

Note The more often designers use CSS to format text, the less they have any need to convert headings and other special text to pictures. For more information about CSS, refer to Chapter 21, "Managing Appearance with Cascading Style Sheets."

When you overtype a graphic with text, FrontPage remembers the file name of the original picture, the text string you enter, and the font characteristics you specify. It then derives a new picture from the original plus your text, saves the results using a derived file name, and displays the derived picture rather than the original.

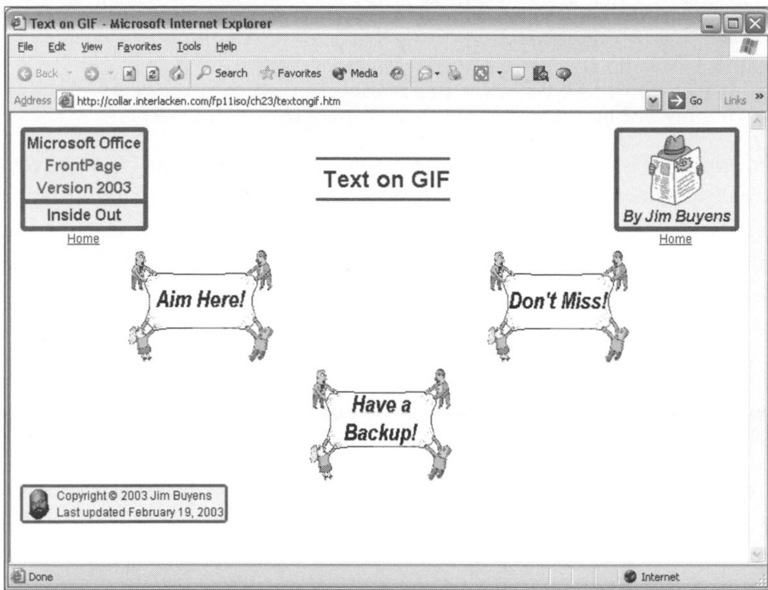

Figure 23-1. This Web page displays three Text On GIF components. The text remains fully editable even between editing sessions.

In general, you shouldn't worry about the name, or even the existence, of derived pictures. In FrontPage, you simply work with the Text-On-GIF component and consider the file name as a component property. There are however, a few quirks and precautions you should understand.

- If you right-click a Text-on-GIF component and select Picture Properties from the shortcut menu, the Picture Properties dialog box displays the original picture's file name (such as ../images/jump2net.gif). This file, however, isn't the one the browser displays. The file name you see in the Picture Properties dialog box is the *input* to the Text-On-GIF component, and not its result.
- If you display the Web page in a browser, right-click the picture, and choose Properties from the shortcut menu, you'll see a derived file name such as _derived/textongif.htm_txt_jump2net_3.gif. (FrontPage automatically creates the _derived subfolder within the folder where you web ape resides.)
- Don't modify, move, delete, or otherwise manipulate the derived file. If you do, the Text-On-GIF component will stop working, overwrite your changes the next time you save the page, or both.

  If you need to make changes, modify the original picture, reconfigure the Text-On-GIF component, or both.
- If you publish your site manually rather than through Remote Site View, be sure to publish the contents of any _derived folders.
- If the background picture is a transparent GIF file, you must format your text with a different color than the GIF file's transparent color. Otherwise, you'll end up with

transparent text. Note that a GIF file's transparent color isn't readily apparent because, by definition, it's invisible.

- Don't add text to a picture you've resized but not resampled. Otherwise, the derived picture may not have enough pixels to display your text clearly.

To understand this last point, suppose that your page displays a 1x1 pixel spacer picture. In the picture Properties Dialog box, however, you configure the HTML to display the picture at larger than its natural size, such as 100 pixels wide and 50 pixels high. This is a common practice because delivering a 1x1 pixel picture to the browser consumes very little bandwidth, and loss of resolution from magnifying a picture at the browser has no effect on a completely transparent picture.

Suppose, however, that you use the Text-On-GIF component to add some text over the spacer picture. The text appears normally in Design view, but comes out blank in Preview mode and in the Browser. What happened?

Because the original picture is physically 1x1 pixel in size, the derived picture is physically 1 pixel as well. Unless your text consisted of one gigantic period, one pixel is clearly insufficient to display the text accurately (or at all).

To resolve this problem, you would need to select the 100 pixel by 50 pixel spacer area, click the Resample button on the Pictures toolbar, and only then click the Text button on the Pictures toolbar. Resampling a picture sets its physical size equal to its display size, which in this case provides enough pixels to legibly display your text.

The section "Resampling Pictures," later in this chapter, explains more about resampling.

Saving Changes to Picture Files

Whenever you change a picture using any of the methods described in this chapter and then save the Web page, FrontPage displays a Save Embedded Files dialog box. This dialog box asks you to confirm the file name and other details for a new version of each picture you changed. To change the proposed Save properties for any file you're about to save, first select the file, and then click one of these buttons:

- **Rename** Click this button to open the file name to editing. Change the file name to whatever you want, and then press Enter.
- **Change Folder** Click this button to save the file in a different folder. Select a folder from the resulting dialog box, and then click OK.

> **Tip** If a file's Folder column is blank, FrontPage saves the file in the same folder as the Web page itself.

- **Set Action** Click this button to change handling of the selected file to Save, Don't Save, Overwrite, or Use Existing.

  In most cases, you should create a new file. This gives you the option to open the original file later and redo or undo your changes if you find them unsatisfactory.

- **Picture File Type** Click this button to change a picture's format from GIF to JPEG or to change other format properties.

Click OK when all these options are set the way you want them.

Caution The Save Embedded Files dialog box offers you a default file name option for each picture you changed. With some picture changes, such as AutoThumbnail, the default is the original file name followed by *_small* (before the file extension). With others, such as brightness and contrast, the default is the original file name. Always double-check the default file name before choosing it.

For more information about using the Save Embedded Files dialog box, refer to "Using the Save Embedded Files Dialog Box," on page 255.

Creating Thumbnail Pictures

FrontPage can replace full-sized pictures in any Web page with miniaturized versions called *thumbnails*. In the browser, clicking the thumbnail displays the full-sized picture.

For more information about the Auto Thumbnail feature, refer to "Organizing Pictures with Thumbnails," on page 283.

Positioning Pictures

The Pictures toolbar has three buttons that support absolute positioning of pictures. *Absolute positioning* means that you can specify the exact xy-coordinates of the location where the picture will appear. These coordinates are measured from the top left corner of the picture's container (usually the browser window) to the top left corner of the picture.

Absolute positioning requires the following short process:

Position Absolutely

1. Select the picture, and click Position Absolutely on the Pictures toolbar.
2. Drag the picture into position.

After you flag a picture as absolutely positioned, you can drag it whenever it's selected, even during a subsequent editing session.

Absolute positioning works in three dimensions. Not only can it position objects up and down or right and left, it can also position them forward and backward relative to each other. This involves a property called *z-index*. A *z-index* can be positive or negative, but in either case, objects with higher *z-index* vales appear in front of objects with lower values. If two objects have the same *z-index*, the one defined later in the HTML comes out on top. The default *z-index* value is zero. To arrange overlapping pictures:

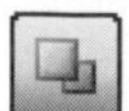

Bring Forward

1 Apply absolute positioning to each picture you want to arrange.

2 Select one picture, and on the Pictures toolbar, click Bring Forward or Send Backward.

Repeat this for other pictures as necessary. You can set positioned pictures in front of or behind both regular page content and each other. Figure 23-2 shows a Web page with seven overlapping pictures. If you open this page in Page view, you can drag the pictures around at will.

Send Backward

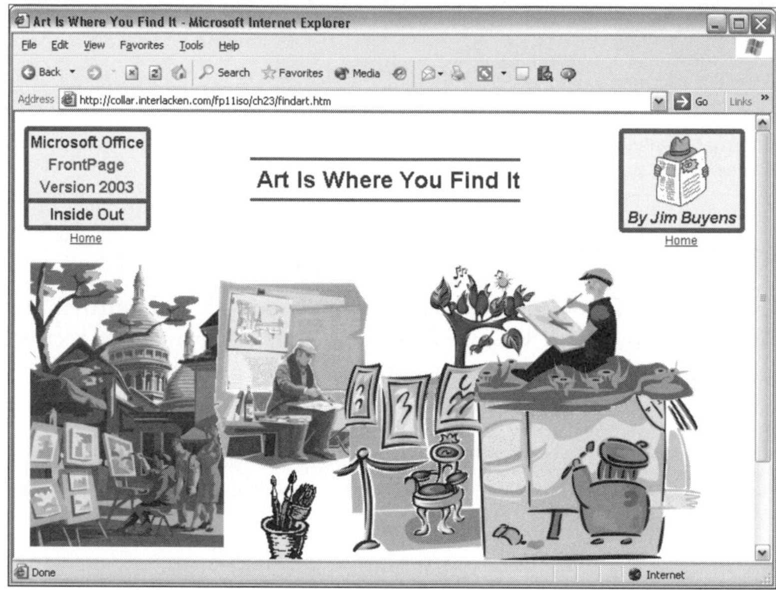

Figure 23-2. The montage on this Web page actually consists of seven pictures, each positioned absolutely in three dimensions.

Tip **Insert Positioned Pictures in Order.**

Using the Bring Forward and Send Backward buttons to arrange pictures can become confusing when you're working with many different pictures on the same page. Try to plan ahead: First insert and position the pictures you want in the background, and then insert your foreground pictures.

Microsoft Internet Explorer 4 was the first browser to support CSS2 positioning, which is the technology FrontPage uses for positioning pictures. Browsers that don't support absolute positioning will still display your page elements, but not in the expected layout. As always, test your pages in every browser environment you care about.

For more information about CSS2, refer to Chapter 22, "Positioning Content with Cascading Style Sheets."

Rotating and Flipping Pictures

The Pictures toolbar provides four toolbar buttons for rotating pictures: two to rotate right or left in 90-degree increments, and two more for flipping top to bottom and right to left. To see their effects, look at Figure 23-3 Rotating a picture merely reorients it, whereas flipping creates a mirror image of the original picture. You can flip or rotate the same picture any number of times.

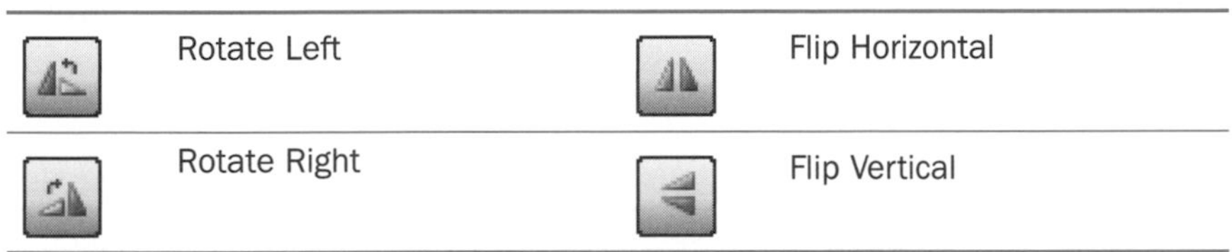

	Rotate Left		Flip Horizontal
	Rotate Right		Flip Vertical

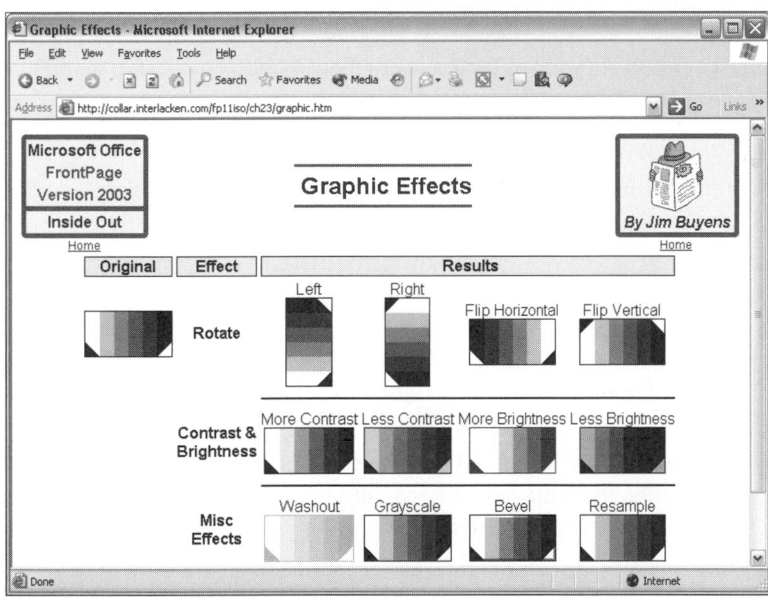

Figure 23-3. This page displays various picture transformations you can apply directly within FrontPage.

Controlling Contrast and Brightness

The Pictures toolbar contains two pairs of buttons for modifying brightness and contrast. Clicking these buttons repeatedly intensifies their effect:

- **More Contrast** Makes high intensities higher and low intensities lower (that is, it darkens a picture's dark colors and brightens its light colors).
- **Less Contrast** Makes high intensities lower and low intensities higher (that is, it pushes all the colors in your picture toward gray).

- **More Brightness** Adds white to every color in the picture; the darker the color, the more white is added. Eventually, the picture becomes pure white.
- **Less Brightness** Adds black to every color in the picture; the lighter the color, the more black added. Eventually, the picture becomes pure black.

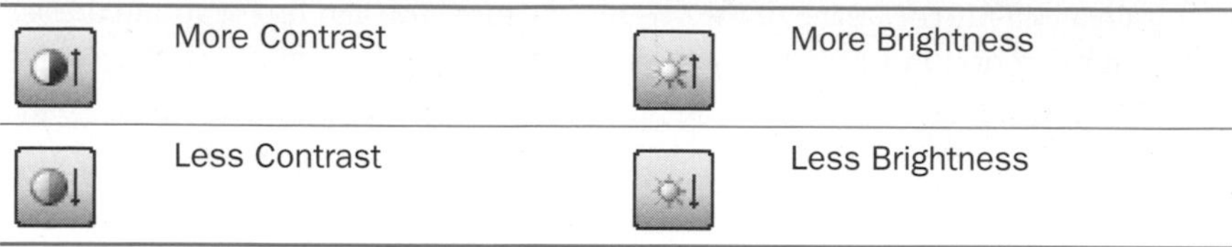

More Contrast
More Brightness
Less Contrast
Less Brightness

Figure 23-3 previously illustrated sample results from using these buttons.

Cropping and Resizing Pictures

Cropping is the process of making a picture smaller by choosing part of it and discarding the rest. To crop a picture in FrontPage:

Crop

1. Select the picture, and click Crop on the Pictures toolbar.
2. Within the selected picture, FrontPage draws a bounding box with handles. Move the handles so that the bounding box encloses the part of the picture you want to retain.
3. Click Crop again, or press Enter. FrontPage discards any pixels outside the bounding box.

> **Tip** It's best to keep all your pictures in an /images folder rather than the root folder. FrontPage helpfully provides such a folder when you create your Web site.

To resize a picture, simply select it and drag its handles. Dragging the corner handles resizes the picture proportionately; the height and width are forced to change by the same percentages. Dragging the top or bottom handle changes only the height, whereas dragging the left or right handle changes only the width.

Resizing a file with its handles doesn't alter the size of the picture file itself; it changes only the amount of screen space the picture occupies. Reducing the size of a picture in this way saves the Web visitor nothing in download time.

- To resample a picture you've just resized, open the drop-down menu on the Picture Actions button and select resample picture to match size. Figure 23-4 shows this action in progress.
- To resample any picture any time, select it and then click the Resample button on the Pictures toolbar.

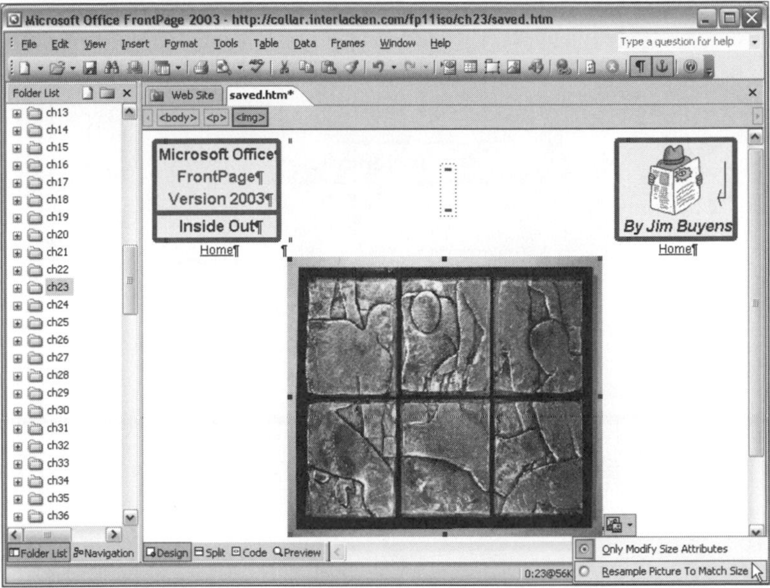

Figure 23-4. After you resize a picture, FrontPage displays a Picture Actions button like the one shown here at the lower right. To resizes the picture physically as well as visually, open the drop-down menu and choose Resample Picture To Match Size.

The section titled, "Resampling Pictures," later in this chapter will have more to say about resampling.

Setting Transparency

All GIF and JPEG pictures are rectangular. Most real-life objects aren't. One solution to this dilemma, although a poor one, is to enclose all pictures in borders. This often produces unattractive results. A second and better approach is coloring the unused portions of the picture to match its surroundings—the Web page background. However, this solution also has drawbacks:

- It requires a different picture version for each background color.
- Smoothly matching a textured background picture generally isn't possible.
- Web visitors can instruct their browsers to ignore background pictures, background colors, or both.

The best solution is to make portions of the picture transparent, as if the picture (but not its background) were printed on a sheet of clear plastic. Figure 23-5 provides an example of this technique. The picture on the left, with a white background, doesn't blend with the textured background. The picture on the right has a transparent background that lets the page's background show through.

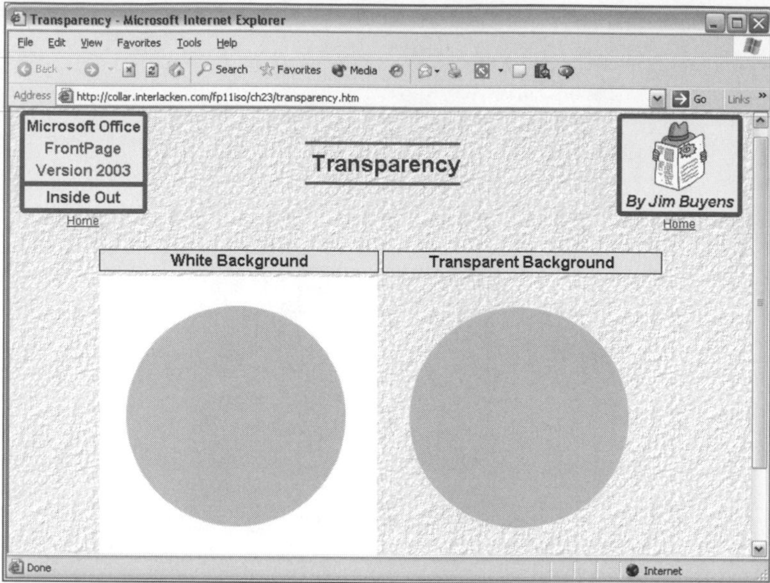

Figure 23-5. The picture on the left has a white background; the one on the right has a transparent background.

Most GIF file editors have features for handling transparency, although you can also control transparency from within FrontPage. The FrontPage procedure is as follows:

1. Add the picture to your Web page, if you haven't already.
2. Make sure the Pictures toolbar is displayed.
3. Click the picture to select it, and then click the Set Transparent Color button on the Pictures toolbar.

Set Transparent Color

4. Move the mouse pointer over the selected picture, and click any pixel of the color that should become transparent. All pixels matching that color in the picture will immediately become transparent.
5. To make a different color transparent, repeat steps 4 and 5. Only one color of a GIF can be transparent at a time.

To turn off transparency for a picture, repeat steps 3 and 4. However, in step 4, click the area that's already transparent.

> **Caution** If you're setting transparency for an image with text, make sure that the texture or color of your Web page's background won't interfere with the text's readability.

Applying Monochrome and Washouts

Color

Clicking the Color button on the Pictures toolbar displays a drop-down menu that contains four commands. Despite the button name Color, each of these commands modifies the amount of black and white in the current picture. Here are descriptions of each command:

- **Automatic** Displays a picture in its natural state. This command applies only to pictures contained within VML codes, such as pictures copied out of Microsoft Word and pasted into FrontPage. It doesn't apply to pictures (including VML drawings) that you create using FrontPage alone.
- **Grayscale** Removes all color from a picture (that is, it converts the color to continuous shades of gray). You can undo this operation by clicking the button again, but not after you save the picture.
- **Black & White** Converts every pixel to either black or white, sometimes producing a silhouette effect. Like the Automatic command, this command applies only to pictures contained within VML codes.
- **Wash Out** Lightens every pixel in a picture. This makes it more suitable, for example, for use as a background. You can wash out a picture only once before saving your changes.

  To doubly wash out a picture, wash it, save it, and then wash it again.

Figure 23-3 previously showed these picture effects.

Beveling Edges

Bevel

This feature lightens the top and left edges of a picture while also darkening the bottom and right edges. This creates the effect of a three-dimensional button.

To create this effect, select the picture and then click the Bevel button on the Pictures toolbar.

Resampling Pictures

Resample

To physically resize a picture, you must both resize *and* resample it in FrontPage. First resize the file, and then click Resample on the Pictures toolbar. Resampling creates a larger or smaller file than the original, rescaled by mathematically averaging pixels. Unlike resizing, resampling *does* change the file stored in your Web site.

Restoring Pictures

Restore

Until you save a picture file, FrontPage can always revert to the version it originally loaded from your Web site or other location. To return to this version, click Restore on the Pictures toolbar. Don't use Restore to reverse only the most recent of several changes; if you want to do that, instead choose Undo from the Edit menu.

Creating Line Art Within FrontPage

As you lay out and construct Web pages, it's inevitable that sooner or later, you'll feel the need to draw a line. Or a box. Or maybe an arrow. To satisfy such urges, FrontPage includes a collection of drawing tools and a selection of predesigned shapes that you can easily add to any page. To access these tools and shapes, display the Drawing toolbar.

Creating AutoShapes

Auto-Shapoes

FrontPage comes with dozens of predesigned shapes from which to choose. Clicking AutoShapes on the Drawing toolbar presents the following categories:

- **Lines** Contain six basic line choices.
- **Basic Shapes** Lists choices such as Octagon, Right Triangle, Cube, and even Smiley Face. There are 32 basic shapes.
- **Block Arrows** Presents 28 block-outlined arrow shapes.
- **Flowchart** Contains shapes similar to those found in Microsoft Visio. Use these shapes to create a flowchart site map, for example. There are 28 flowchart shapes to work with.
- **Stars And Banners** Calls attention to a certain area of content on a page. For example, a star could highlight a new sale item. There are 16 stars and banners available.
- **Callouts** What some people call speaking bubbles. To create that sophisticated Sunday morning comics look, select one of the 20 callout shapes.
- **More AutoShapes** Displays the Clip Art task pane.

Troubleshooting

Drawing, AutoShapes, and WordArt options on the Insert menu and various toolbars are dimmed

If, for reasons of browser compatibility, you've configured FrontPage not to create VML graphics, features that use VML are unavailable and appear dimmed on menus and toolbars. This includes drawings, AutoShapes, and WordArt.

To check your compatibility settings, choose Page Options from the Tools menu, and select the Authoring tab. This will display the Page Options dialog box, shown in Figure 23-6.

Here are some guidelines for using this dialog box:

- To make the drawing, AutoShapes, and WordArt options available, make sure that the VML Graphics (Office Drawing) check box is selected.
- To create ordinary picture files for the benefit of browsers that don't support VML, make sure that the Downlevel Image File check box is selected.

Editing Pictures in FrontPage

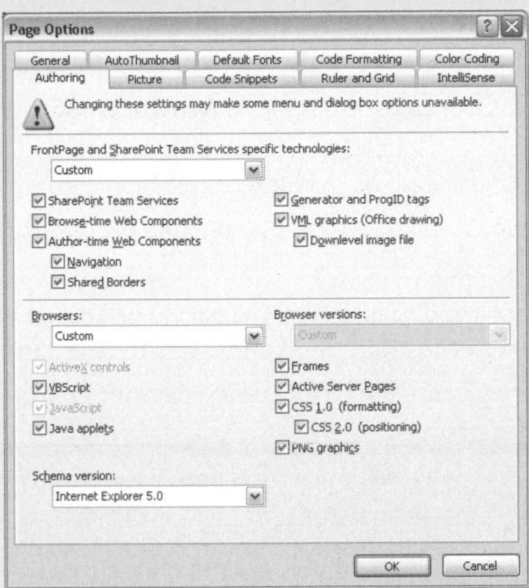

Figure 23-6. If the VML Graphics (Office Drawing) check box on the Authoring tab isn't selected, the drawing, AutoShapes, and WordArt features won't be available when you edit a Web page.

For more information about the Page Options dialog box, refer to Chapter 46, "Configuring Page Creation Options."

To add an AutoShape to a page:

1. Select the desired shape from any AutoShape category.
2. Position the crosshair mouse pointer on the page.
3. Click the left mouse button to insert the shape. Hold down the left mouse button and drag the shape to the dimensions you want.

For more information about using clip art, refer to "Inserting Clip Art," on page 259. For more information about AutoShapes, refer to "Inserting AutoShapes," on page 270.

Creating Drawings

To use any FrontPage drawing tool, click the appropriate button on the Drawing toolbar. The mouse pointer then becomes the drawing tool; you click and drag on the page in the location where you want the drawn object to appear. Choose from the following drawing tools:

- **Draw** Displays an extensive menu of commands and subcommands for grouping, ungrouping, ordering, aligning, and performing other operations on elements in a drawing. These commands generally follow the conventions of standard drawing programs.

- **Select Objects** Prepares the mouse pointer for selecting objects by clicking them or by dragging the mouse across an area.
- **AutoShapes** Displays a shortcut menu with submenus for various categories of predesigned shapes. The submenus include Lines, Block Arrows, Flowchart, Stars And Banners, and so forth.
- **Line** Draws a straight line of any length at any angle.
- **Arrow** Works the same as drawing a line, except that the line ends with an arrowhead.
- **Rectangle** Creates rectangles of any dimension on the page. Hold down the Shift key while dragging out the rectangle to constrain the shape to a perfect square.
- **Oval** Works the same as drawing a rectangle. Hold down the Shift key while dragging out the oval to constrain the shape to a perfect circle.
- **Text Box** Creates a rectangle with a blinking insertion point. You can type text into a text box and then format it just as you would any other text on a page.

For more information about working with text, refer to Chapter 8, "Adding and Formatting Text."

- **Insert WordArt** Displays the WordArt Gallery dialog box, shown in Figure 23-7.

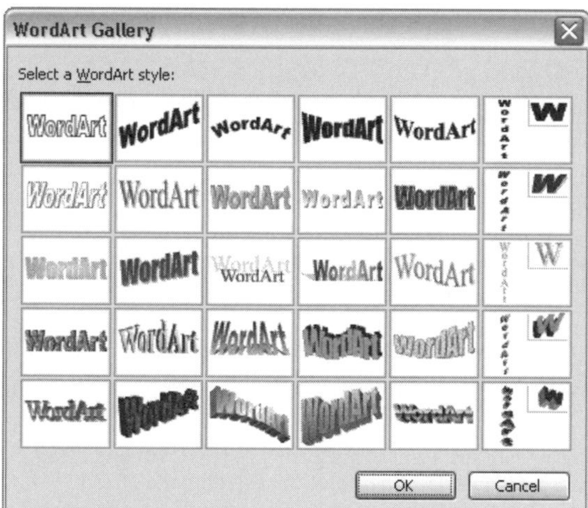

Figure 23-7. The WordArt Gallery dialog box shows the various text formatting options available.

- **Insert Clip Art** Displays the Insert Clip Art task pane so that you can add a clip art picture to the composition.

For more information about using clip art, refer to "Inserting Clip Art," on page 259.

- **Insert Picture From File** Displays the Picture dialog box so that you can add an existing picture from your Web site or from your hard drive to the composition.

> For more information about adding pictures to a Web page, refer to Chapter 10, "Adding and Formatting Pictures." For more information about drawings, refer to "Inserting Drawings," on page 267.

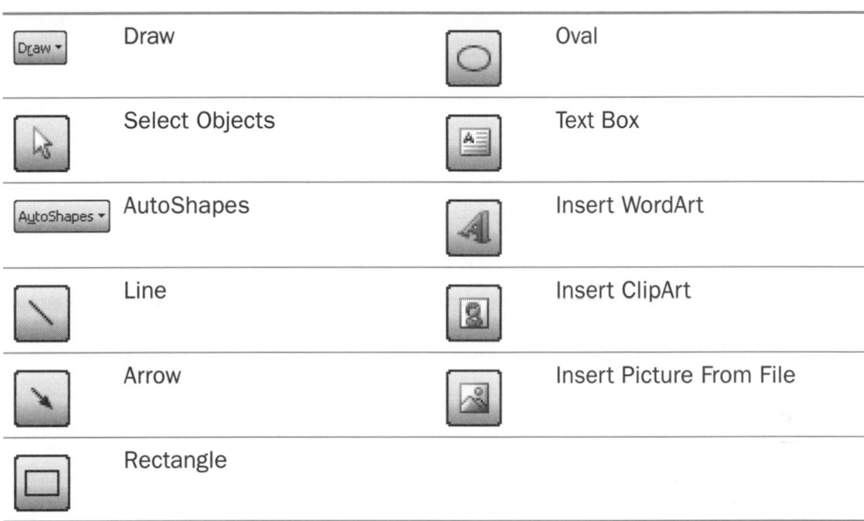

Button	Name	Button	Name
Draw	Draw		Oval
	Select Objects		Text Box
AutoShapes	AutoShapes		Insert WordArt
	Line		Insert ClipArt
	Arrow		Insert Picture From File
	Rectangle		

> For information about additional buttons on the Drawing toolbar, refer to the section "Formatting and Modifying Line Art," later in this chapter.

Creating WordArt Objects

To add special effects to a line of text, such as a three-dimensional effect, a curve, a drop shadow, or a color gradient, try this:

1. Click Insert WordArt on the Drawing toolbar.
2. Select the WordArt option of your choice, and click OK.
3. When the Edit WordArt Text dialog box appears, specify these options:
   - **Text** Type the text that you want formatted.
   - **Font** Choose a font to style the text. Because WordArt is designed for headlines, a heavy font such as Impact produces the best results.
   - **Size** Choose the size of the headline from the drop-down list. Click the Bold or Italic button, or both, to apply those attributes as you want.
4. Click OK to make the new headline appear in Design view. Figure 23-8 shows some typical results.

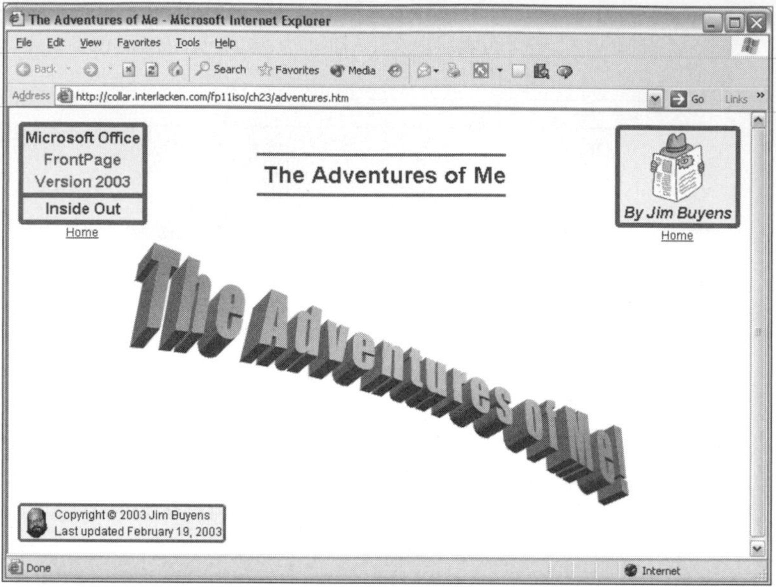

Figure 23-8. The FrontPage WordArt feature created and then modified this headline.

Caution WordArt is best suited for single lines of text, such as a headline. It's not intended to format paragraphs of text.

Formatting and Modifying WordArt

After you place a WordArt headline on a page, you can use many options to customize its appearance. Selecting an existing WordArt headline brings up the WordArt floating toolbar, which contains the following options:

- **Insert WordArt** Displays the WordArt Gallery dialog box, shown previously in Figure 23-7, for creating a new WordArt headline.
- **Edit Text** Displays the Edit WordArt Text dialog box, already described.
- **WordArt Gallery** Displays the WordArt Gallery dialog box, shown previously in Figure 23-7. To choose a different style, select the new style, and then click OK.
- **Format WordArt** Displays the Format WordArt dialog box, which changes the appearance of the current WordArt headline. Options in this dialog box control the color of the text, its transparency, its size, and other aspects of its appearance, as well as the alternative text for the picture. This button also appears on the Picture toolbar.
- **WordArt Shape** Displays a drop-down list; options on this list change the curve that the headline follows. For example, select Inflate Bottom to make the headline appear to bend out from the bottom. You can choose from 40 shapes.

- **WordArt Same Letter Heights** Adjusts the letters so that they all have the same height. Click this button again to restore the original formatting.
- **WordArt Vertical Text** Draws the headline vertically from top to bottom. Click this button again to restore the original formatting.
- **WordArt Alignment** Controls the alignment of the headline on the page, or in relation to adjacent elements. Select Left Align, Center, Right Align, Word Justify, or Stretch Justify.
- **WordArt Character Spacing** Adjusts the space between the letters of the word. Select from standard options of Very Tight, Tight, Normal, Loose, or Very Loose. Or type a percentage in the Custom box to create a nonstandard spacing option. If you've previously adjusted the kerning, select Normal to return the headline to its original spacing.

	Insert WordArt	Aa	WordArt Same Letter Heights
Edit Text...	Edit Text	Ab b	WordArt Vertical Text
	WordArt Gallery		WordArt Alignment
	Format WordArt	AV	WordArt Character Spacing
	WordArt Shape		

For more information about WordArt, refer to "Inserting WordArt," on page 272.

Formatting and Modifying Line Art

After you place a drawing on a page, whether it's a rectangle, text box, WordArt object, or any other creation, the Drawing toolbar provides many options for adjusting the drawing's appearance. Certain options might not be available with some types of art.

- **Fill Color** Displays a relatively standard FrontPage color selection menu. However, the menu also includes a Fill Effects option so that you can specify gradients, textures, patterns, and picture backgrounds.

For more information about using the standard FrontPage Color dialog boxes, refer to "Using FrontPage Color Dialog Boxes," on page 509.

- **Line Color** Displays a relatively standard FrontPage color selection menu. However, there's also a Patterned Lines option so that you can select line patterns.
- **Font Color** Displays a standard FrontPage color selection menu that controls the color of text.

This control has no effect on WordArt text. To modify the color of WordArt text, right-click the WordArt, and choose Format WordArt from the shortcut menu, or click the Format WordArt button on the WordArt toolbar.

- **Line Style** Displays a list of styles, including various thicknesses, double scores, triple scores, and so forth. This button also appears on the Pictures toolbar.
- **Dash Style** Displays a list of dash patterns, including solid, fine dots, coarse dots, fine dashes, coarse dashes, and so forth.
- **Arrow Style** Displays a list of arrowheads.
- **Shadow Style** Applies one of 20 various shadow effects to the selected picture. Select No Shadow to return the selected picture to its original state. Shadow Settings displays the Shadow Settings floating toolbar, where you can make adjustments to the shadow's color and distance from the picture.
- **3-D Style** Displays a list of 20 three-dimensional effect options. These options can, for example, transform a plain circle into a shaded cylinder or cone. Select No 3-D to return the selected picture to its original state. 3-D Settings displays the 3-D Settings floating toolbar, where you can make incremental adjustments to the degree of tilt applied to the picture. On this floating toolbar, you can also adjust the depth, lighting, surface, and color of the three-dimensional effect.

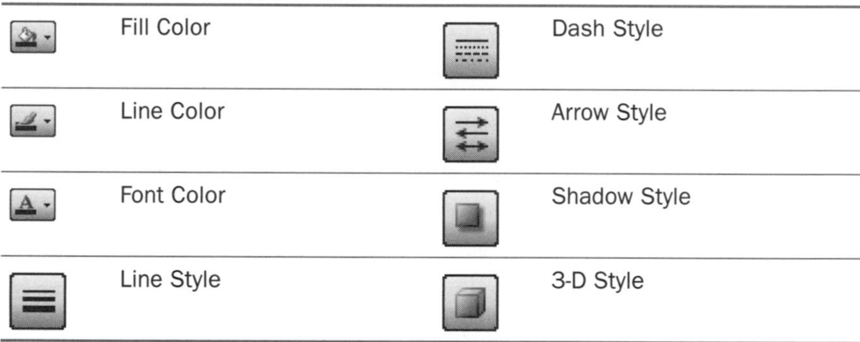

	Fill Color		Dash Style
	Line Color		Arrow Style
	Font Color		Shadow Style
	Line Style		3-D Style

Figure 23-9 illustrates a number of line art and WordArt effects. Notice the curved text, three-dimensional objects, and overlapping elements.

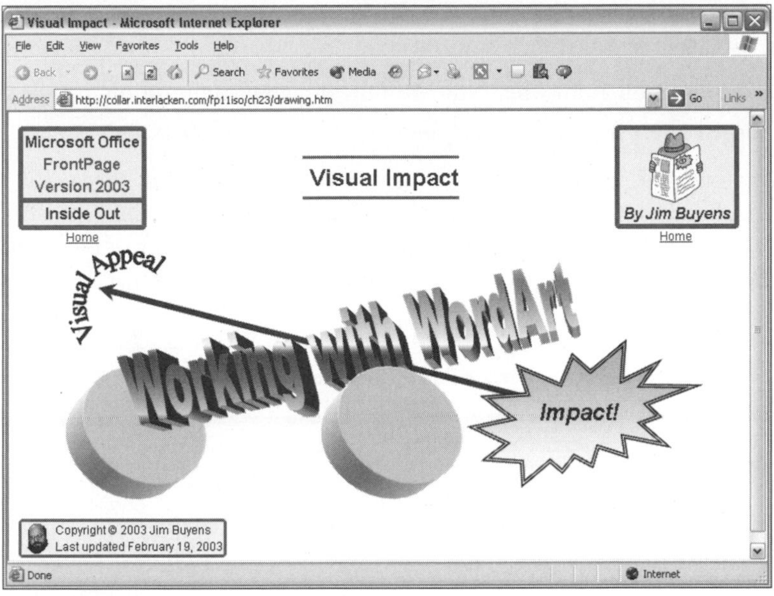

Figure 23-9. This page features various WordArt and line art creations.

Selecting any picture displays selection handles that can rotate, skew, and stretch the picture to just about any shape or size you want. When working with art created within FrontPage, the key is experimentation. Try various shapes, sizes, and colors to get the perfect effect that meets your Web site's needs.

Displaying Line Art in the Browser

When you create artwork that uses the Drawing, AutoShapes, and WordArt components, FrontPage stores them as a compact collection of lines, curves, and other shapes rather than as pictures. The specific format FrontPage uses is VML, which in turn stores the information in XML format.

Transmitting VML data to the browser is much faster than transmitting an ordinary picture file that produces the same display. Of course, the VML data is useless to browsers that don't support it. Currently, only Internet Explorer 5 and later can display VML.

For the benefit of browsers that don't support VML, FrontPage can also save GIF versions of every drawing, AutoShape, and WordArt object you create. Then, in the midst of the VML code, FrontPage inserts the HTML to display the GIF picture. Browsers that display VML will do so and, because of some special coding, never request or use the GIF file. Browsers that don't support VML will ignore it and display the GIF picture instead.

For more information about options that control the use of VML and substitute GIF files, refer to the Troubleshooting sidebar, "Drawing, AutoShapes, and Word Art Options on the Insert Menu and Various Toolbars Are Dimmed," earlier in this chapter.

If your drawing is at all complex, it's often wise to first create a drawing area (or *canvas*) and then add objects to it. To create a drawing area:

1 Set the insertion point where you want the drawing composition to appear.
2 Choose Picture from the Insert menu, and choose New Drawing.

The canvas sets aside an area of the page for your drawing. To resize the canvas, select it and drag its handles. Browsers that don't support VML have a much easier time displaying compositions drawn inside a drawing area than compositions consisting of individual objects. This is because the GIF file FrontPage creates for such browsers consists of one large picture for the entire canvas.

For more information about this and related topics, refer to "Adding Pictures to a Page," on page 251.

In Summary…

This chapter reviewed the tools built into FrontPage for editing pictures. Although it isn't a complete picture-editing program, FrontPage can make many kinds of common changes to pictures. This chapter also explained how to create drawings, AutoShapes, and WordArt in FrontPage.

The next chapter explains how to use the Photo Gallery component, which organizes snapshot collections for presentation on the Web.

Chapter 24

Using FrontPage Photo Galleries

Regardless of the interest level of their audience, most people enjoy showing off their snapshot collections. This is as true in business and government institutions as it is in schools, in clubs, and for individuals. To support this playful indulgence, Microsoft Office FrontPage 2003 includes a component designed specifically for displaying collections of photos. Its name, as you might suspect, is the Photo Gallery component.

A Photo Gallery component accepts a series of full-sized pictures as input and displays a thumbnail version of each one. When a Web visitor clicks one of these thumbnails, the browser requests and displays the full-sized picture. A Photo Gallery component displays pictures in the order you want, in the size you want, with the captions and descriptions you want, and with a page layout you select. As with other components, FrontPage does all the programming work for you, behind the scenes.

Creating a New Photo Gallery

The first step in creating a new photo gallery is displaying the Photo Gallery Properties dialog box, shown in Figure 24-1.

There are three ways to do this. Here's the most straightforward procedure:

1. Open a new or an existing Web page that you want to contain a photo gallery.
2. Set the insertion point where you want the photo gallery to appear.
3. Choose Picture from the Insert menu, and then choose New Photo Gallery.

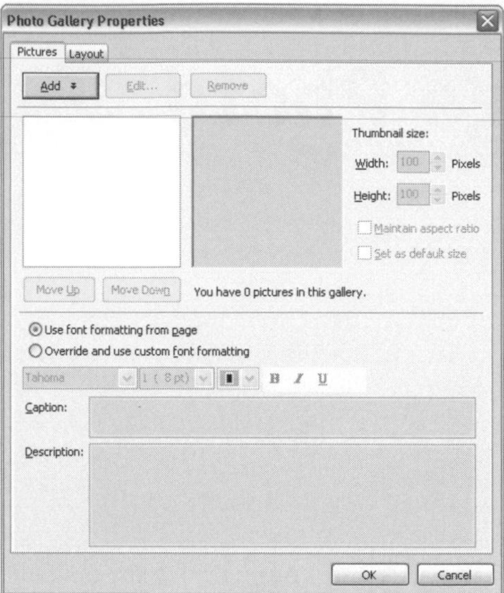

Figure 24-1. This is the Pictures tab of the Photo Gallery Properties dialog box.

To use the second procedure, perform steps 1 and 2 from the first procedure, and then continue with these steps:

1. Choose Web Component from the Insert menu, or click the Web Component button on the Standard toolbar.
2. Choose Photo Gallery from the Component Type list.
3. The right side of the Insert Web Component dialog box is titled Choose A Photo Gallery Option and displays four thumbnail layouts: Horizontal, Vertical, Montage, and Slideshow. Choose the layout you want, and then click Finish. Don't obsess about your selection—you can change it later.

The third procedure creates a new Web page and a new photo gallery in one fell swoop, and even supplies an initial collection of pictures. Of course, you can delete these pictures later. Here's the procedure.

1. Display the Page Templates dialog box using either of the following methods:
   - Choose New from the File menu to display the New task pane, and then click More Page Templates.
   - Click the Create a New Normal Page down arrow on the Standard toolbar, and then choose Page.
2. When the Page Templates dialog box appears, on the General tab, double-click Photo Gallery, or select Photo Gallery, and click OK.

This third procedure creates a new Web page containing some commented instructions and a Photo Gallery configured with default pictures and a default layout. To modify this photo gallery, double-click it, or right-click it and choose Photo Gallery Properties.

In the Photo Gallery Properties dialog box, you'll probably want to add your own pictures. There are two procedures for doing this: one for picture files already on hand, and another for pictures you get from a scanner or digital camera.

Adding Pictures from Files

Here's the procedure for adding a file from a local disk, from a file server, or from the Web to a photo gallery:

1. In the Photo Gallery Properties dialog box, click Add.
2. Choose Pictures From Files from the resulting drop-down menu. This displays the standard FrontPage File Open dialog box. All of the picture file formats that FrontPage supports will be available.

> **Note** If you add a picture in a format other than GIF or JPEG, FrontPage converts it to one of those formats when you save the page.

3. Locate and select one or more picture files that you want in the gallery, and then click Open. Each picture file you selected appears in the Photo Gallery Properties dialog box, as shown in Figure 24-2.

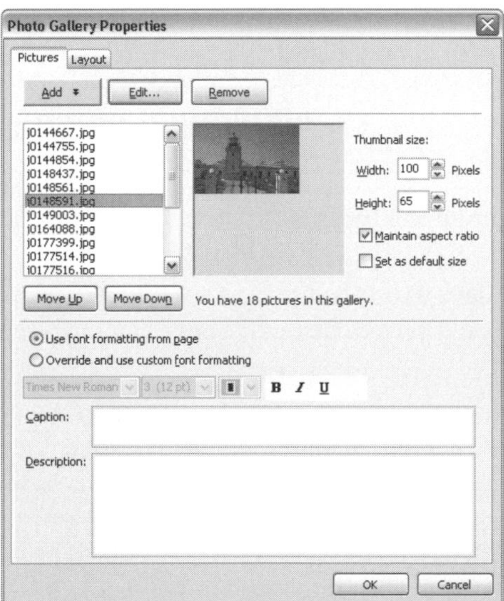

Figure 24-2. This dialog box configures the list of pictures in a photo gallery, the size of the thumbnails, and a caption and description for each picture. The Layout tab controls the photo gallery's overall appearance.

To select multiple files in the File Open dialog box, hold down the Shift or Ctrl key while clicking the file names.

FrontPage makes a new full-sized copy and a new thumbnail of any picture you add to a photo gallery. This has three important ramifications:

- There's no reason to add files to your Web site before adding them to a photo gallery.
- Changing the original version of a file has no effect on the copy in the photo gallery.
- Changing the photo gallery version of a file has no effect on the original.

Adding Pictures from a Scanner or Camera

A Photo Gallery component can also accept pictures from a scanner or digital camera connected to your computer. Here's the procedure:

1. In the Photo Gallery Properties dialog box, click Add.
2. Choose Pictures From Scanner Or Camera from the resulting drop-down menu. This displays the Insert Picture From Scanner Or Camera dialog box, shown in Figure 24-3.

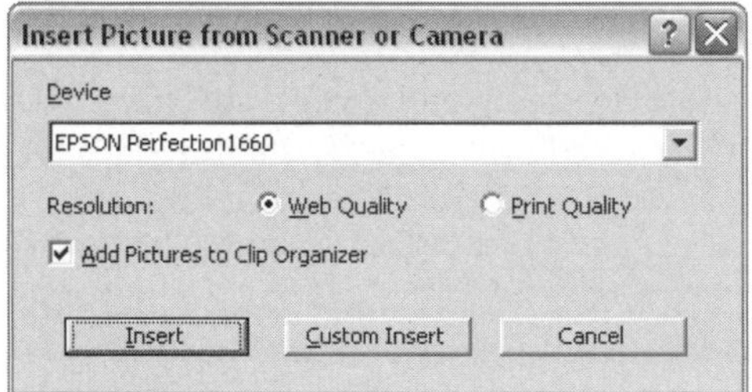

Figure 24-3. The Insert Picture From Scanner Or Camera dialog box lists available connected devices.

3. Configure the following options in the Insert Picture From Scanner Or Camera dialog box:
   - **Device** Select the device you want to use for capturing pictures. The drop-down list will show only devices currently connected to your computer and working.
   - **Resolution** Specify the resolution (and hence the file size) of the pictures you import: Web Quality or Print Quality. Web Quality keeps the file size down when FrontPage imports the picture. The resulting lower-resolution image will be perfectly adequate for Web viewing but won't take a long time for visitors to download. Choose Print Quality if you expect visitors to print the picture. Selecting this results in a higher-resolution image that will take longer to download.
   - **Add Pictures To Clip Organizer** Select this check box to add the pictures you're importing from the scanner or camera not only to the photo gallery, but also to the FrontPage Clip Organizer on your hard disk.
4. The procedure from this point forward depends on the software that came with your scanner or camera. As a result, the procedure will vary depending on how that software works.

For starters, try clicking the Insert button. This generally acquires the picture with few, if any, additional prompts.

To gain more control over the scanning process, click the Custom Insert button. This generally provides options to change image properties and preview the image before you scan.

5. If your scanner or camera software displays any dialog boxes or prompts, respond to them following the instructions that came with the scanner or camera software.
6. Unless your scanner or camera software sends pictures directly to FrontPage (that is, without intervention) it probably had a command named Place Image, Insert Picture, or something similar. Choose this command to close the program and add the picture to the photo gallery.
7. The picture appears in the Photo Gallery Properties dialog box, as shown in Figure 24-2.

Arranging Photo Gallery Pictures

Once the Photo Gallery Properties dialog box contains a list of pictures, you can preview the appearance of any picture simply by clicking it. A thumbnail of that picture will then appear in the preview box at the right of the list of files.

Web visitors will see thumbnails of your pictures in the order that the Photo Gallery Properties dialog box displays them. To move a picture up or down, select it, and click the Move Up or Move Down button. To move several pictures up or down as a group, hold down the Shift or Ctrl key while selecting them.

Removing Photo Gallery Pictures

To remove a picture from the gallery, select the picture in the file list in the Photo Gallery Properties dialog box, and then click Remove. This deletes both the full-sized and thumbnail file from the photo gallery, but not the source file you originally added.

Checking Photo Gallery Appearance

Once your photo gallery contains at least a preliminary list of pictures, you'll no doubt want to view them as Web visitors will. To do this:

1. Click OK to close the Photo Gallery Properties dialog box.
2. Save the Web page as you normally would. If the Save Embedded Files dialog box appears, make any adjustments you want to the name, folder location, and file type of the pictures it displays. You should, however, save all the files.

For more information about using the Save Embedded Files dialog box, refer to, "Using the Save Embedded Files Dialog Box," on page 255.

3 Choose Preview In Browser from the File menu, then select the browser you want to test. Alternatively, click the Preview In Browser button on the Standard toolbar.

4 When the browser window appears, check the appearance of your page.

After you complete step 1, another option is to simply click the Preview tab at the bottom of the Page view window. However, because the Preview window is often too small to display the entire component, previewing in the browser is usually a better choice.

Controlling Photo Gallery Layout

The main advantage of using a photo gallery is that it automatically displays multiple pictures in a professionally designed layout. You do, however, have some control over how those pictures appear on the page. The Layout tab of the Photo Gallery Properties dialog box, shown in Figure 24-4, controls this.

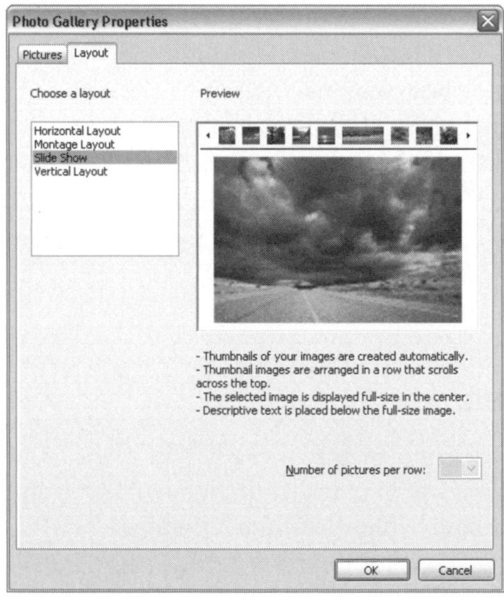

Figure 24-4. This is the Layout tab of the Photo Gallery Properties dialog box.

To display this tab:

1 Use one of these methods to display the Photo Gallery Properties dialog box:
   - Double-click the photo gallery in Design view.
   - Right-click the photo gallery in Design view, and then select Photo Gallery Properties from the shortcut menu.

2 Click the Layout tab.

Note If you used the Insert Web Component dialog box to create your photo gallery, the Layout tab displays the selection you made at that time.

On the Layout tab, a list box titled Choose A Layout offers four ways of displaying your pictures. Selecting any layout displays a preview in the Preview box and a description just below it. Here are the layout options:

- **Horizontal Layout** Select this layout to display pictures in rows across the screen, with descriptive text below each picture. Specify a value in the Number Of Pictures Per Row box to control how many pictures appear in each row of the layout.
- **Montage Layout** Select this layout to arrange pictures in a circular pattern much like a collage. The caption text appears when a visitor moves the mouse pointer over the picture. This layout doesn't display Description text.
- **Slide Show** Select this layout to display a full-sized picture in the center of the page. Thumbnail pictures scroll across the top of the page, where visitors can select them. Caption and Description text appears below the full-sized picture. This option doesn't work properly in Netscape Navigator, at least through version 7.
- **Vertical Layout** Select this layout to display pictures in columns with Description text arranged to the right of the pictures. Specify a value in the Number Of Pictures Per Row box to control the number of pictures that appear in each row of the layout.

Choose the type of layout you want, specify a value in the Number Of Pictures Per Row box if it's available, and then select the Pictures tab or click the OK button.

Figure 24-5 shows a fully configured photo gallery displayed in Internet Explorer. This photo gallery uses the Slide Show layout: Clicking any thumbnail picture at the top of the page displays the corresponding full-sized picture at the bottom. The arrows to the left and right of the thumbnails scroll the list to the left and right.

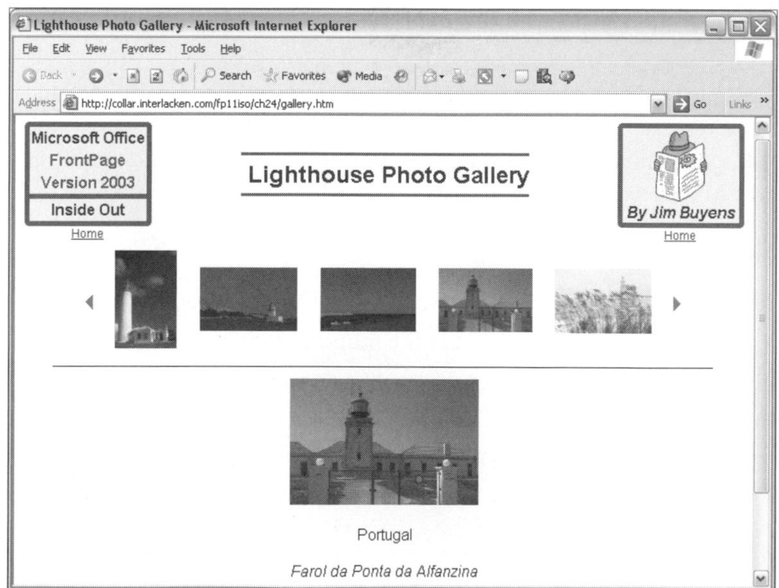

Figure 24-5. This figure shows a slide show photo gallery as a browser displays it.

As a general rule, you should choose a layout that doesn't make your visitors scroll left or right. Determine the screen resolution you're designing for, such as 800 by 600 pixels, and then make sure that the width of your layout doesn't exceed the width of your target resolution. (In the case of 800 by 600, the target width should be about 750 pixels, accounting for the window borders.)

Editing Photo Information

To control the appearance of the thumbnails a photo gallery displays, use the options that appear in the Thumbnail Size section of the Pictures tab of the Photo Gallery Properties dialog box. This tab appears in Figure 24-6.

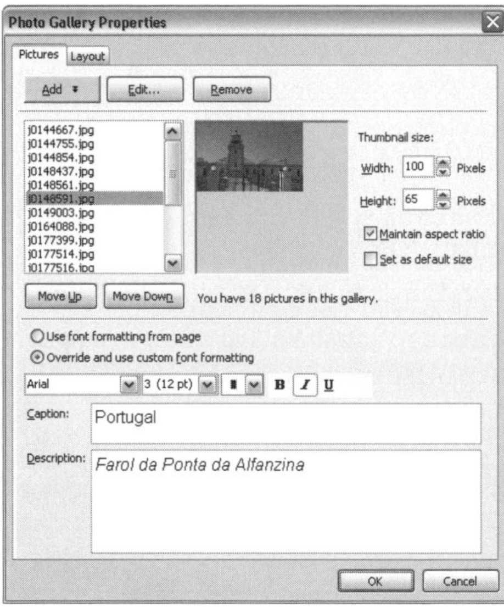

Figure 24-6. Use the Photo Gallery Properties dialog box to add formatted captions and descriptions to your pictures.

Here's how to configure these settings.

- **Width** Specify how wide you want the thumbnail to be.
- **Height** Specify how tall you want the thumbnail to be.
- **Maintain Aspect Ratio** Select this check box to retain the proportions of the thumbnail when resizing it.
- **Set As Default Size** Select this check box to make all thumbnails the same approximate size.

The bottom half of the Pictures tab specifies and formats captions and descriptive text for each picture in the gallery. Here are the options:

- **Use Font Formatting From Page** Choose this option if you want the photo gallery to display text in the same font as the rest of the Web page that contains it.

  If you want the photo gallery to display text in a custom font, select the Override And Use Custom Font Formatting option.
- **Override And Use Custom Font Formatting** Choose this option to format specific characters in the Caption or Description text.

  After choosing this option, select the text you want to modify, and then use font, font size, color, boldface, italics, and underlining controls in the usual way.
- **Caption** Use this option to give the picture a short, meaningful title.
- **Description** Use this option to provide a sentence or two describing the picture.

Some gallery layouts display both captions and descriptions, whereas others show only one text item.

For information about which photo galleries display text, and how, refer to the section, "Controlling Photo Gallery Layout," earlier in this chapter.

Inside Out

Photo Gallery Custom Fonts Are Piecemeal

Custom font formatting is a rather disappointing feature. If you want typography to differentiate photo gallery captions and descriptions from the rest of the page, you must individually display, select, and format the caption and description for each picture in the gallery. Perhaps some new release will provide a way to specify default fonts for all captions and descriptions in a photo gallery.

Editing Picture Properties

If you're not satisfied with the appearance of a photo gallery picture, you might be able to correct it directly from the Photo Gallery Properties dialog box. Here's the procedure:

1. Open the Photo Gallery Properties dialog box, and select the file name of the picture you want to change.
2. Click the Edit button. This displays the Edit Picture dialog box, shown in Figure 24-7.

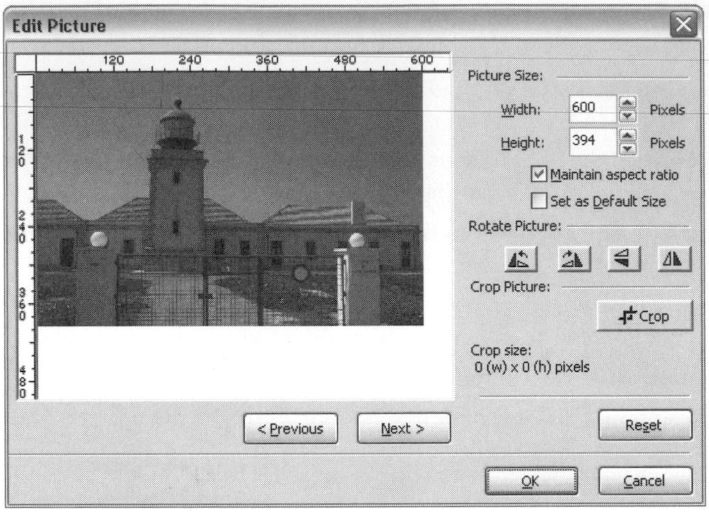

Figure 24-7. The Edit Picture dialog box presents options for changing the appearance of a picture.

At this point, a preview of the picture you selected in step 1 will appear in the Edit Picture dialog box, as shown in Figure 24-7. Use any of these commands to change the appearance of the picture:

- **Picture Size** Shows the current pixel width and height of the full-sized picture. The rulers in the preview window indicate the same size.
  - **Width** Specify how wide you want the full-sized picture to be.
  - **Height** Specify how tall you want the full-sized picture to be.
  - **Maintain Aspect Ratio** Select this check box to retain the proportions of the full-sized picture when resizing it.
  - **Set As Default Size** Select this check box to make all full-sized pictures the same approximate size.
- **Rotate Picture** Changes the orientation of the selected picture. Click the appropriate button to rotate the picture left or right, or to flip it horizontally or vertically.
- **Crop Picture** Discards unneeded areas of the picture. To crop the selected picture, click Crop. Within the picture, FrontPage draws a bounding box with handles. Move the handles so that the bounding box encloses the part of the picture you want to retain, and then click Crop a second time. FrontPage discards any pixels outside the bounding box.
- **Previous and Next** Move backward and forward through all of the pictures in the current photo gallery.
- **Reset** Removes any changes you've made since opening the Edit Picture dialog box.

When you've finished, click OK to save your changes and return to the Photo Gallery Properties dialog box.

Inside Out

The Edit Picture Dialog Box Is Unavailable Outside Photo Gallery

When you're not working in a photo gallery, all the editing commands in the Edit Picture dialog box (and more) are available on the Pictures toolbar, in the Picture Properties dialog box, or by clicking and dragging handles. Nevertheless, it would be a nice improvement to make the Edit Pictures dialog box available for all pictures, perhaps as a right-click menu option or configurable editor.

Using Windows SharePoint Services Picture Libraries

If the FrontPage Photo Gallery component doesn't provide all the flexibility you need, a Microsoft Windows SharePoint Services picture library might provide a closer fit. This type of library can hold far more pictures than a FrontPage Photo Gallery component. Any number of authorized Web visitors can upload pictures, and those pictures immediately become available to other visitors. Windows SharePoint Services picture libraries provide a wide variety of viewing formats, one of which appears in Figure 24-8.

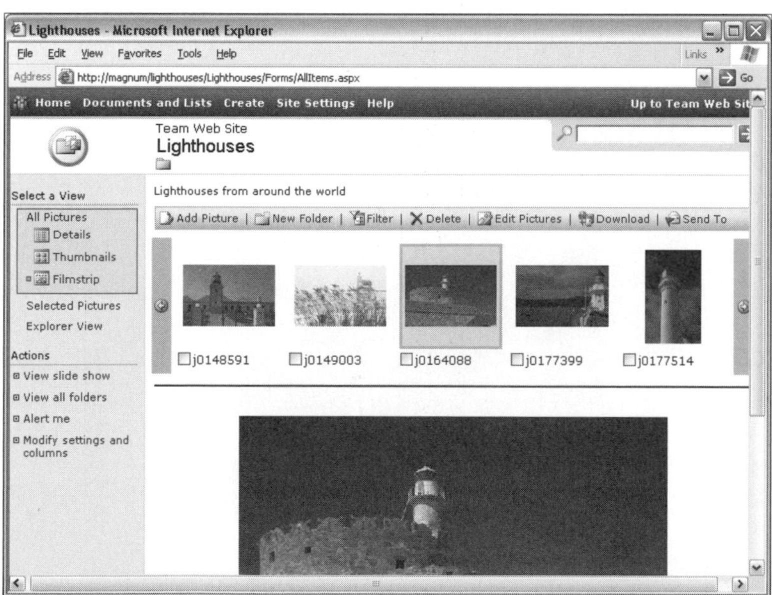

Figure 24-8. A SharePoint Team Services picture library is a great way for groups of people to collect and share photos.

Authorized people can also view and modify Windows SharePoint Services picture libraries by using the Microsoft Picture Library program included with Microsoft Office 2003. This is a Microsoft Windows desktop program, and thus has a richer user interface than any Web page can provide. For example, it's easy to upload large batches of pictures through this program.

The primary disadvantages of Windows SharePoint Services picture libraries is that you must have a Windows SharePoint Services Web server available, and SharePoint Sites are generally more suited for use as corporate, departmental, or project portal sites rather than as general-purpose Web sites. Of course, a portal of that type might be just what you need!

For more information about Windows SharePoint Services picture libraries, refer to "Using Picture Libraries," on page 937.

Insider Extra: Microsoft ASP.NET Picture Library

If neither a FrontPage photo gallery nor a SharePoint picture library meets your needs, the ASP.NET Picture Library Insider Extra on the companion CD might be worth a look. After copying this application into your Web site, creating a picture library is as easy as filling a folder with pictures. The Picture Library Web page reads your folder contents, creates selection thumbnails, and displays the corresponding pictures, all on the fly. Figure 24-9 shows the application in use. The captions above each picture are cleaned-up versions of the picture file names.

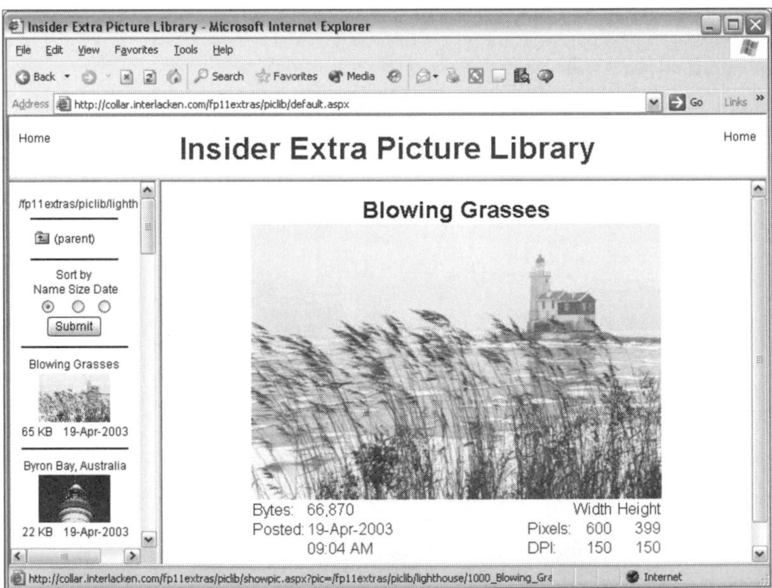

Figure 24-9. This picture library application is an Insider Extra you can copy from the cmpanion CD.

To run the ASP.NET Picture Library, your Web server must be capable of running ASP.NET pages. This capability is automatic starting with Microsoft Windows Server 2003 but requires installing a free download with Microsoft Windows XP Professional or Windows 2000. In addition, to modify or debug the application on your system, you'll need some proficiency in ASP.NET programming.

For more information about the ASP.NET Picture Library, refer to the documentation on the companion CD.

In Summary…

This chapter explained how to use the FrontPage Photo Gallery component to arrange multiple pictures on a Web page. The Photo Gallery component makes it easy to incorporate thumbnails, captions, and descriptions into a professionally designed layout.

The next chapter presents general information, tricks, and techniques for using pictures of all kinds in your Web site.

Part 8

Incorporating Advanced Content

Chapter 25

Using Web Pictures Intelligently

This chapter discusses two important but often overlooked aspects of site design: the color palettes in your pictures and the total download time for your pages. This advice is far from all-encompassing, however. When choosing pictures and positioning the pictures in your Web pages, you should also consider color scheme, page layout, and the tendency for pictures to detract attention from text. In short, you should consider all the design tips sprinkled throughout this book.

Choosing Picture File Formats

Most current Web browsers can display only two picture file formats: Graphics Interchange Format (GIF) and Joint Photographic Experts Group (JPEG). A few browsers also support Portable Network Graphics (PNG), a new high-function alternative. Table 25-1 compares these formats.

Table 25-1. Characteristics of GIF, JPEG, and PNG Formats

	GIF	JPEG	PNG
Colors available	16,777,216	16,777,216	16,777,216
Colors per picture	256	16,777,216	16,777,216
Compression	Lossless	Lossy	Lossless
Transparency	One color	No	Alpha channel
Translucence	No	No	Alpha channel
Animation	Yes	No	No
Remembers gamma	No	No	Yes

Note Microsoft Office FrontPage 2003 can import pictures other formats—BMP, TIFF, MAC, MSP, PCD, RAS, WPG, EPS, PCX, and WMF—and convert them to GIF or JPEG pictures.

Table 25-1 identifies some important differences between GIF, JPEG, and PNG pictures:

- **Lossy vs. lossless compression** Storing a bitmapped picture might require several bytes of information for each pixel and, if the picture is large, might result in a very large file. Most bitmapped file formats therefore include provisions for *compression*. Compression uses complex mathematical formulas to identify and abbreviate repeating patterns in the data.

  GIF compression uses a formula that results in zero loss of data from the compression/decompression process (that is, it provides *lossless* compression). The JPEG format supports varying degrees of compression, but most of them fail to guarantee an exact reproduction of the original. Depending on the creator's choice of settings, the resulting picture typically loses a measure of color fidelity, sharpness, or contrast. This is called *lossy* compression. The more data lost, the smaller the picture file.

- **Transparency** All formats mentioned in this chapter save rectangular pictures. The number of horizontal and vertical pixels can be whatever you want, but there's no way to save a picture in these formats with circular, oval, or irregular borders.

  One way to avoid rectangular picture shapes is to fill the edge with the same color as the background of your Web page. However, this won't work if the page uses a complex picture as a background, or if the visitor has configured the browser to override incoming background colors and pictures.

  A better solution involves specifying a *transparent color* in the picture. Instead of displaying pixels having the transparent color, the browser displays whatever pixels lay behind them—usually the background color or picture.

For information about setting transparency in FrontPage, refer to "Setting Transparency," on page 643.

  Even better is an *alpha channel*, which, for each pixel, specifies 256 levels of transparency as well as a base color.

  The GIF format is well suited for setting a single color to transparent. Typically, GIF pictures have large areas of one color, such as in a clip art picture. Setting one color in the picture as the transparent color lets the page background show through. The JPEG format doesn't support the idea of transparency—but even if it did, JPEG files, which are typically photographs, have so many colors that setting a single color to transparent would be like poking pinholes in the picture. Only a few pixels would be converted to transparent.

- **Animation** The GIF format includes a provision to accommodate multiple pictures in the same file and to specify timing for displaying them sequentially. This provides a way to present simple animations within the browser without requiring the visitor to install additional animation software.

  GIF animation typically loops continuously—in other words, it keeps playing over and over as long as the page is open in the browser. Take care when creating this type of animation so that it doesn't become distracting to the visitor. Every item placed on a page is one more thing that could distract visitors from the content on the page.

- **Gamma** Different computers make different assumptions about the relationship between software color brightness and the resulting monitor brightness. (This relationship, by the way, is nonlinear.) If you save a picture in PNG format, you can specify its *gamma factor*. Visitors' computers can then achieve better rendition.

Working with JPEG files

Every time you open and save a JPEG file, the quality of the picture deteriorates. This is what *lossy compression* means. If you save a picture and then reopen it, you don't get everything back. Each time you save it and reopen it again, you lose more quality.

For this reason, experienced graphic designers usually store original pictures in lossless formats such as TIFF, BMP, or their picture editor's native format. They convert to lossy formats such as JPEG only as a final step in preparing pictures for the Web.

Most Web designers prefer the GIF format for text, line art, and icons because of its lossless compression and transparency. JPEG finds use in backgrounds, photographs, and other areas where maximum compression and color fidelity are more important than sharpness.

The new PNG picture format supports full 32-bit color with an alpha channel, multiple compression methods, gamma information, and additional features that ease cross-platform difficulties. Unfortunately, PNG support in browsers remains far from universal, and PNG pictures tend to be larger than GIF or JPEG pictures.

On the Web For detailed information about PNG, browse *www.w3.org/TR/REC-png-multi.html*.

Tip **Limit the size of your Web pages.**

When creating a top-level page—the beginning page of a section or an area in your Web site—try to keep total file size down to 30 to 40 KB. This measurement includes all of the picture files and the HTML that constitute your page. Pages much larger than that can take a long time to download for visitors who connect to the Internet by modem. It's OK to make secondary pages more than 40 KB because visitors generally won't try to browse those pages unless they're interested in the content. Remember, however, that visitors are impatient and won't wait long, even for information they know they want.

Visualizing Transparency

At times, it's quite desirable for parts of a computer picture to be transparent:

- When the edges of an object are irregularly shaped.
- When parts of a picture must appear translucent
- When parts of a picture should blend gradually into the background

Accommodating Irregular Edges

Figure 25-1 shows a Web page containing two versions of the same picture. The version on the left has a solid white background that clashes with the textured background of the Web page. The version on the right has a transparent background that allows the Web page background to show through clearly.

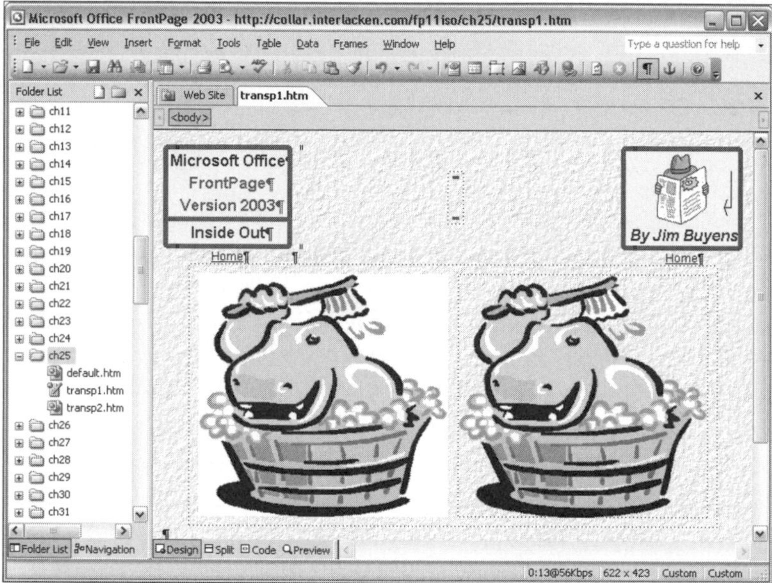

Figure 25-1. Compare the white background in the picture on the left with the transparent background of the picture on the right.

No amount of editing of the left picture will make it look as good as the picture on the right. No solid color can possibly blend evenly with the surrounding texture, and even adding a textured background to the picture will produce slight mismatches as the visitor resizes the browser window.

If your Web page background is solid rather than textured, you can achieve the effect of transparency simply by using pictures whose background color exactly matches the Web page background. The drawback is that if you change the Web page background color, you'll have to change all the pictures as well. Pictures with transparent backgrounds have no such drawback—you can use them on any Web page.

Smoothing Edges with Anti-Aliasing

Another application that greatly benefits from transparency is anti-aliasing. This is a technique that reduces the jagged appearance of curved lines when they're displayed on a computer monitor. Pixels along a curved edge, rather than being either the object's color or the background color, take on a mixture of the two. Figure 25-2 shows the string *abc* dithered on the left and anti-aliased on the right.

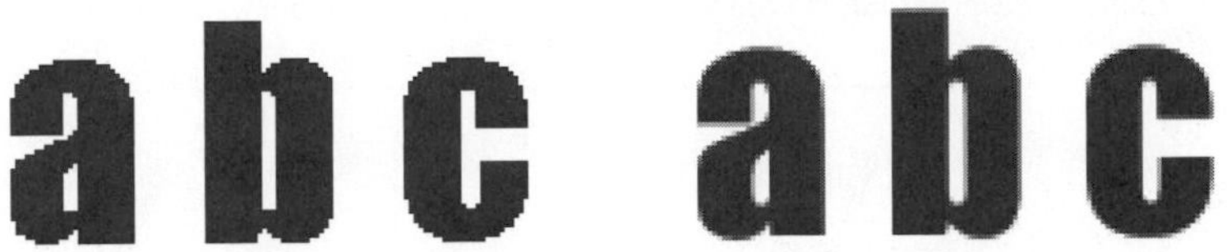

Figure 25-2. Dithering, shown here on the left, colors each pixel on an all-or-nothing basis. Anti-aliasing, shown on the right, colors each pixel proportionately.

The right side of Figure 25-2 provides an enlarged view of anti-aliasing. Pixels entirely in the white area are entirely white, and those entirely in the black area are correspondingly black. Pixels along the border, however, are colored gray in proportion to the amount of black or white space that would be occupied at a much higher resolution.

The use of anti-aliasing isn't confined to black-and-white drawings; the concept of proportionately shading edge pixels can apply to any intersection of two colors.

Many picture editors anti-alias everything by default, but this isn't always desirable. Anti-aliased edges sometimes appear blurry, like a slightly out-of-focus photograph, and sometimes the sharpness of dithered pictures is more important than the elimination of jagged edges. For this reason, it's important to have both dithering and anti-aliasing tools at hand. Figure 25-3 provides an even larger view of anti-aliasing at work.

Figure 25-3. Pixels along the dithered curve are either light or dark. Pixels along the anti-aliased curve use various shades of gray for a smoother effect.

Using Transparency Effectively

Figure 25-4 shows a transparent AutoShape drawing positioned over a WordArt component. To make the WordArt show through, the designer positioned the AutoShape over the Word-Art and adjusted the transparency of the AutoShape circle.

For more information about AutoShape drawings and WordArt components, refer to "Creating Line Art within FrontPage," on page 646.

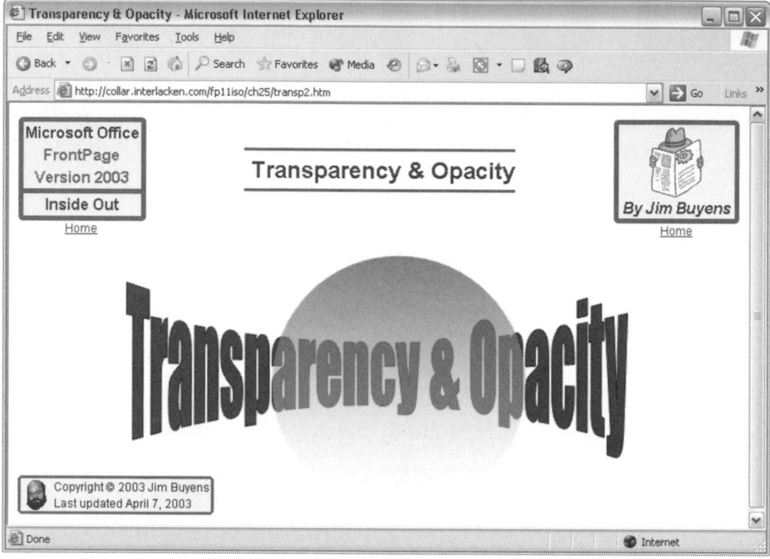

Figure 25-4. Experimenting with the transparency settings of FrontPage drawing features can result in interesting effects that add depth to your page.

A problem arises when preparing anti-aliased pictures (or, for that matter, nonrectangular pictures of any kind) for use on various colored or textured backgrounds. You know one color—that of the picture—but the second color varies depending on where the picture is used. The edge pixels need to be shaded not from one color to another, but from a solid color to various degrees of transparency—degrees that allow background colors to partially show through. To further complicate the problem, each pixel in the picture might require a different amount of transparency.

An *alpha channel* stores a fourth value along with the normal red, green, and blue intensities for each pixel. Each pixel's alpha value indicates the degree of transparency for that pixel, normally with the same precision used for red, green, and blue values. The addition of an alpha channel expands 24-bit color (8 bits each for red, green, and blue) to 32-bit color.

Unfortunately, neither GIF nor JPEG supports a true alpha channel. Advanced picture editors such as Adobe Photoshop *do* support alpha channels, but saving a picture in Web format converts the transparency information to fixed colors based on the editor's current background color. Having alpha channel support in the picture editor and its native file format is less useful than if Web pictures fully supported the feature, but it at least provides an easy way to create multiple versions of a picture with different background colors.

A common problem involves pictures anti-aliased for one background but used on another. This results in a sort of halo around the opaque portions of the picture. Unfortunately, even editing the picture with a program that supports alpha channels won't restore the original transparency information; the alpha channel was lost when the picture was saved with a fixed color background. Pixel-by-pixel editing along the edges is often the only remedy to this halo effect.

The JPEG file format doesn't support transparency at all, but the GIF format does support an all-or-nothing sort of transparency. The creator of a GIF file can designate one color in the picture as transparent. This is better than nothing—but nowhere near as powerful as a full alpha channel.

Of 16,777,216 possible colors, only 256 can exist within any given GIF file. These 256 are the GIF file's palette. Transparency works by designating one palette entry—out of the 256—as transparent. When the browser encounters this palette-entry color, it displays whatever lies behind the GIF picture instead of the palette-entry color.

If two palette entries represent the same color, only one of them can indicate transparency. This might explain why you occasionally get incomplete results when setting transparency on the basis of color.

Managing Picture Download Time

Download time is a constant concern for all Web visitors. Even visitors with high-speed connections—who, by the way, are still a minority on the World Wide Web—don't want to be stuck waiting for huge picture files to download. As a Web designer, you should also be concerned with outbound bandwidth. The larger your pages, the fewer pages your server and your Internet connection can deliver per second (or minute).

In general, the time required to download a page is the combined size of all constituent files divided by the bytes per second of available bandwidth. Managing download time thus becomes an issue of managing download bytes. And because most download bytes occur in picture files rather than the HTML, managing download bytes becomes an issue of managing picture file size.

FrontPage estimates each page's download time for a typical modem visitor and displays that time in the status bar—for example, the *0:13@56Kbps* shown in the lower right corner of Figure 25-1. This indicates that the page would take 13 seconds to load over a 56 kilobit per second modem link. You can use this feature to monitor the effect of pictures you add to a page.

Tip **Monitor your download times.**
To configure the connection speed used for calculating download times, choose Options from the Tools menu, click the Reports View tab, and adjust the Assume Connection Speed Of setting. Although most designers now assume a minimum connection speed of 56 Kbps, it's still a good idea to know what the download time is at a 28.8 Kbps connection.

There are, however, three mitigating factors:

- Most current browsers cache pictures and other files (that is, they keep local copies of recently used files). Before downloading any file, the browser checks for a local copy. If one exists, the browser does *either* of the following, depending on its configuration:
  - Uses the local copy without question, subject to certain timing constraints.
  - Transmits the local copy's date stamp to the server. If the cached copy is outdated, the Web server transmits a new version. If the cached copy is current, the Web server responds with a status code instructing the browser to use the cached version.

  You can maximize the benefits of caching by using stock pictures and not storing them redundantly on your server. This increases caching by reducing the number of different pictures. Storing all pictures in, say, an /images folder ensures that the same picture has the same URL, no matter which page on your site displays it. Storing the same picture in two different server locations forces the browser to download and cache each copy separately.
- To reduce total picture bytes on a Web page, you might be tempted to use many small picture files rather than one large or medium file. This process can go too far, however, because of a factor called *connection overhead.*

  Unless both the browser and the Web server support a feature called *persistent connections*, the HTTP protocol forces the browser to open a new connection for every file it downloads. Thus, a Web page containing 10 pictures forces the browser to open and close 11 server connections: one for the HTML page and one for each picture. Each of these connections requires processing time on both the browser and the server—time that might exceed what's required to download a smaller number of slightly larger files.

  Stringent balancing of download bytes vs. required connections is seldom warranted, given the number of other variables in effect. Nevertheless, it's good practice to avoid large numbers of very small files.
- GIF picture compression works mainly by consolidating horizontally adjacent pixels For example, rather than sequentially storing 100 white pixels on the same line, the file stores a single instruction to display 100 consecutive pixels, all white.

  You can use this information to create pictures that compress well. Just remember that flat horizontal areas compress well but complex horizontal areas don't.

  JPEG compression is more two-dimensional and thus is less affected by the nature of the picture. Flat areas still compress better than highly variegated ones, however. With JPEG files, you can also balance quality against picture size. To do this, vary the Quality setting in the Picture Properties dialog box shown in Figure 25-5.

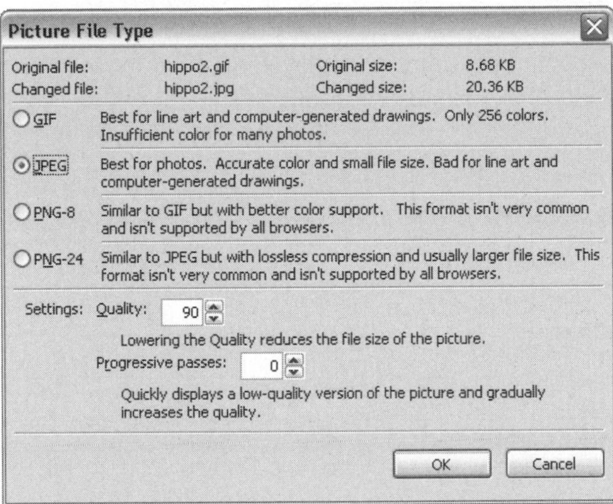

Figure 25-5. A JPEG file's quality setting balances file size against visual degradation. A value of 100 indicates no compression.

Managing Picture Palettes

Pictures that contain large, flat, solid-color areas often appear properly in an editor or a stand-alone viewer but appear grainy in browsers using 256-color display adapters. To correct this problem, you need to convert the picture's *palette*. A palette is simply a collection of colors, and most picture editors can store, edit, and save palettes—both with individual pictures and as stand-alone palette files. If you open a picture with one palette and then open a palette file that defines another palette, most editors provide several options to reconcile the differences. For instance, you can usually convert each pixel in the picture to the nearest color in the new palette. If the palette consists solely of the 216 browser-safe colors, each pixel in the original picture takes on a safe color value. Your visitors' browsers won't perform dithering or color substitution on pictures you convert in this manner.

For more information about the 216 safe colors, refer to "Achieving Accurate Rendition—Safe Colors," on page 507.

Note Because many people have high-resolution display adapters capable of displaying millions of colors, it's nice to reward them with pictures that display well at a higher resolution. When creating a Web picture from a photograph, for example, using the JPEG format provides enough colors to display pictures almost at print quality, but enough compression so that pictures download quickly to the browser. For visitors with a lower resolution, the same pictures display with acceptable quality in most situations.

The fixed 216-color palette explains two other problems Web designers often encounter:

- Black-and-white photograph rendition is usually terrible. This is because the browser has only six levels of gray—four if you exclude black and white. Table 25-2 lists the six gray levels available to visitors who, because of their video equipment, must use the safe palette.

Table 25-2. Shades of Gray in the 216-Color Safe Palette

Color name	Decimal	Hexadecimal
Black	0-0-0	00-00-00
	51-51-51	33-33-33
	102-102-102	66-66-66
	153-153-153	99-99-99
	204-204-204	CC-CC-CC
White	255-255-255	FF-FF-FF

  These six shades of gray aren't enough to display continuous-tone gray-scale pictures, such as black-and-white photographs.

- Screen shots look terrible, because many of the 20 colors reserved by Microsoft Windows aren't in the safe palette. Table 25-3 shows the 16 colors available to early 16-color VGA adapters. These colors were indelibly fixed in VGA hardware, and by default, they're now fixed in the Windows mind-set as well.

Table 25-3. RGB Values in the PC's Original 16-Color Palette

Color name	Bright	Dark
Black	0-0-0	192-192-192 (light gray)
Red	255-0-0	128-0-0
Green	0-255-0	0-128-0
Blue	0-0-255	0-0-128
Cyan	0-255-255	0-128-128
Magenta	255-0-255	128-0-128
Yellow	255-255-0	128-128-0
White	255-255-255	128-128-128 (dark gray)

All the colors in the Bright column appear in the browser-safe palette, but none of those in the Dark column are in the browser-safe palette. This explains why screen shots converted directly to GIF files don't appear as clearly on Web pages as they did when originally displayed. To obtain a clear display, you'll need to use a picture editor to convert the dark VGA colors to their nearest safe-palette equivalents, or configure Windows to use more browser-safe colors.

For more information about choosing colors, refer to Appendix E "Design Tips for Choosing Colors."

Making RGB and Hex Colors Match

Many picture editors use RGB as their color model, just as video adapters do. HTML, however, uses hexadecimal values to display colors in a Web browser. When creating or modifying a picture, you might need to create Web-safe colors in decimal and then translate them to hex for use in HTML.

To make sure that the decimal and hex colors you create are part of the standard browser-safe color palette, choose color components from those listed in Table 25-4. For example, if the hex value in HTML is 99CC66, the matching RGB value is 153, 204, 102. Simply match the corresponding values from Table 25-4.

Table 25-4. Equivalent Browser-Safe Palette Color Values

Type	Equivalent values					
Decimal	0	51	102	153	204	255
Hex	00	33	66	99	CC	FF

This table applies equally whether it's the hex or the decimal value that you already know. If, for example, you need to duplicate a safe background color that appears in a certain Web page, inspecting the HTML would give you a hexadecimal value. If you needed to enter decimal values into a photo-editing software program, you could use Table 25-4 to convert the hex color values.

The Windows Calculator accessory provides a more general way of converting numbers between decimal and hexadecimal. Here's the procedure:

1. From the Windows Start menu, choose Start, and then choose Programs, Accessories, and Calculator.
2. Choose Scientific from the View menu.
3. If the number you want to convert is hexadecimal, select the Hex option. If it's decimal, select the Dec option.
4. Enter the number you want to convert.
5. To convert the number you entered to hexadecimal, select the Hex option. Select the Dec option to convert it to decimal.

In Summary…

Working with pictures inherently involves working with color. The results can be confusing, often resulting in pictures with undesired effects. Remember simply that JPEG pictures work best for photographs and pictures that contain varied tonal ranges. GIF pictures work best with pictures that contain large solid areas of color, and any single color in a GIF can be made transparent.

The next chapter discusses a number of ways that FrontPage can add animation to your Web pages.

Chapter 26

Enhancing Web Pages with Animation

You can use animation in your Web site to call attention to something important. If your site sells designer mouse pads, for example, you could create an animated image of a designer mouse pad with a 3-D rotating effect and use it to promote a sale.

But a spinning logo or image isn't the only form of animation. Animation also controls button images that change when a visitor moves the mouse pointer over them, or pages that fade out as a new page comes in. Video is another form of animation. This chapter explains how to use Microsoft FrontPage to apply these techniques, plus a couple of others.

Animating Page Transitions

Figure 26-1 shows, in frozen form, an animation effect in progress as one Web page replaces another. Instead of just erasing the screen and painting the new page normally—from top to bottom—the browser replaces it in an ever-decreasing circle. In this way, the White On Black page gradually replaces the Black On White page.

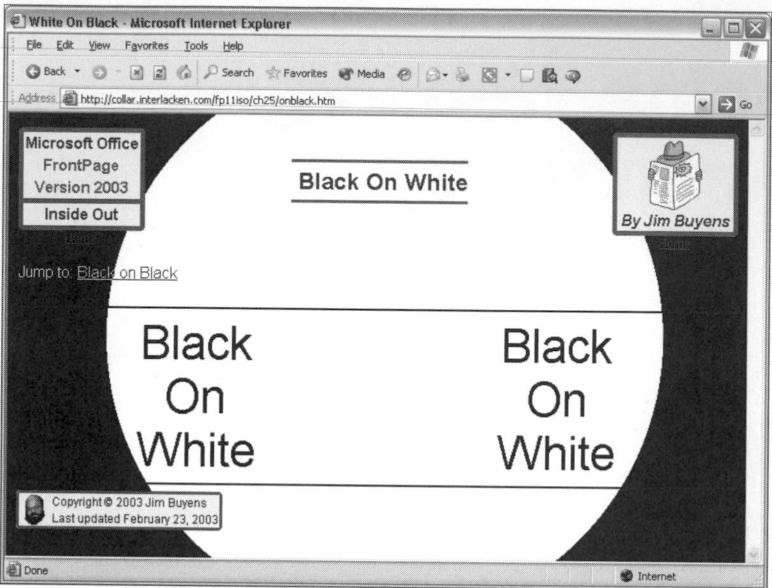

Figure 26-1. The page with the black background is gradually replacing the page with the white background. You control such effects using the Page Transition command on the Format menu.

To set page transitions, choose Page Transition from the Format menu. This opens the Page Transitions dialog box, shown in Figure 26-2.

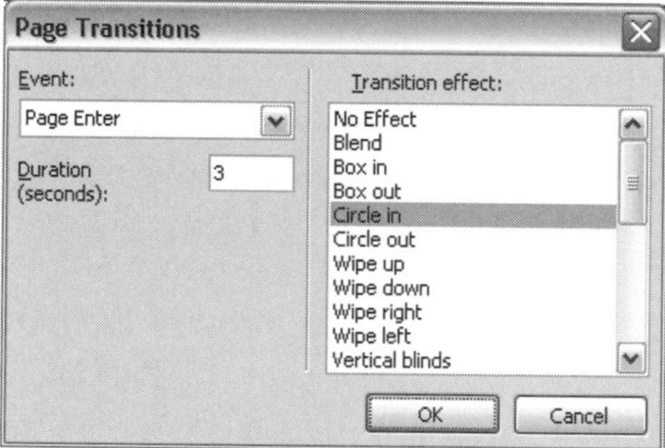

Figure 26-2. The Page Transitions dialog box defines animated transitions for Web pages.

The following options are available:

- **Event** Specifies when the page transition occurs:
  - **Page Enter** Displays a transition effect as the currently edited page appears on the Web visitor's browser.
  - **Page Exit** Displays a transition effect as the currently edited page disappears from the visitor's browser.

- **Site Enter** Displays a transition effect as the currently edited page appears on the visitor's browser, provided that the previous page was from a different Web site.
- **Site Exit** Displays a transition effect as the currently edited page disappears from the visitor's browser, provided that the next page is from a different Web site.

- **Duration (Seconds)** Specifies how long the transition effect lasts.
- **Transition Effect** Controls the animation pattern with more than 20 effects. You can guess from each transition's name the type of effect it produces. But the best way to become familiar with these effects is to simply try them on your own system.

One drawback to page transitions is that the browser must first wait for the *entire* new Web page to arrive and then apply the effect. The visitor has no opportunity to start viewing early content while later content continues to arrive. The time to play the effect further increases the visitor's wait time. Also, the effects work only in Microsoft Internet Explorer. Netscape Navigator ignores them.

Using Interactive Buttons

Graphic buttons are among the most popular user interface elements on the Web. Sometimes, these are the plain gray buttons that HTML itself provides, but more often, they're actually pictures that change appearance when the mouse pointer passes over them and revert when the mouse pointer moves away. Frequently, such buttons also change appearance when the Web visitor clicks them. Earlier versions of FrontPage provided two ways of creating such buttons:

- **Hover Button component** This approach used a Java applet to change the appearance of a button when the mouse passed over it. This component provided only a limited range of effects, the Java applet was sometimes slow, and designers using external FTP programs found it difficult to publish all the files the component required. As a result, Microsoft has removed this component from the FrontPage 2003 user interface.

  If you have existing pages that use Hover Button components, you can still inspect and modify their properties by double-clicking them in Design view. For new buttons, however, Microsoft strongly recommends using the Interactive Button component described in this section.
- **Mouse Over and Swap Picture options on the DHTML toolbar** These options still exist, as do many other options on this toolbar. Nevertheless, if you crave flashing buttons, you'll find the new Interactive Button component much easier to use.

For more information about Hover Button components, refer to Appendix H, "Configuring Hover Buttons And Ad Rotators." For more information about using the DHTML toolbar, refer to "Using DHTML Effects," later in this chapter.

Figure 26-3 shows a Web page that uses four Interactive Button components. Each button looks like a file tab, and the button under the mouse pointer is darker. The button gets even darker if the Web visitor clicks it.

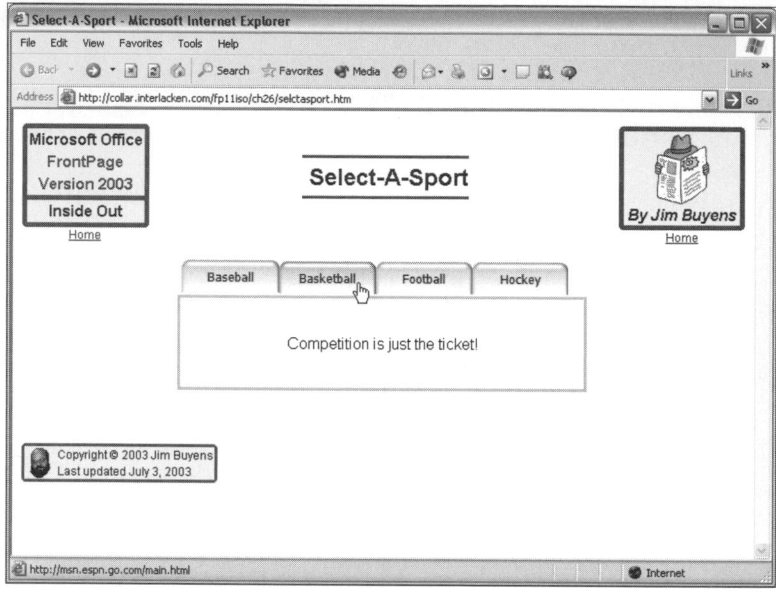

Figure 26-3. Each file tab in this Web page is actually a FrontPage Interactive Button component.

Here's the procedure for adding an Interactive Button component to any Web page. It assumes that you've already opened the page in Design view.

1 Set the insertion point where you want the Interactive Button component to appear.
2 Choose Interactive Button from the Insert menu. Alternatively:
   - Choose Web Component from the Insert menu, or click the Web Component button on the Standard toolbar.
   - When the Insert Web Component dialog box appears, select Dynamic Effects in the Component Type list on the left, and then select Interactive Button in the Choose An Effect list on the right.
   - Click Finish.

Web Component

3 When the Interactive Button dialog box shown in Figure 26-4 appears, select the entries in the Buttons list until you find your favorite. As you click each choice, a sample button appears in the Preview area.

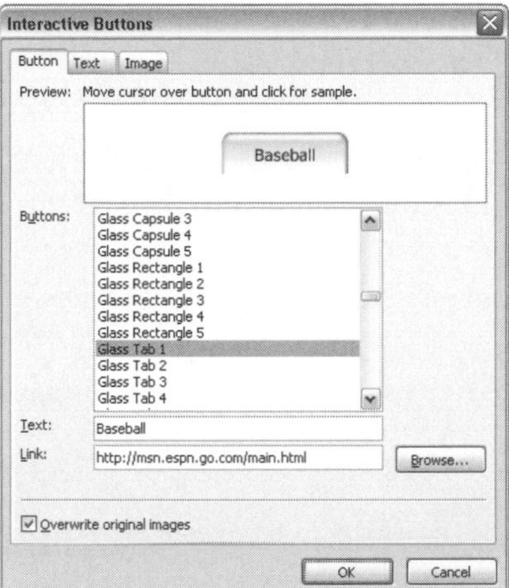

Figure 26-4. The Button tab configures the most essential properties of an Interactive Button component.

4. Enter the button title in the Text box.
5. Enter a hyperlink location in the Link box. (To specify this location by pointing and clicking, click the Browse button.) To make the button submit an HTML form, use a hyperlink such as this (where *[0]* indicates the first HTML form on the page):

   javascript:document.forms[0].submit();
6. FrontPage will dim the Overwrite Original Images check box when you're creating a new button. Click the OK button to create the Interactive Button component with all defaults.

To preview the button, click the Preview tab at the bottom of the Design view window, or save the page and then use the standard FrontPage commands to preview the page in your browser.

When you save a page that includes interactive buttons, FrontPage might display the Save Embedded Files dialog box. This occurs because FrontPage needs to save the three picture files each interactive button might display.

For more information about using the Save Embedded Files dialog box, refer to "Using the Save Embedded Files Dialog Box," on page 255.

Here's the procedure for reconfiguring an existing Interactive Button component in Design view:

1. Display the Interactive Button dialog box using any of these methods:
   - Double-click the Interactive Button component.
   - Right-click the Interactive Button component, and then choose Button Properties from the shortcut menu.

- Open the drop-down menu on the Interactive Button component's Quick Tag Selector icon, and then choose Tag Properties. (The Quick Tag Selector icon will show an <img> tag.)
- Select the Interactive Button component, and press Alt+Enter.

2 Modify the Buttons, Text, and Link settings as you do when creating new interactive buttons.

3 If you intend to change the button pictures, select the Overwrite Original Images check box.

4 To configure additional options, click the Text tab. This will display the fields shown in Figure 26-5.

Chapter 26

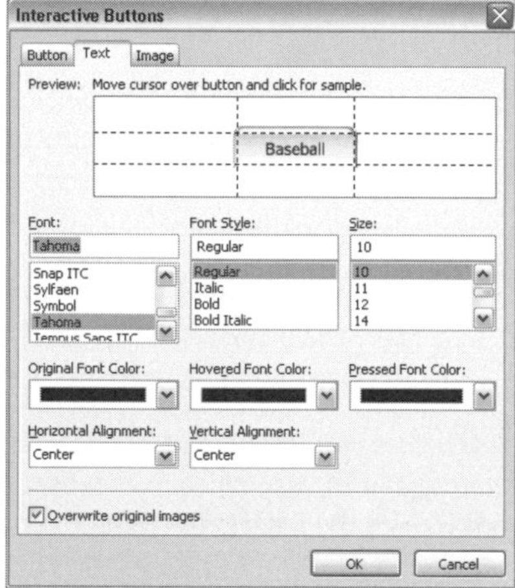

Figure 26-5. This tab controls the appearance of an Interactive Button component's text.

Note The Text and Image tabs are also available when you create a new button.

5 Use the Font, Font Style, and Size boxes to specify the typographical properties of the button text.

6 Use the Original Font Color, Hovered Font Color, and Pressed Font Color controls to specify the button text's normal color, its color when the mouse pointer is over it, and its color after the Web visitor clicks it.

7 Use the Horizontal Alignment and Vertical Alignment controls to position the text where you want it.

As before, the Preview area near the top of the dialog box will show the effects of your changes; you can click OK to save them. However, you might prefer to first modify the button properties that appear on the Image tab, shown in Figure 26-6.

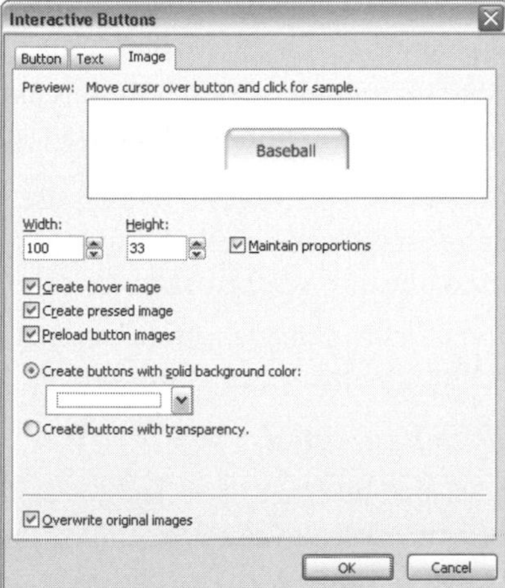

Figure 26-6. The Image tab controls an Interactive Button component's size and effects.

If so, proceed as follows:

1. Use the Width and Height boxes to stretch or shrink the button picture.
   - To change these values proportionately, make sure that the Maintain Proportions check box is selected.
   - To change Height without changing Width (or vice versa) make sure that the Maintain Proportions check box is cleared.
2. Select the Create Hover Image check box if you want the button's appearance to change when the mouse pointer passes over it. Clear the check box if you don't want this effect.
3. Select the Create Pressed Image check box if you want the button's appearance to change when the Web visitor clicks it. If you don't want this effect, clear this check box.
4. Select the Preload Button Images check box if you want the browser to load all the button pictures into memory when it first displays the page. Otherwise, clear this check box.

> **Tip** **Preload your button images**
>
> Preloading button images ensures that changes to a button's appearance occur smoothly. If you don't preload images, the browser retrieves hovered and pressed images only when it first needs them, and this may incur a time delay. Preloading is usually the best choice, but it does have a drawback: The browser has to download all the button images even if it never displays them.

5. To specify the button background, select one of these options:
   - **Make The Button A JPEG Image And Use This Background Color** Select this option if you want the button to have a solid color background. Use the nearby color drop-down list to specify the color you want.

- **Make the Button A GIF Image And Use A Transparent Background** Select this option if you want the button to have a transparent background.

Unfortunately, FrontPage has no built-in facility for adding custom button types to the Interactive Button component. Working around this limitation involves two tasks:

- First, you must provide a copy of the blank button picture you want to use. The default folder for these is C:\Program Files\Microsoft Office\Templates\Buttons. Supply two versions of the file: one in GIF format and one in PNG format.
- Second, you must add some information to a file named ibutton.xml that resides by default at C:\Program Files\Microsoft Office\Templates\1033\buttons:

  1. Open this file in Notepad or any other text editor.
  2. Copy the information about any existing button to the Clipboard. This includes everything between an existing pair of <ibutton> and </ibutton> tags, including the tags themselves.
  3. Paste this information after the last </ibutton> tag in the file.
  4. Modify the button and picture file names and dimensions throughout the information you just pasted.
  5. Test the new button, and refine the remaining tags based on experience.

Because Netscape Navigator 4 doesn't conform to the official W3C DHTML specification, FrontPage Interactive Button components won't display hovered and pressed effects in that browser. Instead, the original button appearance remains in effect. Any hyperlinks on those buttons will, however, work correctly.

Using DHTML Effects

In addition to animating the appearance and disappearance of entire Web pages, FrontPage can animate the way individual elements arrive on screen, react to mouse activity, or both. Headings, pictures, and other objects can fly in from various borders, drop in one word at a time, spiral in, zoom in, and so forth. In addition, an object's appearance can change as the mouse pointer passes over it.

Figure 26-7 shows such a page-load animation in progress. The heading line, including the picture, has already slid in from the right edge of the window. The bookmark hyperlinks Backup, Diskettes, Drink Holder, and Foot Pedal have already dropped in from the top of the window, and the bookmark hyperlink Whiteout is en route.

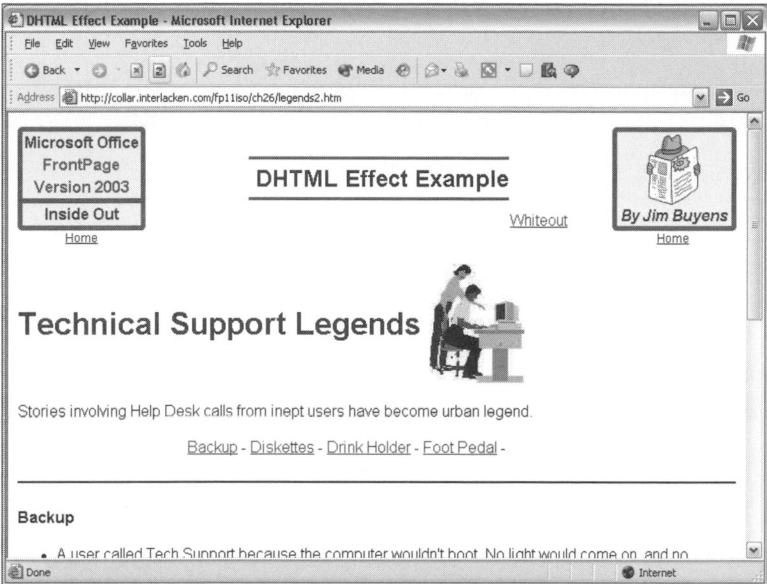

Figure 26-7. The hyperlinks on this Web page are dropping in word by word from the top.

FrontPage creates these effects by adding browser scripts to your Web page. These scripts are short JavaScript programs that use DHTML and CSS Positioning. Internet Explorer began supporting these features in version 4, and Netscape Navigator began supporting them in version 6. Applying DHTML effects in FrontPage is quite simple:

1. Set the insertion point anywhere within the element you want to animate. This will usually be a paragraph or a picture.
2. Locate the DHTML Effects toolbar described in Table A-4 in Appendix A. If this toolbar isn't visible, choose Toolbars from the View menu, and then choose DHTML Effects.
3. Use the Choose An Event drop-down list (labeled On) to specify the event that triggers the effect. There are four options:
   - **Click** Means that the effect occurs whenever the Web visitor clicks the element.
   - **Double-Click** Means that the effect occurs whenever the Web visitor double-clicks the element.
   - **Mouse Over** Means that the effect occurs whenever the Web visitor moves the mouse pointer over the element.
   - **Page Load** Means that the effect occurs whenever the Web visitor loads or reloads the page.
4. Use the Choose An Effect drop-down list (labeled Apply) to choose the effect you want. As illustrated in Table 26-1, the choice of effects varies depending on the trigger event.

5 If the Effect Settings list is enabled, click the drop-down arrow, and choose one of the listed options.

To remove an effect, first select the element, making sure that the DHTML Effects toolbar displays the effect you want to remove. Then click the toolbar's Remove Effect button.

Table 26-1. Effects Available for DHTML Events

Event (On)	Effect (Apply)	Description	Settings
Click, Double-Click	Fly Out	Moves the animated element off-screen	Direction of movement
Click, Double-Click, Mouse Over	Formatting	Changes the appearance of text	Fonts (including font colors) and borders
Page Load	Drop In By Word	Moves text on screen from the top, a word at a time	(none)
	Elastic	Moves the entire element on screen from the right or bottom overshoots and then corrects	From right or from bottom
	Fly In	Moves the element on screen from any side or corner	Side or corner, entire element or a word at a time
	Hop	Moves the element slightly up, right, down, and then left	(none)
	Spiral	Moves the element from the upper-right corner to its proper place, using a spiral motion	(none)
	Wave	Moves the element slightly down, right, up, and then left	(none)
	Wipe	Gradually reveals the element	Left to right, top to bottom, or from middle
	Zoom	Text starts out either very large or very small and then zooms to normal size	In (reduced text becomes normal) or out (enlarged text becomes normal)

Highlight Dynamic HTML

FrontPage can visually indicate elements with DHTML effects by showing them with a light blue background. This occurs only in Design view, and not in the Web visitor's browser. However, if you find the blue background in Design view distracting, you can toggle it on or off by clicking the Highlight Dynamic HTML Effects button on the DHTML Effects toolbar.

The various DHTML Effects animations run only once. There's no way to make them run continuously, and that's probably a good thing. After loading your page, you want Web visitors to read your content and not to sit there watching cartoons.

Highlighting hyperlinks is a common use for Mouse Over effects. When the mouse pointer passes over hyperlinked text, the text can change color, get larger, change font, and so forth. FrontPage calls this a *rollover effect*.

For information about configuring rollover effects for all hyperlinks on a Web page, refer to "Advanced Page Properties," on page 498.

Swapping Pictures with DHTML Effects

When you select a picture and then use the DHTML Effects toolbar, the toolbar offers the effects listed in Table 26-2.

Table 26-2. Picture Effects Available for DHTML Events

Event (On)	Effect (Apply)	Description	Settings
Click	Fly Out	Moves the picture off the screen	Direction of movement
	Swap Picture	Replaces the picture with another picture	Location of the replacement picture
Double-Click	Fly Out	Moves the picture off the screen	Direction of movement
Mouse Over	Swap Picture	Replaces the picture with another picture	Location of the replacement picture
Page Load	Refer to Table 26-1		

The Swap Picture effect offers a flexible alternative to interactive buttons if you proceed as follows:

1. Create two versions of a picture you want to use as a button. Both pictures should be the same size.
   - One is the picture as it normally appears.
   - The other is an alternative version that appears when the Web visitor passes the mouse pointer over the picture area.
2. Add the "normal" picture to your Web page, and build the desired hyperlink.
3. Select the normal picture, and then display the DHTML Effects toolbar.

4 On the DHTML Effects toolbar:
   - Set the On drop-down list to Mouse Over.
   - Set the Apply drop-down list to Swap Picture.
   - Set the third drop-down list to Choose Picture.

5 Use the resulting Picture dialog box to specify the "alternative" picture.

Scripting DHTML Behaviors

The W3C DHTML specification mentioned in the preceding sections describes a wide selection of changes that you can make to a Web page already on display—Interactive Button components and the DHTML Effects toolbar only scratch the surface. Full use of DHTML requires in-depth programming skills, but FrontPage 2003 provides a new Behaviors task pane that handles most requirements without making you look at programming code at all. Figure 26-8 shows an example of this task pane.

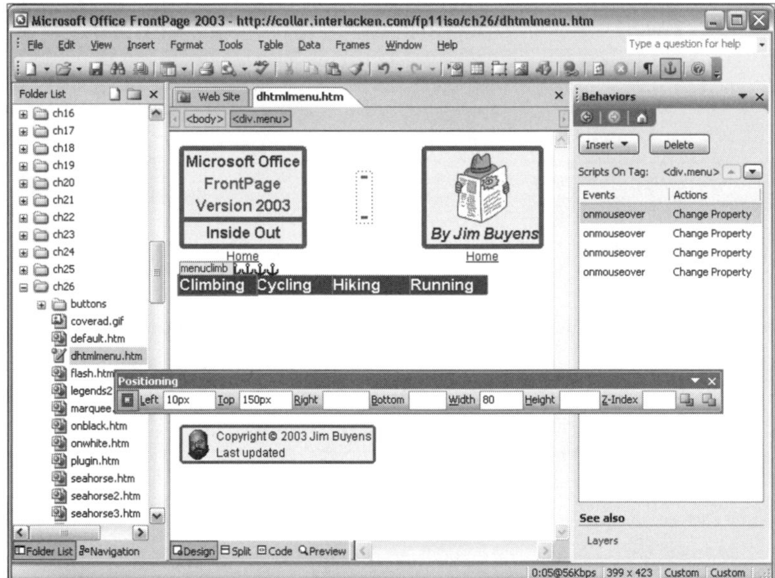

Figure 26-8. The Behaviors task pane can program a wide variety of Web page effects without exposing you to any program code.

Behavior actions can take many kinds of actions. For example, they can jump to another URL, play a sound, or display a message box. In addition, an event on one page element can run a script that modifies that element, or even a different page element.

If you want an event on one element to modify a different page element, the modified element must have an *id* attribute. (Otherwise, the script has no way of telling the browser which element to modify.) To find or assign the *id* attribute for a page element, proceed as follows:

1. Make sure that the Quick Tag Selector is displayed. If it isn't, choose Quick Tag Selector from the View menu.
2. Select the page element you want a DHTML effect to modify. This will probably be a picture or a layer, but it could be almost anything on the page.
3. Selecting a page element will also select its Quick Tag Selector icon. Click the down arrow on this icon, and choose Edit Tag from the drop-down menu. This will display a Quick Tag Editor dialog box that looks like this:

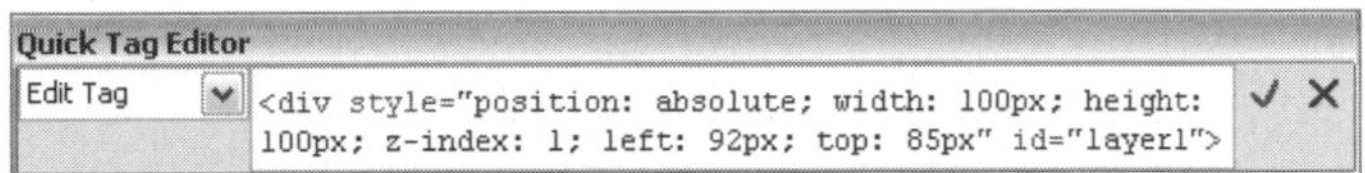

   Review the tag attributes, and make sure that one of them is an *id*. In this example, the *id* attribute is *id="layer1"*.

   - If you find an *id* attribute, write down or remember its value, and then click the X button on the right of the Quick Tag Editor dialog box.
   - If no *id* attribute is present, set the insertion point between any existing attributes and supply one, taking care not to assign the same *id* value as any other element on the page. Record the new *id* value, and then click the check mark button on the right in the Quick Tag Editor dialog box.

Tip The X button closes the Quick Tag Editor dialog box without saving any changes you've made. The check mark button saves your changes before closing the dialog box.

For many page elements, the following procedure might be easier. However, it only works for elements that have Property dialog boxes containing a Style button.

1. Display the element's Properties dialog box. For example:
   - Right-click the element and choose its Properties command from the shortcut menu.
   - Open drop down menu on the element's Quick Tag Selector icon, and then choose Tag properties.
2. Click the Style button on the Properties dialog box. (If the dialog box has no Style button, revert to the first procedure.)
3. When the Modify Style dialog box appears, type the *id* you want into the ID text box. *Don't* choose an existing *id* from the drop-down list!
4. Click OK twice to close the Modify Style dialog box and the Properties dialog box.

Here's the procedure to actually specify the event you want the browser to detect and the effect you want it to have:

1. Display the Behaviors task pane. There are two ways of doing this:
   - Chose Behaviors from the Format menu.
   - Press Ctrl+F1 to display the task pane you used most recently. Then, if necessary, choose Behaviors from the drop-down menu in the task pane title bar.
2. Select the page element you want to trigger the action. To do this, use either of these methods:
   - Click the element in Design view.
   - Click the element's tag icon in the Quick Tag Selector.

   In the Behaviors task pane, a message above the central list box will confirm the tag you selected. In this example, the message *Scripts On Tag: <div>* confirms that you're working on a <div> tag.
3. Click the Insert button in the Behaviors task pane, and then select the type of action you want the browser to take. Some of these choices include:
   - **Call JavaScript** Runs a JavaScript function you coded elsewhere in the page.
   - **Change Property** Modifies the properties of some page element.
   - **Check Browser** Jumps to another page depending on the visitor's browser.
   - **Go to URL** Unconditionally jumps to another page.
   - **Swap Image** Replaces one picture with another.

Selecting any listed action displays a dialog box in which you configure the details of what you want to occur. If the name of an action doesn't clarify what it does, the fields on the resulting dialog box probably will. If not, consult the FrontPage Help files.

As an example, suppose you want clicking on one layer to make another layer visible. This is a common requirement when constructing drop-down menus. In step 2, you would have selected the menu title; now you want to reveal the menu command. Continue as follows:

1. Click the Insert button in the Behaviors task pane, and then choose Change Property.
2. When the Change Property dialog box shown in Figure 26-9 appears, select the Select Element option. This tells FrontPage that you want to select which element the script will modify.

   Specifying Current Element means that the script will modify the element that receives the event (for example, the element that the Web visitor clicks).
3. In the Element Type drop-down list, select the type of element you want to modify. In order for an element type to appear, it must be present in your Web page and have an *id* attribute.
4. In the Element Id drop-down list, select the *id* of the element you want to modify. This list will display only elements of the type you specified in step 3, and that have *id* attributes.

Figure 26-9. This dialog box specifies a list of property changes that a Behavior action will make.

5 To modify the *Font*, *Position*, or *Border* attributes of an element, click the Font, Positions, or Borders button on the right in the dialog box. These buttons display standard FrontPage dialog boxes that you've seen in earlier chapters.

6 To change the visibility of an element, click the Visibility button. This displays the Visibility dialog box, shown in Figure 26-10.

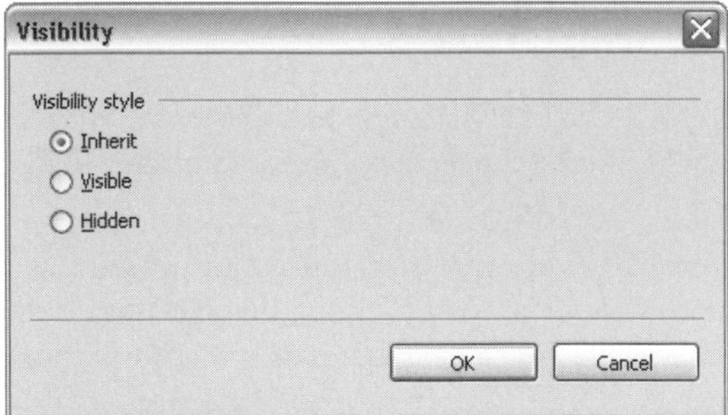

Figure 26-10. This dialog box specifies the visibility a Behavior action should assign to a page element.

Choose one of these options, and then click OK:

- **Inherit** The element will have the same visibility as the element that structurally contains it. This is the default behavior.
- **Visible** The element will be visible.
- **Hidden** The element will be invisible.

7 To specify property changes directly, click the Add button. This displays the Insert Property dialog box, shown in Figure 26-11. Specify the attribute name and value you want, and then click OK.

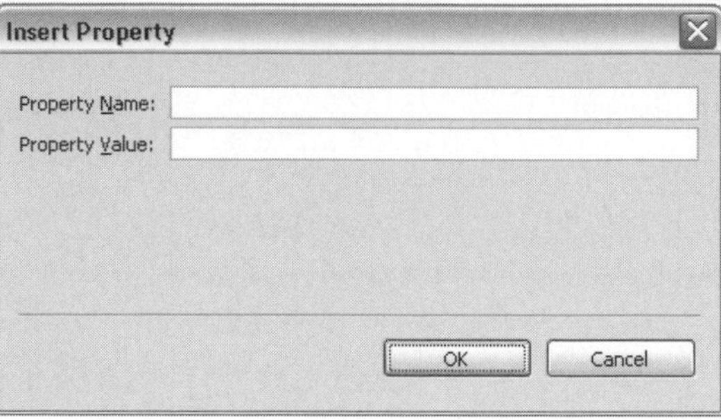

Figure 26-11. This dialog box can control any DHTML property of any element.

Specifying attribute names in this dialog box is somewhat tricky, because you must specify the programming attribute names. These aren't the same names you'd use in ordinary HTML or CSS code. For the most part, they're the same as CSS names except that initial capping replaces hyphens. The attribute name for *font-family*, for example, would be *styles.fontFamily*.

8 Without leaving the Change Property dialog box, you can specify changes to as many properties as you want. The list in the center of the dialog box will continue to show more entries. To change an existing attribute entry, select it, and click Modify. To remove an attribute, select it, and click Remove.

One thing the Change Property dialog box can't do is specify change to more than one element. In fact, if you specify changes to one element, and then change the selection in the Element Type or Element ID list, the dialog box will *erase* your entries for the first element! This argues strongly for the following rules:

- Once you've specified property changes for an element, don't modify the Element Type or Element ID selections unless you want to discard the existing changes.
- To change the properties of more than one element, finish configuring the changes for the first element, then click the Insert button on the Behaviors task pane and configure changes to the second element. Repeat until satisfied.

When you've specified all the properties you want, click OK.

9 When a script appears for the first time in the Behaviors list box, it usually has an event type of *onclick*. This is fine if you want a mouse click to trigger the script, but a tragedy in any other case. To recover:

- Click the incorrect event name (for example, *onclick*).
- Click the down arrow that appears next to the incorrect event name.
- Select the event you want from the resulting list. For example, *onmouseover* events generally trigger the scripts that make drop-down menus visible or hidden.

Refer again to Figure 26-8. In addition to a Behaviors task pane, this figure shows a Web page that displays drop-down DHTML menus. Figure 26-12 shows the same page as it appears in a browser. The page has eight absolutely positioned layers: one for each of the four menu titles and one for each corresponding list of commands.

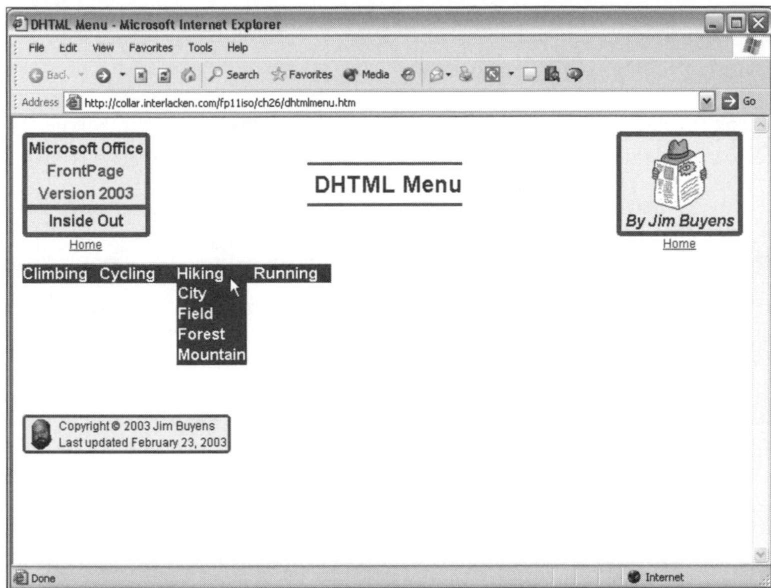

Figure 26-12. Actions in the Behaviors task pane control the drop-down menus in this Web page.

The presence of the positioning toolbar in Figure 26-8 is a reminder that all eight layers are absolutely positioned. This is what keeps the menu commands properly aligned below the menu titles, and what superimposes the menu commands over the page background. Each list of menu commands is a layer that contains an HTML table. Normally, the menu commands would be hyperlinks, but in this example, for simplicity, they're ordinary text.

Initially, the four menu titles are visible, and the four menus are hidden:

- When the mouse pointer passes over the Climbing menu title, Behavior actions make the Climbing command list visible and the Cycling, Hiking, and Running menu commands hidden.

  The Behaviors task pane in Figure 26-8 shows four actions for the Climbing menu title: one for making the Climbing list visible, and one each to hide the Cycling, Hiking, and Running menu commands (in case one happens to be visible).
- When the mouse pointer passes over the Cycling menu title, Behavior actions make the Cycling command list visible and the Climbing, Hiking, and Running menu commands hidden.
- This pattern continues for the Hiking and Running menus.

The Behaviors task pane generally creates results that work will in Internet Explorer 4 and later and in Netscape Navigator 6 and later. Even so, you should test your results in each browser you care about. If a script failure produces obnoxious error messages or leaves visitors with no way to navigate the site, you might need to develop alternative pages and use Check Browser scripts to switch among them.

Inserting Sound Files

The browser can play a background sound while Web visitors view your page. To add this feature, follow the instructions given in Chapter 18 for the Page Properties dialog box.

The procedure for setting up a hyperlink that plays a sound file is the same as that for linking to any other type of file. Chapter 11 explains how to build hyperlinks.

For more information about playing a background sound, refer to "General Page Properties," on page 493. For more information about building hyperlinks of any kind, refer to Chapter 11, "Building Hyperlinks."

Keep in mind that although Microsoft Windows environments provide very good support for .wav files, other operating systems might not. Browsers on virtually all operating systems can play sound files in a format named .au, which originated on UNIX, but finding software that converts .wav files to .au format can be difficult.

Musical Instrument Digital Interface (MIDI) files (which on PCs often have the file extension .mid) also enjoy wide support and tend to be small in size. However, because MIDI files essentially record the musician's actions rather than the resulting sound, creating a MIDI file generally requires playing music on a synthesizer or scoring notes in a specialized music program. (This isn't a problem, of course, when you download a MIDI file that someone else has created.)

Presenting Video

FrontPage can create Web pages that display video clips as easily as it creates pages that display still pictures. The most common video formats on the Web are:

- Windows Media Video (WMV) from Microsoft.
- Motion Picture Experts Group (MPEG), an independent standard.
- QuickTime (formerly called Active Movie [MOV]) from Apple.
- RealVideo (RAM) from RealNetworks.
- Audio Visual Interleaved (AVI) from Microsoft. Use of this format is declining.

Delivering video requires no special software in FrontPage or on your Web server, but displaying it requires a player on the visitor's browser. Visitors can obtain player software from these companies' Web sites, or through their browser suppliers. It's good practice and common courtesy to provide hyperlinks that download players for video clips or other multimedia elements used on your Web pages

For information about downloadable Microsoft browser features, browse: *www.microsoft.com/windows/ie/download/default.asp*. For information about downloadable Netscape browser plug-in features, browse *www.netscape.com/plugins/index.html*. For more information about QuickTime, including download locations, browse *www.apple.com/quicktime/*.

Inserting Video Files

Displaying video files on the Web presents several challenges. First, video files are generally quite large. Second, they come in many different formats. And third, many of these formats support an unlimited number of coding-decoding (codec) schemes.

Note A *codec* is a scheme for translating analog video signals to and from digital format. Most of these schemes also provide compression, which reduces the size of the encoded file. To view the file, a Web visitor must use the same codec as the person who encoded it, and therein lies the rub. There are many, many codecs in use, and more seem to emerge everyday.

To address these challenges, most Web designers don't display video files in Web pages in the same way as they might a picture. Instead, they simply provide a text hyperlink that states the title of the video, its size, and its format. The target of such a hyperlink is the video file you want to deliver.

If the Web visitor has a viewer for the given file format and is willing to wait for the download, he or she clicks the link. When the download is complete, the browser starts the viewer and tells it which file to play.

For more information about building hyperlinks, refer to Chapter 11, "Building Hyperlinks."

Streaming video is another technique that minimizes the length of time a Web visitor must wait to see a video. Basically, this involves initiating a download, observing the download speed, and starting the video when it seems likely that the end of the file will arrive before the time comes to display it. The server sending the video and the client receiving it also exchange status messages and can adjust the quality of compression to maintain a smooth rate of play. To deliver streaming video, you need special server software such as Microsoft Windows Media Services, Apple QuickTime Streaming Server, RealNetworks Helix Universal Server, or Darwin Streaming Server for Windows, Linux, and Solaris. After putting your video on such a server, you lead Web visitors there by once again providing a simple hyperlink. Consult your streaming media server documentation for details.

If you do want to display video clips directly in a Web page, FrontPage can do this in three distinctly different ways. Here are the possibilities:

Broken Picture

- **Display the video as a picture file** This is the easiest and most direct way to add video using FrontPage, but it creates HTML that Netscape Navigator doesn't understand. Instead of the video, Netscape displays a Broken Picture icon.

  Internet Explorer displays a video inserted this way, but without any playback controls such as Play, Pause, and Stop, or a Playback bar.
- **Display the video using an ActiveX control** This method creates HTML that tells the browser to load a specific Microsoft ActiveX control—usually the Windows Media Player—and have the ActiveX control display the video. This method can either display or suppress playback controls in Windows versions of Internet Explorer, but displays nothing in any other browser.

For more information about using ActiveX controls, refer to "Incorporating ActiveX Controls," on page 785.

- **Display the video using a plug-in** This method tells the browser to retrieve the video file from your Web server and then display it using whatever program the browser associates with the video's file type. This means that the Web visitor controls—by configuring the browser—what program displays your video. Although you have no control over which, if any, program displays the video, this method works with all current-day browsers.

For more information about using plug-ins, refer to "Incorporating Plug-Ins," on page 711.

Frequently Asked Questions About Video Files

What guidelines exist for distributing video on the Web?

Exercise restraint when placing video files on Web pages. These files are extremely large by Web standards and might take several minutes to download, possibly frustrating or angering some visitors.

Place warnings on hyperlinks that lead to such downloads so that viewers have a chance to avoid starting a lengthy download.

If you're using a plug-in to display the video, tell your visitors which plug-in you expect them to have and provide a hyperlink to its download location.

What's the procedure for displaying an animated GIF file?

Animated GIF files don't qualify here as video. Insert animated GIFs using the Picture dialog box, as you would for any other GIF or JPG picture.

Here's the procedure for enhancing your Web page with a video that will be displayed as a picture file:

1. If the video file doesn't reside in the current Web site, drag it from its current location and drop it into the FrontPage Folder List or Folders view. The images folder is a good place to store such files.
2. Open the Web page that should display the video.
3. Set the insertion point where you want the video to appear.
4. Choose Picture from the Insert menu, and then select Video. This will display a standard FrontPage file open dialog box titled Video.
5. Select the video file you want to display. Normally, this will be a file with an .avi file extension. Click Open.

Tip Dragging a video file from the Folder List and dropping it onto an open Web page accomplishes the same results as steps 3, 4, and 5 of this procedure.

The WYSIWYG editor in Design view doesn't display video files in full animation and sound. Instead, to avoid distractions, FrontPage displays the first video frame as a still picture. If you want to see the video file actually play, click the Preview tab at the bottom of the Design view window. Figure 26-13 shows how the page should look.

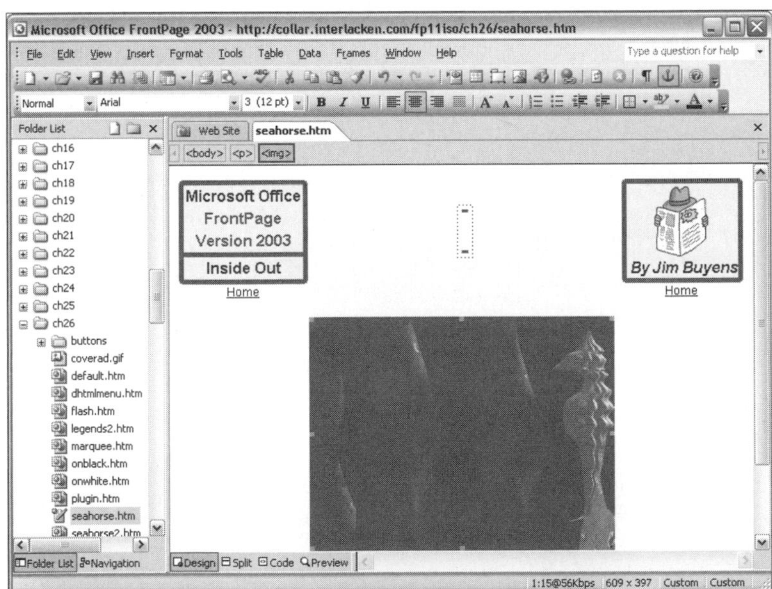

Figure 26-13. Adding a video like this to any Web page is as simple as dragging it from the Folder List and dropping it into the page.

To modify the playback properties of a video on any open Web page, first double-click it to display the Picture Properties dialog box, and then select the Video tab. Right-clicking the video and then choosing Picture Properties accomplishes the same end.

For more information about configuring video properties, refer to the next section, "Modifying Video Properties."

Here's the procedure for inserting an ActiveX control that displays a video:

1. If the video file doesn't reside in the current Web site, drag it from its current location and drop it into the FrontPage Folder List or Folders view. The images folder is a good place to store such files.
2. Open the Web page that should display the video.
3. Set the insertion point where you want the video to appear.
4. Choose Web Component from the Insert menu.
5. When the Insert Web Component dialog box appears, choose Advanced Controls from the Component Type list on the left.
6. Choose ActiveX Control from the Choose A Control list on the right, and then click Next.
7. When the Insert Web Component dialog box shown in Figure 26-14 appears, make sure Windows Media Player is selected, and then click Finish.

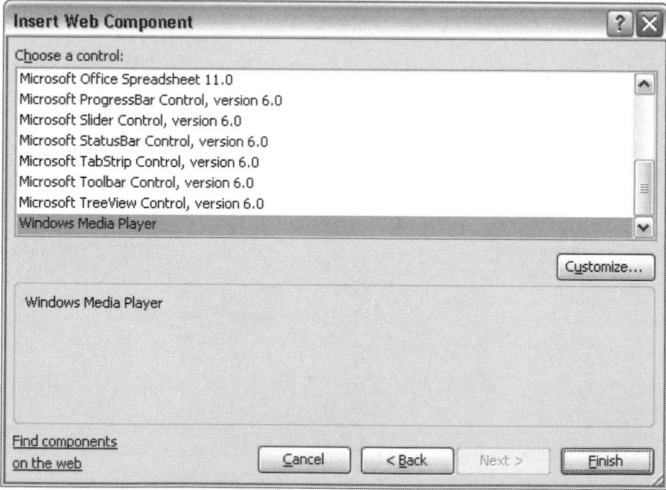

Figure 26-14. From this dialog box, select the control you want to insert.

8. You must now tell the *Windows Media Player* object which video file to play. To do this, double-click the control (or right-click it and choose ActiveX Control Properties from the shortcut menu).

9 When the Windows Media Player Properties dialog box shown in Figure 26-15 appears, click the click the Browse button to locate the video file you want to display. When the associated box shows the correct file name, click Open.

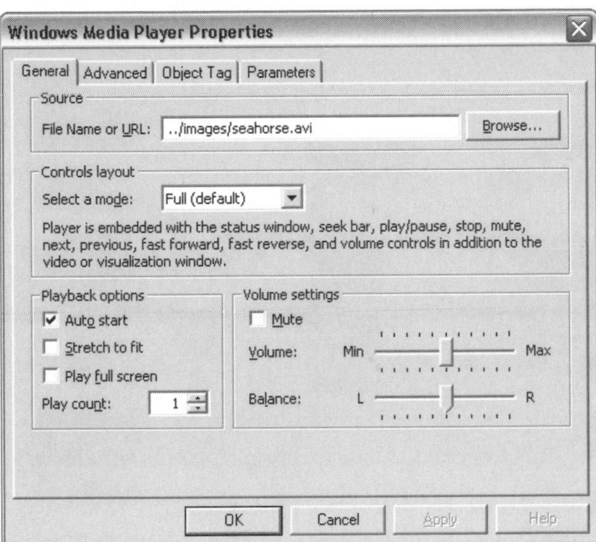

Figure 26-15. These general-purpose dialog boxes configure the properties of most ActiveX controls. Here, they're configuring a *Windows Media Player* object.

10 Configure any other settings you want in the Windows Media Player Properties dialog box, and then click OK.

For more information about using ActiveX controls, refer to "Incorporating ActiveX Controls," on page 785. For instructions on inserting a plug-in that displays a video, refer to "Incorporating Plug-Ins," on page 711.

Modifying Video Properties

The Video tab of the Picture Properties dialog box, shown in Figure 26-16, controls the display and playback of video files added to a Web page as a picture.

The options on this tab control the following:

- **Video Source** Specify the location of the file containing digitized video. This location can be in the current Web site, on your local hard disk, on a file server, or on the World Wide Web. You can use the Browse button to locate the file.

Note If the Picture Properties dialog box contains both a Picture Source and a Video Source entry, the browser first displays the static picture and then, when possible, replaces it with the first frame of the video.

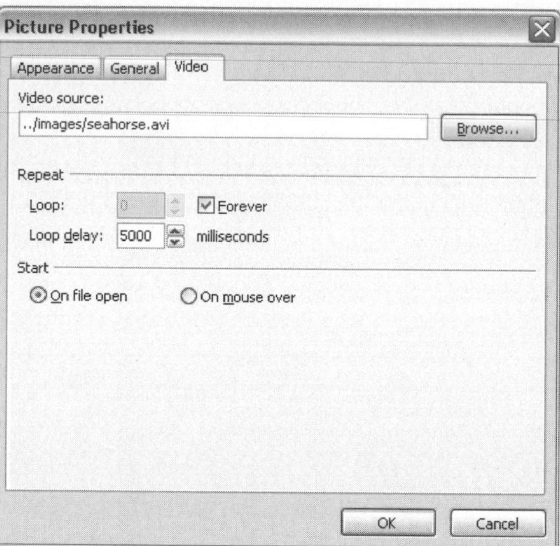

Figure 26-16. This tab controls presentation of full-motion video files.

- **Repeat** Settings in this section control the replaying of the video:
  - **Loop** Controls the number of times the browser should replay the video.
  - **Forever** Overrides the Loop setting and repeats the video continuously.
  - **Loop Delay** Causes a delay between repeat playings. The default is zero; any other value is milliseconds. To specify a 5-second delay, for example, you would type 5000.
- **Start** This section controls when the browser plays the video:
  - **On File Open** Plays the video as soon as the browser opens the file.
  - **On Mouse Over** Plays the video when the mouse pointer passes over the display area.

Incorporating Movies in Flash Format

Macromedia Flash is a popular program that creates audiovisual content (movies) for the Web. Movies in Flash format generally have the following file extensions:

- **SPL** Short for Macromedia Splash. This file format originated with an earlier version of Flash named Splash.
- **SWF** Short for Macromedia Shockwave Flash. This the most common format for Flash movies.
- **SWT** Short for Macromedia Shockwave Template. This type of file processes instructions that dynamically assemble Flash movies from other files.

Movies in Flash format are usually line-oriented rather than bitmap-oriented and are therefore much smaller than true video files. FrontPage 2003 makes quick work of adding such movies to your Web page. Figure 26-17 shows a Web page displaying a movie in Flash format; the panes of the Windows logo fall in from the top of the picture.

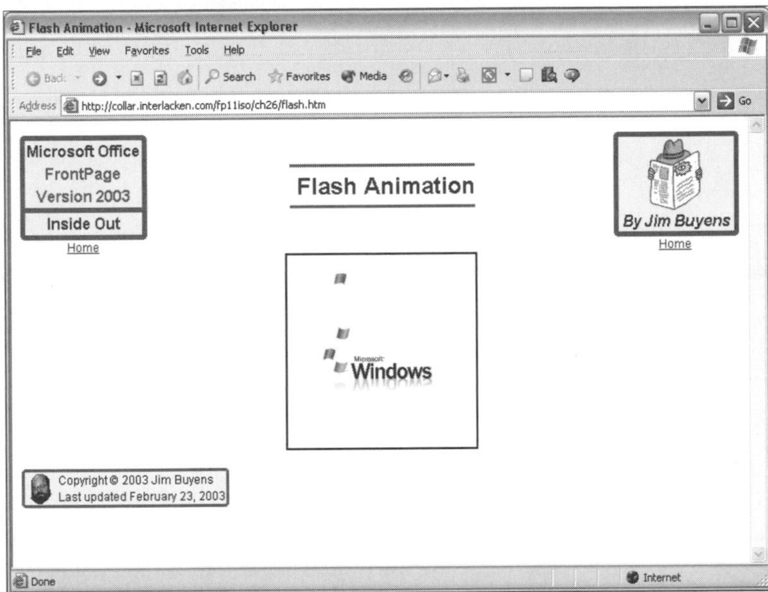

Figure 26-17. The movie in the center of this Web page comes from a Macromedia Flash file.

Here's the easiest way to configure a Web page to display a Flash format movie. It's basically the same procedure you would use to display an ordinary picture.

1. Add the .spl, .swf, or .swt file to your Web site. For example, drag the file from Window Explorer and drop it into your Web site's images folder.
2. Open the page that will display the Flash format movie.
3. Drag the Flash format movie file out of the Folder List and drop it into the Web page.

This configures the Flash format movie to run with all defaults. The following methods provide more control:

- Choose Picture from the Insert menu, and then choose Movie In Flash Format.
- Display the Insert Web Component dialog box by choosing Web Component from the Insert menu, or by clicking the Web Component button on the Standard toolbar. Then, when the Insert Web Component dialog box appears:

Web Component

   1. Select Advanced Controls in the Component Type list on the left.
   2. Select Movie In Flash Format in the Choose A Control list on the right.
   3. Click the Finish button.

Both methods display the Movie In Flash Format Properties dialog box, shown in Figure 26-18. The same dialog box appears when you modify the properties of an existing Flash format movie (for example, by double-clicking it in Design view, or by right-clicking it and choosing Move In Flash Format Properties from the shortcut menu).

Figure 26-18. This dialog box configures the appearance of a Macromedia Flash picture.

The Movie In Flash Format Properties dialog box offers two tabs: Appearance and General. The Movie settings on the Appearance tab control the movie's display properties.

- **Quality** Choose the display quality you want:
  - **Low** Favors playback speed over appearance.
  - **Auto Low** Emphasizes speed at first but improves appearance if data arrives rapidly.
  - **Auto High** Emphasizes playback speed and appearance equally at first but sacrifices appearance if data arrives slowly.
  - **Medium** Produces a better quality than the Low setting, but worse than High.
  - **High** Always favors appearance over playback speed.
  - **Best** Provides the best display quality regardless of playback speed.
- **Scale** Specify the display characteristics you want:
  - **Default (Show All)** Displays the movie in the available area without distortion, maintaining the original aspect ratio. If the available area is the wrong shape, borders will appear on two sides.
  - **No Border** Scales the movie to fill the available area, without distortion but possibly with some cropping.

  - **Exact Fit** Displays the movie in the available area without preserving the original aspect ratio. Distortion might therefore occur.
- **Background Color** Specify the background color you want the movie to have, or select the Transparent check box. This overrides settings within the Flash format file itself.
- **Alignment** Specify how you want the Flash Player to position the animation within the available space:
  - **Default (Center)** Centers the movie in the browser window and crops edges if the available space is too small.
  - **Left, Right, Top, and Bottom** Align the movie along the given edge of the browser window, cropping the remaining sides as necessary.
  - **Top Left, Top Right, Bottom Left, and Bottom Right** Align the movie into the given corner of the browser window, cropping the remaining sides as necessary.

The Layout settings control page positioning.

- **Alignment** Specify where you want the browser to position the movie. Left and Right position the movie at the left or right page margin and wrap any adjacent text around it. The remaining settings position the movie vertically, relative to any surrounding text.
- **Border Thickness** Specify the thickness of a border that will surround the movie. For no border, specify zero.
- **Horizontal Spacing** Specify how much blank space should appear to the left and right of the movie.
- **Vertical Spacing** Specify how much blank space should appear above and below the movie.

The Size settings control the screen space the movie will occupy:

- **Specify Size** Select this check box to control the amount of screen space available to the movie. Clear it to display the movie at its original size.
- **Width** Specify how wide you want the movie to appear. This can be a specific number of pixels or a percentage of available space.
- **Height** Specify how tall you want the movie to appear. Again, this can be in pixels or a percentage.
- **Keep Aspect Ratio** Select this check box if you want FrontPage to adjust the Height box when you change the Width box (or vice versa). This preserves the movie's original proportions.

Clicking the General tab of the Movies In Flash Format Properties dialog box displays the controls shown in Figure 26-19.

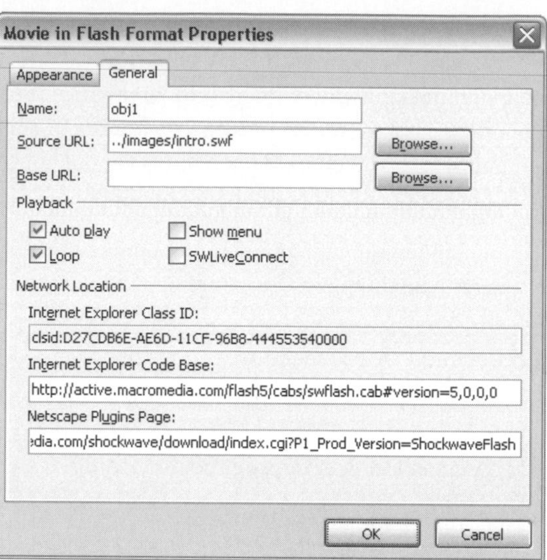

Figure 26-19. This tab configures the name, location, and other attributes of a movie in Flash format.

Here's an explanation of each one:

- **Name** Specify a name suitable for referencing the movie programmatically (for example, from Behavior actions). This name will become the movie's *id* attribute.
- **Source URL** Specify the location of the movie file, relative to the folder where the Web page resides. To locate the file graphically, click the accompanying Browse button.
- **Base URL** Specify a base folder that applies to relative path statements in the movie. If you leave this setting blank, the player will look for auxiliary files in the same folder as the movie itself. Click the accompanying Browse button to locate this folder graphically.
- **Playback** Use these settings to control how the movie plays:
  - **Auto Play** Select this check box if you want the movie to start playing automatically.
  - **Loop** Select this check box if you want the movie to continually repeat itself.
  - **Show Menu** Select this check box to display a full menu of options the Web visitor can use to enhance or control playback. This menu appears when the visitor right-clicks the movie.
  - **SWLiveConnect** Select this check box to enable communication in Netscape Navigator between the Flash plug-in and JavaScript.
- **Network Location** Use these settings to specify the location of Flash Player components:
  - **Internet Explorer Class ID** Identify the ActiveX control that the browser should use. FrontPage supplies a default that you probably shouldn't override.

- **Internet Explorer Code Base** Specify a download location that the browser can use to install the Flash Player ActiveX control (provided, of course, that the control isn't already installed on the Web visitor's computer).
- **Netscape Plugins Page** Specify a download location for the Flash Player plug-in. The browser can use this if the Web visitor's computer lacks the plug-in.

Incorporating Plug-Ins

A *plug-in* is a piece of software that takes over a section of the browser window and displays something in it. Usually the display is from a file obtained from the Web server, and most often it's some kind of multimedia file. Netscape Communications originally devised plug-ins, and Internet Explorer now supports them. Plug-ins generally aren't as configurable (with HTML) as other approaches to multimedia, but support by both browsers is a strong point. Displaying a given file with a plug-in requires three things:

- The file has to be specially marked in the HTML.
- When the Web server delivers the file, it must properly identify the file type.
- The Web visitor's browser must have a plug-in available for the given file type.

Some plug-ins come with the browser itself. Web visitors can install more from various Internet sites. In general, a Web designer doesn't know which, if any, plug-in software will process a given file type. This can vary considerably, depending on the type of computer, the type of browser, and the browser's configuration.

FrontPage can't install plug-ins on the Web visitor's browser or perform browser configurations. It can, however, flag files in a Web page for plug-in processing. To begin:

1. Choose Web Component from the Insert menu, or click the Web Component button on the Standard toolbar.
2. In the Component Type list, select Advanced Controls.
3. In the Choose A Control list, choose Plug-In.
4. Click Finish to display the Plug-In Properties dialog box, shown in Figure 26-20. This figure shows some typical values filled in.

When the Plug-In Properties dialog box appears, all its options are blank or set to their defaults. Supply the following properties as required:

- **Data Source** Specify the relative or absolute URL of the file that the plug-in should process, or click the Browse button to locate the file.

  Although FrontPage accepts a blank value in this text box, telling the browser to process a missing file name as a plug-in is rather pointless. Therefore, you should consider this option mandatory.

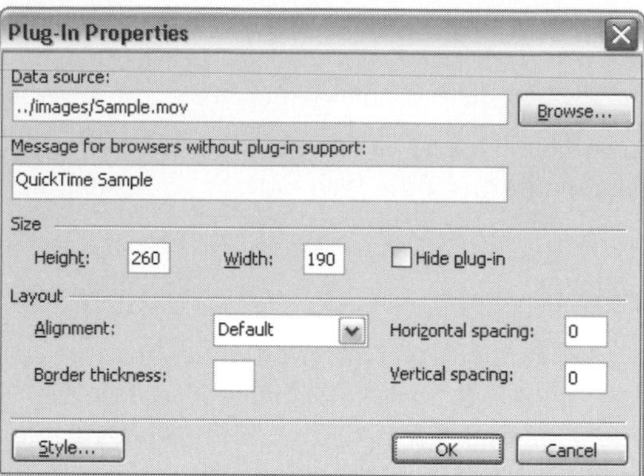

Figure 26-20. This dialog box creates instructions for the browser, telling it to display the named file using a plug-in.

- **Message For Browsers Without Plug-In Support** Supply any text you want to appear if the browser doesn't support plug-ins. For example, if the plug-in displays a clown saying "Hello," you might enter **A clown says Hello**.
- **Size** Specify how much window space the plug-in should consume:
  - **Height** Specify a height in pixels. You can also modify this property by selecting the plug-in in Design view and dragging its handles.
  - **Width** Specify a width in pixels. This is another property you can modify by dragging the plug-in's handles in Design view.
  - **Hide Plug-In** Select this check box if you don't want the plug-in to occupy any window space. This can be appropriate for nonvisual files such as sound clips.
- **Layout** Specify how you want the plug-in to appear on the Web page:
  - **Alignment** Specify how the browser should position the plug-in relative to surrounding text. This works just as Chapter 10 described for picture placement.
  - **Border Thickness** Specify the thickness, in pixels, of a black border that will surround the plug-in. For no border, specify zero.
  - **Horizontal Spacing** Specify the number of pixels that should separate the plug-in from the nearest left and right elements on the same line.
  - **Vertical Spacing** Specify the number of pixels that should separate the plug-in from the nearest elements above and below it.

For more information about picture placement, refer to "Modifying Size and Placement Properties," on page 274.

- **Style** Click this button to apply CSS properties to the plug-in display.

Figure 26-21 shows Netscape Navigator using a plug-in to display the AVI file configured in Figure 26-20.

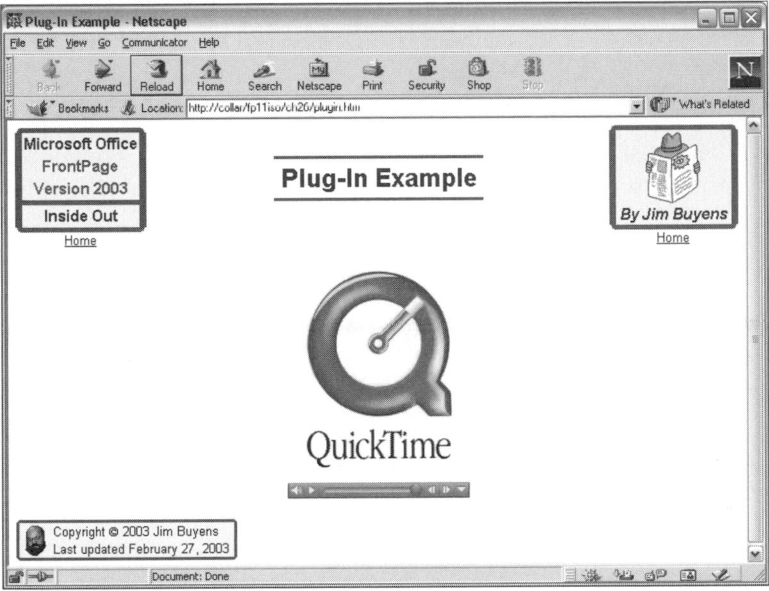

Figure 26-21. Netscape Navigator uses a plug-in to display the MOV file configured in Figure 26-20.

Troubleshooting

Plug-in doesn't play correctly in browser

A common plug-in problem involves MIME types. The file type a browser uses for selecting a plug-in usually isn't a file extension; it's a MIME type that the Web server assigns. The MIME type for an AVI file, for example, is usually *video/x-msvideo*. Correctly displaying the file requires a two-step translation:

1. The Web server translates the file extension to a MIME type.
2. The browser uses the server-supplied MIME type to select a plug-in.

For more information about MIME types, refer to "MIME Types and Other Curiosities," in Appendix N. For information about configuring MIME tables in Microsoft Web servers, refer to Appendix O, "Installing and Configuring a Web Server."

Incorrect Web server configuration is a common cause of plug-in files that fail to appear properly. After eliminating browser configuration as the source of a problem, ask the Web server's system administrator to check the server's MIME type table. Be sure to provide the file extensions you're using and the MIME type you'd like assigned.

Displaying a Marquee

The Marquee component displays a line of text that scrolls automatically across the browser window. Browsers lacking built-in marquee support display the marquee text statically.

To add a marquee to your Web page:

1. Open the page in FrontPage.
2. To convert existing text to a marquee, select the text. To create a marquee that uses new text, just set the insertion point where you want the marquee to appear.
3. Choose Web Component from the Insert menu.
4. Make sure that Dynamic Effects is selected in the Component Type box on the left, and then select Marquee from the Choose An Effect list on the right. Click Finish to display the Marquee Properties dialog box, shown in Figure 26-22.

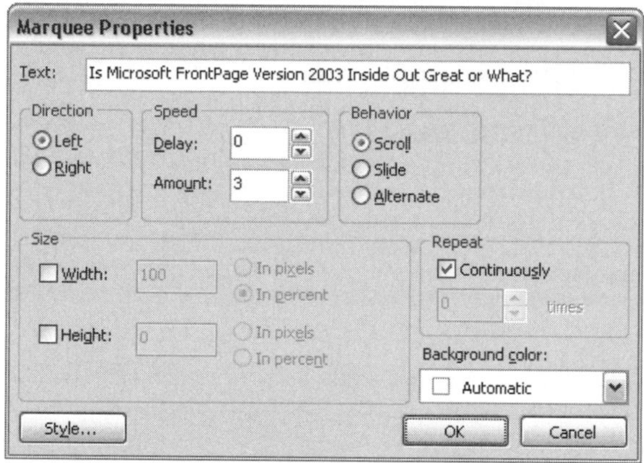

Figure 26-22. This dialog box configures a FrontPage marquee.

5. Configure the marquee by setting the dialog box options as described below, and then click OK.

Inside Out

Distracting Attention with Marquees

Use of the marquee has fallen out of favor because no single rate of scrolling is right for all Web visitors, and because the constant motion distracts the visitor from other content. Use of marquees on Web pages has therefore dropped to near zero. If you want your Web site to have a professional appearance and deliver a satisfying experience, you should probably avoid using this component.

The Marquee Properties dialog box provides the following options:

- **Text** Specifies the message that the marquee animates. Any text you selected before starting the marquee command appears here.
- **Direction** Controls how the marquee text moves—toward the left (the usual choice) or toward the right.
- **Speed** Controls how quickly the marquee moves:
  - **Delay** The number of milliseconds between each motion of the marquee.
  - **Amount** How many pixels the marquee shifts in each step.
- **Behavior** Determines the type of motion:
  - **Scroll** Advances the marquee continuously across the screen in accordance with the Direction setting. Motion continues until the trailing edge of the text reaches the end of the marquee area.
  - **Slide** Like Scroll, advances the marquee continuously across the screen. Motion continues until the leading edge of the text reaches the end of the marquee area, where it stops.
  - **Alternate** Moves the marquee text back and forth within the available area. In this method the marquee text is always completely visible, for maximum impact.
- **Size** Determines the screen area occupied by the marquee:
  - **Width** Controls the marquee's horizontal dimension. The default is to occupy all available width: the entire browser window, table cell, frame, or other container.

  To choose a specific width, select the check box, enter a value, and then indicate the unit of measure as either pixels or percent.
  - **Height** Controls the marquee's vertical dimension. The default is to accommodate only the marquee text, including its formatting.

  To choose a specific height, select the check box, enter a value, and then indicate the unit of measure as either pixels or percent.
- **Repeat** Controls how often the marquee redisplays the moving text:
  - **Continuously** Means that the marquee continues moving text as long as the visitor's browser displays the Web page.
  - **Times** Specifies how many times the marquee effect repeats.

Caution If you specify the Behavior setting as Scroll and then set Repeat to a specific number of times, little or no text might be visible in the marquee area when movement stops.

- **Background Color** Gives the marquee its own background color. The default is the Web page's background color.
- **Style** Assigns CSS attributes to the marquee.

To modify an existing marquee, either select it and choose Properties from the Format menu, or right-click it and choose Marquee Properties from the shortcut menu. To change a marquee's font, font size, text color, or other text properties, either select the marquee and use the normal format menus, or open the Marquee Properties dialog box and click Style to apply CSS attributes.

Figure 26-23 shows a marquee in an Internet Explorer browser window. Assigning a Behavior setting of Scroll makes the text scroll from behind the icon on the right, travel across the screen, and then disappear behind the icon on the left. This effect results from placing the two icons and the marquee in the left, right, and center cells of a one-row, three-column table.

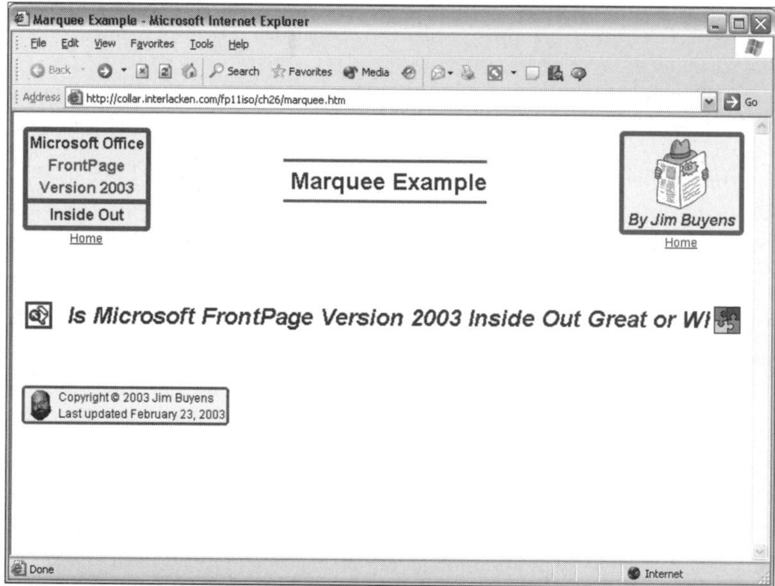

Figure 26-23. The marquee in this Web page scrolls from behind the icon on the right and then disappears behind the icon on the left.

In Summary...

FrontPage features a number of exciting animated elements to spice up your Web pages. Using components such as hover buttons, page transitions, and DHTML effects, you can make your pages look like you spent a million dollars on technology.

The next chapter describes components that use information from a FrontPage-based Web to generate Web content.

Chapter 27

Displaying Derived Content

Wouldn't it be great if you didn't have to create your own Web content? What if Microsoft Office FrontPage 2003 could do it for you? Well, that's exactly what the components described in this chapter endeavor to do.

Of course, these components don't really create new content; they merely derive it from other content. The Hit Counter component displays a number that increases by 1 each time a visitor requests your page. The Date And Time component reports the date and time when you, someone else, or an automated process updated a Web page. The Table Of Contents For This Web Site component creates a table of contents based on an analysis of hyperlinks in your Web site. The Table of Contents Based On Page Category component creates a table of contents based on category codes you assign to your Web pages.

Using the Hit Counter Component

Simple hit counters are a favorite way to measure visits to a given Web page—and to publicly brag (or moan) about the results. Hit counters involve three components:

- A count kept in a small file on the Web server. For FrontPage, this is a file in the _private folder of your Web site.
- A program on the Web server that increments the count and creates a displayable version for output. For FrontPage, this is part of Microsoft Windows SharePoint Services or the FrontPage Server Extensions.
- HTML that triggers the server-side program and indicates where to insert the displayable output. This is what the Hit Counter component in FrontPage creates.

Figure 27-1 shows a page displaying a typical FrontPage hit counter. The displayed count is actually a picture whose source—rather than being a GIF or JPEG file—is a program that increments a count and generates data in GIF format. Each execution of the program increments the count by 1 until you reset the counter.

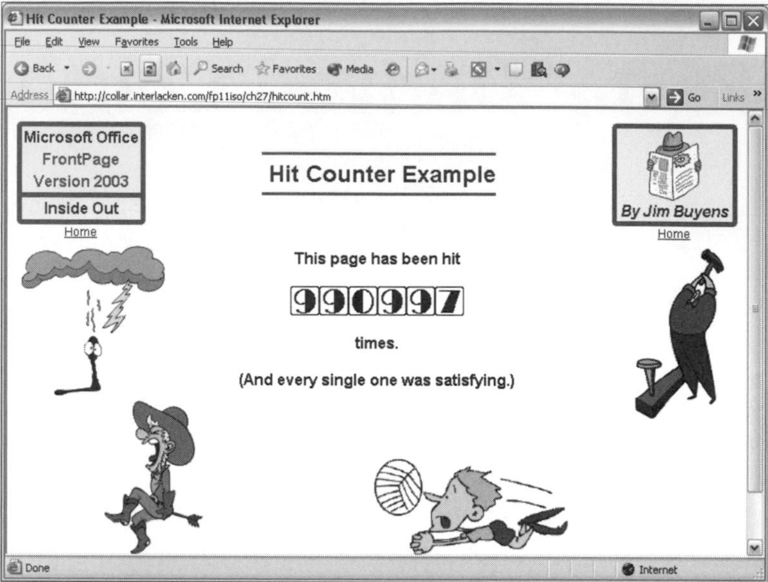

Figure 27-1. Show Web page activity using the FrontPage Hit Counter component.

Adding a hit counter to your page is enjoyable, simple, and rewarding. Here's the procedure:

1. Choose Web Component from the Insert menu.
2. In the Insert Web Component dialog box, select Hit Counter in the Component Type list that appears on the left, and the select the hit counter appearance you want from the Choose A Counter Style list on the right.
3. Click Finish to display the Hit Counter Properties dialog box, shown in the foreground of Figure 27-2.

To configure the options in the Hit Counter Properties dialog box, proceed as follows:

- **Counter Style** Select the style of digits that will display the hit count.
- **Custom Picture** Select this option to specify a digit style you designed or obtained yourself. Specify a file location relative to the root of your FrontPage-based Web site, such as /images/decocnt.gif. This should be a picture file containing the digits 0 through 9, in left-to-right order. The hit counter will use the leftmost 10 percent of this picture to represent 0, the next 10 percent to represent 1, and so forth. Obviously, the width of the entire picture should be a multiple of 10 pixels.

> **Tip** **Create a Hit Counter Only You Can See.**
>
> To create an invisible hit counter, specify a custom picture that's completely transparent or the same color as the background of your Web page. To view the counts accumulated by such a counter, refer to Insider Extra 12, "Accessing Hit Counts with Scripts."

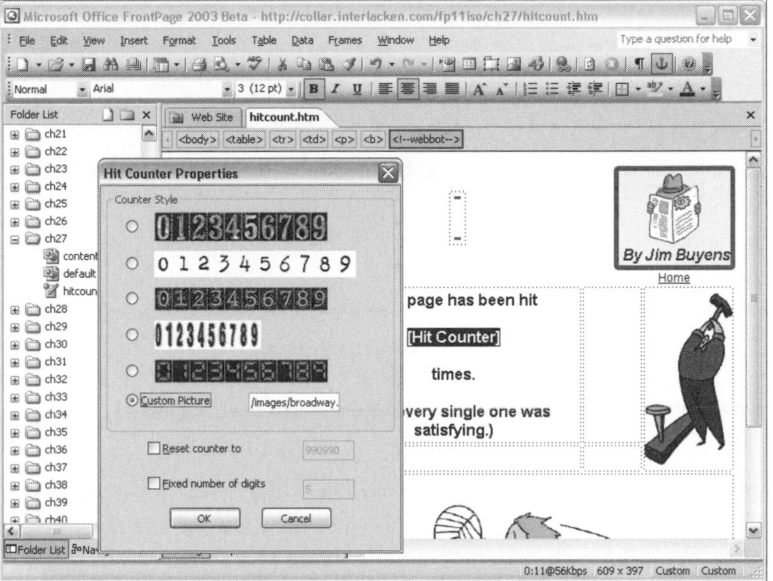

Figure 27-2. Use this dialog box to create or configure your hit counter.

- **Reset Counter To** Select this check box to set or reset the hit counter's starting value. To set a new start value, select the check box, specify the new starting count, and then save the Web page.

> **Tip** **Avoid Resetting a Hit Counter Accidentally**
>
> After resetting the counter to a new value, save the page, clear the Reset Counter To check box, and save again. Otherwise, FrontPage will keep resetting the counter every time you save the page.
>
> When FrontPage publishes a Web site, it doesn't copy hit counts from the local Web site to the remote Web site. Therefore, to reset hit counts on the remote Web site, you must open it in FrontPage and reset the counter yourself.

- **Fixed Number Of Digits** Select this check box to control how many digits the counter will display. If the check box is cleared, FrontPage displays as many digits as necessary to represent the count without leading zeros. If the check box is selected, FrontPage always displays the number of digits you specify.

FrontPage doesn't display hit counters interactively; instead, as you can see in the background in Figure 27-2, it simply displays the text *Hit Counter*. To see the hit counter in action, view the page in your browser, using an http:// URL.

As usual, there are four ways to display the Hit Counter Properties dialog box for an existing hit counter:

- Double-click the Hit Counter component.

- Right-click the counter, and then choose FrontPage Component Properties from the shortcut menu.
- Select the counter, and then choose Properties from the Format menu.
- Select the counter, and then press Alt+Enter.

If the counter doesn't work, the problem usually lies on the Web server. Verify that all of the following are true:

- Either Windows SharePoint Services or the FrontPage Server Extensions are installed. If they aren't, ask your server administrator to install them. If you administer the Web server yourself—perhaps because it runs on your own computer—try using the FrontPage Server Health features on the server or reinstalling the FrontPage Server Extensions.
- Anonymous visitors have security permission to execute the server extensions, as well as to update the _private directory in your Web.
- The hidden folder /_vti_bin in your Web site contains a program named fpcount.exe, and that the folder is executable by anonymous visitors.

Note In some versions of the FrontPage Server Extensions, the /_vti_bin folder physically resides within each Web site. For others, the /_vti_bin folder in each Web site is only a pointer to a single shared copy of all the programs.

For more information about installing and configuring the FrontPage Server Extensions, refer to Chapter 50, "Understanding the FrontPage Server Extensions." For more information about FrontPage security, refer to "Controlling Web Site Security Through FrontPage," on page 1146.

Troubleshooting

Can't add multiple hit counters to a single page

When you add multiple hit counters to a single page, one of the following situations could occur:

- If you use the same counter style, both hit counters display the same number.
- If you use different styles, each hit counter increases once per page hit. If a page contains two hit counters, they'll display 1 and 2 on the first page hit, 3 and 4 on the second hit, and so forth. As to which counter increases first, this is random.
- Resetting the counter on one Hit Counter component resets the counter on any other Hit Counter components on the same page to the same number.

The Hit Counter component in FrontPage isn't designed for multiple uses on a single page. To resolve such problems, use only one hit counter per page.

Using the Date And Time Component

The Date And Time component displays the date anyone (or any FrontPage process) last saved a page. FrontPage maintains these dates automatically, and they don't necessarily correspond to the file system date of the page.

To insert a Date And Time component, set the insertion point, and then choose Date And Time from the Insert menu. Figure 27-3 shows the Date And Time dialog box that appears.

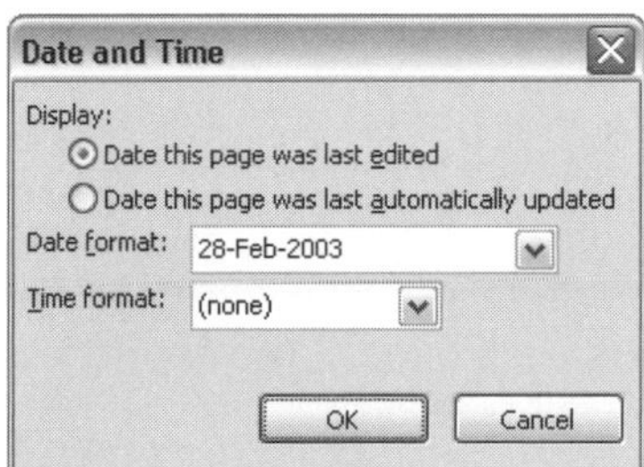

Figure 27-3. This dialog box configures the Date And Time component.

To modify the appearance of a Date And Time component, configure the following options in the Date And Time dialog box:

- **Display** Use this group of controls to specify which date to display:
  - **Date This Page Was Last Edited** Select this option to display the date you or someone else last saved the page with FrontPage.
  - **Date This Page Was Last Automatically Updated** Select this option to display the date a page last changed because of either manual editing or automatic updating caused by a change elsewhere in your Web site.
- **Date Format** Select a date format or (none) from the drop-down list.
- **Time Format** Select a time format or (none) from the drop-down list.

> **Tip** Avoid date formats that use numbers for months. The expression 2/10/2004 means February 10 in some parts of the world and October 2 in others.

A common use for the Date And Time component is to indicate a version date at the bottom of a Web page.

Frequently Asked Question

How can I make a Web page display its file system date?

The following script displays the date and time of the last update to a file as indicated in the Web server's file system:

```
<script language="JavaScript">
<!--
document.write(document.lastModified)
// -->
</script>
```

To use this script in a Web page, follow these steps:

1. Open the page in Design view.
2. Set the insertion point where you want the date to appear.
3. Click the HTML tab at the bottom of the Design view window, and make sure that the insertion point isn't inside another HTML tag.
4. Enter the script as just shown.
5. Click the Normal tab at the bottom of the Design view window.

This script, like any other, won't execute in FrontPage. To see it display a date, switch to Preview mode or load the page into a browser.

This technique, by the way, doesn't work correctly with ASP or Microsoft ASP.NET pages. For those page types, the *document.lastModified* property contains the date that the page executed on the Web server, which is usually the current date.

Using the Table Of Contents For This Web Site Component

The Table Of Contents For This Web Site component generates a hyperlinked table of contents based on any starting page in your Web site. The first level of headings reflects all hyperlink targets referenced in the starting page. Below each of these page entries, indented, are its hyperlink targets. This process continues through any number of levels. Each entry is a hyperlink to the page it represents.

The Table Of Contents For This Web Site component lists pages in the current Web site only. Hyperlinks to locations outside the current Web site don't appear. Page titles, and not hyperlink text or file names, identify each listed page. To change the title of a page, open it in Design view, choose Properties from the File menu, and update the Title box.

You can create a Table Of Contents For This Web Site component in either of two ways. The first method adds the component to any new or existing page:

1. Set the insertion point where you want the Table Of Contents For This Web Site component to appear.
2. Choose Web Component from the Insert menu.
3. In the Insert Web Component dialog box, choose Table Of Contents from the Component Type list on the left.
4. Choose For This Web Site from the Choose A Table Of Contents list on the right, and then click Finish.

The second method of creating a Table Of Contents For This Web Site component creates a new page using the Table Of Contents template:

1. Use either of these methods to display the Page Templates dialog box:
   - Choose New from the File menu, and choose Page Or Web. Then, when the New Page Or Web Site task pane appears, click the Page Templates in the Other Templates section.
   - Click the New Page drop-down arrow on the Standard toolbar, and then choose Page.

New Page

2. When the Page Templates dialog box appears, select the Table Of Contents template, and then click OK.
3. When a new page appears in Design view, double-click the Table of Contents For This Web Site component. (Figure 27-5 shows an example of this component.)

Using either of these methods displays the Table Of Contents Properties dialog box, shown in Figure 27-4.

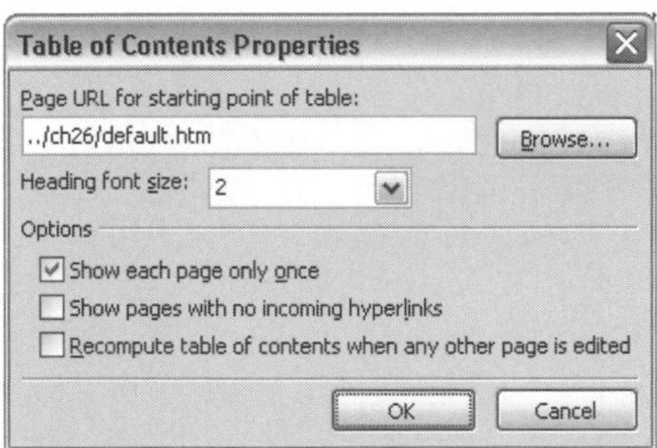

Figure 27-4. This dialog box configures the Table Of Contents For This Web Site component.

To configure a Table Of Contents For This Web Site component, set the controls in the Table Of Contents Properties dialog box as follows:

- **Page URL For Starting Point Of Table** Identify the page whose hyperlinks will become first-level headings in the table of contents, provided those hyperlinks point within the current Web site. To display an entire FrontPage-based Web site, specify its home page.

- **Heading Font Size** Specify a heading style for the table of contents heading. Selecting 1 specifies the Heading 1 style, selecting 2 specifies the Heading 2 style, and so on. The title of the starting-point page provides the heading text.

  To omit the heading, specify None. This is generally desirable when the page that contains the table of contents is also the starting point. The heading, in that case, would represent a page linking to itself.
- **Show Each Page Only Once.** Select this check box to prevent pages from appearing more than once in the table of contents. Clear the check box if you want the table of contents to show a complete list of hyperlinks for each page.
- **Show Pages With No Incoming Hyperlinks.** Select this check box to display any orphan pages at the end of the table of contents. An orphan is a page that can't be reached by clicking any combination of your site's hyperlinks. If this check box is cleared, no orphan pages will appear.
- **Recompute Table Of Contents When Any Other Page Is Edited.** Select this check box to make FrontPage re-create the table of contents every time a page in the Web site changes. This can be time-consuming. If you'd rather re-create the table manually—by opening and saving the Table Of Contents page—leave this box cleared.

Unfortunately, the Design view window shows only a mock-up of the actual table. Figure 27-5 provides an example.

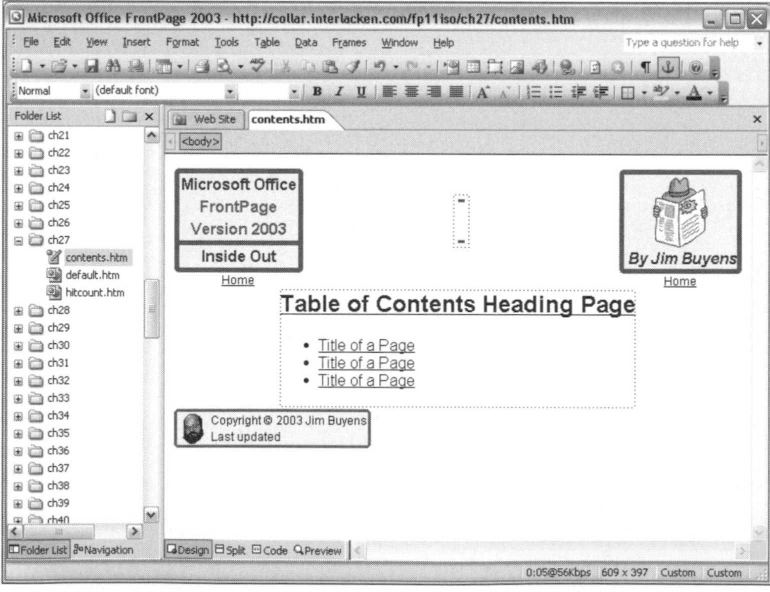

Figure 27-5. The Table Of Contents For This Web Site component appears in FrontPage as a mock-up.

To see the actual table, you must open the page with your browser, as shown in Figure 27-6.

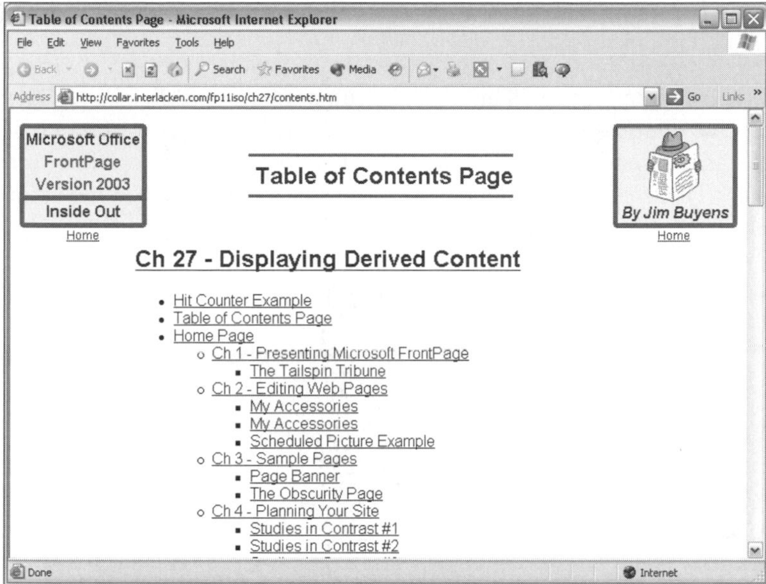

Figure 27-6. A browser displays a Table Of Contents For This Web Site component in full detail.

Inside Out

Relentlessly Correct

Figure 27-6 illustrates one of the most frustrating aspects of the Table Of Contents For This Web Site component. The Web designer told the component to produce a table of contents for the ch27 folder, and in doing so, the component itemized all the pages in the Web site. This was because the starting page ch27/default.htm had a hyperlink to the Web site's home page. There's no real fix for this behavior other than removing the hyperlink to the Web site's home page, an action the designer might rightfully be reluctant to take. Hyperlinks back to the home page are useful things.

This problem isn't limited to links targeting the home page. If you want the Table Of Contents For This Web Site component to produce a useful site map, you must avoid creating any hyperlinks that violate the structure of that map.

A *recursive hyperlink* is any pair of pages with links to each other, such as a home page with a hyperlink to a topic page that contains a hyperlink back to the home page. Not only are recursive hyperlinks possible on the Web, they're common. To avoid infinitely nested entries, the Table Of Contents For This Web Site component stops expanding hyperlinks for any page found subordinate to itself.

The Table Of Contents For This Web Site component has an almost punitive approach to errors, omissions, and tricky approaches. If you've forgotten to give any of your pages meaningful titles, for example, you might find yourself with a table full of pages with names like New Page 3 or with blank entries.

Also, the Table Of Contents For This Web Site component works by analyzing ordinary hyperlinks. Anything ingenious you've done with JavaScript, ASP, or frames is likely to disturb this analysis and produce a table that's, shall we say, surprising. Tossing a Table Of Contents For This Web Site component into your Web site is no substitute for careful organization.

Inside Out

Site Map or Site Mess?

Approach the Table Of Contents For This Web Site component realistically. The concept of automatically creating a site table of contents is appealing, but few sites have pages so tightly organized that they automatically produce a well-organized table of contents. You might find that constructing a table of contents manually is easier than reorganizing your site so that the Table Of Contents For This Web Site component produces satisfactory results.

On the CD

If you're looking for a more automated way of browsing through the content of a FrontPage-based Web site, the techniques in Insider Extra #6, "Scripting Dynamic Menus and Tables of Contents," might provide just the ticket. This Insider Extra describes several Web pages that read, format, and display the file and folder content of a Web site.

Troubleshooting

Applying fonts to a Table Of Contents component has no effect

Using the Font dialog box—which appears after you select Font from the Format menu—to modify a Table Of Contents component has no effect. Both FrontPage and the browser display the table of contents in a default font. (This occurs with both the For This Web Site and Based On Page Category components.)

This occurs because FrontPage uses a variety of HTML tags to format a table of contents and doesn't propagate conventional font attributes to each tag. To work around this problem, set up a CSS style sheet that modifies the tags present within the Table Of Contents component:

- To modify the Table Of Contents heading, use a type selector in the range *H1* through *H6*, corresponding to the Heading Font Size setting you specified in the Table Of Contents Properties dialog box.

  For example, if you specified a Heading Font Size of 2, an *H2* type selector would modify its appearance.
- Use an *LI* type selector to modify the appearance of the individual page listings.

For more information about CSS, refer to Chapter 21, "Managing Appearance with Cascading Style Sheets."

Using the Table Of Contents Based On Page Category Component

Link bars and the Table Of Contents For This Web Site component are two very convenient ways to let FrontPage do the work of connecting pages in your Web site. They both, however, take a rather structured, hierarchical view. Often, the pages you want to group cut across other boundaries, and then you're back to maintaining lists of hyperlinks by hand. Fortunately, the Table Of Contents Based On Page Category component provides an alternative.

Caution The Table Of Contents Based On Page Category component works only with disk-based Web sites and with server-based Websites using the FrontPage Server Extensions version 2000 and later.

Using the Table Of Contents Based On Page Category component is a two-step process:

1. Assign Category codes to all like pages in your Web site. You can define as many of these categories as you want, and you can assign any number of categories (or none) to any page in the same Web site.
2. Wherever you want a list of all Web pages in a certain category, insert a FrontPage Table Of Contents Based On Page Category component. Tell the component what categories to list, and when you save the Web page, FrontPage does the work of finding and listing all pages with matching categories.

To perform the first step—assigning categories to Web pages—follow this procedure:

1 Right-click the page in the Folder List or in Folders view, choose Properties from the shortcut menu, and then select the Workgroup tab. A dialog box like the one shown in Figure 27-7 appears.

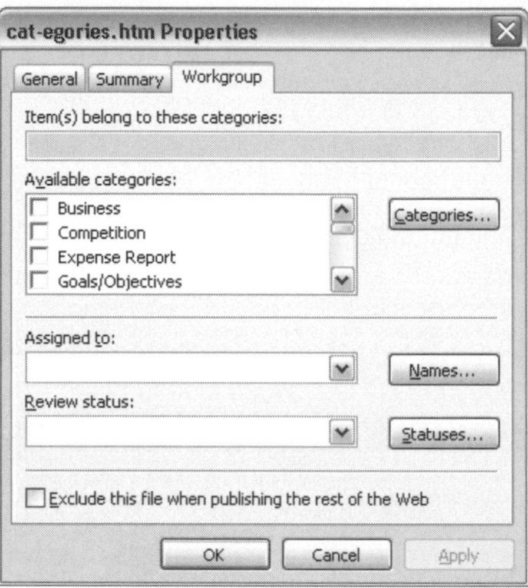

Figure 27-7. Define categories for a file on the Workgroup tab of the Properties dialog box.

Alternatively, open the page in Design view, choose Properties from the File menu, and then click the Workgroup tab. Except for its exterior shape, this tab is identical to the tab shown in Figure 27-7.

2 If the category you want to assign already exists, select its check box in the Available Categories list.

3 If you need to create a new category, click the Categories button to display the Master Category List dialog box, shown in Figure 27-8, and choose from the following options:

- To add a new category, type it in the New Category box, and then click Add.
- To remove a category, select it, and then click Remove.
- To undo all changes made since opening the dialog box, click Reset.
- Click OK to save your changes and exit.

4 After you've selected all the appropriate categories, click OK.

Figure 27-8. Clicking the Categories button shown in Figure 27-7 displays this dialog box, where you can alter the list of valid categories.

To use the category codes you just assigned in a Table Of Contents Based On Page Category component, proceed as follows:

1. Open a Web page and set the insertion point where you want the table of contents to appear.
2. Choose Web Component from the Insert menu.
3. Choose Table Of Contents from the Component Type list on the left in the Insert Web Component dialog box.
4. Choose Based On Page Category from the Choose A Table Of Contents list on the right in the dialog box, and then click Finish.

Figure 27-9 shows the resulting Categories Properties dialog box.

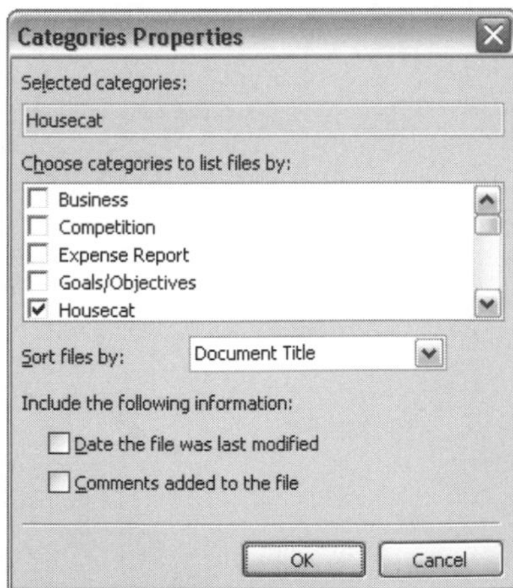

Figure 27-9. The Table Of Contents Based On Page Category component creates a hyperlinked list of all pages in a Web site that are coded with given category codes.

Configure each option in the Categories Properties dialog box in accordance with these instructions:

- **Choose Categories To List Files By** Select the check box for each category you want included in the list of Web pages. If you select multiple check boxes, a match to any one of them will include the page. For example, if you select both the Planning and the Waiting categories, the list will include any Web page coded Planning, Waiting, or both.
- **Sort Files By** Indicate how you want the list sorted: by Document Title or by Date Last Modified. Document Title arranges pages alphabetically from A through Z. Date Last Modified lists the most pages recent first.
- **Date The File Was Last Modified** Select this check box if you want the list of matching pages to include the date someone last modified each page.
- **Comments Added To The File.** Select this check box if you want the list of matching pages to include comments made regarding each page.

> **Note** The comments that the Table Of Contents Based On Page Category component display are those you enter in the Folder List or Folders view. For more information about entering such comments, refer to "Working with Folders View," on page 180

As with the Table Of Contents For This Web Site component, FrontPage displays only a mock-up of the finished Table Of Contents Based On Page Category component. Figure 27-10 provides an example.

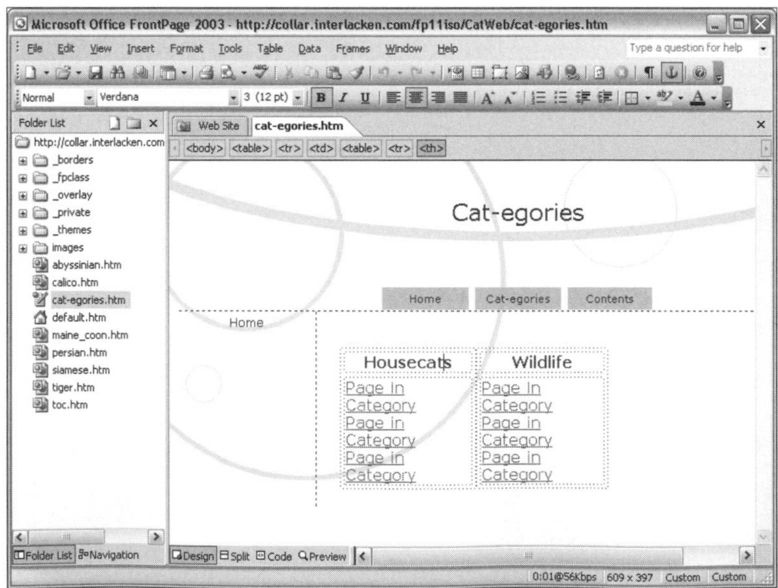

Figure 27-10. Table Of Contents Based On Page Category components appear as mock-ups when FrontPage displays them.

Saving the page and viewing it in a browser displays the actual list, as shown in Figure 27-11.

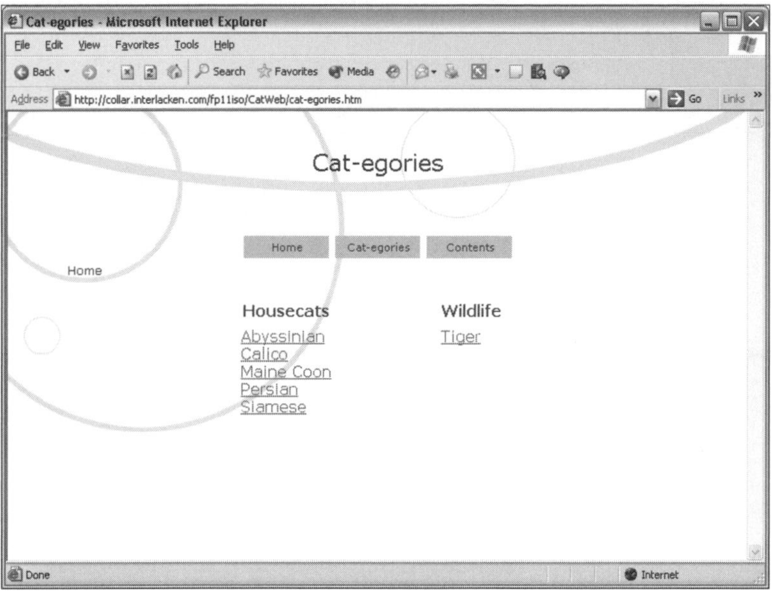

Figure 27-11. Table Of Contents Based On Page Category components appear as expected when you save them in a Web site and display them in your browser.

Table Of Contents Based On Page Category components are great for displaying lists of Web pages selected by product line, responsible person, type of status report, or almost any sort of criteria you can imagine. Any time you need to select and list Web pages, doing so with category codes will almost certainly ease maintenance over time.

Troubleshooting

Table Of Contents Based On Page Category component doesn't reflect new categories you assign to a page

Simply changing the category of a Web page might not update all the Table Of Contents Based On Page Category components in the same Web site. If you encounter this problem, run the Recalculate Hyperlinks command from the Tools menu.

In Summary...

This chapter explained several components that generate Web content based on analysis of information tracked by or contained in a FrontPage-based Web site.

The next chapter explains how to provide a text search capability that Web visitors can use for locating content within your Web site.

Chapter 28

Providing a Text Search Capability

Text searching is one of the most common and popular means for Web visitors to find content on the Web. No matter how well organized a site's Web pages and menus are, some visitors will always prefer entering a few keywords, reviewing a list of matching pages, and cutting to the chase.

This chapter explains several techniques that search all or part of a Web site, an entire Web server, or the entire World Wide Web for given keywords. One of these techniques will almost surely be right for any requirement.

Using the Web Search Component

The Web Search component provides a text search capability for an entire Web server, a single Web site, or a folder tree within a Web site. This makes the Web Search component less powerful than the large Internet search engines, but limited searching has advantages as well:

- If you've done a good job of organizing your Web sites and servers, each Web site represents a specific body of knowledge. Searching that realm might very well be a reasonable thing to do.
- Searching only your Web site limits the opportunities for visitors to wander off and visit other sites.
- If you want to search an entire group of servers, many other tools are available for that purpose. The Search The Web With MSN feature described later in this chapter is a case in point.

An additional limitation of the Web Search component is that it doesn't work on Windows SharePoint Services. On SharePoint sites, you should use the full-text-search component described later in this chapter.

Scanning large numbers of files for every query would simply consume too much time. Fortunately, building an index ahead of time and using it later to satisfy queries are both practical operations. Virtually all full-text search engines therefore use a text index—a database of word locations—to satisfy queries. Microsoft FrontPage uses one of two markedly different text indexes, depending on your Web site's operating environment.

The first text index is a server-based catalog that a service called Microsoft Indexing Service keeps up-to-date. If you have a server-based Web site that runs on a Microsoft operating system and Indexing Service is installed on the same server, FrontPage will use the Indexing Service catalog as its full-text index.

Note In the parlance of Indexing Service, a *catalog* is a database of words and the file locations where they occur. Indexing Service builds the catalog initially by examining every file in a list of folder trees. Subsequently, it rescans any new or changed files and deletes information about files that disappear. A low-priority background task makes all this occur.

In any other case, FrontPage uses its own built-in full-text index. This index has fewer features and more restrictions, but it's more universal. Information later in this chapter will indicate how and when differences between these two indexing techniques affect the Web Search component.

Note Regardless of other settings, searches configured in FrontPage don't search hidden folders (that is, folders whose names begin with an underscore). Such folders aren't available for normal Web browsing.

Performing a Web search requires running a program on the Web server—a program that's part of the FrontPage Server Extensions. Therefore, for the Web Search component to work, the Web page that contains it must be part of a server-based Web, and you must load the page by giving your browser an HTTP URL.

Adding a Web Search Component

You can add a Web Search component to your Web site using two different methods. The first method adds a Web Search component to any new or existing page. This process is much the same as for other Web components:

1. Set the insertion point where you want the Web Search component to appear.
2. Choose Web Component from the Insert menu. This displays the Insert Web Component dialog box.
3. Select Web Search from the Component Type list on the left, and select Current Web from the Choose A Type Of Search list on the right. Click Finish.

The second way to start using the Web Search component involves creating a new page with the Search Page. Here's the procedure for this method:

1. Use either of the following methods—the choice is yours—to display the Page Templates dialog box.
   - Choose New from the File menu. Then, when the New task pane appears, click the More Page Templates link in the New Page section.
   - Click the New Page drop-down arrow on the Standard toolbar, and then choose Page.

2. When the Page Templates dialog box appears, select the Search Page template, and then click OK.
3. When the new page appears in Design view, locate the Web Search component (an HTML form with a Search For box, like that shown in Figure 28-1), and then double-click it.

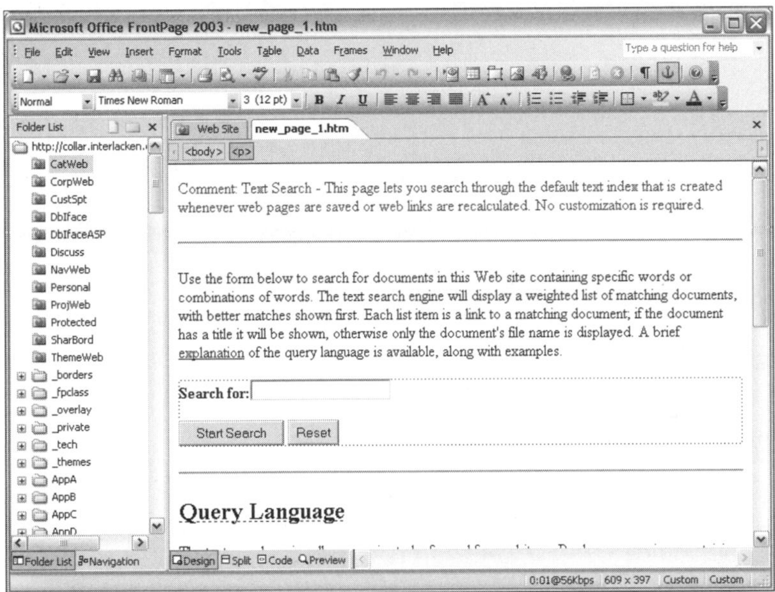

Figure 28-1. The Search Page template produces a Web page like this. The Web Search component is the HTML form containing the Search For box.

Following either procedure opens a two-tabbed dialog box named Search Form Properties. The first tab, shown in Figure 28-2, controls the appearance of the input form.

Here are the available options for controlling the appearance of the input form:

- **Label For Input** Supply the phrase that prompts visitors to enter keywords.
- **Width In Characters** Specify the width, in typical characters, of the text box provided for entering search terms.
- **Label For "Start Search" Button** Supply a caption for the button that initiates the search.
- **Label For "Reset" Button** Supply a caption for the button that reinitializes the search form.

The second tab, Search Results, controls the presentation of items found in the search. There are two versions of this tab: one for IIS running with Indexing Service, and one for all other environments.

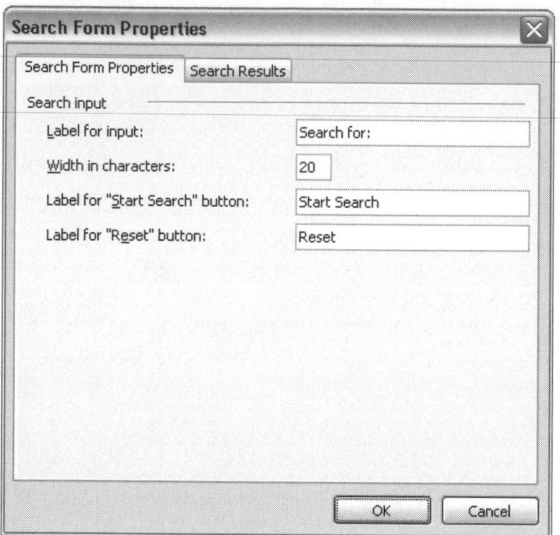

Figure 28-2. Use this dialog box to configure your search page.

Searching with Indexing Service

Figure 28-3 shows the Search Results tab of the Search Form Properties dialog box as it appears when Indexing Service is installed on the computer where a server-based Web site resides.

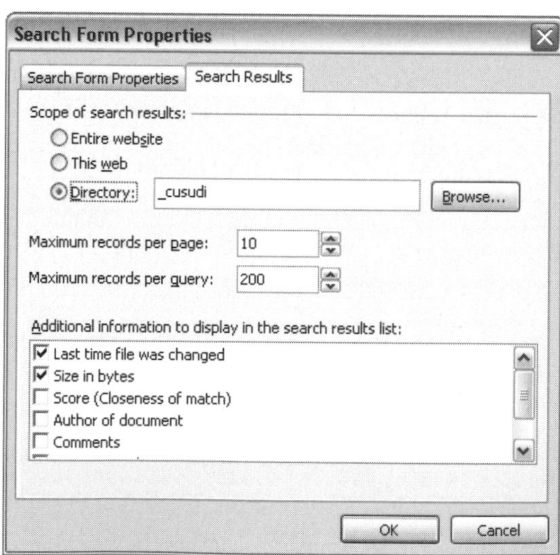

Figure 28-3. This dialog box controls the format of search results when Indexing Service is present.

This tab contains the following options:

- **Scope Of Search Results** Use this group of options to limit the range of Web pages to search:
  - **Entire Website** Select this check box to search the entire Web server where the Web site resides. This includes the root Web site and all other Web sites on the same server.
  - **This Web** Select this check box to search only the current Web site and any subwebs it might have.
  - **Directory** Select this check box to search a single folder (plus its subfolders) in the current Web site. Specify the folder in the text box provided.
- **Maximum Records Per Page** Specify the maximum number of matching pages reported on one page of search output. The visitor must click a Next button to see each additional page of results.
- **Maximum Records Per Query** Specify the maximum number of matching pages reported by an entire search.
- **Additional Information To Display In The Search Results List** Specify what information should be presented with search results. Scroll down for more selections. Here are the options:
  - **Last Time File Was Changed** Select this check box to display the date and time that matched pages were last modified.
  - **Size In Bytes** Select this check box to display the size of each matching page.
  - **Score (Closeness of Match)** Select this check box to display a number indicating match quality.
  - **Author Of Document** Select this check box to display the name of the person who created the document (if known).
  - **Comments** Select this check box to report any notes recorded with each matching file.
  - **Document Subject** Select this check box to report the names of matched documents. For Web pages, this is the title field. (This field and the next don't appear in the figure. To display them, scroll down the Additional Information To Display In The Search Results List.)
  - **Matches** Select this option to report the number of matching documents found.

Indexing Service detects *all* file changes—whether made by FrontPage or by other means—and updates its indexes as soon as the Web server has processing time available. This means that text searches will always be up-to-date, with little or no time lag.

On the CD

If the user interface or the results from the Web Search component don't suit your taste, you might prefer programming your own Web Search page. For more information on this possibility, refer to Insider Extra #7, "Scripting Web Searches."

Troubleshooting

Search returns results from wrong Web site

Searches performed with the Web Search component sometimes return a list of pages from the wrong Web site. This occurs on Web sites that use Indexing Service, and most often on new or physically relocated virtual Web servers. This occurs because the Web Search component is using a different Indexing Service catalog than the one that indexes the current Web site. Here's how to resolve this problem:

1. Open the Web site where the problem occurs, choose Recalculate Hyperlinks from the Tools menu, and then click Yes. Try the search again after the recalculation is complete.
2. If the problem persists, ask the server administrator to verify that an Indexing Service catalog exists for your virtual Web server:
   - If it doesn't, ask the administrator to create one. Microsoft Knowledge Base article 203796, "Configuring FrontPage 2000 to Search Using Index Server," provides instructions.
   - If it does, ask the administrator to reapply the catalog to the virtual Web server. Consult Microsoft Knowledge Base article 214835, "Search Returns Results From Wrong Web," if necessary.

   In either case, ask the administrator for the name of the catalog and its starting location.
3. Repeat step 1.
4. If the problem persists, gain file system access to the area where the problem Web site resides. Locate the Web site's root folder, and then look for a subfolder named _vti_script. Use Notepad to examine any files in this folder that have a file extension of .idq. If you find any line that begins *cicatalog*= and doesn't point to the starting location identified in step 2, correct it and save the file.

For more information about configuring Indexing Service, refer to "Configuring Home Directory Settings," in Appendix O, and "Locating an Indexing Service Catalog," in Insider Extra 7.

Suppose, for example, that you open an IDQ file and discover that it contains the following line:

```
cicatalog=C:\InetPub
```

Any searches performed by this IDQ file will refer to files that reside within the C:\InetPub folder tree. If your Web site doesn't physically reside in this folder tree, the IDQ file will return results from the wrong Web site. If you decide to update the *cicatalog* location, be sure to specify the starting location of an existing catalog.

Normally, FrontPage identifies and inserts the correct catalog name automatically. However, FrontPage doesn't detect changes or make corrections in this area until you run the Recalculate Hyperlinks command. This is the reason for recommending step 1.

Of course, running the Recalculate Hyperlinks command won't help if no suitable catalog exists, or if the registry information for the correct catalog is incomplete. These are the reasons for recommending steps 2 and 3. Step 4 mainly provides information but also provides a manual fix.

Searching with the FrontPage Text Index

If your Web site doesn't reside on a server with Indexing Service installed, the FrontPage Server Extensions use a text index that FrontPage updates incrementally whenever it saves Web pages or en masse whenever it recalculates hyperlinks. Changing a Web site with tools other than FrontPage might therefore result in incorrect search results until someone runs the Recalculate Hyperlinks command.

Note The built-in FrontPage text index uses a public domain technology called Wide Area Information Service (WAIS). If you encounter FrontPage documentation that refers to the WAIS search engine, it means the built-in FrontPage text index.

Within a Web that uses the FrontPage text index, the Search Results tab looks like Figure 28-4. The properties you can configure are different from those available with Indexing Service.

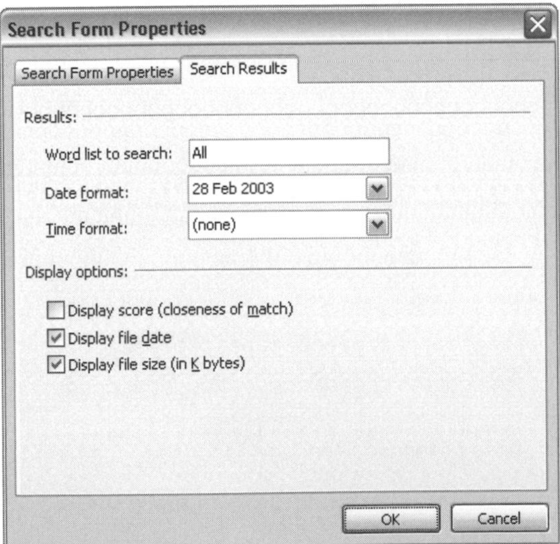

Figure 28-4. This dialog box controls the format of search results not produced by Indexing Service.

The following are the properties you can configure on the Search Results tab:

- **Word List To Search** Specify either All, to search all pages in the current Web site, or the name of a subfolder. For example, to search the contents of a Discussion Web site, you would specify the folder where that Web site resides.
- **Date Format** Specify the format for displaying file dates. This field will be dimmed unless the Display File Date check box is selected.
- **Time Format** Specify the format for displaying file times. This field will be dimmed unless the Display File Date check box is selected.

Tip **Use date formats that don't confuse international visitors.**

It's always best to use 4-digit year, alphabetic month, and 24-hour time formats on the Web. These are less confusing to international visitors. Depending on the country, 01/02/03 can be January 2, 2003; February 1, 2003; or February 3, 2001.

- **Display Score (Closeness Of Match)** Select this check box to display a number indicating match quality.
- **Display File Date** Select this check box to display the date and time that matched pages were last modified.
- **Display File Size (In K Bytes)** Select this box to display the size in KB of each matching page.

Troubleshooting

Search component returns no results

If the FrontPage Web Search component returns no results when you know that matching pages are present, the Web Search component might be trying to use the wrong search engine. This is especially common after publishing the Search page from a server where Indexing Services is present to as server where it's not, or vice versa. To resolve this problem:

1. Use FrontPage to open the Web site where the Web Search component is failing.
2. Open the Web page that contains the failing Web Search component.
3. Display the Search Form Properties dialog box by double-clicking the Web Search component or by right-clicking it and choosing Search Form Properties from the shortcut menu.
4. Review the settings on both tabs of the Search Form Properties dialog box, make corrections if you wish, and then click OK to close it.
5. Save the page, even if you didn't make any changes.
6. Choose Recalculate Hyperlinks from the Tools menu.

If these steps don't resolve the problem, or if running a Web search returns the message *Service is not running*, it's likely that Microsoft Indexing Service is present on the same computer as the Web site but not properly configured. Typical configuration problems include the following.

Indexing Service is installed but not running

To investigate this possibility, proceed as follows:

1. Install the Insiders Extras Web site from the companion CD.
2. Open the Insider Extras Web site, and then copy either of these pages into the failing Web site:
   - The selfdiag.asp page from the selfdiagasp folder.
   - The selfdiag.aspx page from the selfdiagnet folder.

   Before deciding to use the selfdiag.aspx page, make sure that the Web server has the Microsoft .NET Framework installed. If you're not sure about this, just use the selfdiag.asp page from the selfdiagasp folder.
3. Run the Web page you copied in step 2, taking care to specify an *http://* URL. Figure 28-5 shows some typical results.

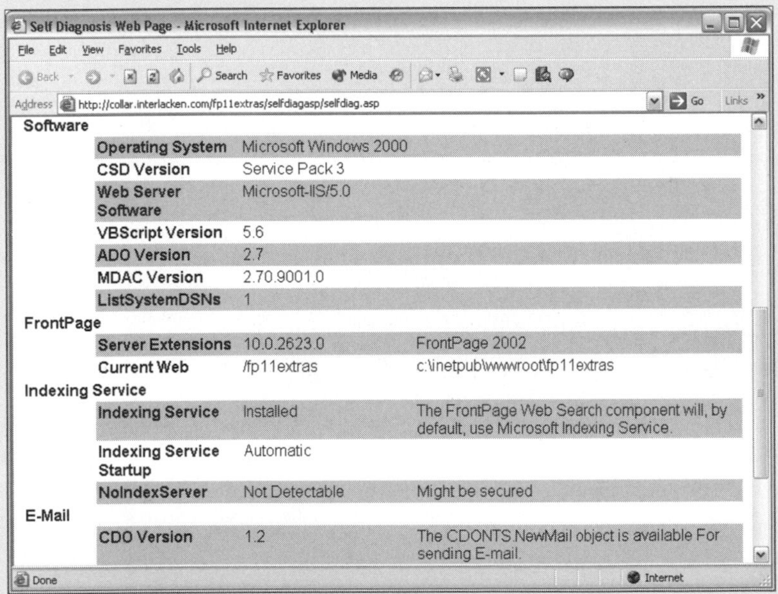

Figure 28-5. The Self Diagnosis Web Page in Insider Extras #1 and #2 can be useful in diagnosing Web Search Component problems.

4. Inspect the Indexing Service line. The information that appears to the right of this title can have four possible values:
   - **Unavailable** This indicates that Indexing Service isn't installed. The Web Search component will use the built-in FrontPage search engine.

- **Installed** This indicates that Indexing Service is installed, but that—most likely for security reasons—the self-diagnosis Web page can't determine whether it's running.
- **Running** This indicates that Indexing Service is installed and running.
- **Stopped** This indicates that Indexing Service is installed but not running.

In the latter three cases, the Web Search component will use Indexing Service unless a registry value named *noindexserver* has a value of *1*. This value appears two lines down, to the right of the noindexserver line.

If Indexing Service is installed, not running, and the *noindexserver* registry entry is absent or equal to anything but 1, the Web Search component will try to use Indexing Service and fail.

5 Inspect the Indexing Service Startup line. The value to the right of this title shows whether Indexing Service is configured to start automatically when the Web server boots:

- **Not Detectable** This indicates that the self-diagnosis Web page—probably because of security restrictions—can't determine the startup status for Indexing Service.
- **Automatic** This indicates that the computer will try to start Indexing Service each time it boots. This means that Indexing Service will normally be available.
- **Manual** This indicates that the computer won't try to start Indexing Service when it boots. This usually means that Indexing Service won't be available.
- **Disabled** This setting prevents Indexing Service from starting, even if another service tries to start it. Again, this means that Indexing Service won't be available.

Indexing Service is installed and running, but it has no catalog that includes your Web site

This possibility is more difficult to investigate, because it requires administrator-level access to Indexing Service. If you have such privileges, refer to these Microsoft Knowledge Base articles which the previous Troubleshooting sidebar also mentioned:

- **203796** Configuring FrontPage 2000 to Search Using Index Server.
- **214835** Search Returns Results From Wrong Web

Insider Extra #7, "Scripting Web Searches," which you can install from the companion CD, also contains information about configuring indexing service catalogs.

Using The Full-Text Search Component

If your Web site runs on Windows SharePoint Services, the Web Search component that the previous section described will be of little use. If you try adding a Web Search component to such a site, you'll receive an error message.

If your site is a SharePoint Team Site, this may be no great loss. The home page and many other standard pages already contain search boxes, and visitors can just use those. If you want to add the same capability to a page you create yourself, proceed as follows.

1. Open the page that should provide a search capability.
2. Set the insertion point where you want the search form to appear. Don't choose a location inside any other form, or inside a Web Part Zone.
3. Choose Web component from the Insert menu, or from the Standard toolbar. This displays the Insert Web Component dialog box.
4. In the Component Type list box at the left, choose Web Search.
5. In the Choose A Type Of Search list box at the right, choose Full-Text Search.
6. Click Finish.

This creates a simple search form like the one Figure 28-6 shows inside the centered box. The page banner, the Enter Search Term prompt, and the centered box, were all present before inserting the Full-Text Search form.

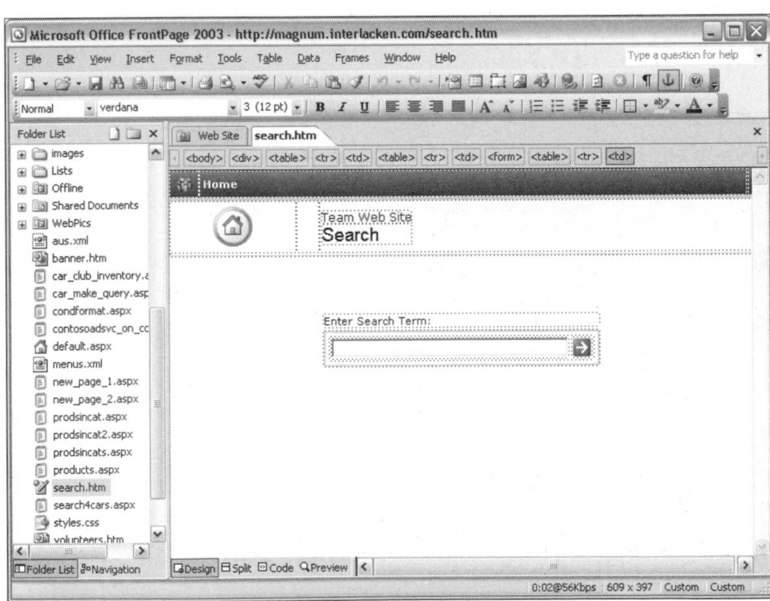

Figure 28-6. Use the full-text search component to create a search form that works on a Windows SharePoint Services site.

The form itself is neither a FrontPage component nor a Web Part. It's an ordinary HTML form that submits the contents of the text box to a SharePoint search program. The arrow button is a standard HTML picture button. In terms of function, the full-text search form works exactly like any other search form you find on a Windows SharePoint Services site.

Searching the Web with MSN

The Search The Web With MSN component displays an HTML form that your visitors can use to search the World Wide Web for a given string. A page that contains this component appears in Figure 28-7.

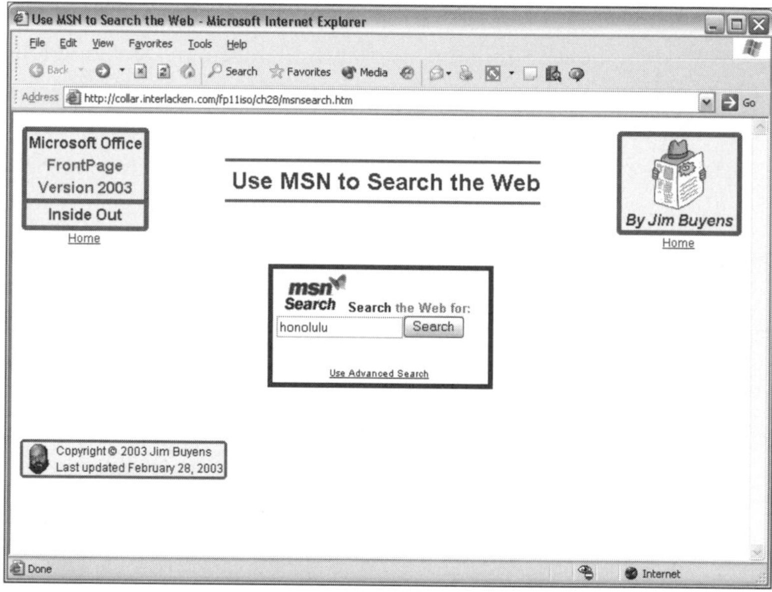

Figure 28-7. The Search The Web With MSN component in the center of this Web page submits search terms to the public MSN search engine. The border around the search form is actually a one-cell table added later.

Entering search terms and clicking the Search button submits a request to the MSN search engine, at *http://search.msn.com*. Figure 28-8 shows some typical results.

Here's the procedure for adding this component to a page in your Web site:

1. Set the insertion point where you want the component to appear.
2. Choose Web Component from the Insert menu. This displays the Insert Web Component dialog box.

3 Select MSN Components from the Component Type list on the left, and select Search The Web With MSN from the Choose A MSN Component list on the right. Click Finish.

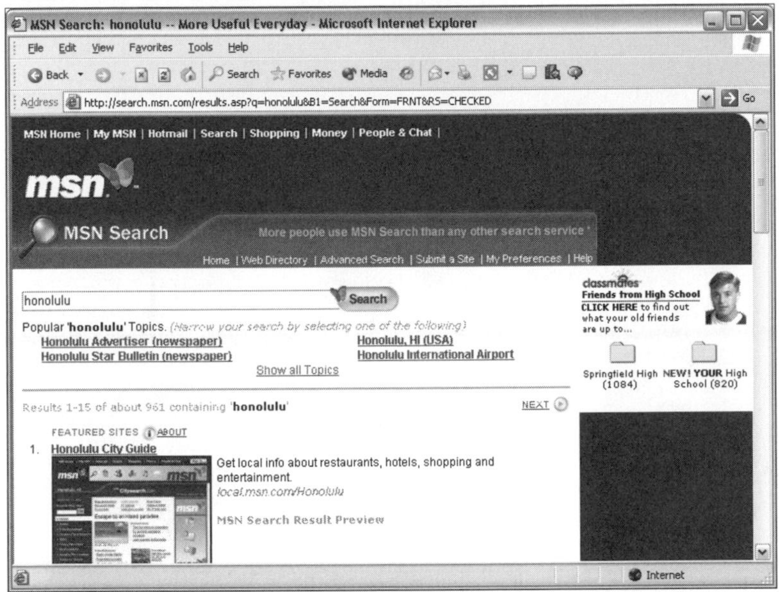

Figure 28-8. Submitting a request using the form shown in Figure 28-7 produced these results.

Unlike most other Web components, Search The Web With MSN doesn't have a persistent identity or a custom dialog box for configuration. Instead, the result of inserting this component is some ordinary HTML that appears in your Web page. Right-clicking this area doesn't offer a Search The Web With MSN Properties choice, for example. Instead, it offers a Form Properties choice that directly configures the properties of the HTML form.

For more information about HTML forms, refer to Chapter 34, "Creating and Using Forms."

Two details of the MSN Search form are critical. As long as you preserve these details, you can modify the MSN Search form as much as you like:

- Submitting the form sends a request to the location *http://search.msn.com/results.asp*, as shown in the Action box of the Options For Custom Form Handler dialog box in Figure 28-9. This is the location of the MSN search engine.
- The *Name* property of the text box for entering the search terms must be *q*. This is the form field name that identifies the list of search terms to the MSN search engine.

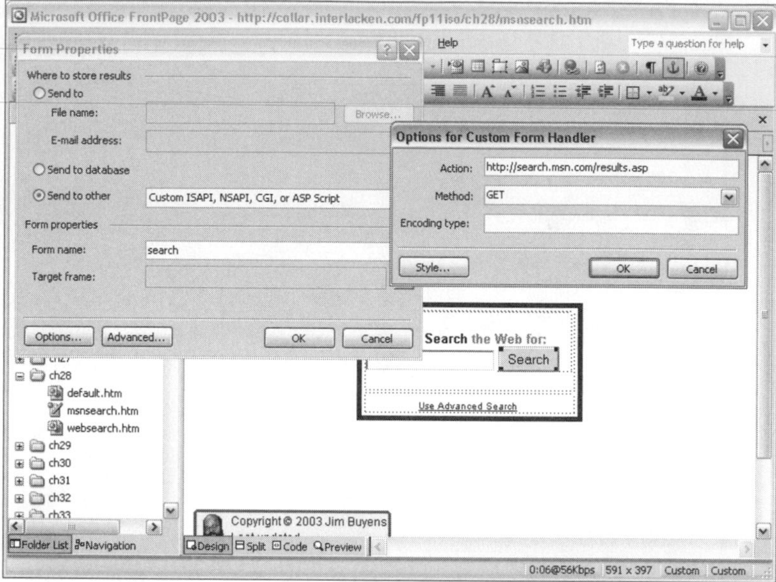

Figure 28-9. The Search The Web With MSN component doesn't have its own Properties dialog box. To configure it, just modify its HTML form properties. If you want, click Options to display the Options For Custom Form Handler dialog box.

One drawback of using this component is that it sends visitors away from your Web site. One minute a visitor is happily browsing your Web site; the next minute, the visitor discovers the MSN Search form; and the minute after that, your visitor is browsing some other site. One way of reducing this effect is to make the MSN search results appear in a new window instead of yours. Here's the procedure:

1. Right-click anywhere in the MSN Search form, and choose Form Properties from the shortcut menu to display the Form Properties dialog box.
2. Click the Target Frame button (the pencil button that appears at the far right of the Target Frame button) to display the Target Frame dialog box.
3. Select New Window from the Common Targets list, and then click OK. Click OK again to close the Form Properties dialog box.

You might want to make a similar change to the Use Advanced Search hyperlink, which also jumps to a page outside your Web site.

> **Tip** **Don't send visitors away!**
>
> Hyperlinks that point outside your Web site are a sure way to lose visitors. Many Web designers therefore avoid such links, or at least open them in a new window. That way, the window displaying the designer's Web site remains on the visitor's desktop and eventually regains the visitor's attention.

In Summary...

This chapter explained several techniques that provide a full-text search capability for visitors to your Web site. This helps visitors find the information they want without traversing a series of hyperlinks.

The next chapter describes some additional components that, like the Search The Web With MSN component, enhance your Web site with real-time information from public sources.

Chapter 29

Organizing Reusable Web Site Content

Most Web sites contain a great deal of repetitive content. This includes standard headers, footers, menu bars, names, dates, and places that occur on multiple pages or perhaps on every page in a Web site. Coding this sort of content into every page is time-consuming and error-prone, and the pages become difficult to maintain over time. Therefore, Microsoft Office FrontPage 2003 provides components that replicate a single copy of whatever content you want in as many pages as you want. This ensures that all copies look the same, and that they remain synchronized whenever you make changes to the original.

The most popular such component is named Include Page. This component copies the contents of one Web page (preferably a short one) into another. Subsequently changing the source page automatically updates all the other pages that include it.

Scheduled Include Page, a closely related component, displays the included content for a period of time specified by the designer. A Scheduled Picture component provides the same service for individual graphical elements.

The Substitution component provides the same service for words, names, and phrases that the Include Page component provides for pages. First you set up a *Site Parameter* that stores any word, name, or phrase as a named constant. The Substitution component can then display those values wherever you want. Changing a Site Parameter automatically updates each Substitution component that uses it.

Shared borders replicate identical content to the top, left, right, or bottom edges of all or selected pages in your Web site. This would be boring and mundane if not for the fact that shared border content can be self-customizing. This means that the content automatically changes depending on the properties of each page that uses the shared border. Web sites organized using Navigation view are the most common place to use shared borders—but there are no restrictions on using them elsewhere if appropriate.

This chapter explains how to use each of these components. Another option for replicating content or formatting to many pages is the Dynamic Web Template feature that Chapter 12 described.

For more information about Using Dynamic Web Templates, refer to, "Using Dynamic Web Templates," in page 322.

Using the Include Page Component

FrontPage's Include Page component merges the content of one Web page into another. This is a very useful feature for coding repetitive page segments once and using them on many pages. The concept is similar to that of boilerplate text in word processing.

Included pages usually contain page segments rather than full-blown page layouts—segments that appear on several or all pages in a site. Including the same segment on several pages guarantees that it will look the same everywhere. Later, if you must change the segment, you'll need to update only one location.

Figure 29-1 shows three typical candidates for the Include Page component.

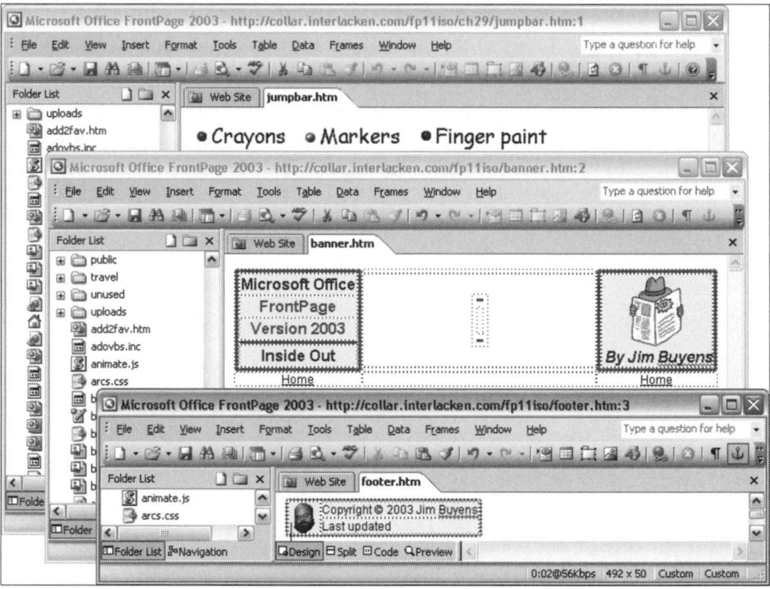

Figure 29-1. FrontPage displays three pages suitable for inclusion in other pages.

You've seen at least two of them before:

- The upper page, named jumpbar.htm, contains a picture with hotspots.
- The middle page, named banner.htm, contains the page banner that appears in most of the Web pages in this book.
- The lower page, named footer.htm, contains the copyright notice that appears at the bottom of most of the Web pages in this book.

> **Tip** **For simultaneous viewing, open pages in separate windows.**
> To view several Web pages simultaneously—each in its own window—start by opening the first page normally. Then right-click each additional page in the Folder List or in Folders view, and choose Open In New Window from the shortcut menu.

Each segment is an ordinary, freestanding Web page, but its primary purpose is to appear as part of other pages. To include a segment in another Web page:

1 Construct the segment as its own page, just as you would any other Web page.

> **Note** The _private folder in a FrontPage-based Web site is an excellent place to keep Web page segments for the Include Page component. This folder (thanks to the leading underscore in its name) is accessible to you while editing but not to Web visitors when browsing.

2 In Design view, open the page that will include the segment.

3 Set the insertion point where the included content should appear.

Web Component

4 Choose Web Component from the Insert menu, or click the Web Component button on the Standard toolbar. This displays the Insert Web Component dialog box.

5 Select Included Content in the Component Type list on the left, and then select Page in the Choose A Type Of Content list on the right.

6 Click Finish to display the Include Page Properties dialog box, shown in Figure 29-2.

Figure 29-2. Specify the page segment to be displayed at the insertion point in your currently open page.

7 Use either of these procedures to complete the Include Page Properties dialog box:

- Click the Browse button, locate the page you want to include, and then click OK to confirm the page selection.
- Type the path and file name directly into the Page To Include box.

8 Click OK to insert the included content in your current page.

> **Tip** When you add an Include Page component to an ASP.NET or Web Part Page, the component may appear correctly in Design view but come up missing when a Web visitor browses your site. If you encounter this problem, use an ASP.NET User Control or a Web Part rather than an Include Page component.

Figure 29-3 shows a Web page that includes all three segment files shown in Figure 29-1. Included content takes on the properties of the page that includes it—background, color scheme, and so forth. The included portions look as though a designer created them directly in the parent page.

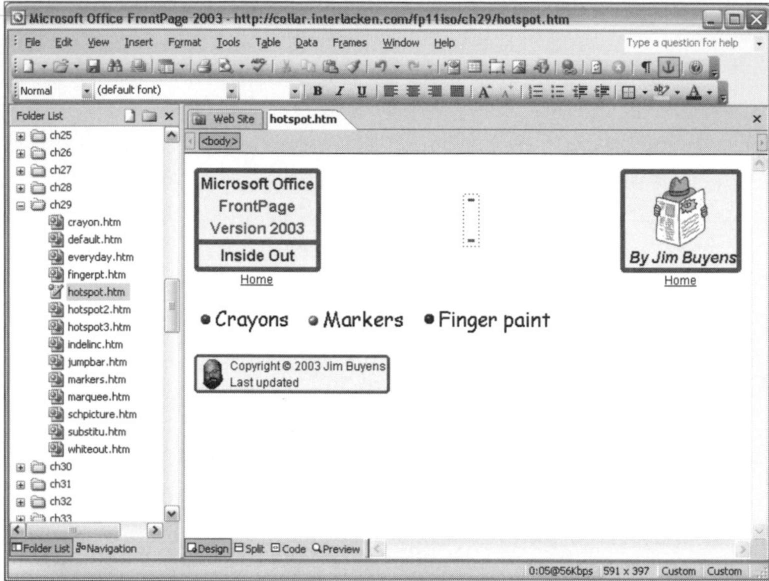

Figure 29-3. Included portions of a Web page take on the look of the parent page.

There's an implied line break before and after every Include Page component (that is, the included content occupies the entire display width and doesn't flow continuously with surrounding content). If this presents a problem, locate the included content in a table cell, or expand the amount of included content. Include entire paragraphs, for example, and not single words. Alternatively, use the Substitution component for words or phrases.

To change the included content, edit the source page. To change the properties of this or any FrontPage component, do any of the following:

- Double-click any area the component occupies.
- Right-click the component, and choose Properties from the shortcut menu.
- Select the component, open the drop-down menu for its <!-- webbot --> tag in the Quick Tag Selector, and choose Tag Properties from the resulting menu.
- Select the component, and then choose Properties from the Format menu.
- Select the component, and then press Alt+Enter.

The Include Page component places a full copy of the included content in each Web page that uses it, for two reasons. First, merging content at browse time would consume more resources on the Web server. Second, merging content at authoring time produces pages that display correctly even if the Web server that delivers them doesn't have the Microsoft FrontPage Server Extensions installed.

Of course, when you update a page that's included in other pages, you expect all the pages to reflect the new content. To accomplish this, FrontPage maintains, for each page, a list of other pages that include it. Then when you save the included page, FrontPage updates all of the host pages.

This indexing information is just the sort of thing you might expect to find in a FrontPage-based Web site. The Include Page component can include only other pages in the same Web site.

Updating an included page without going through FrontPage (or Web Folders, or an HTTP location in My Network Places) won't update FrontPage's various indexes and won't propagate changed pages to others that include them. These are functions of the FrontPage software only. If you make changes to your Web site using means beyond the control of FrontPage, open the Web site in FrontPage, and run the Recalculate Hyperlinks command.

Frequently Asked Questions

How much of a page does the Include Page component actually include?

When an Include Page component merges content into a Web page, it merges only the portion between the included page's <body> and </body> tags. It discards the <body> and </body> tags themselves, plus anything that appears before or after them.

I want to include several noncontiguous but repetitive elements in every page in my Web site. How can I do that?

There are three solutions:

- For each contiguous area, add a separate Include Page component to each Web page.
- If the noncontiguous areas occupy the edges of the Web page, use the Shared Border feature, described later in this chapter.
- Use Dynamic Web Templates. For more information about this feature, refer to "Using Dynamic Web Templates," on page 322.

What are server-side includes?

Most Web servers have a feature called Server-Side Include (SSI) that searches outgoing Web pages for specially formatted comment lines. Each such comment line specifies the name of another file that resides on the Web server. The server transmits the contents of that file instead of the content line. The following statement, for example, replaces itself with the contents of a file named promo.inc, which resides in the parent folder of the current Web page:

```
<!-- #include file="../promo.inc" -->
```

FrontPage neither assists nor resists the use of SSIs. Lack of assistance means that there's no Insert SSI menu anywhere; if you want to add an SSI statement to your Web page, you must do so in Code view. Lack of resistance means that FrontPage will blissfully ignore the SSI and let it remain in place undisturbed.

By default, Microsoft Web servers perform SSI processing only on pages having an .stm or .asp file extension. The .stm extension is the three-letter equivalent of .shtml, which is the extension that usually triggers SSI processing on UNIX-based Web servers.

Note FrontPage isn't the only program that can maintain the integrity of a FrontPage-based Web site while making changes. The Web Folders feature in Microsoft Windows 98, Microsoft Windows Me, and Microsoft Windows NT is actually a front end to parts of FrontPage that correctly update Web sites, as are any HTTP locations that appear under My Network Places in Microsoft Windows 2000 and Windows XP. For more information about this topic, refer to the Frequently Asked Question, "How can programs other than FrontPage safely update a FrontPage-based Web site?" on page 481.

Troubleshooting

Include Page component interferes with other FrontPage features

Because of the way they propagate content, the Include Page component and its close cousin, the Scheduled Include Page component, are occasionally troublesome when used together with certain other FrontPage features. Here are some situations to avoid:

- Don't mix shared borders and Include Page components. For example, don't add Include Page components to shared border areas, and turn off shared borders on any page you're using as a segment to appear in other pages.

  Adding an Include Page component to a shared border sets up a sort of "double include" situation—ordinary pages include the shared border page, and then the shared border page includes the Include Page segment. FrontPage has a history of bugs in this situation—and even if it didn't, this practice can lead to very messy situations, such as pages including themselves.

- Don't use text animations on any page you're using as an included segment. FrontPage will include the page with the text animation, but it won't include the Dynamic HTML script that makes the animation work.

  You can work around this limitation by applying the same animation to something (for example, a space character) on each page that includes the page with the original animation. However, the need to specially configure each page that uses an Include Page component defeats the reason for using the Include Page component at all.

- Put all image maps (pictures with hotspots) in the same physical page.

  Hotspots assign different hyperlink targets to different parts of a single picture. The collection of all such links for a single picture is called an *image map*, and each image map on the same page must have a different name. FrontPage normally assigns unique image map names by numbering them FPMap0, FPMap1, FPMap2, and so forth. However, if an included page and the page that includes it each contain one image map, both image maps will have the name FPMap0, and one of them won't work properly.

Using the Scheduled Include Page Component

Given how often content on the Web changes, it's not surprising that designers frequently need to make scheduled changes. Figure 29-4, for example, shows two Web page segments that might appear on the same page at different times—the upper during January, and the lower during other months.

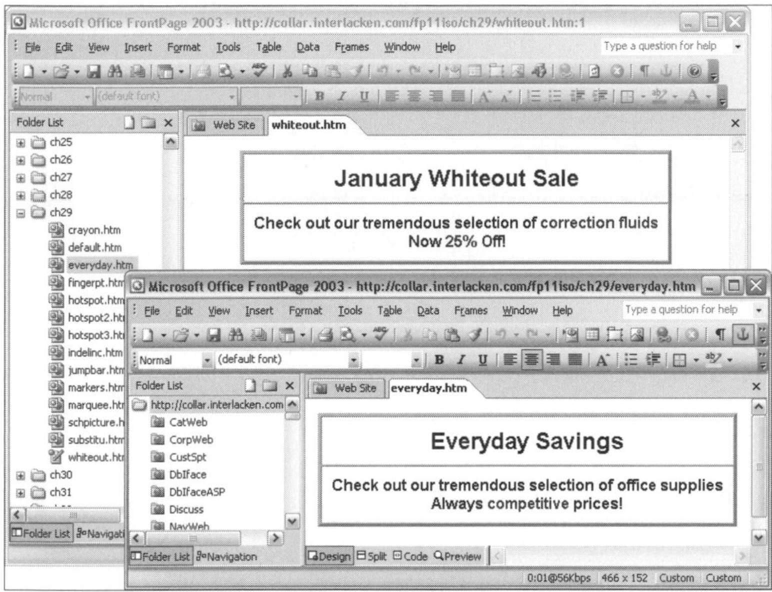

Figure 29-4. Here are two segments that might appear on the same Web page at different times.

FrontPage supports scheduled changes with the Scheduled Include Page component. This component resembles the Include Page component, but adds three features:

- A start date
- A stop date
- An optional URL

Inserting a Scheduled Include Page component is much like inserting an Include Page component:

1. Set the insertion point.
2. Choose Web Component from the Insert menu, or click Web Component on the Standard toolbar. This displays the Insert Web Component dialog box.

Web Component

Chapter 29

3. Select Included Content in the Component Type list on the left, and select Page Based On Schedule in the Choose A Type Of Content list on the right.
4. Click Finish to display the Scheduled Include Page Properties dialog box, shown in Figure 29-5.

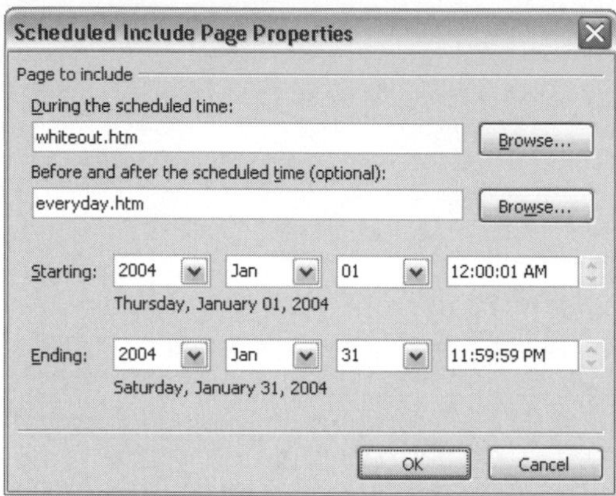

Figure 29-5. This dialog box controls the properties of a Scheduled Include Page component.

Configure the Scheduled Include Page Properties dialog box as follows:

- **Page To Include** Use these two options to specify the Web pages you want to include based on the date and time:
  - **During the Scheduled Time** Enter the Web location of the content you want Web visitors to see during the scheduled period.
  - **Before And After The Scheduled Time (Optional)** Enter the Web location of the content you want Web visitors to see before and after the scheduled period. If you leave this box blank, nothing will appear.
- **Starting** Specify the year, month, day, and time Web visitors should begin seeing the scheduled content. To start showing the content immediately, enter a past date.
- **Ending** Specify the year, month, day, and time Web visitors should stop seeing the scheduled content. To keep showing the content indefinitely, enter a date far in the future.

Figure 29-6 shows Microsoft Internet Explorer displaying the Scheduled Include Page component configured in Figure 29-5.

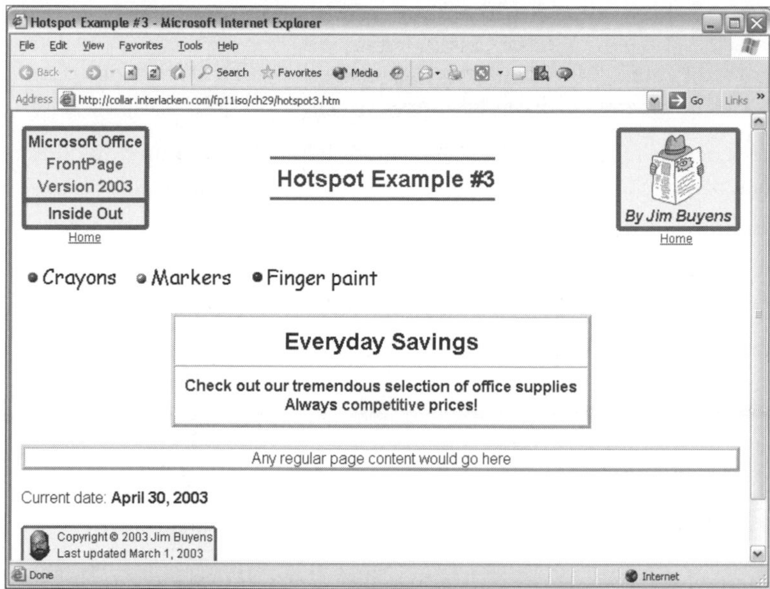

Figure 29-6. This is the Web page configured in Figure 29-5. The everyday.htm segment appears because the current date isn't January 2004.

Troubleshooting

Scheduled Include Page content doesn't change on schedule

The Scheduled Include Page component and the Scheduled Picture component both suffer one nagging flaw: The scheduled change isn't completely automatic. Even on a Web server running the FrontPage Server Extensions, there's no automatic process that inserts, replaces, or removes scheduled content at the given time. To ensure proper timing of Scheduled Include Page components, you must do *either* of the following:

- Make some change to your FrontPage-based Web site every day. (For example, change the value of some configuration variable.)
- Arrange with your server administrator to recalculate hyperlinks in batch mode on a nightly basis.

A scheduled batch file can run the owsadm.exe program to recalculate hyperlinks. For more information about this command, refer to "Administering the FrontPage Server Extensions," Appendix P.

As a practical matter, most Web designers use ASP or JavaScript code to display or hide scheduled content. For information and examples regarding this technique, refer to Insider Extra 6, "Scripting Dynamic Menus and Tables of Contents."

Using the Scheduled Picture Component

The Scheduled Picture component works almost exactly like the Scheduled Include Page component. The differences are as follows:

- The Scheduled Picture component conditionally displays a single picture rather than a block of content.
- Conditionally displayed pictures flow in line with text. There are no automatic paragraph breaks before and after a scheduled picture.

Figure 29-7 shows the Scheduled Picture Properties dialog box. This dialog box and the procedure for invoking it parallel exactly those for the Scheduled Include Page component.

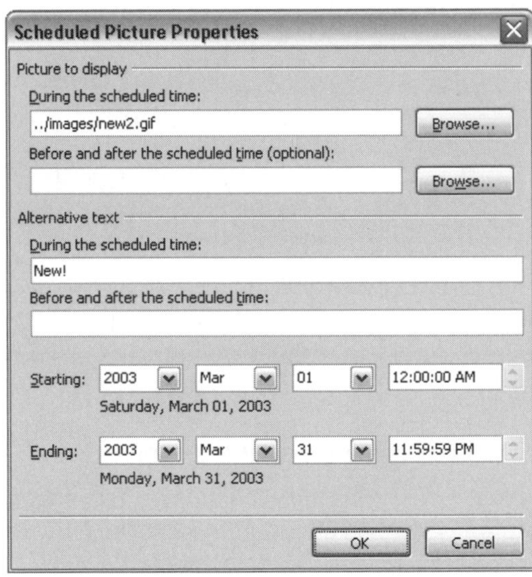

Figure 29-7. This dialog box sets the properties of a Scheduled Picture component.

There are two additional settings, both in the Alternative Text section:

- **During The Scheduled Time** Enter the text you want Web visitors to see in possible lieu of the picture that appears during the scheduled period.
- **Before And After The Scheduled Time** Enter the text you want Web visitors to see in possible lieu of the picture that appears before and after the scheduled period.

If you leave either of these boxes blank, no alternative text will appear. Refer to the previous section for details on the remaining settings.

Scheduled Pictures suffer the same timing nuisance as Scheduled Include Pages; for date changes to take effect, you must initiate a hyperlink recalculation.

Using Site Parameters and the Substitution Component

Site Parameters are commonly occurring character strings you can establish centrally and then reference by name throughout a Web site. Like included page segments, site parameters provide uniformity and eliminate redundant maintenance. If the value of a site parameter changes, you need to update it in only one place.

Suppose, for example, that the names of key people at your site change from time to time. You could:

1. Set up a site parameter for each key position in your organization chart (say, *veepmktg* for your vice president of marketing).
2. Assign each site parameter a value. (Assign *veepmktg* the value *Janet Leverling*, for example, if she's the vice president of marketing.)
3. Have each page in the site reference the parameter *veepmktg* rather than the explicit name *Janet Leverling*.

When someone new takes over the vice president of marketing position, you can then change the value of the *veepmktg* parameter rather than finding and updating each affected page by hand, possibly missing some in the process.

Figure 29-8 shows the Site Settings dialog box for adding and maintaining site parameters. To display this dialog box, choose Site Settings from the Tools menu, and then click the Parameters tab.

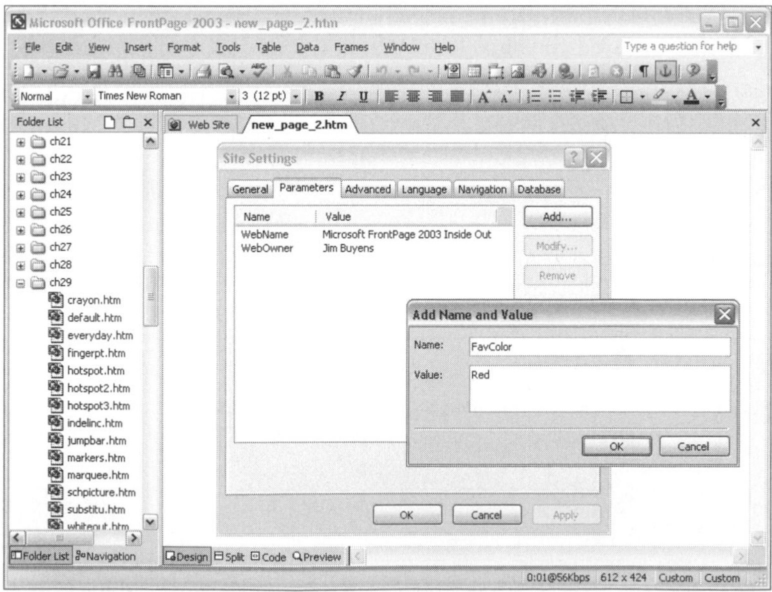

Figure 29-8. FrontPage can accommodate any number of global parameters for a site.

The Substitution component displays site parameter values in a Web page. You configure the component with the site parameter's name, and the component displays the parameter's value. Any text that will appear on multiple pages and be subject to occasional change is a candidate to become a Site Parameter. Here's how to display Site Parameter values in a Web page:

1 Open the page in Design view.
2 Set the insertion point where you'd like the Site Parameter value to appear.
3 Choose Web Component from the Insert menu, or click Web Component on the Standard toolbar. This displays the Insert Web Component dialog box.

Web Component

4 Select Included Content in the Component Type list on the left, and then select Substitution in the Choose A Type Of Content list on the right.
5 Click Finish to display the Substitution Properties dialog box, shown in Figure 29-9.

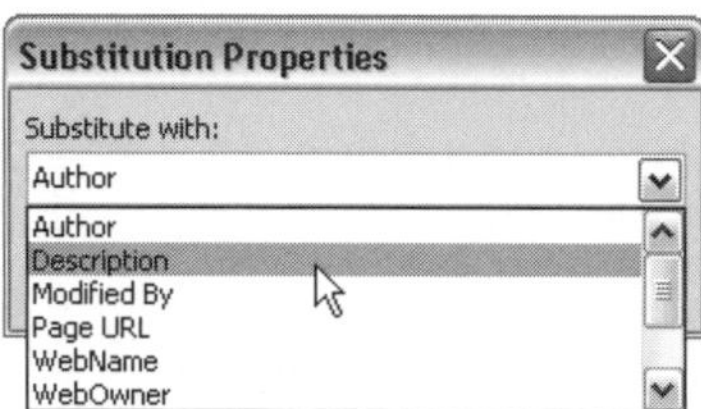

Figure 29-9. The Substitution Properties dialog box lists all the Site Parameters you've defined in the Site Settings dialog box.

6 Choose the Site Parameter you want to insert, and then click OK.

After you click OK, FrontPage will insert a marker for the selected parameter. If you redefine the parameter later (from the Parameters tab of the Site Settings dialog box), FrontPage will update the value displayed on your Web pages everywhere the site parameter appears.

Figure 29-9 shows four built-in Site Parameters: Author, Description, Modified By, and Page URL. FrontPage maintains these values on a page-by-page basis, as shown in Table 29-1. The only built-in parameter you can modify directly is Description; it displays any comments you enter on the Summary tab of the Properties dialog box displayed in the Folder List or in Folders view. A Web designer manually created the site parameters WebOwner and WebName.

Table 29-1. Site Parameters Maintained by FrontPage

Substitution name	FrontPage property	Description
Author	Created By	The user name of the person who created the page
Description	Comment	Comments entered in a page's Properties dialog box in the Folder List or in Folders view
Modified By	Modified By	The user name of the person who most recently modified the page
Page URL	Location	The location of the page, as seen from a browser

Figure 29-10 shows a Web page with six Substitution components—one component for each of the four built-in parameters, plus two that display parameters configured under Tools, Site Settings: WebName and WebOwner.

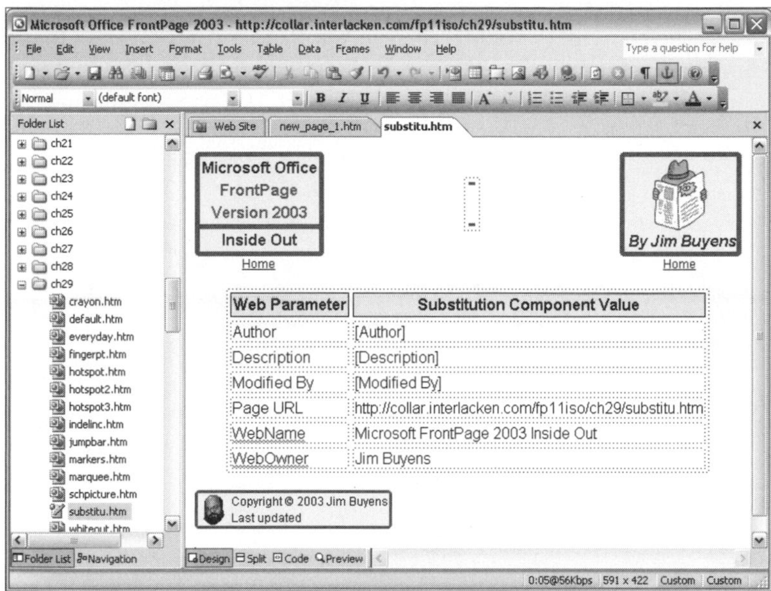

Figure 29-10. FrontPage shows system-maintained Site Parameters as placeholders but displays developer-defined Site Parameters as values. Browsers display the final values in either case.

The Substitution component for Description displays the placeholder *[Description]* in Figure 29-10 because the parameter is empty. In a browser, however, empty values appear blank.

The Description parameter displays a file's Comment property, as entered in the Folder List or in Folders view. For more information about entering information in this parameter, refer to "Working with Folders View," on page 180.

The Component Errors report lists all cases where Substitution components refer to missing or empty Site Parameters. For more information about the Component Errors report, refer to "Component Errors," in Appendix D.

Using Shared Borders

This section discusses another FrontPage facility that standardizes content and appearance across an entire Web site. *Shared borders* provide a way to insert standard content at the upper, lower, left, or right edges of any or all pages in the same Web site.

Shared borders appear between your Web page's normal content and the upper, left, right, or lower edge of the browser window. You can put whatever you want inside the shared border area, but the *same* content appears in the *same* border for *every* page in your Web site. The lower shared border for one page can't be different from the lower shared border of any other page, for example. When Microsoft decided to call these borders "shared," they weren't kidding!

A typical use of shared borders would include a Page Banner component in the upper shared border; a Link Bars component in the left shared border; and copyright, contact, or date and time information in the lower shared border. Figure 29-11 illustrates such a page.

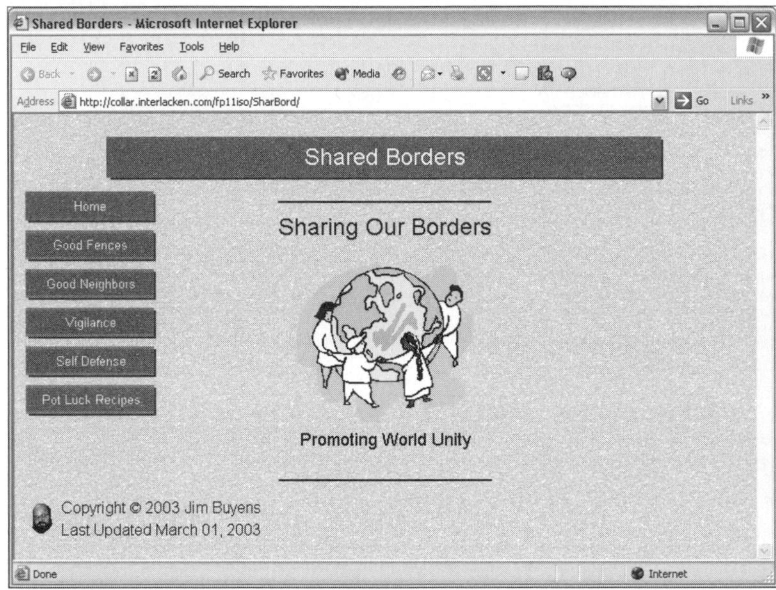

Figure 29-11. This page uses a Page Banner component in the upper shared border, a Link Bars component in the left shared border, and a Date And Time component in the lower shared border.

A Page Banner or Link Bars component included in a shared border produces different results in each page where the shared border appears. The same is true for other components, such as Date And Time or Substitution, that display values stored outside the Web page itself.

For more information about the Date And Time component, refer to "Using the Date And Time Component," on page 721.

To apply shared borders, choose Shared Borders from the Format menu. This will display the dialog box shown in Figure 29-12.

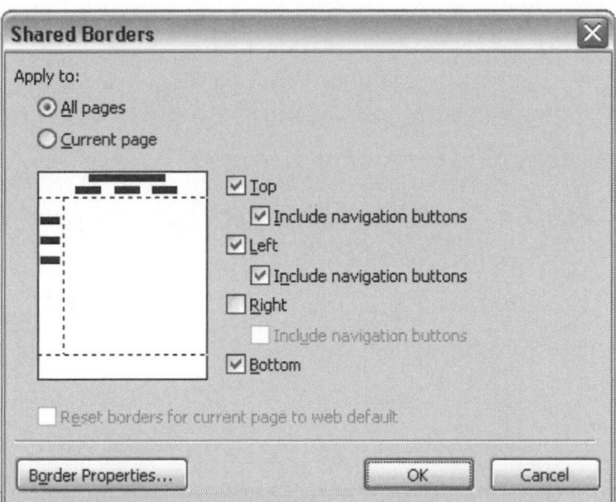

Figure 29-12. This dialog box controls the application of shared borders to any or all pages in a Web.

This dialog box controls the following settings:

- **Apply To** Choose All Pages to apply shared borders to an entire Web site. Choose Current Page to override the Web site's default for this page.
- **Top, Left, Right, and Bottom** For each side of the page where you want a shared border to appear, select the corresponding check box:
  - **Include Navigation Buttons** Select this check box if you want FrontPage to include a Link Bars component within the shared border.
- **Reset Borders For Current Page To Web Default** Select this check box if you want to remove all shared border overrides from the current page.
- **Border Properties** Click this button to display the Border Properties dialog box, shown in Figure 29-13.

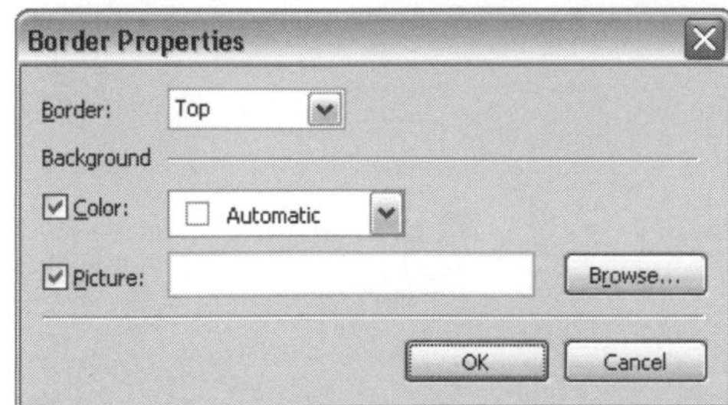

Figure 29-13. This dialog box modifies the background properties of any shared border.

The Border Properties dialog box modifies the background color and background picture of any shared border you select. Here's how to use the controls in this dialog box:

- **Border** Choose the shared border you want to modify: Top, Left, Right, or Bottom.
- **Background** Specify the background content of the shared border:
  - **Color** Select this check box, and then select a color from the drop-down list to specify a background color.
  - **Picture** Select this check box, and select a picture that will fill the background.

The first time you use shared borders in a FrontPage-based Web site, FrontPage will take these actions:

- Creates a folder named _borders
- Creates Web pages named top.htm, left.htm, right.htm, and bottom.htm (or whichever of these you chose to use) within the _borders folder
- Surrounds the content of each existing Web page with an HTML table
- Includes the top.htm, left.htm, right.htm, and bottom.htm files within the table cells along the corresponding borders

Figure 29-14 shows FrontPage displaying the shared borders page from Figure 29-11. The visible boundaries around each shared border aren't visible when the page appears in a browser. You can edit information in the borders, but any changes will affect *every* page in the same Web site that uses shared borders. That's the point of shared borders: to show zones of identical or self-customizing content on every page.

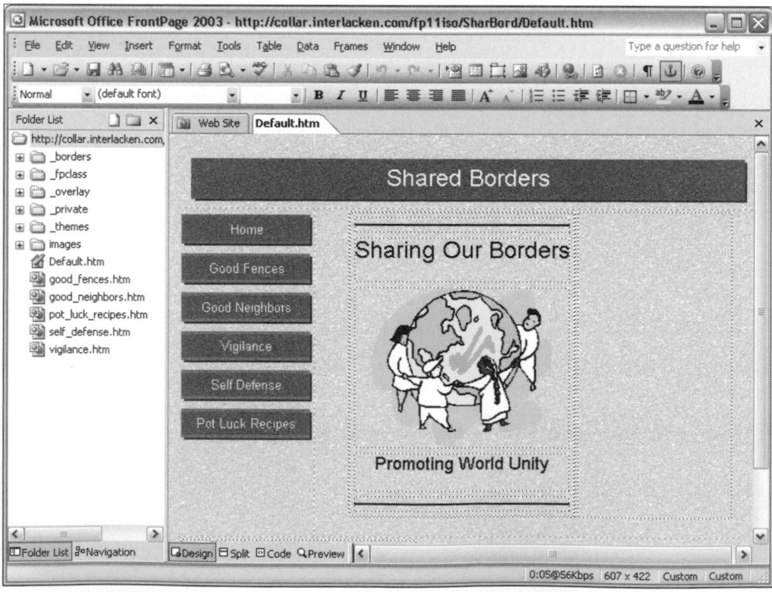

Figure 29-14. Shared borders can provide standard content along the edge of any or all pages in a Web site. The choice of edges is configurable.

To override a Web site's shared border settings for a specific page, first open the page in Design view, and then choose Shared Borders from the Format menu. In the Shared Borders dialog box, make sure that Current Page is selected, and then do either of the following:

- Indicate which shared borders the current page should use.
- To return a page to its Web site's default shared border settings, select the Reset Borders For Current Page To Web Default check box.

In Summary…

This chapter explained how to use several FrontPage components that replicate standard content to one or many pages. This decreases initial development time, but the real payoff comes during maintenance, when changing a single master copy updates all locations that use it.

The next chapter describes components that enhance your Web site with real-time information from public sources.

Chapter 30

Using Automatic Web Content Components

In the past, developing new Microsoft Office FrontPage 2003 components was a complex job that required the skills of a professional programmer. Even simple problems required a complex solution. With Web Components, however, FrontPage now provides a simple solution for simple problems.

From a designer's point of view, a Web Component is a selection that appears in the Insert Web Components dialog box. Choosing a Web Component adds a block of HTML at the current insertion point. There are two kinds of Web Components, each with different capabilities:

- **Noninteractive** These Web Components create exactly the same block of HTML each time you run them. They have no configuration options and no persistent identity. You can edit the HTML that a noninteractive Web Component creates just as you would edit HTML that you hand-typed.
- **Interactive** These Web Components display a dialog box or series of wizard pages to collect information and then customize their results accordingly. Interactive Web Components retain their identity as components. You can't directly change them in Design view; instead, you must use one of the normal procedures for modifying FrontPage components—for example, by right-clicking the component and choosing FrontPage Component Properties from the shortcut menu, by double-clicking the component, and so forth.

The dialog box or wizard pages that an interactive Web Component displays are actually Web pages. These Web pages can reside on the designer's local disk or anywhere on the Web. If they're on the Web, the dialog box or wizard can prompt the designer for information, verify it remotely, and then add valid results to the designer's Web page, all within the FrontPage user interface. This is very cool.

Web Components are so useful and so easy to develop that they'll probably start popping up all over. They'll arrive with FrontPage, with Microsoft Office System updates, and as downloads from a variety of online services. In addition, you can develop custom Web Components for yourself or your organization. Therefore, you should consider the Web Components described in this chapter as examples rather than a comprehensive list.

On the CD Inside Extra

Insider Extra 11, "Developing Custom Web Components," provides five Web Components written specifically for this book, as well as instructions for creating such components yourself.

Using Expedia Web Components

The Expedia online travel service provides two Web Components that display maps for a given address or public place:

- **Link To A Map** Displays a text address or place name, with a hyperlink to a dynamic map. (A *dynamic map*, in this sense, is one that you can enlarge, reduce, zoom in, zoom out, and move to the north, south, east, or west.)
- **Static Map** Displays a static map hyperlinked to the same dynamic map as the first component.

Both components are interactive and involve essentially the same configuration procedure. If you'd like your Web site to provide maps (and other travel assistance) to specific locations, proceed as follows:

1. Make sure that your connection to the Internet is working.
2. Open the Web page that should contain the text hyperlink or static map, and set the insertion point where you want it to be.
3. Choose Web Component from the Insert menu, or click the Web Component button on the Standard toolbar.

Web Component

4. When the Insert Web Component dialog box appears, choose Expedia Components from the Component Type List on the left.
5. In the Choose An Expedia Component list on the right, select one of these options, and then click Finish:
   - **Link To A Map** Displays a hyperlink containing a physical address or place name. Clicking the hyperlink displays a map of that place.
   - **Static Map** Displays a clickable map.
6. When the Find A Map On Expedia.com page appears, click Next.
7. When the What Would You Like To Locate? wizard page shown in Figure 30-1 appears, take either of these actions, and then click Next:
   - **Search For An Address Or Intersection** Select this option if you want to specify a physical location. Then enter a street address or intersection, city, state, and zip code. If you don't know the value for a field, leave it blank.
   - **Search For A Place** Select this option if you want to specify the name of a public place. Continue by selecting a region and then typing a place name. This can be the name of a city, province, country, continent, island, natural landmark, historic place, or almost anything else. Easter Island, Mount Everest, North Prairie, Parthenon, Smithsonian Institution, Stonehenge, and Zanzibar are all acceptable, for example.

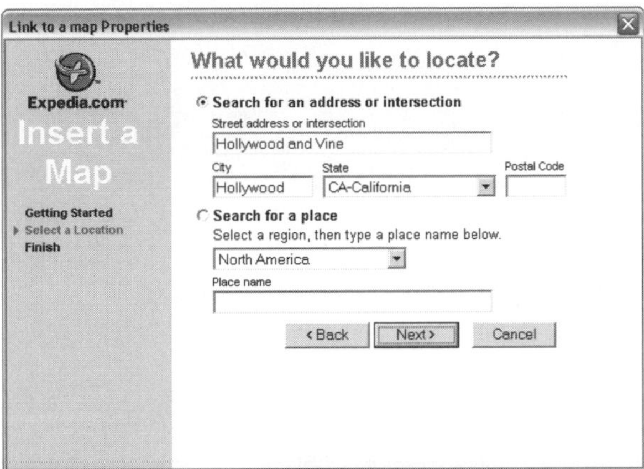

Figure 30-1. This wizard is actually a series of Web pages that come from Expedia's Web site.

8 Unless you were incredibly precise in step 6, the What Would You Like To Locate? page will take on the appearance of Figure 30-2. This occurs because Expedia's database contains more than one place matching your description. Either correct your original entry or choose an item from the Best Matches list, and then click Next.

This step clearly shows the power of using Web pages as wizard pages. The page you see in Figure 30-2 comes from Expedia's Web server, and it validates input against Expedia's geographic database.

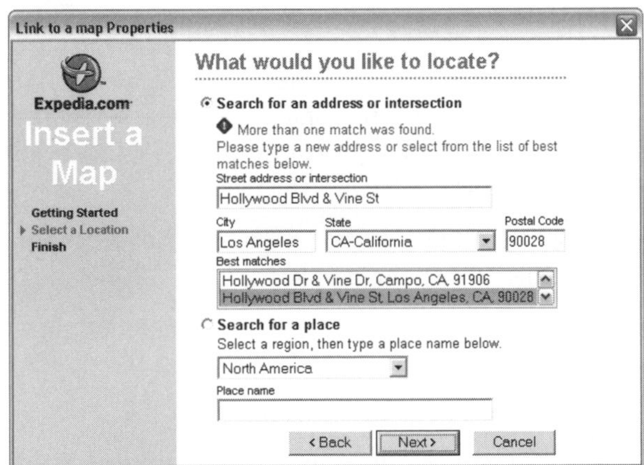

Figure 30-2. The wizard validates your input against databases that reside at Expedia.

9 When the You Are Finished! wizard page appears, don't take it as an omen of doom. Instead, celebrate your success by clicking the Finish button.

Figure 30-3 shows the default Expedia map for Hollywood Blvd. & Vine St., Los Angeles, CA, 90028. This is exactly the text that a Link To A Map component would display. The Static Map component displays the map you see in the figure, but not the movement controls and of course not the surrounding Web page. Clicking the static map displays the complete Expedia Web page.

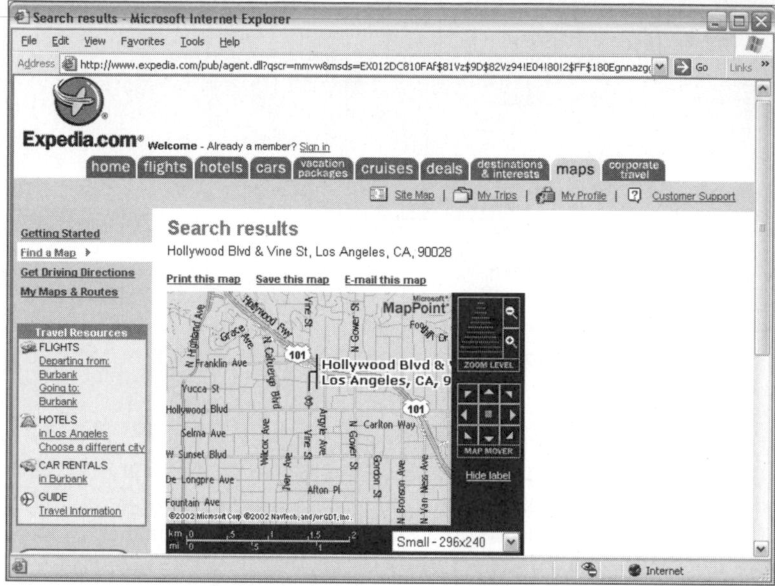

Figure 30-3. Clicking either type of Expedia Web component displays a map page like this.

Using the MSN Stock Quote Component

This component creates an HTML form where your visitors can enter a stock exchange symbol and receive the current price and other statistics for that stock. The form submits the request to *http://moneycentral.msn.com* for processing, and MSN MoneyCentral sends back the stock quotation Web page shown in Figure 30-4.

Because this is a noninteractive component, it accepts no configuration parameters. The procedure for inserting it is therefore quite simple:

1. In Design view, open the Web page that will contain the stock quote request form.
2. Set the insertion point where you want the request form to appear.
3. Choose Web Component from the Insert menu.
4. When the Insert Web Component dialog box appears, choose MSN Components from the Component Type list on the left.
5. Select Stock Quote in the Choose A MSN Component list on the right, and then click Finish.

These actions insert the HTML form titled MoneyCentral Stock Quote that appears in the Web page in Figure 30-5. This is just an ordinary HTML form, not a full-fledged component with a Stock Quote Properties dialog box and other accoutrements.

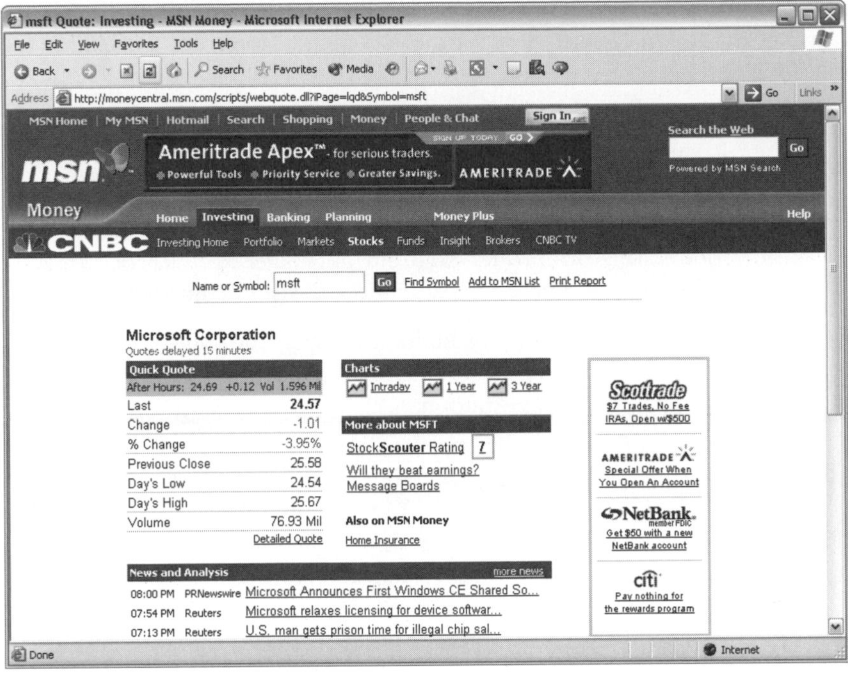

Figure 30-4. The Stock Quote component provides stock quotes like this for your Web visitors.

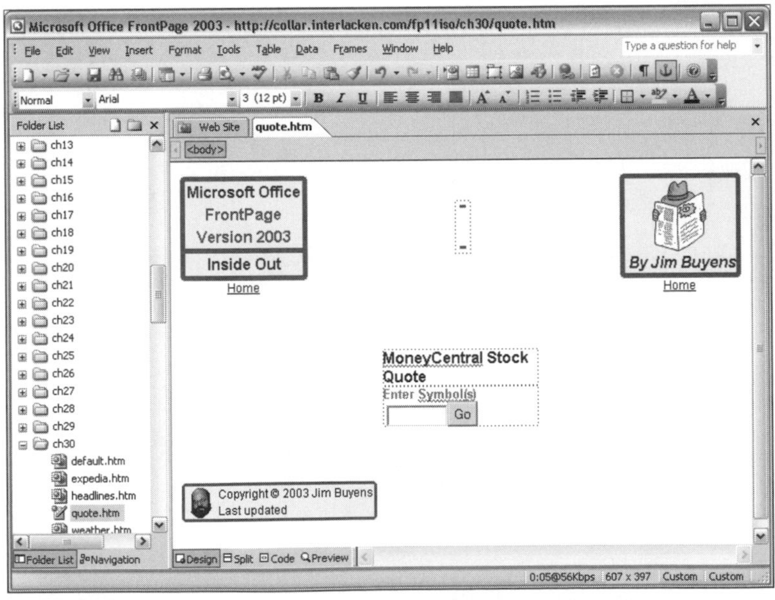

Figure 30-5. Inserting a Stock Quote component adds a form like this to your Web page.

Chapter 30

To change the properties of this form, right-click anywhere within the dotted rectangle, and choose Form Properties from the shortcut menu. However, *don't* change either of the following options:

- After opening the Form Properties dialog box and clicking Options, don't disturb the URL in the Action box. Changing this URL prevents MSN MoneyCentral from receiving and processing the visitor's request.
- After right-clicking the MoneyCentral Stock Quote box and choosing Form Field Properties, don't change the Name field to anything other than *SYMBOL*. If you do, MSN MoneyCentral won't know what stock the Web visitor requested.

By default, the Stock Quote component doesn't display the quote in a new window. To modify this behavior, right-click the HTML form, choose Form Properties from the shortcut menu, and click the Target Frame button.

Using MSNBC Components

These components all retrieve and display information from the MSNBC Web site. This provides current information for your visitors and perhaps more visitors for MSNBC.

Using the Headlines From MSNBC Components

These components, shown in Figure 30-6, display current headlines from news categories.

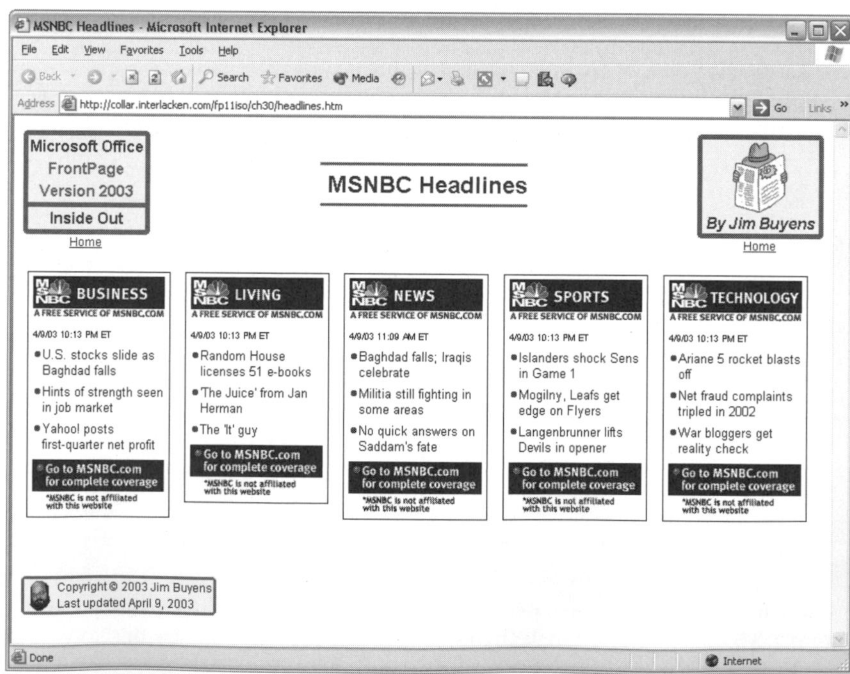

Figure 30-6. This Web page illustrates all five types of MSNBC headline components.

Because these are noninteractive components, the procedure for inserting them strongly resembles the procedure for inserting any other noninteractive component:

1. Set the insertion point where you want the component to appear.
2. Choose Web Component from the Insert menu, or click the Web Component button on the Standard toolbar.
3. In the Web Components dialog box, choose MSNBC Components from the Component Type list on the left. Then select one of the following choices from the Choose A MSNBC Component list on the right:
   - Business Headlines From MSNBC
   - Living And Travel Headlines From MSNBC
   - News Headlines From MSNBC
   - Sports Headlines From MSNBC
   - Technology Headlines From MSNBC
4. Click Finish to insert the component.

Each headline component is actually a hyperlinked picture. By default, these hyperlinks don't open in a new window, and therefore some visitors might leave your site prematurely. To prevent this:

1. Right-click the headline component, and then choose Hyperlink Properties from the shortcut menu.
2. When the Edit Hyperlink dialog box appears, click the Target Frame button.
3. When the Target Frame dialog box appears, select New Window, and then click OK.

Using the Weather Forecast From MSNBC Component

This component displays the current and forecasted weather conditions for any city you select, again courtesy of the MSNBC Web site. Like the headline components, it displays its results in the current Web page. To view some typical results, refer to Figure 30-7.

Unlike the headline components, Weather Forecast From MSNBC is an interactive Web Component that validates your configuration settings against databases at the MSNBC Web site. Therefore, your computer must be connected to the Internet any time you insert or modify the component.

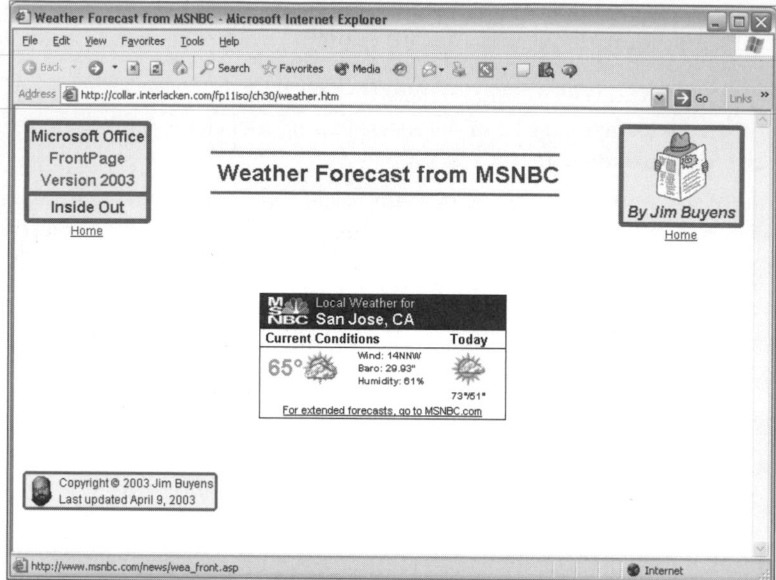

Figure 30-7. With the Weather Forecast From MSNBC component, a weather forecast like this can appear on any Web page you want.

Here's the procedure for adding a Weather Forecast From MSNBC component to your own Web page:

1. Make sure that your connection to the Internet is working.
2. Open the Web page that will contain the weather forecast.
3. Set the insertion point where you want the weather forecast to appear.
4. Choose Web Component from the Insert menu.
5. When the Insert Web Component dialog box appears, choose MSNBC Components from the Component Type list on the left.
6. In the Choose A MSNBC Component list on the right, select Weather Forecast From MSNBC.
7. Click Finish.

   FrontPage connects to the MSNBC Web site and begins running a configuration wizard. The wizard's exact form and content might change over time, but at some point, you should receive a prompt like the one shown in Figure 30-8.

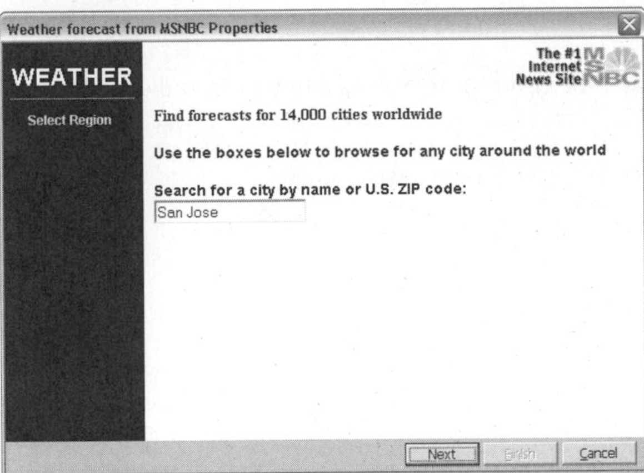

Figure 30-8. This dialog box prompts you for a city.

8 Enter the name or, for the U.S., the ZIP code of the city you want, and then click Next.

9 The wizard queries the MSNBC Web site and responds with a list of matching cities, as shown in Figure 30-9. Select the city you want, and then click Finish.

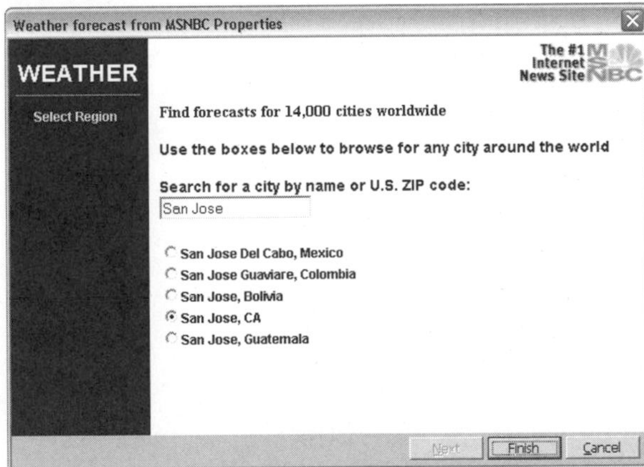

Figure 30-9. Choose the exact city you want from the list provided.

At this point, MSNBC sends FrontPage the HTML to retrieve and display the current weather for the city you requested. FrontPage adds this HTML to your Web page, but it won't actually run it. Instead, FrontPage displays an imitation weather forecast for Seattle, Washington. (55° Fahrenheit, damp, and dreary—what a surprise.)

Because the Weather Forecast From MSNBC component is interactive, right-clicking it and choosing FrontPage Component Properties from the shortcut menu reruns the wizard.

In Summary…

This chapter explained the concept of Web Components and explained how some typical components work.

The next chapter explains how FrontPage can make usage statistics for your Web site available to Web visitors.

Chapter 31

Monitoring and Reporting Site Activity

All modern Web servers create log files containing a detailed record of each visitor request. Each record typically contains the date and time, the requested page, the visitor's IP address, the visitor's browser identification string, and additional data. As individual records, this information can be useful for investigating events in progress at a specific time.

Most site operators, however, find usage information far more useful in aggregate. They want to know how many hits (requests) the site is receiving per day, per week or per month; which are the most and least popular pages; which browsers are used the most; and many other statistics. This chapter explains how to retrieve and display such statistics.

Locating and Monitoring Usage Reports

A variety of commercial applications are available for summarizing and reporting Web server log statistics. If your provider has installed one of these, the provider's Help pages will probably explain how to display the resulting statistics.

The Microsoft FrontPage Server Extensions and Microsoft Windows SharePoint Services can both analyze Web server logs, too. This capability is inactive by default but an administrator can activate it by configuring a single Web page.

For information about configuring the FrontPage Server Extensions or Windows SharePoint Services to perform usage analysis, refer to the section, "Displaying Data in a Top 10 List," later in this chapter.

Once the server extensions or SharePoint are collecting usage statistics, you can view the results in Microsoft Office FrontPage 2003. Chapter 17, "Keeping Your Web Site Up-to-Date," explained how to do this. Unfortunately, that procedure requires that anyone who views statistics for a Web site must also have authority to open the site in FrontPage: that is, to create, modify, and delete pages.

The remainder of this chapter describes how the Top 10 List component can display the same data to Web visitors, even if they can't open the site in FrontPage.

Creating Top 10 Lists

Top 10 Lists provide a quick and easy way to display Web site statistics to Web visitors with no special authority. Seven Top 10 Lists are available, and you can provide all, some, or none of them to visitors as you choose. Here are the seven lists:

- **Top 10 Visited Pages** Displays the 10 pages in your Web site that visitors requested the most. Figure 31-1 provides a sample of this report.
- **Top 10 Referring URLs** Displays the 10 most common pages outside your Web site that directed visitors into your Web site. Figure 31-2 illustrates this report.

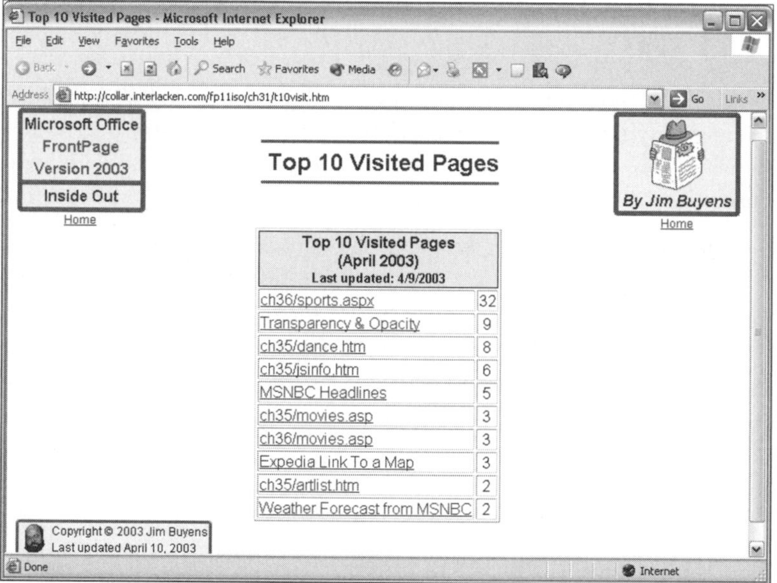

Figure 31-1. The Top 10 Visited Pages report lists the 10 most popular pages in your Web site for the current month.

- **Top 10 Referring Domains** Displays the 10 most common Web servers (other than yours) that directed visitors into your Web site. Figure 31-3 illustrates this and the remaining four reports. In a real-life situation each report would, of course, display more than one line.
- **Top 10 Operating Systems** Displays the 10 most common operating systems that visitors to your Web site were using.
- **Top 10 Browsers** Displays the 10 most common browsers that visitors to your Web site were using.
- **Top 10 Visiting Users** Displays the user names of the 10 visitors who accessed your Web site most frequently.
- **Top 10 Search Strings** Displays the 10 most common keywords that visitors used to locate your site on one of the large Internet search engines.

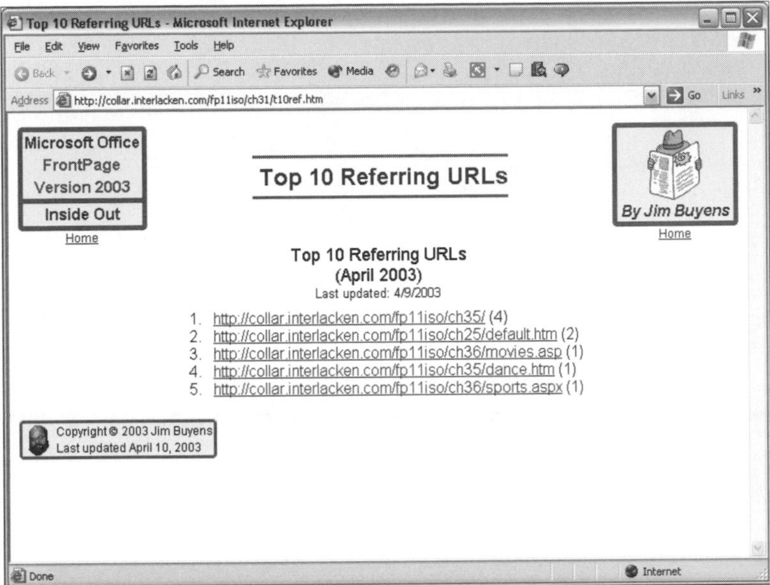

Figure 31-2. The Top 10 Referring URLs report displays the 10 pages outside your Web site that most frequently sent visitors into your Web site.

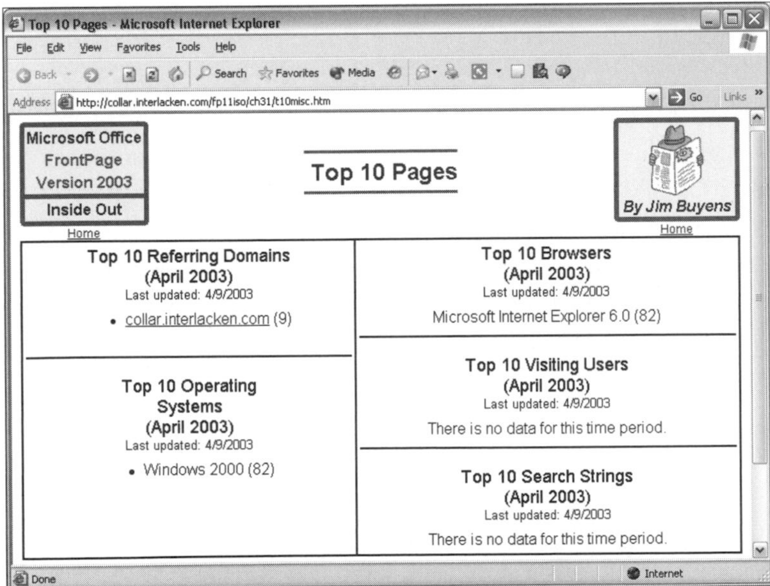

Figure 31-3. These Top 10 Lists report various centers of high activity.

Figure 31-4 shows the Reports view Usage reports that correspond to the Top 10 Referring Domains and Top 10 Operating Systems reports shown in Figure 31-3.

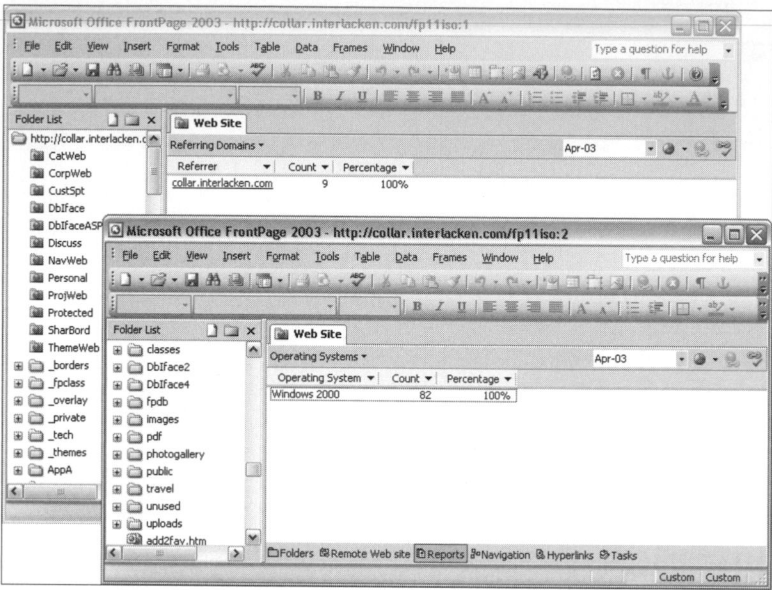

Figure 31-4. Top 10 Lists are essentially extracts of the Usage reports that FrontPage itself provides.

Here's the procedure for making any of these reports available to your visitors:

1. Set the insertion point where you want the Top 10 List to appear.
2. Choose Web Component from the Insert menu. This displays the Insert Web Component dialog box.
3. Select Top 10 List in the Component Type list on the left and the type of list you want from the list on the right.
4. Click Finish to display the Top 10 List Properties dialog box, shown in Figure 31-5.

Figure 31-5. This dialog box configures the properties of a Top 10 List.

5 Specify the options in the Top 10 List Properties dialog box as follows:

- **Title Text** Enter the heading you want to appear at the top of the Top 10 List.
- **Include Date Usage Processing Was Last Run** If you select this check box, the Top 10 List will display the most recent date that Windows SharePoint Services or the FrontPage Server Extensions collected usage statistics from the Web server. In effect, this is the "current as of date" for the statistics in the list.
- **List Style** Select the presentation format you want. Table 31-1 summarizes the options.

6 Click OK to insert the Top 10 List.

Table 31-1. Top 10 List Styles

List style	Description
Table	Select this icon if you want the statistics displayed in an HTML table. Figure 31-1 provides an example of this format.
Numbered	Select this icon if you want the statistics displayed as a numbered list. Figure 31-2 provides an example.
Bulleted	Select this icon if you want the statistics displayed as a bulleted list. See the lists on the left in Figure 31-3.
Text	Select this icon if you want the statistics displayed as plain text. The lists on the right in Figure 31-3 use this format.

After you've created the Top 10 List, Design view displays a mock-up to show where the component resides. After you save a page containing a Top 10 List component, browsing the page will display the most recent statistics Windows SharePoint Services or the FrontPage Server Extensions have collected.

Getting the Top 10 List component to display data can be a long, strange journey. As the next section explains, both the Web server and Windows SharePoint Services or the FrontPage Server Extensions (whichever the server runs) require proper configuration.

Frequently Asked Questions About the Top 10 List Component

Can the Top 10 List component show more than one month of data or data other than the current month's data?

No.

Can the Top 10 List component show more or fewer than 10 report details?

No, unless there are fewer than 10 lines of information to report.

Can an existing Top 10 List component display a different statistic?

No, you must delete the existing Top 10 List and create a new one in its place.

Displaying Data in a Top 10 List

The Top 10 List component displays a mock-up of itself in both the normal and preview modes of Page view. In addition, browsing a page that contains a Top 10 List and resides in a disk-based Web site displays the following message:

Publish this Web site to a server that supports the FrontPage Server Extensions to see usage data here.

To understand the reasons for this, you must understand where the usage data comes from. Almost all Web servers keep a log of every request they receive—one log record per request. This log record contains the date and the time of the request, the requested Web page, the status code, the visitor's IP address, and so forth. On a scheduled basis, Windows SharePoint Services or the FrontPage Server Extensions scan these logs and accumulate the data that appears in Top 10 Lists, the Usage reports in Reports view, and so forth.

Of course, if you don't have a Web server, you don't have a Web server log. Even if you did have a log, you wouldn't have the FrontPage Server Extensions to summarize it. Therefore, the Top 10 List component displays data only when the following requirements are met:

- The Web page that contains the Top 10 List component resides in a server-based Web site.
- The Web server is running Windows SharePoint Services or the FrontPage Server Extensions 2002. Earlier versions of the server extensions don't collect usage statistics.
- The Web server logs the data you're interested in seeing. There are two aspects to this requirement:
  - If the Web server isn't configured to keep a log, your statistics will obviously be zero.
  - If the Web server isn't configured to log the data for a particular Top 10 List, that list will be empty. On IIS, the log should include at least the following information: Date, Time, Client IP Address, User Name, Method, URI Stem, HTTP Status, Bytes Sent, User Agent, Referrer. This list of fields is something you must configure in the Web server and not in FrontPage.

For more information about configuring Web server log options, refer to "Configuring Site-Level and Folder-Level Options," in Appendix O.

- If your Web server runs Windows SharePoint Services, the Web page shown in Figure 31-6 must be configured to perform usage analysis.

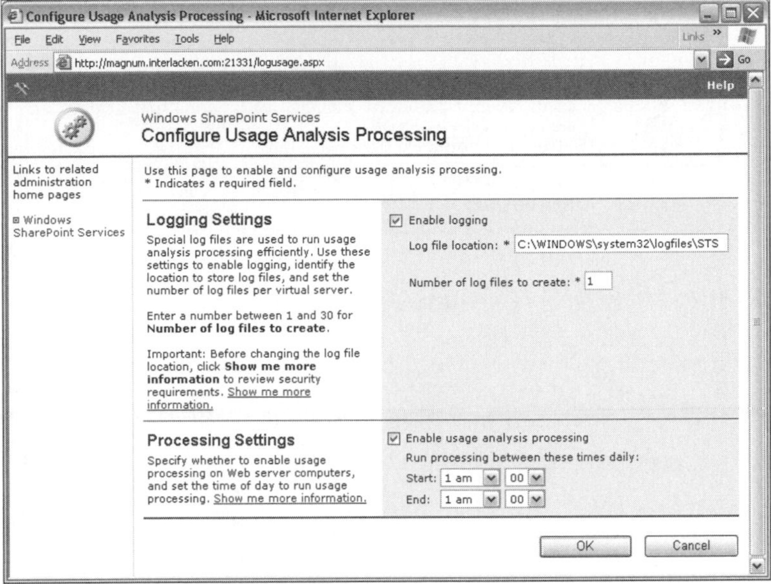

Figure 31-6. This Web page controls whether Windows SharePoint Services collects and analyzes log files.

To display this page:

1. Open the server's Windows SharePoint Services Central Administration page. If you don't know the page's URL, connect to the server using the Internet Information Services management console, open its Web Sites category, right-click SharePoint Central Administration, and choose Browse from the shortcut menu.
2. Scroll down to the Component Configuration section, and then click the Configure Usage Analysis Processing link.

Usage analysis will run only if, on this page, both of the following are true:

- The Enable Logging check box in the Logging Settings section is selected.
- The Enable Usage Analysis Processing check box in the Processing Settings section is selected.

- If your Web server runs the FrontPage Server Extensions, the Web page shown in Figure 31-7 must be configured to perform usage analysis.

To display this page:

1. Open your Web server's root Web site in FrontPage.
2. Choose Server from the Tools menu, and then choose Administration Home from the submenu.
3. When the FrontPage Server Extensions 2002 Site Administration page appears, scroll down to the Configure Usage Analysis Settings section, and then click the Change Usage Analysis Settings link.

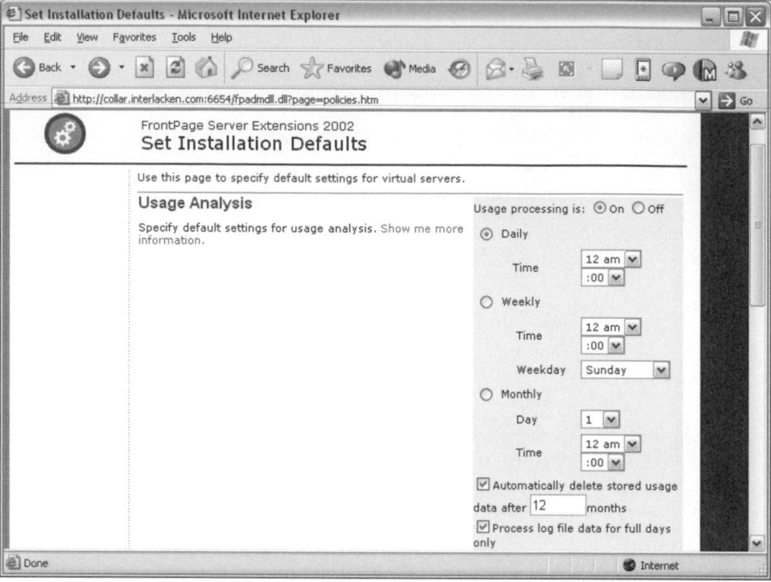

Figure 31-7. This Web page controls how often, if ever, the FrontPage Server Extensions update usage statistics.

The settings on this page apply to the entire Web server; you can't configure them on a site-by-site basis. Chapter 50 explains how to configure this page but the setting titled Usage Processing Is warrants particular attention.

- If the Usage Processing Is option is set to Off, no data will appear.
- If the Usage Processing Is option is set to On and you have a new Web site, no data will appear until the next time the server extensions run usage analysis log processing. This might require waiting a day, a week, or a month.

For more information about configuring the frequency of Web server usage analysis, refer to "Administering Installation Defaults, and "Administering Server-Level Settings," in Appendix P.

In Summary...

This chapter explained the Top 10 List component, a FrontPage component that displays Web site usage statistics on a Web page.

The next chapter explains how to add Java applets and ActiveX controls to a Web page.

Chapter 32

Using ActiveX Controls and Java Applets

The astounding growth of the World Wide Web is a testament to the power and practicality of HTML. Even so, HTML remains basically a static medium. The designer lays out a page and hopes that visitors will look at it. Extending the functionality of HTML is difficult because designers can't count on visitors upgrading their browsers until years have passed.

Fortunately, current-day browsers can display various kinds of programmed objects in the browser window, and these objects can provide functions not present in the browser itself. This chapter describes how to use two types of such objects:

- **Microsoft ActiveX controls** These are Microsoft Windows software components that provide standardized interactive and background services. Many such controls are capable of operating in a Web page, provided, of course, that the Web browser supports Active X controls. Currently, only Windows versions of Microsoft Internet Explorer provide such support.
- **Java applets** These are another kind of program that takes over part of the browser window. These applets can run on any type of computer that has a Java Virtual Machine interpreter installed, and so this encompasses a wide range of computers. Compared to ActiveX controls, Java applets are limited in capability. This reduces the security risk of running downloaded code on the visitor's computer, but it also reduces their capability for useful work.

Incorporating ActiveX Controls

Microsoft's vision of uniting Windows and the World Wide Web naturally involves a merger of Windows programming objects and active Web pages. This section explains how to incorporate such objects, called ActiveX controls, into your Web page.

Introducing ActiveX

ActiveX controls are reusable software modules that provide functions other software can exploit. Because ActiveX controls are easy to distribute and use, they've become a very popular way to package and distribute software. Microsoft designed ActiveX controls with Windows in mind, but the concept extends to almost any other platform.

Physically, ActiveX controls are Windows dynamic link libraries (DLLs), but they often have an .ocx file extension. They come from a variety of sources: Some come with the operating system, some come as parts of other software installed on your computer, and others come from Web pages that use them and provide a download location.

Each ActiveX control provides one or more software objects. These objects might or might not display anything on the screen, but they all have *properties*, *methods*, and *events*:

- **Properties** These are data values accessible by external processes as well as by the control. Depending on how a control is written, an external process might or might not be able to update a given property.
- **Methods** These are software routines, programmed into the control, that external processes can trigger.
- **Events** These are external incidents that trigger code to execute. Event routines run in response to external stimuli, such as mouse clicks, keystrokes, or incoming data.

Using ActiveX Controls on the Web

A typical Windows computer has hundreds—or even thousands—of ActiveX controls installed on it. Of these, only a fraction provide functions that are useful on a Web page. However, if a particular control is useful, a browser can run the control just as easily as any other piece of software can. Some ActiveX controls, of course, exist specifically for use in Web browsers. ActiveX controls have many capabilities, but the important ones that pertain to Web pages are these:

- ActiveX controls can display preset data. Chapter 26, "Enhancing Web Pages with Animation," for example, showed how the Microsoft Windows Media Player control can display a video.
- ActiveX controls can interact with script code also contained within the Web page. *Scripts*, in this sense, are small blocks of program code delivered with the Web page, and they run on the Web visitor's browser. They're usually written in JavaScript and VBScript. Scripts can read and modify ActiveX properties, invoke their methods, and respond to their events.
- The HTML for an ActiveX control can specify a download location. Then, if a Web visitor doesn't have all the ActiveX controls that a given page uses, the browser can download and install those controls on the fly.
- ActiveX controls running in a Web browser can make any changes to the local system that the Web visitor could make.

The last capability is, of course, a potentially dangerous one. Browsing the Web could expose your system to any number of malicious, intrusive, or privacy-invading software components. A digital signature scheme ensures that whoever downloads an ActiveX control knows who created it and thus whom to prosecute if the control is mischievous or destructive! Figure 32-1 shows the Security Warning dialog box that appears before Internet Explorer downloads and installs any ActiveX control from the Web.

Figure 32-1. This dialog box asks for permission to install and run a new ActiveX control used in a Web page.

Lack of browser support is probably the greatest impediment to using ActiveX controls on the Web. Currently, Windows versions of Internet Explorer are the only browsers that support ActiveX controls. All other browsers simply ignore the controls and display a presupplied message or nothing in their place. Here, then, are some strategies for using ActiveX controls:

- Use ActiveX controls only in situations where you know all the Web visitors will be using a Windows version of Internet Explorer:
  - If you're delivering a specialized service over the Internet, for example, you can simply tell your clientele what browser to use.
  - On an intranet, a Windows version of Internet Explorer might be your corporate standard.
- Design your Web page to degrade gracefully if the browser can't run ActiveX controls. You might provide two different mechanisms for entering a quantity—for example, an ActiveX slider or gauge as well as an ordinary text box. This provides Web visitors with the best experience possible given their browsers' capabilities.
- Design two different Web pages, one for Internet Explorer users and another for everyone else. Before you recoil at the thought of doing twice the work, consider the following:
  - A number of forces are, in any event, driving a trend toward multiple representations of the same content. Wireless devices, personal digital assistants (PDAs), and Microsoft WebTV are cases in point.

- Technologies that separate presentation from content—technologies such as database-driven and XML-driven Web sites—often make platform-dependent Web pages practical. For example, instead of handcrafting 1000 Web pages to display 1000 catalog items, modern designers develop one Web database page that displays any item in a catalog database. That way, supporting five platforms requires creating five Web pages and not 5000. And for those five, you need to do the database development—which is usually the hard part—only once.

Inserting ActiveX Controls

Here's the procedure for adding an ActiveX control to a Web page that's already open in Design view:

1. Set the insertion point where you want the ActiveX control to appear.

Web Component

2. Choose Web Component from the Insert menu, or click Web Component on the Standard toolbar. This displays the Insert Web Component dialog box.
3. In the Component Type list on the left, select Advanced Controls. Then, in the Choose A Control list on the right, select ActiveX Control.
4. Click Next to display the Insert Web Component dialog box shown in Figure 32-2. If the control you want appears in the Choose A Control list, select it, and then click Finish.

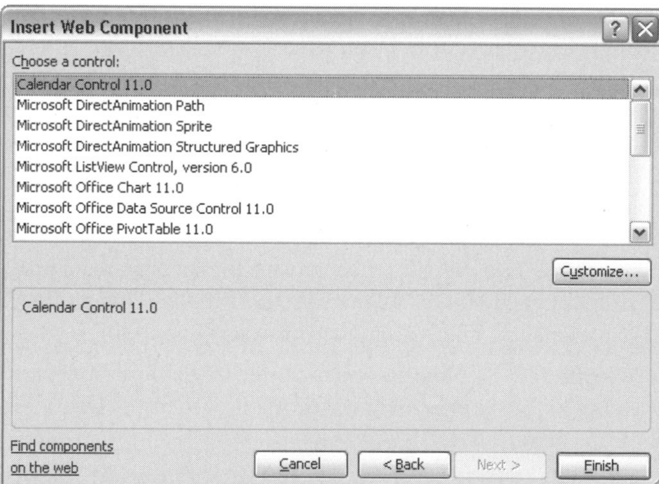

Figure 32-2. To add an ActiveX control to your Web page, select it from this list, and then click Finish.

5. If the Choose A Control list doesn't include the control you want, click Customize to search for the control on your system. This displays the Customize ActiveX Control List dialog box, shown in Figure 32-3.

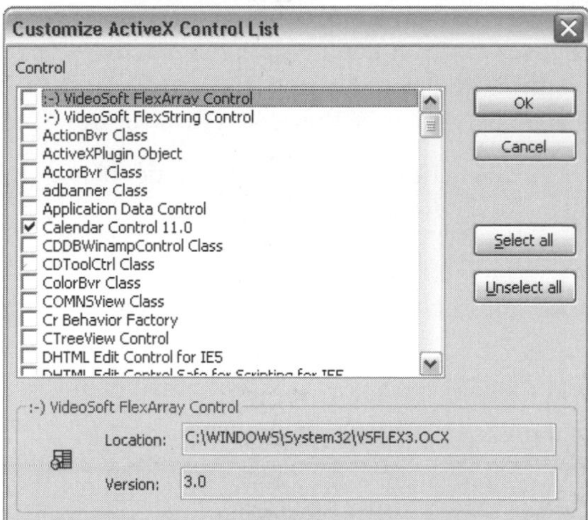

Figure 32-3. Click Customize in the Insert Web Component dialog box to include or exclude controls from the Choose A Control list.

This dialog box displays a complete list of the ActiveX controls installed on your system. You'll probably discover many more controls than you expect; the list includes all controls you've downloaded from Web pages, plus those installed by other software. The check box to the left of each control name specifies whether that control appears in the Choose A Control list shown in Figure 32-2.

If the control you want is present in this list, select its check box, click OK, and go back to step 4.

> **Important** The Location box in Figure 32-3 displays the file name and path of any control you select. This is important if you want to provide a copy of the control in your Web site for visitors to download. You can't copy something into your Web site if you don't know where it is!

6. If you still can't find the control you want, click the Find Components On The Web link in the lower left corner of the Insert Web Component dialog box (shown in Figure 32-2). This closes the dialog box but starts Internet Explorer so that you can find the control on the Web. After you've found the control, download and install it on your system, and then return to step 1.

   This step assumes, of course, that your default browser is Internet Explorer. Starting a browser such as Netscape Navigator that can't install Active X controls serves little purpose. It's almost as though your computer went on strike.

FrontPage adds any new ActiveX control to your Web page at the current insertion point. If the control generates a display, Design view displays it. If not, the control just occupies a blank space. Either way, FrontPage surrounds the area with sizing handles. You can drag, cut, copy, paste, and resize the area in all the usual ways.

ActiveX controls don't execute in Design view—objects in FrontPage need to "hold still" for editing. This means that ActiveX controls don't respond interactively, as they would in a browser situation. Some controls don't even display in WYSIWYG mode. To see the control in action, switch to Preview mode, or choose Preview In Browser from the File menu.

As you might expect, there's a dialog box that sets the properties of any control on a Web page. Any of the following methods displays this dialog box:

- Double-click the ActiveX control.
- Right-click the control, and choose ActiveX Control Properties from the shortcut menu.
- Click the control, and choose Properties from the Format menu.
- Click the control, and press Alt+Enter.

All of these techniques produce a dialog box resembling the one shown in Figure 32-4. However, because no two ActiveX controls have the same properties and capabilities, no two of their Properties dialog boxes look the same.

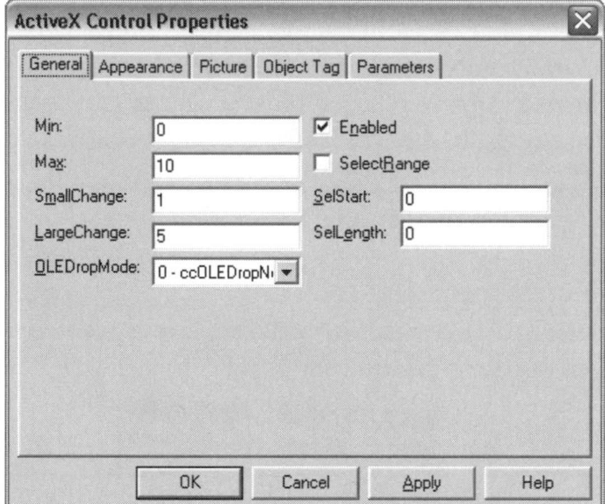

Figure 32-4. The Microsoft Slider control displays this ActiveX Control Properties dialog box. Other controls might display more or fewer tabs, but nearly all controls display the Object Tag and Parameters tabs.

The last two tabs in Figure 32-4, Object Tag and Parameters, are generic and appear for nearly all ActiveX controls. The rest are specific to the particular control. The Object Tag tab is shown in Figure 32-5.

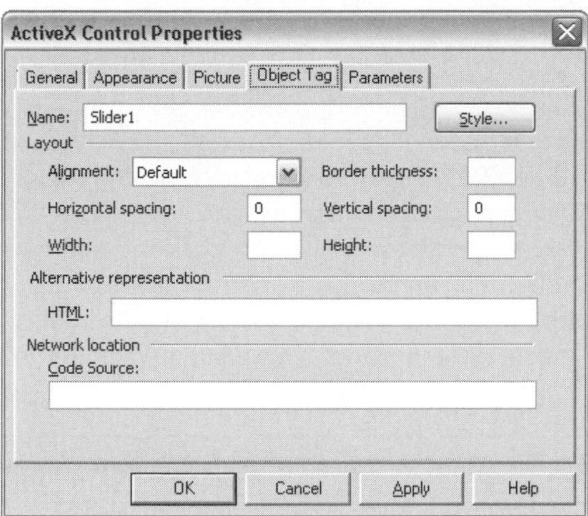

Figure 32-5. The Object Tag properties for an ActiveX control pertain to size and placement on the Web page and to download location. The browser, and not the ActiveX control, uses this information.

Chapter 32

The Object Tag tab contains these settings:

- **Name** Specify a name by which scripts on the same Web page can reference the control.
- **Layout** Use these options to specify the control's page placement and appearance:
  - **Alignment** Specify the control's position relative to surrounding text. Table 10-3, on page 275, describes the possible values.
  - **Border Thickness** Enter a nonzero value to surround the control with a border. The specified value controls the border's thickness in pixels.
  - **Horizontal Spacing** Enter the number of pixels that should separate the control from neighboring elements on the same line.
  - **Vertical Spacing** Enter the number of pixels that should separate the control from any text or pictures above and below it.
  - **Width** Specify, in pixels, the amount of horizontal space available to the control.
  - **Height** Specify, in pixels, the amount of vertical space available to the control.

> **Note** You can also resize the area available to an ActiveX control by selecting the control in Design view and then dragging its handles.

- **Alternative Representation** Specify what a browser should display if it doesn't support ActiveX controls:
  - **HTML** Supply any HTML that should appear if a browser doesn't support ActiveX controls. This can be plain text, HTML tags, or both.

- **Network Location** Use this option to specify a network location for the control and its data. This feature allows capable browsers such as Internet Explorer to fetch and install the control on demand:
  - **Code Source** Provide the URL of the file containing the ActiveX control. If a control isn't installed on a Web visitor's computer, browsers such as Internet Explorer can download and install it using this URL. If you want Web visitors to download an ActiveX control from your site, copy the control into your Web site from the location shown in Figure 32-3, and then specify its URL in the Code Source box. Alternatively, you might want to specify a Code Source location at a supplier's Web site rather than your own to ensure that Web visitors will get the most current version.

Note Be sure to observe copyright restrictions when distributing ActiveX controls.

The Parameters tab, shown in Figure 32-6, provides a general-purpose way to establish settings for the control. Whether default entries appear depends on the control. Any entries that do appear might be redundant with settings on tabs other than Object Tag and Parameters. With luck, any parameters you need to work with will appear on control-specific tabs or with recognizable names on the Parameters tab. If good luck eludes you, you'll have to locate and consult documentation from the control's supplier. The next two sections in this chapter address these issues in greater detail.

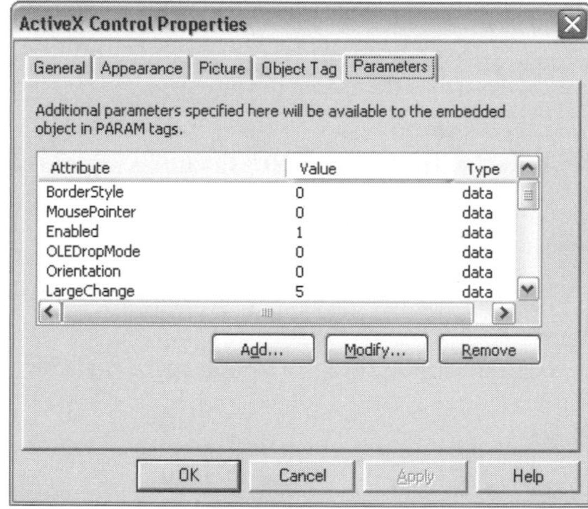

Figure 32-6. The Parameters tab lists values that the ActiveX control expects and uses.

Using Local-Property Editing

If an ActiveX control is installed on your computer and supports local-property editing, its property sheet displays three or more tabs. Figure 32-7 shows the General tab displayed for the Microsoft Calendar control. The Object Tag and Parameters tabs follow as usual.

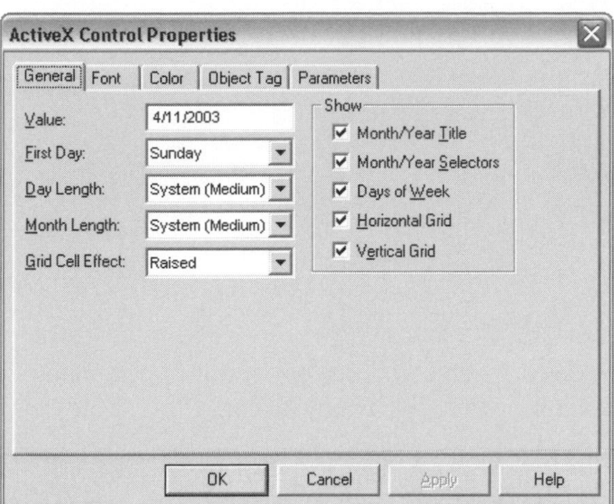

Figure 32-7. This is the local-property editing dialog box for the Microsoft ActiveX Calendar control.

The General, Font, and Color tabs list the Calendar control's available properties and current values. Use standard Windows dialog box procedures to modify these settings. When you've finished, click OK.

Each control that supports local-property editing displays its own set of tabs and properties. Recall, for example, the total of five tabs displayed for the Microsoft Slider control, shown previously in Figure 32-4.

As you can imagine, local-property editing is a much-appreciated feature among Web developers who use ActiveX controls, and most new controls include it. Local-property editing does increase the size of the control, however, making it bulkier and thus slower for the Web visitor to download.

Editing Object Parameters

Most ActiveX controls now support local-property editing. However, for those that don't (or aren't locally installed), FrontPage displays only the Object Tag and Parameters tabs. Initially, the parameters list is blank, and you have to add all required parameters manually, one by one. Here's the procedure for adding a parameter:

1. Obtain a list of the control's required and optional parameters. This information usually comes as documentation from the control's supplier.
2. Open the ActiveX Control Properties dialog box for the given control, and click the Parameters tab.
3. Click Add. The dialog box shown in Figure 32-8 appears.

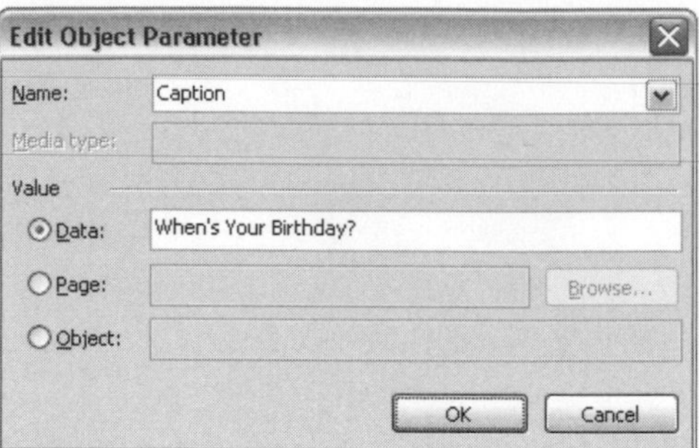

Figure 32-8. The Edit Object Parameter dialog box specifies parameters of ActiveX controls that don't support local-property editing.

4. Specify parameters using the following options:
   - **Name** Enter the name of the parameter, spelled exactly as shown in the control's documentation.
   - **Media Type** Specify the MIME type of the specified value. You can specify a Media Type only if you select the Page option in the Value section in the lower part of the dialog box.
   - **Data** Select this option if the parameter's value consists of data. Type the data into the associated text box.
   - **Page** Select this option if the parameter's value is the URL of a file. Enter the URL in the associated text box, or click Browse to locate the URL.
   - **Object** Select this option if the parameter's value is the name of another ActiveX control on the same page. Type the name of the control in the associated text box.
5. Click OK to close each dialog box.

To modify an existing parameter:

1. Select the parameter from the list shown in Figure 32-6, and then click Modify. (Alternatively, double-click the parameter.)
2. Change whatever settings require correction, and click OK to close each dialog box.

To remove a parameter setting, select it and click Remove.

Inserting and using ActiveX controls needn't be complex. Chapter 26, for example, explained how to use the Microsoft Media Player control for displaying video files. In many cases, however, the reason for putting a software component in a Web page is so that the Web visitor can interact with it. If this is your intent, you should know that connecting an ActiveX control to the rest of the Web page normally requires a small amount of program code that you must write yourself. The next two sections explain Web pages that use ActiveX controls exactly this way.

For more information about the Microsoft Media Player control, refer to "Inserting Video Files," on page 701.

Scripting the Microsoft Slider Control

The Microsoft Slider control displays a graduated scale that represents a range of numbers. A Web visitor can select any number within the given range by dragging a *slider* or *thumb* along the scale. The Volume Control applet in the Windows operating system, for example, uses Slider controls. The Slider control is an ActiveX control that's part of the Windows operating system; therefore, it's installed and ready for use on every Windows computer.

Note This section explains how a slider control can enhance a very simple HTML form. For more information about HTML forms, refer to Chapter 34, "Creating and Using Forms."

For more information about HTML code, refer to Chapter 40, "Working with HTML Code." For more information about scripting, refer to Chapter 41, "Working with Script Code."

Figure 32-9 shows a Web page that uses the Microsoft Slider control. The Web visitor can choose a quantity either by dragging the slider left or right or by typing a value in the text box. No matter which control the visitor uses, a bit of script code keeps the other control in sync.

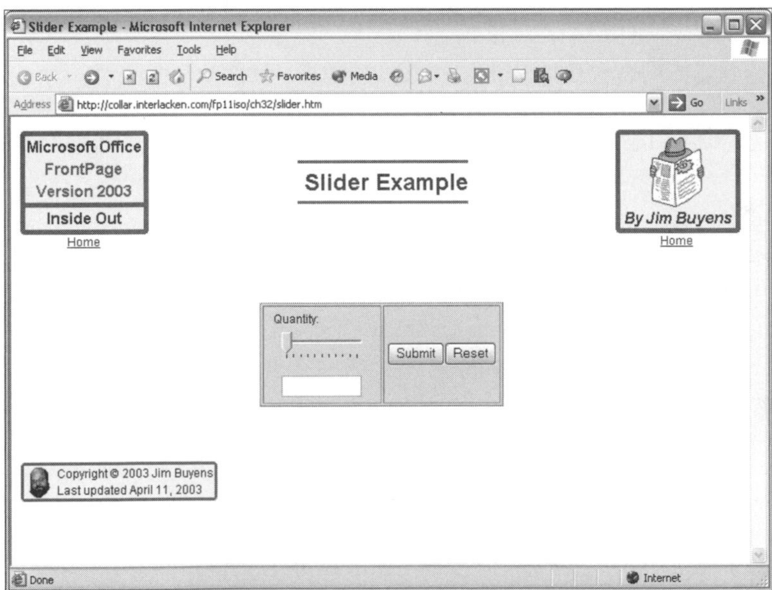

Figure 32-9. An ActiveX control displays the slider on this Web page. This particular slider selects a value between 0 and 10.

Clicking the Submit button submits the HTML form to the Web server for processing. Because the slider control isn't a standard HTML form element, the browser doesn't transmit its value. However, the browser does transmit the text box's value, and that's just as good.

Scripts that run in the same Web page as an ActiveX control can access the control's properties using a very simple notation: *<element name>.<attribute name>*. The *<element name>* is whatever appears in the Name box of the Object Tag tab in the ActiveX Control Properties dialog box. The object represented in Figure 32-5, for example, is named Slider1. The *<attribute name>* values appear on the Parameters tab in the same dialog box.

Scrolling down the list of attributes shown in Figure 32-6 reveals an attribute named *Value*. This attribute contains the value the Web visitor selects by dragging the slider. A script can use the expression *Slider1.value* to access or modify the current value of this attribute.

The Web page shown in Figure 32-9 contains two scripts:

- One script updates the text box whenever the Web visitor moves the slider.
- The other script moves the slider whenever the Web visitor changes the value in the text box.

The following script updates the text box whenever the Web visitor moves the slider. This script can appear almost anywhere in the Web page, but somewhere in the <head> section is probably best.

```
1 <script LANGUAGE="JavaScript" FOR="Slider1" EVENT="Change">
2 if (navigator.appName.substring(0,9) == "Microsoft") {
3   form1.qty.value = Slider1.value
4 }
5 </script>
```

Chapter 41, "Working with Script Code," provides an overview of script code, but here are the details for this example:

- Line 1 denotes that this is the start of a script, that the programming language is JavaScript, that the script pertains to the *Slider1* element, and that the script should run whenever any property of the *Slider1* element changes.
- Line 2 verifies that the browser is Internet Explorer.
- If the browser *is* Internet Explorer, line 3 copies the *value* property of the *Slider1* ActiveX control into the *value* property of the text box. The name of the text box is *qty*, a fact you could confirm by double-clicking the text box in Design view and inspecting the Name box in the Text Box Properties dialog box. The name of the form is *form1*, which you could verify by right-clicking anywhere in the form, choosing Form Properties from the shortcut menu, and again checking the Name box.
- Line 4 terminates the range of the *if* statement begun on line 2.
- Line 5 marks the end of the script.

The script that updates the slider control whenever the Web visitor updates the text box is slightly more complicated. It starts with the following line, which is the HTML for the text box itself:

```
<input type="text" name="qty" size="10"
onChange="qtyChange(qty.value)">
```

The *onChange* attribute in this tag specifies a single JavaScript statement that executes whenever the value of the text box changes. As coded, that statement calls a function named *qtyChange* and passes the new value *qty.value* as an argument. Here's the code for this function:

```
1 <script>
2 function qtyChange(aqty){
3   if (isNaN(aqty)) {
4     alert("Quantity " + aqty + " is invalid.")
5   }else{
6     if (navigator.appName.substring(0,9) == "Microsoft") {
7       form1.Slider1.value = aqty;
8     }
9   }
10 }
11 </script>
```


- Line 1 marks the beginning of a block of script code. The default language is JavaScript.
- Line 2 marks the beginning of the *qtyChange* function. The function takes one argument, named *aqty*.
- The *isNaN* function in line 3 returns *true* if *aqty* is not a number. (*isNaN* is "is not a number," get it?)
- If *aqty* is not a number, line 4 displays an error message.
- Otherwise, *aqty* must be a number, and:
  - Line 6 verifies that the browser is Internet Explorer.
  - Line 7 copies the *aqty* value into the *Slider1* control.
  - Line 8 terminates the range of the *if* statement begun on line 6.
- The remaining lines close out the first *if* statement, the function definition, and the block of script code.

Submitting the form requests a Web page named sliderqty.asp from the Web server. This is an ASP page containing script code that runs on the Web server as well as ordinary HTML code. The inner workings of ASP is beyond the scope of this discussion, but at a high level, the sliderqty.asp page retrieves the values submitted with the HTML form and adds them to the outgoing Web page for display. Figure 32-10 shows a typical result.

For more information about ASP, refer to Appendix J, "Processing Form Data with ASP and ASP.NET Pages."

To view this page in FrontPage, open the sample Web site you installed from the companion CD, and then open ch32/slider.htm.

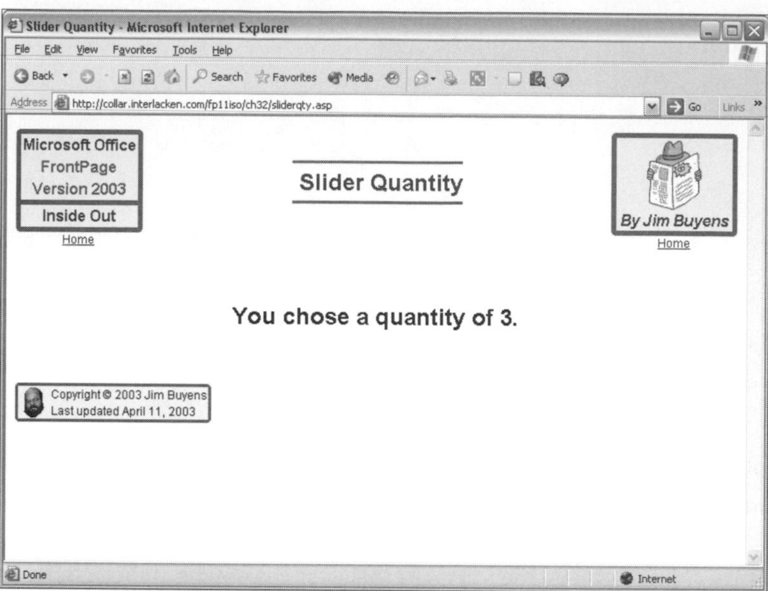

Figure 32-10. Submitting the HTML form shown in Figure 32-9 produces a Web page that incorporates the specified value.

To actually submit the form and see the results shown in Figure 32-10, you must satisfy all of the following requirements:

- The sample Web site must reside on a FrontPage-enabled Web server capable of running ASP.

For more information about using server-based Web sites, refer to "Using Server-Based Web Sites," on page 146.

- The sample Web site (or at least the ch32 folder) must be marked as executable.

For more information about marking Web server folders as executable, refer to "Reviewing Folder Settings," on page 1144, or "Configuring Home Directory Settings," in Appendix O.

- Even if the Web server is running on your own computer, you must use an HTTP URL to load the slider.htm page. Loading the slider.htm page directly from disk won't work because the browser will then try to load sliderqty.asp from disk as well. And *that* won't work because:
  - Loading an ASP page from disk doesn't execute any script code that's marked to run on the Web server.
  - Even if you changed the server-side script code to browser-side script code, none of the software resources present on the Web server would be available.

Of course, a real Web page of this type would contain more than one field. The ASP page or other process on the Web server would perform more complex processing than simply echoing values back to the Web visitor. Nevertheless, this example illustrates the use of ActiveX controls to enhance the Web visitor's experience.

This Web page, by the way, works perfectly well in Netscape Navigator. For proof, inspect Figure 32-11. Netscape ignores the slider object, and the script code bypasses any references to *Slider1* when Netscape is the browser. The page therefore functions as a perfectly normal HTML form.

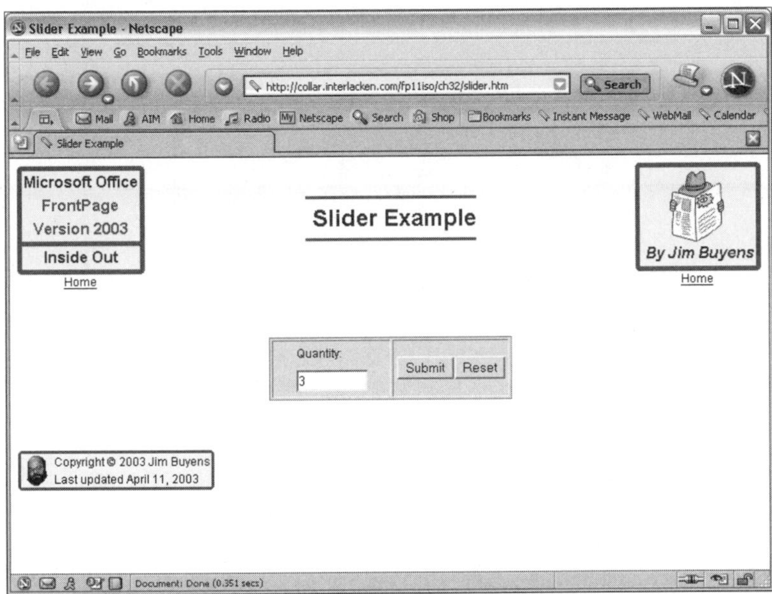

Figure 32-11. Netscape Navigator ignores ActiveX controls in Web pages. However, with suitable precautions, the page can still be functional.

Scripting the Microsoft Calendar Control

Figure 32-12 shows FrontPage displaying another ActiveX control: a Calendar control. When the Web visitor uses the list boxes at the upper right to select a month and a year, the grid of days changes to reflect the proper dates. Clicking any day makes the month, day, and year available to scripts and other elements in the Web page.

The Calendar control is an attractive way to collect dates from Web visitors, but as with the Slider control, clicking an HTML form's Submit button doesn't transmit the Calendar control's values to the Web server. To overcome this limitation, this Web page's Submit button is actually a push button that runs a small script. The script copies the Calendar control's currently selected year, month, and day values into three hidden form fields and then submits the form. This transmits the three copied values to the Web server for processing.

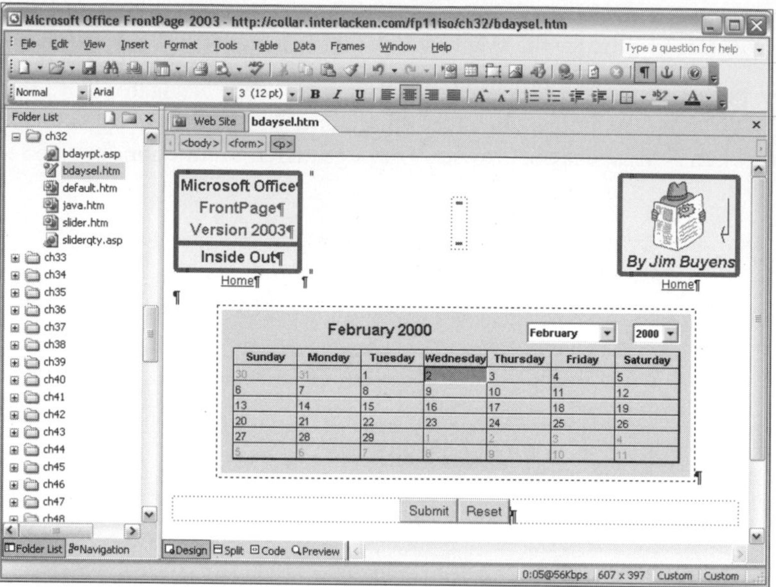

Figure 32-12. A Calendar ActiveX control displays the interactive calendar on this page.

You can create most of the HTML code for the push button by choosing Form from the Insert menu and then choosing Push Button. The button's name isn't important, but if you want it to be *btnSub*, display the button's Properties dialog box and change the Name field. The code is as follows:

```
<input type="button" value="Submit" name="btnSub"
onClick="subForm();">
```

Notice that this button isn't a Submit button. Clicking it doesn't submit the form. Instead, the *onClick* attribute runs a function named *subForm* whenever the visitor clicks the button. You must add this attribute to the button's HTML code manually, in Code view.

> **Tip** If you select a button (or any other page element) in Design view, it will still be selected when you switch to Code view.

The following information will help you understand the code for the *subForm* function:

- The Calendar control's name is *cal01*.
- Whenever the Web visitor selects a date, the Calendar control's *month*, *day*, and *year* attributes reflect that selected date. If no date is selected, all three attributes contain *0*.
- The HTML form's name is *form1*.
- The HTML form contains three hidden form fields named *qmon*, *qday*, and *qyr*. These fields have no visual presence on the Web page, but the browser nevertheless submits their values when it submits the form.

To view the definition of these hidden form fields:

1. Right-click anywhere in the HTML form (the Submit button is a good spot) and choose Form Properties from the shortcut menu.
2. When the Form Properties dialog box appears, click Advanced. Figure 32-13 shows the results.

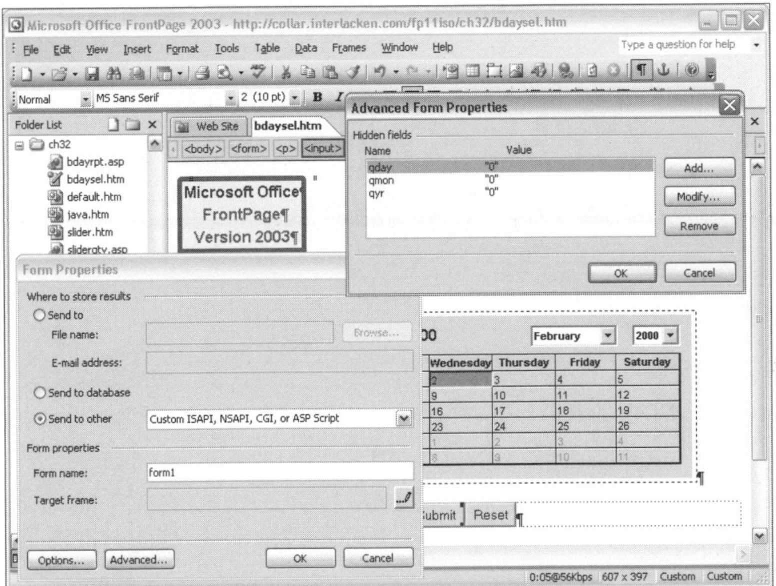

Figure 32-13. The HTML that creates the Submit button on this Web page has three hidden form fields.

When the Web visitor clicks Submit, the *subForm* function first checks to see whether *cal01.day*—the Calendar control's day of the month value—is greater than zero. If so, it copies the *cal01.month*, *cal01.day*, and *cal01.year* values to the hidden form fields *qmon*, *qday*, and *qyr* and then submits the form. Otherwise, it displays a message to the Web visitor and then exits. The following is the actual code for this function:

```
function subForm() {
  if (cal01.day > 0) {
    form1.qmon.value = cal01.month;
    form1.qday.value = cal01.day;
    form1.qyr.value = cal01.year;
    document.form1.submit();
  }else{
    alert("You must select a date!");
    return;
  }
}
```

To view this page in a browser, open the sample Web site, select ch32/bdaysel.htm, and then choose Preview In Browser from the File menu. Figure 32-14 shows the results.

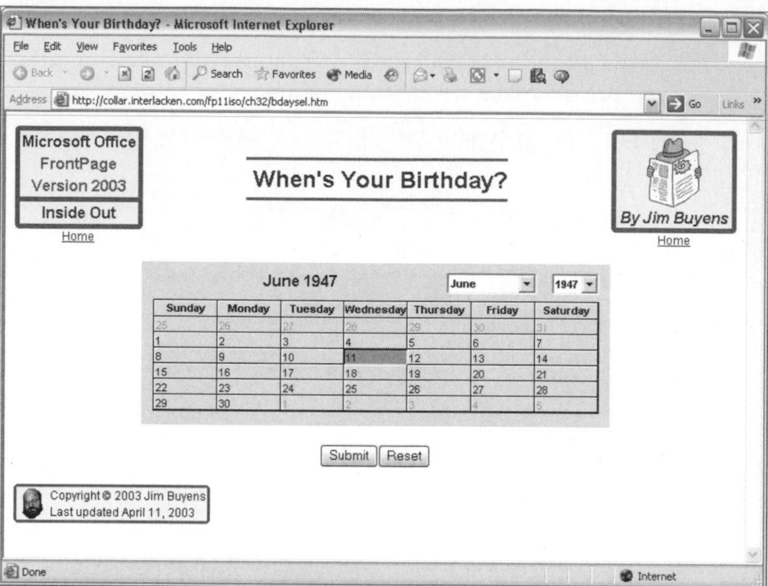

Figure 32-14. Internet Explorer correctly displays the page edited in Figure 32-12.

As in the slider example, submitting the form shown in Figure 32-14 runs an ASP page that displays the submitted data back to the Web visitor. All the requirements regarding a server-based Web site, executable folders, and HTTP URLs apply. Figure 32-15 shows the results.

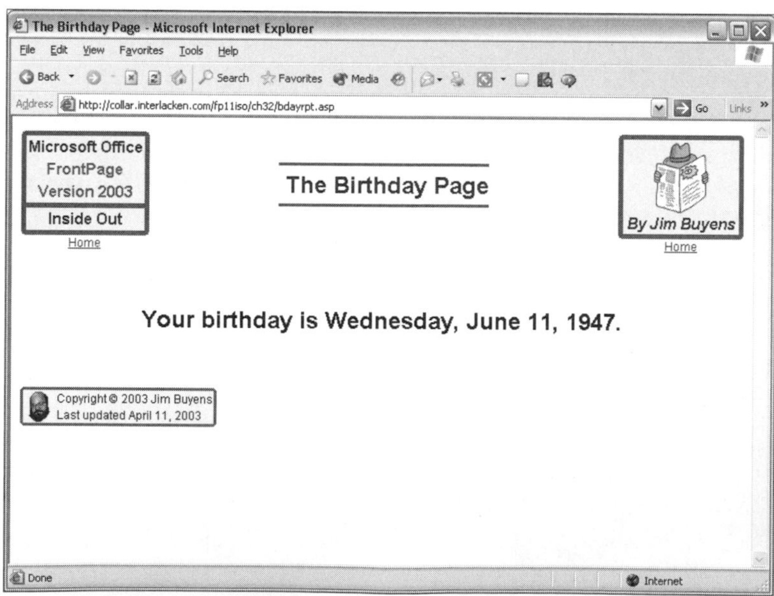

Figure 32-15. Submitting the HTML form shown in Figure 32-14 produces a Web page that incorporates the specified date.

Incorporating Java Applets

Java is a popular programming language closely resembling C++, but with restrictions that help the innocent avoid frustration. A team at Sun Microsystems invented Java, and Sun remains its guiding authority.

Java programs don't compile to a processor's native instruction set; instead, they compile to the instruction set of an imaginary computer called the *Java Virtual Machine*. Java programs are portable to any type of computer and any operating system that has a virtual machine emulator. The emulator is a piece of software that carries out Java Virtual Machine instructions using local native instructions so that the compiled Java program can run.

Java applets are small Java programs that run as part of a Web page. Applets are considerably less capable than ordinary programs—even ordinary Java programs. Applets can take up space on the screen, play sounds, modify the browser window, interact with scripts, and open various connections to the machine that delivered the applet to the visitor's browser. Applets can't, however, make changes to the local machine's files or hardware settings. The collective name for these restrictions is the *Java sandbox*. The idea is that an applet, playing within its sandbox, can't do anything at all to your computer; therefore, it can't do anything bad.

Applets reside on a Web server. You can locate many freeware or shareware applets on the Web, download them to your own site, and use them in your pages. Browsers download applets just as they do pictures or other files used on a Web page, but of course the browser runs the applet rather than displaying it as a picture.

Note The examples in this section use a freeware Java applet named GraphicsButton. This applet displays a button with a specified picture on its face and jumps to a specified Web location when a Web visitor clicks the button. In addition, the edges of the button depress when the visitor clicks it.

To obtain GraphicsButton, its documentation, and other information about Java, visit Pineapplesoft at *www.pineapplesoft.com/goodies/*.

Applets, like ActiveX controls, have properties and methods. The ActiveX distinction between methods and events is discarded in Java; both are simply considered methods. To add a Java applet to one of your Web pages:

1. Obtain a copy of the applet and its documentation.
2. Use FrontPage to open the Web page that will contain the applet.
3. Import the applet file, which normally has a file extension of .class, into your Web site. You'll probably find it convenient, as many Web developers do, to place all Java applets in a folder named classes.
4. Choose Web Component from the Insert menu, or click Web Component on the Standard toolbar.

Web Component

5 When the Insert Web Component dialog box appears, select Advanced Controls in the Component Type list on the left, and select Java Applet in the Choose A Control list on the right.

6 Click Finish to display the dialog box shown in Figure 32-16, which shows some typical values filled in.

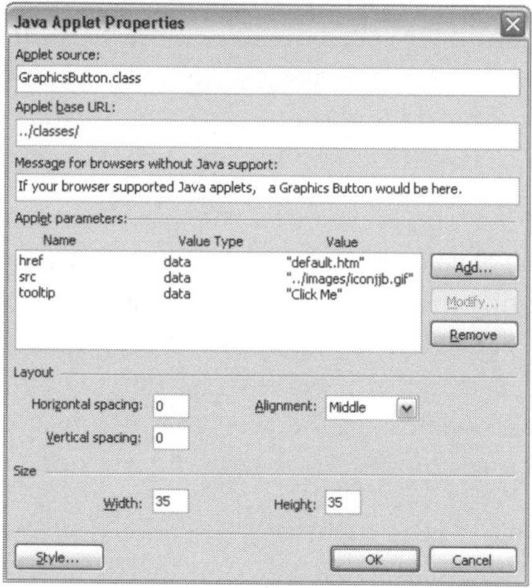

Figure 32-16. This dialog box adds a Java applet to a Web page.

7 When the Java Applet Properties dialog box appears, all its properties are blank or set to their defaults. Supply the following options as required:

- **Applet Source** Specify the name of the Java applet file. Don't specify a complete URL or a path of any kind.
- **Applet Base URL** Specify the URL path to the applet file. Don't include http://, the computer name, the port number, or the name of the applet file itself.
- **Message For Browsers Without Java Support** Specify any text the browser should display if it doesn't support Java applets.
- **Applet Parameters** Use this list to specify any settings the applet requires for proper operation. Click the Add button to specify a name and value for each required applet parameter. Step 8 describes this process in detail. Consult the applet's documentation for a list of mandatory and optional parameter names and data values.
- **Layout** Specify how you want the applet to appear on the Web page. Horizontal Spacing specifies the number of pixels that should separate the applet from the nearest left and right elements on the same line. Vertical Spacing specifies the number of pixels that should separate the applet from the nearest elements above and below it. Alignment specifies how the browser should position the applet relative to surrounding text. For a list of possible values, consult Table 10-3, on page 275.

- **Size** Specify how much window space the applet should consume. Width specifies a width in pixels. Height specifies a height in pixels. You can also modify these properties by selecting the applet in Design view and dragging its handles.

8 Clicking Add in the Applet Parameters section of the dialog box (Figure 32-16) produces the Set Attribute Value dialog box, shown in Figure 32-17.

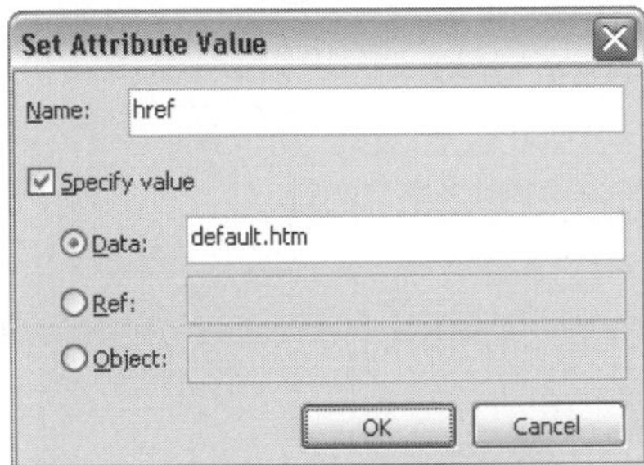

Figure 32-17. This dialog box sets parameter values for Java applets.

Configure a parameter by filling in these settings:

- **Name** Specify the name of the parameter, spelled exactly as described in the applet's documentation.
- **Specify Value** Select this check box for parameters that take a value. Clear it for keyword parameters.
- **Data** Select this option and fill in the accompanying text box if the value you want to specify is a string.
- **Ref** Select this option and fill in the accompanying text box if the value you want to specify is a URL.
- **Object** Select this option and fill in the accompanying text box if the value you want to specify is the URL of an Object element in the same Web page.

To modify a parameter setting:

1. Select its entry in the Applet Parameters list (Figure 32-16), and click Modify. (Alternatively, double-click the desired parameter.)
2. Change whatever settings require correction, and click OK.

To remove a parameter, select it and click the Remove button.

Figure 32-18 shows the GraphicsButton applet open in both FrontPage and Internet Explorer. Like ActiveX controls, Java applets don't execute within FrontPage; this accounts for the difference in their appearance.

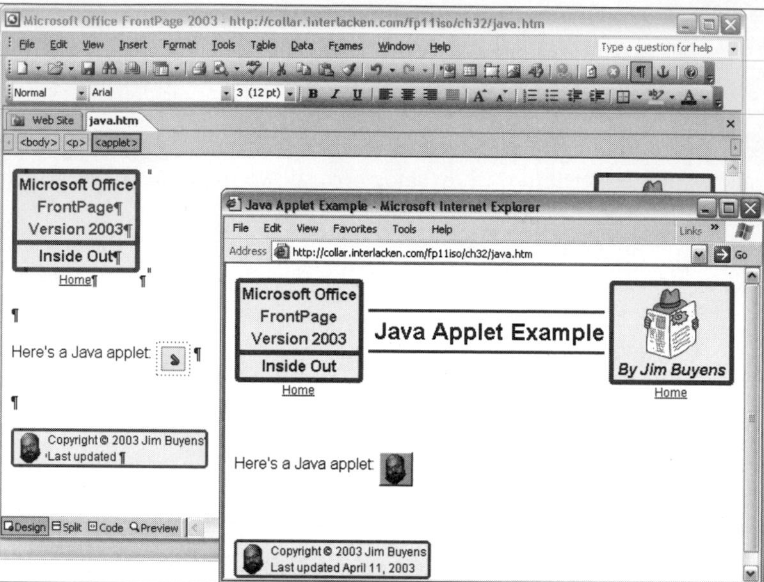

Figure 32-18. Because Java applets don't execute in FrontPage, you display their true appearance only by browsing them.

In Summary…

This chapter explained how to enhance Web pages with ActiveX controls and Java applets. These are programmed objects that operate within the browser window. Making full use of such objects might require writing small amounts of script code.

The next chapter explains how to create FrontPage discussion groups and how to make visitors register themselves on non-Microsoft Web servers.

Chapter 33

Discussion Web Sites and Self-Registration

People love to talk, and people on the Web are no exception. The Web offers lots of ways to talk, including e-mail, newsgroups, chat rooms, and message boards. FrontPage supports this urge by providing a message board of its own called a *Discussion Web Site.*

A FrontPage Discussion Web Site works by creating a Web page out of each message a visitor enters on an HTML form. Microsoft Office FrontPage 2003 indexes the discussion by means of a table of contents that's organized either chronologically or by thread. (A *thread* is an initial message with responses listed and indented below it.) In addition, visitors can search messages using the Web Search component.

Related to Discussion Web Sites is the issue of self-registration. This feature provides a way for Web visitors to identify themselves and then create logon accounts for using a Web site with restricted access.

As you might suspect, self-registration involves security risks. Just because someone enters a name on a form doesn't mean that the name is real; you'd be surprised at how often the names of historical figures and cartoon characters show up in such accounts. Because of this, and because Microsoft Web servers use Microsoft Windows system logon accounts for Web authentication, the FrontPage Self-Registration feature doesn't work on those Web servers. This chapter therefore concludes with a brief overview of alternative self-registration systems.

Creating and Managing Discussion Web Sites

A Discussion Web Site accumulates messages that Web visitors submit through a special HTML form. The Microsoft FrontPage Server Extensions perform the following tasks:

- Save each message as a Web page
- Build Next and Previous hyperlinks between pages
- Maintain an index page of all articles

In some respects, Discussion Web Sites resemble Usenet newsgroups. Discussion Web Sites can also incorporate the Search component to locate articles containing specified text and the Registration component to identify Web visitors.

Discussion Web Sites work only on Web servers running the FrontPage Server Extensions. If your server runs Microsoft Windows SharePoint Services, you should use the Discussion Boards feature of a SharePoint Team Site.

For more information about SharePoint team site discussion boards, refer to "Using Web Discussions," on page 933

Creating a New Discussion Web Site

Here are the steps required to create a Discussion Web Site:

1. Open the Web site where the Discussion Web Site will reside. If you're creating a new site, open its parent. Log in as an administrator.
2. Display the Web Site Templates dialog box using either of these methods:
   - Choose New from the File menu. When the New task pane appears, under New Web Site, click More Web Site Templates.
   - Click the Create A New Normal Page drop-down arrow on the Standard toolbar, and then choose Web Site.

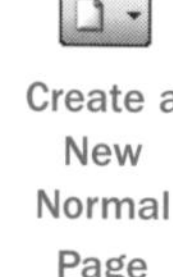

Create a New Normal Page

3. When the Web Site Templates dialog box appears, make sure that the General tab is selected, and then select Discussion Web Wizard.
4. In the Options section, either specify a location for the Discussion Web Site, or select the Add To Current Web Site check box. The FrontPage Server Extensions must be installed on any server you specify.
5. If the Web server at the given location requires Secure Sockets Layer (SSL) communication, select the Encrypted Connection Required check box.
6. Click OK.

At this point, FrontPage will start the Discussion Web Site Wizard. The following steps explain how to complete this wizard:

1. When the Discussion Web Site Wizard displays its welcome page, click Next.
2. On the second page of the Discussion Web Site Wizard, shown in Figure 33-1, select options as follows:.
   - **Submission Form (Required)** This option is mandatory. It provides the form for discussion participants to enter messages.
   - **Table Of Contents (Suggested)** Make sure that this check box is selected if you want an index page containing hyperlinks to each message in the discussion.
   - **Search Form** Make sure that this check box is selected to allow visitors to search all messages for a word or phrase.
   - **Threaded Replies** Make sure that this check box is selected if your index will sort messages by thread, with replies indented below each main topic. Clear this check box to keep all messages in chronological order.
   - **Confirmation Page** Make sure that this check box is selected if Web visitors should receive confirmation after posting discussion entries.

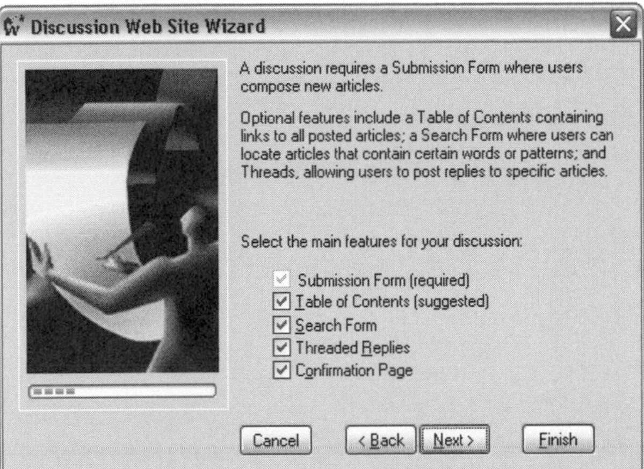

Figure 33-1. Choose the major features of your Discussion Web Site using this dialog box.

3 Click Next to display the wizard page shown in Figure 33-2.

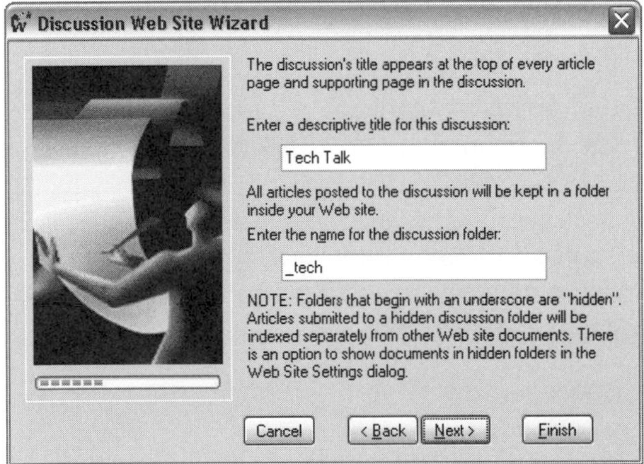

Figure 33-2. Give the Discussion Web Site an external title and an internal folder name.

On this page, specify:

- A descriptive name (that visitors will see) for the Discussion Web Site.
- A name for the folder that will contain the posted messages. This is a folder within your Web site, and not the Web site's root folder. The name must be two to eight characters long and begin with an underscore.

> **Tip** The short name of a Discussion Web Site must conform to the rules for naming folders on the system that hosts the Web site. Pithy, intuitive names are usually better than verbose ones. You can provide a more descriptive name later.

4 Click Next, and then use the wizard page shown in Figure 33-3 to choose the fields you want on the input form. The Category and Product fields are drop-down lists. You can add more fields later by editing the form directly in FrontPage. When you're satisfied with your entry, click Next.

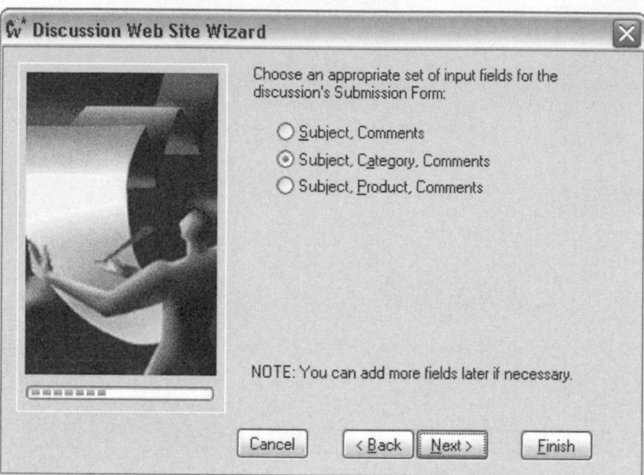

Figure 33-3. Choose the fields you want included in the Discussion Web Site's submission form.

5 If your Discussion Web Site will be restricted to registered visitors, select Yes on the next wizard page, shown in Figure 33-4. Click Next to continue.

Caution Before selecting this option, review the restrictions regarding self-registration described in "Enabling User Self-Registration," later in this chapter.

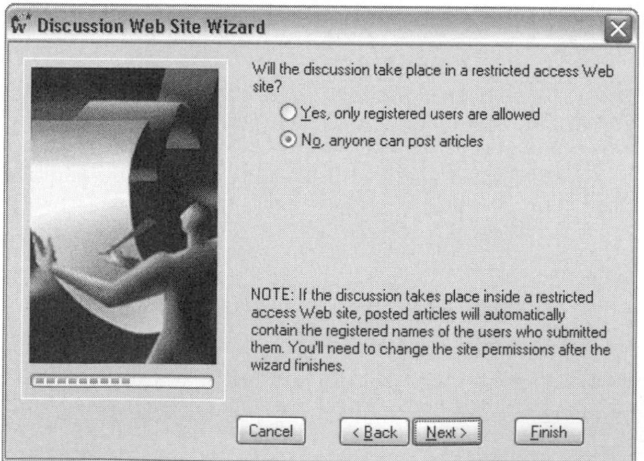

Figure 33-4. Select Yes to restrict the Discussion Web Site to registered visitors.

6 The next wizard page, shown in Figure 33-5, controls the order for displaying posted articles. After selecting Oldest To Newest (Default) or Newest To Oldest, click Next to continue.

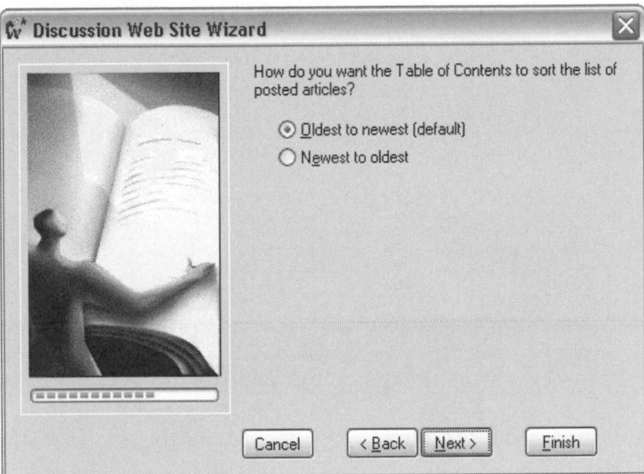

Figure 33-5. Specify the order in which posted articles should appear.

7 When the wizard page shown in Figure 33-6 appears, specify whether you want the discussion's table of contents to be the home page for the Discussion Web Site.

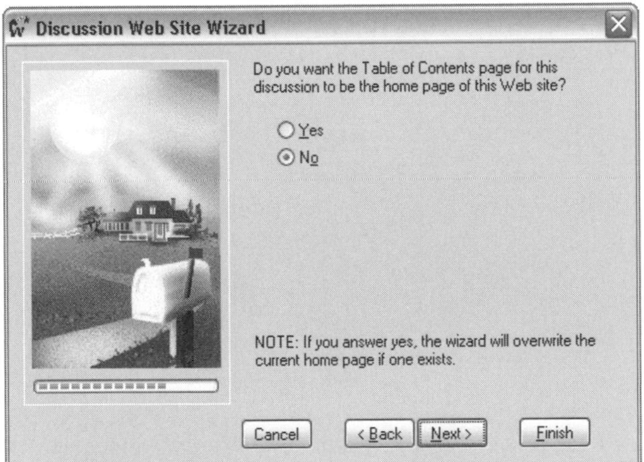

Figure 33-6. Selecting Yes makes the table of contents the home page for the Discussion Web Site.

- If you're creating the discussion in a new site, it's probably best to select Yes.
- If you're adding the discussion to an existing Web site, selecting Yes overwrites the Web site's existing home page. To prevent this, select No.

8 If you chose in step 2 to have a search form, the wizard page shown in Figure 33-7 appears next. Choose the combination of fields a search of the discussion should report, and then click Next.

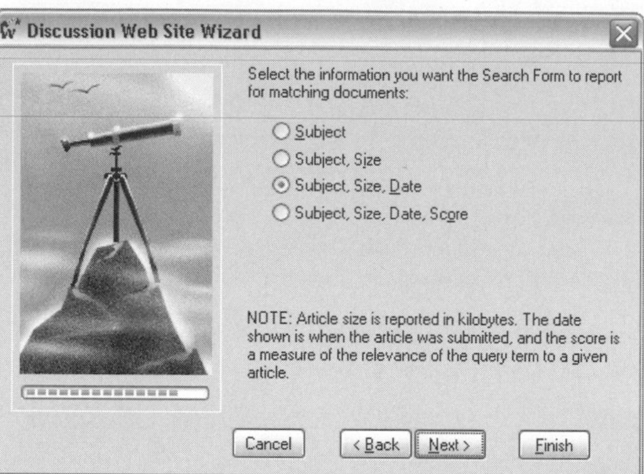

Figure 33-7. Specify the result fields a search of the discussion should display.

9 Use the wizard page shown in Figure 33-8 to control the use of frames. As you select different settings in the Frame Options section, the diagram to the left changes to show the resulting appearance. You can adjust the relative frame sizes by dragging their borders.

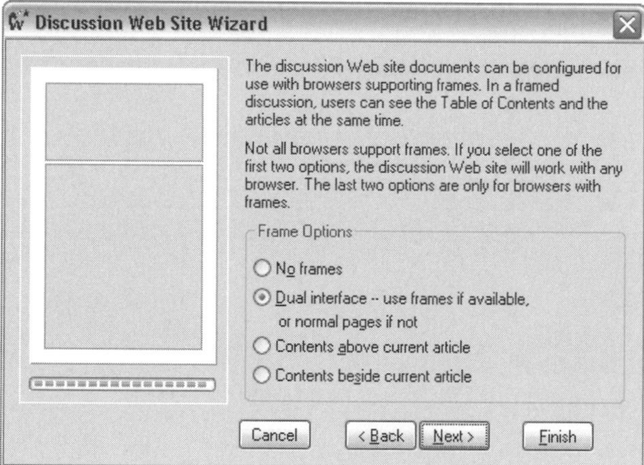

Figure 33-8. Choose a frame design, or none, for the Discussion Web Site.

10 The final wizard page in the Discussion Web Site Wizard has no input options—just a reminder that you can use the Back and Next buttons to review and modify any settings. The wizard saves nothing until you click Finish. When you're satisfied with your entries, click Finish, and let the wizard create your Discussion Web Site.

Even if you created the discussion in a new Web site and chose in step 5 to restrict the Web site to registered visitors, FrontPage won't automatically restrict access to the discussion. The new

Web site, if you created one, will have default permissions. To restrict access, do either of the following:

- Use the Permissions Administration Web page to modify permissions for the Web Site. To display this page, choose Server from the Tools menu, and then choose Permissions.

For more information about the Permissions Administration Web page, refer to "Administering User Rights," in Appendix P.

- Activate self-registration, as described later in this chapter.

Examining a New Discussion Web Site

A typical discussion contains the following folders and files. (The prefix *tech_* varies, depending on naming conventions within your Web site.)

- **tech_frm.htm** The home page for the discussion. If you chose in step 7 of the previous procedure to make the discussion's table of contents the home page for the Discussion Web Site, this page will be named with the Web server's default file name —for example, default.htm or index.htm.

  The page itself is a frames page with the tech_tocf.htm table of contents page and the tech_welc.htm welcome page as frame sources.
- **tech_cfrm.htm** A confirmation page that provides feedback after a visitor contributes a message.
- **tech_post.htm** The form that posts messages.
- **tech_srch.htm** The form that initiates a text search for messages.
- **tech_toc.htm** A table of contents page formatted for freestanding use.
- **tech_tocf.htm** A table of contents page formatted for use within the home page.
- **tech_welc.htm** A welcome page formatted for use within the home page.

Figure 33-9 shows the tech_frm.htm frames page displaying the tech_tocf.htm table of contents page in the upper frame and the tech_welc.htm welcome page in the lower. Indentations in the table of contents indicate threading—that is, responses to an article are indented under it.

Clicking an article in the table of contents displays it as shown in Figure 33-10. The article frame includes a menu bar for displaying the table of contents, searching the entire discussion for words or phrases, posting a new article, posting a reply to the current article, jumping to the next or previous articles, or jumping to a higher article in the thread hierarchy. The discussion form handler constructs these pages from a combination of submitted data and included templates.

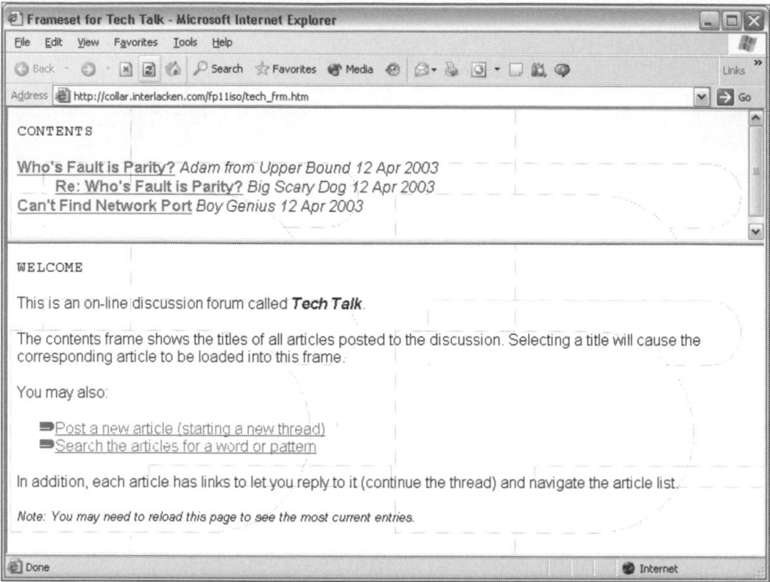

Figure 33-9. The default frames page displays the discussion's contents at the top and a welcome page below.

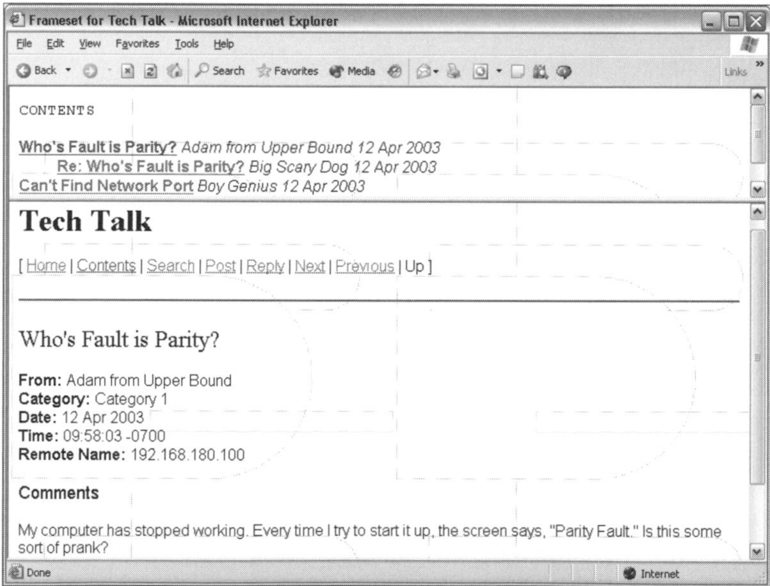

Figure 33-10. Displaying an article with frames combines the table of contents with the article text and details.

Figure 33-11 shows the discussion group submission form open in FrontPage. This page, like the others, provides more function than style. You'll almost certainly want to update the Category drop-down list with meaningful choices, include a site logo, add hyperlinks to other pages, and so forth.

For more information about configuring drop-down list properties, refer to "Setting Drop-Down Box Properties," on page 840.

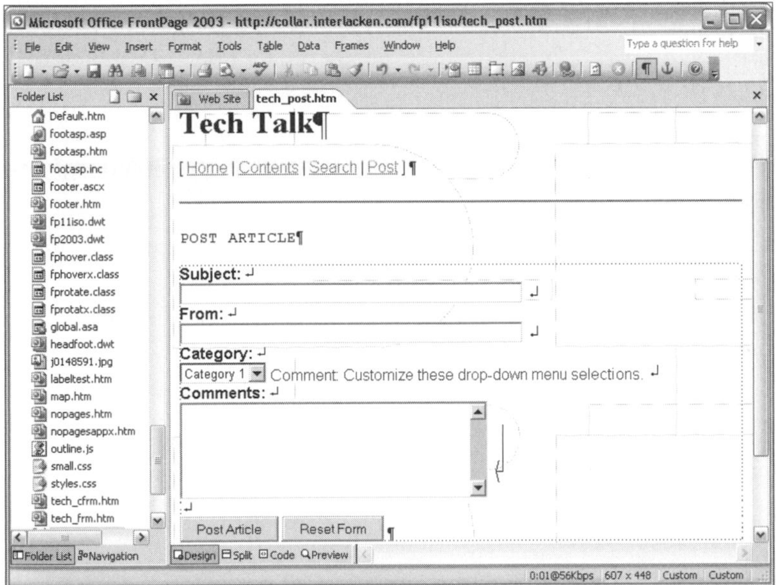

Figure 33-11. FrontPage displays a Discussion Web Site's submission form.

Enhancing Your Discussion Web Site's Appearance

The Discussion Web Site Wizard creates pages that—except for themes—are spartan at best. You'll almost certainly want to modify the styles, page layouts, and colors to make your Discussion Web Site distinctive and attractive. Be careful, however, to make cosmetic changes with these points in mind:

- Take care not to delete or modify hyperlinks, form fields, or form properties involved in making the Discussion Web Site work. You can change the Category drop-down list to an option button group, for example, but you must retain the element name Category.
- Don't delete any included sections. If you do, FrontPage will only include them again when it constructs future pages. Instead, change the content of the included sections.
- FrontPage makes frequent use of FrontPage components when constructing discussion group pages. View this as a help, and work within the structure provided. The FrontPage components provide a degree of centralized control impossible with self-contained pages.

Caution Like most pages in a FrontPage Discussion Web Site, the header and footer sections are included with the Include Page component. To modify these sections, *don't* delete the Include Page component and enter something in its place; instead, modify the included file.

Modifying Discussion Web Site Properties

The submission form stores most operational settings for a Discussion Web Site. Submissions are, after all, a Discussion Web Site's primary update transactions. So, to view or modify the properties of an existing Discussion Web Site:

1. Open the Discussion Web Site's article submission page in Design view. To find it, look for a page named <discussion-prefix>_post.htm or a page with the title Submission Form.
2. Right-click the HTML form on the submission page, and choose Form Properties from the shortcut menu.
3. In the Form Properties dialog box, Send To Other should be selected, and Discussion Form Handler should be specified as the location.
4. Click Options to display the properties of the Discussion Form Handler.

The Options For Discussion Form Handler dialog box has three tabs. The first of these is the Discussion tab, shown in Figure 33-12.

Figure 33-12. This is the Discussion tab of the Options For Discussion Form Handler dialog box.

You can configure the following settings on this tab:

- **Title** Supply a name for the discussion group. This name will appear on article pages.
- **Directory** Name the folder in the Discussion Web Site that will contain the article pages. This name must be two to eight characters long and begin with an underscore.
- **Table Of Contents Layout** Use this section to control which fields appear in the table of contents:
  - **Form Fields** Enter the names of one or more form elements, separated by spaces. Together, the contents of these fields will become the article's subject in the table of contents.
  - **Time** Select this check box if you want the table of contents to include the time the Web visitor submitted the article.
  - **Date** Select this check box if you want the table of contents to include the date the Web visitor submitted the article.
  - **Remote Computer Name** Select this check box if you want the table of contents to include the name or IP address of the submitting Web visitor's computer. Whether you get the computer's name or IP address depends on the configuration of your Web server. If you get the name, it might serve to identify the Web visitor's organization. IP addresses are considerably less interesting.
  - **User Name** Select this check box if you want the table of contents to include the name of the Web visitor who submitted each article.

> **Caution** The user name will be blank unless you set the Discussion Web Site's permissions to block anonymous access. To do so, choose Server from the FrontPage Tools menu, and then select Permissions.

- **Order Newest To Oldest** Select this check box to make new postings appear at the beginning of the table of contents. If this check box is cleared, new articles appear at the end.
- **Get Background And Colors From Page (Optional)** Specify the location of a Web page whose background color, background picture, and text colors will apply to all pages in the Discussion Web Site.
- **Browse** Click to select the background and colors page from the current Web Site.

The Article tab of the Options For Discussion Form Handler dialog box, shown in Figure 33-13, controls the page layout of discussion group articles.

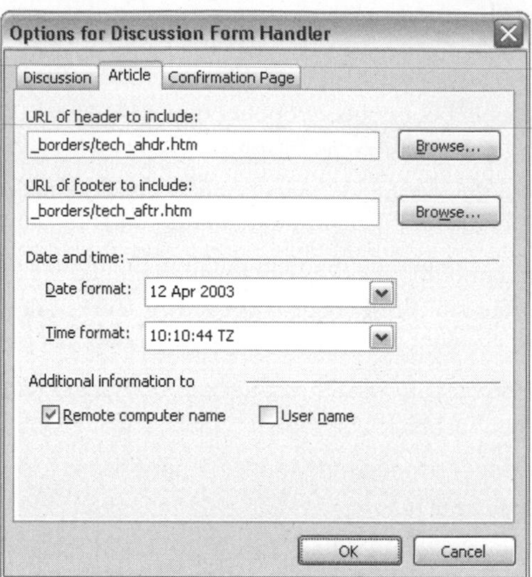

Figure 33-13. The Article tab controls the format of pages the Discussion Form Handler creates.

This tab controls the following properties:

- **URL Of Header To Include** Specify the location of a page you want FrontPage to include as the header of each article, or click the Browse button to select the header page from the current Web site.
- **URL Of Footer To Include** Specify the location of a page you want FrontPage to include as the footer of each article, or click Browse to select the footer page from the current Web site.
- **Date And Time** Choose a format (or None) in each of the following drop-down lists:
  - **Date Format** Choose a date format to display the date the Web visitor submitted the article.
  - **Time Format** Choose a time format to display the time the Web visitor submitted the article.
- **Additional Information To** Select either of the check boxes in this section to include the corresponding information about each article page:
  - **Remote Computer Name** The name of the submitting Web visitor's computer.
  - **User Name** The name of the Web visitor who submitted the article.

Figure 33-14 shows the Confirmation Page tab of the Options For Discussion Form Handler dialog box.

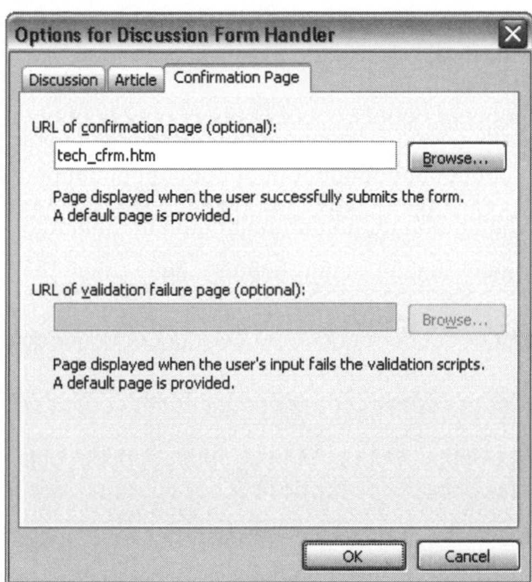

Figure 33-14. The Confirmation Page tab optionally specifies a page that provides feedback to visitors who post discussion articles.

Chapter 33

This tab contains two input fields, namely:

- **URL Of Confirmation Page** Specify the location of a page that provides feedback to Web visitors who post articles. If you leave this field blank, The discussion form handler will create a default page on the fly.

For more information about confirmation pages, refer to "Configuring Confirmation Page Options," on page 868.

- **URL Of Validation Failure Page** This field is always dimmed fro the discussion form handler.

The Search facility is optional. If included, it uses the same Search facilities as any other Web Site.

For more information about the FrontPage Search facility, refer to "Using the Web Search Component," on page 733.

Managing Discussion Web Sites

Discussion Web Sites are an add-only facility. There's no automatic mechanism to purge old articles or offensive postings.

- To delete old articles:
  1. Open the Web site in FrontPage.
  2. Open the discussion folder. This is the folder you specified under Enter The Name For The Discussion Folder in Figure 33-2.
  3. Delete the article files you no longer want. Each article resides in a separate Web page, and you can delete these just as you would any other Web page. For example, select one or more pages and then press Delete.
  4. To regenerate the discussion's table of contents, choose Recalculate Hyperlinks from the Tools menu.
- To correct an article, update it as you would any other Web page.

FrontPage Discussion Web Sites can be useful and convenient tools, but their lack of an automatic purge mechanism for old articles is a serious limitation. Discussion Web Sites are best suited to topics requiring permanent retention or topics where the entire Discussion Web Site can be deleted after some period.

The Discussion Boards facility in a SharePoint Team Site is superior in virtually every respect to a FrontPage Discussion Web Site. If this facility is available to you, or could be, investigate it fully before deploying a Discussion Web Site.

For more information about SharePoint Team Site Discussion Boards, refer to "Using Web Discussions," on page 933.

Enabling User Self-Registration

The FrontPage Registration feature lets Web visitors create their own accounts for access to a Web site. An HTML form gathers the new visitor's name and password, plus any other desirable fields. The Registration component adds the visitor name and password to the Web site's authentication database and uses the Save Results component to store submitted data for other purposes.

A common use for the Registration component is requiring Web visitors to identify themselves before they're granted access to a given subweb. This supports any later follow-up you want to perform and, combined with a log analysis tool, supports analysis of usage by individuals.

Two major restrictions affect use of the Registration component:

- You must locate the Registration form in the root Web site of the server that hosts the restricted subweb. Administrators of restricted subwebs can't configure the Registration component unless they're also administrators of the root Web site.

Note A Registration form can't reside within the Web site to which it provides access. Before registering, Web site visitors have no access there!

- The Registration component won't operate at all on any Microsoft Web server. Microsoft Web servers use Windows system logon accounts for user identification, and allowing unknown Web visitors to create their own Microsoft Windows NT accounts would be a major security breach.

To activate the Registration component for a Web on a supported server:

1. Open the server's root Web site in FrontPage.
2. Use either of the following methods to display the Page Templates dialog box:

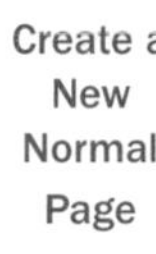

Create a New Normal Page

   - Choose New from the File menu. When the New task pane appears, under New Page, click More Page Templates.
   - Click the Create A New Normal Page drop-down arrow on the Standard toolbar, and then choose Page.
3. Select the User Registration template from the General tab, and then click OK.
4. When the new registration page appears in Page view, choose Replace from the Edit menu. Then change all occurrences of the following string (including the brackets) to the textual name (without brackets) of the Web site that will have self-registration:

   [Name of your sub site]
5. Scroll to the bottom of the page, and locate the HTML form shown in Figure 33-15.

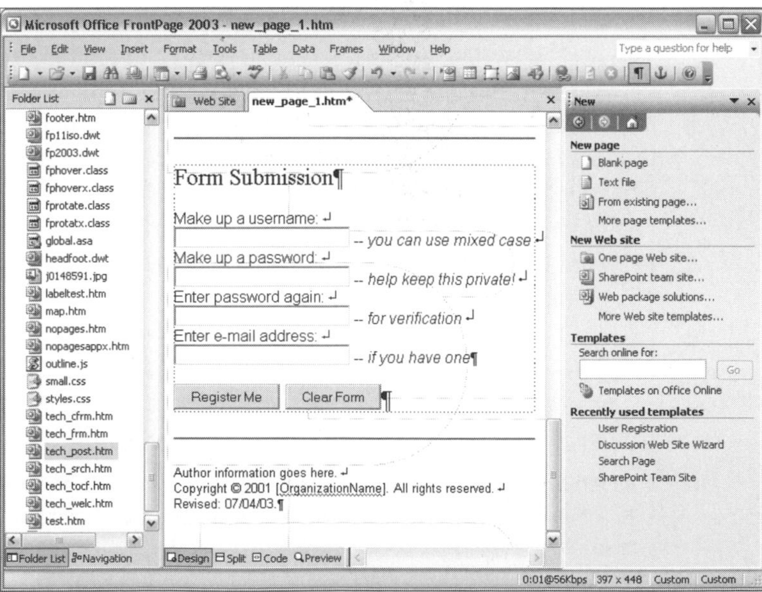

Figure 33-15. This HTML form is the significant part of the Web page produced by the User Registration template.

6 Right-click anywhere in the form, and choose Form Properties from the shortcutmenu.

7 When the Form Properties dialog box appears, verify that the Send To Other option is selected and set to Registration Form Handler. Clicking the Options button displays the dialog box shown in Figure 33-16.

Figure 33-16. This dialog box controls settings for the Registration Form Handler.

8 Configure or verify the following options on the Registration tab:

- **Web Site Name** Enter the name of the Web site visitors will register to use. This must consist of a leading slash (/) followed by the internal (short) name of the Web site. Don't use a trailing slash or the Web site's name in words.
- **Username Fields** Enter the names of one or more form fields, separated by commas or spaces. The form handler constructs the user name by joining these fields. By default, the User Registration template creates a one-line text box named Username for this purpose.
- **Password Field** Name the form field where the visitor enters a new password. The default text box is named Password.
- **Password Confirmation Field** Name the field where the visitor retypes the new password to confirm it. The default text box is named PasswordVerify.
- **Require Password** Select this check box to require that new passwords be at least six characters long and not partially match the user name.
- **URL Of Registration Failure Page (Optional)** Enter the relative or absolute URL of a page the form handler displays if it can't register the user for the Web site. You can type the URL or click Browse to locate it.

9 If desired, use the File Results, Confirmation Page, and Saved Fields tabs to accumulate data about each registration in a Web page or text file. These tabs work exactly like the corresponding tabs in the Save Results component, described in Chapter 35, "Processing Data Submitted from Forms."

Tip **Specify the correct path to a registration info file.**

If you want the Save Results component to save the registration information within the same Web site that visitors are registering for, be sure to specify the file location as a local file, such as C:\InetPub\wwwroot\fp-iso_private\regdb.txt, and not a relative URL, such as *fp-iso/_private/regdb.txt*.

10 Click OK three times to close both dialog boxes, as well as the subsequent reminder that the registration page for the subweb must be saved in the root Web site. Add any extra fields or make any desired changes to the registration form or Web page.

Caution If you rename the *Username*, *Password*, or *PasswordVerify* form elements in the Form Field Properties dialog box for each field, be sure to adjust the field names in the Options For Registration Form Handler dialog box (shown in Figure 33-16) as well.

11 Choose Save As from the File menu, and save the Web page in the root folder of the root Web site. This implies, of course, that you have permission to update the root Web site.

Each Web site supporting user registration will have its own registration page, so be sure to adopt a workable naming scheme, such as *reg* followed by the Web site name and then the .htm file extension.

12 Open the Web site that visitors will register for, logging in as an administrator.

13 Choose Server from the Tools menu, and then choose Permissions.

14 Follow these steps if your Web server is running the FrontPage Server Extensions 2002. (Otherwise, go to step 15.)

  1 When the Permissions Administration Web page appears in your browser, click the Change Permissions link.

  2 When the Change Subweb Permissions Web page appears, select the Use Unique Permissions For This Web Site option, and then click Submit.

  3 When the Permissions Administration Web page reappears, click the Administration link in the top navigation pane, and then click the Change Anonymous Access Settings link.

  4 When the Change Anonymous Access Settings Web page appears, locate the Anonymous Access Is option and select Off.

  5 Click Submit, and then click OK to confirm.

15 Follow these steps if your Web server is running an older version of the FrontPage Server Extensions:

  1 On the Settings tab of the Permissions dialog box, select Use Unique Permissions For This Web Site, and click Apply.

  2 On the Users tab, select Only Registered Users Have Browse Access, and click OK.

  3 If the Web server allows you to configure the Web page that appears in case of login failure, specify the registration page saved in step 11.

Note After you complete step 14 or 15, every Web visitor will need to enter a valid user name and password before accessing any page in your Web site.

After you have registration working, you can make further changes to the registration page. However, you must have form elements for the user name, password, and password confirmation fields, and you must also specify their names in the Options For Registration Form Handler dialog box (shown in Figure 33-16).

For more information about Web site security settings, refer to "Controlling Web Site Security Through FrontPage," on page 1184.

Using Alternative Self-Registration Systems

If your Web site resides on a Windows-based Web server, the FrontPage Self-Registration feature is essentially useless. Fortunately, however, this doesn't stop you from implementing self-registration in other ways.

If you're on an Intranet, it's frequently possible to bypass the need for self-registration. In all likelihood, everyone in your company or office already has a Windows username and password, and you can use these accounts to control access to your Web site (discussion or otherwise). Chapter 46 explains how to do this.

For more information about using Windows user accounts to control access to a Web site, refer to, "Controlling User-Level Web Site Access," on page 1148.

In the case of Internet applications, it's quite common to make registration and authentication parts of the application, and not an external service. An e-commerce application, for example, grants access to itself based on its own customer database, and not on some other database that the Web server uses. Microsoft calls this approach *forms-based authentication* because it uses HTML forms for login as well as for application processing.

The main drawback of using forms-based authentication is that to make it work, you have to write a bit of program code. Insider Extra 14, "Building Your Own Self-Registration System," provides some guidance on performing this task.

For information about using forms-based authentication to control access to a web site, refer to Insider Extra 14, "Building Your Own Self-Registration System."

In Summary…

This chapter described the Discussion Web Site and Self-Registration features of FrontPage. It also provided a brief overview of a self-registration system you can create or modify yourself.

The next chapter is one of three that discuss how FrontPage can create HTML forms, process form submissions, and work with databases.

Part 9

Using Forms and Databases

Chapter 34

Creating and Using Forms

Pages that collect input data are a familiar feature of the Web. Visitors use forms to identify themselves, submit search terms, make purchases, file comments or complaints, and perform virtually any kind of task that requires entering data and submitting it for processing. If you've ever used a Web page that included text boxes, check boxes, drop-down lists, submit buttons, and the like, you've used an HTML form.

Microsoft Office FrontPage 2003 can create HTML forms as easily as it creates any other sort of Web content. You just set the insertion point, choose the type of object you want from a menu, and move on to the next task. Each form field does require configuration, of course, as does the entire form. This chapter and the next two explain all these details.

This chapter deals primarily with individual form fields: what types are available, what types are best for a given job, and what configuration each type of field requires. Chapter 35, "Processing Data Submitted from Forms," explains how to tell the Web server what to do with any data that Web visitors submit. Chapter 36, "Accessing Databases with FrontPage," explains how to use the database capabilities built into FrontPage.

Creating and Modifying HTML Forms

An *HTML form* is a bounded area of a Web page that contains objects for data input and buttons for data submission. Figure 34-1 provides an example.

Here are some useful facts about HTML forms:

- Each form occupies a specific area on a Web page. A single Web page can contain one or more forms.
- Within each form are one or more form elements. Table 34-1 lists the available types.
- Each element on the form has a name and a value. The name internally identifies the input field, whereas the value reflects its current value.
- One element in the form—either a push button or a picture form field—must act as the submit button. When the Web visitor clicks this element, the browser:
  - Encodes all the element names and values in the form.
  - Transmits the data to a Web server for processing. The form's *Action* property contains a URL (referred to as the *Action URL*) that starts the necessary program on the Web server.

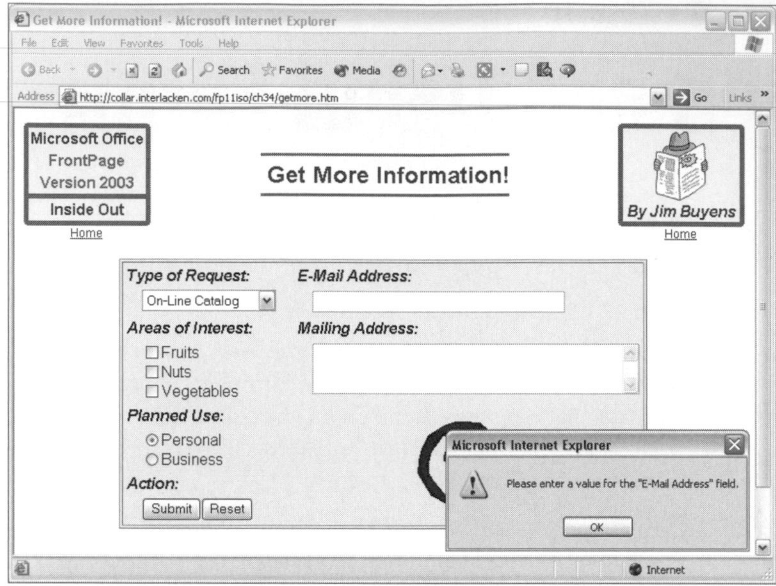

Figure 34-1. This page shows a typical HTML form. It collects data from the Web visitor and submits the data to some process. The warning box appears whenever the visitor clicks Submit without specifying an e-mail address; this typifies the FrontPage form field validation feature.

Table 34-1. Form Element Types

Element type	Description
Text Box	Used for entering short, one-line text strings.
Text Area	Used for entering multiple-line text, such as suggestions or comments.
File Upload	Used for uploading a file. The visitor types a file name by hand or uses a Browse button to locate the file.
Check Box	Contains independent fields having only two values, such as yes/no or true/false.
Option Button	Presents a list of choices of which only one can be selected at a time.
Group Box	A titled border that surrounds a group of related fields.
Drop-Down Box	Presents a list of choices. A Web visitor can select one listed item or several, depending on restrictions set by the page creator. If the menu is sized so that only one choice is visible, a drop-down arrow on the right drops down the menu to permit selection. If the menu is sized so that two or more choices are visible, a scroll bar replaces the drop-down arrow.
Push Button	A button that transmits the form contents to the Action URL, clears the form, or invokes a script.

Table 34-1. Form Element Types

Element type	Description
Advanced Button	A that can display HTML content on its face, but that otherwise behaves like an ordinary push button.
Picture Form Field	A picture that, when clicked, transmits the form contents to the Action URL.
Label	An invisible element that surrounds a form field and its title. Clicking the title is then equivalent to clicking the form field.
Hidden	An invisible element that the browser transmits with the Action URL.

Figure 34-2 illustrates the appearance of the visible form fields with one exception: the picture form field. A picture form field looks like any other picture.

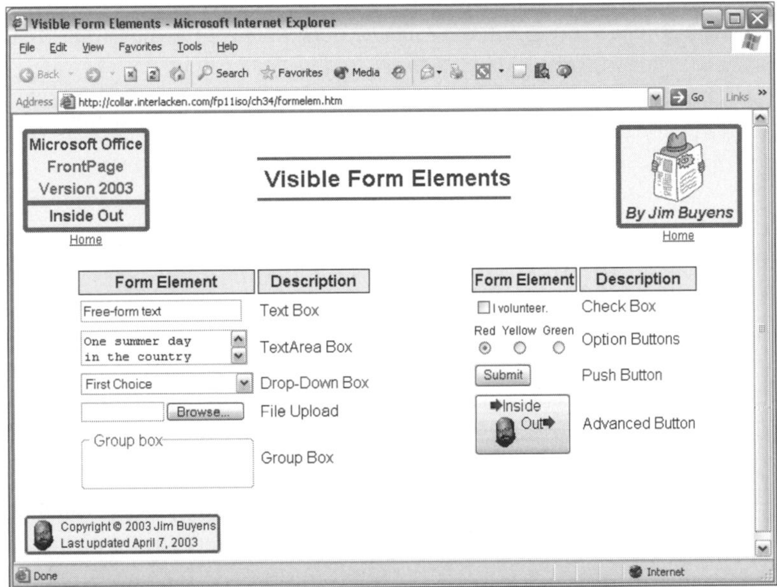

Figure 34-2. This Web page shows the appearance of each visible form field element.

The original—and still the most common—way of processing HTML forms is submitting them to programs that run on a Web server. More recently, script languages like Microsoft VBScript and JavaScript have also gained access to form elements. Script code can respond to form element events such as gaining focus, losing focus, mouse pointer movements, and clicking. (Scripts running on the browser can't directly access resources or update files on the server, but they *can* send requests to the server, just as clicking a push button can.)

For more information about using browser scripts, refer to "Scripting Web Pages on the Browser," on page 1056.

Note *Browser scripts* are small blocks of program code that appear within HTML and execute on the Web visitor's computer. The capabilities of browser scripts are intentionally limited for security reasons, but two capabilities they retain are setting form element properties and responding to form element events.

Drawing Forms in FrontPage

FrontPage can easily add forms and form elements to your Web pages. To add an HTML form to any Web page:

1. Set the insertion point where you want the first form element to appear, choose Form from the Insert menu, and then choose Form from the resulting submenu. This creates a form that FrontPage indicates with dashed lines, and that contains only a Submit button and a Reset button.
2. For each element you want in the form, choose Form from the Insert menu, and then choose the type of form element you want.

Tip If you add a form element outside an existing HTML form, FrontPage will normally create a new form that surrounds the new form element. To prevent this, choose Page Options from the Tools menu and then, on the General tab, clear the check box titled Automatically Enclose Form Fields Within A Form.

Form elements appear in line with text. To put two form elements on different lines, you must insert a paragraph break or line break between them. To line up form elements horizontally or vertically with others—or with surrounding HTML objects— organize them into a table. One common approach is to place field captions and corresponding form elements in adjacent columns. Another is to place each caption and field element pair within a single cell.

To expand the form, simply add more content—whether it's text, pictures, tables, more form elements, or any other valid objects. You can add content by direct insertion, by dragging, or by cutting and pasting. To create a second, separate form, insert a form element *outside* the boundaries of the existing form.

Figure 34-3 shows the form from Figure 34-1 open in FrontPage. The gray background and raised edges come from an HTML table and not from the form itself.

Creating an HTML form visually is only part of the job. You must also:

- Configure the properties of both the form itself and each form element. The next section in this chapter describes how.
- Provide a way to process the data after it reaches the Web server. Chapters 35 and 36 will provide the details.

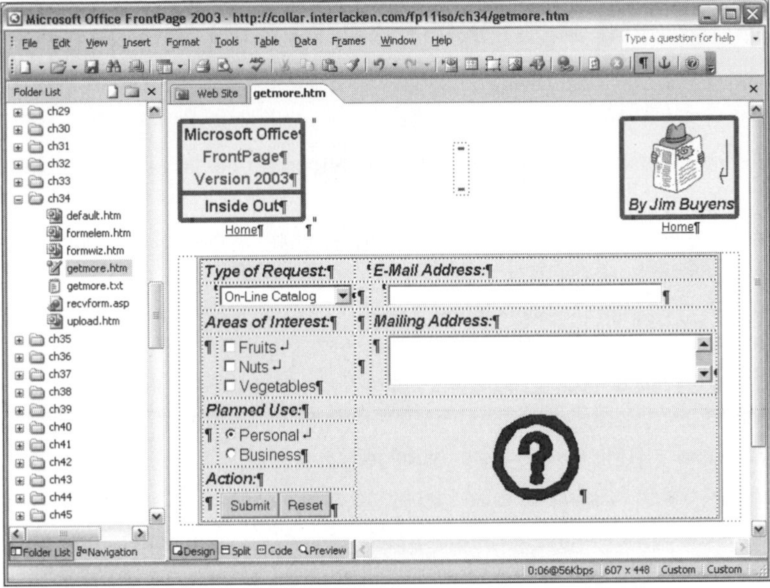

Figure 34-3. FrontPage created the form pictured in Figure 34-1.

FrontPage won't stop you from adding two or more HTML forms to a single Web page. This is perfectly valid from an HTML point of view. There are, however, several reasons for limiting the number of forms per Web page to one:

- Submitting a form transmits only the form field values inside that form. If you want a submit button to transmit all the form field values on a Web page, all the form elements must be within the same form.
- The programming model for Microsoft ASP.NET Web pages requires one and only one form per page. If you want an .aspx page to process your form input, you must heed this limitation.
- Crowding several functions into a single Web page is likely to be confusing for visitors. Give them a menu page for choosing the function they want, and then a separate page for each function.
- A single HTML form can contain any number of submit buttons. A program on the Web server can tell which button the visitor clicked—based on the button's *Name* property—and then take the proper action.

Choosing and Arranging Form Elements

Some general guidelines will help you choose form element types and arrange them effectively:

- Place required fields, key fields, and other important fields near the upper left in the form to give them prominence.
- Group fields in naturally expected sequences such as Name, Address, City, State/Province, ZIP Code/Postal Code.
- Group related fields by placing them close together. Make the groups distinct by using white space, indentation, or picture elements.
- Put lengthy fields—such as comments or special instructions—at the bottom of the form.
- Use ordinary HTML text for field captions.
- Use text boxes for single fields consisting of plain text.
- Use text areas for multiple lines of free-form text, such as comments.
- Use check boxes for yes/no or true/false choices; a selected check box means yes or true. For a list of yes/no items, use a series of check boxes.
- Use option buttons for lists in which the visitor should select only one item at a time.
- Use drop-down boxes that allow multiple selections as a substitute for check boxes.
- Use drop-down boxes that permit only single selections as a substitute for option buttons.
- Use HTML tables to align captions and form elements horizontally and vertically.
- If groupings appear repeatedly—such as an order form requiring a similar group of fields for each item ordered—create an HTML table with a row for each grouping and a column for each field.
- Put the Submit and Reset buttons at the bottom of the form. This provides some assurance that the visitor has reviewed the entire form before submitting it.

Setting Form Element Properties

There are five ways to modify the basic properties of a form element:

- **Double-clicking** Double-click the element you want to modify.
- **Right-clicking** Right-click the element you want to modify, and then choose Form Field Properties from the shortcut menu.
- **Quick Tag Selector** Select the element you want to modify, click the down arrow on its Quick Tag Selector icon, and then choose Tag Properties from the drop-down menu.

- **Clicking** Select the element you want to modify, and then choose Properties from the Format menu.
- **Using keystrokes** Select the form element you want to modify, and then press Alt+Enter.

The dialog box you see depends on the type of form element. The section "Controlling Form Element Properties," later in this chapter, discusses the dialog boxes for each type of form element.

Validating Form Input

Most applications involving HTML forms require constraints on form input. Quite often, for example, it's an error to leave certain fields blank. Other fields must conform to certain patterns—a U.S. Postal Service ZIP code, for example, should consist of five numeric digits.

FrontPage supports these requirements with a feature called *validation*. In FrontPage, the page designer specifies value constraints using convenient dialog boxes. FrontPage then enforces these constraints by adding JavaScript or VBScript code to the Web page. If the visitor violates the constraints, the browser transmits no data to the server but instead displays an error message. Figure 34-1 provides an example of this.

Validation is available for text boxes, drop-down boxes, and option buttons. Check boxes have only two values, both presumably valid, and therefore need no validation. Similarly, there's no validation for either push buttons or picture form fields because there's no wrong way to click them.

The Advanced tab of the Site Settings dialog box controls the language FrontPage uses when creating script code. The setting that governs validation script code is the Client drop-down list in the Default Validation Script Language section. Choosing JavaScript or VBScript instructs FrontPage to create validation scripts in those languages.

For more information about the Advanced tab of the Web Settings dialog box, refer to "Controlling Advanced Site Settings," on page 1139.

Caution VBScript validation scripts won't work in Netscape Navigator versions 7 and earlier. Check later versions for compatibility.

To specify validation rules for a form element that supports them, open the form field's Properties dialog box, and click Validate. The next section describes each form element and discusses the applicable validation rule settings.

FrontPage form field validation makes no use of the Validation features that are part of ASP.NET. If you decide to use one of these approaches, don't try using the other on the same form.

Inside Out

FrontPage Form Field Validation Isn't Bulletproof

Be aware that because FrontPage form field validation runs on the browser, it isn't completely reliable. Very old browsers ignore browser-side scripts, and newer browsers can turn them off. A persistent visitor could use the browser's View Source command to obtain, modify, and save your HTML, and then use the modified version to submit invalid requests.

This doesn't mean that browser-side form field validation is useless; but it does mean that your form-handling program on the Web server should check the validity of every input field. The FrontPage Save Results form handler, for example, does this.

Controlling Form Element Properties

You can change the position of an existing form element by dragging or by cutting and pasting. For other kinds of changes, however, you'll need to display the element's Properties dialog box by right-clicking the element and choosing Form Field Properties from the shortcut menu.

The following fields appear in nearly every dialog box that controls the properties of a form element:

- **Name** For a given field to be processed, you must give it the name that the script or server-side program expects. If you—rather than the programmer—get to name the field, use short, lowercase names with no special characters or hyphens.
- **Tab Order** Many form elements have a Tab Order field. This property controls the order in which fields receive the focus when the visitor presses the Tab key. The current field receives the focus after any fields with lower tab-order values, but before any fields with higher values. It's a mark of good design when form fields receive the focus in sensible order.
- **Style** Click this button to specify CSS properties for the element.

Inside Out

Design view supports ASP.NET forms as HTML forms

FrontPage has no special support for designing ASP.NET forms. For example, it has no built-in features for quickly adding *id="<element-name>"* and *runat="server"* attributes to form elements. You can use Code view or the Quick Tag Selector's Edit Tag feature to enter these attributes, but doing so in Microsoft Web Matrix or Microsoft Visual Studio will be much easier.

Once you have the form elements designed, FrontPage is still a great editor for titling and arranging them in an awe-inspiring way.

On the Web
Web Matrix is a free graphical development environment for ASP.NET pages. To learn more about Web Matrix and download the current version, browse *www.asp.net/webmatrix/*.

The following sections describe the available settings and validation rules for each type of HTML form element.

Setting Text Box Properties

Figure 34-4 displays the Properties dialog box for a text box.

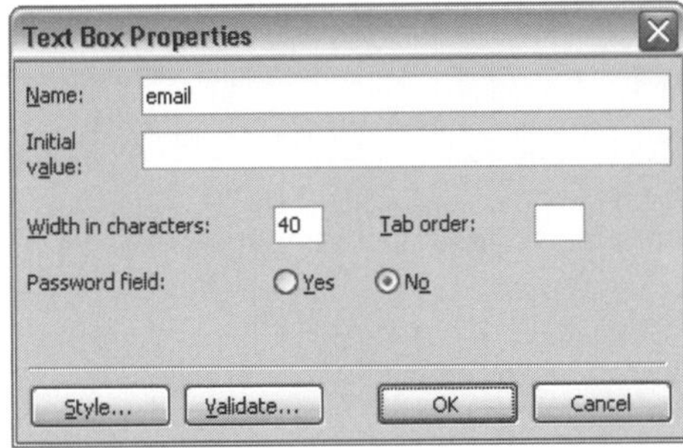

Figure 34-4. Use this dialog box to modify the properties of a text box.

In addition to the Tab Order and Style controls, which the previous section described for all Form elements, this dialog box provides the following options:

- **Name** Specify an internal name for the text box.
- **Initial Value** Supply a data value that should appear when the browser initially displays the form or when the Web visitor clicks the Reset button.
- **Width In Characters** Specify the width of the field in typical display characters. You can also change the width of a text box by selecting it and then dragging the handles on its left or right side.
- **Password Field** Select Yes if you want the browser to display asterisks in place of whatever characters the visitor actually types. Otherwise, select No.

Clicking the Validate button in the Text Box Properties dialog box displays the Text Box Validation dialog box, shown in Figure 34-5. This figure is actually a composite shown with all fields active, for clarity; in practice, one or more fields will be dimmed, depending on the Data Type you select.

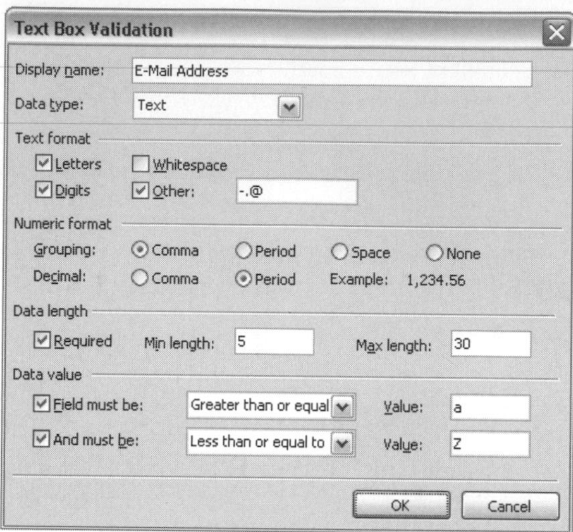

Figure 34-5. This dialog box sets constraints on values entered in a text box.

These are the available properties:

- **Display Name** Enter a name that will appear in error messages. Normally, this should agree with the text box's caption on the Web page. If you don't specify a display name, error messages will use the internal name from the Text Box Properties dialog box, shown previously in Figure 34-4.
- **Data Type** Specify the type of data the text box can contain:
  - **No Constraints** Select this option if the text box can contain any type of data.
  - **Text** Select this option if the text box can contain alphanumeric or linguistic expressions.
  - **Integer** Select this option if the text box can contain only whole numbers.
  - **Number** Select this option if the text box can contain only whole or decimal numbers.
- **Text Format** Indicate what kinds of text characters are valid. FrontPage enables this section only if the Data Type is Text.
  - **Letters** Select this check box if alphabetic characters are valid.
  - **Digits** Select this check box if numeric characters are valid.
  - **Whitespace** Select this check box if spaces, tabs, carriage returns, and linefeeds are all acceptable.
  - **Other** Select this check box if any additional characters are acceptable. Enter the acceptable characters in the text box provided.

- **Numeric Format** Set the format of numbers. FrontPage enables this section only if the Data Type is Integer or Number.
  - **Grouping** Indicate which characters, in addition to numeric digits, are valid in a numeric field. The options are:

Option	Meaning	Example
Comma	The comma character is permissible	12,345,678
Period	The period character is permissible	12.345.678
Space	The space character is permissible	12 345 678
None	No punctuation is permissible	12345678

  - **Decimal** Indicates which character is acceptable as a decimal point. FrontPage dims this field if Data Type is Integer. Note that the grouping character and the decimal character can't be the same.

Option	Meaning
Comma	The comma character is acceptable as a decimal point
Period	The period character is acceptable as a decimal point

- **Data Length** Set the length restrictions on data entered in the text box:
  - **Required** Select this check box if the visitor can't leave the text box blank.
  - **Min Length** Specify the fewest characters the text box can contain.
  - **Max Length** Specify the most characters the text box can contain.
- **Data Value** Use these properties to set range constraints on the text box values. If Data Type is Number or Integer, FrontPage uses numeric comparisons. If Data Type is Text or No Constraints, FrontPage uses alphabetic comparisons.
  - **Field Must Be** To set a range limit on the value Web visitors enter, select this check box, and then specify a comparison and a boundary value. The available comparisons are Less Than, Greater Than, Less Than Or Equal To, Greater Than Or Equal To, Equal To, and Not Equal To.
  - **Value** Specify the boundary value. Comparison against this value must be true or an error occurs. If, for example, Field Must Be reads *Greater Than 10* and the visitor enters *9*, the visitor gets an error message.
  - **And Must Be** Select this check box and specify a comparison to enforce a second range limit on the value in the text box. The Value property on this line works as it does with the Field Must Be drop-down list.

Setting TextArea Box Properties

The dialog box for changing the properties of a TextArea box appears in Figure 34-6.

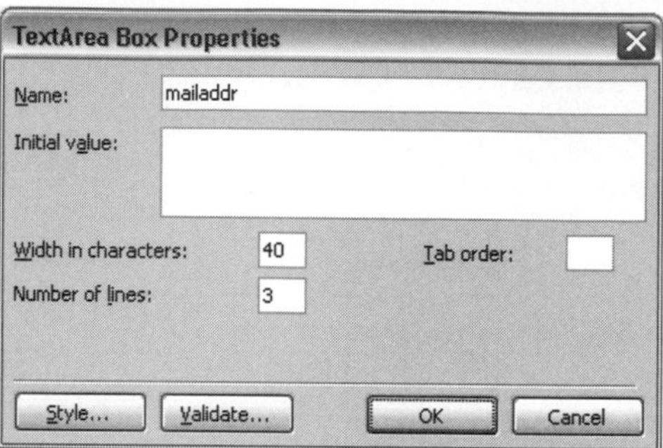

Figure 34-6. Use this dialog box to modify the properties of a TextArea box.

Use these property settings to configure the operation and appearance of a TextArea box:

- **Name** Designate an internal name for the TextArea box.
- **Initial Value** Supply a data value that appears when the browser first displays the form or when the visitor clicks the Reset button.
- **Width In Characters** Set the width of the TextArea box in units of typical display characters.
- **Number Of Lines** Set the height of the TextArea box in lines.
- **Validate** Click this button to display the same Text Box Validation dialog box that appears for text boxes. Refer to the previous section for details.

Tip You can change the Width In Characters and Number Of Lines properties of a TextArea box by selecting the box and then dragging its handles.

Setting Check Box Properties

The dialog box shown in Figure 34-7 controls the properties of a check box.

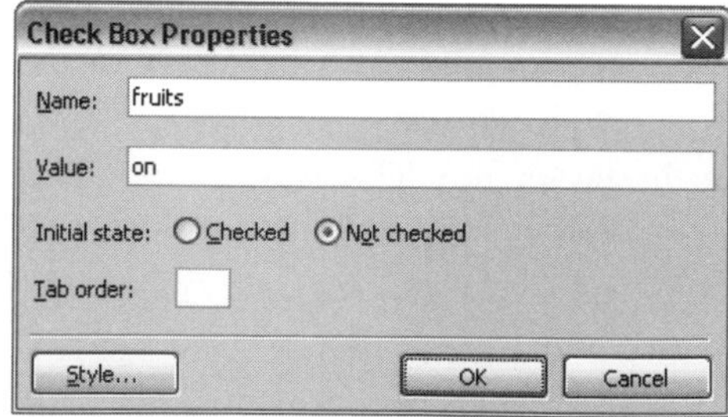

Figure 34-7. This dialog box controls the properties of a check box.

The following properties are available:

- **Name** Give the check box an internal name.
- **Value** Specify a string that the browser will transmit to the server or script if the check box is selected. If the check box configured in Figure 34-7 is selected when the visitor clicks Submit, the browser transmits *fruits=on*. If not, the browser sends neither the name nor the value.
- **Initial State** Specify how the browser should initialize the check box—selected (Checked) or cleared (Not Checked)—when it first displays the form or later responds to the click of a Reset button.

Setting Option Button Properties

Like lobbyists, heartaches, and rock-band aficionados, option buttons , which in HTML are officially called radio buttons, appear in groups. Only one option button in a group can be selected at a time. No other HTML form elements interact this way.

The grouping mechanism for option buttons within a form is quite simple: All buttons with the same name are in the same group. Conversely, to group a set of option buttons, give them all the same name.

Assigning duplicate names to form elements is usually an error, but in the case of option buttons, it's a necessity. Each like-named option button, however, must have a different value so that the server can determine which button was selected when the Web visitor clicked Submit. The browser transmits the selected option button's value and no others. Figure 34-8 shows the Properties dialog box for option buttons.

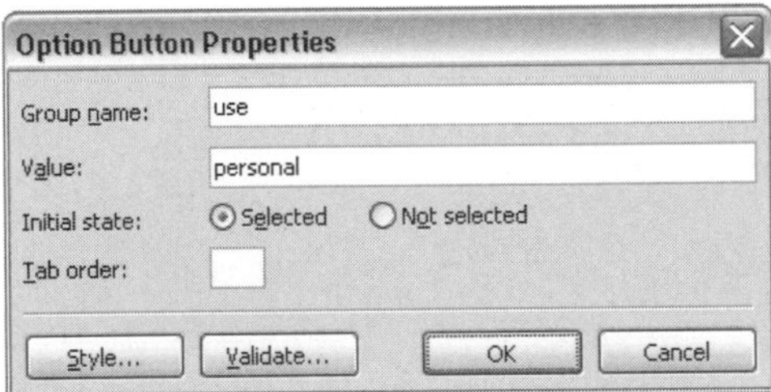

Figure 34-8. This is the Option Button Properties dialog box.

To configure the behavior and appearance of an option button, use the following settings:

- **Group Name** Specify an internal name for the option buttons. Be sure to give each option button in the same group the same name.
- **Value** Designate the string that the browser will transmit if the visitor selects this option button before clicking Submit. Be sure to give each option button in the same group a different value.
- **Initial State** Specify how to initialize the option button—Selected or Not Selected—when the browser first displays it or when the visitor clicks the Reset button.

Note Setting the initial state of one option button to Selected sets the initial state of all other buttons in the same group to Not Selected.

- **Validate** Displays the Option Button Validation dialog box, shown in Figure 34-9:
  - **Display Name** Gives the button group a name that will appear in error messages. This option is dimmed unless the following check box is selected.
  - **Data Required** Displays, if selected, an error if the visitor clicks Submit and no option buttons in the group are selected.

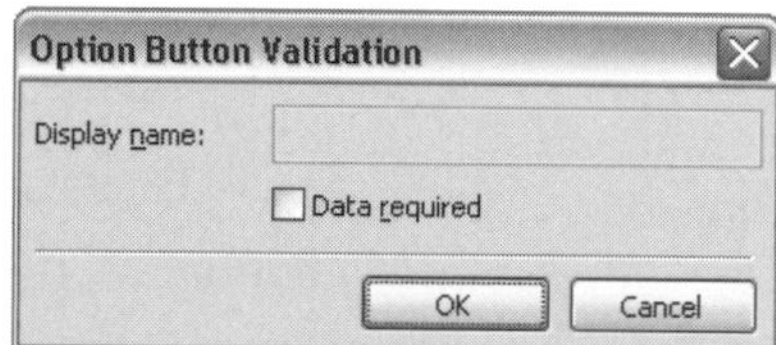

Figure 34-9. This is the Validation dialog box for option buttons.

Normally, a visitor can't clear all the option buttons in a group. The only way to clear a button is to select another button in the same group. It's possible, however, to have all option buttons in a group cleared when first displayed. This, together with the Data Required validation rule, ensures that the visitor made a choice and didn't accept the default. Changing the validation rules for one option button automatically changes them for all buttons in the same group.

Setting Drop-Down Box Properties

The Properties dialog box for drop-down boxes is shown in Figure 34-10.

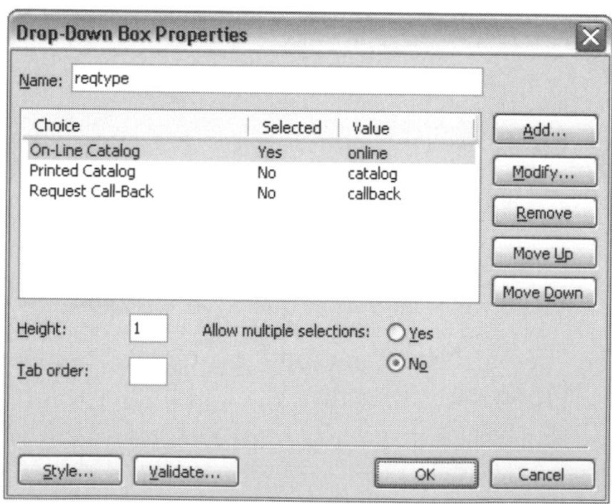

Figure 34-10. Use this dialog box to control property settings of drop-down boxes.

To control the configuration of a drop-down box, review and adjust the following settings:

- **Name** Assign an internal name to the drop-down box.
- **Choice-Selected-Value** This table contains a row for each entry in the drop-down box. Use the five buttons to the right to make changes:
  - **Add** Click this button to display the Add Choice dialog box, which appears in Figure 34-11.

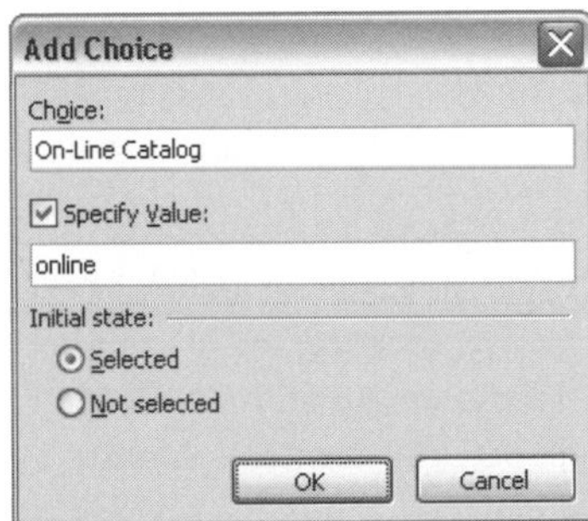

Figure 34-11. The Add Choice and Modify Choice dialog boxes contain identical fields for adding or modifying entries in a drop-down box.

Configure the following options:

Option	Meaning
Choice	Specify the text that the browser will display to the Web visitor.
Specify Value	Select this check box if you want the browser to transmit the value in the associated text box. Clear if you want the browser to transmit the value in the Choice text box.
Initial State	Click Selected if you want the browser to select the current choice when it first displays the drop-down box or when the visitor clicks Reset. Click Not Selected if you don't want the browser to select the current choice. If the Allow Multiple Selections option described and shown in Figure 34-10 is No, setting the initial state of one choice to Selected also sets the initial state of all other choices to Not Selected.

- **Modify** Click this button to alter the currently selected choice. When a Modify Choice dialog box similar to Figure 34-11 appears, make any desired changes, and then click OK.
- **Remove** Click this button to delete the currently selected choice.
- **Move Up** Click this button to move the currently selected choice one position higher in the list.

- **Move Down** Click this button to move the currently selected choice one position lower in the list.
- **Height** Specify the height of the displayed list in lines. A one-line list has a drop-down arrow on the right. Lists containing two or more lines have scroll bars on the right.

  You can also change the height of a drop-down box by selecting it and then dragging the handles on its top or bottom side.

Note When an HTML drop-down box has a height of 1 line, the browser provides a drop-down arrow for viewing multiple items. Windows calls this a drop-down list.

When an HTML drop-down box has a height of 2 or more lines, the browser displays a scroll bar rather than a drop-down arrow. Windows calls this a scrollable list box.

- **Allow Multiple Selections** Select No if the visitor should select only one choice at a time. Select Yes if the visitor can select two or more items simultaneously.
- **Validate** Click this button to display the Drop-Down Box Validation dialog box, shown in Figure 34-12.

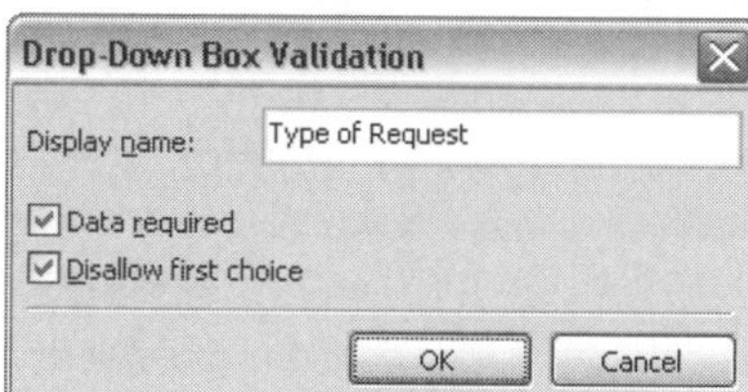

Figure 34-12. This is the Validation dialog box for drop-down boxes.

The Drop-Down Box Validation dialog box provides these options:

- **Display Name** Give the drop-down box a name that will appear in error messages.
- **Data Required** Select this check box if the browser should display an error message when the visitor clicks Submit and no choices in the drop-down box are selected. A drop-down box can have zero selections in two circumstances:
  - When the browser initially displays the form and if you didn't set any Selected values to Yes in the Drop-Down Box Properties dialog box.
  - When you set Allow Multiple Selections to Yes and the visitor Ctrl+clicks the last selected choice.
- **Disallow First Choice** Select this check box if the browser should display an error message when the visitor clicks Submit and the first choice in the drop-down box is selected.

  This setting is appropriate when the first menu choice is actually a prompt to select a different choice. This ensures that the visitor makes a conscious choice and doesn't simply accept the default.

Setting Push Button Properties

Figure 34-13 shows the dialog box for push buttons.

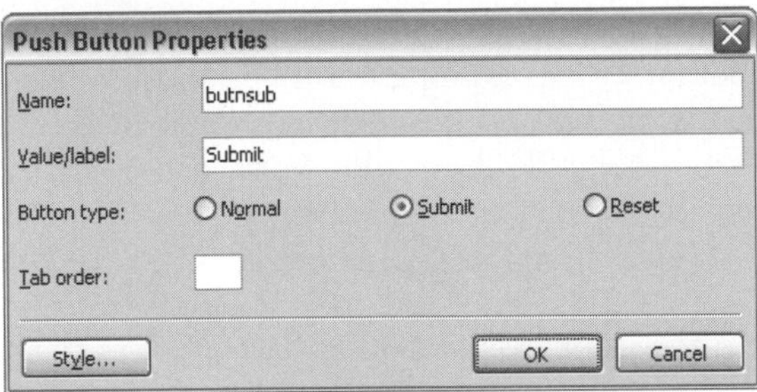

Figure 34-13. This dialog box controls push button properties.

The following options are available:

- **Name** Give the push button an internal name.
- **Value/Label** Enter the text, if any, for the button's visible caption.

  If the push button has both a Name and a Value/Label, the browser transmits the *name=value* pair when the Web visitor clicks the button. This tells the Web server which of several buttons the visitor clicked.
- **Button Type** Specify the type of push button:
  - **Normal** Select this option if clicking the button neither submits nor resets the form. This is normally the correct choice when a browser-side script will respond to the button. Choosing this button type sets the default label to Button.
  - **Submit** Select this option if clicking the button should submit the form. Choosing this button type sets the default label to Submit.
  - **Reset** Select this option if clicking the button should reset the form to its initial state. Choosing this button type sets the default label to Rese

There are no validation features for push buttons—either you click a push button or you don't.

Setting Picture Form Field Properties

A picture form field works much like a Submit push button. Clicking a picture form field submits the form's data using the form's Action URL. To insert a picture form field:

1. Choose Form from the Insert menu, and then choose Picture.
2. When the Picture dialog box appears, choose the picture you want and then click OK.

Tip Choosing Picture from the Insert menu doesn't create a picture form field, even if the insertion point is within an HTML form. After inserting a picture this way, you can't configure it to submit a form.

Figure 34-14 shows the dialog box for setting the properties of a picture form field. The Name property on the Form Field tab identifies the picture form field; the browser transmits this name to the server when the Web visitor clicks the picture. No validation is available. The remaining tabs are the same as those shown in the Picture Properties dialog box that Chapter 10 described.

For more information about the Picture Properties dialog box, refer to "Modifying Picture Properties," on page 273.

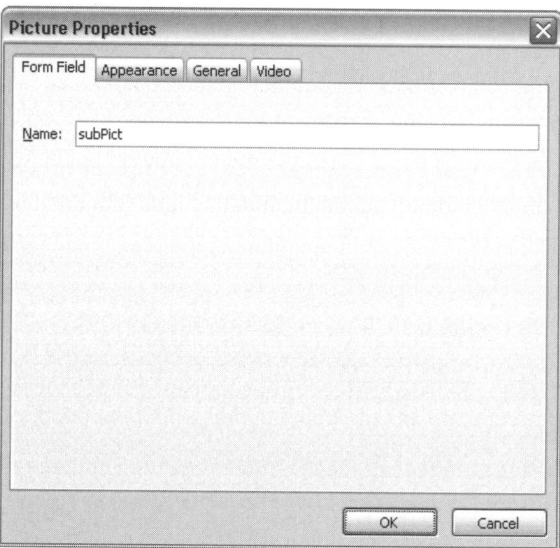

Figure 34-14. This dialog box controls the properties of picture form fields.

Setting Label Properties

Normally, the text that visually identifies form elements to the Web visitor is just that: ordinary text. Only visual proximity associates the label with its control.

HTML *labels* associate a form field's descriptive text with the form field itself. Clicking the descriptive text then has the same effect as clicking the form field. To "officially" designate text as the label of an HTML form element:

1 Enter the label text inside the HTML form and directly adjacent to the form element. If you want the label above or below the form element, separate them with a line break.

2 Select both the text and the form element.

3 Choose Form from the Insert menu, and then select Label.

This designates the selected text as the selected control's label. Design view displays a thin dotted line surrounding the text. In Code view, you'll see a <label> tag preceding the text you selected and referencing the internal name of the form element. To remove the label designation, select the label, choose Form from the Insert menu, and then select Label as you did before.

Note Support for the HTML <label> tag began with Internet Explorer 4 and Netscape Navigator 6.

Setting Advanced Button Properties

If plain text labels on push buttons don't satisfy your needs (or your tastes), consider creating an advanced button. An advanced button can contain any HTML content you want on its face; otherwise, it works exactly like an ordinary push button.

When you first add an advanced button to a form, it looks like this:

Type Here

The black highlighting indicates that the Type Here text is selected. Typing in this area modifies the button's caption just as though you were typing in any other area. You can also modify text styles, insert tables and pictures, and so forth. Figure 34-2, shown previously, and Figure 34-16 (shown later in this section) both show highly stylized advanced buttons.

Right-clicking an advanced button and choosing Advanced Button Properties from the shortcut menu displays the Advanced Button Properties dialog box, shown in Figure 34-15.

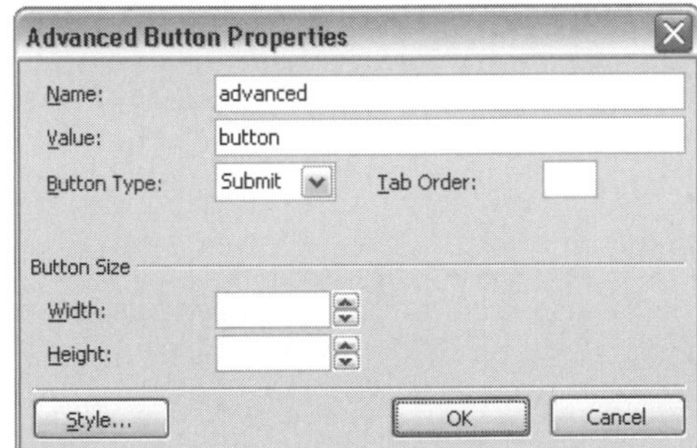

Figure 34-15. The properties of an advanced button are very similar to those of an ordinary push button.

This dialog box controls the following properties:

- **Name** Supply an internal name for the advanced button.
- **Value** Enter the value that should identify the button when the submission reaches the server. However, Internet Explorer and Netscape Navigator work differently in this regard:
  - Netscape Navigator version 4 ignores the Advanced Button tag but does display the HTML inside the button.
  - Netscape Navigator versions 6 and 7 send the button name and the contents of its *Value* attribute to the Web server.
  - Internet Explorer versions 4 and later send the Web server the button name and all the HTML inside the Advanced Button tags.
- **Button Type** Specify what function the advanced button performs:
  - **Normal** Select this option if the button neither submits nor resets the form.
  - **Submit** Select this option if clicking the button should submit the form. This is the default.
  - **Reset** Select this option if clicking the button should reset the form to its initial state.
- **Button Size** These two properties are optional. If you leave them blank, the browser makes the advanced button just large enough to surround your content.
  - **Width** Give the advanced button a specific width in pixels.
  - **Height** Give the advanced button a specific height in pixels.

You can also change the width of an advanced button by selecting it and then dragging the handles on any side.

Figure 34-16 shows an HTML form that contains two advanced buttons. Unfortunately, Netscape Navigator versions 4 and earlier don't display advanced buttons. They display any HTML you put on the button face, but not the button. Ordinarily this would limit use of advanced buttons to environments that run Microsoft Internet Explorer exclusively. There is, however, a workaround: Simply code a conventional button *inside* the advanced button.

Here's the reason this works:

- When Internet Explorer versions 4 or later displays an advance button, it ignores any regular buttons that reside within it.
- Netscape Navigator versions 6 and 7 displays both the advanced button and any conventional buttons it contains. This is a bit unsightly, but both buttons still work.
- Browsers that can't display advanced buttons still detect and display all the HTML you supply for the button face. This includes any regular buttons.

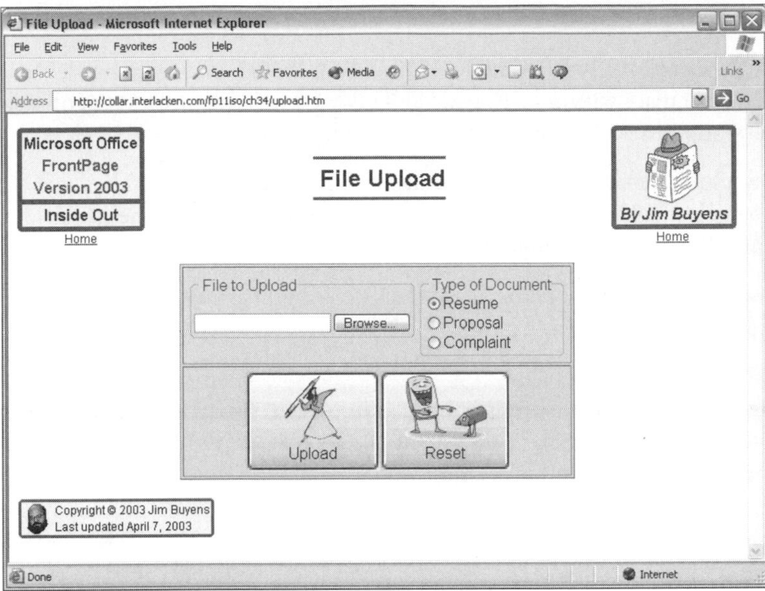

Figure 34-16. This Web page illustrates a File Upload element, two Group Box elements, and two Advanced Button elements.

Figure 34-17 shows the same Web page in FrontPage, which displays the advanced button and the regular button. If you decide to do this, Configure the standard and advanced button with the same properties. The standard button *doesn't* inherit the properties of the advanced button.

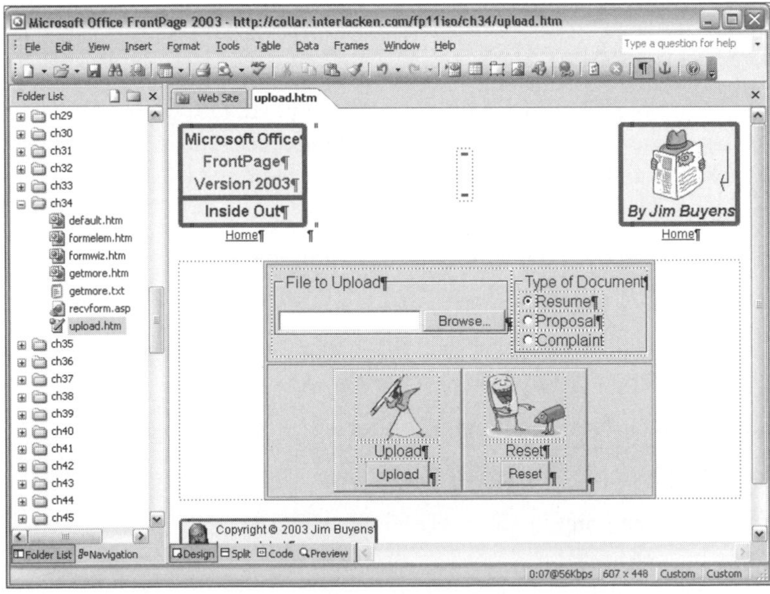

Figure 34-17. Notice the ordinary push buttons within the two advanced buttons.

Setting Group Box Properties

This form element is entirely cosmetic. It provides a shaded and titled border that surrounds any content you place within it. The File To Upload and Type Of Document boxes in Figure 34-16 are group boxes.

Internet Explorer versions 4 or later can display group boxes, as can Netscape Navigator versions 6 or later. Older browsers don't display the group box, but they do display the group box text and the group box contents.

When you first insert a group box, it contains no content. You can add content by dragging elements into it, by cutting and pasting, or by setting the insertion point within the group box and using any of the standard FrontPage insert commands.

To change the title of a group box, set the insertion point inside the text, and edit as usual. To change the title, CSS style, or text alignment of a group box, right-click it, and choose Group Box Properties from the shortcut menu.

Inside Out

Control Group Box Widths

The group box has one annoying habit: It fills the entire space—from left to right—that contains it. This means that if you insert a group box normally on a Web page, it fills the entire width of the page. To make the group box narrower, place it inside a table cell. That way, the group box fills the table cell instead of the entire width of the page.

Setting File Upload Properties

This component provides a way for Web visitors to upload files to your Web site. In a Web page or in Design view, the File Upload element looks very much like two form elements together: a text box and a push button titled Browse. Figures 34-2 and 34-16 both show examples of File Upload elements.

Getting file uploads to work requires four configurations:

- A File Upload form element
- A destination folder setting for the HTML form that contains the File Upload element
- An Enclosure Type setting for the HTML form
- Security settings for the destination folder

To insert a File Upload element, proceed as follows:

1. Set the insertion point inside an HTML form.
2. Choose Form from the Insert menu, and then choose File Upload.

3 If you previously configured a file upload destination folder for the current form, FrontPage will add the File Upload element to the form. Otherwise, it displays the Destination Folder dialog box shown in Figure 34-18.

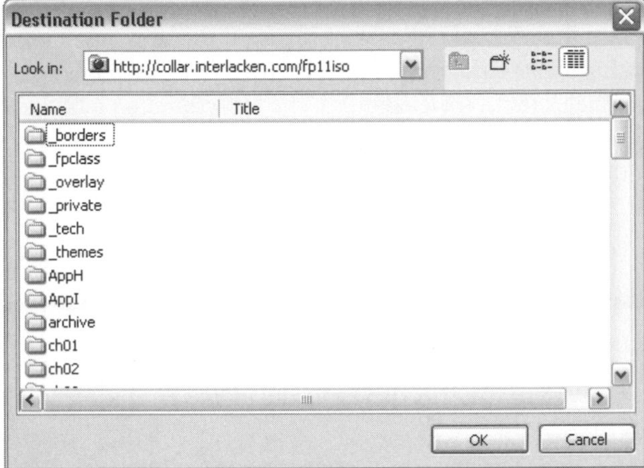

Figure 34-18. This dialog box specifies where the Save Results component should save files that visitors upload from an HTML form.

If this dialog box appears, select the folder where you want uploaded files to appears, and then click OK to add the File Upload element. If you click Cancel, FrontPage won't add the File Upload element.

4 Use any method you want to display the File Upload Properties dialog box that appears in Figure 34-19. For example, right-click the File Upload element, and then choose Form Field Properties from the shortcut menu.

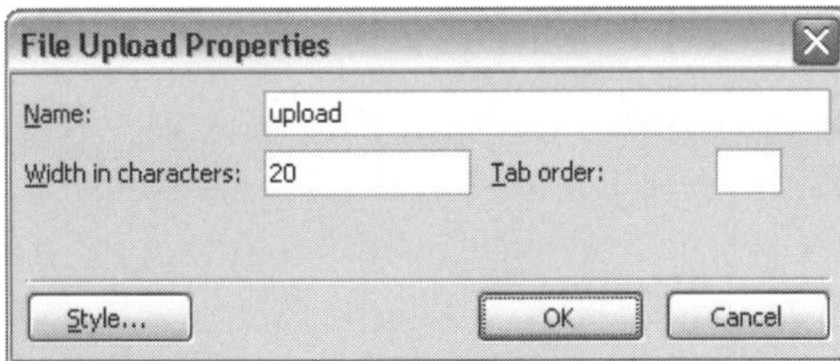

Figure 34-19. This dialog box controls file upload properties.

5 When the File Upload Properties dialog box appears, configure these settings:

- **Name** Specify an internal name for the File Upload element.
- **Width In Characters** Specify the width of the File Upload element in typical display characters.

6 Click OK to close the File Upload Properties dialog box.

> **Tip** You can also change the width of a File Upload element by selecting it and then dragging the handles on its left or right side.

Notice that when you configure a File Upload element, you must specify a destination folder where the uploaded files will appear. Strange as it may seem, FrontPage considers this a property of the HTML form, and not of the File Upload element. All File Upload elements in the same form use the same destination folder.

When the Save Results form handler receives a form submission that includes uploaded files, it reads the destination folder from the original HTML file that resides on the Web server, and not from some parameter that's traveled out to the browser and back. This is important. If the HTML specified the file upload location, Web visitors could create their own HTML and update any folder they wanted. In no time at all, they'd be overwriting legitimate pictures, running unauthorized programs, and generally wreaking havoc on your site.

If the original HTML file doesn't specify a destination folder, the Save Results component rejects the file and displays a message like this:

Form Validation Error

Please correct the information you provided by following these steps, then submit the information again:

'<file-name>' does not refer to a page or folder in this web. It may be a page or folder in a subweb, or it could be a badly formed URL.

If you wish to check of modify the destination folder for a form that accepts file uploads, proceed as follows:

1. In Design view, right-click the form that contains the File Upload element, and then select Form Properties from the shortcut menu.
2. When the Form Properties dialog box shown in the background of Figure 34-20 appears, look under the Where To Store Results heading and make sure that the Send To option is selected.

   Here's the reason:

   - If you choose Send To Database, the FrontPage Save Results form handler doesn't handle the form submission. Instead, FrontPage adds ASP or ASP.NET form-handling code to your Web page, and this code ignores file uploads.
   - If you choose Send To Other combined with Discussion Form Handler or Registration Form Handler, FrontPage will once again ignore file uploads.
   - If you choose Send To Other combined with Custom ISAPI, NSAPI, CGI, Or ASP Script, it's entirely your responsibility to verify that the custom form handler you specify can handle file uploads. If it can't, the Web server will discard any files that visitors try to upload through the current form.

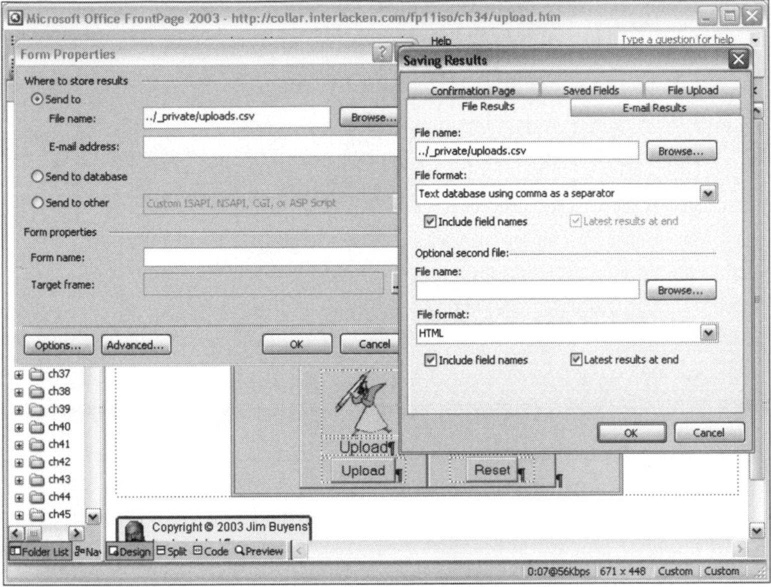

Figure 34-20. For a File Upload element to work, you must configure the Destination setting with a valid folder name.

3. Click the Options button.
4. When the Saving Results dialog box appears, click the File Upload tab. This tab appears in the foreground of Figure 34-20.
5. In the Destination box, specify the folder that should contain any files that visitors upload through File Upload elements in the current form.
6. Click OK twice to close the Saving Results and Form Properties dialog boxes.

For more information about configuring form properties for the File Upload element, refer to "Configuring File Upload Options," on page 870.

Finally, you should be aware that HTML forms are incapable of uploading files unless the <form> tag include the attribute enctype="multipart/form-data".

- When you configure the File Upload tab with a destination folder, FrontPage automatically adds this attribute to the <form> tag.
- If you process the form with a custom form handler (such as an ASP or ASP.NET page), you might have to specify this attribute yourself. To do this, display the options for Custom Form Handler dialog box, and then set the Encoding Type property to *multipart/form-data*.

For more information on Using a Custom Form Handler, refer to, "Using a Custom Form Handler," on page 874.

For file uploads to work, you must also configure the file upload destination folder with proper security. Here are the necessary steps:

1 Right-click the file upload destination folder in the Folder List and choose Properties from the shortcut menu.
2 When the Properties dialog box shown in Figure 34-21 appears:
   - If the Allow Programs To Be Run check box is enabled and selected, clear it.
   - If the Allow Scripts To Be Run check box is enabled and selected, clear it.
   - If you want, select the Allow Anonymous Upload To This Directory check box. This will dim the Allow Programs To Be Run and Allow Scripts To Be Run check boxes.
   - If you want Web visitors to overwrite existing files in the destination folder, select the Allow Uploaded Files To Overwrite Existing Filenames check box.

Note If you don't allow anonymous file upload, Web visitors who want to perform uploads will need to enter a Windows username and password having sufficient authority to open the same Web site and modify the same files in FrontPage.

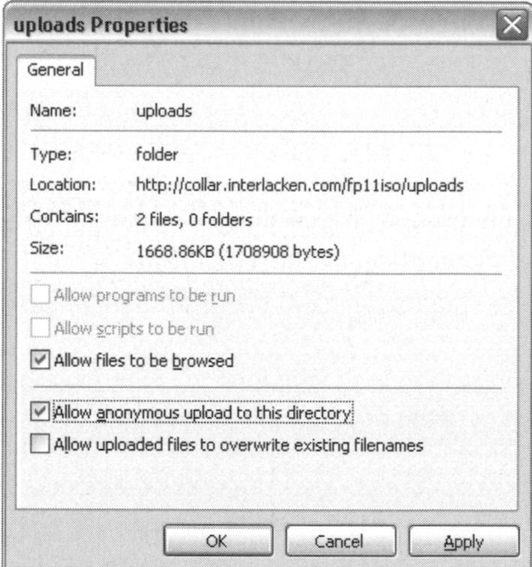

Figure 34-21. When you configure a file upload destination folder, you must clear the Allow Programs To Be Run check box in this dialog box.

3 Click OK to close the Properties dialog box.

Notice that FrontPage stops you from letting anonymous visitors upload files to folders that can execute scripts or programs. If anonymous visitors had this capability, they could upload and run any program they liked, with disastrous results.

On the CD Insider Extra

If the FrontPage File Upload element doesn't provide all the flexibility you need, you might need to develop custom programming that receives and stores an uploaded file. For an example of such programming, refer to Insider Extra #9, "Receiving File Uploads with ASP.NET."

Using Hidden Form Fields

Hidden form fields have both their names and their values hard-coded into the HTML. The Web visitor can neither see nor alter these fields; they're totally under the page designer's control. Hidden fields usually contain application data that's constant or parameters that control the actions of a server-side program. This permits changing the behavior of the server-side program through changes to the HTML—an easier process than changing the program itself.

Here's the procedure for adding, changing, and deleting hidden form fields:

1. Display the Form Properties dialog box in any of the usual ways. For example:
   - Right-click anywhere in the form, and then choose Form Properties from the shortcut menu.
   - Select anything in the form, choose Form from the Insert menu, and then choose Form Properties.
2. Click the Advanced button in the Form Properties dialog box. This displays the Advanced Form Properties dialog box, shown in Figure 34-22.

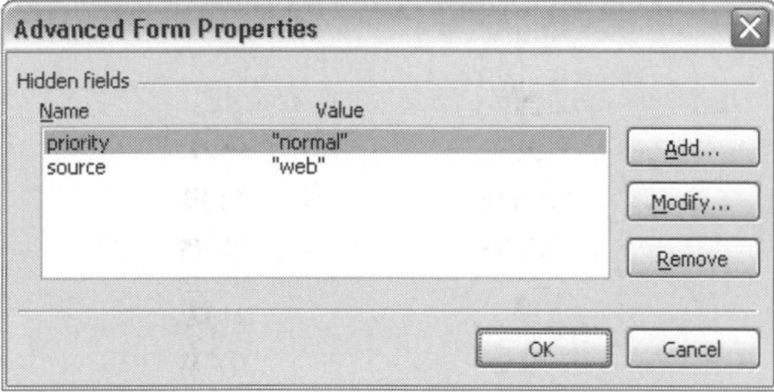

Figure 34-22. This dialog box maintains hidden fields on an HTML form.

To use this dialog box to add a hidden field:

1. Click Add.
2. When the Name/Value Pair dialog box appears, enter the hidden field's name and value in the respective text boxes, and click OK.

To change a hidden field:

1. Select the field to change, and click Modify.
2. When the Name/Value Pair dialog box appears, correct the field value, and click OK.

To delete a hidden field, select it, and then click Remove.

Chapter 34

Using the Form Page Wizard

FrontPage provides a wizard to help you get started creating HTML forms. This wizard has so many options that only a representative sample appears here.

The Form Page Wizard is unlikely to produce a finished page tailored to your complete satisfaction, but it can give you a good starting point, or at least some quick ideas. If you don't like the initial results, keep rerunning the wizard with different options until results improve. To run the wizard:

1 Display the Page Templates dialog box using either of these methods:

- Choose New from the File menu. When the New task pane appears, under New Page, click More Page Templates.
- Click the New Page drop-down arrow on the Standard toolbar, and then choose Page.

New Page

2 When the Page Templates dialog box appears, choose Form Page Wizard on the General tab, and then click OK.

3 When the Form Page Wizard displays its first page, click Next to display the next page of the wizard, shown on the left in Figure 34-23. This page contains a list of the major questions the form asks. To add questions, click Add; the wizard page shown on the right in Figure 34-23 will appear.

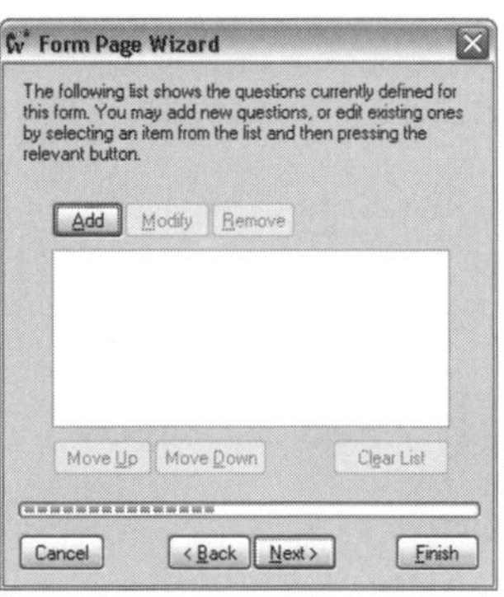

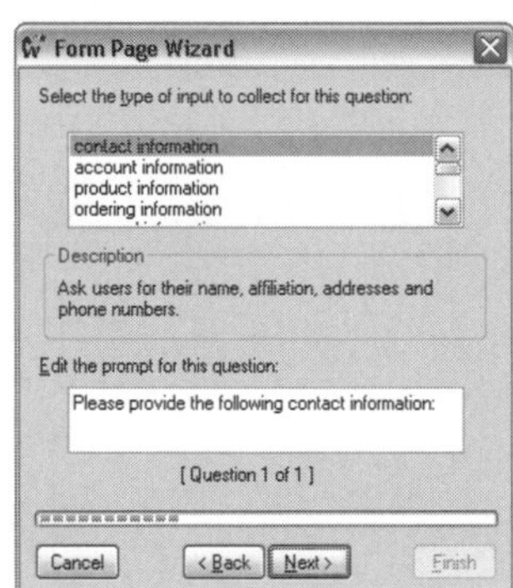

Figure 34-23. These wizard pages build a list of major questions for the Web visitor and prompt the designer for the type of input to collect for each question.

4 From the list at the top of the page on the right in Figure 34-23, select the type of input to collect for the current question. In the text box at the bottom of the page, review the suggested prompt, and make any necessary changes. Click Next.

5 The left side of Figure 34-24 shows a typical page that the wizard might display next. Each type of input in the previous step results in a different page with different options. Select the items you want to collect, revise the base name for those items if necessary, and then click Next.

Chapter 34

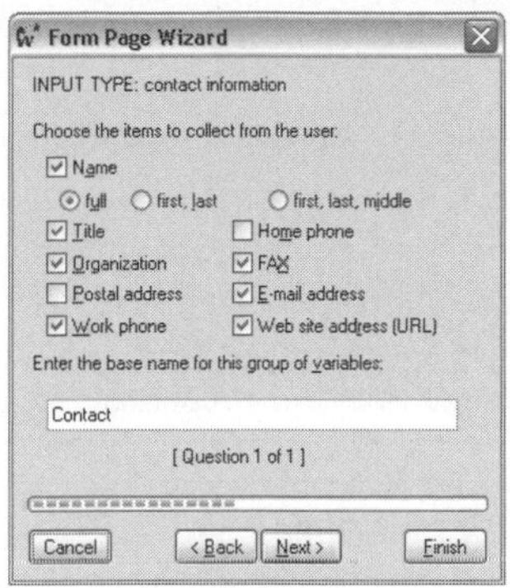

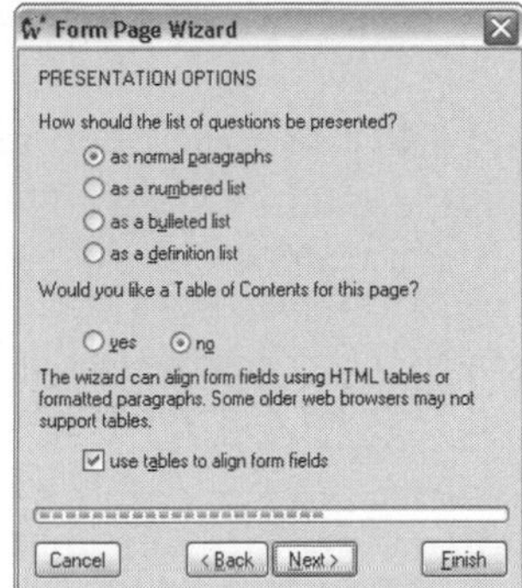

Figure 34-24. The wizard page on the left controls the data elements a form collects from the visitor. The wizard page on the right controls high-level aspects of form page layout.

6 Repeat steps 3, 4, and 5 as often as necessary to collect all the input you need. To start over, click Clear List in the page shown on the left in Figure 34-23. When you've finished, click Next.

7 When the page shown on the right in Figure 34-24 appears, indicate how you want the list of questions presented, whether you want a table of contents, and whether to use tables for form field alignment. Click Next when you've finished.

8 The next page, shown in Figure 34-25, controls how the input fields are captured.

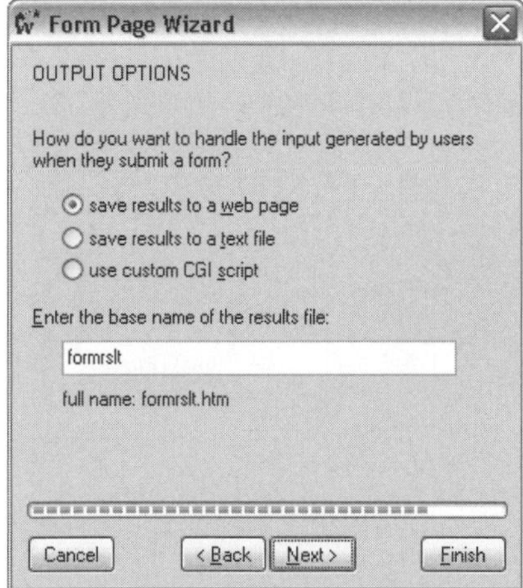

Figure 34-25. This wizard page controls how form data is saved.

The following options are available:

- **Save Results To A Web Page** Appends the data to a Web page whenever a visitor submits the form.
- **Save Results To A Text File** Saves submitted data in a text file on the server. Various programs can import data from such files at a later time.

- **Use Custom CGI Script** Assumes that a Web programmer will write a custom process to store the data.
- **Enter The Base Name Of The Results File** Designates the name of the Web page or text file (no .htm or .txt file extension) where the Web server saves the data. Specify a relative location inside your Web site or an absolute path in the Web server's file system. If you selected Use Custom CGI Script, this field is dimmed.

For details on saving form results, refer to "Setting HTML Form Properties," on page 859.

Caution The Save Results To A Web Page and Save Results To A Text File options use facilities in the FrontPage Server Extensions. Make sure that the server extensions are installed on any Web servers you plan to use, and check that your application is properly configured.

9 Clicking Next once more displays the final page of the Form Page Wizard, which has no input fields. You can use the Back and Next buttons to review and correct your work. When you've finished, click Finish to create the page as specified.

10 FrontPage will display the new page in Design view but won't save it. Make any further edits you think are necessary, and then either discard the work and start over or save the page in the usual way.

Figure 34-26 and Figure 34-27 show typical results from running the Form Page Wizard. Rerun the wizard as often as necessary to optimize results, and then finalize layout and appearance by editing the page directly. It's a good idea to test data collection features often. This makes it easy to localize and correct any errors.

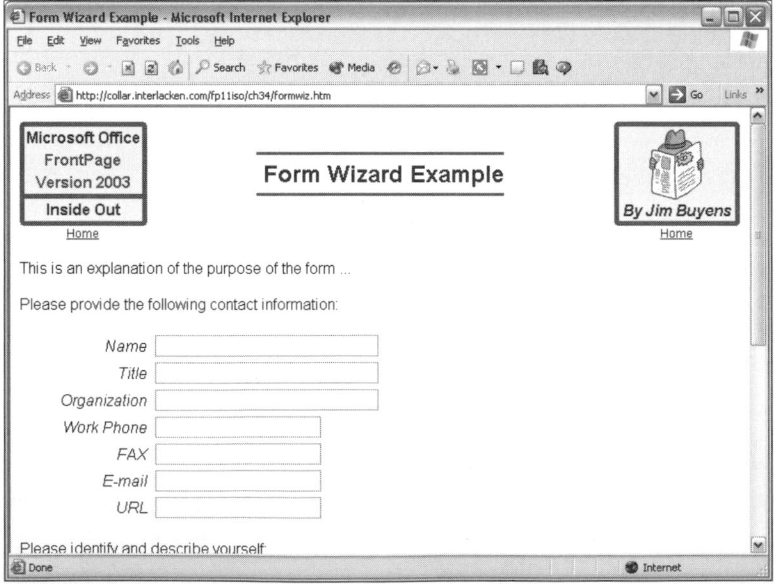

Figure 34-26. This is the top half of a page that the Form Page Wizard created.

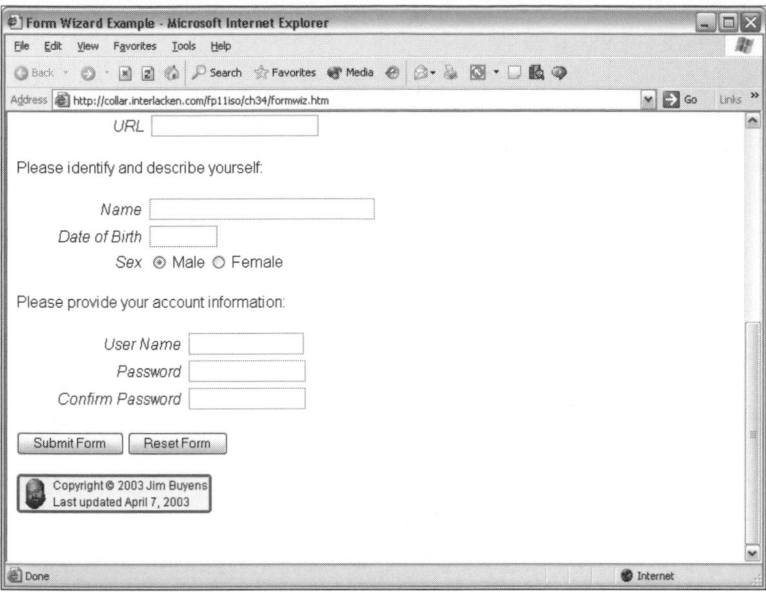

Figure 34-27. This is the lower half of the page shown in Figure 34-26.

In Summary...

This chapter explained how to create HTML forms that display input fields in a Web visitor's browser and how to submit the visitor's entries to the Web server for processing.

The next chapter explains how to configure the form so that the Web server provides the type of processing you want.

Chapter 35

Processing Data Submitted from Forms

Designing an HTML form (and, presumably, imagining how it will work) in Microsoft Office FrontPage 2003 is an interesting and satisfying exercise, but it's only half the battle. The remaining half involves configuring the Web server so that it does something useful after the visitor submits the form. That's the topic of this chapter.

Programming the Web server to save form data in files, in a database, or as mail isn't particularly difficult—unless, of course, you're not a programmer. In that case, you'll be glad to know that the Microsoft FrontPage Server Extensions and Microsoft Windows SharePoint Services provide an assortment of prewritten server-side programs that satisfy most requirements with no programming required on your part. Instead, you describe your requirements by clicking through some dialog boxes, and FrontPage does the rest.

If you do have some programming skills, you'll probably find ASP or ASP.NETa very easy way to get started with server-side programming. Appendix J, "Processing Form Data with ASP and ASP.NET Pages," explains how ASP and ASP.NET pages receive data from forms.

Setting HTML Form Properties

An HTML form is only a data-entry template and does no processing on its own. To process or save data entered on HTML forms, you'll need to follow one of these approaches:

- Correctly invoke features of the FrontPage Server Extensions or SharePoint Team Services.
- Write ASP or Microsoft ASP.NET pages to process the data exactly as you want.
- Obtain server-side programs or scripts from another vendor and correctly invoke them.
- Arrange for custom script or custom server-side programming.

In the first case, your job consists of making sure that the FrontPage Server Extensions or SharePoint Team Services are available on your Web server and then using dialog boxes in the FrontPage desktop software to specify the kind of processing you want. For the other approaches, you'll need to configure your form so that it asks the Web server to run the correct program. In all cases, the properties of the HTML form provide the necessary configuration. To view or modify the properties of an HTML form, use any of the following procedures:

- Right-click anywhere in the form, and choose Form Properties from the shortcut menu.
- Set the insertion point anywhere within the form, choose Form from the Insert menu, and then choose Form Properties.
- Click drop-down arrow on the <form> icon in the Quick Tag Selector, and then choose Tag Properties from the shortcut menu.

Both procedures display the Form Properties dialog box, shown in Figure 35-1.

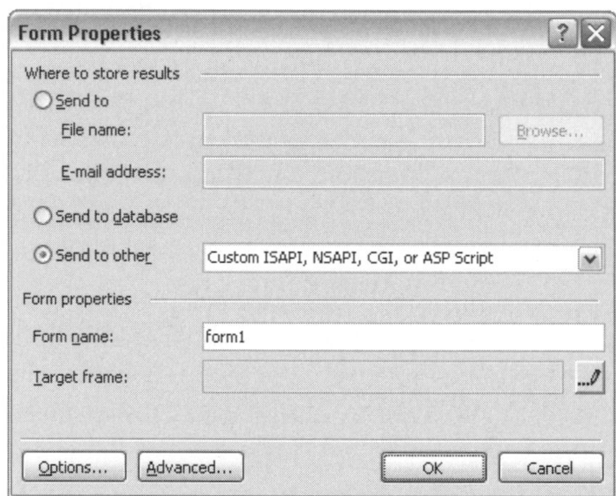

Figure 35-1. This is the Form Properties dialog box.

The Form Properties dialog box controls the following properties:

- **Where To Store Results** Use this group of controls to select a type of processing for the data in the form:
  - **Send To File Name** Adds the form data to a file on the Web server. This file can be either a Web page that gets longer and longer with each submission or a data file suitable for later processing in Microsoft Excel, Microsoft Access, or some other offline program. The associated text box specifies the name of the file—on the Web server—that will receive the data.
  - **Send To E-Mail Address** Sends the form data as an e-mail message. Each time a Web visitor clicks the form's Submit button, the Web server generates one message. Enter the receiving e-mail address in the associated text box.

- **Send To Database** Appends the form data to a database on (or accessible to) the Web server. This can be a Microsoft Access database that resides within your Web site or any database accessible to the Web server via ODBC.
- **Send To Other** Sends the form data to the destination you specify in the drop-down list:

Here are the options you can specify after selecting Send to Other:

- **Custom ISAPI, NSAPI, CGI, Or ASP Script.** Sends the form data to a server-based program that's not part of FrontPage. You must consult the program's documentation or designer to determine what input it requires for proper operation.
- **Discussion Form Handler.** Adds the information from the Web visitor to a discussion site.
- **Registration Form Handler.** Collects registration data from visitors to a site.

For more information about sending form results to a file or as e-mail, refer to "Saving Form Results as Files or E-Mail," later in this chapter. For more information about saving form submissions in a database, refer to "Saving Form Results to a Database," on page 879. For more information about custom scripts, refer to "Using a Custom Form Handler," later in this chapter. For more information about discussion sites, refer to "Creating and Managing Discussion Web Sites," on page 807. For more information about self-registration, refer to "Enabling User Self-Registration," on page 820.

- **Form Properties** Controls the form's name and, if it appears with a frames page, the frame where results of its processing should appear:
  - **Form Name** Gives the form a name. This text box is optional unless a script or custom form handler needs a name to process the form.
  - **Target Frame** Specifies the name of a frame in which output from the server-based program should appear. This property is optional.
- **Options** Displays different dialog boxes, depending on your choice in the Where To Store Results section.
- **Advanced** Displays the Advanced Form Properties dialog box, which configures hidden form fields.

For more information about frames pages, refer to Chapter 15, "Creating Web Sites with Frames." For more information about hidden form fields, refer to "Using Hidden Form Fields," on page 853.

Saving Form Results as Files or E-Mail

The FrontPage Save Results component receives data from an HTML form and then saves it on a Web server, sends it by e-mail, or both. Save Results can format data as Web pages or as simple ASCII text, build data files ready for importing into database or spreadsheet applications, or add information directly to databases.

For more information about HTML forms, refer to Chapter 34, "Creating and Using Forms."

The Save Results component requires the presence of the FrontPage Server Extensions or SharePoint Team Services, both on the Web server you use for testing and on the server your visitors use. If this is a problem, you'll have to get your system administrator to install the server extensions or SharePoint, find another provider, or choose a different approach.

The Save Results program that actually saves or mails your form data runs on the Web server, and not as part of the FrontPage desktop software or the Web visitor's browser. As a result, you can't test this component by switching FrontPage to preview mode or by loading the Web page into your browser from a disk location.

> **Note** The Save Results component is extremely powerful and flexible—so powerful and so flexible that it never appears in FrontPage at all. For example, the Send To File Name and Send To E-Mail Address options both use the Save Results component.

There are two ways to start using the Save Results component:

- Use the Feedback Form template to create a new Web page. This creates a working Save Results page that you can modify to suit your requirements.
- Create or modify your own form, choosing and configuring the Send To option in the Where To Store Results section of the Form Properties dialog box.

Figure 35-2 shows a form that the Feedback Form template created, along with its Form Properties dialog box. The setting Send To File Name is the sole unique feature of pages created with this template; you can discard or modify anything else on the page. You can also choose this setting on existing forms or forms you create yourself.

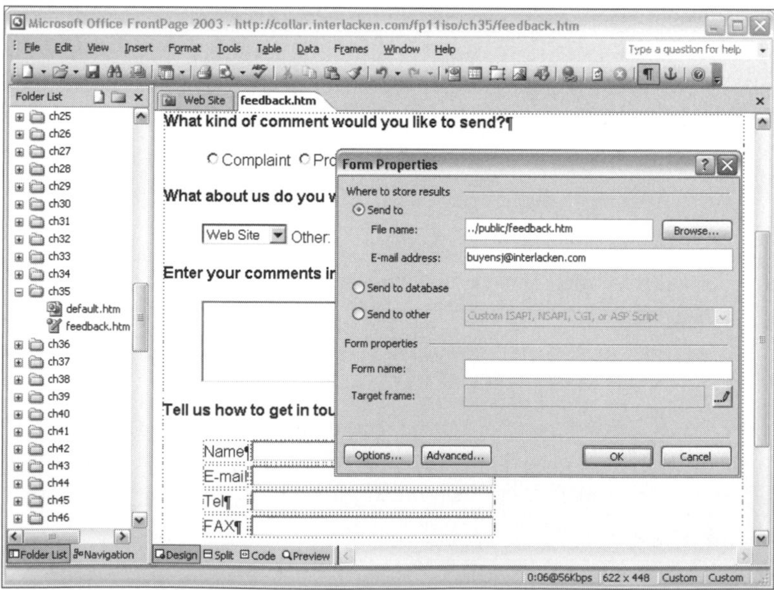

Figure 35-2. The Feedback Form template creates a Web page that, using the Save Results component, accumulates data in files on the server.

Tip To display the Form Properties dialog box shown in Figure 35-2, right-click anywhere on the form, and select Form Properties from the shortcut menu.

To configure the Save Results component, click the first Send To option (for either a file name or an e-mail address) in the Form Properties dialog box shown in Figure 35-2, and then click Options. This displays the Saving Results dialog box, which includes the following tabs:

- **File Results** Specifies the format and location of files that collect the form data.
- **E-Mail Results** Specifies the format and destination of e-mail messages that transmit the form data.
- **Confirmation Page** Optionally specifies a custom page that assures the Web visitor that the Web server has accepted the data.
- **Saved Fields** Specifies which form fields to save.
- **File Upload** Tells the server extensions or SharePoint how to handle any files uploaded along with the form submission. (This tab appears only if your form contains a File Upload component.)

Refer to the following sections for screen shots and descriptions of each tab.

Configuring File Results Options

The first Saving Results configuration tab controls the format and location of text files that accumulate the data. This tab appears in Figure 35-3.

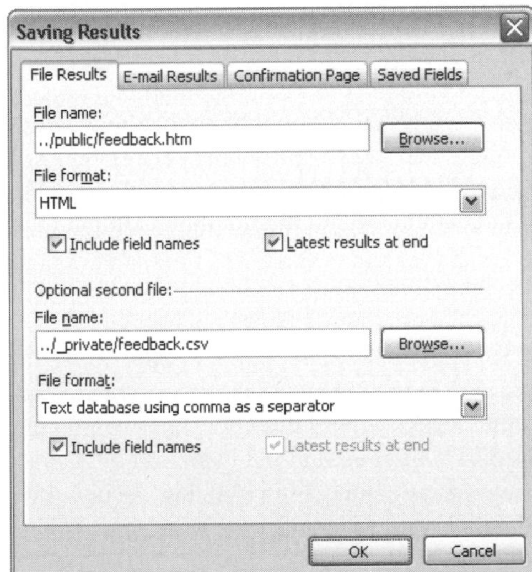

Figure 35-3. This dialog box configures settings for the Save Results component.

Set the options on the File Results tab as follows:

- **File Name** Specify the name and location of the data collection file:
  - For locations within the current Web site, specify a relative URL.
  - For locations outside the current Web site, specify a file name and folder in the server's file space. Specify the folder as a UNC or a drive-letter path. If the file doesn't exist, the FrontPage Extensions or SharePoint Team Services create it when the first data arrives.
  - If File Format (the next option) specifies HTML, use an .htm file extension and a folder location that Web visitors can browse.
  - If File Format specifies text, use a .txt or .csv file extension. To locate the file within your Web site but hide it from Web browsers, specify a location in your Web site's _private folder.

Caution Think carefully before saving form results to a location accessible by HTTP. This makes it very easy for you to view or download results, but equally easy for ordinary Web visitors to do so. If you consider form results confidential, save them in a file location on the server that's within a password-protected Web or FTP area.

- **File Format** Choose a format for the results file. Table 35-1 lists the choices.
- **Include Field Names** Select this check box to save both the name and the value of each form field. If this check box isn't selected, FrontPage saves only the values.
- **Latest Results At End** Select this check box to append data to the end of a Web page. Clearing the check box adds new data at the top of the page. FrontPage ignores this setting if the File Format isn't one of the HTML types; new data in such cases always appears at the end of the file.
- **Optional Second File** In this section, specify the name, format, and other settings for a second file in which the component can save results. This permits saving form results twice in different formats, such as HTML and comma-separated, or in two different file locations to reduce the risk of loss. Configure this section with the same four fields just described.

Table 35-1. Format Options for the Save Results Component

File format	Description
XML	The component formats the name of each form field name and its data as an XML tag, surrounds all the field tags with <record> and </record> tags, and adds the entire structure to an XML file. To use this format, your Web server must be running SharePoint Team Services.
HTML	The component appends the data to a Web page, formatting the data as normal text with each field on a new line. This is the default.
HTML definition list	As above, but the component formats the *name=value* pairs as a definition list.

Table 35-1. Format Options for the Save Results Component

File format	Description
HTML bulleted list	As above, but the component formats the data as a bulleted list.
Formatted text within HTML	As above, but the component formats the data as Formatted (monospaced) text.
Formatted text	The component saves a plain text file formatted for easy reading.
Text database using comma as a separator	The component writes all data values on one line, separating them with commas. This is useful for databases, spreadsheets, and other programs that can import the comma-separated values (CSV) format.
Text database using tab as a separator	As above, but tab characters separate the data values.
Text database using space as a separator	As above, but spaces separate the data values.

Figure 35-4 shows the effects of saving results with the HTML file format setting. The Save Results component keeps appending form results to the same HTML page indefinitely in the manner shown.

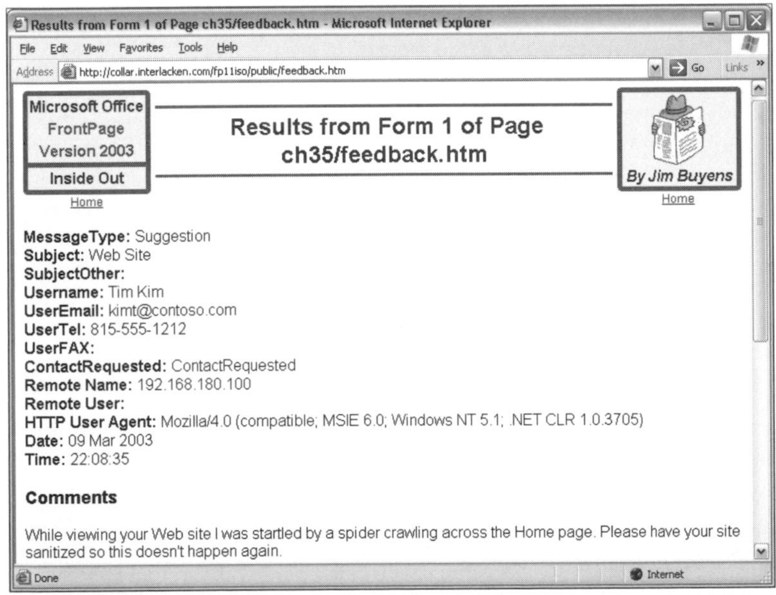

Figure 35-4. Saving form results as HTML produces an ever-growing Web page formatted like this.

The following is the identical data (numbered for clarity) in the format Text Database Using Comma As A Separator. Notice that the first data record contains field names rather than data; this is a common convention and very useful when performing spreadsheet and database imports.

```
1 "MessageType","Subject","SubjectOther","Comments",
  "Username","UserEmail","UserTel","UserFAX",
  "ContactRequested","Remote Name","Remote User",
  "HTTP User Agent","Date","Time"

2 "Suggestion","Web Site","","While viewing your Web
  site I was startled by a spider crawling across the
  computer screen. Please have your site sanitized so
  this doesn't happen again","Phil","phil@localhost",
  "1-555-555-5555","1-555-555-5556","ContactRequested",
  "192.168.180.102","",
  "Mozilla/4.0 (compatible; MSIE 5.5; Windows NT 5.0)",
  "07 Jan 2003","14:55:09"

3 "Problem","Web Site","","My pet rock abandoned me
  after five years of faithful service holding up the
  corner of my bookcase. Do you know of a detective agency
  that can track him down?","Herman from Huron",
  "herman@deadletter.msn.com","","","","192.168.180.102","",
  "Mozilla/4.0 (compatible; MSIE 5.5; Windows NT 5.0)",
  "07 Jan 2003","15:01:38"
```

Tip **Don't delete *FormInsertHere* components.**

If you decide to edit a Web page that the Save Results component updates, don't delete the component that displays *Form Results Inserted Here*. This is an internal component named *FormInsertHere* that marks the location where FrontPage inserts any additional data it collects from forms.

Configuring E-Mail Results Options

Figure 35-5 shows the E-Mail Results tab of the Saving Results dialog box.

Set the options as follows:

- **E-Mail Address To Receive Results** Enter the e-mail address that receives the mailed data.
- **E-Mail Format** Select a data format for the mailed data. Formatted Text is the most universally readable and is the default.
- **Include Field Names** Select this check box if you want to include field names in the message as well as field values.

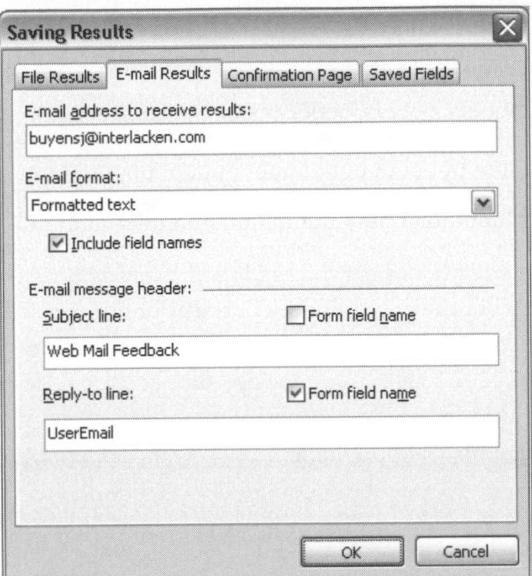

Figure 35-5. Use this tab to send HTML form data as an e-mail message.

The options in the E-Mail Message Header section control the Subject line and Reply To address of the mailed data:

- **Subject Line** This property is optional but recommended. You have two options:
  - If the associated Form Field Name check box is cleared, type some text to serve as the message's Subject line.
  - If the check box is selected, enter the name of a form field. Any data entered in that field then becomes the Subject line of the message.
- **Reply-To Line** This property is optional; it adds a Reply To header to the message that transmits the form data. If the recipient of the form data replies to that message, the reply will be delivered to the address you specify here. You have two options:
  - If the associated Form Field Name check box is cleared, enter the e-mail address of a person who will receive all such replies.
  - If the check box is selected, enter the name of a form field. Any data entered in that field then becomes the Reply To address.

> **Note** Saving results to a file and sending e-mail aren't mutually exclusive. If the need arises, the Save Results component can send e-mail as well as saving zero, one, or two result files.

> **Note** Saving form results as e-mail won't work unless your Web server's administrator has identified a Simple Network Management Protocol (SNMP) mail server to the FrontPage Server Extensions or SharePoint Team Services. For more information about this configuration, refer to "Changing Configuration Settings," in Appendix P

On the CD Insider Extra
For information about creating ASP or ASP.NET pages that send mail based on information from HTML forms, refer to Insider Extra 9, "Sending Custom E-Mail."

Configuring Confirmation Page Options

Figure 35-6 shows the Confirmation Page tab of the Saving Results dialog box. If the URL Of Confirmation Page (Optional) box is blank, the Save Results component generates a confirmation page like that shown in Figure 35-7. If this format isn't acceptable, you can design your own page and specify its URL on the Confirmation Page tab.

For more information about creating confirmation pages, refer to "Managing Confirmation Pages," later in this chapter.

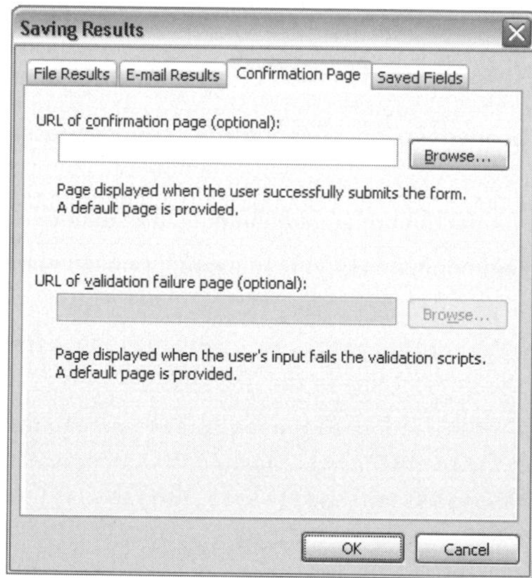

Figure 35-6. The Confirmation Page tab specifies the URL of a custom confirmation page.

In some cases, you can also specify the relative or absolute URL of a validation failure page. The Save Results component displays this page if any submitted fields fail validation. If you don't specify a validation failure page, the Save Results component creates one on the fly.

For more information about creating validation failure pages, refer to "Managing Confirmation Pages," later in this chapter.

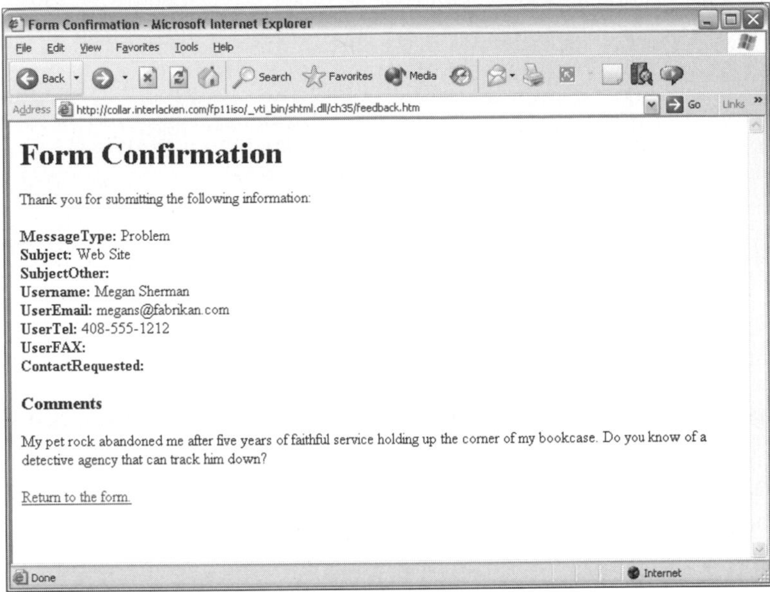

Figure 35-7. By default, the Save Results component generates form confirmation pages such as this.

Configuring Saved Fields Options

The fourth tab in the Saving Results dialog box, Saved Fields, is shown in Figure 35-8.

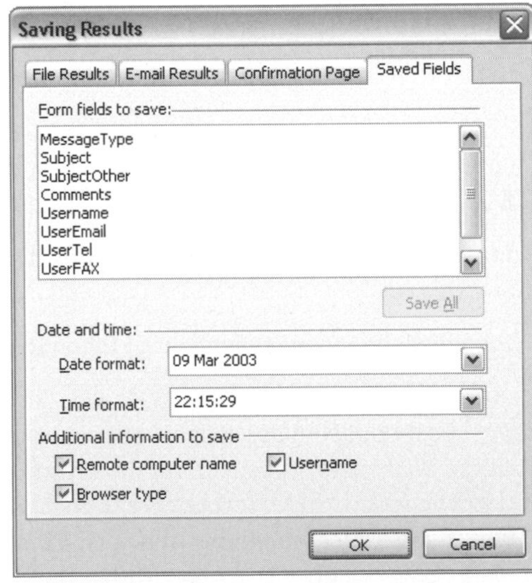

Figure 35-8. Use the Saved Fields tab to control which HTML form fields and system fields the Save Results component saves.

The upper half of the Saved Fields tab specifies which fields to save and in what order. Clicking Save All lists all fields defined in the current form. To remove a field, select it, and then press the Delete key.

> **Tip** The field names you must use on the Saved Fields tab are the names you assigned in the *Name* property of each field in your form. If your form fields still have default field names like T1 and R3, now is the time to regret it and fix them.

To reposition a field:

1. Select the field (including the carriage return at the end), and then press Ctrl+X or Shift+Delete to cut it.
2. Set the insertion point at the beginning of a line elsewhere in the list.
3. Press Ctrl+V or Shift+Insert to paste the field.

The remaining options record data not derived from the form itself. Activating any of these options appends the relevant information to the form data:

- **Date Format** Select (None) or a date format. If you specify a format, the form results will contain the date the visitor submitted the form.
- **Time Format** Select (None) or a time format. If you specify a format, the form results will contain the time the visitor submitted the form.
- **Remote Computer Name** Select this check box to record the name or IP address of the computer that submitted the form.
- **Username** Select this check box to record the name of the visitor who submitted the form. This data will be blank unless the Web page containing the form resides in a restricted Web site and the visitor was prompted for both a name and a password.
- **Browser Type** Select this check box to record the type of browser the visitor used to submit the form.

Configuring File Upload Options

If your form contains a File Upload component, the Saving Results dialog box displays a fifth tab titled File Upload. Figure 35-9 shows this tab.

Configure the properties of the File Upload tab in accordance with the following instructions. All these entries are optional:

- **Destination** Specify the folder where uploaded files will reside. FrontPage retains the file name base and extension that the Web visitor specified but discards the file's original path, instead using the location you specify here. If you leave this option blank, FrontPage stores the uploaded files in the folder where the Web page resides. This default is usually a very poor choice, because it gives the Web visitor a chance to replace your Web page!

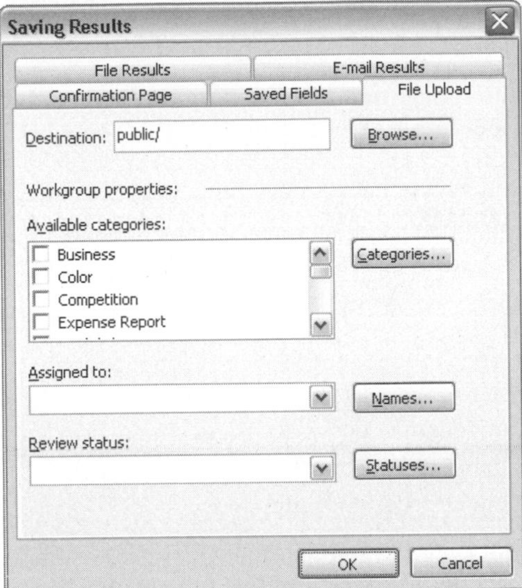

Figure 35-9. The File Upload tab configures the destination folder and other attributes of uploaded files.

- **Available Categories** Specify any workgroup categories FrontPage should assign to uploaded files. A Table Of Contents Based On Page Category component can then display a categorized list of uploaded files. Click the Categories button to modify the list of available categories.

For more information about workgroup categories, refer to "Using the Table of Contents Based On Page Category Component," on page 727.

- **Assigned To** Type or select the name of the person who's assigned to any files that the current form uploads. Click Names to update the selection list.
- **Review Status** Type or select the current review status of any uploaded files. Click Statuses to update the selection list.

On the CD Insider Extra

If you need more flexibility or greater security for uploading files than FrontPage natively provides, and if you're willing to do some programming, refer to Insider Extra 10, "Receiving File Uploads with ASP.NET."

Managing Confirmation Pages

Certain FrontPage components prompt your Web visitors for data and then submit the data to a Web server for processing by the FrontPage Server Extensions or Windows SharePoint Services. Three of these components—Save Results, Registration, and Discussion—confirm successful server-side processing by echoing the data back to the person who entered it. A Web page that echoes submitted data this way is called a *confirmation page*. The same three components also support *validation failure pages*—pages that report failures caused by invalid input.

If you don't specify a confirmation page or a validation failure page, the component's form handler generates default pages as required.

Enabling Confirmation Prompts

The dialog boxes for the Save Results, Registration, and Discussion components each contain a Confirmation Page tab, as shown previously in Figure 35-6. This tab has the following properties:

- **URL Of Confirmation Page (Optional)** Specify the location of a page for FrontPage to use as a template when it reports successful processing. If you leave this option blank, the form handler generates a default format. You can click Browse to select a confirmation page from the current Web site.
- **URL Of Validation Failure Page (Optional)** Specify the location of a page FrontPage should use when informing the visitor of rejected input. This option is dimmed if none of the form's elements has validation rules. If it's left blank, the form handler generates a default format. Again, you can click Browse to select a validation failure page from the current Web site.

For more information about form field validation, refer to "Validating Form Input," on page 833.

A validation failure page appears only when the Web server, rather than the browser, detects a validation failure. This is rare because validation usually occurs on the browser, before the visitor submits the page. However, if the visitor's browser doesn't support scripting, bad data can still arrive at the Web server. The Save Results component therefore validates input on both the browser and the Web server. If the server detects an error, it displays a validation failure page.

Using the Confirmation Field Component

You can design a confirmation page as you would any other Web page, but you need some means to tell the server extensions or SharePoint where to display the submitted data values. The Confirmation Field component provides this. Each Confirmation Field component contains the name of one data field. The server extensions or SharePoint replace each component with its named data value during transmission to the visitor.

Figure 35-10 shows a confirmation page created for a FrontPage Discussion Web site. The Discussion Form Handler sends this form to the visitor whenever an article is submitted successfully. The visible text *[Subject]* is actually a FrontPage component that will, on output, display whatever the visitor typed in the form field named Subject.

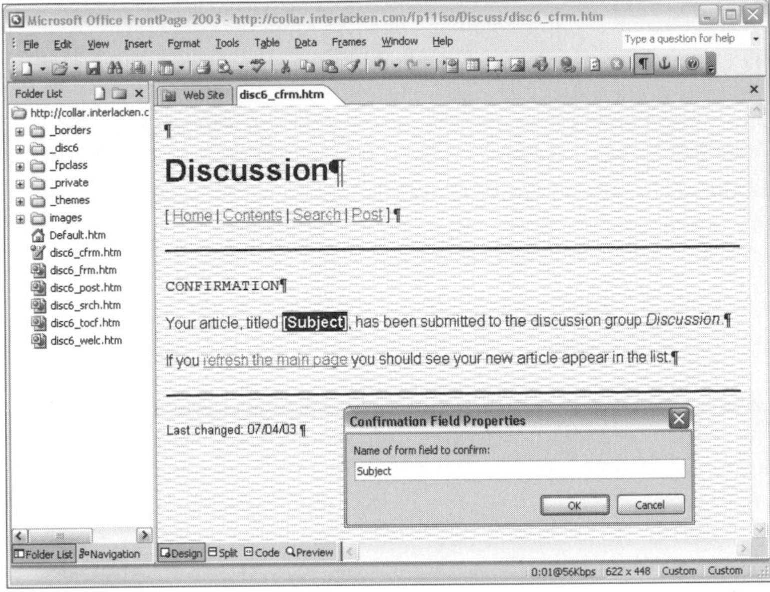

Figure 35-10. Confirmation pages generally contain form field components that the form handler replaces with visitor input values, such as *[Subject]* in this figure.

To help you get started with confirmation pages, FrontPage provides a Confirmation Form template. There's nothing terribly unique about this template; it contains some sample text and a few sample Confirmation Field components. If you find creating something from something easier than creating something from nothing, take the following approach:

1. Use FrontPage to open the Web site where the confirmation page will reside.
2. Use either of the following methods to display the Page Templates dialog box:

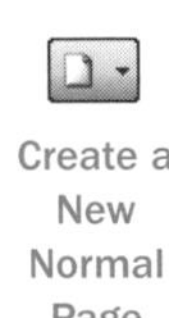

Create a New Normal Page

   - Choose New from the File menu. When the New task pane appears, Under New Page, click More Page Templates.
   - Click the Create A New Normal Page drop-down arrow on the Standard toolbar, and then choose Page.
3. Choose Confirmation Form from the General tab, and then click OK.

To add a Confirmation Field component (that is, an object that the server replaces with a submitted data value) to any Web page, proceed as follows:

1. Set the insertion point where you want the component to appear.
2. Choose Web Component from the Insert menu.
3. When the Insert Web Component dialog box appears, select Advanced Controls in the Component Type list on the left, and then select Confirmation Field from the Choose A Control list on the right. Finally, click Finish.
4. When the dialog box shown in Figure 35-10 appears, enter the name of the input field and click OK.

Tip **To find the name of a form element, open its Properties dialog box.**

To find the name of a submitted field, open the Web page containing the HTML form, and then double-click the form element. The Name option in the element's Properties dialog box contains the name that the Confirmation Field component expects.

Normally, the name you enter in the Confirmation Field Properties dialog box should be the name of an element on the form the visitor submits. However, for the Registration component only, the following names are also valid:

- **Registration-Username** The name of the visitor attempting to register.
- **Registration-Password** The password the visitor requested.
- **Registration-Error** A text explanation of a run-time error condition.

You can include any text, pictures, hyperlinks, or other Web page objects you want on a confirmation page. Confirmation pages are normal Web pages in every way, except that a form handler replaces any Confirmation Field components you insert with data that your visitors submit. You can format the page in any style and with any text or pictures you want.

Resetting Submitted Data

The Save Results component has no facilities to modify submitted data, to send submitted data to other processes, or to delete old data. If you want to perform one of these tasks, take the following actions:

- To correct or delete data saved as HTML, open the Web page in Design view, make your changes, and save.
- To correct data saved as text, right-click the file in Folders view or in the Folder List, choose Open With from the shortcut menu, and open the file with FrontPage (Open As Text) or Notepad. Make your changes and save.
- To download text data for use in other programs, locate the file in Folders view or in the Folder List, and then choose Export from the File menu.
- To delete a text file that contains data you no longer need, select it in Folders view or in the Folder List, and then press the Delete key. FrontPage will create a new file the next time a visitor submits data.

Using a Custom Form Handler

Just because you used FrontPage to create an HTML form doesn't mean you must use the FrontPage Server Extensions or Windows SharePoint Services to process it. In fact, you can use any type of server-side program you want. Here's how to configure an HTML form for processing by a custom program that runs on the Web server:

1 Open the Web page that contains the HTML form.

2 Use either of the following procedures to display the Form Properties dialog box:
   - Right-click anywhere in the form, and choose Form Properties from the shortcut menu.
   - Set the insertion point anywhere within the form, choose Form from the Insert menu, and then choose Form Properties.

3 Under Where To Store Results, select the Send To Other option, and make sure Custom ISAPI, NSAPI, CGI, Or ASP Script is selected in the accompanying drop-down list.

4 Click Options to display the Options For Custom Form Handler dialog box, shown in Figure 35-11.

Figure 35-11. Use this dialog box to specify a custom program for processing form data.

Here's how to specify the settings in the Options For Custom Form Handler dialog box:

- **Action** Must contain the URL of the server-side program. It's your responsibility to provide this program or ensure that it exists. Server-side programs usually have file names that end in .exe, .dll, .cgi, .asp, or .aspx. If you leave this field blank, the browser will send the form data to the URL of the current Web page. This is a common practice with custom ASP and ASP.NET pages.
- **Method** Specifies POST or GET, whichever the server-side program requires. These are two different ways of transmitting form data to a Web-server program. POST, which transmits data in the HTTP request body, is newer, less restrictive, and generally preferred. GET is subject to length limits and other restrictions because it transmits the form data as part of the URL.
- **Encoding Type** Indicates the encoding method used for passing form data to a server-side program. This method permits transmission of reserved characters such as carriage returns and slashes. The only valid entries are as follows:
   - **Blank** The default; means that the body of the request contains data from ordinary form elements.
   - **application/x-www-form-urlencoded** Has the same effect as Blank.
   - **multipart/form-data** Means that the body of the request contains multiple sets of form data. Normally, the first set contains data from ordinary form elements, and any additional sets contain files being uploaded.

Of course, the HTML form must collect the form elements that the server-side program expects and identify them by the correct names. Otherwise, it's like mailing the government a magazine subscription form instead of your annual tax statement. Something's not going to work correctly.

For more information about processing form data with ASP and ASP.NET pages, refer to Appendix J, "Processing Form Data with ASP and ASP.NET Pages."

In Summary…

This chapter explained how to configure an HTML form to request the correct services from a Web server (that is, the services that fulfill the purpose of the form).

The next chapter explains how to use the database capabilities built into FrontPage. This includes the ability to save form results in a database and to develop simple reporting and updating capabilities without programming.

Chapter 36

Accessing and Updating Databases with FrontPage

As Web use evolves from passive viewing to interaction between Web visitor and server, databases are critical and inevitable building blocks. If your applications involve Web visitors querying, entering, or updating persistent data, you need Web access to database services.

Unlike earlier releases, Microsoft Office FrontPage 2003 supports two distinctly different approaches to using databases on the Web:

- A conventional approach that creates ASP or Microsoft ASP.NET program code to manipulate and display the database. This approach first appeared in FrontPage 2000. It works with the FrontPage 2000 or 2002 Server Extensions, but it *doesn't* work with Microsoft Windows SharePoint Services.

- A new approach that transforms information from XML data sources into HTML for display in a Web page. This approach is new in FrontPage 2003, and it works *only* with Windows SharePoint Services.

This chapter deals exclusively with the FrontPage 2003 version of the conventional database features introduced in FrontPage 2000. Chapter 37, "Using SharePoint Team Sites," explains the new, XML-based approach that requires Windows SharePoint Services.

Neither of these approaches—or even both together—qualify FrontPage as a full-featured development environment for Web database applications. If your needs tend in that direction, Microsoft Visual Studio .NET is probably a better match, at least for the programming chores. Chapter 43, "Using FrontPage 2003 and Visual Studio .NET Together," explains how to use FrontPage 2003 for the visual design and Visual Studio .NET for the programming aspect of the same project.

Reviewing Conventional Database Features

The conventional database features in FrontPage 2003 are very similar to those in FrontPage 2000 and FrontPage 2002. Here's a complete list:

- **Save Results To Database** An enhancement to the Save Results component described in Chapter 35, "Processing Data Submitted from Forms." This feature appends form data directly to a database table rather than, as previously described, to Web pages or a text file.
- **Database Results Wizard** A tool for creating Web-based database queries. This wizard prompts you for the name of the database, the name of a table or query, the columns you want to list, and formatting options. It then creates Web pages that look up and display the requested data on demand.
- **Database Interface Wizard** A means to create a series of Web pages that can display, add, change, and delete records in any database you decide to support.

Database Requirements and Restrictions

Creating Web database pages requires that you work in a FrontPage-based Web site. For a disk-based Web site, the database must be accessible from your computer. For a server-based Web site, the database must be accessible from the computer where the Web site physically resides.

You need to use a FrontPage-based Web site because FrontPage stores certain information about databases at the Web site level, and not within each page. The database needs to be readable during design so that FrontPage can retrieve the table names and field names for various selection lists.

For database pages to actually run against the database (that is, to insert records, make queries, and display results) a disk-based Web site won't suffice. Instead, you'll need a server-based Web site running on a Web server that supports either ASP or ASP.NET pages, as well as ActiveX Data Objects (ADO). This includes Microsoft Windows 2000, Microsoft Windows XP Professional, Microsoft Windows Server 2003, and later versions.

> **Note** None of the features in this chapter will work on a Web server running Windows SharePoint Services. If you need to develop database pages that run in that environment, refer to the next chapter.

As for database types, FrontPage database features can access any of the following:

- File-oriented databases (such as Microsoft Access) located in the same Web site.
- Any database defined as an ODBC system data source on the Web server.
- Other network databases such as Microsoft SQL Server and Oracle, provided that they have drivers installed on the Web server.

If you don't already have a database, FrontPage can create an Access database for you. The next section explains how.

Saving Form Results to a Database

Chapter 35, "Processing Data Submitted from Forms," discussed using the FrontPage Save Results component to save data from HTML forms as a file on the server or to transmit it as e-mail messages. This section explains how to save the same sort of data directly to a database.

Figure 36-1 shows a simple HTML form designed for reporting sightings of birds.

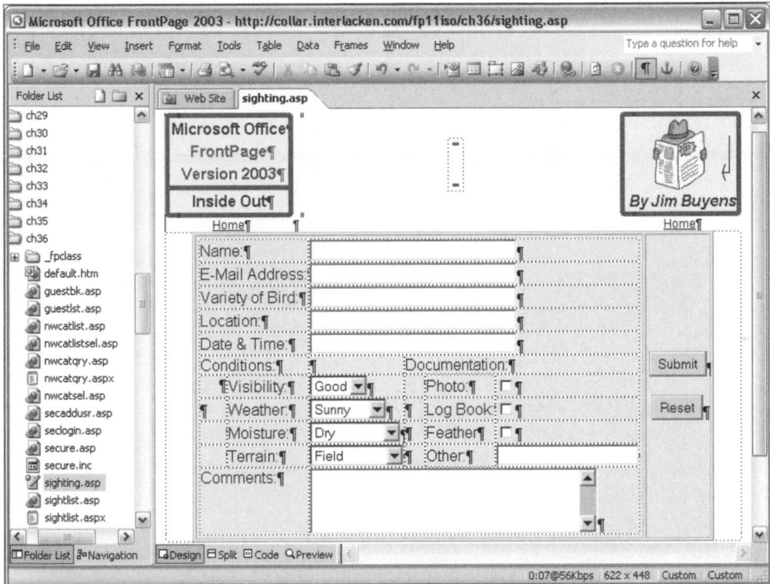

Figure 36-1. This data collection form is a candidate for saving results directly to a database.

Here are the steps required to save this data directly to a database:

1 Design the HTML form, making sure to give each form field an intuitive name.

> **For more information about creating HTML forms and naming form fields, refer to Chapter 34, "Creating and Using Forms."**

2 Save the page containing the HTML form with an .asp file extension. In this example, the file name is sighting.asp.

> **ASP pages contain program statements (scripts) that execute on the Web server whenever a Web visitor requests that page. For more information about ASP, refer to "Scripting Web Pages on the Server," on page 1075.**

3 Right-click anywhere in the form area, and choose Form Properties from the shortcut menu.

4 When the Form Properties dialog box appears, select the Send To Database option, and then click Options. FrontPage displays the Options For Saving Results To Database dialog box, shown in the foreground of Figure 36-2.

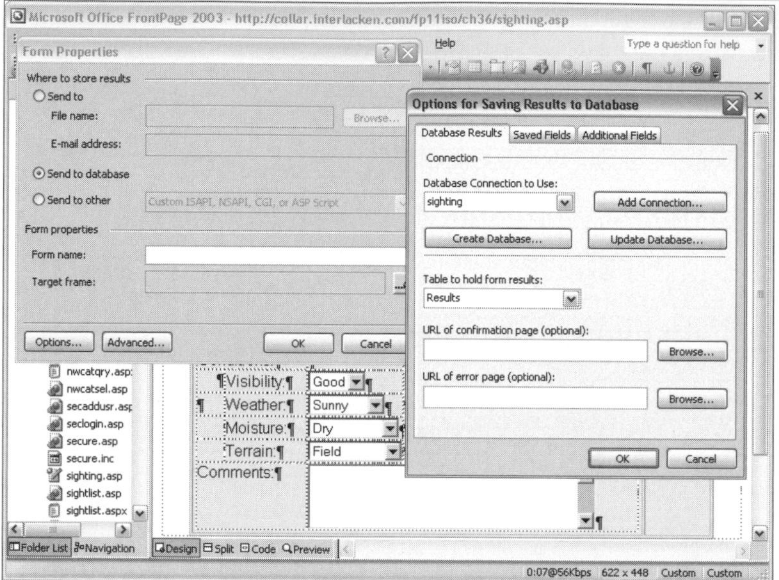

Figure 36-2. The Database Results tab of this dialog box controls basic options for saving form data to a database.

Notice the four options in the Connection section of the Database Results tab:

- **Database Connection To Use** Selects an existing database connection to use for storing the collected data.

> **Note** A *database connection* is a pointer to a database—a pointer defined at the Web site level. For more information about database connections, refer to "Configuring a FrontPage Data Connection," later in this chapter.

- **Add Connection** Creates a new connection to an existing database. In essence, this is a shortcut to choosing Site Settings from the Tools menu and then displaying the Database tab.
- **Create Database** Creates a new database to store the form results. In that database, FrontPage creates a new table with a column for each element in the form. FrontPage also creates a connection to the new database.
- **Update Database** Revises the structure of an existing database to reflect the current collection of form fields.

5 To follow along with this example, click Create Database.

> **Note** Clicking Create Database in step 5 constitutes the One Button Database Publishing feature promoted as part of FrontPage. Although FrontPage provides additional features related to saving HTML form data to a database, they're all optional.

6. When you click Create Database, FrontPage creates a database named sighting.mdb in the Web site's /fpdb folder and creates a database connection named *sighting*. The string *sighting* comes from the name of the Web page: sighting.asp.
7. Clicking the Saved Fields tab displays the dialog box pictured on the left in Figure 36-3. The Form Fields To Save list itemizes which form fields will be saved in the database, and in what database fields.

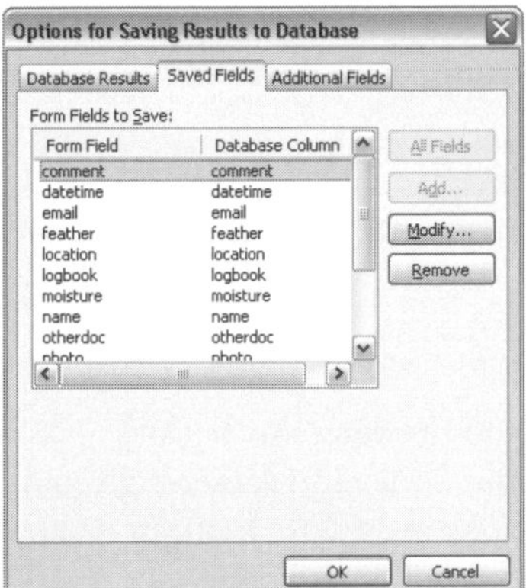

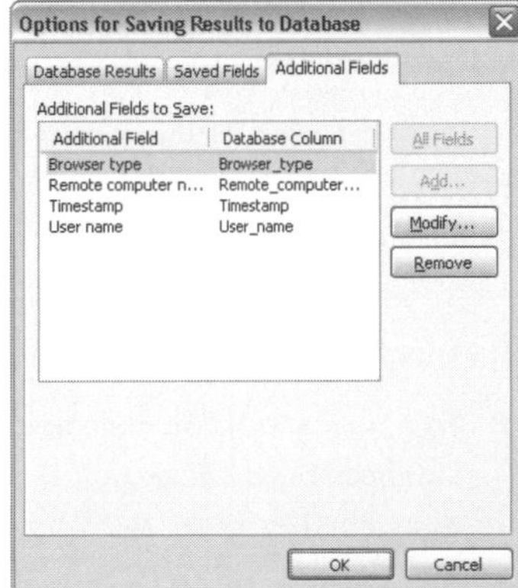

Figure 36-3. The Saved Fields tab displays each field in the HTML form and the database field, if any, that will receive its values. The Additional Fields tab controls fields received not from the HTML form, but from the HTTP transaction that submits it.

The four buttons along the right edge of this tab provide these functions:

- **All Fields** Adds every field in the HTML form to the list.
- **Add** Adds one field from the HTML form to the list. A dialog box prompts for the specific field.
- **Modify** Selects the database field that receives data from the currently selected form field. A Modify Field dialog box displays the form field name and a drop-down list of available database columns.
- **Remove** Stops recording data from the currently selected field.

If you're entering data from a new form into an existing database table, you must display the Saved Fields tab and correlate your form fields to database field names. Otherwise, the Save Results component won't save any fields. Likewise, if you've changed either the database structure or the HTML form, once again you'll need to display the Saved Fields tab and hook up the correct form fields to the correct database fields.

8 The Additional Fields tab, shown on the right in Figure 36-3, saves up to four additional fields in the database. The data for these fields isn't part of the HTML form; instead, the browser transmits it as HTTP headers along with the form data. Again, you can remove or reinsert these fields as you want.

9 Looking back at Figure 36-2, notice these additional options:

- **Table To Hold Form Results** Names the table that will receive the data from the HTML form you selected in the Database Connection To Use box. Clicking Create Database in step 4 creates a table named Results.
- **URL Of Confirmation Page (Optional)** Provides the URL of a page that the Web visitor will receive if the server can successfully update the database. If you leave this option blank, FrontPage will construct a default confirmation page.
- **URL Of Error Page (Optional)** Provides the URL of a page that the Web visitor will receive if the server fails to update the database. Leaving this option blank tells FrontPage to construct a default error page.

For more information about confirmation pages, refer to "Managing Confirmation Pages," on page 871.

10 When all three tabs are configured to your satisfaction, click OK twice.

To actually run the page and add data to the database, both the Web page and the database need to be on a server that meets the requirements given in the previous section. Furthermore, the Web page must be in a folder that can execute ASP scripts.

Executable Web Folders

Programs that run on Web servers present a significant security risk. Allowing Web designers (or Web visitors!) to store and execute programs on the server grants them the capability to do *anything* a program can do. This could be useful work, certainly, but it could also interfere with normal server operation or invade the privacy of others. For this reason, most server administrators allow programs to execute only if they reside in certain folders that only a few trusted individuals can update.

ASP files contain source code rather than executable programs, but because they trigger executable processes, they too must reside in an executable folder. For FrontPage database development, the executable folder can reside on any enterprise, workgroup, or personal Web server that has access to a test or production copy of the database.

For information about configuring Web folders as executable, refer to Appendix O, "Installing and Configuring a Web Server."

Chapter 36

Figure 36-4 shows the Bird Sighting Report form after a visitor has entered some data. Figure 36-5 shows the default confirmation page sent after FrontPage added this information to the database.

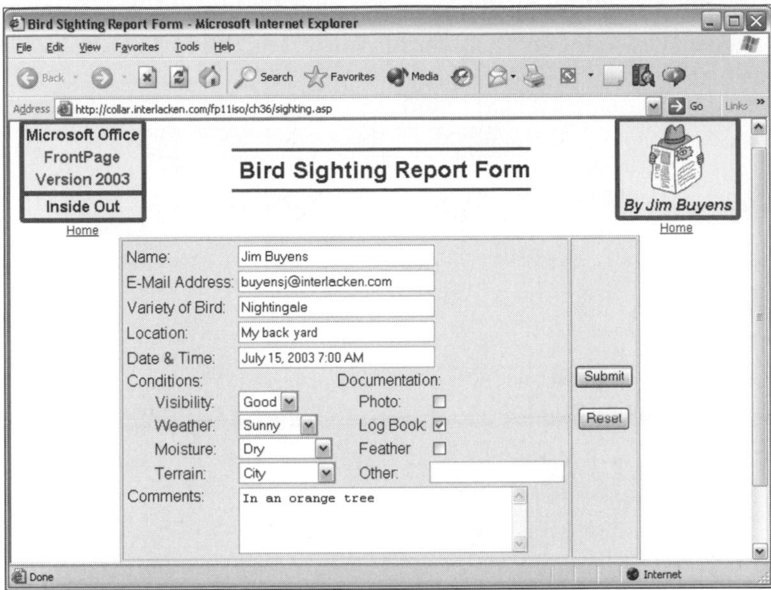

Figure 36-4. This is how the HTML form shown in Figure 36-1 appears in a browser. A fictitious visitor filled out the form.

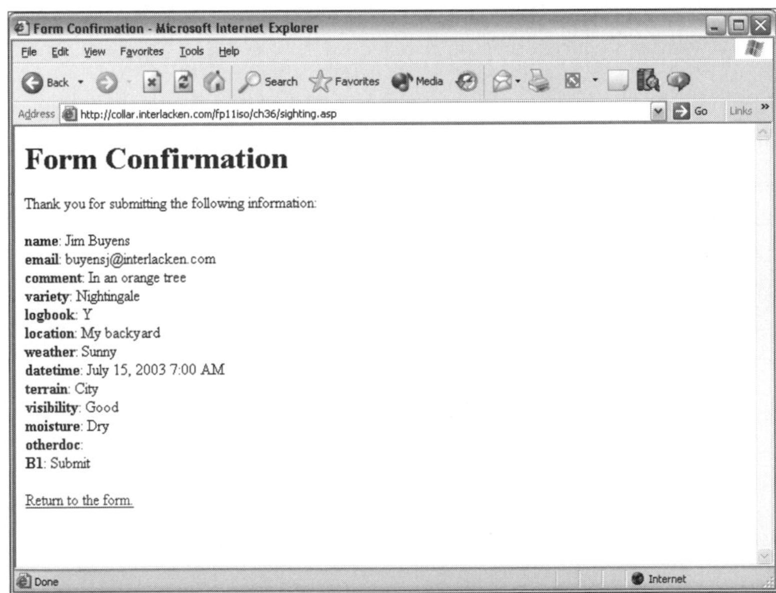

Figure 36-5. Clicking Submit on the Bird Sighting Report page adds a record to the database and displays this confirmation page.

Figure 36-6 shows Microsoft Access 2002 displaying some data collected from the Bird Sighting Report form. To process the database with Access, you would download the database to your computer, open it through a file-sharing connection to the Web server, or run Access directly on the server. Of course, you're free to process the data with additional Web database pages as well.

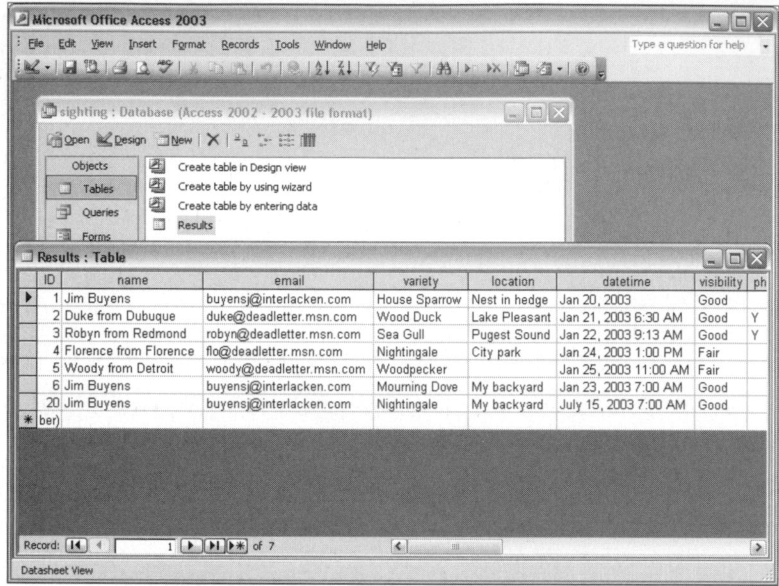

Figure 36-6. Access displays some data collected from the Bird Sighting Report form.

Using the Database Results Wizard

The previous section showed how to use the database features of the Save Results component to add records to a database. This section explains how to use another component—the Database Results Region component—to query and display database information. To create this component, you run (what else?) the Database Results Wizard.

It's easy to confuse the names Database Results Region and Save Results To Database. Here are some hints to help you keep these straight:

- The Save Results component—which has the word *Save* in its name—accepts and saves data from an HTML form, optionally in a database.
- The Database Results Wizard—which doesn't contain the word *Save*—queries a database and formats the results.

Displaying a Simple Query

To illustrate the Database Results Wizard, this section will create a Web page that displays data collected by the Bird Sighting Report page. This example displays selected fields from the table, using a custom sort order. Figure 36-7 shows the finished product as an ASP page. The ASP.NET version appears in Figure 36-8. The two versions are different because the ASP.NET version uses less custom code and more features built into the Microsoft .NET Framework.

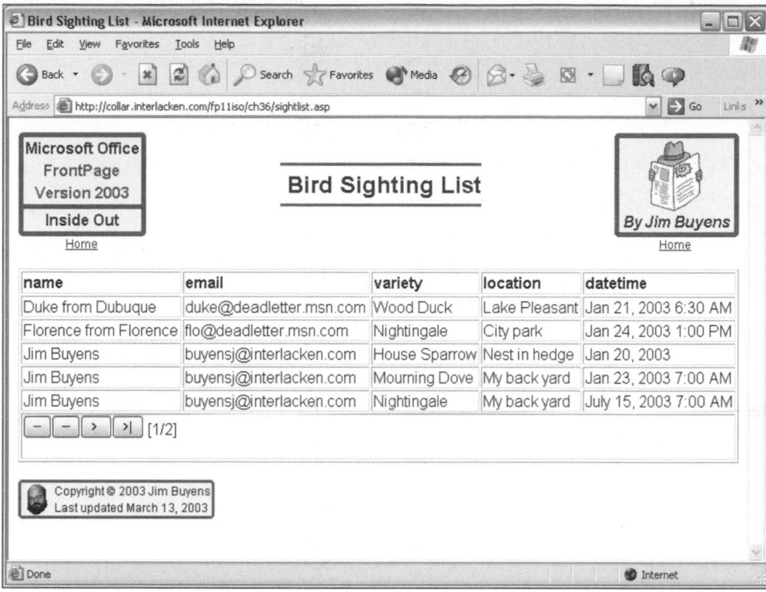

Figure 36-7. This Web page queries and displays the bird sighting database constructed in the previous section.

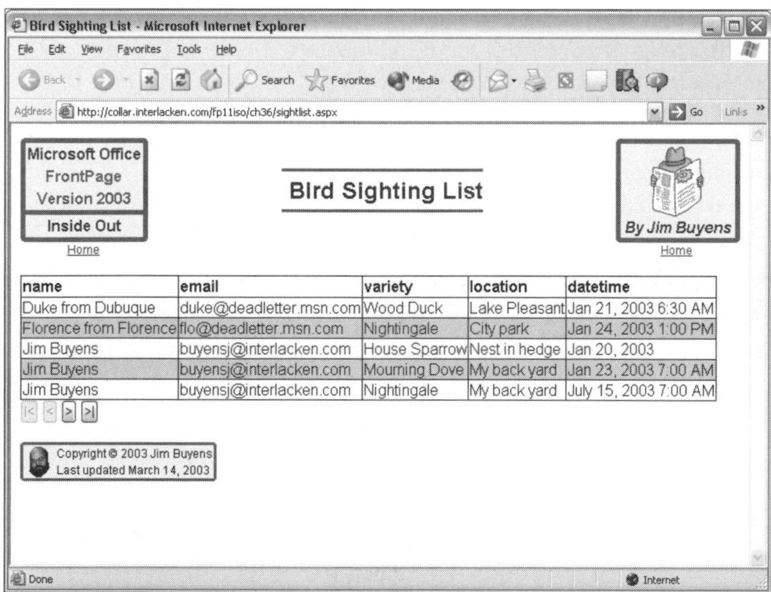

Figure 36-8. The specifications that created the ASP page in Figure 36-7 produce a slightly different appearance in ASP.NET. The data content, however, is the same.

> **Note** The Web page in Figure 36-7 incorporates the same formatting enhancements as most of the other Web pages in this book. The designer added a standard header and footer and applied a standard linked style sheet.

Here's the step-by-step procedure to create either version of this Web page:

1. Create a new, blank Web page in Page view.
2. Choose Database from the Insert menu, and then choose Results to launch the Database Results Wizard. The wizard's first page is shown on the left in Figure 36-9.

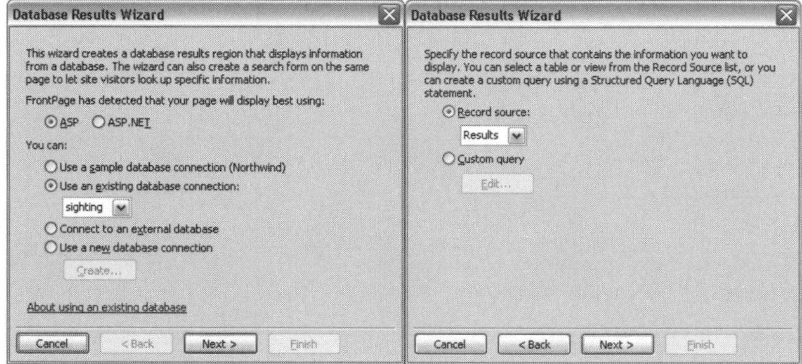

Figure 36-9. The first page in the Database Results Wizard selects the database connection that provides the displayed data. The second page specifies the table or query that provides the data.

This page offers the following choices:

- **FrontPage Has Detected That Your Page Will Display Best Using** Tells FrontPage to create either ASP or ASP.NET program code for displaying the database information. ASP.NET is the newer of these technologies, but it might not be available.
  - **Use A Sample Database Connection (Northwind)** Adds a sample database to your Web site, builds a connection to it, and selects that connection.
  - **Use An Existing Database Connection** Selects a database connection already defined within the current Web site.
  - **Use A New Database Connection** Enables the Create button, which displays the Database tab of the Site Settings dialog box, shown later in this chapter on the left in Figure 36-31.

For this example, use the existing database connection *sighting*, created in the previous section.

> **Tip** **Check your Server for ASP.NET Capability**
>
> To check the availability of ASP.NET on your Web server, copy the selfdiag.aspx page to the server, and browse it using an *http* URL. Insider Extra 2, "ASP.NET Self-Diagnosis Web Page," describes this page. The page itself resides in the selfdiagnet folder you installed with the Insider Extra files from the companion CD.

3 Click Next to display the second page of the Database Results Wizard, shown on the right in Figure 36-9. This page offers the following choices:

- **Record Source** Selects a table or query from the database connection you specified in the previous page.
- **Custom Query** Enables the Edit button, which displays a dialog box in which you can enter a SQL statement. For more information about this option, refer to the next section, "Refining Database Queries."

For this example, choose the Results table as the record source for this query, and click Next. Results is the one and only table in the sighting database.

4 Figure 36-10 shows the wizard's third page, which includes two options:

- **Edit List** Controls which fields the Web page displays.
- **More Options** Controls selection criteria, sequence, default criteria values, and some additional display options.

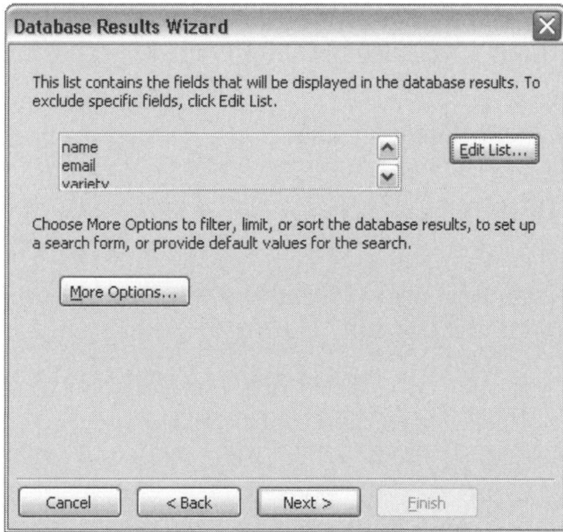

Figure 36-10. Click the Edit List button to control which table fields the Web page will display. Click the More Options button to control record selection and sorting.

5 Click Edit List to display the Displayed Fields dialog box, on the left in Figure 36-11.

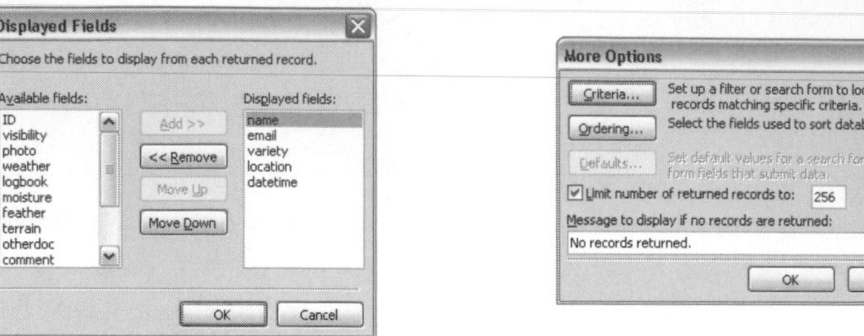

Figure 36-11. Click Edit List in the third page of the Database Results Wizard (Figure 36-10) to display the Displayed Fields dialog box, which selects and orders fields for appearance on the Web page. To display the More Options dialog box, click More Options.

This dialog box configures the following options:

- **Available Fields** Lists fields from the database table that don't currently appear on the Web page.
- **Displayed Fields** Lists fields that do appear on the Web page, and specifies their order.
- **Add** Moves any selected fields out of Available Fields and into Displayed Fields.
- **Remove** Moves any selected fields out of Displayed Fields and into Available Fields.
- **Move Up** Moves any selected field one position higher in the Displayed Fields list.
- **Move Down** Moves any selected field one position lower in the Displayed Fields list.

For this example, select and arrange the fields as shown on the left in Figure 36-11.

6 Clicking the More Options button displays the More Options dialog box, shown on the right in Figure 36-11. The More Options dialog box has the following options:

- **Criteria** Controls which database records the Web page will display, based on their data values.
- **Ordering** Controls the order in which records appear—from top to bottom —on the Web page.
- **Defaults** Dimmed unless you specify criteria. In the presence of criteria, it provides substitutes for any criteria the Web visitor leaves blank.
- **Limit Number Of Returned Records To** If selected, limits the number of records retrieved from the database. This option provides no way to view additional records beyond the given limit. This option exists to prevent runaway queries (that is, queries that retrieve thousands or tens of thousands of records). This is far more records than the Web visitor can assimilate and is thus a

considerable waste of resources. The Split Records Into Groups option described in step 10 shows the Web visitor a few records at a time to and provides buttons for moving forward and backward through the result set. However, the result set can't be larger than any limit you specify here

- **Message To Display If No Records Are Returned** Specifies the text FrontPage will display if there are no database records to display.

This example uses only the Ordering option. Later sections in this chapter explain the remaining options.

For more information about using advanced query settings, refer to "Using Advanced Query Settings to Select and Sort Records," later in this chapter.

7 Click Ordering in the More Options dialog box (on the right in Figure 36-11) to display the Ordering dialog box, shown in Figure 36-12.

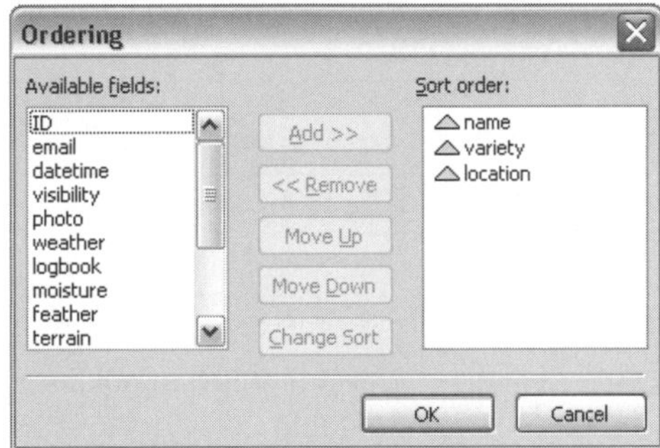

Figure 36-12. The Ordering dialog box specifies which data fields control the order of query results.

Each field in the current database query initially appears in the Available Fields column, and initially has no effect on sorting the results of the query. The Sort Order column lists fields that do affect the order of query results.

Fields higher in the column have precedence over fields below them, and an up or down arrow indicates ascending or descending sequence for each field.

The Ordering dialog box contains the following buttons:

- **Add** Moves any selected fields out of the Available Fields column and into the Sort Order column.
- **Remove** Moves any selected fields out of the Sort Order column and into the Available Fields column.
- **Move Up** Moves one selected Sort Order field one position higher in the list. This and the next two buttons will be dimmed unless one and only one Sort Order field is selected.
- **Move Down** Moves one selected Sort Order field one position lower in the list.
- **Change Sort** Toggles one selected Sort Order field between ascending and descending sequence.

8 For this example, select and arrange the fields as shown in Figure 36-12. Click OK twice, and then click Next.

The fourth page of the Database Results Wizard appears in Figure 36-13. This page controls the layout of the displayed data:

- **Choose Formatting Options For The Records Returned By The Query.** Determines how FrontPage will display each record the query returns. There are three overall formats, each with variations:
- **Table—One Record Per Row** Means that FrontPage will create an HTML table in which each column corresponds to a field in the database and each row contains these fields from a different record. (Figure 36-13 shows this option selected.) Table 36-1 lists the additional options for this format.

Note For an ASP.NET Database Results Region, a DataGrid—One Record Per Row option replaces Table – One Record Per Row. In addition, the List—One Field Per Item and Drop-Down List—One Record Per Item options are absent.

Table 36-1. Formatting Options for Table—One Record Per Row

Option	Effect (if selected)
Use Table Border	Specifies that the table will have borders.
Expand Table To Width Of Page	Sets the table's width to 100 percent.
Include Header Row With Column Labels	Provides a row of column headings above the table. The captions are the field names.

- **List—One Field Per Item** Means that FrontPage will display each field on a separate line, with formatting breaks between records. Table 36-2 lists the additional options. This setting is unavailable if you chose ASP.NET in step 2.

Table 36-2. Formatting Options for List—One Field Per Item

Option	Effect (if selected)
Add Labels For All Field Values	Precedes each field value with the corresponding field name
Place Horizontal Separator Between Records	Separates the records with a horizontal rule
List Options: Paragraphs, Line Breaks, Bullet List, Numbered List, Definition List, Table, Formatted Text Fields, Scrolling Text Fields	Specifies the paragraph style used for fields within a record

- **Drop-Down List—One Record Per Item** Means that FrontPage will populate a drop-down list with choices from the selected database records. The list then works like any other drop-down list in an HTML form. Table 36-3 lists additional options for this setting. This setting is unavailable if you chose ASP.NET in step 2.

Table 36-3. Formatting Options for Drop-Down List—One Record Per Item

Option	Effect
Display Values From This Field	Select the field that contains the values the visitor will see in the drop-down list.
Submit Values From This Field	Select the field that contains the values the form will submit to the Web server.

Typically, the reason for displaying one field and submitting another is to display an option to the visitor in words (such as employee name) but to send the Web server a code (such as employee number).

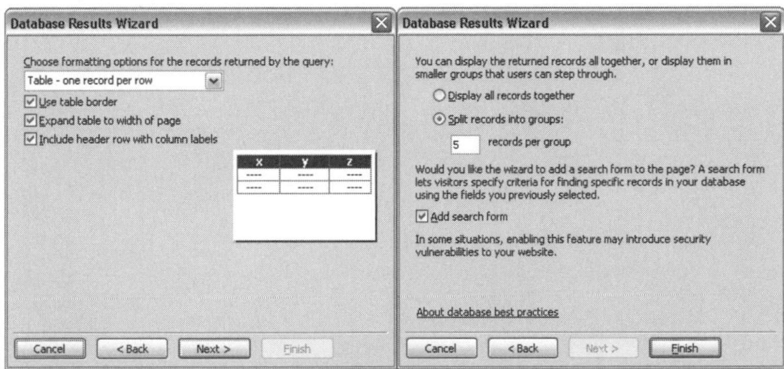

Figure 36-13. The fourth page of the Database Results Wizard (on the left) controls the arrangement of the displayed data. The wizard's last page (on the right) displays either an unlimited number of records per Web page or a set number with Forward and Back buttons.

9 Click Next after you've selected the formatting options you need.

10 The Database Results Wizard's final page (shown on the right in Figure 36-13) provides another way of limiting the number of records displayed per page.

This dialog box provides the following options:

- **Display All Records Together** Displays all selected records on one Web page.
- **Split Records Into Groups** Displays a limited number of records per Web page. FrontPage creates first, last, forward, and back buttons so that the Web visitor can move through the database. The Records Per Group box specifies the number of records per page.

- **Add Search Form** If selected, creates an HTML form that prompts for and submits any form field values you specified as record selection criteria. (The next section in this chapter describes how to do this.) If you didn't specify any criteria involving form fields, this option will be dimmed.

For this example, specify 5 records per group.

If you chose in step 2 to create an ASP page, clicking Finish in the final Database Results Wizard page will create the Web page shown in Figure 36-14. The two shaded table rows are just for information and don't appear on the Web visitor's browser. The middle row is the Database Results region, which repeats once per record displayed.

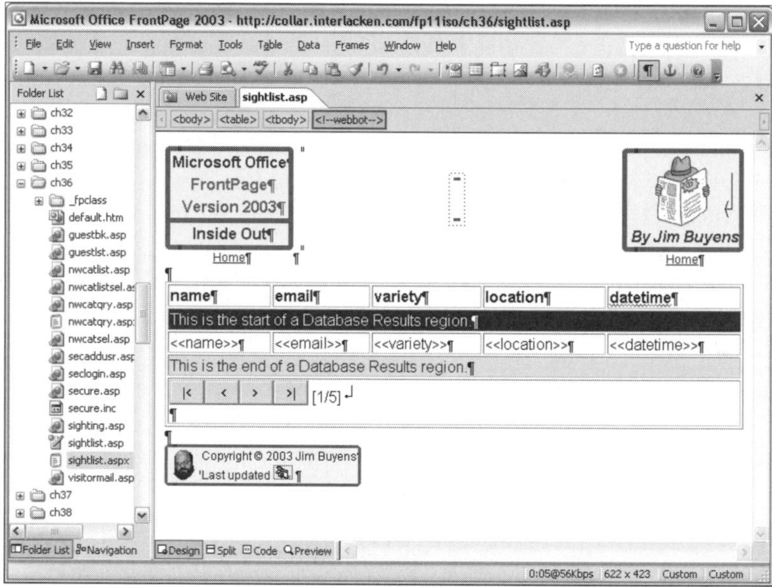

Figure 36-14. This Web page is typical of ASP pages that the Database Results Wizard creates.

Figure 36-15 shows how Design view displays the ASP.NET Web page that creates the results shown previously in Figure 36-8. This page contains four ASP.NET components, and as you can see, FrontPage is unable to display three of them. The top and bottom components display the page banner and page footer, respectively. The visible component in the middle line is an ASP.NET DataGrid control, which actually displays the data. FPDB:DBRegion is a custom FrontPage component that retrieves the data and loads the DataGrid control.

Accessing and Updating Databases with FrontPage

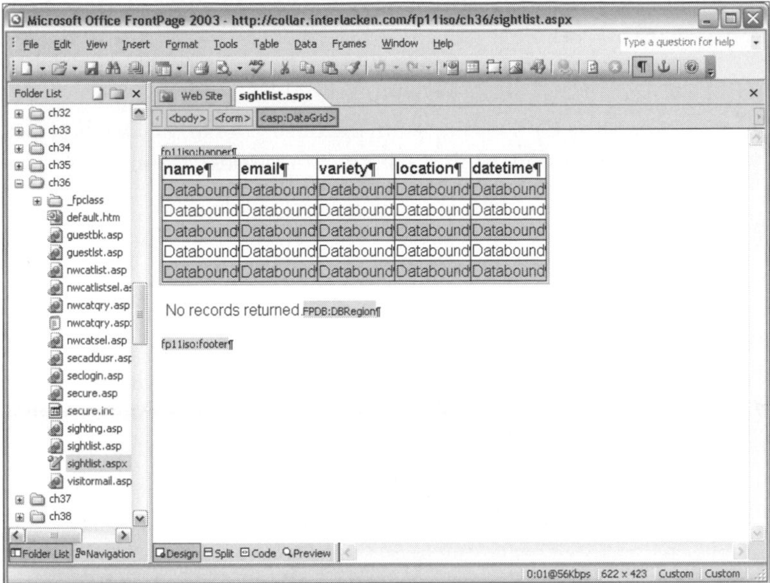

Figure 36-15. FrontPage displays an ASP.NET Database Results region as two gray bars: one for an ASP.NET DataGrid control and another for a custom control that runs the database query.

FrontPage preview mode won't display data in pages containing Database Results regions; preview mode actually displays Web pages temporarily saved to disk and doesn't have access to all the facilities of a Web server. To view the page in action, save it with the appropriate file extension (.asp or .aspx) in an executable folder in a server-based Web site, and then choose the Preview In Browser command from the File menu or the Standard toolbar. Figure 36-7 and Figure 36-8 show Web pages that these actions display.

Refining Database Queries

Selecting Record Source in the second page of the Database Results Wizard (on the right in Figure 36-9) generates the simplest possible database query—it selects all fields from all records in the given table and presents them in the table's default sequence. FrontPage provides two alternatives that query the database with more specific options:

- Using the Custom Query option in the second page of the Database Results Wizard (again, on the right in Figure 36-9), you can query the database any way you want by writing your own SQL statement.

> **For more information about SQL, refer to "Introducing SQL," in Appendix K.**

- To specify more complex queries:
  1. Choose the Record Source option in the second page of the Database Results Wizard.
  2. Click the More Options button in the third page of the Database Results Wizard (shown in Figure 36-10). This displays the More Options dialog box, shown on the right in Figure 36-11.
  3. Click the Criteria button to select records based on comparisons to either form fields or constants.
  4. Click the Ordering button to control the sequence in which the records will appear.

Figure 36-16 shows the type of Web page these techniques can produce. Entering a Category ID in the text box and clicking Submit Query displays products in that category, in Product ID order. The next two sections will describe each alternative in detail.

> **Note** A designer manually formatted the Web page shown in Figure 36-16 using a combination of table attributes and CSS properties. For clarity in this example, the column headings remain equal to the database column names. This is the default, but it's something you'd want to change in a real application. Changing the column headings is a simple matter of editing them as text in FrontPage.

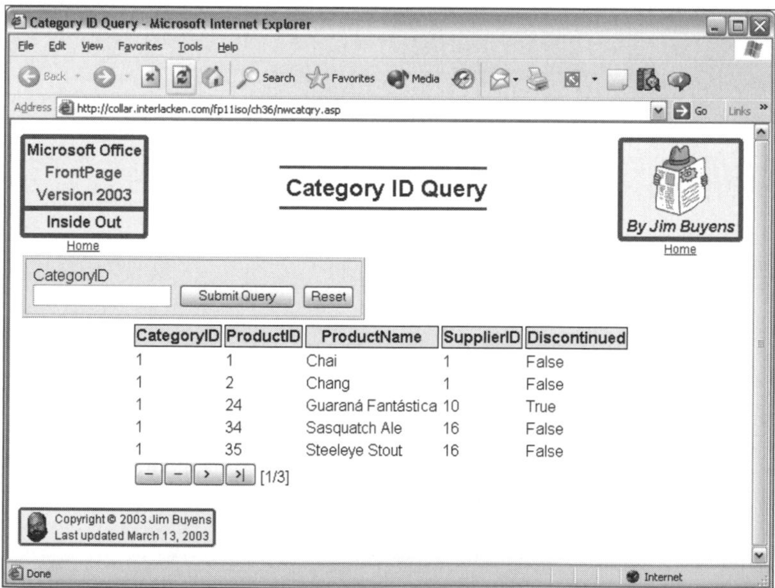

Figure 36-16. Entering a Category ID and clicking Submit Query displays matching records in Product ID order.

Using a Custom Query to Select and Sort Records

Selecting Custom Query and clicking the Edit button in the second page of the Database Results Wizard (on the right in Figure 36-9) displays the dialog box shown on the left in Figure 36-17. This dialog box provides great flexibility by accepting any SQL statement you want to enter, but it requires knowledge of SQL.

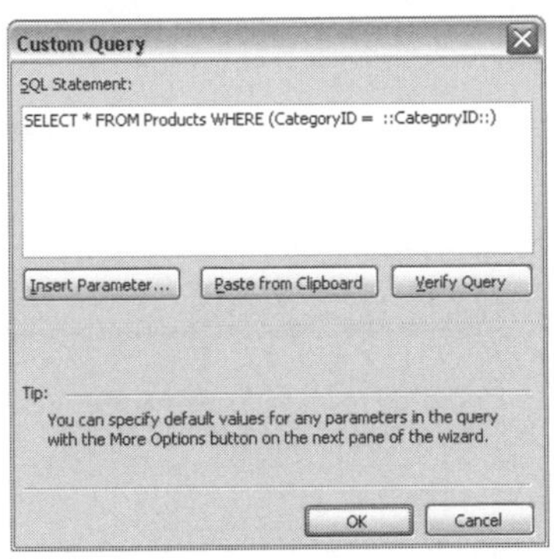

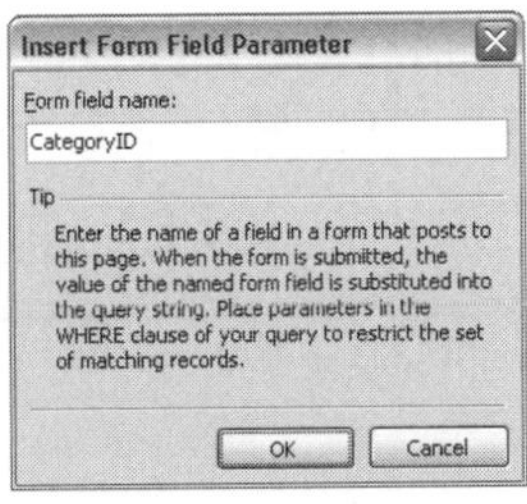

Figure 36-17. The Custom Query dialog box accepts a SQL statement typed by hand or pasted from the Clipboard. The Insert Form Field Parameter dialog box specifies the name of an HTML form field whose value will become part of the SQL statement.

The Custom Query dialog box contains the following options:

- **SQL Statement** Contains a SQL command that tells the database software what data to retrieve.
- **Insert Parameter** Displays the dialog box shown on the right in Figure 36-17. Here you can enter the name of an HTML form field.
- **Paste From Clipboard** Copies any text currently in the Clipboard to the SQL Statement box.
- **Verify Query** Submits the current SQL statement to the database software and reports any errors. Use this button to test the query before closing the dialog box.

Be sure to set the insertion point properly before clicking the Insert Parameter button—usually where a constant would appear in a HAVING or WHERE expression. FrontPage inserts the HTML form field name based on the insertion point's location.

For more information about using form fields to supply query values, refer to "Using Search Forms to Specify Query Values," later in this chapter.

If you want, you can skip clicking the Insert Parameter button and insert the form field code yourself. Just type two colons, the name of the form field, and two more colons wherever you want the form field's value to appear.

Tip Be sure to surround any form field parameters with the usual delimiters required by SQL. Values compared to character fields must be enclosed in apostrophes, whereas values compared to numeric fields must not.

You can create and debug queries in Microsoft Access and then transfer them to FrontPage using the Paste From Clipboard button. Here's the procedure:

1. Open the database (or a copy of it) in Access.
2. Open or create a query that displays the data you want. Use constants in place of any form field values you plan to use.
3. Choose SQL View from the View menu, the View drop-down menu on the Query Datasheet toolbar, or the View drop-down menu on the Query Design toolbar.

   Figure 36-18 shows this operation in progress.

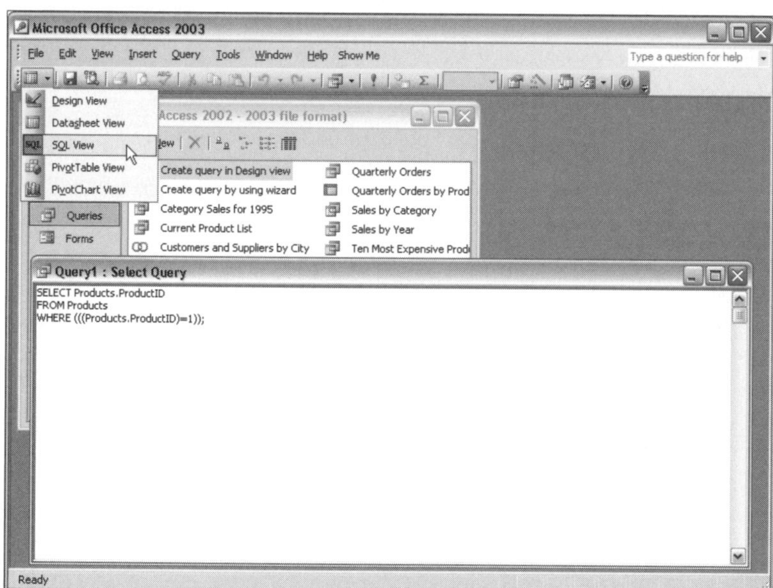

Figure 36-18. After you get a query working in Access, you can display the SQL code and copy it to the Clipboard for pasting into the Database Results Wizard.

4. Select all the text in the SQL statement, and then copy it to the Clipboard by choosing Copy from the Edit menu, pressing Ctrl+C, or pressing Ctrl+Insert.
5. Switch to FrontPage, and display the Custom Query dialog box (shown on the left in Figure 36-17).
6. Click Paste From Clipboard to insert the SQL statement.
7. If, in step 2, you used any constants in place of form field values, select each one and then use the Insert Parameter button to insert the form field name.
8. Change any quotation marks (") to apostophes (')

Using Advanced Query Settings to Select and Sort Records

Writing SQL statements gives you total control over the selection of records from a database table and the order in which they appear. The catch, of course, is that you have to know SQL. This section describes another way to control record selection and ordering—a way that's slightly less flexible but that requires no SQL proficiency.

To use this method, advance to the third page of the Database Results Wizard (shown in Figure 36-10), and then click More Options. This displays the More Options dialog box (shown on the right in Figure 36-11).

> **Note** If you select the Custom Query option in the second page of the Database Results Wizard (shown on the right in Figure 36-9), and then click the More Options button in the third page of the wizard, you'll find that the Criteria, Ordering, and Defaults buttons are dimmed. This is because a SQL statement in a custom query might contain options that these buttons can't preserve. To control criteria and ordering for a custom query, work directly with the SQL statement.

Clicking the Criteria button in the More Options dialog box displays the Criteria dialog box, shown on the left in Figure 36-19. The list in the Criteria dialog box shows the criteria currently in effect.

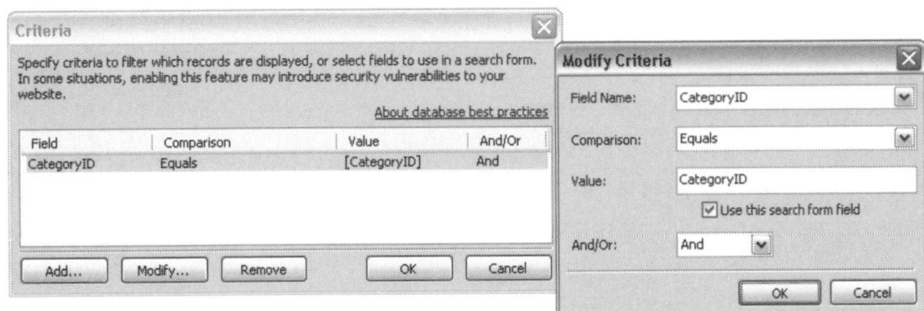

Figure 36-19. Clicking the Criteria button in the More Options dialog box displays the Criteria dialog box, which controls selection of database records for display. The Modify Criteria dialog box specifies selection criteria for database records.

These buttons modify the list:

- **Add** Click this button to display an Add Criteria dialog box very similar to the Modify Criteria dialog box shown on the right in Figure 36-19. The Add Criteria dialog box adds a new criterion to the list.
- **Modify** Click this button to display the Modify Criteria dialog box. This dialog box changes the properties of an existing criterion.
- **Remove** Click this button to delete the currently selected criterion.

Here's how to use the options in the Add Criteria and Modify Criteria dialog boxes:

- **Field Name** Select the field whose value you want to test.
- **Comparison** Specify the operator for the comparison: Equals, Not Equal, Less Than, and so forth.
- **Value** There are three ways to use this option:
  - If you want to select records based on the value of an HTML form field, enter the name of the form field, and then select the Use This Search Form Field check box.
  - If you want to select records based on a fixed value, enter the value, and then clear the Use This Search Form Field check box.
  - If you chose a Comparison operator of Is Null or Not Null, the Value option will be dimmed.

Note A null value in a database field means that the field currently has no value. This is different from a numeric field being zero or a character field containing a zero-length string—in both those cases, the field *has* a value. A field whose value is null has no known value—not even zero or an empty string.

- **And/Or** Select And if other criteria, as well as this one, must be true for the record to be selected. Select Or if this is one of several criteria, any one of which, if true, is sufficient to select the record.

Clicking the Defaults button in the More Options dialog box (shown on the right in Figure 36-11) displays the Defaults dialog box, shown in Figure 36-20. This dialog box specifies default values for criteria received from HTML forms (that is, if the HTML form value is blank or missing, the default supplied here takes effect).

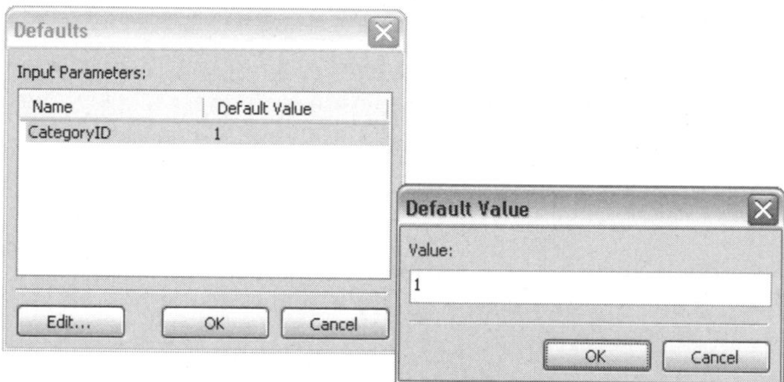

Figure 36-20. The Defaults dialog box lists each database field.

Initially, the Input Parameters list contains each field having defined criteria based on an HTML form value. To supply a default value for any field, either double-click it or select it and click Edit. The result will be the dialog box shown on the right in Figure 36-20. Enter the default value, and then click OK.

The Ordering button in the More Options dialog box controls the sequence of records listed in the reports. For details on using this option, refer to step 7 in the section "Displaying a Simple Query," earlier in this chapter.

Using Search Forms to Specify Query Values

If you specified database selection criteria based on HTML form fields—either by entering parameters in the Custom Query dialog box (shown on the left in Figure 36-17) or by entering criteria in the Criteria dialog box (shown on the left in Figure 36-19)—the final page of the Database Results Wizard (shown on the right in Figure 36-13) will contain a check box titled Add Search Form. Selecting this check box adds an HTML form to the page that contains the Database Results component. Figure 36-21 shows the result as it appears on an ASP.NET page.

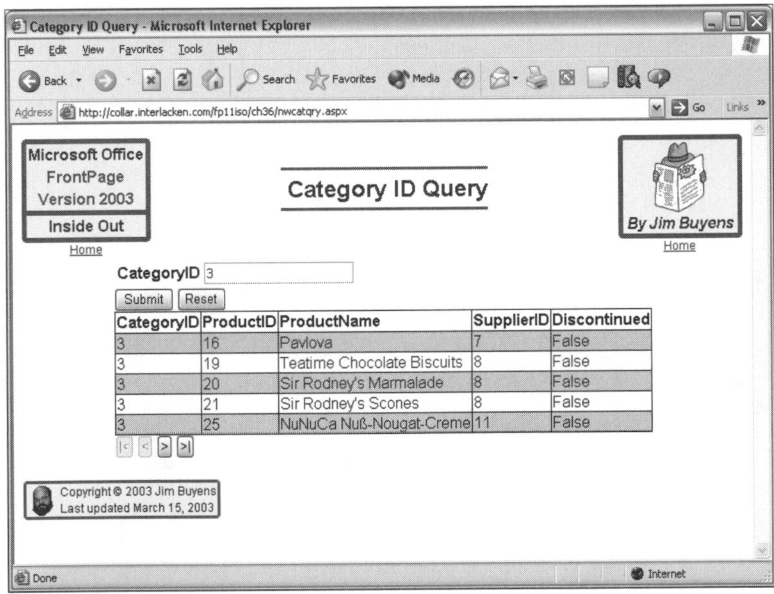

Figure 36-21. The Database Results Wizard created the HTML form on this Web page. It specifies a value for filtering the query results.

This Web page handles both input and output of database queries. The Web visitor enters a Category ID, clicks Submit, and receives a listing of products in that category.

Working with ASP.NET Database Result Search Forms

If you're using ASP.NET, the search form will appear in Design view as a one-row, two-celled HTML table. The first cell will contain the field name as a title, and the second row will contain two ASP.NET controls: a TextBox control and a Regular Expression Validator control. Design view has no facilities for modifying such controls. If you're not happy with the way they look or act in the browser, you'll need to use the Quick Tag Editor, Code view, or another editor to modify them. The rest of the material in this section won't apply.

Inside Out

Design in FrontPage. Develop ASP.NET code in something else.

The ASP. NET version of the Database Results component requires that a search form be on the same page as the Database Results component it controls. In addition, this version can't display query results as lists or drop-down lists.

ASP Database Results components can provide both of these features, and so, at least initially, these omissions from the ASP.NET version might seem unfortunate. However, if you're attempting to provide these kinds of database features, you're bound to be writing program code in the near future anyway. You might as well jump into Visual Studio or Web Matrix at the start. FrontPage is a design and Web site management tool, not a programming environment.

Working with ASP Database Result Search Forms

If you're using classic ASP, FrontPage will use classic HTML to build a Database Result search form. In this case, Design view displays the form as shown near the top of Figure 36-22.

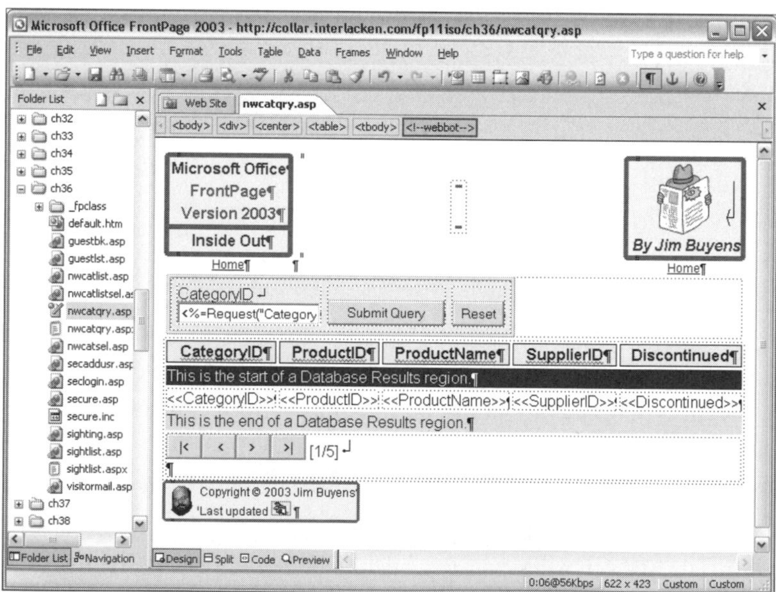

Figure 36-22. The HTML form at the top of this page collects and submits input that controls data displayed by the Database Results region below it.

Figure 36-23 shows the properties of the text box from Figure 36-22. This text box is named CategoryID, the same as the name of the database field it selects. The use of similar names is a convention followed by the Database Results Wizard, and not a firm requirement.

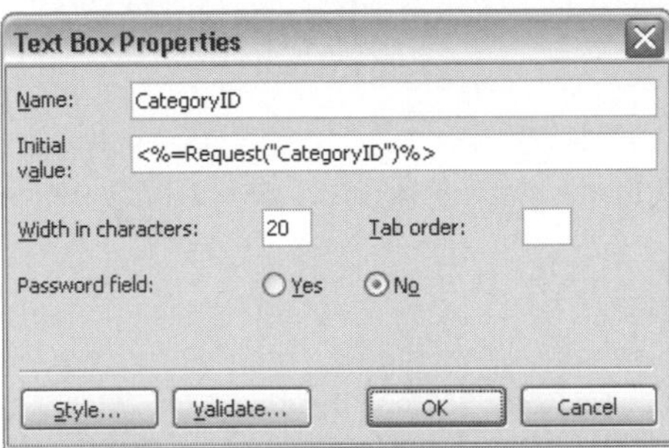

Figure 36-23. The CategoryID text box in Figure 36-22 has these properties.

The Initial Value field might look a bit peculiar until you realize that it's a piece of ASP code. Whenever the Web server processes the ASP page, the inline expression *<%=Request("CategoryID")%>* obtains the form field value named *CategoryID* and writes it out as part of the Web page. Thus, the text box is always initialized to its previous value.

When using the ASP version of the Database Results component, nothing stops you from putting the HTML form and the Database Results region on different Web pages. To make them separate pages, just cut the HTML form out of the Database Results page and paste it wherever you want. Adjust the relative URL in the form's *Action* property if necessary.

Figure 36-24 shows a Web page with an HTML form that submits input to the nwcatqry.asp page. However, instead of using a text box for the *CategoryID* field, this page uses an ASP Database Results component configured to display a drop-down list. The list contains one entry for each record in the Categories table, a table that defines the list of valid categories for the nwind.mdb database. The Database Results drop-down list displays the alphabetic *CategoryName* field, but it submits the numeric *CategoryID* field.

Troubleshooting

Page containing HTML form and Database Results component returns an error when first displayed

If you create a Database Results component that receives criteria from an HTML form on the same Web page, displaying the page might return a message such as the following:

Database results error
The operation failed. If this continues, please contact your server administrator.

Older versions of the component might display a message like this:

Database Results Error
Description: [Microsoft][ODBC Microsoft Access Driver] Extra) in query expression '(CategoryID =)'.
Number: -2147217900 (0x80040E14)
Source: Microsoft OLE DB Provider for ODBC Drivers
One or more form fields were empty. You should provide default values for all form fields that are used in the query.

Such messages occur because the database query in a Database Results component runs every time a visitor requests the Web page—including the first time, before the Web visitor has entered any query fields. With missing criteria values, the database query fails. To avoid this problem, do either of the following:

- Put the HTML form and the Database Results region on different pages.
- Use the Defaults dialog box (shown on the left in Figure 36-20) to assign defaults for all input fields used in the query.

Assigning default values to the forms field has no effect. The browser fills in form field defaults after receiving the Web page, which is after the reported error occurs.

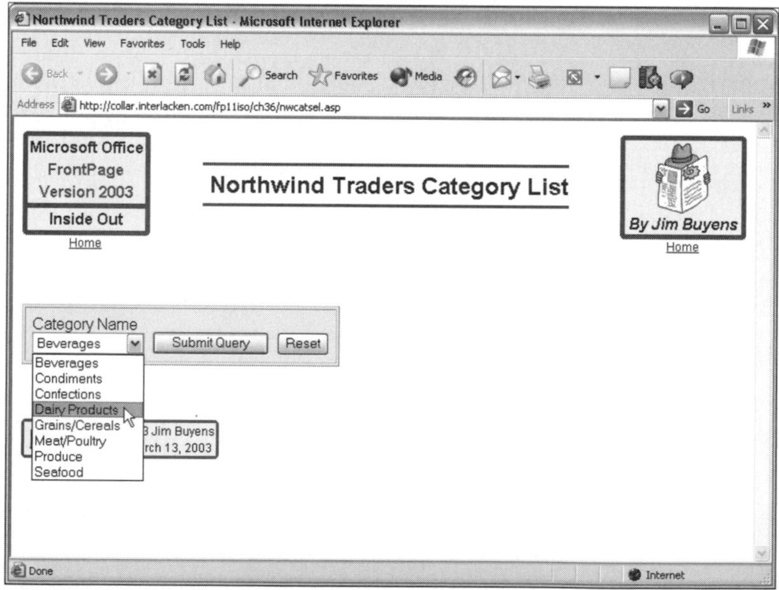

Figure 36-24. The Database Results component populated the drop-down list in this Web page with values from a database.

Inside Out

Database Results drop-down lists don't preserve selections

When a Database Results drop-down list appears in a form that, as shown in Figure 36-16, uses the same Web page for input and output, visitors who select a value, click Submit, and receive a new version of the page expect their selection to remain in effect. In fact, a Database Results drop-down list always positions the list at the first entry. This limits the usefulness of Database Results drop-down lists.

To learn how to create a database-driven drop-down box that retains its value, refer to "Recycling Form Element Values," in Appendix J.

Configuring Database Results Columns

The objects displayed as *<<CategoryID>>*, *<<ProductID>>*, *<<ProductName>>*, *<<SupplierID>>*, and so forth in Figure 36-22 are Database Column Value components. These components are valid only inside the ASP version of a Database Results region, and each one contains the name of a database field to display. Whenever the Database Results region has a record to display, it replaces each Database Column Value component with the value of its corresponding field.

Because Database Column Value components exist only within the ASP version of a Database Results region, you can't use the techniques in this section to modify an ASP.NET version of a Database Results region. Instead, you must modify the ASP.NET DataGrid control that the Database Results Wizard creates. To do this in FrontPage requires working in Code view and therefore requires intimate knowledge of the DataGrid control.

For more information about the ASP.NET DataGrid control, browse *msdn.microsoft.com* and search for the terms *framework*, *DataGrid*, and *class*.

Configuring Database Column Value Components

Here are the steps to insert a new Database Column Value component:

1. Set the insertion point where you want the component to appear. Remember, the component must be within a Database Results region.
2. Choose Database from the Insert menu, and then choose Column Value. The Database Column Value dialog box, shown in Figure 36-25, will appear.

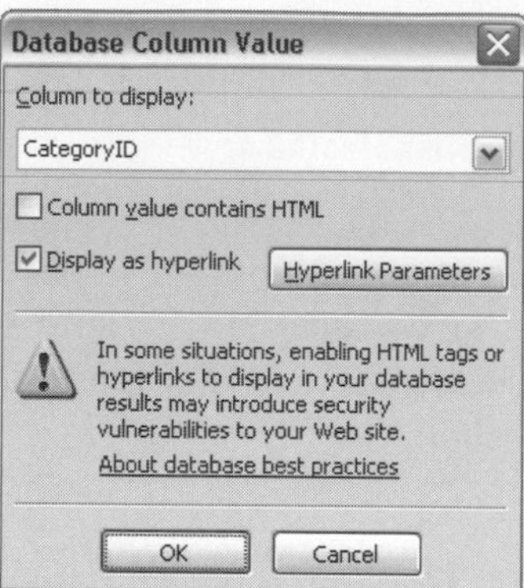

Figure 36-25. This dialog box configures the database field that a Database Column Value component will display.

Use the options in this dialog box as follows:

- **Column To Display** To specify or modify the database field you want to display, select the field you want from the drop-down list.
- **Column Value Contains HTML** Select this check box if the database field you specified contains HTML that you want the browser to display. This choice is appropriate if, for example, the field contains the HTML to display a hyperlink or a picture.

  Normally, the Database Results component translates HTML characters such as < and > to symbolic equivalents like *<* and *>*. This keeps the browser from misinterpreting these characters when they appear in normal text—in a description field, for example. However, it interferes with display of HTML you've purposely included in the query results. Selecting this option turns off the translation.
- **Display As Hyperlink** Select this check box if the database field contains URLs that the visitor should be able to click. FrontPage will display a hyperlink that uses the field contents as both the displayed text and the hyperlink location.

  Suppose, for example, that one row of a database table contained a field with the value *http://www.microsoft.com*. A Database Column Value component with the Display As Hyperlink option selected would use the following HTML to display the field:

  ```
  <a href="http://www.microsoft.com">http://www.microsoft.com</a>
  ```

  This HTML displays the text *http://www.microsoft.com* underlined like any other hyperlink, and clicking it would jump to Microsoft's Web site.

  Although the example shows a fully qualified URL, relative URLs work equally well.
- **Hyperlink Properties** Click this button to append database values to the URL as query string parameters. Chapter 11 explained how to use the resulting Hyperlink Parameters dialog box.

3 Click OK.

To modify a Database Column Value component, double-click it; right-click it and choose Database Column Value Properties from the shortcut menu; or select it and choose Properties from the Format menu. This again displays the dialog box shown in Figure 36-25.

Creating Query Columns That Contain HTML

The previous section explained how, if some column in a database table or query contains HTML, you can select the Column Value Contains HTML check box in the Database Column Value dialog box to display the HTML as Web content instead of odd-looking text. However, it didn't explain how the HTML got there. Not many database tables contain columns full of HTML.

In many cases, the tables that physically reside in the database don't contain HTML at all. Instead, the query that retrieves the records surrounds ordinary column values with HTML code. Figure 36-26 shows a Web page that uses just such a query.

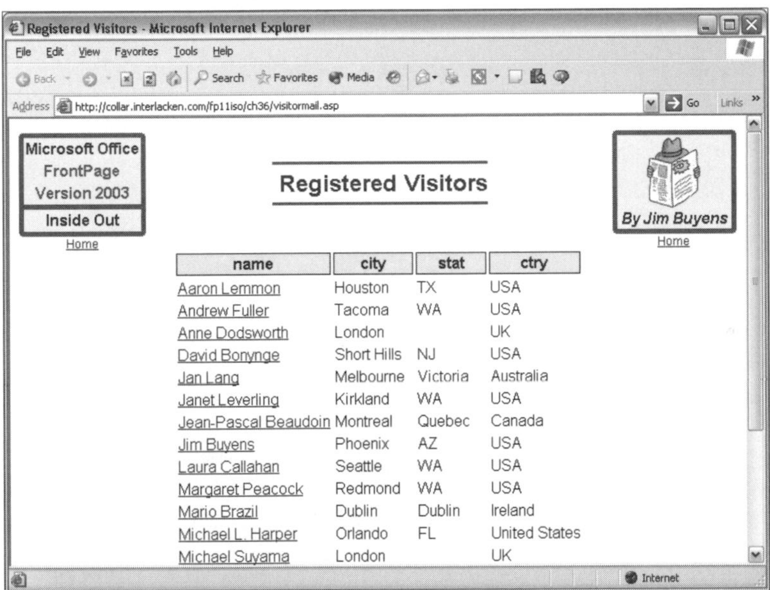

Figure 36-26. A database query generated the HTML for the clickable names in the *mailto* column of this Database Results page.

The *city*, *stat*, and *ctry* fields are part of an ordinary table named visitors. The *mailto* column, however, isn't physically part of the database at all. Instead, it contains a string that Microsoft Access assembles, based on a formula, for each row in the query. Here's the formula:

```
mailto: "<a href=" & Chr(34) & "mailto:" & [mail] & Chr(34) & ">" & [name] & "</a>"
```

This formula contains five types of elements:

- The initial expression *mailto:* assigns a column name to the calculated field.
- Expressions in quotation marks appear verbatim in the results.
- The *Chr* function accepts a numeric argument and returns the corresponding ASCII character. *Chr(34)* returns a quotation mark character.
- Expressions in square brackets return the values of other fields in the same row. The expression *[mail]* returns the value of the *mail* field in the current table row.
- The ampersand (&) joins two strings together.

Notice that the expression includes values from two different columns in the table: *[mail]* and *[name]*. In fact, you can include values from as many fields as you want. This isn't a requirement, but it's certainly a powerful feature.

Figure 36-27 shows this formula entered as a column specification in Microsoft Access Design view. The designer saved the query as vismailto. Figure 36-28 shows the same query in Access Datasheet view. There's no distinction between the *mailto* field, which is calculated, and the other fields, which reside physically in the database.

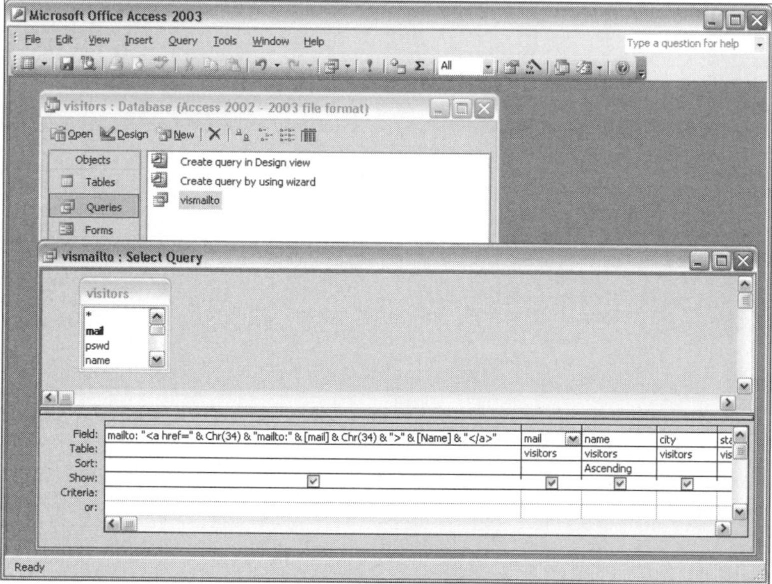

Figure 36-27. This query defines a field named *mailto* that comes from a formula rather than from a physical field in a table.

Accessing and Updating Databases with FrontPage

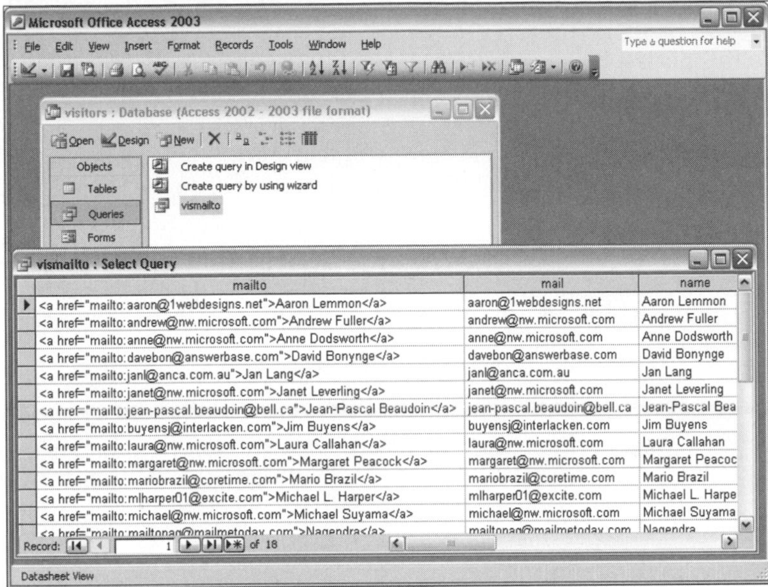

Figure 36-28. Running the query shown in Figure 36-27 produces these results. You can treat the calculated column like any other.

To run this query and produce clickable hyperlinks like the ones shown in Figure 36-26:

1. Set up a database connection to the database that contains the data (and the saved query)—unless, of course, you already have one.
2. Open a Web page, and set the insertion point.
3. Choose Database from the Insert menu, and then choose Results.
4. In the first page of the Database Results Wizard (shown on the left in Figure 36-9), specify the database connection you set up in step 1.
5. In the wizard's second page (shown on the right in Figure 36-9), specify the query that contains the calculated expression. (The Record List will include a choice for the query name, plus the word *VIEW*.)
6. In the wizard's third page (shown in Figure 36-10), be sure to include the calculated field in the output.
7. In the fourth page, *don't* specify Drop-Down List—One Record Per Item.
8. When the wizard finishes:
    1. Right-click the Database Column Value component titled <<*mailto*>>, and choose Database Column Value Properties from the shortcut menu.
    2. Select the Column Value Contains HTML check box, and click OK.

The same general technique works for all sorts of HTML: <a href=...> tags for hyperlinks, <img src=...> tags for pictures, and so forth. In the case of an <img> tag, the database would contain the name of the picture file and not the picture itself.

If for some reason you don't want to create a stored query, you can use calculated fields in a custom query. To do this, include the expression that defines the calculated field in the SQL statement you enter in the Custom Query dialog box (shown on the left in Figure 36-17).

Creating an Ordinary Hyperlink for a Database Column Value

Figure 36-29 shows another way of adding hyperlinks to a Database Results region.

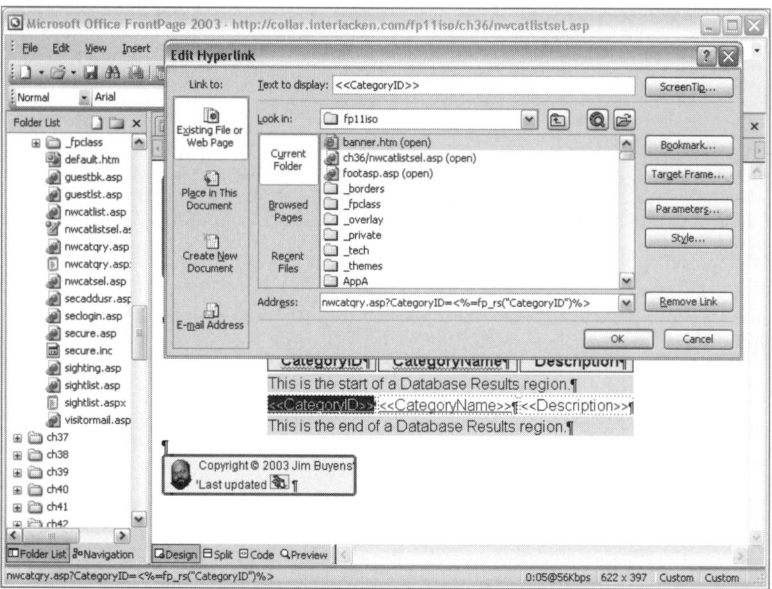

Figure 36-29. You can build ordinary hyperlinks that surround Database Column Value components and, if you want, include database values from the same record.

Here's the full procedure:

1. Create an ordinary Database Results region that displays the text you want to use as a hyperlink as well as all the field values you want to include in the hyperlink URL.
2. Right-click the Database Column Value component that shows the desired text, and choose Hyperlink or Hyperlink Properties (whichever appears) from the shortcut menu.
3. Enter any address you want in the Address box of the Insert Hyperlink or Edit Hyperlink dialog box.
4. Wherever you want a value from the database to appear in the URL, enter an expression such as the following:

   ```
   <%=fp_rs("CategoryID")%>
   ```

   Replace *CategoryID* with the name of the field you actually want.

Figure 36-30 shows the Web page from Figure 36-29 in use. Notice that the mouse pointer is over the *CategoryName* field for category 4 and that the status line at the bottom of the window displays a URL that includes the query string *CategoryID=4*. The digit *4* comes from the *CategoryID* field listed in the first Database Results column. Clicking this hyperlink displays the nwcatqry.asp page (previously shown in Figure 36-16), instructing that page to display products with a *CategoryID* of 4.

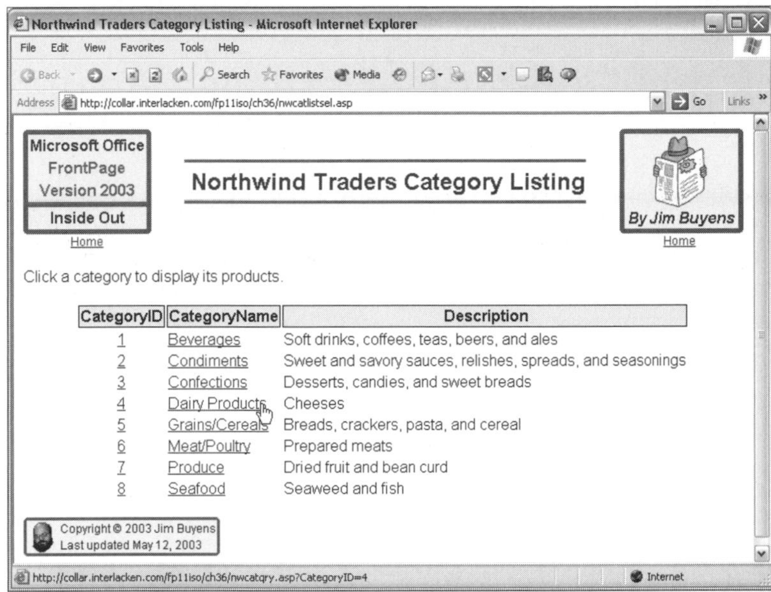

Figure 36-30. The hyperlinks in the *CategoryName* column of this Web page jump to the nwcatqry.asp page and tell it to display records with a specified CategoryID code.

Two additional points regarding this approach are worth noting. The first point concerns the expression *<%=fp_rs("CategoryID")%>*:

- The <% and %> tags mark the beginning and end of a block of ASP code. In other words, the code between these tags is going to execute on the Web server.

  Note that the code that reads the database and formats the contents as HTML runs on the Web server and not on the browser. This is because the database resides on the server.
- The equal sign is a shortcut that tells the ASP processor to evaluate the subsequent expression and write it into the outgoing HTML.
- The string *fp_rs* is the name of the *recordset* object that contains the records the database region will display. FrontPage automatically generates code that positions the recordset to each available record and then reports that record.

  A *recordset*, as you might suspect, is an object that contains the results of a database query.

- The string *CategoryID* is the name of the field that contains the value you want to retrieve. Be sure to include this field in the third page of the Database Results Wizard (shown in Figure 36-10).

The second point regards the query string variable name *CategoryID*. This actually refers to the name of the text box in the upper left corner of Figure 36-16, and not directly to the name of the database field. When FrontPage creates a form like the one shown in Figure 36-16, it just happens to use the same name for the form field as the corresponding field in the database.

Re-Creating and Formatting Database Results Regions

You can rerun the Database Results Wizard at will simply by double-clicking any part of the Database Results region that isn't another FrontPage component or HTML element. You can also rerun the wizard by right-clicking the Database Results region and choosing Database Results Properties from the shortcut menu, or by selecting the region and choosing Properties from the Format menu.

You can format Database Results regions and their accompanying forms as much as you want, but keep in mind that rerunning the wizard might discard your formatting when it overwrites the Database Results region. You can never solve this problem completely, but here are some ways to minimize it:

- First get the Database Results region working as you want it, and then worry about formatting.
- As much as possible, format the Database Results region using CSS styles. Because CSS styles appear in the <head> section and not intermixed with the HTML, overwriting the HTML won't overwrite the CSS styles.
- FrontPage uses a fake HTML attribute named *BOTID* to associate the HTML form with its Database Results region. When called upon to generate an input form, the wizard inserts *BOTID="x"* into the <form> tag, where *x* is an arbitrary number. The *BOTID* attribute isn't an official attribute of the <form> tag, so browsers and other programs will ignore it. However, the Database Results Wizard uses this attribute to locate and replace the correct HTML form.

  If you have trouble with the Database Results Wizard replacing the wrong form (or not replacing the correct one), view the page in HTML view, and look for BOTID attributes.

Using the Database Interface Wizard

Chapter 14, "Creating Web Sites with Templates and Wizards," described the basic procedure for creating a set of Web pages known collectively as a database interface. To briefly reiterate, this procedure uses a wizard you select from the Web Site Templates dialog box to create any combination of the following Web pages:

- **Results page** This is an ordinary Web page that contains a Database Results component. You could create exactly the same page using the procedures described in the "Using the Database Results Wizard" section, earlier in this chapter. Furthermore, you can use any of the techniques described in that section to modify any results page that the Database Interface Wizard creates.
- **Submission form** This is another ordinary Web page, but it contains an HTML form that uses the Save Results component for adding records to the database. You could create the same page, or modify a page created by either method, by following the instructions in the "Saving Form Results to a Database" section, earlier in this chapter.

  Despite the similarity in results, there's a difference in mind-set between creating a Save Results To Database page using the technique described in this chapter and creating a Save Results To Database page using the Database Interface Wizard described in Chapter 14:

  - The procedures in this chapter assume that you want to first create an HTML form and then hook it up to a database.
  - The Database Interface Wizard technique assumes that you want to select or create the database first and then have FrontPage create an HTML form for the database fields you select.

For more information about using the Database Interface Wizard, refer to "Using the Database Interface Wizard," on page 379.

- **Database Editor page** This is a frames page that displays, adds, changes, and deletes records in whatever database you selected when you ran the Database Interface Wizard. The target pages that display and add information are, of course, based on your old favorites—the Database Results component and the Save Results To Database component.

Surprisingly, the pages that modify and delete records also use the Database Results component. Both of these pages—update.asp and delete.asp—contain Database Results components that run custom queries and select no fields for display:

- The custom query in the update.asp page uses the SQL command UPDATE to locate the record with the key you selected, copy your form field values into the record, and save the record in the database. The wizard specifies no fields for display because the UPDATE command doesn't produce any records to display.
- Similarly, the custom query in the delete.asp page uses the SQL command DELETE to delete the record having the key you selected.

You can modify any Database Editor pages you want—the wizard puts them in a folder named <*connection*>_interface/Results/editor—but try to keep your changes cosmetic. Major changes are likely to update the page itself or the way it interacts with other pages in the same frames page.

If, while running the wizard, you decided to protect the Database Editor with a password, the editor remembers that the visitor is logged in by sending the visitor a cookie. As long as the visitor's browser keeps sending the cookie back, the Database Editor won't ask that visitor to log in again.

Configuring a FrontPage Data Connection

FrontPage reads and writes database information through named *connections*. A database connection names a Microsoft Access database located in the current Web site, an ODBC data source on the Web server, or a direct connection to some other database. Connections might initially strike you as yet another obstacle between you and your data, but they provide a number of advantages:

- You can define all the information about a database once and then use that definition in multiple Web pages.
- You can create or upload databases to your Web site and then access them with Web pages, without assistance from the server administrator. For example, you don't need the administrator to set up an ODBC data source.
- You can access databases in your Web site, ODBC data sources on the Web server, and any other databases available to the Web server, all in a uniform way.

> **Tip** Whenever you drag and drop an Access file into the Folder List or Folders view, FrontPage offers to create a database connection.

If you're planning to use an Access database stored within the same Web site, first create it or upload it to the desired location—somewhere your Web site visitors won't find it by accident. The /fpdb folder is a good choice. Then:

1. Choose Site Settings from the Tools menu.
2. Click the Database tab. This displays the dialog box shown on the left in Figure 36-31.
3. Click the Add button to display the New Database Connection dialog box, shown in the top right corner of Figure 36-31.

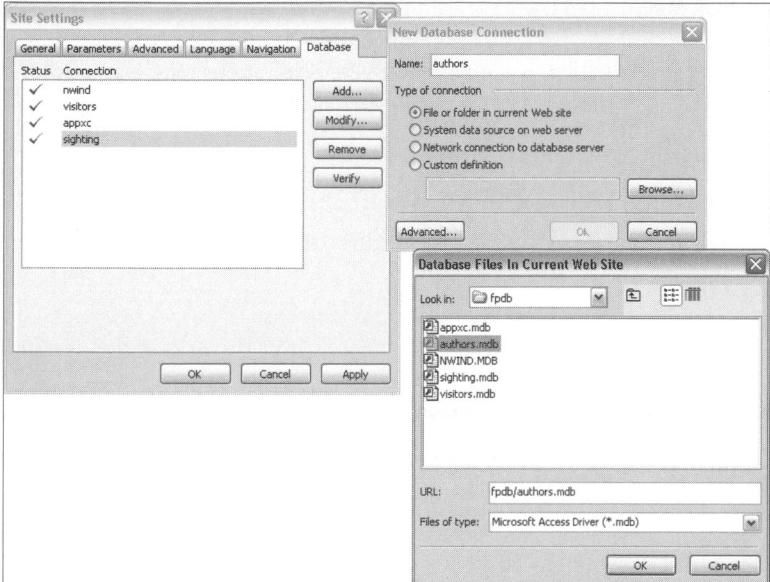

Figure 36-31. The Database Site Settings tab lists a Web site's currently defined database connections. The New Database Connection dialog box adds a new database connection to a Web site. The Database Files In Current Web site dialog box locates a database in the current Web site.

The following options are available:

- **Name** The identifier you plan to use when accessing the connection from a Web page. Simple names of six to eight characters are best. Using the name of the database as the name of the connection is usually a good choice because it gives you one less thing to remember.
- **File Or Folder In Current Web site** Connects to a database in the current Web site.
- **System Data Source On Web Server** Connects to an ODBC system data source name defined on the Web server.
- **Network Connection To Database Server** Connects to another database driver installed on the Web server.
- **Custom Definition** Connects to either a data source name (.dsn) or a universal data link (.udl) file that you designate by clicking Browse and choosing the file you want in the Connection Files In Current Web Site dialog box, similar to the one shown in the bottom right corner of Figure 36-31.
- **Browse** Displays a dialog box for selecting the specific database.

4 Click OK.

The Browse button in the New Database Connection dialog box displays different dialog boxes depending on the Type Of Connection selection. Clicking the Browse button after selecting File Or Folder In Current Web Site displays the Database Files In Current Web Site dialog box, shown in the bottom right corner of Figure 36-31.

The following options are available:

- **Look In** Selects folders in the current Web site.
- **URL** Specifies the database for this connection. Making a selection in the file list updates this box.
- **Files Of Type** Specifies the type of database. This can be Access, dBase, FoxPro, Paradox, or any file-oriented database with a driver installed on the Web server.

If you click Browse after selecting System Data Source On Web Server, FrontPage displays the System Data Sources On Web Server dialog box, shown on the left in Figure 36-32. The listed items are ODBC system DSNs defined in the Data Sources (ODBC) administrative tool on the computer where the Web resides. Select the data source you want, and then click OK.

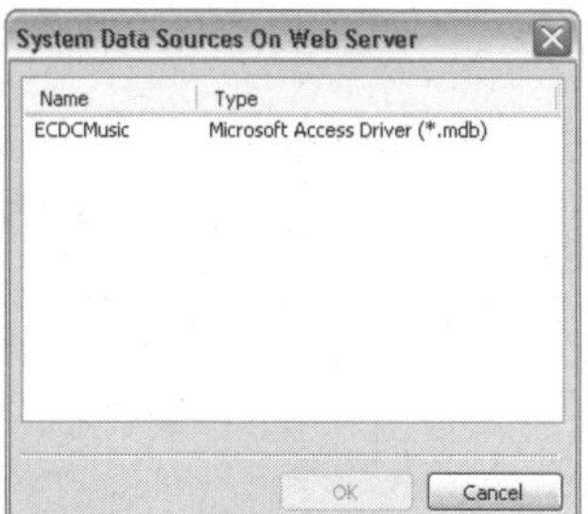

Figure 36-32. The System Data Sources On Web Server dialog box locates an ODBC System DSN defined on the Web server. The Network Database Connection dialog box locates a database through another database driver installed on the Web server.

Clicking Browse after choosing Network Connection To Database Server displays the Network Database Connection dialog box, shown on the right in Figure 36-32. Select the type of database driver, specify the server where it runs, and enter the name of the database on that server.

Clicking the Advanced button in the New Database Connection dialog box (shown in the top right corner of Figure 36-31) is seldom necessary, especially with file-oriented databases, but doing so displays the dialog box shown in Figure 36-33.

Troubleshooting

Can't Browse System Data Sources

Sometimes after choosing System Data Source On Web Server in the New Database Connection dialog box, the Browse option is dimmed or produces the following error message:

```
Server error: This web server does not allow a client to list the server's
data sources. Contact your system administrator for more information.
```

This behavior occurs when the *ListSystemDSNs* registry key is set to zero on the Web server. Many administrators choose this setting to stop users from listing the names of all the data sources on the server. (There's no setting that allows each user to view their own data sources and no others.)

To confirm this situation, log on to the Web server and display the following registry setting:

HKEY_Local_Machine\Software\Microsoft\Shared Tools\Web Server Extensions\All Ports\ListSystemDSNs

Alternatively, you can run the selfdiag.asp page in Insider Extra 1 or run the selfdiag.aspx page in Insider Extra 2.

If you know the name of an existing system DSN and want to use it even though *ListSystemDSNs* is set to zero, proceed as follows:

1. Choose Site Settings from the Tools menu, and then click the Database tab.
2. Click Add to add a new database connection.
3. Select the Custom Definition option, and then click the Advanced button.
4. In the Connection String box, type the DSN, as shown in this example:

   ```
   DSN=ECDCMusic;DRIVER={Microsoft Access Driver (*.mdb)} ).
   ```

5. Click OK twice, verify the connection, click Apply, and then click OK again.

Alternatively, eschew using the system DSN, and specify the database location using one of the other options in the New Database Connection dialog box.

You can obtain this information from the creator of the database or, in enterprise environments, from the database administrator:

- **Authorization** Specifies the logon credentials needed to access the database:
  - **Username** A logon account permitted to use the database.
  - **Password** The authentication code assigned to the given account.

- **Timeouts** Specifies time limits that, if exceeded, will cancel a database operation:
  - **Connection** Specifies the number of seconds allowable for opening a connection to the database.
  - **Command** Specifies the number of seconds allowable for completing a database command—a query, for example.
- **Other Parameters** Provides a list of named values required by the database driver. The Add, Modify, and Remove buttons control individual parameters. The Move Up and Move Down buttons reorder selected items in the list, and the Clear List button removes all entries.

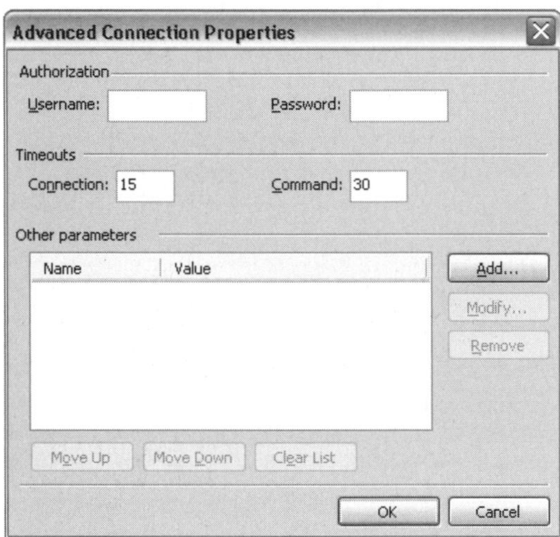

Figure 36-33. Clicking the Advanced button in the New Database Connection dialog box (shown in Figure 36-31) displays the additional options in this dialog box.

The remaining buttons on the Database tab of the Site Settings dialog box (shown on the left in Figure 36-31) are described here:

- **Modify** Displays a Database Connection Properties dialog box identical to the New Database Connection dialog box (shown in the top right corner of Figure 36-31) in which you can update an existing database connection.
- **Remove** Deletes the database connection.
- **Verify** Attempts a connection to the database and reports the results. A check mark means that the connection succeeded, whereas a broken link means that the connection failed. Unverified connections have a question mark.

> **Tip Set up database connections for every Access database.**
> It's a good idea to set up FrontPage database connections for every Access database in your Web site, even if you plan to use a certain database for custom development only. Existence of a database connection tells FrontPage to set up (and preserve) correct file system security for the database.

In Summary...

This chapter explained how to use the capabilities built into FrontPage for creating Web pages that access and update databases. Using databases on the Web has become a popular practice because it's much more accurate and much less time-consuming than creating Web pages for each item in a collection (for each product, department, or employee, for example).

The next chapter explains how you can use FrontPage to create Web pages that use the new XML-based database features that Windows SharePoint Services provides.

Part 10

Collaborating with Teams and Workgroups

Chapter 37

Using SharePoint Team Sites

This chapter and Chapter 38 explain two of the most poorly defined technologies to come along in quite a while: *portals* and *data-driven Web sites.* Nearly everyone who works in or around the Web is rushing to embrace these technologies, despite the fact that (or perhaps because) they mean something different to almost everyone you ask.

Portals generally provide a variety of tools that Web visitors can use to find, collect, record, display, and organize information. Among these tools is a home page—or perhaps a group of top-level pages—customized to the needs and preferences of each visitor. This avoids confusion and information overload.

Custom-developing all the tools and services required to build a high-function portal would be a daunting task. As a result, Microsoft and other vendors have developed general-purpose software that makes it easy to develop portal sites. Microsoft Office FrontPage 2003 has specific features to work with one such product, Microsoft Windows SharePoint Services, a no-cost feature included with Microsoft Windows Server 2003.

Windows SharePoint Services is a general-purpose Web server environment that can run applications of many different kinds. One such application is SharePoint Team Sites, which help groups of people work together by providing an easy-to-use repository of project documents, discussions, and lists of virtually anything the group needs to share and retain. FrontPage provides additional applications, and developers can create more using Microsoft Visual Studio .NET.

This chapter describes how to create, use, and customize SharePoint Team Sites in FrontPage 2003. Chapter 38 will then explain additional database features in FrontPage 2003 that leverage features built into Windows SharePoint Services. If you understand both these chapters, you'll also understand the FrontPage 2003 concept of *data-driven Web site.*

Introducing Portals

To some people, a portal is nothing more than a home page. To others, it's a piece of software that constructs home pages on the fly based on visitor identification or preferences. Another group defines portals as document libraries configured so that Web visitors can find the information they need by using keyword indexing and search facilities rather than hard-coded hyperlinks. In fact, all of these definitions are partially correct.

A portal is a special type of Web site that helps visitors avoid information overload. It does this in several ways:

- It provides a main menu—or perhaps a series of menu pages—that displays only the information and choices that the Web visitor needs or wants.
- It provides ways of searching for and accessing information.
- It provides ways of entering and saving information that others might need.
- It provides entry points to corporate information or e-business systems.

Microsoft offers two general-purpose solutions for building portal sites, both of which use the same underlying technology:

- **Windows SharePoint Services** Is a collection of software components that in some ways expand and in some way constrain the capabilities of an IIS Web server, all in the interest making portals easier to create and use. Windows SharePoint Services comes with Windows Server 2003 at no additional charge

  A SharePoint Team Site is one of several sample applications that come with (and run on) Windows SharePoint Services. This type of Web site supports collaboration within individual teams
- **SharePoint Portal Server** Extends the capabilities of Windows SharePoint Services with features suited to large-scale enterprise portals.

Compared to Windows SharePoint Services, SharePoint Portal Server provides features such as these:

- With SharePoint Portal Server, administrators can configure and manage groups of SharePoint sites as a unit. For example, an administrator could configure all SharePoint sites owned by the Marketing department to display a summary of year-to-date sales.

  With only Windows SharePoint Services, administrators must configure and manage each site individually. If the Marketing department controlled ten SharePoint sites, the administrator would have to add the year-to-date sales summary ten times.
- With SharePoint Portal Server, authorized visitors can make information in one SharePoint site available to others. A Public Affairs department, for example, could add company announcements to its own SharePoint site, and make those announcements available to every other SharePoint site in the company.

  With only Windows SharePoint Services, the information in a SharePoint site is only available by browsing that site. In the case of company announcements, for example the choices would be:

  - Setting up a SharePoint site for company announcements only, and asking everyone in the company to occasionally browse that site.
  - Duplicating the announcements once for every SharePoint site.
  - Using a non-SharePoint technology to share the data.

FrontPage 2003 can create, modify, and enhance SharePoint Team Sites on any Web server running Windows SharePoint Services. Such sites provide the following services to anyone with a Web browser, connectivity to your server, and the necessary permissions. The clients for these features are either a browser (for the Web-based tasks) or standard Office applications (for document creation and retrieval).

- **Document Libraries** A SharePoint Team Site document library has two components: a folder tree full of documents and a list that describes them. You can search for documents using either the document content itself or the data in the list.
- **Web Discussions** After a Microsoft Office 2000, Office XP, or Office 2003 user saves a document to a Web server as HTML (and remember that this is an integrated, one-step process), Web visitors browsing that document can make comments using a *Discuss toolbar*. Windows SharePoint Services stores these comments separately from the document itself. Then, when the document creator opens the document, all the comments appear seamlessly merged.
- **Search page** This feature uses Microsoft Indexing Service to search for documents within the current SharePoint Team Site.
- **Picture Libraries** This type of library incorporates a folder tree full of pictures and a list containing one descriptive record for each picture. Built-in features provide several ways of locating, viewing, and modifying pictures. For example, you can display pages full of clickable thumbnails, full-sized pictures, or slide shows.
- **Discussion Boards** This is the sort of feature most people call a *threaded discussion group*. Within a SharePoint Team Site, you can create as many discussion boards as you want, and each board can accommodate an almost unlimited number of threads and messages. You can sort and present the messages any way you want and purge old messages automatically.
- **Lists** These are the basic unit of storage in a SharePoint Team Site. Lists can contain announcements, upcoming events, scheduled tasks, team members or contacts, excuses, or anything else you want. The number of lists and the fields they contain are totally at your discretion.
- **Alerts** With this feature, team members can ask to be notified whenever a specified document or folder changes. Windows SharePoint Services detects such changes and sends the notifications by e-mail.
- **Administration** This Web-based tool provides control over the preceding applications.

Lists are central to the operation of a SharePoint Team Site. Physically, a list is just a database table. But the power of lists comes from the fact that you can create them, update them, display them, and if necessary delete them using standard Web pages that team members can quickly learn to use. Lists can record any combination of fields you configure.

Most pages in a SharePoint-based Web site are *Web Part Pages*. This is a special type of page that might provide some content of its own, but more importantly defines one or more *Web Part zones*. These are areas on the page where smaller units called *Web Parts* can reside.

A single Web Part zone can display any number of Web Parts, and a given Web Part can appear in any number of Web Part Pages.

Figure 37-1 shows the home page from a typical SharePoint Team Site located in the Web server's root folder. This is a Web Part Page. The Windows SharePoint Services logo and the areas titled Announcements, Events, and Links are each Web Parts that instantly retrieve and display up-to-date information from lists (which, you recall, are database tables).

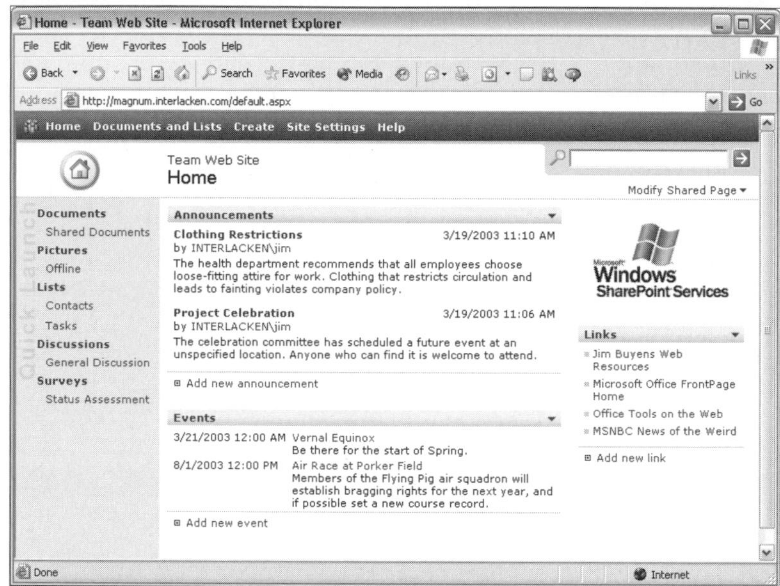

Figure 37-1. The home page for a SharePoint Team Site is highly configurable, but this version is fairly typical for a new site.

Figure 37-2 shows the same page open in FrontPage.

The Quick Launch bar on the left contains a number of specialized FrontPage-style Web components, and several Microsoft ASP.NET components appear as gray bars near the top of the page. They're titled SharePoint ProjectProperty and SharePoint PortalConnection. In addition, notice these two elements:

- The box titled Left that surrounds the Announcements and Events Web Parts
- The box titled Right that surrounds the Site Image and Links Web Parts

These boxes designate two Web Part zones named, of course, Left and Right.

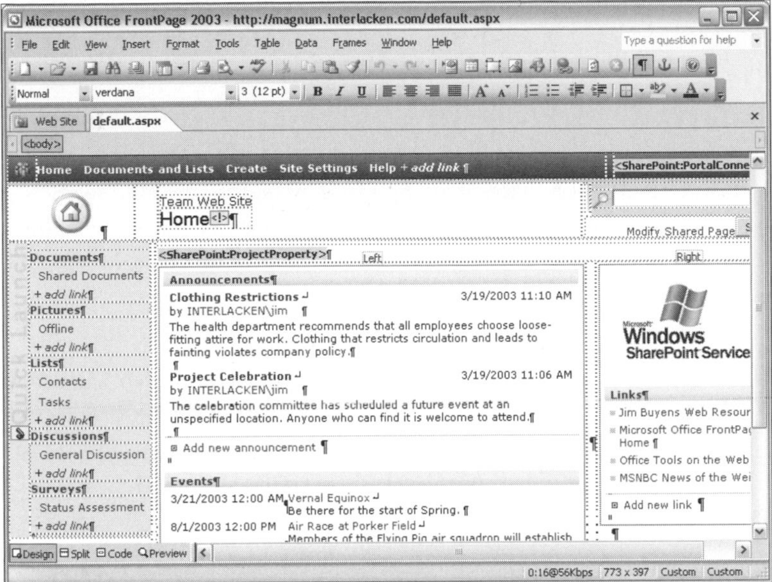

Figure 37-2. When you open a Web Part Page in Design view, you can modify it much as you would an ordinary Web page.

Functionally, here's what the various elements in a SharePoint Team Site home page provide:

- The menu bar at the top of the page provides access to all features in the site.
- The Quick Launch bar on the left provides hyperlinks to whatever high-usage features you select.
- The Announcements and Events areas provide links to the Announcements and Events lists and display recent additions to those lists.
- The Links area provides hyperlinks that team members might frequently use. This data resides in a list called, logically enough, Links.
- The Modify Shared Page link above the Windows SharePoint Services logo displays a page that can add, remove, or rearrange the Web Parts each visitor's version of the home page displays. (Figure 37-2 shows the Modified Shared Page Web part that displays this link.)
- The search form above the Modify Shared Page link locates text anywhere within documents that the site contains.

In general, it's best to block anonymous access to SharePoint Team Sites. Otherwise, the Web server won't prompt team members for user names and passwords, and none of the data in the SharePoint Team Site will be identified by team member.

For more information about controlling access to SharePoint Team Sites, refer to "Administering SharePoint Team Site Settings," later in this chapter.

Windows SharePoint Services bears some resemblance in both features and appearance to SharePoint Team Services 1.0, which was included with FrontPage 2002. Internally, however, these two products are quite different:

- SharePoint Team Services 1.0 used the FrontPage Server Extensions as its base platform.
- Windows SharePoint Services is an independent feature of Windows Server 2003. You can, if you wish, use Windows SharePoint Services without ever installing or using the FrontPage desktop software or the FrontPage Server Extensions. However:
  - The FrontPage desktop software is one of several clients that can create and modify Windows SharePoint Services sites.
  - Windows SharePoint Services can emulate most features of the FrontPage Server Extensions.

Because of this difference, there's no direct upgrade between the two versions. At a minimum, you'll need to re-create any visual customizations, including ASP.NET features, Web Parts, navigation, and layouts.

You should also be aware that Windows SharePoint Services is a very secure, tightly locked system. For example:

- It won't run classic ASP pages.
- It won't run ASP.NET pages that contain code render blocks or code declaration blocks.
- It runs only precompiled (code-behind) ASP.NET pages that contain a digital signature and that an administrator has specifically authorized.
- It stores Web pages, pictures, library documents, and most other files in a SQL Server or MSDE database rather than as files in the Web server's file system.
- It stops anyone from adding common file types that contain executable code. This applies to files that you try to publish via FrontPage as well as files that visitors try to upload to document libraries.

If you want a SharePoint environment, test or production, you'll need a copy of Windows Server 2003. If you want capabilities beyond what the supplied Web Parts or FrontPage 2003 can deliver, you'll need to start developing and digitally signing Web applications in Visual Studio .NET.

You should also know that some SharePoint Team Site pages display correctly only in Windows versions of Microsoft Internet Explorer and that some pages require the presence of Office 2003 as well. Microsoft has made an effort to support other browsers and platforms in the pages that team members would use on a daily basis, but anyone performing advanced or administrative tasks should definitely be running a Windows version of Internet Explorer.

None of this should dissuade you from investigating or using SharePoint Team Sites or any other application that requires Windows SharePoint Services. It should encourage you, however, to embark with both eyes open, and it should reassure you that the FrontPage Server Extensions will be around for some time.

Creating a New SharePoint Team Site

Windows SharePoint Services runs only on computers with Microsoft Windows Server 2003 and Microsoft IIS 6 installed. To install Windows SharePoint Services, you must be an administrator on the target server. At a high level, here are the tasks required:

1. Install Windows Server 2003, or any later version.
2. Install IIS. It's a component of the Application Server role
3. Run Windows Update, download the Windows SharePoint Services feature, and install it using the instructions provided.
4. Open Internet Information Services management console, then expand the computer name and the Web Sites nodes on the left.
5. Right-click the virtual server named SharePoint Central Administration, and then choose All Tasks and SharePoint Central Administration from the shortcut menu.
6. When the Central Administration page shown in Figure 37-3 appears, under Virtual Server Configuration, click the Extend Or Upgrade Virtual Server link.

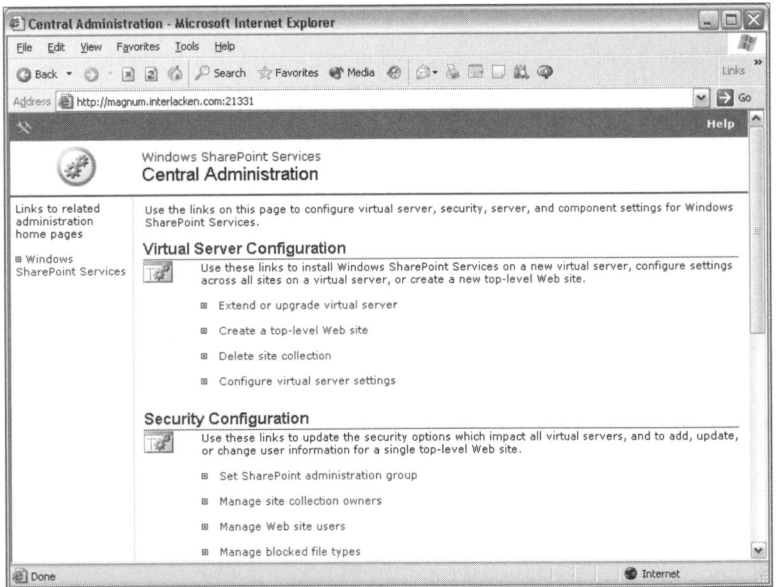

Figure 37-3. This Web page is the focal point for administering a Windows SharePoint Services virtual server.

7. When the Virtual Server List page shown in Figure 37-4 appears, click the link for any server you want to run SharePoint Team Services.

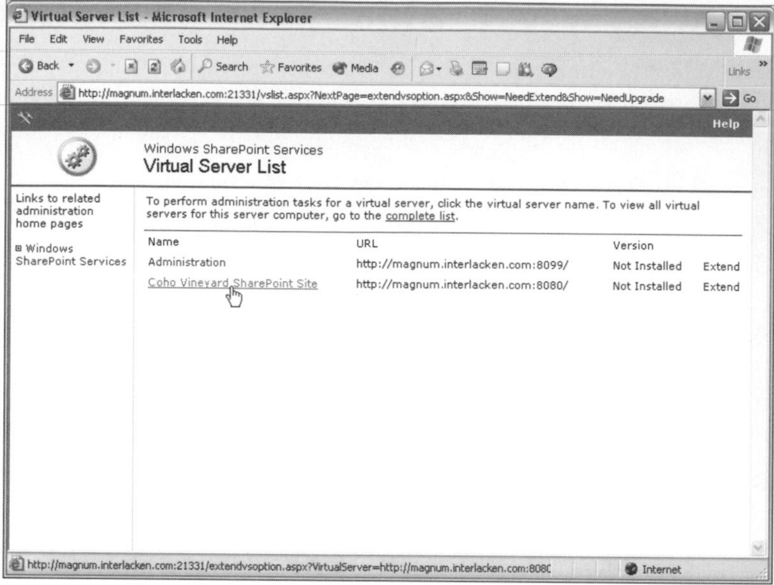

Figure 37-4. This page adds Windows SharePoint Services to a virtual server.

On a single virtual server, you can create as many SharePoint Team Sites as you want. To do this from an existing SharePoint Team Site's home page, proceed as follows:

1. Click the Site Settings link at the top of the page.
2. When the Site Settings page appears, under Administration, click Manage Sites And Workspaces.
3. When the Manage Sites And Workspaces page appears, click the Create link.
4. When the New SharePoint Site page appears, specify the new site location and other details, and then click Create.

To use FrontPage for creating a new SharePoint Team Site, use the procedures previously described in Chapter 14. This involves the following general steps:

1. Start FrontPage, open the New task pane, and click More Web Site Templates.
2. When the Web Site Templates dialog box appears, select the General tab, select SharePoint Team Site, and specify a folder location on the server running Windows SharePoint Services.

For more information about using FrontPage to create a new SharePoint Team Site, refer to "Creating a SharePoint Team Site," on page 393.

Using SharePoint Built-In Features

The following sections explain how to use the built-in features of a SharePoint Team Web Site. Most of these procedures use Web pages that come with SharePoint, and don't use any FrontPage software. This is valuable information, however, because if you don't understand SharePoint itself, you won't understand the SharePoint features in FrontPage.

Using Document Libraries

To work with a SharePoint Team Site document library, click Documents And Lists on the menu bar of any page in the same site. This displays the Documents And Lists page, shown in Figure 37-5. By default, this page displays an icon representing each document library or list in the current SharePoint Team Site. To view a list of document libraries only, click the Document Libraries link in the Select A View area on the left.

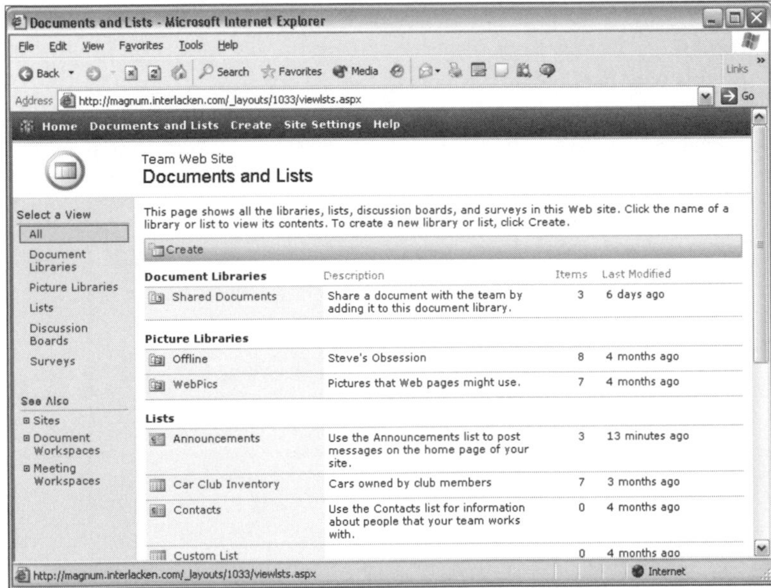

Figure 37-5. This page provides a selection list of SharePoint Team Site document libraries. The one library shown here appears by default in every new SharePoint Team Site.

The one document library shown in Figure 37-5—Shared Documents—appears automatically in every new SharePoint Team Site. However, a single site can have as many document libraries as you want. The Create link jumps to a Create page that has options to create new document libraries and other SharePoint Team Site objects.

How Document Libraries Work

SharePoint Team Site document libraries have three major components:

- A folder tree where all the documents reside
- A SharePoint Team Site list that records additional information about each document in the library
- A series of Web pages that update the document library, perform queries against it, and so forth

Adding a document to the library requires updating two of these components in unison: the folder tree and the SharePoint list. That's why you should always update SharePoint Team Site document libraries through the Web pages provided or directly from Office 2003 using My Network Places.

Click the icon for any library to display a document library view page like the one shown in Figure 37-6. This page lists the documents in the library.

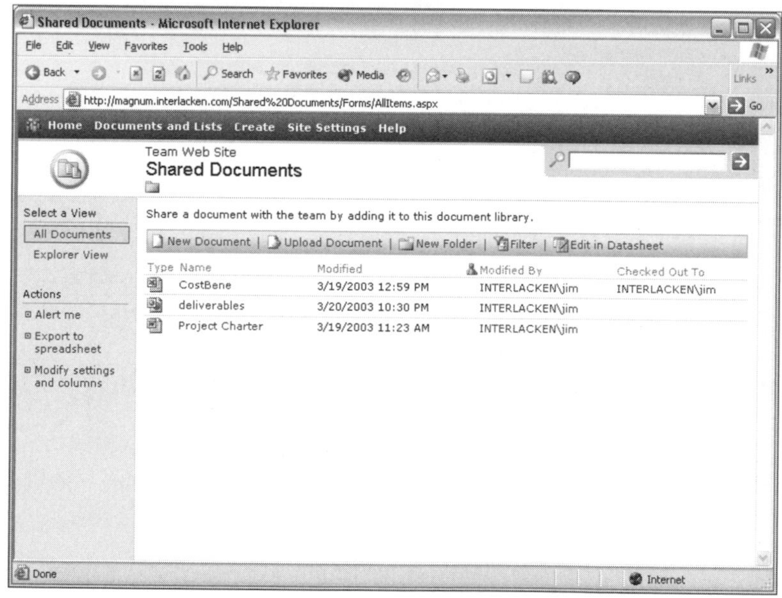

Figure 37-6. Click a library name or icon in the Documents And Lists page (Figure 37-5) or click the Shared Documents link to display a list of documents like this.

Here are the page's notable features:

- **Main document area** This is the large area with a white background that appears in the center of the Web page. It lists all the documents in the current library. To sort this listing on any field, click the field's column heading (that is, click Type, Name, Modified, Modified By, or Checked Out To). It also provides a menu bar with these links:
  - **New Document** Opens a new document you plan to store in the current library. If the library specifies a template, the Web page downloads it, starts the appropriate editor, and specifies the current library as the default save location. If the library has no defined template, the Web page starts Microsoft Word.

> **Tip** **Save SharePoint library documents in HTML format.**
> When saving documents into a SharePoint Team Site library (or saving them to disk in preparation for upload to a SharePoint Team Site library), it's usually best to save them in HTML format. That way, other team members can view and annotate the document directly in their browsers. If you save or upload a non-HTML document in its native format, other team members will have to download the document, open it with another program, and then upload it again if they've made any changes.

  - **Upload Document** Displays an Upload Document page that uploads a document from your computer and adds it to the library.
  - **New Folder** Displays a New Folder page for creating an additional folder within the current library.
  - **Filter** Redisplays the current Web page, adding selection controls above each selectable column heading. These controls limit the list of documents based on criteria you specify.
  - **Edit In Datasheet** Displays the list of documents as an editable table that resembles a spreadsheet.
- **Select A View** This area in the top left corner selects among all available formats for listing documents in the library. By default, there are two such formats:
  - **All Documents** Displays one line of text for each document in the library. Figure 37-6 illustrates this format.
  - **Explorer View** Lists the library contents in a format resembling Microsoft Windows Explorer.
- **Actions** This area provides additional commands for working with the library:
  - **Alert Me** Displays a New Alert page. This page tells Windows SharePoint Services to send you an e-mail message whenever someone changes the contents of a document or folder within the library.

> **Note** Alert is a pervasive feature. You can ask to receive alerts regarding almost any aspect of a SharePoint Team Site.

- **Export to Spreadsheet** Downloads an Excel query file that points to the library content list. After opening this file in Excel, authorized Web visitors can download, modify, or export the content list.
- **Modify Settings And Columns** Displays a Customization page that modifies the name of the library, its available views, its assigned template, its presence or absence on the Quick Launch bar, and so forth. Significantly, clicking this link also provides options that add or remove columns (that is, fields) from the document listing. You can use these extra columns to record anything you want about the documents in the library and then to sort or filter documents on that basis.

Each line in the main document area of a document library view page (Figure 37-6) contains the following clickable fields:

- **Type** Opens a file for viewing. If the file is a type that the browser can display, the browser displays it. Otherwise, the browser treats it as a download and starts the application on your computer that's associated with the file type.
- **Name** Displays a drop-down menu with these choices:
  - **View Properties** Displays all available information about the document.
  - **Edit Properties** Displays a page where you can modify the document's name or title.
  - **Edit In <application>** Downloads the document and opens it in the associated application on your computer.
  - **Delete** Removes the document from the library.
  - **Check Out** Stops anyone but you from updating the document. (After you choose this option, it changes to Check In.)
  - **Version History** Displays a history of updates to the document. This includes date, time, modified by, document size, and comments.
  - **Alert Me** Displays a New Alert page where you can request e-mail notification when someone changes or electronically discusses the document.
  - **Discuss** Displays the document, including comments from other team members and with a toolbar that you can use to make comments yourself.
  - **Create Document Workspace** Creates a specialized SharePoint site for the sole purpose of organizing material related to the current document. This site contains a document library for the primary document and supporting files, a task list for assigning to-do items, and a links list for resources related to the document.

Note The URL path to a document workspace is the path to the SharePoint Team Site that originally contained it, plus the document's file name base. If a SharePoint Team Site at *www.cpandl.com/luge* contained a document named rules.doc, the URL of that document's workspace would be *www.cpandl.com/luge/rules*

- **Modified By** Displays a Personal Settings page that provides information about the team member who last modified the document.
- **Checked out to** Displays a Personal Settings page that provides information about the team member who checked out document.

These options are relatively straightforward, with two exceptions: Discuss and Alert Me. The next two sections discuss these options.

Using Web Discussions

The Discuss option is what most Office applications call *Web Discussions*. Despite the similarity in names, this option has nothing to do with SharePoint Team Site Discussion Groups. Web Discussions provide a way to add yellow "sticky notes" to a document and to share those notes with others—all without actually updating the document itself. This is possible because the sticky note information resides in a database on a *discussion server*. This can be any SQL Server or MSDE database that services a SharePoint Team Site.

This is a very useful approach, because several people can review and annotate the same document simultaneously, and then the document owner can see all their suggestions merged together. There are no concerns about someone accidentally updating the document itself, because no one can update the document at all.

Figure 37-7 shows Internet Explorer accepting discussion comments for a document.

In this figure, the Web visitor:

1. Displayed the Shared Documents page shown in Figure 37-6.
2. Hovered the mouse over the file name deliverables.
3. Opened the resulting drop-down menu, and chose Discuss.

Because the deliverables file is in HTML format, Internet Explorer directly displays that document and the Discuss toolbar shown at the bottom of Figure 37-7. If the document had been in some other Office format, Internet Explorer would have downloaded the document, started the appropriate Office application, and told that application to display its own Discuss toolbar.

Tip To show or hide the Discuss toolbar in Internet Explorer, choose Explorer Bar from the View menu, and then choose Discuss.

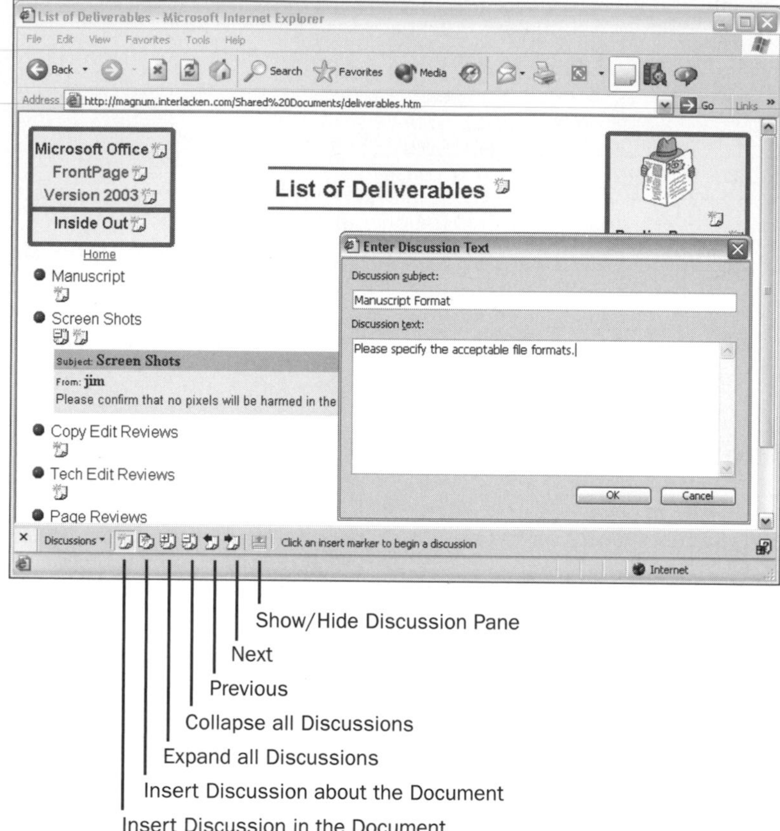

Figure 37-7. The sticky note icons show where you can append comments to the document. Click one to display the Enter Discussion Text dialog box.

Here's how to use the buttons on the Discuss toolbar. (Note that some buttons might be dimmed, depending on the type of document.)

- **Discussions** Click this button to display a menu containing the following options:
  - **Insert In The Document** Choose this command to display or hide all possible locations for inline sticky notes (those that appear inline with the document text). There's basically one sticky note location per paragraph. To add text to a new or an existing sticky note, click it.
  - **Insert About The Document** Choose this command to display an Enter Discussion Text dialog box in which you can enter discussion comments about the document in general.
  - **Refresh Discussions** Choose this command to retrieve a current set of discussion comments from the discussion server. Your display will then reflect changes other visitors might have made after you first displayed the page.

- **Filter Discussions** Choose this command to display discussion comments from only a certain participant, or within a certain time span.
- **Discussion Options** Choose this command to select the discussion server and the discussion fields to display.

Tip **Host discussions across multiple servers**

To host discussions on one server about documents on another, first open the document, and then, on the Discuss toolbar, choose Discussion Options from the Discussions drop-down menu. Finally, select the server that records discussion items from the Select A Discussion Server drop-down list.

- **Insert Discussion In The Document** Click this button to perform the same function as the Insert In The Document menu command just described.
- **Insert Discussion About The Document** Click this button to perform the same function as the Insert About The Document menu command just described.
- **Expand All Discussions** Click this button to display the title, text, and all other fields for each discussion comment.
- **Collapse All Discussions** Click this button to hide the contents of all discussion comments. A sticky note with a plus sign appears in place of each comment. To expand a particular comment, click the plus sign.
- **Previous** Click this button to display the previous discussion comment.
- **Next** Click this button to display the next discussion comment.
- **Show/Hide Discussion Pane** Click this toggle button to display or hide the discussion pane.
- **Close** Click this button to close the Web discussion.

Discussion text also appears—in almost identical format—when the document creator opens the HTML file in Word. In fact, all discussion text from all contributors is merged seamlessly into place. (If no discussions appear, choose Online Collaboration from the Tools menu, and make sure that the correct discussion server is specified.)

Using Alerts

Click any Alert Me link on a SharePoint Team Site page (such as the document library view page shown in Figure 37-6) to display the New Alert page, shown in Figure 37-8. On this page, you can ask to receive change notices for the current document or for any document in a specified folder (subject to filters); set notification criteria; specify your e-mail address; and indicate how long Windows SharePoint Services should accumulate changes before sending them.

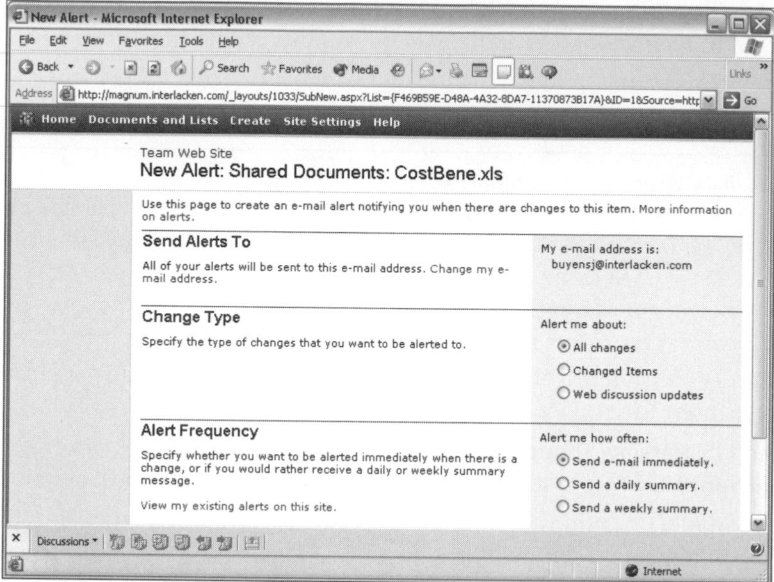

Figure 37-8. This Web page requests e-mail notification of changes to a given document or folder.

Figure 37-9 shows a typical alert message. Although the message in the figure provides only one notification, a single message can report multiple changes.

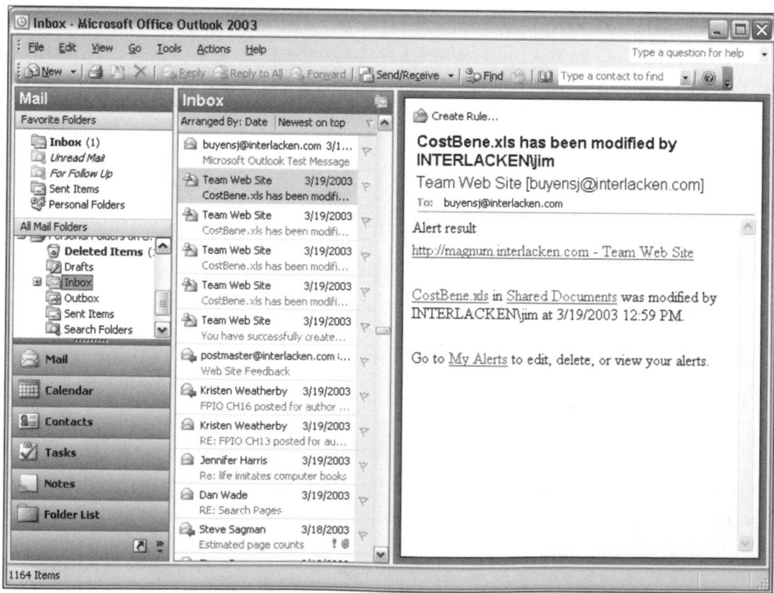

Figure 37-9. A SharePoint Team Site sent this alert automatically.

The notification process periodically scans a database and combines all notifications to the same recipient. The less often you choose to receive messages, the more notifications each message will contain.

The Alert feature of a SharePoint Team Site isn't limited to Web Discussion comments that team members make using Internet Explorer. On the contrary, team members can request notification of almost any change to a SharePoint Team Site.

Troubleshooting

Members don't receive SharePoint Team Site alerts

SharePoint Team Site members who request alerts might not receive the expected mail for any of the following reasons:

- **Not enough time has passed** SharePoint Team Sites send notifications at specified intervals, even if a team member selected Send E-Mail Immediately. These intervals apply to the entire Web server and are thus something an administrator must control. The following settings are the defaults, but your server's configuration might vary:
    - **Immediate Notifications** Every five minutes.
    - **Daily Notifications** Midnight.
    - **Weekly Notifications** Sunday midnight.
- **Server settings might be incomplete** The server administrator must configure Windows SharePoint Services with the name of an SMTP mail server and an address that will appear in the From and Reply To fields of each outgoing message.
- **The Web Alerts feature might be disabled** The server administrator can turn off the Web Alerts features at the server level. Obviously, this inhibits the transmission of notification messages.

Using Picture Libraries

Typically, most of the results and working documents that teams collect are textual in nature. Some, however, are visual. SharePoint Team Sites therefore provide picture libraries to efficiently handle the storage, viewing, and retrieval of visual information.

A new SharePoint Team Site doesn't contain any picture libraries, but you can easily create as many as you want. Here's the procedure:

1. Open the SharePoint Team Site in Internet Explorer, and click the Create option on the menu bar of any page.
2. When the Create page appears, click the Picture Library link.

3 When the New Picture Library page shown in Figure 37-10 opens, specify these options:

- **Name** Specify a short name that will identify the library throughout the SharePoint Team Site.
- **Description** Briefly characterize the library's content or purpose.
- **Display This Picture Library On The Quick Launch Bar?** Select Yes if you want a link to this library from the Quick Launch bar of the SharePoint Team Site home page.
- **Create A Version Each Time You Edit A File On This Web Site?** Select Yes if you want SharePoint to store a backup copy and history record every time someone updates a picture in this library.

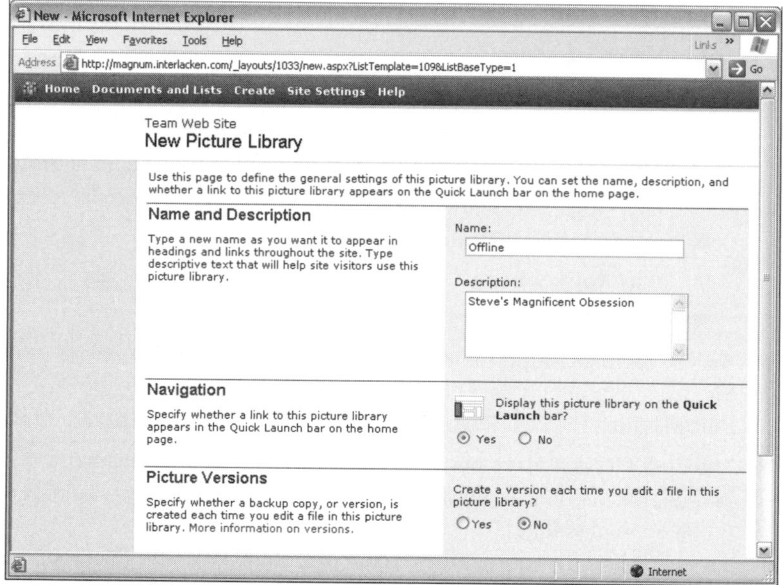

Figure 37-10. Use this page to create a new SharePoint Team Site picture library.

4 To create the library, click the Create button at the bottom of the page.

At this point, SharePoint will display an empty contents page for the new picture library, in a format similar to that of a document library. To begin adding pictures, click the Add Picture link. This displays the Add Picture page, shown in Figure 37-11.

Tip **Use Office Picture Library to update SharePoint picture libraries**

Microsoft Picture Library is a new Windows application included with Microsoft Office 2003. If this application is installed on your computer, an Upload Multiple Files link will appear in the Add Picture page shown in Figure 37-11. Clicking this link starts Picture Library and points it to the SharePoint picture library you were browsing. Among its other features, Picture Library can perform batch uploads and downloads.

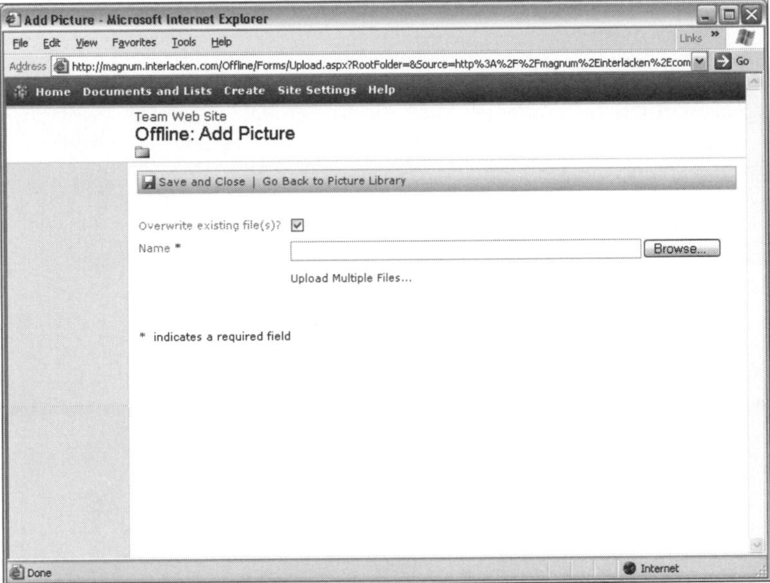

Figure 37-11. This is the page that adds pictures to a SharePoint Team Site picture library.

Click the Browse button to locate a file on your computer, and then click Save And Close to upload the file and add it to the library. To display a library as shown in Figure 37-12 click Details under All Pictures in the Select A View area.

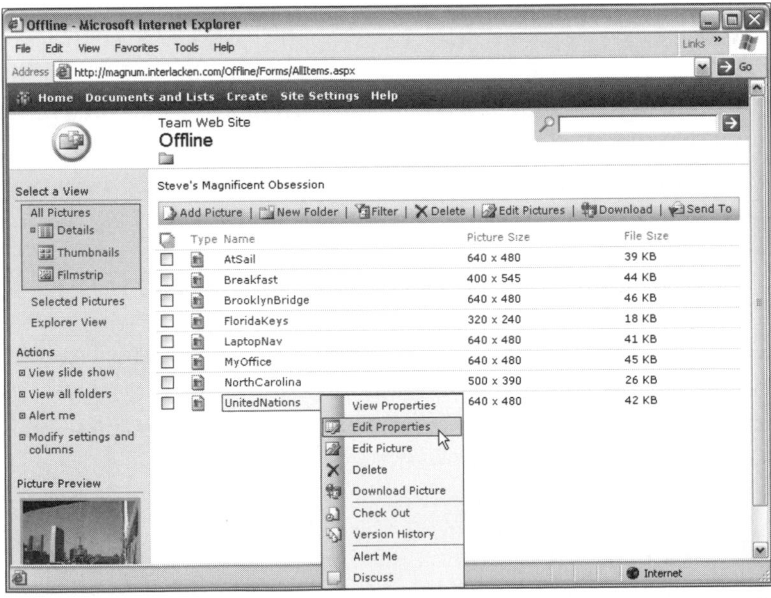

Figure 37-12. The contents listing for a picture library resembles that for a document library, but contains additional controls for working with pictures.

To display the library contents in a different format, click one of these links in the Select A View area:

- **Thumbnails.** Displays a miniature version of each picture in the library. Figure 37-13 illustrates this view.

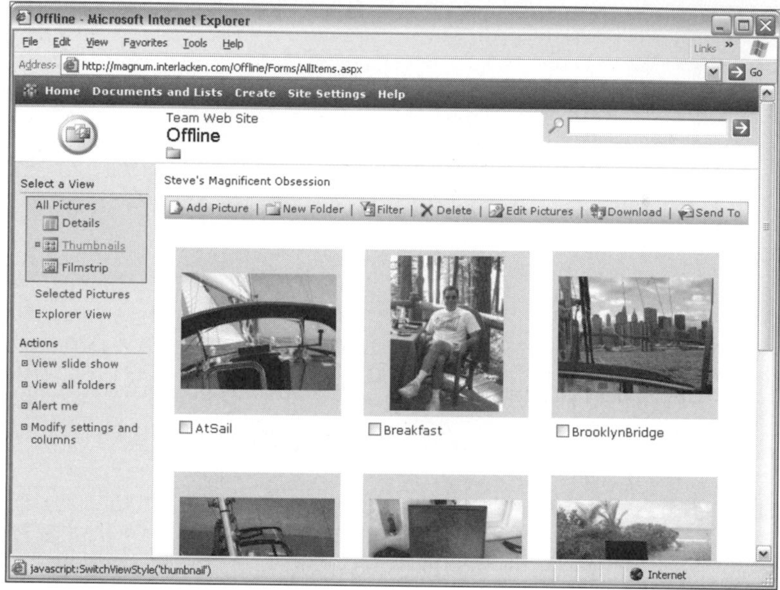

Figure 37-13. This page lists the contents of a SharePoint Team Site picture library.

- **Filmstrip.** Displays a horizontal series of thumbnails representing each picture in the library. Clicking any thumbnail displays the corresponding full-sized picture on the same page.
- **Selected Pictures.** Displays only those pictures whose check boxes you selected.
- **Explorer View.** Lists the library contents in a format resembling Windows Explorer.

Here are some common actions you can perform from Details view. Many of these actions are available in other views as well.

- Selecting the check box for any picture displays a thumbnail in the Picture Preview area in the lower left corner.
- Clicking the Type icon for any picture displays the full-sized picture—and nothing else—directly in the browser window.
- Clicking the name of any picture displays the full-sized picture in a formatted SharePoint Team Site page. Figure 37-14 provides an example.

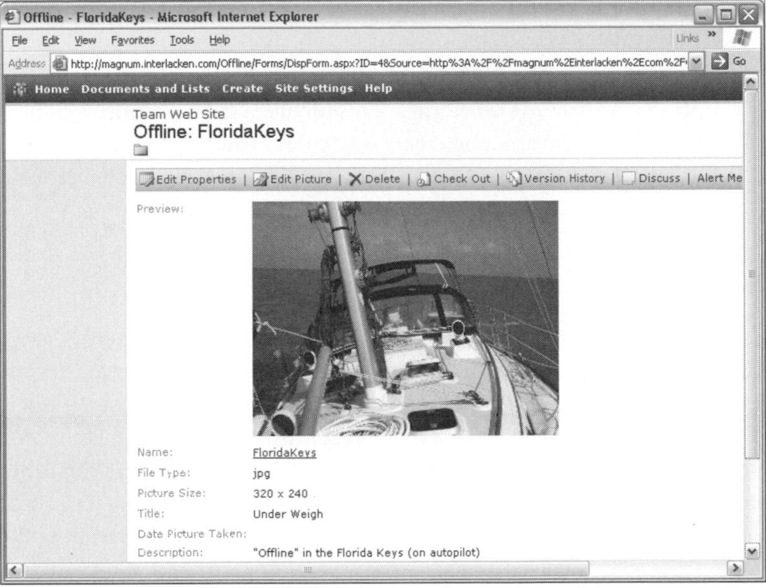

Figure 37-14. This page displays all current information for an entry in a picture library.

- Hovering the mouse over the name of any picture reveals a drop-down menu with these choices:
  - **View Properties** Displays all available information about the picture.
  - **Edit Properties** Displays a page where you can modify the picture's name or title.
  - **Edit Picture** Starts Microsoft Picture Library and tells it to open the picture for editing.
  - **Delete** Removes the picture from the library.
  - **Download Picture** Downloads the picture to your computer.
  - **Check Out** Stops anyone but you from updating the picture. (After you choose this option, it changes to Check In.)
  - **Version History** Displays a history of updates to the picture. This includes date, time, modified by, picture size, and comments.
  - **Alert Me** Displays a New Alert page where you can request e-mail notification when someone changes or electronically discusses the picture.
  - **Discuss** Displays the picture, including comments from other team members and with a toolbar that you can use to make comments yourself.

The Actions area, which appears on the left, provides these additional capabilities:

- **View Slide Show** Opens a new window that displays the first picture in the library and buttons to displays additional pictures automatically.
- **View All Folders** Displays a selection list of folders in the library.

- **Alert Me** Displays the New Alert page so that you can request e-mail notification when someone changes or electronically discusses anything in the library.
- **Modify Settings And Columns** Displays a Customization page with links to change options in effect for the library. This includes the capability to add new columns, reorder existing columns, and create new views. You might use new columns to record who took each picture, when the picture was taken, and so forth. A new view could then filter on those criteria.

Using Discussion Boards

A SharePoint Team Site discussion board works a lot like an Internet newsgroup or a FrontPage Discussion Web. Team members can post new messages, respond to existing messages, and view messages in their entirety or in condensed lists. Whoever administers the SharePoint Team Site can purge and correct messages, alter discussion board settings and defaults, and so forth. If security settings permit, team members can initiate and control their own discussion boards, and whoever posts a message can subsequently revise or delete it. Figure 37-15 shows a summary view of a typical discussion board.

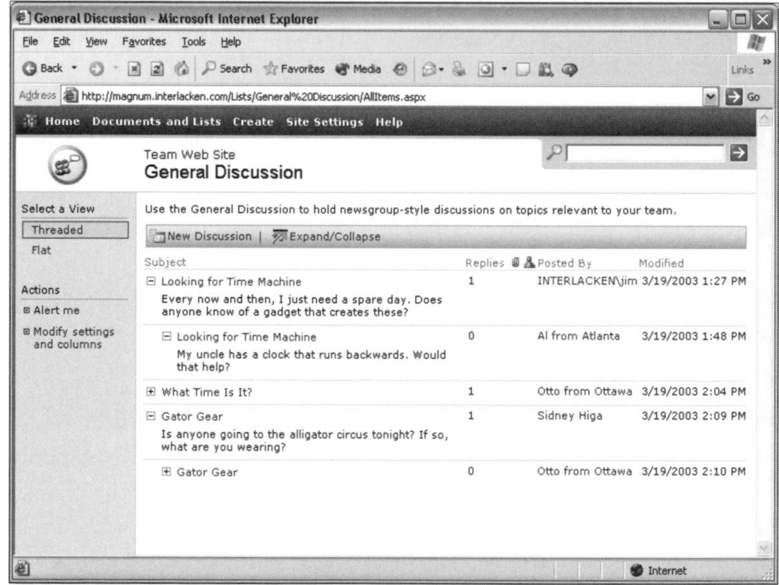

Figure 37-15. Click a discussion board name or icon in Figure 37-16 to display a list of messages like this.

To display this Web page, choose Discussion Boards from the menu bar of any page in the SharePoint Team Site. This displays the Discussion Boards page, shown in Figure 37-16, which shows the name and description of each available discussion board. The General Discussion board appears by default as part of every new SharePoint Team Site.

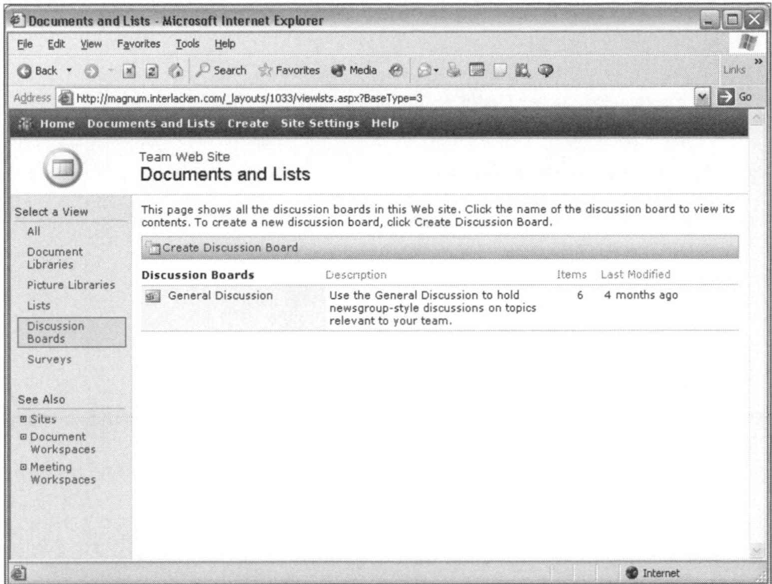

Figure 37-16. This page provides a selection list of SharePoint Team Site discussion boards. The single discussion board shown here appears by default in every new SharePoint Team Site.

To view or modify the contents of an existing discussion board, click its icon or title to display a discussion page like the one shown in Figure 37-15. Here's how to use this page:

- **Select A View** Click any link in this area (on the left) to display the discussion board in the format you want. Threaded view, the default, is the view shown in Figure 37-15. Flat view displays each article independently, regardless of its relationship to other articles.
- **Actions** Click Alert Me to sign up for e-mail notifications whenever someone updates the board. Click Modify Settings And Columns to reconfigure the board or create additional views.
- **New Discussion** Initiates discussion on a new topic (that is, creates a new top-level message). Figure 37-17 shows the Web page that supports this function. (Remember, to create a new discussion board, you click the Create link at the top of the page.)
- **Expand/Collapse** This link appears only in Threaded view. Click it to toggle between a display of all messages and a display of top-level messages only.
- **Filter** This link appears only in Flat view. Click it to redisplay the current Web page, adding selection controls above each selectable column heading. These controls limit the list of messages based on criteria you specify.
- **Subject, Posted By, and Modified** In flat view, click any of these column headings to sort the display on that column.
- **Posted By** Click any entry in the Posted By column to display information about that person.

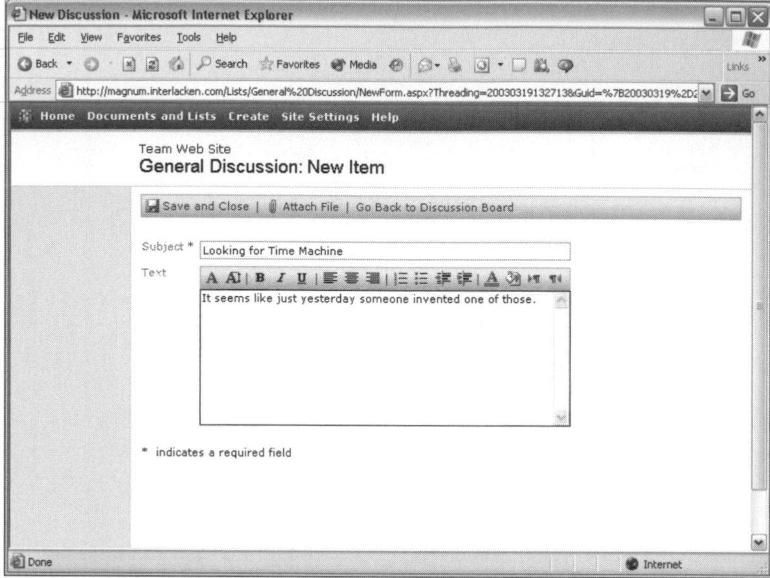

Figure 37-17. This Web page starts a new discussion thread. To display it, click any New Discussion link.

Clicking on the Subject text of any message displays the message itself and all related details. Figure 37-18 provides an example.

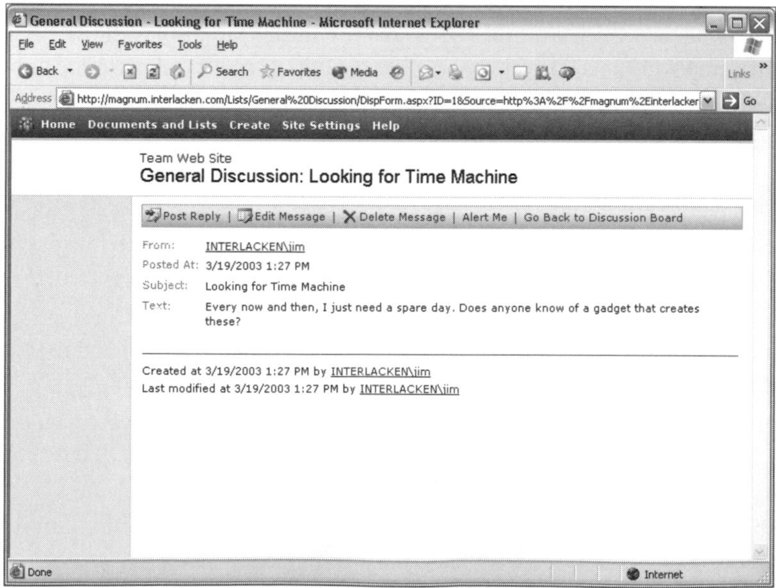

Figure 37-18. This is how a SharePoint Team Site displays an individual discussion message.

The menu bar on this page contains the following links:

- **Post Reply** Creates a new message that responds to the current one. The page for posting a reply strongly resembles the one shown previously in Figure 37-17.
- **Edit Message** Modifies the current message. Depending on the settings in effect for the discussion board, this might be possible only for an administrator or the person who originated the message.
- **Delete Message** Deletes the current message. Again, this might be possible only for an administrator or the person who originated the message.
- **Alert Me** Displays a New Alert page where you can request notification whenever someone changes the current message.
- **Go Back To Discussion Board** Backs up one screen (usually to the Discussion Board View page, shown in Figure 37-15).

To create a new discussion board, click the Create link on the menu bar of any SharePoint Team Site page. When the SharePoint Team Site Create page appears, scroll down to Discussion Boards, and then click Discussion Board.

Using Lists

Clicking the Documents And Lists link on the menu bar of any SharePoint Team Site page displays the Documents And Lists page, shown in Figure 37-19. This is basically a list of all the lists in the current SharePoint Team Site.

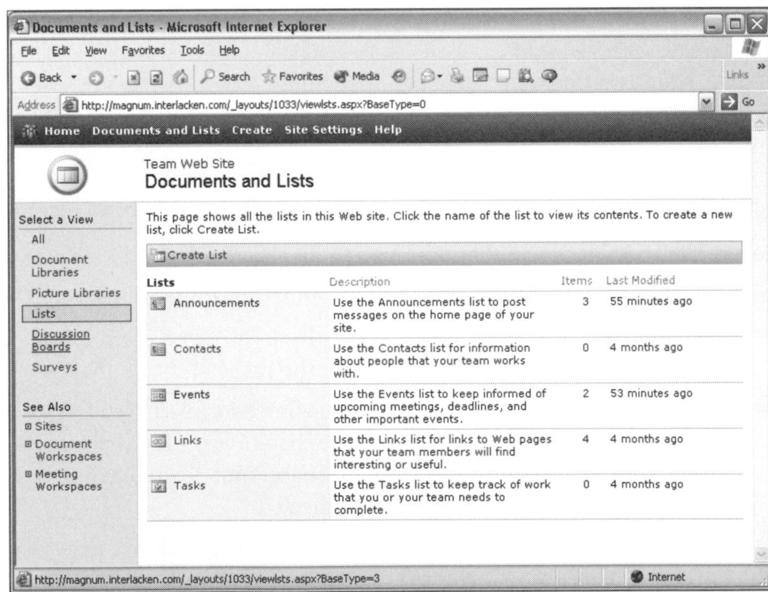

Figure 37-19. This page identifies the lists in a SharePoint Team Site. The lists shown here appear by default in every new SharePoint Team Site.

The choices in the Select A View area filter the list based on type: all lists, document library lists, picture library lists, and so forth. The Lists choice displays all list that aren't document libraries, picture libraries, discussion boards, or surveys. This is the setting in effect in Figure 37-19; the five lists shown here appear by default in any new SharePoint Team Site.

To display the contents of a specific list, click its entry in the Documents And Lists page. For ordinary lists, this displays a List View page like the one shown in Figure 37-20.

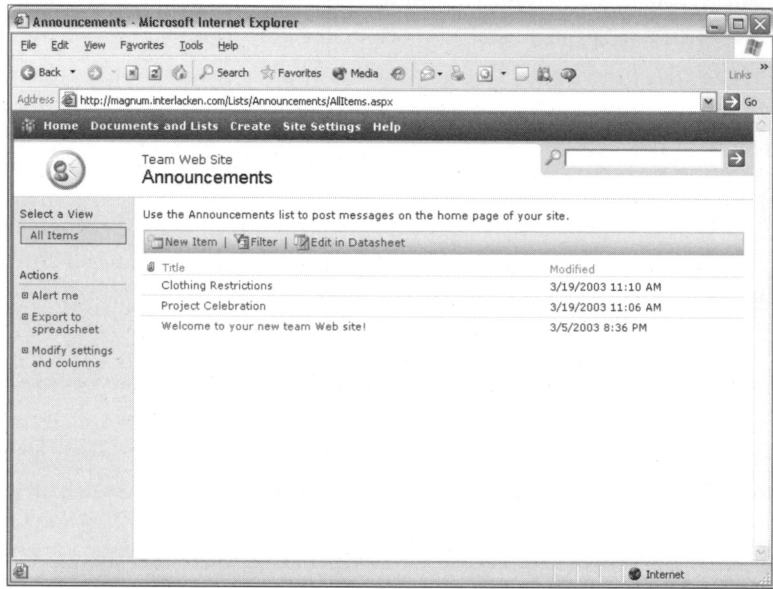

Figure 37-20. Click a list name or icon in a Documents And Lists page (Figure 37-19) to display the items in the list.

The links on this page work much like those already described for document libraries, picture libraries, and discussion boards (are you noticing a pattern?), but here's a brief summary:

- **Select A View** Click any link in this area to display the list in the format you want.
- **Actions** This area provides the following commands for working with the list:
  - **Alert Me** Displays a New Alert page where you can request e-mail notification when someone changes the contents of the list.
  - **Export To Spreadsheet** Downloads a Microsoft Excel Web Query file that downloads the data in the list. Such files have a .iqy file extension. When you open such a file, Excel connects to the SharePoint Team Site database and downloads the data for the list you requested.
  - **Modify Settings And Columns** Displays a Customization page that modifies the name, description, columns, views, and other settings.

- **New Item** Displays a page named New Item Form that adds a new item to the list.
- **Filter** Limits the displayed messages based on criteria you specify.
- **Edit In Datasheet** Displays the list in an editable table that resembles a spreadsheet.

Inside Out

Downloading Web Query files rather than data

An Export To Spreadsheet link in a SharePoint Team Site doesn't download the actual contents of a list; instead, it downloads an Excel Web Query file that tells Excel to open the database and retrieve the data itself.

This is a very useful approach. If you save the Web Query file on your computer, opening it causes Excel to connect to the database server and download a fresh copy of the list data. This saves you from logging onto the SharePoint Team Site and downloading fresh copies of the data manually. If you want to save a copy of the data as of some specific point in time, copy it from the query region and paste it into another spreadsheet.

A list is the basic unit of information in a SharePoint Team Site. Physically, a list is a table in an MSDE or a SQL Server database. Each list item that you see in a Web page is a row in a database table. The columns that you see in Web pages are columns in those database tables. The Web pages in a SharePoint Team Site that create new lists actually create new database tables, and the pages that add, modify, and delete columns in lists actually modify the layout (the schema) of the corresponding tables.

The five lists shown in Figure 37-19 all contain different combinations of fields and different views. Nevertheless, they're all simple database tables that operate using the same basic principles.

Creating a New Survey

Surveys are a particularly interesting type of list. Creating a survey requires four basic steps:

1. Decide what questions you want to ask.
2. Design a form that people can use to record their answers.
3. Let the survey population fill out the form.
4. Analyze the results.

Although a SharePoint Team Site can't choose questions for you, it does most of the work for the three remaining steps. This section explains how to create a survey and, along the way, how to perform a myriad of tasks useful for creating other lists as well.

Here's the procedure:

1. Click the Create link on any SharePoint Team Site menu bar. This displays the Create Page page, shown in Figure 37-21, Figure 37-22, and Figure 37-23.

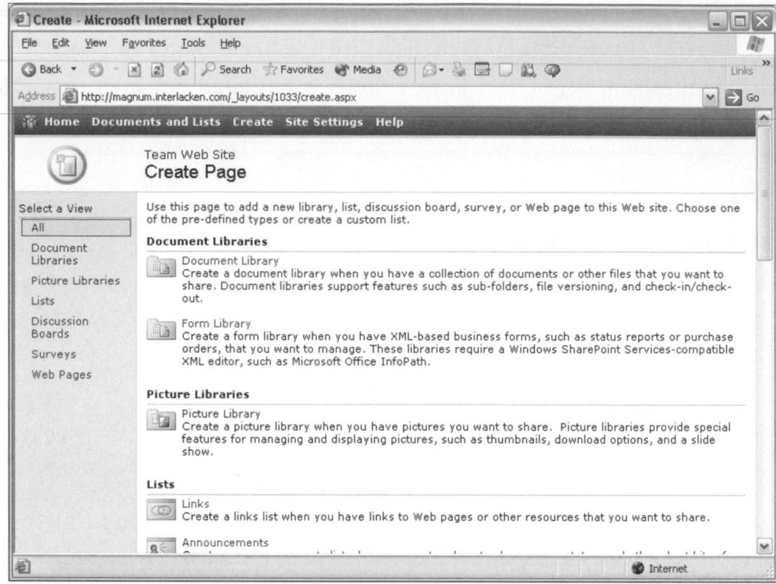

Figure 37-21. This Web page has links for creating lists, discussion boards, and document libraries of all kinds.

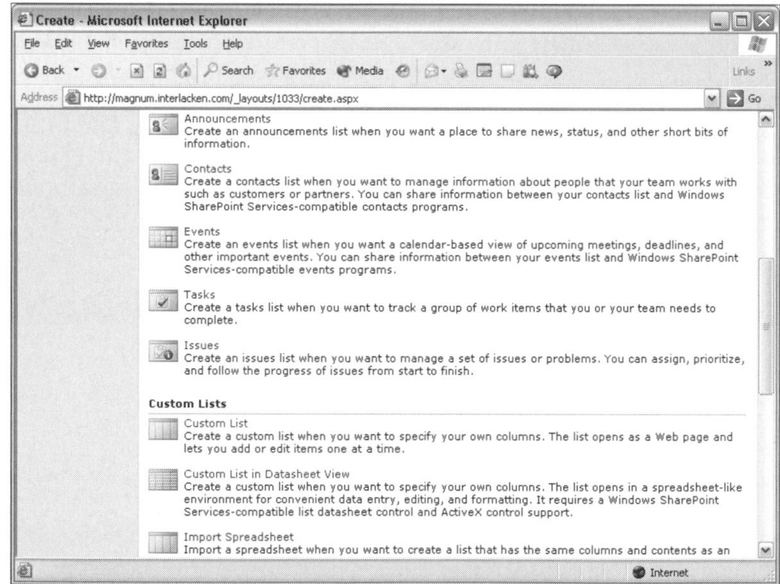

Figure 37-22. This is the middle third of the Web page that starts in Figure 37-21.

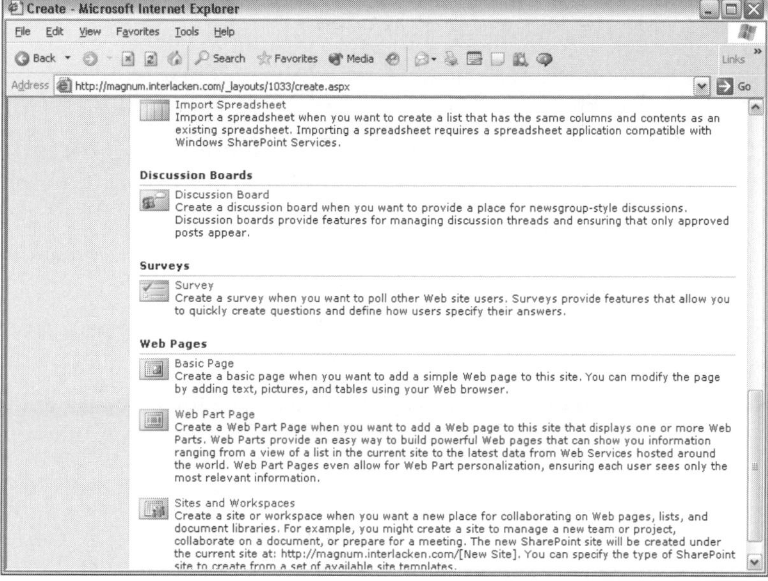

Figure 37-23. This is the bottom third of the Web page that starts in Figure 37-21.

2 Click the Survey link shown in Figure 37-23. This displays the New Survey page, partially shown in Figure 37-24.

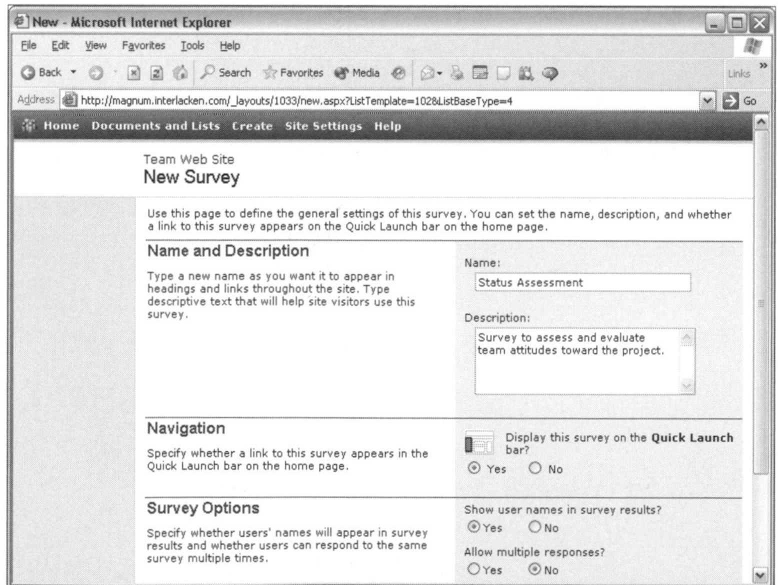

Figure 37-24. Click the Survey link in the Create Page page (Figure 37-23) to display this Web page for creating a new survey.

Fill out the input options as follows:

- **Name** Give the survey a short, descriptive name.
- **Description** If you want, enter some text that explains the survey and its purpose.
- **Display This Survey On The Quick Launch Bar?** Select Yes if you want all Quick Launch bars in the current SharePoint Team Site to contain a link to this survey.
- **Show User Name In Survey Results?** Select Yes if displays of survey results should include the name of each respondent.
- **Allow Multiple Responses?** Select Yes if the same person can fill out the survey multiple times.

3 Click the Next button to display the Create New Question page, shown in Figure 37-25 and Figure 37-26. This Web page constructs the first survey question.

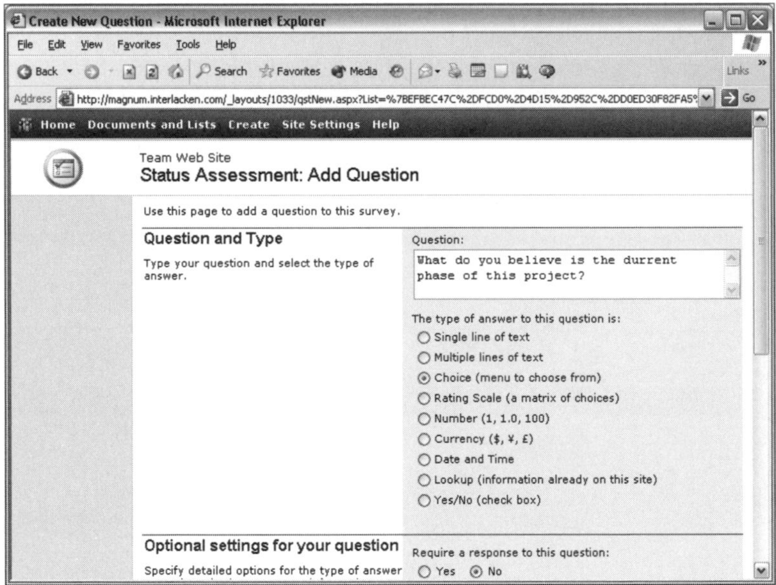

Figure 37-25. This page adds a question to a SharePoint Team Site survey.

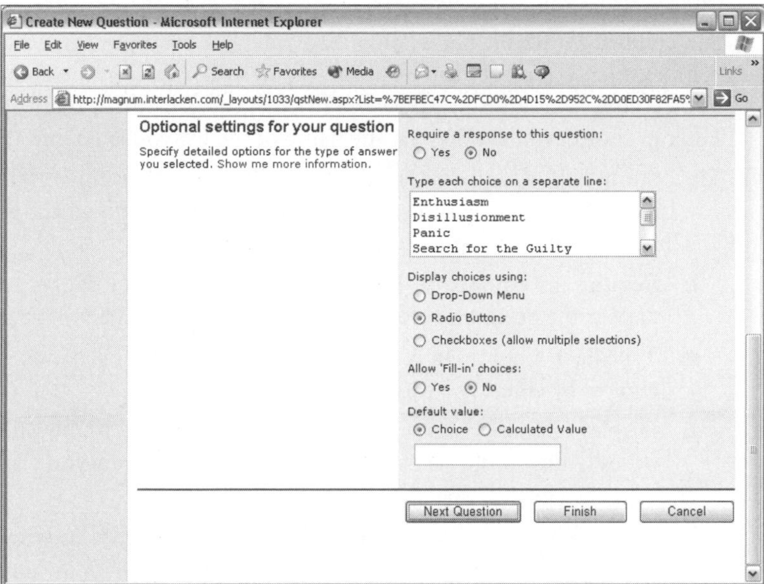

Figure 37-26. This is the bottom half of the Web page that begins in Figure 37-25.

Here's how to use the input options provided:

- **Question** Enter the text for the first question in the survey.
- **The Type Of Answer To This Question Is** Indicate what type of data constitutes the survey answer. Table 37-1 summarizes the result of each choice.

Table 37-1. SharePoint Team Site Survey Answer Types

Type of answer	Input form
Single Line Of Text	Text box
Multiple Lines Of Text	Text area box
Choice (Menu To Choose From)	Drop-down menu, radio buttons, check boxes, or fill-in choices.
Rating Scale (A Matrix Of Choices)	A row of radio buttons (for example, 1 through 5 and N/A) for each of several choices.
Number (1, 1.0, 100)	Text box
Currency ($, ¥, £)	Text box
Date And Time	Combination of text box (for date) and drop-down lists (for hour and minute)
Lookup (Information Already On This Site)	Drop-down list
Yes/No (Check Box)	Check box

The Lookup choice populates a drop-down list with all values that occur in a given list and column within the SharePoint Team Site. For example, this could include all Full Name values in the User Information list, all Title values in the Shared Documents library, all E-Mail Address values in the Contacts list, and so forth. To configure a Lookup choice, you specify first the name of the list you want and then the column.

4 The bottom half of the Edit Question page changes depending on the type of answer you specify. Figure 37-26 shows the format that appears if you choose Choice (Menu To Choose From). Configure each option as follows:

- **Require A Response To This Question** Select Yes if the respondent must answer the question before proceeding. Select No if answering is optional.
- **Type Each Choice On A Separate Line** Enter the list of choices. Separate choices by entering a carriage return.
- **Display Choices Using** Select Drop-Down Menu, Radio Buttons, or Checkboxes (Allow Multiple Selections), depending on how you want respondents to view the choices.
- **Allow 'Fill-In' Choices** Select Yes if respondents can enter text in lieu of choosing one of the standard answers.
- **Default Value** Enter the name of the choice that will be selected when the respondent first displays the Web page that contains this question.

5 If this is the last question in the survey, click Finish. Otherwise, click Next Question, and go back to step 3.

6 Clicking Finish in step 5 displays the Customization page, partially shown in Figure 37-27.

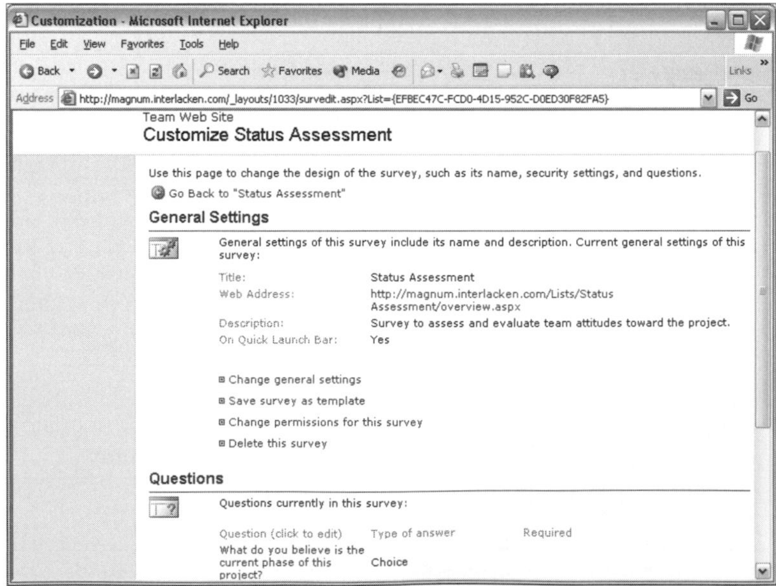

Figure 37-27. This page modifies the overall properties of a survey.

Review the following links in the General Settings area, and modify them as necessary:

- **Change General Settings** Displays a Change General Settings page very similar to the one shown previously in Figure 37-24. This provides a way to update these settings without re-creating the survey.
- **Save List As Template** Saves a copy of the survey for use in creating additional surveys in the future.
- **Change Permissions For This Survey** Controls who can complete, modify, and view the survey.
- **Delete This Survey** Removes the survey forms, links, and data from the SharePoint Team Site.

7 Under the Questions heading, review these settings and make any necessary changes.

- **Question (Click To Edit)** Click the text of any question listed under this heading to change the text or format of that question, or to delete the question completely.
- **Add A Question** Adds the questions in the survey. You must click this link and repeat steps 3 and 4 once for each question.
- **Change The Order Of The Questions** Displays a list of current questions and question numbers. The question numbers appear in drop-down lists that you can manipulate to put the questions in any order.

Figure 37-28 shows how the Status Assessment survey appears to a survey respondent. This is a custom survey created by using the procedure just described; it's not a standard element of every new SharePoint Team Site.

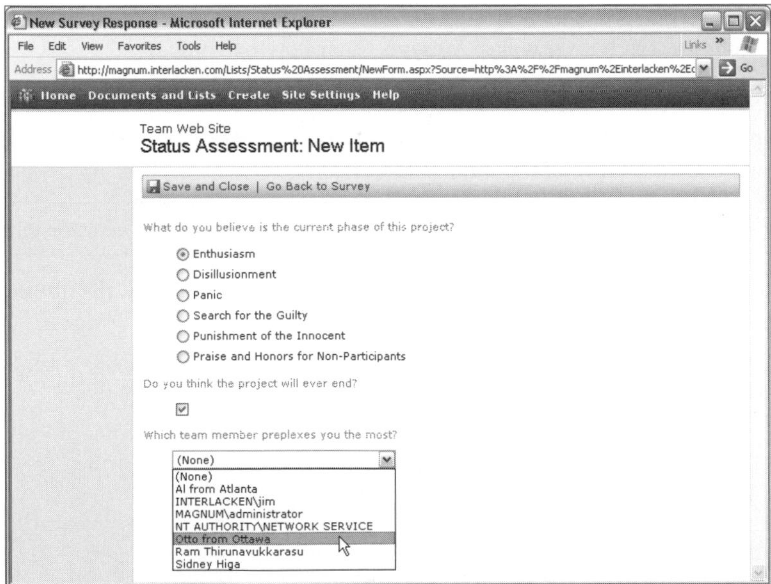

Figure 37-28. This is how the survey looks to a survey respondent. The survey itself is just a list with a column for recording each answer.

Here's how to display this page:

1. Click the Documents And Lists link on the menu bar of any page in the site.
2. Click the survey's list title or icon. This displays the Overview page, shown in Figure 37-29.

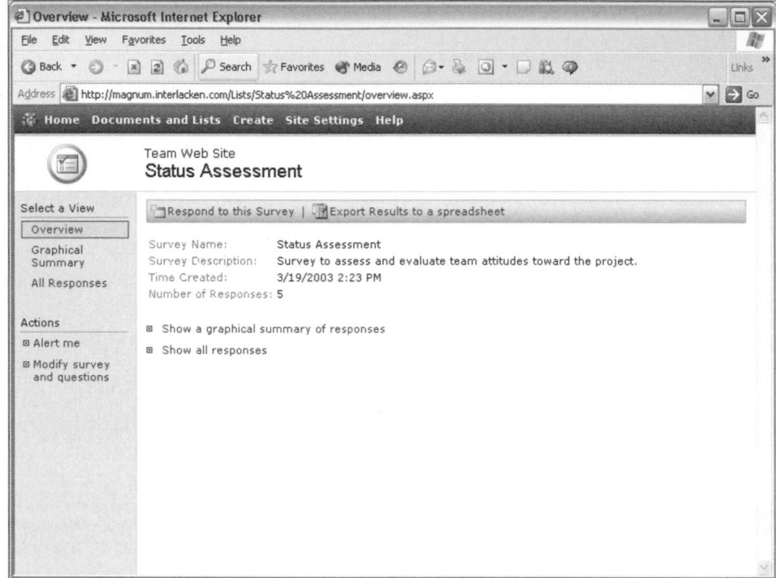

Figure 37-29. The entry point for analyzing survey results is this Web page.

The body of a survey Overview page presents the following choices:

- **Respond To This Survey** Opens the survey so that you can answer the questions.
- **Export Results To A Spreadsheet** Downloads an Excel Web Query (.iqy) file that downloads the survey data into a spreadsheet.

For more information about downloading list data, refer to "Using Lists," earlier in this chapter.

- **Show A Graphical Summary Of Questions** Displays a graphical summary of survey responses similar to the one shown in Figure 37-30.
- **Show All Responses** Displays a textual listing of survey responses similar to the one shown in Figure 37-31.

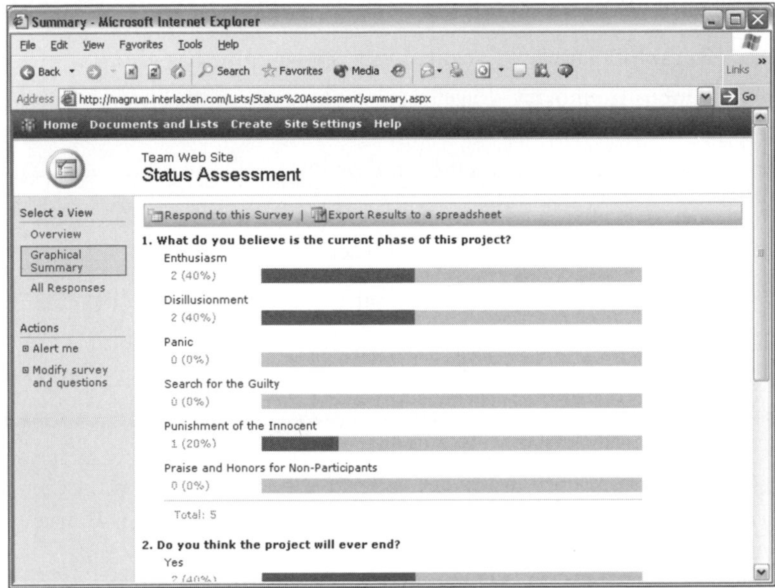

Figure 37-30. The graphical summary of survey responses looks like this.

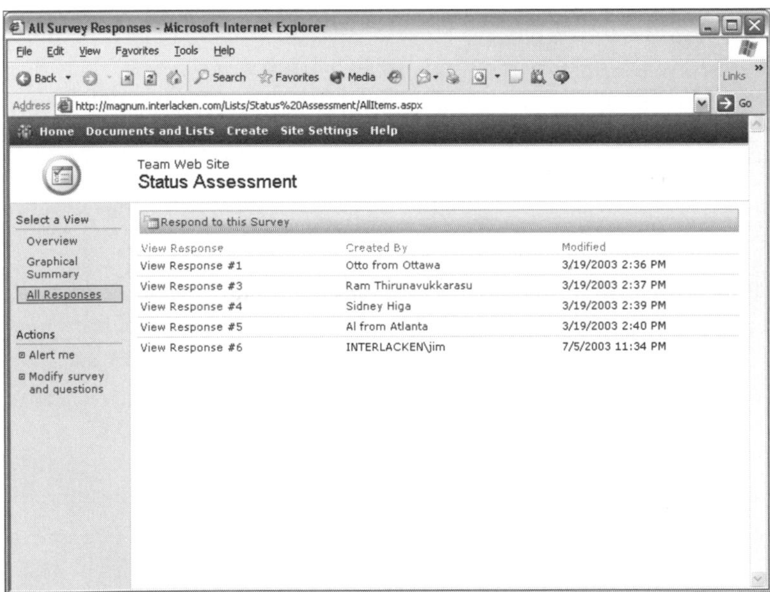

Figure 37-31. This Web page displays all responses to a survey.

The Select A View area provides access to three views:

- **Overview** Displays the initial view shown in Figure 37-29.
- **Graphical summary** Displays the same view as the Show A Graphical Summary Of Responses link in the main body.
- **All responses** Displays the same view as the Show All Responses link in the main body.

The Actions area provides these two choices:

- **Alert Me** Click this link if you want to receive e-mail notification whenever someone completes or changes the survey.
- **Modify Survey And Questions** Changes the properties of the survey. This includes the survey name, description, questions, and other settings. In short, it displays the Customization page (shown previously in Figure 37-27).

Creating other kinds of lists follows basically the same pattern as creating a survey. This is because, in fact, a survey is nothing but a list in which each row is a survey response and each column is an answer.

Creating New Libraries, Discussions, and Lists

The procedure for creating a new survey is a special case of the procedure for creating any other sort of SharePoint Team Site list. To begin creating a SharePoint Team Site list of any kind, click the Create link on any SharePoint Team Site page menu bar. This displays the Create page, shown previously in Figure 37-21, Figure 37-22, and Figure 37-23. To create any standard type of list, click the corresponding link and follow the prompts.

For maximum power and flexibility when creating a new list, choose one of the links under the Custom Lists heading. These links are:

- **Custom List** Creates a list with only one column: Title. After the list exists, of course, you can display it and then click Modify Settings And Columns to add more columns, delete the Title column, or make any other changes you want.
- **Custom List In Datasheet View** Displays a New List page where you supply a name and description, and then displays a spreadsheet-like grid where you define each field you want the list to contain. This works very much like Design view for tables in Microsoft Access, or the Design Table window in SQL Enterprise Manager.
- **Import Spreadsheet** Creates a list from data contained in a spreadsheet. Each row of spreadsheet data becomes one list record, and each column of spreadsheet data becomes a list column. The values in the first row will become the column names in the list.

Clicking any of these choices displays the New List page, shown in Figure 37-32.

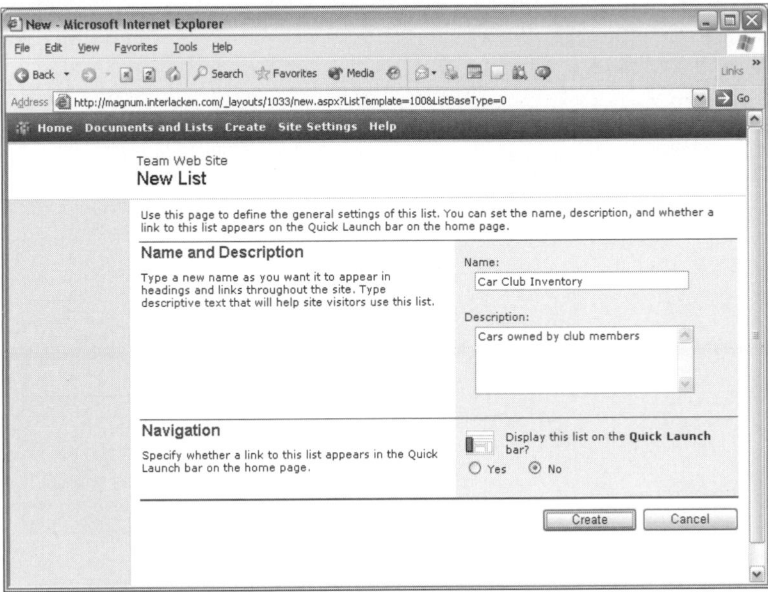

Figure 37-32. Use this page to name and describe a new SharePoint Team Site list.

Configure these settings:

- **Name** Enter a name that will identify this list throughout your SharePoint Team Site.
- **Description** Briefly describe the list's content or purpose.
- **Display This List On The Quick Launch Bar?** Select Yes if you want the Quick Launch bar of the SharePoint Team Site home page to display a link to this list.

When these entries are complete, click the Create button. The next three sections explain how to proceed, depending on which type of custom list you're creating.

Chapter 38, "Leveraging Windows SharePoint Services," explains how FrontPage can access SharePoint lists and other data sources with even more flexibility than SharePoint itself.

Creating a Basic Custom List

If you originally chose Custom List, clicking the Create button will display the list page shown in Figure 37-33. The list contains one column, named Title, and no records.

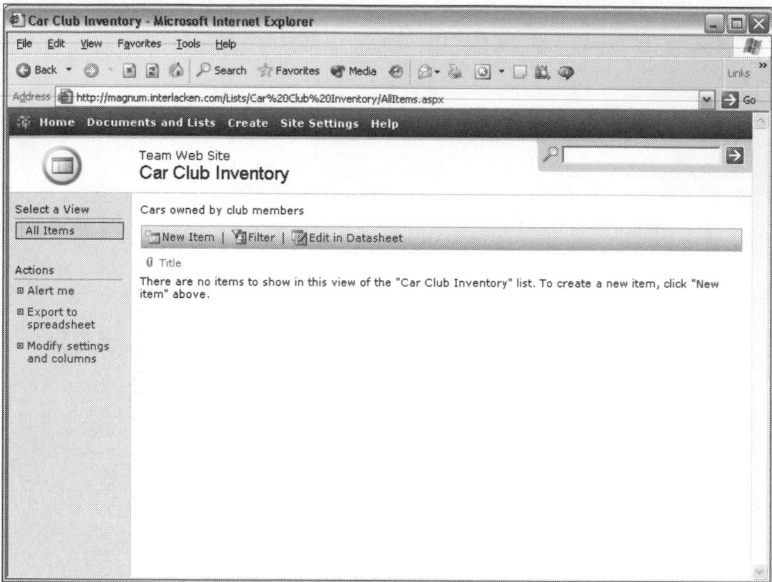

Figure 37-33. This new list has no items yet.

In all likelihood, you'll want your list to contain more or different fields. To make such changes, proceed as follows:

1 Under Actions, click the Modify Settings And Columns link. This displays the Customization page, shown in Figure 37-34 and Figure 37-35.

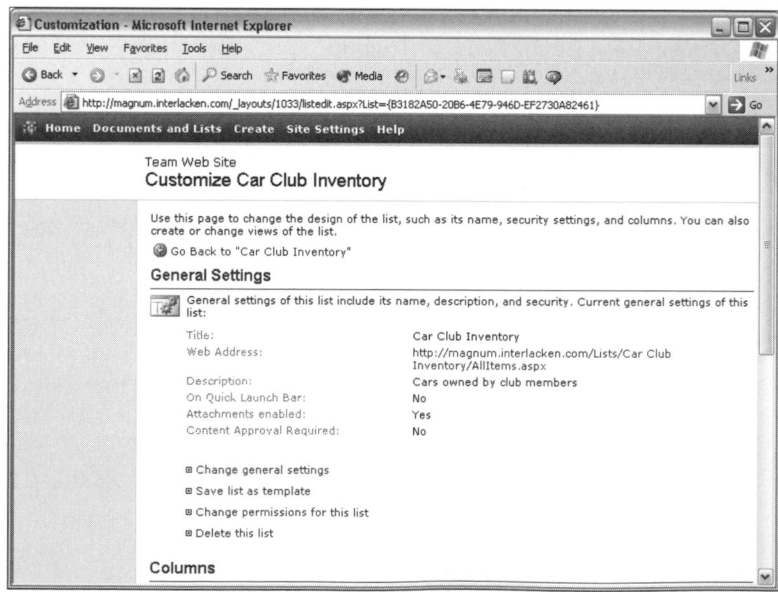

Figure 37-34. This page displays the configuration of a SharePoint Team Site list.

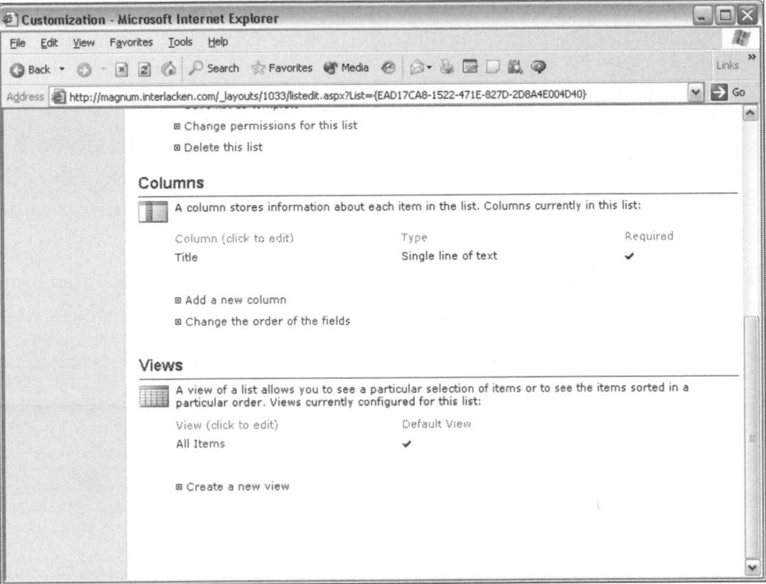

Figure 37-35. This is the bottom half of the Web page shown in Figure 37-34.

2 To modify the Title field, scroll down to the Columns heading, and then, under Column (Click To Edit), click Title. This will display an Edit Column page similar to the one shown in Figure 37-36. Overtype whatever settings you want to change, and then click OK.

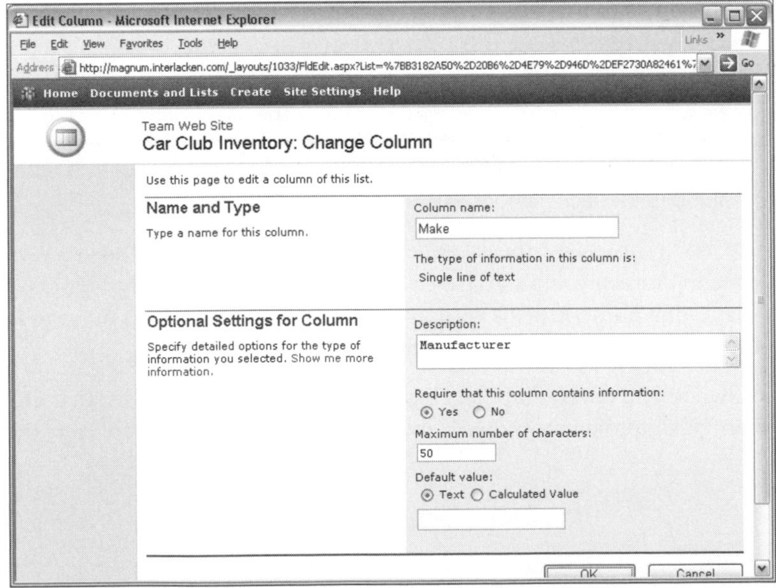

Figure 37-36. Use this page to change the properties of a list column.

3. To include more columns in the list, click the Add A New Column link on the Customization page. This displays a Create New Column page similar to the Create New Question page shown in Figure 37-25 and Figure 37-26. Give the column a name, choose a format, specify optional settings, and click OK.
4. When the list contains all the columns you want, click the Go Back To link near the top of the Customization page. This will display the list page shown previously in Figure 37-33, but the page will now include the new columns you defined. To enter some data, click the New Item link.
5. When the New Item page shown in Figure 37-37 appears, enter some data, and then click the Save And Close link. To enter more data, click the New Item link again.

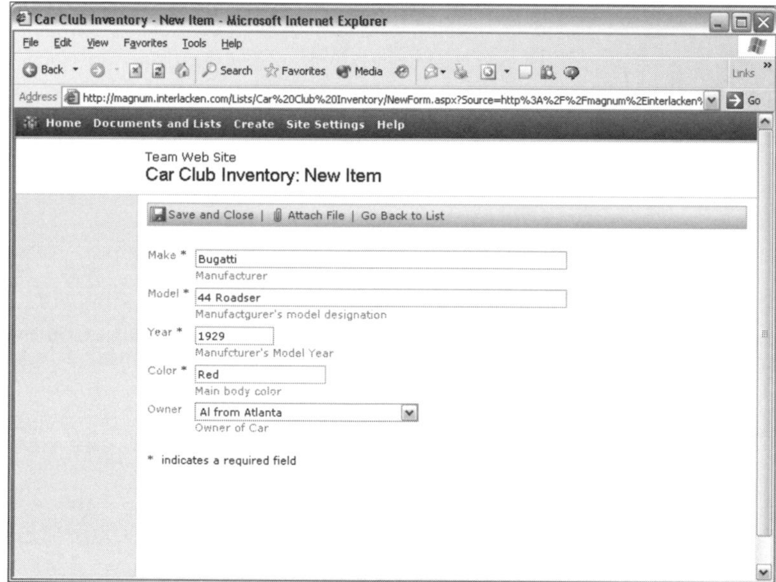

Figure 37-37. A SharePoint Team Site automatically creates a data entry page like this for each custom list.

Figure 37-38 shows how the list page appears after the list contains six records. It's a bit odd for data in the Year column to have a comma, but unfortunately, SharePoint has no options for displaying numeric fields without commas. You could avoid the commas by using two-digit years or by making Year a text field.

The Owner field is a Lookup field based on a User Information list that the SharePoint Team Site provides automatically. Basically, this is the list of authorized team members.

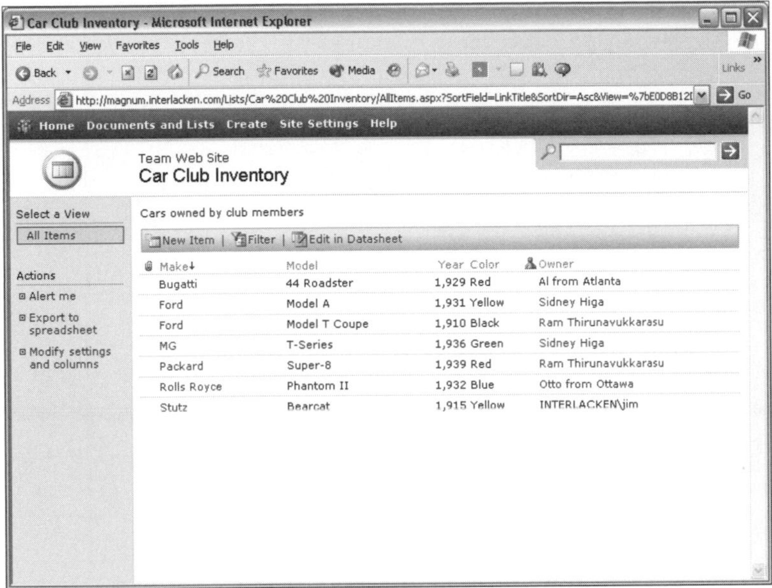

Figure 37-38. This is how Windows SharePoint Services displays the contents of a custom list. To sort the display on any column, click its heading.

Once the list exists, team members can view it or update it using any of these methods:

- Click its entry in the Quick Launch bar (provided, of course, that you chose to display this list on the Quick Launch bar when you created or later modified the list).
- Click the Documents And Lists link on the menu bar of any page in the SharePoint Team Site, and then, under Lists, click the list name.
- Add the list to a Web Part Page. The section, "Configuring Web Part Pages," later in this chapter, will explain how to do this.

All in all, creating and using a custom list is much more modern and much more convenient than using the FrontPage Save Results component. The custom list, of course, requires that your server be running Windows SharePoint Services and that everyone who accesses the list be a team member.

Creating a Custom List in Datasheet View

If you chose Custom List In Datasheet View on the Create page, clicking Create on the New List page will display the list as shown in Figure 37-39.

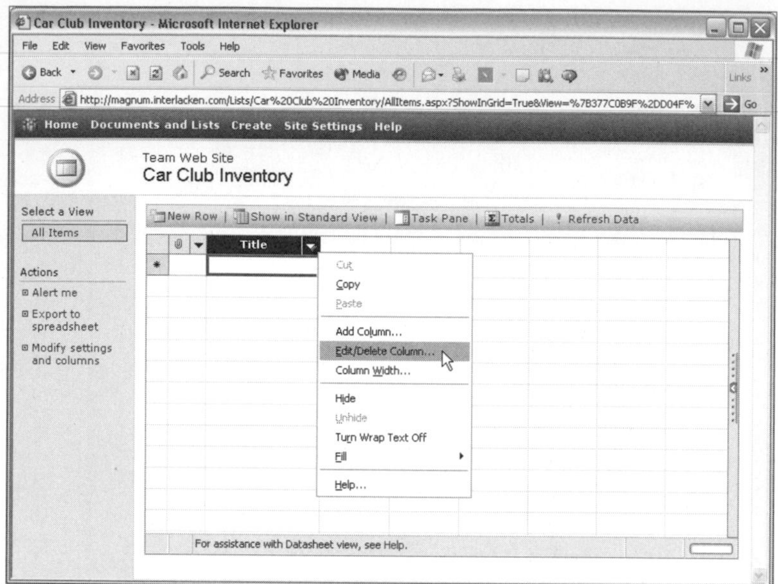

Figure 37-39. In Datasheet view, you can enter data and modify list properties as well.

Here's how to work with this view:

- To modify a column, right-click the column heading, and then choose Edit/Delete Column from the shortcut menu. This displays the Edit Column page shown previously in Figure 37-36.
- To add a new column, right-click anywhere in the datasheet, and then choose Add Column from the shortcut menu. As before, this displays a Create New Column page very similar to the Create New Question page shown in Figure 37-25 and Figure 37-26.
- To add a row of data, type the data into the row that begins with an asterisk.
- To modify the data in any row, simply type over it.
- To delete one or more rows, select the rows, right-click the selection, and then choose Delete Rows from the shortcut menu.

Creating a Custom List by Importing a Spreadsheet

If you chose Import Spreadsheet on the Create page, the process of creating a list works like this:

1. Make sure that the data in your spreadsheet is organized in contiguous rows and columns and that the first row contains the field names you want the SharePoint Team Site list to use.
2. When the New List page shown in Figure 37-32 appears, it will include an Import Spreadsheet heading. Under this heading is a File Location box. Enter the location of the spreadsheet in this box, either by typing or by clicking the nearby Browse button.

3 Click OK. SharePoint will then start Excel, load the spreadsheet you specified, and display the Import to SharePoint Team Services List dialog box, shown in Figure 37-40.

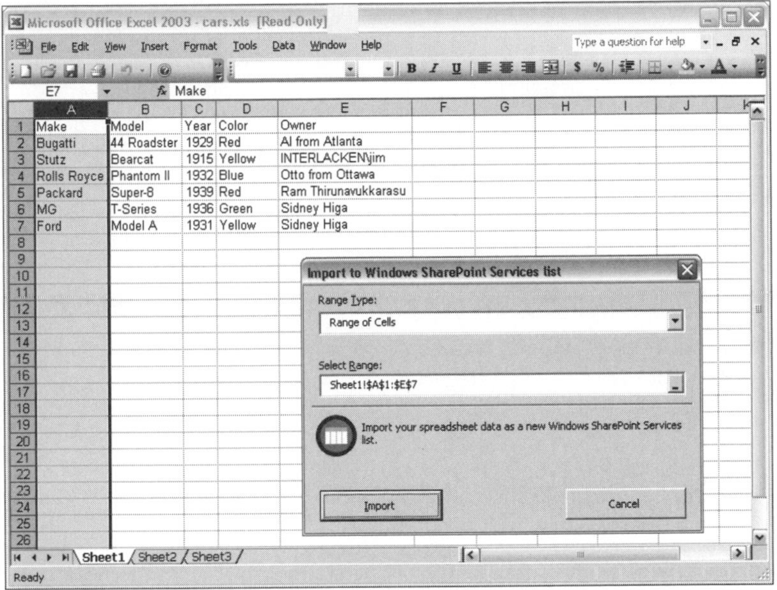

Figure 37-40. When you create a list based on a spreadsheet, Windows SharePoint Services starts Excel and tells it to upload the column headings and data.

Configure these settings:

- **Range Type** Select the type of range that encloses the data you want to import. This will be a range of cells, a list range, or a named range.
- **Select Range** Specify the range that encloses the data. This must conform to the range type you selected.

4 Click Import to create the list and import the data.

Configuring Web Part Pages

The home page of a SharePoint Team Site is probably the most familiar Web Part Page you'll encounter. A Web Part Page contains one or more Web Part zones, and each of these zones can contain one or more Web Parts. A Web Part is an independent unit of content.

To see the Web Part zones in a SharePoint Team Site home page, click the Modify My Page link near the top right corner, and then choose Add Web Parts and Browse from the shortcut menu. The display will now resemble the page shown in Figure 37-41.

Modifying the Layout of a Web Part Page

Clicking the Modify My Page link on a Web Part Page displays not only an Add Web Parts option, but the following choices as well:

- **Design This Page** Shifts the page into an editable view where you can rearrange Web parts by dragging.
- **Modify My Web Parts** Displays a submenu with one choice for each Web Part on the page. Selecting any Web Part displays a task pane where you can modify the Web Part's appearance and layout.
- **Shared View** Displays the Web Part Page as configured for the SharePoint Team Site as a whole.
- **Personal View** Displays the Web Part Page using your personal settings.
- **Reset Page Content** Resets all personal settings to the default for new members.

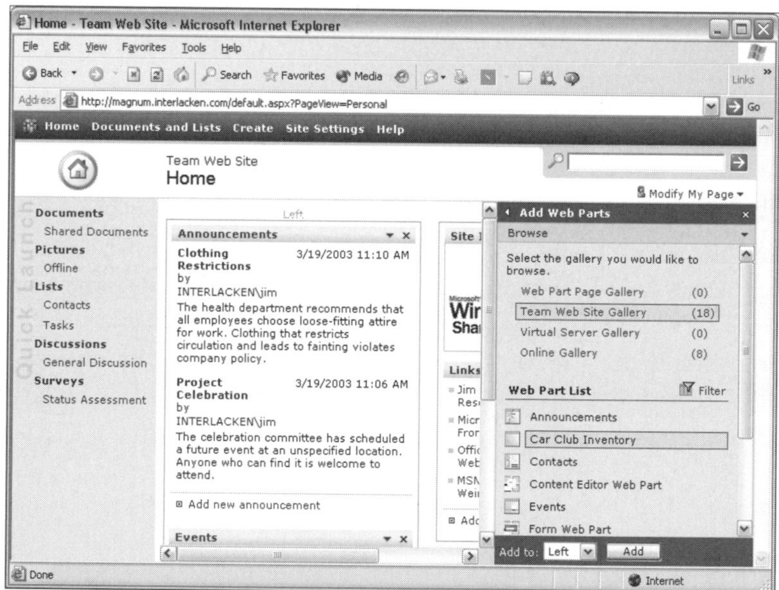

Figure 37-41. You can add Web Parts to a Web Part Page using only Internet Explorer.

The Left heading above the Announcements list identifies a Web Part zone named, logically enough, Left. This is a name and not a keyword; whoever created this page could have named the zone Middle, Abigail, or Fluffy. A gray box shows the limits of the zone, which extends below the browser window.

At the right of the Left zone is a second zone, named Right. (Figure 37-41 shows part of the gray box surrounding this zone, but the task pane hides its title.)

The top half of the task pane lists four libraries of Web Parts: the Web Part Page gallery, the Team Web Site gallery, the Virtual Server gallery, and the Online gallery. In this example, not all of these libraries contain Web Parts, but they could. Here's the procedure for adding a Web Part to any Web Part Page:

1. Select the gallery that contains the Web Part you want. If you're not sure which gallery this is, select them one by one.
2. Select the Web Part you want from the Web Part List area in the bottom half of the task pane. Notice that the custom list created in the previous section appears automatically as a Web Part.
3. In the Add To drop-down list at the bottom of the task pane, specify which Web Part zone should display the Web Part, and then click Add.
4. To close the task pane, click its close box. As shown in Figure 37-42, the Web Part now appears in your version of the SharePoint Team Site home page.

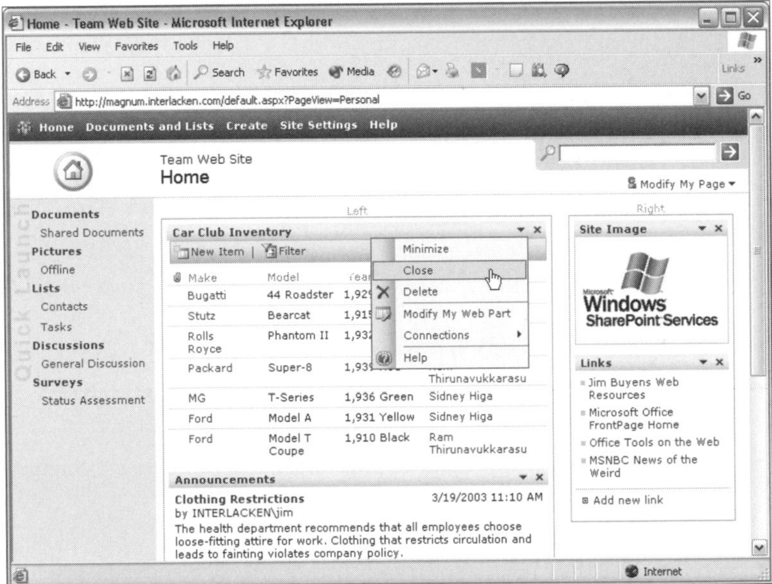

Figure 37-42. Each Web Part on a page has its own drop-down menu.

Click the drop-down arrow in each Web Part title bar to reveals these options:

- **Minimize** Shrinks the Web Part so that only its title bar is visible.
- **Close** Makes the Web Part disappear.
- **Modify My Web Part** Displays a task pane that controls a Web Part's view, toolbar, appearance, layout, and advanced settings.
- **Help** Displays helpful information about the Web Part.

Chapter 38, "Leveraging Windows SharePoint Services," explains how FrontPage can create and configure Web Part Pages with even more flexibility than SharePoint itself.

Administering SharePoint Team Site Settings

To modify settings for a SharePoint Team Site, click the Site Settings link on any SharePoint Team Site page. This displays the Site Settings page, shown in Figure 37-43 and Figure 37-43.

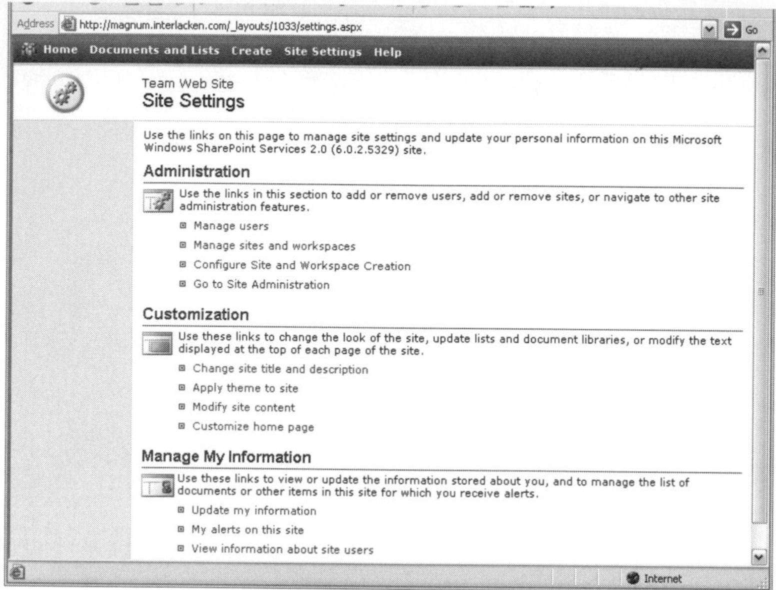

Figure 37-43. The Site Settings page controls properties for an entire SharePoint Team Site.

This page contains the following headings and links:

- **Administration** These links add or remove users, add or remove sites, and link to additional administration pages:
  - **Manage users** Displays a page that adds, removes, or changes the roles of users who have access to the current site.
  - **Manage Sites And Workspaces** Displays a page with links to each site located within the folder tree for the current site and to which you have access.
  - **Allow Site And Workspace Creation** Displays a page that controls who can read, update, reconfigure, and administer the current SharePoint Team Site.
  - **Go To Site Administration** Displays the Administration page for the SharePoint Team Site.
- **Customization** These links change the appearance of a site, update lists and document libraries, and modify the text displayed at the top of each page:
  - **Change Site Title And Description** Displays a page that modifies the SharePoint Team Site's title and description.
  - **Apply Theme To Site** Displays a page that changes the SharePoint Team Site's fonts and color scheme.

- **Modify Site Content** Displays a page with links to customize each document library, discussion board, and list in the current SharePoint Team Site.
- **Customize Home Page** Displays the home page with the Add Web Parts task pane visible.

- **Manage My Information** These links display or update your personal information and alerts.
  - **Update My Information** Displays a Personal Settings page that shows and modifies your own user account information.
  - **My Alerts On This Site** Displays all alerts you currently have in effect and provides a way to delete those you no longer want.
  - **View Information About Site Users** Displays a list of users who have access to the current SharePoint Team Site.

In Summary…

This chapter explained how team members can use the features of a SharePoint Team Site to share documents and coordinate their activities. It also explained how to create custom lists and custom pages that perform standard functions, and it briefly explained how to administer such a site.

The next chapter explains how FrontPage can develop content for SharePoint Team Sites, including the use of Web Parts and database access.

Chapter 38

Leveraging Windows SharePoint Services

Chapter 37, "Using SharePoint Team Sites," explained the concepts of Microsoft SharePoint Web sites, how to use them, and some ways to modify them. That material, however, only scratched the surface of what Microsoft Windows SharePoint Services can do. This chapter explains how you can use Microsoft Office FrontPage 2003 to create not only SharePoint Team Sites, but other kinds of SharePoint applications as well. It then explains how to create your own Web Part Pages, how to access data sources located both inside and outside a SharePoint application, and how to display and otherwise integrate such data with the rest of the application.

None of this, by the way, requires that you write even a single line of program code.

As you read this chapter, keep in mind the question of what constitutes a *data-driven Web site*. Almost every feature this chapter describes would be useless without an underlying database to accept, store, and deliver information. This kind of dependency on databases is certainly a major factor in declaring a site data-driven.

Creating SharePoint Team Sites

Creating the first SharePoint Team Site on a Web server affects the entire virtual server and is therefore a job for the server's administrator. Chapter 37 briefly explained how an administrator would do this. Basically, the administrator first installs Windows SharePoint Services on the computer and then "SharePoint-extends" one or more virtual Web servers on that machine. The administrator would typically choose a new, empty server to extend, but in any event, SharePoint-extending a virtual server creates one SharePoint site in the server's root. In practice, most SharePoint-extended servers support many groups of people or applications, each of which requires its own site or group of sites.

For more information about adding Windows SharePoint Services to a Web server, refer to "Creating a New SharePoint Team Site," on page 927.

Authorized visitors can create additional sites using only a browser. These can be complete SharePoint Team Sites or more specialized sites for planning a meeting, developing a complex document, or coordinating other tasks requiring team input.

FrontPage 2003 offers three additional ways of creating new Windows SharePoint Services sites of various kinds and capabilities. The next three sections describe these approaches.

Creating Sites from SharePoint Templates

Chapter 14, "Creating Web Sites with Templates and Wizards," described one way that FrontPage can create additional sites on a SharePoint server. Here are the basic steps:

1. Choose New from the File menu.
2. When the New task pane appears, under New Web Site, click SharePoint-Based Team Web Site. (Actually, any template will do. They all display the Web Site Templates dialog box.)
3. When the Web Site Templates dialog box appears, make sure that the General tab and the SharePoint Team Site option are selected.
4. In the Specify The Location Of The New Web Site box, enter the URL where you want the new SharePoint Team Site to reside. The host name must specify a server running Windows SharePoint Services, and the path should specify a new folder on that sever.
5. Click OK to create the site.

For more information about creating a SharePoint Team Site from a Web template, refer to "Creating a SharePoint Team Site," on page 393.

This procedure creates a standard SharePoint Team Site. Typically, the next step would be to browse the site, click Site Settings on any menu bar, and authorize the appropriate team members.

Creating Sites from SharePoint Packages

Chapter 14 also described how to create SharePoint Team Sites from packages. Packages have two characteristics that ordinary templates lack:

- They consist of a single file, which is easy to transport.
- They can create libraries, lists, and other database objects as well as ordinary Web content such as Web pages and picture files.

Figure 38-1 shows the home page that results from installing the News And Reviews package that comes with FrontPage 2003.

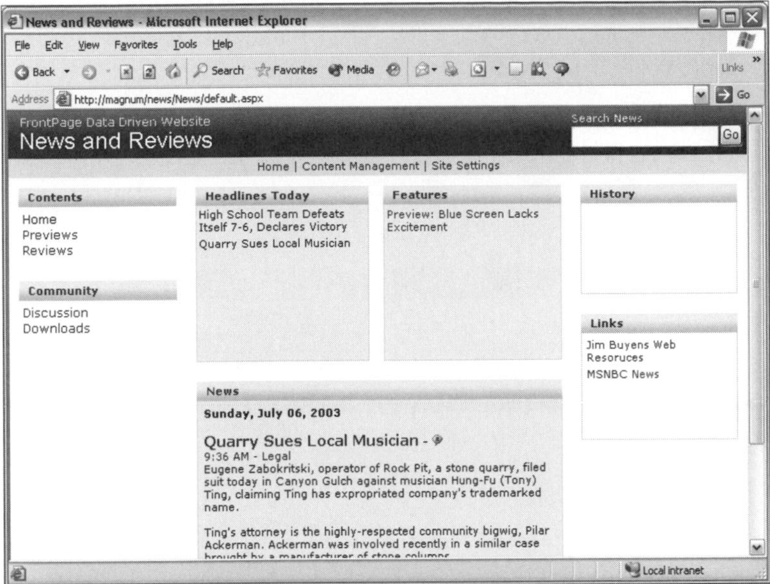

Figure 38-1. Installing a News And Reviews package creates a Windows SharePoint Services site with a home page like this. This isn't a SharePoint Team Site, but it uses many of the same Web Parts.

Despite some visual similarities, this site differs considerably from an ordinary SharePoint Team Site:

- The Contents and Community areas provide ordinary Web content through a Dynamic Web Template.
- The Headlines Today, Features, News, History, and Links areas are Data View Web Parts. They all display information, in various levels of detail, that resides in SharePoint lists.
- The Content Management link on the menu bar jumps to a page where you can add, modify, or delete articles or features.
- Each article in the News Web Part contains a "bubble" icon that jumps to a page where visitors can enter discussion comments about that article.

For more information about creating Windows SharePoint Services sites from packages, refer to "Creating Web Sites from Packages," on page 396.

Figure 38-2 shows the home page of a site that FrontPage can build from its Web Log package. This is a sort of online diary that you update, and that Web visitors can read and comment upon. This page differs visually from a standard SharePoint Team Site not only because it uses a different arrangement of Web Parts, but also because it uses a non-default theme.

Tip To change the theme for any SharePoint site, click the Site Settings link on any menu bar. When the Site Settings page appears, look under Customization, and click Apply Theme To Site.

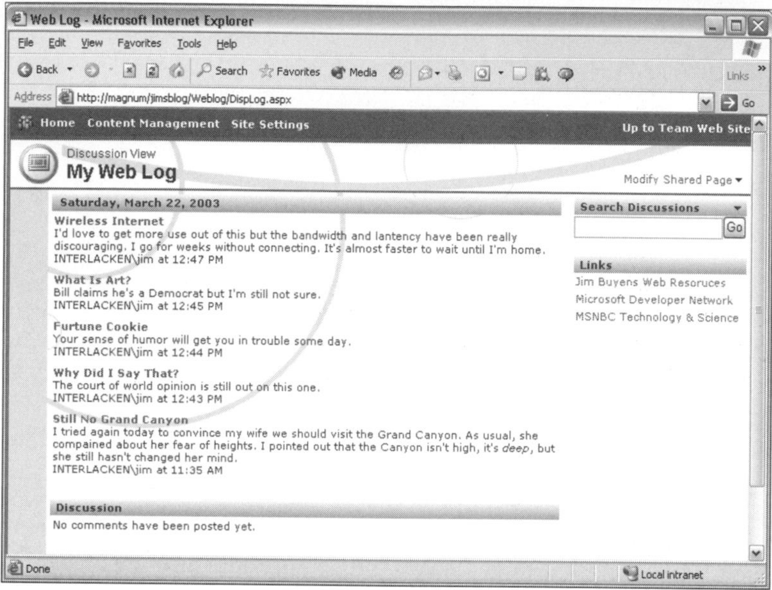

Figure 38-2. This home page shows another type of SharePoint site that FrontPage can create from a package.

Here's the procedure for creating a News And Reviews site, a Web Log site, or any other type of site for which FrontPage provides a package:

1. If you want to add the package to an existing site, open that site.
2. Choose New from the File menu.
3. When the New task pane appears, under New Web Site, click Web Package Solutions. (Again, any template link will do.)
4. When the Web Site Templates dialog box appears, make sure that the Packages tab is selected.
5. In the Specify The Location Of The New Web Site section, do either of the following:
   - Enter the URL where you want the new site to reside. The host name must specify a server running Windows SharePoint Services, and the path should specify a new folder on that server.
   - Select the Add To Current Web Site check box.
6. Click OK to process the package. Within a few moments, the Import Web Package dialog box, shown in Figure 38-3, should appear.

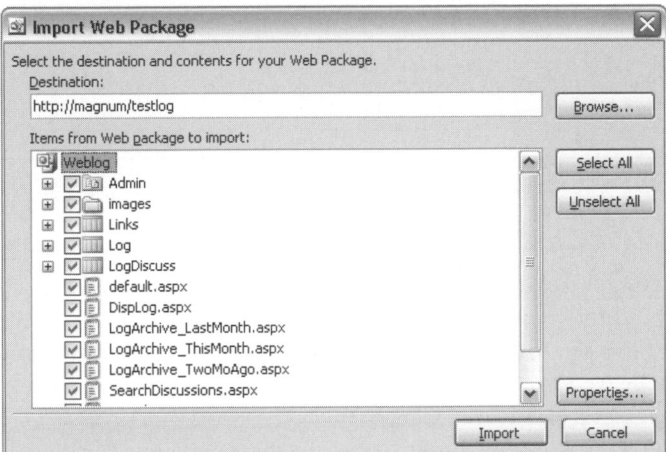

Figure 38-3. When you import a package, you have considerable flexibility in choosing which parts of the package you want.

Review the following settings:

- **Destination** Verify that this box correctly specifies the Web address you want for the new site. If you selected the Add To Current Web Site check box in step 5, the destination will be the address of the current site plus (usually) a folder name. You can change the folder name if you want. If you chose in step 5 to create a new site, this box specifies its root location.

> **Tip** To install several packages in the same site, specify a different folder location for each one.

- **Items From Web Package To Import** Confirm each item in the package you want to import. If the check box to the left of an item is selected, SharePoint will import it; otherwise, it won't. Normally, you should import all the items in the package. If a plus sign precedes any item, clicking the plus sign shows dependent items. In the case of lists, for example, the pages that process the list are dependent on the list itself. If you don't import a list, you don't import the pages that process it either.
- **Select All** Click this button to select every item in the Items From Web Package To Import list.
- **Unselect All** Click this button to clear the selection for every item in the Items From Web Package To Import list.
- **Properties** Click this button to view the Title, Description, Author, Company, Size, and External Dependencies of the package.

Note An external dependency is a file that the package requires but doesn't include. Usually these are files that appear in the root Web site when an administrator installs SharePoint.

Note Notice that in Figure 38-3, Links, Log, and LogDiscuss are SharePoint lists rather than files.

After completing these steps, click the Import button in the Import Web Package dialog box. If you get any security warnings or other prompts, respond to them. FrontPage will display an Importing Package dialog box that contains a progress bar and that might seem to freeze occasionally. Be patient—eventually, you'll receive a *Deployment Complete* message. Open your new site, and have fun exploring.

Creating Sites from SharePoint Services

This method of creating a SharePoint site occurs almost completely on the SharePoint server. FrontPage merely sends the server a command to create a site from a template already on the server. These might be Microsoft templates that come with SharePoint or custom templates an administrator provides for widespread use.

Follow these steps to create a SharePoint site from a template on the sever:

1. Display the Web Site Templates dialog box, as you did in the previous sections.
2. Click the SharePoint Services tab, select a template, and fill in the Specify The Location Of The New Web Site box. Then click OK to create the site.

The only tricky part of this procedure is getting the correct set of templates to appear on the SharePoint Services tab. The list of templates *should* come from the server you specify in the Specify The Location Of The New Web Site box, but updating that box might not update the list of templates. To work around this quirk, click the Browse button.

Creating and Modifying Web Part Pages

Every site on a Web server extended with Windows SharePoint Services has access to several libraries of Web Parts. Most of these Web Parts are highly configurable, and in total, they provide great power, elegance, and utility. The topics in this section explain how you can leverage all this power and flexibility to your own ends.

Creating Web Part Pages

Any page can contain a Web Part, but it takes a special kind of page to contain two or more Web Parts—it takes a Web Part Page. The most direct way to create a Web Part Page is to use a page template. Here's the basic procedure:

1. Open the site that will contain the Web Part Page. Remember that this site must reside on a server extended with Windows SharePoint Services.
2. Choose New from the File menu. Then, in the New task pane, under New Page, click More Page Templates.
3. When the Page Templates dialog box appears, click the Web Part Pages tab.
4. Single-click each template listed on the Web Part Pages tab, observing the template's effect in the Preview area at the lower right. The rectangles in the Preview area represent Web Part Zones.
5. Select the page template that provides the arrangement closest to what you want, and then click OK.

Inside Out

Web Part Zones and Web Parts needn't be 1:1

As you review the templates on the Web Part Pages tab, keep in mind that a single Web Part Zone can accommodate any number of Web Parts. If you want your page to display six Web Parts, you needn't look for a template with six zones. Remember as well that you can add or remove Web Part Zones once the new page is open in Design view.

Another, even more flexible way of creating Web Part Pages is to first create a perfectly normal page (that is, a Normal page from the General tab) and then use Design view to add some Web Part Zones. The next section will explain how to do this.

One consequence of using FrontPage's Web Part Page templates is that they automatically supply the same title bar, menu bar, and color scheme as a normal SharePoint Team Site page. This can be handy when you're adding a page to a SharePoint Team Site, but a nuisance in other situations. In those other cases, you might find it simpler to start by opening an existing page and saving it under a new name.

No matter how you create a Web Part Page, you must give it the file extension .aspx when you save it.

For more information about using templates to create Web Part Pages, refer to "Selecting Web Part Pages Templates," on page 317.

Creating Web Part Zones

Adding a Web Part Zone to any Web page is extremely simple. Here's the procedure:

1. In FrontPage, open the Web page that should contain the Web Part Zone, and set the insertion point where you want the zone to appear.
2. Display the Web Parts task pane by doing either of the following:
   - Choose Insert Web Part from the Data menu.
   - Click the drop-down arrow in the title bar of any other task pane, and then choose Web Parts.
3. Click the New Web Part Zone button at the bottom of the task pane.

Figure 38-4 shows a new Web page that contains nothing but a new Web Part Zone. The title Zone 1 identifies the zone.

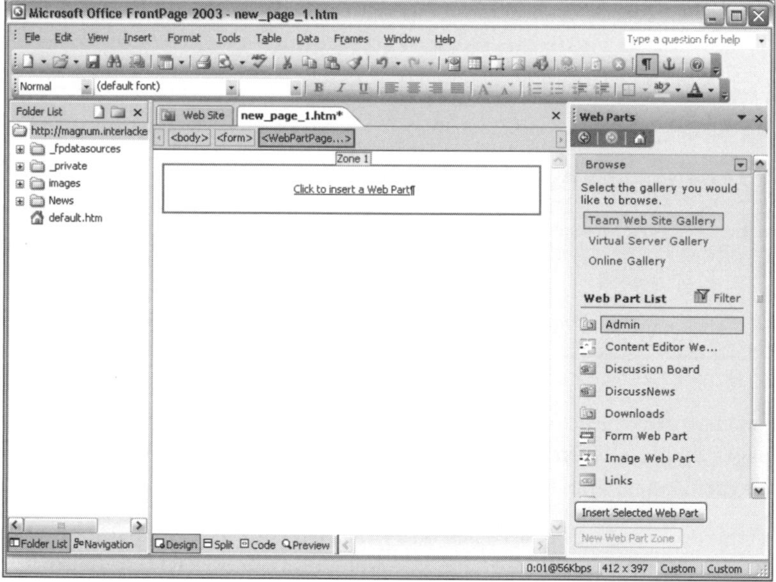

Figure 38-4. The area titled Zone 1 is a Web Part Zone ready to receive Web Parts.

To inspect or modify the zone's properties, take one of the following actions. They all display the Web Part Zone Properties dialog box, shown in Figure 38-5.

- Right-click the zone, and choose Web Part Zone Properties from the shortcut menu.
- Select the zone, and choose Web Part Zone Properties from the Data menu.
- Select the zone, click the drop-down arrow on its Quick Tag Selector icon ("*<WebPartPages:WebPartZone>*"), and then choose Tag Properties.

Figure 38-5. This dialog box configures the properties of a Web Part Zone.

Here's how to configure the settings in the Web Part Zone Properties dialog box:

- **General Settings** Specify these overall properties for the current zone:
  - **Zone Title** Assign a short but descriptive name that will identify the zone.
  - **Frame Style** Choose a style. Table 38-1 itemizes your choices.
- **Layout Of Web Parts Contained In The Zone** Specify how SharePoint should arrange multiple Web Parts in the current zone:
  - **Top-To-Bottom (Vertical Layout)** Select this option if, when the zone contains more than one Web Part, they should appear above and below each other.
  - **Side-By-Side (Horizontal Layout)** Select this option if multiple Web Parts within the zone should appear to each other's left and right.
- **Browser Settings For Web Parts Contained In The Zone** Specify the extent that Web visitors can reconfigure Web Parts in the current zone:
  - **Allow Users To Add, Remove, Resize, And Move Web Parts** Select this check box to let Web visitors add, remove, resize, and rearrange Web Parts.
  - **Allow Users To Change Personal Web Part Settings** Select this check box to let Web visitors change personal settings for Web Parts.
  - **Allow Users To Change Web Part Settings For All Users** Select this check box to let any Web visitor change Web Part settings that apply to all visitors.

Table 38-1. Web Part Zone Frame Styles

Frame style	Description
Default	Web Parts in the zone default to the standard frame style. This is normally Title Bar And Border.
None	No visible frame will surround Web Parts in the zone.
Title Bar And Border	A visible frame will surround the title bar and contents of each Web Part in the zone.
Title Bar Only	A visible frame will surround the title bar of each Web Part in the zone.

Adding Web Parts to Zones

Once your page contains a Web Part Zone, you'll no doubt want the zone to contain one or more Web Parts. There are two ways to begin:

- If the zone contains no Web Parts, it will display a link titled Click To Insert A Web Part. Click this link to set the insertion point inside the zone and to display the Web Parts Gallery task pane.
- If the zone already contains one or more Web Parts:
  1. Set the insertion point inside the zone, making sure that neither the zone nor any existing Web Part is selected.
  2. Choose Web Part from the Insert menu, or choose Web Parts from the drop-down menu on any other task pane's title bar.

Inside Out

Setting the insertion point inside a Web Part Zone can be tricky

Clicking an existing Web Part selects the Web Part, as indicated by an orange border.

Clicking a Web Part Zone selects the Web Part Zone, as indicated by a blue border.

If either of these objects is selected when you insert a Web Part, the new Web Part will replace the selection. To avoid this, press the arrow keys until the insertion point is inside the Web Part Zone, but no blue or orange borders appears.

To continue inserting the Web Part, proceed as follows:

1. In the Web Parts task pane, under Browse, select a gallery. If in doubt, try the Team Web Site Gallery first.

2 In the Web Part list, select the Web Part you want to insert. Notice that the task pane displays only 10 Web Parts at a time:
   - To view and potentially select additional Web Parts, you might need to click the Next link that appears after the tenth item.
   - To view the tenth item and the Next link, you might need to scroll down the Web Part list.

3 Click the Insert Selected Web Part button.

Within a few moments, the Web Part you selected should appear, complete with current data. Web Parts that display lists might appear blank if the list is empty.

Tip Don't forget to assign the file extension .aspx when you first save any page that contains a Web Part.

To inspect or modify the Web Part's properties, use any of the following methods to display the Web Part's properties dialog box, shown in Figure 38-6. This dialog box has no title other than the name of the Web Part.

- Right-click the Web Part, and choose Web Part Properties from the shortcut menu.
- Select the Web Part, and choose Web Part Properties from the Data menu.
- Select the Web Part, and click the drop-down arrow on the Web Part's Quick Tag Selector icon ("*<WebPartPages:ListViewWebPart>*"), and then choose Tag Properties.

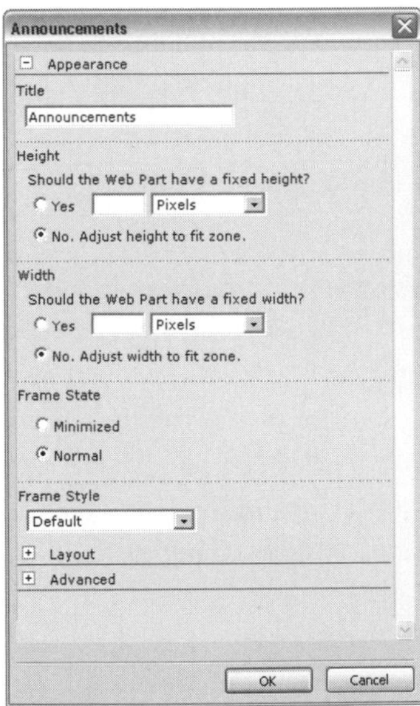

Figure 38-6. This dialog box configures the properties of a Web Part. To configure settings in the Layout and Advanced sections, click the plus icons that precede their titles.

The properties dialog box for a Web Part contains three collapsible sections: Appearance, Layout, and Advanced. Figure 38-6 shows the Appearance section, which exposes these settings:

- **Title** Enter the text that should appear in the Web Part's title bar.
- **Height. Should The Web Part Have A Fixed Height?** If you want the Web Part to always appear with the same height, select Yes, enter a value, and select a unit of measure. Otherwise, select No, Adjust Height To Fit Zone.
- **Width. Should The Web Part Have A Fixed Width?** If you want the Web Part to have a constant width regardless of conditions, select Yes, enter a value, and select a unit of measure. Otherwise, select No. Adjust Height To Fit Zone.
- **Frame State** Select Minimized if only the title bar should be visible when the Web Part first appears. Otherwise, select Normal.
- **Frame Style** Choose one of the settings shown previously in Table 38-1. Default inherits the frame style of the surrounding Web Part Zone; the remaining values override it.

Expanding the Layout section of a Web Part's properties dialog box exposes the following settings:

- **Include On Page** Select this check box if you want the Web Part to remain active. Clear it to disable the Web Part (that is, to retain the Web Part in Design view but bypass all processing and transmission to the Web visitor).
- **Visible On Page** Select this check box to make the Web Part visible to the visitor. Clear the check box to process the Web Part on the server but suppress its display.
- **Direction** Overrides the reading order of elements in the Web Part's text and frame. Choose Default, Left To Right, or Right To Left.

Controls to inspect and modify the following properties appear after you expand the Advanced section:

- **Allow Minimize** Select this check box if it's all right for visitors to switch the Web Part display between minimized and normal. Generally, a minimized view displays only the title bar.
- **Allow Close** Select this check box if it's all right for visitors to close the Web Part display. This removes the Web Part completely from view.
- **Allow Zone Change** Select this check box if it's all right for visitors to move the Web Part to a different zone on the same page. They do this by changing the Web Part's Zone ID property.
- **Detail Link** Specify a URL that displays a full-page view of the information in the Web Part. Clicking the title bar title jumps to this location. This is optional.
- **Description** Explain what the Web Part does. This text often appears in search results or Web Part catalog views.
- **Help Link** Specify the URL of a page containing information that helps the visitor interact with the Web Part. This is optional.

- **Icon File (Large)** Enter the URL of a large icon that will visually represent the Web Part. This is generally a GIF file no larger than 32 by 32 pixels
- **Icon File (Small)** Enter the URL of a small icon that will represent the Web Part. This icon is usually 16 by 16 pixels.
- **Missing Assembly Error** Specify an error message that will appear if SharePoint can't locate the run-time files for the Web Part. If you leave this field blank, a system message will appear.

Connecting Web Parts

Normally, developers construct Web Parts as freestanding units of content. This means that Web Parts have no dependencies and place no requirements on the page that contains them (other than, of course, the ability to display Web Parts). Windows SharePoint Services does, however, provide a Connections facility by which Web Parts on the same page can interact.

The ability for two Web Parts to connect and interact obviously requires the cooperation and compatibility of both. There's no guarantee that any two Web Parts can interact at all, let alone in the way you want. However, the possibility of connecting Web Parts is still worth investigating, and FrontPage provides a wizard that makes this easy.

To illustrate how this works, suppose that you want to create a form that filters the Car Club Inventory list from the previous chapter by Make. Suppose as well that for some reason, you don't want to rely on Web visitors clicking the Change Filter link in the Data View Web Part that displays the Car Club Inventory list. Proceed as follows:

1. Open the Windows SharePoint Services site that contains the Car Club Inventory list.
2. Use the Full Page, Vertical template to create a new Web Part Page.
3. Within the FullPage Web Part Zone, click the Click To Insert A Web Part link.
4. When the Web Parts task pane appears, select Team Web Site Gallery.
5. In the Web Part List, select Form Part. Then click the Insert Selected Web Part button.

> **Tip** **Modify form elements in a Form Web Part**
>
> You can add, modify, and delete the elements of a Form Web Part using the same commands you would use for a regular HTML form. To add a form field, for example, set the insertion point, choose Form from the Insert menu, and then select the type of element you want to add. To modify an element in a Form Web Part, right-click it, and choose Properties from the shortcut menu.

6. When the Form Web Part appears in Design view, it should contain a text box and a button titled Go. Select the text box, and then press the right arrow key four times. This should set the insertion point outside the Form Web Part, but still within the FullPage Web Part Zone.

   When you've set the insertion point correctly, it should appear just outside the lower right corner of the Form Web Part. To observe this, you might need to scroll the Design view window fully to the right.

7 In the Web Parts task pane, click the Car Club Inventory Web Part, and then click the Insert Selected Web Part button. Design view should now display both the Form Web Part and the Card Club Inventory Web Part, as shown in the background of Figure 38-7.

> **Note** This procedure works with any SharePoint library or list, including the Announcements, Contacts, Events, Links, Members, and Shared Documents lists.

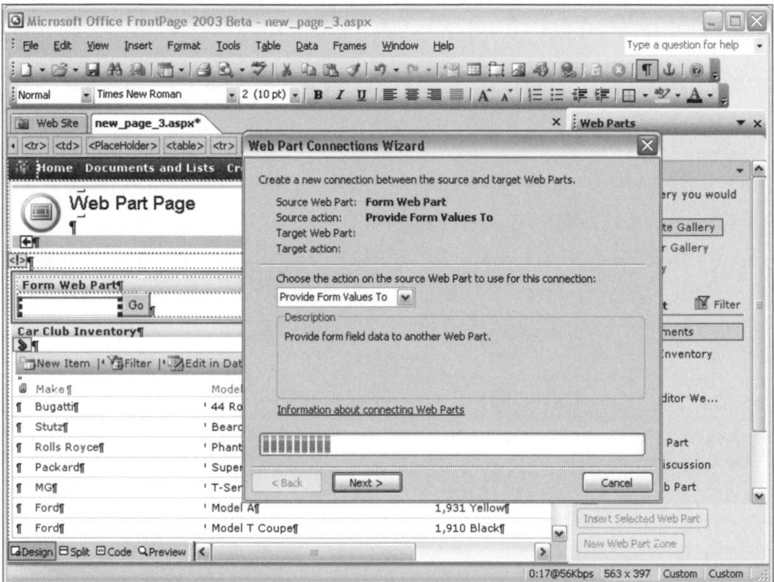

Figure 38-7. The first step in configuring a Web Part Connection is choosing what to send.

8 Take one of these actions:

- Right-click the Form Web Part, and choose Web Part Connections from the shortcut menu.
- Select the Form Web Part, and choose Web Part Connections from the Data menu.

9 When the Web Part Connections Wizard page shown in the foreground of Figure 38-7 appears, open the Choose The Action On The Source Web Part To Use For This Connection drop-down list. The actions listed will vary depending on the type of Web Part you originally chose.

For this example, you originally chose a Form Web Part, so the only action will be Provide Form Field Data To. Select this action, and then click Next.

10 Figure 38-8 shows the second page of the wizard. Because the Form Web Part will control the Car Club Inventory Web Part, and because both of these Web Parts are on the same page, select Connect To A Web Part On This Page, and then click Next.

Figure 38-8. Use this wizard page to specify where a Web Part Connection should send data.

11 Figure 38-9 shows the third page of the wizard.

Figure 38-9. Use this wizard page to specify which Web Part should receive data from the connection, and what action it should take.

Review these two settings, and then click Next:

- **Target Web Part** Select the Web Part that should respond to the action you chose in step 10. In this example, Car Club Inventory is the only other Web Part on the page and is therefore the only choice.

- **Target Action** Choose the action you want the target Web Part to perform. The wizard will show only actions that the target Web Part can perform when the source action from step 10 occurs. In this example, Get Sort/Filter From is the only choice. Take it.

12 At this point, depending on the options you previously chose, the wizard might diverge from the screen shots you see in this example. For this example, however, the fourth page of the wizard will resemble Figure 38-10.

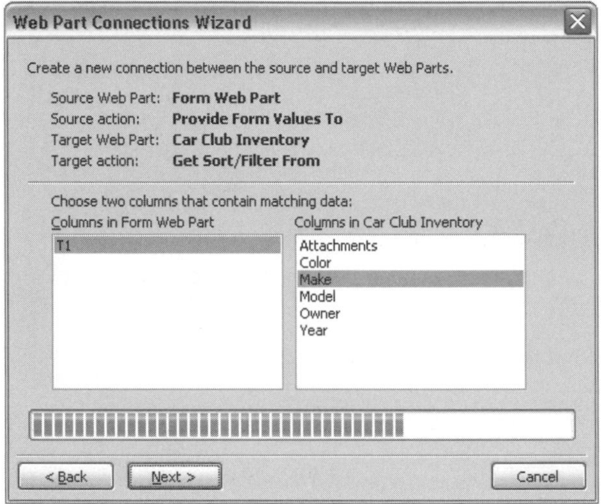

Figure 38-10. This wizard page specifies which elements from one Web Part should filter the contents of another Web Part.

To complete this page, you must associate the text box in the Form Web Part with the Car Club Inventory column you want to filter:

- The text box has the default name T1, so select that name in the Columns In Form Web Part list.
- The object of the example is to filter the Make column, so select Make in the Columns In Car Club Inventory list.

13 Click Next to display the final page of the wizard, which appears only for confirmation. If the page contains the following information, click Finish. Otherwise, click the Back button and correct your work.

- **Source Web Part** Form Web Part.
- **Source Action** Provide Form Field Data To.
- **Target Web Part** Car Club Inventory.
- **Target Action** Get Sort/Filter From.

14 Choose Properties from the File menu, set the Title field to Cars By Make, and click OK.

15 Right-click the Web Part named Web Part Page Title Bar, choose Web Part Properties from the shortcut menu, set the Title field to Cars By Make, and click OK.

16 Right-click the Web Part named Web Part Form, choose Web Part Properties from the shortcut menu, set the Title field to Enter Make and click OK.

17 Save the Web page, taking care to use the .aspx file extension. Then choose Preview In Browser from the File menu. Figure 38-11 shows the results.

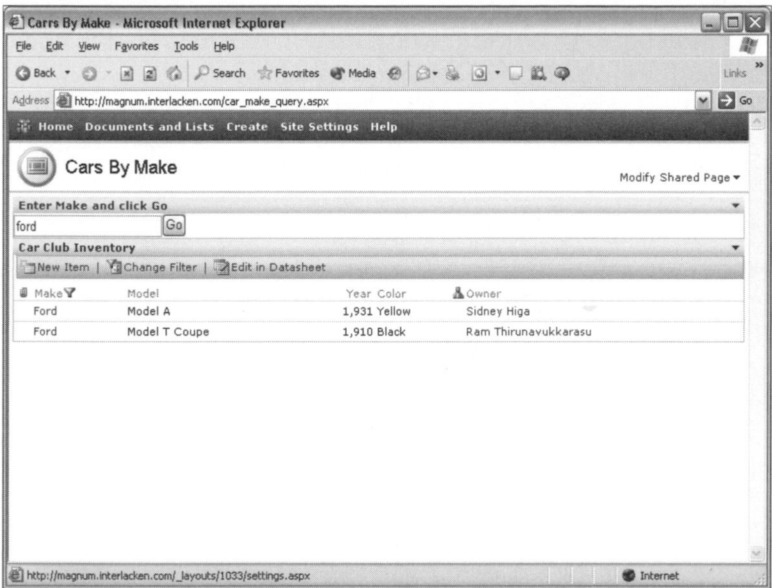

Figure 38-11. In this page, a Web Part Form connects to a Data View Web Part and controls the extent of a query.

Troubleshooting

FrontPage might report existing views as nonexistent

When you use FrontPage to add a Web Part to a Web Part Page, the Web Part might contain the following message rather than the usual sample content:

View may not exist. The page you selected refers to a view that does not exist. It may have been deleted by another user. Click "home" at the top of the page to return to your Web site.

In some cases, despite the error message, the view actually exists. To work around this apparent bug, save, close, and reopen the Web Part Page.

In Figure 38-11, the visitor wanted to see only Ford cars, and therefore typed **Ford** in the text box and clicked Go. The display then changed to display only Ford cars.

Once a Web Part is either the source or the target of a connection, right-clicking it and choosing Web Part Connections displays the Web Part Connections dialog box, shown in Figure 38-12.

- To add a new connection, click the Add button. This starts the Web Part Connections Wizard.
- To modify an existing connection, select it, and then click the Modify button. This reruns the Web Part Connections Wizard.
- To delete an existing connection, select it, and then click the Delete button.

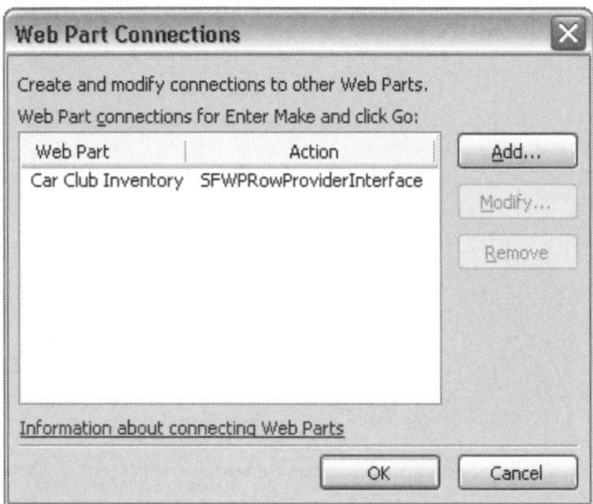

Figure 38-12. This dialog box configures Web Part Connections for Web Parts that have one or more connections already.

Creating Data Sources and Data Views

As you've already seen, Windows SharePoint Services makes easy work of displaying almost any data stored within a SharePoint site. This is true regardless of whether you're accessing SharePoint with a browser or creating Web Part Pages in FrontPage.

Inevitably, however, you're sure to want some additional flexibility in what data you can access, and in what formats you can display it. SharePoint—and therefore FrontPage—provides two features, named Data Sources and Data Views, that do exactly that.

Accessing the Data Source Catalog

The first step in using a Data View is to tell SharePoint where the data resides. You do this by recording its location in a *Data Source Catalog*. To view the Data Source Catalog in any Windows SharePoint Services site, perform these steps:

1. Open the site in FrontPage, and then open any page in the site.
2. Choose Insert Data View from the Data menu, or choose Data Source Catalog from the title bar drop-down list of any task pane.

This displays the Data Source Catalog task pane, shown in Figure 38-13.

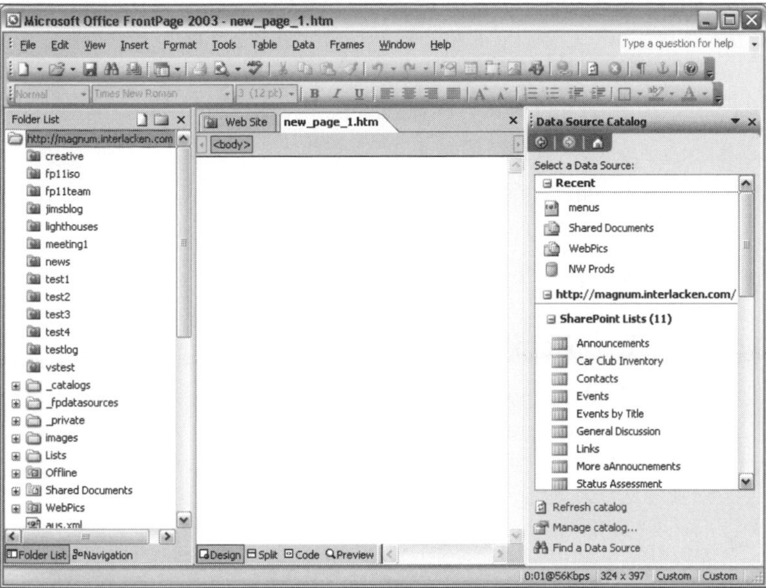

Figure 38-13. The Data Source Catalog lists all data sources available within a Windows SharePoint Services site.

The Data Source Catalog task pane groups data sources into seven general categories. These are:

- **Recent** The last few data sources you've used. This makes them easy to locate, should you need to use them again.
- **SharePoint Lists** Lists in the current SharePoint site, such as Announcements, Events, Links, and custom lists.
- **SharePoint Libraries** Document and picture libraries in the current SharePoint site.
- **Database Connections** Databases and tables located outside the current SharePoint site. These can be SQL Server databases and tables located at any accessible network location, or any other database accessible by OLE DB. Examples in this latter category include Microsoft Access and Oracle.
- **XML Files** Files that store data in XML format.
- **Server-Side Scripts** Web locations that return data in XML format.
- **XML Web Services** Online services that use Simple Object Access Protocol (SOAP) to handle information requests.

To view the data sources within each category, click the plus sign to the left of the category name.

To search for a data source by name:

1. Display the Find A Data Source task pane.
2. Use the Search drop-down list to select the site that contains the data source. For sites hosted on Windows SharePoint Services, the current site will be the only choice.
3. In the For box, enter any string of characters that the name of the data source contains.
4. Click the Search Now button.
5. To work with any data source that appears in the Search Results list, right-click it, and choose a command from the shortcut menu.

The following sections explain how to use each type of data source.

Working with SharePoint Lists and Libraries

SharePoint lists and libraries appear automatically in their respective categories. If you need a new list or library, you can create it using either a browser or FrontPage. To create a SharePoint list in FrontPage, proceed as follows:

> **Tip** To create a list or library while browsing a SharePoint site, click Create on the menu bar of any page.

1. Display the Data Source Catalog task pane.
2. If a plus sign appears to the left of the SharePoint Lists category, click it.
3. Click the Create New SharePoint List link at the bottom of the category list. This displays the SharePoint List dialog box, shown in Figure 38-14.

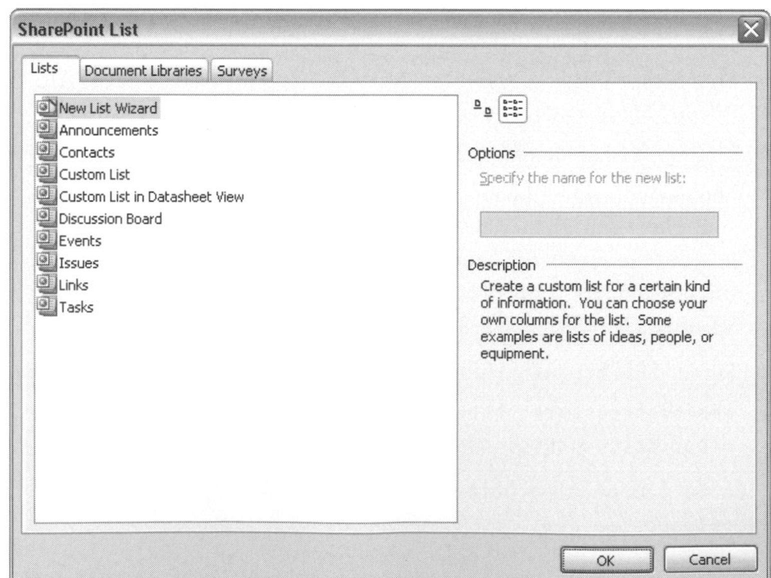

Figure 38-14. FrontPage can create SharePoint lists as easily as the normal Web pages, but with more flexibility.

4. To create a standard list type, click any entry on the Lists tab except New List Wizard. Under Options, on the right in the dialog box, give the new list a name, and click OK.
5. To create a custom list, select New List Wizard, and then click OK. The wizard will prompt you for a list name, description, features, fields, and security settings.

The procedure for creating a new document library or survey is quite similar. To create a new library:

1. Click the Create A New Document Library link that appears within the SharePoint Libraries category.
2. When the SharePoint List dialog box appears, make sure that the Document Libraries tab is selected.
3. To create a standard library type, click any entry on the Document Libraries tab except New Document Library Wizard. Under Options, on the right in the dialog box, give the new library a name, and click OK.
4. To create a custom library, select New Document Library Wizard, and then click OK. The wizard will prompt you for a list name, description, features, fields, and security settings.

To create a new survey, click either link, select the Surveys tab, and then select New Survey Wizard or Survey. The new survey will appear in the SharePoint Lists category.

Creating a SharePoint list or library automatically creates a corresponding data source. To view all the properties of any list or library and change some of them:

1. Right-click the list or library, and then choose Properties from the shortcut menu. This will display the Data Source Properties dialog box, shown on the left in Figure 38-15.

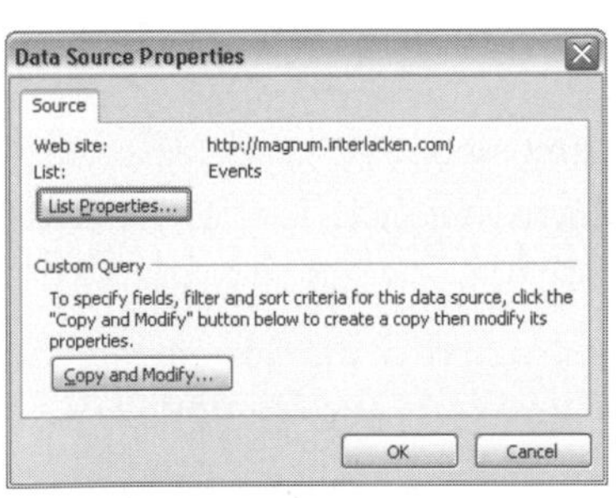

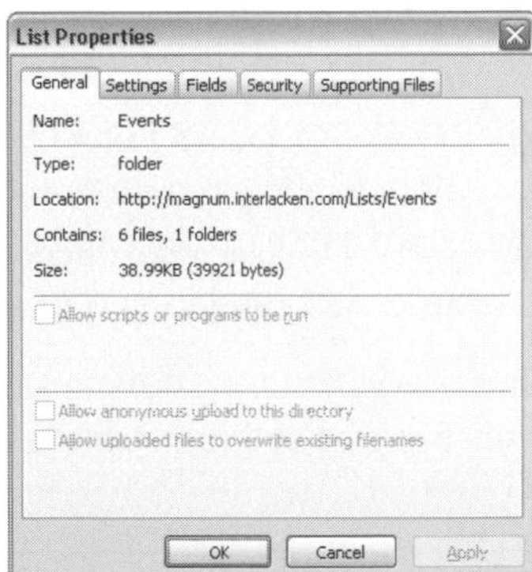

Figure 38-15. The Data Source Properties dialog box on the left provides options to modify an existing data source or create a new, similar one. Clicking the List Properties button displays the dialog box on the right.

2. Click the List Properties button to display the List Properties dialog box, shown on the right in Figure 38-15. The Settings, Fields, Security, and Supporting Files tabs display list settings, many of which you can modify.

If you find that you can't modify the data source property you want to change (or if you're working with a library, in which case the List Properties button will be dimmed), you might need to create a new data source that accesses the existing list in a new way. To pursue this approach, click the Copy And Modify button in the Data Source Properties dialog box. This displays the Data Source Properties dialog box shown in Figure 38-16.

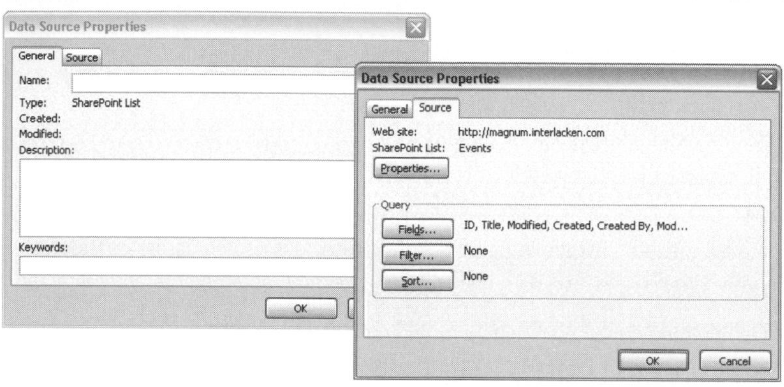

Figure 38-16. This figure shows both tabs in the Data Source Properties dialog box. The General tab provides identifying information, and the Source tab provides entry to detailed configuration.

Initially, the Source tab will be selected. Use the following buttons to configure the new data source as you want it:

- **Properties** Displays the List Properties dialog box shown on the right in Figure 38-15.
- **Fields** Displays an Included Fields dialog box where you can add or remove fields from the data source.
- **Filter** Displays a Filter Criteria dialog box where you can specify criteria for displaying some records and bypassing others.
- **Sort** Displays a Sort dialog box where you can specify which fields determine the order of display.

When you've finished configuring these settings, click the General tab, shown on the left in Figure 38-15, give the new data source a name, enter any description or keywords you want, and click OK.

> **Tip** The Name field on the General tab of the Data Source Properties dialog box shows the modified name of the data source. The SharePoint List field on the Source tab shows which SharePoint table actually contains the data.

You can also perform a Copy And Modify operation by clicking any data source in the Data Source Catalog and then choosing Copy And Modify from the shortcut menu.

Data sources you create by using either Copy And Modify command don't appear as lists or libraries when Web visitors browse the site. They're strictly for use in development environments like FrontPage. Of course, the data is fully visible on any Web pages you create using the data source.

Working with Database Connection Data Sources

The Database Connections section of the SharePoint Data Source Catalog provides access to data that resides in databases outside of SharePoint. Such databases might be part of mission-critical or *ad hoc* systems within your organization. They can also provide a "middle ground" where several SharePoint sites can share data.

Note Unlike Windows SharePoint Services, SharePoint Portal Server 2 has built-in facilities whereby multiple SharePoint sites can share data and otherwise interact.

Initially, a SharePoint site won't contain any database connections. To use such a connection, you or someone else with sufficient privileges must explicitly create it. Here's the procedure:

1. Open the site in FrontPage, open a Web page, and display the Data Source Catalog task pane.
2. Scroll down to the Database Connections section, and then click the Add To Catalog link.
3. When the Data Source Properties dialog box shown in Figure 38-17 appears, click the Configure Database Connection button. This displays the Configure Database Connection dialog box shown on the left in Figure 38-18.

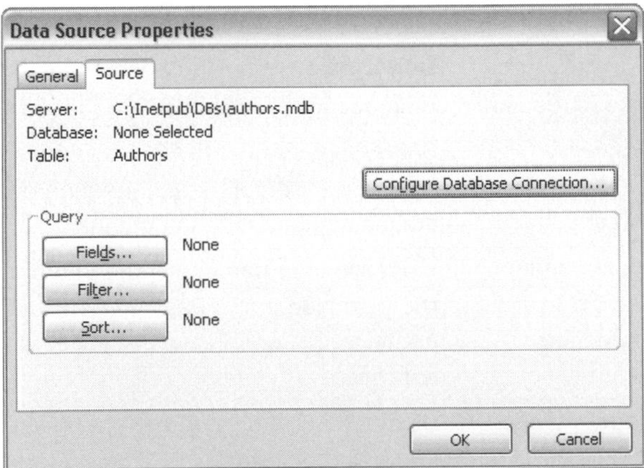

Figure 38-17. Notice the difference between this Source tab and the one on the left in Figure 38-16. This tab applies to a database connection. The Query frame won't appear until you configure a connection.

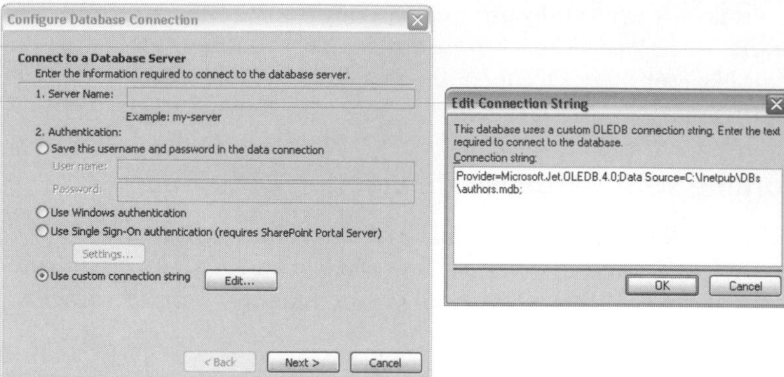

Figure 38-18. To configure a connection to a SQL Server database, fill in the Server Name and Authentication areas. To create an OLE DB database connection, click the Edit button, and fill in the Edit Connection String dialog box on the right.

4 To access a SQL Server database, make the following entries:

- **Server Name** Enter the name of the server where the database resides and, if necessary, a backslash and the instance name. Typically, you need to specify an instance name when two or more copies of SQL Server are running on the same computer, or for MSDE databases. The syntax in that case is <server-name>\<*instance-name*>. By default, SharePoint Setup installs an MSDE database with the instance name *SharePoint*
- **Authentication** Choose one of the options described in Table 38-2.

Table 38-2. Data Source Authentication Options

Option	Description
Don't Attempt To Authenticate	Uses the same credentials as the SharePoint site itself. (This option isn't available for database connection data sources.)
Save This Username And Password In The Data Connection	Uses the user name and password in the User Name and Password boxes, no matter which team member accesses the database.
Use Windows Authentication	Uses the current team member's user name and password.
Use Single-Sign-On Authentication (Requires SharePoint Portal Server 2)	Instructs SharePoint Portal Server to supply the user name and password for accessing the database.

5 To access a non–SQL Server database, select the Use Custom Connection String option, and click the Edit button.

When the Edit Connection String dialog box shown on the right in Figure 38-18 appears, enter the OLE DB connection string required to access the database. This figure shows a typical connection string for a Microsoft Access database. The general format for an Oracle connection string is shown here:

```
Provider=SDAORA;Data Source=<service-name>;
User ID=<username>, Password=<password>
```

Click OK to close the Edit Connection String dialog box.

6 Click Next to display the Configure Database Connection dialog box shown in Figure 38-19, and then configure these options:

- **Database** Select the database that contains the data you want. (For Access databases, root will be the only choice.)
- **Use Custom Query** Select this check box and click the Edit button to enter a SQL statement that returns the data you want. This option and the next are mutually exclusive.
- **Table, View, Or Stored Procedure** Select the listed item that contains the data you want.

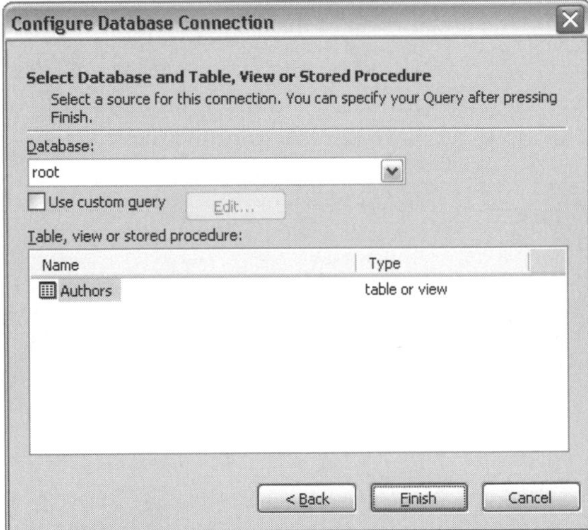

Figure 38-19. Selecting a database and a table or query is the last step in creating a database connection.

7 Click Finish to return to the Data Source Properties dialog box shown previously in Figure 38-17. Configure the Fields, Filter, and Sort options if you want.

8 Click the General tab of the Data Source Properties dialog box (shown previously in Figure 38-15). Enter at least a name—and possibly a description and keywords—and then click OK to add the connection to the Data Source Catalog.

For information about filtering and sorting information in a data source, refer to "Filtering Data Views" and "Sorting and Grouping Data Views," later in this chapter.

Note that the connection string for an Access database specifies a file location accessible to the Web server. This excludes locations within a SharePoint site, because everything within a SharePoint site physically resides in database records. This includes Web pages, lists, document libraries, and any other files you see in FrontPage. If the Access database resides on a file server elsewhere in your network, specify a UNC file name (\\<*servername*>\<*sharename*>\...), and ask the Web server administrator to configure your site so that ASP.NET impersonates a domain account with Update permissions on that UNC name.

For Oracle databases, the computer running your SharePoint site must contain both the Microsoft Oracle driver and the client software that Oracle provides (that is, SQL*NET).

Working with XML File Data Sources

If your SharePoint site has access to suitably formatted XML files, you can add the files to the Data Source Catalog and display their contents almost as if they were databases. Here's the procedure:

1. Display the Data Source Catalog of the SharePoint site that needs access to the data.
2. Scroll down to the XML Files portion of the catalog, and then click its Add To Catalog link.
3. When the Data Source Properties dialog box shown in Figure 38-20 appears, click the Browse button, and locate the XML file you want to access.

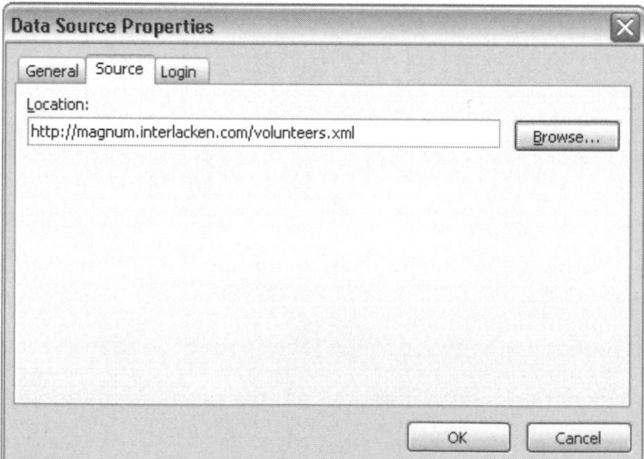

Figure 38-20. An XML file data source can reside in the current site or at a file location.

4. If accessing the XML file requires logon credentials beyond those of the SharePoint site, select the Login tab, shown in Figure 38-21, and choose one of the options described previously in Table 38-2.

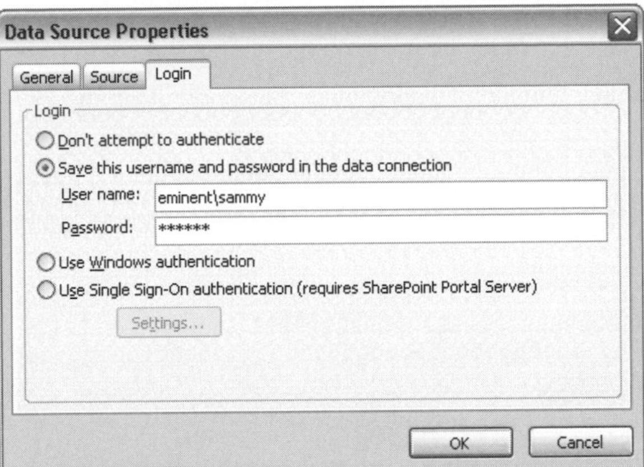

Figure 38-21. Use the Login tab to specify any special credentials required to access a data source.

5 Select the General tab, give the data source a name, and click OK to save it as you did for the preceding data source types.

Troubleshooting

The XML file, server-side script, or XML Web service data source appears empty

When you define a data source that refers to an XML file, a server-side script that delivers XML, or an XML Web service, the data source might fail to operate and might seem empty, even though data exists. This could occur for any of the following reasons:

- The XML source fails to contain both a schema section and a data section.
- The schema section doesn't conform to the W3C's XML-Data specification.
- The data in the data section fails to conform with the schema in the schema section.

Here are two ways of creating acceptable XML files. Unfortunately, both require programming skills:

- Use the .NET Framework *XMLWriter* class to save the contents of a .NET Framework *DataTable* object as XML.
- Save the contents of a classic ADO *Recordset* object by using its *Save* method with a *PersistFormat* of *adPersistXML*.

Working with Server-Side Script Data Sources

The Server-Side Script section of a Data Source Catalog identifies Web-based programs that send XML rather than HTML in response to a Web visitor's request. Such programs might be ASP or ASP.NET "pages," but the results are essentially useless for human interpretation.

Are you starting to discern a pattern to this process? Open the Data Source Catalog, scroll down to Server-Side Scripts, and click the Add To Catalog link. Yet another variation of the Data Source Properties dialog box will appear, this time resembling Figure 38-22.

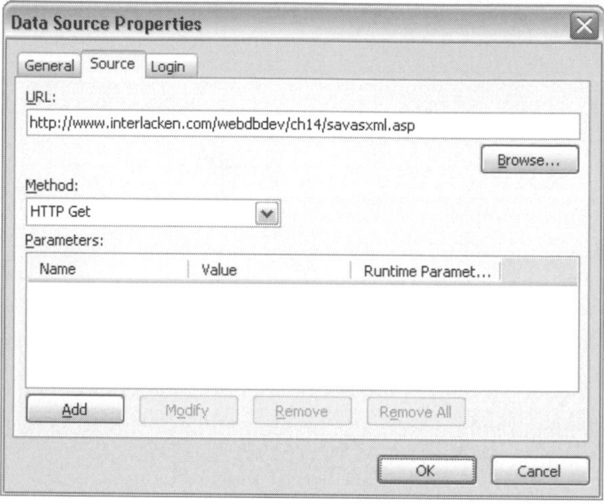

Figure 38-22. When retrieving XML from a server-side script, you might also need to specify an HTTP request method and parameters.

Configure these options:

- **URL** Specify the URL of the server-side script. To do this by pointing and clicking, click the Browse button.
- **Method** Specify the type of request the server-side script expects to receive. The GET method appends any parameter names and values to the URL, whereas the POST method sends them in the body of the request.
- **Parameters** Use the Add, Modify, and Remove buttons to specify any parameters that the server-side script needs to operate. These might be key values, for example.

As before, use the Login tab to specify access credentials and the General tab to give the data source a name and save it.

Working with XML Web Service Data Sources

An XML Web Service is a specialized program on a Web server that both receives requests and transmits responses in XML format. To configure such a service, click the Add To Catalog link in the XML Web Services section of the Data Source Catalog to display the version of the Data Source Properties dialog box shown in Figure 38-23.

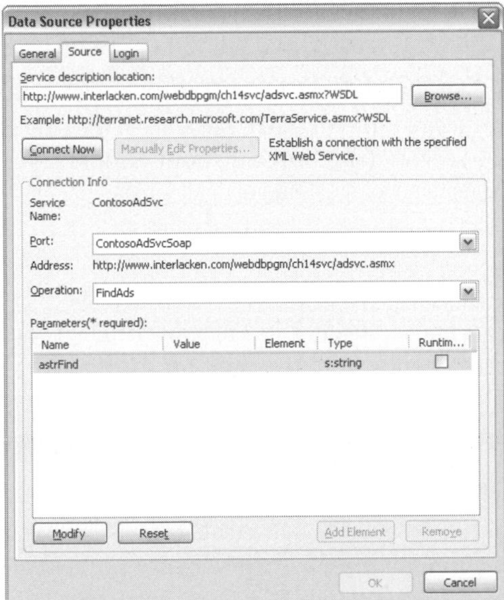

Figure 38-23. This figure is a composite. The portion above the Connection Info area appears before you click Connect Now, and the portion below appears after.

To use this dialog box, you must know the URL that requests the Web Service Description Language (WDSL) description of the XML Web service. This is a description, in XML format, of the Web service's capabilities. For Web services running on a Microsoft server, it's usually the address of the Web service plus *?WDSL*. For services running on other operating systems, it might be a URL with a .wsdl file extension. Armed with this information, continue as follows:

1 Enter the WSDL URL in the Service Description Location box, and then click Connect Now.

2 Within a moment or two, the title on the Connect Now button should change to Disconnect, and various controls in the Connection Info area will change from dimmed to enabled. Configure these settings:

   - **Port** Select the application protocol you want to use for accessing the Web service. The choices listed are those that the Web service's WSDL claimed will work. If there's a choice that involves SOAP (such as the ContosoAdSvcSoap choice in this figure), that should be your preference.
   - **Operation** Select what you want the Web service to do. Again, the choices listed are those that the Web service's WSDL identified.
   - **Parameters** The dialog box will automatically display the name of any parameter the Web service requires or accepts for the operation you specified. Again, this information comes from the Web service's WSDL. To configure the permanent or default value of any parameter, select it and click the Modify button near the bottom of the dialog box.

Once again, use the Login tab to specify access credentials, and use the General tab to give the data source a name and save it.

For an XML Web service to work as a SharePoint data source, it must return data in the same specific XML format that SharePoint sites require for XML file and server-side script data sources. If you configure an XML Web service data source without error and yet receive no data, this is probably the reason.

Accessing Data Source Details

To modify and test a data source, locate and right-click its entry in the Data Source Catalog task pane. Then choose one of these commands from the shortcut menu:

- **Insert Data View** Adds a Data View Web Part to the current Web page—a Web Part that displays information from the current data source. For more information about using Data View Web Parts, skip to the next section.
- **Show Data** Displays a Data View Details task pane that summarizes the properties of the data source and displays the contents of a record. Figure 38-24 shows an example. The row that reads roughly *(N) Row [2/3] < >.* *[2/3]* means that the current row is number 2 of 3. Click the arrows to move forward or backward one record.

> **Tip** The Show Data command provides a quick and easy way to test any data source. Just right-click the data source, choose Show Data from the shortcut menu, and see whether any data results. Then verify that the data is what you expect.

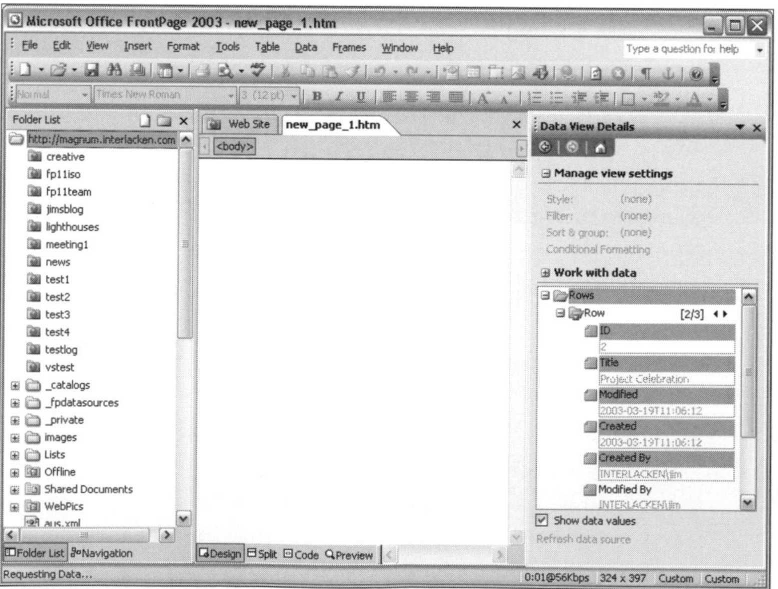

Figure 38-24. The Data View Details task pane summarizes the settings for one view of a data source. It can also query and display the underlying data one record at a time.

- **Copy And Modify** Create a new, modified version of the data source.
- **Move To** Moves the data source definition to another SharePoint site. This is only possible if the Web server is running SharePoint Portal Server 2.
- **Save As** Saves a copy of the data source definition as an XML file. However, this isn't possible for SharePoint lists and libraries.
- **Mail Recipient (As Attachment)** Starts Microsoft Office Outlook and creates an e-mail message that includes the data source definition as an attachment. To complete the operation, enter the recipient's e-mail address, compose a message body, and click Send. Again, this isn't possible for SharePoint lists and libraries.
- **Remove** Deletes the data source definition but not any lists, libraries, databases, XML files, server-side scripts, or XML Web services it refers to.
- **Properties** Displays the Data Source Properties dialog box so that you can review and modify the data source definition.

Creating and Configuring Data View Web Parts

As interesting as creating Data views might or might not be, they add nothing to your SharePoint site by themselves. The payback comes when you use them to create *Data View Web Parts*. A Data View Web Part makes the contents of a data source visible in a Web Part Page.

> **Note** Data View Web Parts use XML style sheets (XSL) to transform the XML from a data source into HTML for display. Some people refer to this process as "using an XSL Transform" or "using XSLT." The format for an XML style sheet is, of course, XML. To view all this XML, or even modify it, open the Web Part Page in FrontPage, and then switch to Code view.

Adding a Data View Web Part to a Page

Here's the procedure for adding a Data View Web Part to a page in the simplest possible way:

1. Open your SharePoint site. If no data source exists for the data you want to display, create one as described in the section "Creating Data Sources and Data Views," earlier in this chapter.
2. Open a new, empty Web page. To take maximum advantage of the styles built into a Data View Web Part, this page should use one of the templates from the Web Part Pages tab of the Page Templates dialog box. The Full Page, Vertical template is usually a good choice.
3. Click the spot where you want the displayed data to appear. In you started from a Web Part Pages template, this would be the Click To Insert A Web Part link in any Web Part Zone.
4. If no task pane is displayed, choose Web Part from the Insert menu, or press Ctrl+F1. Then select Data Source Catalog from the drop-down menu in the task pane's title bar.
5. Right-click the data source you want to display, and then choose Insert View from the shortcut menu.

Within a few seconds, Design view should display your new Web Part, complete with a representative amount of data. The task pane will also change to show the Data View Details task pane for the data source you selected. Figure 38-25 shows the FrontPage window after a designer created a Data View Web Part that displays the site's Announcements list.

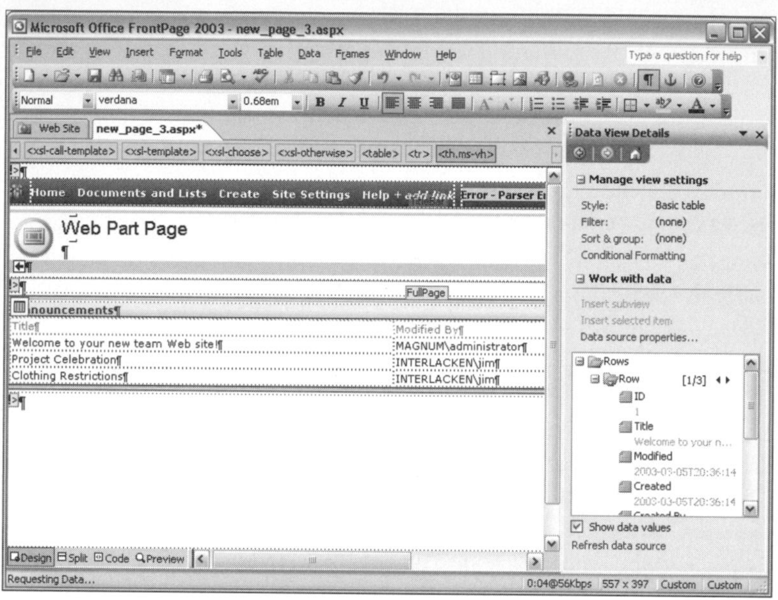

Figure 38-25. Data View Web Parts display data even in Design view. This makes it easy to visualize what a Web visitor would see.

You can also create Data View Web Parts directly from the Data View Details task pane. This method is interesting because is provides more control over the initial results. Proceed as follows.

1. In the Data Source Catalog task pane, right-click the data source you want to use, and then choose Show Data from the shortcut menu.
2. In the Data View list box, select the columns you want to appear in the Web page:
   - To select all the columns, click either the Rows or the Row line.
   - To select specific columns, click the first one, and then Ctrl+click each additional column.
3. In the open Web page, set the insertion point where you want the Data View Web Part to appear.
4. In the Data View Details task pane, click the Insert Data View link just under the Work With Data heading. (This link appears as Insert Subview in Figure 38-25 because in that figure, the Data View already exists.)

To refresh the data in a Data View Web Part that appears in Design view, select it, and then choose Refresh from the Data menu.

Adding, Deleting, and Formatting Data View Columns

Because a Data View Web Part is such special component, you might think that you couldn't manipulate its details using ordinary FrontPage commands. In fact, you can. To format the data in a column, for example, select the contents of any cell in that column, and then use commands from the Format menu or the Formatting toolbar. Any change you make to data in one row will apply to all rows. Here are some additional; actions you can perform:

- To delete a column, select all its cells, and then choose Delete Columns from the Table menu.
- To relocate a column, select all its cells, and then drag it to the location you want.

The procedure for adding a new column is a little more complicated. Proceed as follows:

1. Take either of these actions:
   - Select the Data View Web Part, and then display the Data View Details task pane.
   - Right-click the Data View Web Part, and then choose Data View Properties from the shortcut menu. This also displays the Data View Details task pane.
2. Create a blank column where you want the new column values to appear. For example, right-click the column to the right of where you want the new column to be, and then choose Insert Columns from the shortcut menu.
3. Set the insertion point inside any detail cell in the new column. (A *detail cell*, in this sense, is a cell in a row that displays data values.) Don't set the insertion point inside the header row, for example.
4. To display data from any column as text, select the column name in the Data View Details task pane, and then click the Insert Selected Item link in that task pane.
5. To specify a format for the column data, right-click the column name in the Data View Details task pane, and then choose one of these commands from the shortcut menu:
   - **Insert As Text** Formats the data as ordinary text.
   - **Insert As Rich Text** Formats the data as rich text (that is, with features such as boldface, italics, and fonts intact).
   - **Insert As Boolean** Format the data as True or False.
   - **Insert As Hyperlink** Formats the data as a hyperlink. This requires that the data itself be a URL.
   - **Insert As Picture** Displays the data as a picture. This requires that the data itself be a picture.

Enhancing Data View Web Parts

Once the Data View Web Part exists, you can use the Data View Details task pane to modify its properties. To begin, right-click the Data View Web Part you want to configure, and then choose Data View Properties from the shortcut menu. Finally, click one of the following links. Additional subtopics will describe the first five links in more detail.

- **Style** Changes the appearance and capabilities of the Data View Web Part.
- **Filter** Restricts the records that the Data View Web Part displays.
- **Sort & Group** Controls the order and groups in which the Data View Web Part displays records.
- **Conditional Formatting** Applies special formatting based on data values.
- **Insert Subview** Adds a Data View Web Part to each row of another Data View Web Part. This is useful for displaying data in a header/detail relationship.
- **Insert Selected Item** Adds a column to an existing Data View Web Part.

For more information about adding columns to an existing Data View Web Part, refer to "Adding, Deleting, and Formatting Data View Columns," earlier in this chapter.

- **Data Source Properties** Displays the Data Source Properties dialog box for the current data source.
- **Show Data Values** If selected, the list box displays data values as well as data structures. If cleared, the list box displays data structure only.
- **Refresh Data Source** Reloads the list box, taking into account any changes to the data source that might have occurred.

Controlling Data View Styles

To modify the general appearance of a Data View Web Part, first select it, and then take one of these actions:

- Click the Styles link in the Data View Details task pane.
- Choose Style from the Data menu.

This will display the View Styles dialog box, shown in Figure 38-26.

Use these guidelines to choose the style you want on the General tab:

- **Choose A View Type** On the Web, HTML view is usually the only choice. Datasheet view displays data in an Excel-like table, and Calendar view displays dated information in calendar format. Both of these latter views require the use of special ActiveX controls.
- **HTML View Styles** Choose the data arrangement you want. SharePoint provides over a dozen options, which you can view by scrolling down the list of previews. Clicking any preview displays a verbal description near the bottom of the dialog box.

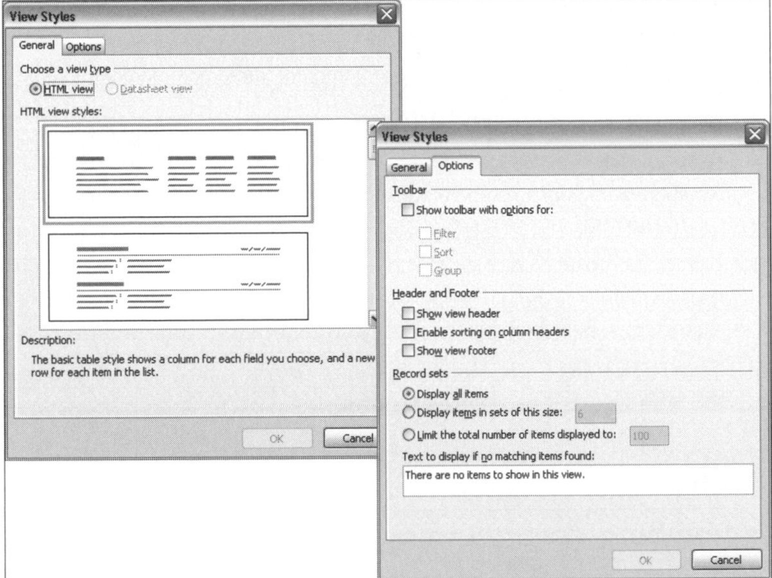

Figure 38-26. The General tab of the View Styles dialog box controls the overall arrangement of elements. The Options tab controls toolbar, header and footer, and paging options.

The Options tab controls these additional settings:

- **Show Tool Bar With Options For** Select this check box to display a toolbar between the Web Part's title bar and its column headings:
  - **Filter** Select this check box to provide a toolbar button that visitors can use to restrict the records on display.
  - **Sort** Select this check box to provide a drop-down list of column names. When the visitor selects a column name, SharePoint sorts the data on that column.
  - **Group** Select this check box to provide another drop-down list of column names. When the visitor selects a column name, SharePoint sorts and groups the data on that column. (If the visitors also choose a sort field, SharePoint sorts the data within each group on that field.)
- **Header And Footer** Use these controls to modify the arrangement of header and footer lines:
  - **Show View Header** Select this check box to provide an extra line above the column headings. This line can contain whatever text you want—just be sure to enter the text in Design view.
  - **Enable Sorting On Column Headers** Select this check box if it's all right for Web visitors to sort the display on any column by clicking its heading.
  - **Show View Footer** Select this check box to display an extra line after the last row of data. Again, this line can contain whatever text you want.

- **Record Sets** Use these settings to control settings related to the number of records available for display:
  - **Display All Items Together** Select this check box to display all available records in one continuous list.
  - **Display Items In Sets Of This Size** Select this check box to display a fixed number of records at a time. SharePoint will provide Next and Previous links to scroll through all the records.
  - **Limit The Total Number Of Items Displayed To** Specify the maximum number of records to display. (Displaying thousands or even hundreds of records can be very slow in terms of transmission time and in formatting time.)
  - **Text To Display If No Matching Items Found** Enter a message that informs the Web visitor if no records are available.

Filtering Data Views

To restrict the display to records with certain data values, select the Data View Web Part, and then do either of the following:

- Click the Filter link in the Data View Details task pane.
- Choose Filter from the Data menu.

This displays the Filter Criteria dialog box, shown in Figure 38-27.

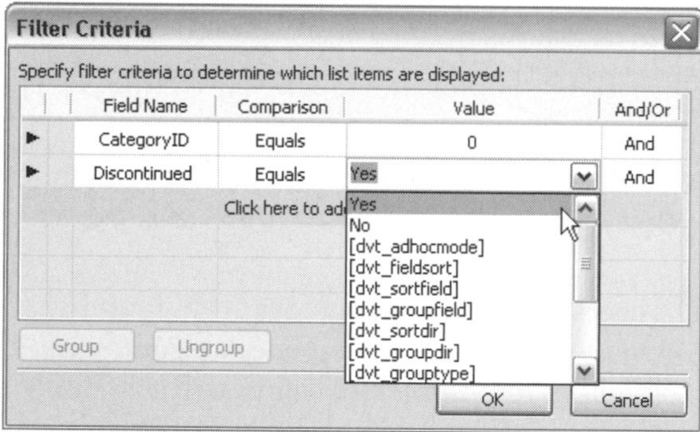

Figure 38-27. To configure criteria, specify a field name, comparison, and value for each comparison. The value can be a constant or any field name from the drop-down list.

This dialog box displays any number of filter clauses (that is, any number of comparisons). Here's the procedure for adding a filter clause:

1. Click the Click Here To Add A New Clause line. This will appear in the first line of the grid that doesn't already contain a clause.
2. FrontPage will add a line to the grid and display a drop-down list in the Field Name column. Select a field name from the drop-down list.

3 Selecting a field name will set the Comparison column to Equals. If this isn't acceptable, click the cell in the Comparison column, and choose a different condition from the resulting drop-down list. The possibilities include Equals, Not Equals, Is Null, Not Null, Less Than, Greater Than, and so forth.
4 Click the cell in the Value column, and then hand-type a value or choose one from the drop-down list. To compare against the value of another field, select its name from the drop-down list.
5 Choose a grouping condition from the And/Or column.

The effect of multiple clauses is fairly obvious if you join them all with And conditions or join them all with Or conditions. The effect of mixing And and Or conditions is much less obvious. To avoid any confusion, select two or more criteria you want SharePoint to evaluate first, and then click the Group button. In Figure 38-28, for example, the designer entered all three conditions, then selected the last two (by Shift+clicking their arrows), and then clicked the Group button. This makes it fairly obvious that SharePoint should display only records with a *UnitPrice* value greater than 10, and a *CategoryId* value of 0 or 1.

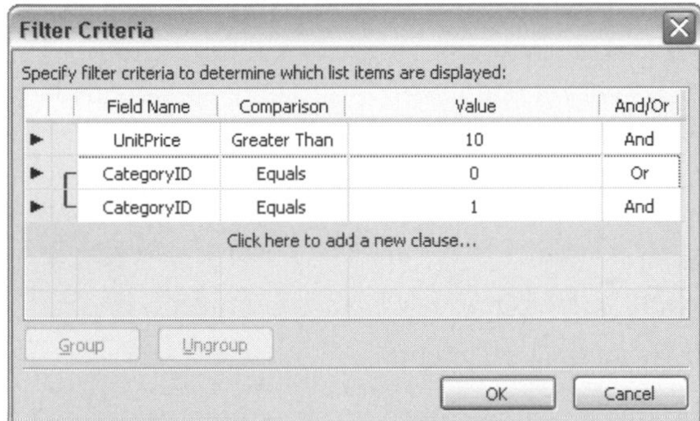

Figure 38-28. To group a series of comparisons, as if surrounding them in parentheses, select all the comparisons, and then click Group. This view shows the result of grouping two comparisons.

Sorting and Grouping Data Views

Figure 38-29 shows how a Data View Web Part appears to the Web visitor when common grouping options are in effect.

- Because this page groups by *SupplierID*, it sorts by *SupplierID* as well.
- A gray bar called the *group header* denotes the start of each group.
- Another gray bar called the *group footer* denotes the end of each group.
- The Web visitor can expand or collapse the group (that is, display or suppress the individual records) by clicking a plus or minus sign in the group header.
- Within each group, the records appear in *ProductName* order.

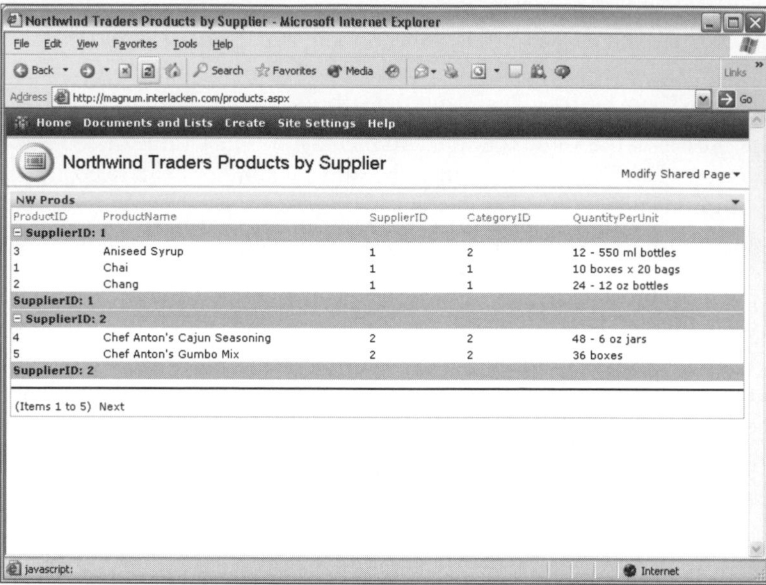

Figure 38-29. Grouping displays header and footer bars like these around all records with equal values in designated fields.

To configure options such as these, select the Data View Web Part, and then take either of these actions:

- Click the Sort & Group link in the Data View Details task pane.
- Choose Sort And Group from the Data menu.

This displays the Sort And Group dialog box, shown in Figure 38-30.

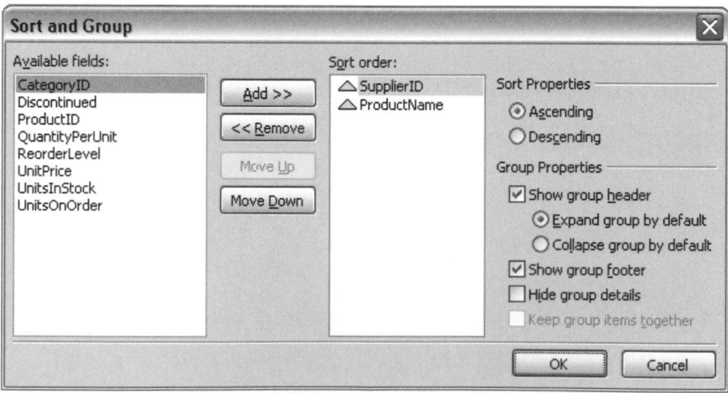

Figure 38-30. This dialog box controls which fields participate in sorting and grouping.

Here's how to use the controls in this dialog box:

- **Available Fields** This list itemizes all fields not currently involved in sorting or grouping. To involve a field in sorting or grouping, either double-click it or select it and click the Add button.
- **Sort Order** This list itemizes all fields currently involved in sorting or grouping:
  - To remove a field, select it and click the Remove button.
  - To increase the significance of a field, select it and click the Move Up button. This moves the field one position higher in the list.
  - To decrease the significance of a field, select it and click the Move Down button.
- **Sort Properties** Use these options to change the direction of sorting:
  - **Ascending** To sort on a field in increasing order, select the field in the Sort Order list, and then select this option.
  - **Descending** To sort on a field in decreasing order, select the field in the Sort Order list, and then select this option.

Tip Double-clicking any field in the Sort Order list toggles its Sort property between Ascending and Descending.

The settings in the Group Properties section apply individually to each field in the Sort Order list. To view or modify the settings for a specific field, select that field. Here are the available settings:

- **Show Group Header** Select this check box to display a gray bar at the beginning of each group:
  - **Expand Group By Default** Select this option if you want each record in a group to be visible when the display first appears.
  - **Collapse Group By Default** Select this option if you want each record in a group to be hidden when the display first appears.
- **Show Group Footer** Select this check box to display a gray bar at the end of each group.
- **Hide Group Details** Select this check box to display group headers only, with no possibility of viewing the individual records in each group.
- **Keep Group Items Together** Select this check box to display all records in the same group on the same Web page. This might result in some pages displaying more items than the limit you specified in the Options tab of the View Styles dialog box shown previously in Figure 38-26.

Applying Conditional Formatting to a Data View

This feature changes the appearance of a field value based on its contents. For example, you can make negative numbers appear in red, specified values appear in boldface, or values outside a certain range invisible. To make use of conditional formatting:

1. In any Data View Web Part:
   - Right-click any instance of the field you want to format, and then choose Conditional Formatting from the shortcut menu.
   - Select any instance of the field you want to format, and then display the Conditional Formatting task pane.
   - Select any instance of the field you want to format, and then choose Conditional Formatting from the Data menu.

Note Don't try any of these procedures with a column heading; they won't work.

2. When the Conditional Formatting task pane appears, click the Create button, and choose one of these commands from the shortcut menu:
   - **Show Content** Choose this command to specify conditions under which column values will be visible.
   - **Hide Content** Choose this command to specify conditions under which columns values will appear empty.
   - **Apply Formatting** Choose this command to specify when values should have an alternative appearance.
3. When the Condition Criteria dialog box shown in Figure 38-31 appears, configure the condition or conditions you want to detect. For details, refer to the procedure for configuring the Filter Criteria dialog box, shown previously in Figure 38-27.

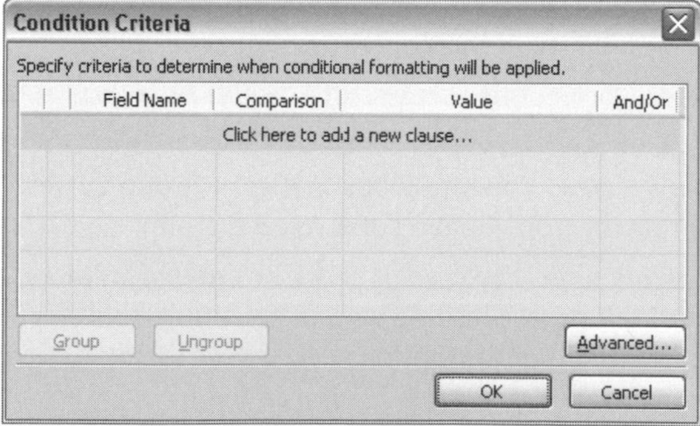

Figure 38-31. Setting criteria for conditional formatting involves the same process as setting filtering criteria.

You can base conditional formatting of one field on the value of the same field, a different field, or several fields.

4 Click OK. If you chose the Apply Formatting command in step 2, FrontPage will display the Modify Style dialog box, shown in Figure 38-32. To apply styles, click the Format button, and then choose Font, Paragraph, Border, Numbering, or Position.

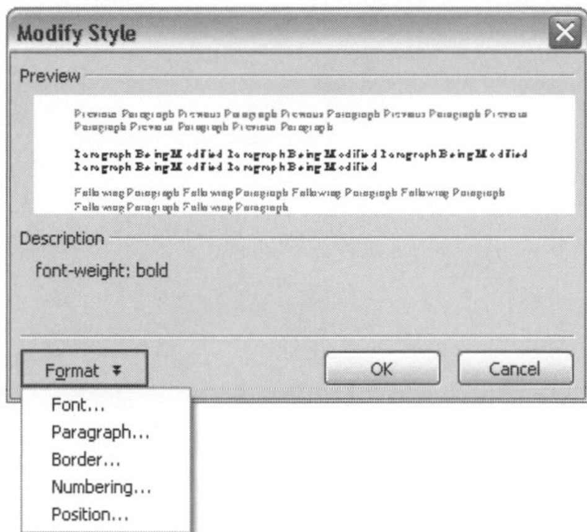

Figure 38-32. Conditional formatting can apply any CSS style attribute to the data on display.

This dialog box works exactly like the Modify Style dialog box that configures CSS styles for a normal HTML element, except that you can't apply named styles such a style selectors, class selectors, and ID selectors. You can only configure inline styles.

For more information about configuring CSS style properties, refer to "Assigning Style Sheet Properties," on page 602.

5 When you've finished applying styles, click OK.

The Conditional Formatting task pane will display each conditional formatting rule you define. Figure 38-33, for example, shows the display for two rules: one that applies formatting and one that hides content. Any data that Design view displays will reflect the rules in effect, as will the entire Web page if you view it in your browser.

A single Data View Web Part can contain as many conditional formatting rules as you want. To create more, just repeat the preceding procedure. However, if you create multiple rules for the same field, try to avoid overlaps. It's fine, for example, to create two rules on the same field, one for values of 0 to 10 and another for values of 11 to 50. But if you create one rule for 0 to 10 and another for 0 to 50, the Web Part might not apply them in the order you expect.

Clicking any rule displays a drop-down menu with these choices:

- **Edit Condition** Redisplays the Condition Criteria dialog box so that you can modify the criteria for the rule.
- **Modify Style** Redisplays the Modify Style dialog box so that you can modify the styles that an Apply Formatting rule assigns.
- **Delete** Eliminates the rule.

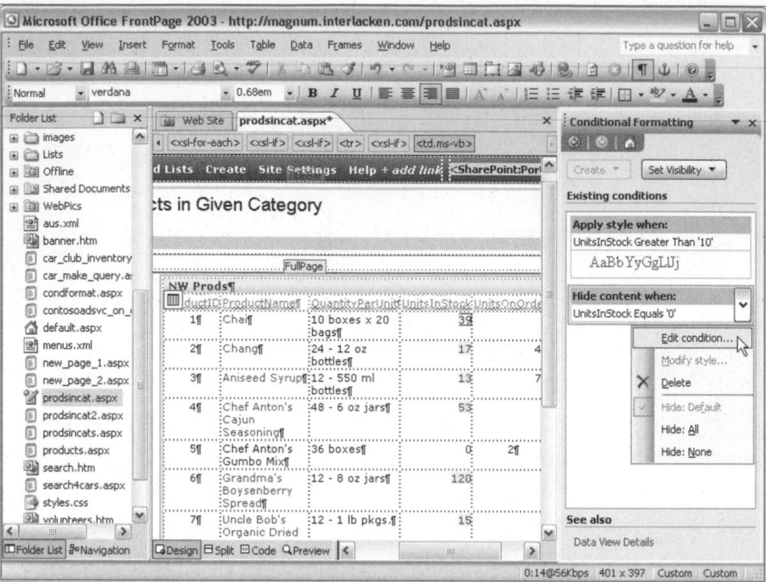

Figure 38-33. The Conditional Formatting task pane displays each conditional formatting rule in effect for a page.

The next three commands on the drop-down menu override or restore the rule's condition or effect. This can be helpful for seeing the effect of a rule even if no matches occur in the current data and for checking the values of a field that a rule hides. The exact commands vary according to the type of rule.

- For Show Content rules, the three commands are:
  - **Show: Default** The rule will display data in accordance with the condition you specified.
  - **Show: All** The rule will ignore the condition you specified and display data in all cases.
  - **Show: None** The rule will ignore the condition you specified and hide data in all cases.
- For Hide Content rules, the following commands will appear:
  - **Hide: Default** The rule will hide data in accordance with the condition you specified.
  - **Hide: All** The rule will ignore the condition you specified and hide data in all cases.
  - **Hide: None** The rule will ignore the condition you specified and show data in all cases.

- For Apply Formatting rules, the following commands will appear:
  - **Apply: Default** The rule will format the data in accordance with the condition you specified.
  - **Apply: All** The rule will ignore the condition you specified and apply the formatting you specified in all cases.
  - **Apply: None** The rule will ignore the condition you specified and never apply the formatting you specified.

The Set Visibility button at the top of the Conditional Formatting task pane provides more global control over the effect of rules. To use this facility, click the button, and then choose one of these commands from the resulting drop-down menu:

- **Default** All rules will operate in accordance with their current settings.
- **All Formatting Hidden** No rules will apply. The Web Part will display data as if no rules existed.
- **All Formatting Visible** All rules will apply, regardless of conditions.

Again, these options are for testing. It's difficult, for example, to verify that a Hide rule is working properly when you can't see the data. To see what data the Hide rule is suppressing, you could choose either All Formatting Hidden from the Set Visibility menu or Hide: None from the rule's menu. Afterward, of course, you would choose Default from the same menu so that the rule would resume normal operation.

Inserting Subviews

Normally, each row of a Data View Web Part displays one value in each column. In most cases, this is quite adequate, but it presents a problem if your data source contains repeating regions of XML data within other repeating regions. This would be the case if, for example, your data source provides information about book authors, and the record for each author contains a list of the books written by that author.

A Subview is essentially a Data View Web Part that appears inside one cell of another Data View Web Part. To display repeating data in a Subview, proceed as follows:

1. Open a new or an existing Web Part Page.
2. Add a Data View Web Part that displays the ordinary columns from the data source. (*Ordinary columns*, in this sense, are those that contain a single data value in each row.)
3. Add a new column to the Data View Web Part. For example, right-click anywhere in an existing column, and then choose Insert Columns from the shortcut menu.
4. Set the insertion point inside the new column, but not inside the header row.

5 Right-click the existing Data View Web Part, and choose Data View Properties from the shortcut menu. This will display the Data View Details task pane.

6 Select the field or fields you want the Subview to display, and then, under the Work With Data heading, click the Insert Subview link. Within a few moments, Design view will display data in the Subview column.

> **Note** If the Insert Subview link is dimmed, the Data View Details task pane is probably displaying a different data source than the current Data View Web Part. A Subview and the Data View Web Part that contains it must use the same data source.

7 To change the appearance of the Subview, select any column value and then choose Style from the Data menu. This displays the View Styles dialog box, shown previously in Figure 38-26. Configure the style you want, and then click OK.

Figure 38-34 shows a Web Part Page displaying a data view web part that includes a Subview.

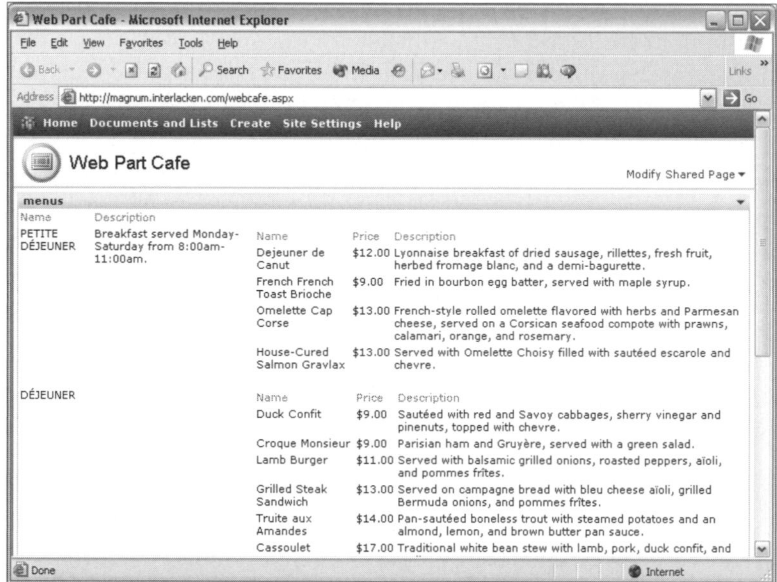

Figure 38-34. The data in the three leftmost columns of this Data View Web Part come from a Subview. There are zero to many Subview items for each main item at the left.

Using Web Part Connections to Display Header/Detail Structures

The fact that a Subview must use the same data source as the Web Part that contains it is a major limitation. It prevents you, for example, from displaying header and detail data from separate tables. If this is what you want to do, proceed as follows:

1. Add separate Data View Web Parts for the header and detail tables.
2. Set up a Web Part Connection from the header Web Part to the detail Web Part.

Figure 38-35, shows an example of this technique. Clicking any category in the Data View Web Part on the left displays products in that category in the Data View Web Part on the right.

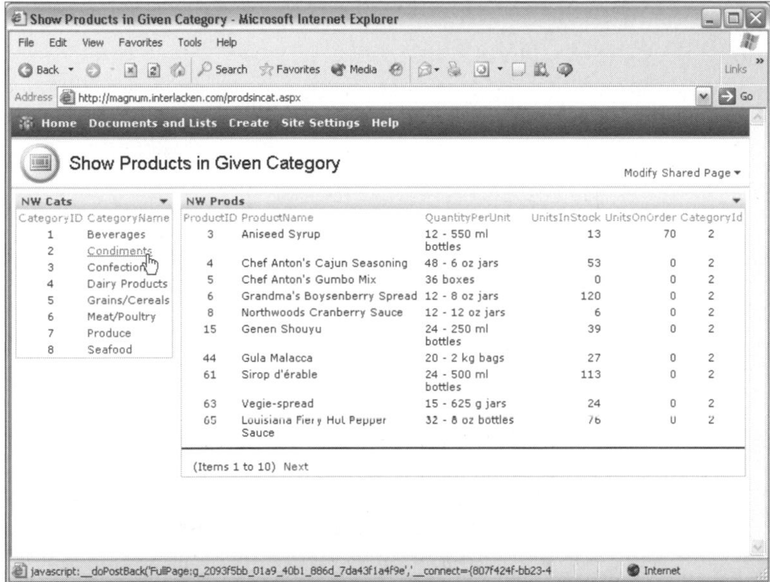

Figure 38-35. When you click any category in the NW Cats Web Part, a Web Part Connection tells the NW Prods Web Part to filter its display by that category.

The Web Part Connection settings in this page are:

- **Source Web Part** NW Cats.
- **Source Action** Provide Data Values To Another Web Part.
- **Target Web Part** NW Prods.
- **Target Action** Filter This View Using Data Values.
- **Columns That Contain Matching Data** CategoryID = CategoryID.

For more information about configuring Web Part Connections, refer to "Connecting Web Parts," earlier in this chapter.

In Summary...

This chapter explained how to create and use a variety of Windows SharePoint Services resources, including Web sites, Web Part Pages, Web Part Zones, data sources, and Data views. In addition, it explained how to add Web Parts to a Web Part Page, and how to use Data View Web Parts for displaying data from a variety of sources. Combining the powerful features of Windows SharePoint Services with the ease and familiarity of FrontPage for designing Web pages results in a powerful development environment for many kinds of applications.

The next chapter will explain how FrontPage can help you manage the activities of several designers working on the same Web site.

Chapter 39

Managing Design Teams

Every day, it seems, Microsoft FrontPage–based Web sites and Web sites in general get larger and larger. Couple that with the natural law that says, "The more work you have to do, the sooner it needs to get done," and eventually you find yourself working in a group rather than alone. Of course, this leads to the minor chaos and pandemonium that groups everywhere seem to experience.

If you have a server-based Web site or a disk-based Web site residing on a file server, several people can access the same Web site at the same time. This is far from being a problem; in fact, it's something Microsoft Office FrontPage 2003 has special features to support:

- **Tasks view** Maintains a list of pending work items for the current Web site. FrontPage can create such tasks as part of other functions, associate these tasks with specific Web pages, and prompt for task status when a designer saves the associated page.
- **Workflow status and reporting** Records the following items for each page in a FrontPage-based Web site: Assigned To, Assigned By, Assigned Date, Review Status, Reviewed By, and Review Date. By viewing reports that display these fields, you can instantly check on the status and progress of assigned changes.
- **Document control over publishing** Provides a Publish/Don't Publish indicator for each file in a FrontPage-based Web site. This is useful when some parts of a Web site, but not others, are ready for publication.
- **Document Check-In and Check-Out** Reserves a file on behalf of one designer so that others can't make conflicting updates.

Although less powerful than full-scale project management and source control systems, these features are highly integrated with FrontPage and provide all the functions many small projects need. At the very least, they can record the status of each Web page in process so that team members working on the same site can avoid stepping on each other's work.

Working with Tasks View

Developing and maintaining any Web site involves a multitude of small, interrelated tasks. Changes made to one page require updates on another. New pages require links from others. Errors in spelling, missing pictures, and hyperlinks to nowhere require follow-up and correction. To keep track of these pesky details, you need a task list.

As shown in Figure 39-1, FrontPage provides an automated, highly integrated Tasks view, which displays a list of pending tasks for the current site. You can create tasks either manually as you think of them or automatically as a result of other processes.

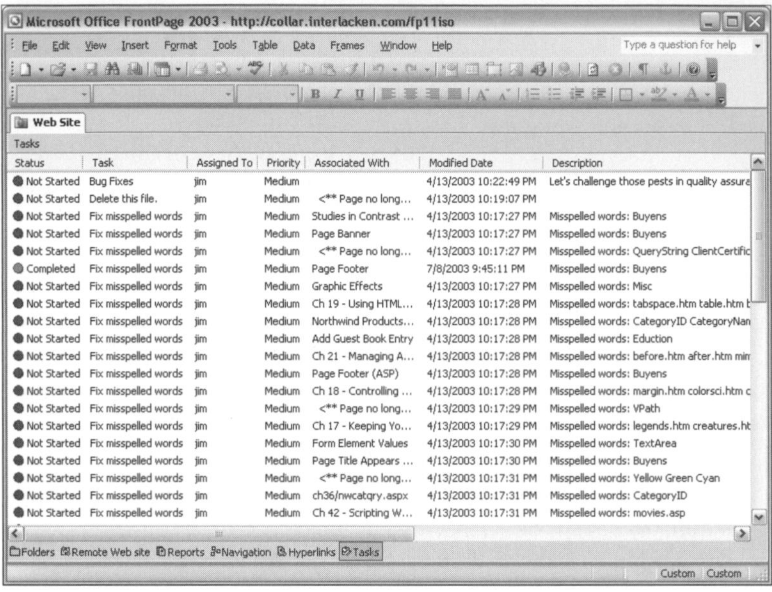

Figure 39-1. FrontPage's Tasks view helps you remember unfinished tasks in a highly integrated way. As you resolve each issue, you can mark the task complete.

The Tasks view column headings are straightforward. Clicking any column heading sorts the list on that column. To display the Tasks List, click the Tasks icon on the Views bar.

Creating Tasks Manually

FrontPage provides a variety of convenient ways to create tasks. Here's how to create a task manually:

1. Display the New Task dialog box, shown in Figure 39-2, using any of these methods:
   - In any FrontPage view, choose Tasks from the Edit menu, and then choose Add Task.
   - In any FrontPage view, click the down arrow for the Create A New Normal Page button on the Standard toolbar, and then choose Task.
   - In Tasks view only, right-click any blank area in the main Tasks window, and choose Add Task from the shortcut menu.

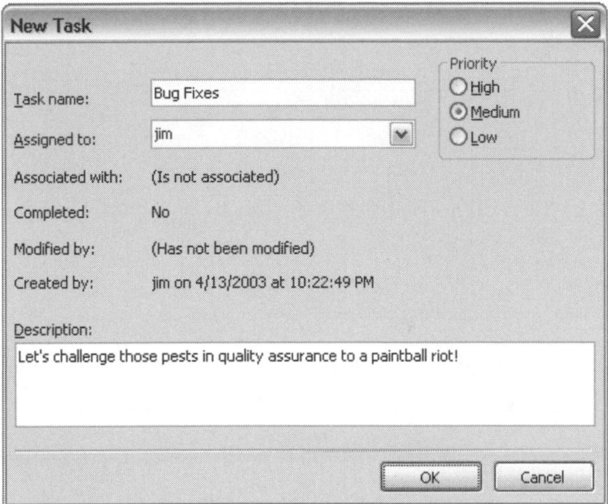

Figure 39-2. Use this dialog box to create new tasks.

2 When the New Task dialog box appears, enter a title in the Task Name box.
3 In the Priority section, select High, Medium, or Low.
4 Choose a name from the Assigned To drop-down list.
5 Optionally, enter a comment in the Description box, and then click OK.

Creating Tasks Associated with a Specific File

Notice that in Figure 39-2, the Associated With field indicates no link. This is because no file was selected when the designer created the task. To manually create a task associated with a specific file, you must select the file before creating the task. For example:

- Locate and select the page in the Folder List or anywhere in Folders, Remote Web Site, Reports, Navigation, or Hyperlinks view.
- Open the page in Design view, and set the focus in the open page.

In addition, in the Page Templates dialog box, you can create a New Page task rather than the new page itself.

Creating Tasks Automatically

Certain global FrontPage operations also create tasks. For example, you can check the spelling in your entire Web site and, rather than stopping at each error, simply create tasks pointing to any pages that contain errors. Here's a complete list of the ways FrontPage can create tasks automatically:

- **Pages that contain spelling errors.** Set the insertion point anywhere outside the Design view editing window, and then choose Spelling from the Tools menu. This displays the Spelling dialog box shown here. If you select Add A Task For Each Page

With Misspellings, FrontPage creates a task for each page containing so much as a single misspelled word.

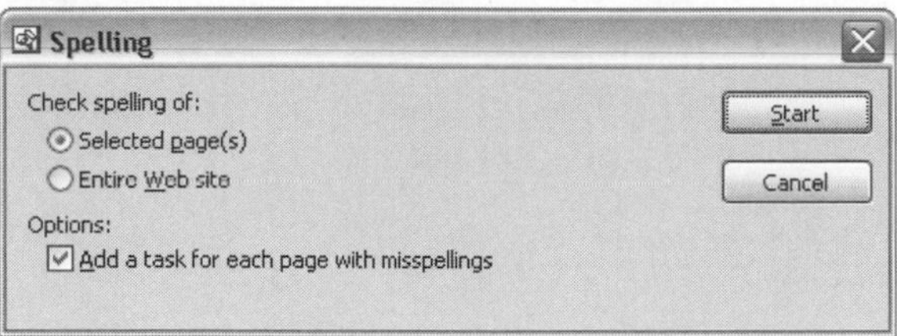

- **New pages that need detail filled in** When FrontPage creates a new page, it can either open the page immediately or create a blank page and a task reminding you to edit the page later. Figure 39-3 shows how a designer might create a hyperlink to a new page. (Notice that the designer selected the Just Add Web Task check box.)

For more information about creating new pages, refer to "Creating a New Web Page," on page 187.

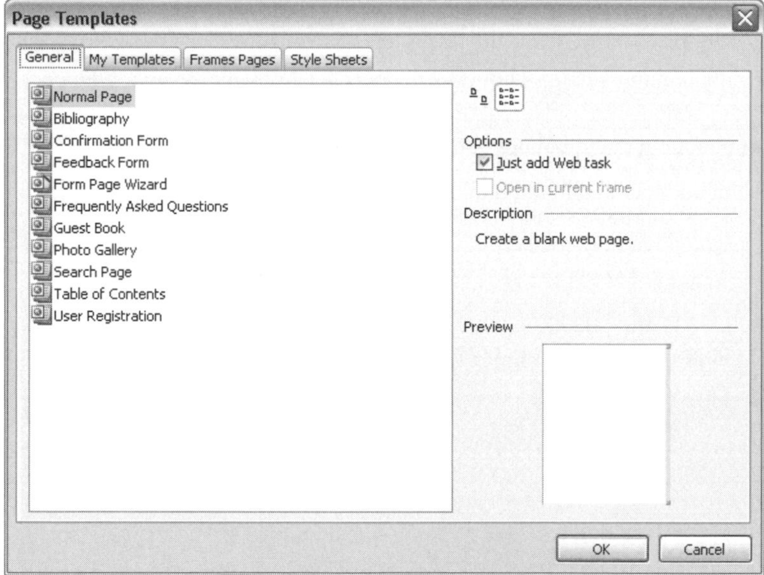

Figure 39-3. FrontPage uses the Page Templates dialog box to create new Web pages. The Just Add Web Task option adds an entry to the Tasks List rather than opening the new page.

Working with Tasks

Tasks view behaves in most respects like any report in Reports view. Clicking the column headings sorts the report on that heading. Single-clicking the Task, Assigned To, Priority, and Description fields in any row opens those fields to editing.

By default, Tasks view displays only tasks that are Not Started or In Progress. To display completed tasks as well, choose Tasks from the Edit menu and then choose Show History, or right-click a blank area in the main Task window and choose Show History from the shortcut menu. Right-clicking a task in Tasks view displays the shortcut menu shown here:

The commands on this menu work as follows:

- **Edit Task** Displays the Task Details dialog box, which is similar to the New Task dialog box shown in Figure 39-2. Here you can modify the properties of a task. You can display this dialog box by doing either of the following:
  - Double-click the task you want to edit.
  - Choose Tasks from the Edit menu, and then choose Edit Task.
- **Start Task** Opens a task's associated file, if any, with the appropriate editor, such as Design view for an HTML page. You can also perform this action by doing either of the following:
  - Click the Start Task button in the Task Details dialog box
  - Choose Tasks from the Edit menu, and then choose Start Task.
- **Mark Complete** Changes the task's status to Completed. You can also make this change by choosing Tasks from the Edit menu and then choosing Mark Complete.
- **Delete Task** Removes a task from the list after you confirm your choice. Pressing the Delete key accomplishes the same result.

Choosing the Start Task command by any means tells FrontPage to open the associated file (if there is one). Then, after you change and save the file, FrontPage displays the message box shown here, asking whether your changes satisfy the task's requirements. Clicking Yes instructs FrontPage to mark the task completed.

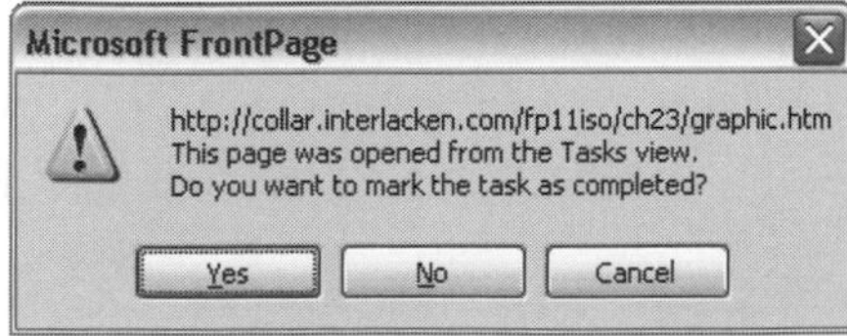

Chapter 39

Controlling and Reporting Workflow Status

Tasks view records who's assigned to various tasks involving pages, but it doesn't show overall responsibility, overall status, review responsibility, or review status. FrontPage includes several features related specifically to these areas. All involve data that you enter in the Properties dialog box for files in a FrontPage-based Web site. Figure 39-4 shows this dialog box.

Figure 39-4. The Workgroup tab in a file's Properties dialog box specifies the file's assigned designer and review status.

To display this dialog box:

1 Right-click any file in the Folder List or in Folders, Remote Web Site, Reports, or Hyperlinks view, and choose Properties from the shortcut menu.
2 Click the Workgroup tab.

For pages open in Design view, you can display an equivalent tab by choosing Properties from the File menu and then selecting the Workgroup tab.

Here are the properties available on the Workgroup tab:

- **Available Categories** Lists the category names defined within the current Web site:
  - If the current page already belongs to a given category, FrontPage automatically selects the corresponding check box.
  - To assign additional categories, select the corresponding check box.
  - To create or delete categories, click the Categories button.

  A list of all categories assigned to the current file appears in the Item(s) Belong To These Categories box.

For more information about the use of categories, refer to "Categories," in Appendix D, and "Using the Table of Contents Based On Page Category Component," on page 727.

- **Assigned To** Specifies who's assigned to work on this file. You can either type the name by hand or select it from the drop-down list. Clicking the Names button displays the dialog box shown on the left in Figure 39-5, which adds designers to or deletes them from the list.

Figure 39-5. To add or remove names in the Assigned To list for a file's workgroup properties, click Names to display the dialog box on the left. To modify the Review Status choices, click Statuses to display the dialog box on the right.

Whenever it changes the Assigned To field for a file, FrontPage records the name of the designer making the change, the date, and the time. This is where the Assigned Date and Assigned By columns in Figure 39-6 come from.

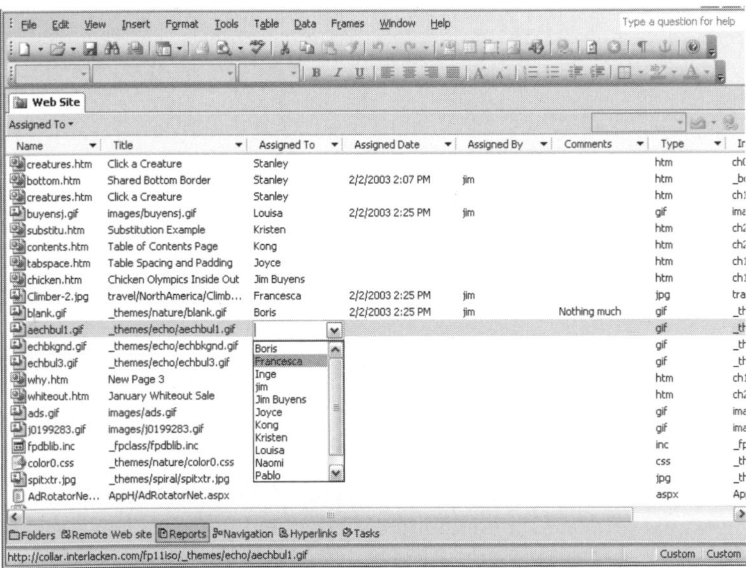

Figure 39-6. The Assigned To report lists each file in a FrontPage-based Web site, showing who is currently assigned, by whom, and when.

Figure 39-6 shows the FrontPage Assigned To report. To locate all files assigned to a specific person, click the Assigned To column heading, and then scroll down to that name. You can also change the Assigned To field directly in this report by first selecting the correct line and then single-clicking the Assigned To field.

On the CD

For more information about the Assigned To report, refer to “Assigned To,” in Appendix D.

- **Review Status** Records the results of the most recent review for the current file. As with Assigned To, either type the review status or select it from the drop-down list. FrontPage records the given status, plus the user name, date, and time.

  Clicking the Statuses button in the dialog box shown in Figure 39-4 displays the dialog box shown on the right in Figure 39-5. As with the Usernames Master List dialog box, in this dialog box, you can add statuses, remove them, or reset the list.

  Figure 39-7 shows the Review Status report, which summarizes the review status of each file in the current Web site.

For more information about the Review Status report, refer to “Review Status,” in Appendix D.

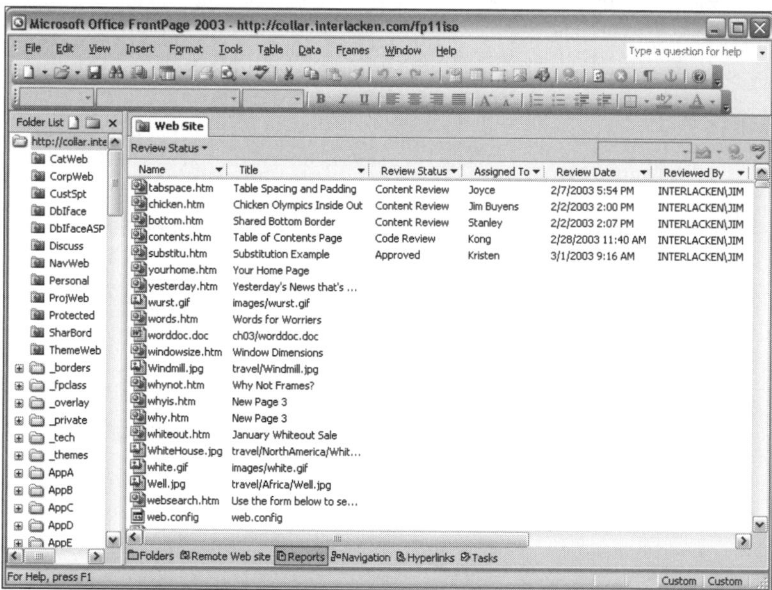

Figure 39-7. The Review Status report lists the status, reviewer, and date for each file in a FrontPage-based Web site.

- **Exclude This File When Publishing The Rest Of The Web** Prevents (if selected) or permits (if cleared) publication of the current file when you run the Publish Web Site command. The next section explains this further.

Controlling Publishing at the Document Level

The Exclude This File When Publishing The Rest Of The Web check box, on the Workgroup tab of a file's Properties dialog box (Figure 39-4), prevents publishing of the current file to another FrontPage-based Web site. To prevent publishing of the current file, select this check box. To allow publishing, clear the check box. You can also control this setting by right-clicking any file in the Design view Folder List, in Folders view, in Remote Web Site view, or in Reports view, and then choosing the Don't Publish option on the shortcut menu.

This feature doesn't affect your ability to import, move, or copy the given file, even among different FrontPage-based Web sites or servers. It affects only the operation of the FrontPage Publish feature.

For more information about the Publish feature, refer to Chapter 16, "Publishing Your FrontPage-Based Web Site."

The Publish Status report, shown in Figure 39-8, shows which files are enabled and disabled for publishing. You can also update publishing status directly in this report. In this figure, an update is in progress where the drop-down list appears.

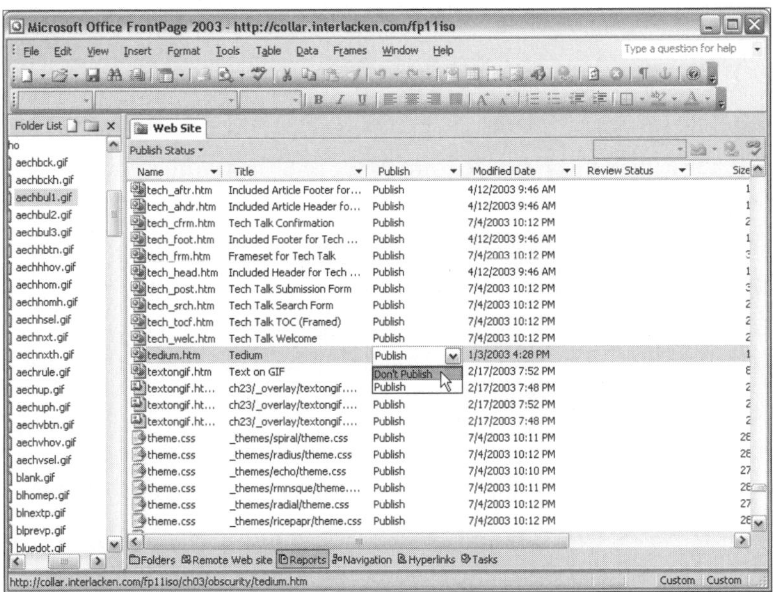

Figure 39-8. The Publish Status report shows which pages in a Web site are enabled or disabled for publishing to another FrontPage-based Web site or server.

On the CD

For more information about the Publish Status report, refer to "Publish Status," in Appendix D.

Using Document Check-In and Check-Out

When several people work on the same Web site, there's always a chance that two people might start working on the same page at the same time. The result is a duel between versions; whoever saves the file last overlays the first person's updates.

To compound the problem, changing a Web site page can take days or weeks if the change is part of a general site upgrade or requires multiple approvals. Of course, that doesn't mean that someone's going to keep the page open in FrontPage all that time, but it does mean that the designer wants the file safe from being updated by other people during that interval.

Document Check-In and Check-Out provides an answer to this problem. Here's how this feature works:

1. The Web site's administrator turns on the Document Check-In and Check-Out feature. The procedure for doing this appears later in this section.
2. Before a designer begins changing a file, he or she checks the file out (that is, takes ownership by using a shortcut menu option). This does two things:
   - It prevents any other designer from making changes to the file.
   - It saves a copy of the file for possible restoration.
3. After the file is checked out, it shows up as locked to other designers and administrators of the same Web site. If they try to open the file, they'll get an error message with two options: either give up editing the file or open a read-only copy. They can save the read-only copy under another name, but they can't update the checked-out original.
4. When the designer who checked out the file is finished with any updates, he or she can take either of two actions:
   - Check the file in, which relinquishes ownership and deletes the backup copy.
   - Undo the checkout, which restores the backup copy (undoing all changes) and then relinquishes ownership.

Document Check-In and Check-Out is optional for the following environments:

- Disk-based Web sites
- Server-based Web sites using the FrontPage 2000 Server Extensions
- Server-based Web sites using the FrontPage Server Extensions 2002

In addition, Document Check-In and Check-Out is always in effect for Web sites running on Microsoft Windows SharePoint Services.

For environments where Document Check-In and Check-Out is optional, the options that control it appear on the General tab of the Site Settings dialog box. To display this dialog box, choose Site Settings from the Tools menu, and then click the General tab. Figure 39-9 provides an example.

Figure 39-9. The Use Document Check-In And Check-Out option in this dialog box makes the use of source code control for a FrontPage-based Web site available or unavailable.

To configure Document Check-In and Check-Out, specify these settings:

- **Use Document Check-In And Check-Out** Select this check box to activate Document Check-In and Check-Out. Clear the check box to disable it.
- **Check Out Files From The Remote Web Site** Select this option if the current Web site is actually a local copy of a shared site.

  To appreciate this option, imagine that you and several other designers are working on the same Web site. A single remote site contains the master copy of the site in progress, but each designer works on a local copy. Checking out a file on the local site accomplishes nothing, because no other designers access the local site. But if FrontPage records checkins and checkouts on the remote site, they apply to all designers who configure their local sites to check out files from that remote site.

  This option will be dimmed if you haven't configured a remote Web site location that corresponds to the current Web site. To configure the location of a remote site, close the Site Settings dialog box, switch to Remote Web Site view, and click the Remote Web Site Properties button.
- **Check Out Files From The Local Web Site** Select this option if you and several other developers update the current site directly.

  This option is always in effect for Windows SharePoint Services sites.

- **Prompt To Check Out File When Opening A Page** Select this check box if you want FrontPage to display the following prompt whenever you open a page that you haven't already checked out:

  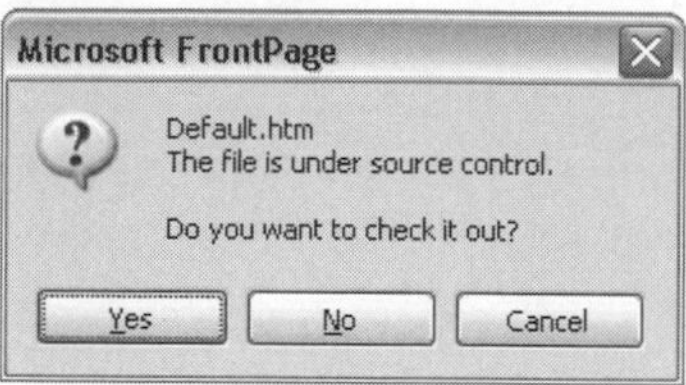

  Clicking Yes checks the file out and then opens it. Clicking No opens the file and permits saving it, but with no source code control in effect. (This might be acceptable for making quick, simple changes.) Clicking Cancel abandons the edit.

When you click OK in the Site Settings dialog box, FrontPage prompts you that it needs to recalculate the Web site's hyperlinks. Click Yes to continue.

> **Tip** The user name FrontPage uses for Document Check-In and Check-Out is normally the one that provides access to the FrontPage-based Web site. For Web sites with no user-level security, FrontPage uses your Windows user name.

When Document Check-In and Check-Out is in effect, all FrontPage Folder Lists may display these icons in front of a file name:

- **Green check mark** Means that the file is checked out to you.
- **Gray padlock** Means that the file is checked out to someone else.

Figure 39-10 shows a typical FrontPage Folder List with Document Check-In and Check-Out in effect. Both icon types are visible. The designer has right-clicked the file members.htm and can use the Check Out option on the shortcut menu to take ownership.

If you try to open a file someone else has checked out, you'll see the following message box. Clicking Yes opens the file despite the fact that the user Mary has checked it out but won't let you update Mary's version. To save your version, you'll have to use another file name. Clicking No abandons the edit.

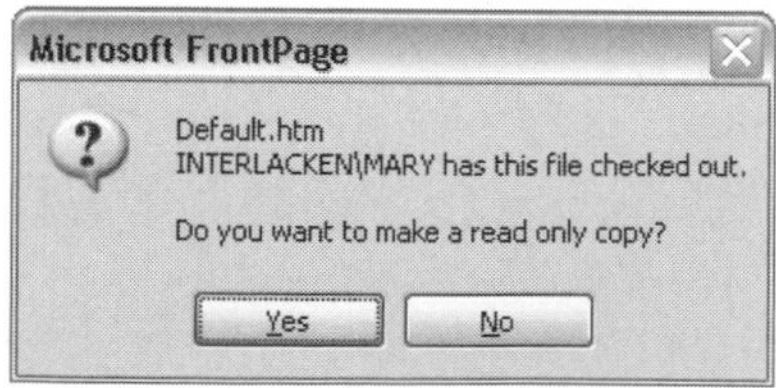

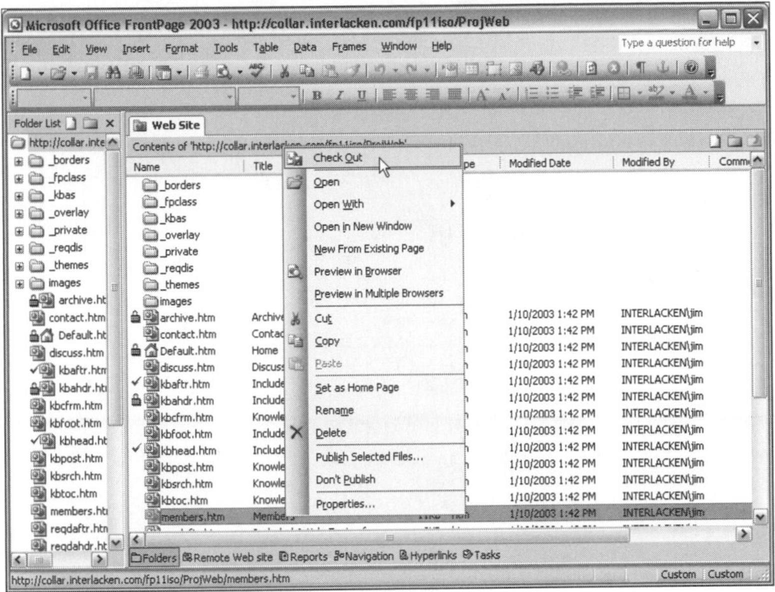

Figure 39-10. With Document Check-In and Check-Out in effect, a green check mark denotes files checked out to the current user, and a gray padlock denotes files checked out to someone else.

Attempting to save a file that's checked out to someone else produces the following message box. There are no real options here other than clicking the OK button and saving the file under another name, or talking to Mary and asking her to incorporate your change with hers.

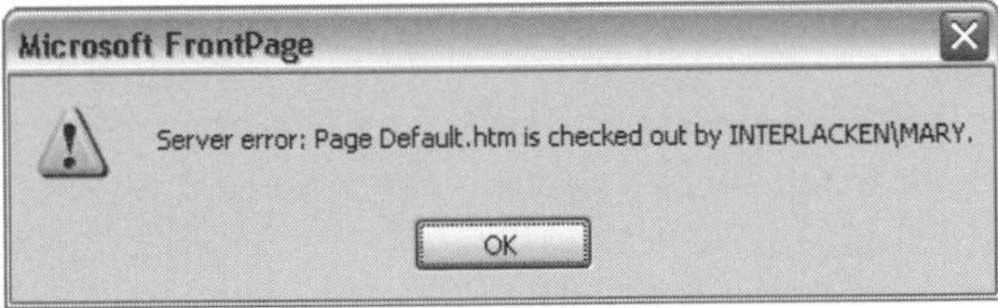

The Checkout Status report, shown in Figure 39-11, shows the checkout status of every file in a Web site. To find all files checked out by a specific person, sort the report by clicking the Checked Out By column heading. To look for files that have remained checked out for a suspiciously long period, sort the report by Locked Date.

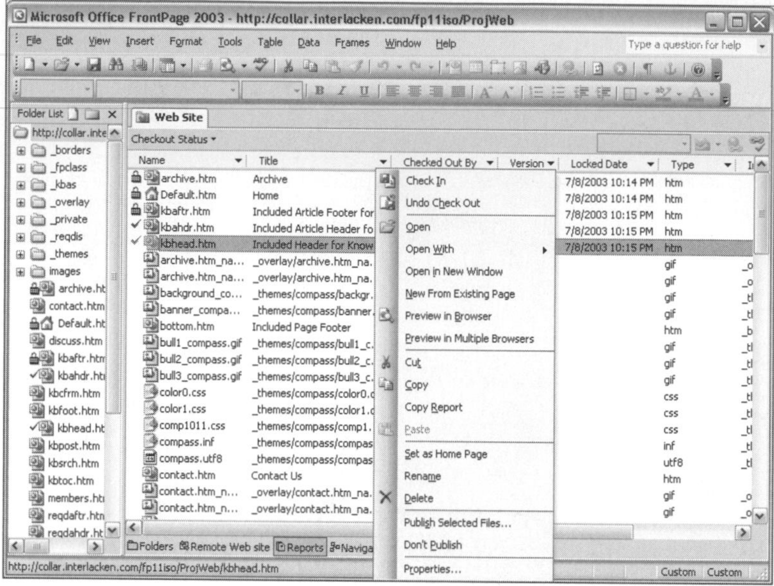

Figure 39-11. The Checkout Status report shows who checked out each file in a Web site, and when.

Figure 39-11 also shows the shortcut menu for a file checked out to the current designer. Choosing Check In relinquishes control of the file and deletes the backup copy made at checkout. Choosing Undo Check Out restores the backup copy—in effect reversing all changes—and then relinquishes control.

There are two additional precautions related to creating and deleting files in a Web site with Document Check-In and Check-Out in effect. First, creating a new file doesn't automatically check it out to you. If you want the file checked out, you have to do it yourself. Second, you can't delete a file checked out to someone else. To delete a file checked out to someone else, you must first ask that person to check it in.

On the Web Even greater source code control, including backout through multiple versions, is available by installing Microsoft Visual SourceSafe on a server-based Web site. For details, *consult* the Visual SourceSafe documentation.

In Summary…

This chapter explained four FrontPage features that help coordinate the actions of a design team working on a single Web site: Tasks view, Workflow Status, Document Publishing, and Document Check-In and Check-Out.

The next several chapters explain how to use FrontPage for working directly with various kinds of code. The first of these chapters, Chapter 40, deals with HTML code.

Part 11

Working Directly with Code

Chapter 40

Working with HTML Code

Despite the powerful Design view editor in Microsoft Office FrontPage 2003, some designers simply can't be happy without directly viewing and modifying HTML code. In this chapter, you'll learn how to do just that.

The chapter begins with a very brief review of HTML and then continues with a look at methods for working with HTML in Design view. The chapter then explains the basic and advanced features of the Code view editor.

Reviewing HTML Basics

HTML consists of tags and ordinary text. Tags begin and end with angle brackets (< >), and they contain instructions that control the appearance and operation of the page. Everything outside the angle brackets is ordinary text.

The first word inside the angle brackets specifies the type of tag: <p> is a paragraph tag, <img> is an image tag, and <table> is the tag that defines a table, for example. Additional expressions within the angle brackets specify *attributes* (that is, characteristics of the page element that the tag defines). The following <hr> tag, for example, defines a horizontal line. The attribute *width="80%"* tells the browser to make the line 80 percent of the width of its container.

```
<hr width="80%">
```

Tip An element's *container* surrounds the element and limits its size. The browser window is the most common container, but frame windows, table cells, and other elements are also containers for the elements within them.

Spaces, tab characters, or line endings separate attributes within the same tag. The number of such characters is irrelevant; one space is as good as 100 as far as HTML is concerned. Most attributes consist of a keyword, an equal sign, and a value although some consist of a keyword alone. The value must be enclosed in quotation marks if it contains any characters other than letters, numbers, percent signs, and hyphens.

Some tags, like <hr> (horizontal rule) and
 (line break), stand alone. Many other tags occur in pairs: one like <b> (bold) to start an effect, and another like </b> (cancel bold) to end it. The end tag always has the same identifier as the start tag, preceded by a slash (/). End tags have no attributes.

Text in HTML tags isn't case-sensitive. The tags <p align=center> and <P ALIGN=CENTER> are perfectly equivalent. Some designers prefer HTML tags in all uppercase so that the tags stand out from content in the code. The more recent trend, however, has been toward all lowercase tags.

The following six lines of HTML appear in nearly all Web pages:

```
<html>
  <head>
  </head>
  <body>
  </body>
</html>
```

- <html> and </html> mark the beginning and end of a Web page.
- <head> and </head> mark the beginning and end of the head section, a block of code guaranteed never to appear to Web visitors. The head section typically contains entries such as:
  - The page's title (enclosed by <title> and </title> tags)
  - Style sheets (enclosed by <style> and </style> tags)
  - Scripts (enclosed by <script> and </script> tags)
  - <meta> tags, which generally describe the page and provide keywords for Internet search engines
- <body> and </body>, which mark the Web page's displayable area.

A complete course in HTML, complete with listings, descriptions, and examples of every defined tag, is clearly beyond the scope of this book. Fortunately, hundreds of other references are available to fill the vacuum. Visit your local bookstore and browse a number of them, searching for one or two that start at your level of expertise and explain whatever you're ready to learn next. There are also many HTML sites online. You can find them using your favorite search engine. It's never a bad idea for any Web developer to have at least a working knowledge of HTML—how it works, and what its limitations are.

Hopefully, FrontPage will create all the HTML you'll ever need so you'll never have to deal with the code directly. The rest of this chapter is for those who want to fine-tune their Web pages, for the curious, and for those who already know how to do something in HTML and simply prefer not to learn another approach.

Revealing Tags in Design View

Figure 40-1 shows a page displayed in Design view with the Reveal Tags feature in effect.

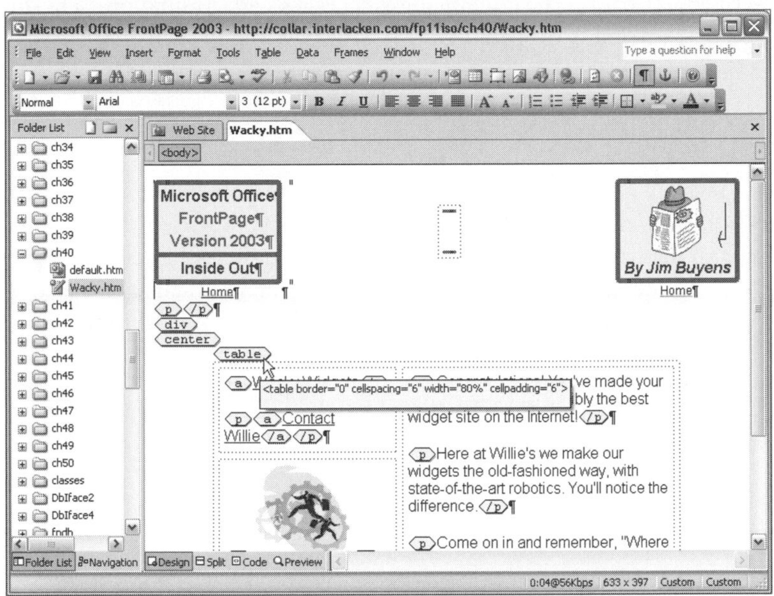

Figure 40-1. The Reveal Tags feature shows the location and type of HTML tags in the body of a Web page in the normal pane. For details about a specific tag, hover the mouse pointer over it, and wait for a ScreenTip to appear.

There are two ways to turn Reveal Tags on and off:

- Choose Reveal Tags from the View menu.
- Press Ctrl+Slash (/).

Reveal Tags doesn't give you any additional editing capability; it just keeps you informed about the HTML that FrontPage creates. It's also useful for locating HTML that has no visible appearance, such as paragraphs with nothing in them.

Show All

There's something else Reveal Tags doesn't do: It doesn't reveal tags that FrontPage indicates another way. Notice the table in Figure 40-1, for example. The <table> start tag is visible, but not the <tr> and </tr> tags that delimit each row, and not the <td> and </td> tags that bound each cell. The lines around each table cell, however, provide the same information. The </table> end tag is below the displayable portion of the window.

Show Layer Anchors

Don't overlook the following commands, which control the visibility of the elements that Reveal Tags doesn't display:

- The Show All button on the Standard toolbar controls the visibility of block endings, line endings, table cells, and anchor icons that show the physical position of repositioned content.

- The Show Layer Anchors button on the Standard toolbar displays anchor icons where the HTML that defines a layer physically resides.

Highlight Dynamic HTML Effects

- The Highlight Dynamic HTML Effects button on the DHTML Effects toolbar is described in Chapter 26, “Enhancing Web Pages with Animation.” This button controls the visibility of spans and divisions involved in such effects.

Using the Quick Tag Selector

The Reveal Tags option shows the location of many common HTML tags, but it doesn’t help you select or modify those tags. What’s more, it obstructs your view of the normal Web page content. For all these reasons, the Reveal Tags features hasn’t achieved much popularity among FrontPage designers. The need remains, however, to visualize and modify HTML code even though you’re working in Design view. To meet this need, FrontPage 2003 provides a new user interface element called the Quick Tag Selector.

In Figure 40-2, the Quick Tag Selector appears immediately above the Design view window; it looks like a row of HTML tags.

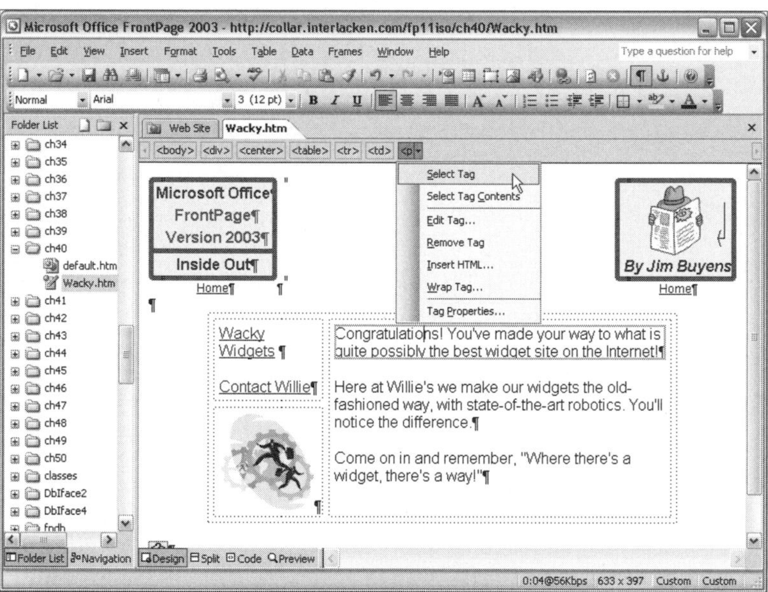

Figure 40-2. The Quick Tag Selector not only displays the hierarchy of tags that surrounds the current selection, but can also select any tag it displays.

It’s more useful, however, to think of these as icons:

- The rightmost icon, <p>, indicates that paragraph tags (<p> and </p>) enclose the current selection.
- The next icon to the left, <td>, indicates that table cell tags (<td> and </td>) enclose the paragraph tags.

Chapter 40

- The next icon, <tr>, indicates that table row tags (<tr> and </tr>) enclose the table cell tags, and so forth.
- The leftmost icon is always <body>, indicating that <body> and </body> tags enclose the entire visible portion of the page.

As you select different elements in Design view, the Quick Tag Selector changes to show the hierarchy of tags enclosing the current selection. If the series of tag icons is wider than the Design view window, scroll buttons appear on each side of the Quick Tag Selector.

The Quick Tag Selector also works in reverse, and this accounts for its name. Clicking any icon in the Quick Tag Selector quickly selects the corresponding content in Design view. This makes it very easy to select any HTML element you want, even if you're working with nested tables or other elements that are very close together.

Clicking the down arrow on any Quick Tag Selector icon displays a menu offering these commands:

- **Select Tag** Selects the start tag, the end tag, and everything between. This is also what occurs when you simply click the tag icon.
- **Select Tag Contents** Selects any content between the start and end tags, but not the tags themselves.
- **Edit Tag** Displays the Quick Tag Editor for the purpose of updating the current tag. (The next section explains the Quick Tag Editor.)
- **Remove Tag** Deletes the start and end tags but not any content between them.
- **Insert HTML** Displays the Quick Tag Editor for the purpose of adding text or HTML code just before the tag you selected.
- **Wrap Tag** Displays the Quick Tag Editor for the purpose of surrounding the current start and end tags with a new pair of matching tags.
- **Tag Properties** Displays the FrontPage dialog box for configuring the current tag type. If, for, example, you click the Quick Tag Selector icon for an <img> tag, this command will display the Picture Properties dialog box.

Tip The Quick Tag Selector and the Quick Tag Editor also work in Code view.

Using the Quick Tag Editor

The Quick Tag Editor works in Design view, but it provides direct access to the text that constitutes an HTML tag. To invoke this feature, click a Quick Tag Selector down arrow, and then choose the Edit Tag, Insert HTML, or Wrap Tag command. Figure 40-3 shows a typical display.

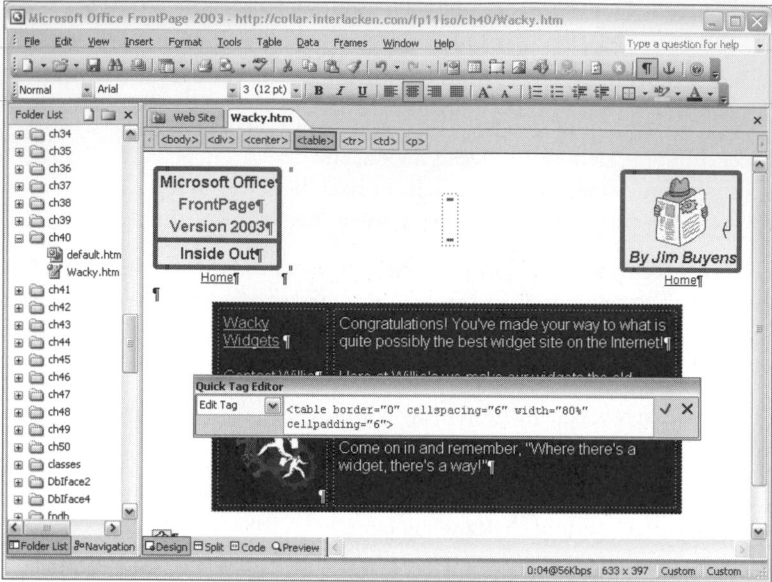

Figure 40-3. The Quick Tag Editor operates in Design view but can modify the HTML for any tag.

When the Quick Tag Editor first appears, the drop-down list on the left will specify one of these editing modes, corresponding to the command you chose in the Quick Tag Selector:

- **Edit Tag** The Quick Tag Editor displays the text of the start tag you chose. Make any changes you want, and then click the check mark button to save your changes and close the Quick Tag Editor.
- **Wrap Tag** The Quick Tag Editor displays an empty pair of angle brackets. Between these brackets, enter the text for any HTML tag you want. When you click the check mark button, the Quick Tag Editor will surround the tag you originally selected (and its matching end tag) with the new tag you entered and *its* matching end tag.

  Suppose, for example, that you clicked the <p> icon for a paragraph consisting of `<p>Hello.</p>` and then chose Wrap Tag. Suppose further that you entered **<a href="hello.htm">** in the Quick Tag Editor and then clicked the check mark button. FrontPage would change the original HTML to `<a href="hello.htm"><p>Hello.</p></a>`.
- **Insert HTML** Again, the Quick Tag Editor displays an empty pair of angle brackets. Clicking the check mark icon, however, saves your input just before the Design view selection or insertion point. If you don't supply an end tag, FrontPage creates one for you.

You're perfectly free to change the editing mode drop-down menu—and therefore the editing mode itself—at any time. The Quick Tag Editor then behaves as if you'd chosen a different command from the Quick Tag Selector.

To close the Quick Tag Editor without saving, click the X button.

Working with HTML Code

Editing in Code View

Up to now, this chapter has skirted the issue of viewing and editing a Web page in its entirety as HTML code. Well, the buck stops here. To view all the HTML for a Web page in one editable window, select the Code tab at the bottom of the Design view window. A display like that shown in Figure 40-4 will result.

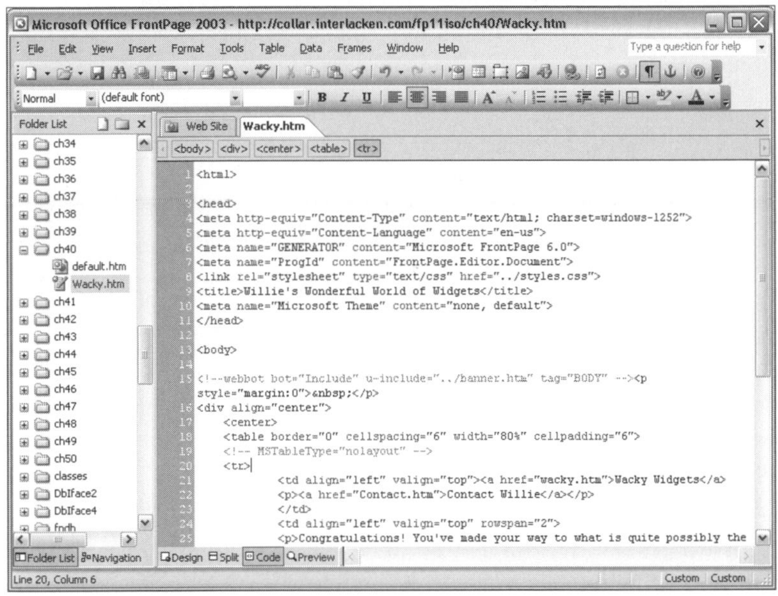

Figure 40-4. FrontPage readily displays an HTML version of the current Web page. Any changes you make take effect when you close the window.

Of course, the display in Figure 40-4 is fully editable as text; you can cut, copy, paste, delete, find, replace, undo, open, and save using the normal FrontPage commands and keystrokes. But as a bonus, almost all of FrontPage's menu commands are available as well! You can insert tables, hyperlinks, pictures, FrontPage Web components, and other elements using the same commands you learned in Design (that is, WYSIWYG) view. Simply set the insertion point within the HTML, and then use the menu bar as usual.

> **Caution** Be sure to set the insertion point correctly before inserting a new element. For example, don't try to insert a new picture inside the HTML for an existing picture.

In some cases, you can modify the properties of existing Web page elements with FrontPage menus, even though you're working in Code view. There are three ways to use this facility:

- Right-click the element, and then choose Tag Properties from the shortcut menu.
- Set the insertion point within the element, and then choose Properties from the Format menu.
- Set the insertion point within the element, and then press Alt+Enter.

Chapter 40

Caution In Design view, where FrontPage creates all the HTML for you, HTML errors are extremely rare. In Code view, you create the HTML, and errors are quite possible. FrontPage doesn't check your HTML for accuracy as you work.

If you choose Code view while editing a frames page, FrontPage will display the HTML for the frames page. To edit the HTML for a target page:

1. Right-click the target page, and choose Open Page In New Window from the shortcut menu.
2. Click the Code tab in the new editing window that appears.

Tip **Select in Design view, edit in Code view**
Finding the correct location to insert HTML can be difficult in Code view, especially if you're not a whiz at HTML. To make this job easier, first select an element in Design view, and then switch to Code view. FrontPage will select the same element in Code view and position the display so that the element is visible.

If you click the Split tab at the bottom of the FrontPage editing window, FrontPage divides the window in half, showing Code view in the upper half and Design view in the lower half. Both views remain fully editable, and the Code view pane will immediately reflect changes you make in the Design view pane. Changes you make in the Code view pane, however, won't be visible in the Design view pane until that pane regains focus.

Each copy of FrontPage includes a copy of Microsoft Script Editor, a second tool for working intelligently with code. To open a page in Script Editor, first open the page in Design view, and then take any of these actions:

Microsoft Script Editor

- Switch to Code view, and then click the Microsoft Script Editor button on the Code View toolbar.
- Choose Macro from the Tools menu, and then choose Microsoft Script Editor from the submenu.
- Press Alt+Shift+F11.

For more information about using Microsoft Script Editor, refer to "Using Microsoft Script Editor," on page 1066.

Configuring the Code View Display

The following options modify the way FrontPage displays your code, but not the code itself:

- **Line Numbers** With this option in effect, FrontPage numbers each line in the current file; the first line is 1, the second line is 2, and so forth. These numbers appear in the margin to the left of each line. (A *line*, in this sense, is everything up to and including a linefeed.)

- **Word Wrap** When a line would otherwise extend beyond the right margin of the editing window, this option inserts extra implied line breaks. This makes the whole line visible without scrolling. Lines 15 in Figure 40-4 show this option in effect. Notice that only one line number appears per physical line, regardless of the number of on-screen lines.
- **Selection Margin** This option displays an extra margin immediately to the left of each line. Clicking this margin selects the entire line.

  If you have line numbers in effect, clicking a line number has the same result as clicking the selection margin. Other than appearance, there's no reason to have both options in effect.

There are two ways to turn these options on or off:

Options

- Open the Options drop-down menu on the Code View toolbar. Choosing a command on the drop-down menu toggles the corresponding option on and off.
- Choose Page Options from the Tools menu, and then click the General tab. The Code View Options section provides check boxes that control each option.

Both of these methods also display an Auto Indent option. Because this option affects the physical content of your code, its description appears in the next section.

Code view color-codes the unique elements of HTML and script code. By default, for example, HTML tags are purple, HTML attribute names are red, and attribute values are blue. To change the colors assigned to any element:

1. Choose Page Options from the Tools menu, and click the Color Coding tab. Figure 40-5 illustrates this tab.

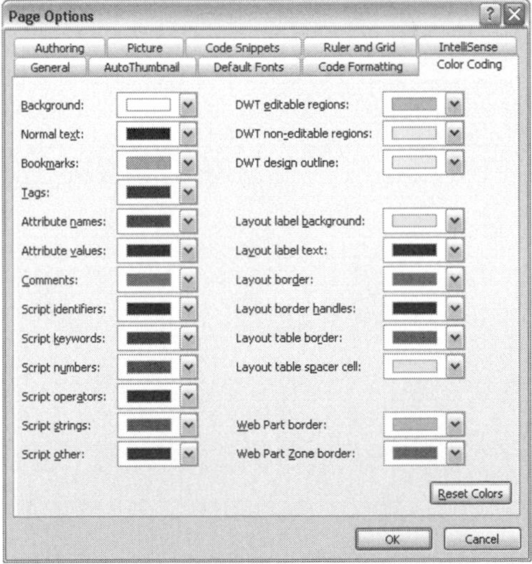

Figure 40-5. This tab specifies the Code view color for each listed element type.

Chapter 40

2 Click the drop-down arrow for any element type, and then use the resulting color picker to specify the color you want.

Personalizing HTML Format

If you're accustomed to maintaining HTML by hand, you've probably developed indentation styles and other conventions to make the HTML more readable. FrontPage can either preserve the format of your existing code or adopt whatever conventions you prefer. FrontPage helps in two ways:

- FrontPage remembers the order, capitalization, and surrounding white space for each tag in the page. As a result, opening and saving any Web page produces no change in formatting. When you edit pages in Design view, FrontPage does its best to maintain formatting of the code it modifies, and it tries to use comparable styles for the code it inserts. In short, FrontPage tries to write code that follows the same conventions as the rest of the page.
- FrontPage can also reformat HTML code using rules that you control. To prevent accidental reformatting, this is never automatic: You must issue a specific Reformat HTML command. If you maintain HTML code that's inconsistently or badly formatted, this command provides relief. It's also useful if you like entering HTML without regard to format and then letting the computer line up the results. Just right-click anywhere in the Code view display, and choose Reformat HTML from the shortcut menu.

To set the options for reformatting HTML code, choose Page Options from the Tools menu, and then click the Code Formatting tab. Figure 40-6 shows this tab.

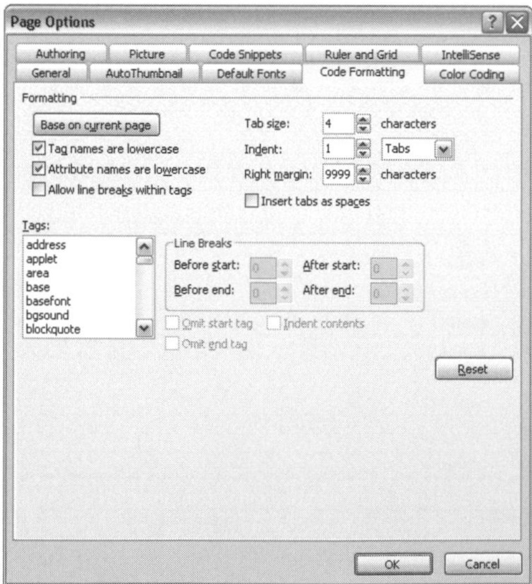

Figure 40-6. The Code Formatting tab in the Page Options dialog box provides control over the formatting of HTML code edited by FrontPage.

The Code Formatting tab provides these options:

- **Base On Current Page** Click this button if you want FrontPage to analyze the current page, determine its formatting styles, and set all the Formatting fields on the Code Formatting tab accordingly.
- **Tag Names Are Lowercase** Select this check box if you want FrontPage to use lowercase letters for the names of HTML tags—for example, <p> and </p> rather than <P> and </P>.
- **Attribute Names Are Lowercase.** Select this check box if you want FrontPage to use lowercase letters for HTML attributes—for example, *src="trans5x5.gif"* rather than *SRC="trans5x5.gif"*.
- **Allow Line Breaks Within Tags** Select this check box if, when an HTML tag would extend beyond the right margin, you want FrontPage to add line breaks inside the tag. Otherwise, FrontPage won't split tags onto multiple lines, regardless of how long the tag becomes.

> **Note** FrontPage will insert line breaks only where white space is valid.

- **Tab Size** Specify how many space characters are equivalent to one tab character.
- **Indent** Specify how many tabs or spaces FrontPage should insert when it indents a line. This measurement consists of an amount and a unit of measure (spaces or tabs), and it applies in two situations:
  - During a Reformat HTML operation, when FrontPage detects a tag flagged Indent Contents. (More on this in a moment.)
  - When you select one or more lines and then press Tab or Shift+Tab.

> **Note** For readability, experienced HTML coders usually indent complex, multiline structures such as tables and lists. All <tr> (table row) tags, for example, might begin on a new line, indented two more spaces than their parent <table> tag. <td> (table detail) tags might also start on a new line, indented two spaces more than their preceding <tr> tags. This produces an indented code listing that's easy to read.

- **Right Margin** Specify the maximum number of characters on a line. FrontPage will insert a line break rather than create lines longer than this setting.
- **Inserts Tabs As Spaces** Select this check box if you want FrontPage to insert spaces rather than a tab character when you press the Tab key. The Tab Size setting specifies the number of spaces.
- **Tags** Use this list to select Reformat HTML settings for each valid HTML tag. FrontPage remembers the following settings on a tag-by-tag basis:
  - **Line Breaks** Specify how many line breaks FrontPage should insert before and after the start tag and before and after the end tag. Table 40-1 describes the available settings.

Table 40-1. Automatic Line Break Settings

Setting	Description	Example
Before Start	The number of line breaks to insert before an element's start tag	Before <TABLE>
After Start	The number of line breaks to insert after an element's start tag	After <TABLE>
Before End	The number of line breaks to insert before an element's end tag	Before </TABLE>
After End	The number of line breaks to insert after an element's end tag	After </TABLE>

  - **Omit Start Tag** Select this check box if you want FrontPage to suppress an element's start tag. This is valid for only a few tags, such as <html>.
  - **Omit End Tag** Select this check box if you want FrontPage to suppress an element's end tag. This pertains to certain tags, like <p> (paragraph), whose end tags are optional.
  - **Indent Contents** Select this check box if you want FrontPage to indent each occurrence of this tag relative to its parent. The Indent properties described earlier specify the amount of indentation.
- **Reset** Restores all Formatting settings to their original values.

FrontPage can also reformat HTML so that it conforms to the rules of XML. Primarily, this involves proper use of case, the mandatory use of quotation marks around attribute values, and end tags for each start tag. The result is a format called Extensible Hypertext Markup Language (XHTML). To apply such formatting, right-click anywhere within the Code view window, and choose Apply XML Formatting Rules from the shortcut menu.

Typing Code

FrontPage 2003 presents a number of new features that make it easy to add code. Except for the Auto Indent features, each of these features is always available. To turn Auto Indent on or off, select it from the Options menu on the Code View toolbar, or select its check box on the General tab of the Page Options dialog box.

Here's the complete rundown:

- **Auto Indent** With this option in effect, FrontPage adds enough spaces to the beginning of each new line that the first character you type appears under the first visible character in the preceding line.
- **Code indentation** Selecting one or more lines and pressing Tab or Shift+Tab changes the indentation of those lines.
- **Improved paste** Pasting code into Code view now works the way you probably expect. For example, if you copy some code shown in a Web page and paste it into

Code view, FrontPage discards any formatting and pastes characters such as < and > rather than mnemonics like *>* and *<*

- **Typing shortcuts** New hot keys and commands on the Code View toolbar can insert start tags, end tags, and comments automatically. Here's a list:
  - **Insert Start Tag (Ctrl+comma)** Inserts the characters <> and sets the insertion point between them.
  - **Insert End Tag (Ctrl+.)** Inserts the characters </> and sets the insertion point after the /.
  - **Insert Comment (Ctrl+/)** Inserts the characters <!-- --> and sets the insertion point between the two interior spaces.

Insert Start Tag 

Insert End Tag 

Insert Comment 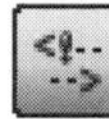

  - **Tab setting** The Code Formatting tab of the Page Options dialog box configures whether pressing the Tab key inserts tab or space characters, and how many.

Inside Out

Freed from the tyranny of Notepad!

In earlier releases of FrontPage, pasting formatted code frequently required first pasting it into Notepad, then copying it from Notepad, then pasting it into Code view. Microsoft has fixed FrontPage 2003 so that you can achieve the same results by pasting formatted code directly into Code view.

Using the IntelliSense Feature

Microsoft IntelliSense is a technology that displays pop-up selection lists that show and explain whatever parameters are valid at the current point in the code. This makes writing code much easier and less prone to errors. FrontPage Code view provides IntelliSense for HTML, CSS, XSL, and JavaScript, and for ASP.NET built-in objects. Chapter 2, "Editing Web Pages," described the key points of this feature.

For an overview of the IntelliSense feature, refer to "Automating Code Entry with IntelliSense," on page 64.

Essentially, IntelliSense displays pop-up lists of potential code elements as you type. When you're working with HTML and type <, for example, IntelliSense displays a pop-up list of tags that are valid at the current location. If you type **<table><**, IntelliSense offers choices of caption, col, colgroup, tbody, tfoot, thead, and tr because, according to the rules of HTML, only those tags can directly follow a <table> tag. Figure 40-7 illustrates this situation.

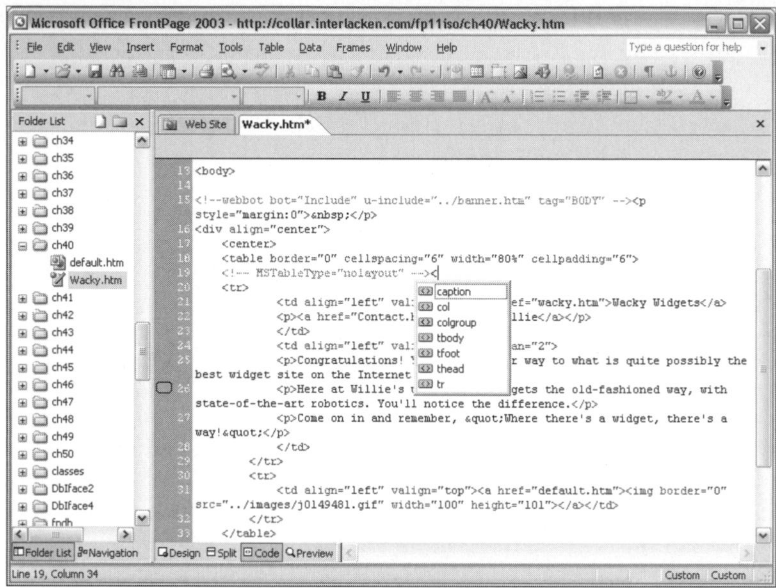

Figure 40-7. IntelliSense automatically displays selection lists of element types, attribute types, attribute values, and programming objects.

There are three ways to insert the text from any IntelliSense list:

- Double-click the entry.
- Select an entry by clicking it, pressing the Up or Down Arrow keys, or partially typing the entry. Then press Tab or Enter.
- Type enough characters to uniquely identify the choice, and then press Ctrl+Spacebar or click the Complete Word button on the Code View toolbar.

When you're working with program code and coding a function or method call, IntelliSense will also display helpful information about each parameter. If you're working with JavaScript, for example, and enter **document.write(**, IntelliSense displays *write(sText)* as a ToolTip. This reminds you that the *write* method expects a *String* value containing any text as its first parameter.

At first, IntelliSense menus might seem to appear at random. They make more sense, however, when you realize that they appear in response to a lead-in character. For example:

- The lead-in character for a choice of HTML tags is a left angle bracket (<).

- The lead-in character for a choice of HTML attributes is the space that follows a tag name or an attribute value.
- The lead-in character for a choice of HTML attributes values is the equal sign that follows the attribute name.

Thus, the following procedure would create the tag <td align=center>:

1. Type <. IntelliSense displays a list of tag names.
2. Select the tag name *td* either with the mouse or by pressing the Down Arrow key, and then press Tab. The characters *td* appear in your code.
3. Type a space, the lead-in character for an HTML attribute. IntelliSense displays a list of the valid attributes for a <td> tag.
4. Select *align* from the IntelliSense list, and then press Tab. The characters *align* appear in your code.
5. Type =, the lead-in character for an HTML attribute value. IntelliSense displays a list of the values an *align* attribute can have.
6. Select *center*, and then press Tab. The characters *center* appear in your code.
7. Type > to complete the tag.

Although this procedure saves some typing, its greatest value comes from the list of valid choices. This saves you from consulting your HTML reference, from spelling errors, and from entering a tag in the wrong place.

The Code View toolbar provides the following commands related to IntelliSense. Corresponding hot keys appear in parentheses.

- **List Members (Ctrl+L).** Displays the IntelliSense list of choices that are valid at the insertion point or current selection. Selecting any choice will add the corresponding text at the insertion point or replace the current selection.

  This command makes it easier to use IntelliSense with existing code. Otherwise, to get the IntelliSense list, you would have to set the insertion point and retype the lead-in character.
- **Parameter Info (Ctrl+Shift+Spacebar).** Displays the IntelliSense ToolTip for a function or method parameter at the insertion point.
- **Complete Word (Ctrl+Spacebar).** Replaces a partially typed entry with a complete word, provided you've typed enough characters to uniquely identify one and only one entry. If you haven't typed enough characters, IntelliSense selects the first matching entry but doesn't add it to your code.

List Members 

Parameter Info 

Complete Word 

To activate or disable IntelliSense features, choose Page Options from the Tools menu, and then click the IntelliSense tab shown in Figure 40-8.

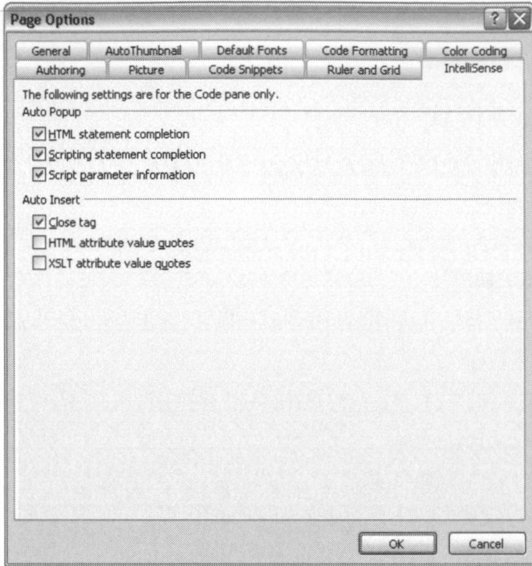

Figure 40-8. This tab controls which selection lists IntelliSense displays automatically, and which tags and elements it inserts automatically.

The IntelliSense tab of the Page Options dialog box provides these options:

- **Auto Popup** Use these options to control when IntelliSense displays pop-up selection lists and information:
  - **HTML Statement Completion** Select this check box if you want IntelliSense lists to appear as you work with HTML.
  - **Script Statement Completion** Select this check box if you want IntelliSense lists to appear as you work with browser-side scripting languages.
  - **Script Parameter Information** Select this check box if you want IntelliSense to display ToolTip information about subroutine and function parameters.
- **Auto Insert** Use these options to control when IntelliSense automates typing for you:
  - **Close Tag** Select this check box if you want IntelliSense to create an end tag whenever you type the closing bracket of a start tag. If this option were in effect and you typed **<td>**, IntelliSense would automatically add *</td>*.
  - **HTML Value Attribute Quotes** Select this check box if you want IntelliSense to supply quotation marks every time you finish typing an HTML attribute name. If this option were in effect and you typed **align=**, IntelliSense would add two quotation marks (" ") and set the insertion point between them.
  - **XSLT Attribute Value Quotes** Select this check box if you want IntelliSense to supply quotation marks every time you finish typing an XSLT attribute name.

Using Code View Bookmarks

Despite the fact that in Code view, you edit HTML code, Code view bookmarks have nothing to do with HTML bookmarks. A Code view bookmark is an editing spot you designate so that you can return to it later. This is handy if, for example, you're working on several disparate parts of a long Web page at once. Bookmarking each location makes it easy to jump among them.

FrontPage provides four commands for using Code view bookmarks. All four appear on the Code View toolbar, and three have hot keys, as follows:

- **Toggle Bookmark** (Ctrl+F2) Sets or clears a bookmark on the line that contains the insertion point or current selection. A rounded rectangle in the left margin identifies each line that currently has a bookmark. In Figure 40-7, for example, line 25 has a bookmark.
- **Next Bookmark** (F2) Positions the display at the first subsequent bookmark. The search starts at the insertion point or current selection, proceeds to the end of the page, and continues from the top of the page to the starting point.
- **Previous Bookmark** (Shift+F2) Positions the display at the next prior bookmark. This works like the Next Bookmark command, except in the opposite direction.
- **Clear Bookmarks** Removes all Code view bookmarks in the current page.

Toggle Bookmark 

Next Bookmark 

Previous Bookmark 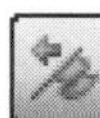

Clear Bookmarks 

FrontPage remembers Code view bookmarks only for the duration of one editing session. After you close a Web page, FrontPage forgets them.

Selecting Code Elements

FrontPage has several advanced commands for selecting code elements intelligently. You can select each of these commands in three different ways:

- By pressing a hot key.
- By clicking a button on the Code View toolbar.
- By right-clicking a location in the code and then choosing the command you want from the shortcut menu.

Here's the list:

Select Tag

- **Select Tag (Ctrl+Shift+;)** This command selects the first pair of start and end tags that enclose the insertion point or current selection, plus everything between those tags. Each time you rerun the command, it selects the next enclosing pair of start and end tags.

Find Matching Tag

- **Find Matching Tag (Ctrl+;)** This command has three possible outcomes.
  - If the insertion point or current selection is inside a tag, the command selects the whole tag.
  - If the current selection is an entire start or end tag, the command selects the matching end or start tag.
  - If the insertion point or current selection isn't within a tag, the command does nothing.

Select Block

- **Select Block (Ctrl+')** This command is useful only when you're dealing with program languages that use curly braces ({}) to denote blocks of code. In that case, it selects everything inside the current pair of curly braces. Each time you rerun the command, it selects everything within the next outward pair of curly braces.

Find Matching Brace

- **Find Matching Brace (Ctrl+])** This is another command with three possible outcomes:
  - If the character just to the right of the insertion point or current selection is neither an opening nor a closing curly brace ({ or }), the command sets the insertion point just before the next closing brace.
  - If the character just to the right of the insertion point or selection is a closing brace, the command sets the insertion point just before the matching opening brace.
  - If the character just to the right of the insertion point or selection is an opening brace, the command sets the insertion point just before the matching closing brace.

  This command takes nested pairs of curly braces into account. Because of this, the next brace you see isn't necessarily the matching brace. For example, in this series:

```
{ { } { } }
```

  the first and last brace are matching, as are the second and third, and the fourth and fifth.

The following command is available only on the Code View toolbar:

- **Function Lookup** Displays a list of functions or subroutines defined within the current file. Selecting any entry selects the corresponding function or subroutine and positions the display to that location.

Storing and Inserting Code Snippets

FrontPage 2003 can store chunks of code in a code snippet library and then insert them into any document you edit. FrontPage treats these snippets as plain text, with no restrictions as to what they contain or where you insert their contents. Here's the procedure to insert a snippet:

1. Open the file you want to modify, and switch to Code view.
2. Set the insertion point where you want the snippet text to appear.
3. Click the List Code Snippets button on the Code View toolbar, or press Ctrl+Enter. This will display a pop-up list like the one below.

List Code Snippets

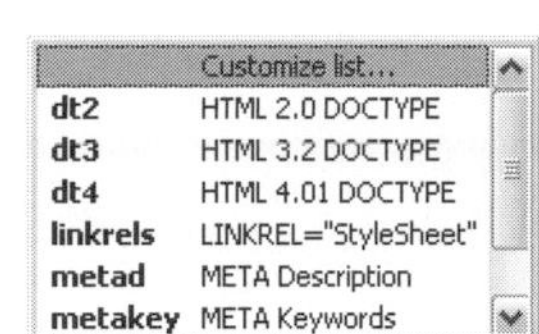

4. Locate the snippet you want, and then use either of these procedures to add the corresponding text to you file:
   - Double-click the snippet you want.
   - Select the snippet you want, and then press Enter or Tab.

To modify the list of snippets, proceed as follows:

1. Use either of these procedures to display the Code Snippets tab of the Page Options dialog box, which appears in the background in Figure 40-9:
   - Repeat steps 1 through 3 above, and then double-click the Customize List choice at the top of the pop-up list.
   - Choose Page Options from the Tools menu, and then click the Code Snippets tab.
2. To add a snippet, click the Add button. This displays the Add Code Snippet dialog box, shown in the foreground in Figure 40-9. Enter the following data, and then click OK:
   - **Keyword** Enter a single word or acronym that will identify the snippet in the pop-up list.
   - **Description** Enter a longer explanation that will appear in the pop-up list.
   - **Text** Enter the text you want FrontPage to insert whenever you select the snippet.

   By default, FrontPage will set the insertion point at the end of any snippet it inserts. If you want the insertion point to be somewhere inside the snippet, enter a pipe character (|) at that location. If you want FrontPage to select part of the snippet, enclose that part with pipe characters. In Figure 40-9, the pipe characters enclosing *Jim Buyens Web Resources* tell FrontPage to mark that phrase as the current selection each time it inserts the snippet.

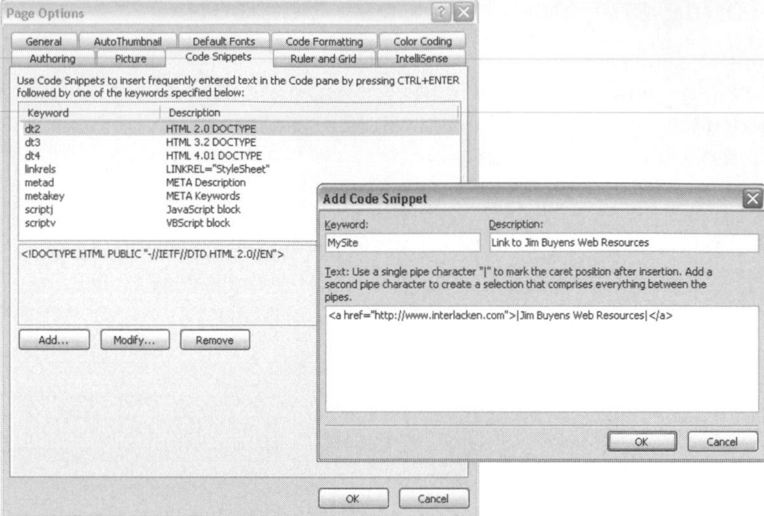

Figure 40-9. Each snippet you add to the code snippet library is available whenever the FrontPage editor is in Code view mode.

3 To modify a snippet, select it in the list, and then click the Modify button. This displays a Modify Code Snippet dialog box that's remarkably similar to the Add Code Snippet dialog box, and that requires the same input.

4 To remove a snippet, select it in the list, and then click the Remove button.

Using the HTML Markup Component

FrontPage makes every effort to support every feature of HTML and to save Web pages with all the formatting and features they had when opened. Occasionally, however, it might be necessary to insert pieces of HTML that FrontPage absolutely won't touch. This isn't as crazy as it sounds, for the following reasons:

- Keeping up-to-date with every new HTML feature is an extremely difficult task, especially given the constant succession of browser and HTML version upgrades.
- Accommodating obsolete features is difficult as well.
- Pages newly imported into FrontPage might contain syntax errors or incorrect codes, especially if someone previously maintained them by hand.
- Something about the HTML is trickier than FrontPage expects. For example, the page might contain incomplete HTML fragments joined together later by scripts.

Working with HTML Code

The HTML Markup component inserts a block of HTML directly into your Web page. FrontPage doesn't check this HTML at all, doesn't display it, and doesn't integrate the HTML with neighboring objects. To use this feature:

1. Open the Web page in Design view.
2. Set the insertion point where you want the new HTML to appear, and then choose Web Component from the Insert menu.
3. When the Insert Web Component dialog box appears, select Advanced Controls in the Component Type list on the left, and then select HTML in the Choose A Control list on the right.
4. Click the Finish button to display the HTML Markup dialog box, shown in Figure 40-10.

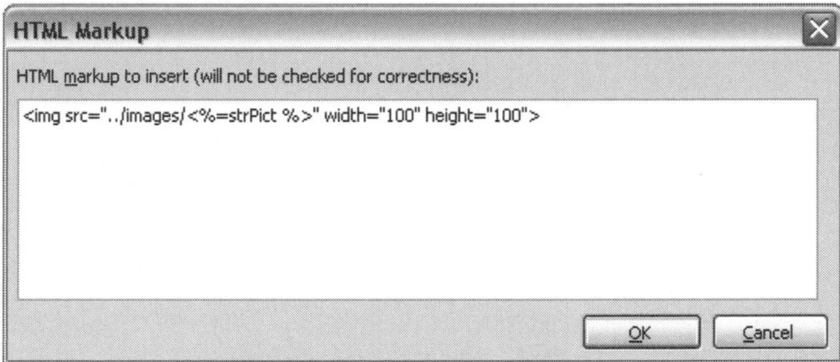

Figure 40-10. The HTML Markup component inserts and modifies HTML outside the control of FrontPage.

5. Type or paste the HTML you want, and then click OK.

If Reveal Tags is in effect, Design view displays HTML Markup components appear as question-mark icons. The HTML will appear as written if you display the page in your browser or click the Preview tab at the bottom of the editing window.

- To modify an HTML Markup component, double-click the question-mark icon. Alternatively, select the icon, and then choose Properties from the Format menu.
- To delete an HTML Markup component, select its icon, and then either press the Delete key or choose Delete from the Edit menu.

It's not unusual to find HTML Markup components in newly imported HTML code. These often reflect marginal or incorrect syntax in HTML that someone previously maintained by hand. You can view the incorrect code by double-clicking the icon. To correct the bad HTML, either fix the code in the HTML Markup dialog box or delete the bad HTML and re-create it using FrontPage tools.

If there's no need to isolate the code in an HTML Markup component, you can convert it to regular HTML through the following procedure:

1. Open the HTML Markup component (by double-clicking, for example).
2. Select the HTML code you want to remove.

3 Cut the HTML code to the Clipboard by pressing Shift+Delete or Ctrl+X, or by right-clicking the selection and choosing Cut from the shortcut menu.
4 Click OK to close the HTML Markup dialog box.
5 Set the insertion point where you want the HTML code to appear. This will probably be just to the right or left of the HTML Markup component.
6 Choose Paste Special from the Edit menu, select Do Not Convert, and then click OK.
7 If the HTML Markup component is now empty, select it, and press the Delete key to delete it.

If someone gives you a piece of HTML code, such as the code to use a non-FrontPage hit counter or mailer:

1 Copy the HTML to the Clipboard.
2 Set the insertion point where you want the HTML to appear.
3 Choose either of these methods:
   - Click the down arrow for the rightmost icon in the Quick Tag Selector, and then choose Insert HTML. When the Quick Tag Editor appears, clear its contents, press Ctrl+C to paste the new HTML, and click the check mark button to save it.
   - Choose Paste Special from the Insert menu, and then, when the Convert Text dialog box appears, select Do Not Convert and click OK.

If this works, it permits a much better WYSIWYG display than using the HTML Markup component. It also facilitates editing and provides much better integration with your other content. If it doesn't work, there's always the HTML Markup component to fall back on.

Overuse of the HTML Markup component generally indicates a problem. Except in rare cases, FrontPage should handle your HTML well enough that the "hands-off" aspect of HTML Markup isn't necessary.

In Summary...

More than any earlier version, FrontPage 2003 has powerful features for working with code of all types, including and especially HTML. These include the Quick Tag Selector, the Quick Tag Editor, code formatting preservation and reformatting, and powerful new editing features in Code view.

The next chapter will introduce the concept of browser-side scripting and explain how to use Microsoft Script Editor as an adjunct to FrontPage Code view.

Chapter 41
Working with Script Code

The use of "under construction" phrases and icons on the World Wide Web has become an almost comical cliché; in reality, everything on the Web changes *constantly* or quickly becomes obsolete. Inevitably, making all these changes becomes tiresome. As a result, savvy designers, wearing their construction hard hats, search for ways to automate the work. Script languages meet this need.

In the most general sense, a *script* is a set of instructions that describes how certain entities are to interact. The script for a stage play, for example, describes in some detail what the actors should say, their interplay, and when they should enter and exit the scenes. In a computer sense, scripts are lines of high-level programming code that control the interaction of software components. Scripts in Web pages can coordinate useful activities such as these:

- Provide a customized display for each visitor.
- Display and update databases.
- Create self-modifying HTML based on a variety of environmental factors.
- Provide a measure of interactivity for the visitor without the delay of sending data back to the server and waiting for a response.

Code that runs during Web page transmission can insert HTML at the location that triggers the script. This makes any aspect of the page programmable; indeed, you could create a Web page that consisted of a script only. Such a script would need to write all the HTML required to display what you wanted the Web visitor to see. More common, however, is to author the static (unchanging) parts of the page in an HTML editor such as Microsoft Office FrontPage 2003 and to code only the variable portions as scripts.

Special HTML tags mark parts of ordinary Web pages as script code, specify the script language, and control whether the script runs on the server or within the browser. In either case, the server or browser examines, compiles, and runs the code immediately.

- Scripts that run on the server access server-based resources and modify the HTML sent to the browser.
- Scripts that run on the browser access resources internal to the browser and modify HTML received from the server. They can also respond to events on the browser and—if the browser permits—modify a Web page already on display.

As interesting as this introduction might (or might not) be, this book is about creating Web pages with FrontPage and not about the details and nuances of writing scripts. To gain true proficiency in writing scripts, you should obtain one or more books dedicated to that subject alone. FrontPage does have the capability to create certain kinds of scripts without programming, however, and to enter script code from within FrontPage. The remainder of this chapter will discuss how to use these scripting facilities at the browser. The next chapter will address scripting on the Web server.

Introducing Script Languages

Various computer languages have come into use for scripting: awk, sed, Perl, REXX, VBScript, and JavaScript are a few examples. These languages are more general than macro languages tied to a specific program, yet less formal than large-scale development languages such as C and Pascal. Because most scripts are short bits of code connecting other objects and methods, programmers generally view great rigor in a scripting language as excess baggage. Instead, *quick* and *dirty* are the watchwords.

A full explanation of script language programming is beyond the scope of this book. Still, the increasing use of such languages makes FrontPage's support of them a critical feature. Web pages commonly use either of these script languages:

- **JavaScript** Was developed by Netscape Communications and first appeared in Netscape Navigator. Originally called LiveScript, this language has little in common with the Java programming language except that both bear a general resemblance to C++.

  JavaScript runs under both Netscape Navigator and Microsoft Internet Explorer, subject to slight implementation differences.

> **Note** Other names for JavaScript include ECMAScript and JScript. The European Computer Manufacturers Association (ECMA) is the standards body that holds the official language specification. JScript is Microsoft's official name for its implementation of JavaScript.

- **VBScript** Was developed by Microsoft and first appeared in Internet Explorer. VBScript is a subset of Microsoft Visual Basic for Applications, which is a subset of Microsoft Visual Basic. Curiously, VBScript has no visual aspect of its own; instead, it runs within the visual interface of the application that invokes it.

  VBScript runs under the Internet Explorer browser and, on the server side, under Microsoft IIS. Because of differences in their environments, the resources available to VBScript on the server differ from those available on the browser.

> **Note** In this chapter, the acronym *IIS* refers to Internet Information Services for Microsoft Windows 2000, Windows XP Professional, and Windows Server 2003.

On the Web

For more information about the JavaScript and VBScript programming languages, browse *msdn.microsoft.com/scripting*.

Introducing JavaScript

Figure 41-1 shows FrontPage editing some JavaScript in a Web page. The script appears between the <script> and </script> tags. The *document.write* method writes data into the Web page as if it had come from the server. The expression *document.lastModified* supplies the Web page's date and time stamp—the date recorded in the Web server's file system.

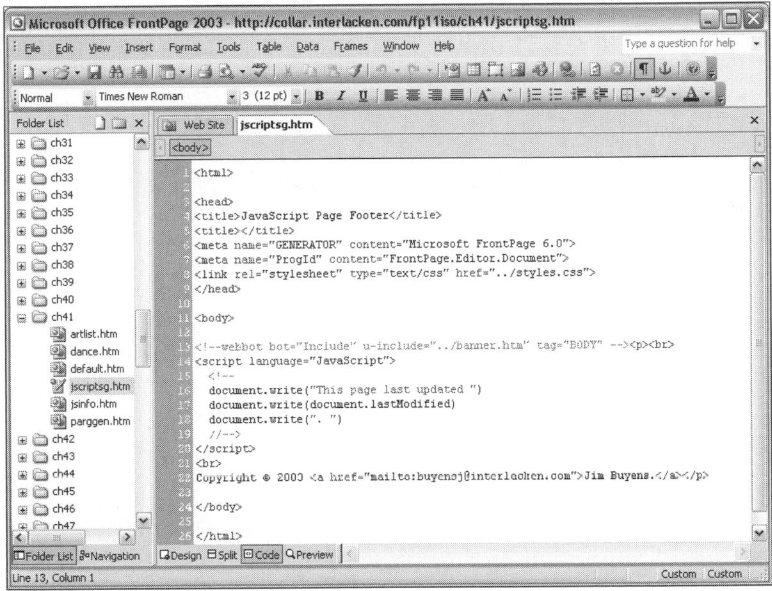

Figure 41-1. FrontPage can insert JavaScript or VBScript into Web pages. This script displays the date the page was last updated.

FrontPage does nothing with any such code you insert; if you switch back to Design view, FrontPage merely displays a J icon where the code resides. FrontPage doesn't verify the code for correctness or try to execute it. To see the code run, switch to preview mode, or open the page with a browser.

Early versions of the JavaScript language were definitely works in progress; various bugs and limitations appeared and disappeared with every browser version. Newer versions are more uniform and reliable, but still not identical. Be sure to test your scripts under all recent versions of each browser you care about. As long as JavaScript remains the only script language available on both Netscape Navigator and Internet Explorer, it will probably remain the preferred language for populations of mixed browsers.

Introducing VBScript

The VBScript language serves all the same purposes and objectives as JavaScript, but it uses a subset of Microsoft Visual Basic. VBScript lacks many familiar Visual Basic features such as a GUI development environment, GUI run-time displays, file input and output, and the ability to call system services. However, its syntax is very familiar to countless Visual Basic developers, and it interfaces very well with Microsoft ActiveX controls.

On a browser, VBScript provides roughly the same capabilities as JavaScript. All versions of Internet Explorer 4 and later support VBScript, but as of version 7, Netscape Navigator provides no support at all. This severely limits the usefulness of browser-side VBScript in environments where Netscape Navigator is common.

On IIS, however, ASP provides server-side support for VBScript. Although scripts running on the server can't interact directly with the visitor, they can produce "plain vanilla" HTML as output and thus operate the same with any browser. They can also interact with server-side components and with such services as database systems.

Scripting Web Pages on the Browser

All modern browsers have features for running program code that arrives nestled inside Web pages. Such code might customize the page based on the date, based on the type of browser, or on other factors. In addition, it can respond to events—like button clicks—that occur after the page is loaded. These features can significantly enhance your Web pages.

Scripts have access to a variety of built-in objects belonging to the browser: the current window, the current URL, and HTML objects such as form elements, hyperlinks, and pictures. Each of these objects has an assortment of properties, some of which the script can modify.

Developers place script statements within <script> and </script> tags in the HTML. The browser executes script statements as it loads the page, and those statements can write data into the browser's input stream. If the browser finds a function or subroutine defined within <script> and </script> tags, the browser stores it for future use. Code found later in the page can then execute the routine.

Events on the page can also trigger script code. There's an *onClick* event, for example, that occurs when the Web visitor clicks a button. If the Web page creator supplied code for that event, the code executes whenever the visitor clicks that button.

Support for browser scripts varies widely. Some browsers support no scripting at all, some support only JavaScript, and some support both JavaScript and VBScript. In addition, the level of support varies with the browser version. Even among browsers that do support scripting, most provide a way for Web visitors to turn scripting off.

If you decide to use scripting on a Web page, be sure to:

- Test the script with all common browsers.
- Note (perhaps at the bottom of the page) the minimum browser version the visitor should have.
- Provide a way for visitors to navigate your site even if they lack script support.

Because JavaScript is the only scripting language Internet Explorer and Netscape Navigator have in common, it's the predominant language for browser-side scripting. JavaScript is the default scripting language for both browsers (that is, <script> defaults to <script language="JavaScript">).

> **Note** All recent versions of Internet Explorer and Netscape Navigator support some level of scripting. Browsers with no scripting support at all are generally very old or experimental.

Browsers that don't support scripting easily ignore <script> and </script> tags, but what of the code between them? An older browser can easily ignore unknown tags, but it has no reason to ignore content between unknown start and end tags. In the case of <script> tags, the old browser will generally try to interpret the script code as HTML, and this can get ugly fast. To prevent this, experienced coders often enclose script code in HTML comments, as shown here:

```
<script language="JavaScript">
<!--
alert("Your message could appear here.");
//-->
</script>
```

The <!-- and --> tags mark the beginning and end of an HTML comment. Script languages successfully ignore the start <!-- tag, but the end --> tag presents a problem: a double minus sign is a valid JavaScript operator. Prefixing the closing tag with a double slash (//) marks it as a JavaScript comment as well as an HTML comment.

Generating Browser Scripts

The section "Validating Form Input," in Chapter 34, has already described one method of generating browser scripts. Establishing validation rules for form elements generates script routines that the browser runs when the Web visitor clicks the form's Submit button. If the script detects no form element fields having values outside the prescribed range, it submits the form normally. If the script detects an incorrect value, it displays an error message to the visitor and submits nothing.

The features on the DHTML Effects toolbar and those in the Behaviors task pane also generate JavaScript code that runs on the browser. Both of these features modify the browser display in response to visitor actions.

For more information about using the DHTML Effects toolbar, refer to "Using DHTML Effects," on page 690. For more information about scripting page element behaviors, refer to "Scripting DHTML Behaviors," on page 694.

If any of these facilities meet you needs, you should by all means use them. However, don't expect FrontPage to generate code you can customize. The JavaScript code that FrontPage creates is strictly for machine consumption.

Displaying Current Information (Coding Example 1)

Figure 41-1 showed a script that obtains and displays real-time information each time a Web visitor loads a page. Figure 41-2 shows the same page in preview mode.

> **Note** Preview mode displays the current Web page using whatever version of Internet Explorer is installed on your system.

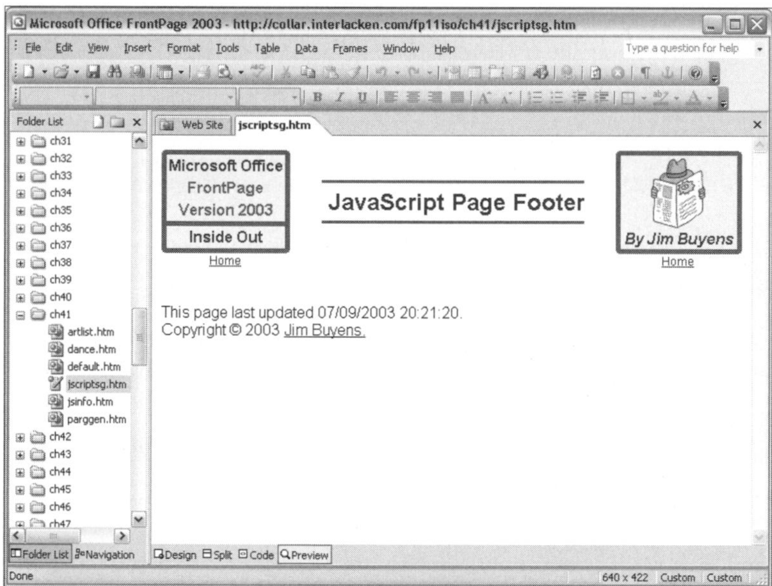

Figure 41-2. Here, in preview mode, FrontPage runs the script shown in Figure 41-1.

Of course, the information available to a script isn't limited to Date Last Modified. Figure 41-3 shows a Web page displaying a selection of more useful information.

Each property value displayed in Figure 41-3 comes from a one-line script such as the following:

```
<script>document.write(document.title)</script>
```

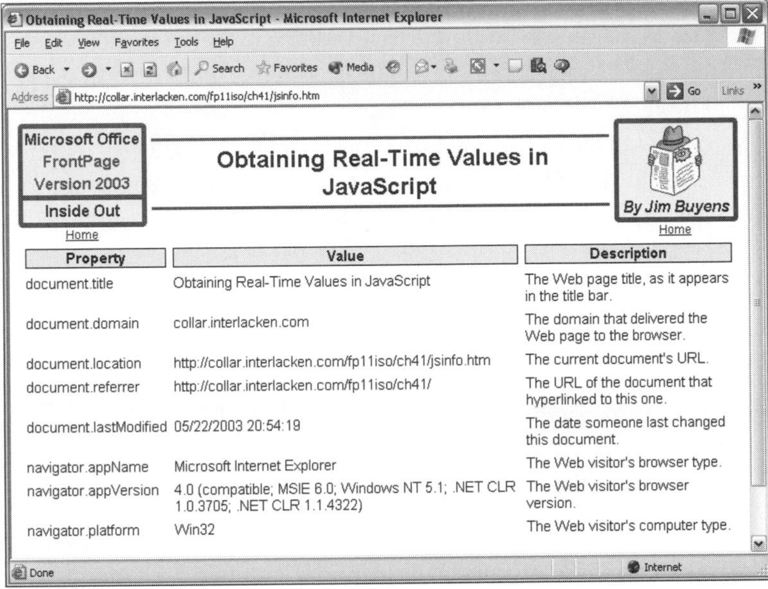

Figure 41-3. Scripts written in JavaScript obtain and display all the information in the center column of this HTML table.

As you can see in the background of Figure 41-4, a J icon represents each <script>…</script> tag pair.

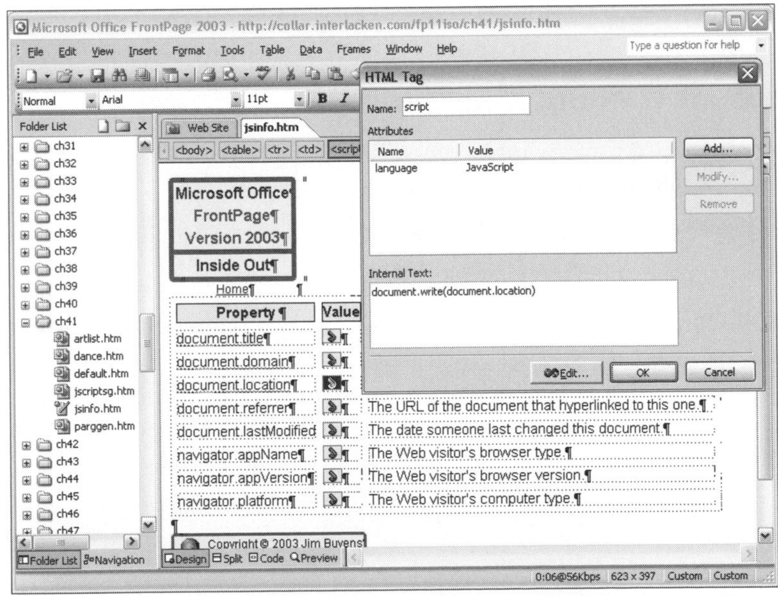

Figure 41-4. Each property value displayed in Figure 41-3 comes from its own script, and each script shows up in Design view as a J icon in the Value column.

Double-clicking one of these J icons displays the HTML Tag dialog box, shown in the foreground in Figure 41-4. You can do simple script editing in the Internal Text box. If you click the Edit button, FrontPage will start another program, called Microsoft Script Editor, and load your Web page into it.

The section "Using Microsoft Script Editor," later in this chapter, discusses Microsoft Script Editor in some detail. This is basically a stripped-down version of the editor professional programmers use in Visual Studio 6. In the meantime, this section assumes that you'll edit script code by switching to Code view or by using the HTML Tag dialog box.

Scripts aren't limited to just writing static values into the HTML stream. They can define variables, make comparisons, branch, manipulate text, perform arithmetic, run subroutines, and all the other things that programming languages do. They aren't limited to writing simple values into table cells, either; you can write any sort of HTML you want, and the browser will interpret it just as if the HTML had arrived from the server. You could even check the date, the browser version, or any other value and create different HTML accordingly. The possibilities boggle the mind.

If a script can create customized HTML as the Web page loads, you might wonder whether a script can change a Web page already on display—for example, add, modify, or remove things like text, pictures, hyperlinks, and table cells. The answer is yes, and this is what DHTML is all about. The catch is that DHTML first showed up in Netscape Navigator 4 and Internet Explorer 4, and the two implementations were quite different. DHTML conventions have since converged, but differences among browsers still exist (as do those old browsers!). This, plus the inherent complexity of the task, can make DHTML programming a daunting task. The section "Responding to Events (Coding Example 3)," later in this chapter, explains a simple DHTML script.

Changing Content (Coding Example 2)

This example performs some simple comparisons and produces different HTML as a result. It flags items as follows:

- With a New! or Upd! (updated) icon if they're less than 14 days old
- With a picture bullet if they're more than 14 days old

Figure 41-5 shows how a browser displays this Web page; Figure 41-6 shows the FrontPage Code view.

Working with Script Code

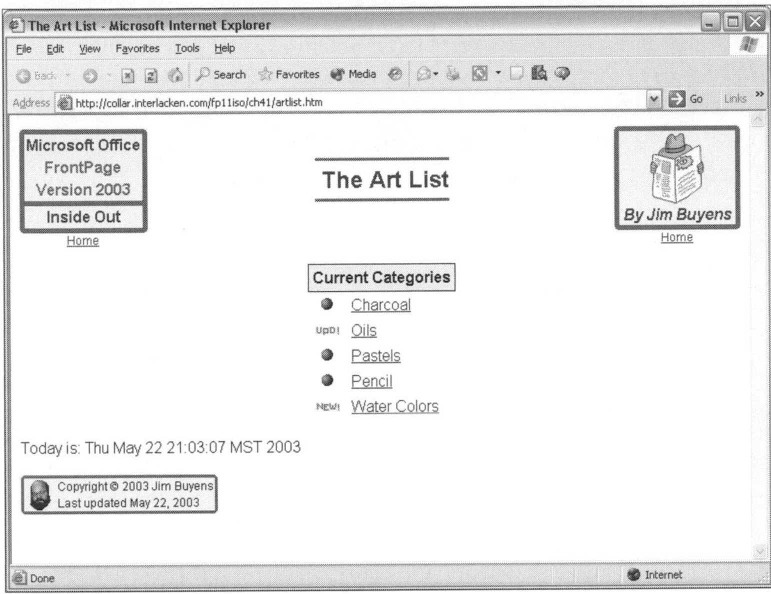

Figure 41-5. JavaScript programming in this page's HTML displays a New! or Upd! (updated) icon for items less than 14 days old but displays a picture bullet for items that are older.

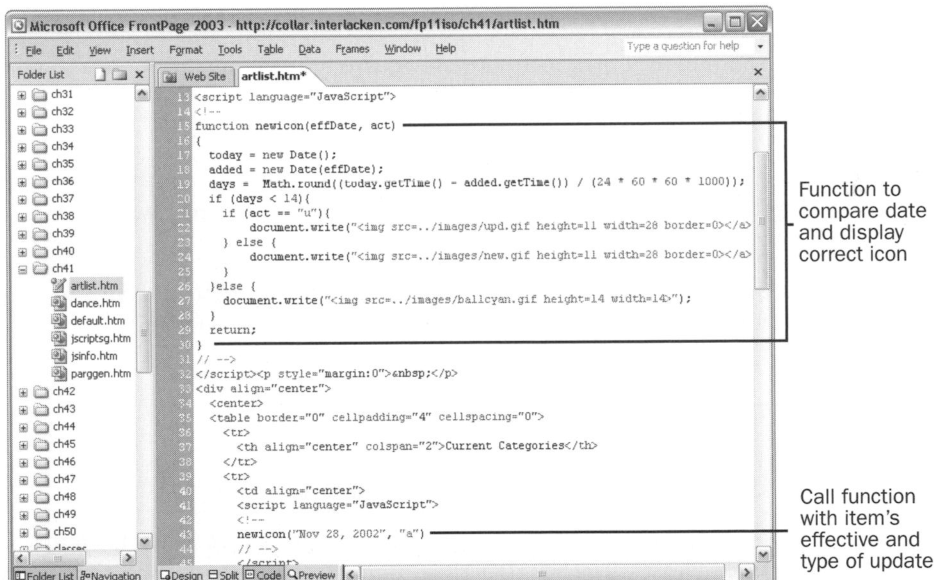

Figure 41-6. Here's the Web page shown in Figure 41-5 as it appears in FrontPage's Code view.

The <script> block at the top of Figure 41-6 defines a function named *newicon*. This function accepts two arguments, *effDate* and *act*. The *effDate* argument accepts the effective date of the listed item. The *act* argument accepts an action code—*a* for added items and *u* for updated ones. The function then creates two date objects and computes their difference. The date object named *today* contains the current date, and the one named *added* contains the date received in *effDate*.

JavaScript dates are actually very large integers that count time in milliseconds. Subtracting two dates therefore produces a difference in milliseconds. To convert milliseconds to days, the script divides the number by 24 × 60 × 60 × 1000 (24 hours times 60 minutes per hour times 60 seconds per minute times 1,000 milliseconds per second). The script saves the result in days to the variable named *days*.

- If the variable *days* is less than 14 and *act* is *u*, the script writes the characters `<img src=images/upd.gif height=11 width=28 border=0>` into the HTML stream as if they had come from the server. This is the function of the *document.write* statement. The characters shown constitute an HTML <img> tag, which is the tag that displays pictures.
- If the variable *days* is less than 14 and *act* is not *u*, the script writes an <img> tag that displays the new.gif icon.
- If the variable *days* isn't less than 14, the script writes an <img> tag that displays cyanball.gif.

The table cell preceding each menu choice contains another script component, the first of which appears at the bottom of Figure 41-6. These scripts are one line each, as in

```
newicon("Nov 28, 2002", "a")
```

This statement runs the *newicon* routine with a value of *Nov 28, 2002* for *effDate* and *a* for *act*. The appropriate icon will appear in place of each such JavaScript statement when the browser displays the Web page.

The last script component on the page displays the current date. It consists of the following two statements, which use concepts explained earlier in this section:

```
today = new Date();
document.write (today);
```


Responding to Events (Coding Example 3)

Figure 41-7 shows a simple Web page that responds to events. When the mouse passes over the area titled Please Click The Hyperlink Above, the browser replaces the picture with the one of three, chosen at random. One choice is shown in Figure 41-8. When the mouse passes out of that area, the browser restores the original picture.

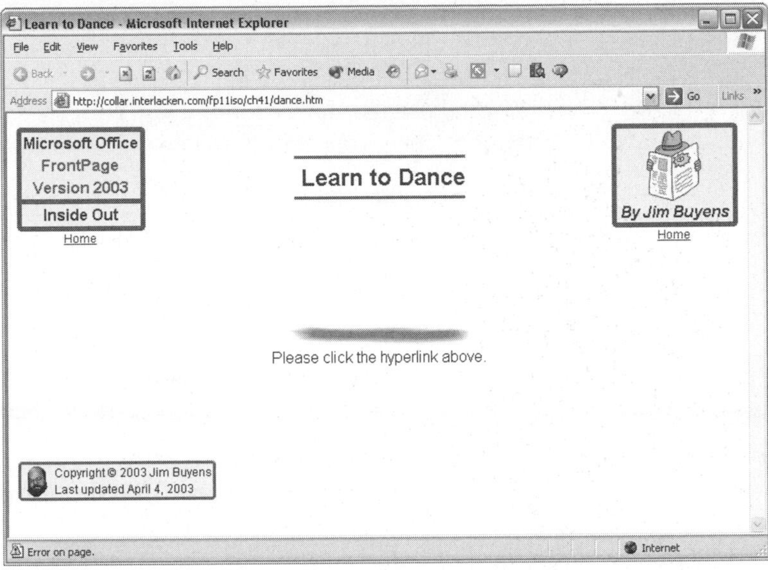

Figure 41-7. This Web page initially displays a nearly empty picture above the prompt.

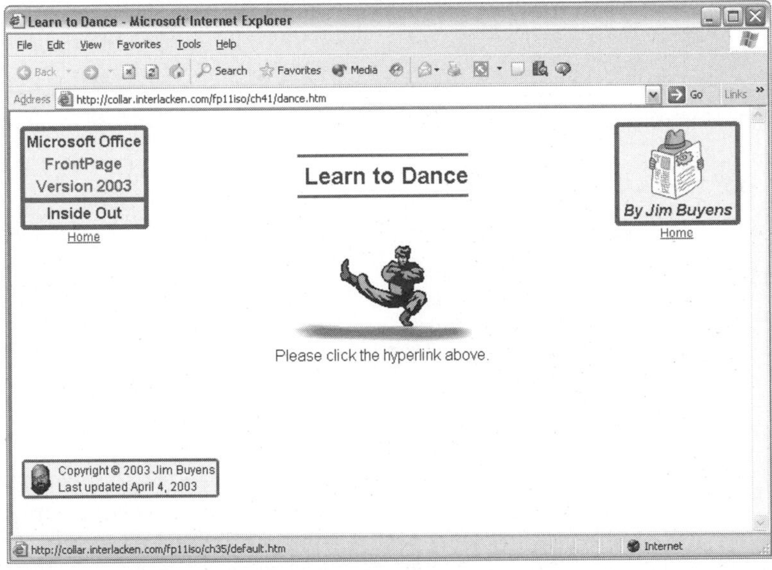

Figure 41-8. Moving the mouse over the picture area activates a script that displays a different picture. Another script displays the first picture when the mouse leaves the picture area.

FrontPage can achieve similar results—using essentially the same method—with no script programming on your part at all. Basically, you insert and select the first picture, display the DHTML Effects toolbar, choose On Mouse Over, choose Apply Swap Picture, and then click <Choose Settings> to select the second picture. However, this doesn't display one of three pictures chosen at random, and it doesn't illustrate how to write scripts that respond to browser events.

For more information about the Swap Picture DHTML effect, refer to "Using DHTML Effects," on page 690.

Here's how to write the script:

1. Prepare the four pictures you want to swap. Make sure that they're all the same size.
2. Add the first picture to the Web page where you want the swapping to occur.
3. Assign a hyperlink to the picture you inserted in step 2. If you don't want the hyperlink to display a different Web page, specify *javascript:void(0);* as the hyperlink address. (This calls a JavaScript function that does nothing.)
4. Select the picture you added in step 2, and then switch to Code view. The <img> tag for your picture should be on-screen and selected.
5. Add the following attribute to the <img> tag for the picture. This assigns an internal name to the picture so that scripts can refer to it.

   ```
   name="dance"
   ```

6. Enter a block of code such as the following anywhere before the picture you added in step 2. Just after the <head> tag, just before the </head> tag, and just after the <body> tag are three good choices.

   ```
   <script LANGUAGE="JavaScript">
   <!--
   var dancer1 = new Image(); dancer1.src = "../images/dancer1.gif";
   var dancer2 = new Image(); dancer2.src = "../images/dancer2.gif";
   var dancer3 = new Image(); dancer3.src = "../images/dancer3.gif";
   var dancer4 = new Image(); dancer4.src = "../images/dancer4.gif";
   // -->
   </script>
   ```

   The first two lines mark the beginning of a script block, and the last two mark the end. The third line contains two statements: one that creates an *Image* object named *dancer1* and another that loads the picture ../images/dancer1.gif into it. The fourth line creates an *Image* object named *dancer2* and loads the picture ../images/dancer2.gif into it, and so forth.

   The reason for loading these pictures into memory is to make them available for instantaneous display.

7 Enter the following function just after the last *var* statement from step 6, and before the closing comment and </script> tag:

```
function swapRandom(){
  curDate = new Date();
  curSec = curDate.getSeconds() % 3;
  if (curSec == 0){
    document.dance.src = eval('dancer2.src');
  }else{
    if (curSec == 2){
      document.dance.src = eval('dancer3.src');
    }else{
      document.dance.src = eval('dancer4.src');
    }
  }
}
```

The first statement marks the beginning of the function and gives it a name. The second creates a *Date* object containing the current date and time. The third statement uses the *getSeconds* method to get the current second, divides this by 3, and saves the remainder in a variable named *curSec.*

The first *if* statement tests the remainder in *curSec.* If it's zero, the script replaces the picture on the Web page with the second picture from step 6. Otherwise, the second *if* statement again tests the remainder in *curSec.* If it's 2, the script displays the third picture from step 6; otherwise, it displays the last picture from step 6.

8 Locate the anchor tag (that is, the <a> tag) for the hyperlink you added in step 3, and then add the following attributes:

```
onmouseover="swapRandom();"
onmouseout="document.dance.src = eval('dancer1.src');"
```

The first attribute specifies a JavaScript statement that runs whenever the visitor moves the mouse pointer over the picture. That statement runs the *swapRandom* function from step 7.

The second attribute specifies a JavaScript statement that runs whenever the visitor moves the mouse pointer off the picture. That statement copies the picture in the *Image* object named *dancer1* into the visible picture.

9 Save the Web page, and then try browsing it in both Internet Explorer and Netscape Navigator. To view a working example, browse the file ch41/dance.htm in the sample Web site installed from the companion CD.

All the machinations with hidden picture objects, by the way, aren't the real point of this example. The real point is the availability of attributes like *onMouseOver* and *onMouseOut* that trigger script code when events occur on the browser.

Internet Explorer versions 4 and later recognize a wide variety of events, and you can code them on any HTML tag. Netscape Navigator 4 recognizes fewer events, and only for hyperlinks and form elements. That's why the example in this section had to use a hyperlink; Netscape 4 supports the *onMouseOver* and *onMouseOut* events for hyperlinks but not for pictures.

Hopefully, complications caused by browser differences will decrease over time. Meanwhile, exercise care and be sure to test with every browser you're concerned about.

For more examples of scripts that respond to events on the browser, refer to "Responding to Form Events on the Browser," in Appendix I.

Using Microsoft Script Editor

The quickest and often easiest way of adding script code to a Web page is to simply click the Code tab at the bottom of the editing window. This provides direct editing of all HTML and script code in the current page

For more stringent requirements, FrontPage includes a tate-of-the-art code editor called Microsoft Script Editor. You can display this editor (shown in Figure 41-9) in four ways:

- Double-click any script icon to open the HTML Tag dialog box. Then, when the HTML Tag dialog box shown previously in Figure 41-4 appears, click Edit.
- Click the Microsoft Script Editor button on the Code View toolbar.
- Choose Macro from the Tools menu, and then choose Microsoft Script Editor.
- Press Shift+Alt+F11.

Microsoft Script Editor

HTML portion of Toolbox window provides objects for dragging into main window

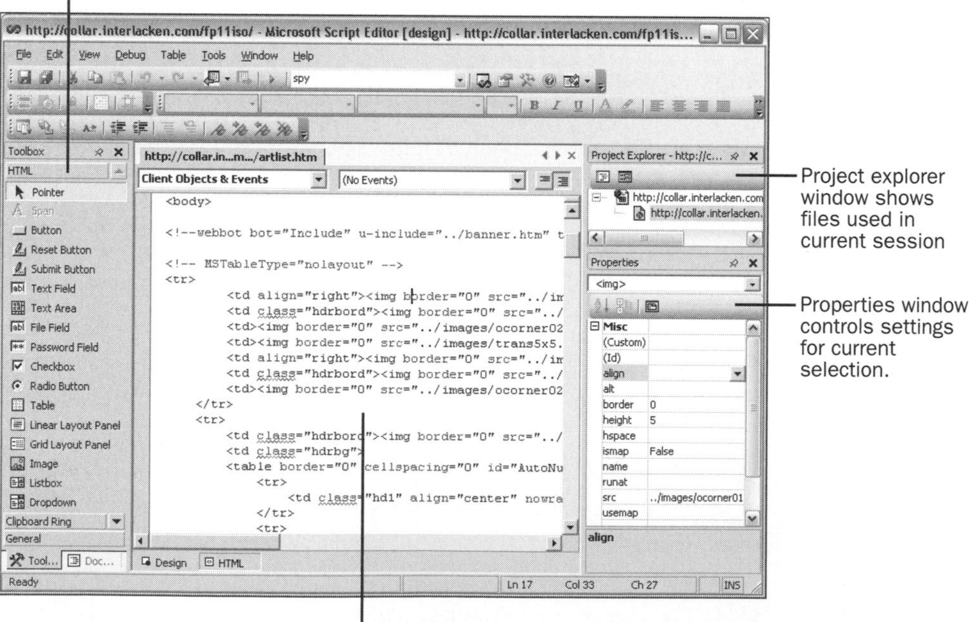

Figure 41-9. This is Microsoft Script Editor, an advanced development environment for Web coding.

Script Editor is a power tool for working with Web pages as lines of code. Working with code might have been something you hoped to avoid when you bought FrontPage, so this section will provide just an overview. If you're a coder at heart, a coder in hiding, or in fact any sort of coder at all, this will probably be enough to get you started.

Strictly speaking, Script Editor isn't part of FrontPage; it's a tool developed separately for use in various Microsoft products. Don't be surprised when Script Editor and FrontPage have different ways of doing things.

Examining the Main Document Window

The large center area in Figure 41-9 is the main document window. This is where the code for your Web page appears. You can modify the code by typing, by using the Edit menu, by using shortcut keys, and so forth.

Source code in the document window is color-coded: tag names are dark red, attribute names are bright red, attribute values are blue, and so forth. You can change the source code color scheme, font, and size by choosing Options from the Tools menu, choosing Environment, and then choosing Font And Colors.

Notice the two tabs at the bottom of the window. One of these works, and one doesn't.

- **The HTML tab** Displays your HTML code. This is the default view and the one that works.
- **The Design tab** Displays a graphical design view of the current document; this is the tab that doesn't work. When Script Editor is bundled with Microsoft Office applications such as FrontPage, it depends on the host application for graphical design view. In other words, use FrontPage, not Script Editor, for WYSIWYG editing.

> **Note** If Script Editor appeals to you and you want the Design tab to work, consider purchasing its successor, Microsoft Visual Studio .NET.

Examining the Toolbox Window

The Script Editor toolbox is a source of generic elements you can add to your Web page by dragging. It appears by default on the left in the main window, as shown in Figure 41-9. If the toolbox isn't visible, choose Toolbox from the View menu.

To add any element in the toolbox to your Web page, drag the element from the toolbox to wherever in your HTML it should appear. Script Editor will insert a basic set of tags and attributes. You'll need to fill in attribute values by hand or by using the Properties window, as described shortly.

Examining the Project Explorer Window

The Project Explorer window shows the files that make up the current Web page. As you might expect, there's usually only one file listed here—your HTML, ASP, or ASP.NET file. This window appears in the upper right corner in Figure 41-9.

Examining the Properties Window

The Properties window, located just below the Project Explorer window, is more interesting. This window displays a property sheet for most Web page elements you select in the main document window. If no properties are available for a given element, the Properties window applies to the document as a whole.

Figure 41-10 zooms in on the Properties window. There are three views, corresponding to the three toolbar icons: Alphabetic, Categorized, and Property Pages. The box above the toolbar indicates that an <img> tag is selected in the main window. The property list below the toolbar includes only those properties appropriate to the type of tag.

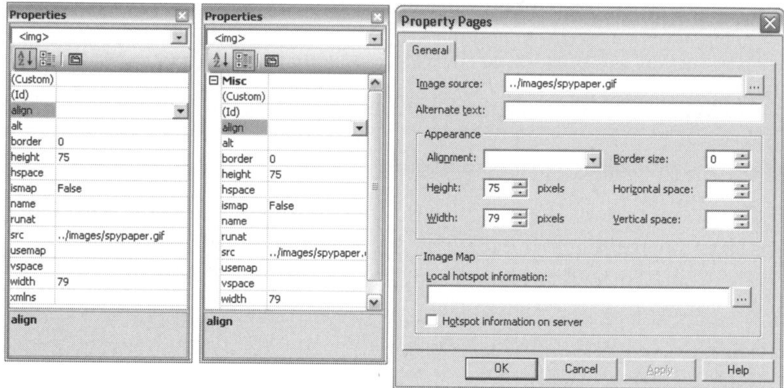

Figure 41-10. The Properties window displays settings appropriate to the item selected in the main Script Editor window. This figure shows the three views corresponding to the three toolbar icons.

- **Alphabetic view** Lists the element's properties in alphabetical order.
- **Categorized view** Lists the same properties, but grouped by category. In practice, all Web page properties fall into the same category—Misc—so sorting them by category accomplishes nothing.
- **Property Pages dialog box** Provides another view of the same properties. In general, these aren't the same dialog boxes that FrontPage uses.

To set property values in Alphabetic or Categorized view, first select the property name, and then enter the value. You can enter most values by hand, and many by drop-down list or dialog box. If a drop-down list is available, a drop-down arrow will appear when you select the property name. If a dialog box is available, an ellipsis button will appear.

Figure 41-11 and Figure 41-12 show the four tabs in Script Editor's Color Picker dialog box.

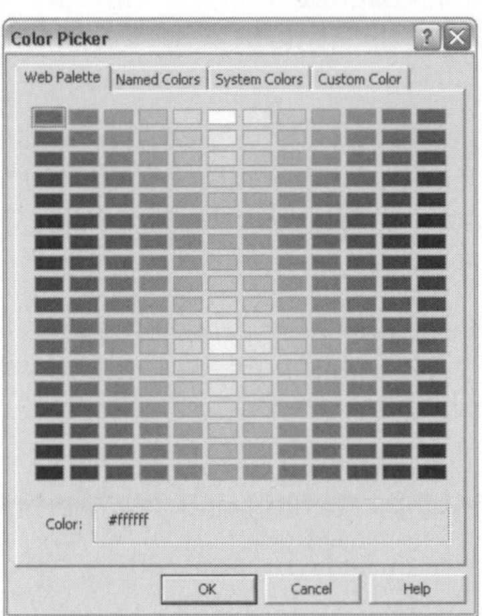

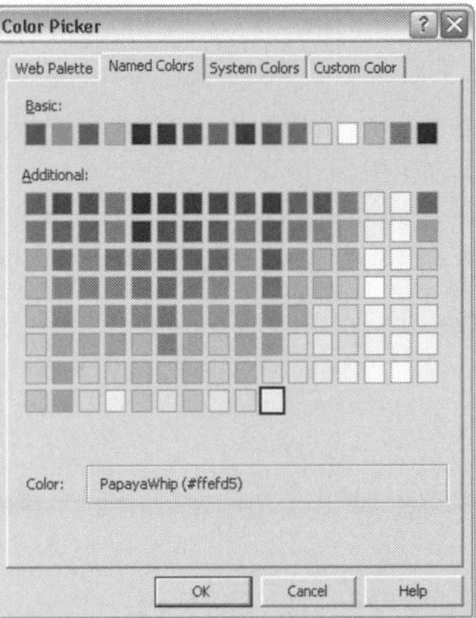

Figure 41-11. The Web Palette tab selects colors that browsers can display without dithering or substitution on 256-color display systems. The Named Colors tab selects colors that browsers recognize by name.

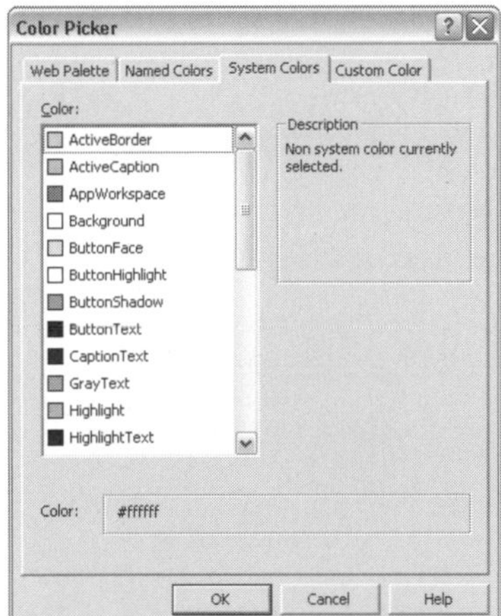

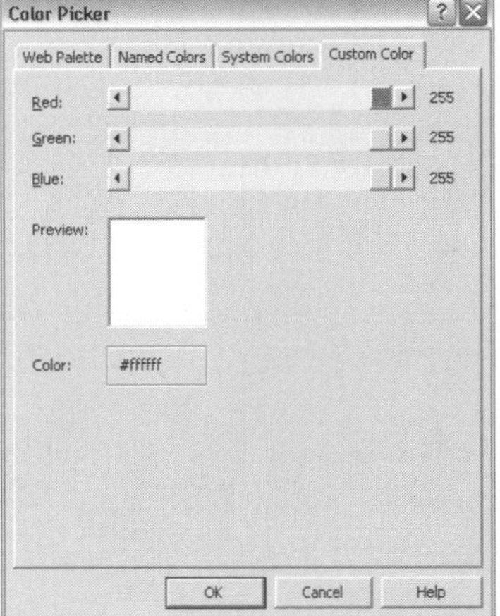

Figure 41-12. The System Colors tab assigns system colors to Web page elements. The Custom Color tab specifies colors in terms of Red, Green, and Blue components.

Here's how to use each tab in the Color Picker dialog box.

- **Web Palette** This tab, shown on the left in Figure 41-11, displays the 216 safe colors first discussed in Chapter 18. Color arrangement is roughly by hue: blues and violets to the left, greens and yellow in the center, and reds to the right.

> **Note** For more information about safe colors, see "Achieving Accurate Rendition—Safe Colors," on page 507.

- **Named Colors** This tab, shown on the right in Figure 41-11, displays the colors most browsers recognize by name. Most browsers recognize *bgcolor="PapayaWhip"* as equivalent to *bgcolor="#ffefd5"*, for example. The Named Colors tab shows all colors for which such an equivalence exists.

  The origin of this list of colors seems lost in antiquity. You might think that the named colors are better supported in some ways than in others, but if so, you'd be wrong. The Web Palette colors (also called the safe colors) are really the best supported, and very few of those have browser-recognized names.
- **System Colors** This tab, shown on the left in Figure 41-12, displays color choices based on the system colors in effect on the visitor's computer. However, colors specified this way work properly only on Internet Explorer.
- **Custom Color** This tab, shown on the right in Figure 41-12, is nothing more than another RGB color picker, with sliders for the three colors and a preview box.

Examining the Document Outline Window

The Document Outline window ,as shown in Figure 41-13, displays a condensed, structured diagram of the elements in your Web page. When you click an element in the outline, Script Editor highlights and positions its code in the main editing window. This window doesn't appear by default; to display it, choose Other Windows from the View menu, and then choose Document Outline.

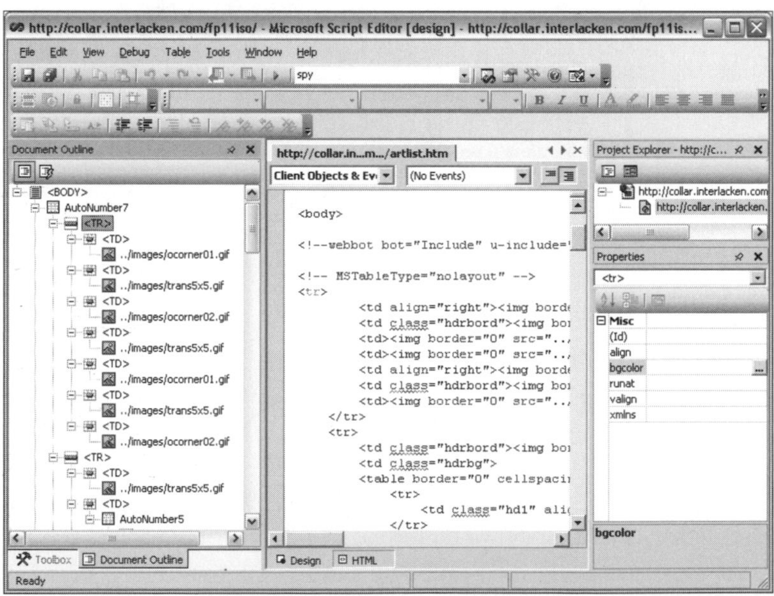

Figure 41-13. The Document Outline window shows the structure of your Web page in terms of HTML elements. Selecting an item in the Document Outline window positions and selects the corresponding code in the main document window.

Editing Script Code

As interesting as all these HTML editing features might be, Script Editor's major strength lies in entering and debugging script code. Figure 41-14 shows an example of Microsoft IntelliSense, a major advance in code editing.

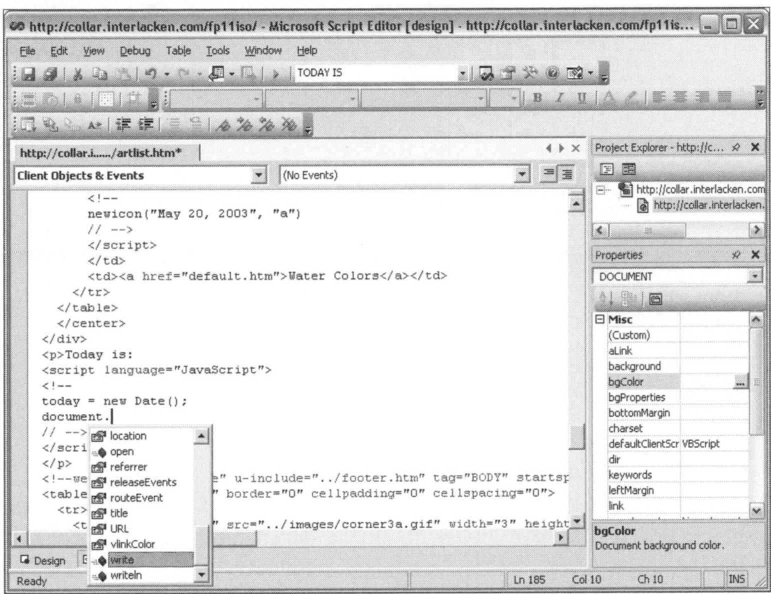

Figure 41-14. Whenever you type a period after the name of a known object, Script Editor presents a list of valid properties and methods. Here, the developer is choosing the document object's *write* method.

As in FrontPage Code view, IntelliSense kicks in whenever you type the name of an object known to Script Editor followed by the lead-in character for another element. Instantly, IntelliSense displays a drop-down list of that object's valid properties and methods. If you type additional characters, IntelliSense positions the drop-down list accordingly. Pressing the Tab key enters the complete property or method name.

Debugging Browser Scripts with Script Editor

The most impressive feature Script Editor has to offer is its ability to debug browser scripts and ASP pages interactively. This means that you can start a script, let it run one line at a time, inspect variables and objects as the script progresses, set breakpoints, and generally poke around while the script is running.

For information about debugging ASP code with Script Editor, refer to "Debugging Server Scripts with Script Editor," on page 1082.

To enable browser-side script debugging:

1 Start Internet Explorer and choose Internet Options from the Tools menu.
2 On the Advanced Tab of the Internet Options dialog box, locate the Disable Script Debugging check box, and make sure that it *isn't* selected. Figure 41-15 shows the correct setting.

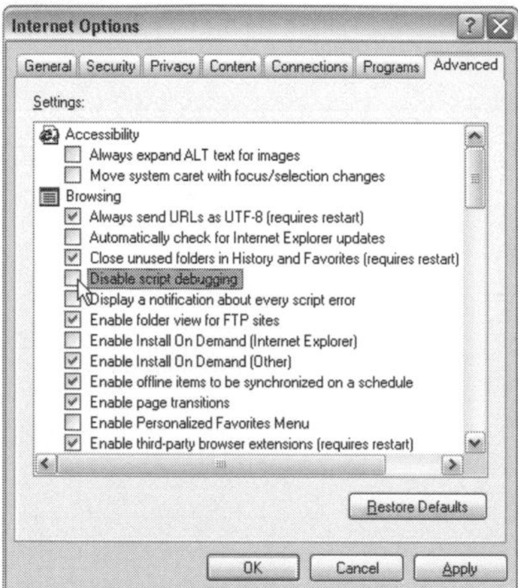

Figure 41-15. You can enable or disable browser-side scripting by configuring this dialog box in Internet Explorer. To enable or disable server-side debugging, use the Internet Information Services management console on the Web server.

Figure 41-16 shows Script Editor debugging a simple script. The arrow in the left margin shows the current statement, and the Locals window shows the values of all current local variables (local to the script in the current browser window, that is).

Here's what's happened so far:

1 The Web designer opened the file parggen.htm in Design view.
2 The designer chose Macro from the Tools menu and then chose Microsoft Script Editor.
3 In Script Editor, the designer chose Step Into from the Debug menu to load the Web page into the browser, execute the first line of script code, and highlight it in the main document window. That first line of code was:

```
cnt = 1;
```

Tip If the only option on the Debug menu is Install Web Debugging, choose that option, and then close and reopen Script Editor.

4 Each time the designer pressed F11, Script Editor executed the next sequential line of code.

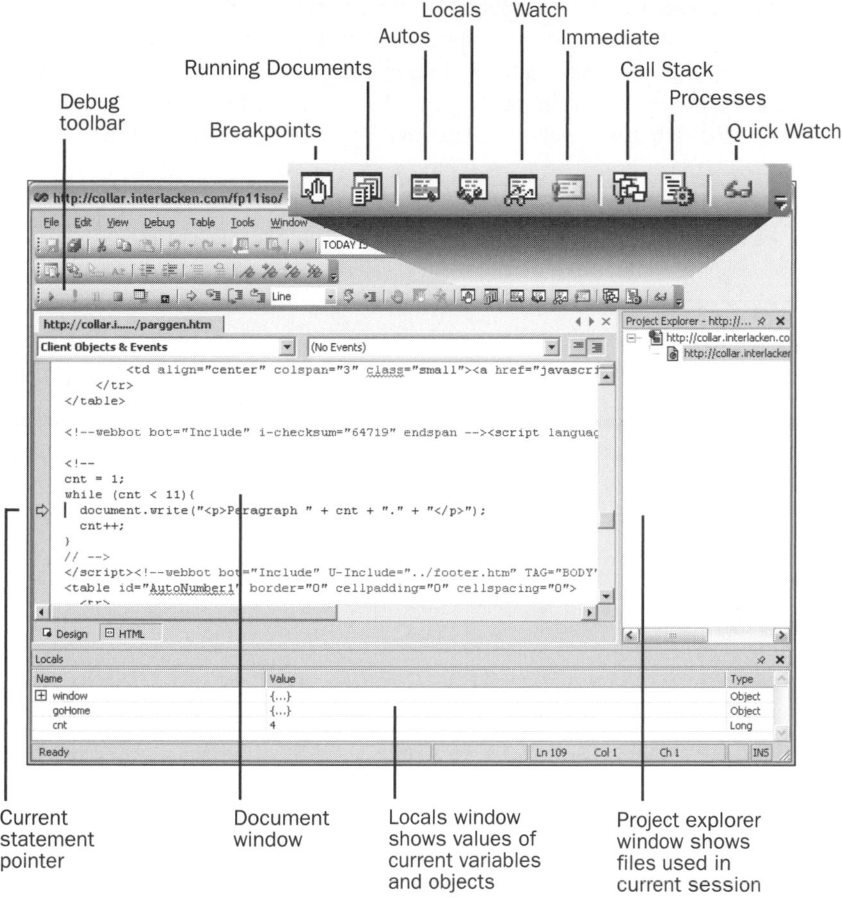

Figure 41-16. Here Script Editor is single-stepping through a browser script written in JavaScript. The highlighted statement is the next to be executed, and the value of *cnt*—in the Locals window—shows that this is the fourth iteration through the *while* loop.

The Locals window shows the values of all current, local variables (that is, of all variables available to the current script procedure). In this case, there's only one, *cnt*, and its value is 4. You can change the current value of any variable by typing over it in the Locals window.

Features like this are great for figuring out why your script is doing what it's doing, or not doing what you think it should. Repeatedly pressing the F11 key quickly becomes boring and mundane, however, especially for long and complex scripts. In such cases, it's usually preferable to set a breakpoint where a suspected problem exists, and then press the F5 key to runs the script until it reaches the breakpoint

A breakpoint flags a script statement so that whenever it's about to be executed, execution of the entire script stops. To set a breakpoint, select the statement in Script Editor, and then choose Insert Breakpoint from the Debug menu. Script Editor will flag the statement by placing a red dot in the left margin of the document window, and it will halt execution whenever that statement is about to execute. You can flag as many statements as you want as breakpoints.

Tip You can also set and remove breakpoints by double-clicking the left margin of the main document window.

To cancel a breakpoint, select the statement, and then choose Remove Breakpoint from the Debug menu. To leave the breakpoint defined but ignore it, choose Disable Breakpoint. To cancel all breakpoints, choose Clear All Breakpoints.

Script Editor is a remarkably full-featured and complex application with advanced features beyond those described here. Describing it completely would require a book this size, with no space left for FrontPage. Hopefully, however, this introduction will be enough to get you started.

In Summary...

This chapter explained how to add simple groups of programming statements called scripts to a Web page and then have those scripts execute on the browser as it receives the Web page or responds to events.

Scripts can also execute on the Web server as it transmits the page. The next chapter will explain how to create and debug Web page scripts that run on the Web server.

Chapter 42

Scripting Web Pages on the Server

Web sites built only of HTML pages and browser-side scripts are one-way conduits. They send information to your Web visitors but receive almost nothing in return. If you want your site to receive, process, save, and react to information from your Web visitors, you'll need to either sit by your Web server 24 hours a day (and be a very fast typist) or develop some sort of program to handle the interactions for you. Of course, most developers choose the latter option and learn to write programs that run on the Web server.

In terms of capabilities, programs on a Web server can do anything more conventional programs can do: check security, query and update databases, send e-mail, capture pictures, read hot tub temperatures, ring bells, toot whistles, and whatever else you can imagine. In terms of interaction with the Web visitor, however, the techniques are fairly rigid:

- The browser sends a request to a program on the Web server. Typically, this includes information from an HTML form or appended to the program's URL.
- The Web server runs the program that the browser requested.
- The program does whatever work the application requires and then, as a response, sends a customized Web page to the visitor.

Designing the HTML for these customized responses involves a dual mind-set. Typically, most of the HTML is the same for each response, and designers prefer a visual editor like Design view in Microsoft Office FrontPage 2003 for this part of the work.

From a programming point of view, server-side scripting eliminates many browser compatibility issues. There's no need to write code that works on many different browsers; you only need to write code that runs on one computer: your Web server. In addition, control is greater. All Web visitors receive information on the same basis—the server's date, for example—and visitors never see script code. Visitors can't turn off the script in their browsers.

This brief chapter can't possibly take the place of a complete book (or library) on Web programming techniques, but it should at least get you into the mind-set and help you understand where FrontPage fits in.

Introducing Server-Based Scripting

Given the wide range of other technologies found on the Web, it's no surprise that a variety of server-side programming approaches have arisen. Table 42-1 lists some of the most common, along with their proponents and typical programming languages.

Table 42-1. Web Server Programming Technologies

Acronym	Name	Proponent	Typical programming languages	Works with visual editors
ASP	Active Server Pages	Microsoft	VBScript, JavaScript	Yes
ASP.NET	Active Server Pages .NET	Microsoft	Visual Basic .NET, C#	Yes
JSP	Java Server Pages	Sun	Java	Yes
PHP	PHP: Hypertext Preprocessor	Apache Software Foundation	PHP	Yes
ISAPI	Internet Server Application Programming Interface	Microsoft	C++	No
NSAPI	Netscape Server Application Programming Interface	Sun	C, C++	No
CGI	Common Gateway Interface	National Center for Supercomputing Applications	C, C++, Perl	No

In this table, notice that ASP, ASP.NET, JSP, and PHP can all make use of visual editors like FrontPage. The developer uses a visual editor to create the overall page design and any fixed elements and then writes code to generate HTML for the variable portion of each response. Of course, the visual design must provide some sort of object or placeholder to indicate where the variable output should appear.

ISAPI, NSAPI, and CGI programs consist entirely of code and must therefore generate every scrap of HTML they send to the Web visitor. Use of these technologies to develop individual Web pages is rare; they're best suited for system software that extends the overall capabilities of Web servers.

Regardless of how you write them, server-side scripts must reside in an executable directory, and for reasons of security and resource consumption, many server administrators tightly control access to such directories.

> **Tip** If you don't administer your own Web server, you might need to contact the server administrator to get permission to run server-side scripts.

The remainder of this chapter will describe the ASP and ASP.NET approaches to developing server-side programs and explain how FrontPage fits into that process.

Developing JSP and PHP Pages in FrontPage

It should come as no surprise that FrontPage supports the Microsoft ASP and ASP.NET technologies better than competing technologies like JSP and PSP. With suitable precautions, however, FrontPage and these other technologies *can* work together. Here are some tips to get you started:

- **Disable features that use the FrontPage Server Extensions.** Unless the Web server that runs your JSP or PHP pages has the FrontPage Server Extensions installed:
  - Choose Page Options from the Tools menu, and then click the Authoring tab.
  - Clear the Windows SharePoint Services and Browse-Time Web Components check boxes.
- **Disable features that create ASP or ASP.NET code.** Unless the Web server that runs your JSP or PHP pages can also run ASP:
  - Choose Page Options from the Tools menu, and then click the Authoring tab.
  - Clear the Active Server Pages check box.
- **In the case of PHP, enable and use ASP-style <% and %> code delimiters.** To do this, open the Web server's php.ini file, and set `asp_tags="1"`. Then use ASP-like <% %> tags rather than the usual <?php ?> tags. This stops FrontPage from reformatting your PHP code.
- **Configure the JSP and PHP file extensions to open in Design view.** To do this:
  - Choose Options from the Tools menu, and then click the Configure Editors tab.
  - Locate and select the file extension you want to use, select FrontPage (Open as HTML), and then click the Make Default button.

  If the extension you want doesn't appear, click the New Extension button above the Extensions list. Then, when the Open With dialog box appears, type the extension you want, select FrontPage (Open as HTML), and click OK.

  If you later find that the Design view editor corrupts your JSP or PHP files, repeat this procedure, but set the default to FrontPage (Open As Text).

Introducing Active Server Pages

This technology was Microsoft's first attempt to make scripting on the Web server as easy as scripting on the browser. By almost any measure, it's been spectacularly successful. ASP pages quickly achieved number one status as the leading technology for writing server-side scripts that run on Microsoft Web servers.

> **Caution** ASP is available only on Microsoft Web servers. If your Web server uses different software, contact the server's administrator for information about alternative approaches. Third-party implementations of ASP are available for UNIX, but they aren't 100% compatible with Microsoft ASP.

The basic ASP paradigm is quite simple. When the server gets a request for an ASP Web page, it processes the page, executes the server-side script, and sends only the results to the visitor. The results consist of plain HTML and not the original script statements.

The script code can appear anywhere in the Web page, but it must be within either of these special tags:

- **<script runat="server"> and </script>** These tags delimit a *code declaration block.* The server saves up any script statements you enclose with these tags and runs them when it encounters the end of the Web page.

  Few, if any, developers use these tags in ASP pages. This is because any code the tags enclose runs after the body of the page has left the server, and that's too late to customize the page.
- **<% and %>** These tags delimit a *code render block.* Any statements they enclose execute immediately. Virtually all real-world ASP code resides between such tags.

Each ASP page executes as one program. This means that in general, any variables you declare in one <% %> block are available in all subsequent <% %> blocks. (Of course, any variables you declare within a subroutine or function are available only within that subroutine or function.)

The default and most popular programming language for ASP pages is VBScript. Microsoft also supports its implementation of JavaScript (called JScript) on ASP pages, and other languages such as Perl are available from third parties. Remember that the Web server executes this code and that the browser sees only the results, so there's no need to choose a server-side programming language that browsers support.

> **Tip** **Server-side scripts and browser-side scripts can co-exist.**
> There's no restriction against using server-side and browser-side scripts on the same page. The two script types are identified differently in the HTML, allowing the server-side script processor to pass browser-side script statements to the browser unmodified. Server-side scripts can even generate browser-side scripts by writing the necessary statements to the outbound HTML stream.

Whenever an ASP page is running, it automatically has access to the five objects listed below. A high percentage of the work that ASP pages perform involves manipulation of these objects.

- *Request* Provides information about the Web visitor's current request.
- *Response* Sends a Web page or other response back to the Web visitor.
- *Server* Provides access to information and resources located on the Web server.
- *Session* Stores information about multiple requests from the same Web visitor.
- *Application* Provides shared information for all visitors using the same application (that is, using ASP pages in the same designated folder tree).

VBScript has no built-in capability to access databases, read and write files, or send e-mail. To perform these tasks, ASP programmers generally use objects from these collections:

- **ActiveX Data Objects (ADO)** Objects from this collection access and update databases.
- **Scripting.FileSystemObject** Objects from this collection access and update files on the Web server.
- **Collaboration Data Objects (CDO)** Objects from this collection send e-mail.

> **For information about configuring Microsoft Web servers to run scripts, see Appendix O, "Installing and Configuring a Web Server."**

Changing Content with ASP Code (Coding Example 1)

This section will illustrate a server-side solution to one of the problems posed in the previous chapter—the problem of displaying New! and Upd! icons for a specified period of time. This solution uses VBScript and the ASP feature of IIS. Figure 42-1 shows the results.

The code to set the first item's picture is shown here:

```
<% maxdays = 14 %>
<% If (now - #5/15/2003# < maxdays) Then %>
     <img src="../images/new.gif">
<% Else %>
     <img src="../images/cyanball.gif">
<% End If %>
```

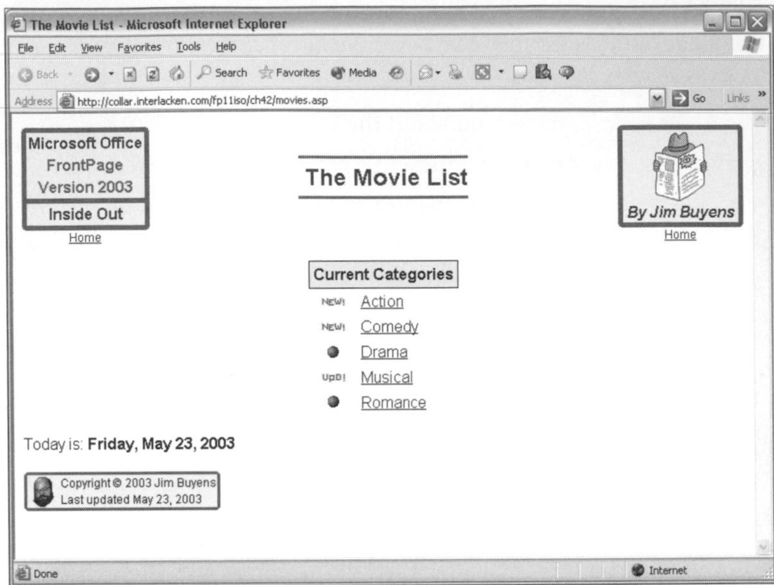

Figure 42-1. This Web page is very similar to the page shown in Figure 41-5, but it uses server-side scripting. The file extension is .asp rather than .htm, and the page resides in an executable directory.

Four features of VBScript make this code somewhat simpler than the Java Script version:

- The *now* function in VBScript returns the current date and time.
- Dates and times in VBScript are stored as whole numbers for days and fractions of a day for time—6:00 AM is 0.25, 12:00 noon is 0.5, and 6:00 PM is 0.75, for example. Subtracting two dates immediately provides the difference in days.
- VBScript directly supports date values. VBScript treats anything you enclose in pound signs (#) as a date.
- VBScript supports a *response.write* method that's similar to JavaScript's *document.write* method.

Given these features:

- Line 1 in the listing above defines a variable that gives the cutoff period in days: 14.
- Line 2 subtracts the date 5/15/2003 from the current date, giving the difference in days, and then compares the difference to the cutoff period.
- Line 3 is ordinary HTML that the server transmits to the browser only if the *If* condition is true (that is, only if 5/15/2003 is within 14 days of the current date).
- Line 4 is an *Else* statement that negates the *If* statement on line 2.
- Line 5 is ordinary HTML that the server transmits to the browser only if the *If* condition on line 2 is false.
- Line 6 terminates the *If* condition.

The code on lines 2 through 6 can be repeated to generate the bullet for each item in the jump list. Because there's less code to repeat than in the JavaScript example, it isn't so tempting to create a procedure. Not creating a procedure also avoids the complexity of passing the item date and the add-or-update indicator as arguments. Instead, you can simply hard-code the date and icon (New! or Upd!).

Figure 42-2 shows the Web page of Figure 42-1 open in FrontPage. Line 1 from the preceding listing resides in the <head> section and doesn't appear in WYSIWYG view. Each category row begins with three VBScript components containing the *If*, *Else*, and *End If* statements from lines 2, 4, and 6, respectively. Lines 3 and 5 of the listing appear as ordinary HTML, which accounts for the appearance of the picture bullets.

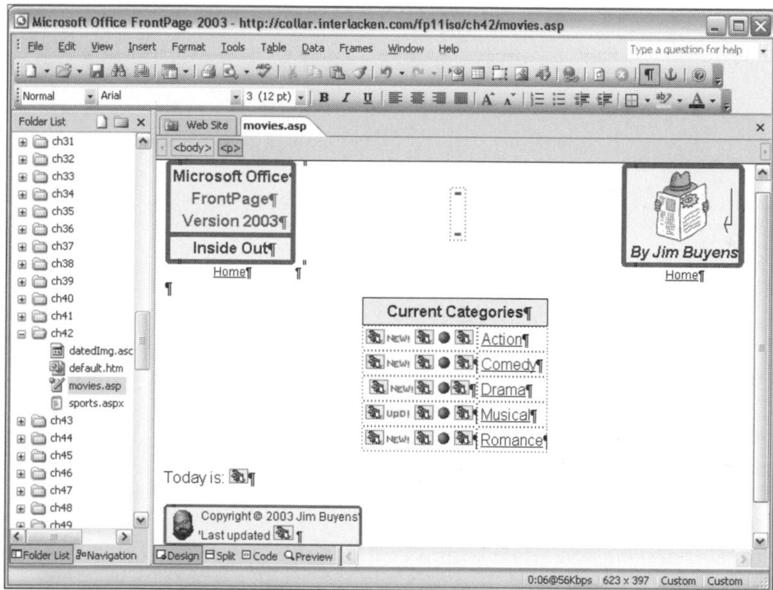

Figure 42-2. This is how the Web page from Figure 42-1 appears in FrontPage. The three VBScript components preceding each category item contain *If*, *Else*, and *End If* statements so that visitors see only one icon.

Figure 42-3 shows the same Web page open in Code view. You can see the *maxdays = 14* statement just before the *</head>* statement, and one of the *If...Else...End If* sequences that control the bullets.

To add additional categories, the designer would copy a set of three VBScript components and two icons from an existing row, double-click the first icon to set the date, and change the icon file name to new.gif if necessary. To flag a category as updated, the author would change the icon file name to upd.gif if necessary and then double-click the first component to reset the date.

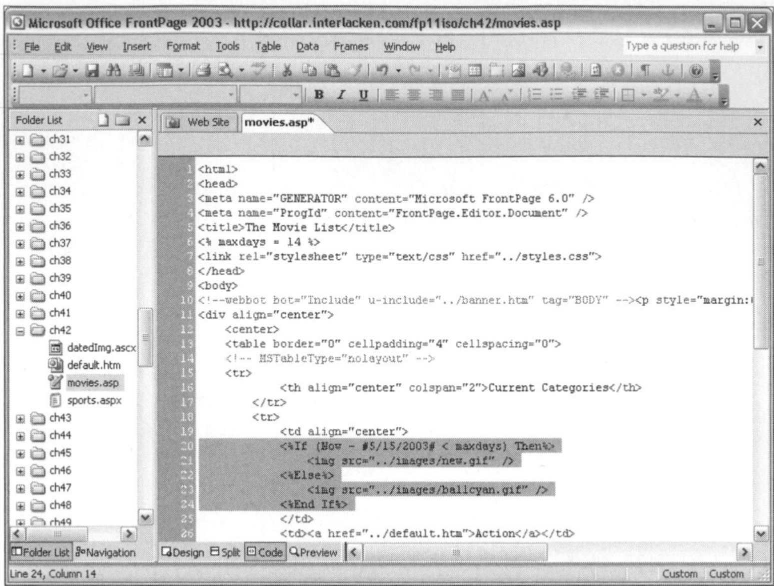

Figure 42-3. Here are the contents of the first VBScript component in row 1, column 1 of the category table in Figure 42-2.

The last Script component on the page displays the current date. The code required to do this is quite simple:

```
<%=formatDateTime(Now, vbLongDate) %>
```

Within an ASP page, an expression containing a start <% tag, an equal sign (=), a VBScript expression, and an end %> tag all on the same line is equivalent to one line of code that begins with a *document.write* statement. (That is, it evaluates everything between <%= and %> as a VBScript expression and inserts the result into the HTML stream.) Type conversion is automatic in VBScript, so *<% = now %>* would display the current date and time in a default format. The expression shown displays the current day and date with the month in words. The name *vbLongDate* is a constant built into VBScript.

Debugging Server Scripts with Microsoft Script Editor

Microsoft Script Editor can interactively debug server-side scripts, but it has no remote debugging capability. To interactively debug an ASP page, you must run Internet Explorer, Script Editor, and IIS all on the same computer. In practical terms, the best platform for debugging ASP scripts interactively is likely to be Microsoft Windows XP Professional.

> **Note** **Save ASP files before opening them in Script Editor**
> Script Editor activates IntelliSense for ASP code only when the file extension is .asp. If you create a new ASP page and switch to Script Editor before saving the page for the first time, the file name will be new_page_1.htm, and IntelliSense for ASP code won't be available. To avoid this situation, always save ASP files before opening them in Script Editor.

To enable server-side debugging, the server's administrator must select the Enable ASP Server-Side Script Debugging check box on the Debugging tab of the Application Configuration dialog box, as shown in Figure 42-4. This dialog box is part of the IIS snap-in for Microsoft Management Console (MMC).

For more information about the settings in the Application Configuration dialog box, refer to "Configuring Home Directory Settings," in Appendix O.

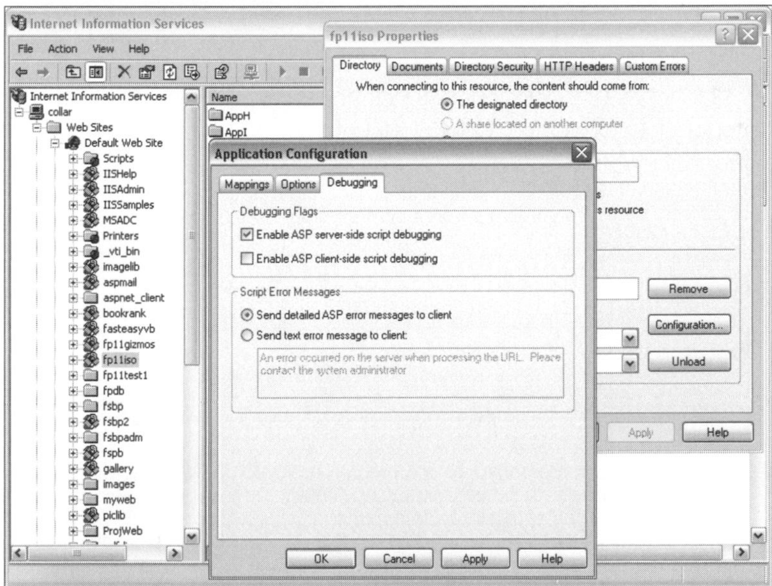

Figure 42-4. To debug a server-side script, you must enable debugging on the Web server.

To start a debugging session for an ASP page, you must first use a browser to request the page. Then one of two things must happen that interrupt script processing:

- **A script command** In VBScript, the *Stop* command will open the debugger, tell it to open the current page, and position it at the current statement. In JavaScript, the equivalent command is *debugger*.
- **An error** If the ASP processor detects a server-side scripting error and debugging is enabled, it starts Script Editor immediately.

In either case, Script Editor will automatically display the page and the statement that caused the interruption.

Script Editor can display several specialized debugging windows in addition to those that appear automatically. You can hide or display these windows by choosing options on the View menu or by clicking toolbar buttons. Figure 42-5 shows how to locate these options.

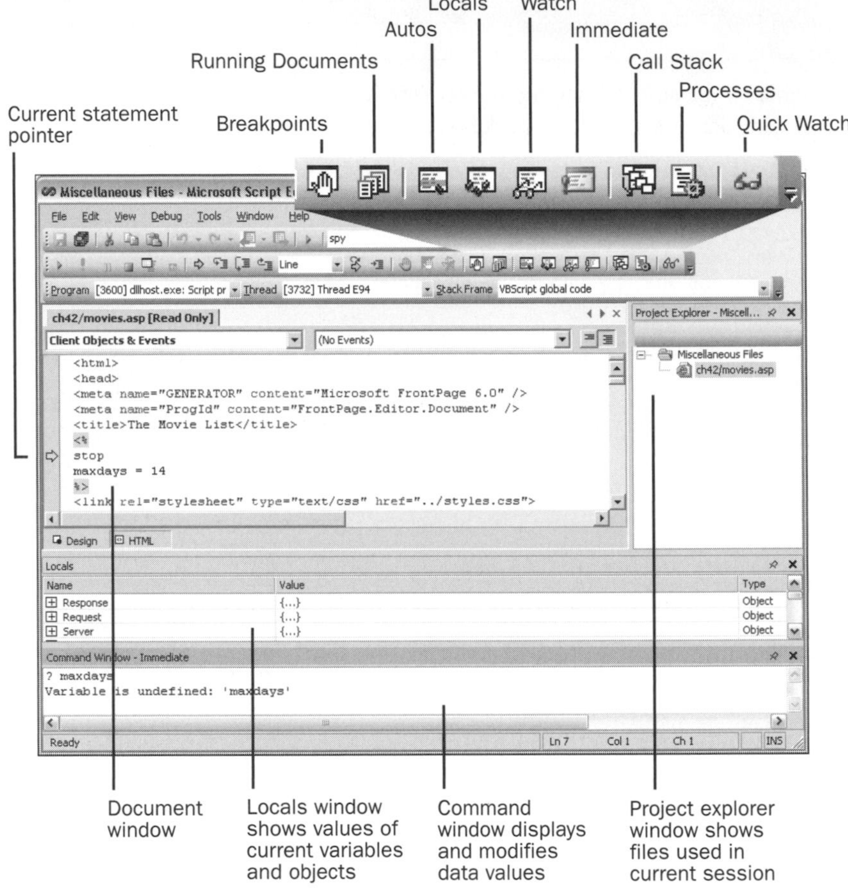

Figure 42-5. Microsoft Script Editor can interactively display values, modify values, and trace the flow of execution in an ASP page.

- **Breakpoints** Displays a current list of statements where script processing will halt.
- **Running Documents** Lists two groups of Web pages. To debug any listed document, double-click its entry:
  - **Microsoft Active Server Pages** Lists any ASP pages that the server is currently executing. Note that an ASP page will appear under this entry only if the Web server temporarily suspends execution of that page. The Web server does this only if debugging is in effect for the given executable folder and the Web page either fails or executes a *Stop* or *debugger* statement (in VBScript and JavaScript, respectively).

- **Microsoft Internet Explorer** Lists any Web pages currently displayed in your browser. Note, however, that double-clicking an ASP page under this entry loads only the code that Internet Explorer receives (that is, the response HTML and any browser-side scripts it contains).

- **Autos** Lists the name, value, and type of each value in the current statement and the previous statement.
- **Locals** Displays the values of all variables available to the current script.
- **Watch** Displays a list of all variables you've instructed the debugger to monitor.
- **Immediate** Accepts typed commands and displays the results. You can use this window to query or modify variables and properties in your script or to run hand-entered script statements.

  The Command Window always uses the language of the currently executing statement. If you're running a block of VBScript code, the Command Window expects VBScript statements. If you're running a block of JavaScript code, it expects JavaScript statements.

  To display a variable or property in VBScript, enter a question mark, a space, and the name of the variable or property.

  To display a variable or property in JavaScript, simply enter its name.
- **Call Stack** Lists any subroutine or functions that are currently running.
- **Processes** Displays a list of applications currently running on the server.
- **QuickWatch** Displays the value of the currently selected expression.

Starting an ASP debugging session is a somewhat indirect process, and it might cause the browser to time out. To understand why this is so, consider the flow of control:

1. The browser requests the page.
2. The Web server detects a serious error or a *Stop* statement and finds that server-side debugging is in effect.
3. The Web server halts the script.
4. The Web server looks for a running copy of Script Editor. If it finds one, it tells Script Editor to start a debugging session. If it can't find a running copy of Script Editor, it starts one and proceeds as before.
5. The developer debugs the Web page.
6. The browser either times out or displays the resulting Web page, depending on how long the developer spends debugging.

Introducing ASP.NET Web Forms

As part of its .NET Framework initiative, Microsoft has released a major upgrade to ASP. This is, of course, Microsoft ASP.NET. The new version reflects several years of experience and enhancement, and it differs considerably from the older ASP technology. Here are some of the limitations ASP.NET resolves:

- VBScript isn't suited for developing reusable modules. To use the same code in several pages, you must copy it into each page.
- Neither ASP nor VBScript has access to the full functionality of the underlying Windows operating system.
- The practice of putting program code where its output should appear in a Web page doesn't scale well. In complex pages, code can end up in all sorts of odd places.
- At many large sites, Web page designers and Web page programmers are two very different groups of people. With the page design and the program code both residing in the same file, conflicts and confusion inevitably arose.

ASP.NET resolves these issues in the following ways:

- ASP.NET uses the full Visual Basic .NET programming language. This is the most capable and most feature-complete version of Visual Basic ever released. You can also code ASP.NET pages in C# or any other language that has a .NET compiler.
- Visual Basic .NET, C#, and other supported languages have access to the entire set of .NET system-level objects. Essentially, this means that an ASP.NET page can do anything Windows can do.
- All .NET programming languages are fully object-oriented. This means that they have access to class libraries and other forms of reusable code.
- ASP.NET clearly separates program code from Web page layout code. You can even store the two kinds of code in different files and then change one without changing the other. You can still mix program code and HTML code if you want to, but after you become accustomed to the new structure, you'll seldom if ever have the desire.
- With ASP.NET, you can create your own program objects—with methods, properties, and all the other accoutrements you want—in essentially the same way that you create Web pages.

ASP.NET also changes the fundamental paradigm for running server-side code. ASP ran code in (and inserted content into) each part of the Web page as it left the server. ASP.NET, on the other hand:

- Reads the whole page into memory, storing each HTML tag you want to modify as an object.

  More specifically, ASP.NET loads any tag containing a *runat="server"* attribute into memory as an object. This can be any type of tag, regardless of whether it normally supports a *runat="server"* attribute.
- Fires a series of events. Some of these occur because of something the Web visitor did, such as clicking a button, and some occur every time a page runs. Designated

subroutines (event handlers) in your code respond to these events and can raise additional events of their own. Table 42-2 list the events that occur during each execution of a page.

- Converts the page from a collection of objects back to HTML and transmits this result to the Web visitor. Each object has the opportunity to send whatever HTML it wants to the Web visitor, regardless of the HTML that created the object. For example, none of the objects send the *runat="server"* attribute to the browser.

Table 42-2. ASP.NET Page Events

Event	Event handler	Description
Init	Page_Init	Occurs when ASP.NET initializes the page. No page elements are available at this time.
Load	*Page_Load*	Occurs when ASP.NET has loaded all server controls into memory.
PreRender	*Page_PreRender*	Occurs when ASP.NET is ready to render the page as HTML.
Unload	*Page_Unload*	Occurs after ASP.NET has removed all server controls from memory.

Another unique aspect of ASP.NET pages is that by default, every page is an HTML form, and that <form> tag has the *runat="server"* attribute. This is because ASP.NET uses hidden form fields to remember the state of the page from one execution to the next. The presence of <form> and </form> tags when you don't expect them might be a surprise, but they do little harm, and you shouldn't remove them. The way ASP.NET uses forms does, however, lead to two restrictions:

- Each page can contain only one HTML form.
- Each HTML form must request the page that contains it. You can't, for example, use one Web page for data entry and another for processing.

If you want your application to behave as if these restrictions weren't present, you can do so using other techniques. Upon receiving a request, for example, the server-side code for one page can transfer control to another page. These techniques, however, are beyond the scope of this book.

Changing Content with ASP.NET Code (Coding Example 2)

To visualize how some of this works, consider the task of displaying the current date on a Web page, as the Art List example in the previous chapter did, or as the Movie List example in this chapter does. Both of those examples included a line of code where the date was supposed to appear. To use the ASP.NET approach for this task, you would add a tag like the following where you wanted the date to appear:

```
<asp:literal id="litTodayIs" runat="server" />
```

Because this tag contains a *runat="server"* attribute, ASP.NET loads it as an object each time the page executes. The *id=* attribute gives the object a name. The slash (/)just before the closing angle bracket (>) takes the place of an </asp:literal> end tag.

When ASP.NET sends the page to the visitor, this object supplies the contents of a property named *Text*. So, if the page contains this statement:

```
litTodayIs.Text = Now()
```

the Web visitor will receive the current date and time in place of the <asp:literal> tag shown above. The *Page_Load* event handler is a common place for such a statement, because *Page_Load* occurs after ASP.NET has loaded all the objects in the page, and before ASP.NET sends any output to the Web visitor. The first few lines in the Web page might therefore be:

```
1 <%@ Page Language="vb" %>
2 <script runat="server">
3 Sub Page_Load (sender As Object, e As EventArgs)
4     litTodayIs.Text = Now()
5 End Sub
6 </script>
```

Line 1 is a @ *Page* directive, which sets compile and run-time options for the page. Lines 2 and 6 mark the limits of a code declaration block (that is, an area that contains executable code). Lines 3 and 5 mark the beginning and end of the *Page_Load* subroutine, which, by virtue of its name, runs every time the *Page_Load* event occurs. The *sender* argument points to the object that raised the event (in this case, the *Page* object), and the *e* argument points to an object that contains any special information related to the event (in this case, none). Line 4, of course, does the work.

The task of conditionally displaying a New! or an Upd! icon rather than a round bullet is more interesting. Wouldn't it be great to have an HTML tag that displays either of two pictures, based on the interval from some starting date? Well, how about a tag like this?

```
<fp11iso:datedImg id=" dimgBaseball" runat="server"
    src1="ballcyan.gif" src2="new.gif"
    start="4/4/2003" duration="14" />
```

The *src1* attribute specifies the name of the picture that the tag will normally display. The *src2* attribute specifies an alternative picture. The *start* attribute specifies when to start showing the alternative picture, and the *duration* attribute specifies the number of days to continue displaying it.

As it happens, ASP.NET is great at this sort of thing. The preceding tag is a perfect example. The tag name <fp11iso:datedImg> came from the following statement, which defines an *ASP.NET user control*:

```
<%@ Register TagPrefix="fp11iso" TagName="datedImg"
Src="datedImg.ascx" %>
```

This is a directive that associates the tag prefix and name fp11iso:datedImg with the file datedImg.ascx. (The *c* in the third position of the file extension denotes *control.*) At a summary level, the datedImg.ascx file consists of these statements:

```
<%@ Control Language="vb" %>
<script runat="server">
Public src1 As String = ""
Public src2 As String = ""
Public duration As String = ""
Public start As String = ""

Private Sub Page_Load(sender As Object, e As EventArgs)
'   Program code goes here.
End Sub
</script>
<img border="0" src="ballcyan.gif" id="imgPic" runat="server">
```

The *@ Control* directive sets options for a user control, just as the *@ Page* directive sets options for a complete page. The <script runat="server"> and </script> tags create a code declaration block as before. The four public variables *src1*, *src2*, *duration*, and *start* automatically receive the corresponding attribute values from the tag that loads the control.

The <img> tag on the last line is a template for the HTML that the control will create. It has a *runat="server"* attribute so that ASP.NET will load it as an object and an *id=* attribute so that code in the *Page_Load* subroutine can refer to it by name. Program code can read and modify the value of the *src* attribute by using the expression *imgPic.src*.

Here's the program code that goes inside the *Page_Load* subroutine:

```
Dim dteStart As Date              ' Working copy of start date.
Dim intDuration As Integer = 0    ' Working copy of duration.
Dim strSource As String = ""      ' Hold area for picture name.

If IsDate(start) Then             ' Is start date valid?
    dteStart = CDate(start)       ' If so, convert to .NET Date.
    If IsNumeric(duration) Then        ' If duration is valid
        intDuration = CInt(duration) ' Convert to .NET Integer,
    Else                               ' Otherwise
        intDuration = 14               ' Default to 14.
    End If
                                  ' Get difference between
                                  ' start date and today's date.
    Select Case DateDiff(DateInterval.Day, dteStart, Now.Date)
        Case < 0                  ' If negative, use src1
            strSource = src1      ' use src1,
        Case < intDuration        ' If 0 through duration
            strSource = src2      ' use src2,
        Case Else                 ' Otherwise
            strSource = src1      ' use src1.
    End Select
Else                              ' If start date is invalid
    strSource = src1              ' use src1.
End If
```

```
imgPic.Src = Request.ApplicationPath ' Initialize path.
If Not imgPic.Src.EndsWith("/") Then ' If / is missing
   imgPic.Src &= "/"                 ' append it.
End If
imgPic.Src &= "images/" & strSource  ' Append images folder
                                     ' and picture file name.
```

On the CD   To view the complete code for this page and for the datedlgm custom control, open the ch42/sports.aspx and ch42/datedImg.ascx files you installed from the companion CD.

There are just two additional points worth mentioning:

- Dates in the .NET Framework are very large integers that count the number of 100-nanosecond ticks since midnight on January 1 of the year 1. This would make data arithmetic difficult, were it not for the availability of built-in functions like *DateDiff*. The *DateDiff* function returns the difference between two dates in any unit of measure you want.
- FrontPage doesn't automatically adjust the URLs in a custom server control as it does in ordinary HTML code. There's simply no way for FrontPage to figure out the difference between a URL and ordinary text. To provide some portability between pages in different locations, this control therefore builds an absolute path based on the current application root, plus the images folder, plus the picture file name. The expression *Request.ApplicationPath* returns the URL of the current application root.

Figure 42-6 shows how the sports.aspx page looks in a browser: perfectly normal. If you browse this page and choose Source from the View menu, you'll find ordinary <img> tags where <fp11iso:datedImg> tags appeared in the source file.

Because code for built-in ASP.NET controls like <asp:literal> and for custom controls like <fp11iso:datedImg> differs so markedly from the code that the Web visitor sees, you might wonder how FrontPage displays such controls. Figure 42-7 provides the answer: It displays them as gray boxes annotated with the type of control. This reflects the fact that the source code has no appearance until it runs and that each time it runs, the results might be different.

Inside Out

Include Page components might not appear correctly in ASP.NET pages

The page banner and page footer are not visible in Figure 42-7 because of an apparent bug (or bug-like feature) in early versions of FrontPage 2003. This bug or feature displayed Include Page components correctly in FrontPage but didn't save the included HTML as part of the page. The sports.aspx page therefore uses custom controls to display the page banner and footer, and these of course appear in FrontPage as gray boxes.

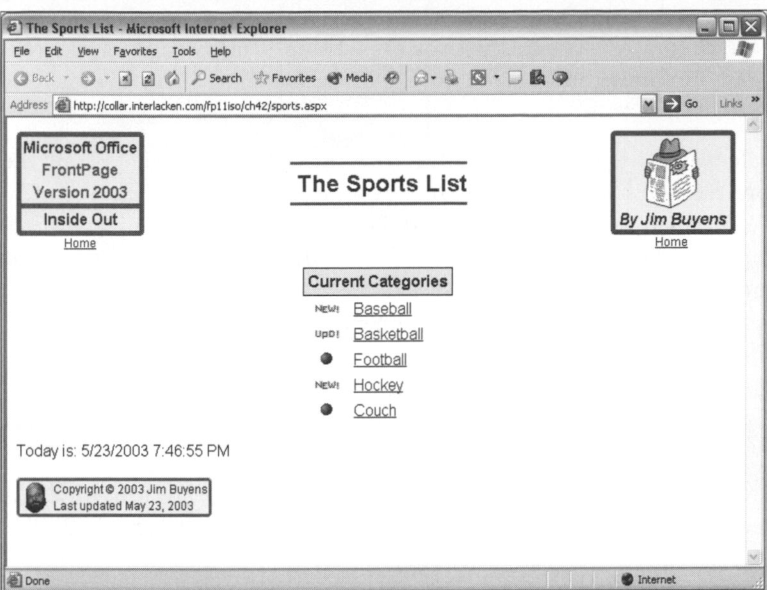

Figure 42-6. An ASP. NET custom control displays the ball, New!, or Upd! bullet pictures in this Web page based on attributes in the HTML and on the current date.

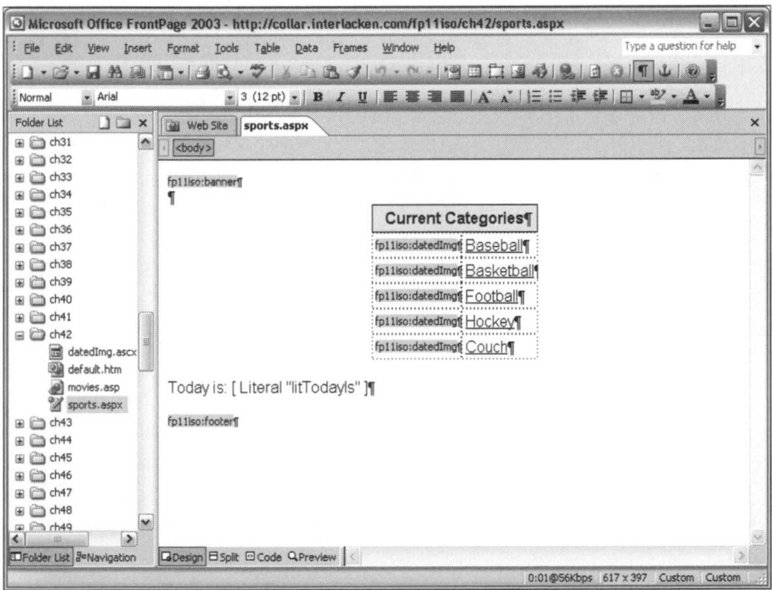

Figure 42-7. FrontPage displays ASP. NET controls as simple gray boxes.

Custom controls are one way that ASP.NET facilitates reuse of code. Once you have a custom control working, you can use it as often as you want in as many pages as you want, and never worry about duplicating code. If you do find a bug someday, fixing it in one place will fix it everywhere.

The sample files sports.aspx and datedImg.ascx contain both the HTML and the program code in one file. ASP.NET calls this the *inline code model.* When you create ASP.NET pages in Visual Studio .NET, the program code and the HTML reside in separate files. Visual Studio then compiles all the code files for a site into one DLL and adds directives to each Web page so that the page runs the correct code. This is the *code-behind model*, and it's also the technique that lets programmers and page designers work with separate files. The next chapter will discuss this technique in greater detail.

In Summary...

This chapter explained the fundamentals of using script code that runs on the Web server rather than on the browser and showed examples using both ASP and ASP.NET.

The next chapter will explain how to leverage the design and site management power of FrontPage and the programming power of Visual Studio .NET in one project.

Chapter 43

Using FrontPage 2003 and Visual Studio .NET Together

Compared to earlier versions, Microsoft Office FrontPage 2003 provides more and better features than ever for working with code. Even so, FrontPage makes no claims of being a complete and integrated software development environment. That distinction goes to Microsoft Visual Studio .NET 2003.

Visual Studio is Microsoft's top-tier platform for developing software of all kinds, and that includes software that runs on Web servers. Specifically, Visual Studio .NET is the preferred development environment for Microsoft ASP.NET Web pages. Visual Studio includes not only a full-bore programmer's code editor, but a graphical HTML editor as well. Unfortunately, this HTML editor lacks many of the tools and conveniences that FrontPage provides.

Because each product has different strengths, Web designers typically prefer FrontPage, and Web programmers usually prefer Visual Studio, even if people with both specialties are working on the same project. Individuals who perform both roles might prefer to switch between products, depending on the task at hand. This chapter explains how these two pieces of software (and their corresponding approaches to creating Web pages) can coexist peacefully.

This chapter isn't an introduction to Visual Studio, or to programming in general. It presumes that you already know how to use both Visual Studio and FrontPage, and that you now want the freedom to choose between them for a particular task.

Choosing the Correct Version of Visual Studio .NET

Product packaging is subject to frequent change, but the initial release of Visual Studio .NET 2003 included four editions designated as Standard. These standard editions include most of the Visual Studio development environment, but only one programming language. In addition, the graphical database tools that Visual Studio provides will work only with Microsoft Access databases and with local MSDE databases.

Note The Microsoft Data Engine (MSDE) is a run-time version of SQL Server that includes only rudimentary administration tools.

The four packages are:

- **Microsoft Visual Basic .NET Standard** BASIC is one of the most widely known programming languages in the world. In addition, most developers who wrote classic ASP applications did so in VBScript. Visual Basic .NET is the most powerful and sophisticated version of BASIC ever released.
- **Microsoft Visual C# .NET Standard** Visual C# is a professional programming language similar in syntax to JavaScript, Java, and C++, but tailored specifically for .NET programming.

  Visual Basic .NET and Visual C# .NET are by far the most popular languages for developing ASP.NET pages.
- **Microsoft Visual J# .NET Standard** Visual J# .NET provides an implementation of the Java programming language, but frankly, most programmers who want to work in Java do so on a non-Windows platform.
- **Microsoft Visual C++ .NET Standard** Visual C++ is by far the most difficult of these four languages to use for ASP.NET programming. As a result, and despite a bit of a learning curve, most C++ programmers switch to Visual C# for ASP.NET development.

The greatest attraction of these single-language editions is their low price. Typically, you can purchase them for about the same price as a copy of FrontPage. If you need only one programming language and you require only simple database features, purchasing one of these editions is an excellent way to get started.

If you need multiple programming languages or full graphical database features, the following editions of Microsoft Visual Studio .NET will provide a better match. Each includes all four of the languages mentioned earlier, plus an increasing number of design, database, and testing tools.

- Microsoft Visual Studio .NET Professional
- Microsoft Visual Studio .NET Enterprise Developer
- Microsoft Visual Studio .NET Enterprise Architect

Many companies and consultants purchase Video Studio as part of a Microsoft Developer Network (MSDN) subscription. For an annual fee, an MSDN subscription provides licensing for a designated bundle of Microsoft applications, operating systems, and development tools, including Visual Studio.

Of the many editions of Visual Studio .NET, at least one will almost certainly be cheap enough or full-featured enough to meet your needs. The information in the rest of this chapter applies to all editions of Visual Studio .NET, including the single-language Standard editions.

Collocating ASP.NET Projects and FrontPage-Based Web Sites

To create ASP.NET Web pages in Visual Studio, you must first create an ASP.NET *project.* This is a group of ASP.NET pages and related files that Visual Studio manages as a unit. ASP.NET projects and FrontPage-based Web sites are quite analogous, and both can exist in the same physical folder tree.

Here's the procedure for creating a new ASP.NET project:

1. Choose New from the Visual Studio .NET File menu, and then choose Project from the submenu. (Alternatively, click New Project on the Visual Studio .NET Start Page.) This will display the New Project dialog box, shown in Figure 43-1.

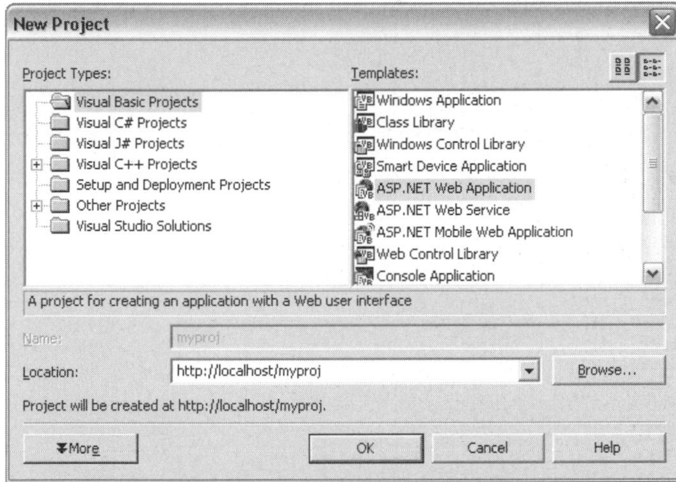

Figure 43-1. This dialog box creates a new Visual Studio project. An ASP.NET Web application can also be a FrontPage-based Web site.

2. Configure the New Project dialog box as follows:
   - **Project Types** Select the entry that corresponds to the programming language you want to use for your project. In most cases, this will be Visual Basic Projects or Visual C# Projects.
   - **Templates** Select ASP.NET Web Application.
   - **Location** Specify the http:// URL, file sharing location, or local drive and path where you want the project to reside.
3. Click OK.

Note When you create a Visual Studio project, Visual Studio also creates a *solution*. This is simply a file (with a .sln file extension) that contains the location and overall settings for one or more projects. Opening a solution opens each project it names. If you directly open a project file (which has a file extension such as .vbproj), Visual Studio will create a solution that refers to that project.

Even if you specify a file sharing location or local drive and path in step 3, the location you specify must reside within the content tree of an IIS Web server and the server must have the Microsoft .NET Framework installed. If Visual Studio can't verify both of these conditions, it won't accept the address. If it *can* verify both conditions, Visual Studio will save both the physical path and the *http://* URL path as project properties.

Using Visual Studio with Microsoft Windows SharePoint Services

Visual Studio can't create ASP.NET projects on Web servers running Windows SharePoint Services. There are two reasons for this:

- By default, Windows SharePoint Services blocks many of the file extensions that usually appear in ASP.NET projects. This stops ordinary visitors from uploading executable files that might interfere with smooth operation.
- Ordinary ASP.NET pages won't run under Windows SharePoint Services.

To create your own applications that run on Windows SharePoint Services, you must create them as Web Parts. For instructions on doing this, browse *msdn.microsoft.com/library*, and then perform one of these actions:

- Open the URL*msdn.microsoft.com/library/en-us/dnspts/html/sharepoint_webparttemplates.asp*.
- Search for the article "Web Part Templates for Microsoft Visual Studio .NET."
- Open the following sequence of topics:
  - Web Development
  - Server Technologies
  - SharePoint Products and Technologies
  - Technical Articles
  - Web Part Templates for Microsoft Visual Studio .NET

Regardless of the type of location you specify, Visual Studio will use the physical path if possible. In Figure 43-2, for example, the full path to the styles.css file shows up as c:\inetpub\wwwroot\myproj\styles.css, even though in Figure 43-1 the designer specified an *http://* location for the entire project.

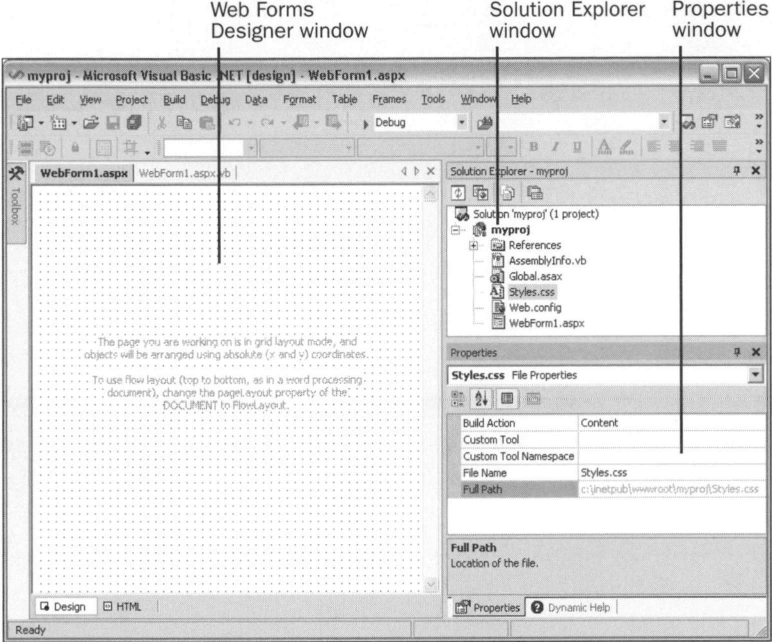

Figure 43-2. Solution Explorer shows the files in a Visual Studio project. The Properties window shows the attributes of the current file or element.

If you want, you can create a disk-based, FrontPage-based Web site at the same physical location as an ASP.NET project (or vice versa). In this configuration, however, the disk-based, FrontPage-based Web site has no way of knowing what changes you make in Visual Studio. If you add, change, or delete any files in Visual Studio, FrontPage won't correct any hyperlinks or FrontPage components in the site. You can avoid this situation by telling Visual Studio to access the project via the FrontPage Server Extensions. Here's the procedure:

1. Verify that the FrontPage Server Extensions are installed on the Web server where the ASP.NET project resides. If not, install them.
2. Open your ASP.NET project in Visual Studio, using an http:// URL.
3. Choose <*project-name*> Properties from the Project menu, or right-click the project in Solution Explorer, and then choose Properties from the shortcut menu. This displays the <*project-name*> Property Pages dialog box, as shown in Figure 43-3.
4. Under Common Properties, select Web Settings.
5. Under Web Access Method, select FrontPage.
6. Click OK to close the dialog box, and then close and reopen the entire project.
7. Repeat steps 3 and 4, and then, under Web Access Method, make sure that the FrontPage Link Repair check box is selected.
8. Click OK to close the dialog box.

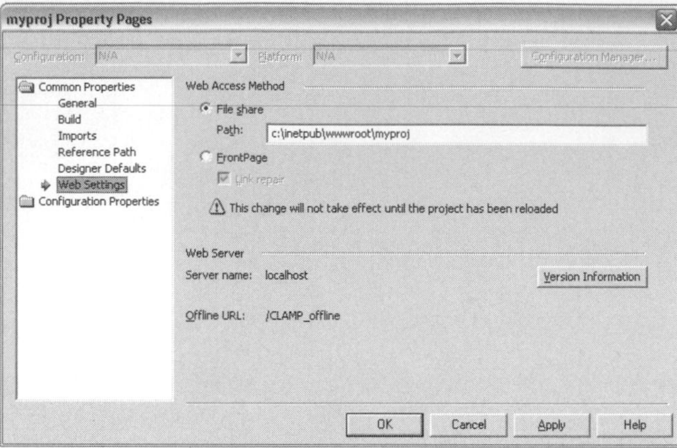

Figure 43-3. Use this panel of the project Property Pages dialog box to specify that Visual Studio should use the FrontPage method for accessing files in a project.

If you specify an *http://* location for a new ASP.NET project and Visual Studio can't determine the project's physical file location, the Web Access Failed dialog box shown in Figure 43-4 will appear. If the Web server is running the FrontPage Server Extensions, you can proceed by selecting Try To Open The Project With FrontPage Server Extensions and then clicking OK. If this succeeds, Visual Studio will thereafter access the project via FrontPage, and you won't have to worry about FrontPage indexes, cross-references, hyperlinks, and components getting out of date.

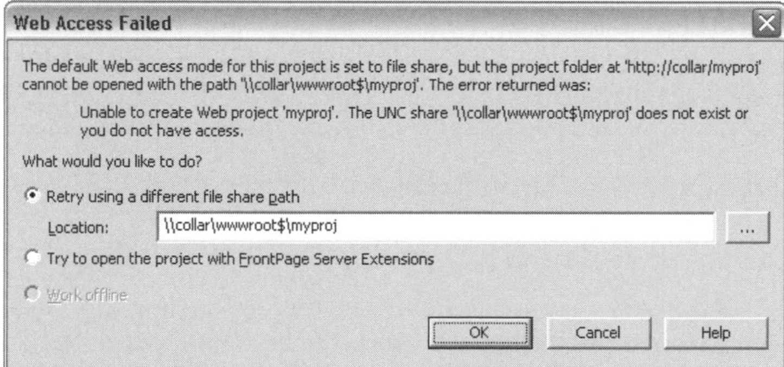

Figure 43-4. If Visual Studio can't use a file share to access a project, it displays this dialog box offering FrontPage as a second option.

Once both FrontPage and Visual Studio can open the same site, you should take care not to open the same file in both programs at the same time. If you do, and make changes and then save the file in both programs, you'll lose the set of changes you saved first.

You should also take special care when organizing files or folders in a FrontPage/Visual Studio site:

- Never use FrontPage to move, rename, or delete files that are part of a Visual Studio project. The relationships among files in a Visual Studio project are complex, and FrontPage lacks the capability to keep these relationships up-to-date. If you must perform file maintenance to Visual Studio files, do so in Visual Studio.
- Before using either program to move, rename, or delete files, close *all* files in the other program.

  Suppose, for example, that you rename a file in FrontPage. This starts a ripple effect that can modify hyperlinks or other content in dozens of other files. If, when this occurs, one of the affected files is open in Visual Studio, saving the Visual Studio file at a later time will overwrite the change that FrontPage made.

  Similar problems can occur if you move, rename, or delete files in Visual Studio when the same (or related) files are open in FrontPage.

Aligning FrontPage-Based Web Sites and IIS Applications

Whenever you're using FrontPage to work with ASP.NET pages, the FrontPage-based Web site should be an IIS application. At a high level, here are three ways you can designate a Web site as an IIS application:

- In FrontPage, choose Site Settings from the Tools menu, click the Database tab, and create a database connection. The FrontPage Server Extensions (which, remember, run on the Web server) will then mark the root of the FrontPage-based Web site as an IIS application.
- In Visual Studio .NET, create an ASP.NET Web Application project on a server running the FrontPage Server Extensions. This creates a FrontPage-based Web site and an IIS application at the same location.
- In Internet Information Services Manager, right-click the folder where the FrontPage-based Web site begins, and then choose Properties from the shortcut menu. When the folder's Properties dialog box appears, under Application Settings on the Directory tab, click Create.

Reconciling the FrontPage Folder List and the Visual Studio Solution Explorer

Visual Studio has a Solution Explorer window that displays the projects within a solution, and all the files within each of those projects. A Solution Explorer window appears in the upper right corner in Figure 43-2.

At first glance, you might think that the list of files in Solution Explorer and the list of files in the FrontPage Folder List ought to be the same. In fact, these lists are generally quite different. For proof, compare the Folder List in Figure 43-5 to Solution Explorer in Figure 43-2.

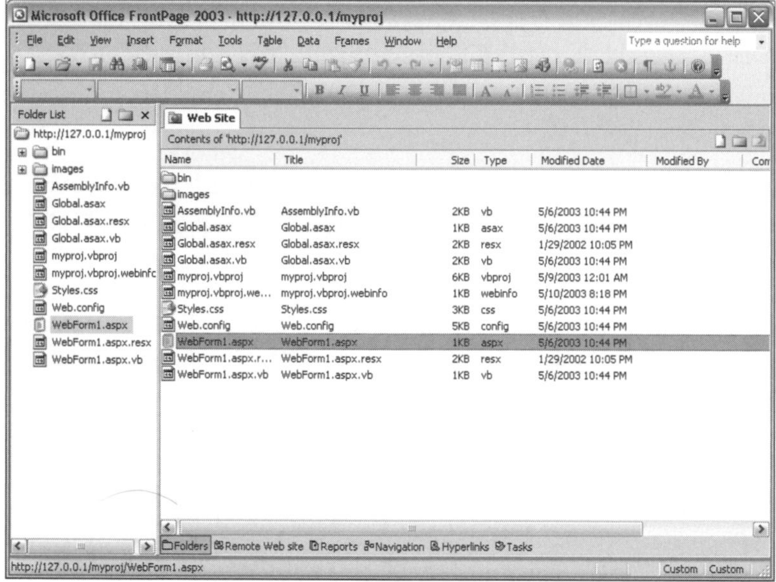

Figure 43-5. The Visual Studio Solution Explorer doesn't display all the files in a project folder. FrontPage displays many files that Visual Studio doesn't.

According to FrontPage, this site contains two subfolders and eleven files. According to Visual Studio, it contains a References node, no folders, and five files!

In fact, the information that Solution Explorer displays is distinctly *not* a folder listing. Instead, it's a list of files that Visual Studio will need when it compiles the project. Visual Studio keeps this list in the project file (in this case, myproj.vbproj).

> **Tip** If you're a longtime programmer, it might help to think of a Visual Studio project file as a *make file* and Solution Explorer as a *make list*.

Notice that Visual Studio shows one file named WebForm1.aspx, but FrontPage shows three files named WebForm1.aspx, WebForm1.aspx.resx, and WebForm1.aspx.vb:

- The .aspx file contains the HTML.

- The .aspx.resx file contains any messages or other text strings that the programmer cares to define.
- The aspx.vb file contains the program code for the page.

Visual Studio treats these three files as one ASP.NET Web form, and therefore displays only one icon. FrontPage sees them as three files, and therefore displays three icons. Similar thinking applies to the global.asax file and the myproj.vbproj file.

The images folder that FrontPage displays requires no compilation, and therefore doesn't appear as part of the Visual Studio project. When Visual Studio compiles the project, it places the resulting DLL (and possibly a debugging file) in the bin folder. Solution Explorer doesn't display this folder because the programmer doesn't (and shouldn't) manipulate these files directly in Visual Studio.

The References node contains a list of programming components set up for ready access throughout the project. These can be .NET class libraries, COM components, or Web services, but they aren't files in the ordinary sense and won't appear in FrontPage.

In most cases, the fact that Solution Explorer displays only files having programming relevance decreases clutter and makes Visual Studio easier to use. If, however, you really need to see a complete file and folder listing, try this procedure:

1. In Solution Explorer, select the node for your project.
2. Choose Show All Files from the Project menu.

This will display all the files and subfolders in the folder where the project begins. Files that are part of the project will appear normal, and others will be dimmed. If the display seems out-of-date, select the project node, and then choose Refresh from the Project menu.

> **Tip** In Visual Studio, the F5 key doesn't mean Refresh. Instead, it means Start Debugging. To perform a refresh operation, choose Refresh from the Project menu.

If you add a file in Visual Studio and then display the file area in FrontPage, the new file might not appear. If this happens, click anywhere in the FrontPage Folder List or Folders view, and then press F5 (Refresh).

If you add a file in FrontPage and want to make it part of a Visual Project, use either of these procedures:

- If Show All Files is in effect, right-click the dimmed file in Solution Explorer, and choose Include In Project from the shortcut menu.
- If Show All Files is off, right-click the project node in Solution Explorer, choose Add from the resulting shortcut menu, and then choose Add Existing Item.

  This displays a standard Open File dialog box titled Add Existing Item. Select the file you want to add, and then click Open.

To remove a file from a project, right-click its name in Solution Explorer, and choose Exclude From Project from the shortcut menu.

Comparing the Inline and Code-Behind Models for Code

If you ever used FrontPage to work with ASP pages, you probably put your ASP code inside <% and %> tags. These tags define a *code render block*, meaning a block of code that executes when the Web server creates the HTML code for the page (that is, when the Web server *renders it*). The Web server scans the page as it leaves the server and executes code render blocks at the time it encounters them.

Code declaration blocks provide a second way of adding program code to a Web page. A code declaration block begins with a <script runat="server"> tag and ends with a <script> tag. The Web server doesn't execute code declaration blocks immediately; instead, the Web server saves the code until another piece of code calls it.

> **Note** ASP.NET pages generally use code declaration blocks (<script runat="server"> and </script> tags) rather than code render blocks (<% and %> tags). Standardized events cause specially named subroutines inside the code declaration blocks to run.

Code render blocks and code declaration blocks both reside in the same file as the HTML. This is convenient when the same person develops both the visual design and the program code for a page, and it's the only model FrontPage supports for working with ASP and ASP.NET code. However, this *inline code model* has drawbacks as well:

- It leads to confusion when different people perform design and programming tasks.
- It requires that your program code be present in the Web site that your visitors access. This makes your source code vulnerable to theft by intruders.
- Neither FrontPage nor Visual Studio provides Microsoft IntelliSense support for inline ASP.NET code.

To avoid these drawbacks, Visual Studio manages source code using a *code-behind model*. In this model, the HTML and the program code reside in separate files. Before you test your site or cut it to production, you compile all the program code for all the pages and other modules in a project and link the results into one executable file (a .dll file in the bin folder, to be exact). This DLL contains, among other things, a class for each Web page in the project. When a Web page runs, it inherits its corresponding class and thereby gains access to its program code.

If it seems like quite a chore to manage all these separate files (and the relationships among them), you're right. Fortunately, it's a chore that Visual Studio does very well and with very little intervention from you. Just take heed of this advice:

- Visual Studio provides two views of any Web page you open: Design view and HTML view. These are generally analogous to Design view and Code view in FrontPage, and you switch between them in much the same way. Just click the Design or HTML tab that appears at the bottom of the Web Forms Designer window (and in Figure 43-2).

If you're accustomed to working with ASP pages, it might surprise you that your source code doesn't appear in HTML view. To enter, view, or correct source code, right-click the Web Forms Designer window (either Design view or HTML view will do), and then choose View Code. This displays your source code in a new window that has its own tab at the top of the Visual Studio editing window.

Note In Figure 43-2, the WebForm1.aspx.vb tab identifies the source code for the WebForm1.aspx page.

- You can edit source code files in FrontPage, but neither IntelliSense nor compilation features will be available. As a result, most developers prefer Visual Studio for working with source code.

Tip To open source code files in FrontPage, open the .vb or .cs file you want as text.

- When publishing your site, you *must* include the DLL that Visual Studio creates in your site's bin directory. There's generally no reason, however, to publish .vb, .cs, .resx, and other source code files.

Choosing Compatible Page Design Features

Visual Studio includes a graphical HTML editor called the Web Forms Designer that, at a high level, is generally analogous to FrontPage Design view. Nevertheless, at a detail level, these two editors are completely different. Most Web designers will probably prefer FrontPage Design view, whereas most programmers will likely opt for the integration and object support that the Visual Studio Web Forms Designer provides.

This section describes some of the most significant differences between these two programs and how to reconcile them.

Choosing a Compatible Browser Schema

Both FrontPage and Visual Studio mark each Web page with the browser you had in mind when you designed the page. If, for example, you target Microsoft Internet Explorer 5 when you design a page, both FrontPage and Visual Studio will add the following meta tag to that page:

```
<meta name=vs_targetSchema content="http://schemas.microsoft.com/intellisense/
ie5">
```

The setting in this tag controls the options that IntelliSense displays and, to some extent, the kind of HTML that FrontPage and Visual Studio create. In addition, Visual Studio displays warning messages for any HTML that's not compatible with the schema you specify.

FrontPage assigns the same target schema to all pages that a given Web designer creates using a given computer. To review or modify the setting in effect for you:

1. Choose Page Options from the Tools menu, and then click the Authoring tab.
2. Use the Browsers drop-down list to specify the browser you want, and then click OK.

Visual Studio controls the target schema setting at either the page or the project level. To change the target schema for a specific page:

1. Open the page in the Visual Studio Web Forms Designer.
2. Right-click anywhere in the page background, and then choose Properties from the shortcut menu. This displays the Document Property Pages dialog box, shown in Figure 43-6.

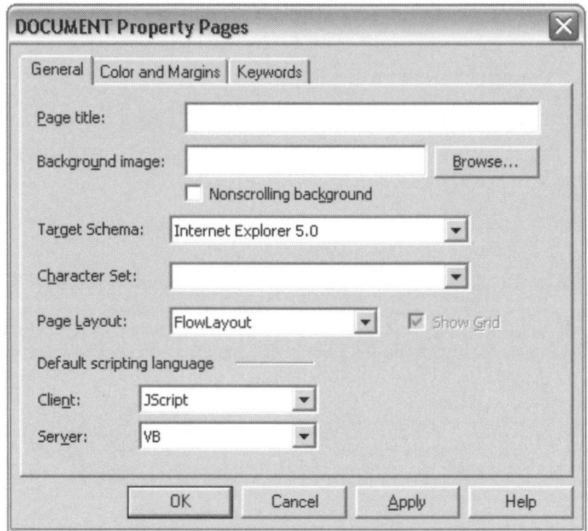

Figure 43-6. Use this dialog box to set the target schema and page layout mode for a Web page.

3. Select the browser you want from the Target Schema drop-down list, and then click OK.

Visual Studio's default target schema is Internet Explorer 3.02/Netscape Navigator 3.0. To choose a different default for any new pages you add to a project, proceed as follows:

1. Choose Properties from the Project menu. Or, if you prefer, right-click the project node in Solution Explorer, and then choose Properties from the shortcut menu.
2. When the <*project-name*> Property Pages dialog box shown in Figure 43-7 appears, open the Common Properties node, and then select Designer Defaults.
3. Select the browser you want in the Target Schema drop-down list, and then click OK.

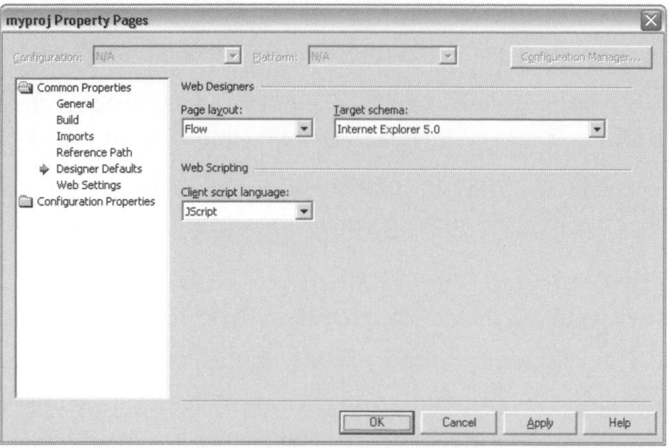

Figure 43-7. Use this panel of the *<project-name>* Property Pages dialog box to set the default target schema and page layout mode for a project.

Choosing a Compatible Page Layout Mode

The Visual Studio Web Forms Designer offers two distinct methods for placing content on a Web page:

- **Grid layout** Uses CSS positioning to specify exact xy-coordinates for every element on the page. This makes the job of designing Web forms very much like that of designing Windows forms, but it places great demands on browser compatibility. This mode is the Visual Studio default.
- **Flow layout** Arranges content from left to right and from top to bottom within the browser window. This is the longtime HTML and FrontPage default.

Most Web designers prefer flow layout, and this requires overriding the Visual Studio default. To do this for a single page:

1. Open the page in the Visual Studio Web Forms Designer.
2. Right-click anywhere in the page background, and then choose Properties from the shortcut menu.
3. When the Document Property Pages dialog box shown in Figure 43-6 appears, select FlowLayout in the Page Layout drop-down list, and then click OK.

To change the default page layout mode for all new pages you add to a project, use this procedure:

1. Right-click the project node in Solution Explorer, and then choose Properties from the shortcut menu. (Alternatively, choose Properties from the Project menu.)

   This displays the *<project-name>* Property Pages dialog box shown in Figure 43-7.

2. Under Common Properties, select Designer Defaults.
3. Select Flow from the Page Layout drop-down list, and then click OK.

Changing a project's default page layout mode to flow layout doesn't affect any pages that already use grid layout. It affects only pages that you add to the project.

If you use grid layout in Visual Studio and then open the same page in FrontPage, you should specify absolute positioning for any page elements you add. To do this:

1. Add the element you want to the page.
2. With the new item selected, take either of these actions:
   - Click the Position Absolutely button on the Positioning toolbar.
   - Choose Position from the Format menu. When the Position dialog box appears, under Positioning Style, select Absolute, and then click OK.

Once absolute positioning is in effect for an element, you can drag the element into any position you want.

For more information about absolute positioning, refer to Chapter 22, "Positioning Content with Cascading Style Sheets."

Controlling HTML Format

FrontPage takes great care to preserve the formatting of existing HTML and provides detailed control over the format of any new HTML it creates. It never reformats an entire page of HTML unless you issue a specific, manual command.

For more information about personalizing HTML format in FrontPage, refer to "Personalizing HTML Format," on page 1040.

Visual Studio takes a much more cavalier attitude toward HTML formatting. It reformats HTML at will, makes no effort to preserve existing HTML formatting, and provides little control over the results. To exercise what control Visual Studio does provide, take these steps:

1. Open Visual Studio, and then choose Options from the Tools menu.
2. When the Options dialog box shown in Figure 43-8 appears, open the Text Editor node, and then open the HTML/XML node.
3. Configure the resulting settings, and then click OK.

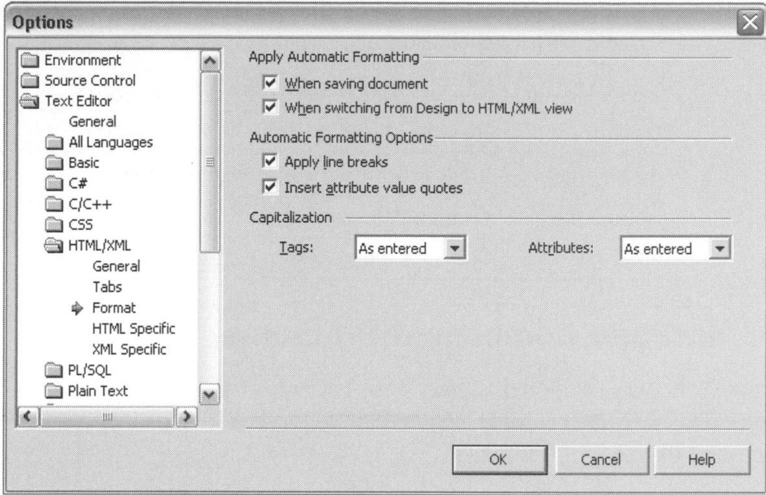

Figure 43-8. This panel of the Options dialog box controls HTML formatting options. Other panels in the HTML/XML category control additional HTML view and formatting options.

Here are the available HTML/XML options:

- **Apply Automatic Formatting** Specify when, if ever, you want Visual Studio to reformat your HTML code:
  - **When Saving Document** Select this check box if you want Visual Studio to reformat your HTML code whenever you save a Web page.
  - **When Switching From Design To HTML/XML View** Select this check box if you want Visual Studio to reformat your HTML code whenever you switch from Design view to HTML view.

> **Tip** To deliberately reformat HTML code, first switch to HTML view. Then choose Advanced from the Edit menu, and then choose Format Document.

- **Automatic Formatting Options** Specify the following formatting options:
  - **Apply Line Breaks** Select this check box if you want Visual Studio to insert line breaks before and after certain HTML tags.
  - **Insert Attribute Value Quotes** Select this check box if you want Visual Studio to add or retain quotation marks around attribute values (for example, align="center").
- **Capitalization** Specify how you want Visual Studio to capitalize tag and attribute names when it reformats HTML:
  - **Tags** Specify how you want Visual Studio to capitalize tag names when it automatically reformats HTML. Table 43-1 lists the available options.

- **Attributes** Specify how you want Visual Studio to capitalize attribute names when it reformats HTML. Again, Table 43-1 lists the options.

Table 43-1. HTML Capitalization Settings

Option	Result
As Entered	Retains element case exactly as you entered it
Uppercase	Changes element names to uppercase
Lowercase	Changes element names to lowercase

Avoiding FrontPage Component Problems

Many FrontPage components that operate at browse time don't work in ASP.NET pages. This particularly affects components that use the FrontPage SmartHTML Interpreter—components like Save Results.

The SmartHTML Interpreter is a program named shtml.dll that comes with the FrontPage Server Extensions. This program examines each normal Web page that a FrontPage-extended Web site delivers and customizes the content of certain components. Unfortunately, this process doesn't work on ASP or ASP.NET pages. Such pages follow a different path out of the server: a path that bypasses the shtml.dll program.

Generally, this lack of compatibility is a lesser problem than you might suspect. If the FrontPage Save Results component could meet your needs, you probably wouldn't have written an ASP.NET page in the first place. Nevertheless, if you have an ASP.NET page that needs to save form results in a file or send them as e-mail, you should plan on writing your own ASP.NET code to do the job.

Components that format and arrange page content are less troublesome, but you should still be cautious. Although FrontPage stops you from modifying certain kinds of content, such as the non-editable portion of Dynamic Web Templates and the individual appearance of elements controlled by themes, Visual Studio enforces no such restrictions. At first, this might seem wonderfully liberating, but there's a reason FrontPage stops you from editing such content: The next time FrontPage updates all pages using that template or theme, it will overwrite any changes you've made to areas that the template or theme supposedly controls.

The best advice is to tread carefully when using such components, or to avoid them completely. For example, use ASP.NET user controls rather than Include Page components or Dynamic Web Templates, and use shared style sheet files rather than FrontPage themes.

Selecting the FrontPage or Visual Studio .NET Publishing Model

Visual Studio has a Copy Project command that serves much the same purpose as the Publish command in FrontPage. The Copy Project command, however, has much different options. If you want Visual Studio to copy an ASP.NET project from one location to another, proceed as follows:

1. Open the ASP.NET project in Visual Studio.
2. Choose Copy Project from the Project menu. This displays the Copy Project dialog box, shown in Figure 43-9.

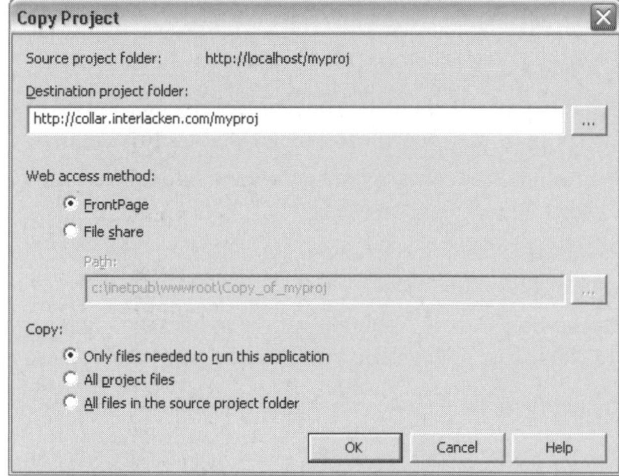

Figure 43-9. The settings in this dialog box control the way Visual Studio copies a project from one location to another.

3. Use the Destination Project Folder box to specify the target of the copy operation. You can enter this location either by typing or by clicking the ellipsis (...) button to the right of the text box.
4. Choose a Web access method. The possibilities are:
   - **FrontPage** Select this option to publish the files though the FrontPage Server Extensions.
   - **File Share** Select this option to copy the files to a local disk or network file sharing location. Then, in the Path box, enter the location that corresponds to the Destination Project Folder location you specified in step 3.
5. In the Copy section, select which files you want to copy. Here are the possibilities:
   - **Only Files Needed To Run This Application** Select this option to copy compilation output such as DLLs and references from the bin folder, plus any files that have a Build Action property of Content.

- **All Project Files** Select this option to copy compilation output and all files in the project. This copies the same files as the previous option, plus the project file and all source files.
- **All Files In The Source Project Folder** Select this option to copy all files in the project folder tree.

6 Click OK to initiate the copy operation.

Interpreting Build Action Values

The Build Action property indicates what Visual Studio .NET does with a file when you build (that is, compile) a project. To view or modify a file's current Build Action property, select the file in Solution Explorer, and then, in the Properties window, scroll down to the entry titled Build Action. Here are the possible values:

- **None** The file requires no compilation and needn't be present for the project to run. A text file that contains only documentation would have this value.
- **Compile** The file requires compilation but needn't be present for the project to run. Source code files typically have this value.
- **Content** The file requires no compilation, but must be present for the project to run. Web pages typically have this value.
- **Embedded Resource** The file becomes part of the project build output as a DLL or an executable. Resource files usually have this value.

The default Build Action for a file depends on its file extension.

The Visual Studio Copy Project command behaves like a normal Windows Copy command, and not like a FrontPage Publish command. It doesn't compare date stamps on the source and destination files for example, and it doesn't delete files in the target folder that don't exist on the source. It does, however, prompt before overwriting any files.

The FrontPage Publish command, on the other hand, supports not only the FrontPage and file sharing connections, but also FTP and WebDAV access. It's also more intelligent with regard to incremental file publishing and detecting file conflicts. To take advantage of these features but not publish source code:

1. Display the site's content in a FrontPage All Files report.
2. Sort the All Files report on file extension.
3. Select all files having the extensions .vb, .cs, .resx, .vbproj, and .csproj.
4. Right-click the selection and choose Don't Publish from the shortcut menu.

For more information about publishing a FrontPage-based Web site, refer to Chapter 16, "Publishing Your FrontPage-Based Web Site."

Inside Out

Parallel lines never meet

It's unfortunate that so many features that do the same thing in FrontPage and Visual Studio work so differently.

To some extent, this occurs because the two products come from different groups within Microsoft. In addition, both products address the needs of different people. Even so, it seems that Microsoft could make the various FrontPage and Visual Studio editors plug-in components that designers could select in either program at will.

In Summary…

This chapter explained how programmers using Visual Studio and designers using FrontPage can work on the same physical copy of a Web site. These two programs take a markedly different view of Web site development, but with care, you can take the best advantage of each.

The next chapter will explain how to configure FrontPage options to suit your way of working.

Part 12

Customizing Your Copy of FrontPage

Chapter 44

Configuring FrontPage Options

Like most software programs, Microsoft Office FrontPage 2003 provides a variety of ways for you to make it work the way you want—not just the way it comes from the factory. For example, you can adjust the options FrontPage invokes on startup and the editor FrontPage invokes for various file types.

This chapter explains how to create a personalized work environment within FrontPage.

The most global options for controlling the FrontPage user interface appear, logically enough, in the Options dialog box, a choice on the Tools menu. The next four sections cover the five tabs in this dialog box: General, Configure Editors, Reports View, FTP, and ASP.NET.

Note In earlier releases of FrontPage, a Publishing tab also appeared in the Options dialog box. In FrontPage 2003, these settings appear in the Remote Web Site Properties dialog box, whose options you configure in Remote Web Site view.

Controlling General Options

The General tab is displayed in Figure 44-1.

This tab contains the following options, which you can set by selecting or clearing each check box:

- **Startup Task Pane** Select this check box if you want FrontPage to display the Getting Started task pane every time you open FrontPage.
- **Open Last Web Site Automatically When FrontPage Starts** Select this check box if you want FrontPage, when starting up, to open the Web site you most recently worked on.
- **Check If Office Is The Default Editor For Pages Created In Office** Select this check box if you want FrontPage to verify at startup that file types belonging to Microsoft Office System applications are, in fact, associated with those applications. (Non-Microsoft applications sometimes overwrite file-type associations upon installation.)

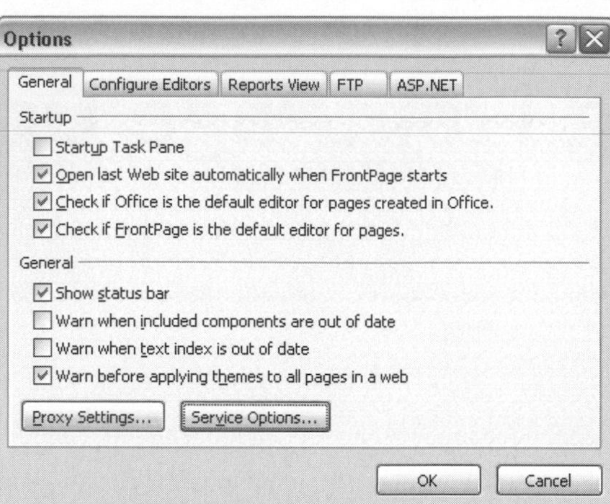

Figure 44-1. This tab of the Options dialog box controls settings at the most global level.

- **Check If FrontPage Is The Default Editor For Pages** Select this check box to tell FrontPage to verify, every time it starts, that it's registered as your standard editor for Web pages.
- **Show Status Bar** Select this check box to display a status bar along the bottom edge of the FrontPage window.
- **Warn When Included Components Are Out Of Date** Select this check box if you want FrontPage to inform you whether the content of any FrontPage components in your Web pages is out of date. If FrontPage gives you such a warning, choose Recalculate Hyperlinks from the Tools menu to update the components.
- **Warn When Text Index Is Out Of Date** Select this check box if you want FrontPage to notify you when the text index for a Web site is out of date. FrontPage displays a warning when you open any such Web site and asks whether you want to recalculate the index.
- **Warn Before Applying Themes To All Pages In A Web** Select this check box if you want FrontPage to display an Are You Sure? dialog box before permanently applying a theme to a site. (Applying a theme permanently overwrites existing formatting in your Web pages. There's no way to undo a theme.)
- **Proxy Settings** If your network is connected to the Internet (or some other network) through a proxy firewall, click this button to display the Connections tab of the Internet Properties dialog box, and then verify your computer's firewall settings.

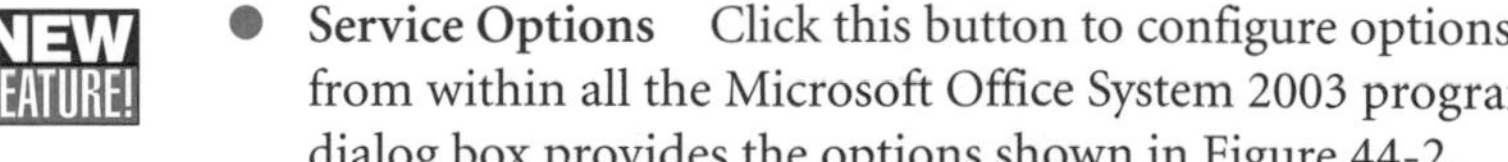

- **Service Options** Click this button to configure options for using network services from within all the Microsoft Office System 2003 programs. The Service Options dialog box provides the options shown in Figure 44-2.

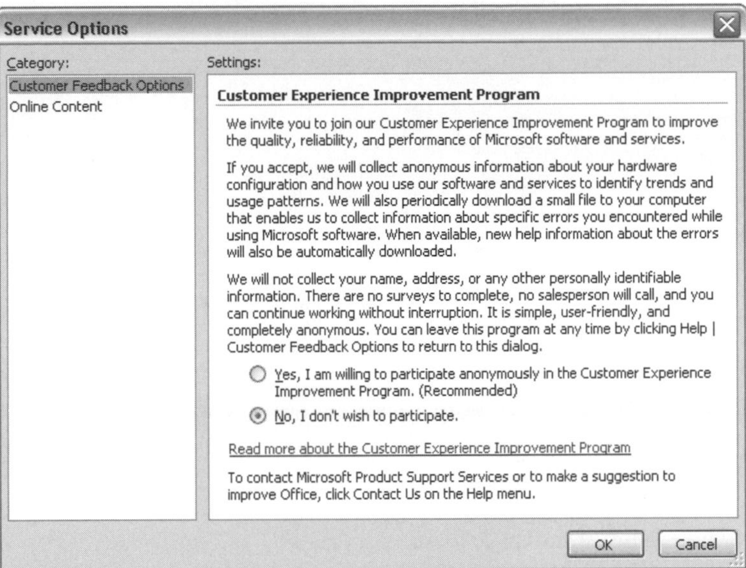

Figure 44-2. Customer Feedback Options refers to a program whereby Microsoft retrieves usage profiles from your system.

Dealing with Proxy Servers

A *proxy firewall* receives HTTP requests from client computers on a local network, satisfies the requests using an outside network, and then sends the responses back to the client computer. This allows *inside* computers to access *outside* resources, but prevents *outside* computers from accessing *inside* resources. Consult your network administrator to determine what settings are required at your site.

FrontPage uses the same software, and therefore the same proxy settings, that Microsoft Internet Explorer uses for connecting to the Internet. If Internet Explorer can get to the Internet, so can FrontPage, and vice versa.

For more information about using a proxy server refer to, "Using a Proxy Server," in Appendix N.

The Customer Feedback Options category gives you a way of contributing to the further development of Microsoft software through the Customer Experience Improvement Program. If you select the Yes option in the Settings pane, Microsoft will periodically collect anonymous information about your computer, about which software options you use, and about software failures that occur. Microsoft uses this information to improve its products and to update the Help information on your computer. If you're more concerned about privacy than helping Microsoft, select No. (The default is No.)

Selecting the Online Content category displays the settings shown in Figure 44-3.

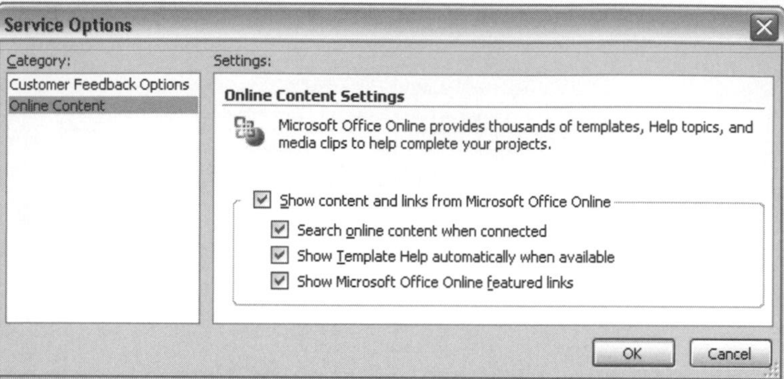

Figure 44-3. This dialog box determines which Office Online services appear automatically in Microsoft Office applications.

Configure these settings as follows:

- **Show Content And Links From Microsoft Office Online** Select this check box if you want links to Microsoft's Office Online Web site to appear throughout your copy of Microsoft Office. If you clear this check box, no such links will appear, and the next three options will be dimmed.
- **Search Online Content When Connected** Select this check box if you want features such as the Type A Question For Help and Clip Art Search For boxes to search for content on the Office Online site as well as on your local computer (provided, of course, that your connection to the Internet is active). Clear this check box to search for local content only.
- **Show Template Help Automatically When Available** Select this check box if you want Help information from the Office Online Web site to appear automatically when you open a template (provided, of course, that such information is available). Clear this check box to prevent automatic Help display.
- **Show Microsoft Office Online Featured Links** Select this check box if you want the Office Online section of the Getting Started task pane to display links to new or interesting pages on the Office Online Web site. Clear this check box to display only the Office Online Search box.

Configuring External Editors

You can configure FrontPage to associate any editor you want with any type of file you plan to use. This results in a highly integrated Web development environment.

If you're not happy with the way FrontPage opens a particular type of file, choose Options from the Tools menu, and then click the Configure Editors tab. This displays the dialog box shown in Figure 44-4.

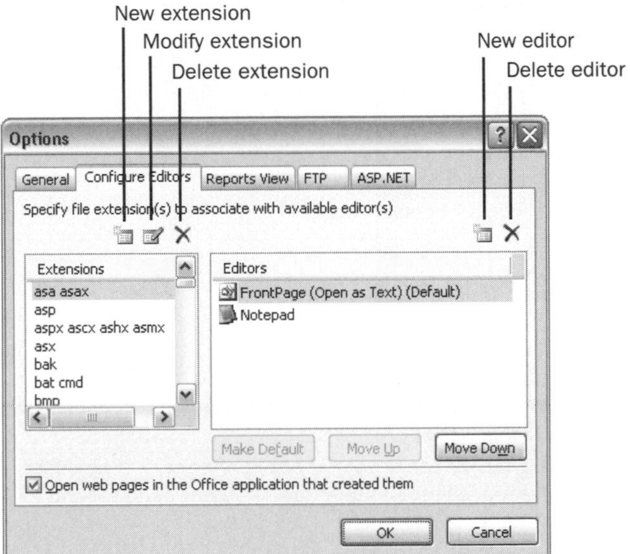

Figure 44-4. FrontPage can associate a different editor with each file extension.

> **Tip** If you double-click a picture in Page view and get the message *No picture editor is configured*, it's probably because Configure Editors has no editor associated with the picture file type GIF or JPG.

The Extensions list on the left of the Configure Editors tab shows groups of file extensions. Selecting any group of extensions displays the currently associated editors in the Editors list on the right. One of these editors will be the default; this is the editor that FrontPage starts when you double-click the file in the Folder List, Folders view, Reports view, and so forth, or when you right-click the file and choose Open from the shortcut menu. The other editors appear as selections after you right-click a file and choose Open With from the shortcut menu.

To add an extension that doesn't appear in the list:

1. Click the New Extension button above the Extensions list. This displays the Open With dialog box, shown in Figure 44-5.
2. In the Extension box, enter the new file extension.
3. If the program you want FrontPage to run when it opens the file appears in the Choose The Program You Want To Use To Open This File list, select it, and then click OK.

   If the program you want doesn't appear, click the Browse For More button. This displays a Browse dialog box. Find and select the startup file for the editor you want, and then click Open.

Figure 44-5. This dialog box associates one application with a new file extension. You can associate additional applications after you click OK.

To add, rename, or remove an existing extension:

1 Select the group that contains the extension or others like it.
2 Click the Modify Extension button above the Extensions list. This opens all the text in that group of extensions to editing:
   - To add an extension, set the insertion point before or after any existing extension, and start typing. Make sure that a space separates each pair of extensions.
   - To rename an extension, set the insertion point within it, and type normally.
   - To remove an extension, backspace over it, or select it and press the Delete key.

To delete an entire group of extensions, select the group, and then click the Delete Extension button above the Extensions list.

To add an editor for an existing group of extensions:

1 Select the group of extensions that needs another editor.
2 Click the New Editor button above the Editors list. This displays an Open With dialog box very similar to the one shown in Figure 44-5, except that fixed text replaces the Extension text box.
   - If the new editor you want appears in the Choose The Program You Want To Use To Open This File list, select it, and click OK.
   - Otherwise, click the Browse For More button, locate the startup file for the program you want, and then click OK.

To remove an editor for an existing group of extensions, select that editor, and then click the Delete Editor button above the Editors list box.

To designate a different editor as the default for a group of extensions:

1 Select the group of extensions with the wrong default editor.
2 In the Editors list, select the correct default editor.
3 Click the Make Default button.

To change the editors for one extension in a group, you must:

1 Select the group that contains the extension.
2 Click the Modify Extension button, and delete the extension from the group.
3 Click the New Extension button, and define one editor for the extension.
4 Select your new entry in the Extensions list, and then click the New Editor button to define any additional editors.

The last option on the Configure Editors tab (Figure 44-4) is the Open Web Pages In The Office Application That Created Them check box. Leave this check box cleared if you want FrontPage to open all Web pages in the FrontPage Editor, regardless of which Office application created them. Select this check box if you want FrontPage to pass Web pages to the application originally used to create them.

Customizing Reports View

The Reports View tab, shown in Figure 44-6, controls the settings for Reports view.

For more information about Reports view, refer to "Working with Reports," on page 481.

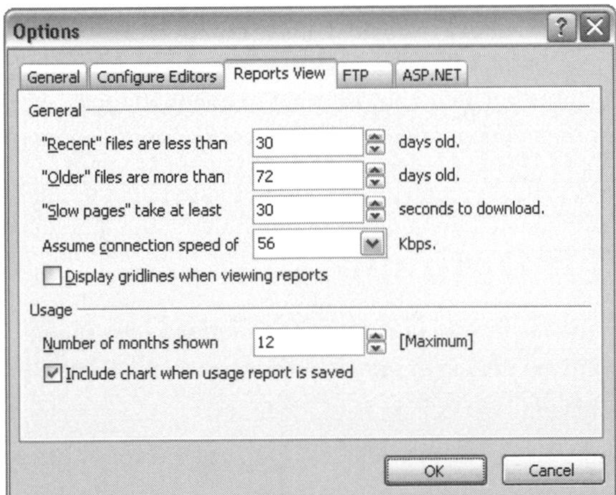

Figure 44-6. This tab in the Options dialog box controls settings that pertain to Reports view.

- **"Recent" Files Are Less Than *X* Days Old** Select a value to determine which files appear in the Recently Added Files report.

- **"Older" Files Are More Than X Days Old** Select a value to determine which files appear in the Older Files report.
- **"Slow Pages" Take At Least X Seconds To Download** Select a value to specify the download time that qualifies a Web page for inclusion in the Slow Pages report.
- **Assume Connection Speed Of X Kbps** Select a connection speed from the drop-down list. To compute total download time, FrontPage divides the total number of bytes for a Web page and all its constituent files by this connection speed.

Note You can also see the download time in Design view; it appears at the bottom of the main FrontPage window, near the right edge of the status bar. Click the displayed download time to change the assumed connection speed.

- **Display Gridlines When Viewing Reports** Select this check box if you want FrontPage to draw row and column gridlines whenever it displays reports.
- **Number Of Months Shown** Specify the maximum number of past months for which you want FrontPage to show usage reports.
- **Include Chart When Usage Report Is Saved** Select this check box if, when you save a FrontPage Usage report, you want FrontPage to save not only the usage data, but also any charts you have on display.

  This setting warrants a bit of explanation. When a FrontPage report is displayed, you can save a snapshot of the data by choosing Save or Save As from the File menu. FrontPage then saves the data in a Web page that looks as if Microsoft Excel had created it. That way, you can use the same file for display to Web visitors or for additional analysis in Excel.

  When FrontPage displays a Usage report, you can chart the data by clicking the Usage Chart button on the Reports toolbar. If such a chart is displayed when you choose Save or Save As from the File menu, FrontPage needs to know whether it should save the data and the chart or just the data. This option tells FrontPage whether to save the chart.

Customizing FTP Options

In PC text files, two characters mark the end of each line: a carriage return (ASCII 13) and a linefeed (ASCII 10). The convention on UNIX systems, however, is that only the linefeed character appears at the end of a line. Therefore:

- When FTP programs transfer files from UNIX to a PC, they convert linefeeds to a carriage return/linefeed combination.
- When FTP programs transfer files from a PC to UNIX, they convert any carriage return/linefeed combinations to linefeeds.

These conversions, of course, are appropriate only for text files. If you apply them to binary files like executables, compressed archives, or pictures, the conversion corrupts the file.

When FrontPage uses FTP to publish a Web site to a UNIX server, it obviously needs to know which files are text. To make this determination, it uses information from the FTP tab of the Options dialog box, shown in Figure 44-7.

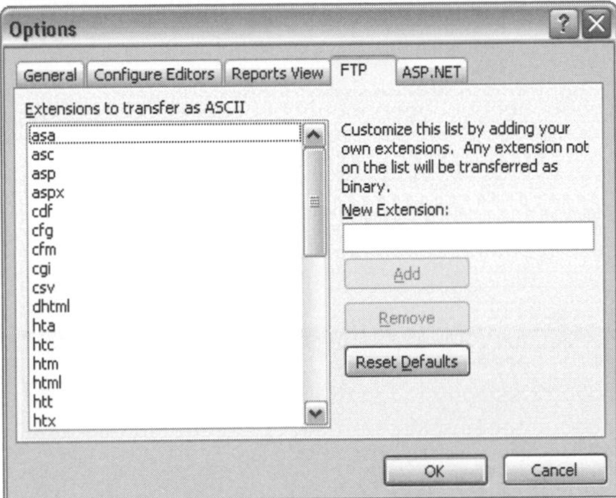

Figure 44-7. Use this dialog box to specify file extensions that identify text files when publishing a Web site by FTP.

If a file extension appears in the Extensions To Transfer As ASCII list, FrontPage will treat files having that extension as text when it publishes them to a UNIX server. If a file extension doesn't appear in that list, FrontPage publishes the file as binary (that is, without conversion). If you publish by FTP and find that handling of some file extension is incorrect, display this dialog box, and then proceed as follows:

- To treat a new file extension as text, enter it in the New Extension text box, and then click Add.
- To stop treating a file extension as text, select it in the Extensions To Transfer As ASCII list, and then click Remove.
- To restore the entire list to its installation default, click the Reset Defaults button.

After making such changes, be sure to click the OK button when you close the Options dialog box. Clicking Cancel discards all changes.

Customizing ASP.NET Options

Figure 44-8 shows the ASP.NET tab of the Options dialog box. This dialog box configures two settings applicable to Microsoft ASP.NET pages in your Web site.

Chapter 44

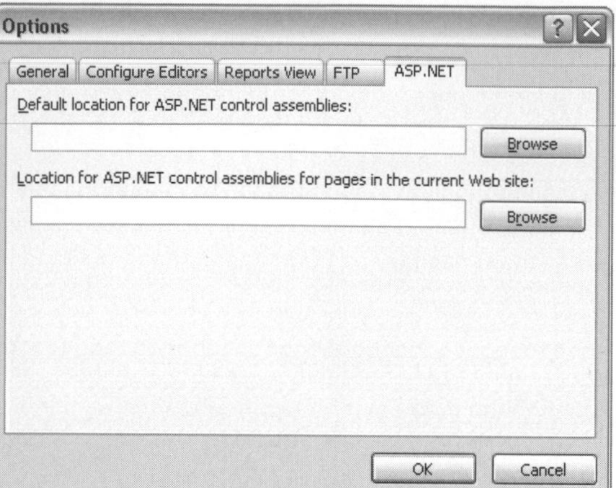

Figure 44-8. This dialog box overrides system locations for ASP.NET user controls.

These settings are:

- **Default Location For ASP.NET Control Assemblies** Specify the folder that contains compiled versions of ASP.NET user controls available to the entire Web server. This includes Microsoft SharePoint Web Parts, which are a type of user control.

  To use the system default, leave this box blank.

- **Location For ASP.NET Control Assemblies For Pages In The Current Web Site** Specify the folder that contains compiled versions of ASP.NET user controls available to the current Web site only. This includes SharePoint Web Parts.

  To use the system default, leave this box blank.

In Summary...

This chapter explained the various options available to customize options within FrontPage. These changes affect any Web site that you open.

The next chapter explains how to customize the FrontPage settings that control the appearance of new Web pages.

Chapter 45

Configuring Page Creation Options

Because the primary business of Microsoft Office FrontPage 2003 is creating Web pages, it should come as no surprise that FrontPage has more settings to control the creation of such pages than it has for any other purpose. In fact, FrontPage 2003 has more page-related options than any earlier version.

The following sections describe the 10 tabs that appear in the Page Options dialog box. To display this dialog box, choose Page Options from the Tools menu.

Configuring General Options

Figure 45-1 shows the General tab—the most far-reaching tab in the Page Options dialog box.

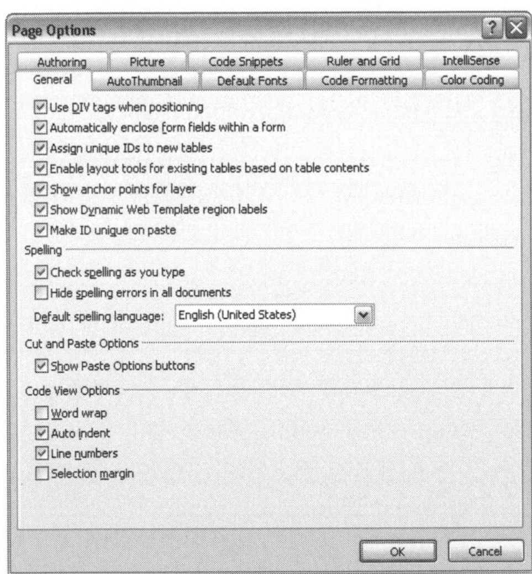

Figure 45-1. This tab controls settings that affect the general appearance of Web pages.

The available options work as follows:

- **Use DIV Tags When Positioning** Select this check box if you want FrontPage to surround positioned elements with DIV tags rather than add positioning attributes to normal tags. This makes your HTML a little larger but improves compatibility with older browsers.
- **Automatically Enclose Form Fields Within A Form** Select this check box if you want Front Page to automatically build a new HTML form around any form field you insert on the page. (Naturally, this option doesn't apply to fields you insert within an existing HTML form.)

  Form fields originally had no use outside an HTML form. As a result, older browsers such as Netscape Navigator 4 ignore such fields. Now that form fields can interact with scripts, however, they do have a use outside HTML forms. This option gives you a choice between compatibility with older browsers (check box selected) and simpler HTML (check box cleared).
- **Assign Unique IDs To New Tables** Select this check box if you want FrontPage to assign a unique ID to each table you create.

- **Enable Layout Tools For Existing Tables Based On Table Contents** Select this check box if you want FrontPage to display layout tools whenever you select a table whose purpose seems to be page layout. Clear the check box if you want FrontPage to display layout tools only for tables you've specifically designated as layout tables.

- **Show Anchor Points For Layer** Select this check box if you want Design view to display an anchor icon where the HTML code for a layer physically resides. Clear the check box to suppress these icons.

  You can also toggle this setting by clicking the Show Anchor Layers button on the Standard toolbar.

- **Show Dynamic Web Template Region Labels** Select this check box if you want Design view to display the names of each editable region in a Dynamic Web Template. These names appear in a shaded rectangle in the upper left corner of the region. Clear the check box if you don't want such labels to appear.

- **Make ID Unique On Paste** Select this check box if you want FrontPage to change the id= attribute of any tag you paste from the Clipboard if the receiving Web page already contains a tag with that id value.

Show Layer Anchors

  Suppose, for example, that you paste a tag having an *id="myself"* attribute, and the page already contains a tag identified with *id="myself"*. If this check box is selected, FrontPage will change the *id* value of the pasted tag to *myself0*. If you paste the tag again, FrontPage will identify it as *myself1*, then *myself2*, and so forth.
- **Spelling** These settings control background spelling features:
  - **Check Spelling As You Type** Select this check box if you want FrontPage to immediately check the spelling of each word you type.

- **Hide Spelling Errors In All Documents** Select this check box if you don't want Design view to highlight misspelled words. Clear the check box if you want Design view to show misspelled words by drawing squiggly lines beneath them.
- **Default Spelling Language** Select the default spelling language from the drop-down list.

- **Cut And Paste Options** This option controls the operation of Cut, Copy, and Paste commands:
  - **Show Paste Options Buttons** Select this check box if you want FrontPage to display a Paste Options button after you paste an item from the Clipboard into a Web page. Such buttons provide a drop-down menu of options like the one shown here:

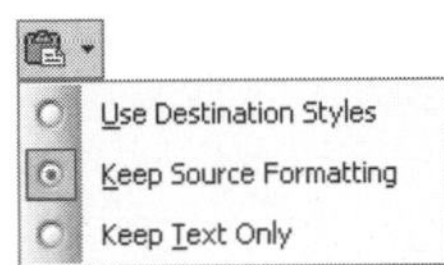

- **Code View Options** These options control features that pertain to Code view:
  - **Word Wrap** Select this check box if you want Code view to visually wrap lines within the Code view window. Clear the check box if you want Code view to hide the excess portion beyond the right margin of the editing window.
  - **Auto Indent** Select this check box if you want Code view to add enough spaces at the beginning of each new line that the first character you type appears under the first visible character in the preceding line. Clear the check box if you want to always start typing at the left margin.
  - **Line Numbers** Select this check box if you want Code view to display line numbers for each line in the current file. These numbers appear in the left margin that precedes each line. Clear the check box if you want no such numbers to appear.
  - **Selection Margin** Select this check box if you want FrontPage to display extra blank space at the left of each line in Code view. Clicking this area selects the entire corresponding line. (Clicking a line number has the same effect.) Clear the check box if you want no such margin.

Options

Options

You can also toggle these options by clicking the Options drop-down arrow on the Code View toolbar.

Configuring AutoThumbnail Options

The AutoThumbnail tab controls the creation of thumbnail pictures. Figure 45-2 shows this tab.

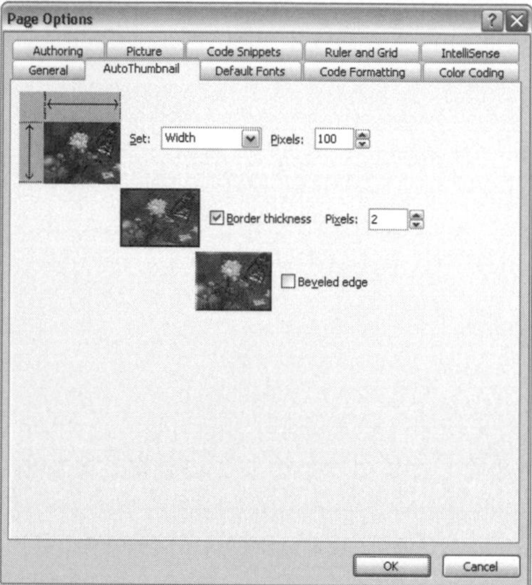

Figure 45-2. This tab in the Page Options dialog box controls how FrontPage creates thumbnail pictures.

For more information about creating thumbnail pictures, refer to "Creating Thumbnail Pictures," on page 639.

Here's how to specify the options that appear on the AutoThumbnail tab.

- **Set** Controls the size of the thumbnail pictures. You should specify both a sizing strategy and a measurement. The accompanying Pixels box specifies the fixed size applied to the edge you choose with the Set option. The Set sizing strategies are:
  - **Width** Select this option if you want FrontPage to make all thumbnail pictures the same width and calculate a height proportional to that of the full-sized picture.
  - **Height** Select this option if you want FrontPage to make all thumbnail pictures the same height and calculate a width proportional to that of the full-sized picture.
  - **Shortest Side** Select this option if you want FrontPage to make the shortest side of each thumbnail picture a uniform size and make the longest side proportional to that of the full-sized picture.
  - **Longest Side** Select this option if you want FrontPage to make the longest side of each thumbnail picture a uniform size and makes the shortest side proportional to that of the full-sized picture.

- **Border Thickness** Select this check box to create borders around each thumbnail picture. The accompanying Pixels box controls the border width.
- **Beveled Edge** Select this check box to create bevels around the edges of each thumbnail picture.

For more information about setting AutoThumbnail properties, refer to "Setting AutoThumbnail Properties," on page 285.

Configuring Default Font Options

The Default Fonts tab, shown in Figure 45-3, specifies the character set and font that FrontPage displays in the absence of any specifications within a Web page. These specifications don't appear in the HTML, and thus they have no effect on what your Web visitors see. They affect only the way FrontPage display pages. Figure 45-3 shows the available options.

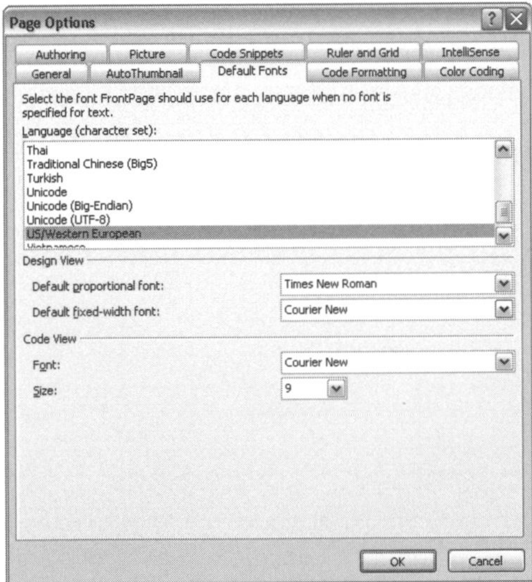

Figure 45-3. The Default Fonts tab controls the way FrontPage displays text when the Web page itself provides no guidance.

- **Language (Character Set)** Select the national language character set you want FrontPage to use for displaying text.
- **Design View** Use these settings to control the default fonts in Design view:
  - **Default Proportional Font** Specify the font you want Design view to use when it displays normal text and the HTML doesn't specify a font.
  - **Default Fixed-Width Font** Specify the font you want Design view to use when it displays fixed-character-width text and, again, the HTML doesn't specify a font. This pertains, for example, to text formatted with the <PRE> (Formatted) HTML tag.

- **Code View** Use these settings to control the default fonts in Code view:
  - **Font** Specify the font you want Code view to use when it displays (what else?) code.
  - **Size** Specify the font size you want Code view to use when displaying code.

Configuring Code Formatting Options

The Code Formatting tab shown in Figure 45-4 controls the formatting of HTML source code. By default, this affects only code that FrontPage adds to your page. To reformat all the HTML in a page, you must open the page, switch to Code view, right-click the editing window, and choose Reformat HTML from the shortcut menu.

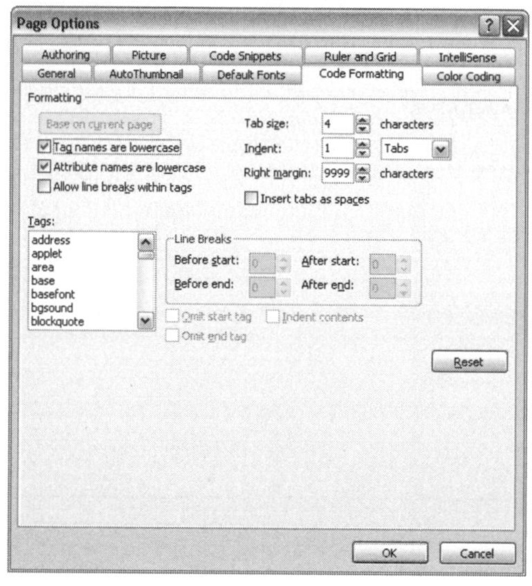

Figure 45-4. This tab controls the format of any HTML code FrontPage creates.

Chapter 40, which addressed the general issue of working with HTML code, has already explained the options on this tab.

For more information about personalizing HTML format, refer to "Personalizing HTML Format," on page 1040.

Configuring Color Coding Options

When FrontPage displays code in Code view, it shows different types of code in different colors. By default, for example, HTML tags are purple, HTML attribute names are red, and attribute values are blue. The Color Coding tab, shown in Figure 45-5, specifies these colors. It has no effect on any colors your Web visitors see.

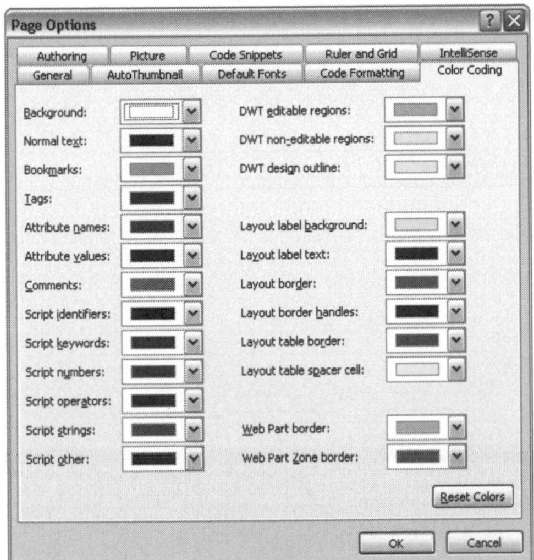

Figure 45-5. This tab controls the color of source code that FrontPage displays in Code view.

To change the colors assigned to any element, click its drop-down arrow, and then use the resulting color picker to specify the color you want.

For more information about using FrontPage color dialog boxes, refer to "Using FrontPage Color Dialog Boxes," on page 509.

Configuring Authoring Options

On the Authoring tab, shown in Figure 45-6, you can specify what technologies are available in your production Web environment. FrontPage then dims any commands, toolbar buttons, and so forth that would produce incompatible results.

The options in the FrontPage And SharePoint Technologies section specify the features you expect your Web server to have. The options in the Browsers section specify the least capable browser you expect your Web visitors to have, and can also suppress various features you might not want to use.

Note Some options in the FrontPage And SharePoint Technologies section might be dimmed because of browser and server choices you made earlier in the dialog box.

Chapter 17 includes a compete explanation of each option on this tab. Refer to that chapter for further information.

For more information about managing browser compatibility, refer to "Managing Browser Compatibility," on page 470.

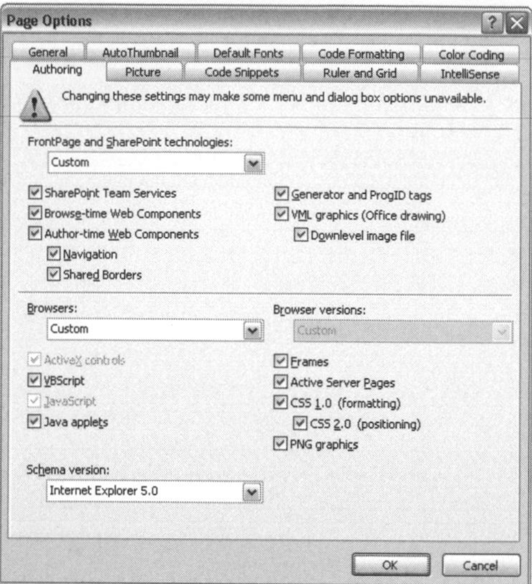

Figure 45-6. On this tab, you can specify the technologies you want your site to support. FrontPage then dims all options that would be incompatible.

Configuring Picture Options

The Picture tab, shown in Figure 45-7, specifies the file formats and other settings rules that FrontPage uses when it creates picture files. This applies, for example, to pictures that you paste from the Clipboard or obtain as clip art and that FrontPage later saves as file in your Web site.

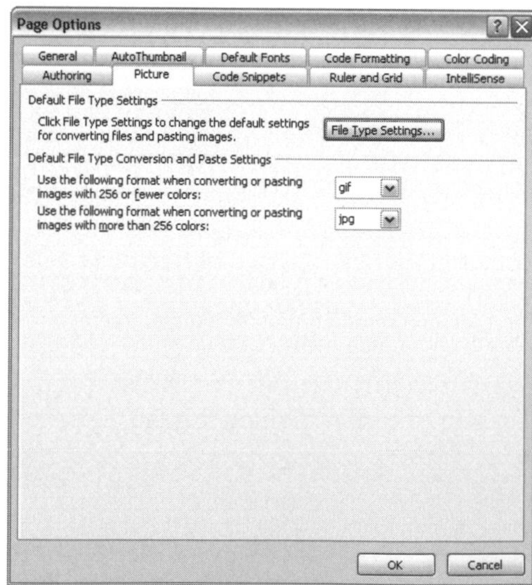

Figure 45-7. This tab specifies the default characteristics of picture files that FrontPages creates.

Use these settings to configure the way FrontPage saves new or modified picture files:

- **Default File Type Settings** Click the File Type Settings button to change the way FrontPage normally saves converted or pasted pictures. This displays a Picture File Type dialog box; Chapter 10 explained how to configure this dialog box.

For more information about using the Picture File Type dialog box, refer to "Using the Save Embedded Files Dialog Box," on page 255.

- **Default File Type Conversion And Paste Settings** Use these settings to choose the picture file format that FrontPage should use when saving pictures:
  - **Use The Following Format When Converting Or Pasting Images With 256 Or Fewer Colors** Choose GIF, JPEG, or PNG. The default (and usually best) choice is GIF.
  - **Use The Following Format When Converting Or Pasting Images With More Than 256 Colors** Choose GIF, JPEG, or PNG. The default (and usually best) choice is JPG.

For more information about choosing picture file formats, refer to "Choosing Picture File Formats," on page 671.

Configuring Code Snippet Options

The Code Snippets tab, shown in Figure 45-8, maintains a library of text fragments (*snippets*) that you can select by name and then insert in Code view. This saves you from repeatedly typing that text. The tab contains the usual Add, Modify, and Remove buttons.

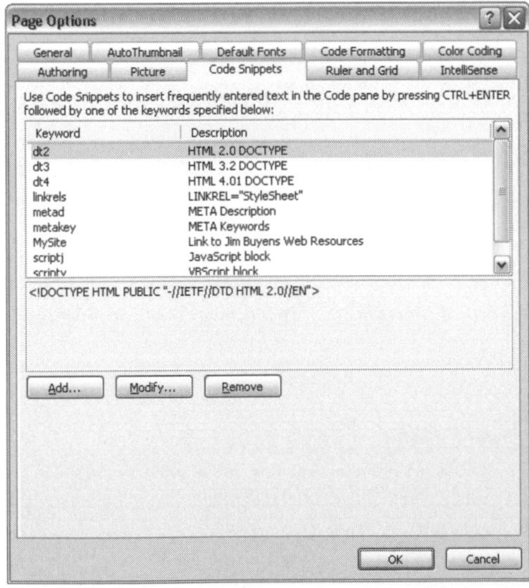

Figure 45-8. The Code Snippets feature stores fragments of text that you can select by name and then insert in Code view; this saves typing.

Chapter 40 explained how to use this tab in some detail. Please refer to that chapter for more information.

For more information about storing and inserting code snippets, refer to "Storing And Inserting Code Snippets," on page 1049.

Configuring Ruler and Grid Options

The Ruler And Grid tab, shown in Figure 45-9, controls the units of measure, size, and snap-to precision of rules and grids that appear in Design view.

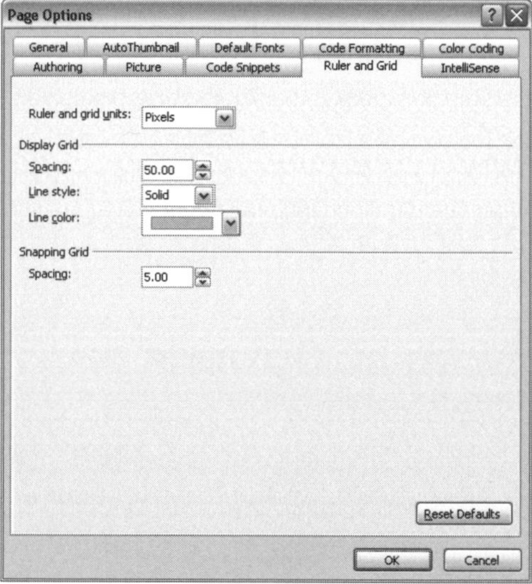

Figure 45-9. The Ruler And Grid tab controls the dimensions of layout guides that appear in Design view.

Rulers and grids provide points of reference as you work in Design view, but they have no direct effect on what Web visitors see. Chapter 19, "Using HTML Tables for Page Layout," explains how to use rulers and grids.

For more information about displaying rulers and grids, refer to "Displaying Rulers and Layout Grids," on page 58.

Configuring IntelliSense Options

Microsoft IntelliSense is the feature in Code view that anticipates your typing, provides selection lists of valid keywords, and displays tool tips for subroutine and function arguments. Figure 45-10 shows the IntelliSense tab, which controls this feature.

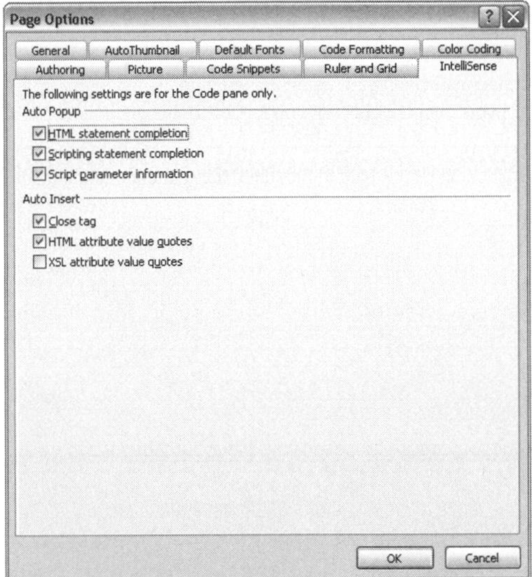

Figure 45-10. The settings on this tab control when IntelliSense offers context-sensitive assistance in Code view.

The IntelliSense tab provides these options:

- **Auto Popup** Specify when you want IntelliSense to display pop-up selection lists and information:
  - **HTML Statement Completion** Select this check box if you want IntelliSense to display selection lists as you type HTML.
  - **Scripting Statement Completion** Select this check box if you want IntelliSense to display selection lists as you type browser-side scripts.
  - **Script Parameter Information** Select this check box if you want IntelliSense to display Help information about subroutine and function parameters.
- **Auto Insert** Specify when you want IntelliSense to enter text automatically:
  - **Close Tag** Select this check box if you want IntelliSense to create an end tag whenever you type the closing bracket of a start tag.
  - **HTML Attribute Value Quotes** Select this check box if you want IntelliSense to enter a pair of quotation marks every time you finish typing an HTML attribute name.
  - **XSL Attribute Value Quotes** Select this check box if you want IntelliSense to supply a pair of quotation marks every time you finish typing an XSL attribute name.

For more information about using the IntelliSense feature, refer to "Using the IntelliSense Feature," on page 1043.

In Summary...

This chapter described the options available in the Page Options dialog box, which customizes the way FrontPage applies many page-creation features.

The next chapter explains how to control FrontPage settings that apply to entire Web sites.

Chapter 46

Configuring Web Site Settings

Because you can configure properties for Web pages, pictures, and other individual elements of a Web site, it should come as no surprise that you can also change properties that affect the site as a whole. This chapter describes the various site-level options that you can control with Microsoft Office FrontPage 2003, including settings for language, security, and user and administrative access. Before you begin working on your Web site, it's almost certainly worthwhile to review the options that control your work environment.

Reviewing Site Settings

The Site Settings command on the Tools menu of FrontPage governs settings that apply globally to the current Web site. There are six tabs in the Site Settings dialog box: General, Parameters, Advanced, Language, Navigation, and Database.

Controlling General Site Settings

Figure 46-1 shows the General tab of the Site Settings dialog box for a server-based Web site.

This tab contains controls for two configurable options:

- **Web Name** Specify the identity of the current Web site. To rename a site, you must be an administrator of its parent site.
- **Use Document Check-In And Check-Out** Select this check box to activate source code control for the current Web site. If this box is selected, FrontPage prompts you to check out (that is, take control of) any file you want to edit. This way, FrontPage prevents anyone else from checking out or modifying the file until you check it in (that is, relinquish control of it). This stops designers from interfering with each other when they want to work on the same file.

Figure 46-1. The General tab of the Site Settings dialog box specifies the Web site's textual name and controls document checkin and checkout.

For more information about source code control, refer to "Using Document Check-In and Check-Out," on page 1023.

In addition, the General tab displays the Web server's URL (or the file location, for disk-based Web sites). If you've opened the Site Settings dialog box in a server-based Web site, the General tab also displays the version number of the Microsoft FrontPage Server Extensions on that server, and the name and version of the Web server itself.

Table 47-1 correlates the first digit of the FrontPage Server Extensions version number to the corresponding product name.

Table 46-1. Major Versions of the FrontPage Server Extensions

First digit	Server extensions version
1	FrontPage 1.1
2	FrontPage 97
3	FrontPage 98
4	FrontPage 2000
5	FrontPage 2002
6	Microsoft Windows SharePoint Services

Controlling Site Parameters

The Parameters tab, shown in Figure 46-2, displays a list of site parameters (that is, of variables and their current values). After defining these variables once, you can use them in any number of Web pages by choosing Web Component from the Insert menu, selecting Included Content in the Component Type list, and then selecting Substitution.

For more information about the Substitution component, refer to "Using Site Parameters and the Substitution Component," on page 759.

Figure 46-2. You can define any number of variables from the Parameters tab of the Site Settings dialog box.

Here's how to use the buttons on this tab:

- **Add** To define an additional variable, click Add, enter the desired name and value in the Add Name And Value dialog box, and then click OK.
- **Modify** To change the value of a variable, first select the variable in the list, and then click Modify. When the Modify Name And Value dialog box appears, make your edits, and then click OK.
- **Remove** To remove a variable, select it, and click Remove.

Controlling Advanced Site Settings

The Advanced tab, shown in Figure 46-3, controls settings for scripting languages, display of hidden directories, and temporary files.

Figure 46-3. The Advanced tab of the Site Settings dialog box contains settings for such advanced items as validation scripts and hidden directories.

The following settings control the programming language that FrontPage uses for writing scripts that validate form field input on the browser:

- **Client** This setting controls the programming language that FrontPage will use to generate script code that runs on the Web visitor's browser. The choices are:
  - **VBScript** Only Microsoft Internet Explorer supports this scripting language.
  - **JavaScript** Both Internet Explorer and Netscape Navigator support this scripting language.
  - **<None>** FrontPage won't create validation scripts that run on the browser.
- **Show Hidden Files And Folders** Select this check box to display files in hidden folders. Such folders contain system information and files generated by FrontPage. They usually have names beginning with an underscore (_).
- **Display A Web Page View Of Available Document Libraries To Office Users Who Open From Or Save To The Web Site** This check box appears only when the current Web site runs on Windows SharePoint Services. Select it if you want File Open, File Save, and File Save As dialog boxes to initially display the Document Libraries view of this Web site, as shown in Figure 46-4. Clear the check box if you want Microsoft Office programs to display an ordinary files and folders view.

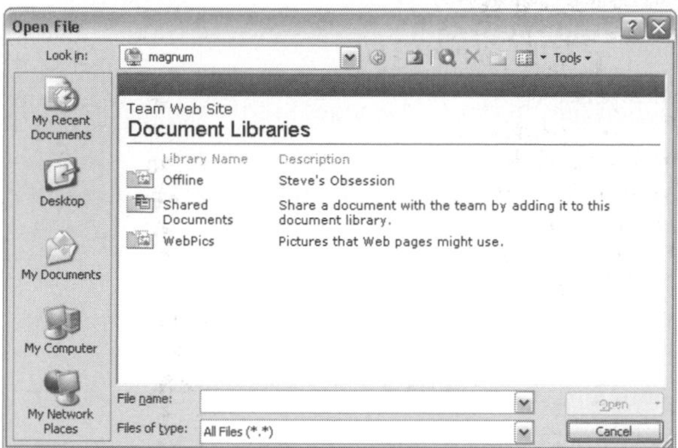

Figure 46-4. This is the Web site view of a SharePoint Team Site document library that Office programs can display for opening or saving files.

Views

In either case, the dialog box includes a Views button that can override the default view.

- **Delete Files** Click this button to delete any temporary files that are no longer in use.

Controlling Language Settings

The Language tab, shown in Figure 46-5, controls language defaults for your Web site.

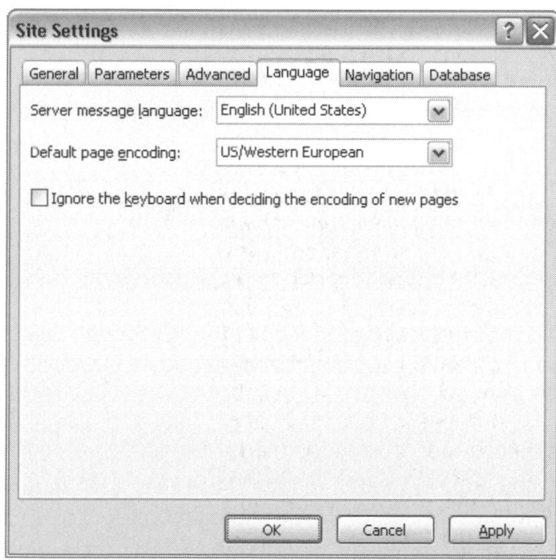

Figure 46-5. The Language tab of the Site Settings dialog box controls whether server error messages appears in English or another available language. This tab also establishes the default character set for saving pages.

The following options are available:

- **Server Message Language** This setting controls the language the FrontPage Server Extensions use when sending error messages to the Web browser. Match this setting to your audience.
- **Default Page Encoding** Specify the character set you want FrontPage to use for all new Web pages it creates. If you prefer using Unicode rather than a specific language, choose Multilingual (UTF-8).
- **Ignore The Keyboard When Deciding The Encoding Of New Pages** This setting controls what happens when your computer's keyboard language (as specified in the Keyboard component of Control Panel) makes the keyboard incompatible with the language you specified in Default Page Encoding:
  - If this check box is cleared, FrontPage sets the language of the new page to that of the keyboard.
  - If this check box is selected, FrontPage always uses the site's default page encoding for new pages.

To override the default page encoding for a single page, open the page, choose Properties from the File menu, click the Language tab, and configure the HTML Encoding settings.

To override the page encoding for a portion of a page, select that portion, and then choose Set Language from the Tools menu.

Note Configuring software to accept different languages is only half the battle; you also need to configure your keyboard to type the necessary characters. The Keyboard component in Control Panel configures natural-language settings for keyboards. Of course, you must also obtain a keyboard with the necessary keys and key caps, but that's a hardware issue.

Understanding Web Pages and Language Encoding

Because the Web is worldwide, it must accommodate character sets for languages used all around the world. Yet because the Web is bandwidth-constrained, it uses single-byte character sets.

A single-byte character set provides only 256 different codes, which isn't nearly enough to represent all the characters in all the languages that appear on the Web. As a result, each language uses the 256 codes in its own way. To display a Web page properly, a browser must know what character set its author intended. The following HTML, for example, indicates the US/Western European character set:

```
<meta http-equiv="Content-Type" content="text/html; charset=iso-8859-1">
```

The Default Page Encoding setting in FrontPage specifies the character set that FrontPage assigns to new pages created in the current Web site. The setting for most Western languages is US/Western European.

Specifying an *HTML Encoding* value causes some browsers to display the resulting Web pages twice, as if they notice the *charset=* parameter on the first pass and then apply it on the second pass. To avoid this behavior, specify *HTML Encoding* = *<none>*. Specifying *<none>*, however, implies complete trust that the default character set on the visitor's browser will display your page correctly.

Configuring Other Site Settings

The Navigation tab, shown in Figure 46-6, specifies the titles that FrontPage will use for four standard link bar entries: Home Page, Parent Page, Previous Page, and Next Page.

For more information about link bars, refer to "Working with Navigation View," on page 331, and "Using Link Bars with Navigation View," on page 348.

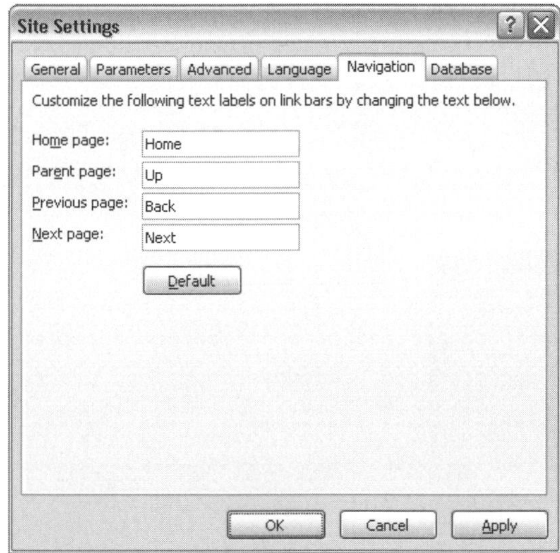

Figure 46-6. The Navigation tab controls the link titles of standard targets that appear in link bars based on Navigation view.

The Database tab, shown in Figure 46-7, lists and configures named connections between your Web pages and databases that reside on the Web server.

For more information about using the Database tab, refer to "Configuring a FrontPage Data Connection," on page 912.

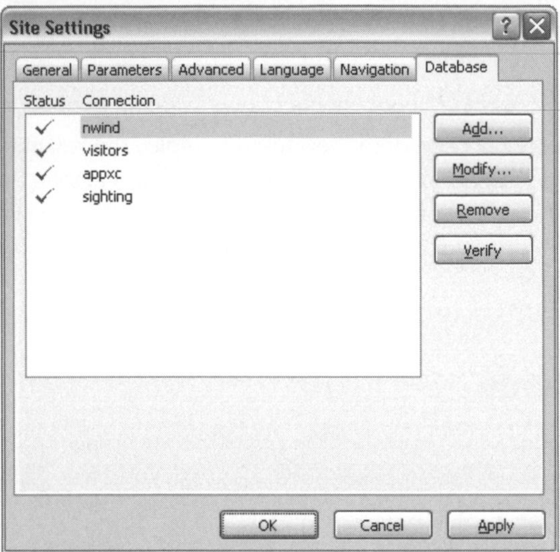

Figure 46-7. The Database tab creates, modifies, and deletes FrontPage database connections.

Reviewing Folder Settings

To view or change the properties of a folder, select the folder, and choose Properties from the File menu. FrontPage displays the Properties dialog box for that folder, as shown in Figure 46-8.

Figure 46-8. This is the Properties dialog box for a folder in a FrontPage-based Web site.

Here are the properties you can view or configure in this dialog box:

- **Name** Displays the current folder name.
- **Type** Displays the type of item selected (in this case, a folder).
- **Location** Reports the current location of the folder.
- **Contains** Shows the number of files and folders that the folder contains.
- **Size** Lists the total file size of the elements within the folder.
- **Allow Scripts Or Programs To Be Run** Select this check box if it's all right for the Web server to run scripts or executable programs that reside in the selected folder.

  Programs primarily include CGI and ISAPI programs, which in Windows usually have an .exe or a .dll file extension.

  Scripts, on the other hand, aren't executable in themselves; they're interpreted by other programs—script processors—that the server administrator authorizes and approves. This provides an extra layer of control and security. Three common script types are ASP pages, Microsoft ASP.NET pages, and Perl programs.

  This option appears only on disk-based Web sites (where it is always dimmed) and on server-based Web sites where the server doesn't provide separate control of program and script execution.
- **Allow Programs To Be Run** Select this check box to allow the Web server to run executable programs in the selected folder. This check box doesn't appear for folders in disk-based Web sites.

  This option and the next appear only on server-based Web sites where the Web server provides separate control of program and script execution.
- **Allow Scripts To Be Run** Select this check box to allow the Web server to run scripts from the selected folder. This check box doesn't appear for folders in disk-based Web sites.
- **Allow Files To Be Browsed** Select this check box to permit file access from Web browsers. Clear this check box to prevent ordinary visitors from accessing the folder. This check box is absent from Web servers that don't support it and from disk-based Web sites.
- **Allow Anonymous Upload To This Directory** Select this check box to allow Web visitors to upload files to the folder anonymously. This check box appears as unavailable for folders in disk-based Web sites.

Caution It's extremely dangerous for any folder to have both anonymous upload and execute permissions. This combination gives anyone on the Web permission to upload scripts, programs, or both to your Web server and then run them. If you allow this sort of activity, it's only a matter of time until one of those scripts or programs does something unpleasant.

- **Allow Uploaded Files To Overwrite Existing Filenames** Select this check box if it's all right for an uploaded file to replace, or overwrite, an existing file with the same name in this folder. This check box appears as unavailable for folders in disk-based Web sites.

Controlling Web Site Security Through FrontPage

Security is a constant concern on the Internet. Most Web sites allow any and all visitors to view Web pages but restrict editing and administration to a few authorized individuals.

FrontPage-based Web sites depend largely on the Web server's security functions for control. Security commands issued within FrontPage communicate with FrontPage software on the server and instruct it to implement the required settings. Working though FrontPage isolates Web designers from many of the security differences among Web servers.

Installing FrontPage Server Extensions, initializing security, and creating new FrontPage-based Web sites are tasks that system administrators usually perform. Administrators are responsible for the overall stability and performance of the server. If you're running a personal Web server, this is probably as far as you'll go by way of security. It's like being the president, chief engineer, and janitor of a one-person company.

In a multi-user environment, however, the system administrator usually turns ongoing maintenance over to the new Web site's owner. The owner then designates any additional administrators and authors.

To change permissions via FrontPage on a particular Web server, you must open the applicable Web site *on that server*. This requires the presence of the FrontPage Server Extensions. If the server extensions aren't installed, you or an administrator will have to control permissions using the server's native security system.

Updating a Web site's permissions on your development server and then publishing your Web site to a production server doesn't affect security on the production server. This is because, in most scenarios, security on the two servers *ought* to be different. You might be an administrator of your personal Web server, for example, but only an author (allowed to change content but not permissions) on the production server. In a shared development environment, many Web authors could have permission to update the group's authoring server, although only the project leader or librarian might have rights to publish content on the production server.

Controlling Web Site Security on Back-Level Server-Based Web Sites

Server-based Web sites running the FrontPage 2000 Server Extensions or an earlier version control security on the basis of user names, passwords, and three levels of access:

- **Browse** People with this level of access can view the Web site with browsers such as Internet Explorer, but they can't open the site in FrontPage or make changes.
- **Author And Browse** People with this level of access can open the Web site and change its content, but they can't modify site settings or permissions.
- **Administer, Author, And Browse** People with this level of access can change content, settings, and permissions.

To change permissions for a FrontPage 2000 or earlier server-based Web site, the Web site's administrator opens the Web site in FrontPage and then chooses Permissions from the Tools menu. This displays the Permissions dialog box, shown in Figure 46-9. The tabs available will vary, depending on the capabilities of the Web server and the installed version of the FrontPage Server Extensions.

Note The Permissions choice on the Tools menu will be disabled for servers having no security in effect, or for those whose security isn't configurable through the FrontPage Server Extensions.

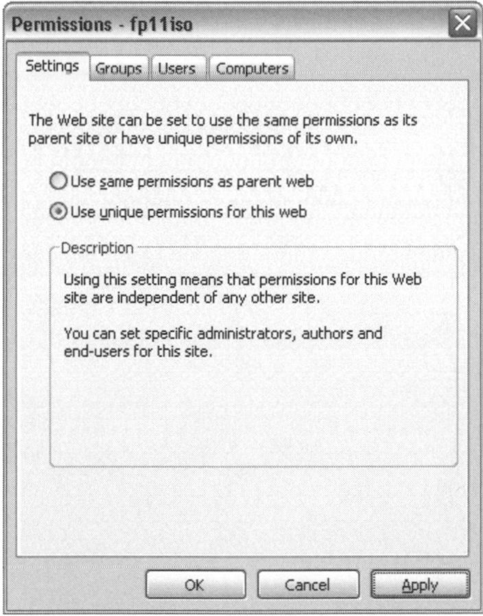

Figure 46-9. The Permissions dialog box in FrontPage lets administrators establish permissions for the current Web site that differ from those of the root Web site.

The Settings tab controls whether the current Web site will use the same permissions as the root Web site or unique permissions of its own. Although new Web sites always inherit permissions from the root Web site, this is seldom appropriate for ongoing use. In all but the simplest environments, different people will maintain the root Web site and subordinate Web sites. Therefore, after creating a new Web site, the root Web site administrator will generally activate unique permissions so that the appropriate users or groups can begin setting their own permissions and creating content.

Selecting the Use Unique Permissions For This Web option and clicking Apply unlocks the remaining tabs in the Permissions dialog box. These tabs might include Groups, Users, and Computers, depending on the Web server.

Controlling User-Level Web Site Access

There are two main variations of the Users tab:

- One for Web servers that use Windows 2000 Active Directory or a Microsoft Windows NT 4.0 user account database. Microsoft IIS takes this approach.
- Another for servers that maintain site-specific user lists. Most Web servers other than IIS use this method.

Figure 46-10 shows the Users tab for Web sites that reside on IIS.

Figure 46-10. This Users tab is typical for Web sites running on servers that support Windows 2000 or Windows NT security.

The list at the top of the Users tab shows which users have permission to access the current Web site and what rights each uses has. To begin adding a user to the list, click the Add button to display the Add Users dialog box, shown in Figure 46-11.

If the server supports multiple user account databases, the Obtain List From drop-down list can retrieve user names from the database you want. In Figure 46-11, for example, NS44 is the name of the local computer, and the Names list lists user accounts local to that computer.

- If the Web site resides on a stand-alone Windows 2000, Windows XP, or Windows Server 2003 computer, the Obtain List From drop-down list will contain the stand-alone machine's computer name.
- If the Web site resides on a Windows 2000 or Windows Server 2003 Domain Controller, the Obtain List From drop-down list contains the name of the local domain as well as the names of any other domains it trusts.

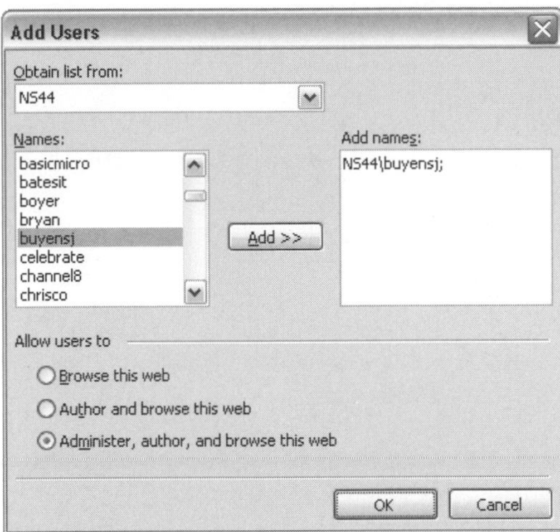

Figure 46-11. This dialog box grants users with Windows NT accounts access to a FrontPage-based Web site.

- If the FrontPage-based Web site resides on a stand-alone Windows 2000, Windows XP, or Windows Server 2003 computer that's a *member* of a Windows 2000 or Windows Server 2003 domain, the Obtain List From drop-down list will include entries for the stand-alone server or workstation, plus the local domain name, plus the names of other domains that the local domain trusts.

To continue granting Web site access to an existing Windows 2000, Windows XP, or Windows Server 2003 user, follow these steps:

1. In the Add Users dialog box (shown in Figure 46-11), select one or more users in the Names list, and then click the Add button. You can also add users by double-clicking their entries in the Names list.
2. Select the most appropriate privilege in the Allow Users To section, and click OK.

You can add as many users as you want before clicking OK, but they all receive the same permissions. To give various users different permissions, close and reopen the dialog box. FrontPage can't create, modify, or delete Windows users, nor can it change passwords. Instead, tools provided with the operating system perform these functions.

To change permissions for a user already listed on the Users tab (shown previously in Figure 46-10), first select the user, and then click the Edit button. This displays the Edit Users dialog box, shown in Figure 46-12, where you can change a group's level of access. Clicking Remove on the Users tab deletes the selected group from the authorized list.

Figure 46-12. This dialog box adds existing Windows NT users to the list of those permitted to access the current FrontPage-based Web site.

Notice the Valid Username And Password Required To Browse This Web check box on the Users tab of the Permissions dialog box (Figure 46-10):

- **Cleared** Means that anyone with network access to your Web server can browse the Web site, using programs such as Internet Explorer or Netscape Navigator.
- **Selected** Means that Web browsing is available only to authorized users and to members of authorized groups. To verify authorization, the Web server will prompt visitors for a qualifying user name and password.

> **Note** Password-protected Web pages are accessible only if the browser and Web server use the same authentication scheme. If the server and browser come from different providers, they might not reveal their security algorithms to each other for security reasons. If you have trouble getting valid passwords accepted, change or add authentication schemes until you find a compatible set.

Most non-Microsoft Web servers have site-specific user lists that are quite distinct from the operating system's list of login accounts. This avoids the security concerns of granting Web users system-wide login accounts, but it also means that people needing both types of access will have to remember an additional user name and password.

In many of these cases, you can maintain site-specific user lists directly from within FrontPage. The Users tab and the Add Users dialog box, however, take on a different appearance.

Controlling Web Site Access by Group

Groups are simply collections of users granted identical security privileges. Grouping all users from a certain department, with a certain job classification, on a client site, or from another category makes it easy to grant or revoke privileges for the whole group. Granting privileges by group also eases maintenance as individuals enter and leave the group—rather than updating their access in many different locations, you update only the membership of the group.

Support for groups varies from one Web server to another, as does the ability to create, delete, and modify groups from within FrontPage. In Figure 46-13, the Web server is IIS, and the groups listed are local to the server. The operating system provides tools that create, modify, and delete these groups. Other Web servers maintain groups in their own way and might permit maintenance via FrontPage. The Add, Edit, and Remove buttons in Figure 46-13 work very much as they do in the Permissions dialog box shown in Figure 46-10.

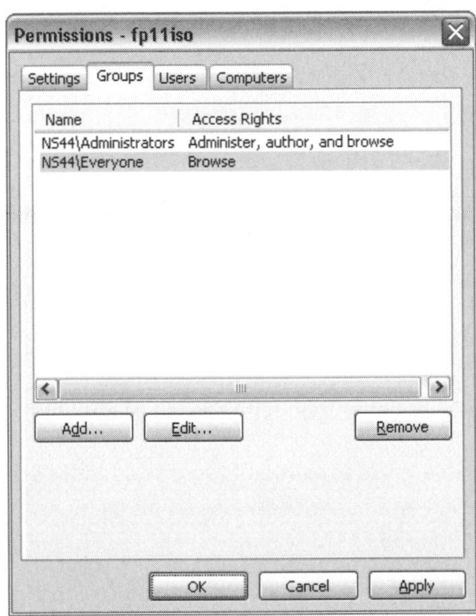

Figure 46-13. This dialog box sets the access level for groups of users.

Controlling Web Site Access by Network Address

Some Web servers can control access based on a remote user's IP address. Because IP addresses are typically assigned to organizations in blocks, granting or denying access based on IP address can provide a form of security broadly grounded in organizational membership.

The Computers tab, shown in Figure 46-14, controls access to a FrontPage-based Web site based on the IP address of the browsing computer. This tab is available only for Web servers that support this feature.

An Add Computer dialog box grants access to a specific computer or range of network addresses. To use this dialog box, click the Add button on the Computers tab, enter the computer's IP address in the IP Mask field, choose the level of access, and then click OK. The access levels work the same as those for users and groups, except, of course, that you can exercise no direct control over who might be sitting at the computer to which you're granting Web site access.

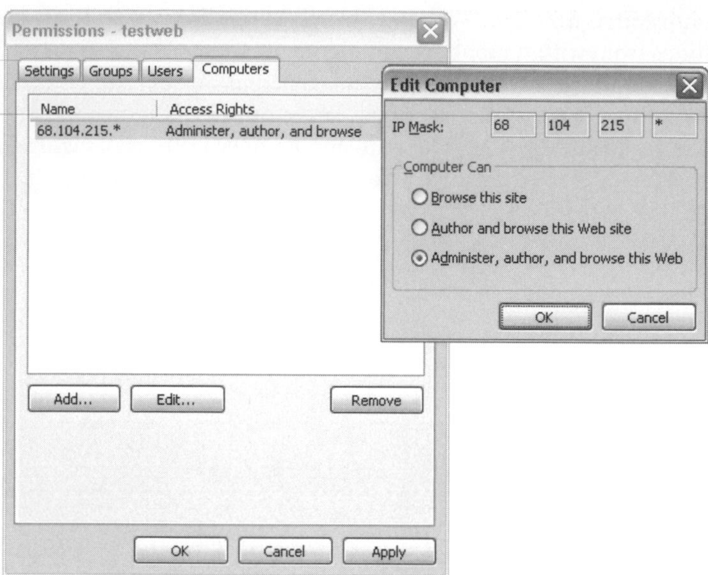

Figure 46-14. The Computers tab grants or limits Web site access based on IP address.

To control access for a range of IP addresses, enter asterisks (*) in one or more boxes in the IP Mask field. In Figure 46-14, the Web server will allow browsing by all users having IP addresses 68.104.215.0 through 68.104.215.255.

The Edit button on the Computers tab (shown in Figure 46-14) modifies the permissions of an existing IP address entry. The Remove button deletes the selected entry from the list.

Controlling Web Site Security on FrontPage 2002 Server-Based Web Sites

If your Web server is running the FrontPage 2002 Server Extensions, a series of Web pages (rather than a series of dialog boxes) manages user security. To display the initial Web page, choose Server from the Tools menu, and then choose Permissions. Your browser should then display the Permissions Administration page, shown in Figure 46-15. Chapter 50 explains how to use this Web page and its hyperlinks.

For more information about managing users and roles in a FrontPage 2002 server-based Web site, refer to "Administering Web Settings," in Appendix P.

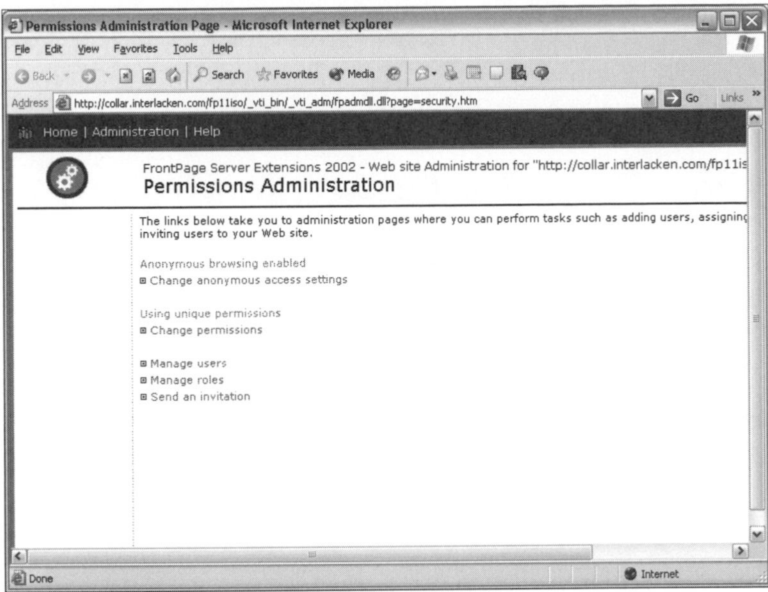

Figure 46-15. This Web page controls user-level access to a FrontPage-based Web site.

Securing Web Page Delivery with IIS

In addition to storing file and folder information, the Windows NT file system (NTFS) stores *access control lists* (ACLs) that specify which visitors can access a given file or folder, as well as what permissions they have. If a file or folder's ACL doesn't authorize a visitor to perform an operation, NTFS blocks the attempt and returns an error message.

When retrieving pages for Web delivery, IIS normally first accesses the file with an Anonymous account. If that access succeeds, IIS delivers the page. If it fails, IIS prompts the Web visitor for a user name and a password. If the visitor responds with a user name and a password that provide access, IIS delivers the requested page. If not, IIS repeats the prompt.

FrontPage establishes the following NTFS permissions for the various FrontPage access levels:

- **Browse This Web** Visitors and groups at this access level have Read permissions in NTFS.
- **Author And Browse This Web** Visitors and groups in this category have Change permissions in NTFS.
- **Administer, Author, And Browse This Web** Web administrators have Full Control permissions over their Web files; they can update both files and permissions.

It's best to use FrontPage to set permissions for Web sites, rather than using native Windows NT dialog boxes. This prevents problems caused when FrontPage finds permissions in an unexpected state.

Security administration is a complex, critical task that requires case by case judgment. It always involves trade-offs among the degree of protection, ease of administration, and ease of access for authorized visitors. There aren't any universal answers or pat solutions—but FrontPage at least provides a start.

Changing FrontPage Server Administration Settings

To change settings of all kinds for the current Web site, open the Web site in FrontPage, choose Server from the Tools menu, and then choose Administration Home from the submenu. This displays the Site Administration page, shown in Figure 46-16, in your browser. Appendix P explains how to use this Web page.

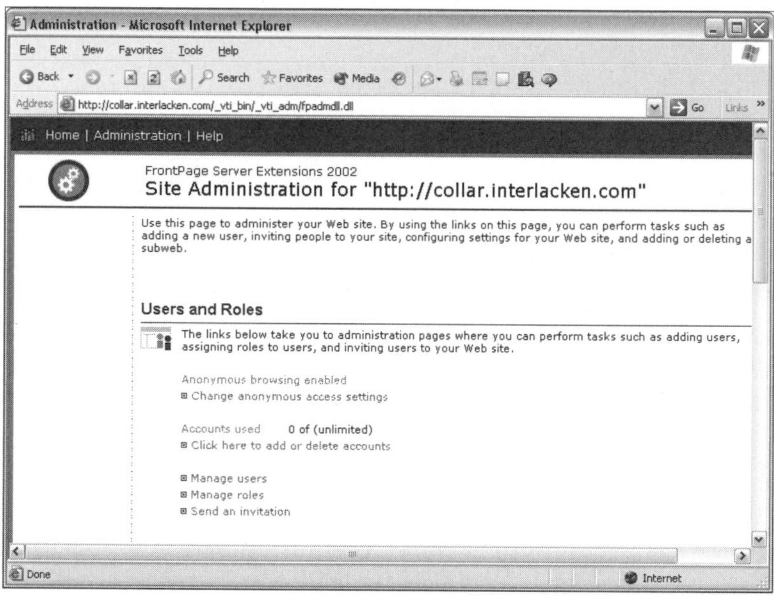

Figure 46-16. This Web page provides access to all server-based options for a Web site.

In Summary…

This chapter explained how to configure FrontPage settings that affect an entire Web site. This included Site settings, folder settings, and security configuration.

This book has attempted to explain everything FrontPage can do. This, of course, is an impossible task, because no book can predict the creativity, skill, and hard work you bring to every site you create or maintain. In the end, these are more valuable than any piece of software. Hopefully, FrontPage 2003 will be the most effective possible conduit between your thoughts and finished results of the highest caliber. Good luck with your site and I hope we meet again.

Index to Troubleshooting Topics

Index

Page numbers with the prefix A refer to Appendixes on the companion CD. Page numbers with the prefix IE refer to Insider Extras on the companion CD, as follows:

A3–A24 .... Appendix A
A25–A32 .... Appendix B
A33–A44 .... Appendix C
A45–A70 .... Appendix D
A71–A78 .... Appendix E
A79–A86 .... Appendix F
A87–A92 .... Appendix G
A93–A106 .... Appendix H
A107–A110 .... Appendix I
A111–A120 .... Appendix J
A121–A128 .... Appendix K
A129–A158 .... Appendix L
A159–A168 .... Appendix M
A169–A192 .... Appendix N
A193–A216 .... Appendix O
A217–A245 .... Appendix P
IE3–IE8.................. Insider Extra 1
IE9–IE16................ Insider Extra 2
IE17–IE22.............. Insider Extra 3
IE22–IE28.............. Insider Extra 4
IE29–IE34.............. Insider Extra 5
IE35–IE40.............. Insider Extra 6
IE41–IE50.............. Insider Extra 7
IE51–IE54.............. Insider Extra 8
IE55–IE60.............. Insider Extra 9
IE61–IE64.............. Insider Extra 10
IE65–IE74.............. Insider Extra 11
IE75–IE92.............. Insider Extra 12
IE93–IE108............ Insider Extra 13
IE109–122 .... Insider Extra 14

B

D

F

G

M

N

O

S

T

U

V

W

Z

About the Author

Jim Buyens has been professionally involved with the World Wide Web since its inception, including roles as a server administrator, Web master, content developer, and system architect. He currently develops Web-based business systems for the telecommunications industry, and is also an acclaimed Microsoft Most Valuable Professional (MVP) who contributes extensively to the Microsoft Online FrontPage Communities.

Jim received a Bachelor of Science degree in Computer Science from Purdue University in 1971 and a Master of Business Administration from Arizona State University in 1992. When not enhancing the Web or writing books, he enjoys traveling and attending professional sports events—especially NHL hockey. He resides with his family in Phoenix.

Other books by Jim Buyens include:

- Faster Smarter Beginning Programming, November, 2002, Microsoft Press
- Web Database Development Step by Step .NET Edition, June, 2002, Microsoft Press
- Troubleshooting Microsoft FrontPage 2002, May, 2002, Microsoft Press
- Microsoft FrontPage Version 2002 Inside Out, May , 2001, Microsoft Press
- Web Database Development Step by Step, June, 2000, Microsoft Press
- Running Microsoft FrontPage 2000, June, 1999, Microsoft Press
- Stupid Web Tricks, July, 1998, Microsoft Press
- Running Microsoft FrontPage 98, October, 1997, Microsoft Press
- Building Net Sites with Windows NT—An Internet Services Handbook, July 1996, Addison-Wesley Developers Press

Contacting the Author

Hearing from happy readers is always a welcome and pleasant experience, and hearing from the less-than-satisfied is important as well. Please note that I can respond only if you write in English. My e-mail address is

buyensj@interlacken.com

I'm most interested in your impressions of this book: what you liked or disliked about it, what questions it did or didn't answer, what you found superfluous and what you'd like to see added in the next edition. I'll post errors, omissions, corrections, and frequently-asked questions on my Web site at

www.interlacken.com/fp2003/

I can accept enhancement requests only for this book, and not for the Microsoft software. To suggest product enhancements, send e-mail to:

mswish@microsoft.com

or browse the Web page at

www.microsoft.com/mswish

Please understand that I'm just one person and I can't provide technical support or debugging assistance, even for readers. Please try other channels, including the following newsgroups

microsoft.public.frontpage.client
microsoft.public.frontpage.programming

and the Microsoft Search page at

www.microsoft.com/search/

If you're getting an error message or error number, try searching for that exact phrase or number. If this produces too many hits, try searching within the results for the word FrontPage. If you're having trouble with a specific feature or component, try searching for the name of the component and again, if that produces too many hits, searching for FrontPage within those results.

If all else fails, please write. While I can't promise to answer each message, I'll try to provide at least a useful suggestion. Even when I can't answer your e-mail messages directly, I find it instructive to learn what problems users like you are experiencing—and therefore how I can make this and future books more useful to everyone.

Proof of Purchase

Use this page as proof of purchase if participating in a promotion or rebate offer on this title. Proof of purchase must be used in conjunction with other proof(s) of payment such as your dated sales receipt—see offer details.

Microsoft® Office FrontPage® 2003 Inside Out

0-7356-1510-1

CUSTOMER NAME

Microsoft Press, PO Box 97017, Redmond, WA 98073-9830